General Oregon Re

What they say about *The Oregon Book*

"You want to know more about Oregon? Consult with Connie Battaile through her incredibly complete and aptly titled *The Oregon Book: Information A to Z*, perhaps *the* Oregon book. For an encyclopedic review of our state, read on...

> **Gerry Frank**, businessman, political advisor, Oregon booster, restaurateur, author, *Oregonian* columnist, and chocolate cake expert.

"*The Oregon Book: Information A to Z* is a remarkable compilation. It covers a vast variety of material of interest to Oregonians concerned with a vast variety of professions and avocations. The book should shine as a quick source volume combining short factual items with extensive cross-references, and the huge bibliography points the reader directly to the primary source or sources. It should be of inestimable value to the individual who has no clue where to turn to find that one bit of elusive information we all so often seek."

> **Lewis L. McArthur**, *Oregon Geographic Names*

"Almost everything you ever wanted to know about Oregon. A cornucopia for fact-seekers and browsers. An indispensible book for all Oregon libraries."

> **Harold Otness**, scholar, reviewer for *Library Journal*, and reference librarian, Southern Oregon University.

"*The Oregon Book: Information A to Z* by Connie Hopkins Battaile promises to be an invaluable resource and reference guide to anyone with the slightest degree of interest in Oregon's history, geography, economy, demographics, etc. It is one of those books that will occupy an important niche on my bookshelf along with other similar richly fact-filled published works about Oregon. I only wish it would have been available some years ago when I was busy researching material for my book, *This Day in Oregon: A Daybook of Oregon History*. It would have saved me hours and hours of seeking out the information needed to fill my book. I am sure that future researchers into Oregon's past or present will be indebted to Ms. Battaile's perserverance in her striving to collect, record, and publish such a comprehensive array of facts and figures about this great state of Oregon."

> **James Cloutier**, *Orygone I, II, III*, and *IV*, *This Day in Oregon*, *The Alpine Tavern*,...

"Connie Battaile has compiled an exceptional and unique encyclopedia of information, fact, and fancy about the state of Oregon. The more than 3,500 entries in this volume and the extensive bibliogrpahy will be valuable to librarians, local, county, and state officials, and literally anyone else searching for historical and contemporary information about the place called Oregon. *The Oregon Book* should occupy a prominent place on every reference shelf."

> **William G. Robbins**, Distinguished Professor of History, Oregon State University, and author of *Landscapes of Promise: The Oregon Story 1800-1940*.

The Oregon Book
Information A to Z

by

Connie Hopkins Battaile

First Edition
1998

Saddle Mountain Press
425 Coast Hwy SW
Newport OR 97365
800-668-6105

Publisher's Cataloging-in-Publication data
Battaile, Connie.
    The Oregon book: information A to Z/by Connie Hopkins
    Battaile. -- 1st Edition.
        p. cm.
    Includes bibliographical references.
    Preassigned LCCN: 98-090263
    ISBN: 0-9657638-2-X (pbk)
    ISBN: 0-9657638-3-8 (hardcover)
    1. Oregon--Encyclopedias. I. Title
F874.B38 1998   917.95'03
                    QBI98-434

Printed in the United States of America
Published by:
Saddle Mountain Press
425 Coast Hwy SW
Newport, OR 97365
800-668-6105

Cover designed by Anderson McConaughy Design, Portland, Oregon.
Cover photo by Ray Atkeson

The paper used in this publication meets the minimum requirements of American
National Standard for Information Sciences. ANSI Z 39.48-1984

To the authors, writers, and reporters of Oregon,
whose dedicated endeavors have provided the basis for this work
and laid the foundation for our shared sense of Oregon identity.

Contents

Preface

A state is a happenstance kind of thing.

Oregon, for instance, happened into being out of a brew of Spanish and Russian, British and American tuggings and jostlings for the "unclaimed" - though long inhabited - regions of western North America. Its boundaries were eventually defined by water - the Pacific, Columbia, and Snake rivers - and by that artifice of human invention, the straight line, striped arbitrarily across mountain and valley and defined by another human artifice, latitude and longitude.

For those living in the northern Willamette Valley, i.e., half of the state's population, living in Oregon is rather like living in a house on a large corner lot. The house faces the main street, the Columbia, with another, and less crossable, side street along the west edge. If the resident meanders back through the long back yard and climbs the fence he can get into neighbor California's yard. The side yard to the east is really his empty lot, offering little but weeds and a place to play.

For the rest of those living in Oregon, the state is a less easily defined place. Those living outside the WIllamette Valley, which has been the heartland of Oregon from the beginning of settlement, are marginalized by geography and mindset. For them to be Oregonian takes a different, broader, deeper commitment. Those from the edges who contribute to the state by serving on state boards or commissions arrive at meetings (nearly always in the Willamette Valley, of course) bleary from early risings and hours in the car, and can look forward to long hours and late arrival home - or can spend extra, hard-to-spare, days in travel. Oregon is big. Rough. Travel takes time. And it takes a lot to knit a sense of state out of such distances and differences.

Yet it has happened. There is a sense of Oregon abroad in the land that defies expectations. Somehow that pioneer anticipation of Oregon as a land of promise, a better, more fruitful place, has settled into the psyche of those who came later. Oregon's specialness is affirmed by its stunningly varied landscape, its wide array of weather, its tolerant and diligent peoples, and its traditional assumption that the state, its government, belongs to the people of the state - and we, the people, can make it better.

So out of a misspelled name for a Wisconsin river and a 19th century brew of politics, we have a state, and those attached to that state feel a sense of belonging and quiet pride. The Oregon way, the Oregon style, the Oregon system, the Oregon plan... Those words carry more than just a definition.

It is to honor that resonating sense of what it is to be an Oregonian that this work was compiled.

Acknowledgments

Just think how many hands it has taken, how many writers and reporters moved by professional pride or passionate interest to document some part of Oregon, how many courteous workers in agencies and organizations answering mail and telephone inquiries, how many cartographers making the maps, how many statisticians gathering the data, how many lives, making the stories of Oregon.

The numbers are countless, and I am grateful to them all. I carry special appreciation for help from Monty Elliott who read the geology entries and George Taylor who read the weather entries, from Deb Hollens and Anne Richards who run a gem of a documents collection at Southern Oregon University library, Harold Otness for suggesting the title and for faith in the project, Darlene Dube' of Oregon Books for midwifing its launching, and Julian Battaile for unwavering support, for preparing several massive mailings, - and for careful readings of the entire manuscript more times than devotion or sanity should allow.

About the author-

Connie Hopkins Battaile (pronounced Battle) has lived in Oregon most of the time since she was 9. She attended Waldport schools, Oregon State University, and the University of Oregon, where she graduated. Her Masters of Library Studies degree is from the University of Hawaii. She has been a reference librarian with Jackson County, Southern Oregon University, and, for a few misplaced years, at Colgate University in upstate New York. Her earlier book, Circulation Services in a Small Academic Library, has not been made into a movie, either.

Introduction

The Oregon Book is designed to be used for the quick look-up of some bit of information, to answer questions such as, When was the Roseburg explosion?, or, What is Measure 5?, or, What does the air pollution index mean?. To that end, the articles have been kept short. Articles are arranged alphabetically, except that a few numeric titles come first. "See" references direct the user from a title that is not used to a title that is used.

Each article consists of a heading, an explanatory text, one or more citations when appropriate, and often one or more "See also" references to other entries. If the text includes a word or phrase that is also the title of another entry, it is **bolded** if the compiler thought the reader might find pertinent information in that entry - though if that word appears more than once, it is bolded only the first time. City names are consistently bolded, but other words may or may not be bolded. For example, there is an article about the legislature, but the word legislature is not always bolded when it is used in other articles.

Coverage

The Oregon Book includes information about most aspects of Oregon except that there are no personal-name entries and few about popular culture or sports.

Cities: The city recorder in each of Oregon's 240 incorporated cities was sent a copy of the proposed entry and asked for corrections and additions. Many replied, and their information was added. Unincorporated communities are entered if an interesting source appeared.

State agencies: Each state agency was sent a letter asking for information, especially statistical information and annual reports. Some responded generously, and some not at all. Budget constraints have restricted the amount of data collection that state agencies are doing, and some have had to abandon even annual reports.

Elevations: Elevations are from the Oregon Official State Map 1995-96. The Oregon Department of Transportation prepared the map in cooperation with the Department of Geography at the University of Oregon. The map includes officially recalculated elevations, some of them considerably changed from familiar older figures.

Sources

The Oregon Book is based on written work. Indeed, one way of thinking about it is as an index to what has been written about Oregon, though some information has come by phone and letter, especially from agencies and organizations.

Most of the time, if a written source was used as the basis for an entry or portion of an entry, it is listed at the end of the article, though occasionally an article was compiled from so many sources that there was no point in listing them. If the entry is about an organization or governmental unit or agency, its address and phone number are listed at the end of the entry. The intent was to give the reader a source of further information, if possible, at least for some portion of the entry.

Books and articles are cited by title and then listed by title in the Bibliography. However, if the full citation for a newspaper or magazine article, including date and page number, is provided in the article, it is not further listed in the Bibliography. The *Oregonian* is cited frequently, based on the edition received in Corvallis until October 1996 and then on the edition received in Ashland until the book closed on April 11, 1998. The pagination in the edition of the *Oregonian* preserved on microfilm or CD-ROM may be different from that in the paper edition that was used.

The Bibliography is extensive but far from exhaustive. For example, how many dozen guidebooks have been published about Oregon or some part of Oregon? Though most of them are fine, indeed, few have been included.

Because of word-processing limitations, the initial articles "A," "An," and "The," have been highhandedly removed from titles in the Bibliography.

Although every effort has been made to assure accuracy, the author and publisher do not assume and hereby disclaim any liability for loss or damage caused by errors or omissions.

Readers who have corrections, requests for changes or additions, or books or articles to suggest are encouraged to contact the author in care of the publisher or by e-mail to oregonbk@mind.net.

The Oregon Bookshelf

What are the basic Oregon reference books? Although that depends somewhat on users' interests, there are five that I have found so useful that I keep them right at hand - and I hope that readers will find that <u>The Oregon Book: Information A to Z</u> deserves to join them.

The first is that Oregon classic, <u>Oregon Geographic Names</u> by Lewis A. and Lewis L. McArthur. First published in 1928, it is now in its 6th edition (1992). The book is a compilation of information about 5,473 Oregon place names. The thorough research, the history that is both explicit and implicit in the entries, and the dry commentary make the book a pleasure and a treasure.

Next is the <u>Oregon Blue Book</u>, a biennial reference book issued by the Secretary of State and sold by that office and through bookstores. It includes not only information about Oregon government, agencies and elected officials past and present, but also offers an eminently readable history of the state, information about the state's economy, natural resources, arts, sciences, colleges and universities, media, local governments, and federal offices in Oregon, plus a listing of all the ballot measures Oregonians have ever voted on and the full text of the state Constitution.

The <u>Dictionary of Oregon History</u>, compiled during the 1930s as a Work Projects Administration effort under the editorship of Howard McKinley Corning, though not without error, is useful for quick information on many of the events of Oregon's history, and is handy for identifying the men important to Oregon's first hundred years of settlement. Note that it is the work of another era, one in which women received slight notice.

The <u>Oregon Atlas and Gazetteer</u> provides a happy and inexpensive compromise between having only a highway map for the state and having the full set of U.S.G.S. topographic maps for the entire state. It is frustrating, of course, to have the river or road you are following disappear off the edge of the page, or to find that the power line on one page does not continue on the next, but it is nonetheless a wonderfully useful tool.

A guide book is useful. I find that the <u>Oregon Washington AAA TourBook</u> (free to members) provides handy, accurate information about many Oregon places and attractions. There are a number of other good guide books available.

The Oregon Book
Information A to Z

Bolded words in the articles are the titles of related articles.

4-H Clubs. A national program of youth groups sponsored by the **Extension Service**. In Oregon 43,000 students in grades four to twelve, plus 8,000 adult leaders, are involved annually in the program, which originated in the federal Smith Lever Act of 1914. The traditional focus on homemaking and agricultural skills has expanded to include recreational, personal, and leadership skills. The name comes from the member pledge "I pledge my Head to clearer thinking, my Heart to greater loyalty, my Hands to larger service, and my Health to better living for my Club, my Community, and my Country." Corvallis Gazette-Times 5/30/94:A6.

45th parallel. A line of latitude, parallel to the equator and halfway between it and the North Pole. It crosses Oregon from near Oxbow on the **Snake River**, across **Interstate 84** between **Baker City** and **North Powder**, through central Oregon near **Fossil** and **Shaniko**, across **Interstate 5** on the north edge of **Salem**, to Roads End, just north of **Lincoln City**. Other places around the world on the 45th parallel include the northern tip of Japan, northern China, Mongolia, northern Italy, France, the northern border of Vermont and the southern border of Montana. Oregonian 9/28/97:L1. See also **Latitude and longitude**.

200 Market Street. See **Black Box**.

911. See **Emergency Management Division**.

1000 Friends of Oregon. A non-profit membership organization founded in 1975 to advocate for responsible planning for growth. Priorities include fighting urban sprawl and promoting sensible development while protecting farm and forest lands and other natural resources. Nine land-use watchdog groups around the state are affiliated with it. Former governor Tom McCall was a co-founder. 534 SW 3rd Ave., #300, Portland 97204. 503-497-1000. See also **Land use planning**.

1972 Downtown Plan. A plan adopted in 1972 as the guideline for redeveloping downtown **Portland** that had been described by a notable visiting architect two years before as a collection of "towers, bunkers and bombsites." The bold, visionary, and simple plan was put together after two years of public involvement. Among the features that resulted from the plan were **Governor Tom McCall Waterfront Park**; **Pioneer Courthouse Square**; and the **transit malls**. Oregonian 8/10/97:E1.

2040 plan. See **Region 2040 plan**.

A. C. Gilbert's Discovery Village. A multi-building children's museum on the **Salem** riverfront that includes the Toy Hall of Fame in the 1871 Parrish House, the 1883 Rockenfield House, and the 1887 Gilbert House. The buildings house interactive, hands-on exhibits in the humanities, arts, and sciences, and outdoor play/science areas are planned. A. C. Gilbert invented the Erector Set; Gilbert House was his uncle's home. 116 Marion St. NE. 503-371-3631.

Abalone. A genus, *Haliotis*, of edible, rock-clinging **shellfish**. Two species, red and flat, are found off the southern Oregon coast where they are harvested by recreational divers. The bag limit is 1 abalone, minimum shell width of 8 inches, with an annual limit of 5. Red abalone grow well over the size limit, though it takes 22 years for them to reach it. Flat abalone don't reach the 8" size requirement so are protected. Oregonian 10/30/95:B2.

Abbey Bach Festival. A three-day festival of classical and church music held at **Mount Angel Abbey** in late July. It opens on a Wednesday evening with vespers, picnic, and concert. 503-845-3321.

Abernethy Elm. A five-foot-diameter elm **tree**, probably *Ulmus americana*, on Clackamette Drive in **Oregon City** near the **Interstate 205** bridge. It was planted in 1850 by George Abernethy (1807-1877) on the north side of his home; on the south the home looked upriver to **Willamette Falls**. Abernethy served as the first and only **governor**, 1845-1849, for the **provisional government** in what was then called the **Oregon Country**.

Abernethy Rocks. Rocks used for currency in the **Oregon City** area in 1845. A shortage of coins led merchant (and later governor) George Abernethy to use chips of flint left from Indian spear making at **Willamette Falls**. He marked each piece with his name and a value. The currency was honored because of his known integrity. Dictionary of Oregon History. See also **Money**.

Abert Lake. See **Lake Abert**.

Abert Rim. A 2,500-foot high, 30-mile long **fault** scarp in **Lake County**, the largest exposed geologic fault in North America.. The west face rises abruptly from **Lake Abert** and is topped by a 600' cliff (which has a viewpoint on top reached by a dirt road), while the east side slopes gradually down to **Warner Valley**. The rim is a northern extension of the **Warner Mountains**. It was first reported by John C. Fremont, who discovered it while looking for the reputed **Buena Ventura River** in 1843.

Abiqua Battle, 1848. One of the few conflicts between settlers in the **Willamette Valley** and **Indians** took place on Abiqua (AB ih kwah) Creek east of **Silverton** along a major Indian trail to central Oregon. The battle occurred on March 5 and 6, 1848, while most of the men of the area were off at the **Cayuse War**, a war triggered by the **Whitman massacre** and feared by settlers to presage a general Indian uprising. Area residents became even more nervous when they discovered that the local Molalla Indians were being visited by two Cayuse Indians as well as a number of **Klamath Indians**, so attempted to arrange a meeting. The Indians, however, attacked. One white was injured and thirteen Indians were killed. Dictionary of Oregon History; Oregon Geographic Names. See also **Indian conflicts, Willamette Valley**.

Abiqua Creek Falls. A 70-foot falls on Abiqua Creek in **Marion County** north of **Silver Falls State Park**. The waterfall, located in a spectacular columnar basalt canyon, is owned by **Mount Angel Abbey**. Access is over a private logging road that may be locked. Oregonian 4/6/95:B7.

Abortion. In 1995, 14,078 abortions were performed in Oregon, over 10,000 of them in **Multnomah County**. Residents of all 36 counties obtained abortions, but there were providers in only eight counties. In 1994 the ratio was 307 abortions to 1,000 live **births**. As of 1995, Oregon required no waiting period, and did not require minors to have parental consent. The state had outlawed abortion in 1854 and it remained illegal until the U.S. Supreme Court's Roe vs Wade decision in 1973. Some abortionists practiced quite openly, however, until a 1951 police raid. Ruth Barnett, who began her abortion practice in 1918, was one of those jailed several times over the next few years. She was imprisoned for five months in 1968 at age 73, the oldest woman ever incarcerated in Oregon. Anti-abortion ballot measures were defeated in 1986 and 1990. Oregon: A Statistical Overview; Oregonian 11/6/94:D4, 7/18/96:A1, 1/24/97:D6. See also **Pregnancy**; **Teen pregnancy**.

Abraham Lincoln. A bronze statue that stands in **Portland**'s **Park Blocks**, sculpted by George F. Waters in 1928. It was one of four statues donated to the city by Dr. Henry Waldo Coe, noted neurologist and psychiatrist. Portland, An Informal History; Portland's Public Art.

Abuse. See **Child abuse**; **Domestic disturbance**.

Accountancy, Board of. A board of seven members, five of them Certified Public Accountants (CPAs), that is responsible for examining and registering Oregon's 7,000 CPAs, public accountants, and municipal auditors. It conducts twice-yearly CPA examinations. 3218 Pringle Rd. SE, Suite #110, Salem 97302-6307. 503-378-4181. Oregon Blue Book.

Acid rain. Rain in Oregon has a pH of about 5.4, which is within the normal range for rain. Because there are no major sources of atmospheric oxides of sulfur or nitrogen in or upwind from Oregon, acid rain has not been a problem in the state. Oregon's mountain lakes would be especially susceptible if the rain were to become more acidic, because they lack the alkalinity that could neutralize some of the acids. Oregon Environmental Atlas. See also **Air pollution**.

Acre. A measure of land area equal to 43,560 square feet. If square, an acre would be just under 209' on each side. A 40-acre square is 1/4 mile on each side. A **section** contains 640 acres and is a mile long on each side. A million acre square is just under 40 miles on a side. See also **Land description**.

Acre-foot. A measure of water volume, specifically, the amount needed to cover an acre of land with one foot of water. One acre-foot of water can supply the domestic needs of one or two families for a year. River volume and the storage capacity of irrigation **reservoirs** are measured in acre feet, with **Lake Owyhee**, the largest reservoir in the state, containing over one million acre-feet of water. For comparison, **Upper Klamath Lake** (Oregon's largest freshwater lake) contains 850,000 acre-feet and **Crater Lake** (the state's deepest lake) contains 14 million acre-feet. The number of acre-feet needed to grow a crop depends upon the soil, climate, and crop being grown. The drainage from a river basin, expressed in this work as acre feet per acre (of drainage basin), correlates to some extent with rainfall, though losses occur through evaporation, incorporation into biomass, and recharging of underground aquifers. Oregon rivers vary in their annual flows from .1 acre foot/acre from the arid **Owyhee** drainage basin of southeast Oregon to around 4 acre feet/acre in the **Willamette Valley** to the **Chetco River**'s 9 acre feet/acre on the south coast. Atlas of Oregon Lakes.

ACT. The American College Testing national college entrance test of English, math, reading, and science, required primarily by colleges in the Midwest. Eleven per cent of Oregon high school seniors took the test. In 1994, and again in 1995, Oregon high school seniors had the highest scores in the country. The national average was 20.9 out of 36; Oregon students scored 22.6. Oregonian 8/15/ 96:B3. See also **SAT.Act of Admission**. See **Admission Act**.

Act of Congress Admitting State of Oregon into The Union. See **Admission Act**.

Acupuncturists. See **Medical Examiners**.

Adair Village. A **Willamette Valley** residential community in **Benton County** seven miles north of **Corvallis** that was incorporated in 1976 on the site of **World War II**'s **Camp Adair**. The E. E. Wilson Game Reserve, also on part of the old camp, lies north of the town. Population 1980 589; 1995 565. Elevation 328'. 6030 NE Wm. R. Carr Ave., 97330. 541-745-5507. Oregon Geographic Names.

Adams. A northeast Oregon farm community in **Umatilla County**, 13 miles northeast of **Pendleton**, with an economy based on grains, hay, peas, cattle, and canola. The town was founded as a railroad town in 1883 and named for John Adams who homesteaded the land. The city was incorporated in 1893. During the bitterly cold winter of 1907 the town ran out of fuel and the whole town agreed to hold up a train loaded with coal. After their successful holdup and distribution of the coal, they untied the engineer, paid market value for the coal, and told him to be on his way. The Adams Ladies Club has published three volumes of the history of Adams, 1883 through 1913. Population 1980 240; 1995 260. Elevation 1,526'. PO Box 20, 97810. 541-566-9380. Oregon Geographic Names.

Address tiles. See **Portland address tiles**.

Administrative Rules (OAR). See **Oregon Administrative Rules**.

Administrative Services, Department of (DAS). A department of Oregon government through which the **Governor** provides leadership to state government. DAS is responsible for, among other things, central printing plants, central accounting, hiring, labor relations, and the motor pool. It includes the offices of **Economic Analysis** and **Health Plan Administrator**, and the divisions of Controller, Budget and Management, Facilities, Human Resource Services, Information Resource Management, Internal Support, Risk Management, and Transportation, Purchasing and Print Services, plus a number of boards and commissions. 155 Cottage St. NE, Salem 97310-0310. 503-378-3104. Governing Oregon; Oregon Blue Book.

Admission Act. An act, officially entitled "The Act of Congress Admitting State of Oregon into The Union," passed by Congress on February 14, 1859. It describes the state's **boundaries**, regulates navigable waters, prescribes representation in Congress, offers that **section**s 16 and 36 in every township be granted to the state for schools, that 72 sections of land be set aside for support of a state university, that 10 sections be set aside for public buildings, that up to 12 **salt springs**, each with 6 sections of land, become state property, that 5% of the net proceeds of Congressional sale of lands in Oregon go to the state, that Oregon never tax U.S. owned lands within Oregon, and that the rest of the **Oregon Territory** become the Territory of Washington. The full text is in the Oregon Blue

Book. See also **Land grants**.

Adoption. In 1994, 470 children were adopted through the State Office for Services to **Children and Families**. 250 children were in **foster care** awaiting adoption, and it was expected that another 700 in foster care would be freed for adoption. Information on adoption 800-331-0503. Oregon Adoptive Rights Association, PO Box 882, Portland 97207. See also **Celebration Family**; **Foster care**; **Holt International Children's Services**.

Adrian. An agricultural community in far eastern Oregon on the **Snake River** in **Malheur County** 25 miles south of **Ontario**. Adrian was platted along the Oregon Short Line Railroad in 1893 by Reuben McCreary, who named it for his birthplace in Illinois. It was incorporated in 1972. The local Future Farmers of America have developed a business selling signs to farmers nationwide. Population 1980 162; 1995 130. Elevation 2,220'. PO Box 226, 97901. 541-724-5014. Oregon Geographic Names.

Adult and Family Services Division (AFS). A division of the Department of **Human Resources** that provides temporary cash, food stamps, and child care benefits for low-income families. It operates the "**JOBS** for Oregon's Future" program, and helps families obtain **child support** payments. The office has 51 field offices that served some 22,000 single- and two-parent families in 1997, down from 55,000 families four years before. About half of the money for welfare benefits and all of the money for food stamp coupons comes from the federal government. AFS has been a national leader in welfare reform. In 1997 about 15% of the division's employees were former aid recipients. 500 Summer St. NE, Salem 97310-1013. 503-945-5601. Oregon Blue Book. See also **JOBS**; **Oregon Health Plan**; **Oregon Option**; **Welfare**.

Adult foster-care homes. Homes licensed by the state to provide care for up to five adults who are unable to care for themselves. They serve as an alternative to nursing homes. As of June 1997 over 2,080 had been licensed by the Oregon Department of **Human Resources** (800-232-3020), up from the 86 licensed the first year in 1986. Concerns raised in 1994 about the level of care and abuse in a few of the homes resulted in increased monitoring. Over half of the homes in **Multnomah County** are operated by **Romanians**. See also **Long term care ombudsman**.

Advertising. A **Portland** ad agency, Wieden & Kennedy, has won multiple awards for creative excellence, including being cited twice by Adweek as its agency of the year. In 1991 a team of three **Portland State University** students won the top Citibank/Clio College Advertising Award. Will Vinton's Claymation® characters, the California Raisins™, were recognized by the Smithsonian for their significant role in pop culture. Facts of Life; Oregonian 4/20/96:B1.

Advertising Museum. See **American Advertising Museum**.

Aeronautics Section. A state agency founded in 1921, the first government aviation agency in the U.S. Now part of the Oregon Department of **Transportation**, it is responsible for planning Oregon's aviation system, owning and operating 32 Oregon **airports**, licensing or registering 400 other airports and landing areas, registering all **pilots** and civilian **aircraft** based in Oregon, and coordinating rescue missions. It is funded primarily by user fees; no state general fund revenue is used. 3040 25th St. SE, Salem 97310. 503-378-4880. Oregon Blue Book.

Affirmative Action Office. A state office responsible for directing the affirmative action programs in all state agencies. It reports to the **governor**. 155 Cottage St. NE, Salem 97310. 503-373-1224. Oregon Blue Book. See also **Civil Rights Division**.

Afro-Americans in Oregon. See **Blacks in Oregon**.

Agates. Translucent stones that form as chemically precipitated microcrystalline quartz in holes in rocks, and are released as the rock weathers. They are deposited in river gravels and are found in many areas of the state and along ocean **beaches**, especially in the late winter after storms have moved the beach sand out to sea, leaving the agate-bearing gravels exposed. Gem Trails of Oregon. See also **Gemstones; Thundereggs**.

Agency Lake. See **Upper Klamath Lake**.

Agency Plains. An extensive irrigated flat land in central Oregon between **Madras** and the **Deschutes River** at an elevation of 2,400 feet. **Highway 26** crosses the area northwest of Madras. It was named for the nearby **Warm Springs Indian Reservation** agency; Little Agency Plains lies just to the south of it, beyond Willow Creek.

Aging. See **Senior and Disabled Services Division**.

Agricultural commodity commissions. Oregon's 29 commodity commissions conduct promotional, educational, production and market-research projects. The director of the Department of **Agriculture** appoints the members of some of the commissions, while producers of six commodities elect their commissioners. Each commission is funded by an assessment on its products, and each hires its own employees. The commissions include those for **alfalfa seed**, bartlett **pears**, beef **cattle, blueberries**, clover, **dairy** products, dungeness **crab**, fine fescue, fryers, grains, **hazelnuts**, highland bentgrass, **hops, mint**, orchard**grass seed**, pota-**toes**, processed prunes and plum growers, processed vegetables, **raspberries** and **blackberries**, ryegrass, **salmon, sea urchins, sheep, strawberries**, sweet **cherries**, tall fescue, trawl fisheries, western Oregon **onions**, and **wheat**. There is also a **wine** advisory board. Oregon Blue Book.

Agricultural Experiment Station. Oregon's principal agricultural research agency, established in 1888 in accordance with the Hatch Act of 1887. It conducts research at **Oregon State University** and at ten branch stations located in the major crop and climate areas of the state, including the Coastal Oregon Marine Experiment Station **Seafood Laboratory**. 138 Strand Agriculture Hall, Oregon State University, Corvallis 97331. 541-737-4251.

Agricultural exports. About 80% of Oregon's agricultural production leaves the state, half of it exported to other countries. In 1994, **wheat** and wheat products were Oregon's leading agricultural export (26%), followed by vegetables (including **potatoes**) and preparations (25%), **seeds**, and fruits and preparations. In 1993 agricultural and fish exports from Oregon ports totaled $2.4 billion, half of it produced in Oregon. Oregon Agriculture.

Agricultural Marketing Center. A two-building, public/private project being built in the **River District** in **Portland**. The two are the Oregon Agricultural Center which provides quarters for agriculture-related companies and agencies, and the Food Innovation Center where researchers will develop new products using Northwest farm commodities and will provide assistance to the food industry with marketing, packaging, and distribution. **Oregon State University**, Washington State University, and the University of Idaho all participate. The Center is near Albers Mill, where the Wheat Marketing Center is housed. Oregonian11/15/96:E9.

Agricultural societies. See **State Agricultural Society**.

Agricultural Stabilization and Conservation Service. See **Farm Service Agency**.

Agriculture. Oregon's diversified agriculture produces some 230 commodities with a total 1995 production value of $3.1 billion from 3 million acres. A fourth of the state's economy is related to agriculture. Agricultural receipts for the top 10 counties in Oregon for 1995 (in millions) were **Marion** $404, **Umatilla** $256, **Clackamas** $217, **Linn** $189, **Washington** $184, **Malheur** $167, **Yamhill** $150, **Lane** $130, **Klamath** $123, and **Morrow** $122. Over 200 agricultural commodities are produced in Oregon, more than in any other state, and Oregon leads the nation in production of a variety of specialty crops, including **grass seed**, **Christmas trees**, **hazelnuts**, cane **berries**, peppermint, potted florist **azaleas**, English holly, bearded **iris**, and flowering trees. The state is a major producer of **pears**, sweet **cherries**, **hops**, and **onions**, as well as **peas**, **beans**, and **corn** for processing. In 1995 greenhouse and nursery products were Oregon's top commodity with $352 million in sales, followed by **cattle**, $340 million. **Grains**, **seed crops**, field **crops**, **vegetable crops**, and **dairy** products each brought in over $200 million. About 80% of Oregon's production is marketed outside the state, and about half of that is exported overseas. **Wheat** is the leading agricultural export. 1995 Oregon; Agriculture; Oregon Agriculture. See also **Conservation Reserve Program**; **Farmers**; **Farms**; **Food processing**; **Gleaning**; **Livestock**; **National Germplasm Repository**; **Pesticides**; **Poultry**.

Agriculture history. See **Cattle history**; **Farming history**; **Fruit crops history**; **Horses**; **Nursery history**; **Ranches**.

Agriculture, Oregon Department of. The Oregon department responsible for regulating food production and processing, ensuring food safety, developing product markets, and protecting the natural-resource base for future generations. The director is appointed by the **governor**. The department includes **agricultural commodity commissions** plus a number of other commissions, committees, and advisory groups, and eight divisions: Agricultural Development and Marketing; Animal Health and Identification; Commodity Inspection; Food Safety; Laboratory Services; Measurement Standards; Natural Resources; and Plant Division. 635 Capitol Street NE, Salem 97310-0110. 503-986-4552. Oregon Blue Book.

Agriculture Visitors Center. See **Norpac**.

AIDS. A **disease**, caused by the HIV virus, that first appeared about 1980. It is spread by having sex with or using injection drugs with HIV-infected individuals. In 1997, though there was no known cure, expensive treatments had effectively stopped or reversed some cases. As of January 1997, 3,877 persons in Oregon had been diagnosed with AIDS since the epidemic began and of those, 2,355 had died. In 1996, 315 new cases were reported, down 26% from 1995. Oregon AIDS Hotline 800-777-2437. Oregonian 11/30/95:B9.

Air disasters. See **Plane crashes**.

Air inversion. See **Inversion**.

Air permits. Approximately 1,400 industrial and commercial businesses in Oregon have permits from the Department of **Environmental Quality** governing their release of air pollutants. A special permit program monitors major industrial sources of **air pollution** (those with the potential to emit 100 tons of any regulated air pollutant) and of hazardous air pollution (10 tons of any hazardous pollutant or 25 tons of any combination of hazardous air pollutants).

Air pollution. Emissions of air pollutants in Oregon in 1996 totaled 207,000 tons of fine **particulates** (PM_{10}), 64,000 tons of **sulfur dioxide** (SO_2), 1,423,000 tons of **nitrogen dioxide** (NO_2), 1,495,000 tons of **carbon monoxide** (CO), and 219,000 tons of volatile organic compounds (VOC). 15% came from industry, 41% from cars and trucks, 23% from nonroad engines (lawn and garden, boats, construction), and 21% came from household and other produces (hairsprays, air fresheners, paints and solvents, dry cleaners, gas stations, auto body shops). The Natural Resources Defense Council reports that 307 deaths in the **Portland** area are attributable to air pollution, 89 in the **Eugene** area, and 96 in the **Medford** area. In 1951 Oregon became the first state to adopt statewide air pollution control laws. Air quality in the Medford area improved after controls were placed on open burning and **wood stoves**, oxygenated **gasoline** was required in the winter, and **vehicle inspection** was instituted. The federal government is instituting tougher standards for extremely small particles, under 2.5 microns, most common in smoke and exhaust. Oregon Air Quality; Oregon Environmental Atlas; Oregonian 11/26/96:A8. See also **Acid rain**; **Air permits**; **Air quality**; **Environmental Quality, Department**; **Field burning**; **Greenhouse gases**; **Inversion**; **Ozone**; **Pollution**; **Radon**; **Slash burning**; **Toxic pollutants**; **Vehicle inspection**; **Visibility**.

Air pollution index (API). Figures reported twice a day by the Oregon Department of **Environmental Quality** for **Portland**, **Eugene**, **Medford**, and **Bend**. The five measured pollutants are fine **particulates**, **carbon monoxide**, **ozone**, **sulfur dioxide**, and **nitrogen dioxide**. The data for each is reduced to an index value using a procedure established by the U.S. Environmental Protection Agency. For each area the largest index value and the pollutant responsible for that reading are reported as the API. The API descriptors (and range) are Good (0-50), Moderate (51-100), Unhealthful (101-300), Hazardous (301-500), and Very Hazardous (500+). An Air Pollution Alert may be signaled at 200, a Warning at 300, and an Emergency at 400. Oregon Air Quality.

Air quality. Oregon's air normally meets clean air standards for nitrogen oxides and **sulfur dioxide**, but there have been problems meeting **ozone**, **carbon monoxide**, and **particulate** standards, especially in **Portland, Eugene, Medford, Salem**, and **Grants Pass**. Since **vehicle inspection** programs began in the Portland and Medford metropolitan areas, carbon monoxide emissions have been reduced 30% per vehicle mile. Oregon Environmental Atlas.

Aircraft. In 1995, the Oregon **Aeronautics Section** listed over 4,000 registered aircraft. The first aircraft in Oregon was seen on March 11, 1889, when **Portland** inventor Elija Morton unveiled his "alleged flying machine." During the 1906 **Lewis and Clark Exposition**, a dirigible flew over Portland. In both **World**

Wars, massive efforts enabled Oregon to supply material for constructing planes, **spruce** during **World War I**, and **aluminum** during **World War II**. Oregonian 11/9/96:C2; Organic Machine; This Day in Oregon. See also **Aviation history**; **Pilots**; **Spruce Goose**.

Airlines. The top carriers at **Portland International Airport** in 1995 were Alaska, United, Delta, Southwest, and Horizon. Alaska carried 2.3 million passengers during the year, or 22% of the airport's total. Oregonian 1/26/96:D1.

Airplanes. See **Aircraft**; **Aviation**; **Plane crashes**.

Airports. In 1997 there were 99 commercial and general aviation airports in Oregon with revenues of $11.5 billion a year. Eight had regularly scheduled passenger service: **Astoria** and **North Bend** on the Coast, **Portland** and **Eugene** in the Willamette Valley, **Medford** and **Klamath Falls** in southern Oregon, **Redmond** in central Oregon, and **Pendleton** in northeast Oregon. The state owns and operates 32 airports, and licenses more than 400 other airports and landing areas. The **Port of Portland** opened **Swan Island** Airport in 1927, replaced in 1940 by the Portland Airport (now the **Portland International Airport**). The Port also owns three other airports. Tongue Point Naval Air Station was dedicated in 1939. Over 100 airports are pictured from the air and described in Oregon Airport Directory. Oregonian 6/30/97:B4. See also **Aeronautics Section**.

Alaskan. A side-wheel steamer that foundered and sank off **Cape Blanco** on May 13, 1889 while en route to San Francisco for repairs. Thirty-one of the 47 men aboard died. Shipwrecks of the Pacific Coast.

Albacore. See **Tuna**.

Albany (ALL bah nee). A **Willamette Valley** city 73 miles south of **Portland** lying between **Interstate 5** and the **Willamette River**, named by the founding Montieth brothers in 1848 for their former home town in New York state. The city, incorporated in 1864, is the county seat of **Linn County.** It was at one time a busy river port and later a railroad node. Three of its historic areas are on the National Register of Historic Places; self-guided tour information is available. Other attractions include the 4th of July **Albany World Championship Timber Carnival**, October Apple Festival and Fall Fruit Show, November 11th **Veteran's Day** parade, Albany Civic Theater, and free summer River Rhythms concerts. Oregon Metallurgical, with 650 workers in 1997, is the largest employer. Several major industries are located in neighboring **Millersburg**. Albany, Australia, is its sister city. Population 1980 26,511; 1995 36,205. Elevation 210'. PO Box 490, 97321. 541-917-7500. Visitors Association 800-526-2256. Oregon Geographic Names.

Albany College. A one-time college in **Albany** that began as the Albany Academy in 1858. In 1867, under the auspices of the **Presbyterian Church**, it became Albany College. It operated in and near Albany until 1937, when it was moved to **Portland** and renamed **Lewis and Clark College**. Dictionary of Oregon History.

Albany World Championship Timber Carnival. An annual **Albany** 4th of July weekend festival. Loggers compete in a series of events that test strength, skill, and endurance. The winner of the most events is awarded the All Around Logger title; Melvin Lentz of **Creswell** held the title for 16 years, 1981-1996, until he was injured in a logging accident in 1997. The festival began in 1941 but skipped the **World War II** years to resume in 1946. PO Box 1540, Albany 97321. 541-928-2391.

Albatross. An American sailing ship that the three Winship brothers sailed up the **Columbia River** in early June, 1810. They and their 22-man crew attempted to establish a settlement and **trading post** near the present site of **Rainier** but were thwarted by heavy rain and flooding. After 8 days they reloaded the ship and left. It was the first attempt to establish a settlement in Oregon. Dictionary of Oregon History.

Albina. An area in north and northeast **Portland** where 68,000 people live in 13 neighborhoods. Albina, named for the wife of developer William Page, was a separate, incorporated city from 1887 until it and East Portland consolidated with Portland in 1891. The area has been home to many of Portland's immigrants and, following **World War II**, to much of its black community. Real estate values have risen dramatically during the 1990s. Oregonian 9/8/96:A1,16-19.

Alcohol. Sales of distilled alcoholic beverages in Oregon in fiscal year 1994/95 averaged $56.74 per capita, but ranged from a low of $30 in **Morrow County** to a high of over $111 dollars per capita in **Lincoln** and **Clatsop** counties. Oregon: A Statistical Overview. See also **Liquor Control Commission; Prohibition; Temperance**.

Alcohol and Drug Abuse Programs, Office of. A state agency in the Department of **Human Resources** which, through the Governor's Council on Alcohol and Drug Abuse Programs, assesses the impact of alcohol and drug abuse in Oregon, and the prevention, intervention, and treatment programs of 16 state agencies. 500 Summer St. NE, Salem 97310-1016. 503-945-5763. Oregon Blue Book. See also **Police, Oregon State**.

Alcohol and drug treatment. A study released in 1996 of the cost benefits of alcohol and drug treatment found that in the three years following treatment those who had completed treatment had 70% fewer incarcerations than those who left treatment early, they used 1/3 the amount of foods stamps, and had substantially lower medical expenses and child welfare problems. For every dollar spent on completed alcohol or drug treatment, taxpayers saved $5.60 on reduced welfare, food stamps, Medicaid, crime, courts and imprisonment. Oregonian 3/14/96:E5.

Alcohol use. Over 10% of Oregon sixth-graders and nearly 30% of eighth-graders reported alcohol use in the previous month in a 1994 survey. In 1995, 30% of Oregon eighth graders said they had drunk alcohol, up from 23% in 1990, while in 1996 70% of 11th-graders reported using alcohol during the year. A survey of adults found that an estimated 253,000 residents (6.3% of the state's adults) abuse or are dependent on alcohol or drugs, and 44% of them admit to engaging in risky behavior while under the influence of intoxicants. Oregonian 1/13/95:A1, 3/14/96:E5, 10/22/96:B1, 1/29/97:E1 See also **Liquor Control Commission; Prohibition; Temperance**.

Alder. Shrubs or small deciduous **trees** that have small woody cones called strobiles. Four species of alder grow in Oregon, but the most common is red alder, *Alnus rubra*, which grows in western Oregon, especially along **Coast Range** streams. It has splotchy white bark, serrated leaves that drop in the fall while still green, and 1" brown strobiles. Alder roots fix nitrogen from the air, adding fertility to the soil. The wood is used for furniture, firewood, and pulp. Trees to Know.

Aldrich Mountains. A 30-mile-long range of mountains south of Highway 26 between Dayville and **John Day**. Fields Peak, 7,360', is the highest point; Aldrich Mountain is 6,988'. Geologically, the mountains are made up of the Izee terrane, composed of layers of shallow ocean deposits that are 12 miles thick. These **fossil**-rich deposits were laid down beginning nearly 250 million years ago, during the **Triassic** and **Jurassic**. They were then folded, refolded, and intruded by **granitic** rocks. Much of the area lies within the **Malheur National Forest**. Elmer Aldrich, son of rancher Henry Aldrich, was killed during the **Bannock War** in 1878. Geology of Oregon; Oregon Geographic Names. See also **Blue Mountains**; **Cedar Grove Botanical Area**.

Alfalfa seed. In 1995 Oregon growers produced 6.3 million pounds of alfalfa seed, worth $7.3 million, on 10,220 acres. The crop is also an important source of honey. Oregon Agriculture. See also **Hay**.

Algae. Non-vascular plants with chlorophyll; most are aquatic. Among the many kinds found in Oregon are **seaweeds**, **mare's eggs**, and a blue-green alga, *Aphanizomenom flos-aquae*, that has been harvested from **Upper Klamath Lake** since 1982 in what has become a multimillion-dollar business. It is freeze-dried, powdered, and sold through distributors as a health supplement by Cell Tech, a company that uses multilevel marketing, and by other companies. Oregonian 8/26/95:E1.

Alkali Lake. See **Bacteria**.

Allow Me. A life-size statue of a courteous man with an umbrella located in **Portland**'s **Pioneer Courthouse Square**. The 1984 bronze by J. Seward Johnson is sometimes known as Mr. Portland. Portland Guidebook.

Aloha. An unincorporated Portland-area suburban community in **Washington County** just west of **Beaverton** on Highway 8. The post office was established in 1912. It was named Aloah for a small resort on Wisconsin's Lake Winnebago. The post office department transposed the last two letters so the name looks Hawaiian. However, it is pronounced as if spelled Aloah. Oregon Geographic Names.

Aloha apartment fire. A fire on June 28, 1996, at Oakwood Park Apartments in **Aloha** that killed 8 Mexican immigrants, 3 adults and 5 children. The fire was set by a an 11-year-old boy.

Alpenfest. A Swiss-style festival held in late September at **Wallowa Lake**. 541-432-4704.

Alsea Bay Bridge Interpretive Center. See **Waldport**.

Alsea River. A 49-mile long river that flows from the central **Coast Range** to the ocean at **Waldport**. It drains 474 square miles with an average annual flow of 1,055,000 acre feet, or 4.9 acre feet/acre, as measured at river mile 21. The name derives from that of the band of Yakonan Indians who lived at its mouth. Oregon Geographic Names.

Alternative architecture. A number Oregonians are promoting alternative building materials and techniques, including cob (earth) and **straw-bale houses** and clay ovens. Cob Cottage Company, PO Box 123, Cottage Grove 97424. 541-

942-2005.

Altitude. See **Elevation**.

Aluminum. In 1997 two aluminum smelters were located in Oregon, Reynolds Metals Company at **Troutdale** and Northwest Aluminum Company near **The Dalles**. When operating, they process imported ore, primarily from Australia. They and smelters in Washington state were built by the Defense Plant Corporation in the 1940s during **World War II** to supply aluminum for airplanes, using **hydroelectric power** from the recently-completed **Bonneville Dam**. In 1998 another company, Columbia Ventures, announced plans to build a smelter near **Boardman**. Bauxite, the ore from which aluminum is extracted, is found in scattered locations in the **Coast Range** of northern Oregon and southern Washington. In some places white lumps of almost pure aluminum hydroxide are found, some as large as potatoes. However, despite the high aluminum content, Oregon's bauxite is not commercially usable at this time because the red iron oxide it contains makes it too costly to refine. Mineral Industry of Oregon; Oregonian 3/3/98:C1; Organic Machine. See also **Direct service industries; Energy shortage**.

Alvord Basin. A stark area east of **Steens Mountain** in **Harney County** with a rainfall averaging 5 inches a year, the lowest in Oregon. It includes the vast Alvord Desert, one of the largest **playa**s in the world, used by land sailors in the summer, and site of a 1976 land-speed world record attempt. The basin lies at 4,025 feet, and is surrounded by mountain ranges, most notably the jagged Steens Mountain scarp which towers a mile above it. The historic Alvord Ranch is located in the basin, as are alkaline Alvord and **Borax Lake**s and **Mickey Hot Springs**. A 22-megawatt **geothermal** energy plant has been proposed south of Borax Lake. Brigadier-General Benjamin Alvord was in command of the Department of Oregon 1861-1865. Oregon's Great Basin Country. See also **Mud cracks**.

Amazon. A temporary **University of Oregon** married student housing project built in 1947 to provide housing for returning **World War II** veterans and their families. The 240-unit project was designed by noted architect Pietro Belluschi. Efforts in 1994-95 to raze the dilapidated buildings and replace them with new housing were opposed by a coalition of historic preservationists and low-income housing advocates.

American Advertising Museum. A museum in **Portland** that is the nation's first devoted to the history of **advertising**. Its exhibits range from Burma Shave signs through graphics to radio and TV commercials. 50 SW Second Avenue. 503-226-0000. Portland Guidebook.

American College Testing. See **ACT**.

American Society for Encouraging the Settlement of the Oregon Territory. An organization formed in 1829 by Hall Jackson Kelley of Boston, "the Prophet of Oregon", to spread his conviction that Americans should be settling in the **Willamette Valley**. Kelley's efforts provided information and vision for the first settlers, though he, himself, made only a brief, unsatisfactory trip to Oregon. Empire of the Columbia.

AmeriCorps. A federal program established in 1992 though which high school graduates work in public works and social service jobs in exchange for higher education vouchers and a small living stipend. Members in Oregon have, among other things, tutored children, helped restore watersheds, and built trails.

Amity. A small **Willamette Valley** agricultural city in **Yamhill County**, six miles south of **McMinnville** on **Highway 99W**. The area was settled early and Amity was the name given in 1849 to the first school after the amicable resolution of a dispute about where it would be located. The city was incorporated in 1880. For 40 years the city has held a pancake breakfast on the 4th Sunday in July which several thousand attend, and it also hosts a daffodil festival in March. Area attractions include Amity Vineyards and the Brigittine **Monastery of Our Lady of Consolation**. Population 1980 1,092; 1995 1,190. Elevation 161'. PO Box 159, 97101. 503-835-3711. Old Yamhill.

Amphibians. Cold-blooded **animals** that have gilled aquatic larvae and air-breathing adults. Oregon's amphibians include 15 species of **salamanders**, 8 of **frogs**, and 2 species of **toads**. Field Guide to Western Reptiles and Amphibians.

Amtrak. Federally sponsored passenger rail service that runs on lines owned by **railroad** freight companies. Oregon is served daily by the Empire Builder between **Portland** and **Chicago**, by the Coast Starlight between Seattle and Los Angeles, the Cascadia between **Eugene** and Seattle, and the Mount Adams between Portland and Seattle. Amtrak provides thruway motor coach connections from Portland to **Ashland, Bend**, and **Boise**, and from **Albany** through **Corvallis** to **Newport**. Oregon officials estimate that Amtrak saved more than 43 million miles of driving, mostly along **Interstate 5**. 800-USA-RAIL (800-872-7245).

Amusement parks. **Portland** once had four amusement parks: **Oaks Amusement Park, Council Crest, Jantzen Beach**, and Lotus Isle. Only Oaks is still operating. Jantzen Beach (on **Hayden Island**) was dismantled in 1970 and turned into a shopping center. Thrillville, south of **Salem**, operates next door to the **Enchanted Forest**. See also **Carousels; Ferris wheels; Roller coasters**.

Anadromous fish. Fish that hatch in fresh water, migrate to the ocean for part of their lives, and then return to fresh water to spawn. Oregon's anadromous fish runs include **salmon, steelhead** (sea-run rainbow **trout**) as well as a few sea-run cutthroat trout, **shad, smelt**, and **lamprey**. White **sturgeon** may spend time in the ocean but it is apparently not necessary to its spawning cycle. There are no migratory fish in central and southeast Oregon. Oregon's Migratory Fish.

Anarchists. See **Firebrand**.

Ancient people. See **Indians, prehistoric**.

Andesite. A common volcanic rock intermediate in silica content between the fluid **basalt** and the pasty **rhyolite**. Andesite **volcanoes** are typically high and steep; **Mount Hood** is an example. Andesite sometimes forms shrinkage columns as it cools.

Andre Berger Awards. Annual awards of $1,000 given to writers of fiction, nonfiction, and poetry. The awards were established in 1994 by Andre Berger, a **Lake Oswego** poet, writer, and retired psychologist. Northwest Writers, Inc., organizes the judging. PO Box 3437, Portland 97208.

Anglerfish. An ocean fish, *Cryptotsaras couesi*, that normally lives at depths of 6,000 feet. However, in 1989 a shrimp fisherman off **Reedsport** caught an anglerfish in his nets at 636 feet; it is now in the **Oregon State University** collection. As is characteristic of the species, the 12-inch female had a 2-inch male fused to her head. The angler fish, also called the warted she-devil, feeds on small fish that are attracted to worm-like appendages dangling from a long filament that arches over her head. Great Northwest Nature Factbook.

Anian Strait. See **Northwest Passage**.

Animal Damage Control Program. See **Wildlife Services**.

Animal Forensics Laboratory. See **Forensics Laboratory**.

Animal rights. Animal rights concerns in Oregon have focused on the case of Vicki Kittles, convicted of animal abuse in **Astoria** in 1994. As a result, the 1995 **legislature** changed the malicious killing of animals from a **misdemeanor** to a **felony**. An on-line magazine concerned with animal-rights issues, The Ark, is published in **Portland** by Paige Powell. Oregonian 5/7/95:E1.

Animals, domestic. See **Cats**; **Dogs**; **Livestock**; **Veterinary Medical Examining Board**.

Animals, invertebrate. See **Butterflies**; **Crawfish**; **Crickets**; **Fleas**; **Grasshoppers**; **Gypsy moth**; **Insects**; **Mosquitoes**; **Poisonous animals**; **Sea creatures**; **Slugs**; **Snails**; **Spiders**; **Spruce budworm**; **Zebra mussel**.

Animals, vertebrate. 68 species of **fish** are found in Oregon, 29 species of **amphibians**, 29 species of **reptiles**, 261 species of breeding **birds**, and 140 species of **mammals**. Of the total, 37 species are listed as **endangered** and 116 as sensitive. See also **Bigfoot**; **Exotic animals**; **Fishing**; **Forensics Laboratory**; **Hunting**; **Poisonous animals**; **Protected animals**; **Wild horses**.

Animators. Matt Groening, creator of an animated TV cartoon series, "The Simpsons," grew up in **Portland**, graduating from Lincoln High School in 1972. Chris Bailey, creator of the Mickey Mouse animated short, "Runaway Brain" (nominated for an Academy Award in 1996), also grew up in Portland. "Pinto" Colvig from **Jacksonville**, noted as a **clown**, was also an early animator. See also **Cartoonists**.

Antelope. An isolated ranching community on the high desert of central Oregon 30 miles northeast of **Madras** in **Wasco County**. Originally just a stage stop on **The Dalles** to **Canyon City** route, by 1887 a resident wrote, "There is enough of a town so you can see it with the naked eye." It was incorporated in 1901 and named for the many **pronghorn antelope** once found in the area. **Pulitzer Prize** winning author H. L. Davis grew up in Antelope where his father was the high school principal. In the 1980's the followers of Bhagwan Shree Rajneesh incorporated the town of **Rajneeshpuram** on the **Big Muddy** Ranch, 20 miles to the east. On September 18, 1984, some of his followers who were living in Antelope outvoted the other residents of the town to change the name of Antelope to Rajneesh. After the Rajneeshi community fell apart in 1985, residents voted to change the name back to Antelope. Population 1980 39; 1995 65. Elevation 2,631'. PO Box 105, 97001. 541-489-3239. Antelope; East of the Cascades.

Antelope (animal). See **Pronghorn antelope**.

Anthony Lake. A small, 22-acre mountain lake 20 miles west of **North Powder**, one of several lakes in the Anthony Lakes Recreation Area in the **Elkhorn Mountains** of northeast Oregon. The rugged alpine area is noted for late summer wildflower displays, including Indian paintbrush, Jacob's ladder, monkey flowers, and mountain arnica. The lake and creek are named for William "Doc" Anthony, a circuit-riding doctor and rancher who settled there in 1864. Atlas of Oregon Lakes; Oregon Geographic Names; Oregonian 4/5/95:E2.

Anthony Lakes Ski Area. A ski area noted for its powder snow, located between **La Grande** and **Baker City**, 19 miles west of **Interstate 84** at **North Powder**. The area, with a 900-foot vertical drop from a top elevation of 8,000 feet, is served by a chair lift and also has a 13K Nordic track. PO Box 1046, Union 97883. 541-562-1039. Snow conditions 541-856-3277. Oregonian11/16/97:T7.

Anthropology. See **Archeology**; **University of Oregon Museum of Natural History**.

Anti-Catholic sentiment. Catholic-Protestant contention in Oregon began in 1841 with strife between missionaries, and was exacerbated by inflammatory publications following the **Whitman massacre**. It became a political issue during the 1850's with the appearance of the **Know Nothing party**, during the 1890's with the activities of the American Protective Association, during the 1910's with the Guardians of Liberty and the Federation of Patriotic Societies, and was fanned again by the **Ku Klux Klan** during the 1920's. William H. Gray's inaccurate and virulently anti-Catholic History of Oregon was published in 1870. "Bigot Disclosed." See also **Catholic Church**; **Schools, private**.

Anti-Chinese sentiment. In the state **Constitution** adopted by Oregonians in 1859 **Chinese** were denied the right to own real property or to work mining claims; the provision was repealed by Oregon voters in 1946. In the 1870s and '80s, anti-Chinese sentiment, fanned by a **Presbyterian** minister and a U.S. **Senator**, grew until it erupted in violence on February 28, 1886, when masked men drove 180 Chinese woodcutters from the Albina area in **Portland**. Despite law and order efforts, assaults and dynamitings continued until October. Riots also occurred in **Oregon City** and **Salem** with parades and masked men who drove the Chinese from their jobs. "Bigot Disclosed." Dictionary of Oregon History. See also **Chinese massacre**; **Intermarriage**; **Poll tax**; **Segregation**.

Anti-Japanese sentiment. In 1922 the U.S. Supreme Court ruled that Japanese immigrants were not eligible for citizenship, and in Oregon exclusionary pressures by the **Ku Klux Klan**, the American Legion, and Governor Walter Pierce, led to the passage of the 1923 Oregon Alien Land Law which limited their ability to own land. The act was in effect until nullified by the Oregon Supreme Court in 1949. On July 12, 1925, a mob of 75 persons in **Toledo** forcibly evicted 35 Japanese sawmill employees and their families from the town. During **World War II**, before Japanese-Americans were deported to **relocation centers**, a drunken mob in **Tillamook** attacked a group of Japanese American oystermen. "Anti-Japanese Legislation." See also **Segregation**.

Antique Auto Portland Swap Meet. A **Portland** swap meet for old cars and parts, begun in 1965, which, with 6,000 stalls and 60,000 attendees, is the largest on the West Coast. Six local car clubs sponsor the meet, held on an April weekend at the **Exposition Center** and **Portland International Raceway**. 503-684-3391. Oregonian 4/7/95:C1.

Antique Powerland Museum. A display of steam-powered tractors and other vintage farm equipment, located north of **Salem**, 1/4 mile west of Interstate 5, Brooks exit 263. The Pacific Northwest Truck Museum (503-678-5108) and

Oregon Electric Railway Society are also located on the grounds. 3995 Brooklake Road, Brooks 97303. 503-393-2424. See also **Great Oregon Steamup**.

Appaloosa. A breed of spotted horses developed by the **Nez Perce** Indians from the Spanish horses brought to the southwest by Coronado around 1540. They were outstanding buffalo and war horses and remain popular today as show and cattle horses. Oregon Desert.

Appeals Court. See **Court of Appeals**.

Applegate Lake. A flood-control reservoir on the Applegate River in southern Oregon, built by the **Army Corps of Engineers** as part of the **Rogue Basin Project**. Water releases in the summer help cool the Applegate and Rogue Rivers, thus providing better fish habitat. The dam, completed in 1980, is 242 feet high, and at maximum pool, the lake covers 988 acres. The speed limit for boats is 10 mph. Migrating **salmon** and **steelhead** are collected just below the dam and taken to the hatchery at **Lost Creek Lake** for spawning; the juvenile fish are released in the Applegate River to maintain the runs. The **Forest Service** maintains campsites and an 18-mile hiking trail around the shoreline, but trail bikes and horses may use only designated side trails. USFS Star Ranger Station, 6941 Upper Applegate Road, Jacksonville 97530. 541-899-1812.

Applegate Partnership. An award-winning **forest resource organization** working to end land management gridlock in the half-million acre **Applegate River** watershed in southwest Oregon and to achieve a sustainable economy and ecology in the area. The group, organized in 1992, includes local residents, environmentalists, and timber industry members. Federal officials from the **Forest Service** and **Bureau of Land Management** have also been affiliated with it. Box 277, Applegate 97530. 541-846-6917.

Applegate River. A tributary of the **Rogue River** that rises in the **Siskiyou Mountains** near the California border and flows north to join the Rogue west of **Grants Pass**. It was named for Lindsay Applegate, one of three pioneering Applegate brothers, after he and a party of others prospected for gold along it in 1848 while on their way to the California **gold rush**. Oregon Geographic Names; Ruch.

Applegate Trail. A **wagon road**, also called the Scott-Applegate Trail or South Road, that left the **Oregon Trail** at Fort Hall (eastern Idaho), followed the California Cutoff (opened in 1844) down the Humboldt River in Nevada, left it to cross the deserts south of **Goose Lake**, entered Oregon near **Malin**, crossed the **Cascade Mountains** near **Highway 66**, then followed close to present **Interstate 5** west and north into the **Willamette Valley** to end in **Polk County**. Jesse and Lindsay Applegate had each lost a 10-year old son while rafting their wagons down the **Columbia River** on their 1843 trek to Oregon, and were among the most active promoters of an alternative route. The route was explored in 1846 by a party of 15 Oregon settlers known as the South Road Company, led by Captain Levi Scott and the Applegates. Some members of the party then guided the first wagons over the trail from Fort Hall that year. The route was grueling, especially over the mountains of southern Oregon (the first year only one wagon made it to the **Umpqua River** unbroken), and some of the users criticized the trail's promoters for years afterwards. In 1848 Oregon travelers to the California gold fields drove 46 wagons south over the Applegate Trail to Tule Lake and then helped Peter Lassen open a route southwest to the Sacramento Valley, making them the first wagons to travel between Oregon and California. In 1852 Modoc Indians killed a number of immigrants on the trail at Bloody Point, near Tule Lake, California. Wagon ruts can still be seen from Dole Road near **Myrtle Creek**, and at Tub Springs on Highway 66 east of **Ashland**. Interpretive centers are located at several sites. Applegate Trail; Dictionary of Oregon History; Plains Across. See also **Broadside**; **Mother of Oregon**; **Siskiyou Trail**; **Sunny Valley**.

Apples. In 1995 Oregon growers produced 4 million boxes of apples, worth $25.5 million, on 9,525 acres. The first apples in the Oregon country grew from seeds planted at **Fort Vancouver** in 1825. In **Oregon City** in 1840 another productive planting began by accident from some discarded apple cores. In 1847 Iowa nurseryman Henderson Luelling brought, with considerable hardship, rooted stock across the plains to **Milwaukie** where he established the first nursery. The first box of fruit sold in **Portland** brought a profit of $75. Apple orchards were planted in the **Hood River** valley in 1853 and in the **Medford** area in 1885. Commercial production boomed in both districts at the turn of the century, spurred by the development of **railroads**, refrigerator cars, and cold storage. In **Wasco County** in 1911 the **Dufur** Orchard Company planted 4,000 acres of apples, making it the world's largest single apple orchard. The trees were pulled out about 10 years later and the land was converted to a wheat ranch. Several communities, including **Molalla** and **Albany**, host apple festivals in the fall. Dictionary of Oregon History; Empire of the Columbia; 1995 Oregon; Oregon Oddities; Tracking down Oregon. See also **Fruit**.

Appraiser Certification and Licensure Board. A board that licenses and certifies real estate appraisers in Oregon. Its nine voting members are appointed by the governor. 200 Labor & Industries Building, Salem 97310. 503-373-1505. Oregon Blue Book.

Apprenticeship and Training Division. A division of Oregon's Bureau of **Labor and Industries** that administers the state's apprenticeship programs, veteran's on-the-job training, dislocated workers programs, and **Job Corps** training The state has over 420 apprenticeship programs serving 6,000 apprentices. A 10-member council sets policy. 800 NE Oregon St. #32, Portland 97232, 503-731-4072. Oregon Blue Book.

Appropriations. See **Budget**.

Aquariums. Oregon's major aquarium is the **Oregon Coast Aquarium** in **Newport**. The oldest (1927) privately-owned aquarium in the world is located in **Depoe Bay**; it features a performing seal.

Aquifer. A water-bearing layer of permeable rock, sand, or gravel. About half of Oregon is underlain with aquifers having moderate to large potential yields of **groundwater**. Aquifers are often interconnected, which increases the potential for contamination, and the risk of contamination is greatest from shallow sources, such as alluvial or basin-fill aquifers, which supply about 77% of Oregon's groundwater. Atlas of the Pacific Northwest; Water Resources.

Arbor Day. A day designated for planting and appreciating trees. It began in 1872 in Nebraska and was first observed in Oregon in 1889. The state legislature has since designated the first full week in April as Arbor Week, and the Oregon Department of **Forestry** publishes a guide for schools to use. Nationally, Arbor Day falls on the last Friday of April. See also **Tree City USA.**

Arboretums. See **Gardens; Hoyt Arboretum** (Portland); **Mount Pisgah Arboretum** (Eugene); **Peavy Arboretum** (Corvallis); **Rogue River.**

L'Arbre Seul. See **Lone Pine.**

Archeological Conservancy. An organization, headquartered in New Mexico, that had, as of 1998, acquired 145 sites in 25 states for preservation. One of its four Oregon sites is **Fort Rock Cave.** 5301 Central Ave. NE, Suite 1218, Albuquerque NM 87108. 503-266-1540.

Archeology. The scientific study of the material remains of past human life and activities. In Oregon archeologists have found artifacts dating back 11,500 years, while some carbon from **Fort Rock Cave** has been dated to 13,200 years ago. Four of the five cultural areas of Oregon represent the major cultural areas of the West: the Northwest Coast, Plateau, Great Basin, and California. The fifth major cultural area in Oregon, the Willamette Valley, had a hybrid Plateau/ California character. The people of all areas were hunter-gatherers; the only agriculture was an occasional tobacco patch. The Northwest Coast people lived close to the ocean and rivers in plank-house settlements; fishing and woodworking were important. Life for the Plateau people of north-central Oregon focused on the salmon runs; villages were of substantial pit houses. The people of the Great Basin area of eastern Oregon were highly mobile, living in lightly-built wickiups or in pit houses; they hunted rabbits and other game, gathered seeds and roots, and wove mats, baskets, nets, and sandals. The California culture of Oregon's southwestern mountains utilized salmon, game, and acorns; they lived in small clusters of streamside pit houses, and developed a local pottery. The Willamette Valley people used a variety of seasonal food sources; their spring and summer sites featured large earth ovens for roasting camas roots. Despite federal and state legal protection of cultural sites, archeological study has been much hindered by the destruction of prehistoric sites by construction, hobby collectors, and commercial pillage. The sites are non-renewable; once gone they are lost forever. The Oregon Archeological Society sponsors classes. 503-644-2144. Archaeology of Oregon. See also **Artifacts; Indians, prehistoric.**

Architects. In 1994 Oregon had 2,300 registered architects. The State Board of Architect Examiners prescribes qualifications, conducts examinations, and issues certificates of qualification. 750 Front Street NE, Suite 260, Salem 97310. 503-378-4270. Oregon Blue Book.

Architects, notable. Ellis F. Lawrence, founder of the School of Architecture and Allied Arts at the **University of Oregon**, designed over 50 homes in the Arts and Crafts Style in the early 1900s. Pietro Belluschi, whose designs include 12 Oregon churches, the **Portland Art Museum** (1936), and the **Equitable Building** in **Portland** (1948), became dean of the MIT School of Architecture in 1951. John Yeon, along with Belluschi, helped define the **Northwest Regional Style.** In **Portland** Skidmore, Owings and Merrill won awards for their **urban renewal** designs in the 1960s and 70s. In 1991 the American Institute of Architects gave their highest award for design to the Portland firm of Zimmer Gunsul Frasca Partnership for their work in reshaping the city, including the **Oregon Convention Center**, the **Justice Center**, and KOIN Center. "Architecture in Oregon, 1845-1895", Frozen Music; Oregon Style; Pietro Belluschi; Zimmer Gunsul Frasca. See also **Mount Angel Abbey**.

Architecture and city planning. See **1972 Downtown Plan**; **Oregon Experiment**; **Portland Center**; **Urban renewal**.

Archives. A division of state government, supervised by the **Secretary of State**, that is responsible for preserving the official records of Oregon state government. The Archives also includes records from the **provisional government, 1843-1849** and the **territorial government, 1849-1859**. Records of the **legislature** have been included since 1947. The Archives Division also codifies and publishes the **Oregon Administrative Rules**. Controversy swirled around the Cecil Edward's Archives Building when it was being built in 1992 because of the high quality of its fixtures and furnishings. 800 Summer Street NE, Salem 97310. 503-373-0701. Governing Oregon; Oregon Blue Book.

Arctic Museum. See **Paul Jensen Arctic Museum**.

Area. Oregon covers 97,060 square miles of land area (62,120,000 acres, larger than the United Kingdom) plus 889 square miles of inland water area for a total area of 97,949 square miles. See also **Size**.

Area Agencies on Aging. See **Senior and Disabled Services Division**.

Arlene Schnitzer Concert Hall. A 2,700-seat **Portland** concert hall at SW Broadway and Main, popularly called The Schnitz. It was remodeled and renamed from the opulent 1928 Paramount Theater in 1984, and is now home for the **Oregon Symphony**. It is part of the **Portland Center for the Performing Arts**. 503-796-9293, for event information recording. Emergencies (during events only), 503-274-6564.

Arlington. A town on the **Columbia River** in **Gilliam County**, 52 miles east of **The Dalles** on **Interstate 84**. Originally called Alkali, the name was changed to honor the home of Robert E. Lee, though it was later learned that Arlington was also the middle name of the man who proposed it. Arlington was incorporated in 1885. Much of the town was wiped out by a flood following a cloudburst on July 23, 1927. In the 1950s the town was relocated to higher ground to make way for the lake formed by the **John Day Dam**. Carl "Doc" Severinsen (1927-), popular trumpeter and band leader, is from Arlington, and an annual Big River Band Festival is held in June. Population 1980 521; 1995 460. Elevation 285'. PO Box 68, 97812. 541-454-2743. History of Gilliam County; Oregon Geographic Names.

Armstrong nugget. A large **gold nugget** found in 1913 in northeast Oregon near Susanville in **Grant County**. It weighs 80.4 troy ounces (2,500 grams, or 5.5 avoirdupois pounds), and is valued at over $30,000. It and other nuggets are on display in the **Baker City** branch of the U. S. Bank.

Army Corps of Engineers. A unit of the U.S. Army whose first work in Oregon was building **military roads**. In 1867, as the federal agency mandated by the government to have jurisdiction over navigable waterways, the Corps undertook civilian projects in Oregon, **dredging** the **Columbia** and **Willamette Rivers**, removing underwater snags, blasting rocks and constructing wing dams and dikes to improve channels, constructing **canals and locks**, building **jetties** and boat **har-**

bors, and, beginning in the 1930s, constructing multi-purpose **dams** on the Columbia, the Willamette and its tributaries, and the **Rogue River**. The Corps has recreational facilities on 19 of its lakes in Oregon, including four created by dams on the Columbia River. Military activities of the Corps of Engineers in the state have included building **Fort Stevens** and fortifications at the mouth of the Columbia, and, during **World War II**, constructing airports and military bases. U.S. Army Engineer District, PO Box 2946, Portland 97208-2946. 503-326-6021. Army Engineers.

Arnold Ice Cave. A **lava tube** cave southeast of **Bend** where ice was mined commercially in the nineteenth century. The ice in the cave is advancing, covering the stairs and making access hazardous without crampons and rope. The cave has had many names, the current one apparently the result of the association of two road signs that pointed down the same road. Central Oregon Caves. See also **Ice caves**; **Lava tubes**.

Arrowhead plant. See **Wapato**.

Arrowheads. See **Artifacts**; **Projectile points**.

Art. See **Art** entries; **Basketry**; **Calligraphy**; **Murals**; **One Percent for Art**; **Orlo**; **Petroglyphs and pictographs**; **Photographers**; **Portland Art Association**; **Portland Institute for Contemporary Art**; **Sculpture**; **Salem Art Fair and Festival**; **Washington Park Fences Project**.

Art and the Vineyard. A three-day **Eugene** arts festival held in early July at Alton Baker Park on the **Willamette River** as a benefit for the Maude Kerns Art Center. The festival, begun in 1984, includes art exhibits, arts marketplace, participatory art, children's activities, an entertainment stage with a variety of music, an international food court, and a wine tasting area. 541-345-1571.

Art Fair and Festival. See **Salem Art Fair and Festival**.

Art galleries. Shops that sell original art. Those in **Portland** that reported sales of over a million dollars in 1994 are The Real Mother Goose, Gango Gallery, Savage Fine Arts, and Laura Russo Gallery. Business Journal 5/19/95:11. See also **First Thursday**.

Art in the Pearl. A Labor Day weekend outdoor fair of juried art and crafts, focused on the work of local artists, first held in 1997 on **Portland's** North Park Blocks in the **Pearl District**. Oregonian 8/31/97:D7.

Art museums. See **Maryhill Museum of Art**; **Portland Art Museum**.

Art schools. See **Oregon School of Arts and Crafts**; **Pacific Northwest College of Art**; **Sitka Center**.

Artifacts. Products of human activity. Any artifact, Indian or pioneer, that is over 100 years old cannot be removed from federal lands, but a property owner can legally sell those found on his own land except that all trade in human remains and funerary and ceremonial materials is illegal. Both state and federal laws forbid disturbing graves, whether on public or private land. Artifacts or objects of historical significance can be reported to the state **Historic Preservation Office** at 503-378-6508. Oregonian 4/26/95:E1. See also **Archeology**; **Pot hunting**; **Projectile points**.

Artists. Notable Oregon artists include Michele Russo (ca 1910-), and Carl Morris, 1911-1993. Artists of the Pacific Northwest.

Artists Repertory Theatre. A major **Portland** theater company begun by six actors in 1982. In recent years the company has dominated the Portland Drama Critics Circle awards. In 1997 it moved into a new home in the intimate Reiersgaard Theatre, a flexible black-box style theater with movable seats and stage, and began operating as a partial Equity company. 1516 SW Alder Street, 97205. 503-241-1278. Oregonian 10/5/97:G1.

Artquake. A onetime downtown **Portland** arts festival that was held on Labor Day weekends from 1977 through 1995. It featured juried art and craft sales, arts organizations, art exhibits, folk arts, street performances, events for children, gourmet food booths, a film festival, literary events, and performances of music, drama, and dance. Oregonian 2/24/96:D1. See also **Art in the Pearl**.

Arts Commission, Oregon. A commission under the state Department of **Economic Development**, established to work with arts-producing and service organizations to support and extend the role of the arts in Oregon. It sponsors the annual **Governor's Arts Award** and the Community Service Award for community service. It also administers the **One Percent for Art** program. The nine members of the commission are appointed by the governor to four-year terms. 775 Summer St. NE, Salem 97310. 503-986-0088. Oregon Blue Book.

Arts organizations. Organizations promoting the arts employ more than 21,000 people in Oregon. The Oregon Blue Book lists local arts agencies and regional councils from throughout the state.

Asbestos. A fibrous mineral that was used for fire-proofing and insulation until it was found to be a carcinogenic air pollutant in even the smallest exposure and was banned in the late 1970s. The Department of **Environmental Quality** certifies and licenses asbestos abatement contractors and enforces the laws regarding the removal and disposal of asbestos-containing materials. At one time there was an asbestos mine in **Grant County** north of **Mount Vernon**. After the mine opened, the hotel operator at Mount Vernon Hot Springs brought in some ladies of the night for the miners and placed a sign on the highway that read ASS-BEST-OS MINE AHEAD with an arrow pointing to his establishment. Experiences.

Ashland. A southwest Oregon cultural and outdoor recreation center at the foot of the **Siskiyou Mountains** in **Jackson County**. It is located 16 miles southeast of **Medford** on **Interstate 5**. Abel Helman laid out the town in 1855 and named it for the Ohio county in which he was born; it was incorporated in 1874. The city owns its own electric utility, airport, ski area, and cemeteries, and operates its famed 100-acre Lithia Park with a voter-approved dedicated tax levy. It is noted for the **Oregon Shakespeare Festival, Southern Oregon University**, **Lithia water**, nearby mountains, mountain lakes, and **Ski Ashland Ski Area**. Guanajuato, Mexico, is its sister city. Population 1980 14,943; 1995 17,985. Elevation1,895'. 20 E. Main St., 97520. 541-482-3211. Chamber of Commerce 541-482-3486. Ashland, the First 130 Years; Land in Common.

Ashland Academy. See **Southern Oregon University**.

Ashwood. An unincorporated central Oregon community in **Jefferson County** 40 miles north of **Prineville**. It was platted in 1899 by the Wood family, and was named for them and the nearby ashy volcanic butte. Though the area had been used for sheep and cattle grazing since 1874, it was the discovery of gold in

1897 that prompted settlement. **Gold, silver**, and **mercury** mines operated for a time. Paulina, the legendary **Paiute** marauder, was killed nearby in 1867. "Ashwood"; East of the Cascades; Oregon Ghost Towns.

Asians in Oregon. The 1990 census counted 69,000 Asians and Pacific Islanders, 2.4% of the state's population, in Oregon. The largest groups were **Chinese** (14,000) and **Japanese** (12,000). There were also 9,000 Koreans, 9,000 Vietnamese, and 7,000 **Filipinos**. The proportions were highest in **Benton County** (5.5%), **Multnomah County** (4.7%), and **Washington County** (4.3%).

Assessed value. Assessed value of real property and business personal property in Oregon totaled $150 billion in 1994-95, or $48,770 per capita. The per capita values ranged from a low of $31,830 in **Malheur County** to a high of $112,390 per capita in **Gilliam County**. Exempt property includes publicly-owned real estate, a portion of the value of agricultural and forest lands, and churches, lodges, hospitals, and the property of other social welfare organizations. Oregon: A Statistical Overview. See also **Property tax; Tax exemptions**.

Assisted living facilities. See **Long term care ombudsman**.

Associations. See **Organizations**.

Astor Column. A 125-foot high monument on Coxcomb hill in **Astoria**, dedicated in 1926. An interior circular staircase of 166 steps leads to an observation platform near the top, and a sgraffito frieze depicting Oregon's early history spirals up the outside. The column was constructed with funds donated by John Jacob Astor's great grandson who intended it to be a monument to the western terminus of the Great Northern Railroad. John Jacob Astor had himself been responsible for the establishment of Astoria. New York architect Electus Ritchfield designed the monument, and Italian artist Attilio Pusterla executed the frieze. In 1995 the column was restored at a cost of $800,000. Dictionary of Oregon History; Oregonian 11/20/95:B4.

Astor Overland Expedition. An expedition of 60 persons dispatched by John Jacob Astor of the **Pacific Fur Company** from Montreal, Canada, in July, 1810, to the mouth of the **Columbia River** where it was to join with another Pacific Fur Company group arriving by sea. The groups were to establish a fur **trading post** to be known as **Astoria**. After extraordinary hardships, the members of the overland group straggled into Astoria in early 1812, the second overland trip to Oregon. On the trip Marie Dorion, wife of the expedition's Canadian interpreter, gave birth to her third child near **North Powder**. Astoria; Dictionary of Oregon History.

Astoria. "Astoria is for Explorers." A historic ocean port at the northwest corner of Oregon, located on a peninsula between the **Columbia River** and **Youngs Bay**, and at the junction of **Highway 101** and **Highway 30**. The city, with a varied economy based on fish, timber, and tourism, is the seat of **Clatsop County**. In 1811 the Pacific Fur Company established a fur **trading post** at what is now 15th and Exchange streets, and named it Astoria in honor of company founder John Jacob Astor. The trading post was the first permanent American settlement west of the Rockies. The post was taken over by the British in 1813 and renamed **Fort George**, but was later restored to the U.S. The first U.S. post office (1847) and customhouse (1849) west of the Rockies were established at Astoria. The city, incorporated in 1856, had a major fire in 1883, and another in 1922 burned 32 downtown blocks, which were soon rebuilt. Between 1870 and 1900 the town prospered from salmon canneries. The annual Midsummer Scandinavian Festival in June celebrates the city's heritage, and the first Fisherman's Poetry Festival was held in 1998. Attractions include the 125-foot **Astor Column**, the **Columbia River Maritime Museum**, Uppertown Firefighters Museum, Clatsop County Heritage Museum and Flavel House, many Victorian homes, Columbia Riverfront Parks and Riverwalk, Maritime Memorial, and nearby **Fort Clatsop National Memorial**. Walldorf, Germany, is its sister city. Population 1980 9,998; 1995 10,100. Elevation 19'. Rainfall 70". 1095 Duane St., 97103. 503-325-5821. Chamber of Commerce 800-875-6807. Astoria; Astoria and Empire; Oregon Geographic Names. See also **Knappton Cove Heritage Center**.

Astoria (trading post). The first American settlement in Oregon was an 1811 **trading post** established by the American **Pacific Fur Company** on the present site of the city of **Astoria** near the mouth of the **Columbia River**. The 33 men who arrived on the *Tonquin* built the fort before the **Astor Overland Expedition** arrived a year later. In the fall of 1813 the Pacific Fur Company, pressed by the loss of supplies due to the War of 1812 with Great Britain, sold the fort to the Canadian **North West Company** which renamed it **Fort George**. Astoria. See also **Gardens**.

Astoria and Columbia River Railroad. A rail line along the **Columbia River** between **Goble** and **Astoria** completed in 1898 after complex difficulties. From Goble on in to **Portland**, the trains ran on **Northern Pacific** track. The line, with various owners through the years, carried freight and, until 1952, vacationers heading for the beach. In 1997 the Albany-based Portland and Western Railroad bought the line, but it does not plan to restore service all the way to Astoria until business justifies clearing a 1,000-foot long **landslide** 27 miles east of Astoria. Oregonian 6/17/97:E2. See also **Great Northern**; **Willamette and Pacific Railroad**.

Astoria fire. A fire on December 2, 1922, that burned 34 blocks, killing two persons and wiping out the entire Astoria business district. Property losses were estimated to be over $12,000,000. Dictionary of Oregon History. See also **Disasters**.

Astoria post office. In 1847 the federal government appointed a postmaster for **Astoria**, giving it the first post office on the Pacific coast. At the same time the post office and the custom house were designated as a federal enclave, as was sometimes done to provide sanctuary for shanghaied sailors who jumped ship. Because it still has federal enclave status, local police officers are commissioned as deputy U.S. marshals so they can enforce laws there. Oregonian 1/24/96:C2. See also **Postal service history**.

Astronauts. Oregon astronaut Air Force Lt. Col. Susan J. Helms of **Portland** has made three space flights, including a 16-day flight in 1996 as flight engineer and payload commander on the *Columbia*. Her first space flight was aboard *Endeavor* in January 1993, and her second in September 1994 was a nine-day *Discovery* flight. She graduated from Parkrose High School in Portland in 1976. Donald R. Pettit of **Silverton** was selected in 1996 to be a shuttle mission specialist astronaut. Oregonian 9/7/94, 6/6/96:B9, 6/27/96:A20.

Astronomy. The largest of the astronomy groups in Oregon is the **Rose City Astronomers**. A complete listing of all groups in Washington and Oregon is available from The Northwest Region Astronomical League, 15600 NE 8th B1-243, Bellevue WA 98008. See also **Observatories**; **Oregon Star Party**; **Pine Mountain Observatory**; **Planetariums**.

Athena. A northeast Oregon farming community in **Umatilla County** 17 miles northeast of **Pendleton**. It is located on Highway 11 at the western base of the **Blue Mountains**. Originally called Centerville because it was about half way between Pendleton and Walla Walla, the name was changed in 1889 because of confusion with other Centervilles. Athena was suggested because the rolling hills around the town are similar to those surrounding Athens, Greece. The city was incorporated in 1905. The community hosts Caledonian Games (**highland games**) on the second weekend in July. Population 1980 965; 1995 1,080. Elevation 1710'. Precipitation 12". PO Box 686, 97813. 541-566-3862. Oregon Geographic Names. See also **Weston**.

Athletic trainers. In 1997 there were 98 athletic trainers voluntarily registered with the Oregon **Health Division Licensing Programs** office. Oregon Blue Book.

Atlantic Pacific Highways and Electrical Exposition. A world's fair proposed for **Portland** in 1925. Plans were suddenly deflated when state voters defeated a tax measure to pay for it at the November 1922 election. An alternative and also unsuccessful plan for a World's Electrical, Industrial, and Highways Exposition, to be held in 1927, surfaced briefly.

Atlases. See **Maps**.

Attorney general, Oregon. The chief legal officer of the state and head of the **Justice Department**. Other duties include supervising all legal proceedings in which the state has an interest, providing the legal counsel to state departments, boards, and commissions, and providing written opinions on questions of law when requested by a state official. Pay as of 1998 was $72,000 per year. The position, created by the legislature, is filled by statewide election every four years in years divisible by four (1996, 2000,...). There are no listed qualifications, and the attorney general is not in the line of **succession** to governor. Most of the other 190 attorneys in the Justice Department are known as assistant attorney generals. Justice Building, Salem 97310. 503-378-6002. Governing Oregon; Oregon Blue Book. See also **Recall**; **Term limits**.

Attorney general, U.S. A member of the President's cabinet and head of the U.S. Department of Justice. Oregon offices are located in **Portland** and **Medford**.

Attorneys. Oregon had 10,851 active attorneys in 1996. The oldest functioning law firm in Oregon is Wood, Tatum, Sanders & Murphy, established in 1870. Oregon's first woman lawyer was Mary Leonard, admitted to the bar in 1886 - after having been acquitted of the 1878 murder of her husband. Oregon Blue Book; "Letter to the Editor." See also **Bar Examiners**.

Auburn mining district. A **mining district** about eight miles southwest of **Baker City** where **gold** was discovered in 1861 on Griffin Creek. The next year a town called Auburn was laid out in Blue Canyon. By 1864 it had 5,000 people and was the **second largest city** in the state. Though a wide-open, roistering town, it also served as **Baker County** seat from 1862 to 1867. The post office operated from 1862 until 1903. Now all that is left of the town is three cemeteries: two Chinese and one white. "Cynthia Stafford"; Oregon Ghost Towns; Oregon's Golden Years.

Auctions. See **Livestock auctions**.

Audiology. See **Speech-Language Pathology and Audiology State Board of Examiners.**

Audits Division. A division under the **Secretary of State** that is responsible for evaluating the financial condition and operations of state agencies and for administering the Municipal Audit law. It encourages citizens and government workers to report waste and misuse of tax dollars by calling its hot line, 800-336-8218. Public Service Building, 255 Capitol St. NE, Suite 500, Salem 97310. 503-986-2255.

Aumsville. A **Willamette Valley** city in **Marion County**, 10 miles southeast of **Salem**. First called Hoggum for the number of pigs about, the name was changed to Aumsville in 1868 by farmer Henry Turner to honor his deceased son-in-law, Amos (Aumus) Davis. The city was incorporated in 1911. It is home to the annual Corn Festival. Population 1980 1,432; 1995 2,285. Elevation 363'. PO Box 227, 97325. 503-749-2030. Oregon Geographic Names.

Aurora. A **Willamette Valley** town in **Marion County** 13 miles south of **Oregon City** on **Highway 99E**. It was established in 1857 by Dr. William Keil, founder of the **Aurora Colony**. The city was incorporated in 1893. In 1993 it sponsored a covered wagon that traveled the **Oregon Trail** from Independence, Missouri, to **Independence**, Oregon. The Old Aurora Colony Museum is a five-building complex of restored buildings portraying life in the 19th century. Population 1980 523; 1995 650. Elevation 132'. PO Box 100, 97002. 503-678-1283. Chamber of Commerce 503-678-5754. Oregon Ghost Towns.

Aurora borealis. Oregon newspapers reported sightings of the aurora borealis, also called northern lights, on September 28, 1909, March 12, 1929, June 21, 1936, February 4 and May 5, 1937, September 21, 1941, March 2, 1942, September 5,14, and 23, 1957, and August 5, 1972.

Aurora Colony. A Utopian communal settlement established in 1856 by Wilhelm Keil and a group of his followers. They had organized in 1844 in Missouri and come across the **Oregon Trail** to Willapa Bay, Washington, in 1855; the lead wagon carried the body of Keil's recently deceased 19-year-old son, immersed in alcohol in a coffin. The group soon moved to a location south of **Oregon City**, between Mill Creek and the Pudding River. The colony, named for Keil's daughter, had 14,000 acres and 600 residents, and thrived until Keil's death in 1877. The industrious and self-sufficient group included many fine artisans and musicians, and hosted Oregon's first classical music concerts. The community disbanded, but the town of **Aurora** remains. The Old Aurora Colony Museum is located at Second and Liberty streets. 503-678-5754. Oregon Historical Quarterly 92(4), Winter 1991-92. Special issue.

Australian ballot. A form of secret ballot that Oregon adopted in 1891 to reduce corruption and coercion at elections. Before its adoption each political party printed and distributed its own ballots, usually in an identifiable color, and voters had to ask for the ballots they wanted. Characteristics of the Australian ballot are that it is printed by the government rather than by political parties, the same kind and color of paper is used for all ballots, and the ballot is marked in secret by the voter. Empire of the Columbia.

Authors. The Oregon Authors Committee of the Oregon Library Association has published Oregon Authors annually since 1974. It lists authors who were living in Oregon at the time they wrote their work. See also **Children's literature**; **Literature**; **Novels**; **Oregon Literature Series**; **Poets**.

Auto emissions testing. See **Vehicle inspection**.

Auto racing. Auto races in Oregon include the annual June **Portland IndyCar Race** at **Portland International Raceway**, one of the largest spectator events in Oregon. The Oregon Region of the Sports Car Club of America (503-697-9649) sponsors seven races each year at Portland International Raceway, including the Rose Cup races in June. The International Conference of Sports Car Clubs (503-629-8798) sponsors races each year at PIR in **Portland** and at **Port Orford**. In 1905 the first **transcontinental** auto race (and the first transcontinental crossing), **From Hellgate to Portland**, ended at the **Lewis and Clark Exposition**. The first nationally sanctioned auto race was held in Portland in 1909, two years before the Indianapolis 500 races began. See also **Portland Historical Races**; **Portland Speedway**.

Auto theft. In 1997, reported auto thefts in major Oregon cities ranged from one per 50 residents in **Portland** to one per 700 residents in West Linn. Oregonian 3/31/97:B4.

Automobiles. In 1996, Oregon (population 3.1 million) had 3.1 million registered vehicles. In 1995 Oregonians bought 164,000 new vehicles, over half of them **trucks**. Ford trucks led, with 28,000 sold. Oregonian 10/17/96:F1. See also **Imports**.

Automobiles, history. In 1899 the first automobile in Oregon arrived in **Portland** by rail. By 1910 Meier and Frank Company had switched deliveries from horses to trucks, and by 1920 there were 100,000 motor vehicles in Oregon. Two cars have been built in Oregon, a Benson in 1904, and two to four Beaver Sixes, built by the Beaver State Motor Company between 1914 and 1918 in **Gresham**. All have disappeared. Oregonian 12/28/94:D2; Round the Roses. See also **Antique Auto Portland Swap Meet**; **Concours d'Elegance**; **From Hellgate to Portland**; **Good Roads**; **Portland Historical Races**.

Aviation history. Charles Hamilton of Los Angeles flew the first airplane in Oregon at a **Portland** exhibition on March 5, 1910. In 1912 Oregon's own famed aviator Silas Christofferson took off from the roof of the **Multnomah Hotel** in **Portland** and flew to Vancouver, Washington, a feat replicated on September 16, 1995. The first commercial airline was formed in 1919, **airports** and airmail service appeared in 1926, and regular passenger service began in 1928. On September 14, 1927, Charles Lindbergh landed the Spirit of St. Louis, the plane in which he had made his famous flight to Paris four months earlier, in Portland to open the new Swan Island Airport. "Exhibition Era"; Dictionary of Oregon History; Oregonian 9/17/95:D1; Round the Roses. See also **Aeronautics Section**; **Aircraft**;

Captain Michael King Smith Evergreen Aviation Educational Center; Oregon Aviation Museum; Plane crashes;.

Awards. See **Andre Berger Awards**; **Drammy awards**; **Earle A. Chiles Award**; **Governor's Arts Award**; **MacArthur Fellowships**; **National Book Awards**; **Nobel Prize**; **Oregon Book Awards**; **Pulitzer Prize**.

Awbrey Hall fire. See **Forest fires**.

Azalea. An unincorporated community in **Douglas County** in the upper Cow Creek Valley near **Interstate 5**. The post office was known as Starvout when it was established in 1888. In 1907 it became Booth, and in 1914 was renamed Azalea for a local wild shrub. Oregon Geographic Names.

Azaleas. Flowering shrubs related to **rhododendrons**. The deciduous fragrant Western **azalea**, *Rhododendron occidentale*, is native to southwestern Oregon. Oregon growers produce 28% of the nation's potted florist azaleas. Oregon Agriculture.

Bach Festival. See **Oregon Bach Festival**.

Bachelor Butte. See **Mount Bachelor**.

Back Country Byways. A **Bureau of Land Management** (BLM) program that identifies certain country roads as interesting recreational drives. The BLM has designated 14 in Oregon: Christmas Valley (93 miles), Lakeview to Steens (90 miles), Steens Mountain (66 miles), Diamond Loop (64 miles), Leslie Gulch/Succor Creek (50 miles), Snake River/Mormon Basin (150 miles), Lower Deschutes River (36 miles), Lower Crooked River (43 miles), South Fork John Day River (50 miles), Nestucca River (48 miles), South Fork Alsea River (11 miles), Galice-Hellgate (39 miles), Grave Creek to Marial (33 miles), and Cow Creek Road (45 miles). Only Diamond Loop, Galice-Hellgate, and Cow Creek roads are paved the entire way. BLM Facts. See also **Scenic Byways**.

Bacteria. In 1989 David R. Boone of the **Oregon Graduate Institute** discovered a new bacterium 10 feet below the surface at Alkali Lake northeast of **Lake Abert** and named it *Methanohalophilus oregonense*, the first microbe to be named after a state. It is an anaerobic organism, and, as its name indicates, is methane-making and salt-loving. Oregonian 12/17/97:D18.

Badger. A heavy-bodied nocturnal animal of the **weasel** family, *Taxidea taxus*, widespread in the deserts of eastern Oregon. It may be up to 29 inches long and weigh 25 pounds, is grizzled with a white stripe down the head, and has a flattened look. Badgers use their powerful digging ability to unearth rabbits, rodents, and other prey and to dig their own burrows; their burrow entrances are a hazard to horsemen on the open range. A dog that rashly attacks a badger will be seriously injured if not killed, but humans can usually outrun them. **Wolves** were their major predator. In 1994-95, 180 were trapped with an average value of $9 each. Atlas of Oregon Wildlife; Mammals and Life Zones of Oregon; Mammals of the Northwest.

Baha'i faith. A religious movement, emphasizing the spiritual unity of mankind, that originated in Iran in the 19th century. There are 40 Spiritual Assemblies in Oregon. Spiritual Assembly of the Baha'is of Portland, PO Box 83297, 97283-0297. 503-289-6331.

Bailey Mountain. See **Mount Bailey**.

Bailey Gatzert. A fast and popular stern-wheel excursion **steamboat** that operated on the **Columbia River** from 1892 until 1917, making daily round trips between **Portland** and **The Dalles** for much of that time. It was pictured on U.S. 32 cent postage stamp in 1996. Blow for the Landing.

Bakeoven. A location on the east side of the **Deschutes River** in **Wasco County**. During the 1862 **gold rush** a German baker was taking a pack load of flour from **The Dalles** to **Canyon City**. Indians drove off his horses at night, so he built an oven of clay and rock at the spot and baked bread that he sold to passing miners and prospectors. The oven lasted for years after it was abandoned. Bakeoven Creek and Bakeoven Road commemorate the same oven. Oregon Geographic Names.

Baker City. A historic eastern Oregon city on the **Powder River** 300 miles east of **Portland** on **Highway 84**. It is the county seat of **Baker County** from which it takes its name. Originally a gold mining center, it was established as Baker City in 1866 and incorporated in 1874. Between 1911 and 1989 its name was just Baker, but is now again Baker City. **Wallowa-Whitman National Forest** headquarters are in the city. Attractions include a recently restored historic downtown featuring the 1889 **Geiser Grand Hotel** and other 19th century buildings, a display of gold including the **Armstrong Nugget** at the U.S. National Bank, the Oregon Trail Regional Museum with a rock and mineral collection, the nearby **Oregon Trail Interpretive Center**, and the **Blue** and **Wallowa** mountains. The mid-July Miners Jubilee Celebration, originated in 1934, is the city's major festival. Population 1980 9,471; 1995 9,730. Elevation 3,449'. PO Box 650, 97814. 541-523-6541. Visitor information 800-523-1235. Oregon Geographic Names; Oregonian 3/22/98:A1. See also **Anthony Lakes Ski Area**.

Baker County. A ranching, timber, and **gold mining** county in northeast Oregon centered around the **Powder River**. Incorporated cities are **Baker City** (county seat), **Greenhorn, Haines, Halfway, Huntington, Richland, Sumpter**, and **Unity**. In addition to the Powder River, the Burnt River drains the south end of the county, **Elkhorn Mountains** and the **Blue Mountains** rim it on the west, and the **Wallowa Mountains** rise on the northeast. The county is bounded by **Wallowa, Union, Grant**, and **Malheur** counties and by **Idaho** across the **Snake River** on the east. Elevations range from 1,720' on the Snake River up to 9,000' peaks in the Wallowa and the Elkhorn ranges. Agriculture, lumber, recreation, and mineral industries - including **cement** - support the county, which has a 1995 taxable assessed value of $699,000,000, or $42,000 per capita. Attractions include **ghost towns**, the **Oregon Trail Interpretive Center, Sumpter Valley Railroad**, skiing, and other outdoor recreations. The county was formed from **Wasco County** during the **gold rush** of 1862, and was named for Colonel Edward D. Baker (1811-1861), one-time law partner of Abraham Lincoln and later U.S. Senator from Oregon, who was killed in the **Civil War**. Population 1980 16,134; 1995 16,500. Area 3,089 square miles. Density 5/sq.mi. Annual precipitation 11"; average temperature January 25°F, July 67°F. Courthouse, 1995 3rd St., Baker City 97814. 541-523-8200. Visitor information 800-523-1235. History of Baker County; Oregon Blue Book.

Baker Project. A U.S. **Bureau of Reclamation** project in **Baker County**

that provides irrigation from **Philips Lake** for 18,500 acres near **Baker City** and for 7,300 acres along the **Powder River** from the Thief Valley Reservoir.

Balanced Rocks. An area along the **Metolius River** where massive rocks, each weighing over a ton, perch on more slender 20 to 30 foot pinnacles. The Button Head Rocks are nearby. The fragile formations are the result of differential weathering. The area was discovered by John Newberry in 1855. Geology of Oregon.

Bald eagle. See **Eagles**.

Baldock Freeway. A brief name for the section of **Interstate 5** between **Portland** and **Salem**. In 1961 the completed stretch was dedicated to Robert "Sam" Baldock (1889-1968) who had been Oregon State Highway Engineer during the early stages of freeway design and construction until his retirement in 1956. It was discovered, however, that state law did not allow naming things for a person still living, and the name faded from use. Oregonian 11/23/96:B2.

Balloon bombs. **World War II** explosive devices launched from Japan between November 1944 and April 1945. They were designed to be carried to North America on the jet stream (of which America was as yet unaware) where they would land and cause forest fires. The bombs were carried by 10-meter-high, hydrogen-filled, paper balloons. Each balloon carried 4 incendiary devices, a high-explosive bomb, and a self-destruction device, all designed to be ignited sequentially. About 300 of the approximately 9,000 balloons were found, some 40 of them in Oregon. No fires were set, but five children and the minister's wife were killed when they came upon a bomb while on a Sunday School picnic near **Bly** in **Lake County**. Silent Siege. See **Incendiary bombs**; **Mitchell monument**.

Ballooning. On November 10, 1889, Prof. P. H. Redmon made a balloon ascension in **Portland**, then, from an altitude of 2,000 feet, he parachuted from the balloon, performing stunts on his descent and thrilling the 3,000 spectators. This Day in Oregon.

Ballot measure 5, 47. See **Measure 5, 47**.

Ballot measures. Oregonians vote on all proposed changes to the state **constitution**, whether the proposal originated with the **legislature** or through an **initiative** petition. Oregonians also vote on statutory measures adopted by the legislature that they have referred to the voters for a final decision, measures adopted by the legislature that have been referred to the voters through a **referendum** petition, and measures that were initiated by voters through initiative petition. Oregonians adopted the initiative and referendum in 1902. Between then and the end of 1996, 712 measures were placed on the ballot. 363 were referred by the legislature (206 passed), 61 were legislative measures that were referred by petition (25 passed), and 288 were placed on the ballot through initiative petition (99 passed). All statewide ballot measures since 1902 are listed in the Oregon Blue Book. Governing Oregon. See also **Australian ballot**.

Baltimore Colony. A well organized group from Maryland under the leadership of Dr. Henry Hermann that, in 1859, settled along the Coquille River near what is now **Myrtle Point**. The group included men of many professions and trades, as well as their families. Many of the settlers and their heirs have been important in **Coos County** and Oregon affairs. Century of Coos and Curry.

Bamboo. A member of the grass family with woody stems and evergreen leaves. It is grown commercially in Oregon for its edible fresh shoots and as nursery stock, and researchers are investigating its potential for timber and fiber products and for bioremediation of sewage sludge. Oregon Bamboo Company, 541-863-6834.

Banana. A fossil banana, genus *Ensente*, was found in the **Clarno formation** and dated to 43 million years ago. It is one and a half inches long and half inch wide, with seeds. Oregonian 3/16/95:A1. See also **Fossils, plant**.

Bandon. A south coast city in **Coos County** at the mouth of the **Coquille River**, 23 miles south of **Coos Bay** on **Highway 101**. The town, settled by Irish, was named in 1873 for Bandon, Ireland, and incorporated in 1891. Most of the town was destroyed in the **Bandon fire** in 1936, but was later rebuilt. Attractions include the Old Town Harbor District with its galleries, shops, and cafes, cheddar **cheese** from the Bandon Creamery, the Cranberry Festival in September (**cranberry** bogs are both north and south of town), and **rock hounding** on the beaches. Population 1980 2,311; 1995 2,610. Elevation 0'. PO Box 67, 97411. 541-347-2437. Chamber of Commerce 541-347-9616. "Bandon"; Oregon Geographic Names. See also **Grandmother Rock**.

Bandon Fire. A fire that burned 145,000 acres and destroyed the city of **Bandon** on September 26, 1936. It was fueled by Scotch **gorse**, an introduced spiny, oily shrub that had all but engulfed the town and could not be effectively breached in the pre-bulldozer era. Eleven persons died, and all but 20 homes were destroyed, leaving 1,500 persons homeless. Dictionary of Oregon History. See also **Disasters**; **Forest fires**.

Bandon Lighthouse. See **Coquille River Lighthouse**.

Bands. Brass bands were formed in many Oregon towns in the 1850s, the one from the **Aurora Colony** being the most famous, although the first band to reach Oregon came overland in 1849 with the American Rifle Regiment. In 1863 the **State Fair** began offering a prize for the best brass band performance. Dictionary of Oregon History.

Banfield Freeway. **Interstate 84** through **Portland** to **Interstate 205**. The first portion opened on October 1, 1955 as the Banfield Expressway, dedicated to Thomas Harry Banfield (1886?-1950), Portland industrialist and civic leader, and chairman of the State Highway Commission from 1943 to 1950. Oregonian 9/1/50:1, 9/2/50:6, 11/23/96:B2.

Banking. In 1994 Oregon had forty-four state-chartered banks with 363 branches and $17.7 billion in assets, plus seven national banks with 332 branches and $18.7 billion in assets. In 1997 82% of deposits were controlled by U.S. Bancorp, Wells Fargo, BankAmerica, Washington Mutual, and KeyCorp. After several mergers and acquisitions, the largest remaining Oregon-based/Oregon-owned banks were Klamath First with assets of $935 million, West Coast Bancorp (Lake Oswego) $604 million, and Centennial Bancorp (Eugene) $405 million. The number of banks and banking jobs is expected to decrease due to the mergers. State-chartered financial institutions are regulated by the state **Finance and Corporate Securities** Division. See also **Credit unions**; **Federal Reserve Bank**.

Banking, history. Oregon's first banking services were offered by various merchants and express companies until 1859 when Ladd and Tilton in **Portland** became the first bank organized in Oregon. Ladd and Bush (now owned by U.S. Bank) was founded in **Salem** in 1868. Other banks were organized throughout the state and bank assets increased steadily except for major drops in 1893, 1921, and 1930-35. The Portland Clearing House was organized in 1889. U.S. Bank opened a branch in **The Dalles** in 1933, the first branch bank in the nation, and in 1966 was the first to offer drive-through banking. Dictionary of Oregon History; Gold and Cattle Country; Gold in the Woodpile; Oregonian 3/27/97:C1, 4/20/97:D4. See also **Express services**; **Money**.

Bankruptcy. Personal bankruptcies in Oregon declined from a high of 12,842 in the recession of 1991 to 11,877 in 1994, but then climbed to 16,738 in 1996. U.S. Bankruptcy Court, 1001 SW 5th, Portland 97204. 503-326-2231

Banks. A **Willamette Valley** community in **Washington County**, 12 miles northwest of **Hillsboro**. Though among the areas settled early, the post office wasn't established until 1902, and the city was incorporated in 1921. The town was named in honor of two pioneer settlers, John Banks and his son Robert. Population 1980 489; 1995 575. Elevation 250'. PO Box 428, 97106. 503-324-5112. Oregon Geographic Names; Oregonian 9/22/96:H1.

Banks-Vernonia Linear State Park. A park being developed along 21 miles of logging railroad right-of-way (abandoned in the 1960s) in **Washington** and **Columbia Counties** as part of the **Rails to Trails** program. The park is only 60 to 100 feet wide except for the four trail heads at **Vernonia**, Beaver Creek four miles south of Vernonia, Tophill eight miles from Vernonia, and Buxton 13.5 miles from Vernonia. Three more trailheads are planned. The several miles of pavement have an adjacent bark trail for horses. No motorized vehicles are allowed. It became a state park in 1990. 503-378-6305. Oregonian 9/14/95:E4, 12/5/97:B2.

Bannock War, 1878. An **Indian war** that consisted of a series of encounters between the U.S. First Cavalry under General O. O. Howard and the Bannock and **Northern Paiute** Indians. It began May 30, 1878, in Idaho where the Bannocks were going hungry because settlers' hogs were destroying the **camas** patches that had been guaranteed to the Indians by treaty. After several skirmishes and raids, the Bannocks joined with Northern Paiutes at **Steens Mountain**. The combined Indian forces of some 1,500 warriors and their families rode north, pursued by the military. There were further battles and skirmishes, with a major encounter at Battle Mountain (now a state park) 18 miles south of **Pilot Rock** on July 7. The Indians then rode toward the **Umatilla Reservation** where the Umatillas tricked the Paiute chief and killed him. The Indians scattered, as did the pursuing troops. The Paiutes surrendered in August, and the Bannocks a month later. In all, 9 soldiers, 6 settlers, and 78 Indians were killed. It was the last Indian war in Oregon. Chronicle of the Indian Wars; Feelin' Fine; History of Grant County.

Baptist Church. The first Baptist Church west of the Rockies was organized at West Union in **Washington County** in 1844; the building was dedicated in 1853. By 1856 there were 26 churches in the Willamette Association. A school begun by Baptists in **McMinnville** in 1855 later became **Linfield College**. The Baptists established the first church in **Prineville** in 1873 and an 1894 Baptist Church still stands in **Mitchell**. Guide to Early Oregon Churches. See also

Churches; Religion.

Bar Examiners, Board of. A 14-member board appointed by the Oregon **Supreme Court** to conduct examinations of those applying to become **attorneys** and to screen them for character and their fitness to practice law. The board recommends to the Supreme Court those it finds qualified to be admitted to the **Bar** to practice law in Oregon. The **Bar** handles disciplines. PO Box 1689, Lake Oswego 97035-0889. 503-620-0222. Oregon Blue Book.

Bar, Oregon State. An association of **attorneys**, organized in 1891, that in 1935 became the State Bar, a public corporation. It licenses and disciplines lawyers, operates a lawyer referral service and **Tel-Law**, publishes a wide variety of legal and public service materials, provides services for lawyers, and supports public service programs through the Oregon Law Foundation. The Bar can investigate and try lawyers and recommend reprimand, suspension, or disbarment to the **Supreme Court**. Records of complaints against lawyers are available from the Bar. Membership in 1997 was about 12,000. No tax money is used to support it. PO Box 1689, Lake Oswego 97035-0889. 503-620-0222. 800-452-8260. Governing Oregon; Oregon Blue Book.

Barbers and hairdressers. Oregon has approximately 25,000 barbers, hairdressers, facial technicians, and nail technicians. They and their businesses are licensed by the Board of Barbers and Hairdressers, 700 Summer Street NE, Suite 100, Salem 97310-1351. 503-378-8667. Oregon Blue Book.

Barley. In 1995, Oregon growers produced 59 million bushels of barley, worth $22.3 million, on 106,550 acres. 1995 Oregon.

Barlow. A **Willamette Valley** community in **Clackamas County** ten miles southwest of **Oregon City** on **Highway 99E** south of **Canby**. Barlow was named for pioneer William Barlow who owned the land where the railroad station was built in 1870. The city was incorporated in1903. Population 1980 105; 1995 130. Elevation 101'. 106 N. Main St., 97013. 503-266-1330. Oregon Geographic Names.

Barlow Road. The first wagon road over the **Cascade Range**, which went from **The Dalles** around the south side of **Mount Hood** to **Oregon City**. The route was pioneered by the Barlow party in 1845 as an alternative to the harrowing trip down the **Columbia River**, but they had to leave their wagons in the mountains. The next year the **provisional government** gave Samuel K. Barlow ("God never made a mountain but what he provided a place for man to go over or around it") and Philip Foster permission to develop the route into a toll wagon road with tolls of $5 per wagon and $.10 per head of livestock. 152 wagons and 1,500 head of livestock crossed in 1846 alone. The steep, rugged route took **wagon trains** about eight days. Since the **Oregon Trail** pioneers didn't reach the area until autumn, they usually traversed the road in cold, snow, rain, and mud. It operated as a toll road until 1919. Barlow Road. See also **Estacada**.

Barnacles. Small marine crustaceans that attach themselves to rocks, piling, boats, and other floating objects. They significantly decrease the speed of boats. Two kinds, acorn and goose barnacles, occur on the Oregon coast. Acorn barnacles attach themselves to their substrate with some of the strongest adhesive known. Goose barnacles have bodies on leathery stalks. There are several species of each; all of them feed on minute sea life that they catch with feathery cirri. Acorn barnacles may live seven years or more. Seashore Life.

Barns. One of the oldest surviving barns in Oregon is the 1853 Richard A. Forrest English-Style barn in **Douglas County**. Oregon barn styles evolved to meet local needs. Probably the most famous barn in the state is the Round Barn, built by Pete French on the P Ranch, now on the **Malheur Wildlife Refuge**. Cattle Country; "A Guide to Historic Barns in Douglas County Oregon"; Style & Vernacular.

Barometric pressure. Air pressure, usually measured as inches of a column of mercury. The standard pressure at 32°F at sea level is 29.92". At **Astoria** during the **Columbus Day Storm** the barometric pressure dropped to 28.62", and during a major storm on December 12, 1995 it dropped to 28.51", the lowest ever recorded in the state. **Portland**'s lowest, 28.556", was recorded on January 9, 1880. Wind moves from areas of high pressure to areas of low pressure; the greater the difference, the greater the wind speed. Oregonian 2/12/96:B7.

Barrels. About half of Oregon's **wine** production is of varieties that are aged in barrels, traditionally using imported French oak barrels. Oregon white **oak** is now being cut into staves in **Yamhill County** and air-dried for two years before being made into barrels in California. It is not yet known whether it will satisfactorily replace the French barrels. Oregonian 9/5/95:B10.

Barter Fair. See **Southern Oregon Barter Fair**.

Basalt. A fine-grained volcanic rock with low silica content formed by the partial melting of rocks from the earth's interior. It is extremely fluid when molten (like molasses), so that a basalt or shield **volcano** may pour out a huge volume of basaltic **lava** that spreads over great areas but builds little height. If basalt is extruded under water, it forms pillow basalt. Some basalt fractures into columns as it cools. Basalt is the most common rock in Oregon; examples include **Jordan Craters**, some of the **Cascade** peaks (such as **Belknap Crater**), the vast flows of **Columbia River Basalt**, and old sea floors. See also **Andesite**.

Baseball, amateur. Baseball came to Oregon in 1866 when the Pioneer Base Ball Club of East Portland was organized. After some months, the nine members elected by ballot to play their first game against another team defeated the new Clackamas Club 77-46. One early team in Yamhill County consisted of William D. Fenton and his eight sons.

Baseball, professional. In 1997, the Class A Northwest League included (with their affiliated teams) the **Portland** Rockies (Rockies), the **Eugene** Emeralds (Braves), the **Salem-Keizer** Volcanoes (Giants), and the **Medford** Timberjacks (A's). The Bandits, charter members of the Western Baseball League, were organized in **Bend** in 1995.

Baseball, professional, history. Oregon's first professional baseball team, the **Portland** Gladiators, was organized in 1890 but lasted only three seasons. However, after the Webfooters appeared in 1901, professional baseball persisted in Portland, though with only one pennant (1983) since 1945. Play was at Vaughn Field (24th and Vaughn) until the team moved into the **Civic Stadium** in 1956. "For the Love of the Game"; Round the Roses.

Basic rule. A state rule that Oregon used instead of highway **speed limits**

until 1974 when it was displaced by federal speed limits triggered by the gas short-ages of 1973. Under the basic rule a suggested speed limit was posted, but if conditions were safe motorists could exceed it, and if conditions were unsafe po-lice could ticket even a driver going slower than the suggested limit. Oregonian 1/10/96:D7. See also **Traffic fines.**

Basin and range physiographic province. A region in the western interior of the United States, including the vast portion of south-central Oregon lying be-tween the **Cascade Range** on the west, the **high lava plains** on the north, and the **Owyhee uplands** on the east. It is characterized by north-south trending **fault-**block mountain ranges alternating with broad, usually land-locked, basins, often with a **playa** in the bottom. **Steens Mountain** at 9,670' is the highest of Oregon's fault block ranges and is one of several marked by spectacular scarps. Most of the rocks are volcanic rocks from the **Miocene** (11 to 25 million years old), though much older rocks from the Jurassic (150 million years old) occur in the **Pueblo** and **Trout Creek Mountains** as well as in Nevada. The only rivers in the Oregon portion that drain to the ocean are the **Klamath River** on the southwest and the **Owyhee River** on the eastern edge of the area. The meager precipitation over the rest of the area drains into land-locked alkaline lakes, remnants of the once huge **Pleistocene lakes.** Geologically, the **Basin and range** province has been stretched east-west, perhaps doubling in extent, and has also been rotated 60° clockwise. Geology of Oregon. See also **Gearhart Mountain; Great Basin.**

Basketball, men's. See **Bellfountain; Trail Blazers.**

Basketball, women's. In 1997, after winning three national championships in a row, the **Oregon City** High School Pioneers basketball team was featured on Cheerio cereal boxes. The **Western Oregon State College** women's basketball team has been ranked first in the nation in the NAIA Division II. The Power, a women's professional team in the new American Basketball League, opened in **Portland** in 1996. Oregonian 3/16/96:C8, 9/10/96:D1.

Basketry. The Indians along the **Columbia River** were noted for their well-made and handsome basketry, which included twined bags used when digging roots, as well as twined flat carrying bags and twined hats, coiled cedar root bas-kets with imbricated designs, and folded cedar bark baskets. Columbia River Bas-ketry. See also **Indian hemp; Ititamat.**

Basques in Oregon. An ancient and linguistically unique group of people from the Pyrenees Mountains in Spain. The first came to southeast Oregon as sheepherders in the 1870s. In the **Jordan Valley** area two-thirds of the population is of Basque ancestry. An annual Basque Festival has been held at **Hines** since 1994. The one-day June celebration features a pit barbecue, Basque dancers, car-rying contests, and bota-bag drinking contests. Amerikanuak; "Basque Folklore in Southeastern Oregon." See also **Four Rivers Cultural Center.**

Bass. See **Warmwater fish.**

Bassist College. An accredited private college in **Portland** that specializes in apparel, interior and industrial design, and retail management. It enrolled 103 students in 1995. 2000 SW 5th Ave., Portland 97205. 503-228-6528. Oregon Blue Book.

Bats. Small, furry flying mammals. Fifteen species, three of them classed as

protected animals, are found in Oregon. Their body lengths range from 3 to 5 1/2 inches, and the largest have 16-inch wingspans - though the wings are actually membranes stretched between elongated toes. All fifteen species live on flying insects that they find through echolocation, using their large ears. Bats occasionally carry **rabies**, though it is found in fewer than 1 in 20,000 animals. Because of their insect-eating capacity, bats are being encouraged to roost around dwellings. Instructions for building bat houses are available from the Audubon Society of Portland, 5151 N.W. Cornell Road, Portland 97210. 503-292-9453. Atlas of Oregon Wildlife; Mammals and Life Zones of Oregon; Mammals of the Northwest.

Battle of the Gorge. A two-year, $25 million race between the **Oregon Trunk Line** (owned by James Hill's **Great Northern Railroad**) and the **DesChutes Railroad** (owned by Edward Harriman's **Union Pacific**) to build a rail line up the **Deschutes River** to **Bend**. It began on July 26,1909, with the lines building up opposite sides of the narrow, rocky canyon. Disputes and feuds complicated the harrowing construction activity; the Oregon Trunk Line triumphed and Hill drove a golden spike at Bend on October 5, 1911. The two parallel lines gradually consolidated their operations so that by 1936 both operated on one line. East of the Cascades.

Battle Rock, 1851. A basalt rock islet just offshore in a cove south of **Port Orford**. There, on June 10, 1851, nine men who had been left by William Tichenor to establish a settlement at the area were besieged by several hundred Indians. During the battle some 20 Indians were killed. Two weeks later, as hundreds more Indians gathered, the party managed to escape and made a harrowing trip overland to the **Umpqua River**. **Fort Orford** was then established later the same year to protect settlers. Hero of Battle Rock. See also **Rogue River War**.

Battleship *Oregon* Monument. See *Oregon*.

Bawnmore. A 279' steam freighter that went aground 700' offshore from **Floras Lake** on the southern Oregon coast in a dense fog on August 28, 1895. The crew was saved and goods were salvaged for several months from the disintegrating ship. The salvage included trolley cars that residents used as outbuildings, gallons of yellow paint happily applied to many area structures, and some bulls that were said to have given rise to the *"Bawnmore* breed" among the local dairy herds. Oregon's Seacoast Lighthouses.

Bay City. A northwest Oregon city in **Tillamook County**, located on **Tillamook Bay** and **Highway 101**, five miles north of **Tillamook**. Bay City was established in 1888 by Winfield Cone who gave it the appropriate name of his home town in Michigan. The city was incorporated in 1910. Population 1980 986; 1995 1,100. Elevation 17'. PO Box 3309, 97107. 503-377-2288. Oregon Geographic Names.

Bayocean. A town, advertised as "The Queen of Oregon Resorts," that was developed on the then wooded south spit at **Tillamook Bay** beginning in 1907. The town included homes, stores, hotels, bowling alley, and a salt-water natatorium with a waterfall illuminated with colored lights and a gallery for 1,000 spectators. The spit started to erode following completion of the north Tillamook **jetty** in 1917 and the town began falling into the sea. Several times after 1939 the ocean washed completely across low areas of the spit, finally cutting a mile-wide opening in 1952. A breakwater was built to reconnect the spit in 1956, but the last house washed out in 1960. The beach has been gradually rebuilding following construction of the south jetty in 1974. Bayocean; "Ocean processes and hazards along the Oregon coast;" Tillamook.

Bays. See **Estuaries**.

Beach Cleanup. See **SOLV**.

Beachcombing. A pastime of gleaning interesting, useful, or salable items from the beach. Finds range from lumber, wrecked ships, whales, and Japanese glass floats to bottles with notes in them. Some coastal towns have beachcombing festivals. Beachcombing; Uncle Mike's Guide. See also **Beeswax**; **Nike shoe spill**; **Ship spills**.

Beaches. Two areas are included in the legal definition of Oregon beaches. The first, the area below high tide line, was declared part of the state highway system in 1913 and was used by cars until **Highway 101** was completed in the 1930s. The other area, the 262 miles of dry sand above high tide line, belonged to the state, which had, by 1966, sold 112 miles of it to private owners even though the beaches were historically considered to be public. The public use of dry sand beaches to a fixed line (set more or less at the vegetation line, approximately 16 feet above sea level) was confirmed by the state Beach Bill in 1967 and its amendments in 1969, by the Oregon Supreme Court in 1969, and by the U.S. Supreme Court in March 1994. However, the public has no legal right to cross private land to get to the beaches. 54% of the land along the coast is in public ownership. The Official State Map, published by the Department of **Transportation**, has a sidebar showing where and when vehicles are allowed on the beach. Fire at Eden's Gate.

Beaches - geology. Beach sand comes from the erosion of sea cliffs supplemented by materials transported by rivers; the sands along almost the entire Oregon coast contain sand from the **Klamath Mountains**. During winter storms beach sand is washed north and out to offshore submerged bars; during the summer the sand is moved south and redeposited on the beaches. The slope of the beach increases as the size of the sand grains increases. **Dunes** build when moving sands are trapped behind headlands as well as in some other areas. Along the Oregon coast **jetties** do not normally significantly alter the flow of sand. However, between the time the north jetty was built at **Tillamook Bay** in 1917 and the south one in 1974, the town of **Bayocean** washed away as Tillamook Spit eroded. Beach erosion also occurs when property protection structures such as walls or rock revetments rob the beach of its sand source. Permits from the **Oregon Parks and Recreation Department** are now required for such structures. The strong **El Niño** in 1982-83 resulted in the mouth of the Alsea River moving north, threatening homes on the **sand spit** at **Waldport**. Rising **sea levels** due to global warming are also expected to erode beaches. Geology of Oregon; "Ocean processes and hazards along the Oregon coast." See also **Agates**; **Black sand**; **Coast**; **Driftwood**; **Landslides**; **Rip current**; **Tar balls**; **The Capes**.

Beachside State Park. A **state park** located next to a long beach four miles south of **Waldport**. It has 81 campsites that are open year-round. Reservations, 800-452-5687. PO Box 693, Waldport 97394. 541-563-3220.

Beacon Rock. A large monolith 838 feet high that stands on the Washington shore of the **Columbia River** four miles below **Bonneville Dam**. It was bought by Henry J. Biddle in order to keep it from being turned into a rock quarry, and he, at his own expense, built a 3/4 mile trail to the top for public use. After Washington State refused it as a park, Sam Boardman proposed in 1931 that the State of Oregon accept it as an Oregon park. However, chagrined by the outrage of its own citizens, the State of Washington relented and accepted it. Treasures of the Oregon Country.

Beans. In 1995, Oregon growers produced 153,000 tons of snap beans for processing, worth $26.8 million, on 24,735 acres, which is 18% of U.S. production. Over half of the production was in **Marion County**. An additional 6,050 tons of edible dry beans, worth $3 million were produced on 6,320 acres. 1995 Oregon.

Bear Creek. A southwest Oregon stream that rises at the juncture of the **Cascade Range** and **Siskiyou Mountains** and flows northwest 33 miles to the **Rogue River**. **Ashland**, **Talent**, **Phoenix**, **Medford**, and **Central Point** lie in the valley, noted for its winter **pear** orchards. The creek was once known as Stuart Creek for Captain James Stuart who died nearby in 1851 from wounds received in a battle with Indians. The name Bear Creek came from an episode in which three grizzly bears were killed along its bank. Oregonian 11/9/1913:Sec. 5? p.9.

Bear Creek Greenway. A proposed park and trail corridor planned to extend 18 miles from **Ashland** north down **Bear Creek** through **Talent**, **Phoenix**, and **Medford** to **Central Point**. By 1997 nearly all of the land needed for the trail was in public ownership, and portions of the trail had been built, though much was damaged by a flood that year. The trail had been incorporated in a master plan in the 1960s and authorized by state legislation in 1973. 200 Antelope Road, White City 97503. 541-776-7268.

Bear Creek Valley. A 27-mile-long southern Oregon valley along Bear Creek in **Jackson County**. The creek, which heads near **Siskiyou Pass**, flows into the **Rogue River** near Central Point. The valley has been a corridor for north/south traffic since the **Siskiyou Trail** was explored by fur trappers in the 1820s. Now **Interstate 5** passes through, past **Central Point**, **Medford**, **Phoenix**, **Talent**, and **Ashland**. The valley is noted for its pear orchards.

Bear Essentials. See **Orlo**.

Bear Valley. A large, open valley in southern **Grant County** along the Silvies River, south of the **Aldrich Mountains**. **Highway 395** goes through the valley, which is over 10 miles long and five miles wide. **Seneca** is at the south end, near the confluence of Bear Creek and the Silvies River.

Bears. Large, furry omnivores. Grizzly bears, perhaps *Ursus horribilis*, although there may have been three species in Oregon, were at one time found throughout the state, but the last known was killed in **Wallowa County** in 1937. Grizzlies weigh up to 1,000 pounds and are noted for their fearless aggressiveness. Black bears, *U. americanus*, (which are sometimes brown), are found in forested areas throughout the state. They grow to six feet long and 450 pounds. In 1930 there were 9,000 bears in Oregon; there are now thought to be 25,000. The black bear is classified as a **game animal**. Some 17,000 **hunting tags** are issued annually and about 1,000 bears are killed. Illegal bear hunting (**poaching**) for gall bladders and paws for export also occurs. In the spring, black bears can destroy fifty 10" diameter conifers a night by scraping off the outer bark and eating the inner bark; artificial feeding reduces the damage. Atlas of Oregon Wildlife; Big Game History; Mammals and Life Zones of Oregon; Mammals of the Northwest; Oregon Hunting Guide. See also **Imnaha; Old Reelfoot**.

Beaver. The largest North American rodent, *Castor canadensis*, weighing 30 to 60 pounds. The beaver is the official Oregon **state animal**. It has a broad, flat, scale-covered tail and webbed hind feet. The large, chisel-like front teeth grow continuously; constant use in cutting down trees and gnawing the barks and twigs on which it lives keeps them from becoming too long. In 1994-95, 4,538 beaver with an average value of $12 each were trapped in Oregon. Beaver were trapped intensively between 1807 and the mid 1840s; over 100,000 pelts a year were collected by the **Hudson's Bay Company** at **Fort Vancouver**. The fur was shaved off the pelts and felted to make men's top hats until silk hats came into vogue. Later, the near extermination of beaver led to drought in areas downstream from former beaver ponds, areas that earlier had been verdant all summer. The beaver's ingenious dams and ponds sometimes damage roads and farms. An inexpensive water-level maintenance invention has significantly reduced the damage; information is available from the **Extension Service**. Atlas of Oregon Wildlife; Mammals and Life Zones of Oregon; Mammals of the Northwest.

Beaver. See **Steamboats**.

Beaver Boards. See **Historical markers**.

Beaver money. Gold coins, featuring the imprint of a beaver, minted at **Oregon City** in 1849. They were authorized by the **provisional government** because of a severe shortage of coins, but ended up being minted under private auspices. The company produced 6,000 $5 coins and 2,850 $10 coins, for a total value of $58,500. After coins from the San Francisco U.S. mint became more available in 1854, the government bought up most of the beaver coins. Earlier the Northwest Fur Company had issued tokens bearing the image of a beaver that were used in place of money. Dictionary of Oregon History; Oregon Oddities. See also **Money**.

Beaver (power plant). An **electric power plant** west of **Rainier** in **Columbia County** owned by **Portland General Electric**. The plant, fueled by **natural gas**, became operational in 1974. It has a nameplate capacity of 583.2 **megawatts**. Inventory.

Beaver Six. See **Automobiles, history**.

Beaver State. A sobriquet for Oregon, derived from the official **state animal**.

Beaverton. A **Portland** area suburb and the fifth largest city in Oregon, located in **Washington County**. The area was agricultural, with the first **Donation Land Claim** in 1847. The town was established in 1868 as a shipping point on the **Oregon Central** railroad and named for the many beaver in the area. It was incorporated in 1893. **High tech** industries and the headquarters for **Nike** (shoes) are located in the city. Population 1980 31,962; 1995 61,720. Elevation 189'. PO Box 4755, 97076. 503-526-2222. Chamber of Commerce 503-644-0123. Chakeipi.

Bed and breakfast lodging. Overnight lodging in homes with breakfast included in the price. Oregon has some 350 licensed B&Bs; about 80 of them belong to the Oregon Bed & Breakfast Guild, a voluntary professional group. Their directory is free by sending a legal-size SASE to PO Box 3187, Ashland 97520. 800-944-6196.

Beer. Oregon's first commercial brewery was established in **Portland** in 1852. The state has since licensed another 125, though only a few of the older breweries survived **Prohibition**. Blitz-Weinhard (now owned by Stroh) in **Portland**, founded 1856, is the oldest brewery in the west, and was the only brewery in the state from 1953 until BridgePort opened the first microbrewery in 1984. Oregon now has some 70 microbreweries, more per capita than any other state. Many have pubs that serve food along with their brew. Oregon Brewers Guild, 510 NW Thurman Street, Portland 97209. Brewed in the Pacific Northwest; Oregonian 3/1/96:D1. See also **Erickson's**; **Hops**; **Oregon Brewers Festival**.

Bees. Insects related to wasps that feed on pollen and nectar. Oregon is home to 998 species of native bees, plus the introduced honeybee, *Apis mellifera*, that was brought to North America from Europe 300 years ago and to Oregon from California in 1849. In 1854, a settler successfully brought a swarm across the **Oregon Trail** in a wire-sided hive. About $400 million worth of Oregon crops are now dependent on pollination by honeybees, and the bees produce 150,000 gallons of honey annually, worth $1.7 million in 1994. A healthy colony contains 50,000 to 75,000 bees and one queen. Oregon's 50 commercial beekeepers own 45,000 hives, and another 25,000 hives are owned by hobbyists and smaller operators. While beekeepers treat their hives for parasites, wild honeybee colonies, which once numbered 75,000, were decimated in the 1990s by introduced mites. Oregon State Beekeepers Association, 1874 Winchester NW, Salem 97304. 503-364-8401. Dictionary of Oregon History; Nectar and Pollen Plants of Oregon; Oregonian 5/16/96:D1, 1/24/97:D4. Oregon's Agricultural Progress 41(1/2):14-17. Summer/Fall 1994.

Beeswax. Quantities of beeswax, much of it in 20-pound blocks stamped I.H.S., have been found along the beach south of **Neahkahnie Mountain**. Legend and evidence indicate that it was from a Manila galleon that shipwrecked in the area with wax from the Philippines that was bound for Catholic missions in Mexico. The ship may have been the *San Francisco Xavier*, lost in 1705, or the *San Jose*, lost in 1789. Beeswax has also been found on **Clatsop Spit**, possibly from the same wreck or from the wreck of a **Japanese junk** in 1820. Lost Mines and Treasures; Oregon Shipwrecks; Tillamook; Wrecks of Japanese Junks. See also **Ozokerite**.

Belknap Crater. A **basalt** shield **volcano**, elevation 6,877', north of **McKenzie Pass**. It rises 400 feet above the surrounding lava field, and has two craters; the larger is 1,000' wide and 250' deep. Tree molds that have been dated to 360 A.D. are visible at the edges of extensive Belknap **lava** flow. J. H. Belknap was an early resident along the **McKenzie River**. Geology of Oregon.

Bell tower. A bell tower and plaque at Lamb's Marketplace at the corner of SW Oleson and Garden Home roads honors Cpl. Lyle S. "Toad" Tate (1946-1967) who was killed in the **Viet Nam war**. As a boy Tate would ring the bell which hung in the Community Church of Garden Home from 1918 to 1966. Oregonian 11/11/97:A1.

Bellfountain. An unincorporated community northwest of **Monroe** in **Benton County**. When first settled in 1848 it was known as Belknaps Settlement for a pioneer family, and the community was an early **Methodist** center and site of camp meetings. The post office, established in 1895, was called Dusty, but its name was changed in 1902 to Bellfountain, probably for a town in Ohio. In the winter of 1936-37 the high school basketball team defeated Portland's Franklin and Lincoln high schools to become state champions. The four-year high school had 2 teachers and 29 students at the time. Dictionary of Oregon History; Oregon Geographic Names; Other Side of Oregon.

Benchmarks. As part of **Oregon Shines**, Oregon established 259 (reduced to 100 in 1997) benchmarks, 31 of them classed as critical, by which to measure progress toward goals set for the year 2010. They call for the state to: 1) build the world's best work force by the year 2010; 2) preserve Oregon's superior quality of life; and 3) adopt a strong commitment to an international perspective. The Oregon **Progress Board** reports to the legislature every two years on the status of the benchmarks. Oregon Blue Book.

Bend. A rapidly growing city in central Oregon, the county seat of **Deschutes County**. It is located on the **Deschutes River** near the intersection of **Highway 20** and **Highway 97**. Its name comes from Farewell Bend Ranch, established in 1877 at a crossing of the Deschutes long used by **Indians** and pioneers. The city was platted by a promoter in 1903 and incorporated in 1905. Rail lines were completed in 1911 after the **Battle of the Gorge**. Bend grew from 500 people in 1910 to 5,000 in 1920 after two major pine mills were built. One of the mill sites on the west riverfront is now the focus of an extensive redevelopment effort called the Old Mill District. The headquarters office for the **Deschutes National Forest** is located in the city. Ranching, irrigated farming, and, more recently, tourism are important to its economy. Bend has become a popular retirement area and year-round recreation destination because of its dry, sunny climate and many outdoor attractions, including Drake Park, **Mirror Pond**, **Pilot Butte**, **Cascade Lakes Highway**, **Mount Bachelor Ski Resort** (22 miles west), **Newberry National Volcanic Monument** (11 miles south), and the **High Desert Museum** (6 miles south). Population 1980 17,260; 1995 30,630. Elevation 3,623'. 710 NW Wall St., 97701. 541-388-5505. Chamber of Commerce 541-382-3221. East of the Cascades; Frontier Doctor.

Benedictine monasteries. See **Mount Angel Abbey**; **Queen of Angels Monastery**.

Benham Falls. Falls on the **Deschutes River** that mark the region in which an earlier channel of the river, 137 feet below the present, was blocked by lava flows some centuries ago. Silt dropped over the years by the impounded river created great flat meadows upstream from the falls. East of the Cascades. See also **Dillon Falls**.

Benson fountains. Twenty drinking fountains donated to **Portland** in 1912 by teetotaling lumber tycoon Simon Benson so that his loggers could quench their thirst without public drunkenness. The city has since added more of the same four-armed bubblers, designed originally by noted Portland architect A. E. Doyle. One of the fountains is featured in a small plaza at the north end of the **Park Blocks**.

Portland, An Informal History.

Benton County. A **Willamette Valley** county on the west side of the **Willamette River**, bounded by **Polk, Linn, Lane**, and **Lincoln** counties. Incorporated cities are **Corvallis** (the county seat), **Adair Village, Monroe**, and **Philomath.** Elevations range from 160' at the river to 4,097' **Marys Peak** in the **Coast Range.** Major employers are Hewlett Packard and **Oregon State University**, with grass seed, Christmas trees, and timber also important. Taxable assessed value in 1995 was $3,861,000,000, or $51,000 per capita. It has Oregon's most highly educated population; 90% are high school graduates and 41% have a bachelor's degree or more. The county was created in 1847 from Polk County, and was named for Missouri Senator Thomas Hart Benton (1782-1858), an advocate for the development of the **Oregon Territory.** Population 1980 68,211; 1995 75,500. Area 679 square miles. Density 111/sq.mi. Annual precipitation 43"; average temperature January 39°F, July 66°F. Courthouse, 120 NW 4th, Corvallis, 97330. 541-757-6800. History of Benton County; Oregon Blue Book.

Bentonite. A **clay** mineral, formed from chemically altered volcanic ash, that is mined in **Crook** and **Malheur Counties.** It is used for sealing dams and landfills because it swells greatly when it absorbs water. Geology of Oregon.

Berger Awards. See **Andre Berger Awards.**

Berlin. An unincorporated community on Hamilton Creek seven miles southeast of **Lebanon.** Horse races in the vicinity were so popular that the home of a Mr. Burrell, who extended hospitality, became known as Burrell's Inn. This was shortened to Burl Inn when the post office was established, and then to Berlin. During **World War II**, the U.S. government, without consulting the residents, decided to change the name to Distomo. The residents, however, protested so vigorously that the proposal was abandoned. Oregon Geographic Names.

Bernard Daly Educational Fund. A scholarship fund established in 1922 for **Lake County** students, funded by a bequest from Dr. Bernard Daly (1858-1920) of **Lakeview.** The Irish-born Dr. Daly, legendary for his miserly ways, was also a member of the legislature, lawyer, and judge. The fund, now valued at over $2 million, has awarded over 1,400 scholarships, all based solely on merit, to Lake County students. Dictionary of Oregon History; Oregonian 12/16/94:A31.

Berries. In 1994 Oregon produced 100% of the country's **blackberries**, black raspberries, and **loganberries**, 75% of its **boysen** and youngberries, 32% of its red **raspberries**, 13% of its **blueberries**, 7% of its **cranberries**, and 4% of its **strawberries.** See also **Huckleberries; National Germplasm Repository.**

Berry Botanic Garden. A private, five-acre **Portland** garden where, beginning in 1932, Mrs. A.C.U. Berry grew rare plants from the Orient. A membership organization has maintained the garden since 1978. The garden, with 3,000 kinds of plants, now specializes in Pacific Northwest natives, alpines, and species of *Lilium, Primula*, and *Rhododendron.* It is open to the public by appointment, March through October. 11505 SW Summerville Avenue, Portland 97219. 503-636-4112.

Bethel. A **natural gas** fueled **electric power plant** at **Salem** owned by **Portland General Electric.** The plant, with a nameplate capacity of 113.4 **megawatts**, became operational in 1973. Inventory.

Better Business Bureau of Oregon and Washington. 800-488-4166.

Better Government Competition. A biennial contest sponsored by the **Cascade Policy Institute** since 1994 to solicit ideas for improving state and local government in Oregon. Winners are given funding to turn their suggestions into reports which are then submitted to the appropriate levels of government for consideration. Several winning ideas have been implemented. 503-242-0900. Oregonian 3/5/98:D8.

Beulah Reservoir. An irrigation reservoir in dry ranch land created in 1935 as part of the **Vale Project** and now operated by the Vale Oregon Irrigation District. It was formed by 121-foot high Agency Valley Dam on the North Fork of the **Malheur River**, 15 miles north of **Juntura**. The three-mile long, 2,060-acre lake has a maximum depth of 85 feet, and is popular for boating, water skiing, and fishing; camping is allowed. Beulah Arnold was the daughter of the first postmaster in the nearby community of Beulah. Atlas of Oregon Lakes.

Beverly Beach State Park. A **state park** with 279 campsites seven miles north of **Newport** near a miles-long beach. The campground is open all year. Reservations, 800-452-5687. 198 NE 123rd Street, Newport 97365 541-265-9278.

Beverly Cleary Sculpture Garden. A **Portland** grouping of fountains and bronze statues erected in 1995 as a tribute to Beverly Cleary, much-honored author of **children's literature**. It is located in Grant Park (NE 33rd and Thompson), in the neighborhood where the stories in fifteen of her books, written between 1950 and 1984, take place. The larger-than-life statues depict her characters Ramona Quinby, Henry Huggins, and Henry's dog Ribsy. "Memories"; Oregonian 10/8/95:F1.

Bicycle paths. Oregon's first bicycle paths were authorized in 1901, to be paid for by a bicyclers' fee. In 1971 Oregon became the first state to dedicate state money for the construction of bike paths when the legislature passed the Bicycle Bill, requiring that projects financed through the State Highway Fund allocate not less than 1% of total project costs to establish foot paths and bicycle trails. 530 miles were established during the next 20 years. Casual and Factual Glimpses; First 75 Years. See also **Columbia River Scenic Highway**.

Bicycling. The popularity of bicycling during the 1890's led to organized demand for better **roads** in Oregon. Now there are some 40 cycling clubs in the state, a number of communities publish guides for bicyclists, and the Oregon Department of **Transportation** (503-986-4000) publishes a series of free maps. A 1993 inventory found that of the total 632 miles of Oregon urban highways, 6% had bikeways and sidewalks on both sides of the road. 30% had sidewalks on both sides, and 32% had bikeways (shoulders or bike lanes) on both sides. **Eugene**, noted as a leading bicycling community, had 52 miles of on-street bike lanes plus 25 miles of separated paths. **Corvallis**, with 95% of its arterial and collector streets bicycle friendly, had the highest rate of bicycle commuting in the state at 8.2% in 1990. Community bikes in **Portland** (yellow) and **Ashland** (green) were available in 1996/97 for anyone to use. Bicyclists under the age of 16 are required to wear helmets. The **Portland** Bike Show in March, held annually since 1988, is one of the country's largest. 503-235-8771. Bicycle Federation of Oregon, PO Box 3552, Eugene 97403. 541-683-7225. Bicycle Transportation Alliance, PO

Box 9072, Portland 97207. Oregon Bicycle and Pedestrian Plan. See also **Bicycle paths**; **Cycle Oregon**; **Good Roads movement**; **Rail biking**; **Trails**.

Big Blow. See **Columbus Day Storm**.

Big game animals. Nine animal species are classified as big game under Oregon law and are regulated by the Oregon Department of **Fish and Wildlife**: **bear, bighorn sheep, cougar, deer, elk, moose, mountain goat, pronghorn antelope**, and silver gray **squirrel**. Records for many are in the Record Book for Oregon's Big Game Animals. See also **Hunting**; **Poaching**; **Protected animals**.

Big Hole. A mile-wide **maar** depression 45 miles south of **Bend** and just south of Highway 31 that was created about 20,000 years ago by a steam explosion. It was later covered by several feet of pumice from the eruption of **Mount Mazama**. A pine forest in the crater makes it less obvious than nearby **Hole-in-the-Ground**. Geology of Oregon.

Big Muddy. A 64,229-acre ranch on the **John Day River** southeast of **Antelope** that was bought by the followers of the Bhagwan Shree Rajneesh in 1981 for $5.7 million and renamed Rancho Rajneesh. During their four years there the commune spent $60 million developing 2,000 acres into **Rajneeshpuram**. In 1995 Dennis Washington, who bought the ranch in 1991 for $3.65 million, offered it to **OMSI** and to the state (both said no) and then to Texas-based Young Life Ministries for a youth-family camp. Residents of the area had wanted it to continue as a working cattle ranch. Oregonian 12/19/95:D2.

Big Pink. The U.S. Bancorp Tower, 111 SW Fifth in downtown **Portland**, a 43-story building of pink granite and rose glass, also known as the Tower of Power. In 1983, the year it was built, Portlanders voted it their favorite building, in part for the way its surface appearance changes with changing light conditions. It was designed by Skidmore, Owings and Merrill along with Pietro Belluschi. Frozen Music.

Big trees. **Trees** that are the largest of their species, as measured by a system of points: total circumference in inches, plus total height in feet, plus 1/4 of the crown spread in feet. The Oregon Department of **Forestry** (ODF) maintains Oregon's Register of Big Trees, while the National Register is maintained by American Forests of Washington, DC. Oregon's champion trees - and an application form - are listed periodically in the Forest Log, published by the ODF. Of the 81 listed in the May/June 1994 issue, 44 were also national champions. The tallest tree in Oregon is the national champion **Douglas-fir**, 329 feet high. The largest in circumference is the national co-champion **Sitka spruce**, 673 inches around, or 17.9 feet in diameter. Trees to Know. See also **Heritage Tree Program**.

Bigfoot. A legendary large ape, sometimes called Sasquatch. Recent Oregon sightings have been reported in areas southeast of **Molalla** and **Estacada**. To report a sighting call 800-BIGFOOT. The Western Bigfoot Society met monthly at Ray's Used Books in Portland, owned by C. Ray Crowe, until it was sold 1997, and there had been a bigfoot museum in the basement. Oregonian 6/3/95:C1, 6/8/97:L1.

Bigfoot (Indian). A Snake River Indian said to have weighed 300 pounds and been seven feet tall, and to have had a footprint that was 18 inches long and six inches wide. He traveled on foot, sometimes covering 50 to 80 miles a day, as he and a few other Indians attacked **wagon trains** and homesteads in eastern Oregon and southern Idaho. In August 1866 three Indian fighters camped near the head of the **Malheur River** woke to find his footprints nearby and gave chase, hoping to claim the $1,000 bounty on him. Though they rode rested horses, Bigfoot outran them for 30 miles to the **Snake River** and escaped by swimming the river and disappearing into the willows along its banks. However, two years later one of the men succeeded in killing him after lying in ambush for four days. Tales out of Oregon.

Biggs. An unincorporated community at the junction of **Highway 97** and **Interstate 84**. Before the **Sam Hill bridge** opened in 1962, traffic crossed the **Columbia River** between Biggs and Maryhill, Washington, by **ferry**. The community has some traveler accommodations. W. H. Biggs was an 1880 settler in the area. Oregon Geographic Names.

Bighorn sheep. A large, gray, wild sheep, *Ovis canadensis*, somewhat smaller than a **mountain goat**. Males average 225 pounds. Both males and females have heavy, curved horns weighing up to 40 pounds. Bighorn sheep were once abundant in the **Siskiyou Mountains** and through much of Oregon east of the **Cascade Range**. The subspecies known as the California Bighorn roamed the high desert canyons of southeast Oregon, but it had disappeared by 1916 because of competition and diseases from domestic sheep. The subspecies in northeast Oregon, the Rocky Mountain Bighorn, disappeared by 1945. One source says that both have been reintroduced, beginning in 1954, and that by 1990 there were 1,900 California bighorn sheep at 18 sites and 455 Rocky Mountain bighorns at eight sites, but another source says all of the introduced sheep were from California populations. *Pasturella multosida*, a bacterial pneumonia, and/or *P. hemolytica*, a strain found in domestic sheep, killed a number of bighorns in **Hells Canyon** in the winter of 1995-1996. A few **hunting tags** are issued, but a hunter may receive only one in his lifetime. Big Game History; Mammals and Life Zones of Oregon; Oregon Hunting Guide.

Bigotry. See **Anti-Catholic sentiment**; **Anti-Chinese sentiment**; **Anti-Japanese sentiment**; **Blacks in Oregon history**; **Braceros**; **Homosexuals**; **Intermarriage**; **Know Nothing party**; **Ku Klux Klan**; **Oregon Citizens' Alliance**; **Poll tax**.

Bike paths. See **Bicycle paths**.

Bill. A proposed **law** that has been placed before the **legislature** for consideration. The legislative process begins when the bill is introduced in either the **Senate** or **House of Representatives** by one or more legislators. Budget bills are always given a 5000 number, while other Senate bills are numbered from 1 up and House bills from 2000 up. The presiding officer refers the new bill to a committee. The committee may let it die or may hold hearings, may or may not amend it, and may or may not vote on it. If it passes the committee it is brought before the entire chamber ("sent to the floor") for a vote where it must be voted on as submitted since no floor amendments are allowed. Before the floor vote the entire bill must be read aloud unless the requirement is suspended (as it usually is) by a two-thirds vote. If the bill passes, it is sent to the other chamber where the entire process is repeated. If the bill is amended by committee in the second chamber and passes that chamber, the originating chamber must vote on it again so that an identical bill is approved by both houses. If the two chambers are unable to agree on the wording, a conference committee is appointed to work out wording that both chambers will approve. Once passed by both chambers, the bill is sent to the **governor** who may sign it into law within five working days, let it become law without signing it, or **veto** it. A law may be referred to the voters before it goes into effect unless an emergency clause has been attached to it. The emergency clause may not be attached to revenue measures. The legislature may approve amendments to the **constitution**, but they also must always be approved by voters before becoming official. There is no limit to the number of bills that can be introduced, but each chamber has a cutoff date. By the end of each session about 30% of the several thousand introduced bills have passed and become law. During legislative sessions the daily Legislative Calendar lists the status of each bill and its history. Governing Oregon; Oregon Blue Book; Oregon Legislative Guide. See also **Initiative**; **Referendum**.

Billboards. Advertising signs along state highways are regulated by the Oregon Motorist Information Act of 1971, which limits the number to 2,271 (after the state bought and removed 2,031 in 1975) and regulates their placement and content. Only 1,608 permitted billboards are standing, though a number of illegal billboards have been erected and left standing while lawsuits continue. Billboards rent for $500 to $2,500 per month, or about $3 per 1000 viewers, compared to $18 per 1000 viewers for newspaper advertising. Mail Tribune 12/28/97:1A.

Billy Chinook. See **Lake Billy Chinook**.

Bingham Springs. A warm springs on the Umatilla River 30 miles east of **Pendleton** in **Umatilla County**. It was a stage station and later a resort, complete with swimming pool and bowling alley. It has also been known as Warm Springs, Purdy Springs, and Wenaha Springs. Oregon Geographic Names.

Bingo and raffles. In 1994 the Charitable Activities Section of the Oregon Department of **Justice** issued 386 charitable bingo licenses and 394 raffle licenses. Players spent $86 million on bingo, of which 88% was returned to them and $9.7 million went to the sponsoring organizations. $2.9 million was spent on raffles of which $1.7 went to the sponsoring groups. Lodges, veterans groups, programs for the elderly, and Catholic organizations held the most bingo licenses. 503-229-5725. Oregonian 10/22/95:A18.

Biofuels. Fuels of biological origin, including **wood**, **methane**, methanol, and garbage. Biofuels supplied 7% of Oregon's energy in 1994. 13% was used for residential heating and the rest by industry. State Energy. See also **Ogden Martin**.

Biographical sources. Biographies of many pioneers and government officials to 1956 are included in the Dictionary of Oregon History. Other sources include Oregon Biography Index, Who's Who in Oregon (1929), Capitol's Who's Who for Oregon (1938, 1942, 1948), and Who's Who in the West (1949-1988). Capitol Names provides biographical sketches of the 158 persons whose names are inscribed in the house and senate chambers in the state **capitol**. See also **Vital records**.

Biotechnology Innovation Center. See **Oregon Biotechnology Innovation Center**.

Birds. Oregon's variety of terrain, climate, and vegetation provides for a corresponding richness of bird life; 477 species have been recorded in the state and some 260 breed in the state. The Atlas of Oregon Wildlife includes maps of the distribution of each breeding and wintering species as well as a checklist of wintering birds. All birds, except **game birds** and European starling, house sparrow, and rock dove, are **protected animals**. Since 1926, the Audubon Society has sponsored an annual Christmas bird count. The highest count, in1966, included a flock of 1,100,000 starlings in East Portland. The Portland Audubon Society sponsors a rare bird alert, 503-292-0661. **Oregon Field Ornithologists** is a state-wide birding organization. Atlas of Oregon Wildlife; Birder's Guide to Oregon; Birds of Oregon. See also **Animals; California condor; Endangered animals; Great blue heron; Osprey; Owls; Pacific flyway; Sandhill crane; Sea birds; State bird; Swifts; Turkeys; Water ouzel**.

Birds on a Wire. An outdoor sculpture at the **Oregon Museum of Science and Industry** in **Portland**. It is a series of long tubes that fill with water, tip to spill the water into a pool at the base of the wall, and then rise to be refilled. The sculpture is illuminated at night. Hydraulic and pneumatic chambers in the tubes, a maze of wiring, and a computer program control the movements. David Curt Morris designed and installed it in 1995 on the south wall of a power substation opposite the entrance. Oregonian A&E 4/28/95:16.

Birth control, history. Both possession and dissemination of birth control information and supplies were outlawed in 1873 and didn't become legal in the U.S. until 1936 court decisions. In 1916 Margaret Sanger, birth control advocate, spoke in Portland where she was arrested on obscenity charges. In the 1930s she worked with Walter Pierce, Oregon's U.S. Representative from the 2nd District, former governor, and advocate of eugenics, who led an unsuccessful campaign to make it legal for doctors to dispense birth control information and supplies. "Walter M. Pierce and the Birth Control Movement"

Births. Oregon recorded 42,715 births (and 28,190 **deaths**) in 1995. 12,007 of the births were to unmarried mothers. Over 5% of the pregnant women (2,376) had inadequate prenatal care, and over 5% (2,217) of the babies weighed less than 5 pounds. 18% of the mothers had used tobacco while pregnant and 3% had used alcohol. In 1994 the Oregon birth rate averaged 13.6 births per 1,000 residents, the lowest since 1936. (The rate had peaked at 25.4 in 1947 during the post **World War II** baby boom.) 1994 birth rates ranged from a low of 5.3 in **Sherman County** to a high of 18.5 in **Jefferson County**. In the **Metro** area, the birth rate was 12.9 in **Clackamas Country**, 14.4 in **Multnomah County**, and 16.2 in **Washington County**. In 1996 there were 5.6 infant deaths per 1,000 births, down from 1947 when the infant death rate was 24.8 per 1,000 births. The maternal death rate per 100,000 births dropped from 96.7 in 1947 to 6.8 in 1996. Oregon: A Statistical Overview; Oregon Blue Book; Oregonian 1/29/97:E6, 10/29/97:A10. See also **Abortions; Midwives; Names; Obstetricians; Pregnancy; Teen pregnancy; Vital records**.

Bishops Close. See **Elk Rock**.

Bison. Wild woods bison, *Bison athabascae*, also called buffalo, were found in southeast Oregon until the early 1800s. A hard winter was said to have killed them off, but their numbers may already have been diminished due to hunting by **Indians** mounted on recently-acquired **horses**. The Indians of northeast Oregon also made annual trips through the Rocky Mountains to hunt bison on the plains. However, the vast herds there, numbering over 60,000,000, were slaughtered between 1872 and 1878 for hides, leaving just 1,091 bison in all of North America in 1889. Their descendants now number 100,000; some are being raised commercially for meat on Oregon ranches. Mammals and Life Zones of Oregon; World of the Bison.

Bite: A Taste of Portland. A three-day festival, one of Oregon's largest gatherings, that features wine-tasting and food samples from Portland area restaurants. It is held in **Governor Tom McCall Waterfront Park** in August, and is a benefit for Oregon Special Olympics. 200,000 attended in 1997. 503-248-0600.

Black Bird. A much-photographed 29-foot-high **Medford** bird caricature that stands in front of Black Bird, a general merchandise store. The bird, made of fiberglass over wire and rods, was created by Lee Hobbs in 1965, the year he opened the store. It is clothed appropriately for holidays. Mail Tribune 10/6/96:1E.

Black Box. The popular name for a **Portland** building at 200 Market Street that is entirely wrapped in a reflective black glass skin. It is also called the Darth Vadar Building, and some liken it to the science fiction monolith in book and film "2001". The building, designed by Rudat/Boutwell and Partners and built in 1973, has no 13th floor. Frozen Music.

Black ice. A thin layer of ice on a paved surface that is, since it is too thin to cause a reflection, essentially invisible. It is, however, thick enough to create a driving hazard and is frequently the cause of winter highway accidents, especially where it persists in cold, shady spots.

Black sand. Heavy dark sand found at scattered locations along the southern Oregon coast. It contains grains of **chromite**, garnet, **gold**, magnetite, platinum, and zircon. The sands have been mined, sometimes successfully. Geology of Oregon.

Black walnut. A tree, *Juglans nigra*, native to the eastern U.S. but widely planted as a shade tree. The national champion tree grows at 22236 NW Gillihan Road on **Sauvie Island**. It is 130' tall and 23'2" in circumference (7'4" in diameter). Oregon Blue Book.

Blackberries. In 1995, Oregon growers produced 100% of the nation's commercial blackberries. Production was 35 million pounds, worth $19.2 million, on 5,100 acres, almost half of them in **Marion County**. Oregon's only native blackberry, *Rubus vitifolius*, sometimes called dewberry, has trailing vines and sought-after berries of distinctive flavor. The naturalized Himalaya and Evergreen blackberries, thought to be native to Europe, form impenetrable thickets in western Oregon. The Evergreen was introduced by James Stephens in 1850. 1995 Oregon; Oregon Oddities; Plants and Animals of the Pacific Northwest. See also **Boysenberries**; **Loganberries**.

Blacks in Oregon. The 1990 census counted 46,000 blacks in Oregon, or 1.6% of the state's population. The highest proportion (6%) was in **Multnomah County**. The Oregon Commission on Black Affairs works to implement economic, social, legal, and political equality for blacks in Oregon. Room M-319, Smith Center, Portland State University, PO Box 751, Portland 97207. 503-725-4646. Oregon Blue Book. See also **Homowa Festival of African Arts; Million Man March; Minority, Women and Emerging Small Business Office**.

Blacks in Oregon history. The 1850 census counted 207 free colored in Oregon, a number which may have included Hawaiians. In 1857 Oregonians adopted the state **Constitution** which banned both **slavery** and free Negroes from Oregon; the measure was repealed in 1926. However, **Roseburg**'s **sundown law** was on the books until the 1960s. The Oregon legislature ratified the 14th amendment to the U.S. Constitution in 1866 but repealed the ratification two years later. It refused to ratify the 15th amendment giving blacks the right to vote until 1959. Blacks accounted for 0.6% of **Portland**'s population in 1940; this increased to 2.6% in 1950 following the influx of shipyard workers during **World War II**. In 1990, the 46,000 black Oregonians accounted for 1.6% of the state's population. Peculiar Paradise; "Slaves and Free Men"; This Side of Oregon; "Unwelcome Settlers". See also **Cockstock affair; Exclusion laws; Intermarriage; Knights of the Golden Circle; Lynchings; Poll tax; Segregation; Slavery; Sundown laws**.

Blaine. See **James G. Blaine Society**.

Blair Lake Meadows. Meadows at 5,000' elevation in the **Cascade Range**, about 20 miles northeast of **Oakridge** along Forest Service Roads 24 and 1934, that are notable for their early-summer displays of **wildflowers**, including wild orchids, columbine, and scarlet gilia. Oregonian 4/5/95:E2.

Blazermania. See **Trail Blazers**.

Blimps. Nonrigid airships. Their ability to cruise at 35 mph and stay aloft for long periods makes them ideal for shooting footage of outdoor sporting events. In 1997 there were 53 nationwide, of all sizes, licensed by the Federal Aviation Administration. American Blimp Corporation in **Hillsboro** manufactures a 130-foot blimp. Larger blimps were used during **World War II** to patrol the Oregon coast looking for submarines. Each ship was 252 ft long, 59 ft. in diameter, and had a volume of 425,000 cubic feet. They were housed south of **Tillamook** in two 7-acre hangars built in 1942. One of the hangars, the largest wooden buildings in the world, burned, but the other remains and now houses a museum. A 160' blimp housed at Tillamook has been recently used by University of Washington scientists for research on ocean surface characteristics.

Blind. Oregon has at least 7,500 legally blind persons. The Oregon Commission for the Blind has offices in **Portland, Salem, Eugene**, and **Medford** through which it provides vocational and other services to enable blind persons to live and work independently. 535 SE 12th Ave., Portland 97214-2488. 503-731-3221 or toll-free 888-20-BLIND. Services are also provided by the Oregon School for the Blind which serves students from ages 5 through 21 through a residential program at no cost to their families. 700 Church St. SE, Salem OR 97301-3714. 503-378-3820. The Talking Book & Braille Services department of the **Oregon State Library** provides free materials to over 6,000 blind and physically handicapped Oregonians. State Library Building, Salem OR 97310. Salem: 503-378-3849. Portland 503-224-0610. 800-452-0292. Oregon Blue Book.

Blitzen River. See **Donner und Blitzen River**.

Blizzards. See **Snowfall records**.

BLM. See **Bureau of Land Management**.

Bloch Music Festival. See **Ernest Bloch Music Festival**.

Bloodhounds. On October 9, 1954, a man, his pregnant wife, and her 13-year old son, all dressed in street clothes, went into the Coast Range west of **Falls City** to hunt deer. On the 15th their car was noted and it was discovered that they were missing. Hundreds of men and a helicopter searched unsuccessfully. Norman Wilson, a Californian with three bloodhounds, heard about the search and offered to help. His dogs found the first body the next day, and the other two were found soon after. The search set a record for success in following a cold trail. The old mark had been 105 hours, while Wilson's dogs followed a scent that was 315 hours (over 13 days) cold. Tales out of Oregon. See also **Search dogs**.

Blue Back Speller. A 96-page abridgment of Noah Webster's Elementary Spelling Book. Two thousand copies, bound in blue, were printed at **Oregon City** in 1847, the first English-language book printed on the Pacific Coast Dictionary of Oregon History. See also **Book publishing**.

Blue Book. See **Oregon Blue Book**.

Blue Book Controversy. See **Organic laws**.

Blue Bucket Mine. Somewhere in eastern Oregon during the 1845 wanderings of the **Lost Wagon Train**, the immigrants collected some yellow pebbles, later lost, and placed them in a blue bucket. When some members of the party later saw **gold nuggets** at Sutters Fort in California, they realized that the pebbles had been gold and undertook an unsuccessful search for their source. Further legions have also searched, all without luck, though the explorations led to the discovery of other gold in Eastern Oregon. Gold and Cattle Country; Lost Mines and Treasures. See also **Canyon City mines**; **Lost mines**.

Blue heron. See **Great blue heron**.

Blue Lake, Jefferson County. The bluest of Oregon's eleven Blue Lakes, sometimes called the Crater Lake of the Central Cascades. It lies south of **Highway 20** between the **Santiam Pass** and **Suttle Lake**. Though only 54 acres in size and 1/2 mile long, the lake is 314 feet deep. Blue Lake lies in an explosion crater formed 3,500 years ago when underground water came in contact with hot volcanic rock. Springs 240 feet below the surface near the east shore feed the lake; some of these may be mineral springs. About half of the shoreline is owned by a private party which, in 1996, closed off public access to the lake. After the closure, the Oregon Department of **Fish and Wildlife** discontinued stocking the lake with fish. Atlas of Oregon Lakes; Oregonian 4/23/96:B1.

Blue Lake, Multnomah County. A small lake that has long been an important recreation area for the east **Portland** metropolitan area. It is one mile long, 24-feet deep, covers 61 acres, and lies on the **Columbia River** floodplain where it was formerly connected at high water to **Columbia Slough**. Extensive development in the area, plus lack of circulation, shallowness, and heavy use, all contribute to water quality problems. The south shore is lined with residences, and a county park lies along the north shore where, for six weeks in the summer, concerts are presented on Thursday evenings. Atlas of Oregon Lakes.

Blue Mountain Community College. A public two-year college in **Pendleton** that serves over 3,000 students from **Umatilla** and **Morrow** counties. It offers a complete lower-division transfer program as well as 14 occupational programs, and is home to one of the nation's top intercollegiate rodeo teams. It was founded in 1962. 2410 NW Carden Ave., PO Box 100, Pendleton 97801-0100. 541-276-1260. Oregon Blue Book. See also **Community colleges; Small Business Development Centers**.

Blue Mountain Observatory. A sophisticated seismological station built in 1997 by Boise State University 20 miles east of **Baker City**. The unmanned station, one of two in the United States, has 13 monitors, arranged in a circle four miles across, that record and study earth vibrations in order to determine which are caused by explosions, which by **earthquakes**, and which by nuclear weapons tests. Oregonian 11/19/96:B4, 5/5/97:B6.

Blue Mountain physiographic province. A roughly triangular region of northeast Oregon that includes a cluster of mountain ranges: the **Ochoco, Aldrich**, and **Strawberry** mountains on the south, the **Blue, Greenhorn** and **Elkhorn** mountains in the center, and the **Wallowa Mountains** on the east. It is bounded on the northwest by the **Deschutes Columbia plateau**, on the southwest by the **high lava plains**, and on the east by the **Snake River** and the **Owyhee uplands**. The mountains of the region are geologically complex, built by the accretion of **terranes** beginning about 200 million years ago, though the rocks are up to 380 million years old, the oldest in the state. **Granitic** rocks intruded between 120 and 160 million years ago. The **fossil** record is documented at **John Day Fossil Beds National Monument**. **Gold** and other minerals have been mined extensively in a 50 by 100 mile belt northeast of **John Day** and from around **Canyon City**. Geology of Oregon. See also **Serpentinite; Shoshone**.

Blue Mountain University. A one-time **Methodist**-sponsored college in **La Grande** that was the first institution of higher learning in eastern Oregon. It opened in 1876 in a new brick building that was used the next year as a fort during the **Bannock War**. Financial problems led the school to close in 1886. Dictionary of Oregon History.

Blue Mountains. Broadly, an extensive mountainous area of northeast Oregon and southeast Washington, but more narrowly, the forested mountain ranges north and south between **Pendleton** and **La Grande**. Rock Creek Butte, elevation 9,097', is the high point; it is 12 miles west of **Baker City**. Tributaries of the **John Day River** and **Snake River** drain the area, much of it in the **Umatilla** and **Wallowa Whitman** national forests. Forest Dreams; Geology of Oregon. See also **Elkhorn Ridge; Mount Emily; Shoshone**.

Blue River. An unincorporated community 42 miles east of **Eugene** on the **McKenzie River**. Its free library, operated on the honor system, was founded by Frances O'Brien (1902-1995) in the 1940s, and received national publicity for her policies, namely, that the library was always open, the doors always unlocked, and no library cards were required. The state's tallest living **Christmas tree** is in Blue River. The 130-foot tall Douglas fir stands behind a Christmas gift shop whose owners light it. Oregonian 5/23/97:C1.

Blue River Reservoir. A narrow six-mile-long reservoir north of the

McKenzie River 45 miles east of **Eugene**. It was formed in 1968 by a 320-foot-high embankment dam built by the **Army Corps of Engineers** to provide flood control. The reservoir covers 935 acres and has a maximum depth of 248 feet; it is drawn down in late summer in preparation for flood runoff. Steep forested sides limit recreational use, though it is used for boating and fishing, and there is a campground at the north end. Army Engineers.

Blue schist. See **Grandmother Rock**.

Blueback. A U.S. submarine launched May 16, 1959, and decommissioned in October 1990. It is moored at **OMSI** where it is open for tours. The 219-foot long vessel has both diesel and electric motors, and contains six torpedo tubes plus storage for 18 torpedoes. It carried a crew of 77 sailors.

Blueberries. In 1995, Oregon growers produced 17 million pounds of blueberries, worth $7.6 million, on 2,050 acres, nearly all in the **Willamette Valley**. This was 13% of the nation's commercial crop. 1995 Oregon.

Blues. See **Waterfront Blues Festival**.

Bly. An unincorporated community in **Klamath County**, population 700 "more or less" says the sign. It is on the Sprague River 57 miles east of **Klamath Falls** on **Highway 140**. The post office was called Sprague River when established in 1873. The name was changed to Bly, a **Klamath Indian** word for up or high (as in up-river), in 1883. On May 5, 1945 a Japanese **balloon bomb** exploded on nearby Gearhart Mountain, killing a woman and five children who were on a church picnic. Oregon Geographic Names. See also **Mitchell Monument**.

Board foot. A measurement traditionally used for logs and lumber. A board foot measures 1 foot wide by 1 foot long by 1 inch thick. It takes about 16,000 board feet of lumber to build a 2,000-square-foot house. In 1997 the **Bureau of Land Management** began to use 100 cubic feet (CCF) as a measure instead of board feet, since the cubic measure more accurately represents the full volume of a log.

Board of Control. A board, composed of the **governor**, **secretary of state**, and the state **treasurer**, that supervised state institutions (prisons and hospitals) from 1913 until the legislature eliminated it, effective July 1, 1969, and, in a major reorganization of state government, put the institutions under department heads who were answerable to the governor instead of to three different elected officials. Oregonian 5/14/69:1.

Board of Education. See **Education, State Board of**.

Board of Forestry Lands. Cut-over timber lands foreclosed by Oregon counties for non-payment of property taxes during the **depression**, and then deeded to the state Board of Forestry to be managed by the Oregon Department of **Forestry**. The counties receive two-thirds of net revenue from the 654,000 acres, over half of it in the **Tillamook State Forest**.

Boarding schools (public). Several school districts in eastern Oregon communities have recently opened small boarding programs as a way to keep their local high schools open. In 1996 programs were operated at Harper in **Malheur County**, **Mitchell** and **Spray** in **Wheeler County**, **Paisley** in **Lake County**, **Ukiah** in **Umatilla County**, and **Unity** in **Baker County**. Crane Union High School, 27 miles southeast of **Burns**, has been a boarding school since 1928 for students from its own vast district in **Harney County** and had about 80 boarding students in 1996. **Chemawa Indian School** is the oldest boarding school in the country. Oregonian 1/7/96:L6.

Boardman. A rapidly-growing north central Oregon industrial and recreation center in **Morrow County**, located 45 miles west of **Pendleton** between **Interstate 84** and the **Columbia River**. It is named for Samuel H. Boardman (1874-1953) who homesteaded the area in 1903, and who later developed Oregon's famed **state parks** system as its first superintendent. The city was platted in 1916 as a station on the **Union Pacific** railroad and incorporated in1927. In the 1960s the town was relocated because the **John Day Dam** would flood the original townsite. The economy is based on agribusiness including **onion** processing plants, 35,000 acres of **poplars**, Columbia River water sports, **Boardman power plant**, **solid waste** disposal, a U.S. Navy Bombing Range to the south, and the **Umatilla Chemical Depot** to the east. Population 1980 1,261; 1995 2,550. Elevation 298'. PO Box 229, 97818. 541-481-9252. Visitor information 541-481-3014. Oregon Geographic Names.

Boardman power plant. A **coal**-fueled **electric power plant** in **Morrow County** owned by **Portland General Electric**. The plant, which became operational in 1980, has a nameplate capacity of 560.5 **megawatts**. Inventory.

Boardman State Park. See **Samuel H. Boardman State Park**.

Boards and Commissions. Oregon government structure includes nearly 200 boards and commissions with some 2,000 members, usually appointed by the governor. They advise on matters from higher education to historical records to health services, and include 29 **agricultural commodity commissions**. On most boards members serve without pay and on some without reimbursement for their expenses. Among the paid boards are those for **SAIF** and the **Parole Board**. Most of the boards are financed by assessments and fees rather than by tax money.

Boat building. RiversWest Small Craft Center in **Oaks Amusement Park** in **Portland** teaches a variety of small boat construction methods and also promotes recreational use and history of low impact boats. 503-636-7344. Oregonian 8/25/94:NO 4. See also **Cow scow**; **Ship building**.

Boating. The state **Marine Board** reported that some 190,000 boats were registered in the state in 1995, up from 143,000 in 1985. In 1997 recreational boating was a $1 billion-a-year business in the state. Over the past ten years there have been an average of 104 reported boating accidents and 18 fatalities a year. Oregonian 5/31/96:D1, 4/1/97:B16; Willamette River Recreation Guide. See also **Drownings**; **White water boating**.

Bob Day. An annual celebration held in **Talent** 1995, '96, and '97 that honored those named Bob - as well as those who had ever shaken hands with a Bob or known a Bob. The festival had a variety of events and entertainment, including the Parade of Bobs and the Thingamabob Contest. In 1997 the organizers talked of opening The Bob Museum and Interpretive Center. Ashland Daily Tidings 11/13/97:2.

Bobbie. See **Silverton Bobbie**.

Bobcat. A spotted, short-tailed, 30-pound wild cat, *Lynx rufus*, found nearly throughout Oregon. Its diet is much like the coyote's: rabbits, squirrels, rodents, birds, fawns, and lambs. Though bobcats are quite common, they are rarely seen. 2,066 were trapped in 1994-95, with an average value of $24 each. Atlas of Oregon Wildlife; Mammals and Life Zones of Oregon; Mammals of the Northwest.

Body piercing. By 1997 the state **Health Division Licensing Programs** office had licensed 107 body piercing facilities and registered 215 body piercing technicians. The program is supported by fees and fines. Oregon Blue Book.

Bohemia mining district. A **mining district** southeast of **Cottage Grove**, named for James "Bohemia" Johnson who discovered **gold** in the area in 1863. **Gold mining** was most active between 1891 and 1910. Dictionary of Oregon History; Tracking down Oregon.

Boiler Bay. A bay on the central Oregon coast in **Lincoln County**, a mile north of **Depoe Bay**. A boiler from the 1910 shipwreck of the *J. Marhoffer* is visible at low tide. The burning ship, the victim of a gasoline torch explosion, was steered toward shore and all but the cook made it safely to land. The south side of the bay, including Government Point, is a **state park**. Oregon Geographic Names.

Boletes. Mushrooms that have pores instead of gills on the under side. There are a number of genera and species, some poisonous. However, the King bolete, *Boletus edulis*, also called Cep, Steinpilz, and Porcini, is a choice edible and is gathered commercially. Mushrooms Demystified.

Bomber. A landmark on McLoughlin Boulevard south of **Milwaukie** where, after **World War II**, a Boeing B-17 bomber was mounted over a gas station, later a restaurant. The plane cost $1,500.

Bombs. In 1996 state **police** responded to 307 bomb reports, most of them for real devices. The rest were for hoaxes and suspicious packages. The number has been increasing yearly, perhaps due to the availability of information on the Internet. Mail Tribune 8/12/97:2A. See also **Balloon bombs; Incendiary bombs**.

Bonanza. A south central Oregon ranching community in **Klamath County**, 27 miles east of **Klamath Falls**. The name, Spanish for prosperity, is said to have been prompted by the area's good springs, now in a park in the center of the town. The city was incorporated in 1901. Population 1980 270; 1995 365. Elevation 4,200'. PO Box 297, 97623. 541-545-6566. Oregon Geographic Names.

Bond rating. In 1996 Standard and Poor's Corporation raised the rating on Oregon general obligation **bonds** from AA- to AA, and raised the rating on Certificates of Participation from A to A+. The improved ratings were expected to save up to $50 million in interest costs on bonds to be issued within the year. Oregonian 9/10/96:B14.

Bonds. At the end of 1995 Oregon state government had a total of $5,818 million in outstanding bonded debt. Of that, $3,868 million was in general obligation bonds, all authorized by the voters. $758 million was in revenue bonds, another $837 million was in conduit revenue bonds for **economic development** projects and other purposes, and $353 million was in Certificates of Participation (insured certificates that are based on anticipated legislative appropriations). Local governments in Oregon carried an aggregate of $7,058 million in bonded indebtedness, half of it in revenue bonds, such as for water or sewer projects, to be paid off from the income generated. All general obligation bonds require a vote of the people, but not all revenue bonds do. Voters have authorized state bond issues for veterans home loans, reforestation of the **Tillamook Burn**, higher education buildings, pollution control facilities, elderly housing, and small scale local energy loan fund. Debt Management Division, Oregon State **Treasury**. 503-378-4930. See also **Bond ratings**; **Property tax**.

Bonneville Dam. A dam on the **Columbia River** 40 miles east of **Portland** built for power generation and navigation enhancement. It was the first dam built on the Columbia, and is the westernmost. Though the dam is 146 miles from the ocean, the river is tidal to its base. The dam, built by the **Army Corps of Engineers**, flooded the **Cascades of the Columbia** and created Lake Bonneville. The lake, famous for **wind surfing**, extends 45 miles to **The Dalles Dam**. The completed spillway was dedicated September 28, 1937, by President Franklin D. Roosevelt and the official opening was on July 9, 1938. The spillway dam is a concrete gravity structure 1,090 feet long and 170 feet high; 18 spillway gates control the water level. The powerhouse structure is 1,027 feet long and 190 feet high. Overall length of the dam is 4,500 feet. A second powerhouse, which necessitated the controversial move of the Washington community of North Bonneville, was completed in 1986, doubling nameplate generating capacity to 1,093 **megawatts.** The Corps of Engineers is responsible for power generation, while the **Bonneville Power Administration** distributes and markets the power. One result of increased winter river flows (the result of meeting seasonal power demands) is that the river no longer freezes across at **Portland**. Cascade Locks, 97014-0150. Inventory; Water Power in the "Wilderness". See also **Cascade Locks**; **Frozen rivers**.

Bonneville landslide. See **Cascade landslide**.

Bonneville Lock. A navigation **lock** on the south shore of the **Columbia River** at **Bonneville Dam**, completed in 1938 to replace the original **Cascades Canal and Locks**. The single-lift lock had a maximum lift of 70', was 500' long, 26' in depth over the sills at low water, and could handle ships weighing up to 8,000 tons. Its original 76' width made possible the use of large barge tows on the river, enabling river shipping rates to compete with railroad rates. It is being replaced with a new lock that is 675' long and 86' wide. Army Engineers.

Bonneville Power Administration (BPA). A federal power marketing agency, one of five in the U.S. Department of Energy, created in 1937 to market electricity from **Bonneville Dam**. It now markets the electricity from 29 federal Northwest dams and a **nuclear power** plant owned by **Washington Public Power Supply System** (WPPSS). By law public utilities have first right to the power. BPA also operates a distribution system of 15,000 miles of high-voltage transmission lines. The federal dams and distribution system together are known as the Federal Columbia River Power System. In 1996 it sold 102 million **megawatt** hours of electricity for revenues of $2.4 billion, about 45% of the power consumed in the Northwest. BPA also funds the region's efforts to save **salmon** (capped at $435 million a year) as well as measures for conserving energy. To cut costs, BPA reduced the number of employees from 3,755 in 1994 to 2,905 in 1997. 905 NE 11th Ave., PO Box 3621, Portland 97208-3621. 503-230-3000; 800-622-4519. Oregonian 9/21/97:E5. See also **Electric power plants**; **Indego**; **Northwest Power Planning Council**; **Public Power Council**; **Western Intertie**.

Bonneville Power Administration finances. The BPA Annual Report for 1996 reported revenues totaling $2.43 billion. Of that, 42% was from sale of power to **people's utility districts**, 17% to investor owned **electric utilities**, 16% to **direct service industries**, 3% from power sold to other regional buyers, 14% from sales outside the Northwest, and 8% was from wheeling (transmission) and other sales. Debt totaled $16.4 billion, which included $2.5 billion of long-term U.S. bonds for conservation and fish and wildlife measures, $6.8 billion owed to the federal government to repay generating system and transmission system construction costs, and $7.1 billion owed to non-federal sources for financing three **Washington Public Power Supply System** nuclear plants (two of them abandoned) and several smaller projects. Combined, the debt service on the non-federal debt of $498 million and interest on the federal debt of $384 million took 36% of the budget. In 1996 and 1997 Bonneville paid $175 million to abandon five uncompleted projects it was involved with, the most expensive being the Tenaska natural gas project near Tacoma, Washington. A six-year funding plan allows $252 million a year for fish and wildlife programs plus the costs of hydro operation adjustments. Oregonian 9/14,15,28/97:A1. See also **Salmon management**.

Book publishing. The first printing press in the Northwest arrived by ship in 1839 for use at **Lapwai Mission** (in present-day Idaho) where it was used to print booklets in the **Nez Perce** language. The first book published in what is now Oregon was the **Blue Back Speller** in 1847, and in 1854 the first novel, Margaret Jewett Bailey's Ruth Rover, was published. However, book publishing did not become a major enterprise, and there were fewer than ten book publishers before 1910. Binfords and Mort in **Portland** has been publishing since 1930 and is still active. The **Oregon Historical Society** and **Oregon State University** Press are also major publishers. With desk-top publishing, there are now thought to be hundreds of publishers presently in Oregon. There was no publishers association as of 1997. History of Oregon Literature.

Bookstores. **Portland** is one of the most bookish cities in the country with over a hundred bookstores in the Portland area, or 1.7 bookstores per 10,000 population. Powell's City of Books is the largest new-and-used bookstore in the country with 500,000 titles in 43,000 square feet.

Boomer. A seldom seen, nocturnal, furry, short-tailed rodent, *Aplodontia rufa*, the size of a small cat, found west of the **Cascades** from British Columbia to northern California. Its burrows are common near streams in areas of dense vegetation and loose soil; it feeds on plants such as salal, ferns, and young conifers. **Bobcats** and long-tailed **weasels** are its main predators. It is sometimes called sewellel or mountain beaver, though it is not a true beaver. Atlas of Oregon Wildlife; Mammals and Life Zones of Oregon; Mammals of the Northwest. See also **Fleas**.

Boone. See **D. Boone Tree**.

Boones Ferry. A ferry across the **Willamette River** near what is now **Wilsonville**, operated from 1847 to 1872 by Col. Alphonso Boone and his son, Jesse. A ferry continued to operate at the site until Boone Bridge on **Interstate 5** was completed in 1954. Col. Boone (1796-1851), grandson of Daniel Boone, had been a member of the 1846 wagon train that made the harrowing first crossing of the **Applegate Trail**. Dictionary of Oregon History. See also **D. Boone tree**.

Boot camp. The state operates a boot camp for juvenile offenders called Tillamook Youth Accountability Camp, opened in 1997. The boys volunteer to attend the 18-week camp, giving up privileges at MacLaren or Hillcrest in exchange for shorter sentences and harder work. The boys, who also serve an intense eight month parole after their time at the camp, can be sent back to **juvenile corrections** at any time if they break the rules. The state may open a second youth boot camp and also operates an adult boot camp called Oregon Summit. Oregonian 5/11/97:D1, 7/15/97:E11.

Boots. Some 30,000 pairs of logging boots, specialty boots, and boots for motorcycle riders are manufactured annually by the West Coast Shoe Company in **Scappoose**. The company was founded in 1918 by John Shoemaker and is still operated by the Shoemaker family. Oregonian 7/9/95:F2.

Borax. A mineral with a variety of uses that was mined in Oregon at the turn of the century at **Borax Lake** in the **Alvord Basin**. **Chinese** laborers scraped up the white crusts that coated the ground around the lake and extracted the borax in boilers fired by **sagebrush** until both the borax and sagebrush gave out in 1907. About 400 tons of borax was shipped annually by 16-mule team 130 miles to the railroad in Winnemucca, Nevada. Borax was also mined along the coast 5 1/2 miles north of **Brookings** in the 19th century. Century of Coos and Curry; Oregon's Great Basin Country.

Borax Lake. A 10-acre hot lake located in the **Nature Conservancy**'s 320 acre Borax Lake Preserve about four miles north of Fields in the **Alvord Basin**. The lake sits about 40 feet above the surrounding wind-eroded basin floor. Waters in the lake are heated by a 100-foot deep spring of 170°F water in the center; surface temperature ranges from 65°F to 105°F. A unique 2" fish, the Borax Lake chub, *Gila boraxobius*, thrives in the hot waters, and the lake is used by a variety of waterfowl. **Borax** was mined from its deposits. No camping or swimming is allowed. A controversial 23 megawatt geothermal energy development has been proposed by Anadarko Petroleum Corporation on **Bureau of Land Management** land a mile away. Oregonian 11/15/94:B1, 4/2/96:B2.

Boring. An unincorporated community in **Clackamas County** 18 miles northeast of **Oregon City**. The townsite was platted in 1903 and called Boring Junction for W. H. Boring, an old-time resident of the area. Oregon Geographic Names.

Boring lavas. **Lavas** that erupted about 5 million years ago in the north **Willamette Valley** from over 100 small vents, cones, and shield volcanoes, including **Mount Tabor**, Mount Defiance, **Larch Mountain**, Mount Sylvania, and Highland Butte. Many of the other hills and buttes in and east of **Portland**, around **Oregon City**, and south to La Butte near **Wilsonville** are from these eruptions. Geology of Oregon.

Boston Men. A term used in **Chinook jargon** for Americans, as opposed to "King George Men," the term used for the British. The term derived from the ship *Boston* which the Nootka Indians burned in 1803. They kept the two survivors, a blacksmith and a sail maker, as slaves until the ship *Lydia*, also from Boston, rescued them in 1805. Dictionary of Oregon History.

Boston Roller Mills. The oldest continuously operating water-powered mill on the west coast, founded in 1858 on the Calapooia River. The mill was converted from stone grinding to a roller mill in 1890, and ten years later generated the first electricity in the area, lighting a light on top of the mill. It now operates as a feed mill and generates 100 kilowatts of power. PO Box 71, Shedd 97377.

Bottle bill. A law that mandated a refundable deposit for beer and soft drink containers. At the time it passed in 1971, following several years of intense politicking, it was the first effective bottle return legislation in the nation. In 1996, over 90% of all soda and beer bottles were returned and recycled, reducing both roadside litter and the volume of garbage going to **landfills**. Richard Chambers of Salem, a publicity-averse logging equipment salesman from **Salem**, originated the idea and pushed it through, aided by Governor Tom McCall. Fire at Eden's Gate; Oregon Environmental Atlas.

Bottom fish. Fish, also called groundfish, found near the floor of the ocean, especially those which are commercially important. In 1995 Oregon's bottom-fish catch brought $38.7 million. It included cod, lingcod, rockfish (snapper), thornyheads, rockfish, sablefish, sole, flounder, halibut, sanddab, and **whiting**. Conservation measures have been implemented after commercial catches of some species declined in recent years and commercial quotas were sharply reduced in 1997. In 1996 an artificial reef made up of 750,000 pounds of concrete pipe was placed on the sandy ocean floor about a mile off the mouth of the **Siuslaw River** near **Florence** to provide groundfish habitat. Oregonian 2/22/96:B1, 9/25/96:D4, 2/21/97:D2, 11/9/97:B10.

Boundaries, state. Oregon is bounded by **California** and **Nevada** on the south, **Idaho** on the east, **Washington** on the north, and the Pacific Ocean on the west. The boundaries of Oregon were set by the **Admission Act** of February 14, 1859: "Beginning one marine league at sea, due west from the point where the forty-second parallel of north latitude intersects the same, thence northerly, at the same distance from the line of the coast lying west and opposite the state, including all islands within the jurisdiction of the United States, to a point due west and opposite the middle of the north ship channel of the Columbia River; thence easterly, to and up the middle channel of said river, and, where it is divided by islands, up the middle and widest channel thereof, to a point near Fort Walla Walla, where the forty-sixth parallel of north latitude crosses said river, thence east, on said parallel, to the middle of the main channel of the Shoshone or Snake River; thence up the middle of the main channel of said river, to the mouth of the Owyhee River; thence due south, to the parallel of latitude forty-two degrees north; thence west, along said parallel, to the place of beginning..." The Oregon **Constitution** provides for extension of the boundary seaward as authorized by Congress. Because the **Snake River** loops into Oregon south of the Owyhee, a few acres of Oregon lie on the Idaho side of the river. South of the Snake, the border lies just west of longitude -117°W. Irregularities in the southern border are due to surveying errors. Oregon Blue Book. See also **Exclusive Economic Zone**; **Latitude and longitude**; **Size**.

Boundary commissions. Commissions authorized by state law to guide the creation and growth of **cities**, **special service districts**, and privately owned water and sewer systems. The 1969 law also specifically authorized the seven-member

Lane County Local Government Boundary Commission, the **Marion-Polk** Boundary Commission (dissolved in November 1980), and the 13-member **Portland** Metropolitan Area Local Government Boundary Commission (abolished effective 12/31/98). Governing Oregon; Oregon Blue Book; Oregonian 6/25/97:B15. See also **Metro**; **Region 2040 plan**; **Urban growth boundaries**.

Boundary question. The question for uneasy early settlers of Oregon was whether the **Oregon Country** would end up British, American, or as an independent nation. After festering for years, the British/American question was finally settled peacefully by the **Oregon Treaty of 1846**, which set the border between British and American interests at 49°, the present boundary with Canada. Dictionary of Oregon History; Empire of the Columbia. See also **Champoeg**; **Fifty-four Forty or Fight**; **Joint Occupancy**; **Oregon Question**; **Provisional government**.

Bounty. An amount paid to a person who kills an animal defined as destructive. The first bounties in Oregon were paid in 1843 for wolves that were attacking livestock in the **Willamette Valley**; the money was raised through a voluntary tax. The amounts were 50 cents for a small **wolf**, $3 for a large wolf, $1.50 for a **lynx**, $2 for a **bear**, and $5 for a **cougar**. No state bounties have been offered since 1961, though some counties may still offer bounties for **coyotes** or other animals that damage livestock or crops. Dictionary of Oregon History. See also **Wolf meetings**.

Box Car Rapids. A section of the **Deschutes River** near **Maupin**. One night in 1956 a northbound freight train rounded the curve in the steep canyon and ran headlong into a rock slide. The diesel locomotive, with engineer and brakeman, careered off into the river and disappeared. It was finally located more than a hundred yards downstream. During the next three weeks hundreds of spectators watched the dangerous but ultimately successful effort to recover the bodies of the two men and the locomotive. Oregonian 3/1/97:C1.

Boxing and Wrestling Commission. A five-member commission created in 1987 by the Oregon Legislature to supervise, license and control professional boxing and **wrestling** in order to protect boxers and prevent anyone with criminal links from getting involved. The members are appointed by and report to the superintendent of the Oregon State **Police**. The Commission is credited with reducing corruption and violence in the sport. 9450 SW Commerce Circle, Suite 315, Wilsonville 97070. 503-682-0582. Oregon Blue Book; Oregonian 8/19/96:B6. See also **Casinos**.

Boysenberries. In 1994, Oregon growers produced 2,800 metric tons of boysen and youngberries, worth $3.9 million, on 1,210 acres. This was 75% of the nation's supply, and was produced in the **Willamette Valley**. 1994-1995 Oregon Agriculture.

Braceros. Mexican contract workers who were brought into the U.S. during **World War II** to provide farm labor under an agreement signed with Mexico in August 1942. The Bracero Program, officially called the Emergency Farm Labor Supply, brought over 15,000 braceros to Oregon during the next five years. They worked and lived under harsh conditions and faced widespread anti-Mexican sentiment. **Migrant** workers replaced them after the program was phased out at the end of the war, though it didn't end officially until 1964. Bracero means "strong-armed ones." Nosotros.

Brands. In Oregon the ownership of both livestock and logs is indicated by brands registered with the state. Cattle brands are registered with the Oregon Department of **Agriculture** and log brands with the Oregon Department of **Forestry**. The first cattle brand in Oregon was the "D" brand, first used in 1849 by Russell Dement of **Myrtle Point** who is said to have also used it on some **elk** cows. Dictionary of Oregon History.

Breakwaters. Rock structures built to protect harbors from large waves. The **Army Corps of Engineers** has built ocean breakwaters at **Depoe Bay** and at **Port Orford**. See also **Jetties**.

Breast implants. See **Juries**.

Breitenbush Hot Springs Retreat and Conference Center. A center located in the **Cascade Range** 10 miles northeast of **Detroit** on the Breitenbush River. The center, operated by a workers cooperative, focuses on being an ecologically aware community. It offers workshops, conference space, and individual accommodations. The river, a tributary of the North **Santiam**, was named for Lewis Breitenbusher, an 1849 pioneer. PO Box 578, Detroit 97342. 503-854-3314. Oregon Geographic Names; Reflections Spring 1995:14. See also **Environmental organizations**.

Brethren. See **United Brethren Church**.

Bretz floods. See **Pleistocene floods**.

Breweries. See **Beer**.

Bricks. Bricks have been made in Oregon since 1841-42 when George Gay built his farm home near Wheatland, north of **Salem**, from bricks made on the site. On-site clay was also used in 1846 for the first brick church in Oregon, **Saint Paul Catholic Church**, for **Philomath College**, and for other **Willamette Valley** buildings. A commercial brickyard operated at **Willamina** from 1910 to 1971. There is currently a brickyard at **Monroe**. Dictionary of Oregon History. See also **Alternative architecture**; **Clay**.

Bridal Veil Falls. An easily viewed double waterfall in the **Columbia River Gorge** located in Bridal Veil Falls State Park one mile west of exit 28 from **Interstate 84**. The upper portion drops some 60 feet and the lower portion 40 feet. Waterfall Lover's Guide.

Bridge of the Gods. **Klickitat** Indian legend reported that a natural bridge across the **Columbia River** collapsed as a result of a violent conflict involving three mountain deities - Wyeast (**Mount Hood**) and Pahto (Mount Adams), contending for the love of Loowit, also called Tahonelatclah, (**Mount Saint Helens**) - and that its ruins formed the **Cascades of the Columbia**. Geologists say that the mammoth **Cascade Landslide** near Bonneville in 1260 AD blocked the river for a time and may have been the source of the legend. In 1926 the Bridge of the Gods highway toll bridge opened at **Cascade Locks**. Bridge of the Gods (novel); "Frederick Homer Balch"; Geology of Oregon.

Bridges. In 1997 there were 6,473 state, county, and city **bridges** in Oregon. Longest is the four-mile long (21,474') **Columbia River** Bridge on **Highway 101** at **Astoria**. The highest is 345' above Thomas Creek on Highway 101 in **Curry**

County, followed by the 295'-high **Crooked River** Bridge (1927) on **Highway 97** (being replaced 1997-2000. The old bridge will remain as a pedestrian bridge.). The first recorded bridge in Oregon was built across Dairy Creek in **Washington County** in 1846. The oldest highway bridges still in use are two spans that were part of the 1894 Burnside Bridge. When that bridge was replaced in 1926, the two spans were moved to **Clackamas County** where they are in use on Bull Run County Road and on Lusted Road over the **Sandy River**. Conde McCullough was the famed designer of 900 Oregon highway bridges, including the handsome reinforced concrete arch bridges built on the Oregon coast in 1936 to complete **Highway 101**. **Ferries** were used until bridges were built. Dictionary of Oregon History; Historic Highway Bridges of Oregon; Oregonian 9/23/96:B6. See also **Covered bridges**; **Railroad bridges**.

Bridges, Columbia River. Nine highway bridges and one **ferry** cross the Columbia River between Oregon and Washington in 1997. The 4.1-mile-long **Astoria**-Megler Bridge (1966) on **Highway 101**, is the longest bridge in Oregon. The next crossing upstream is a ferry operating between **Westport** and Puget Island, Washington. The other eight bridges are the Lewis and Clark Bridge (1930, scheduled for replacement about 2006 by the Port of St. Helens) between **Rainier** and Longview; **Interstate 5** Bridge (the northbound span is the original 1917 Interstate Bridge, southbound was built in 1958) between **Portland** and Vancouver; Glenn Jackson Bridge on **Interstate 205** (1983); **Bridge of the Gods** (1926) from **Cascade Locks** to Stevenson, Washington; Hood River Interstate Bridge, originally called the Waucoma Interstate Bridge (1924); The Dalles Interstate Bridge (1954) on **Highway 197**; Sam Hill Bridge (1962) on **Highway 97** between **Biggs** and **Maryhill**; and Umatilla **Interstate 82** Bridge (eastbound 1955, westbound 1988). Historic Highway Bridges of Oregon; Oregonian 8/3/96:C2. See also **Portland bridges**; **Railroad bridges**.

Bridges, Willamette River. The Willamette River was first bridged at **Harrisburg** in 1871. Three **ferries** and twenty four highways now cross the river, sometimes with a bridge each way. Five of **Portland**'s ten Willamette River bridges are owned by **Multnomah County**. They are Morrison Bridge, the first (1887, 1905, 1958); Hawthorne (1910), which is the oldest operating vertical-lift highway truss bridge in the U.S.; Broadway (1913); Sellwood (1925); and Burnside (1926). The state owns Ross Island Bridge (1926); the innovative and lovely steel suspension St. John's Bridge (1931), designed by D. B. Steinman of Golden Gate bridge fame who considered St. John's his masterpiece; the two-level Marquam Bridge (1966) on **Interstate 5**; and Fremont Bridge (1973) on **Interstate 405**, the country's longest tied-arch bridge. In 1973 its 902-foot-long, 6,000-ton mid span was floated into place and lifted 170 feet into position in the biggest lift ever made. The double-decker Steel Bridge (1888, 1912), leased by the state from **Southern Pacific**, carries cars, trains, and **MAX**, and is the world's only telescoping double-deck vertical lift bridge. In 1910, when Portland had half its present population, 30,000 people walked across the city's four bridges each day. Now about 1,000 a day cross on foot. Dictionary of Oregon History; Historic Highway Bridges of Oregon; Oregonian 4/18/96:A1; Portland, An Informal History; Portland Bridge Book. See also **Portland bridges**; **Railroad bridges**.

Brigittine monastery. See **Monastery of Our Lady of Consolation**.

Britt Music Festivals. A summer series of outdoor music and dance concerts in southern Oregon's **Jacksonville**. The classical, jazz, country, pop, and dance events are held on the grounds where the Peter Britt home used to stand. The Swiss-born Britt (1819-1905) was the first photographer in the area and extensively documented its people and landscapes. 800-882-7488.

Broadside. The most famous broadside issued in Oregon was published in 1847 by James Nesmith, champion of the **Applegate Trail**. Jessy Thornton, a member of the first party to use the trail, had been filling Oregon papers with diatribes against the Applegates and their trail. Nesmith had challenged Thornton to a duel which he refused. Nesmith then had a broadside printed and posted which read, "To the World!! J. Quinn Thornton, Having resorted to low, cowardly and dishonorable means, for the purpose of injuring my character and standing, and having refused honorable satisfaction, which I have demanded; I avail myself of this opportunity of publishing him to the world as a reclaimless liar, an infamous scoundrel, a blackhearted villain, an arrant coward, a worthless vagabond, and an imported miscreant; a disgrace to the profession and a dishonor to his country." Plains Across.

Broccoli. In 1995, Oregon growers produced 12,200 tons of broccoli for processing, worth $4.8 million, on 2,580 acres. 1995 Oregon.

Broken Top. A deeply eroded 9,152' peak in the central Oregon **Cascade Range** southeast of the **Three Sisters**.

Bronze. An alloy of copper, usually with tin, used especially for cast sculptures. **Joseph** in northeastern Oregon is a center of bronze casting with several foundries and shops, and in 1996 a bronze foundry was established in **Nesika Beach** on the south Oregon coast.

Brookings. "Home of the Winter Flowers." A coastal town in **Curry County** in the southwest corner of Oregon, located on **Highway 101** near the California border. It began about 1908 as the **company town** for Brookings Lumber & Box Company, owned by Robert Brookings; it was incorporated in 1951. During **World War II**, the only Japanese bombs dropped from a plane on the U.S. mainland fell on Mount Emily, 8 miles east of town. In the past lumber and fishing were important to its economy. Both are now in decline, but 90% of the country's Easter lilies are raised in the area, and the town is growing because retirees like its mild climate. The Azalea Festival is held Memorial Day weekend. Population 1980 3,384; 1995 5,220. Elevation 129'. 898 Elk Drive, 97415. 541-469-2163. Chamber of Commerce 800-535-9469. Oregon Geographic Names. See also **Incendiary bombs**.

Brother Jonathan. A 220' wooden side-wheel steamer with augmenting sails that became a scheduled carrier between San Francisco and Pacific Northwest ports in 1857, carrying freight, gold, and as many as 1,000 passengers at a time. The news of Oregon's statehood was first carried to **Portland** on her. In one of the west coast's worst sea disasters, the overloaded ship sank after hitting a reef near the Oregon/California line during a storm on July 30, 1865; 166 of the 185 persons aboard drowned. Among the dead were General George T. Wright, newly appointed commander of the Department of the Columbia military district, and James Nisbet, editor of the San Francisco Bulletin. Also lost were freight, mail, the

$250,000 payroll for **Fort Vancouver**, and two camels destined for the Owyhee country. Salvage efforts began after the wreck was located in 1993 in 250 feet of water. "Brother Jonathan" was a jocular name for the United States. Oregonian 3/ 17/96:A17, 10/27/96:D8; Shipwrecks of the Pacific Coast; Treasures of the Oregon Country.

Brothers fault zone. An area with a multitude of overlapping **faults** and volcanic centers that mark a deep and active shear in the earth's crust in the **high lava plains.** The fault zone extends 130 miles across eastern Oregon from **Bend** southeast to **Steens Mountain.** The lava plateau south of the fault is broken by the large fault-blocks of the **basin and range** area while north of it there is little faulting. The community of Brothers, located on **Highway 20,** is near the north edge. Geology of Oregon.

Brownlee Dam. A clay-core earth dam on the **Snake River** between Oregon and Idaho, upstream from **Oxbow Dam.** It was built by the **Idaho Power Company** in 1959 for power generation. The 395-foot high, rock-fill dam is 1,380 feet long, and backs up the Snake River in Brownlee Reservoir for 58 miles. The plant has a generating capacity of 585.4 **megawatts,** though full production can be realized only during high water in late spring. Idaho Power operates Woodhead Park on the Idaho side. **Huntington** sponsors a Catfish Tournament, but the Oregon **Health Division** has issued a warning about eating certain fish from the reservoir because of **mercury** levels. The Brownlee family settled on the Idaho side in 1862. Recreation report 800-422-3143.

Brownsville. A historic **Linn County** town on the Calapooia River in the **Willamette Valley** 20 miles southeast of **Albany.** The town, laid out in 1853 in an area that had been first settled in 1846, was named for Hugh Brown, owner of the first store, and incorporated in 1876. Many pioneer homes and buildings survive, and the Linn County Museum includes a 19th-century railroad depot. Oregon's oldest celebration, the Brownsville Pioneer Picnic, is held in Pioneer Park on the third weekend in June. The Pope and Talbot pulp and paper mill is a major employer. Population 1980 1,261; 1995 1,390. Elevation 265'. PO Box 188, 97327. 541-466-5666. Brownsville; Oregon Geographic Names.

Brunk House. A restored 1861 farm house with gardens and farm tool display. It is located west of **Salem** on Highway 22 at Highway 51. PO Box 67, Monmouth 97361. 503-838-1807.

Bubonic plague. See **Plague.**

Buchanan. An unincorporated community 23 miles east of **Burns** on **Highway 20.** Joseph and Hattie Buchanan established the post office in 1911; the office closed in 1919. Oard's Museum, a free museum of Indian art and artifacts, antique guns, and antique clocks, is at 1604 Buchanan Road. 800-637-0252. Oregon Geographic Names.

Buckaroo. See **Vaqueros.**

Buckskin scrip. In 1932 **Wallowa County** government ran out of **money** and issued warrants to its creditors. In order to get some circulation out of them, the merchants of **Enterprise** resolved to print their own scrip, fully backed by warrants, on buckskin. They issued one buck, 1/2 buck, and 1/4 buck scrip. The plan received so much publicity that about a third of the issue was bought by collectors nationwide. The local bucks had all been redeemed by 1935; the profit was used to build a tennis court. **Heppner**, facing the same problem, used sheepskin scrip. History of Wallowa County.

Budget growth. The state **budget** has increased from $4.647 billion in 1989-91 biennium to $9.599 billion in 1997-99. However, when the costs of voter-mandated programs are taken out and the budget is adjusted for inflation and population growth, the amount spent per capita has decreased during the same period from $2,032 to $1,641. Since 1979, spending has declined 53% on **state parks**, 80% on **higher education**, and 56% on Oregon State Police patrols. The voter-mandated programs include **Measure 5** and **Measure 47** which resulted in an increase in the state's share of school financing from 27% in 1990 to 71% in 1999; Measure 11 in 1994 which imposed tougher sentencing requirements and resulted in increased prison and corrections costs; and Measure 44 in 1996 which added $249 million to the budget from a tobacco-tax increase to expand the **Oregon Health Plan**. Oregonian 11/13/97:D1.

Budget, state. The Oregon state budget governs state government spending for two years beginning on July 1 of odd-numbered years. The budget process begins in the fall of even numbered years with state agencies submitting proposed budgets to the **governor** who, by December 1, submits the governor's proposed budget to the **legislature**. The **Joint Ways and Means Committee** of the legislature reviews and revises it before sending a series of appropriations bills out to the **Senate** and **House of Representatives** for final votes. Major appropriations are not usually acted on until the legislature receives the mid-May revenue projections (based on April **income tax** receipts). Though the Oregon **Constitution** provides that the state must not spend money in excess of revenue, voters have amended it a number of times to authorize **bonds**. The **General Fund** accounts for about a third of the state budget and is the only part that can be spent wherever it is needed. The rest of the budget is made up of dedicated funds, including federal revenues (about 18%) and payments for unemployment insurance, gas taxes, tuition, user fees, and retirement funds. The 1997-99 General Fund budget of $9.4 billion ($1,500 per capita per year) included $3.2 billion in replacement revenue to schools for money lost under **Measure 5** and **Measure 47**. Governing Oregon; Oregon Blue Book; Oregonian 12/18/96:C2. See also **Audits Division**; **Employees, state**; **Kicker**.

Buena Ventura River. See **Buonaventura River**.

Buena Vista. An unincorporated community on the west bank of the **Willamette River** in **Polk County**. It was founded by Reason Hall who settled the area in 1847 and whose name for it was inspired by the Mexican battle of Buena Vista ("beautiful view") in which some of his relatives had participated. Hall started a **ferry** across the Willamette River in 1850, and one still operates there. The Oregon Pottery Company, the first in Oregon, operated there from 1866 to 1896. Oregon Geographic Names.

Buffalo. See **Bison**.

Building Codes Division. A division of the Oregon Department of **Consumer and Business Services** that is responsible for adopting and enforcing a uniform statewide building code. It also administers seven specialty codes, regulates construction related activities, licenses 11 professions and trades, and issues

operating permits for three industries. It maintains full-service field offices in
Coquille, Pendleton, Salem, and **The Dalles**. 1535 Edgewater Street NW, Salem
97310. 503-378-4133. Oregon Blue Book.

Building materials. See **Alternative architecture**; **Bricks**; **Cast iron architecture**; **Siding**; **Straw-bale buildings**; **Tree houses**.

Building permits. The 1995 per capita value of residential and commercial
building permits averaged $1,058 statewide. The highest value, $3,260, was in
Union County with **Washington** and **Deschutes** counties also recording high values. Oregon: A Statistical Overview.

Buildings, historic. See **Barns**; **Buildings, oldest**; **Buildings, notable**;
Camp Rilea; **Capitol**; **Crater Lake Lodge**; **Crown Point**; **Crystal Ballroom**;
Deady Hall; **Edgefield**; **Erickson's**; **Forestry Building**; **Hotels and lodges**;
Houses, historic; **Mission Mill Village**; **New Market Theater**; **Pioneer Courthouse**; **Portland City Hall**..

Buildings, most expensive. The **Mark O. Hatfield Federal Courthouse** in
Portland, completed in 1997 for $94 million, is the most expensive building in
Oregon history. Oregonian 5/4/97:E1.

Buildings, notable. See **Big Pink**; **Black Box**; **Bomber**; **Equitable Building**; **Justice Center**; **Mark O. Hatfield Federal Courthouse**; **Memorial Coliseum**; **Norm Thompson headquarters**; **Pioneer Place**; **Portland Building**;
Rose Garden.

Buildings, oldest. The first structures put up by non-Indian settlers in Oregon were log cabins - and they are still being built, often in more elaborate versions. The oldest surviving log structure in Oregon is the Baker House, built around
1856 near Carver in **Clackamas County**. The oldest surviving frame houses in
Oregon include the **Jason Lee House** and Methodist Parsonage, 1841, in **Salem**;
the **McLoughlin House**, 1846, and the Ainsworth House, 1851, both in **Oregon
City**; the Van Duyn House,1848, and the William Steven House, 1851, both in
Lane County; and the **Monteith House**, 1849, in **Albany**, The tiny 1853 Lane
County Clerk's Office, now part of the county museum, is one of the state's oldest
public buildings. The two-room **Butteville** Schoolhouse, 1855, is perhaps the oldest school still standing. **Saint Paul Catholic Church**, 1846, was the first **brick**
church in Oregon. The frame **Oaks Pioneer Church**, (formerly St. John's Episcopal Church), 1851, in **Portland** is probably the oldest surviving Protestant church
in the state. A surprising number of buildings have been moved from their original
sites. Oregon Style. See also **Buildings, historic**; **Houses, historic**.

Buildings, tallest. The tallest building in Oregon is the 546-foot, 41-story
First Interstate Bank (later Wells Fargo) tower in **Portland**. Others, all in Portland,
include the U.S. Bancorp Tower (**Big Pink**) at 536', 39 stories; KOIN Tower Plaza
509', 35 stories; Standard Insurance Center 367', 27 stories; Pacwest Center 356',
31 stories, and **Mark O. Hatfield Federal Courthouse**, 343', 17 stories. The
control tower at **Portland International Airport** is 266 feet tall. Oregon Blue
Book.

Bulbs. See **Dahlias**; **Iris**; **Lilies**; **Melridge, Inc.**; **Tulips**.

Bull Run Lake. A 466-acre lake, perhaps the most important lake in Oregon. It and the two Bull Run Reservoirs 35 miles east of **Portland** supply municipal water to over one-fourth of Oregon's population through 20 water districts in the metropolitan area. The water is so pure that it does not have to be filtered. (Governor Pennoyer took a drink of the first water from the system on January 2, 1895, and declared, "No body.") The basalt and moraine barrier at the outlet of the 225-foot-deep, mile-long natural lake was augmented in 1917 by a concrete dam that raised the water level 20 feet. Although the lake lies only 9 miles west of **Mount Hood**, it is separated from it by deep canyons so no Mount Hood water drains into it. The lake is fed instead by 110" of annual rainfall in its drainage basin. Bull Run Reservoir #1, built in 1929, covers 442 acres and is 175' deep, while Bull Run Reservoir #2, completed in 1962, covers 469 acres, and is 110 feet deep. **Portland General Electric** has installed power generating facilities at both reservoirs and operates a day-use park at Roslyn Lake at the lower end of the project. A third reservoir has been proposed. The U.S. **Forest Service** established the surrounding 142,000 acre, limited-entry Bull Run Reserve in 1892, though logging has been allowed within it. Bull Run River was named for some cattle that escaped from pioneers. Atlas of Oregon Lakes; "Bull Run Watershed"; Oregonian 1/2/95:D1, 2/25/96:A1, 8/19/96:B1; Round the Roses. See also **Columbia South Shore Well Fields**.

Bullards Beach State Park. A **state park** at the mouth of the **Coquille River**, two miles north of **Bandon**. The park includes the historic Coquille River Lighthouse, a boat ramp, a horse camp, and picnic areas. Its 192 campsites are open all year. Reservations, 800-452-5687. PO Box 2483, Bandon 97411. 541-347-2209.

Bullfrog. A non-native frog, *Rana catesbeiana*, that grows up to 8 inches long, making it the largest frog found in Oregon. It was introduced about 100 years ago and has spread widely, to the detriment of smaller animals, including other species of **frogs** that it has, in some places, exterminated. It is classed as a **game fish**, and an angling license is required, though there are no restrictions on when or how many may be taken. Atlas of Oregon Wildlife.

Bully Creek Reservoir. A curving, three-mile long impoundment nine miles northwest of **Vale** on a tributary of the **Malheur River**. The lake covers a thousand acres when full, and has a maximum depth of 75 feet. The 121-foot high dam that formed the lake was built in 1963 as part of the **Vale Project** for irrigation and flood control and is now operated by the Vale Oregon Irrigation District. The lake is also used for fishing and camping. Bully Creek was apparently named for an incident in which a man fell into the creek and his companions stood around and cried "Bully! Bully!" Atlas of Oregon Lakes.

Buonaventura River. A mythical river, sometimes called the Buena Ventura, that in the early 1800s was thought to flow from the west slope of the Rockies to the Pacific. The **Hudson's Bay Company** (HBC) instructed Peter Skene Ogden, leader of an 1826-1827 fur trapping expedition into the unknown country between the **Snake** and Sacramento, to search for the Buonaventura. By the time another HBC brigade traveled south to the Sacramento in 1829, it became apparent that there was no such river. First Over the Siskiyous.

Bureau of Labor and Industries. See **Labor and Industries Bureau**.

Bureau of Land Management. A U.S. agency, part of the Department of

Interior, created in 1946 by the merger of the **General Land Office** and the Grazing Service. It manages 15.7 million acres of land in Oregon, including 13 million acres, primarily in eastern Oregon, available for livestock grazing, and heavily timbered, revested **O&C lands** in western Oregon. It also manages four **wilderness areas**, 17 heritage areas, and 18 **Wild and Scenic Rivers** (766 miles). The BLM is also responsible for regulating **wild horse** herds in the state, for determining the boundaries of all public lands in the U.S., and for administering mineral management laws on all federal lands. Its recreational and interpretive activities include **Back Country Byways** and the **Oregon Trail Interpretive Center**. It has nine district offices in Oregon: the **Burns, Coos Bay, Eugene, Lakeview, Medford, Prineville, Roseburg, Salem,** and **Vale districts**. BLM Oregon Office, 1515 SW 5th Avenue, Box 2965, Portland 97208. BLM Facts. See also **Federal Forest and Resource Policy Team, Governor's; Forest management agencies; Forestry, Oregon Department of (ODF)**.

Bureau of Reclamation. A federal agency in the Department of Interior established by the Newlands Act of 1902 to implement major **irrigation** projects - which were to be self-liquidating. The first projects in Oregon were the **Umatilla Project** and **Klamath Project**, with main components completed by 1912, while the **Vale Project** and **Owyhee Project** were constructed in the late 1920's and early 30's. Of the many projects it constructed, it still owns and operates just three storage reservoirs, **Gerber Reservoir** in the **Klamath Project, McKay Reservoir** in the **Umatilla Project**, and **Henry Hagg Lake** in the **Tualatin Project**. The Tualatin was the last major project completed in the state, though the Bureau is involved in some pumping projects and riparian improvements. 503-872-2795. Statistical Compilation.

Burlington Northern. A major **railroad**, officially the Burlington Northern and Santa Fe Railway Company, that operates a line north from **Portland** to Seattle, another, the former **Spokane, Portland and Seattle Railroad**, east along the north shore of the **Columbia River** to Spokane, and the former **Great Northern** line from **The Dalles** south through **Bend** and **Klamath Falls** to California. It also has lines in the **Willamette Valley**. Company headquarters are in Fort Worth, Texas. Offices for Oregon operations are at 1313 W 11th Street, Vancouver, WA 98660. 360-418-6371.

Burns. An eastern Oregon ranching and commercial center at the intersection of **Highways 20** and **395**. It is the county seat of **Harney County** and the location of the Harney County Historical Museum and the planned **Burns Archive Center**. Burns was founded in 1884 by storekeeper George McGowan who named it for Robert Burns, his favorite Scottish poet. The city was incorporated in 1891. Population 1980 3,579; 1995 2,890. Elevation 4,148'. 242 S. Broadway, 97720. 541-573-5255. Chamber of Commerce 541-573-2636. Oregon Geographic Names. See also **Hines**.

Burns Archive Center. A state center authorized in 1997 as a backup storage facility for computer data from state agencies and from the state **lottery**. It will be linked by a fiber-optic cable to **Boise** as well as **Portland**, so may store computer records from other states as well. Burns was chosen because it is the most seismically stable place in the state and is relatively safe from earthquake, flood, fire, and other catastrophes. Oregonian 12/4/97:D2.

Burns District, BLM. A district that covers 3,456,382 acres of **Bureau of Land Management** grazing lands, located primarily in **Harney County**. The district also manages the BLM's **wild horse** and burro program. HC 74-12533, Hwy 20 West, Hines 97738. 541-573-4400. BLM Facts.

Burns Paiute Tribe and Reservation. A group of some 370 enrolled members of the Wada Tika band of **Northern Paiute Indians**. The Burns Paiute Tribe was federally recognized in 1968. In 1935, 771 acres west of **Burns** was set aside for its use. The land, designated as a reservation in 1972, was later enlarged to 11,786 acres. The tribe plans to build a small **casino**. HC 71 100 Pa Si Go St, Burns 97720. 541-573-2088. American Indian Reservations; First Oregonians; Oregonian 6/1/97:A1.

Burnt River. A river in **Baker County** that flows from the south slopes of the **Blue Mountains** east and southeast to the **Snake River**. It drains an area of 1,090 square miles with an average annual flow of 96,000 acre feet or .1 acre foot/acre. The lower Burnt River Valley has served as a corridor for the **Oregon Trail**, the **Union Pacific Railroad**, roads, and **Interstate 84**. The origin of the name is uncertain. Oregon Geographic Names.

Burnt River Project. A **Bureau of Reclamation** project in **Baker County** that supplies supplemental irrigation water to 16,000 acres of land from **Unity Reservoir**. The project, undertaken in the late 1930s, also provides recreation benefits. Atlas of Oregon Lakes.

Burros. See **Wild horses**.

Bus lines. Greyhound Bus Lines is Oregon's only remaining traditional intercity bus line. Pacific Trailways, also called Mount Hood Stages, headquartered in **Bend**, operated from 1929 until the mid 1980s. Green Tortoise Adventure Travel offers low cost bus travel from Seattle through Oregon to Los Angeles, as well as tours through the west; travelers sleep on the bus. See also **Public transit**; **School buses**.

Buses, history. The first intercity bus in the nation was built in 1905 in Oregon for operation on the 90-mile run between **Bend** and the end of the railroad at **Shaniko**. The open-car "road train" had four bench seats and pulled a trailer to carry freight and baggage. However, poor roads led to such damage from rocks, jolts, and sagebrush that the venture lasted only a few weeks. East of the Cascades.

Bush House. An 1878 home in **Salem**, designed by Wilbur F. Boothby for Asahel Bush II, founder of the Oregon Statesman newspaper and of the Ladd and Bush Bank, both of which are still operating. Both the Bush House (503-363-4714) and Bush Barn Art Center (503-583-2228) are located in **Bush's Pasture Park** and are administered by the Salem Art Association. 600 Mission Street, 97302-6203.

Bush's Pasture Park. A 100-acre park on Mission Street in **Salem** that surrounds **Bush House**. The grounds include an 1882 greenhouse, flowering trees, an old rose collection, and other flower and herb gardens. **Deepwood** estate adjoins it on the east.

Business Information Center. A centralized site for obtaining information on starting a business in Oregon. It is operated by the **Corporation Division** under the **Secretary of State**. 255 Capitol St. NE, Suite 151, Salem 97310. 503-986-2222. Oregon Blue Book. See also **Small business**.

Business Retention Service. A program in the Oregon **Economic Development Department** that offers assistance to troubled companies facing national or international competition. In 1996 the Council of State Governments called it one of the most innovative small-business economic development programs in the U.S. 503-986-0197. Oregonian 7/26/97:C9.

Business. See **Corporations**; **Employers**; **Les Schwab Tire Centers**; **Manufacturing**; **Oldest businesses**; **Retail sales**; **Salaries**; **Securities**.

Butte Falls. An isolated southwest Oregon timber community in **Jackson County**, 30 miles northeast of **Medford**. It was established as a mill town in 1878 next to the 15' falls on Big Butte Creek, and incorporated in 1911. It gained brief national attention when "Ripley's Believe It or Not" proclaimed it the only city in the world with a cattle guard at each end. Population 1980 428; 1995 410. Elevation 2,535'. PO Box 268, 97522. 541-865-3262. Land in Common.

Butter. See **Dairy products**; **Dog wheel**; **Margarine**.

Butterflies. Over 200 species and subspecies of butterflies are found in Oregon. The availability of appropriate larval food plants is critical for their survival; some feed on only one species of plant. A few Oregon species migrate long distances (Monarch, Painted Lady, California Tortoiseshell), but most live within a small range. The Oregon swallowtail, *Papilio oregonius*, is the **state insect**. It is found in the **sagebrush** canyons of the **Columbia River** drainage; the larvae feed on tarragon sage, *Artemesia dracunculus*. Butterflies of Oregon. See also **Endangered Species Act (U.S.) animal listings**.

Butterfly fleet. See **Mosquito fleet**.

Butteville. A historic unincorporated community on the east bank of the **Willamette River** in **Marion County**, five miles southwest of **Wilsonville**. The town was laid out about 1845, and named for the nearby hill, known as La Butte. It flourished for about fifty years as a river shipping point, but then faded as railroads came in. Oregon Geographic Names; Oregon Ghost Towns.

By-the-wind sailors. See **Sail jellyfish**.

Bybee-Howell House. A Greek Revival Style farmhouse built in 1858 on **Sauvie Island**. **Multnomah County** bought the house and the surrounding 130 acres in 1959 from the Howell family which had owned it for 100 years. The **Oregon Historical Society** and volunteers have refurbished the house and open it to the public during the summer and for special events, including the Wintering-In Harvest Festival in late September. Architecture Oregon Style; Portland, An Informal History. See also **Howell Territorial Park**.

Bybee Lake. Bybee Lake and Smith Lake are large, shallow (one-foot deep) lakes in the industrial area of north **Portland**. Their waters intermingle with marshes to cover nearly 2,000 acres, forming one of the nation's largest urban freshwater wetlands. The area, including the former **Saint Johns landfill** site just south of Bybee Lake, is managed by **Metro** as wildlife habitat. The lakes are part of the **Columbia Slough** hydrologic system; Bybee lake is affected by tides in the **Columbia River** and both lakes are affected by river high water. Smith Lake often has no standing water by the end of August while Bybee Lake is flushed by tidal changes twice a day. The lakes provide waterfowl habitat and the **Army Corps of Engineers** has modified the hydrology by installing a water control structure to help control outbreaks of avian botulism. A parking lot south of Marine Drive and a one-mile-long interlakes trail provide access. James Bybee was the pioneer owner of the lake. Atlas of Oregon Lakes.

Byways. See **Back Country Byways**; **Scenic Byways**.

Cabbage. See **Sauerkraut**.

Cabinet members from Oregon. See **Presidential cabinet members from Oregon**.

Cable cars. A cable-car line operated in the 1890s in **Portland**'s West Hills where Portlanders of the era had summer retreats and, later, year-round residences. Portland, An Informal History.

Cable networks. See **ED-NET**; **Fiber-optic cable**; **NERO Project**.

Cable television. The cable TV companies serving Oregon are listed in the Oregon Blue Book. Oregon Cable Television Association, 960 Liberty St. SE, Suite 200, Salem 97302-4154. 503-362-8838.

Calapooia River. A river that drains a narrow valley in the **Cascade Range** and flows northwest past **Brownsville** to join the **Willamette River** at **Albany**. The name was that of the Indians living in the area. Calapooya Creek in the **Umpqua** drainage is named for the same Indians; it was at the south end of their home territory. Kalapuyans.

Calapooya Indians. See **Kalapuya Indians**.

Calapooya Mounds. Mounds about four feet high and from 75 to 150 feet in diameter found in the central **Willamette Valley** at the time of white settlement. Most of the 150 mounds were leveled by farmers who, in the process, uncovered bones and artifacts indicating burial and/or village sites. Kalapuyans.

Calapooya Mountains. A western extension of the **Cascade Mountains** lying between the **Willamette** and **Umpqua River** drainages. The mountains were significant as the last barrier to settlers who were coming into the **Willamette Valley** from the south on the **Applegate Trail**. The mountains contain cinnabar ore, and at one time a number of **mercury** mines operated in the area. The Calapooya is a variant spelling of **Kalapuya**, the Indians of the Willamette Valley. Dictionary of Oregon History.

Caldera. A large basin, at least a mile in diameter, created by the collapse of a volcanic summit after the ejection of a large volume of **lava**, ash, and/or **pumice** from the magma reservoir below the peak leads to collapse of the unsupported dome. The most famous example in Oregon is the misnamed **Crater Lake**. **Newberry Crater** with its two lakes is also a caldera. The only other caldera lake in Oregon is **Harney Lake** which occupies a large, low, ancient caldera. Other older and less obvious calderas are found in central and southeastern Oregon in **Harney Basin** and in the **Lake Owyhee** volcanic field, such as the huge McDermitt caldera complex on the Oregon/Nevada border. A large, 25-million-year-old caldera has recently been identified west of Union Creek in **Jackson County**. "Ancient caldera complex revealed"; Geology of Oregon. See also **Volcano**.

California. The state that shares 220 miles of Oregon's southern border. It is almost twice as large as Oregon, with ten times the population and 13 times the gross state product. The first Spanish mission was established in what is now California in 1769 and the area remained Spanish until 1822 when it became a province of Mexico. The Mexican government was wary of American and **Hudson's Bay Company** fur trappers, but contact gradually increased, both by sea and overland along the **Siskiyou Trail**. After the Mexican-American war of 1846, California became part of the U.S. and was made a state in 1850 without having first been a territory. During the **gold rush** of 1848 Oregon settlers flocked to California, and the state remained important to Oregon for decades, both economically and as a communication center. Early **transcontinental connections** to California included the **telegraph** in 1861 and the **railroad** in 1869, fourteen years before Oregon's rail connection to the east. See also **San Francisco**.

California condor. A large vulture, *Gymnogyps californianus*, with a nine-foot wingspan. Condors were reported as common on the lower **Columbia River** in 1806, and a few were seen in southwest Oregon a century later. They are now extinct in Oregon and near total extinction in California. Birds of Oregon.

California laurel. See **Oregon-myrtle**.

California Stage Company. The first **stage line** to operate between **Portland** and Sacramento, beginning in 1860. The 700-mile run took seven days. After the company lost its postal contract in 1865, other companies operated the route until the railroad to California was completed in 1887. Dictionary of Oregon History.

California Trail. See **Siskiyou Trail**.

Calligraphy. In 1972 Governor Tom McCall named **Reed College** professor Lloyd Reynolds (1902-1978) as Oregon's first Calligrapher Laureate. The Calligraphy of Lloyd J. Reynolds.

Calyx. An award-winning, semi-annual journal of art and literature by women, published in **Corvallis**. The journal was founded in 1976, and in 1986 the press began publishing books as well. 216 SW Madison Ave., Corvallis 97333. 541-753-9384. Oregon Quarterly Winter 1994 p.10.

Camas. A flowering bulb, *Camassia sp.*, found in moist meadows throughout the Northwest. Though usually blue-flowered, occasionally white-flowered mutants occur, and around **Roseburg** they have become the dominant form. The one-inch, onion-like bulbs were a staple food for many **Indian** tribes that dug the bulbs during the summer and autumn, then roasted, dried, and stored some of them for winter food and for trade. The white flowered death camas, *Zigadenus sp.*, is easily distinguished from camas when in bloom, but the bulbs are similar. Death camas is also toxic to honeybees. Great Northwest Nature Factbook; Wildflower Genetics; Wildflowers of the West.

Camels. Although camels were used for transport in British Columbia during the **gold rush**, there is no evidence that they were ever used in Oregon. At one time a man who called himself "Lawrence of Florence" offered camel rides in the dunes south of **Florence**. **Fossils** of ancestral camels from the **Miocene** have been found in Oregon. Oregon Historical Quarterly 30(2):125, June 1929. See also **Brother Jonathan**.

Camp Abbot. A central Oregon **World War II** army training camp and engineer replacement center on the **Deschutes River** south of **Bend** where **Sun**

River is now located. The camp, in service for about a year after its dedication in September 1943, had accommodations for 10,000 men. Brigadier-General Henry Larcom Abbot, 1831-1927, was involved in military railroad surveys of the area in 1855 and later served in the **Civil War**. East of the Cascades; Oregon Geographic Names. See also **Oregon Maneuvers**.

Camp Adair. A **World War II** military training camp located north of **Corvallis** and known to many as Swamp Adair. Four infantry divisions trained at the camp, the 70th "Trailblazer" (served in France), 91st "Powder River" (served in Italy), 96th "Deadeye" (served in the Philippines and Okinawa), and 104th "Frontier", later "Timberwolf" (served in Belgium and Germany). The camp site was selected in July 1941 and troop trains began arriving in July 1942. The camp, which displaced 250 families, 414 graves, and the hamlet of Wells (Wellsdale), covered 50,000 acres, cost $27,000,000, and was designed to house 33,000 men at a time. It was, for a time, the **second-largest city** in Oregon. The last troops left in 1944; the camp was then used for Italian and German prisoners of war until May 1946 and for a Navy hospital. **Adair Village** now occupies a portion of the site and part of it is the Wilson Game Management Area. The camp was named for Lt. Henry R. Adair, an Oregonian who was killed in Mexico in 1916. Camp Adair.

Camp Angell. An array of barracks on the Oregon coast south of **Waldport** constructed as a **Civilian Conservation Corps** camp in the 1930s during the **Depression**. From 1940-46 it was used as a **World War II** camp for conscientious objectors. The "CO's," also called "conchies", reforested rugged areas near the camp, published two periodicals and ten volumes of poetry, and established a book press. The origins of Beat Generation poetry have been traced to the camp. Camp Angell has more recently served as the Angell Job Corps camp. Another conscientious objectors camp was located in Wyeth, near **Cascade Locks**. No Silence; Oregonian 2/19/97:B1.

Camp Castaway. The name given to a camp set up on the beach by shipwreck survivors on January 3, 1852. The schooner, *Captain Lincoln*, had been carrying 36 dragoons to **Port Orford** to help defend settlers against Indians when a storm piled it on the beach two miles north of **Coos Bay**. All crew and passengers survived and set up camp on the beach for several months while working out plans to go overland to Port Orford. The temporary camp was the first white settlement in what is now **Coos County**. Shipwrecks of the Pacific Coast.

Camp Polk, 1865-66. A now-vanished military camp on the west bank of Squaw Creek three miles northeast of the present location of **Sisters**. It was established during Indian uprisings and named by the commander for his home county in the **Willamette Valley**. Oregon Geographic Names.

Camp Rilea. A summer training area for the Oregon **National Guard**, located along the sandy shores of the **Clatsop Plains** in northwest Oregon. It was established in 1927 as Camp Clatsop, but renamed in 1959 in honor of Major-General Thomas Rilea, 1895-1959, long-time Adjutant General of Oregon. The Camp Rilea Chateau is a 2,000 square-foot, four-bedroom, log lodge that has served as a retreat for military and civilians since it was built in 1935 by the **Civilian Conservation Corps**. Oregon Geographic Names; Oregonian 6/10/96:B2.

Camp Sherman. An unincorporated resort community near the **Springs of**

the Metolius in **Jefferson County** six miles north of Highway 20. After their harvests, farm families from **Sherman County** used to come by wagon to camp in the area, hence the name. East of the Cascades.

Camp Steele. See **Fort Harney**.

Camp Warner, 1866-1873. A military camp established originally on the east side of **Warner Valley**, but moved the next year to Honey Creek on the slopes of McDowell Peak on the west side of the valley. Its facilities included quarters for officers and enlisted men plus a number of specialized buildings. The camp served as an important center of military activities during the **Modoc War**. It was named for Brevet Captain William Warner who had been killed nearby by Indians in 1849. Dictionary of Oregon History; Oregon Geographic Names.

Camp White. A **World War II** military training camp located six miles north of **Medford** in **Jackson County**. It was named in honor of George Ared White who had been a reporter for the Oregonian before becoming adjutant general for Oregon in 1915. He was major-general in command of the 41st Division at the time of his death in 1941. Camp White was authorized in January 1942 and the first troops arrived six months later. The camp, called by Time magazine "the Alcatraz of training camps," also housed German prisoners of war and had 1,300 buildings by the time it was deactivated in 1946. The hospital facility was retained and turned over to the Veterans Administration for a domiciliary. The area is now known as **White City**. Camp White; Oregon Geographic Names; Oregonian 10/17/96:C6; "Reminiscence".

Camp Withycombe. A 259-acre **National Guard** camp in **Clackamas County** near the community of Clackamas. It was established as the Clackamas Rifle Range in 1909, and renamed about 1918 for James Withycombe who was governor at the time. It also houses the Oregon Military Museum. 10101 SE Clackamas Road. 503-557-5359. Oregon Geographic Names.

Campaign expenditures. The **Elections Division** publication on 1994 campaign expenditures shows that in 1994 candidates for partisan state-wide office (governor and labor commissioner) spent an average of $206,000 each for the **primary election** and $217,000 for the **general election**. Candidates for state **senator** spent an average of $17,000 on the primary and $63,000 in the general election. Candidates for state **representative** spent an average of $12,000 in the primary and $42,000 in the general election. Nonpartisan candidates for statewide positions (Superintendent of Public Instruction, judges) spent an average of $7,300 for the primary and $6,000 for the general election. Expenditures for the 20 ballot measures on the 1994 fall general election ballot totaled $17,563,710.

Campaign finance. From 1980 to 1990, the average cost of campaigning for a seat in the Oregon **House of Representatives** increased from $3,500 to $35,000. In his losing 1995 campaign for Senator Packwood's vacated seat, Gordon Smith spent $4.6 million, or $8 for each "yes" vote that he received. In order to prevent undue influence on matters before the legislature, state legislators are prohibited from soliciting or accepting campaign contributions in odd numbered years (the years the legislature meets) from January 1 until the end of the legislative session. The governor is prohibited from soliciting or accepting campaign contributions from January 1 of odd numbered years until 30 days after the end of the session. The **Elections Division** publishes reports of campaign contributions and expenditures following each election. Governing Oregon; Oregonian 3/11/96:A1.

Campaign finance reform. An **initiative** measure adopted by voters in 1994 limited contributions by individuals, groups and political action committees (PACs); prohibited contributions to candidates by corporations and unions; limited contributions to PACs; banned candidates' personal use of campaign funds; and eliminated tax credits for contributions to candidates who don't set optional campaign spending caps. The limits resulted in a drop in total spending on state legislative races from $7.5 million in 1994 to $3.4 million in 1996. In 1997 the Oregon **Supreme Court** ruled that the limits on contributions were unconstitutional, but that voluntary spending limits could remain. The state also allows a tax credit for political contributions that costs the state about $5.4 million a year. Oregonian 2/25/96:E1, 3/19/96:B7, 2/7/97:A1.

Campgrounds. Campgrounds in Oregon are operated by **state parks** and other state agencies, federal agencies, including the U.S. **Forest Service**, **Bureau of Land Management**, **electric utilities**, and private operators. A number stay open all year, and state parks have reduced winter fees. The Oregon **Tourism Commission**, 800-547-7842, distributes a free Oregon campground guide. Reservations for 70 state parks in Oregon and Washington may be made by phone to Reservations Northwest, 800-452-5687, by fax at 503-378-6308, or by e-mail at res.nw@state.or.us up to 11 months in advance. Some National Forest campgrounds may be reserved through 800-280-CAMP. In 1996 45% of the overnight use of campgrounds was by visitors from out-of-state. See also **Yurt camping**.

Camps. See **Summer camps**.

Camps, military. The military established a series of camps in eastern Oregon during the 1860s to protect settlers and transport. They included Camp Alvord, 1864-66, near Andrews at the eastern base of **Steens Mountain**; Camp Watson, 1864-1869, 55 miles west of **Canyon City**; Camp Currey, 1865-66, on Silver Creek about 30 miles west of **Burns**; Camp Logan, 1865-1868, six miles south of **Prairie City**; Camp Lyon on the **Owyhee River** near the Oregon-Idaho border, later called Camp Three Forks; **Camp Polk**, 1865-66 near **Sisters**; Camp C. F. Smith, 1866, at the present site of **Whitehorse Ranch**; **Camp Warner**, 1866-1873, in the **Warner Valley**; Camp Wright, 1865, at the east end of **Wright's Point**; and Camp Steele, later renamed **Fort Harney**, 14 miles east of **Burns**, 1867-1880. Camp Bidwell was located in northern California near the Oregon/Nevada corner. Camp Baker, 1862-65, was located near **Phoenix**, though most military establishments in the western part of the state were built earlier and were called **forts**. Dictionary of Oregon History; Oregon Geographic Names; Oregon's Great Basin Country. See also **Forts**.

Canadians. See **French Canadians in Oregon**.

Canals. See **Ditches**; **Locks**; **Oswego Canal**; **Panama Canal**.

Canby. "Garden Spot of the Willamette Valley." A city in **Clackamas County** 10 miles south of **Oregon City** on **Highway 99E**. It was named for General Edward Canby who was killed during the southern Oregon **Modoc Indian War** in 1873. The city was incorporated in 1893. It lies in the midst of some of the richest agricultural land in the state, much of it used for **nursery** crops, but the city has also been growing as a suburban residential area. Johnson Controls, a battery manufacturer, is the largest industry. Its sister city is Kurisawa, Japan. Population 1980 7,659; 1995 10,855. Elevation 153'. PO Box 930, 97013. 503-266-4021. Chamber of Commerce 503-266-4600. Oregon Geographic Names.

Cancer. In 1997 the Oregon Cancer Center in **Portland** was designated as part of the elite National Cancer Institute network as the only NCI-designated center between Seattle and Los Angeles. The center, based at **Oregon Health Sciences University**, includes a matrix of 180 researchers and physicians from OHSU, the Veterans Affairs Medical Center, and hospitals throughout the state, doing research and working to translate the latest research into patient care. Oregonian 7/6/97:C1.

Candidates. State law requires that candidates for political office must meet a host of requirements and timelines. These include residency in the district a year before the **general election**, a deadline for filing for election 70 days before the **primary election**, deadlines and guidelines for submitting material for the **Voters' Pamphlet**, and a requirement that candidates give nothing of value, such as pencils, to voters - though the ice water given out by the **Democrats** party at the **State Fair** has been determined to be legitimate. Regulations also cover campaign literature, **campaign finance**, and reporting. See also **Elected officials**; **Elections Division**.

Candlefish. See **Smelt**.

Canemah (kah NEEM uh). A historic community on the **Willamette River**, now within **Oregon City**. It was the south (upstream) end of the portage around **Willamette Falls** where river freight, livestock, and passengers were transferred. Earlier it had been the site of an Indian encampment and place of barter. The name is that of an Indian chief. The name was also given to a side-wheel steamer built in the community in 1851 that was Oregon's first floating post office and that also, in 1853, provided Oregon's first **steamboat** explosion, scalding a passenger to death. Dictionary of Oregon History; In Search of Western Oregon; Oregon Geographic Names. See also *Gazelle*.

Canneries, history. The first commercial salmon cannery in Oregon began operation at **Westport** in 1869. By 1874 there were 13 salmon canneries from **Rainier** to **Astoria**, and others were soon built farther up the **Columbia River** and on coastal rivers. The first cannery for fruits and vegetables was started by Asa Lovejoy in 1870 just north of **Oregon City**. Dictionary of Oregon History. See also **Food processing**.

Cannibal Mountain. A 1,946' peak in the **Coast Range** 10 miles east of **Waldport**. It is notable primarily for its distinctive name, though the origin of the name is unknown. Oregon Geographic Names.

Cannon Beach. "Beach of a Thousand Wonders." A north coast residential and resort city in **Clatsop County** 26 miles south of **Astoria** on **Highway 101**. The beach was named for a small cannon that drifted ashore from the shipwrecked schooner *Shark* in 1846. The city was incorporated in 1956. **Sandcastle Day**, held on an early June weekend, includes a sand sculpture contest. Haystack Rock, 235' high and just offshore, is a much-photographed landmark, and Ecola Beach

State Park is 2 miles north. Population 1980 1,187; 1995 1,365. Elevation 0. PO Box 368, 97110. 503-436-1581. Chamber of Commerce 503-436-2623. Oregon Geographic Names.

Canopy Trail. A proposed mile-long web of elevated trails through the forest canopy in southwest Oregon's **Curry County**. The $19 million project would also include a visitor center. Oregonian 10/31/97:D2.

Canyon City. The county seat of **Grant County**, located up a canyon two miles south of **John Day** on **Highway 395**. It sprang up in 1862 as a gold mining camp called Whiskey Gulch that quickly grew to 5,000 men and was, for a brief time, the state's **second-largest city**, perhaps even the largest. By 1880, $26,000,000 of gold had been taken from the area. The town was incorporated in 1891. A flash flood in 1896 destroyed much of the town, as did fires in 1870, 1898, and 1937, but the 1876 **Episcopal Church** survives. The poet Joaquin Miller (1839-1931) wrote his first poems during his four years at Canyon City; his cabin is preserved. Population 1980 639; 1995 685. Elevation 3,194'. PO Box 276, 97820. 541-575-0509. Chamber of Commerce 541-575-0547. Gold and Cattle Country; History of Grant County; Oregon's Golden Years.

Canyon City mines. Mines that were developed after **gold** was discovered in 1862 at Whiskey Flat in **Grant County** by miners looking for the **Blue Bucket Mine**. Thousands of miners descended on the site, and the town of **Canyon City** sprang up. In the first decade $8,000,000 of gold was taken from the area. Pack trains carried goods to the area from **The Dalles** until replaced by **stage lines** traveling **The Dalles Military Wagon Road**. Oregon's Golden Years. See also **Gold mining**; **Vigilantes**; **Yreka trail**.

Canyon Creek Pass. A pass on **Interstate 5**, elevation 2,015', where the highway crosses a ridge instead of following **Cow Creek** (tributary to the **Umpqua River**) around a large loop to the west. It is the most northerly of the five major passes on Interstate 5 in southern Oregon, and is the highest pass north of **Medford**. The **Applegate Trail** also crossed the pass, the most difficult section of a difficult route.

Canyon Road. Originally a road that crossed **Portland**'s West Hills to the Tualatin Valley. **Sunset Highway** (**Highway 26**) and Highway 8 now follow some of the route. The canyon was the location of the first **plank road** on the Pacific Coast, built by a private company in 1851-53 as a major undertaking at a time when Portland had just 800 people. The road was built in order to entice farmers of the Tualatin and Yamhill valleys to ship their **wheat** through the port of Portland. Its success led to such rapid growth that Portland quickly outstripped its rival communities of **Rainier**, **Saint Helens**, Linnton, **Milwaukie**, and **Oregon City**. Empire of the Columbia; Round the Roses. See also **Oswego Canal**.

Canyonville. A southwest Oregon timber and tourism town on the South **Umpqua River** in **Douglas County**, 23 miles south of **Roseburg** on **Interstate 5**. It was incorporated in 1901. The **Cow Creek** Indian Gaming Center (a **casino**), opened in 1992. Population 1980 1,288; 1995 1,235. Elevation 747'. PO Box 765, 97417. 541-839-4258. Oregon Geographic Names.

Canyonville slide. A **landslide** on January 16, 1974, that buried a small telephone company relay station building and the nine men who were working in it. Their bodies were never recovered. The site of the slide, about a mile south of **Canyonville** on the east side of **Interstate 5**, is marked with a small cross, now nearly hidden in the pines that have grown over the spot. The slide was in the same canyon in which the 1846 pioneers faced extreme hardships as they descended Canyon Creek on the **Applegate Trail**. Oregonian 1/18/74.

Cape Arago. A sandstone promontory 14 miles southwest of **Coos Bay**. Originally named Cape Gregory by Captain Cook in 1778, it was later renamed Cape Arago in honor of a French physicist and geographer. The South Cove is believed to be the "bad bay" where English buccaneer and explorer Francis Drake in the Golden Hind dropped anchor briefly in 1579. Jedediah Smith's expedition camped on the cape in 1828. A **state park**, formerly part of the Simpson estate (as was nearby **Shore Acres State Park**) provides views of Simpson Reef with **sea lions**, **seals**, and **elephant seals**. The nearest camping is at **Sunset Bay State Park**. Oregon Geographic Names.

Cape Arago Lighthouse. An active **lighthouse** three miles west of **Charleston** located on an island just offshore. Despite the name, the lighthouse is actually 2.5 miles north of **Cape Arago**. Two previous lighthouses at the same location eroded into the ocean. The first was built in 1866, the second in 1909. The present light, built in 1934, was automated in 1966. The tower is 44' tall, and the light is 100' above the water. The lighthouse is not open to the public, but can be seen from near **Sunset Bay State Park**. Oregon Lighthouses; Oregon's Seacoast Lighthouses.

Cape Blanco. A south coast promontory of sedimentary rock lying north of **Port Orford**. It is the most westerly point in Oregon (west longitude 124° 33' 46"), extending to within 40 miles of the **Cascadia Subduction Zone**; it is also the southernmost point of the **Coast Range**. The name was in use sometime before 1602 by Spanish explorers, but there is uncertainty as to which cape it referred to. Captain George Vancouver passed what is now called Cape Blanco in 1792 and named it Cape Orford to honor his friend, George, Earl of Orford, but Cape Blanco, perhaps called that for the white (blanco) fossil mollusk shells that wash out of terraces high on the bluffs, is the name in current use. **Cape Blanco Lighthouse** is the most westerly in the 48 states. **Kelp** beds off the point were an important sea **otter** hunting grounds in the 19th century. Oregon Geographic Names. See also **Cape Blanco State Park**; *J. A. Chanslor*.

Cape Blanco Lighthouse. The most westerly and the oldest **lighthouse** in Oregon, in service since 1870. The light, 245' above the ocean, is in a 59' tower made of 200,000 locally-produced bricks. It is the only functioning lighthouse in the state in which visitors are allowed into the lantern room at the top. The six-mile access road from **Highway 101** passes **Cape Blanco State Park** and the historic **Hughes House**. 541-332-6774. Oregon Lighthouses; Oregon Parks 2(3):54, Nov/Dec 1994; Oregon's Seacoast Lighthouses.

Cape Blanco State Park. A **state park** on **Cape Blanco** 9 miles north of **Port Orford**. The park is near an active lighthouse, a black sands beach, and the historic **Hughes House**. A three-mile hiking trail, a 3.5 mile horse trail, a horse camp, and a 58-unit campground are included in the park. Reservations, 800-452-5687. 541-332-6774.

Cape Falcon. A cape on the north Oregon coast a few miles north of **Neahkahnie Mountain**. It was named on August 18, 1775 by Captain Bruno Heceta for the saint of the day, Santa Clara de Montefalco. **Oswald West State Park** encompasses most of the cape. Oregon Geographic Names.

Cape Ferrelo. A rugged cliff on the south Oregon coast seven miles north of **Brookings** that is the first prominent headland north of the California border. It was named in honor of Bartolome Ferrelo, a sailor who had command of Cabrillo's ship in June 1542 when it may have been sailing in the area. Oregon Geographic Names.

Cape Foulweather. A promontory on the central Oregon coast ten miles north of **Newport**. It was named by Captain James Cook on March 7, 1778. Oregon Geographic Names.

Cape Kiwanda. A sandstone point, sometimes known as Sand Cape or Haystack Cape, just north of **Pacific City** and about 25 miles southwest of **Tillamook**. Since it is not of hard rock, its existence may be due to the modest protection that Haystack Rock, about a mile offshore, provides from winter waves; old photos show that it has eroded significantly in the last 100 years. The cape is a favorite site for **hang gliding**. Kiwanda was the name of a local Nestucca Indian chief. Oregon Geographic Names. See also **Three Capes Scenic Loop**.

Cape Lookout. A narrow point that juts over a mile into the ocean southwest of **Tillamook**. It is composed of **Columbia River basalt**, tilted down to the north so that while the cliffs on the north are 400' high, those on the south are 800'. John Meares originally applied the name Cape Lookout to what is now called **Cape Meares**; cartographers mistakenly transferred the name ten miles south to Cape Lookout on 1850 and 1853 charts. There was further confusion between the two when a lighthouse destined for Cape Lookout ended up being erected on Cape Meares. In the 1940s a **World War II** bomber crashed on the Cape. Oregon Geographic Names. See also **Three Capes Scenic Loop**.

Cape Lookout State Park. A **state park** with 250 campsites on a sand spit on Three Capes Scenic Route 12 miles southwest of **Tillamook** Attractions include wildlife, beachcombing, and hiking out 2.5-mile long **Cape Lookout**. The campground is open year round. Reservations, 800-452-5687. 13000 Whiskey Creek Road W., Tillamook 97141. 503-842-4981.

Cape Meares. A projection of **Columbia River basalt** that lies south of **Tillamook Bay**. The Cape was described by John Meares in 1788 when he named it **Cape Lookout**. When the name Cape Lookout was later mistakenly applied to the cape 10 miles south, Cape Meares was renamed for its discoverer. Erosion, probably due to construction of the north Tillamook jetty in 1917, cut the coastline back 320 feet by 1960 and another 75 feet during the winter storms of 1960 and 1961. Geology of Oregon; Oregon Geographic Names. See also **Three Capes Scenic Loop**.

Cape Meares Lighthouse. A **lighthouse** nine miles west of **Tillamook** that was put in service in 1890. In 1963 the light was replaced by an automated light installed in a small building nearby. The original building, 38' high, and 217' above the water, is open for public tours during limited hours; the parking area is where the keeper's house used to stand. For a time around 1900 the lighthouse also served as the Barnegat post office. 503-842-4981. Oregon Lighthouses; Oregon Parks 2(3):54, Nov/Dec 1994; Oregon's Seacoast Lighthouses.

Cape Meares State Park. A day-use only **state park** on the tip of **Cape Meares** 10 miles south of **Tillamook**. The park includes an 1890 **lighthouse**, no longer in use, the **Octopus Tree**, and two-miles of the **Oregon Coast Trail**.

Cape Perpetua. A high headland on the central Oregon coast three miles south of **Yachats**. It was sighted and named in 1778 by Captain James Cook on Saint Perpetua's Day, March 7. A road leads to a stone overlook built by the **Civilian Conservation Corps** on top of the cape, east of the highway. Trails lead to the **Devil's Churn** at the base of the cape, and a **Siuslaw National Forest** campground and interpretive center lie just south. Oregon Geographic Names.

Cape Sebastian. An abrupt headland that rises to 700' on the south Oregon coast six miles south of **Gold Beach**. The name was given by Sebastian Vizcaino on January 20, 1603 in honor of the saint of the day. A side road west off **Highway 101** leads to a viewpoint on the top. Oregon Geographic Names.

CAPITAL Center. A $14.3 million educational center in **Washington County** designed to provide a seamless transition from school to work, especially in **high-tech industry**. The name is an acronym for Center for Advanced Partnerships in Technology and Learning. The center, located at Northwest Walker Road and 185th, is funded cooperatively by business and education groups. A regional high school is also planned for the site. Oregonian 6/28/95:D1.

Capital controversy. **Salem** became the state capital by popular vote in 1864 following 15 years of controversy. The **provisional government, 1843-1849**, had been located in **Oregon City**. In 1849 the first legislative session of the **territorial government** also met in rented quarters in Oregon City but during the session voted to move to Salem. However, in 1851 agitation led to the governor, his appointees, and all but one of the Supreme Court justices sitting in Oregon City, while the rest of the government, including most of the legislature, met in Salem. In 1852 the U.S. Congress designated Salem as the territorial capital, and the legislature met there in 1853, but in 1855 it moved itself to **Corvallis**. The U.S., however, refused to fund a territorial capital unless it was in Salem so the legislature quickly returned there. Later that year, on December 29, the brand new capitol building in Salem burned, and the controversy flared again. After a series of inconclusive votes in the legislature and on statewide ballots, a decisive vote of the people in June 1864 firmly and finally designated Salem as capital. Dictionary of Oregon History.

Capital punishment. See **Death penalty**.

Capitol. The Oregon State capitol building in Salem houses the Oregon **Legislature**, the offices of the **governor**, the **secretary of state**, and the state **treasurer**, hearing rooms, visitor galleries, visitor information desk, gift shop, and restaurant. The Modern Greek Style marble building was designed by Francis Keally of New York, winner of a 1936 nationwide competition, and built of white Vermont marble. The Oregon Pioneer, a 23-foot high gold-covered statue, tops the 106 foot dome. Additional art works in and around the building depict Oregon's history, resources, and spirit. The building was completed in 1938 and enlarged in 1976. Earlier, in 1855 and again in 1935, capitol buildings on the same site had each been destroyed by fire. Damage from the 1993 **Scotts Mills earthquake** required $5 million worth of repair and reinforcement of the dome. Oregon Blue Book. See also **Biographical sources**.

Capitol Planning Commission. A group established under state **land use planning** law to implement long-range planning for development of state-owned properties in **Marion** and **Polk Counties** and to coordinate that development with local communities. The commission includes both government and public members. 895 Summer St. NE, Salem 97310. 503-378-8163. Oregon Blue Book.

Captain Michael King Smith Evergreen Aviation Educational Center. A museum, also called the Evergreen AirVenture Museum, planned to open in **McMinnville** about the year 2000. It will house the huge and renovated **Spruce Goose**, plus other antique aircraft. 3850 Three Mile Lane, 97128. 888-977-7823.

Carbon dioxide. A heavy colorless gas, CO_2, that is a waste product of animal metabolism and of combustion but is needed by plants for photosynthesis. The increasing amount in the atmosphere as the major **greenhouse gas** may change the climate. In 1990 emissions in Oregon totaled 55.3 million short tons, and are forecast to increase to 73.1 million tons in 2015. Most of the increase will come from transportation and increased use of **natural gas** for generating **electricity**. Generating electricity for Oregon produced over 22 million tons of CO_2 emissions in 1996. The 1997 legislature required new gas-fired **electric power plants** to reduce carbon dioxide emissions by 17%, making Oregon the first state to regulate how much CO_2. plants can emit. Plants can meet the goal through more efficient technology, through sharing the energy they produce to fuel a second plant (i.e., steam to a wood products plant), or by supporting the **Oregon Climate Trust**. Oregonian 7/16/97:B15, 4/10/98:D4; Report on Reducing.

Carbon monoxide. A toxic, odorless, colorless gas, CO. A high concentration or prolonged exposure can lead to dizziness, headaches, fatigue, functional impairment, and death. It is a byproduct of the inefficient burning of fuels. especially in car engines. Cars and trucks produce up to 90% of urban carbon monoxide emissions which concentrate during periods of air stagnation. Emissions in Oregon totaled 1,495,000 tons in 1996. Oregon Air Quality. See also **Air pollution**; **Gasoline**; **Vehicle inspection**.

Careers. See **Occupations**.

Carey Act of 1894. A federal law adopted August 18, 1894, that authorized the transfer of a million acres of **public domain** desert lands to each of the western states after each state had submitted a plan for irrigating the land and shown the source of water. The states were then to sell each settler no more than 160 acres of which the settler was to cultivate at least 20 acres. The law was designed to allow states and individuals to develop irrigation projects. Idaho used it the most. See also **Bureau of Reclamation**; **Desert Land Act of 1877**; **Land grants**; **Tumalo Irrigation District**.

Carl Washburne State Park. A **state park** near **Heceta Head** 14 miles north of **Florence**. It is near a long sand beach and a rocky headland, and has a 4-mile nature trail loop. The campground has 64 campsites and is open all year. Reservations, 800-452-5687.

Carlton. A **Willamette Valley** agricultural community in **Yamhill County**

nine miles north of **McMinnville** on Highway 47. In 1874 the railroad station was named for John Carl, Sr., and/or Wilson Carl, early settlers. The city was incorporated in 1899. Population 1980 1,302; 1995 1,400. Elevation 198'. PO Box 458, 97111. 503-852-7575. Old Yamhill.

Carnivorous plants. Plants found in nutrient-poor localities that obtain some of their nitrogen from captured insects. Oregon has four genera of carnivorous plants: sundews (*Drosera sp.*), butterworts (*Pinguicula sp.*), bladderworts (*Utricularia sp.*), and pitcher plants, sometimes called cobra plants, (***Darlingtonia***). Great Northwest Nature Factbook.

Carousels. Oregonians have had a long love affair with carousels (merry-go-rounds). A horse-powered carousel operated in 1909 at **Wallowa Lake**. In **Portland, Oaks Amusement Park** includes a 1911 carousel and **Jantzen Beach** SuperCenter includes a 1917 carousel that was refurbished in 1995. In 1990 Portland had seven operating wooden carousels. Ken Means of **Coquille** builds carousels and teaches carousel carving. Oregonian 8/21/97:B2.

Carp. A large-scaled fish, *Cyprinus carpio*, related to goldfish, that feeds on plankton and vegetation. It has been introduced into Oregon waters from Europe where it is considered a delicacy. After carp were introduced into the Silvies River in the 1920s, they spread to **Malheur Lake** where they multiplied so vigorously that in 1955 one and a half million carp over 20 inches long were killed with rotenone. However, the population rapidly recovered, to the detriment of other species. Carp are thought to have been responsible for the near elimination of the **wapato** plant.

Carrots. In 1994, Oregon growers produced 32,000 metric tons of carrots, worth $7.5 million, on 1,400 acres. **Jefferson County** produces 80% of the U.S. supply of carrot seed. Oregon Agriculture.

Cars. See **Auto** entries.

Cartoonists. Jack Ohman of the Oregonian won the Overseas Press Club award for best editorial cartoons on foreign affairs in 1996. Homer C. Davenport (1867-1912) of **Silverton** was a famous national political cartoonist. Oregon Oddities. Carl Barks, who drew Donald Duck comic book stories for 25 years and was the creator of Uncle Scrooge, was born in **Merrill** in 1901, and retired to **Grants Pass**. Cartoonist "Pinto" Colvig, also well-known as a **clown**, grew up in **Jacksonville**. John Callahan lives in **Portland**. See also **Animators**.

Cascade Festival of Music. A central Oregon summer music festival held in **Bend**. It includes classical, country, and jazz performances. 541-383-2202.

Cascade Head. A grassy headland north of **Lincoln City** that rises abruptly from the sea to the 760' "Penacle", as it was called on old maps, and then continues to climb away from the ocean up to 1,565'. It is formed of **basalt** that erupted from a local volcanic vent during the **Eocene**. Trails lead to the high meadow, though the western edge has been fenced off to protect rare vegetation, and another trail drops down to tiny Hart's Cove. The **Siuslaw National Forest** administers the 9,000-acre Cascade Head Scenic Research Area, bought in the 1970s, and is restoring the Salmon River estuary south of the head. Cascade Head was named in 1869 for the 60- to 80-foot cascades in three gorges on its face. Offbeat Oregon; Oregon Geographic Names.

Cascade Head Music Festival. A series of diverse classical music concerts held at St. Peter the Fisherman Lutheran Church in **Lincoln City** in July. The festival has played in several venues since it was founded in 1986. 541-994-5333.

Cascade Lakes Highway. A 66-mile scenic drive through the **Deschutes National Forest** that runs from **Bend** west and south to **Highway 58**. Parts of it are also called Century Drive. The route provides access to the **Deschutes River**, **Mount Bachelor Ski Resort**, trails, campgrounds, and a hundred mountain lakes and reservoirs, plus views of the snowcapped peaks of the **Three Sisters**. The portion between Bend and Mount Bachelor Ski Resort is kept open all year, but the rest is usually closed by snow from October through March. Eleven miles of the route near Bend have been designated as a **safety corridor**. The entire route was named in 1995 as one of the nation's 10 most important **scenic byways**.

Cascade Landslide. In 1260 AD, in one of North America's largest **landslides**, a three-mile stretch (more than four billion cubic yards of earth) dropped off the south side of Washington's Table Mountain and flowed across the **Columbia River** and 100 feet up the south bank, completely blocking the river for a time. After the river broke through, the three-miles between Bonneville and **Cascade Locks** remained a wildly turbulent stretch, known as the **Cascades of the Columbia**, until it was flooded by **Bonneville Dam**. Before the dam was built, a drowned forest was visible along both banks of the Columbia for forty miles upstream. Oregon Geographic Names. See also **Bridge of the Gods**; **Landslides**.

Cascade Locks. An Oregon city in the **Columbia River Gorge National Scenic Area**. It is located in **Hood River County** where the **Bridge of the Gods** crosses the **Columbia River**, 44 miles east of **Portland** on **Interstate 84**. The town grew as the **Cascades Canal and Locks** were built, beginning in 1878, and was incorporated in 1935. The locks were submerged in 1938 by the rising waters behind **Bonneville Dam**, but the town did not have to be moved. Tourism is replacing timber as the town's economic basis. A free museum and riverfront park document the history of the locks, and house the **Oregon Pony**. The Port of Cascade Locks owns two **sternwheelers** that make daily cruises, and the annual "Sternwheeler Days" is held the third weekend in June. Area attractions include wind surfing from the local beach, hiking trails, **Multnomah Falls** (13 miles west), and the **Columbia Gorge Interpretive Center** (3 miles north). Population 1980 838; 1995 1,045. Elevation 103'. PO Box 308, 97014. 541-374-8484. Oregon Geographic Names.

Cascade Policy Institute. A nonprofit, tax-exempt, privately-funded conservative think tank formed in 1991. The Institute publishes a series of articles and studies that propose market-oriented answers, such as privatizing government services, to Oregon's public policy questions. Since 1994 it has sponsored an annual high school essay contest and a biennial **Better Government Competition**. 813 SW Alder, Suite 300, Portland 97205. 503-242-0900.

Cascade Range. A heavily-forested, north-south mountain barrier that extends from British Columbia south to Mount Lassen in California. In Oregon it is breached only by the **Columbia River** on the north and the **Klamath River** on the south. The Western Cascades are composed of older rocks erupted 10 to 42 million years ago from volcanoes long extinct, while the High Cascades along the eastern edge of the range are composed of active or recently extinct **volcanoes**. The Western Cascades have eroded so that their volcanic origins are not apparent, though they had six times the volcanic activity of the High Cascades. The High Cascades include the five highest peaks in Oregon, all over 10,000 feet: **Mount Hood, Mount Jefferson, South Sister, North Sister,** and **Middle Sister**. Craggy peaks such as **Three-Fingered Jack** have not erupted since the end of **Pleistocene** glaciation 10,000 years ago, while the higher and smoother cone-shaped peaks have been more recently active. The High Cascades create a rain shadow, leaving eastern Oregon much drier than the western third of the state. The forests of the Cascade Range provide wood products and, along with the Cascade lakes and rivers, much of Oregon's outdoor recreation. The **Mount Hood, Willamette, Deschutes, Umpqua, Rogue River,** and **Winema National Forests** cover much of the range. Botanical explorer David Douglas was apparently the first to use the name Cascade Range, named for the **Cascades of the Columbia River** where the **Cascade landslide** created rapids. Geology of Oregon; Oregon Geographic Names. See also **Presidents' Range**.

> **Cascade Range physiographic province**. A strip of Oregon that extends from the **Columbia River** south to the California border. The **Willamette Valley** and **Klamath Mountains** border it on the west, while on the east it is bordered by the **Deschutes Columbia plateau**, the **high lava plains**, and the **basin and range** provinces. It is a complex volcanic chain with a history of intermittent activity that goes back 40 million years. The Cascades are parallel to the **Cascadia subduction zone** where the Pacific Ocean floor is pushing under North America; the leading edge of the sinking seafloor eventually melts and percolates up, creating a line of **volcanoes**. Five **gold mining** districts developed in the Western Cascades around old volcanic cores: North Santiam (**Clackamas** and **Marion** counties), Quartzville (**Linn**), Blue River (**Linn** and **Lane**), Fall Creek and **Bohemia** (**Lane**). Geology of Oregon.

> **Cascade route**. See **Natron cut-off**.

> **Cascades Canal and Locks**. A navigation bypass around the **Cascades of the Columbia River** built by the **Army Corps of Engineers**. The system opened in 1896 after 20 years of difficult work, but was not fully completed until 1914. The project, which cost at least 8 lives and $4 million, was complicated by annual high water and the record-breaking **flood of 1894**. The canal was 3,000' long with an eight-foot depth. The lower lock had a lift of 24'. One lock was 521' long, and the other 314'. The **locks** eliminated the need to portage boat freight and passengers traveling between **The Dalles** and **Portland** and resulted in greatly increased river traffic - as well as more reasonable railroad rates. The backwater from **Bonneville Dam** drowned the locks in 1938; they were replaced by **Bonneville Lock**. Army Engineers; "Engineering the Cascades Canal and Locks."

> **Cascades massacre, 1856**. During the **Yakima War** in Washington state, Yakima and **Klickitat** Indians attacked and occupied the white settlement on the Washington shore at the upper end of the portage at the **Cascades of the Columbia** in March, 1856. They had planned to capture both the upper and lower portage settlements as well as the steamships operating from each end of the portage, but fled two days later when troops arrived from both **The Dalles** and **Fort Vancouver**.

Sixteen civilians and soldiers died; the Indian toll is not known. Blow for the Landing; Dictionary of Oregon History.

Cascades of the Columbia River. A six-mile-long section of extreme turbulence in the Columbia River between Bonneville and **Cascade Locks**, formed by the **Cascade Landslide**. The Cascades blocked upstream navigation and could be traveled downriver only at high water and with peril. In 1851 a portage tramway with a mule drawn car was built on the north shore, and the **Oregon Portage Railroad** was built in 1859 along the cliffs on the south shore. The 146 miles stretch of river below the rapids was called the Lower Columbia, and the 45 mile stretch upstream to **The Dalles** was called the Middle Columbia. **Cascades Canal and Locks**, opened in 1896, provided a water route around the Cascades. **Bonneville Dam** flooded the rapids in 1937. Blow for the Landing.

Cascadia subduction zone. A 750-mile-long undersea trench that extends from British Columbia south past Washington and Oregon to northern California. It is parallel to the coast and 40 to 150 miles offshore at the base of the continental slope. The zone marks the area in which the east-moving Juan de Fuca plate slides under the thicker west-moving North American plate at about 1.5" per year. The plates bind and the edge of the North American plate is **uplifted** until, after several hundred years, there is a sudden release of the accumulated pressures, causing major **earthquakes**, **tsunamis**, and abrupt subsidence. The trench itself is obscured by sediments that accumulate at rates of 8 to 26 inches every 1,000 years. Geology of Oregon; "Field trip guide." See also **Continental shelf**; **Plate tectonics**.

Cascara. A small deciduous **tree**, *Rhamnus purshiana*, found in moist, shady locations in western Oregon. It is also called buckthorn or chittum (variously spelled). Its bark is peeled and sold to pharmaceutical companies for use as a laxative and in other preparations. Trees to Know.

Casinos. Since a 1988 federal law allowed Indian tribes to do so, seven of Oregon's nine recognized tribes had opened casinos by 1998, with total estimated revenues of $210 million in 1996. The **Cow Creek Band**'s Seven Feathers Casino in **Canyonville** was first, opening in 1992. In 1995 the Confederated Tribes of **Umatilla** opened their Wild Horse Gaming Resort five miles east of **Pendleton**; Confederated Tribes of **Grand Ronde** opened Spirit Mountain near Grand Ronde (the state's largest); Confederated Tribes of **Warm Springs** opened Indianhead Gaming Center at **Kah-Nee-Ta**; Confederated Tribes of **Siletz** opened Chinook Winds at **Lincoln City**; and the **Coquilles** opened The Mill in **North Bend**. The **Klamath**'s Kla-Mo-Ya casino (named for the Klamath, Modoc, and Yahooskin Band of Snake Indians) 22 miles north of **Klamath Falls** opened in 1997. The **Burns Paiutes** and the Confederated Tribes of **Coos, Lower Umpqua, and Siuslaw** had no casinos. In 1997 the Grand Ronde agreed to set up a foundation to give 6% of net gaming income to schools, local governments, and charities in the 11 nearest counties in return for permission to offer sports betting and any other games approved by the Nevada Gaming Commission. In 1997 the Cow Creek Band, in agreement with the state **Boxing and Wrestling Commission**, added boxing at Seven Feathers, and the Siletz were adding it in 1998 at Chinook Winds. Mail Tribune 2/2/97: 6B; Oregonian 10/22,23/95, 1/11/97:A1, 1/15/97:A1, 10/14/97:E6.

See also **Gambling**.

Cast iron architecture. Cast iron was used both structurally and decoratively in some 180 commercial buildings constructed in the **Portland** waterfront business district between 1854 and 1889 when steel construction, appropriate for the taller buildings using newly designed elevators, replaced it. After the main commercial district moved several blocks west, most of the cast iron buildings were demolished, many of them around 1940 in order to build **Harbor Drive** (since replaced by **Governor Tom McCall Waterfront Park**). The remaining 20 buildings constitute a collection second only to that of New York City's Soho District. The elaborate cast iron facade from Portland's Ladd & Tilton Bank was salvaged when the building was demolished and in 1967 incorporated into the rebuilt Ladd & Bush Bank (later the U.S. National Bank) in **Salem**, making it the largest cast-iron fronted structure on the west coast. Most of the **iron** for the Portland buildings was locally produced. Grand Era of Cast-Iron Architecture; Oregon Main Street. See also **New Market Theater**.

Castle Crest Wildflower Garden. A stream-side display of monkey flowers, gilia, and lupine in **Crater Lake National Park**, at its peak in July. The area is reached by a short trail from a parking lot 1/4 mile east of the Park headquarters.

Catfish. Whiskered bottom fish. **Huntington** sponsors a Catfish Tournament on Memorial Day weekend in May that, in 1995, produced a 58 pound catfish from **Brownlee Reservoir**. See also **Warmwater fish**.

Catholic Church. The first **Catholic** priest in the Oregon country, Father Francois Blanchet (1795-1883), arrived at **Fort Vancouver** in 1838. On January 6, 1839, he celebrated the first Mass in what is now the state of Oregon at **Saint Paul** in a log church that had been built in anticipation in 1836. Several **missions** were shortly established, beginning in 1840 at **Astoria**. Oregon's first Catholic schools opened in Saint Paul, a boys' school in 1843, and a girls' school the next year. Oregon was made a diocese and Father Blanchet was made Archbishop in 1846. In 1855-57 debts from the church building program led Father Blanchet to make a successful money-raising tour of several South American countries. The diocese was divided in 1903, with Oregon east of the Cascade Range placed in the Diocese of **Baker City**. In **Portland** Saint Patrick's Church was built in 1889, and Saint Mary's Cathedral in 1925. The Archdiocese of Portland, which includes all of Oregon west of the Cascades, had 275,000 members in 1995, and the Diocese of Baker had 34,000. Guide to Early Oregon Churches; Pioneer Catholic History of Oregon. See also **Anti-Catholic sentiment; Catholic Ladder; Grotto; Monasteries; Our Lady of Grace Shrine; Private schools; Saint Paul Catholic Church; University of Portland**.

Catholic Ladder. A widely used visual aid devised in 1839 by Father Blanchet for teaching Christianity to Indians. His first Catholic Ladder was a "sahale stick," a square stick with markings to indicate time intervals and events before, during, and after the life of Christ. (Sahale, pronounced SAH ha lee, was a **Chinook jargon** word meaning above or heaven.) His later, more elaborate, versions were charts. "Mysterious Journey"; Pioneer Catholic History of Oregon.

Cats, domestic. **Multnomah County** had an estimated 121,000 cats (and 102,000 **dogs**) in 1996. There were estimated to be 100,000 feral cats (domestic cats that have been abandoned and gone wild) in the state, including 60,000 in the **Metro** area; the Feral Cat Coalition of Portland has monthly clinics to spay or neuter them. Some areas require cats to have licenses. Oregonian 7/23/95:D2, 1/16/96:C1. See also **Kitty Cat**.

Cats, wild. See **Bob cats**; **Cats, domestic**; **Cougars**; **Lynx**.

Cattle. Beef cattle and calves have historically been Oregon's top agricultural commodity, though recently the **nursery industry** has moved into top spot. In 1994 production of cattle and calves totaled $367.7 million. **Malheur County** led, followed by **Harney**, **Klamath**, **Baker**, and **Lake** counties. There are 1,470,000 animals on over 13,000 farms and ranches. 1994-1995 Oregon Agriculture. See also **Brands**; **Cattle history**; **Livestock auctions**; **Livestock districts**; **Open range**; **Ranches**; **Range wars**; **Rangeland**; **Vaqueros**.

Cattle and sheep wars. See **Range wars**.

Cattle drives. Cattle were herded overland into Oregon beginning with an 1837 cattle drive from California. In the 1860s herds large and small were driven into eastern Oregon from all directions, building great holdings. As the cattle multiplied, and before the railroads reached Oregon in the 1880s, cattle drives, sometimes numbering over 10,000 head, slowly moved the excess animals hundreds of miles east or south across open range to market. A drive might take five months to complete. Two main trails were used. One route led east along the **Oregon Trail** from **Pendleton** to Cheyenne or Laramie, Wyoming. The other ran south past **Steens Mountain** to Winnemucca, Nevada, and then turned east to join the Oregon Trail. Dictionary of Oregon History; East of the Cascades; Feelin' Fine; Tales out of Oregon. See also **Corporations, history**; **Cow Column**.

Cattle history. The first **cattle** in Oregon were two bulls and two heifers brought by ship to **Fort George** in 1814. By 1837, the **Hudson's Bay Company (HBC)**, which had also brought some in by ship, had over 1,000 head at **Fort Vancouver**. They would lend but would not sell cattle to settlers. That year, in a successful effort to discourage Ewing Young's proposal to build a still, the **Willamette Mission** commissioned him to bring in cattle from California, and he drove 600 head of scrawny, ill-natured, long-horned Mexican cattle north over the **Siskiyou Trail** in the first major **cattle drive**. However, there were still no cattle for other settlers, so in 1841 Joseph Gale and a few other farmers built a schooner, the **Star of Oregon**, sailed it to San Francisco, sold it, and invested the money in 1,250 head of cattle and other livestock which they drove back to Oregon. In 1843 the first **wagon trains** arrived, some with their own livestock. By 1850 the Oregon census showed nearly 42,000 head of cattle, 9,000 of them milk cows. Cattle in eastern Oregon came from western Oregon, California, and Texas. Many were brought in during great cattle drives of longhorns in the late 1860's; by 1880 there were at least 800,000 head. The major cattle barons of the era included Henry Miller, Peter French, John Devine, and William Hanley. Cattle spurred the growth of **Burns, Prineville**, and **Lakeview**. Dictionary of Oregon History; Ewing Young; Oregon's Great Basin Country. See also **Brands**; **Cow Column**; **Ranches**; **Vacqueros**.

Cauliflower. In 1995, Oregon growers produced 11,100 metric tons of cauliflower for processing, worth $4.2 million, on 2,200 acres. 1995 Oregon.

Cave Junction. A southwest Oregon city in **Josephine County** 30 miles southwest of **Grants Pass** at the junction of **Highway 199** and the road to **Oregon Caves National Monument**. The area was a busy **gold mining** district in the 1850's; nearby the Josephine County Kerbyville Museum displays pioneer artifacts. The name and post office were established in 1936; the city was incorporated in 1948. Several wineries are located nearby. Population 1980 1,023; 1995 1,265. Elevation 1,350'. PO Box F, 97523. 541-592-2156. Chamber of Commerce 541-592-3326. Oregon Geographic Names.

Caveman. An 18-foot fiberglass statue of a hunchbacked Neanderthal wearing an animal skin and clutching a club. It was erected near the north **Grants Pass** Interstate 5 exit in the mid-1970s. The Oregon Cavemen, a local booster club, encourages tourists to visit Grants Pass on their way to **Oregon Caves**. Oregonian 4/6/97:D4.

Caves. The **lava tube**s in central and southeast Oregon are the most numerous of Oregon's caves, but Oregon also has **limestone** and marble caves such as **Oregon Caves** in the **Klamath Mountains**, and sea caves in sandstone and, as at **Sea Lion Caves**, in **basalt**. See also **Arnold Ice Cave**; **Ice caves**; **Lava River Cave**; **Lost Crystal Cave**; **Officer's Cave**.

Cayuse Indians. A Sahaptian-speaking Indian tribe of northeast Oregon, living in the area now covered by **Umatilla**, **Union**, and **Baker** counties. They were bordered by the **Nez Perce** on the east and the Umatillas on the west. The Cayuse were noted for their pride, ferocity, bravery and their **horses**, which they first acquired about 1750. The teepee, a portable dwelling made of skins stretched over poles, was adopted at the same time. Their tens of thousands of small, tough "Cayuse ponies" were characterized by large heads and long manes and tails. In 1855 the Cayuse were assigned to the **Umatilla Indian Reservation**. Making of Oregon.

Cayuse War, 1847-1850. The first of the Northwest's **Indian wars** began after the November 1847 **Whitman massacre**. The financially strapped **Provisional government** in **Oregon City**, with $43.72 in its treasury, sent volunteers to protect **The Dalles**, to free the captives, and to capture the perpetrators. The 900 troops and volunteers were commanded by the inept Colonel Cornelius Gilliam until he accidentally shot and killed himself a few months later. The campaign was inconclusive. **Hudson's Bay Company** managed to free the captives, and the guilty parties surrendered voluntarily in 1850. The Indian unrest led a few years later to the **Yakima War, 1855-58**, in Washington state. That Balance So Rare.

CCC. See **Civilian Conservation Corps**.

Cedar Grove Botanical Area. An isolated 60-acre area of Alaska-yellow-cedar, *Chamaecyparis nootkatensis*, in the **Aldrich Mountains**. The area is about 12 miles south of the **John Day River**, and is reached by a mile-long trail west from Highway 21. Oregon Atlas.

Cedar Hills. An unincorporated 800-acre **Washington County** community just north of **Beaverton**. At the time it was developed in the late 1940s, it was the second-largest suburban housing project in the U.S. Oregonian 7/23/95:H1.

Cedars. Oregon has four species of native conifer **trees** that are called cedars even though none is a true cedar of genus *Cedrus*. The four are (1) Incense-cedar, *Calocedrus decurrens*, of southern Oregon, with an aromatic wood used for lumber and pencils; (2) **Port-Orford-cedar**, *Chamaecyparis lawsoniana*, of **Coos** and **Curry Counties**, a widely-planted ornamental which has a wood of high value, especially to the Japanese, but which is threatened by an introduced root rot; it is valued for finish lumber and for arrow shafts; (3) the related Alaska-yellow-cedar, *C. nootkatensis*, of the high Cascades; and (4) Western redcedar, *Thuja plicata*, of the damp forests of the **Coast Range** and western Cascades. Its wood was used by **Indians** for canoes, house planks, totem poles, and utensils, while the fibrous inner bark was used for baskets, rope, clothing, and diapers. Its rot-and insect-resistant wood is now used for fences, shakes, and lumber. Trees to Know. See also **Cedar Grove Botanical Area**.

Celebration Family. The family of Diane and Dennis Nason of **Sisters** that in the 1980s included 84 children, all but six of them adopted. Many were from other countries and had physical or mental handicaps. The family was featured on CBS "60 Minutes" in February 1984. In 1991 the family fell apart as donations stopped and the state began investigating abuse charges, including the deaths of three children. A year-long jury trial in **Bend**, from November 1, 1994, until November 22, 1995, found the Nasons guilty of racketeering and forgery but acquitted them of all crimes against the children. Oregonian 11/23/95:A1.

Celebrations, historic. **Portland** celebrated the arrival of the first transcontinental train on September 11, 1883, in the greatest festivities the state had known. In 1905 a million and a half people paid admission to the summer-long **Lewis and Clark Centennial Exposition**. On New Years Eve in 1910, 50,000 revelers thronged Portland streets. The **Brownsville** Pioneer Picnic is the oldest continuing celebration in the state.

Celestials. The name by which **Chinese** were called throughout the west in the 19th century. Portland.

Celilo Canal and Locks. See **The Dalles Canal and Locks**.

Celilo Falls. A horseshoe-shaped falls, also called Tumwater Falls, on the **Columbia River** 12 miles upstream from **The Dalles**, now inundated by the lake behind **The Dalles Dam**. For thousands of years Indians speared **salmon** from narrow platforms built out over the roiling waters at the base of the falls. The falls were the uppermost of three obstructions to navigation within an eight-mile stretch of river known as **The Dalles of the Columbia River**. The origin of the name Celilo is unknown. "Wishram."

Celilo Village. A 30-acre federal Indian reservation near the **Columbia River** that provides Columbia River tribes the opportunity to fish. The government, which had taken title to the lands for construction of **The Dalles Dam**, authorized tribal access in 1947. American Indian Reservations.

Cement. Ash Grove Cement Company, located near a **limestone** source at Durkee in **Baker County**, is Oregon's only producer of Portland cement (named for Portland, England.) The plant, fueled by **natural gas** and old automobile tires, produces 500,000 tons a year, with an increase to 900,000 tons planned for 1998. In the past, Portland cement was also produced at **Lake Oswego** and at **Gold Hill**. Mineral Industry of Oregon; Oregon's Iron Dream.

Cemeteries. Oregon has nearly 400 registered cemeteries. A listing is available from the **Mortuary and Cemetery Board**. National cemeteries include Willamette in **Portland** (98,000 veterans); **Eagle Point** (6,700 veterans and spouses), and **Roseburg** (5,200 veterans). Ethnic cemeteries in the Portland area were noted in Oregonian 6/28/95:B1. Local **genealogy** societies have compiled lists of those buried in many cemeteries. The state's oldest gravestone, located in **Astoria**, is that of Donald McTavish, who drowned May 22, 1814, a month after he arrived as the new governor at **Fort George**. Round the Roses; This Side of Oregon. See also **Cremation**; **Deaths**; **Mortuary and Cemetery Board**; **Oregon Memorial Association.**

Censorship. Oregon's libraries receive on average 35 challenges a year to some item in their collection, approximately half of them for children's or young adult material. Most challenges are directed to **public libraries** and the rest to school libraries. Libraries remove or make less accessible about 10% of the challenged items. The Oregon Intellectual Freedom Clearinghouse and the **Oregon State Library** publish an annual report. See also **Pornography**.

Census. The first census in the **Oregon Country** was taken in 1845 by sheriff Joseph Meek for the **provisional government** and showed a total population of 2,109 whites (1,259 males and 850 females) in the region. A census taken in 1849 by Governor Joseph Lane for the new **Oregon Territory** counted 9,083 whites, all but 98 of whom were American citizens. The first official U.S. census, taken in 1850, listed 13,184 whites and 110 colored. Indians were not counted. A federal population census of the state has been taken every 10 years since then by the Census Bureau in the Department of Commerce. Interim estimates are prepared by the state **Center for Population Research and Census**. See also **Metropolitan Areas**; **Population**.

Center for Population Research and Census. A center established by the Oregon legislature to provide an annual estimate of the July 1 **population** of Oregon counties and incorporated cities, and to provide other population counts and figures as needed. Population figures are used as the basis for the distribution of certain state highway, liquor, and cigarette tax revenues to cities and counties, for the disbursement of common school funds, and by state agencies, businesses, researchers, and students. The center also supplies data from U.S. **census** tapes and provides fee-based consultation and analysis services. Portland State University, 97207-0751. 503-725-3922. See also **Population**.

Center of state. See **Geographic center of the state**.

Center of the United States. See **Geographic center of the United States**.

Central Oregon and Pacific Railroad. A wholly owned subsidiary of RailTex Inc., a national operator of **shortline railroads**, that operates the **Coos Bay** and Siskiyou rail lines. The lines were owned by **Southern Pacific** (SP) until 1994. The Siskiyou line extends from **Eugene** south over the **Siskiyou Summit** to Dunsmuir, California; in 1995 the company began shipping freight over the line, abandoned by SP three years before. The Coos Bay line runs between Eugene and **Coquille**. 303 SE Mosher, Roseburg 97470. 541-957-5966. Oregonian 11/25/94:B1.

Central Oregon Community College. A public two-year college in **Bend** that has been offering courses since 1949. Its district covers **Deschutes**, **Crook**, and **Jefferson** counties, plus portions of three others. 6,640 students enrolled for fall 1996 classes. In addition to two-year transfer and vocational programs, the college hosts the **Central Oregon University Center**. 2600 NW College Way, Bend 97701-5998. 541-383-7700. Oregon Blue Book. See also **Community colleges; Small Business Development Centers**.

Central Oregon University Center. A clearinghouse that coordinates delivery of four-year and advanced-degree programs in the **Bend** area. Seven public and private colleges and universities offer courses, using a variety of techniques. Tuition is paid to the individual college, which also awards the degree. 541-383-7256. Oregonian 6/22/95:D1.

Central Oregon Wagon Route. See **Oregon Central Military Wagon Road**.

Central Point. A rapidly growing southwest Oregon suburban community in **Jackson County**, two miles north of **Medford**. The location was called Central Point in 1852 because of its location at the intersection of two pioneer wagon routes in the center of **Bear Creek** valley. The city was incorporated in 1889. Jackson County Exposition Park is on the edge of town, and tours are available at nearby Crater Rock Museum and **Dogs for the Deaf**. Population 1980 6,357; 1995 9,620. Elevation 1,272. 155 S 2nd, 97502. 541-664-3321. Chamber of Commerce 541-664-5301. Land in Common.

Century Drive. See **Cascade Lakes Highway**.

Century farm. An Oregon farm that has been operated as a working farm by the same family for 100 years or more. If the land has ever been rented or leased, it doesn't qualify. The farm must have grossed at least $1,000 from farm use for three of the five years preceding application and must have family members living on or actively managing the farm. Nearly 900 farms are now enrolled. Agriculture; Oregonian 3/29/98:C4.

Certified Public Accountant. See **Accountancy**.

Challenge course. See **Ropes course**.

Chamber music. A number of groups in Oregon promote small ensemble classical music. The Chamber Music Society of Oregon, 503-287-2175, has several affiliates, including Oregon Sinfonietta in **Portland** and Mid-Columbia Sinfonietta in **Hood River**. Chamber Music Northwest, 503-294-6400, holds a month-long festival of chamber music at Catlin Gabel School and/or Reed College in **Portland** during the early summer and schedules several other concerts during the year. Sinfonia Concertante, 503-231-1421, performs in **Portland**.

Champoeg. A site on the east bank of the **Willamette River** southwest of **Wilsonville** where the first government in the **Oregon Country** was authorized at a meeting on May 2, 1843. Mountain man Joe Meek is said to have broken a deadlock by calling "Who's for a divide? All for the report of the committee and an organization follow me." He stepped into the yard and drew a line in the dirt. The popular - and disputed - account is that 50 **French Canadians** and **Hudson's Bay Company** men moved to one side, while 52 Americans and several French Canadians moved to the other. The American side prevailed. They then elected a legislative committee of nine members to draw up a code of laws. At a meeting on July 5 the laws of the **provisional government** were adopted and officers elected.

Champoeg village had 200 residents when it was destroyed by the **flood of 1861**; **Champoeg State Park** now occupies the site. **Champooick** (Champoeg) **District** was one of Oregon's first four **counties**. The origin of the name is not clear, and pronunciation is disputed with both Sham-POO-ee and Sham-POO-ig in use. Champoeg. See also **French Prairie**; **Joint Occupancy**; **Oregon Country**; **Provisional government**; **Robert Newell House**; **Wolf meetings** .

Champoeg State Park. A **state park** 25 miles south of **Portland** (7 miles east of **Newberg**) on historic **French Prairie**. On July evenings a historical pageant reenacts the early days of the area; 503-678-1649 for tickets. The park includes a visitor center, museum with gift shop, log cabin museum, group meeting hall, picnic shelter, the historic **Robert Newell House**, 10 miles of trails, and a year-round campground with 54 campsites. Reservations, 800-452-5687. 503-633-8170.

Champooick (Champoeg) **District**. The southeast of the four original **districts** (later, **counties**) into which the **Oregon Country** was divided by the **Provisional government** on July 5, 1843, and from which the counties of southeast Oregon were later created. Champooick District was the area between the **Willamette River** and the Rocky Mountains and south from the mouth of the Pudding River to 42° (the present Oregon/California border). The other three districts were **Clackamas** to the northeast, **Twality** to the northwest, and **Yamhill** to the southwest. "Oregon Counties."

Chanterelle. A choice edible **mushroom**, *Cantharellus cibarius* and related species, found in the autumn in western forests. It is gathered commercially in Oregon. Mushrooms Demystified.

Chapman Square. See **Plaza Blocks**.

Char. See **Trout**.

Charette. A process of urban planning in which all involved parties, including the public, meet for several days in an intense series of sessions designed to resolve differences and come up with a workable plan. In 1996 **Forest Grove** developed a city center plan through the charette process. Oregonian 9/25/96:D5.

Charitable giving. In 1993 Oregon ranked 40th in the nation in household giving. The average Oregon household contributed $1,952 to charities, compared with the national average of $2,279, from household income of $30,819 (24th in the nation). R. B Pamplin Corporation donates 10% of its pre-tax profits each year compared to the national average of 2%. The Charitable Activities Section of the state Department of **Justice** registers all charities and professional fund-raisers, including **bingo**, 503-229-5725. About 9,000 charities and trusts were registered as of July 1997. The state **Attorney General** has a consumer hot line for complaints about charitable solicitations. 503-378-4320 (Salem), or 503-229-5576 (Portland). Oregonian 2/16/97:A1, 3/30/97:B10, 10/5/97:A18. See also **Foundations**; **Philanthropy**.

Charleston. An unincorporated port 8 miles west of **North Bend** near the mouth of Coos Bay, named for Charles Haskell, an 1853 settler. It is home to charter fishing boats, a fishing fleet, and the **Oregon Institute of Marine Biology**. Nearby attractions include crabbing and clamming in the bay, **South Shore Estuarine Reserve**, and **Shore Acres State Park and Botanical Gardens**, one of several parks along the six mile highway to **Cape Arago**. Oregon Geographic Names.

Charter. A document describing the basic form of government that the people of a city or county have adopted under the authority granted by the state. It is, in a sense, the local government equivalent of a **constitution**, and can be adopted or amended only by a vote of the residents. See also **Home rule**; **Local government**; **Metro**; **Ordinance**.

Charter schools. Schools that can operate with public funds but without most state regulations so long as they show good academic results. Oregon has no charter school law, but it receives federal grants for charter schools under the state's alternative education law. In 1996 seven charter schools were operating in the state and grants had been distributed to begin or expand 23 charter school programs, and the **Portland** Public School System (92 schools, 57,000 students) proposed becoming the nation's first charter school district in an effort to regain local control. Oregonian 3/22/96:B1.

Chautauqua. A movement begun in New York state in 1868 that produced summer lectures and entertainment. Chautauqua assemblies were founded in **Canby** in 1885, **Gearhart** in 1891, and **Ashland** in 1893. The Willamette Valley Chautauqua Association operated the most successful Chautauqua in the state at its own park in **Gladstone** from 1893 until 1928; its shingled, bee-hive auditorium could hold 5,000 people. **Albany**, **La Grande**, and **The Dalles** also hosted Chautauqua assemblies. The remnant walls of Ashland's beehive now form the perimeter of the **Oregon Shakespeare Festival**'s outdoor theater. Dictionary of Oregon History; "Gladstone Chautauqua". See also **Oregon Chautauqua**.

Cheese. In 1994 Oregon produced 20,900 metric tons of cheese. Cheese was first made commercially in Oregon in **Tillamook County** in 1891, and it is still in Tillamook County that Oregon's largest cheese factory, owned by the Tillamook County Creamery Association, annually produces 40 million pounds of cheese, primarily cheddar. Oregon once had dozens of small cheese factories; now there are just a handful. Bandon Cheese in **Bandon** makes 2 million pounds a year of cheddars and specialty cheeses. The Rogue River Valley Creamery in **Central Point** specializes in a blue-vein cheese that is marketed throughout the west. Rogue Gold in **Grants Pass** makes a variety of cheeses, especially cheddar. Goat cheese is made by Tall Talk Dairy of **Canby**, Juniper Grove Farm of **Redmond**, and Alsea Acre Alpines near **Alsea**.

Chehalem Mountains. A short range of mountains in the northern **Willamette Valley**, north and west of **Newberg**. They lie between the Tualatin River and Chehalem Creek. Bald Peak, elevation 1,629', is the high point. Ewing Young, the first white settler in the area, raised horses on their grassy slopes in the 1830s. The name was that of local Indians who had lived in the area in considerable numbers before **epidemics** killed them. Dictionary of Oregon History.

Chemawa Indian School. A **boarding school** established in 1881 at **Forest Grove** to provide both general and vocational education for Indian children, now the oldest boarding school in the country. Because residents of the Forest Grove area objected to the school, it was moved in 1886 to a less controversial location northeast of **Salem**. The school, operated by the U.S. Bureau of Indian Affairs, now serves about 400 Indian students from the western states. A forerunner was the Indian Manual Labor Training School, established by the Rev. Jason Lee at the **Willamette Mission** in 1834. 3700 Chemawa Road NE, 97305-1199. 503-399-5721. First Oregonians.

Chemeketa Community College. A public two-year college in **Salem** that enrolled 16,302 students in fall 1996. It serves students from **Marion, Polk, Yamhill**, and parts of **Linn** counties with more than 40 occupational programs, personal interest classes, and academic courses leading to an associate degree. 4000 Lancaster Drive NE, PO Box 14007, Salem 97309-7070. 503-399-5000. Oregon Blue Book. See also **Community colleges; Small Business Development Centers**.

Cherries. Both sweet cherries and sour (pie) cherries are grown commercially in Oregon for processing and fresh sales, including export to Asia. In 1995 Oregon growers produced 20% of the country's sweet cherries, 27,400 tons worth $24.5 million, on 11,945 acres. Most of the sweet cherries grown in the Willamette Valley (Royal Annes) are used to make maraschino cherries, developed in the 1920s by an **Oregon State University** food technologist. Oregon's cherry industry goes back to cherry cuttings brought to Oregon by Henderson Luelling in 1847. Later, Black Republican, Bing (named for a Chinese nursery worker), and other varieties were developed at Luelling's **Milwaukie** nursery by his brother, Seth, who spelled his name Lewelling. Dictionary of Oregon History; 1995 Oregon; Oregon Oddities.

Chestnuts. A nut that is being grown commercially in the **Willamette Valley**. In 1996 it was estimated that Oregon had about 250 commercial chestnut trees, and more were being planted. Unlike other nuts, chestnuts must be marketed fresh, like apples. Oregonian 12/4/96:D4.

Chetco and Tu-tut-ni Indians. Indians originally from neighboring areas of the south Oregon coast near **Brookings**. There are estimated to be some 500 scattered members left; they are seeking restoration of their tribal status. The tribes have never had a reservation; the few survivors of the **Rogue River War** were sent to the reservations of other tribes. Oregonian 1/26/96:C5.

Chetco River. A river in southwest Oregon that flows from the west slopes of the **Siskiyou Mountains** 58 miles to the ocean at **Brookings**, draining an area of 359 square miles, with an average annual volume of 1,571,000 acre feet or 9 acre feet/acre as measured at river mile point 10.7. **Jetties** at its mouth help maintain a channel for fishing boats. It is named for the Chetco Indians who lived along its lower reaches. Oregon Geographic Names.

Chewaukan (shoe-WAH-kan). A large prehistoric **Pleistocene lake** in south Central Oregon of which **Summer Lake** and **Lake Abert** are remnants. The Chewaukan River drains the area.

Chicano Movement. See **Hispanics in Oregon history**.

Chickens. In 1995 Oregon growers produced 21.4 million broilers worth $34.3 million and 60 million dozen eggs worth $46.5 million. **Clackamas County** led production, followed by **Marion, Sherman**, and **Jackson** counties. Jenks Hatchery in **Tangent** is the largest and oldest (1910) hatchery in Oregon, producing 30% of the chickens in the Northwest. 1995 Oregon; Oregonian 3/27/90:FD8.

Chief Justice. The head of the Oregon **Supreme Court** and the administrative head of Oregon's **judicial system**, supervising the operations and financial management of the **Supreme Court, Court of Appeals, Tax Court**, and **circuit courts**. The Chief Justice, who is elected to a six-year term by the other justices, selects the chief judge of the Court of Appeals and the presiding judges of local courts, and is responsible for the procedural rules for all courts in the state. The Chief Justice is assisted by the State Court Administrator. Supreme Court Bldg., 1163 State St., Salem 97310. 503-986-5555. Governing Oregon; Oregon Blue Book.

Child abuse. In 1995, 26,765 cases of child abuse were reported in the state and 8,991 of those were confirmed. 36 children died of abuse and neglect. That year the state had 1,398 state staff positions in child protection services serving the state's three million people. In 1971, with one-third the population, 1,556 staff members served in child-protection services and there were 347 confirmed cases of child abuse. Oregon law requires law enforcement officials, health care workers, and social service professionals to report suspected child abuse to the State Office of Services for **Children and Families**. Oregonian 12/2/96:A1. See also **Foster care; Keep Kids Alive**.

Child care. In 1996 both parents or the only parent of 450,000 Oregon children (62%) worked outside the home. Oregon has an average of 16 day-care slots for every 100 children; national standards recommend 25. In 1993 64% of Oregon child care facilities did not meet basic standards. Parents can check for complaints against child care operators by calling the state Child Care Division at 800-556-6616. In 1951 Oregon became the first state to authorize an income tax deduction for child care expenses. Adventures in Politics; Oregon: A Statistical Overview; Oregonian 7/18/96:C1, 8/20/96:A8, 7/23/97:C6.

Child Care Division. A division of the **Employment Department** that is responsible for child care regulations, and for child care resource and referral. In 1996 it monitored 1,100 child-care centers and group homes plus 13,000 family child-care homes. The number of care centers has doubled in ten years while the staff has decreased. 875 Union Street NE, Salem 97311. 503-373-7282. Oregon Blue Book; Oregonian 8/20/96:A8.

Child support. Absent parents are estimated to be at least $580 million in arrears in child support payments in Oregon. The Support Enforcement Division of the Department of **Justice** enforces support obligations for families who receive public assistance. County District Attorneys enforce support obligations for other families in a program coordinated by the state Child Support Administrator in the **Adult and Family Services Division**, 503-986-6148. Recent changes in the law have increased collections. Parents who don't pay may lose their occupational, professional, and driver's licenses. Oregonian 10/15/94:C3.

Childbirth. See **Births; Midwives; Obstetricians**.

Children. Oregon ranked 18th best in the nation for child well-being, according to a 1995 study by the Annie E. Casey Foundation in Maryland. Oregon was fourth best for low birth-weight babies, 23rd best for child death rate, 19th for teen violent-death rate, 20th for juvenile arrest rate for violent crimes, 22nd for rate of births to unmarried teenagers, 34th for high school dropouts, 26th for % of teens not attending school or working, 17th for rate of children living in poverty, and

26th best for families headed by a single parent. Oregonian 4/24/95:B1. See also **Keep Kids Alive; Rose Garden Children's Park; Summer camps**.

Children and Families, Oregon Commission on (OCCF). A 19-member umbrella advocacy group for children and families in Oregon. Members are appointed by the governor for four-year terms. The commission is charged with setting policy and moving control of programs for children and families from the state to local communities through county-level commissions. Among the programs it administers are Great Start to ensure that preschool children reach the first grade with good physical, social, intellectual, and emotional development, Court Appointed Special Advocates (CASA), volunteers who represent the interests of abused and neglected children in court, and **Oregon National Guard Youth Conservation Corps**, a program to provide life and work-skills training for "at-risk" youths ages 16-25. 530 Center Street NE, Suite 300, Salem 97310. 530-373-1283. Oregon Blue Book; Oregonian 11/29/96:A23. See also **Juvenile Justice Advisory Committee**.

Children and Families, Services to. The state agency responsible for protecting abused children and working with their families. Services offered through the 41 branch offices include protective services, foster care, adoptions, parent training, counseling, family sex abuse treatment, and services for children with special needs. 500 Summer St. NE, Salem 97310-1017. 503-945-5651. Oregon Blue Book. See also **Child abuse; Keep Kids Alive**.

Children First for Oregon. A nonprofit statewide advocacy organization for children. It issues an annual report card on the care of children in the state. The overall grade for 1996 was a C minus, down from a C the year before. They graded the overall health of teens as an F, investment in families as a C, early childhood as a B, and childhood safety as a B. 503-294-1456; 800-544-0376. Oregonian 1/29/97:E1.

Children's Farm Home. A private, non-profit residential facility near **Corvallis** for the treatment of teen-agers with severe learning disabilities and psychiatric disorders. Most of the 90 children stay for six to nine months of treatment before being reunited with their families. Prior to 1990 the facility provided residential treatment for delinquent and troubled teens. The Oregon Women's Christian Temperance Union (WCTU) built most of the campus in 1922. 4455 NE Highway 20, 97330-9663. 541-757-1852. Oregonian 1/24/96:C1.

Children's literature. Some of Oregon's many prize-winning authors of books for children include Beverly Cleary, author of a number of books, set in **Portland**, for grade school children; Ursula LeGuin, an author known for her fantasy and science fiction for adults who also writes for children; Walt Morey, who created Gentle Ben and other animal stories; and Eloise McGraw, Ellen Howard, Virginia Wolff, Linda Crew, Cynthia Rylant, and Eric Kimmel. Child's World. See also **Beverly Cleary Sculpture Garden**.

Children's Museum. A **Portland** museum, operated by the Portland Parks Department, that plans to move from its Second Avenue location to a building near the **Washington Park Zoo** as soon as the former **OMSI** building can be renovated. On Second Avenue the museum has two floors of exhibits where children can play store, model clay, and explore the customs of children throughout the world. The museum also includes an infant play room and a water-play area. 3037 SW Second Avenue. 503-823-2227. Portland Guidebook. See also **A. C. Gilbert's Discovery Village**.

Children's theater. Four **Portland** theater companies produce shows for children. Ladybug Theater, the oldest professional theater in Portland, produces shows for preschool children at **Oaks Amusement Park**, 503-232-2346. Northwest Children's Theater produces shows for families at the **Northwest Service Center** and Main Street Playhouse. 503-222-4480. Tears of Joy, one of the nation's largest puppet companies, performs at the **Dolores Winningstad Theatre**, 503-248-0557. Oregon Children's Theatre's productions are presented to school classes and to families at the **Civic Auditorium** and **Portland Community College**, 503-228-9571. Oregonian A&E 9/27/96:52.

Chiles Award. See **Earle A. Chiles Award**.

Chiloquin. A southern Oregon town in **Klamath County** 25 miles north of **Klamath Falls** on **Highway 97**. It was named for the **Klamath Indian** village chief Chaloquenas, and incorporated in 1926. **Collier Memorial State Park,** nearby on **Highway 97**, is an open air museum with a large collection of logging artifacts and a log-cabin village. Population 1980 778; 1995 710. Elevation 4,200. PO Box 196, 97624. 541-783-2717. Oregon Geographic Names.

Chimney swifts. See **Swifts**.

China. In 1996 **exports** to China totaled $79 million (compared to $2,100 million to Japan). High technology accounted for $35 million, wood products for $15, other manufactured goods for $13 million, agricultural goods for $9 million, and nonmanufactured products for $5 million. After Hong Kong became part of China in 1997, the combined entity became Oregon's fifth-largest customer. Oregonian 7/30/97:C1.

China Rapids. A series of rapids on the **Snake River** in the eastern-most bend of **Hells Canyon**. They are at 116°27'43"W and mark the most easterly point of Oregon.

Chinatown. A downtown **Portland** neighborhood in Old Town that is the country's second-largest Chinatown, after San Francisco. In 1885 **Chinese** made up one fourth of Portland's population, and Chinatown extended from Third Avenue to the Willamette River and from Oak Street eight blocks south. Portland, An Informal History. See also **Chinese garden**.

Chinatown Gate. A much-photographed gate in **Portland** that frames the Fourth Street entrance to Chinatown off Burnside. The gate, dedicated on November 8, 1986, honors the contributions of Oregon's **Chinese** immigrants.

Chinese garden. A walled garden to be built in Old Town, **Portland**. Northwest Natural Gas donated the site, a $1.5 million block bordered by NW 2nd and 3rd avenues and Glisan and Flanders streets. The $6.4 million garden will be built in Suzhou, China, Portland's sister city, and then reassembled in Portland. Kuang Zhen Yan of Suzhou is chief designer. Oregonian 9/21/97:L1.

Chinese in Oregon. The 1990 census counted 14,000 Chinese in Oregon. Chinese came early, first as sailors and then as **gold miners**, and by 1870 there were 3,330 in the state. During the next decade "China-boys," most of them from southern China, were brought in by the hundreds to replace the **Irish** on railroad construction, and to work in gold mines, in salmon canneries, and as "grubbers" clearing land for farmers. By 1885 one-fourth of **Portland**'s residents were Chinese, though their numbers decreased following the Chinese Exclusion Act of 1882 and the assaults of 1886. Notable Oregon Chinese include Seid Back (1851-1916), Portland merchant, philanthropist, farmer; Seid Back, Jr., (1878-1933), the first Chinese admitted to the bar in the U.S.; and Lung On (1872-1940) and Doc Hay (1862-1952) of **John Day**. The original 1859 Oregon Constitution prohibited "Chinamen" from voting (Art. II, Sec. 6, repealed 1927) and from owning property or working mining claims (Art. XV, Sec. 8, repealed 1946). Chinese were not allowed to become American citizens until 1943. Dictionary of Oregon History; Empire of the Columbia. See also **Anti-Chinese sentiment; Asians in Oregon; Celestials; Kam Wah Chung**.

Chinese massacre. In 1887, two years after the Rock Springs, Wyoming, massacre in which 28 Chinese were killed, 31 Chinese miners in **Hells Canyon** were killed by several ranch hands for their gold. Three of the accused were tried and acquitted while three others were never apprehended. The massacre created an international scandal and the U.S. paid $275,000 indemnity to China. Hells Canyon; Oregonian 8/15/95:A1.

Chinook jargon. (chih-NOOK or shih-NOOK). A simplified trading language of some 300 words developed by Northwest Indians. It was based on the language of the Chinook Indians, a large and important trading tribe whose members lived along the **Columbia River** near its mouth. Chinook jargon also included some words from other **Indian languages** and, after whites came, words from their languages. It was also widely used by Oregon pioneers and by Indians on multi-tribal **reservations**. Skookum, meaning strong or powerful, is an example of a Chinook jargon word which has come into regional use. TenasWawa, a newsletter in Chinook and English, is published at 19330 Widme Road NE, Poulsbo, WA 98370. Chinook, a History and Dictionary. See also **Boston Men; Indian languages; Siwash**.

Chinook salmon. The largest of Oregon's **salmon**, *Oncorhynchus tshawytscha*, also known as king salmon. It is distinguished by a black lower gumline and small round spots on both lobes of the tail. Mature chinook average 28 to 36 inches long and 15 to 25 pounds, but the Oregon record (from the **Umpqua River** in 1910) is 83 pounds, and the world record is 126 pounds. The chinook is native to all the rivers of the coast where they spawn in gravel bars in large rivers. There are spring, summer, and fall runs, but the major spawning time is August to December. Chinook were the mainstay of the **fish canneries** in the 19th century; the catch peaked at 2.3 million chinook (43 million pounds) in 1883. Runs in the 1990s have been between 200,000 and 300,000 fish. The chinook was designated the **state fish** in 1961. Columbia River Salmon; Fishing in Oregon; Oregonian 9/1/94:NO6, 2/22/95:C1, 10/19/96:C1, 1/23/97:E7; Salmon of the Pacific.

Chinook wind. Popularly, an unseasonably warm winter **wind** blowing in from the southwest. However, the true Chinook is a wind that is descending the lee side of a mountain after condensation has occurred on the windward ascent; the air temperature on the lee side will be warmer than the temperature at the same elevation on the windward slope. Chinook winds are more common and pronounced during the winter and at the base of high mountain ranges. The resulting snow melt can help ranchers and road crews but can also cause **floods** and avalanches. Oregon: Wet, High and Dry.

Chipmunks. Small active squirrels with stripes along both head and body. They are classed as **protected animals**. They live on the ground or in brush, seldom climbing far up trees, and do not hibernate. Five species are found in Oregon. The similar golden-mantled **ground squirrel** has less striping on its head. Atlas of Oregon Wildlife; Mammals and Life Zones of Oregon; Mammals of the Northwest.

Chiropractors. In 1997 over 900 chiropractors held active licenses issued by the Oregon Board of Chiropractic Examiners. The five members of the board are appointed by the governor to three-year terms. 3218 Pringle Road SE, Suite 150, Salem 97302-6311. 503-378-5816. Oregon Blue Book.

Chittum. See **Cascara**.

Chlamydia. A sexually transmitted **disease**, caused by the bacterium *Chlamydia trachomatis*. It is the most common reportable disease in Oregon with over 100 cases a week, most in persons between ages 15 and 25. In women, if not treated with antibiotics, it can lead to infertility, ectopic pregnancies, and pelvic inflammatory disease. Symptoms include painful urination and discharges, but over half of those with the disease have no symptoms. Simpler diagnostic and treatment techniques may decrease the incidence. Oregonian 11/9/95:A22, 7/11/97:B1.

Christian Church. See Disciples of Christ.

Christmas flood. See **Flood of 1964**.

Christmas Lake. A small lake five miles northeast of the community of **Christmas Valley** in Lake County. The name was originally applied to Hart Lake; how it was transferred to the present lake is unknown. The man-made lake at Christmas Valley Lodge is not Christmas Lake; it is known simply as The Lake. Where the Pavement Ends.

Christmas lights. Notable displays of Christmas lights are at **Shore Acres State Park** out of **Coos Bay**, at **Portland International Raceway** and at the **Grotto** in **Portland**, and at **Peacock Lane**, also in Portland. The last is a four-block street of homes that have set up decorations nearly every year since 1929. It is located between SE Stark and Belmont just east of 39th. Since 1956 many private boat owners in the Portland area light their boats and parade on the **Willamette** and **Columbia** rivers on a number of December evenings. Round the Roses. See also **Made in Oregon sign**; **Martini glass**.

Christmas tree industry. Oregon's Christmas tree industry leads the nation, supplying over 8 million of the country's 33.5 million trees. In 1995 sales brought in $85.5 million from 6,600 acres, most in the foothills of the **Willamette Valley**. About 15% of the sales were in Mexico, Hawaii, and Asia. The idea of raising Christmas trees originated in 1954 with Hal Schudel of **Corvallis** whose family remains the largest grower. **Douglas fir** is most common, but Noble **fir** is increasing in popularity. Northwest Christmas Tree Association, PO Box 3366, Salem 97302. 503-364-2942. 1995 Oregon.

Christmas trees. The tallest living Christmas trees in Oregon include a 130-

foot **Douglas-fir** in **Blue River**, a 123-foot giant sequoia in **Monmouth**, a 98-foot tree in **Lebanon**, and an 80-foot tree in **Eugene**'s Oakway Center. A locally cut tree, usually between 75 and 100 feet tall, is set up each year in **Portland**'s **Pioneer Square**. Oregonian 11/24/95:C4.

Christmas Valley. An isolated unincorporated community in the high sagebrush desert of **Lake County** east of **Fort Rock**, between **Lakeview** and **Bend**, and 100 miles from each. In 1961 a California firm purchased 70,000 acres of sagebrush for $10 an acre that it then marketed intensively in smaller parcels for up to $1100 an acre. Several thousand Californians had purchased nearly all the land by mid-1966, but fewer than 100 families ended up settling in the area. Purchase money was refunded to some 25% of the buyers who were disappointed with their purchase after viewing their land. High Desert.

Chromite. A heavy black mineral, a source of chromium, that is found in small amounts in belts of **serpentinite** in the **Klamath Mountains**. A number of small chromite mines operated in southern Oregon during **World Wars I** and **II** and during a government strategic stockpiling program in the 1950's. Geology of Oregon.

Chub. See **Borax Lake**.

Chukar. A partridge, *Alectoris chukar*, native to Eurasia, that was introduced into barren, rocky areas of eastern Oregon as a **game bird** in 1951. The birds have thrived, and have been hunted since 1957. Cheatgrass is a favored food. Atlas of Oregon Wildlife.

Church buildings history. The first church building in Oregon was the **Saint Paul Catholic Church**, built in 1836. In 1844 the **Methodists** built the first Protestant church in Oregon in **Oregon City**; it is no longer standing. Round the Roses. See also **Oaks Pioneer Church**; **Old Church**; **Religion**.

Church of Christ. See **Religion**.

Church of Elvis. A free **Portland** museum, open limited hours, on the second floor at 720 SW Ankeny Street. In 1997 the minister, Stephanie Pierce, was also constructing a coin-operated window. 503-226-3671.

Church of Jesus Christ of Latter-day Saints. See **Religion**.

Church of Scientology. A religion founded in 1952 by L. Ron Hubbard. Though it worships no god, it assists its practitioners to develop their "thetan" or soul. It claims 6,000 members in Oregon. Church of Scientology Celebrity Centre and Dianetics Foundation, 709 SW Salmon, Portland, 97205. 503-228-0116. Oregonian 9/27/96:D1.

Church of the Bride of Christ. A 1902 **cult** created in **Corvallis** by Edmund Creffield who called himself Joshua the Second. Tales of scandalous goings on led the community to tar and feather him before he was sent to the penitentiary for adultery. After his release in 1906 he was shot point blank and killed by George Mitchell whose teen-age sister had been one of those involved with Creffield. A Seattle jury found Mitchell innocent after a long and sensational trial, but two days later Mitchell's sister shot and killed him. Both she and Creffield's wife, also implicated in Mitchell's murder, later committed suicide. Oregon Stater 79(7):32, Dec. 1995; Oregonian 4/21/97:B1.

Church of the Holy Water. A church organized in 1994 to unite Columbia

Basin irrigators against government regulators. By making water a sacrament, they hoped to invoke constitutional guarantees of their rights to it. Oregonian 11/20/94:B6.

Churches, largest. In 1995, the eight largest churches in Oregon were the **Portland** Seventh Day Baptist, 7,500-8,500 members; Table Rock Church of Christ (**Medford**) 6,500-7,500; New Hope Community Church (Portland) 5,500-6,500; **Beaverton** Foursquare Church 5,500-6,500; Southeast Asian Vicariate (Portland) 5,000-6,000; Dayspring Christian Fellowship (**Banks**) 4,700-5,700; Applegate Christian Center (**Jacksonville**) 3,500-4,500; and New Beginnings Christian Center (Portland) 3,500-4,500. Oregonian 7/23/95:L6. See also **Religion**.

Churches, oldest. See **Church buildings history**.

Cinco de Mayo. A Mexican commemoration of the May 5 (Cinco de Mayo), 1862 Battle of Puebla when a small group of Mexican patriots defeated a larger troop of French soldiers. It is celebrated in **Portland** at a fiesta in **Governor Tom McCall Waterfront Park**, sponsored by the Portland-Guadalajara **Sister City** Association. The four-day **festival**, complete with fireworks, is one of the city's largest. Other Mexican communities around the state also commemorate the day with fiestas, including Fiesta Latina in **Eugene**. Other Mexican holidays include Mexican Independence Day on September 16 and Guadalupe Day on December 12. Nosotros; Oregonian 5/3/95:B3.

Cinder cone. A small, steep-sided volcano formed by the eruption of cinders. There is often an associated **lava** flow from the base of the cone. Once stopped, the cinder cone usually does not erupt again. Wizard Island in **Crater Lake**, **Pilot Butte** east of **Bend**, and **Lava Butte** south of Bend are some of the many cinder cones in central Oregon. Geology of Oregon.

Circuit court, federal. Appeals from the U.S. District Court in **Portland** are heard by the 9th U.S. Circuit Court, headquartered in San Francisco. The 9th, largest of the national appellate courts, has as many as 28 active judges and 15 senior judges. A panel of 3 judges, drawn at random, hears each case. The U.S. Supreme Court, during its 1996-97 term, reversed or returned 28 of the 29 cases that it reviewed from the 9th Circuit. First Duty; Oregonian 8/20/97:C5.

Circuit courts, Oregon. State trial courts of general jurisdiction. Circuit courts also have jurisdiction over adoption and juvenile matters, probate, guardianship, and conservatorship except in seven counties with **county courts**. Decisions may be appealed to the **Court of Appeals**. Oregon is divided into 23 judicial districts, served in 1997 by 97 circuit judges. In 1998, after the **district courts** are combined into the circuit courts, Oregon's 63 district court judges will become circuit court judges, and the courts will be divided into civil and criminal departments. The judges are elected for six-year terms on a nonpartisan ballot. They must reside in the judicial district in which they are elected, except in **Multnomah County** where they must live within 10 miles of the county. In January 1995 voters in **Union** and **Wallowa counties** recalled a circuit judge, the first time one has been removed from office. Over 169,000 cases, including juvenile cases, were filed with Circuit Courts in 1995, up from 142,000 in 1990. Confusingly, at the federal level, circuit courts are courts of appeal, while the federal trial courts are called district courts. Governing Oregon; Oregon Blue Book. See also **Courts,**

federal; Courts of record.

Cities. Oregon had 240 incorporated cities as of 1996, 202 of them with fewer than 10,000 persons. In 1995 Oregon's largest incorporated city was **Portland** with a population of 497,600, and its smallest was **Greenhorn**, population 3. Portland has been the state's largest city almost from its founding, but a number of places have briefly claimed **second-largest city** honors. In recent years **Eugene** (121,905) has been second followed by **Salem** (118,355), **Gresham** (77,240), **Beaverton** (61,720), and **Medford** (55,090). In 1880, 15% of Oregon's people lived in cities. By 1910 it was 46%, and in 1995 it was 64%. In Oregon, unlike some other states, the terms city, town, and village have no legal definition, but city is often used for an incorporated place, no matter its size. The incorporated cities and the names of their elected officials are listed in the Oregon Blue Book. **Oregon City**, incorporated in 1844, was the first to incorporate in Oregon. Other early incorporations were **Portland** 1851, **Astoria** 1856, **Corvallis**, **Salem** and **The Dalles** 1857, **Jacksonville** 1860, **Eugene** 1862, **Albany** and **Umatilla** 1864, **La Grande** 1865, and **Harrisburg** and **Scio** 1866. League of Oregon Cities, PO Box 928, Salem 97308. 503-588-6550. Governing Oregon; Oregon Main Street. See also **Charter; Home rule; La Pine; Metro; Metropolitan Statistical Areas; Mystery city; Ordinance; Settlements; Urban growth boundaries**.

Citizens' Representative. A person in the **governor's** office who provides access and help for citizens who have problems, questions, ideas, or suggestions about state government. Volunteers and student interns assist in the program. Governor Tom McCall created the office, then called ombudsman, in 1969, before the Oregon Public Meetings Law (1973) and the Public Records Law made state government somewhat more accessible. State Capitol, Salem 97310. 503-378-4582. Oregon Blue Book; Oregonian 8/30/97:C7.

Citizens' Utility Board (CUB). A non-profit, independent public corporation created by voter **initiative** in 1984. The group represents consumer interests in rate cases and in legislative, administrative, and judicial proceedings. Membership is open to any Oregon resident age 18 or older who makes a contribution of $5 or more. Members elect the 15 members of the Board. 921 SW Morrison St., #550, Portland 97205. 503-227-1984. Oregon Blue Book.

City Club of Portland. A non-partisan group founded in 1916 that meets weekly to discuss and shape public policy, spotlight issues, and develop the leadership capacities of its 2,600 members. It also issues reports, sometimes with controversial recommendations. The club, whose weekly programs are broadcast on public radio, has been called "the most prestigious platform in Oregon." Facts of Life.

City of Roses. A sobriquet applied to **Portland**, originating perhaps with the famous **roses** grown in the late 1800's by Leopold Samuel, publisher of **West Shore**.

Civet cat. See **Skunks**.

Civic Auditorium. A 3,000-seat **Portland** auditorium, located at SW 3rd and Clay. It is home for the **Oregon Ballet Theater**, **Portland Opera**, and the Oregon Children's Theatre Company. The building, erected during **World War I** and remodeled in the 1960s, is administered as part of the **Portland Center for the**

Performing Arts. The site was originally a market square and later the Mechanics Pavilion, used for exhibits, concerts and indoor sports such as football on roller skates. 503-796-9293 event information recording. Emergencies (during events only) 503-274-6560. Portland, An Informal History.

Civic Stadium. A **Portland**-owned facility at SW 20th and Morrison, operated by **Metro**. It is home to the Portland Rockies, a professional **baseball** team, and is used for rock concerts and soccer matches. The stadium, known at one time as Multnomah Stadium, is located at the site of Portland's first tannery. It was built in 1926 by the Multnomah Athletic Club which sold it to the city in about 1966. A 1998 proposal called for a $160 million upgrade to attract a major-league baseball team. 503-248-4345. Oregonian 4/5/98:D1. Portland, An Informal History; Round the Roses.

Civil Rights Division. A division of the Oregon Bureau of **Labor and Industries** that administers and enforces state laws protecting Oregonians against discrimination based on race, color, national origin, religion, sex, marital status, handicap, and age in employment, housing, public accommodation, and vocational and trade schools. It also enforces laws protecting Oregonians from discrimination in employment due to family relationship and personal association; an expunged juvenile record; polygraph and breathalyzer test results; having reported patient abuse; having given legislative testimony; having a job injury; reporting work place safety or health violations; or taking parental, pregnancy, or family medical leave. 800 NE Oregon Street #32, Portland 97232. 503-731-4075. Oregon Blue Book. See also **Affirmative Action Office**.

Civil War, 1861-1865. The war between the northern and southern states over **slavery**. Oregonians had been heatedly arguing the merits of slavery since the first **wagon trains** in 1843 and opinion was fairly evenly divided, but residents were even more concerned with Indian threats and the need to keep the **Oregon Trail** supply line open. After the Army regular troops were recalled in 1861, California volunteers were garrisoned at **Fort Yamhill**, **Fort Hoskins**, and the Siletz Blockhouse. Oregon's contribution of volunteers consisted of six three-year companies (the First Oregon Cavalry) raised in the winter of 1861-62, and the First Oregon Infantry, mustered in June, 1865, three months after General Lee surrendered. Most of the Cavalry served in the west. Civil war re-enactments are held at **Willamette Mission State Park** over the 4th of July by the Northwest Civil War Council. All Quiet on the Yamhill; Dictionary of Oregon History; General History of Oregon. See also **Knights of the Golden Circle**; **Star City Stage Line**.

Civilian Conservation Corps (CCC). A federal agency created in 1933 during the **Depression** to put unemployed young men to work on public land projects. In Oregon the CCC employed nearly 87,000 men, 60% of them from out of state, until **World War II** eliminated the need for the camps in 1942. The crews, housed in 49 camps, fought forest fires, planted 49 million trees, controlled insects and rodents on 2.8 million acres, and built roads, 1,317 bridges, 276 **fire lookouts**, **Silver Falls State Park**, **Jessie M. Honeyman State Park**, and the headquarters buildings still used by the state Department of **Forestry** in **Salem**. Roosevelt's Forest Army. See also **Camp Angell**.

Clackamas Community College. A public two-year college in **Oregon**

City that opened in 1971. 8,647 students enrolled for fall 1996 classes. It offers college transfer courses, occupational training in 40 career areas, continuing education, and developmental education. 19600 S Molalla Ave., Oregon City 97045-9049. 503-657-6958 ext. 2401. Oregon Blue Book. See also **Community colleges; Small Business Development Centers**.

Clackamas County. A diverse county in the **Portland** metropolitan area that extends from the **Willamette Valley** east to the summit of the **Cascade Range**, and is bounded by **Multnomah, Hood River, Wasco, Marion, Yamhill,** and **Washington** counties. Incorporated cities include Oregon's oldest, **Oregon City** (county seat), plus **Barlow, Canby, Estacada, Gladstone, Happy Valley, Johnson City, Lake Oswego, Milwaukie, Molalla, Rivergrove, Sandy,** and **West Linn**. Elevations range from tidewater below **Willamette Falls** to the 11,240' summit of **Mount Hood**. Other points of interest include the **Clackamas** and **Sandy** rivers, **End of the Oregon Trail Visitor Center, Barlow Road,** and the Canby **ferry**. Soils around Canby are some of the most productive in the state, so agricultural crops and nurseries are important to its economy, as are timber, manufacturing, retail services, and wholesale trade. Its 1995 taxable assessed value was $19,128,000,000, or $62,000 per capita. The county, named for the Clackamas Indians, was part of **Clackamas District**, one of Oregon's four original **districts**. Population 1980 241,911; 1995 308,600. Area 1,879 square miles. Density 164/sq.mi. Annual precipitation 48"; average temperature January 40°F, July 68°F. Courthouse, 906 Main St., Oregon City 97045. 503-655-8581. Free Land for Free Men; Oregon Blue Book;. See also **Metro**.

Clackamas District. The northeast of the four original **districts** (later, **counties**) into which the **Oregon Country** was divided by the **Provisional government** on July 5, 1843, and from which the counties of northeast Oregon were later created. Clackamas District was the area north of the mouth of the Pudding River between the **Willamette River** and the Rocky Mountains. The other three districts were **Champooick** to the southeast, **Twality** to the northwest, and **Yamhill** to the southwest. "Oregon Counties."

Clackamas River. A major river that drains 937 square miles of the west slopes of the **Cascade Range** between the **Sandy** and **Santiam** rivers. It flows 84 miles northwest from the mountains to join the **Willamette River** at **Oregon City**, with most of its drainage basin in the **Mount Hood National Forest**. About 10% of Oregonians are supplied with drinking water from the river. **Portland General Electric** has built several power generating dams along it, creating a series of lakes. The largest, and farthest upstream, is **Timothy Lake** on Oak Grove Fork. Below it is Lake Harriet, then North Fork Reservoir, Faraday Lake, and Estacada Lake. Flows of 4.4 acre feet/acre yield a total annual volume of 2,660,000 acre feet. Winter flows are 15 times summer volume, and in the **flood of 1996** the lower river cut major new channels. The Clackamas Indians, a Chinookan tribe, lived along the river. Oregon Geographic Names.

Clam burgers. Spherical concretions found in **sandstone** that contain fossilized clams. Fossil Shells.

Clams. Both freshwater and saltwater clams are found in Oregon. All are edible, though only those found on ocean beaches and tidal bay flats are usually collected for food. These include:

- gapers, Empires, or horsenecks, *Tresus nuttallii* and *T. capax*, large, heavy clams (up to 6" long and five pounds) with a large gape where the neck protrudes, found 12 to 18" deep in sandy mud in the lower reaches of large bays;

- cockles, *Clinocardium nuttalli*, 3" clams with prominent ribbing, found in lower bays near the surface in sandy mud;

- mud or eastern softshell clams, *Mya arenaria*, with thin, brittle shells 2 to 6" long, found about 12" deep in mud flats in the upper reaches of estuaries. It was introduced from the east coast in the late 1800s;

- butter or Quahog clams, *Saxidomus giganteus,* with a heavy shell 2-6" long with concentric lines, found up to a foot deep in mixed pea gravel, shell, and sand beds;

- littleneck, rock, or (confusingly) butter clams, *Venerupis staminea*, 2 to 3" with radiating ribs on the shell crossed with concentric lines so that it looks cross-hatched, found most commonly while raking for cockles;

- **razor clams**;

- and **geoducks**.

Several other clams are found less frequently. The edible Japanese varnish clam, *Nuttallia obscurata*, was first found in Oregon at Nestucca Bay in 1997. The harvesting of all edible shellfish is controlled by state law; sport clamming regulations are included in the annual publication, Oregon Sport Fishing Regulations. Many are also harvested commercially. Clam beaches are sometimes closed because of possible **shellfish poisoning** or because of contaminants such as tributyltin. Bay Clams of Oregon; Clam Digging and Crabbing in Oregon. See also **Shellfish**.

Clark County, Washington. A rapidly-growing county north of **Portland**, across the **Columbia River**, that is part of the **Portland-Vancouver Consolidated Metropolitan Statistical Area**. In the 1990s increasing numbers of Oregonians moved to Clark County because of lower housing costs and lower **property taxes**. While the 1997 median price in the five-county Portland area was $149,900, it was $137,500 in Clark County. County population in 1997 was 316,800, up from 238,053 in 1990. Oregonian 10/19/97:B1, 2/27/98:C1.

Clarno Formation. A colorful formation of rocks covering extensive areas in the **Ochoco** and **Strawberry Mountains**. It is made up of **andesite** and **rhyolite** erupted between 35 to 50 million years ago during the **Eocene**. The formation also includes vast volcanic mud flows, one of them 1,000 feet thick, and volcanic ash sediment. **Fossils** of lush, tropical woodlands and large animals, including crocodiles, are preserved in the deposits. **Mercury** ore (cinnabar) occurs in the formation, associated with intrusive volcanic plugs. The **John Day Formation** lies on top of it. Geology of Oregon. See also **John Day Fossil Beds**.

Class size. See **Student/teacher ratio**.

Clatskanie (KLATS kuh nye). A northwest Oregon city in **Columbia County**, 23 miles northwest of **Saint Helens** on **Highway 30**. The name derives from the Indian name, Tlatskani, for a place in the Nehalem Valley. The Indians also used the name to indicate routes they took to get to Tlatskani; whites then used the name for the Clatskanie River. The city had a post office by 1871, and was incorporated in 1891. Population 1980 1,648; 1995 1,885. Elevation 15'. PO Box 9, 97016.

503-728-2622. Chamber of Commerce 503-728-2502. Oregon Geographic Names; Oregonian 2/1/98:H1.

Clatskanie River. A 28-mile long river in northwest Oregon that drains 96 square miles from the north slope of the **Coast Range** north to the **Columbia River** near the town of **Clatskanie**. The name is a variant on the name of an Indian village, Tlats-kani, on the **Nehalem River**, that the Indians reached by way of the Clatskanie River. Oregon Geographic Names.

Clatsop Community College. A public two-year college in **Astoria**. Founded in 1958, it enrolled 2,720 students in fall 1996. It offers two-year transfer courses and courses in vocational and avocational topics. 1653 Jerome Avenue, Astoria 97103-3698. 503-325-0910. Oregon Blue Book. See also **Community colleges; Small Business Development Centers**.

Clatsop County. A coastal county at the mouth of the **Columbia River** in Oregon's northwest corner, bounded by Washington State on the north (reached by a four-mile-long bridge across the river), **Columbia** and **Tillamook** counties, and the Pacific Ocean. Incorporated cities are **Astoria** (county seat), site of the oldest white settlement in Oregon (1811), **Cannon Beach**, **Gearhart**, **Seaside**, and **Warrenton**. The county ranges in elevation from sea level to 3,283' **Saddle Mountain**. The economy is based on fishing, tourism, lumber, and agriculture, and the 1995 taxable assessed value was $2,864,000,000, or $83,000 per capita. Attractions, in addition to those of its communities, include its beaches, **Fort Stevenson**, and **Fort Clatsop**. The county was created in 1844 out of **Twality District**, one of Oregon's original four **districts**, and named for the local Indians. Population 1980 32,489; 1995 34,300. Area 873 square miles. Density 39/sq.mi. Annual precipitation 70"; average temperature January 41°F, July 60°F. Courthouse, 749 Commercial, Astoria 97103. 503-325-1000. Clatsop County; Oregon Blue Book.

Clatsop Plains. A low area of sand and forest in northwest **Clatsop County** that stretches from the mouth of the **Columbia River** south to **Seaside**. **Clatsop Spit**, the sandbar at the north end, has been the site of many **shipwrecks**. The plains are striped with a number of long, narrow lakes of which **Cullaby Lake** is the largest. The **Methodists** had a **mission** in the area from 1840 to 1845. Dictionary of Oregon History.

Clatsop Spit. A long, low spit of sand extending over two miles north into the mouth of the **Columbia River** from **Point Adams** and the **Clatsop Plains**. The spit has been the scene of a number of **shipwrecks**. See also *General Warren*; *William and Ann*.

Clatsop State Forest. A 154,000 acre **state forest**, Oregon's second largest, located in **Clatsop County** with an additional small tract in **Columbia County**. It was created in 1937 as a result of property tax defaults during the **Depression** and is part of the **Board of Forestry Lands**; by law the state manages the lands and the counties receive two-thirds of net revenues. ODF Astoria District Office, Route 1, Astoria 97103. 503-325-5451.

Clay. A very fine-grained soil. The kind common in the **Willamette Valley** is smectite, derived from weathered volcanic ash. It doesn't work well for pottery, though it is used for **bricks** and ceramic tiles. Common clay is mined in **Baker**, **Multnomah**, **Lane**, **Jackson**, and **Klamath Counties**. Bentonite is mined in

Crook and **Malheur Counties** for use as drilling mud and as a soil sealant for waste disposal sites and ponds. Mineral Industry of Oregon. See also **Buena Vista**.

Clean air. See **Air pollution**.

Clear Lake (Linn County). One of ten lakes of the same name in Oregon, this Clear Lake is a natural mountain lake located 55 miles east of **Eugene** on **Highway 126**, a few miles south of its junction with **Highway 20**. It covers 148 acres, is over a mile long, and is 175 feet deep. The lake was formed about 3,000 years ago when molten lava pouring from the east blocked the **McKenzie River**. The backed-up waters inundated a stand of **Douglas fir** trees; dozens of the still-standing snags can be seen through the clear waters of the lake. The lake is fed by a number of springs; Big Spring, the largest, flows into the lake on the northeast corner. No motorboats are allowed on the lake. Fishing is usually good; a fishing resort and a campground are located on the shore. Atlas of Oregon Lakes.

Clear Lake Cutoff. A 20-mile section of **Highway 126** along the **McKenzie River** from Belknap Springs at the junction with **Highway 242** to **Highway 20**, the Santiam Pass route. Before the Clear Lake Cutoff opened in 1962, the only route from **Eugene** east to **Sisters** crossed **McKenzie Pass**, a narrow, winding route difficult to keep open in the winter. **Sahalie Falls, Koosah Falls,** and **Clear Lake** are along the cutoff.

Clear-cut. An area from which all timber has been removed by **logging**. The Oregon **Forest Practices Act** limits clear-cuts to 120 acres in size. Clear-cuts have been used especially in harvesting the **Douglas-fir** forests of western Oregon where the clearings provide the sunlight needed for **Douglas-fir**, a shade-intolerant species, to reestablish.

Cleary. See **Beverly Cleary Sculpture Garden**.

Cleawox Lake. A popular recreation lake in the sand dunes three miles south of **Florence**. Part of the 87-acre lake lies in **Jessie M. Honeyman State Park**, part in the **Oregon Dunes National Recreation Area**, and part is privately owned. A thin arm extends a mile and a half to the north; maximum depth is 48 feet. More than half of the western side is bordered by active sand dunes that are advancing to the north 15 to 20 feet a year and gradually encroaching on the lake. The lake is heavily used for swimming, canoeing, and picnicking. The park includes a campground. The meaning of the Indian name is unknown. Atlas of Oregon Lakes.

Cleft of the Rock Lighthouse. A small, privately-owned **lighthouse** located between **Yachats** and **Cape Perpetua** built in 1973 by Jim and Cherie Gibbs who continue to operate it. Jim Gibbs is a maritime historian who was at one time the lighthouse keeper of **Tillamook Rock Lighthouse**. Oregonian 12/21/97:B4; Oregon's Seacoast Lighthouses.

Climate. Oregon has nine climatic zones, ranging from mid-latitude rain forest to high desert, but all are characterized by winter precipitation and dry summers. West of the **Cascade Range** the climate is influenced by the Pacific Ocean, with moderate **temperatures** and **precipitation**, and a high degree of cloudiness for much of the year. As weather systems move inland to the east, moisture is squeezed out by the **Coast Range** and by the even higher **Cascade Range**, so that east of the Cascades the climate is continental, with low **rainfall** and greater seasonal and diurnal temperature extremes. The coastal strip receives 60 to 80 inches of rain a year and **snow** is rare, while the **Willamette Valley** receives between 40 and 50 inches of rain with occasional snow, and the winter low, though usually between 15°F and 20°F, occasionally drops to 0°F. Most of Oregon east of the Cascades is at a higher elevation and the climate is drier and harsher, with cold winters and hot summers, and annual precipitation between 5 and 20 inches. Precipitation in all areas increases with elevation. <u>Climatological Data</u>; <u>Oregon: Wet, High and Dry</u>.

City	County	Elev.	Jan. min.	July min.	Precip	*Snow	*#days Precip	*GS
Astoria	Clatsop	10'	36°F	68°F	66"	5"	187	273
Baker City	Baker	3471'	17°F	85°F	11"	35"	103	138
Bend	Deschutes	3650'	22°F	82°F	12"	32"	76	88
Brookings	Curry	45'	41°F	68°F	75"	<1"	130	238
Burns	Harney	4140'	13°F	84°F	10"	46"	89	117
Corvallis	Benton	230'	33°F	80°F	43"	8"	139	183
Eugene	Lane	360'	33°F	82°F	49"	6"	143	205
Hood River	Hood River	500'	28°F	80°F	31"	34"	113	183
John Day	Grant	3060'	21°F	88°F	13"	**19"	**85	**179
Klamath Falls	Klamath	4100'	21°F	85°F	13"	38"	72	134
La Grande	Union	2760'	24°F	86°F	17"	37"	110	160
Lakeview	Lake	4780'	19°F	84°F	16"	54"	71	121
Medford	Jackson	1300'	30°F	89°F	19"	4"	99	160
Newport	Lincoln	140'	37°F	65°F	72"	1"	164	195
North Bend	Coos	10'	39°F	66°F	63"	1"	160	197
Pendleton	Umatilla	1482'	27°F	88°F	12"	18"	100	155
Portland	Multnomah	20'	34°F	80°F	36"	9"	152	251
Roseburg	Douglas	465'	34°F	84°F	32"	7"	133	217
Salem	Marion	200'	33°F	82°F	39"	7"	142	213
The Dalles	Wasco	102'	30°F	88°F	14"	24"	75	196
Vale	Malheur	2220'	18°F	94°F	10"	15"	63	124

Data from <u>The Climate of Oregon, Special Reports 913-921</u>, by George Taylor. Oregon Climate Service, Oregon State University, Corvallis, May 1993.

*Data from <u>Oregon Climates</u> brochure from the Oregon Department of Transportation. GS=Growing season.

**(Canyon City)

Climate - prehistoric. Oregon's climate during the **Miocene** (25-11 million years ago) was wet and warm, as evidenced by tropical fossil sea shells in the north **Coast Range** and tropical leaf fossils in eastern Oregon, and by the red soils in the Coast Range and near **Salem**. By the **Pliocene** (11-2 million years ago) the climate had become much drier and gravels were deposited in the **Willamette Valley**. During the **Pleistocene** ice ages of the last 2 million years, until about 10,000 years ago, **glaciers** repeatedly covered mountains, but there was no ice shield in Oregon. In the last 13,000 years, since the time the first humans are known to have appeared in Oregon, the climate has swung through several major variations. A period of gradual warming and summer rains filled the closed basins of eastern Oregon with **Pleistocene lakes**, and humans and other life thrived around the lakes. Then, about 7,500 years ago, came a long, hot, and very dry period, the lakes dried up, and people disappeared from many of the settlements that they had occupied for four thousand years. Then, about 4,000 years ago, the climate moderated somewhat and some water again flowed into the lake beds.

    Climatologist. Oregon has an official state climatologist who heads the Oregon Climate Service. Responsibilities include collecting and archiving **weather** data from the state, answering some 3,000 to 4,000 weather questions a year, doing research on Oregon's weather, and educating people on current and emerging climate issues. The Climate Service has a web page with weather data at www.ocs.orst.edu. 316 Strand Agricultural Hall, Oregon State University, Corvallis 97331. 541-737-5705.

    Clinical Social Workers, State Board of. A seven-member board, appointed by the governor for four-year terms, created to certify and license clinical social workers. Nearly 2,000 were licensed as of July 1997. 3218 Pringle Road SE, Suite 140, Salem 97302-6310. 503-378-5735.

    Cloud Cap Inn. A rustic inn designed by Portland architects Whidden and Lewis and built in 1889 at the 6,000' level on the north slope of **Mount Hood**. It was a popular vacation destination into the 1920s. The Hood River Crag Rats, a mountain rescue group, leased it from the **Forest Service** in recent years. <u>Dictionary of Oregon History</u>.

    Cloudbursts. See **Floods, eastern Oregon**.

    Clover seed. In 1995 Oregon growers produced 5 million pounds of crimson clover seed worth $2.9 million and 5.7 million pounds of red clover seed worth $5.2 million on 21,250 acres. <u>1995 Oregon</u>.

    Clowns. Vance DeBar "Pinto" Colvig (1892-1967), known as Bozo the Clown, grew up in **Jacksonville**. He was also a **cartoonist**, **animator**, actor, and the voice of Walt Disney's Goofy. <u>Oregon Stater</u> 79(4):17-21. September 1995.

    Coal. A combustible rock formed by the decomposition of plants. In 1994 coal supplied 4% of Oregon's total **energy** needs. Most of the 2.5 million short tons (44.6 trillion Btu), all of it brought into the state, was used at the **Boardman** electric power plant. Low grade deposits around **Coos Bay** in the Coaledo Formation date from about 50 million years ago when tropical marshes and jungles surrounded the **Klamath Mountains**. Coal mining began there in 1854, and three million tons had been produced by 1920. Reserves are estimated to be as much as 51 million tons, but it is of poor quality and the bulk coal will spontaneously ignite if loaded more than four feet deep. The mines were sealed in 1985 as a safety measure. **Wallowa County** has major lignite deposits, and thin layers of low grade coals are also found in southwestern **Clatsop County**, in southern Oregon near **Medford**, and in the **Scotts Mills** Formation in the **Willamette Valley** foothills. Geology of Oregon.

Coast. Oregon's Pacific coast is variously reported to extend from 296 to 362 miles, depending on how it is measured, from the **Columbia River** south to the California border. The tidal shoreline is calculated to be 1,410 miles long. The coast is characterized by rocky headlands interspersed with sand **beaches** and **harbors**, and, along the central coast, 56 miles of sand **dunes**. Geologically, the coast is an area of instability characterized by erosion of beach and cliffs, **landslides**, and infrequent but massive **earthquakes**. Temperatures along the coast are mild, with snow and heat both rare. The hotter the inland areas become in summer, the cooler the coast. Most rain falls during the winter; annual averages are about 60 inches. Dramatic winter storms bring huge **waves** crashing on the rocks, while autumn days are often perfect. **Highway 101** follows the coast, 54% of it in public ownership, with frequent **state parks**, viewpoints, **lighthouses**, and **harbors**. Beaches are owned by the state up to high water line with public use up to the vegetation line. "Ocean processes and hazards along the Oregon coast;" National Atlas; Oregonian 7/6,7,8/97:A1. See also **CoastWatch**; **Terraces**.

Coast Guard. A federal agency under the U.S. Department of Transportation that is responsible for boat safety as well as ocean pollution prevention and response, search and rescue, and law enforcement. The Portland Marine Safety Office on Swan Island has overall responsibility for all of Oregon's coastal waters as well as waters of the **Columbia** and **Willamette** rivers. Group Portland covers the rivers, Group Astoria at **Warrenton** is responsible for the Oregon coast south to **Pacific City**, and Group North Bend covers the Oregon coast from Pacific City south. Stations are maintained at a number of coastal ports. Trained volunteer members of auxiliary units help with rescues and use their own boats to patrol. There are 21 of the volunteer units, called flotillas, in Oregon, with about 400 members. 6767 N Basin Avenue, Portland 97217-3992. 503-240-9310. Emergency 503-240-9300. Oregonian 7/25/97:C2.

Coast Highway. See **Highway 101**.

Coast Range. A range of mountains 30 to 60 miles wide along the coast of Washington and Oregon. In Oregon it extends from the **Columbia River** 200 miles south to **Cape Blanco** and the Middle Fork of the Coquille River where it meets the **Klamath Mountains**. **Marys Peak**, elevation 4,094', is the highest point. The **Umpqua** is the only river to break through the Coast Range south of the Columbia. The Coast Range is one of the prime timber growing regions of the world. **Siuslaw National Forest** covers some of the central portions, but much of the forest land is owned by industrial timber companies. Geologically, its development is complex and not yet well understood, though it is in part volcanic, with the oldest volcanic rocks being the 64-million-year-old **Roseburg** Formation. The north end is more recent, having emerged about 15 million years ago. The entire Coast Range is thought to have rotated some 75° clockwise during the last 50 million years. Mineral resources include **coal**, **natural gas**, and **black sand** placer deposits of **gold** and other minerals. Geology of Oregon. See also **Cannibal Mountain**; **Mount Hebo**; **Neahkahnie Mountain**; **Saddle Mountain**; **Siletz terrane**; **Uplift**.

Coast Range physiographic province. An area of Oregon that includes the **Coast Range**, the area between the mountains and the shore, and the area offshore to the **Cascadia Subduction Zone**. It is bordered on the east by the **Willamette Valley**, on the south by the **Klamath Mountains**, and extends north into Washington. It is 30 to 60 miles wide on land and extends offshore for another 40 or more miles of **continental shelf** and slope. **Cape Blanco** near the southwest corner is the westernmost point in the state. Geology of Oregon.

Coast Reservation. A 1.4-million-acre Indian **reservation** established in 1856 for the Indians who were being forcibly removed from southwest Oregon after the **Rogue River War** and for other Indians from western Oregon and northern California. It was originally a 20-mile wide strip that extended 120 miles along the coast from the **Umpqua River** north to **Cape Lookout**. It was soon reduced by government actions to the much smaller Siletz reservation and was essentially gone by the 1890s. She's Tricky. See **Coos, Lower Umpqua, and Siuslaw Indians**; **Fort Hoskins**; **Reservations, history**; **Siletz Tribes**; **Yachats**.

CoastWatch A program begun by the **Oregon Shores Conservation Coalition** to gather information on the welfare of the 362-mile-long Oregon **coast** and to monitor coastal development. Each volunteer is responsible for a mile and walks it four times a year, monitoring invasive European beach grass, mapping public access, and noting seawalls or rock riprap (which starve the beach of its sand) . 605 SE 37th, Portland, 97214. 503-23-4450. Mail Tribune 10/17/97:1B. See also **Environmental organizations**; **Snowy plover**.

Cob. See **Alternative architecture**.

Coburg. A historic **Willamette Valley** agricultural and suburban community five miles north of **Eugene** in **Lane County**. First called Diamond because it was on John Diamond's land claim, the town was renamed Coburg in 1865 in honor of a fine stallion imported from Coburg, Germany. It was incorporated in 1893. Coburg thrived while a major saw mill operated from 1882 until 1914, supplied by log drives down the **McKenzie River**. Skunk farming and a glass factory were briefer ventures. Population 1980 699; 1995 770. Elevation 400'. PO Box 8316, 97408. 541-485-6266. Coburg Remembered.

Cockstock affair. In March 1844 Cockstock, a Wasco Indian, was promised a horse as payment for work on a black-owned farm near **Oregon City**. He completed the work but was refused the horse because the farm and horse had both been sold, so he appropriated it. After he had been compelled to return the horse he became threatening, brought in four Molalla Indians, and, in an armed confrontation, he and two others, including the clerk of the **provisional government**, were killed. The episode resulted in the formation of the **Oregon Rangers** and the first **Exclusion law**. Dictionary of Oregon History; Peculiar Paradise.

Coho salmon. A **salmon**, *Oncorhynchus kisutch*, also called silver salmon.

The coho is distinguished from other salmon by a white lower gumline and small round spots on the upper lobe of the tail. The Oregon record is 25 lb. 5 oz. from **Siltcoos Lake** in 1966. Coho spawn in the **Columbia River** basin and in coastal rivers and tributaries. The Columbia once hosted annual runs of 1.2 million coho, and coastal runs exceeded 1.9 million fish, dropped to 20,000 by 1990, and climbed to 50,000 in 1995. Five rivers have been designated for coho habitat restoration, the **Nehalem**, **Rogue**, **Siletz**, Tillamook, and North **Umpqua**. Coho was also the name given to the east **wind** in a 1997 contest. Columbia River Salmon; Fishing in Oregon; Oregonian 10/19/96:C1; Salmon of the Pacific. See also **Oregon Plan**.

Cold deck. A big stack of logs, such as at a mill. Woods Words.

Cold spells. One of Oregon's worst winters occurred in 1861-62 following the **flood of 1861**. Thousands of head of livestock were killed in the **Willamette Valley**, some through drowning in the flood and others from exposure during the 14 weeks of snow and bitter cold that followed. **Saint Paul** had two feet of snow on Jan. 9, 1862, and the **Willamette** and **Columbia** rivers froze over, trapping the steamer *Multnomah* in the ice near Cathlamet, Washington. **Gold** miners near **Auburn** in northeast Oregon were stopped by 14 feet of snow. Central Oregon had a grim winter beginning in December 1883 when the temperature in the **Sisters** area dropped to 35 to 40°F below zero followed by six feet of snow that covered the region until mid-March. There was a heavy loss of livestock, and many **juniper** trees were killed when starving animals ate their bark. In December 1884 floods in western Oregon were again followed by cold and heavy snow, and a train with 150 passengers was stranded seven miles west of **Hood River** from Dec.18 until January 6. Other hard winters in Oregon were in 1880/81, January 1888 (-2°F at **Portland** with 8" of snow), 1919 (-24°F at **McMinnville** with 24" of snow), January 1930 (-8°F at **Forest Grove** and -50°F at Blitzen near **Frenchglen**), 1932/33 (statewide, with record lows east of the Cascades), 1955/56 (rain, snow, and ice storms, floods, slides), and 1972 (some record cold temperatures west of the Cascades). Oregonian 1/8/1885:3, 12/27/47:7. See also **Cold, unseasonable**; **Frozen rivers**; **Snowfall**; **Temperature records**.

Cold Springs Reservoir. A large irrigation impoundment five miles east of **Hermiston**, built in 1908 by the **Bureau of Reclamation**, and now operated by the Hermiston Irrigation District. The lake covers 1,517 acres when full, with a maximum depth of 71 feet, though it is drawn down during the summer. The vegetation that springs up on the exposed lakebed attracts a variety of wildlife; Cold Springs National Wildlife Refuge surrounds the lake. Fishing is good, though no motorized boats are allowed and boat launching is difficult. Bird watching and hunting are popular. There is no overnight camping. Atlas of Oregon Lakes.

Cold, unseasonable. In early June, on his 1579 voyage along the southern Oregon coast, the pirate Sir Francis Drake, in the first written comments on Oregon weather, reported severe cold and ice, and noted that the ground appeared covered with snow. He noted that "the rain which fell was an unnatural congealed and frozen substance" and two day later "there followed most vile, thicke and stinking fogges." A frost hit **Tillamook County** in July 1853 that took the leaves from the trees. Areas east of the **Cascade Range** have also experienced killing frosts in July. Empire of the Columbia; Oregonian 2/12/96:B7; Tillamook. See also **Cold spells**.

Colegio Cesar Chavez. A college for **Hispanics** and other minorities that began in **Mount Angel** and graduated its first class of 22 in 1977. The school closed in 1983 due to a variety of problems, primarily financial. Nosotros.

Coliseum. See **Memorial Coliseum**.

Colleges, private. See **Higher education, private**.

Colleges, public. See **Oregon University System**.

Colliding Rivers. A spot just north of **Highway 138** at Glide, 18 miles east of **Roseburg**, where Little River slams into the North **Umpqua River** at right angles. Oregon Atlas.

Collier State Park. A **state park** 30 miles north of **Klamath Falls** on **Highway 97**. The park includes an open-air logging museum, a pioneer log cabin village, gift shop, a day-use horse rest and exercise area, a 1.5 mile hiking trail, and 50 camp sites. Reservations, 800-452-5687. 541-783-2471.

Colossus of Portland. A statue proposed for **Portland** by writer Katherine Dunn as a way to supply the city with a major tourist attraction. She describes her proposal as a huge bronze statue with one foot on each side of the **Willamette River**, with "a kind of Rambo body with Bud Clark's face. It would have elevators up the shaft of each leg, and around about the waistband, an observation deck. And a small, very intimate bar in the headband that would rotate." The legendary Colossus of Rhodes, one of the seven wonders of the ancient world, was a bronze statue of a young god which, according to legend, stood astride the entrance to the city's harbor. Oregonian 6/9/96:E4.

Columbarium. See **Tillamook Rock Lighthouse**.

Columbia Basin Fish and Wildlife Authority. Representatives from two federal agencies, four states, and 12 Indian tribes who coordinate planning and implementation of fish and wildlife issues in the basin. Only consensus positions can be presented. 2501 SW 1st Avenue, Suite 200, Portland 97201. 503-326-7031. Directory of Organizations.

Columbia City. "City of Beauty and Livability." A residential community on the **Columbia River** two miles north of **Saint Helens** on **Highway 30** in **Columbia County**. The city was founded in 1867 in hopes, never realized, of becoming a rail terminus. It was incorporated in 1926. Five snow-capped peaks can be seen across the mile-wide river. The 1870 Caples House is now a museum. Population 1980 678; 1995 1,385. Elevation 24'. 1840 Second St., PO Box 189, 97018. 503-397-4010. Oregon Geographic Names.

Columbia County. A county along the **Columbia River** northwest of **Portland**, bounded by **Washington State** on the north and east (reached by a bridge across the Columbia at Rainier), and by **Multnomah, Washington**, and **Clatsop** counties. Incorporated cities are **Saint Helens** (county seat), **Clatskanie, Columbia City, Prescott, Rainier, Scappoose**, and **Vernonia**. It ranges in elevation from tidewater along the river to 2,082' at Bunker Hill in the **Coast Range**. The economy is based on agriculture, lumber, natural gas, manufacturing, fishing, and tourism. The county's 1995 taxable assessed value was $2,434,000,000, or $61,000 per capita. It was created from Washington County in 1854 and named for the river. Population 1980 35,646; 1995 39,700. Area 687 square miles. Density 58/

sq.mi. Annual precipitation 45"; average temperature January 39°F, July 68°F. Courthouse, St. Helens 97051-0010. 503-397-4322. Homes in the Oregon Forest; Oregon Blue Book; Oregonian 2/22/98:B1.

Columbia Gorge. See also **Columbia River Gorge**.

Columbia Gorge Community College. A public two-year college in **The Dalles** that serves **Wasco** and **Hood River** counties. Fall 1996 enrollment was 1,407. It offers academic transfer courses as well as vocational courses. 400 E. Scenic Drive, The Dalles 97058-2282. 541-296-6182. Oregon Blue Book. See also **Community colleges; Small Business Development Centers**.

Columbia Gorge Interpretive Center. A 23,000-square-foot museum two miles west of Stevenson, Washington, next to the Skamania Lodge and Conference Center. The past and present resources of the river, the forests, and the people of the **Columbia River Gorge** are featured in the exhibits. The building, which opened in 1995, is designed to suggest a sawmill. The private, non-profit building is operated by the Skamania County Historical Society. 990 SW Rock Creek Drive, 98648. 509-427-8211. See also **Gorge Discovery Center**.

Columbia Plateau. See **Deschutes-Columbia Plateau**.

Columbia Region Association of Governments (CRAG). See **Metro**.

Columbia Ridge Landfill. A 2,000 acre regional **landfill** site near **Arlington** that opened in 1990 with a life expectancy of 50 years. It is operated by Oregon Waste Systems Inc. of Arlington, a subsidiary of Waste Management Inc. of Oak Brook, Illinois. **Metro** has a 20 year contract, dating from 1989, to dispose of its garbage there, a 140-mile haul. The landfill is also used by **Sherman** and **Gilliam** counties and by several Idaho and Washington cities, including Seattle. Oregonian 5/9/95:B1.

Columbia River. "Great River of the West." A 1,210-(or 1,248-, or 1,264) mile long river that drains an area of 259,000 square miles, from the summit of the Rocky Mountains west to the Pacific. Most of its drainage basin lies in British Columbia, Idaho, Washington, and Oregon. About 40% of the flow at **Bonneville Dam** comes from Canada. The river discharges 180 million acre feet per year, second largest flow in the U.S. Unlike other Oregon rivers, the Columbia's flow peaks in June due to melting snow in the Rockies, and only 27% of its flow comes during the six months of winter when demand for electricity is highest. The highest flow recorded, 1,200,000 cubic feet per second, was during the **flood of 1894**, while the lowest winter flow, recorded before **dams** were built, was 32,000 cubic feet per second. The **Snake River** and the **Willamette River** are major tributaries. Other Oregon tributaries include **Willow Creek** and the **Umatilla**, **John Day**, **Deschutes**, and **Hood** rivers. The Columbia, which drops 1,288 feet between the Canadian border and the Pacific Ocean (2 to 5 feet per mile) has 40% of the hydropower potential of the U.S., and all but 95 feet of this fall is utilized by 11 dams. The 140 miles from Bonneville Dam to the ocean is tidal, and the deepest natural point, 150 feet deep, is off Tongue Point near **Astoria**. Atlas of the Pacific Northwest; Columbia; Northwest Passage; Organic Machine. See also **Frozen rivers; Wallula Gap**.

Columbia River basalt. Vast **basalt** flows during the **Miocene**, 11 to 25 million years ago, from vents in Oregon, Washington, and Idaho, that formed the

Deschutes-Columbia plateau. The flows spread over 60,000 square miles, second in size only to the flows of the Deccan Plateau in India. The various flows, hot and very fluid, poured out at speeds of up to 30 miles an hour, and spread down the ancestral **Columbia River**, south into the **Willamette Valley**, and along the coast from Grays Harbor, Washington, south to **Seal Rock** on the central Oregon coast. Some vents erupted every 10,000 years, though the average interval was 35,000 years. The flows were too liquid to build volcanic cones. The total volume was over 42,000 cubic miles; at the deepest areas, near Yakima, Washington, the flows are 15,000 feet deep. In central Oregon the flows cover the **John Day Formation**. Geology of Oregon.

Columbia River channel. The Columbia has traditionally been divided into three navigable sections, the Lower Columbia, which extended 146 miles from the ocean upstream to the **Cascades of the Columbia** (flooded by **Bonneville Dam**), the Middle Columbia from the Cascades upstream 45 miles to **The Dalles of the Columbia**, and the Upper Columbia upstream from **Celilo Falls**. Besides the Cascades and The Dalles, other navigational hazards included John Day Rapids, 33 miles above The Dalles, just below where **John Day Dam** now stands, and Umatilla Rapids, 107 miles above The Dalles, located where **McNary Dam** now stands. The **Army Corps of Engineers** blasted rocks out of those rapids in the 1860s and '70s. **Cascades Canal and Locks**, opened in 1896, and **The Dalles-Celilo Canal and Locks**, opened in 1915, created an open river, allowing river travel without portaging. Prior to that time each reach of river had its own captive fleet of steamboats and passengers and goods portaged between them. Now the Army Corps of Engineers maintains a 40-foot deep, 600-foot wide channel from the ocean to the Broadway Bridge in **Portland** by **dredging**, and a 15-foot-deep channel for barges and other boats upriver from Bonneville through the eight lakes created by dams on the Columbia and **Snake River** to Lewiston, Idaho, a distance of 320 miles. Each of the eight dams has a single **lock**, 86 feet wide by 675 feet long. Six-mile-long **jetties** help maintain a channel through the infamous bar at the mouth of the river. Army Engineers; To the Columbia Gateway.

Columbia River dams. The Columbia has 42% of the country's total hydropower capacity, most of which has been utilized through a series of 11 **dams** built on the main stem of the Columbia River in the U.S. The dams on the Columbia and the Snake rivers produce an average of 18,500 **megawatts** of electricity. The first, **Bonneville Dam**, completed in 1938, is the farthest downstream. The next three upstream, **The Dalles Dam**, **John Day Dam**, and **McNary Dam**, are also **Army Corps of Engineers** dams and also lie between Oregon and Washington. Of the seven on up the river in Washington State, Grand Coulee, built by the **Bureau of Reclamation**, is the largest and oldest. Three more dams and storage reservoirs were built on the Columbia in Canada under a complex arrangement with the U.S. They control water flow to the U.S. dams and power plants, increasing winter flows when power demand is highest, and decreasing the height of **floods**. Dams on the Columbia and its tributaries lowered the flood stage at Vancouver, Washington from the 37-foot level of the **flood of 1894** to 26.5 feet in an equivalent situation. Total storage capacity is about 30% of average annual runoff at The Dalles. Six percent of the river's water is diverted for **irrigation**. Dams have altered the 320-mile stretch of the Columbia and Snake rivers between Bonneville Dam and Lewiston, Idaho (465 miles from the ocean), from free-flowing to a series of eight long lakes with a 14-foot-deep barge channel connected by **locks**. Organic Machine.

Columbia River discovery. The first white person to discover the Columbia was an American, Captain Robert Gray, who sailed his ship, *Columbia Rediviva*, across the bar and ten miles up the river on May 11, 1792 and thus gave basis to America's claims to the **Oregon Country**. He named the river for his ship. Five months later British Lt. William Broughton sailed 120 miles up the river, becoming the first white to see any of interior Oregon, and naming **Mount Hood**.

Columbia River estuary. The area along the 146-miles of tidal **Columbia River** from **Bonneville Dam** to the ocean. The estuary, which serves as the settling pond for a basin larger than France, has persistent levels of toxic man-made chemicals and has lost 80% of its 722,000 acres of wetlands. The National Estuary Program has allocated $2.4 million for a cleanup project. Oregonian 11/11/97:D1. See also **Lower Columbia River Estuary Program**.

Columbia River Gorge. A deep, 80-mile-long canyon carved through the **Cascade Range** by the **Columbia River**, from the **Deschutes River** on the east to the **Sandy River** at the west end. The broad river is framed by cliffs, forested mountains, and waterfalls as it cuts through **Columbia River basalts**. Vegetation reflects the climatic changes through the gorge, with dense fir forests at the west end (40" of rainfall) changing to grass, pine, and oak hillsides around **The Dalles** near the east end (14" of rain). The gorge serves to funnel not only the river through the mountains, but also winds and transportation routes. The high winds make it a prime site for **wind power** generation and for **windsurfing** at **Hood River**. The gorge has been historically significant as the only water-level corridor through the Cascades north of the **Klamath River**, even though cliffs and rapids made travel difficult on both land and water. In the winter **freezing rains** sometimes halt all activity. Wildflowers of the Columbia Gorge; Magnificent Gateway. See also **Bonneville Dam**; **Cascade Landslide**; **Columbia Gorge Interpretive Center**; **Columbia River Gorge National Scenic Area**; **Gorge Discovery Center**.

Columbia River Gorge Commission. A bi-state commission created by the states of Oregon and Washington in 1987 to work with the U.S. **Forest Service** in implementing a management plan for the **Columbia River Gorge National Scenic Area**. The commission includes six members from Oregon and six from Washington; the governors each appoint three members and the six affected counties appoint one member each. Oregon's participating counties are **Multnomah**, **Hood River**, and **Wasco**. PO Box 730, White Salmon WA 98672. 509-493-3323. Oregon Blue Book.

Columbia River Gorge National Scenic Area. A 292,615-acre area established by federal legislation in 1986 in the **Columbia River Gorge**. The area is an 85-mile-long ribbon in which development is regulated to protect scenic, natural, cultural, and recreational resources and to encourage sustainable economic growth in appropriate areas. The area is a mix of private (70%) and **National Forest** ownership. The 13 urban areas are exempt from regulation. Policy is established by the **Columbia River Gorge Commission**. Waucoma Center, 902 Wasco Avenue, Hood River 97031. 541-386-2333. Oregonian 2/15/98:L1.

Columbia River Highway. See **Columbia River Scenic Highway**.

Columbia River Inter-Tribal Fish Commission. A commission organized in 1977 by the four tribes with 1855 treaty fishing rights on the **Columbia River** (**Warm Springs**, **Umatilla**, **Nez Perce**, and Yakima). It focuses on improving habitat and on modifying dam operations to improve fish passage in order to increase stocks of **anadromous fish** above **Bonneville Dam**. 729 NE Oregon Street, Suite 200, Portland 97232. 503-238-0667. Directory of Organizations.

Columbia River Maritime Museum. A museum in **Astoria** with exhibits describing the maritime history of the Northwest coast and **Columbia River**, including exploration, fur trade, navigation, fishing, whaling, steam and motor vessels, and U.S. naval history. Visitors may also tour *Columbia River Lightship No. 604* which is anchored at the museum. 1792 Marine Drive, Astoria 97103. 503-325-2323.

Columbia River plume. An enormous tongue of fresh or low salinity water that extends offshore from the mouth of the Columbia River, south in the summer (sometimes to California) and north in the winter. "Years ago sailing vessels coming into the Columbia River would fill their casks with fresh water eight miles off the bar. The taking of fresh water from the surface of the ocean eight miles from shore sounds like a regular sea story, but it is vouched for by good authority." The river also contributes annually approximately three cubic miles of suspended sediments to the ocean, forming the **Astoria** fan, which covers 3,500 square miles on the **ocean floor**. Life-History; Oregon Oceanbook; Oregonian 12/8/96:A22. See also **Estuary**.

Columbia River ports. More than $15 billion worth of cargo is either imported or exported through the Oregon ports of **Astoria** and **Portland** and the Washington ports of Vancouver, Longview, and Kalama. www.portofportlandor.com

Columbia River Scenic Highway. A highway built between 1913 and 1922 through the **Columbia River gorge**, an area that had, up to then, been impassable by road. The highway was the dream of entrepreneur Samuel Hill who said, "We will cash in, year after year, on our crop of scenic beauty, without depleting it in any way," and was championed by a group of notables. Logger Simon Benson (1852-1942) donated $10,000 to begin construction, by a group of convicts, of the first section around the "impassable barrier" of Shell Rock Mountain. The highway was engineered by Samuel Lancaster and built as the first major project of the new State Highway Department, working in cooperation with the counties. Both the engineering solutions and the sensitive design of the highway have earned it fame. Beginning in the 1950s, a freeway (later **Interstate 84**) built at water level destroyed much of the central portion of the Scenic Highway. The remaining portions, also known as old U.S. 30, provide access to **Crown Point**, other scenic vistas, and many waterfalls and trails. In 1983, 55 miles of the old highway were listed on the **National Register of Historic Places**. The state plans to reopen all 74 miles between **Troutdale** and **The Dalles** by 2015, with 55 miles open to vehicles and the rest restricted to foot and bicycle traffic. First 75 Years; Historic Highway Bridges of Oregon; Lancaster's Road; Oregonian 8/24/95:B3; Study.

Columbia River Songs. A collection of 26 songs written by folk singer Woody Guthrie during one month in May 1941. The songs were created for use in a film, *The Columbia,* sponsored by the **Bonneville Power Administration** in order to develop support for public power projects. Woody Guthrie.

Columbia River transportation. Even though the Columbia provides the only water-level route through the **Cascade Range** north of the **Klamath River**, travel through the **Columbia River gorge** has always been a challenge, both by water and on land. Cliffs and boulders along the gorge made early land routes impassable. The first **Oregon Trail** pioneers rafted their wagons down the river and through the perilous **Cascades of the Columbia River**, but after 1846 wagons heading from **The Dalles** to the **Willamette Valley** had the alternative of paying a toll to take the grueling **Barlow Road** around the south side of **Mount Hood.** Rocks and turbulent rapids in the **Columbia River channel** meant that most water traffic between **Portland** and points above **The Dalles** had to portage at least twice. Before **locks** were built around the rapids, each piece of river freight had to be handled 10 times. By 1883 rail service was available through the Gorge. The **Columbia River Scenic Highway** opened in 1915, and a water level freeway, now **Interstate 84**, was completed in 1975. "Oregon Trail."

Columbia Slough. An overflow channel of the **Columbia River** at the north edge of **Portland**. **Bybee Lake**, Smith Lake, Delta Park, the sites of the **Saint Johns landfill** and of **Vanport**, and the **Portland International Airport** all lie north of Columbia Slough on the island it creates. At one time the slough was lined with meat packing plants. Columbia Slough is heavily polluted, and a 1997 study found that cancer-causing PCBs and chlordane, even though no longer used, are continuing to seep into Buffalo Slough, an arm to the south that runs through Broadmoor Golf Course. Oregonian 6/2/97:B1. See also **Blue Lake, Multnomah County**.

Columbia South Shore Well Fields. A system of 24 wells installed by the city of **Portland** in 1984 to provide a backup water supply for the city. The wells lie near the **Columbia River** between **Interstate 205** and **Troutdale**. Though only four are used regularly, all but one were used to supply water during the **flood of 1996** when the city's **Bull Run** water became too muddy to use. They are threatened by underground contamination from industrial waste. Oregonian 2/25/96:A1.

Columbia Southern Railroad. See **Shaniko**.

Columbia University. See **University of Portland**.

Columbium. See **Niobium**.

Columbus Day Storm. A storm that slammed into Oregon on Friday, October 12, 1962, as it moved north along the coast from California to British Columbia. It had meandered across the Pacific as tropical typhoon Freda. The center of the storm stayed over the ocean, but **barometric pressure** dropped to 28.41" at **Astoria**, and **winds** reached 170 mph at **Mount Hebo**, 125 mph in **Corvallis**, and 116 mph in **Portland**, where the storm hit just at evening rush hour. During the height of the storm a religious zealot on his usual Portland street corner was heard exhorting, "Give it to 'em Lord. Show 'em who's boss; they've had it too good for too long!" Damage in Oregon totaled more than $170 million, including six billion board feet of downed timber, much of which was salvaged. Twenty four of the 48 deaths from the storm were in Oregon. Big Blow; Electrifying Eden.

Commissioner of Labor and Industries. An Oregon **elected official**, selected by voters every four years on the same schedule as the **governor** (1994, 1998, 2002...). Salary in 1996 was $61,500. The commissioner heads the Oregon Bureau of **Labor and Industries** and administers state laws relating to employment. Requirements for the office, created by the legislature in 1903, are that the commissioner be a citizen and five-year resident of Oregon. 800 NE Oregon Street, #32, Portland 97232. 503-731-4070. Oregon Blue Book. See also **Recall**; **Term limits**.

Common law court. A "court" operating outside the sanctioned legal system. Participants hear cases by persons who feel wronged and render decisions but have no legal power to enforce their verdicts. Their documents are modeled on those of legal courts which sometimes creates confusion as to their authority. In 1997 common law courts were reported in **Portland**, **Salem**, **Madras**, **Grants Pass**, and **Springfield**. Oregonian 4/30/97:B1. See also **Militias**.

Common School Fund. A state fund with both land and financial assets that is managed by the **State Land Board**. The fund was established in 1859 when the federal **Admission Act** deeded **section**s 16 and 36 of every township, or a total of 3.5 million acres (5.5% of Oregon's land base), to the state to support public schools. Much of the land was sold or lost through **land fraud**; 22% (782,000 acres) remains. Of that, 650,000 acres is grazing and agricultural land, and 132,000 acres is forest land, including **Elliott State Forest**, managed under contract by the Oregon Department of **Forestry**. Common School Fund assets also include 800,000 acres of off-shore land and estuarine tidelands, lands under the state's navigable waterway system, and unclaimed estates and bank accounts. The $280 million fund distributes about $10 million a year of investment earnings to Oregon counties for their public schools. Oregon Blue Book. See also **Investment Council**.

Commons. A 125,000 square-foot plaza in the **Rose Quarter**. It is designed for concerts, fairs, and other cultural events for up to 3,000 people, and is a major **outdoor concert space** in **Portland**. Oregonian 10/8/95:Special section.

Commonwealth Building. See **Equitable Building**.

Commonwealth Federation. See **Oregon Commonwealth Federation**.

Communicable diseases. See **Diseases**.

Communications networks. See **Fiber-optic cable**.

Communists. Oregon's most famous Communist was John "Jack" Silas Reed (1887-1920), born to a wealthy **Portland** family, who became a famed and controversial revolutionary author and journalist before dying of typhus in the Soviet Union. He was honored there with a state funeral and is the only American buried at the Kremlin. The 1981 film "Reds" was based on his life. From Here We Speak; "Portlander John Reed." See also **McCarthyism**.

Community colleges. Public two-year colleges that offer transfer courses (the first two years of a college program), as well as professional and technical courses leading to a one-year certificate or two-year associates degree, plus programs for adults who wish to complete their high school education and other courses of interest to the community. Oregon's **Small Business Development Centers** are located at community colleges. Oregon has 17 community college districts, covering 25 of the state's 36 counties, and serving over 330,000 students a year. Most offer courses in several locations. Each was founded by local voters, is governed by a locally-elected board, and supported by a local **property tax**. They operate under the State Board of **Education** and the Commissioner of Community Colleges rather than under the State Board of **Higher Education**. Community colleges appeal to students of all ages (average age is 37) and backgrounds, many of whom are also working. The 17 colleges and their fall 1996 enrollments are **Blue Mountain** (3,342), **Central Oregon** (6,640), **Chemeketa** (16,302), **Clackamas** (8,647), **Clatsop** (2,720), **Columbia Gorge** (1,407), **Klamath** (445), **Lane** (16,489), **Linn-Benton** (10,155), **Mount Hood** (11,970), **Oregon Coast** (763), **Portland** (35,108), **Rogue** (4,783), **Southwestern** (3,215), **Tillamook Bay** (1,063), **Treasure Valley** (3,007), and **Umpqua** (5,497). Office of Community College Services, 255 Capitol St. NE, Salem OR 97310-1341. 503-378-8648. Oregon Blue Book; Oregonian 12/10/96:B2.

Community Corrections. A division of the Department of **Corrections** that is responsible for supervising felony offenders placed on **probation** by the courts or **paroled** from a state **correctional facility**. It is also responsible for release planning and transition services. As of January 1997, parole/probation officers managed over 19,200 felony offenders on probation and another 10,280 on parole or post-prison supervision at an average daily cost of $2.36 per offender. The system is designed to be a cost-effective method for holding offenders accountable while protecting the public. 60% of those on parole and 80% of those on probation complete their sentences without being revoked to prison. Counties are responsible for offenders who have received sentences of 12 months or less. 2575 Center Street NE, Salem 97310-0470. 503-945-9050. Oregon Blue Book.

Community Service Award for the Arts. See **Arts Commission**.

Commuting. In 1997, 65% of **Portland** area commuters commuted alone, up from 55% in 1980, while carpooling declined over the same period from 16 to 12% and mass transit use decreased from 15 to 10%. In 1990 22% of Oregon workers commuted over 30 minutes one-way, matching the Oregon **Benchmark** Year 2000 goal. Counties with the highest proportion of long-distance commuters were **Clackamas** (32%) and **Yamhill** (29%). Counties with the lowest were **Harney** and **Lake**, each with 8%. In 1997 more than half the workers from **Clackamas** and **Polk** counties worked outside their home counties. The average commuter distance increased from 13 miles a day in 1970 to 21 in 1990. In 1994 Oregonians averaged 9,561 vehicle miles per capita (26 miles a day) for all travel, 31% higher than the 1980 rate. The **Benchmark** Year 2000 goal is 8,778 miles (24 miles a day). Traffic on **Interstate 5** south of **Wilsonville** is expected to increase from 60,000 vehicles a day in 1992 to 99,000 vehicles a day by 2012, and comparable increases are expected in the rest of the valley. Oregon: A Statistical Overview; Oregonian 6/21/97:D7, 10/12/97:A1. See also **Home businesses**; **Public transit**.

Company town. A town owned by a lumber company to provide housing for its workers. Oregon has had a number. **Gilchrist**, the last, was sold to homeowners and others in 1997. **Brookings** and **Westfir** began as company towns, and others, now-vanished, included **Kinzua** and **Valsetz**. Some, such as **Shevlin**, were moved from place to place as needed.

Compensation. See **Income**; **Salaries**; **Wages**.

Comprehensive Review of the Northwest Energy System. A group of 20 experts appointed by the governors of Oregon, Washington, Idaho, and Montana in January 1996. The panel is expected to guide the region from an era of local monopoly to an era in which **electric power** is marketed competitively. 851 SW Sixth Ave., Suite 1100, Portland 97204-1387. 800-222-3355. Oregonian 7/7/96:E1.

Computers. In 1996, half of **Portland**'s adults owned computers, compared to 36% nationwide. See also **High tech industries**.

Concert halls. See **Arlene Schnitzer Concert Hall**; **Civic Auditorium**; **Hult Center for the Performing Arts**.

Concordia College. An accredited private college in **Portland** that enrolled 976 students in 1995. 2811 NE Holman St., Portland 97211. 503-288-9371. Oregon Blue Book.

Concours d'Elegance. A major vintage car show held since 1972 in late June or early July at **Pacific University** in **Forest Grove**. It is sponsored by the Forest Grove Rotary Club with proceeds going to scholarships and community services. Some 300 antique, classic, and exotic cars are judged on quality and authenticity of restoration.

Condon. "It's the People." A north central Oregon agricultural community located 70 miles southeast of **The Dalles** at the junction of state routes 206 and 19. It is the county seat of **Gilliam County**. Condon was named in 1884 for Harvey C. Condon, a non-resident owner of the townsite, and incorporated in 1893. Local attractions include the Gilliam County Historical Museum. **Nobel Prize** winners Dr. William Murphy and Dr. Linus Pauling each lived in Condon for a time. Population 1980 783; 1995 745. Elevation 2,844'. PO Box 445, 97823. 541-384-2711. History of Gilliam County.

Condor. See **California condor**.

Confederated Tribes. See **Coos, Lower Umpqua, and Siuslaw**; **Grand Ronde**; **Siletz**; **Umatilla**; **Warm Springs**.

Conflict resolution. See **Dispute Resolution Commission**.

Congregational Church. The Rev. John S. Griffin organized the first Congregational church in Oregon in 1842 at **Hillsboro**; it moved to **Forest Grove** in 1845. The Rev. George Atkinson arrived in 1848 to become pastor of the **Oregon City** church which had been established in 1844. He also founded a girl's school, co-founded Tualatin Academy (later **Pacific University**), and pushed the legislature to establish a public school system. In 1957 the Congregationalists merged with the Evangelical and Reformed churches to become the **United Church of Christ**. Dictionary of Oregon History; Guide to Early Oregon Churches.

Congressional districts. In the 1990s Oregon has five U.S. congressional districts. District 1 in the northwest corner of the state includes Clatsop, Columbia, Washington, and Yamhill counties. District 2 (traditionally **Republican**) includes all of the counties east of the Cascades plus Jackson and Josephine counties in southern Oregon. District 3 (traditionally **Democratic**) is Multnomah County. District 4 includes the south coast plus Douglas, Lane, Linn, and Benton counties. District 5 includes Tillamook and Lincoln counties on the coast plus Polk, Marion, and Clackamas counties in the Willamette Valley. Oregon had one representative from statehood in 1859 until after the census of 1890, two from 1893 until 1913, three from 1913 until 1943, and the fifth was added at the 1983 election following the 1980 census. Oregon Blue Book. See also **Representatives, U.S.**

Connie Hansen Garden and Interpretive Center. A one-acre garden at 1931 NW 33rd in **Lincoln City** that a group of volunteers has bought and is restoring. Hansen, who died in 1992, described herself as an "incurable collector and compulsive gardener." The garden is open 10-2 Tuesdays and Saturdays. Oregonian 9/2/95:B1.

Conscientious objectors. See **Camp Angell**.

Conser Lake monster. A seven-foot tall shaggy creature that was seen north of **Albany** in the summers of 1959 and 1960. Reported to resemble a white gorilla, it was said to keep pace with a truck going 35 mph. It seemed to have no animosity towards humans but was reported to have shredded a couple of hounds that had been sent in pursuit of it. Oregon's Ghosts and Monsters.

Conservation easements. See **Land trusts**.

Conservation Reserve Program. A federal program, begun in 1985, that paid farmers to remove marginal lands from production and sow them in grass. Nearly 500,000 acres of Oregon land, most of it dry-land wheat and barley fields in the Columbia Basin area, has been in the program. The program, which reduced erosion and flooding, brought income of over $3 million a year to **Wasco** and **Gilliam** counties, $5 million to **Umatilla County**, and $6 million to **Morrow County**. Oregonian 2/22/96:D2.

Consolidation. See **Portland/Multnomah County consolidation**.

Constitution. The document though which the people have authorized the authority and framework of state **government** and which can be changed only by a vote of the people. (The somewhat equivalent document for an Oregon city or county is called a **charter**.) Oregon's constitution was drawn up at a convention of 60 delegates that met from August 17 to September 18, 1857, following years of bitter debate about whether or not **slavery** would be allowed in the proposed state. The constitution was approved by the voters (white males) of the **Oregon Territory** on November 9, 1857, by a count of 7,195 to 3,125. (At the same election the voters rejected slavery, 7,727 to 2,645, and excluded free Negroes from the state, 8,640 to 1,081.) However, it took Congress until February 14, 1859 to admit Oregon to **statehood**. Oregon's constitution is based upon those of several Midwestern states. It provides for legislative, executive, and judicial branches of state government and for **elected officials**. It can be amended only by a vote of the people; the first amendment was in 1902. The complete text is in the Oregon Blue Book. Oregon Constitution; Governing Oregon. See also **Initiative**; **Territorial government**.

Construction Contractors Board. A board of nine members, appointed by the governor for four-year terms, that registers Oregon's 35,500 construction contractors and adjudicates complaints. The board publishes guides for contractors and for the public. PO Box 14140, Salem 97309-5052. 503-378-4621. Oregon Blue Book.

Consular Corps. The Oregon Consular Corps in 1996 included two official

Consul Generals, those for **Japan** and **Mexico**. 17 other countries have unpaid Honorary Consuls who perform many consular functions such as promoting their country and its trade, providing assistance to their country's citizens and shipping interests, and issuing documents and visas. Oregon Consular Corps, One World Trade Center, Suite 1100, Portland 97204. 503-464-8482.

Consumer and Business Services, Oregon Department of (DCBS). A department that the legislature created in 1993 by combining a number of boards and agencies. It includes the **Appraiser Certification and Licensure Board**, the **Building Codes Division**, the Office of **Energy**, the Division of **Finance and Corporate Securities**, **Insurance Consumer Advocacy**, the **Insurance Division**, the Office of **Minority, Women and Emerging Small Business**, **Occupational Safety and Health Division**, the **Small Business Ombudsman for Workers' Compensation**, the **Workers' Compensation Ombudsman**, and the **Workers' Compensation Division**. 350 Winter St. NE, Salem 97310. 503-378-4100. Oregon Blue Book.

Consumer complaints. The top five areas of consumer complaints to the **Attorney General**'s office in 1994-95 were (1) games of chance, contests, sweepstakes, 1,351; (2) used car sales, 439; (3) business vs. business, 394; (4) car repair, 391; (5) telemarketing, 335. Oregon Consumer League, PO Box 1236, Oregon City 97045. Oregonian 10/27/95:D3. See also **Consumer hot line**.

Consumer hot line. A service sponsored by the **Attorney General** which hears consumer complaints and problems, and provides information. It is available M-F, 8:30-noon. 503-378-4320 in Salem and 503-229-5576 in Portland.

Consumer Price Index. An index compiled by the U.S. Labor Department's Bureau of Labor Statistics that tracks monthly changes in the prices urban consumers pay for a fixed basket of goods and services based on seven categories: food and beverages, housing, clothing and upkeep, transportation, medical care, entertainment, and other. In 1994 the Consumer Price Index for **Portland** ("All Urban Consumers") was 148.9 (base year 1982-84), compared to the national CPI of 148.2. It has been going up about 3% a year in the 1990s. CPI Quickline 202-606-6994. Oregon Labor Trends

Contemporary art. See **Portland Institute for Contemporary Art**.

Continental shelf. The **ocean floor** between the **coast** and the continental slope, usually defined as being up to 200 meters (656') deep. The comparatively narrow continental shelf off Oregon varies from 10 to 46 miles wide. At the edge of the shelf, the continental slope drops steeply to the **Cascadia subduction zone** and abyssal seafloor at a depth of 10,000' feet. The continental slope is made up of layers of sediments scraped off the Juan de Fuca Plate as it pushes under the North American Plate. The combined width of the continental shelf and slope is 70 miles off **Astoria** and 40 miles off **Cape Blanco**. The offshore area is marked by features such as **faults**, including the major east-west Blanco fracture zone and the north-south Fulmar fault, ridges, cliffs, basins, canyons, channels, and river out washes, including the 3,500-square-mile **Astoria** fan made up of **Columbia River** sediments. Geology of Oregon; Oregon Oceanbook.

Continuing care communities. Retirement living communities that guarantee life-long care for their residents. There were 15 in Oregon as of July 1997. A list is available from **Senior and Disabled Services Division**, 503-945-5832.

Contractors. See **Construction Contractors Board**.

Convention Center. See **Oregon Convention Center**.

Cony. See **Pika**.

Cooks. Bertha Jorgensen is the only Oregonian to have taken the grand prize in the Pillsbury Bake-Off; she won in 1955 with a **hazelnut** sweetbread called Ring-A-Lings. James Beard (1903-1985) was a nationally-known cooking authority and author from Oregon. Peg Bracken, author of the best-selling I Hate to Cook Book, lives in **Portland**. James Beard; Oregonian 2/27/96:FD4.

Cooley House. A house at 2100 Hillside Drive near **Cottage Grove** that was built in 1865 by 14-year-old Zachary Shields for the Alexander Cooley family. The same year Shields built another a half mile south for John Cooley. Each house features a gallery-like porch with fine detail and, following an east coast tradition, two front doors. Style and Vernacular.

Cooper. See **Hijacking**.

Cooper Spur Ski Area. A ski area on the northeast side of **Mount Hood** 27 miles south of **Hood River**. It has a T-bar and rope tow. Top elevation is 4,500 feet with a 500-foot vertical drop. 11000 Cloud Cap Road, Mount Hood 97041. 541-352-7803. Oregonian 11/16/97:T7.

Coos Bay. A large bay on the south Oregon coast The Coos River, Catching Slough, Isthmus Slough, South Slough, and several creeks flow into it, and the cities of **Coos Bay** and **North Bend** are located on the west side. The bay provides Oregon's only deep-water ocean port south of **Newport**. In 1996 the **Army Corps of Engineers** deepened the 15-mile-long shipping channel from 35 to 37 feet. Oregonian 7/4/96:B2. See also *Czarina*; **Portages**; *Santa Clara*.

Coos Bay (city). A city and seaport on **Highway 101** in **Coos County** that was at one time the world's largest wood products port. The town was founded in 1854 as Marshfield and incorporated in 1874, but voters changed the name to Coos Bay in 1944. Empire and Eastside later joined, though adjacent **North Bend** remains separate. Coos Bay is home to **Southwestern Oregon Community College**. Local attractions include tours of an **Oregon-myrtle** factory, **Golden and Silver Falls** 24 miles northeast, the **Oregon Dunes National Recreation Area** to the north, and the **Charleston** area and coastal parks to the west. A local group, FONSI (Friends of New Sustainable Industry) promotes economic development. Chosi, Japan, is its sister city. Population 1980 14,424; 1995 15,430. Elevation 10'. 500 Central Ave., 97420. 541-269-1181. Chamber of Commerce 800-824-8486. Hard Times in Paradise; Oregon Geographic Names; Oregonian 2/26/98:D1; She's Tricky. See also **Coose (Coos) Bay Commercial Company**.

Coos Bay District, BLM. A 332,862-acre district of **Bureau of Land Management** forest lands in **Curry**, **Coos**, and western **Douglas** counties. The district includes the nation's largest **Douglas-fir**. 1300 Airport Lane, North Bend 97459-2000. 541-756-0100. BLM Facts.

Coos Bay Military Wagon Road. A Congressionally authorized **military wagon road** between **Roseburg** and **Coos Bay**. The private company that built the road in 1873 received 105,240 acres of government land as compensation. However, litigation about land fraud resulted in 93,000 acres, containing an estimated 3.6 billion board feet of timber, being revested in the government in 1919. The lands are now managed by the **Bureau of Land Management** as part of the **O&C lands**. From Roseburg the road (still used) heads west through Lookingglass and down the East Fork of the Coquille River to Dora, then turns northwest over a series of ridges to Sumner and Coos Bay. BLM's Billion-Dollar Checkerboard; Dictionary of Oregon History.

Coos County. A county on the south Oregon coast centered around **Coos Bay** with its international and fishing ports. It is bounded by **Douglas** and **Curry** counties and the Pacific Ocean. Incorporated cities are **Coquille** (county seat), **Bandon**, **Coos Bay** (commercial center), **Lakeside**, **Myrtle Point**, **North Bend**, and **Powers**. The **Coast Range** meets the **Siskiyou Range** in the rugged interior of the county; elevations range from sea level up to 4,319' Mount Bolivar in the Siskiyous in the southeast corner. The economy of the county is based on lumber, fishing, dairying and cheese, cranberries, tourism, and log, wood chip and ore shipping. At one time **coal** was mined in the county. Taxable assessed value in 1995 was $2,660,000,000, or $43,000 per capita. Attractions, in addition to those of its communities, include **Golden and Silver Falls**, **Oregon-myrtle** trees and myrtle wood manufacturing, the **Oregon Dunes National Recreation Area**, the fishing port at **Charleston**, and **Shore Acres** and other state parks along the scenic coastline west of Coos Bay. The county was created in 1853 from parts of **Umpqua** and **Jackson** counties and named for the local Indians. Population 1980 64,047; 1995 62,100. Area 1,629 square miles. Density 38/sq.mi. Annual precipitation 57"; average temperature January 44°F, July 61°F. Courthouse, 250 N. Baxter, Coquille 97423. 541-396-3121. Century of Coos and Curry; Oregon Blue Book. See also **Baltimore Colony**; **Camp Castaway**; **Coose Bay Commercial Company**.

Coos, Lower Umpqua, and Siuslaw Indians, Confederated Tribes of. A confederation of tribes that had originally lived along 100 miles of the central Oregon coast. In 1855 after they signed a treaty with the government (never ratified by Congress) they were forcibly rounded up and marched to **Fort Umpqua** where their food rations were cut off. Three years later the 300 survivors were marched to **Yachats** where more than half died of exposure and starvation. In 1875 Congress closed that part of the **Coast Reservation**, and the Indians went to **Siletz** or returned to Coos Bay. The confederation now has about 600 enrolled members who can trace their lineage to the tribes' 1855 membership rolls. In 1984, the confederation was recognized by Congress based on the 1855 treaty. The confederation does not operate a **casino** and has no reservation except six acres in **Coos Bay**, though it was seeking support in 1997 for transfer of some federal land back to it. 338 Wallace, Coos Bay 97420. 541-888-9577. American Indian Reservations; First Oregonians; Native Peoples; Oregonian 10/22/95:A18, 12/13/97:D1; She's Tricky.

Coos River. A river that drains 415 square miles of the slopes of the **Coast Range** west to **Coos Bay**. It is named for an Indian tribe that lived in the vicinity. **Jetties** at the mouth help maintain the channel for deep-water ships. Oregon Geographic Names.

Coose (Coos) Bay Commercial Company. A company of 19 men from **Jacksonville** recruited and organized by P. B. Marple in 1853 to homestead land in the recently discovered Coos Bay area, prove up on it, and then turn the land over to the company in which they were all participants. $1.9 million of **coal** and **gold** was taken from the area during the next two years. <u>Century of Coos and Curry</u>; <u>Dictionary of Oregon History</u>; <u>Native Peoples</u>.

Copper. A valuable metal found along with **gold** and **silver** in the **Wallowa Mountains** and in southwestern Oregon. The most productive copper mine in the state was the Iron Dyke Mine near Homestead in **Baker County**, where 5 million pounds of copper was produced between 1910 and the 1930's; the next largest was the Queen of Bronze mine near Takilma in **Josephine County**. In 1991 renewed mining operations began at the Silver Peak Mine near **Riddle** where, prior to 1937, 735,000 pounds of copper, plus other minerals, had been produced. Formosa Exploration, Inc. ships the copper and **zinc** concentrates to Japan. <u>Geology of Oregon</u>, <u>Mineral Industry of Oregon</u>. See also **Cornucopia Mine**.

Copperfield affair. A national press sensation created when, on December 30, 1913, Governor Oswald West announced that, since **Baker County** refused to close the saloons of Copperfield, a brawling construction town just below the ox-bow on the **Snake River**, he was sending his young private secretary, the slight Miss Fern Hobbs. On January 2 she and the eager press corps arrived at Copperfield by train (also on the train, it was later discovered, were several burly members of the state militia) and read the governor's request for the resignation of officials to the assembled citizens who had decorated the hall for her arrival. The request was spurned, whereupon she announced the imposition of martial law and the closure of the saloons and ordered the citizens to leave their guns at the door as they left. The militia collected 170 revolvers, and Miss Hobbs, job accomplished, left town on the departing train, 90 minutes after her arrival. The militia stayed to complete the job. The town, which had been established in 1908 to house railroad and dam construction crews, was destroyed by fire the next year. <u>Hells Canyon</u>.

Coquille (koh KEEL). "We're in the Hometown Business." A southwest Oregon city 17 miles south of **Coos Bay** on Highway 42; it is the county seat of **Coos County**. It was incorporated in 1885. In 1892 a fire destroyed most of the business section, as did another on St. Patrick's day in 1918. Lumber, fishing, and government offices support the economy. Attractions include the Sawdust Theatre, where 1890s style melodramas are performed on summer weekends, and a large downtown mural depicting the turn-of-the-century town. Coquille is thought to be the French spelling of an Indian word, but the meaning is unknown. Population 1980 4,481; 1995 4,230. Elevation 40'. 99 E. 2nd, 97423. 541-396-2115. Chamber of Commerce 541-396-3414. <u>Oregon Geographic Names</u>.

Coquille (koh QUELL) **Indian Tribe**. A tribe with some 700 enrolled members. Federal recognition, withdrawn in the 1950's, was restored in 1989, along with the right to acquire **reservation** land in **Coos** and **Curry Counties**. In 1996 Congress allocated 5,400 acres of **Bureau of Land Management** timber land to the tribe. The tribe has another 925 acres of federal trust lands in three parcels. The largest, 907 acres, lies along Cape Arago Highway, south of Coos Bay. The other two are the **Grandmother Rock** site in **Bandon** where the tribe owns and operates the Heritage Place Assisted Living Facility, and an abandoned plywood mill on the waterfront in **North Bend** that has been remodeled into the tribe's Mill

Casino. The last native speaker of Miluk, a tribal language, died in 1961, but a member of the tribe who is an anthropologist has reconstructed it, and others are learning it. PO Box 1435, Coos Bay 97420. 800-622-5869; 541-267-4587. Ameri- can Indian Reservations; First Oregonians; Native Peoples; Oregonian 10/22/ 95:A18, 10/2/96:D1; She's Tricky.

Coquille River. A 36-mile long river in southwest Oregon that drains 1,060 square miles of the **Coast Range** and **Siskiyou Mountains** to the coast at **Bandon**. Major tributaries are the North, East, Middle, and South forks. Though the undammed river frequently floods in the winter, in the summer limited groundwa- ter discharge results in low stream flow. **Grandmother Rock**, a massive haystack rock of blue schist at the mouth of the river, was dynamited in 1903 to provide rock to build the two **jetties**. The end of the south jetty incorporates the steel hull of the 300' *Oliver Olson* which went aground in 1953 and was filled with rock to keep it from further damaging the jetty. The river's name is probably derived from that of a local band of Indians. Oregon Geographic Names. See also **Portages**.

Coquille River Lighthouse. A **lighthouse** on the north side of the Coquille River, across from **Bandon**. The 40' tower is next to the river; ships have several times narrowly missed ramming it. The lighthouse was active from 1896 to 1939, restored in 1976, and symbolically re-lit in 1991 with a solar-powered light. The adjacent building is now an interpretive center open year-round. Tours of the tower must be arranged through **Bullard Beach State Park**. 541-347-2209. Oregon Lighthouses; Oregon Parks 2(3):54, Nov/Dec 1994; Oregon's Seacoast Lighthouses; Shipwrecks of the Pacific Coast.

Corn. In 1995 Oregon grew 12% of the nation's sweet corn for processing, 451,000 tons worth $38 million on 50,490 acres, primarily in the **Willamette Val- ley**. Oregon farmers also grew fresh sweet corn (26.9 million pounds worth $3.9 million on 2,285 acres), corn for grain (3.6 million bushels worth $9.2 million on 18,450 acres), and for silage (652,700 tons worth $4.1 million on 26,100 acres). 1995 Oregon.

Cornelius. A rapidly growing Portland-area suburban community in **Wash- ington County** located on Highway 8 between **Forest Grove** and **Hillsboro**. It was named for pioneer merchant, Indian fighter, and longtime Oregon legislator Colonel Thomas. R. Cornelius. The city was incorporated in 1893. Population 1980 4,402; 1995 7,220. Elevation 175'. PO Box 607, 97113. 503-357-9112. Oregon Geographic Names.

Cornucopia Mine. A group of gold mines with extensive **tunnels** in **Baker County** in what was once the state's richest hard-rock area. Gold was discovered and 41 claims were staked in the early 1880s. In 1903 the mines were consoli- dated, and, by the time they were boarded up in 1941, had produced 322,000 ounces of **gold**, one million ounces of **silver**, 670,000 pounds of **copper**, and 120,000 pounds of **lead**. In the 1950s the mine became known nationwide through a stock swindle operated by Earl Belle who fled to Brazil in 1958. The Trust for Public Land may purchase the area for use as trailheads for the **Eagle Cap Wilderness** area. Oregon Ghost Towns; Oregonian 3/8/95:B2

Corporation Division. A division under the Oregon **Secretary of State** that registers businesses, administers the Uniform Commercial Code, commissions notaries public, and operates the **Business Information Center**. Public Service Bldg., 255 Capitol St. NE, Suite 151, Salem 97310-1327. 503-986-2200. Oregon Blue Book.

Corporations. Six Oregon companies were on the 1997 Fortune 500 list. **Nike** (sports shoes, equipment) with 1996 sales of $6.471 billion; **Thrifty Payless** (drugstores) $4.799 billion; **PacifiCorp** (utilities) $4.294 billion; **Fred Meyer** (retail chain) $3.725 billion; **Willamette Industries** (timber, wood products) $3.425 billion; U.S. Bancorp (banking) $3.069 billion. Oregonian 4/8/97:B16. See also **Business**; **Hewlett-Packard**; **Intel**; **Tektronix**.

Corporations, history. The first corporation in Oregon was the Willamette Cattle Company, organized January 13, 1837 for the purpose of importing cattle from California. It was capitalized at $5,000 and managed by Ewing Young, who, with a party of 14, managed to buy over 800 head of nearly wild cattle in Spanish California and drive them over the **Siskiyou Mountains** to the Willamette Valley. They arrived in the fall with 630 head, having lost 200 en route. The cattle ended up costing about $7.75 each. Dictionary of Oregon History.

Corps of Discovery. See **Lewis and Clark Expedition**.

Corps of Engineers. See **Army Corps of Engineers**.

Correctional facilities, history. The first public building in Oregon was a jail, built after the 1841 death of Ewing Young with the proceeds of his unclaimed estate. The state penitentiary was located in **Portland** from 1851 until 1866 when it was moved to **Salem**. Riots at the penitentiary on March 9, 1968 resulted in 31 injuries and $1.6 million in damage from arson fires. Riots at the **Sheridan Federal Correctional Institution** in September 1993 caused $208,000 damage. The number of state prison inmates doubled in the 1980's, even though the percentage of males in their crime-prone years was shrinking. Dictionary of Oregon History; Fire at Eden's Gate; Oregonian 6/20/96:A10.

Correctional facilities, juvenile. See **Juvenile corrections**.

Correctional facilities, Oregon adult. In 1994 Oregon had 2 city jails, 31 county jails, 12 state facilities for adults, one federal facility, and one tribal facility. In 1996 more than 1,000 inmates were housed in rented prison beds in other states because of crowding in Oregon. In 1998 adult correctional institutions operated by the state provide beds for 9,800 inmates; the number needed is expected to increase to 13,000 by the year 2000 and to 19,000 by 2005 because of **Measure 11**. Seven additional facilities are being planned. A 1995 state law transferred responsibility for offenders with sentences of 12 months or less to the counties with state reimbursement. Inmates are required to work and are not allowed to smoke. The 12 state facilities are:

(1) Columbia River Correctional Institution, minimum security for 500. 9111 NE Sunderland Avenue, **Portland** 97211-1799. 503-280-6646.

(2) Eastern Oregon Correctional Institution, medium security for 1,600. 2500 Westgate, **Pendleton** 97801-9699. 541-276-0700.

(3) Mill Creek Correctional Facility, minimum security for 312 on a 2,000 acre working farm. 5465 Turner Road SE, **Salem** 97301-9400. 503-378-5807.

(4) Oregon Corrections Intake Center, short-term for 200. 2206-B Kaen Road, **Oregon City** 97045-4090. 503-655-8420.

(5) Oregon State Correctional Institution, medium security for 840. 3405 Deer Park Drive SE, **Salem** 97310-9385. 503-373-0100.

(6) Oregon State Penitentiary, maximum security for 2,100. 2605 State Street, **Salem** 97310-0505. 503-378-2445.

(7) Oregon Women's Correctional Center, medium security for 190. 2809 State Street, **Salem** 97310-0500. 503-373-1907.

(8) Powder River Correctional Facility, minimum security for 178. 3600 13th Street, **Baker City** 97814-1346. 541-523-6680.

(9) Santiam Correctional Institution, minimum security for 510. 4005 Aumsville Highway SE, **Salem** 97301-9112. 503-378-5807.

(10) Shutter Creek Correctional Institution, minimum security for 216. 2000 Shutters Landing Road, **North Bend** 97459-0303. 541-756-6666.

(11) Snake River Correctional Facility (after completion of expansion in 1998), medium security for 2,336, minimum security for 154, and special housing for 510. 777 Stanton Blvd, **Ontario** 97914-0595. 541-881-5000.

(12) South Fork Forest Camp, minimum security for 150, 28 miles east of **Tillamook**. Inmates work for the State **Forestry Department**. 48300 Wilson River Hwy., Tillamook 97141-9799. 503-842-2811.

Oregon Blue Book. See also **Boot camps**; **Corrections** entries; **Inmate Work Program**; **Jails**; **Juvenile corrections**; **Parole and Post-Prison Supervision Board**; **Sheridan Federal Correctional Institution**; **Smoking**.

Corrections, costs. Total expenditures for public safety in Oregon have risen from $4.5 billion for the 1987-89 biennium to $10 billion in '95-97, and are projected to rise to $13 billion in the 2001-03 biennium. Total state spending on education is projected to go from $4.5 billion to $8 billion during the same period. Prisons cost Oregonians about $19,600 a year per adult criminal at the same time that educating a student costs the public $5,000 a year for public school or $4,100 for college. Oregonian 8/18/96:A1.

Corrections, Department of. A state department that manages the state's 12 **correctional facilities** for adults and supervises parole and probation services through its **Community Corrections** Division. 2575 Center Street NE, Salem 97310-0470. 503-945-0920. Oregon Blue Book. See also **Board of Control**; **Parole and Post-Prison Supervision Board**; **Youth Authority**.

Corruption. During the 1880s and 1890s corruption, centering around **railroads**, land, and politics, was so blatant in Oregon that reformers organized new political parties - the Union Party and then the People's Party (**Populists**). Reforms led to the **Oregon System**. Empire of the Columbia. See also **Government Standards and Practices Commission**; **Land fraud**; **Swamp lands**; **Venal officials**.

Corvallis. A city on the **Willamette River** 85 miles south of **Portland** on **Highway 99W**; it is the county seat of **Benton County**. The site was first settled in 1846 and called Marysville. In 1853 the name was changed to Corvallis (heart of the valley), and in 1857 the city was incorporated. For a brief time in 1855 it served as the state **capital**. Corvallis College, the forerunner of **Oregon State University**, was founded in 1858. Major employers are the university, Hewlett Packard (electronics manufacturing) and CH2M Hill (engineering). **Siuslaw Na-**

tional Forest is headquartered in the city. Attractions include the refurbished 1913 Majestic Theatre and the Da Vinci Days Festival in July, a three day celebration of arts, science, and technology. Uzhgorod, Ukraine, is its sister city. Population 1980 40,960; 1995 47,485. Elevation 224'. PO Box 1083, 97339. 541-757-6901. Visitors Bureau 800-334-8118. Oregon Geographic Names.

Corvallis and Aquina (Yaquina) Bay Military Wagon Road. A crude **military wagon road** between **Corvallis** and **Yaquina Bay**, opened in 1866. The developing company received a Congressional **land grant** of 81,895 acres as compensation. The land later became an asset of the **Oregon Pacific Railroad**, and, after its bankruptcy, of **Southern Pacific**. The government attempted to recover the land in a suit in 1889, but lost the case. Dictionary of Oregon History.

Corvallis and Eastern Railroad. See **Oregon Pacific Railroad**.

Corvallis College. A co-educational primary and secondary school operated by the Southern **Methodist** Church from 1865-1886 in **Corvallis**. In 1869 the legislature made it the home of Oregon Agricultural College, later **Oregon State University**. Dictionary of Oregon History.

Cottage Grove. A **Lane County** timber, retirement, and recreation town located on **Interstate 5** 18 miles south of **Eugene** at the south end of the **Willamette Valley**. Cottage Grove post office, Lane County's first, was established in 1855 at the post master's home (for which it was named) near what is now **Creswell**. The post office - and name - were moved 16 times, ending at present-day Cottage Grove. A bitter feud ensued between those living near the Cottage Grove post office and those living near the train station 1/2 mile away where another post office, called Lemati, was established. The feud was finally resolved years later when the legislature consolidated Lemati with Cottage Grove in 1899. Cottage Grove had been incorporated in 1887. Area attractions include **Cottage Grove Reservoir** and **Dorena Reservoir**, five **covered bridges**, and the historic **Bohemia mining district**. The **films** "The General" (1926) and "Animal House" were filmed in Cottage Grove. In 1968 it was named an All American City. Population 1980 7,148; 1995 7,745. Elevation 641'. 400 E. Main St., 97424. 541-942-5501. Chamber of Commerce 541-942-2411. Cottage Grove; Oregon Geographic Names. See also **Tornadoes**.

Cottage Grove Reservoir. A lake five miles south of **Cottage Grove** formed in 1942 by a dam across the Coast Fork of the **Willamette River**. It flooded the community of Hebron. The 95-foot-high, earth-fill dam was built by the **Army Corps of Engineers** for flood control. The lake is over three miles long, covers 1,139 acres and has a maximum depth of 73 feet when full; it is drawn down in late summer in preparation for flood runoff. Deposits of **mercury** in the area have led to high mercury levels in the lake's fish; the Oregon **Health Division** has issued warnings about eating them. Five parks provide access for recreational use. Atlas of Oregon Lakes.

Cottonwood. A deciduous broad-leaved **tree**, *Populus trichocarpa*, that is also known as black cottonwood, poplar, or balm because of the fragrance of its springtime leaf buds. It is a fast-growing, river-bottom tree of little value for lumber, but it and its hybrids are being grown for pulp fiber on some 40,000 acres along the lower **Columbia River**, in the **Willamette Valley**, and in the **Boardman**

area. These plantations are mechanically harvested after six to ten years. The nation's largest black cottonwood is in Willamette Mission State Park north of **Salem**. It is 158 feet tall and 320 inches in circumference (8'6" in diameter). The nation's largest narrowleaf cottonwood, *P. angustifolia*, is found in **Malheur County**. The related Quaking aspen, *P. tremuloides*, grows in central and eastern Oregon seeps. Oregon Blue Book; Trees to Know.

Cougar. A large (to 200 pounds), tawny, wild cat, *Felis concolor*, also called puma, panther, or mountain lion, found in increasing numbers throughout Oregon, sometimes in residential areas. From 1843 until 1961 the state paid a bounty for each dead cougar until there were fewer than 200 in the state. In 1968 cougars were given big-game status which gave control over hunting. Their numbers have since increased to over 3,700 and continue to increase some 5% a year. The number of complaints of cougar attacks on pets and livestock in Oregon has increased from 222 in 1993 to nearly 800 in 1996. A limited number of cougar **hunting tags** are issued, though the use of dogs for hunting was outlawed by a ballot initiative in 1994. A single cougar kills major prey, such as a deer or elk about once a week. There have been, as of 1997, no human fatalities in Oregon, though in 1994 cougars killed two women in California in separate attacks, and small children have been attacked in Washington. Atlas of Oregon Wildlife; Big Game History; Mammals and Life Zones of Oregon; Mammals of the Northwest; Oregon Hunting Guide; Oregonian 6/20/97:B4.

Cougar Reservoir. A long, narrow, steep-sided lake on the South Fork **McKenzie River** 46 miles east of **Eugene**. The **Army Corps of Engineers** built the 452-foot-high rock fill dam in 1963 for flood control and power generation; 25 **megawatts** of power can be generated. The six-mile long reservoir covers 1,280 acres and has a maximum depth of 425 feet; it is drawn down in late summer in preparation for flood runoff. The lake is used for boating, fishing, and camping. Army Engineers; Atlas of Oregon Lakes.

Council Crest. The high point, elevation 1073', in the hills south of **Portland**. First called Glass Hill, and later Fairmount (still the name of the encircling scenic drive), it was renamed Council Crest by a group of delegates to the National Council of the Congregational Churches who had an outing on the peak during their convention in 1898. A popular **amusement park**, complete with **roller coaster**, was built soon after and lasted for several decades. The area, obtained by the city in 1937, is now a park notable for its vistas. Oregon Geographic Names; Round the Roses.

Counselors and Therapists, State Board of Licensed Professional. A board of seven members appointed by the governor for three-year terms. The board licenses counselors as well as marriage and family therapists, and investigates complaints. As of August 1997, Oregon had 1,007 licensed counselors and 280 marriage and family therapists. 3218 Pringle Road SE, Suite 160, Salem 97302-6312. 503-378-5499. Oregon Blue Book.

Counties. Oregon has 36 counties, created through the years by the state to provide designated governmental functions in local areas. They are **Baker, Benton, Clackamas, Clatsop, Columbia, Coos, Crook, Curry, Deschutes, Douglas, Gilliam, Grant, Harney, Hood River, Jackson, Jefferson, Josephine, Klamath,**

Lake, Lane, Lincoln, Linn, Malheur, Marion, Morrow, Multnomah, Polk, Sherman, Tillamook, Umatilla, Union, Wallowa, Wasco, Washington, Wheeler, and **Yamhill**. They range from Multnomah, the smallest (465 square miles) and most densely populated (1,347 per square mile) to **Harney County**, the largest (10,228 square miles, 22 times the size of Multnomah County) and most sparsely populated (less than one person per square mile). The first counties were the four **districts** established by the **Provisional government** of the **Oregon Country** on July 5, 1843. Oregon Association of Counties, PO Box 12729, Salem 97309-0729. 503-585-8351. Oregon Blue Book; "Oregon Counties." See also **County government; County seat; Metropolitan Service District; Property tax; Sagebrush Coalition; Tri-county area.**

Counties - population. In 1995, estimated populations for Oregon's 36 counties ranged from **Wheeler County** with 1,550 people to **Multnomah** with 626,500, which is 20% of the total state population of 3,132,000. **Gilliam** and **Sherman** counties also had fewer than 2,000 people, while **Clackamas, Lane,** and **Washington** each had over 300,000. The counties that have grown the most since 1990 are in the **Willamette Valley** where **high-tech** industries are located (**Washington County** had 19% growth) or those with retirement appeal, as in central Oregon (**Deschutes,** 25%, **Jefferson,** 18%,) and along the coast (**Curry,** 15% growth). Population densities ranged from 1,347 per square mile in **Multnomah County** and 508 in **Washington County** down to less than one person per square mile in **Lake** (.9), **Wheeler** (.9), and **Harney** (.7) counties. **Center for Population Research and Census.**

Country Fair. See **Oregon Country Fair.**

County commissioners. See **County courts.**

County courthouse. The building in which the elected county governing body is located. At one time the governing body had judicial responsibilities and so was called the **County Court**; the building housing county government was thus called the courthouse. Five of Oregon's counties have courthouses designed by Portland architect Delos D. Neer. They are **Clackamas County** (1884, razed 1935); **Benton County** (1888); **Polk County** (1893), **Lane County** (1898, razed 1959); and **Baker County** (1908). Those in Baker, Benton and Polk counties are still in use.

County courts. Courts that were presided over by the chair of the board of **county commissioners** who was then called the county judge. There was no requirement that the judge be a member of the **bar**. At one time all 36 Oregon counties had county court authority and county judges, but now only seven counties have some judicial function. In **Gilliam, Harney, Sherman,** and **Wheeler** counties the county judge has both juvenile and probate jurisdiction, in **Morrow County** the judge has only juvenile authority, and in **Grant** and **Malheur** the judge has only probate authority. Oregon Blue Book.

County fairs. Each of Oregon's 36 counties has historically had an annual fair to showcase its agricultural products and provide entertainment. The first county fair in Oregon was sponsored by a newly organized **Yamhill County** agricultural society on October 4, 1853. **Marion, Polk,** and **Washington** Counties quickly followed suit. For years the state provided $40,000 to each county for the fairs, at first from horse racing receipts and later from video poker. **Grant County**'s fair, organized in 1909, is thought to have had the longest uninterrupted record of operation. The **Deschutes County** fairground at **Redmond**, scheduled to open in 1998, will be the largest fairground in the state. Dictionary of Oregon History; Oregonian 3/16/97:C4. See also **State Fair**.

County Forest Trust Lands. See **Board of Forestry Lands**.

County government. Counties are units of local government created by the state and having all of their operations prescribed and controlled by state law. They were originally responsible for roads, law enforcement, courts, care of the needy, and tax collections. Responsibilities added since include social services, parks, pollution control, economic development, county fairs, museums, and others. County governments originally had some court jurisdiction, such as over juvenile and probate matters, so the board of commissioners was called the **county court** and the presiding commissioner was called the county judge. The main county office building is still called the county courthouse but now usually houses the state **circuit court**. By 1996, nine of Oregon's 36 counties had adopted **home rule** charters, which give them greater autonomy than counties operating under traditional state law. Oregon Blue Book. See also **Charter**; **Ordinance**.

County judges. See **County courts**.

County seat. The town in which the county government is located. In many counties, the selection of a county seat has been a long and contentious process, and at times the county seat has been transferred to another town. In **Harney County** armed night riders spirited the county records from Harney to **Burns** in 1890, and in 1917 **Madras** became the **Jefferson County** seat after residents took it upon themselves to move the county records from **Culver**.

Court of Appeals. A ten-member state court, created in 1969, that hears all civil and criminal appeals, except death-penalty cases and appeals from the **Tax Court**. It can also review state administrative agency actions. The ten judges are elected on a statewide, nonpartisan basis for six-year terms, with one of them appointed as the chief judge by the chief justice of the **Supreme Court**. The judges usually sit in panels of three to hear cases. Decisions of the Court of Appeals may be appealed within 35 days to the Supreme Court, which will review the case if three or more Supreme Court judges vote to do so. Over 4,000 cases are filed with the Court of Appeals each year, and, unlike the Supreme Court, the Court of Appeals must hear each appeal that is filed with it. In 1997 the court closed 3,957 cases. 1,384 of them were affirmed without opinion (AWOP). Criminal cases took 431 days to close and other cases took 409 days. Supreme Court Bldg., 1163 State St., Salem 97310. 503-986-5555. Governing Oregon; Oregon Blue Book; Oregonian 3/7/98:D11. See also **Courts, state**.

Courthouse. See **County courthouse**; **Mark O. Hatfield Federal Courthouse**; **Pioneer Courthouse**.

Courthouse Square. A proposed - and troubled - $30 million public/private development of a city block in downtown **Salem**, planned to include a transit mall and **Marion County** offices. It is located across a street from the county courthouse. Oregonian 12/22/97:D2, 3/14/98:B2.

Courts, federal. See **Circuit court, federal**; **District court, federal**; **Mark**

O. Hatfield Federal Courthouse.

Courts of record. Trial courts in which a record is kept of proceedings. The record is then the basis for any appeals. In Oregon the state **circuit courts** are courts of record with a written transcript prepared by a court reporter. **District courts** were also courts of record with tape recordings used as the record. **Municipal courts** and **justice courts** are not courts of record, so an appeal from either entails a new trial in a **circuit court**. Governing Oregon.

Courts, state. Oregon's courts include **municipal courts** and **justice courts** (which are not **courts of record**); the **Tax Court** and **circuit courts** (which are courts of record); and the Oregon **Court of Appeals** and Oregon **Supreme Court** which hear appeals from the decisions of the courts of record based on the record. See also **County courts**; **Courts, federal**; **Dispute Resolution Commission**; **District courts**; **Judges**; **Judicial system**; **Juries**; **Plea bargaining**; **Polygraph**; **Small claims courts**.

Cove. An incorporated community in northeast Oregon on the lower slopes of the **Wallowa Mountains**, 15 miles east of **La Grande** in **Union County**. The post office was established as Forest Cove in 1863, but the name was soon shortened to Cove because of confusion with Forest Grove. The city was incorporated in 1904, and prospered as an orchard and dairy center. The business area was destroyed by fires in 1919 and 1921, though an **Episcopal Church** built in 1876 survived and is still in use. The city park contains an outdoor pool that is fed by a long-popular hot spring. Population 1980 451; 1995 585. Elevation 2,893'. 504 Alder, 97824. 541-568-4566. History of Union County.

Cove Island. See **The Island**.

Cove Palisades State Park. A central Oregon **state park** 15 miles southwest of **Madras** on **Lake Billy Chinook**. Attractions include fishing and boating on the large lake below high cliffs, and watching bald **eagles**, especially in winter when an Eagle Watch is held in late February. The park includes a marina and general store as well as 272 campsites. Reservations, 800-452-5687. Rt. 1, Box 60 CP, Culver 97734. 541-546-3412.

Covered bridges. Wooden bridges that were roofed to extend their life expectancy from 10 to 30 or more years. In the early 1900s Oregon had about 450 covered bridges, but by 1997 there were only 48 remaining and just 21 that were open to vehicle traffic. **Lane County** had 18, more than any county west of the Appalachians. In 1997 the oldest remaining was the 1919 Fisher Bridge on a tributary of the Alsea River. Despite preservation efforts, the numbers continue to decrease due to decay, floods, and the cost of preservation. One of the more recent covered bridges, built in 1962 across the South **Umpqua River** at Milo Academy, is actually a steel bridge with wooden housing. Oregon Covered Bridge Advisory Committee, 329 Transportation Building, Salem 97310. 503-986-4200. Covered Bridge Society of Oregon, 7638 SE Rural Street, Portland 97206. Oregon Covered Bridges; Oregonian 9/28/97:B1.

Covered wagons. See **Oregon Trail**; **Wagon trains**.

Cow Column. The livestock contingent of the first **wagon train** (1843) over the **Oregon Trail**. Because the 2,000 animals traveled more slowly than the wagons, the cow column, captained by Jesse Applegate, brought up the rear, traveling under a pillar of dust. The name was later similarly used by other wagon trains. Day; Dictionary of Oregon History.

Cow Cops. A group of volunteers sponsored by the **Oregon Natural Resources Council** to monitor grazing leases on **BLM** and **Forest Service** lands to ensure that ranchers are conforming to the terms of their leases. This includes documenting stream conditions, and making sure that fences and water troughs are maintained and that cattle have not strayed. Oregonian 5/3/95:B2.

Cow Creek. A long stream in southwest Oregon that heads in the **Cascade Range**, flows southwest along **Interstate 5** from Azalea to **Glendale**, then continues in a large loop west, north, and east before joining the South **Umpqua River** near **Riddle**. A road and railroad thread through its steep canyon, but Interstate 5 goes over **Canyon Creek Pass** instead. An immigrant recovered his cattle, stolen by Indians, in the valley, thus giving the creek its name. Oregon Geographic Names.

Cow Creek Band of the Umpqua Tribe of Indians. A southern Oregon tribe with some 900 members on its rolls. Enrollees must be lineal descendants of those on tribal rolls in the 1800s. In 1980 the tribe received a $1.5 million settlement from the federal government because their 1853 treaty had not been honored by the government and because the Termination Act of 1956 was passed without their knowledge or consent. The entire settlement was invested. The only land the tribe owns is 45 acres in **Canyonville** where the tribe operates the Seven Feathers Gaming Center with bingo hall, **casino**, and hotel. 2400 Stewart Pkwy #300, Roseburg 97470. 541-672-9405. "Cow Creek Band of the Umpqua Tribe"; First Oregonians; Native Peoples; Oregonian 10/22/95:A19.

Cow scow. About 1860 a **Corvallis** man, as an alternative to expensive **steamboats**, designed and built a scow powered by oxen on a treadmill. On the first trip the oxen "walked" the boat ashore in a slough. The oxen ate most of the cargo of hay before a steamer pulled the craft back into the river. It then made it downriver to **Canemah** but lacked the motive power to go back upstream, so the owner sold the oxen and the scow went over **Willamette Falls**. Oregon Oddities.

Cowboys. See **Cattle**; **Ranches**; **Vaqueros**.

Cows. See **Dairy products**; **Milk**.

Coxey's Army. A national "army" of hungry men during the **depression** of the mid 1890s. In Oregon, on April 20, 1894, 439 men, calling themselves the "Fifth Regiment of the Industrial Army," assembled at **Portland**. After drilling for several days they began marching eastward towards Washington, D.C. In **Troutdale** they commandeered a train, but were stopped by army troops at **Arlington** and sent back to **Portland**. Dictionary of Oregon History; Portland Gateway.

Coyote. A wild relative of the dog, *Canis latrans*, found throughout Oregon. Though most common on the **sagebrush** plains east of the Cascades, it has expanded its range since white settlement and the elimination of **wolves** so that there are now estimated to be 150,000 in Oregon. Coyotes are grayish brown, bushy tailed, and the size of a medium dog. Fabled for their wiles, their yipping howl carries the essence of the wild. They are omnivorous, living primarily on **rabbits**, ground **squirrels**, and **rodents**, but they also hunt fawns and young antelope, and in 1994 killed 12,000 **sheep** and lambs in the state. They are classed as a **predator** and managed by the state Department of **Agriculture**. Federal trappers kill an estimated 6,500 a year, and in 1994-95 5,144 were taken for pelts with an average value of $13 each. In 1996, after the central Oregon chapter of the Oregon Hunters Association began paying a $10 **bounty**, they paid out nearly $50,000 in 18 months. Atlas of Oregon Wildlife; Don Coyote; Mammals and Life Zones of Oregon; Mammals of the Northwest.

Coyote Springs. An **electric power plant** at **Boardman** in **Morrow County** that was put into operation in 1995. The plant, owned by **Portland General Electric**, is fueled by **natural gas**. It has a nameplate capacity of 346 **megawatts**. Inventory.

CPA. See **Accountancy**.

Crabs. Marine crustaceans with jointed legs; a number of kinds occur along Oregon's coast. The green crab, *Carcinus maenas*, native to Europe, is a small, prolific, predatory crab first found in Oregon waters in 1997 where it was eating young **oysters**. Hermit crabs of various species live in tide pools; they don't grow their own shells but move into a series of ever-larger empty snail shells. The Dungeness crab, *Cancer magister*, is harvested by sports fishers in Oregon bays and commercially in both bays and ocean; the commercial season runs from December to August with most caught in the first two months. Oregon's annual commercial harvest averages about 8 million pounds which is about 20% of the total Pacific coast catch. The 1994 catch of 10.6 million pounds brought in $14.4 million. Many of the Dungeness shells found on the beach are from molting, since each crab, in order to accommodate its increasing size, grows a new shell twice a year. The molt takes 15 minutes; the crab then hides without eating for two days while its new shell hardens. Before Dungeness crabs reach legal size, the females will already have reproduced several times. They feed primarily on small clams. Sport harvest is regulated by the state; the regulations are published in Oregon Sport Fishing Regulations. Clam Digging and Crabbing in Oregon; Oregonian 4/9/97:C12; Pacific States; Seashore Life. See also **Crawfish**; **Surimi**.

Crack-in-the-Ground. A two-mile long narrow **basalt** fissure located north of **Christmas Lake** and south of Four Craters Lava Field that is several thousand years old. It is 10 to 15 feet wide at the top, narrowing at the bottom, and up to 70 feet deep. "The Crack" was a favorite pioneer picnic spot because of the cool air that lies in the bottom. Geology of Oregon. See also **High lava plains**.

CRAG. See **Metro**.

Cranberries. Oregon grows 7% of the nation's cranberries with most of the state's berries processed for juice. In 1995 Oregon growers produced 170,700 barrels (each 100 pounds), worth $8.2 million, on 1,750 acres, down from the record harvest of 304,000 barrels in 1994. Most are grown by 125 growers on coastal bogland between **Port Orford** and **Bandon** in an area drained by the **New River**, and a few are raised in **Clatsop County**. Since the berries are machine harvested by flooding the bogs, the availability of river flows for irrigating and flooding the bogs is a limiting factor. The first commercial berries in **Coos County** were planted at Hauser in 1887. Oregon Oddities; Oregon's Agricultural Progress 41(1/2):18, Summer/Fall 1994; Oregonian 11/25/95:C7.

Cranberry Festival. Bandon has held an annual Cranberry Festival in late September since 1946. 541-347-2277.

Crane. See **Sandhill crane**.

Crane. An unincorporated **Harney County** community on Crane Creek 27 miles southeast of **Burns**. It was an active cattle-shipping yard for a few years, from 1916 until the railroad was extended to Burns in 1924. Crane Union High School has been a **boarding school** since 1928. Oregon Geographic Names; Tales out of Oregon.

Crane Prairie Reservoir. A lake 30 miles southwest of **Bend** first created in 1922 when a local irrigation district built a rock dam on the upper reaches of the **Deschutes River** in order to serve lands in the **Madras** area. The dam was rebuilt in 1939-40, which further flooded the broad prairie, creating a shallow (20' maximum depth), 4,167-acre, 14-mile long reservoir that is a popular camping and fishing lake. The snags left when rising waters killed some standing timber have become home to the largest **osprey** nesting colony in the Pacific Northwest, now part of the 10,600-acre area Crane Prairie Osprey Management Area. The reservoir is part of the **Deschutes Project** and is operated by the Central Oregon Irrigation District. Atlas of Oregon Lakes.

Crater Lake. Oregon's famous Crater Lake, located in **Crater Lake National Park**, is 1,932 feet deep, making it the deepest lake in the United States, and the seventh deepest in the world. The circular lake covers 13,139 acres, and is 6 miles across. It lies in the caldera of Mt. Mazama, a 12,500' peak that collapsed some 6,900 years ago after 400,000 years of eruptions. During the climactic eruption more than a cubic mile of molten rock, glowing pumice avalanches, and gas shot out, emptying the magma chamber inside the mountain. The top of the mountain then collapsed in on itself. More recent volcanic activity created Wizard Island and other cinder cones now under water. Points on the rim rise almost 2000 feet above the lake's surface elevation of 6,176 feet. The famous Crater Lake blue is due to the unusual transparency of the water, which has both low particulate levels and low nitrate levels, limiting the growth of phytoplankton. By 1978 its clarity had decreased from 142 feet to 92 feet, but after the 1991 removal of a polluting septic tank from the rim, readings were again at 142 feet. Rain and snowfall within the caldera are the only source of inflow for the lake. There is no outlet; water is lost from the lake only through evaporation and seepage. A sightseeing helicopter crashed into the lake on September 23, 1995, in 1,500 feet of water, killing both men on board. Atlas of Oregon Lakes; Oregonian 7/10/97:D9.

Crater Lake Lodge. A four-story building in **Crater Lake National Park** that looks out over the lake from the south rim at an elevation of 7,076 feet. Though owned by the federal government, it is operated by a private concessionaire. The original lodge, never fully completed, opened in 1915. The deteriorating building was closed in 1989, completely rehabilitated at a cost of $18 million, and reopened in May 1995. There are now 71 rooms, each with a bath. 541-830-8700. Great Lodges.

Crater Lake National Park. A 183,180-acre park around **Crater Lake** in the southern Oregon **Cascade Range**. Although the park is open year-round, the north entrance and the 33-mile Rim Road around the lake are closed by snow until June or July. Main access is from **Highway 62**, 72 miles northeast of **Medford**. From the intersection it is four miles to park headquarters and other services, including gas, and 11 miles to the Rim Village (elevation 7100 feet) on the south rim of the lake with views, a visitor center, gift shop, **Crater Lake Lodge**, and food services. Summer visitors can sightsee, hike on 90 miles of trails, picnic, camp, fish, and take boat tours. There is cross-country skiing in winter. In addition to the blue lake in its caldera setting, the park has several peaks over 8,000 feet, most with trails to the top, 200-foot-high pinnacles of welded pumice, and **Castle Crest Wildflower Garden**. The park, Oregon's only National Park, was created in 1902 from 160,290 acres of Forest Reserve and was later enlarged to 183,180 acres. P.O.Box 7, Crater Lake 97604. 541-594-2211.

Crawfish. An edible freshwater crustacean, *Astacus bartoni*, also called crawdad, crayfish, or poor man's **lobster**. They are found in many streams in western Oregon and are raised commercially near **Lake Billy Chinook**. A dozen are normally considered a meal, but the **Tualatin** Crawfish Festival features a crawfish eating contest in which a record of 170 in 15 minutes was set in 1970. Oregonian 8/10/97:C9.

Credit unions. Member-owned financial institutions. The first to really function in Oregon was the Portland Postal Employees Credit Union, which began operation in 1928. By 1970 there were 265. In 1994, 68 federal credit unions were operating in the state. There were also 25 state-chartered credit unions with assets of $2,526 million, regulated by the state Division of **Finance and Corporate Securities**. Oregon Credit Union League, 503-641-8420, 800-688-6098. "Beginnings"; Oregonian 10/31/96:C1. See also **Banking**.

Cremation. In the 1990s about 45% of Oregonians chose cremation instead of burial. Cremation does not require embalming but does require an inexpensive pressboard casket. Remains (called cremains) may be placed in a columbarium, buried in a new or existing grave space, scattered in a cemetery scattering garden, or scattered anywhere that they do not create a public nuisance. On private property, the property owners must give permission, and the **Coast Guard** has requirements for scattering ashes at sea. Information is available from the **Mortuary and Cemetery Board**. Oregonian 5/27/96: Special section p.10.

Crescent. See **Gilchrist**.

Crescent Lake. A large, half-moon shaped, natural lake 29 miles southeast of **Oakridge** on the east side of **Willamette Pass**. Its natural **moraine** dam has been augmented by a 40 foot dam; the water is used by the **Tumalo Irrigation District** to irrigate farmland west of **Bend**. The five-mile long lake covers 4,547 acres and has a maximum depth of 265 feet. Camping and fishing are popular. Atlas of Oregon Lakes.

Creswell. A **Willamette Valley** town in **Lane County** 10 miles south of **Eugene** on **Interstate 5**. It began as a station on the railroad named for U.S. Postmaster General John Creswell. The post office was established in 1872, and the city was incorporated in 1909. A $90 million resort and casino development was proposed in 1996. Population 1980 1,770; 1995 2,610. Elevation 535'. PO Box 276, 97426. 541-895-2531. Chamber of Commerce 541-895-5161. Oregonian 3/20/96:C1.

Cretaceous. The geologic period between the **Jurassic** and the **Paleocene**, 67 to 140 million years ago. At the beginning of the Cretaceous Oregon was under water; during the Cretaceous the Pacific shoreline steadily moved westward from the northeast corner until by the end it curved diagonally across the state. The first home-grown Oregon **fossils**, the first actually deposited in Oregon, date from this period; most are marine in origin. They include the fish-like ichthyosaur and the flying reptile, Pteranodon, with a 10 foot wing span. Geology of Oregon.

Crickets. Early in the summer of 1935 a massive plague of crickets suddenly appeared and devoured everything within a three-mile strip along Parsnip Creek in **Wallowa County**. After a week, thousands of gulls appeared and began feeding on the crickets. Then, as suddenly as they had appeared, both gulls and crickets disappeared. In 1995 a cricket hatchery moved from California to **La Grande**. Its crickets are sold to pet stores and as bait. History of Wallowa County; Oregonian 10/18/95:C2.

Crime. See **Good Government Congress**; **Hostages**; **Lynchings**; **Manhunts**; **Murders**; **Vigilantes**.

Crime prevention. Studies have indicated that the most effective crime prevention method, in terms of the cost per serious crime prevented ($3,881) is to provide graduation incentives for students. Parent training ($6,351) was next, followed by juvenile delinquent programs ($13,899), and prison ($16,000). In Oregon costs for dealing with a juvenile delinquent range from $10,200 a year to put him in a foster home with trained foster parents and ongoing support, to $12,800 in a group home, $31,800 in a juvenile treatment facility, and $43,800 a year in a juvenile prison. Oregonian 8/18/96:A1. See also **Measure 11**.

Crime rates. The Oregon rate on the FBI's index of serious crimes fell from 666.5 per 10,000 persons in 1995 to 606.4 in 1996. The index is composed of four **crimes against persons** (murder, rape, robbery, and aggravated assault) (1996 rate of 46) and four **crimes against property** (burglary, motor vehicle theft, arson, and larceny) (1996 rate of 560). **Portland**'s auto theft rate, which had been third highest in the nation, dropped 33% in 1995. Oregonian 8/21/96:A1, 9/18/96:A7, 1/5/97:A7; Report of Criminal Offenses. See also **Law enforcement**.

Crimes against persons. Reported crimes against persons in Oregon fell from 54,830 in 1995 to 49,388 in 1996, a drop of 9.9% The rate per 10,000 persons fell from 175.1 to 155.3. The reported offenses were willful **murder** 119, negligent **homicide** (non-vehicular) 10, forcible rape 1,262, other sex offenses 6,021, kidnapping 580, robbery 3,933, aggravated assault 9,440, and simple assault 28,023. Report of Criminal Offenses. See also **Domestic disturbance**.

Crimes against property. Reported property crimes in Oregon fell from 268,217 in 1995 to 251,141 in 1996, a drop of 6.4%. The rate per 10,000 persons fell from 856.4 to 789.5. The reported offenses were burglary 31,537, larceny 127,685, motor vehicle theft 17,340, arson 1,580, forgery/counterfeiting 10,237, fraud 10,326, embezzlement 675, stolen property 712, and vandalism 51,049. Embezzlement was the only category that increased, up from 558 in 1995. Report of Criminal Offenses.

Crimes, behavioral. Reported behavioral crimes in Oregon increased from 148,468 in 1995 to 150,416 in 1996, an increase of 1.3%. However, the rate per 10,000 persons fell from 474 to 472.9. The reported offenses were weapon laws 3,845, prostitution 889, drug laws 18,021, gambling 37, crimes against family 2,342, driving under influence of intoxicants (DUII) 23,985 (up 18.5%), liquor laws 12,992 (up 23.3%), disorderly conduct 16,293, curfew 7,800, runaway juveniles 13,923, and all other behavioral crimes 50,289. Report of Criminal Offenses.

Crimes, bias. Reported bias crimes, also called hate crimes, increased in Oregon from 114 in 1994 to 182 in 1996. Incidents prompted by race or color accounted for 49%, sexual orientation for 24%, national origin for 12%, religion for 10%, and political beliefs for 4%. Other reportable categories are labor union, economic/social status, and handicap. 48% of the offenses took place in **Multnomah County**. Report of Criminal Offenses.

Crimes, other. In Oregon in 1996 there were 26,717 traffic crimes reported, up .4% from the 1995 total of 26,623. There were also 5,309 fish and game violations and 720 marine violations. Report of Criminal Offenses.

Criminal Justice Commission. A seven-member commission created by the legislature in 1995. In addition to continuing the duties of its predecessor, the Criminal Justice Council, the commission is to develop a state criminal justice policy and long-range public safety plan for Oregon. It also will provide technical assistance to Local Public Safety Coordinating Councils, also created in 1995. It will continue to adopt sentencing guidelines and serve as an information resource for local, state, and federal agencies. 155 Cottage St. NE, Salem 97310. 503-378-2053. Oregon Blue Book.

Criminal offense. An action that breaks a law and for which the punishment may include imprisonment. **Misdemeanors** and **felonies** are criminal offenses, while **infractions** are not.

Crimp. A person who supplied sailors to man vessels. Crimps often owned boarding houses, and in return for extending credit to a seaman they would arrange for his next berth. The practice, common in **Astoria** and **Portland** from 1870 until after the turn of the century, was characterized by exploitation and corruption by both crimps and ships' captains, and the sailors were often shanghaied. The advent of steam power, with its accompanying reduction in crew size, was instrumental in ending the practice. "Crimping."

Crook County. A central Oregon county of grasslands and pine forests, drained by the Ochoco and **Crooked** rivers. Attractions include **Prineville** and **Ochoco** reservoirs, **Steins Pillar**, and rock hounding. The county is bounded by **Jefferson**, **Wheeler**, **Grant**, **Harney**, and **Deschutes** counties. **Prineville**, the county seat, is the only incorporated city. Elevations rise from 2,700' where the Crooked River leaves the county on the west up to 6,753' Round Mountain in the **Ochoco Mountains**. The economy is based on livestock, lumber, and recreation. Taxable assessed value in 1995 was $701,000,000, or $45,000 per capita. The county was created in 1882 from **Wasco County**, and named for Major-General George Crook (1829-1890) who served in the west both before and after making a brilliant record during the **Civil War**; it is apparently coincidence that Crook County is drained by Crooked River. **Vigilantes** ran the county between 1882 and 1884. Population 1980 13,091; 1995 15,700. Area 2,991 square miles. Density 5/sq.mi. Annual precipitation 11"; average temperature January 32°F, July 65°F. Courthouse, 300 E. 3rd, Prineville 97754. 541-447-6555. East of the Cascades; History of Crook County; Oregon Blue Book.

Crooked River. A 130-mile long central Oregon river that drains 4,330 square miles west from the **Ochoco Mountains** past **Prineville** to join the **Deschutes River** at **Lake Billy Chinook**. It has an average annual flow of 1,124,000 acre feet, or .4 acre foot/acre. Fur trappers gave the river its descriptive name. Oregon Geographic Names. See also **Prineville Reservoir**.

Crooked River Dinner Train. See **Excursion trains**.

Crooked River Gorge. A 300-foot deep cleft cut through 10 to 15 million-year-old **basalt** flows and down into light-colored volcanic sediments by the **Crooked River** north of **Redmond**. A **railroad bridge** built by the **Oregon Trunk Line** in 1910 crosses it, and **Highway 97** crosses on a bridge built in 1927. Peter Skene Ogden State Park provides an overlook on the southwest side.

Crooked River National Grassland. A 174,000-acre area east and south of **Madras** in central Oregon that is Oregon's only National Grassland. The range-land of grass, **sagebrush** and **juniper** is managed by the **Ochoco National Forest**. 2321 East Third, Prineville 97754-9117. 541-447-4120.

Crooked River Project. A U.S. **Bureau of Reclamation** project in **Crook County** that provides irrigation for 20,000 acres of farmland in the **Prineville** area from the **Prineville** and **Ochoco** reservoirs. The project also provides for flood control, recreation use, and wildlife enhancement.

Crooked River Ranch. An unincorporated community, population about 3,500, located a few miles northwest of **Redmond**.

Crop circles. Patterns that mysteriously appear in fields of grain. In 1994 three crops circles were noted west of **Portland**. One was a Celtic cross design next to **Highway 26** in **Aloha**, one was a key pictogram two miles farther west, and the third was a doughnut-shaped circle near **Gaston**. Oregonian 11/14/94:B7.

Crops. See **Bamboo**; **Christmas trees**; **Flax**; **Flowers**; **Fruit crops**; **Hay**; **Hops**; **Meadowfoam**; **Mint**; **Nursery crops**; **Nut crops**; **Seed crops**; **Sugar beets**; **Tobacco**; **Vegetable crops**.

Croquet. Portland Croquet Club, 6990 SW Heath Place, Beaverton 97005.

Cross. A 51-foot lighted steel and concrete cross in a city park on top of **Skinner Butte** in **Eugene** was the subject of litigation for 32 years. Erected without permission in 1964 by a local businessman, it replaced a series of wooden crosses that had been on the butte for decades, one of them burned by the **Ku Klux Klan** in 1922. After the Oregon Supreme Court ordered removal of the cross in 1969, Eugene voters declared it a memorial honoring veterans who had died in war. In 1977 the Oregon Supreme Court ruled that the cross could remain as a war memorial, but, after further litigation, the 9th U.S. Circuit Court of Appeals ruled in 1996 that the cross breached the separation of church and state and must be removed. In 1997 it was moved to the hillside campus of Eugene Bible College. Oregonian 8/21/96:A1, 6/26/97:D7.

Crown Point. A viewpoint, vista house, and **state park** on the old **Columbia River Scenic Highway** six miles east of **Troutdale** and 24 miles east of **Portland**. The bluff, rising 625 feet above the **Columbia River** near the west end of the **Columbia River Gorge**, is formed by a series of **Columbia River Basalt** flows. From Vista House, a two-tiered octagonal stone overlook built in 1918, views extend 50 miles up and down the river. Crown Point has been designated as a **National Natural Landmark** for observing the results of gradual valley formation as down cutting has kept pace with the rise of the **Cascade Range**. Historic Highway Bridges of Oregon.

Crow's Shadow Institute. A nonprofit arts institute on the **Umatilla Indian Reservation** founded in 1992 by artist James Lavadour. It is designed to help artists take the first steps toward professional careers. Oregonian 8/6/97:C2.

Crozet Basin. See **Geographic opposite**.

Cruise lines. Several cruise lines operate on the **Columbia River**, making trips up and down river from **Portland**, including week long cruises to Lewiston, Idaho, and day trips to **Astoria**, which receives over 23,000 visitors a year from cruise line dockings. Ships offering overnight river cruises include the *Spirit of Columbia* with a folding bow, and *Queen of the West*, a diesel-driven stern-wheeler. For legal and logistical reasons, only a few ocean cruise ships make it to Portland, though the 791' *Crystal Harmony* docked at the harbor wall in May 1996. Oregonian 3/26/95:D1, 6/2/96:T4.

Crump Lake. See **Warner Valley**.

Cryptosporidiosis. A **waterborne disease** caused by a microscopic protozoan parasite. 37 cases were reported in Oregon in 1996. A 1992 outbreak in **Medford** caused 15,000 residents to become ill with diarrhea and abdominal cramps; it was traced to the city **drinking water**. An outbreak the next year in Wisconsin resulted in 100 deaths. The organism is not readily killed by chlorine so must be removed by filtration.

Crystal Ballroom. A historic **Portland** ballroom with a mechanically-suspended, adjustable-tension dance floor. It was opened in 1914 as Cotillion Hall, renamed the Crystal Ballroom in 1950, and closed in 1968 because of building code violations. It reopened in 1997 after an extensive restoration by McMenamins, and now features Oregon's longest bar at 117 feet. 1332 W. Burnside Street. Oregonian 2/18/97:C1.

Crystal Springs Rhododendron Gardens. A six-acre garden in **Portland** with one of the world's finest collections of **azaleas** and **rhododendrons** in a wooded, lakeside setting. The city provided the land in 1950 and the Portland chapter of the Rhododendron Society has provided the 2,500 plants and much of the labor. The gardens are located across from **Reed College** on SE 28th Avenue near Woodstock; peak bloom is in May.

CUB. See **Citizens' Utility Board**.

Cullaby Lake. A two-mile long, narrow, 188-acre lake on the east side of **Highway 101** at the base of **Coast Range** foothills 8 miles south of **Astoria**. Cullaby Lake is the largest of the many lakes on the **Clatsop Plains**. It is a shallow lake (maximum depth 12 feet) noted for its warm water fishing. A naturally high nutrient content leads to summer algal blooms and dense beds of water plants. Two county parks provide access. Cullaby was a local Indian. Atlas of Oregon Lakes.

Cults. Oregon is considered to be fertile ground for cults because organized religions are not strongly planted, the state has traditionally had a live and let live attitude, and people depressed by gray winters may be more susceptible. Cult activities in Oregon have included those of the **Church of the Bride of Christ** in 1906, **Heaven's Gate** recruitment in 1975, the development of **Rajneeshpuram**

1981-1985, the **Embassy of Heaven Church**, and the more recent Foundation of Human Understanding in **Grants Pass**, led by radio preacher Roy Masters. The database of the Cult Resource Center, part of the Ecumenical Ministries of Oregon, lists over 200 cults. Oregonian 3/29/97:A12.

Cultus Lake. A natural, three-mile-long mountain lake lying west of **Sun River**. It covers 791 acres with a maximum depth of 211 feet. The lake is only fair for fishing, due to the short growing season, but it is popular for water sports. Campgrounds and a resort provide recreation facilities. Cultus is a **Chinook jargon** word meaning worthless; it probably referred to the poor fishing. Atlas of Oregon Lakes.

Culver. A central Oregon agricultural community in **Jefferson County** 10 miles southwest of **Madras**. The post office, given his family's ancestral name by postmaster O. G. Collver, was established in 1900 about five miles east of the present town site. Culver was the county seat until 1917. It was incorporated in 1946 following completion of an irrigation project. Population 1980 514; 1995 715. Elevation 2,633'. PO Box 256, 97734. 541-546-6494. East of the Cascades.

Curry County. A rugged county at the southwest corner of Oregon, bounded by California on the south, the Pacific Ocean on the west, and by **Coos**, **Douglas**, and **Josephine** counties. Incorporated cities are **Gold Beach** (county seat), **Brookings**, and **Port Orford**. Elevations range from sea level up to 5,098' Pearsoll Peak in the **Siskiyou Mountains**. The economy is based on lumber, agriculture, fishing, recreation, tourism, and retirement. Easter **lilies** are raised south of Brookings. Taxable assessed value in 1995 was $1,487,000,000, or $67,000 per capita. The county was created in 1855 from **Coos County** and named for George L. Curry (1820-1878), governor of the **Oregon Territory** at the time. Population 1980 16,992; 1995 22,200. Area 1,648 square miles. Density 13/sq.mi. Annual precipitation 83"; average temperature January 47°F, July 59°F. Courthouse, 450 N Ellensburg, PO Box 746, Gold Beach 97444. 541-247-7011. Century of Coos and Curry; Oregon Blue Book. See also **World War II**.

Customs Service. The U.S. Customs Service, part of the federal Treasury Department, is responsible for ensuring that all goods entering and exiting the U.S. do so in accordance with all applicable U.S. laws. In 1995, the **Portland** office collected over $303 million, most of it from duty on goods that entered through the **Portland** port and airport, but it also has offices in **Astoria**, **Newport**, **Coos Bay**, and **Medford**. The first U.S. Custom House in Oregon was established in Astoria in 1849. 511 NW Broadway, Room 198, Portland 97209. 503-326-2865. 800-BE-ALERT to report illegal activity, including drug smuggling. Hyas Tyee. See also **Foreign Trade Zones**.

Cyanide. See **Heap-leach mining**.

Cycle Oregon. An annual, week-long bicycle tour the second week of September during which 2,000 cyclists (sometimes known as Lemmings in Lycra) pedal over 400 miles through some part of Oregon. The event, which began in 1988, fills rapidly when applications open in early March. Small towns along the route host the cyclists for meals and camping. Cycle Oregon, a nonprofit group, organizes the tour and makes grants from its proceeds to the hosting communities. 800-CYCLEOR (800-292-5367).

Cyclones. See **Tornadoes**.

Czarina. A cargo steamship that wrecked on the north spit at **Coos Bay** while crossing the bar on November 13, 1910. Hundreds of persons gathered on the beach to watch, but because of savage seas nobody could reach the ship to rescue the 24 sailors who could be seen clinging to the rigging. All 24 died. Shipwrecks of the Pacific Coast.

Czechoslovakians in Oregon. Groups of Czechs settled around **Scio** and later, in 1909, at **Malin**. Bohemia, a region in western Czechoslovakia, was the birthplace of "Bohemia" Johnson for whom several features southeast of **Cottage Grove** were named.

D. B. Cooper. See **Hijacking**.

D. Boone tree. A tree felled near **Hermiston** in the 1960s that was found to have an inscription, grown over by bark, that read "D. Boone" and under that, "1801". Daniel Boone (1734-1820) settled on a land grant in what was then Spanish Missouri in 1799, and was known to have continued his frontier explorations. He would have been 67 in 1801. The present location of the piece of wood is unknown, though it may be stored in Hermiston. Oregonian 4/26/95:E2. See also **Boone's Ferry**.

D River. A short river in **Lincoln City**, said by the Guinness Book of World Records to be the shortest in the world. It drops 20 feet from **Devils Lake** to the Pacific Ocean in a distance of 120 feet, and has a drainage basin of 13 square miles.

Da Vinci Days. A 3-day **Corvallis** festival, named for famed inventor and artist Leonardo da Vinci (1452-1519), held in July to celebrate art, science and technology. 541-757-6363.

Daddy trains. Weekend passenger trains that ran between **Portland** and the coast during the early 1900s. During summers, many women and children stayed at the coast, and the fathers commuted to be with them on the weekends, arriving on the Friday evening train and leaving on the Sunday evening train.

Dahlias. Dahlias are grown commercially in the **Willamette Valley**, providing acres of color for visitors in the late summer. Frey's Dahlias are at 12054 Brick Road southeast of **Turner**, Deer Creek Dahlia Gardens at the corner of Mill Creek Road and Bishop Road east of **Aumsville**, and Swan Island Dahlias at 995 NW 22nd west of **Canby**.

Dairy farms. Oregon has about 500 dairy farms, down from 650 in 1991. Most are members of three major marketing associations: Darigold cooperative, Tillamook County Creamery Association, and Farmers Creamery cooperative. **Tillamook County** leads with nearly 30,000 dairy cows, followed by **Marion County** with 12,000. Many early dairy farms were established on **stump farms** with the cows grazing around the stumps. Tillamook was an early dairy center, shipping out butter (1870s) and **cheese**. The Tillamook Cow Testing Association, organized in 1911, was the first in the state and led to world production records. 1994-1995 Oregon Agriculture; Tillamook. See also **Margarine**; **MEAD**; **Milk**.

Dairy products. In 1994 Oregon processors produced 46 million pounds of **cheese**, 16.8 million pounds of butter, 17.5 million pounds of cottage cheese, 9.5 million gallons of ice cream, and 4.7 million gallons of ice milk. The 150 dairy farmers in **Tillamook County** produce over a third of the state's milk. 1994-1995

Oregon Agriculture. See also **Dog wheel**.

Dallas. A timber and commuter town on the edge of the **Willamette Valley** 14 miles west of **Salem**. The town, after having been made county seat of **Polk County**, was fittingly renamed for George Dallas, U.S. vice-president under President Polk. Earlier it had been called Cynthia Ann. The post office was established in 1852; the city was incorporated in 1874. Attractions include the 1899 courthouse, built from **sandstone** quarried three miles west of town, Polk County Museum, area wineries, and Basket Slough National Wildlife Refuge. Population 1980 8,530; 1995 10,850. Elevation 325'. PO Box 67, 97338. 503-623-2338. Chamber of Commerce 503-623-2564. Oregon Geographic Names.

Dalles. See **The Dalles**.

Daly Scholarships. See **Bernard Daly Educational Fund**.

Dammasch State Hospital. A one-time state adult psychiatric hospital in **Wilsonville** that provided long-term treatment services from 1961 until the last patients were transferred to Legacy Holladay Park Medical Center in **Portland** in 1995. At times Dammasch housed over 400 patients. In 1997 it became the center of a controversy when chosen as the site for a state prison.

Dams. There are over 3,500 dams in Oregon. Of them, 850 would threaten lives and property if they failed. Dams less than 10 feet tall or less than 3 million gallons in capacity are exempt from inspections and engineering approval. Some dams were built by the **Army Corps of Engineers**, some by the U.S. **Bureau of Reclamation**, some by power companies, some by individuals, and many by irrigation districts. Manipulation of water levels behind dams (including those on the **Columbia River** in Canada) is used for **flood control**, though only 27% of the average annual runoff of the **Willamette River** and 30% of the Columbia is controlled or stored by dams. Of the four dams on the Oregon stretch of the Columbia, only the **John Day Dam** has significant storage capacity. The **Oregon Natural Resources Council** proposed in 1994 that 11 dams in Oregon should be removed and 4 proposed dams not be built because of environmental damage. Army Engineers; Oregonian 3/3/96:B1. See also **Columbia River dams**; **Flood of 1964**; **Flood of 1996**; **Milltown Hill Dam**; **Willamette River dams**.

Dance. Oregon's major classical dance company, the **Oregon Ballet Theater**, is located in **Portland**. Contemporary dance performance bloomed from the 1984 until 1994 when **Portland State University** eliminated its dance department and later canceled the Contemporary Dance Series, and several important dance spaces were lost. However, several groups are presenting touring dance companies and local performers. Oregonian 8/24/97:E1. See also **Performance**.

Darlingtonia. A **carnivorous plant**, *Darlingtonia californica*, also called pitcher plant, that grows in nitrogen-poor acidic bogs of southwest Oregon. The plant's tubular green leaves grow up to three feet high. Flying insects are lured into the dome at the top by nectar, and then led to the pool of digesting broth at the bottom by the slick surface and downward-pointing hairs of the inner surfaces; the plant then absorbs the nutrients from the drowned insects. The plants may be seen from a walkway over a bog at the Darlingtonia Botanical Wayside on **Highway 101** five miles north of **Florence**. Great Northwest Nature Factbook.

Davis Lake. A large natural lake on the east slope of the **Cascade Range**

northeast of **Willamette Pass**. It was formed when a lava flow blocked Odell Creek, perhaps 1,000 years ago, flooding a shallow basin. The 3,906-acre lake is three miles long, and has a maximum depth of 20 feet. The water level of the lake drops during the summer due to seepage; since the seeps can't be sealed the lake has not been used for irrigation water storage. It is assumed that springs four miles downstream on Davis Creek and in **Wickiup Reservoir** are the major outflow of the lake. The lake provides excellent fishing (restricted to fly fishing) and water-fowl habitat in the large surrounding meadow, and there are campgrounds. Davis Lake was named sometime before 1878 for "Button" Davis, a local stockman. Atlas of Oregon Lakes.

Day care. See **Child care**.

Day length. Summer day length in **Portland** is 15 hours 41 minutes at the summer solstice in June and decreases by seven hours to just 8 hours 42 minutes at winter solstice in December. In **Medford**, near the south edge of the state, summer day length is 15 hours 17 minutes while winter day length is 9 hours 4 minutes. Thus Portland has 24 minutes more summer sun and 22 minutes less winter sun than Medford. It takes the sun about 30 minutes to cross the center of Oregon, so the sun rises half an hour earlier on the Idaho border than it does on the coast (if both are in the same **time zone**.) See also **Latitude and longitude**; **Sunrise, sunset**; **Twilight**.

Daylight saving time. For daylight saving time, clocks are moved forward an hour from the first Sunday in April through the last Sunday in October ("Spring forward in the spring, fall back in the fall.") In 1918 daylight saving time was already in use in portions of the state. Its use created controversy for decades, and in 1952 Oregon adopted a standard time initiative, making it one of the few states without daylight saving time. However, local option soon prevailed - leading to a decade of massive confusion. In at least one community, the county was on stan-dard time but the city hospital was on daylight time, so there was uncertainty over what time of birth (and for babies born near midnight, what date) to put on birth certificates. As the controversy raged, officials of **Gearhart**, **Seaside**, and **Can-non Beach** notified Governor Hatfield in 1961 that they were seceding from the State of Oregon to establish the "Sovereign Domain of the Sunset Strip" which would be on sundial time. After several heated campaigns that pitted farmers against businessmen, Oregon voters adopted summer daylight saving time via **initiative** in November 1962. It was adopted nationwide in 1967. Oregonian 5/9/61:sec.2 p.5, 4/27/62:16. See also **Time zones**.

Dayton. A **Willamette Valley** agricultural town in **Yamhill County** six miles east of **McMinnville**. It was named in 1848, probably for the Ohio hometown of one of the founders. The post office was established in 1851, and the city was incorporated in 1880. For its first 50 years it was an important grain shipping port on the Yamhill River, though periodic floods did much damage. The **Fort Yamhill** blockhouse was moved to the Dayton city park in 1912. Population 1980 1,409; 1995 1,705. Elevation 160'. PO Box 339, 97114, 503-864-2221. Old Yamhill; Oregonian 1/19/97:H1.

Dayville. An eastern Oregon ranching community in **Grant County** 32 miles west of **John Day** on **Highway 26**. It is located where the South Fork enters the

John Day River and is named for the river. The original post office, established in 1868, was three miles west of the present location. The city was incorporated in 1914. Nearby attractions include **John Day Fossil Beds National Monument**, hiking, hunting, and fishing. Population 1980 199; 1995 185. Elevation 2,348'. PO Box 321, 97825. 541-987-2188. Oregon Geographic Names.

De Moss family. A family entertainment troupe, also known as the Lyric Bards, comprised of James De Moss (1837-1912), a **United Brethren** minister from **Cove**, his wife Elizabeth, and five children. The family started singing and playing in mining camps in 1872, and became popular throughout the west, the U.S., and Europe. After Elizabeth's death, De Moss toured with his second wife and their two children. The four surviving children from his first marriage toured until 1932. Family members composed nearly all of their own music, including "Sweet Oregon" with which they ended their concerts. De Moss Springs wheat ranch in **Sherman County** became the family home. Dictionary of Oregon History; Oregon Oddities; Sweet Oregon; Tracking down Oregon.

Deady Hall. The first building at the **University of Oregon**, a Second Empire Style completed in 1876 and still in use. The architect was William W. Piper who guaranteed that it would last a millennium. Villard Hall was built in the same style in 1886. Style & Vernacular.

Deaf. The Deaf and Hearing Impaired Access Program of the Oregon **Disabilities** Commission works with state agencies to ensure access to the hearing impaired. V/TDD 503-378-3142; 800-358-3117. The Oregon School for the Deaf provides free residential education for deaf children ages 5 through 21. 999 Locust St. NE, Salem OR 97303-5254. V/TDD 503-378-3825. Oregon Blue Book. See also **Dogs for the Deaf**; **Hearing Aid Dealers Advisory Council**.

Death penalty. The Oregon **constitution**, in a section adopted in 1984, allows the death penalty for aggravated murder "upon unanimous affirmative jury findings". The first persons in Oregon to receive an official death sentence were five **Cayuse Indians** hanged at **Oregon City** in 1850 for the **Whitman massacre**. The state constitution, adopted in 1857, authorized the death penalty for murder. The provision was affirmed by Oregon voters in 1912, abolished by an **initiative** amendment to the **constitution** (Article I, Section 36) in 1914; reinstated in 1920; reaffirmed in 1958, abolished in 1964; reinstated as a statute in 1978, found unconstitutional in 1981, and adopted (providing for lethal injection) through the initiative in 1984 (Section 40), along with a provision exempting it from the state constitution's prohibition against cruel punishment. The first execution in 34 years was on September 6, 1996, and as of April 1998, there were 21 persons on death row in Oregon. Dictionary of Oregon History; Governing Oregon; Oregonian 9/3/95:A1, 5/16/97:A1, 11/10/97:E1. See also **Murders**.

Death records. See **Vital records**.

Death with dignity. See **Physician-assisted suicide**.

Deaths. Oregon recorded 27,361 deaths (and 41,832 **births**) in 1994. 525 of the deaths were suicides, 352 were alcohol related, and 6,181 were tobacco related. Statewide the death rate per 1,000 was 8.9 (down from 12.0 in 1936). It ranged from a low of 5.6 in **Benton County** to a high of 12.7 in **Lincoln County**. The rates in the **Metro** area were 6.4 in **Washington County**, 9.6 in **Multnomah**

County, and 7.6 in **Clackamas County**. In 1997, 32% of deaths were at home, 31% in nursing homes, 31% in hospitals, and 6% other. In 1980 the figures were 18% at home, 21% in nursing homees, 50% in hospitals, and 11% other. Oregon: A Statistical Overview; Oregonian 4/1/98:B1. See also **Cemeteries**; **Cremation**; **Mortuary and Cemetery Board**; **Oregon Memorial Association**; **Vital records**; **Worker's Compensation**; **Workplace fatalities**.

DeAutremont brothers. Three brothers, Hugh, 19, and twins Ray and Roy, 23, who held up a **Southern Pacific** passenger and mail train at Tunnel No. 13 at **Siskiyou Summit** south of **Ashland** on October 11, 1923. They dynamited the mail car, killing the mail clerk, and killed the brakeman, engineer, and fireman before escaping empty handed. After four years at large during which 2,583,000 "WANTED" posters had been printed in six languages, they were apprehended, tried in a sensational trial in **Jacksonville**, and given life sentences. Railroading in Southern Oregon.

Declination. See **Magnetic declination**.

Dee Wright Observatory. See **McKenzie Pass**.

Deep Creek Falls. A cataract 30 feet high in a narrow basalt canyon in the sagebrush country along **Highway 140**, 35 miles east of **Lakeview** and 2.7 miles west of Adel. Waterfall Lover's Guide.

Deepest lake. **Crater Lake**, 1,932 feet deep, is the deepest lake in Oregon and in the United States, and the seventh deepest in the world.

Deepwood. An ornate, Queen-Anne Style,1894 **Salem** home designed by William C. Knighton (later the first state architect) for druggist Dr. Luke A. Port. The six-acre grounds include two acres of formal, English-style gardens designed in the 1930s by the Northwest's first female landscape architecture firm, Lord-Schryver. The house and grounds adjoin **Bush's Pasture Park**. The house is reserved for weddings on Saturdays but is open for visitors on some other days. 1116 Mission St. SE. 503-363-1825.

Deer. Two species of deer are found in Oregon. Mule deer, *Odocoileus hemionus*, are found east of the **Cascade Range**, summering at high elevations or in well watered valleys, but wintering in juniper and sagebrush habitat during the winter. The black-tailed deer, a sub-species of the mule deer, is the common species west of the Cascades. Both "bounce" when running. Large bucks may weigh over 400 pounds, though most are under 300. The smaller white-tailed deer, *O. virginianus*, was formerly found throughout most of Oregon. It gallops with a rocking horse gait with its hind feet placed ahead of the forefeet, waves its white tail when excited, and has single-beam antlers with side branching, as opposed to the forked antlers of the mule and black-tailed deer. The white-tail prefers brushy or heavily forested areas, especially along streams. It is now found only in north-east Oregon and as a protected subspecies, the Columbia white-tailed deer, in a few herds along the lower **Columbia River** and near **Roseburg**. Deer may become pests in home gardens; the Oregon Department of **Fish and Wildlife** offers advice on controlling deer damage. A variety of deer hunting seasons are held throughout the state; a hunter must have the appropriate **hunting tag**. Nearly 300,000 hunters take an average of 86,000 deer a year, and historically some businesses closed in early October for the opening day of **deer** season. Atlas of Oregon Wildlife; Big

Game History; Mammals and Life Zones of Oregon; Oregon Hunting Guide.

Defense Force, Oregon State (OSDF). A non-paid, 700 member volunteer state **militia** force under the State of Oregon **Military Department**. It serves as backup to the **National Guard**. If the Guard were mobilized for war, the OSDF would become the state force. 1776 Militia Way, Salem 97309-5047. 503-945-3991. Oregon Blue Book.

Democratic party. One of Oregon's two major **political parties**. For the November 1996 election, 805,286 voters (41%) registered as Democrats, compared to 36% as **Republicans** and 20% as **Independents**. **Multnomah County** had nearly twice as many registered Democrats as Republicans. The party was organized in Oregon in 1852 and it and its **Salem clique** quickly dominated local politics. Democrats of the time tended to be Southerners or Southern sympathizers. After a long period of **Republican** domination, in 1949 Democrats controlled both houses of the legislature for the first time since 1879, a majority made possible by the numbers of Democrats who had moved into the state. Democratic State Central Committee of Oregon, 711 SW Alder, Suite 306, Portland 97205. 503-224-8200. Dictionary of Oregon History; Governing Oregon; Oregon Blue Book. See also **Voter registration**.

Demographer. See **Economic Analysis Office**.

DeMoss family. See **De Moss family**.

Density. See **Population density**.

Dentalium. Shells used by the Indians of northwestern North America for decoration and as a medium of exchange. The shells are white, inch and a half long tapered tubes, are found under 6 feet or more of water on the west side of Vancouver Island, British Columbia, where the local Indians collected them by using a broom-like tool. "Economics of Dentalium."

Dentists. In 1996 Oregon had 2,199 dentists and 1,887 dental hygienists. Dr. Bill Ten Pas of **Corvallis** was named president of the American Dental Association in 1995. Dr. James R. Cardwell (1830-1916) of **Portland** became Oregon's first dentist when he arrived in 1852. Dentists are licensed by the Oregon Board of Dentistry, a nine-member board appointed by the governor for four-year terms. The board also administers the state Dental Practices Act and licenses seven dental specialties and dental hygienists. 1515 SW 5th Avenue, Suite 602, Portland 97201. 503-229-5520. Oregon Blue Book. See also **Fluoride**.

Denturists. In 1997 the Oregon **Health Division Licensing Programs** office had licensed 132 denturists. Oregon Blue Book.

Department of .... See rest of name.

Department stores. See **Oldest businesses**.

Depoe Bay. "Whale Watching Capital of the Oregon Coast." A fishing port on a rocky stretch of central Oregon coast in **Lincoln County**, 13 miles north of **Newport**, with one of the world's smallest natural harbors. Walkways under the **Highway 101** bridge enable viewers to watch boats as they maneuver through the twisting passage between the bay and the ocean. Other attractions include a **spouting horn**, Fleet of the Flowers on Memorial Day which honors those who have lost their lives at sea, the Indian Style Salmon Bake on the 3rd Saturday in September, and nearby scenic state parks. The city, named for Willie Depoe, a **Siletz**

Indian, was incorporated in 1973. Population 1980 723; 1995 1,025. Elevation 58'. PO Box 8, 97341. 541-765-2361. Chamber of Commerce 541-765-2889. Oregon Geographic Names.

Depression (economic). Though the depression of 1893, triggered by the June 27 stock market crash, had large repercussions in Oregon, the Great Depression of the 1930s was felt even more. It began with a stock market crash on October 28 and 29, 1929. During the next three years Oregonians suffered as farm prices dropped 65%, over half the lumber mills closed, farms were foreclosed, retail sales and general prices dropped 50%, two thirds of the savings and loans failed, bank deposits dropped 35% by 1933, many banks closed, tax collections dropped 40%, some salaries were cut in half, per capita income dropped 31%, and 60,000 heads of household were unemployed. Local governments provided emergency employment, especially on roads and other public works. State efforts included the State Employment Relief Administration, funded through newly-legal liquor sales. Federal New Deal programs, including the **Civilian Conservation Corps**, begun by Franklin Roosevelt after his election as president in 1932, brought some relief though the Depression didn't really end until **World War II** began in 1941. "Eugene in the Depression." See also **Coxey's Army**; **Good Government Congress**; **Recessions**.

DEQ. See **Environmental Quality, Department of**.

Deschutes-Columbia Plateau physiographic province. An area that includes the portions of Oregon, Washington, and Idaho covered by **Columbia River basalt** flows. The Oregon portion is a triangle, bounded by the **Cascade Range** on the west, the **Blue Mountains** on the southeast, and the **Columbia River** on the north. It slopes from elevations of about 3000 feet on the south and west down to a few hundred feet along the Columbia, and is mostly covered by **wheat** ranches. Rainfall averages less than 20 inches a year. The **Deschutes**, **John Day**, and **Umatilla** rivers drain through the area to the Columbia. Geology of Oregon.

Deschutes County. A rapidly-growing central Oregon county that extends from the crest of the **Cascade Range** down across the **Deschutes River** and onto the **high desert**. Incorporated cities are **Bend** (county seat), **Redmond**, and **Sisters**. It is bounded by **Jefferson**, **Crook**, **Harney**, **Lake**, **Klamath**, **Lane**, and **Linn** counties. Elevations range from 2,380' where the Deschutes River leaves the county on the north edge to the 10,358' summit of **South Sister** on the west. The economy is based on lumber, agriculture, retirement, and tourism. Taxable assessed value in 1995 was $7,024,000,000, or $75,000 per capita. The county was created in 1916 from part of **Crook County**, and named for the Deschutes River. A fire in 1937 destroyed the courthouse and most of the county records. Population 1980 62,142; 1995 94,100. Area 3,055 square miles. Density 31/sq.mi. Annual precipitation 12"; average temperature January 31°F, July 63°F. Courthouse Ad. Bldg, 1130 NW Harriman, Bend 97701. 541-388-6570. History of the Deschutes Country; Oregon Blue Book.

Deschutes National Forest. A 1,852,497-acre national forest on the east slopes of the central Oregon **Cascade Range**, located primarily in **Deschutes County**. The forest administers the **Newberry National Volcanic Monument**, and includes 120,000 acres of designated wilderness including portions of the Diamond Peak, Mount Jefferson, Mount Washington, and **Three Sisters** wilderness areas. 1645 Hwy 20 E., Bend 97701. 541-388-2715.

Deschutes Project. A project providing irrigation water for lands near **Madras**. 50,000 acres are within the North Unit Irrigation District with supplemental supplies for 47,000 acres in the Central Oregon Irrigation District and Crook County Improvement District No.1. The water comes from **Wickiup, Crane Prairie**, and Haystack Reservoirs, constructed by the U.S. **Bureau of Reclamation**. Atlas of Oregon Lakes.

DesChutes Railroad. See **Battle of the Gorge**.

Deschutes River. A famed, 252-mile long fishing river that drains 10,675 square miles along two thirds of the east slope of Oregon's **Cascade Range**. The river is said to rise from the seeps at **Elk Lake** and heads south through **Crane Prairie** and **Wickiup** reservoirs before turning north to flow through **Bend, Lake Billy Chinook** and **Lake Simtustus** to the **Columbia River**, dropping 4,600 feet in its 240 miles. Other than the **Crooked River**, most tributaries, including the **Metolius**, flow in from the west, carrying runoff from the high Cascades. Much of the river's water comes from groundwater percolating through porous **lava**, providing a remarkably uniform flow throughout the year so that winter flows are normally only two or three times the volume of summer flows. The highest flow ever recorded, 78,500 cubic feet a second, occurred during the **flood of 1996**, and was 10 times the usual winter flow. The annual volume of 4,200,000 acre feet equals .6 acre foot/acre. The lower Deschutes, between **Pelton Dam** and the **Columbia River**, is famed for white-water rafting; access is managed by the **Bureau of Land Management**. The river's name comes from the French fur trappers' name for it, La Riviere des Chutes, or River of the Falls, so named because the Deschutes joins the Columbia near **Celilo Falls**. East of the Cascades; Oregon Geographic Names. See also **Benham Falls; Dillon Falls**.

Desert. About one fourth of Oregon, primarily the southeast quarter, is desert, receiving 10 inches or less of precipitation a year. The rain that does fall sinks in or runs off into alkali lakes with no outlets. It is grazing land of vast distances, covered with grasses and **sage brush**. Reub Long writes that you don't measure distance in a desert by miles but by looks, and Oregon's desert, 200 by 130 miles, is ten good looks across. The Oregon Desert. See also **Basin and range; High Desert**.

Desert Land Act of 1877. A federal law adopted March 3, 1877, that provided for the sale of up to 640 acres (320 acres after 1890) of **public domain** desert lands in western states to any person who could show bona fide plans to irrigate it within three years. The buyer had to pay $1.25 an acre and was to cultivate at least 1/8th of the land. Circular. See also **Carey Act of 1894; Land grants**.

Destination resorts. See **Resorts**.

Detroit. A timber and recreation community in the **Cascade Range** 50 miles east of **Salem** on the **North Santiam Highway** in **Marion County**. Local settlers from Michigan named the town for Detroit, Michigan, in 1891. In 1952 the original townsite, about to be flooded by **Detroit Lake**, was relocated 1/2 mile uphill, and the city was incorporated. Population 1980 367; 1995 365. Elevation 1,564'. PO Box 589, 97342. 503-854-3496. Oregon Geographic Names.

Detroit Dam and Lake. An **Army Corps of Engineers** dam on the North Fork **Santiam River** near the town of **Detroit** and the branched, nine-mile long reservoir it created for flood control and power generation. The concrete dam, completed in 1953, is 360 feet high and 1,580 feet long. Big Cliff dam, a re-regulating dam just downstream, is 191 feet high. The two dams have a power generating potential of 118 **megawatts**. The 440-foot-deep, 3,580-acre lake is one of the most popular in Oregon for camping, fishing, and boating, though it is drawn down in late summer in preparation for flood runoff. A variety of facilities, including **Detroit Lake State Park**, are located around the lake and in the town of Detroit. Atlas of Oregon Lakes.

Detroit Lake State Park. A **state park** two miles west of **Detroit** with moorage docks, boat ramp, bathhouse, and 311 campsites. Reservations, 800-452-5687. PO Box 549, Detroit 97342. 503-854-3346.

Developmental disabilities. Oregon is said to have 10,000 adults who are developmentally disabled. The federally funded Oregon Advocacy Center provides free protection and advocacy services to Oregonians with developmental disabilities or those considered mentally ill. 310 SW 4th Ave., Suite 625, Portland 97204-2309. 800-452-1694. Oregonian 7/8/96:B6. See also **Disabilities**; **Eastern Oregon Training and Psychiatric Centers**; **Fairview Training Center**; **Mental Health and Developmental Disability Services Division**.

Devils Churn. A narrow ocean inlet on **Cape Perpetua**, south of **Yachats**, that was originally a sea cave. The roof has collapsed along most of its length, but the trench still terminates in a small cave beneath the headland. During winter storms a **spouting horn** appears near the upper end of the churn. Trails and stairs lead to it from a parking area on **Highway 101**. Geology of Oregon.

Devils Lake. A three-mile-long, 678-acre, natural lake just east of **Lincoln City** that is heavily used for recreation. **Devils Lake State Park** provides access. The name was inspired by an Indian legend of a monster that lived in the lake and sometimes pulled down boats, especially in moonlight. The lake has a maximum depth of 22 feet; water quality has been poor due to siltation and high inputs of nutrients and bacteria. A weed-eating fish, called the grass carp or white amur, has been introduced to control aquatic weeds. The lake drains to the ocean through the 120-foot long **D River**. Atlas of Oregon Lakes.

Devils Lake State Park. A **state park** located on both sides of **Devils Lake** in **Lincoln City**. The 100-unit campground, open all year, is on the north side (reservations, 800-452-5687), and the day use area is on the south. Each has a boat ramp. Ocean beaches are at the west end of 120-foot-long **D River** which drains the lake. 1452 NE 6th, Lincoln City 97367. 541-994-2002.

Devils Punchbowl. A deep hole in the ground on the Oregon coast at Otter Rock north of **Newport** that formed when the roof at the intersection of two sea caves collapsed. The sea rushes in through holes in the walls. There is a **state park** viewpoint and picnic area at the site.

Dexter Reservoir. A 2.8-mile-long reservoir 22 miles southeast of **Eugene**, just downstream from **Lookout Point Reservoir**. The dam at Dexter, completed in 1954 by the **Army Corps of Engineers**, provides power generation and flood control, and the lake functions as a reregulating basin, designed to even out the surges that result from power generation at Lookout Point dam. When full the lake covers 1,025 acres and has a maximum depth of 56 feet. It is heavily used by sailboats and water skiers, and there is a campground. A **covered bridge**, built originally in 1907 and rebuilt in 1945, crosses the lake to **Lowell**. Dexter post office was named by the first postmaster for the brand name on his cookstove. Atlas of Oregon Lakes; Oregon Geographic Names.

Diamond Craters. An area south of **Malheur Lake** where a series of explosions and intrusions 2,500 years ago formed cinder cones, lava flows, bombs, fissures, domes, depressions, and craters. A third of the 100 cinder cones and craters lie within the Central Crater Complex, a large, 200' deep **caldera**. The Graben Dome is a 7,000' long trench that is 1,250 feet wide and a hundred feet deep. The Diamond name comes from the nearby Diamond Ranch where a diamond brand was used by Mac McCoy. Geology of Oregon. See also **Volcanic eruptions**.

Diamond Lake. A large, natural mountain lake that formed when a **lava** flow from **Mount Thielsen** blocked a glacial valley a million years ago. It lies in the **Cascade Range** five miles north of **Crater Lake National Park**. The lake is three miles long and 3,214 acres in size, with a maximum depth of 52 feet. Heavy year-round recreation use includes swimming, boating, fishing, camping, and snowmobiling. John Diamond discovered the lake from the top of Diamond Peak in 1852. Campgrounds and a resort are located on the shore. Snowcat skiing is available by reservation from a top elevation of 8,300 feet with a 3,000-foot vertical drop. 800-446-4555. Atlas of Oregon Lakes; Oregonian 11/16/97:T7.

Diatomite. An absorbent mineral deposit formed of the glassy skeletons of single-celled aquatic algae. Since diatomite can absorb up to 300% of its own weight, it is used as a cat box filler, absorbent, and filter for water and chemicals. It has been mined periodically since 1917 in **Crook**, **Harney**, **Lake**, and **Malheur Counties**, and along the **Deschutes River** near Terrebonne, where the original 67-foot thick deposits have been nearly exhausted. Geology of Oregon.

Dietitians. The seven-member Oregon Board of Examiners of Licensed Dietitians oversees the licensure of dietitians and investigates complaints. 800 NE Oregon St. #21, Suite 407, Portland 97232. 503-731-4085. Oregon Blue Book.

Dillon Falls. A quarter-mile long chasm ten miles southwest of **Bend** through which the **Deschutes River** froths and drops over 40 feet. The falls are located off the **Cascade Lakes Highway** on Road#41. Lava Island Falls are two miles north of Dillon Falls and **Benham Falls** are three miles south. Leander Dillon homesteaded in the area in about 1890. Waterfall Lover's Guide.

Dimensions of Oregon. See **Size**.

Dinosaurs. The only dinosaur fossil discovered in Oregon was found near **Cape Sebastian** in 1969. The single bone is believed to be part of a duckbill dinosaur that lived perhaps 75 million years ago in California; the shifting of plates of the earth's crust moved it north. In 1994 the fossil was chipped out to be part of the **Museum of Natural History Association** collection. No other dinosaur remains have been recovered in Oregon though the geologic environment is similar to dinosaur-rich locations in nearby states. In 1996 Oregon had two commercial dinosaur parks, Thunderbeast Park 15 miles north of **Chiloquin** on **Highway 97** (541-783-2767), and Prehistoric Gardens 12 miles south of **Port Orford** on **High-**

way 101 (541-332-4463). Geology of Oregon; Oregonian 8/29/94:B1. See also **Fossils, animal**.

Dioxins. Hazardous organic chemicals often found as impurities in chemicals such as wood preservatives and herbicides and in the wastes from bleaching wood pulp. There are some 75 chlorinated dioxins with widely varying toxicity; the most toxic is 2,3,7,8-TCDD. Oregon Environmental Atlas. See also **Water pollution**.

Dipper. See **Water ouzel**.

Direct Legislation League. See **People's Power League**.

Direct service industries (DSIs). Companies authorized to buy power directly from **Bonneville Power Administration**. The DSIs include eight **aluminum** companies (two in Oregon) and eight chemical companies (three in Oregon). The two aluminum smelters in Oregon are Reynolds Metals Company at **Troutdale** and Northwest Aluminum Company near **The Dalles**. Direct Service Industries, Inc. 503-233-4445.

Disabilities. The Oregon Disabilities Commission advocates for services for Oregon's disabled. 1257 Ferry St. SE, Salem 97310. Voice/TDD 503-378-3142; Toll-free in Oregon 800-358-3117. Oregon Blue Book. See also **Blind**; **Deaf**; **Developmental disabilities**; **Mental Health and Developmental Disability Services Division**; **Senior and Disabled Services Division**.

Disasters.
-Car crashes:

Interstate 5	August 3, 1988	7 deaths

-Diseases:

The greatest losses of life known in Oregon occurred during the **epidemics** that swept through the Indian communities between 1780 and 1840, especially the **malaria** epidemic of the early 1830s that killed over 10,000 Indians in northwest Oregon. **Spanish influenza** killed 3,675 Oregonians 1918-1920.

-Explosions:

Gazelle explosion	April 8, 1854	28 deaths
Umatilla Ordnance Depot	March 21, 1944	6 deaths
Roseburg explosion	August 7, 1959	9 deaths

-Fires:

Silver Lake fire	December 24, 1894	43 deaths
Bandon fire	September 26, 1936	11 deaths
Aloha apartment fire	June 28, 1996	8 deaths

-Floods:

Flood of 1861	December	Number of deaths unknown
Heppner flood	June 14, 1903	225 deaths
Flood of 1948 (Vanport)	May, June	32 deaths
Flood of 1964/65	December, January	15 deaths

-Geologic events:

Canyonville slide.	January 16, 1974	9 deaths
Mount St. Helens eruption, Washington		
	May 18, 1980	57 deaths

-Massacres:

Smith massacre	June 1828	15 whites
Whitman massacre	November 29, 1847	14 whites
Rogue River War	October 8, 1855	23 Indians
Rogue River War	February 22, 1856	23 whites
Chinese massacre	1887	31 Chinese

-Mountain climbing:

Mount Hood	May 11, 1996	9 deaths

-Plane crashes:

Cape Lookout, B-17F	August. 1943	9 deaths
Brookings, Navy PBY bomber	Jan. 31, 1945	8 deaths
Lakeview, small plane	Oct. 28, 1947	4 deaths

including the **Governor**, **Secretary of State**, and President of the **Senate**

Portland, United Airlines	Dec. 28, 1978	10 deaths
Ocean, Air Force HC-130	Nov. 22, 1996	10 deaths

-Shipwrecks:

William and Ann.	March 1829	46 deaths
General Warren.	January 28, 1852	42 deaths
Brother Jonathan.	July 30, 1865	166 deaths
Fishing fleet.	May 7, 1880	25 deaths
Alaskan.	May 13, 1889	31 deaths
Czarina.	November 13, 1910	24 deaths
Mimi.	April 6, 1913	17 deaths
Santa Clara.	November 2, 1915	16 deaths
J. A. Chanslor.	December 18, 1919	36 deaths
Erria.	December 20, 1951	11 deaths

A total of 1,500 lives, including some of the above, have been lost over time in shipwrecks at the mouth of the **Columbia River**, known as The Graveyard of the Pacific.

-Storms:

Columbus Day storm	October 12,1962	24 deaths.

-Wars:

Indian wars. Total deaths unknown for either side.

See also **Field burning**; **Plane crashes**; **Shipwrecks**; **Storms**; **Wars**.

Disciples of Christ (Christian). A number of Disciples, also called Campbellites, came to the **Willamette Valley** beginning in 1845 and established congregations. The Amity Church of Christ, established in 1846, is the oldest Christian Church congregation west of the Rockies. The Disciples founded Bethel Academy in **Polk County** in 1855 and transferred classes in 1865 to Monmouth Christian College, which later became **Western Oregon University**. Guide to Early Oregon Churches.

Discoverers. The first humans to arrive in Oregon are thought to have come from Asia over 10,000 years ago. The first Europeans to see Oregon were on Cabrillo's 1542 expedition from Spain which sailed as far north as the **Rogue River** but was prevented from landing by severe storms. Though evidence indicates at least one 18th century Spanish shipwreck on the Oregon coast, the first recorded landfall was by some members of Captain Gray's 1788 voyage which put in at

Tillamook Bay where the black cabin boy was murdered by natives. The first overland travelers to reach Oregon were the members of the **Lewis and Clark Expedition** in late 1805. See also **Explorers**; *San Francisco Xavier*; **Settlers**.

Diseases. In 1996 **chlamydia** was Oregon's most commonly reported infectious disease with 5,347 cases. Hepatitis A followed with 942 cases, down from 2,968 the year before. There were 925 cases of **giardiasis**, 871 cases of gonorrhea, 670 cases of campylobacteriosis (diarrhea), and 469 cases of **AIDS**. Other reported diseases and the number of cases were amebiasis 87, botulism 2, **cryptosporidiosis** 37, E. coli 98, H. influenza 33, hepatitis B 178 (but 536 hepatitis B carriers), hepatitis NANB 46, **influenza** 21, listeriosis 14, **Lyme disease** 19, **malaria** 24, **measles** 14, **meningococcal disease** 123, pertussis 35, **rabies** (animal) 5, rubella 1, salmoneliosis 387, shigeliosis 165, syphilis (early) 17, tuberculosis 190, and yersiniosis 18. Oregonian 1/9/97. See also **Cancer**; **Epidemics**; **Hantavirus**; **Plague**; **Sexually transmitted diseases**.

Dispute Resolution Commission. A commission that supports community dispute resolution programs, establishes program standards and qualifications for mediators, and operates the Public Policy Dispute Resolution Program. The seven members are appointed by the governor to four-year terms. 1174 Chemeketa Street NE, Salem 97310. 503-378-2877. Oregon Blue Book. See also **Courts**.

District court, federal. The federal Oregon District Court, with offices in **Portland** and **Eugene**, is a trial court of general jurisdiction for federal cases arising in Oregon. The President appoints the seven district judges, who serve for life. Appeals are heard by the 9th U.S. **Circuit Court**, headquartered in San Francisco but also with judges in **Portland**. See also **Mark O. Hatfield Federal Courthouse**.

District courts, state. Trial courts that had jurisdiction over less serious cases than the state **circuit courts** until their duties were transferred to circuit courts in 1998. District court jurisdiction was limited to $10,000 in civil cases and to misdemeanor criminal cases in which the penalty is a fine of $3,000 or less and/or imprisonment for one year or less. Geographical jurisdiction was by county. They also operated **small claims courts**. In 1997 there were 63 nonpartisan district court judges, elected by county for six-year terms, who became circuit court judges in 1998. In 1995, 407,000 cases were filed with district courts, down from 518,000 in 1990. Oregon Blue Book. See also **Courts, federal**; **Courts of record**.

Districts. On July 5, 1843, the **Provisional government** of the **Oregon Country** established four districts, later called **counties**. These were the **Twality** (Tualatin) **District** in the northwest, which included all the area west of the **Willamette River** and north of the Yamhill River to $54°40'$ (now the south border of Alaska); **Yamhill District** in the southwest, which included the area west of the Willamette and south of the Yamhill to $42°$ (the present Oregon/California border); **Champooick** (Champoeg) **District** in the southeast, which covered the area east of the Willamette to the Rockies and south of the mouth of the Pudding River to $42°$, and **Clackamas District** in the northeast, which included the area north of the mouth of the Pudding River and from Willamette east to the Rocky Mountains. The four districts and subsequent counties have since been divided and subdivided so that there are now 36 counties within the state. General History of Oregon;

"Oregon Counties."

Ditches. Many Oregon ditches were dug by hand to carry water for **gold mining** or **irrigation**. The first in the **John Day** area was the Rawhide Ditch, dug in 1862, so called because, since there was no lumber available, flumes were made by shingling hides over each other. The 136-mile-long Eldorado Ditch extended east from the headwaters of Burnt River in **Baker County** to carry water to gold mining areas around Malheur City. It was hand dug, beginning in 1863; seven years later 1,000 **Chinese** were hired to speed up the project. The ditch, now dry, was seven feet wide at the top and five feet wide at the bottom. It and the 32-mile-long Sparta Ditch on the south slope of the **Wallowa Mountains** were engineered by William H. Packwood (1832-1917). The 23-mile long Sterling Ditch in **Jackson County** was hand dug by Chinese laborers in 1877. Gold and Cattle Country; Gold and Silver in Oregon; Historical Oregon; In the Ruts; Oregon Ghost Towns; Oregon's Golden Years. See also **Lake Labish Ditch**.

Divorce. In 1995 there were 15,289 divorces in Oregon and 25,292 **marriages**. The divorce rate was 5.5 per 1,000 persons, compared with California's rate of 4.3 and Washington's rate of 5.9. **Baker** and **Crook** counties led, with a 7.2 rate, while **Multnomah County** had a rate of 3.7. Over half of the divorces involved children. Oregon became a no-fault state in 1971. The **provisional government** granted the first divorce in Oregon in July 1845. The first to a woman was on November 2, 1846. In 1854 decrees were granted to Margaret Bailey, Oregon's first novelist, and to the mother of poet-to-be Edwin Markham. Dictionary of Oregon History; Oregon Blue Book; Oregonian 1/26/97:A1; What Trouble I Have Seen. See also **Domestic disturbance; Marriage**.

DLCD. See **Land Conservation and Development Commission**.

DMV. See **Driver and Motor Vehicle Services**.

Do Jump! Extremely Physical Theater. A **Portland** theater company, founded in1977, to pioneer theater-in-motion. It performs at Echo Theater, 1515 SE 37th Avenue, 97214, as well as at schools and on tour in and out of state. 503-231-1232.

Doctor-assisted suicide. See **Physician-assisted suicide**.

Doctors. See **Physicians**.

Dog racing. See **Multnomah Greyhound Park**.

Dog wheel. In about 1890, after four years of experimentation, pioneer C. F. Harder succeeded in making a 32-foot high, dog-powered wheel to operate a butter churn on the family dairy farm near **Astoria**. The dog wheel operated for about ten years. "Reminiscence."

DOGAMI. See **Geology and Mineral Industries** (Department of).

Dogs. **Multnomah County** has an estimated 102,000 dogs. The Best of Show award at the 1995 Westminster Kennel Club show in New York City was won by a Scottish terrier bred by Camille Partridge of **Philomath**. Oregonian 1/16/96:C1; Gazette Times 4/11/96:A1. See also **Bloodhounds; Indian dogs; Multnomah Greyhound Park; Search dogs; Silverton Bobbie; Sled dogs**.

Dogs for the Deaf. A non-profit agency founded in southern Oregon in 1977 by animal trainer Roy Kabat to train dogs to assist the hearing impaired. The group placed over 600 trained dogs in its first 20 years and continues to train and place about 50 dogs a year. Placements are free, supported by contributions. 10175 Wheeler Road, Central Point, 97502. 800-990-3647. TDD 541-826-9220.

Dolores Winningstad Theatre. A 300-seat **Portland** theater in the New Theatre Building (sometimes called the Performing Arts Center) at SW Broadway and Main. It is more intimate than the **Newmark Theatre** that is located in the same building, and features a stage floor that can be raised and lowered. The theater, opened in 1987, is part of the **Portland Center for the Performing Arts**. 503-796-9293 for event information recording. Emergencies (during events only) 503-274-6566. Portland, An Informal History. See also **Children's theater**; **Tygres Heart Shakespeare Company**.

Dolphins. Small, toothed **whales** of the dolphin family. Those with beaks are usually called dolphins, those with blunt heads are called **porpoises**. Several species are infrequent visitors along the Oregon coast. The **orca** is the largest member of the family. Mammals and Life Zones of Oregon; Mammals of the Northwest. See also **Marine mammals**.

Domestic disturbance. There were 29,965 incidents of domestic distur-bance, including 8 homicides, and 18,926 arrests in Oregon in 1996. There were also 3,148 violations of domestic restraining orders. Between 1991 and July 1996, 127 Oregonians were killed by domestic violence. From July 1994 through June 1995, 2,766 women and 3,205 children were taken in by Oregon shelters. During the same period, domestic violence programs received 68,700 calls. Oregonian 12/6/95:C1; Report of Criminal Offenses; What Trouble I Have Seen.

Domestic partnerships. Committed but unmarried couples. **Portland** is among the Oregon communities that recognize domestic partnerships, allowing longtime partners of city employees to share in benefits such as health insurance. Both the **University of Oregon** and **Oregon State University** extend benefits to domestic partners. Oregonian 3/15/96:A20.

Domoic acid. See **Shellfish poisoning**.

Donald. A **Willamette Valley** farming community seven miles north of **Woodburn** in **Marion County**. It began as a station on the **Oregon Electric Railway** and was named for R. L. Donald, an official in the construction company that built the railway. The city was incorporated in 1912. Population 1980 267; 1995 465. Elevation 195'. PO Box 388, 97020. 503-678-5543. Oregon Geo-graphic Names.

Donation Land Act of 1850. A federal law, authored by Missouri senator Lewis Linn, that granted 320 acres of **public domain** land to every white male settler in the **Oregon Territory**, and the same to his wife to be held in her name, if they had been in the Oregon Territory on December 1, 1850 and occupied and worked their claim for four consecutive years. Claims of half that much were available to those who arrived during the next five years. The shortage of women led to a number of child marriages. By the time the act expired in 1855, 7,432 patents had been granted within the **Oregon Territory**, covering 2,500,000 acres, 80% of it in what became the state of Oregon, including nearly all of the flat land of the **Willamette**, **Umpqua**, and **Rogue** valleys. The land was granted without re-gard for Indian claims to it and before any Indian treaties had been ratified. Dictio-nary of Oregon History; Disposition; "Donation Land Act;" Empire of the Columbia. See also **Homestead Act of 1862**; **Indians, historic**; **Land grants**.

Donkey engine. At one time, a small steam engine of less than one horse power, but later a stationary steam, gas, diesel, or electric engine used to haul logs from the woods, and for innumerable other purposes. Several kinds have been manufactured in **Portland**. Woods Words.

Donner und Blitzen River. A river that, with its tributaries, drains the west slope of **Steens Mountain**, running north along the base of the mountain to empty into **Malheur Lake**. The name, German for thunder and lightning, was given in 1864 during the **Bannock War** when troops crossed it during a thunder storm. It is often just called the Blitzen. Oregon Geographic Names.

Donor programs. See **Oregon Donor Program**.

Dorchester Conference. An annual spring gathering of Oregon's moderate **Republicans**. For some years, the conference, founded in 1964 by Bob Packwood, was held at Dorchester House in **Lincoln City**. More recent sessions have been held in **Seaside** in early March. 503-241-4259. Oregonian 2/14/96:B5. See also **Oregon Conservative Convention**.

Dorena Reservoir. A lake formed in 1949 after the **Army Corps of Engineers** completed a flood-control dam across the Row River five miles east of **Cottage Grove**. The earth fill dam is 145 feet high. When full, the five-mile-long reservoir covers 1,840 acres and has a maximum depth of 97 feet, but it is drawn down in late summer in preparation for flood runoff. The lake is heavily used for boating and fishing. Natural mercury deposits have led to elevated mercury levels in the fish, though the levels in 1983 were below the USFDA action levels. The original townsite of Dorena (named for two women named Dora Burnette and Rena Martin) was flooded by the reservoir; the town was reestablished five miles upriver near the head of the lake. Army Engineers; Atlas of Oregon Lakes; Oregon Geographic Names.

Douglas County. A county in southwest Oregon, formed around the drainage of the **Umpqua River**, that extends from the summit of the **Cascade Range** to the ocean. Incorporated cities are **Roseburg** (county seat), **Canyonville**, **Drain**, **Elkton**, **Glendale**, **Myrtle Creek**, **Oakland**, **Reedsport**, **Riddle**, **Sutherlin**, **Winston**, and **Yoncalla**. It is bounded by **Lane**, **Klamath**, **Jackson**, **Josephine**, **Curry** and **Coos** counties and the Pacific Ocean. Elevations range from sea level on the west to 9,178' **Mount Thielsen** on the east. The economy is based on lumber, mining, agriculture, fishing, and recreation; Roseburg Lumber Company with over 3,500 employees, is the largest private employer. Taxable assessed value in 1995 was $4,202,000,000, or $43,000 per capita. The county was created in 1852 from **Umpqua County** and named for U.S. Senator Stephen A. Douglas of Illinois (1813-1861), an ardent advocate for Oregon who later, as a candidate for president, was defeated by Abraham Lincoln. Population 1980 62,142; 1995 97,700. Area 5,071 square miles. Density 19/sq.mi. Annual precipitation 33"; average temperature January 41°F, July 68°F. Courthouse, 1036 SE Douglas, Roseburg 97470. 541-672-3311. Land of the Umpqua; Oregon Blue Book; Umpqua Valley. See also **Fort Umpqua**.

Douglas-fir. An evergreen conifer **tree**, *Pseudotsuga menziesii*, that is Oregon's **state tree**. Nearly pure stands of Douglas-fir blanket the **Coast Range**, where it reaches maximum size. It also is common on the lower slopes of the **Cascade Range**, and grows in mixed stands throughout the west. It is Oregon's most economically important tree, used for **lumber**, **plywood**, **pulp**, and **Christmas trees**. The nation's tallest is the Doerner Fir (also called Brummit Fir) on **BLM** land in **Coos County**, with a height of 329 feet. It has a circumference of 438 inches and is 11.6 feet in diameter. Trees 18 feet in diameter have been reported. The "Mineral Tree" in Washington, which blew down in 1929, had a verified height of 393 feet, which is 27 feet taller than the tallest known redwood, and was over 1,000 years old. A downed Douglas-fir log may take 300 years to rot away. **Old growth** fir is sometimes called yellow fir, while younger, but mature, trees are called red fir. The scientific name, "Pseudotsuga," means false hemlock; Scotsman Archibald Menzies first reported the tree in 1791. Another Scotsman, David Douglas, was a young botanist who described the tree along with his other discoveries in the Northwest in the 1820's. Trees to Know, "Mineral Tree." See also **Big trees**.

Downwinders. Persons who lived in areas that were contaminated by releases of radioactive isotopes from **Hanford Nuclear Reservation**. The releases, which included Iodine-131 and other isotopes, began in 1944 and continued into the 1970s. The national Centers for Disease Control proposes a study of the health of those living in the exposed areas; downwinders say that they also deserve some health benefits for having been unwitting guinea pigs. The areas are in Idaho, eastern Washington, and eastern Oregon Oregonian 6/28/96:C7.

Dragon boat races. Races of colorful boats, each with 16 paddlers, that originated in China 2,400 years ago to commemorate the death of a poet who drowned despite efforts by dragon boaters to speed to his rescue. In 1988 Kaohsiung, Taiwan, one of **Portland**'s sister cities, gave Portland eight dragon boats. Now dragon boat races on the **Willamette River** are featured at the **Rose Festival**, and a Portland team competes internationally. Oregonian 5/9/96:D1.

Drain. "Pacific Gateway." A western Oregon timber town 40 miles north of **Roseburg** on **Highway 99** in **Douglas County**. It was established in 1870 as a station and townsite on the **Oregon and California Railroad**, and named for the Charles Drain family which had deeded the site. A post office was established in 1872, and the city was incorporated in 1887. In 1893 Charles Drain Jr. built an elaborate Queen-Anne style house, known as The Castle, which is used by the school district for administrative offices. Population 1980 1,148; 1995 1,110. Elevation 291'. PO Box 158, 97435. 541-836-2417. Oregonian 2/1/96:E2. See also **Milltown Hill Dam**.

Drammy Awards. Annual drama awards given by the Portland Theater Critics Circle for **Portland** productions of plays, musicals, and children's theater. Oregonian 6/18/96:C4.

Dredging. The process of removing material, especially sand and mud, from underwater. The city of **Portland** bought a dredge in 1865 and used it to remove sand bars on which boats had gone aground daily at **Swan Island** and at the mouth of the **Willamette River**. The **Army Corps of Engineers** took over in 1867 and still dredges to maintain the **Columbia River channel** and the **Willamette River channel**. Each year dredging at the mouth of the Columbia removes 5 to 6 million cubic yards of sand which is dumped offshore in the ocean. The Corps also periodically dredges harbor entrances along the coast, and completed a project in 1997 to deepen the **Coos Bay** channel by two feet. Army Engineers; Oregonian 1/3/97:D4. See also **Gold dredging**.

Drews Reservoir. A large irrigation impoundment on Drews Creek 17 miles west of **Lakeview**. It was formed in 1911. When full, the lake is eight miles long, covers 5,579 acres, and has a maximum depth of 50 feet. A day-use area and boat ramp are located on the southwest side near the dam. Lieutenant-Colonel C. S. Drew was commander of the Owyhee Reconnaissance in 1864. Atlas of Oregon Lakes.

Drewsey. See **Gouge Eye**.

Driftwood. "The world's only driftwood beaches occur on Puget Sound and the Pacific Northwest coast. Such beaches form only where an ample number of trees grow near the water... and only where the winds are onshore, pushing floating objects toward shore, where they strand." Great Northwest Nature Factbook. Some of the driftwood may also have been an artifact of hydraulic **gold mining**, which washed huge quantities of wood (and dirt) down the streams. Oregon **beaches** were piled high with silvered driftwood until the 1960s, when the state began a program of burning it off in order to reduce the hazard to beach users, who were sometimes caught under rolling logs during high waves. The amount of driftwood further declined during the 1970's when, after a sudden increase in oil prices, more Oregonians resorted to burning driftwood for heat. More driftwood appears after major flooding. In the first three months of 1998 over a dozen people were injured and three persons, two of them them children, were killed when small waves moved logs they were standing on. Oregonian 4/10/98:A1.

Drinking water. In 1994 Oregon had 3,551 water systems supplying domestic water. Responsibility for monitoring them for over 80 contaminants is divided between the state **Health Division** Drinking Water Program (888 systems, including the largest community systems), Oregon Department of **Agriculture** (180), and county health departments (2,483). The most rigorous standards are for the 886 community systems. About one third of those community systems are cities or water districts, one-third mobile home parks, and one-third subdivisions, rural associations, or investor-owned enterprises. Other water systems serve schools or factories (333); parks, campgrounds, restaurants, motels, rest areas (1,474); and small systems with 3 to 15 connections (835). In 1994 there were about 3,800 **wells** as well as 400 surface-water intakes supplying Oregon's public water systems. Although most of the systems rely on wells, Oregon's largest water systems, serving most of the state's population, rely on surface water. Four cities, **Baker City**, **Bend**, **Portland**, and **Reedsport**, have surface-water sources so pure that the water does not need to be filtered, although it is chlorinated. Oregon Drinking Water. See also **Fluoride**; **Water quality**; **Waterborne disease**.

Driver and Motor Vehicle Services (DMV). A division within the Department of **Transportation** that registers Oregon drivers and vehicles, licenses driving schools, driving instructors, car dealers, and wreckers, and oversees motor carrier services, including truck weigh stations and public transit. In 1996 Oregon had 2.8 million drivers and 3.1 million registered vehicles. Each year DMV processes 750,000 driver licenses, 1.5 million vehicle licenses, and 1 million vehicle titles. Its computer records are accessed over 40,000 times daily by police, insurance companies, and others. DMV has over 60 local offices, including DMV Express offices that are open evenings and Saturdays at major shopping malls. 1905 Lana Ave. NE, Salem 97314. 503-945-5000. Oregon Blue Book.

Drive-in theaters. In 1958 Oregon had 69 outdoor cinemas, but by September 1998 the number had shrunk to seven, located in **Dallas, Hermiston, Hood River, La Grande, Lebanon, Newberg,** and **Woodburn**. Theaters in **Roseburg** and **Portland** closed in 1997. Oregonian 7/13/97:L1.

Dropouts. In 1994-95 7.4% of all Oregon students in grades 9 to 12 dropped out of school, up from 5.7% two years before. The rates were 17.9% (compared to 10% nationally) for Hispanic students, 11.6% (6.6% nationally) for African-Americans, 11.1% for Native-American students, 6.7% (4.2% nationally) for whites, and 5.6% for Asian Americans. Both the highest and lowest dropout rates came from small school districts. In 1996-97 the rate was 7.5%, though figured under a new definition that no longer included students who go on to get their equivalency (GED) diploma, it was 6.7%. Dropout Rates; Oregonian 3/19/96:B3, 10/3/96: E11, 2/9/97:A1, 2/25/98:E1.

Drought. Oregon's longest period of prolonged statewide drought lasted from 1928 through 1941. It resulted in several major **forest fires**, including the **Tillamook Burn** and the **Bandon fire**, and **Malheur Lake** dried up. In 1939 **Condon**, which normally has 12" of rain, recorded 1.5". **Lake Abert** dried up in 1924, and **Goose Lake** in 1926. Eastern Oregon also went through a period of drought around 1890 and from 1959-64, and western Oregon from 1976-81, with 1976/77 generally the driest year known in the state. Another statewide drought occurred from 1987-1994; **Medford** received 8.87" of rain during the 1993/94 crop year, less than half of its average 19". National Water Summary. See also **Dust storms**.

Drownings. The Oregon Department of **Health** reports that an average of 58 persons a year died in accidental drownings from 1985 through 1994 in the state.

Drug abuse. Nearly 10% of Oregon eighth-graders reported using **marijuana** during the previous month, according to a 1994 study, and 11% used inhalants, while less than 1% used hard drugs. Use of cocaine by 11th graders dropped from 9% in 1986 to 1.1% in 1994. However, a 1996 survey found that illicit drug use among eighth-graders grew from 17.8% in 1992 to 33.9% in 1996. Illicit drug use by 11th-graders increased from 29.2% in 1992 to 39.9% in 1996. Oregonian 1/13/95:A1, 10/22/96:B1. See also **Alcohol; Alcohol and Drug Abuse Programs; Smoking**.

Drug Abuse Reduction through Education (D.A.R.E.). See **Police, Oregon State**.

Drug-related deaths. The number of drug-related deaths in Oregon increased from 39 in 1991 to 205 in 1996. Of the 205 deaths, 155 involved heroin, 57 cocaine, and 31 **methamphetamine**. Some of the deaths involved combinations of drugs. Oregonian 1/12/97:A8.

Dry docks. See **Swan Island**.

Dry River Gorge. A canyon along **Highway 20** about 20 miles east of **Bend**

that once drained a **Pleistocene** lake. An informal trail follows some of the gorge.

Dude ranches. See **Resort ranches**.

Dufur (DEW fur). An agricultural community in north-central Oregon's **Wasco County**, 15 miles south of **The Dalles** on **Highway 197**. The post office was established in 1878 and named for Andrew and Burnham Dufur who owned the land. The city was incorporated in 1893. Attractions include a 10-acre city park with public pool, and the annual Threshing Bee on the 2nd full weekend of August. Population 1980 560; 1995 600. Elevation 1,350' PO Box 145, 97021. 541-467-2349. Oregon Geographic Names. See also **Apples**.

Dumps. See **Landfills**.

Dundee. "Heart of the Wine Country." A **Willamette Valley** town on **Highway 99W** two miles southwest of **Newberg** in **Yamhill County**. Originally a railroad town, it grew at the junction of two narrow-gauge rail lines. The first post office in 1881 was named Ekins, but the next year was changed to Dundee by William Reid of the Oregonian Railway Company to honor the headquarters city of his Scottish investors. Dundee was incorporated in 1895. **Grapes** and **hazelnuts** are displacing prunes and walnuts as the major crops in the area. Population 1980 1,223; 1995 2,300. Elevation 189'. PO Box 220, 97115. 503-538-3922. Old Yamhill.

Dune Mushers Mail Run. An annual two-day event in early March during which **sled dog** teams carry mail 72 miles from **North Bend** to **Florence**. The sleds are on wheels instead of runners, but otherwise are the same. 541-269-1269.

Dunes. Oregon has sand dunes both along the **coast** and in the **desert**. Desert dunes are located near many of the shallow lakes and dry lake beds of eastern Oregon, most notably near **Christmas Valley** and north of **Lake Abert**. Coastal dunes up to 180' high lie between **Highway 101** and the ocean in a strip extending from **Heceta Head** 56 miles south to **Cape Arago**. This area, much of it included in the **Oregon Dunes National Recreation Area**, is the largest complex of coastal dunes in the U.S. Dune buggies are allowed in some of the area; an average of three fatalities a year from vehicle accidents have been reported in the dunes near **Reedsport**. Dunes are also found at several other spots north along the coast, especially at **Pacific City** where they, too, are much used by dune buggies. Several freshwater **lakes** are found in the dunes, sometimes with **quicksand** along the edges. The ecology and character of the coastal dunes has been changed by European beach grass, *Ammophila arenaria*, first planted about 1910 to stabilize encroaching dunes. See also **Beaches**.

Dunes City. A western Oregon recreation community on **Highway 101** five miles south of **Florence** in **Lane County**. It was incorporated in 1963 because local residents wished to avoid being included in a proposed Dunes National Park. The area is served by Westlake post office. Local attractions include **Siltcoos** and **Woahink Lakes** and the **Oregon Dunes National Recreation Area**. Population 1980 1,124; 1995 1,220. Elevation 44'. PO Box 97, Westlake 97493. 541-997-3338. Oregon Geographic Names.

Durham. A Portland-area suburban community on **Interstate 5** between **Tigard** and **Tualatin** in **Washington County**. It was originally called Durham Mills for the lumber and flour mills that Albert Alonzo Durham operated on Fanno

Creek. The **Oregon Electric Railway** later built a railroad station at the site that they called Durham. The city was incorporated in 1966. Population 1980 707; 1995 1,510. Elevation 197'. PO Box 23483, 97281. 503-639-6851. Oregon Geographic Names.

Dust storms. In March of 1906, drifts from a dust and sand storm stalled six passenger trains between Wallula, Washington and **The Dalles**. The dust storm also tangled with a blizzard and resulted in 8" of brown snow over most of Oregon's interior plateau. On April 21-22, 1931, during an especially dry spring, a high pressure area over Montana and a low pressure area over California led to fierce east winds that whipped up an enormous dust storm east of the **Cascade Range**. It blasted across western Oregon and Washington with winds of 50 miles an hour and more, darkening the sky, ripping up standing timber, taking out power and phone lines, and stalling vehicles and planes. Wind, falling trees, and fires damaged or destroyed hundreds of houses, barns, and summer homes, injured a number of persons, and killed five. Humidity dropped to record lows (16% at 5 a.m. in **Portland** and 8% at 5 p.m.), further fanning dozens of forest fires. Ships reported dust from the storm 600 miles from shore. The storm also dropped seeds from eastern Oregon plants, including **Ponderosa pine** and thistles, in new sites west of the mountains. Oregonian 4/22,23,24/31:1, 3/25/56:26, 10/31/97:D5. See also **Wind**.

Eagle Cap Wilderness. A 360,000 acre wilderness area in the **Wallowa Mountains** of northeast Oregon. It includes eight peaks over 9,000 feet high, as well as the Minam and Imnaha Wild and Scenic Rivers. The high country is noted for its summer wildflowers, including buttercups, delphiniums, clematis, and pentstemons. Wallowa-Whitman National Forest, PO Box 907, Baker 97814. 541-523-6391.

Eagle Creek. A waterfall-rich creek that drains the lower north slope of **Mount Hood**, joining the **Columbia River** east of **Bonneville Dam**. Over a dozen waterfalls on Eagle Creek and its tributaries are accessible from the six-mile Eagle Creek Trail which begins at Eagle Creek Park, exit 41 from **Interstate 84**. Waterfall Lover's Guide.

Eagle Point. A historic southwest Oregon town in **Jackson County** 10 miles north of **Medford** on **Highway 62**. The area was first settled in 1852 and the farm community grew soon after. The name was given to the first post office about 1872; it came from a prominent cliff just east of town on which eagles nested. The city was incorporated in 1911. The town boomed during **World War II** from the influx of soldiers from nearby **Camp White**. The Veterans Administration's Eagle Point National Cemetery is nearby. Attractions include a museum and Butte Creek Mill, the only water-powered, stone-ground **grist mill** operating in Oregon. Population 1980 2,764; 1995 3,415. Elevation 1,310'. PO Box 779, 97524. 541-826-4212. Journey Back; Land in Common.

Eagles. Large, powerful, hunting birds. Two species are found in Oregon, the bald eagle, *Haliaeetus leucocephalus*, and the golden eagle, *Aquila chrysaetos*. The bald eagle is found near water, especially along the **coast** and the **Columbia River**. Over a thousand winter in the **Klamath Basin** and dozens winter at **Lake Billy Chinook** where an Eagle Watch is staged in late February at **Cove Palisades State Park**. About 250 pairs nest in Oregon, on cliffs or large trees, using, and adding to, the same nest for up to 40 years so that the nest may eventually weigh over 2,000 pounds. The bald eagle is primarily a scavenger, but sometimes catches fish and birds. It is listed as a threatened species. The golden eagle is found in southern and eastern Oregon where it often nests on rimrock; **jackrabbits** are its main food. Oregon Eagle Foundation, PO Box 1616, Klamath Falls 97601. Atlas of Oregon Wildlife; Birds of Oregon. See also **Endangered species**.

Earle A. Chiles Award. A $10,000 cash award given annually since 1983 to a person who has made significant contributions to the management of natural resources in the **high desert** region. It is funded by the Chiles Foundation of Portland and presented by the **High Desert Museum**. Chiles was an executive at Fred Meyer, Inc.

Earliest people. See **Indians, prehistoric**.

Earnings. See **Wages**.

Earth slides. See **Landslides**.

Earthquake hazard maps. Maps depicting earthquake hazard zones of Oregon show that the south coast area around **Brookings** has the largest potential risk from severe ground shaking while the eastern Oregon area around **Burns** is least at risk. Maps for the seismically active **Portland** metropolitan area and for **Salem** focus on more specific quake hazards based on soil conditions. The maps can be purchased at the **Nature of the Northwest** store in **Portland** and from the Oregon Department of **Geology and Mineral Industries** offices in **Baker City** and **Grants Pass**. Oregonian 11/14/96:A26.

Earthquakes. Research indicates that the **Cascadia subduction zone** off Oregon locks for several hundred years at a time and then releases suddenly, dropping the coastal region 2 to 8 feet; these catastrophic earthquakes also trigger **tsunamis** and **landslides**. At 23 places along Oregon beaches, buried tree stumps, some 4,000 years old, remain as evidence of forests that were drowned when the coastline dropped. Scientists estimate that these earthquakes have occurred at intervals ranging from 200 to 1,000 years. The most recent is thought to have been a Richter magnitude 9.0 event, probably on January 26, 1700, that generated thirty-foot **tsunamis** along the Northwest coast and six-foot waves in Japan. Coastal Indians still spoke of it when whites first came. Forty quakes with a magnitude of four or greater have been recorded in the state since 1841, seventeen of them in the Portland area. The largest was the 6.7 Crescent City quake, November 23, 1873, felt from Portland to San Francisco. Other significant quakes were at **Umatilla** on March 5, 1893, **Milton-Freewater** (magnitude 6.1) on July 16, 1936, **Portland** (5.5) on November 6, 1962, a two-month swarm of quakes (to 5.1) at Adel in the **Warner Lakes** area May-July 1968, **Maupin** (4.8) on April 13, 1976, the **Scotts Mills earthquake** (5.6) on March 25, 1993, that caused $28 million damage, and the **Klamath Falls earthquakes** (5.9, 6.0, 5.1) on September 21 and December 4, 1993 (two deaths and $7.5 million damage). The Pacific Northwest Seismograph Network in Seattle operates 130 seismic-monitoring stations and, for any quake with a magnitude greater than 2.9, automatically sends notices to emergency-management agencies throughout the Northwest. Geology of Oregon; "Field trip guide"; "Look Back"; Oregonian 11/9/94:C2, 8/27/97:A20, 3/7/98:A1. See also **Blue Mountain Observatory**; **Seismic Safety Policy Advisory Commission**; **Uplift**.

East Lake. See **Paulina Lake**.

East wind. See **Wind**.

Easter Seal Society of Oregon. See **Polio**.

Eastern Oregon. A term often used for the arid two-thirds of Oregon east of the **Cascade Range**. The area encompasses some 64,000 square miles, larger than the state of Illinois. The fossil record shows that the climate was wet and tropical until the Western **Cascade Range** rose high enough 15 million years ago to cut off moisture from the west. Both the Indians of the area and later white settlers were noted for their hardiness and for being less occupied with accumulating wealth than were those from the easier-living regions west of the mountains. East of the Cascades. See also **Geography**; **Gold rush, eastern Oregon**.

Eastern Oregon Training and Psychiatric Centers. A state facility that serves developmentally disabled adults and mentally ill adults from central and eastern Oregon counties. It is operated by the Oregon **Mental Health and Developmental Disability Services Division**. 2525 Westgate, Pendleton 97801. 541-276-0991. Oregon Blue Book.

Eastern Oregon University. A state regional university in **La Grande**, founded in 1929. Enrollment in fall 1994 was 1,931. The school, the only four-year college in eastern Oregon, serves ten eastern Oregon counties from its La Grande campus as well as from nine other centers and via **ED-NET**. It offers 21 bachelor degree programs and a master's degree in teacher education. It also offers cooperative degrees with **Oregon Health Sciences University** in nursing and **Oregon State University** in agriculture. 1410 "L" Avenue, La Grande OR 97850-2899. 541-962-3512; 800-452-8639. See also **University System, Oregon**.

Eastern Oregon Visitors Association. 800-332-1843.

Ecclesia Athletic Association. A group formed in the Watts area of Los Angeles in 1975 by basketball player and Pentecostal minister Eldridge Broussard, Jr. It was to lead black children away from violence and drugs through a blend of Christianity, discipline, and athletic excellence. In 1987 Broussard and 100 of the others moved to a **Sandy** farmhouse to get away from the crime and violence of Los Angeles. On October 13, 1988, in Broussard's absence, four of the group's adults beat his eight-year-old daughter to death in front of the other children. Broussard himself died in 1991. Oregonian 10/20/96:B1.

Echo. "An Oregon Trail City." A north-central Oregon agricultural, tourist, and residential community that grew up where the **Oregon Trail** crossed the Umatilla River. It is located near **Interstate 84**, 8 miles southeast of **Hermiston** and 20 miles northwest of **Pendleton** in **Umatilla County**. About 1880 the community, which once had been known as Meadows and later as Brasfield Ferry, was named for three-year old Echo Koontz whose father platted the town. The city was incorporated in 1904. Attractions include a reproduction of **Fort Henrietta**, walking tours past historic buildings (brochure available), views of the Oregon Trail, a historical museum, a railroad museum, and Fort Henrietta Days and Rendezvous, held in September on the weekend after Labor Day. Population 1980 624; 1995 530. Elevation 638'. PO Box 9, 97826. 541-376-8411. Oregon Geographic Names; Oregonian 8/24/97:C4.

Eclipse. See **Solar eclipse**.

Economic Analysis Office. A state agency in the Department of **Administrative Services** that monitors the state's economy. It includes the state **economist** as well as the state demographer who tracks **population** changes. 155 Cottage Street NE, Salem 97310. 503-378-3106. Oregon Blue Book.

Economic Development, Oregon Department of. The mission of the Department of Economic Development is to create more and better jobs for Oregonians in the state's 12 economic regions and 13 key **industries**. A commission of five members, appointed by the governor, guides policy and issues industrial development revenue bonds. About a fourth of the funding for economic development projects comes from the lottery, a fourth from federal funds, and the rest from bond proceeds and repayments from revolving loans. The department includes the **Progress Board**, **Industry Development** Division, **Regional Development** Division, and **Tourism Council**. Regional offices are located in **Baker City**, **Bend**, **Coos Bay**, **Corvallis**, **La Grande**, **Lakeview**, **Medford**, **Oregon City**, **Portland**, **The Dalles**, and **Tillamook**. The state office at is 775 Summer Street NE, Salem 97310, 503-986-0123. Getting it Right; Oregon Blue Book.

Economist. Oregon has a state economist in the Office of **Economic Analysis** whose primary responsibility is compiling the quarterly Oregon Economic and Revenue Forecast. 155 Cottage Street NE, Salem 97310. 503-378-3106. Oregon Blue Book.

Economy. Oregon had one of the nation's most diversified and fastest growing economies in 1996, led by **high-tech industry** and the service sector, though growth was expected to slow somewhat due to a tighter labor supply and higher housing costs. **Manufacturing** provided 21% of the total payroll in the state. In 1939, 60% of the state's economy was based on the **forest products industry**, but by 1991 it accounted for less than 10%. **Tourism** ($4.5 billion in 1996) and **agriculture** ($3.4 billion in farm and ranch sales) are other important components of the state's economy. Oregon is near the bottom in federal defense spending; while Washington received $1,064 per capita in 1993, Oregon received $193. Governing Oregon; Oregon Blue Book.

Ecosystems. See **Oregon Biodiversity Project**.

Ecotopia. The title of a 1975 utopian novel by Ernest Callenbach that portrayed an independent, ecologically based nation in the Pacific Northwest. The name is still sometimes used for the region. Some have claimed that the motto for Ecotopia should be "Leave. Me. Alone."

Ecumenical Ministries of Oregon (EMO). An association of 16 Christian denominations that, in 1997, operated 17 social-service programs. Though it was formed in 1973 by the merger of the Greater Portland and Oregon Councils of Churches, its roots can be traced back to the Home Mission Council, established in 1917. 0245 SW Bancroft Ct., Portland, 97201. 503-221-1054. Oregonian 8/30/97:C5.

ED-NET. A statewide interactive telecommunications network created in 1989 to enhance economic development by providing improved access to education, training, and information throughout the state. The ED-NET office also operates COMPASS, a statewide online computer conference and information dial-up network, which serves education, business, government, and non-profit agencies.

7140 SW Macadam Avenue, Portland 97219. 503-293-1992. Oregon Blue Book. See also **NERO Project**.

Edgefield. The former **Multnomah County** Poor Farm, now the site of a McMenamins brewery and winery. Built in 1911, the poor farm was phased out in the 1950s and turned into a nursing home. McMenamins purchased it in 1990 and have developed gardens, a pub, restaurant, theater, and rooms. Free tours are available. 2126 S.W. Halsey, Troutdale 97060. 503-669-8610.

Education. In 1990, 18% of Oregonians aged 25 and older had less than a high school education, 29% had a high school degree, 32% had some college, and 21% had four or more years of college. **Wheeler County** had the least educated population and **Benton County** the most educated, with over 41% of its population having a college degree. Oregon: A Statistical Overview. See also **Community colleges**; **Education** entries; **Higher education** entries; **Home schooling**; **School** entries; **Schools, private**; **Schools, public**; **Science education**; **Student** entries; **Teacher** entries.

Education Act for the 21st Century. A comprehensive reform of the state's public education adopted by the 1991 legislature when it passed House Bill 3565. The bill's number called attention to the fact that only 35% of Oregon's high school graduates go on to a four-year college or university, leaving 65% who need something other than the traditional college prep education. The goals of the act are to produce the best-educated citizens in the nation by the year 2000 and a work force equal to any in the world by 2010. The program involves raising academic standards, increasing parental involvement, giving schools more freedom from state regulation, encouraging school partnerships with business and communities, and increasing learning readiness of preschool children. Control is being shifted to local schools through site councils that include both parents and teachers. Students must demonstrate an array of proficiencies in order to get a Certificate of Initial Mastery (CIM), usually about the 10th grade, and a Certificate of Advanced Mastery (CAM), usually two years later. Oregon Blue Book. See also **School year**.

Education, Oregon Department of. A department headed by the **Superintendent of Public Instruction** that serves some 550,000 K-12 students through 21 **education service districts** and 250 elementary and secondary school districts. It also operates the Oregon School for the **Blind**, the Oregon School for the **Deaf**, and education programs in state **juvenile corrections** facilities. Policy is set by the State Board of Education. 255 Capitol St. NE, Salem 97310-0203. 503-378-3573. Oregon Blue Book. See also **Education, State Board of**.

Education Reform Act. See **Education Act for the 21st Century**.

Education Service Districts (ESDs). Districts authorized by state law to serve as links between the Oregon Department of **Education** and local school districts and to provide support services, such as **special education**, purchasing, instructional media, and graphics, to local school districts. As of 1997, all local school districts were served by the state's 21 ESDs, each governed by a locally-elected board. ESDs are financed by **property tax** levies plus payments for contracted services, and account for about 5% of statewide school costs. Oregon Blue Book.

Education, State Board of. The State Board of Education is a seven-member unsalaried board established by the legislature in 1951 to set over-all educational policies and standards for Oregon's 250 public school districts, 17 **community college** districts, and 21 **education service districts**. The governor appoints the board members to four-year terms. Board policies are implemented by the Oregon Department of **Education**. 255 Capitol St. NE, Salem 97310-0203. 503-378-3573. Oregon Blue Book. See also **Education, Oregon Department of**; **Superintendent of Public Instruction**; **University System, Oregon**.

Eels. See **Lamprey**.

Egg. A 40-million-year-old **fossil** egg, possibly that of a pelican, was found in 1995 near **Vernonia** in northwest Oregon. It was the first fossil egg found in the state. Oregonian 4/19/97:C1.

Eggs. In 1994 Oregon's 2.6 million hens laid an average of 268 eggs per chicken for a total of 708 million eggs, worth $46.2 million. 1994-1995 Oregon Agriculture. See also **Chickens**.

Eight Dollar Mountain. A prominent conical peak, elevation 3,992', north of **Cave Junction** in the Illinois Valley. It is known for its spring wildflowers, including lilies, gentians, violets, cats' ears, phlox, and Indian paintbrush. The mountain was the site of a battle fought on March 25, 1856 during the **Rogue River War**. The origin of the name is uncertain; one story has it that a man wore out a pair of $8 shoes walking around its rough base. Oregon Geographic Names; Oregonian 4/5/95:E2.

El Niño event. A periodic warming of the **Pacific Ocean** off Peru and Ecuador that is linked to worldwide weather changes, usually including drought in Oregon. There is also ocean warming along the Oregon coast with less upwelling of cold water, thus reducing nutrients for **salmon** and other ocean fish. The winter of 1976-77 began a cycle dominated by El Niños. They normally occur every two to seven years but there were three between 1991 and 1995. The strongest El Niño in 130 years occurred in 1982-83, and another of similar strength began in 1997. Oregonian 5/15/97:A1, 7/4/97:D4.

Eldorado Ditch. See **Ditches**.

Elected officials, executive branch. Oregon's **constitution** provides for the election of four full-time elected administrative officials, **Governor**, **Secretary of State**, **Treasurer**, and **Superintendent of Public Instruction**. The legislature later added two others, **Attorney General** and **Commissioner of Labor and Industries**. The Secretary of State, Treasurer, and Attorney General are elected in November of years divisible by four (1996, 2000, 2004,...), and the Governor, Superintendent of Public Instruction, and Commissioner of Labor and Industries are elected in November of the alternate even numbered years (1998, 2002, 2006,...). Oregon voters also elect a number of local officials. Election requirements for city and county officials are established by local **charter**. The Oregon Blue Book lists present and past elected state executives. See also **Campaign finance**; **Candidates**; **Pompous Twit awards**; **Public Officials Compensation Commission**; **Recall**; **Succession**.

Elected officials, judicial. All **judges** in Oregon's state **judicial system** are elected for six-year terms on nonpartisan ballots, though 80% have first been appointed by the governor to fill a vacancy. They must then run for election within two years. There are no **term limits**. State judges include the seven **Supreme Court** judges, ten **Court of Appeals** judges, and the single **Tax Court** judge, who are all elected on statewide ballots. Each of the 160 state **circuit court** judges is elected by voters in the court district. State **district court** judges were elected by county. Voters in some counties elect members of the **county court** and/or a **justice of the peace** or **municipal judge**. Oregon Blue Book. See also **Courts, state; Judicial Fitness and Disability; Public Officials Compensation Commission.**

Elected officials, legislative. Oregon has 30 state **senators** and 60 state **representatives**. They now run from single-seat districts so that each voter votes for just one state senator and one state representative. Required qualifications are stated in the state **constitution**. Qualifications for city council members and county commissioners are governed by city or county **charter**, while state law governs the election of **special district** board members. The Oregon Blue Book gives information and pictures for current members of the legislature. See also **Campaign finance; Candidates; Pompous Twit awards; Recall.**

Elections. Elections in Oregon may be held on the second Tuesday in March, the third Tuesday in May, the third Tuesday in September, and the first Tuesday after the first Monday in November. In even numbered years the March election is the **presidential primary**, the May election is the **primary election**, and the November election is the **general election**. The general election usually includes the greatest number of ballot measures. A special election may be called in case of emergency. Voters must be registered as of the 21st day before an election. Mailed ballots must reach the county clerk by the end of election day. Oregon Blue Book. See also **Australian ballot; Ballot measures; Project Vote Smart; Third party candidates; Vote by mail; Voter registration; Voters' Pamphlet.**

Elections Division. A division under the **Secretary of State** responsible for application of election laws, including **campaign finance** regulations. It publishes a series of manuals to assist candidates for state and local office and for those promoting ballot measures. It also publishes the **Voters' Pamphlet** for **primary** and **general elections**. Oregon Blue Book. 141 State Capitol, Salem 97310. 503-986-1518.

Electoral votes. Oregon has 7 electoral votes for president because the state has five **U.S. representatives** and two **U.S. senators**.

Electric cooperatives. Nineteen electric cooperatives serve about 10% of Oregon's population distributed sparsely over 65% of the state's area. Some co-ops have fewer than 3 customers per mile of line, compared with over 200 per mile in urban areas. The co-ops range in size from Clearwater Power with 1994 revenues of $133,000 up to Oregon Trail Electric with revenues of $35 million. Oregon Utility Statistics; Oregonian 4/20/97:G1. See also **Public Power Council.**

Electric power. Oregon traditionally has depended on **hydroelectric power** generated at **dams** for its electricity. However, as public opposition to additional dams has increased, thermal plants using **coal** or **natural gas** are being built, often with a cogenerating component that uses the waste heat for industrial processes. In 1994 coal provided 10% of the energy input for electricity generated in the state, natural gas 6%, and hydropower 80%. Another 4% was imported from other states. The annual fuel requirements for a 1,000-**megawatt** power plant are 2.3 million tons of coal; or 10 million barrels of oil; or 64 billion cubic feet of natural gas; or 25,000 acres of solar cells; or 33 tons of uranium. Coal is probably the cheapest, but a 1,000-megawatt coal plant creates 15 tons of carbon dioxide per minute, a ton of sulfur dioxide every five minutes, and a stream of nitrogen oxides equivalent to the exhaust of 200,000 cars. Transmission losses plus the energy lost in converting fuels to electricity total about twice as much as the energy contained in the electricity produced. Oregonian 3/14/97:B2; State Energy. See also **Comprehensive Review of the Northwest Energy System**; **Geothermal energy**; **Northwest Power Planning Council**; **Nuclear power**; **Ogden Martin**; **Public power**; **Renewable energy**.

Electric power plants. At the beginning of 1996 electric utilities and companies in Oregon operated electric generating plants having a total nameplate capacity of 9,814.4 **megawatts**. The largest were the four hydroelectric projects on the **Columbia River**, **Bonneville Dam** (1,093 MW), **The Dalles Dam** (1,819.7 MW), **John Day Dam** (2,160 megawatts), and **McNary Dam** (990.5 MW). Other major power plants include **Brownlee Dam** on the Snake (585.4 MW), **Beaver** near Rainier (natural gas, 583.2 MW), **Boardman** (coal, 560.5 MW), **Hells Canyon Dam** on the Snake (391.5 MW), **Coyote Springs** at Boardman (natural gas, 346 MW), **Round Butte Dam** on the Deschutes (247.2 MW), **Oxbow Dam** on the Snake (190 MW), **Lookout Point Dam** on the Middle Fork of the Willamette (135 MW), **Detroit Dam** on the North Santiam (118 MW), **Pelton Dam** on the Deschutes (116.1 MW), and **Bethel** at Salem (natural gas, 113.4 MW). There are a number of smaller plants, most of them hydroelectric, though at least two burn **methane** from **landfills**, and the **Ogden Martin** facility burns garbage. A 1996 competition sponsored by the state **Energy Facility Siting Council** for the best emission-cutting proposal led to approval of a natural-gas powered plant at **Klamath Falls**, and a reduced-emission gas-fired plant has been approved at **Hermiston**. Inventory; Oregonian 4/10/98:D4.

Electric railways. Oregon's first electric interurban line was operating in **Portland** in 1889, and the line to **Oregon City** opened in 1893. **Southern Pacific** operated an electric rail route from Portland to **Eugene** from 1912 to 1929. The last passenger run on the electrics was made in 1949. Atlas of Oregon; "History of Transportation in the Pacific Northwest;" Red Electrics. See also **Light rail**; **Oregon Electric Railway**; **Portland Traction Company**; **Red Electrics**; **Streetcars**.

Electric utilities. In 1994 electricity was supplied to users in Oregon through six **people's utility districts** (8.4% of KWh sales), 19 **electric cooperatives** (9.6%), 11 **municipal electric systems** (6%), and three investor-owned utilities: **Pacific Power and Light** (32.8%), **Portland General Electric** (42%), and **Idaho Power Company** (1.3%). A total of 1.4 million customers bought 40 million **megawatt-hours** of electricity. Average revenues in Oregon per KWh were between 4 and 6 cents compared to a national average of over 8 cents. Oregon revenues for the investor-owned utilities totaled $1.8 billion. Oregon Utility Statistics. See also **Citizens' Utility Board**; **Comprehensive Review of the Northwest Energy System**; **Public Utility Commission**.

Electrical Parade. A **Portland** parade of the 1920s. It was a nighttime parade in which open streetcars were strung with lights, producing a fairyland effect. "How It Was Then."

Electricity consumption. In 1994, 1.4 million Oregon customers bought a total of 40 million **megawatt**-hours of electricity. Some years the state consumes more than it produces. The private **electric utilities** reported that residential, commercial, and industrial users each accounted for roughly a fourth of their sales, 7% was lost in transmission, and the rest was sold for resale. The average residential customer, 1990-1994, used 12.3 megawatt-hours annually (one MWh per month), though averages ranged from a low of 10.7 MWh for **Ashland** to 16.8 MWh for Lane Electric Cooperative. The national average was under 10 MWh. In the 20 years from 1977 to 1997, utility and state electricity conservation programs curtailed energy use in the state by 5 million MWh each year, but, since 1994, utilities have cut investment in conservation programs by nearly half. Oregon Utility Statistics; Oregonian 5/11/97:A1; State Energy.

Electricity cost. In 1995 the average residential rate in the Northwest was 5.4¢/kWh ($54/month) compared to 8.4¢ nationwide. Fast Facts.

Electrification history. Electric lights came to Oregon for the first time on a ship docked in **Portland** in 1880. After wires were strung from the ship to shore, thousands flocked to see the lights suspended over First Street. In 1889 electric power was generated at **Willamette Falls** (where there are still generators) and carried to Portland in the first commercial long-distance transmission in the U.S. In 1915 six intersections on Third Street were crisscrossed with high decorative arches lined with closely-set light bulbs. **Bend** received electricity in 1910 and most urban areas were electrified by the 1920s, but it was not until 1954, 18 years after the national Rural Electrification Act, that 97% of the state had power. Electrifying Eden; East of the Cascades; "How It Was Then;" Oregonian 4/20/97:G1. See also **Electrical Parade**; **Fremont Power House**.

Electrologists, Permanent Color Technicians and Tattoo Artists, Advisory Council for. A council of five members appointed by the governor for two-year terms to advise the **Health Division** on licensing and regulating the practices of electrologists, permanent color technicians and tattoo artists. About 180 electrologists have been licensed under the program established in 1987, and over 80 tattoo artists have been licensed since the law was extended to them in 1993. 700 Summer Street NE, Suite 100, Salem 97310-1351. 503-378-8667. Oregon Blue Book.

Electronics. See **Semi-conductor industry**.

Elephant seal. A large **marine mammal** with an inflatable proboscis, *Mirounga angustifostris*, of the Pacific coast of North America. Once near extinction, the seals have established several breeding colonies on the California coast, and have tried since 1993 to raise young on Shell Island off **Cape Arago**. However, the pups have been washed to sea from the small beach before they were old enough (8 weeks) to survive in the ocean. Mail Tribune 2/6/97:4A.

Elephants. Asian elephants, *Elephas maximus*, (distinguished from African elephants by, among other things, their smaller ears) are featured at the **Metro Washington Park Zoo** where twenty-seven have been born in the nation's most successful breeding program. The first was the wildly-celebrated Packy, born to

Belle on April 14, 1962, after a 635-day gestation. Oregonian 4/10/97:A1,B1. See also **Pink elephant**.

Elevation. Oregon's lowest elevation is sea level, and its highest point is the summit of **Mount Hood** at 11,240'. The elevations used in this work are taken from the official 1995 Oregon road map, prepared in cooperation with the Department of Geography, University of Oregon, which, in turn, used the most recent figures available. Incidentally, the distance, in miles, to a sea level horizon that can be seen from a given height is calculated by adding 50% to the viewer's elevation (in feet), then taking the square root. Thus a person whose eyes are 6 feet above the level of the ocean beach can see three miles to sea; a person on **Marys Peak**, elevation 4,097', can see 78 miles to the west (26 miles of land and 52 miles of ocean); and a person looking west from the summit of Mount Hood can see about 130 miles.

Elgin. An incorporated city 20 miles north of **La Grande** in **Union County**. It had been known variously as Lochow Lochow, Indian Valley, and Fish Trap Ford before a popular song about the wreck of the steamboat *Lady Elgin* inspired the name for the post office, established in 1885. After the **Oregon Railway and Navigation Co**. rail line arrived in 1890, the city thrived for some time as the shipping point for goods from the north and east; it was incorporated the next year. Lumber mills later sustained the economy. In 1893 and 1896 major fires destroyed businesses along Main Street. The 1912 Elgin Opera House has been renovated to serve as both movie theater and auditorium. Population 1980 1,701; 1995 1,680. Elevation 2,670'. PO Box 128, 97827. 541-437-2253. History of Union County.

Elk. A large (up to 1,000 pounds), antlered animal, *Cervus elaphus*, sometimes called wapiti, that is found in forests through much of the west. The elk found in northeast Oregon were nearly eliminated by hunting, so elk from a Wyoming subspecies called Rocky Mountain elk were introduced in 1911. Elk in the **Coast Range** are of the Roosevelt elk subspecies, as are those of the **Cascade Range** - though they may be a mix. Elk were heavily hunted and populations decreased to a few small herds despite a hunting closure between 1900 and 1932, but numbers have since rebounded, and they are now a major game animal, hunted in late fall. Over 100,000 hunters bring in some 16,000 elk a year. **Indians** on the south Oregon coast captured elk in covered pits 10 or 12 feet deep. Elk may be viewed in the winter near Jewell 10.5 miles north of **Highway 26** in **Clatsop County**, at the Dean Creek Elk Viewing area 3.5 miles east of **Reedsport** on **Highway 38**, and at Long Ranch on **Highway 20** about 24 miles east of **Sweet Home** across from Trout Creek Campground. A herd of over 600 elk is studied at **Starkey Experimental Forest**. Atlas of Oregon Wildlife; Big Game History; Mammals and Life Zones of Oregon; Oregon Hunting Guide.

Elk Creek Dam. A partially-constructed, abandoned dam on a tributary of the **Rogue River** 27 miles north of **Medford**. It was planned as one of the **Army Corps of Engineers'** three dams in the **Rogue Basin Project**. In 1987 a court injunction stopped construction of the dam pending a new environmental impact study, but in 1995 the Corps announced that a new study was not feasible. It was estimated that completing the dam, on which $100 million had been spent, would cost $72 million, while removing it would cost $10 million. The Corps has no plans to remove it, though annual **coho** salmon counts on Elk Creek dropped from 200 to 40 since the dam went in. The proposed **Milltown Hill Dam** in **Douglas County** is also sometimes called Elk Creek Dam. Oregonian 11/7/95:C3.

Elk Creek Falls. A waterfall estimated to be over 80 feet high that is accessible from a short trail 30 miles south of **Myrtle Point** (5 miles south of **Powers**). Another 12 miles south a half-mile trail leads to 40-foot-high Coquille River Falls. Waterfall Lover's Guide.

Elk Lake. A natural lake on the **Cascade Lakes Highway** 25 miles southwest of **Bend** that was formed when **lava** flows blocked several small streams. The lake is a mile and a half long, covers 405 acres, and has a maximum depth of 62'. Most of the water flow, both into and out of the lake, is via seepage, but the lake is still considered to be the headwaters of the **Deschutes River** with the seepage moving south to Lava Lake. Sailing, swimming, and fishing are popular; there are campgrounds and a resort at the lake. Atlas of Oregon Lakes.

Elk Rock. A 13-acre **Portland** garden designed by the famed Olmsted brothers that surrounded the 1916 manor house of the Peter Kerr estate. The estate is now the Bishop's Close of the **Episcopal Church**. The garden is open during daylight hours. Elk Rock is a nearby island in the **Willamette River**. 11800 SW Military Lane. 503-636-5613. Oregonian 5/30/97:A&E3.

Elk statue. A bronze statue in **Portland** that stands between SW Main Street traffic lanes in the **Plaza Blocks** between 3rd and 4th Avenues. The work by Roland Perry was presented to the city in 1900 by David Thompson, onetime shepherd and later mayor. It appropriately stands in an area where a bull elk grazed in Portland's earlier days. Portland, An Informal History; Portland's Public Art.

Elkhorn Mountains. A range of mountains northwest of **Baker City** in the **Blue Mountains** of northeast Oregon. It includes 10-mile-long Elkhorn Ridge, which rises steeply to 9,000', and is drained by the Powder River. Rock Creek Glacier lies in a basin on the ridge. Most of the area is included in the **Wallowa-Whitman National Forest**. **Gold** has been mined in some places.

Elkton. A rural community on Highway 38 in **Douglas County**, 37 miles northwest of **Roseburg** at the junction of Elk Creek and the **Umpqua River**. It is near the site of **Fort Umpqua**, operated by the **Hudson's Bay Company** from 1834 to1862. The town was laid out and named in 1850. A flood in 1893 destroyed the town, but it rebuilt. It was incorporated in 1948. Population 1980 155; 1995 180. Elevation 148' PO Box 508, 97436. 541-584-2547. Dictionary of Oregon History; Oregon Geographic Names.

Elliott Cutoff. See **Free Emigrant Road**.

Elliott State Forest. A 92,000 acre **state forest** located in **Coos** and **Douglas** counties. In 1912 Oregon State Forester Francis Elliott convinced Governor Oswald West that some of the remaining scattered **Common School Fund** forest lands should be traded for **Siuslaw National Forest** lands to create one large block of state forest land. In 1930, just after Elliott's death, the exchanges were finally completed and the forest was named for him. Most of Elliott State Forest is second growth forest growing back after the 1868 Coos Bay **forest fire**. Receipts from timber harvests are returned to the Common School Fund. ODF Coos District, 300 5th Street, Bay Park, Coos Bay 97420. 541-267-4136. Elliott State Forest.

Elowah Falls. A 289-foot waterfall on McCord Creek in John B. Yeon State Park in the **Columbia River Gorge** near exit 37 from **Interstate 84**. A trail leads six tenths of a mile to the base of the falls; another leads up a mile past the top of Elowah Falls to 100-foot Upper McCord Creek Falls. The meaning of Elowah is unknown. Waterfall Lover's Guide.

Elvis. See **Church of Elvis**.

Embassy of Heaven Church. A church that was located near **Sublimity** from 1989 to 1997 on a forested 34-acre site that the members called the Kingdom of Heaven. The church, said to have had as many as 200 members, was headed by pastor Paul Revere (Craig Douglas Fleshman). He and several church members resided in Heaven. The church did not recognize the authority of any government, and issued its own passports, automobile registrations, drivers' licenses, and license plates from "Heaven". The church claimed that Heaven belonged to God and thus was exempt from county property taxes, a position disputed by **Marion County**. On January 31, 1997, the residents were evicted and the property was seized for non-payment of taxes. Oregonian 7/25/93:L1.

Embassy Suites. See **Multnomah Hotel**.

Emergency Board. A committee of 17 members of the Oregon **legislature**, which, between legislative sessions, allocates funds from an emergency fund to state agencies. Its members include the president of the **Senate**, the speaker of the **House of Representatives**, the co-chairs of the **Joint Ways and Means Committee**, six other Senate members and seven other House members, usually also from the Joint Ways and Means Committee. The permanent, non-partisan Legislative Fiscal Office provides staff support for the Emergency Board as well as the Joint Ways and Means Committee. Governing Oregon; Oregon Blue Book. See also **Legislative committees**.

Emergency Management Division. A division of the State **Police** that is responsible for coordinating emergency disaster planning, preparedness, and response and recovery efforts among state and local agencies. It manages, among other things, the Emergency Operations Center, coordinates the Oregon Emergency Response System, coordinates ground search-and-rescue plans, and works for statewide implementation of the 911 emergency telephone service. 503-378-2911. Oregon Blue Book. See also **Disasters**; **Search dogs**.

Emery. An abrasive mineral (basically corundum) that is used for grinding and polishing. It is mined in **Linn County** by the only producer in the U.S. Mineral Industry of Oregon.

Emigrant Lake. An irrigation reservoir six miles southeast of **Ashland** formed in 1926 by a dam on Emigrant Creek as a part of the **Rogue River Basin Project**. It is operated by the Talent Irrigation District. The dam was raised in 1960 to 198 feet; the reservoir now covers 878 acres at full pool, with a maximum depth of 160 feet. In 1996 the district proposed installing a 1.5-megawatt generator on the outlet. The lake is V shaped with each arm about two miles long. **Jackson County** provides a campground, picnic area, swimming area, and boat launch at the lake which is heavily used for boating and fishing until the water level drops in late summer. Emigrant Creek was named for the emigrants on the **Applegate Trail** who followed the stream into the **Bear Creek Valley** after crossing the **Cas-**

cade Range. Atlas of Oregon Lakes; Oregonian 11/19/96:B4.

Emigrant Springs State Park. A **state park** located 26 miles southeast of **Pendleton** near **Interstate 84**. The park, located on a historic **wagon train** camping site, includes an **Oregon Trail** exhibit, horse camp, group facilities, year-round two-unit lodge, and a 51-space campground. Reservations, 800-452-5687. 541-983-2277.

Emissions testing. See **Vehicle inspection**.

Employees, state. The 1995-97 state **budget** called for 41,222 FTE (Full Time Equivalent) state employees, or 1.3 employees per hundred residents. A fourth of them were employed in **higher education**. About 30,000 were represented by unions. See also **Public Employees Retirement System**.

Employers. As of June 1995 Oregon's top 10 private sector employers were **Fred Meyer** (11,500); Safeway Stores (9,286); Sisters of Providence in Oregon (7,676); US Bancorp (7,466); **Intel** Corporation (6,723, and it topped 10,000 in 1997); Barrett Business Services (4,862); Kaiser Foundation Health Plan of NW (4,553); **Tektronix** (4,520); Albertsons (4,363); First Interstate Bank of Oregon (4,305). Oregon Blue Book. See also **Corporations; Payroll**.

Employment. Oregon's total labor force in 1993 numbered 1,587,000, up from 1,295,000 in 1980. Manufacturing employment in Oregon rose from 184,000 to 214,000 jobs between 1972 and 1990, while the service sector soared from 490,000 to 938,000 jobs. By the end of 1995 employment in technology (60,860 jobs) had surpassed employment in the timber and paper industries (60,416 jobs). It is expected that 300,000 jobs will be created in the state by the year 2006, including 80,000 professional and technical jobs paying an average of $35,523 a year and 60,000 service jobs paying $17,000. In 1994 manufacturing employment accounted for 16% of all state employment, wholesale/retail accounted for 25%, service for 21%, and government for 16%. Oregon: A Statistical Overview; Oregon Blue Book; Oregon Labor Trends; Oregonian 9/4/94:B4, 1/17/96:A1, 3/16/96:B1. See also **Employers; Employment, non-farm; Industries; Labor force participation; Wages**.

Employment Department. An Oregon department that assists workers in finding jobs, employers in finding employees, the unemployed in collecting benefits, and parents in finding **child care**. It operates 28 full-service offices around the state plus 16 outreach offices. 875 Union Street NE, Salem 97311. 503-378-3208. Oregon Blue Book. See also **Payroll; Unemployment**.

Employment, non-farm. By industry.

	1947	1996
Wholesale and retail	22.7%	24.8%
Lumber and wood products	17.6	3.5
Government	13.4	16.7
Transportation, communications and utilities	11.0	5.0
Construction	5.9	5.3
Food	5.0	1.8
Finance, insurance, real estate	3.2	6.2
Durable & high tech	0.6	3.3
Services, misc.	20.4	33.5

Oregonian 10/29/97:A10.

Employment Relations Board. A board established in 1977 to determine appropriate bargaining units for state and local governments and for private companies not involved in interstate commerce, to conduct representation elections, and to resolve unfair labor practice complaints. Its Conciliation Service Division provides mediation services for resolving collective-bargaining disputes. Old Garfield School, 528 Cottage Street NE, Salem 97310. 503-378-3807. Oregon Blue Book. See also **Strikes**.

Emu. A large (110 to 140 pounds), flightless bird native to Australia that can run more than 30 miles an hour. Both emus and rheas (from South America) lay their eggs in the winter, and both are smaller than the similar African **ostrich**. Emus are being raised commercially on some 300 emu ranches in Oregon for their low-cholesterol meat, oil (up to 6 liters per bird), feathers, and leather. Oregon Emu Association, PO Box 1144, Sherwood 97140.

Enchanted Forest. A privately operated fairyland theme park seven miles south of **Salem** at exit 248 from **Interstate 5**. 503-363-3060.

End of the Oregon Trail Interpretive Center. A museum at the end of the **Oregon Trail** on Abernethy Green in **Oregon City**, near **Interstate 205**. The museum, opened in 1995, features three buildings that look like giant covered wagons. 1726 Washington Street, Oregon City 97045. 503-657-9336.

Endangered animals. In 1993 the following Oregon species were listed on either or both of the federal and state **Endangered Species Act** lists as threatened or endangered: the Oregon silverspot **butterfly**; nine **fish** (Warner sucker, shortnose sucker, Lost River sucker, Hutton Springs tui chub, Borax Lake chub, Foskett speckled dace, Snake River **chinook** and **sockeye** salmon, Lahontan cutthroat **trout**); seven birds (**peregrine falcon**, Aleutian Canada **goose**, **marbled murrelet**, **Northern spotted owl**, brown pelican, western **snowy plover**, and bald **eagle**); four sea turtles (green, leatherback, loggerhead, Pacific Ridley); three land mammals (Columbia white-tailed **deer**, **wolverine**, and kit **fox**), and seven **marine mammals** (sea **otter** and Steller sea lion plus seven **whales**: right, Sei, blue, finback, gray, humpback, and sperm). Rare, Threatened and Endangered. See also **Extinction**; **Protected animals**.

Endangered plants. As of 1993, four Oregon plant species were listed under the federal **Endangered Species Act** as endangered: Applegate's milk vetch, *Astragalus applegatei*; Bradshaw's desert parsley, *Lomatium bradshawii*; MacFarlane's four-o'clock, *Mirabilis macfarlanei*; Malheur wire lettuce, *Stephanomeria malheurensis*; and one as threatened, *Sidalcea nelsoniana*. The state Endangered Species Act listed an additional eight endangered species and six more threatened species. Plants that are listed under the state act are protected only on state-owned or state-leased lands, except that trafficking in them is regulated. Rare, Threatened, and Endangered. See also **Introduced species**.

Endangered species. Plants or animals that are in danger of becoming extinct throughout their range within the foreseeable future. Species not presently endangered, but which are likely to become endangered within the foreseeable future are designated as threatened under the **Endangered Species Act (U.S.)**. Rarity is frequently an indication of threatened or endangered status. Oregon's threatened and endangered species are found throughout the state, usually where habitat has been significantly altered or eliminated. <u>Rare, Threatened, and Endangered</u>. See also **Endangered animals; Endangered plants; Introduced species**.

Endangered Species Act (Oregon). An act passed by the Oregon legislature in 1987 that governs only the actions of state agencies on state-owned lands. The act gave the Oregon Department of **Agriculture** responsibility for threatened and endangered plants, and the Oregon Department of **Fish and Wildlife** responsibility for threatened and endangered animals. Both departments have cooperative agreements with the U.S. Fish and Wildlife Service for research and conservation programs for species protected under the **Endangered Species Act (U.S.).** The Oregon **Natural Heritage Program** maintains a database of Oregon's rare, threatened, and endangered plants, animals, and ecosystems. <u>Rare, Threatened, and Endangered</u>.

Endangered Species Act (U.S.). An act passed by the U.S. Congress in 1973 to provide protection for plant and animal species threatened with **extinction.** The federal law can affect federal, state, and private lands. <u>Oregon Wildlife</u> 51(3):14; <u>Rare, Threatened, and Endangered</u>. See also **God Squad**.

Endowment funds. See **Higher education endowment funds.**

Energy. 1994 energy consumption in Oregon totaled 1,038.2 trillion Btu. Residential use accounted for 21%, commercial 16%, industrial 34%, and transportation 29%. A third of the energy came from **hydroelectric power**, 15% from **natural gas**, 17% from **gasoline**, 18% from other petroleum products, 6% from **electricity** generated outside the state, 7% from **biofuels**, and 4% from **coal**. <u>State Energy</u>. See also **Home heating**.

Energy conservation. See **Electricity consumption**.

Energy Facility Siting Council. A council of seven members appointed by the governor that represents the state's authority for siting, monitoring, and regulating the location, construction, and operation of major energy facilities, disposal of radioactive waste, and transport of radioactive materials. It is part of the Oregon Office of **Energy**. 625 Marion St. NE, Salem 97310. 800-221-8035 (toll-free in Oregon only), 503-378-4040. <u>Oregon Blue Book</u>. See also **Electric power plants**; **Trojan**.

Energy Office. An office within the Oregon Department of **Consumer and Business Services** that is responsible for promoting energy conservation, developing new electricity sources, siting energy facilities, and cleaning up nuclear wastes. The $22 million budget comes entirely from fees and federal sources, using no state taxes. The office provides staff support for the **Energy Facility Siting Council** and **Hanford** Waste Board, and its conservation programs offer advice, tax credits, and loans for homes, businesses, and local government. 625 Marion St. NE, Salem 97310. 800-221-8035 (toll free in Oregon only); 503-378-4040. <u>Oregon Blue Book</u>.

Energy shortage. In 1973, while a **drought** reduced Oregon's **hydroelectric** capacity, oil shortages led many independent **gasoline** stations to close and others ran out of gas. Governor Tom McCall called for a 55 mph speed limit, banned air conditioning in state buildings and decreed that they close by 6 p.m., required that state cars have at least two people riding in them, and finally, in September, banned illuminated display advertising as well as exterior building and landscape lighting. The order was lifted in December, but many Christmas lighting contests were canceled. In January 1974 he instituted an "odd-even" rationing plan, based on license plate numbers, to eliminate lines at the gas stations. He also opposed a proposed **aluminum** plant at **Warrenton** as too energy consuming. Fire at Eden's Gate.

Engineering Examiners, State Board of. A ten-member board established in 1919 to regulate and register engineers and land surveyors. Registration fees fund the board; no tax dollars are used. 750 Front Street NE, #240, Salem 97310. 503-378-4180. Oregon Blue Book. See also **Land surveys**.

English Only. A national movement against providing bilingual government services, including 911 emergency services, public transportation schedules, hospital translators, foreign language books in libraries, and bilingual education. Oregon's legislature adopted SJR 16 in 1989 which welcomed and encouraged multi-culturalism, but measures have since been introduced in the legislature to require English only. Nosotros.

Enola Hill. An arm of Zig Zag Mountain on the west flank of **Mount Hood**; it rises steeply just east of the community of Rhododendron. **Forest Service** plans to log the area have come into conflict with a number of groups, including **Indians**. They used Enola Hill for hunting and gathering as well as for vision quests. Oregonian 3/18/96:B9, 3/22/96:B9.

Enrollment. See **School enrollment**.

Enterprise. The county seat of **Wallowa County**, located on the Wallowa River 65 miles east of **La Grande**. The site had a natural salt lick that attracted game, so had been an Indian gathering place where they also held horse races. In 1887 entrepreneurs established the town as the potential county seat of their new county and the name was selected at a tent meeting in the still-building town. A post office was established the same year, and the city was incorporated two years later. Many of the buildings, including the 1909 courthouse, are built of a locally quarried gray stone. An annual mule show, Hells Canyon Mule Days, is held on Labor Day weekend. Population 1980 2,003; 1995 2,010. Elevation 3,757'. 108 NE First, 97828. 541-426-4196. From the Wallowas; History of Wallowa County; Oregonian 9/5/95:B2.

Enterprise Zones. An incentive program created by the legislature in 1985 to create investment in thirty-two designated areas of the state that have been lagging economically. Constructing a new facility in an enterprise zone entitles the business to a 100% property tax abatement for three to five years on the new plant and on most of the installed equipment. Regional Development Division, Department of Economic Development, 775 Summer St. NE, Salem 97310. 503-986-0120.

Environmental organizations and centers. See **Breitenbush Hot Springs**; **CoastWatch**; **Institute for Sustainable Culture**; **Northwest Earth Institute**; **Orlo Foundation**; **Oregon Environmental Council**; **Oregon Natural Resources Council**; **Sitka Center**; **SOLV**; **Sustainable Northwest**.

Environmental Quality, Department of (DEQ). A department of state government that is responsible for protecting and enhancing Oregon's **water** and **air quality** and for managing the proper disposal of **solid** and **hazardous wastes**. It was created in 1969 after the State Sanitary Authority (formed in 1938 to clean up the **Willamette River**) was dissolved. The department's first administrator was the legendary L. B. Day. DEQ is 811 SW 6th Ave., Portland 97204. 800-452-4011 (toll free in Oregon only); 503-229-5696. Fire at Eden's Gate; Oregon Blue Book.

Eocene. A geologic epoch between 38 and 55 million years ago, between the **Paleocene** and the **Oligocene**. During the Eocene a complex series of events changed the shape of Oregon. The North American plate, still moving west, collided with a north/south line of volcanic islands; these became the foundation of the future **Coast Range**. Great outpourings of lava (the **Clarno Formation**) 32 to 44 million years ago covered central Oregon. There was a low, wide coastal plain. **Fossils**, including palms, warm water snails, and crocodiles, indicate a moist, tropical climate across the area before the Coast Range and **Cascade Range** began to emerge at the end of the epoch. Geology of Oregon.

Epidemics prior to 1855. The first recorded outbreak of an Old World disease among Northwest Indians was an epidemic of smallpox in the 1770s, introduced from either Spanish ships or Indians traveling over the Rockies on horseback; the latter was the known source of a later smallpox epidemic in 1802-03. Tuberculosis and venereal diseases were introduced soon after by fur traders. Another epidemic, perhaps smallpox again, killed many Indians along the **Columbia River** in 1824-25. In 1830 a devastating outbreak of **malaria** appeared. Influenza was epidemic from 1836 to 1839 along the coast, along with another outbreak of smallpox to both north and south. The immigrant families of the 1840s brought the childhood diseases of chicken pox (1840), scarlet fever (1843), and whooping cough (1844). Dysentery was introduced from Hawaii in 1844. Immigrants frequently had camp fever (louse-born typhus) after 1845. **Measles**, brought inadvertently from California in 1847, led to the **Whitman massacre**. Smallpox reappeared in 1853. Indians apparently did not get scarlet fever or typhus, though they were decimated by some of the other diseases, especially smallpox, malaria and measles. Cholera afflicted many immigrants in the Mississippi Valley but did not spread to Oregon. "Pacific Northwest Measles Epidemic of 1847-1848."

Epidemics since 1855. Among the devastating outbreaks of disease in Oregon have been smallpox in **Jacksonville** in 1868 which killed over 40, **polio** in 1916 and again in 1948 and the early 1950s, and diphtheria in **Jackson County** in 1890, in **Lebanon** in 1891, and in **Cottage Grove** in 1917. See also **Influenza**; **Waterborne diseases**.

Episcopal Church. On May 11, 1851, the Rev. William Richmond arrived in Oregon and in that year established Episcopal churches in **Portland**, **Oregon City**, **Lafayette**, **Champoeg**, and **Milwaukie**. The first Bishop of Oregon, the Rev. Thomas Fielding Scott, arrived in 1854. The church has operated a number of schools in Oregon, beginning in 1856. The 1874 Ascension Episcopal Church in **Cove** and the 1876 St. Thomas Episcopal Church in **Canyon City** are still in use. Diocesan Headquarters, PO Box 467, Lake Oswego 97034. 503-636-5613. Dictionary of Oregon History; Guide to Early Oregon Churches. See also **Elk Rock**; **Oaks Pioneer Church**.

Equalization. A method created by the 1991 legislature for providing financial equity among Oregon school districts since, as a result of **Measure 5**, the state had become the primary funder. Eventually each school district is to receive the same amount of money from the state per student, calculated on a complex formula to recognize differences such as the number of students in special education. Equalization has cut funding for wealthy or high-taxing school districts and boosted funding for poor or low tax-rate districts. In 1990-91 the Nyssa School District spent $3,313 per capita while Clatskanie spent $6,134. By 1993-94 Nyssa's per capita expenditures had increased to $5,033 while Clatskanie's had been cut to $5,180. Oregonian 9/4/94:D6, 3/19/96:A1, 1/26/97:A1. See also **School finance**.

Equitable Building. A 12-story office building at 421 SW Sixth Avenue in **Portland**. The 1948 structure was the first curtain-wall high-rise ever built, the first major building built in the U.S. after **World War II**, the first building with an aluminum skin, the first with air-conditioning, and the first with a traveling tram for washing the windows. Portland's Pietro Belluschi was the architect. It has also been known as the Commonwealth Building. Pietro Belluschi.

Equity theaters. See **Artists Repertory Theatre**; **Oregon Shakespeare Festival**; **Portland Center Stage**.

Equus Beds. See **Fossil Lake**.

Erickson's. A onetime saloon in **Portland**, one of the most famous in the west. The building, located on 3rd Avenue between Couch and Burnside, had a bar that snaked around to reach a length of 684 feet; 50 bartenders presided. Portland, An Informal History.

Ermine. See **Weasels**.

Ernest Bloch Music Festival. A one-week festival in July of traditional and contemporary classical music with concerts held on the central Oregon coast in **Newport**, **Lincoln City**, and **Yachats**. The festival honors Bloch (1880-1959), a Swiss-born composer who lived at Agate Beach, north of Newport, from 1939 until his death. 541-265-2787.

Erosion. Average Oregon erosion rates are 5.7 tons of **soil** lost per acre per year from cropland, 2.8 tons per acre from forest land, 2.1 tons from rangeland, and 1.1 tons from pasture. For most Oregon soils an acceptable average annual rate of soil loss has been set at between 2 and 5 tons per acre, depending on soil depth and other factors. However, almost 2 million acres of Oregon cropland are losing soil at a rate faster than it can be naturally replaced and 3 million acres of rangeland are eroding at unacceptable rates. Oregon's Soil.

Erratics. Rocks found distant from the site of their origin, especially as the result of glacial action. **Pleistocene floods** swept large blocks of glacial ice, some with embedded Montana rocks and sediments, down the **Columbia River** and into the **Willamette Valley**. As the ice floes melted they dropped their loads. A number of Montana erratics have been found scattered across the valley, including 40 boulders over three feet in diameter. The largest, which originally weighed over 160 tons, lies between **McMinnville** and **Sheridan** in Erratic Rock State Park. The **Willamette meteorite** may have originally fallen in Montana and floated to Oregon in a chunk of glacial ice. Geology of Oregon.

Erria. A Danish passenger and cargo liner that burned during the early hours of December 20, 1951 while waiting at anchor off **Tongue Point** for a favorable tide to cross out over the bar of the **Columbia River**. Eleven of the 114 persons aboard died, trapped by smoke and fire. Shipwrecks of the Pacific Coast.

Eskimos. See **Paul Jensen Arctic Museum**.

Essential Forces. An elliptical fountain at the entrance to the **Rose Garden**. It includes a pillar of water and a pillar of fire, plus nearly 500 computer-programmable water jets. Oregonian 10/8/95: Special section.

Estacada. "Christmas Tree Capital of the World." A rural community on the Clackamas River in **Clackamas County**, 16 miles east of **Oregon City**. At a 1903 Portland meeting held by the electric and railroad interests who were developing the town, a number of names were suggested; Estacada, inspired by Llano Estacado, Texas, was the one drawn from the hat. The city was incorporated in 1905. Electric power generation, timber, agriculture, industry, and government provide much of the local employment. Attractions include the historic **Philip Foster** Farm which provided Oregon Trail pioneers respite after their arduous trip across the **Barlow Trail**, a historic museum, river sports, nearby parks, and **Mount Hood National Forest**. Population 1980 1,419; 1995 2,060. Elevation 465'. PO Box 958, 97023. 503-630-8270; Chamber of Commerce 503-630-3483. Oregon Geographic Names.

Estacada Timber Festival. A mid-July weekend festival featuring lumberjack contests, music, and dance at Timber Park, off Highway 224. 503-630-3483.

Estuary. A zone at the mouth of a coastal river where there is a complex mixing of fresh river water with ocean salt water. The fresh water is less dense and tends to flow over the top of the sea water, sometimes not mixing until well into the ocean. The salt water below tends to keep river sediments from reaching the ocean, resulting in the gradual filling in of the estuary. Estuaries are rich in nutrients and serve as important breeding and habitat areas for water birds, fish, marine mammals, and invertebrates, including shell fish. Oregon has 21 significant estuaries, nine of them major, with a total of 132,000 acres of intertidal and subtidal estuarine habitat. The **Army Corps of Engineers** administers a permit program for dredging or filling in estuaries. "Ocean processes and hazards along the Oregon coast"; Oregon's 1994 Water Quality. See also **Columbia River estuary**; **Columbia River plume**; **Wetlands**.

Ethics. Oregon law requires that legislators may not request a fee for speaking but may accept an honorarium. Conflicts of interest must be declared, but legislators are not allowed to abstain from voting. See also **Campaign finance**; **Corruption**; **Government Standards and Practices Commission**; **Lobbyist**.

Ethnic composition. See **Population distribution, racial and ethnic**.

Eugene (eu GENE). A city 110 miles south of Portland on the **Willamette River** and **Interstate 5**. It is the **second-largest city** in Oregon, with a diversified economy supported by agriculture, timber, manufacturing, and education, including the **University of Oregon**. The city is the county seat of **Lane County** and location of the headquarters for the **Willamette National Forest**. Eugene Skinner, who took a land claim at the foot of **Skinner Butte** in 1846, platted the townsite in 1851. The first post office in 1850 was named Skinner's, but the name was soon changed to Eugene. The city was incorporated in 1862. Attractions include the **Hult Center for the Performing Arts**, Maude Kerns Art Center, city parks, and nearby lakes, rivers, and trails. Sister cities are Kakegawa, Japan; Chinju, Korea; Kathmandu, Nepal; and Irkutsk, Russia. Population 1980 105,664; 1995 121,905. Elevation 422'. 777 Pearl St, 97401. 541-687-5010. Visitors Association 800-547-5445. "Eugene in the Depression"; Oregon Geographic Names; Story of Eugene. See also **Metropolitan Areas**; **Spencer Butte**.

Eugene Country Fair. See **Oregon Country Fair**.

Eugene District, BLM. A 316,631-acre forested **Bureau of Land Management** district in **Lane County**. 2890 Chad Drive, P.O. Box 10226, Eugene 97440. 541-683-6600. BLM Facts.

Eugene Water and Electric Board (EWEB). A municipal utility that, in 1996, served 41,000 Eugene-area customers with water from the **McKenzie River**, sold steam to 114 downtown customers, and provided electricity to 73,000 customers. It was founded in 1911 after a typhoid epidemic was traced to the existing private water utility. In 1996 EWEB sold 2.7 million **megawatt** hours of electricity for $102 million. It generated 18% of its power at its plants on the McKenzie River, 6% at plants at **Estacada** and in Idaho, and bought the rest. The McKenzie River system includes the Leaburg plant (1930, 6 MW and 1950, 7.5 MW), the Walterville plant (1949, 8 MW), and the Carmen Smith plant (1963, 90 MW). 500 E. 4th Avenue, PO Box 10148, 97440-2148. 541-484-2411. See also **Municipal electric systems**.

Eulachon. See **Smelt**.

Eureka. A copper and gold mining town that existed between 1900 and 1906 in **Hells Canyon** near the mouth of the **Imnaha River**. There is some evidence that the entire operation may have been a giant fraud, designed to fleece eastern investors. Hells Canyon.

Evel Knievel. A motorcycle daredevil noted for his death-defying leaps. He had apparently practiced his skills as a safe cracker in Oregon in 1963, but the closest he came to Oregon in making one of his famous motorcycle jumps was a failed attempt to leap the 1,765-foot wide, 530-foot deep **Snake River** canyon near Twin Falls, Idaho, on September 8, 1974. Though he survived with just scrapes, he did not try the feat again. Oregonian 9/9/74:sec.3,p.1.

Evening at Giverny. An annual $600-a-ticket event that is the major fundraising effort for the **Portland Art Museum**. The event, usually held in a private home in June, includes dinner and an auction.

Evergreen AirVenture Museum. See **Captain Michael King Smith Evergreen Aviation Educational Center**.

Exclusion Day. See **Immunization**.

Exclusions laws. Laws designed to keep **blacks** out of Oregon. The first was passed by the **provisional government** on June 26, 1844, in response to the **Cockstock affair** and authorized a whip lashing for any black who refused to leave, but it was repealed in 1845 before it took effect. Another exclusion law was passed in 1849 but was inadvertently repealed in 1854. An exclusion clause was adopted by popular vote in 1857 to be included in the state **Constitution**; it was repealed in 1926. Peculiar Paradise. See also **Blacks in Oregon, history**.

Exclusive Economic Zone (EEZ). An area of ocean extending 200 nautical miles from the shore, established by presidential proclamation on March 10, 1983.

Within the "territorial sea" (the first three miles), the state owns and manages the natural resources although the federal government has jurisdiction over navigation, commerce, pollution control, and some other activities. Beyond the 3-mile limit, the federal government has exclusive ownership and jurisdiction. The **Pacific Fishery Management Council** manages most marine fisheries within the EEZ. The high seas and international seabed beyond the EEZ are governed by international customs and conventions. Atlas of the Pacific Northwest.

Excursion trains. In 1995, three excursion trains and two dinner trains were operating in Oregon. On summer weekends, the Fun Run Express runs a 3 1/2 hour round trip from **Garibaldi** through **Wheeler** to the Nehalem Winery and back. 503-355-8667. The Mount Hood Railroad offers a five-hour round trip between **Hood River** and Parkdale. 800-872-4661. The **Sumpter Valley Railroad** operates on summer weekends 30 miles southwest of **Baker City**. 541-894-2268. The Spirit of Oregon Dinner Train takes dinner and Sunday brunch excursions into the **Coast Range** from Roy (near **Banks**) on the **Oregon-Tillamook Railroad** line. 503-324-1919. The Crooked River Railroad Company operates a dinner train on a 35-mile round trip between **Redmond** and **Prineville** on summer weekends. 541-548-8630. Oregonian 8/0/95:B9. See also **Zoo Railway**.

Executive. The branch of Oregon government responsible for carrying out Oregon laws. It is headed by the **Governor** and five other **elected officials (Secretary of State, Treasurer, Attorney General, Commissioner of Labor and Industries**, and **Superintendent of Public Instruction**) who administer the laws through a number of departments, **boards and commissions**. Oregon Blue Book. See also **Oregon Administrative Rules**.

Exotic animals. Non-native animals such as tigers, monkeys, wolves, or wolf hybrids that are kept as pets. Deaths and injuries from dangerous exotic animals have led some cities, including **Troutdale** and **Redmond**, to ban them and to calls for greater state control. As of 1996, Oregonians who owned exotic animals were required to have a $20, two-year permit, to open their facilities for inspection, and to meet other requirements for the animals. Oregonian 11/17/96:A1. See also **Introduced species**.

Exotic species. See **Introduced species**.

Experiment Station. See **Agricultural Experiment Station**.

Exploding whale. A 1970 episode in which the State Highway Department packed 20 cases of dynamite under a beached, 45-foot, dead gray whale and blew it up. Pieces of stinking rotting blubber went flying with unexpected force, including a three-foot-square that flew a quarter mile and demolished a nearly new Oldsmobile hardtop convertible. Oregonian 11/13/70:42.

Explorers by land. The **Indians** were, of course, the first explorers of Oregon. Though the **D. Boone tree** suggests that Daniel Boone may have been in eastern Oregon in 1801, members of the **Lewis and Clark Expedition** are the first documented non-Indians to reach Oregon overland (1805-06). Fur trappers followed after the establishment of **Astoria** in 1811. Especially notable were Peter Skene Ogden's explorations in the 1820s while with the **Hudson's Bay Company**, Jedediah Smith's overland trip in 1828 from California to the **Columbia River**, Captain Benjamin Bonneville's personal explorations, especially of the northeast corner of the state, 1832-35, and General John Fremont's explorations for the government, 1843-1846. See also **Smith massacre**.

Explorers by sea. In 1542, the Spanish sailor Bartolome Ferrelo of Cabrillo's expedition sailed as far north as the **Rogue River** but was prevented from landing by fierce storms. The English buccaneer, Sir Francis Drake, may have landed at Whale Cove in **Lincoln County** in 1579 though **Cape Arago** has been marked as a more likely site. In 1603 Spanish sailor Martin d'Aguilar sailed north to about the present site of **Port Orford** but was unable to land. In 1775 the Spanish explorer Bruno Heceta located the mouth of the **Columbia River** but his crew was too weakened by scurvy to cross the bar. Three years later England's Captain Cook sailed north along the coast and initiated the **fur trade**, though he missed the Columbia River. In 1788, the first Americans set foot in Oregon when Captain Robert Gray landed at **Tillamook Bay** where the natives murdered his cabin boy. On May 11, 1792, Robert Gray again visited the coast, this time as captain of the *Columbia Rediviva*, and became the first to sail into the **Columbia River**, providing a strong argument for America's claim to the region. In the fall of that year British Lieutenant William Broughton of Vancouver's expedition spent three weeks exploring the Columbia as far as the **Columbia River Gorge** and was the first to describe the area, writing "The most beautiful landscape that can be imagined." See also **History time line**.

Explosion crater. See **Maar**.

Expo Center. See **Exposition Center**.

Exports. Exports originating in Oregon totaled $7.2 billion in 1994 and $9.4 billion in 1995, and created 100,000 jobs (10% of all private-sector jobs). Advanced technology accounted for $4.3 billion; agriculture and food products (led by wheat) $2.4 billion; lumber and wood products $1.4 billion; and other, $1 billion. A total of $3.8 billion in Oregon exports went to east Asia, $1.4 billion to southeast Asia, $1.9 billion to Europe, $1.2 billion to North America, and $1.1 billion, other. In 1996 **Japan** was Oregon's leading customer ($2.1 billion), followed by Canada, South Korea, Singapore, and **China**. In 1996 the Portland-Vancouver area exported $9.2 billion worth of goods, especially high tech items, ranking it 10th nationally for exports sold from the area, not just "shipped through." Major bulk-loaded exports from the **Port of Portland** were **wheat** 8.3 million tons, **soda ash** 2.4 million tons, and **potash** 1.5 million tons. In 1996 43% of all U.S. grain exports were shipped from the Portland area. Oregonian 9/30/97:C1. See also **NAFTA**; **Trade offices**.

Expose Yourself to Art. A 1978 poster that appears to show, from the back, a derelict spreading his coat to expose himself to the statue of a voluptuous naked woman. The statue is "Kvinneakt," a 1977 bronze sculpture by Norman Taylor located in **Portland** on Fifth Avenue north of Washington Street. The "derelict" was tavern-owner Bud Clark, later mayor of Portland. The poster, created as a fund-raiser, has sold 680,000 copies. Oregonian 5/26/95:E1; Portland Guidebook.

Exposition Center. A facility, usually called the Expo Center, located at 2060 N. Marine Drive at the Multnomah County Fairgrounds in north **Portland**. It is managed by **Metro**. The center's climate-controlled hall, opened in 1997, is the largest clear-span assembly building west of the Mississippi. 503-285-7756. Portland, An Informal History. See also **North Pacific Industrial Association Exposition Building**; **Pacific International Livestock Exposition**.

Expositions. In 1876 Oregon exhibited a framed scene of moss at the Philadelphia Centennial and in 1878 sent a large cabinet made of 25,000 pieces of wood that contained grains and grasses to the Paris Exposition. Portland: An Informal History. See also **Atlantic Pacific Highways and Electrical Exposition**; **Lewis and Clark Centennial Exposition**.

Express services. Private services that competed with the U.S. **Postal Service** in carrying mail and parcels until legislated out of existence in 1895. They charged more than the postal service, but provided faster and more reliable mail service on the frontier and to gold mining camps. The first express service in Oregon seems to have begun in 1848, and there were soon several, including Wells Fargo in 1852. Some express services had agents throughout the state and provided messengers who carried the mail, packages, or gold by whatever means was available, including scheduled **stage lines**, while others operated their own **pony express** services. Wells Fargo transported millions of dollars worth of gold from the gold fields of Oregon and the Rocky Mountains to **Portland** and on to San Francisco, and also offered banking services. Oregon Express Companies; "Portland: Wells Fargo's Hub."

Extension Service. An education program operated by **Oregon State University** to supply Oregonians information based on research in six major program areas: agriculture, home economics, forestry, **4-H**, energy, and **Sea Grant**. The county extension agents, located in most Oregon counties, are OSU faculty members, and were assisted by 33,000 volunteers who contributed 1.2 million hours in 1995. Funding is cooperatively supplied by federal, state, and county governments. Ballard Extension Hall, Oregon State University, Corvallis 97331. 541-737-2713.

Extinction. Animal species known to have become extinct in recent years in Oregon include Alvord cutthroat **trout**, Miller Lake **lamprey**, **California condor**, sharp-tailed **grouse**, Richardson **ground squirrel**, **fisher**, gray **wolf**, grizzly **bear**, sea **otter**, **bison**, and **bighorn sheep**. Attempts have been made to reintroduce the sharp-tailed grouse, sea otter, fisher, and bighorn sheep, with mixed success. See also **Fossils, animal**.

Factory outlet malls. In 1997 Oregon had six factory outlet malls, in **Lincoln City**, the first (1989) and largest with 64 stores, **Bend**, **McMinnville**, **Phoenix**, **Seaside**, and **Troutdale**. Others have been proposed for **Florence** and **Seaside**.

Fairview. A growing suburban community 12 miles east of downtown **Portland** on **Interstate 84** that prides itself on its small-town atmosphere. The name was used by pioneers, but, to avoid confusion with a Fairview in Coos County, the post office was called Cleone between 1883 and 1914. The city was incorporated in 1908. **Blue Lake** Park lies at the north edge of town. Population 1980 1,749; 1995 4,245. Elevation 114'. PO Box 337, 97024. 503-665-7929. "First Fifty-Five"; Oregon Geographic Names.

Fairview Training Center. A state facility for adults who have severe **developmental disabilities**. It opened in 1908, had 320 residents in 1996, and is slated to be closed in May 2000. The residents will be placed in community group homes where they can be cared for at 20% of the cost. Fairview is operated by the Oregon **Mental Health and Developmental Disability Services Division**. 2250 Strong Road SE, Salem 97310. 503-986-5090. Oregon Blue Book; Oregonian 7/8/96:B6, 11/28/96:B5.

Faith healers. **Ashland**'s Susie Jane "Ma" Jessel (1891-1966) was one of the state's best-known faith healers. Hundreds of people a day would appear at her home where she would treat them with what some called her "X-ray hands". She treated all without fee though many tucked a small bit into her apron pocket. "Susie Jessel."

Falcons. Swift birds of prey that feed chiefly on other birds that they catch on the wing by overtaking them. The prairie falcon, *Falco mexicanus*, nests in eastern Oregon. The endangered **peregrine falcon**, *F. peregrinus*, is making a recovery from its near extinction from DDT. The sport of falconry requires a falconry license from **ODF&W** plus a hunting license. Atlas of Oregon Wildlife; Great Pacific Northwest Nature Factbook; Oregonian 7/1/95:A1.

Fall Creek Reservoir. A flood-control reservoir 25 miles southeast of **Eugene** on Fall Creek, a tributary to the Middle Fork of the **Willamette River**. It was formed in 1966 when the **Army Corps of Engineers** completed the 195-foot high, 5,100-foot long, rock fill and earth embankment dam. The two-armed lake covers 1,860 acres, is nearly seven miles long, and has a maximum depth of 161 feet. The reservoir is drawn down in late summer in preparation for flood runoff. Two campgrounds and several day-use parks provide facilities. Army Engineers; Atlas of Oregon Lakes.

Falls City. A city at the foot of the **Coast Range** 10 miles southwest of **Dallas** in **Polk County**. It was named in 1885 for the 25-foot falls on the Little Luckiamute River just upstream from the town. The city was incorporated in 1893. Population 1980 804; 1995 890. Elevation 365'. PO Box 10, 97344. 503-787-3631. Oregon Geographic Names.

Fareless Square. A 340-block area of downtown **Portland** in which no fares are charged on **Tri-Met** buses or **MAX**.

Farewell Bend State Park. A **state park** between **Interstate 84** and the **Snake River** 25 miles northwest of **Ontario** on a historic **wagon train** camping site near the "catfish capital" of Oregon. The park includes an **Oregon Trail** exhibit, a boat ramp/fishing dock, and 96 year-round campsites. Reservations, 800-452-5687. 541-869-2365.

Farm Home Administration. See **Farm Service Agency**.

Farm income. See **Farms**.

Farm labor. Oregon farms are operated by their 12,000 full-time and 20,000 part-time owners plus 10,000 unpaid family members. In addition, it is estimated that farmers hire from 16,000 (in winter months) to 120,000 workers, most of them **Hispanic**, for full or part-time work. Most Oregon farm workers have no union protection or guarantees about working conditions, overtime, job security and hours, though Northwest Treeplanters and Farmworkers United, known by its Spanish initials, PCUN, has tried for years to organize workers and signed its first contract, covering 20 workers, in 1998. Agriculture; Oregonian 8/25/97:B2, 4/1/98:E1. See also **Migrant labor**; **Pesticide Hot Line**; **Undocumented workers**.

Farm land. A 1987 report found that Oregon had 4.3 million acres of crop-land (14% of the privately-owned land in the state), plus 1.8 million irrigated acres (6%), 1.9 million acres of pasture (6%), and 9.2 million acres of privately-owned **rangeland** (31%). Between 1987 and 1992, the acreage in farm uses declined 1.1%, with **Josephine County** having the greatest loss at 14.7%. Hobby farms producing under $10,000 gross income occupy 13% of the farm land but generate only 3% of sales. Atlas of the Pacific Northwest; Oregon: A Statistical Overview. See also **Farmers**; **Farms**; **Irrigation**; **Land use**; **Soil**.

Farm Service Agency.   A federal agency, formerly known as the Ag-ricultural Stabilization and Conservation Service, that administers farm conserva-tion programs, including cost-reimbursement programs for landowners. The former Farm Home Administration is also now part of the Farm Service Agency. 256 Warner-Milne Road, Oregon City 97045. 503-655-3144.

Farm workers. See **Farm labor**.

Farmers. Oregon has 37,000 full and part-time farmers and ranchers, less than 1% of the state's population. 17,000 farmers are hobby farmers, with under $10,000 a year in farm income, though they own over half of the **horses** and **goats** in the state. The average age of all farm operators is 54 years and of ranchers is 60. Over 35% of the full time farmers and ranchers are 65 years of age or older; 3.3% are under 35. Agriculture. See also **Agriculture**; **Farms**; **Grange**; **Oregonians for Food and Shelter**; **Pesticide Hot Line**;

Farmers markets. About 20 Oregon towns have weekly markets at which growers sell produce directly to the public. Most are held on Saturday mornings from May through October. **Eugene** had the first, opening on May 9, 1970. At some markets WIC-program families can use coupons to buy local produce. Craft markets are sometimes held at the same time. 800-723-3638. Oregonian 4/30/96:FD11. See also **Saturday markets**.

Farming history. The first garden planted in what is now Oregon was laid out at **Astoria** in 1811 on a rich piece of land using seeds brought from New York. Only the radishes, turnips and potatoes matured; one of the turnips grew to 15 1/2 pounds. Legend says that a fur trapper planted seeds the next year at **French Prai-rie**, and others were farming there in the 1830s. The **Hudson's Bay Company** (HBC) developed extensive farms at **Fort Vancouver** beginning in 1825. The HBC also brought in **cattle** by ship in the 1820's, and a more diversified farming was gradually introduced, with **fruit**, **flax**, and **hops** increasingly important. As more settlers came, more **Willamette Valley** land was plowed and planted to **wheat**, so that by 1846 more than 160,000 bushels was produced. All agriculture boomed in the 1850s and '60s because of demand fueled by **gold rushes**. The first wheat east of the **Cascade Range** was harvested in 1863. The first **irrigation** project was in 1902. Shipping costs have long been a problem for Oregon agriculture. General History of Oregon. See also **Agriculture history**; **Century farms**; **Fences**; **Great Oregon Steamup**; **Homestead Act**; **Stump farms**.

Farms. In 1860 Oregon had 5,806 farms; by 1994 there were 38,000 with an average size of 461 acres and average value per acre of $740. Since 1977, the amount of farmland in the state has decreased nearly a million acres, from 18.4

million acres to 17.5 million acres in 1994. Farm and ranch receipts in 1994 totaled $2.7 billion. A third of the farms marketed less than $2,500 a year, and only 4,175 farms grossed more than the $100,000 in annual sales needed to support farm operations and a family. In 1995, the average rate of return for Oregon farmers was 1.69%, the lowest since 1983. It had been 4.67% in 1993. Agriculture; 1994-1995 Oregon Agriculture. See also **Agriculture**; **Farm land**; **Farmers**; **Organic farming**.

Fat City Massacre. The facetious name for a breakfast exchange at the Fat City Cafe in Multnomah Village in southwest **Portland** on April 7, 1987, at which Mayor Bud Clark fired police chief Jim Davis. Clark told Davis that he didn't think Davis had the authority the chief was claiming in taking legal action to get working files of a police audit. Davis said, "Yes I do. Read my lips." Clark responded, "Read my lips. Good-bye." A small plaque reading "Site of the Fat City Massacre" was later mounted on the restaurant booth. Governing Oregon; Oregonian 4/8/87:1.

Father of Oregon. A title the 1957 state legislature bestowed on Dr. John McLoughlin (1784-1857) in recognition of his contributions to the settlement of the Oregon Country. As head of the British **Hudson's Bay Company** at **Fort Vancouver** from 1825 until 1846, McLoughlin, contrary to company policy, provided much assistance to arriving American settlers. He then settled in **Oregon City**, which he had laid out, and became a U.S. citizen and the embittered victim of Oregonians' ingratitude. Dictionary of Oregon History. See also **Mother of Oregon**.

Fault. A crack in the earth's crust with displaced sides. Earth movements along the fault are felt as **earthquakes**. The south and east edges of Oregon are cut by several fault zones that run hundreds of miles from the northwest to the southeast; the area to the west of each fault is moving north and that to the east is moving south. From south to north these major fault zones are the McLoughlin, the Eugene-Denio, **Brothers**, and Vale fault zones plus the Olympic-Wallowa lineament. As the **basin and range** area has stretched, the land along one side of north/south faults has raised while the other side dropped, creating mountains such as **Steens Mountain** and **Abert Rim**. Major faults in the Oregon **Coast Range** are the Kings Valley, Corvallis, Gales Creek, and Portland Hills faults. Geology of Oregon. See also **Cascadia subduction zone**.

Federal Columbia River Power System. See **Bonneville Power Administration**.

Federal Courthouse. See **Mark O. Hatfield Federal Courthouse**.

Federal Forest and Resource Policy Team, Governor's. A team of state agency representatives that reviews and monitors federal land and resource-management actions and coordinates state input and responses to proposed federal actions. 775 Summer St. NE, Salem 97310 503-986-0091. Oregon Blue Book. See also **Bureau of Land Management**; **Forest Service (USFS)**.

Federal government in Oregon. Among the federal agencies of special significance to Oregon are the **Forest Service** and the **Bureau of Land Management** which each manage a quarter of the area of the state. See also **Courts, federal**; **Customs Service**; **Land ownership**; **Military in Oregon**; **National**

entries.

Federal Reserve Bank. An independent agency of the U.S. government that helps to oversee the nation's **banking** system and guide the national economy. There are 12 Federal Reserve Bank districts. Oregon is served by the **Portland** branch of the Federal Reserve Bank of San Francisco at 915 SW Stark, PO Box 3436, 97208-3436. 503-221-5900.

Felony. An action that breaks a law, a more serious offense than a **misdemeanor**, and is punishable by a fine or prison sentence or both. Two Oregonians who served in the U.S. Congress have been found guilty of felonies, Senator (1901-1905) John Mitchell whose conviction for bribery was under appeal at the time he died in 1905, and Representative (1995-96) Wes Cooley in 1997 for lying in the **Voters Pamphlet**.

FEMAT Report. A two volume federal report published as a result of the **Northwest Forest Conference** held in **Portland** April 2, 1993. An assessment team led by Dr. Jack Ward Thomas proposed ten alternatives for the management of west-side federally owned lands within the range of the endangered **Northern spotted owl** in the Pacific Northwest and northern California. The government selected alternative 9. The first volume was entitled Forest Ecosystem Management: An Ecological, Economic, and Social Assessment: Report of the Forest Ecosystem Management Assessment Team, July 1993, and the second was the Interagency SEIS Team's Draft Supplemental Environmental Impact Statement on Management of Habitat for Late-successional and Old-growth Forest Related Species within the Range of the Northern Spotted Owl.

Fences. The first fences in Oregon were palisades, made of upright, pointed logs set in trenches, at **Fort Clatsop** (1805), **Astoria** (1811), **Fort Vancouver** (1825), and later around stockaded homes. They, and split rail fences, had the advantage of not requiring any nails or other scarce iron for construction. Homesteaders needed some 25,000 ten-foot-long wooden rails to enclose a 320 acre farm and divide it into 40 acre fields, so a good homestead had a woodlot as well as open fields. The first picket fence is thought to have been built in 1842 for the **McLoughlin House** in **Oregon City**, and by the end of the 19th century nearly every house had at least a front fence of pickets. Cast metal fencing arrived in the 1860s and was used around a few homes and cemetery plots. Picket Fence in Oregon; St. Paul.

Fences Project. See **Washington Park Fences Project**.

Ferguson Ridge Ski Area. A northeast Oregon ski area 10 miles southeast of **Joseph** with a 640-foot vertical drop from a 5,740-foot top elevation. Facilities include a T-bar and rope tow. Eagle Cap Ski Club, Route 1, Box 143, Joseph 97846. 541-426-3493. Oregonian 11/16/97:T7.

Fern Ridge Reservoir. A large, shallow reservoir 12 miles west of **Eugene** formed in 1941 when the **Army Corps of Engineers** built a 46-foot high, earth-fill dam across the Long Tom River in a swampy area of the valley floor. The reservoir is operated for recreation, flood control, and wildlife habitat. It has an average depth of 11 feet and maximum depth of 33 feet. The lake is over four miles long and nearly as broad and covers 9,360 acres at full pool. It is drawn down in winter for flood control. The lake is the third most-used lake in Oregon with about 800,000 visitors a year. Boating (especially sailing), swimming, fishing, and bird watching are popular activities; there are several public day-use parks and a private campground in the area. Atlas of Oregon Lakes.

Ferns. Leafy plants that reproduce by spores instead of seeds. Oregon has a variety of species. The two most common are the large annual bracken fern, *Pteridium aquilinum*, of abandoned fields, and the clumps of evergreen sword fern, *Polystichum munitum*, in shady forests. New sword fern plants grow five years before becoming recognizable. Pacific Coast Fern Finder; Plants and Animals.

Ferries. Boats, powered in a variety of ways, that carry people, wagons, cars, trains, livestock, and/or freight across rivers. Most have been replaced by **bridges**. In 1826 the **Hudson's Bay Company** established the first ferry across the **Willamette River** two miles northwest of what is now **Saint Paul**. Switzer's Ferry across the **Columbia River** from **Fort Vancouver**, Washington to Oregon began operation in 1846, and **Boones Ferry** began in 1847. **Portland's** first ferry across the Willamette was established in 1848, while the last Portland ferry was displaced by the St. Johns Bridge in 1931. Olds Ferry across the **Snake River** began operation in 1862. Ferries were also used to carry **railroad** trains, the largest being the 338' *Kalama* which carried **Northern Pacific** trains across the Columbia River between Goble, Oregon, and Kalama, Washington, from 1883 until the **railroad bridge** between **Portland** and Vancouver opened in 1908. Only one public ferry still crosses the Oregon portion of the Columbia River, operating between **Westport** and Cathlamet, Washington. Three ferries cross the Willamette River: the **Buena Vista** Ferry in southern **Polk County** (since 1852); the **Wheatland** ferry north of **Salem** (early 1850's) near where Jesse Applegate operated a ferry in 1843-44; and the **Canby** ferry (1915). Dictionary of Oregon History; Ferryboats on the Columbia River; Saint Paul.

Ferris wheels. **Oaks Amusement Park** has a 96-foot Ferris wheel. The Portland Bridge Book.

Festa Italiana. An annual **Portland** celebration of things Italian, held on an August weekend. It has included a grape stomp and pizza toss, along with music, dancing, comedy, bocce ball tournament, and wine tasting.

Festival of Flowers. A 12-day **Portland** festival held at **Pioneer Courthouse Square** in late May and early June. It features a display of 25,000 flowering plants, plus daily music and dance performances. The plants are sold to the public at the end of the festival.

Festivals. Oregon has an estimated 700 fairs and festivals a year. For major festivals in **Portland**, see **Artquake; Bite: A Taste of Portland; Cinco de Mayo; Festa Italiana; Festival of Flowers; Homowo Festival of African Arts; Oregon Brewers Festival; Rose Festival**. For festivals elsewhere in Oregon, see **Alpenfest; Art and the Vineyard; Bob Day Saturday; Celebrations, historic; Cranberry Festival; Da Vinci Days; Fiestas; Highland games; Nesika Illahee Pow-Wow; Oktoberfest; Oregon Country Fair; Salem Art Fair and Festival; Sandcastle Day; Southern Oregon Barter Fair; State Fair**. See also **Celebrations, historic; Music festivals**.

Fiber-optic cable. In 1996 high-speed communications were extended to eastern Oregon with the installation of fiber-optic cables to **Klamath Falls, Burns**

and **Grant County**, and high-speed frame relays were installed on the telephone system to serve state **lottery** locations, schools, and public agencies. Two of the four underwater fiber-optic cables providing telephone links between North America and Japan come ashore in Oregon, one in **Pacific City** (Pacific Telecom Inc. in 1991) and one in **Bandon** (AT&T in 1996). The latter is a TPC-5 cable capable of carrying 240,000 voice lines, four times as much as earlier cables. AT&T will also lay a line from Bandon to China in 1998/99, and WCI Cable proposed that a cable line from Alaska come ashore at **Tillamook**. Commerical fishing is prohibited within a two mile corridor along each cable. Oregonian 4/18/95:B18, 3/17/96:D1, 10/19/97:C1, 3/17/98:D1; 3/22/98:B4.

Field burning. A method of disposing of straw residue that helps to eliminate weeds, insects, and diseases in **grass seed** fields, though the smoke may cause respiratory problems and traffic accidents. A smoke-caused 23-vehicle crash on **Interstate 5** that killed 7 people and injured 38 others on August 3, 1988, was documented in a novel, Ever After, by William Wharton, whose daughter and family were killed in the crash. A 5-car accident near **La Grande** on September 20, 1993, also caused by smoke, injured five people. Field burning in the **Willamette Valley** is being reduced annually under state law to a low of 40,000 acres by 1998, and the timing of burns is controlled to reduce smoke impact. Burning will be used to control diseases and weeds that haven't responded to alternative treatments. Oregonian 5/4/95:D2, 8/27/97:A1. See also **Air pollution**; **Visibility**.

Fiestas. Special celebrations by Oregon's **Hispanic** community include those on Mexican Independence Day on September 16, Guadalupe Day on December 12, and **Cinco de Mayo** on May 5, as well as **Woodburn's** Fiesta Mexicana, dating from 1964, held in early August. Nosotros.

Fifty-four Forty or Fight. The 1844 campaign slogan of presidential candidate James Polk, referring to the line of latitude (54° 40') he advocated as the northern boundary of the western U.S. It was the southern border of Alaska, then owned by Russia. The area of dispute, known as the **Oregon Country**, was claimed by both Great Britain and the U.S. However, two years after his election, Polk quietly agreed to the **Oregon Treaty of 1846**, which set the boundary at 49°, the present Canadian border. The treaty clarified the status of American settlers in the Oregon Country. Empire of the Columbia. See also **Boundary question**.

Filbert. See **Hazelnut**.

Filipinos in Oregon. The 1990 census counted 7,000 Filipinos in Oregon. See also **Asians in Oregon**.

Films. In the mid 1990s, film making, including movies, television shows, and TV commercials, contributed about $40 million a year to the state's economy. The Film & Video office in the Oregon Department of **Economic Development** promotes the industry. 503-229-5832. Oregonian 3/10/96:L1. See also **Northwest Film and Video Center**.

Films - history. A film of a 41-round fight at Carson City between Gentleman Jim Corbett and Bob Fitzsimmons, shown in **Portland** on August 5, 1897, was the first moving picture shown in Oregon. By 1912 nickelodeons were operating in downtown Portland, and a few years later, cinema houses were being built on Broadway and all over the suburbs. One of the first movies made in Oregon was the acclaimed Buster Keaton comedy, "The General," filmed in **Cottage Grove** in 1926. "One Flew Over the Cuckoo's Nest," "Animal House," "My Private Idaho," and "Mr. Holland's Opus" are other notable movies filmed in Oregon. During the 1920s, Portland's daily papers, the Oregon Journal and the **Oregonian** sponsored weekly newsreels of Oregon news and sports to be shown at subscribing theaters. The Premium Picture Company had a lot in **Beaverton** where it made films such as "Flames of Passion" and "Gold." Movie star Jane Powell was from Portland. "How It Was Then;" Oregonian 3/10/96:L6, 10/26/97:L2; "Scooping."

Finance and Corporate Securities, Division of. A division of the Oregon Department of **Consumer and Business Services** that regulates both Oregon's state-chartered financial institutions, securities offerings and dealers, and other agencies and dealers including **pawn shops**. 350 Winter St. NE, Room 21, Salem 97310. Finance Section 503-378-4140; Corporate Securities Section 503-378-4387. Oregon Blue Book. See also **Banking; Credit Unions; Securities**.

Finley Wildlife Refuge. See **William L. Finley National Wildlife Refuge**.

Finns. People from Finland began to settle in **Astoria** in the 1870s, and by 1905 numbered 2,027 (out of a total population of 11,045,) making it the largest Finnish community west of the Mississippi River. "Ethnicity and Radicalism."

Fir. True firs are conifer **trees** with cones that perch upright on their topmost branches like little owls and that shatter when ripe. Though Oregonians are usu-ally referring to **Douglas-fir** when speaking of fir trees, Douglas-fir is not a true fir and has cones that hang down and that drop without shattering. However, six species of true firs, genus *Abies*, do grow in Oregon. True firs account for about 10 percent of the commercial timber in Oregon. Some, especially noble fir, *A. procera*, and red fir, *A. magnifica*, are also popular **Christmas trees**. Trees to Know.

Fire. See **Field burning; Fires, historic; Forest fires; Indian burning; Prescribed burning; Slash burning**.

Fire fighters. Nine members of the **Prineville** Interagency Hotshots fire fighting team were among the 14 fire fighters who died July 6, 1994, in a **forest fire** on Storm King Mountain near Glenwood Springs, Colorado. A monument to them, and to all forest fire fighters, has been erected in Ochoco Creek Park in Prineville. See also **Smoke jumpers**.

Fire hydrants. The first fire hydrant in **Portland** was installed on March 28, 1864, at the corner of Washington and First Streets. This Day in Oregon.

Fire lookouts. Buildings or towers on mountain tops used for spotting **forest fires**. One of the first was built on **Mount Hood** in 1915; it toppled onto Eliot Glacier in 1941. At one time there were 805 lookouts in Oregon, but many have been replaced by airplane patrols. Among those still in use is the 85-foot tower on Black Butte west of **Sisters**, rebuilt in 1995. A restored cupola-style lookout, originally constructed in 1928, has been moved to the grounds of the Tiller Ranger Station on the **Umpqua National Forest**, and **Magness Memorial Tree Farm** includes a lookout tower. The Forest Service rents out several fire lookouts for overnight stays; for information contact **Nature of the Northwest**, 503-872-2750. Fire Lookouts of the Northwest.

Fire Marshal, Office of State. A division of the State **Police** that is respon-sible for reducing the loss of life and property from fire, explosion, and hazardous materials, and minimizing hazards of structures, equipment and materials exposed to fire risks. 4760 Portland Rd. NE, Salem 97305. 503-373-1540. <u>Oregon Blue Book</u>.

Firearms. See **Guns**.

Fireball. Any meteor brighter than the planet Venus. A fireball streaks across the Oregon sky about once a month. The brightest fireball on record in Oregon, the Coos Bay fireball, was observed over southwestern Oregon at 12:11 a.m. on February 24, 1992. It was much brighter than full moon, illuminating over 25,000 square miles as brightly as broad daylight. There were reports of electrophonic sound (sounds emitted by other objects at the same time the fireball is seen) but no sonic boom was heard; this indicates that no **meteorites** reached the earth. "Coos Bay Fireball."

Fireboats. Boats designed to pump river water onto burning docks and boats. Two **Portland** Fire Bureau fireboats were licensed in 1995 as the first marine ambulances in Oregon so that they can offer life-saving services to accident victims and bridge jumpers. <u>Oregonian</u> 4/24/95:B4.

Firebrand. A nineteenth century anarchist weekly of considerable regional influence which urged its readers to ignore marriage laws, blue laws (Sunday restrictions), and labor laws. It was published in **Portland** from 1895 until the arrest, in 1897, of the three principals. They were charged with sending obscene literature through the mail; apparently the magazine's advocacy of free love led to its demise. The charges were later dropped. "Free Love and Free Speech on the Pacific Northwest Frontier".

Fires, historic. See **Astoria fire**; **Bandon fire**; **Disasters**; **Forest fires**; **Portland fire**; **Silver Lake fire**; **Tillamook Burn**.

First humans. See **Discoverers**; **Indians, prehistoric**.

First Interstate Tower. See **Buildings, tallest**.

First Thursday. An open house at **art galleries** in **Portland** on the first Thursday of each month from 6 to 9 p.m. at which time they showcase their new exhibits. Various performing artists have attached themselves to the event since William Jamison founded it in 1987. A brochure, available at the galleries, lists the nearly 60 Portland galleries. 503-288-3420. Other communities have similar events.

Fish. Oregon's ocean fish species include **halibut, salmon, smelt**, and **whiting**. Inland waters include **lamprey**, white **sturgeon**, native and introduced **trout**, and native and introduced **warmwater fish**. <u>Oregon Blue Book</u>. See also **Anadromous fish**; **Anglerfish**; **Bottom fish**; **Carp**; **Chub**; **Endangered Species**; **Fishing**; **Game fish**; **Oregon Coast Aquarium**; **Shad**; **Sharks**; **Squawfish**; **Sucker**; **Tuna**; **Walleye**.

Fish and Wildlife Commission. A state commission of seven members appointed by the governor for four-year terms. It formulates general state programs and policies, establishes seasons, methods, and bag limits for recreational and commercial take, and appoints the director of the Oregon Department of **Fish and Wildlife**. 2501 SW 1st Avenue, PO Box 59, Portland 97207. 503-872-5272. <u>Oregon Blue Book</u>.

Fish and Wildlife Service (U.S.). A federal agency within the U.S. Department of the Interior that is responsible for the conservation, protection and enhancement of wild creatures and their habitats, including migratory birds, endangered species, certain marine mammals, and freshwater and anadromous fish. Its operations include fish hatcheries. 911 NE 11th Avenue, Portland 97232-4181. 503-231-6118. Directory of Organizations. See also **Forensics Laboratory**; **National Wildlife Refuges**.

Fish and wildlife agencies. See **Columbia Basin Fish and Wildlife Authority**; **Columbia River Inter-Tribal Fish Commission**; **Fish and Wildlife Commission**; **Fish and Wildlife, Oregon Department of**; **Fish and Wildlife Service (U.S.)**; **National Marine Fisheries Service**; **National Wildlife Refuges (NWRs)**; **Northwest Power Planning Council**; **Pacific Fishery Management Council**; **Pacific States Marine Fisheries Commission**.

Fish and Wildlife, Oregon Department of. The Oregon Department of Fish and Wildlife (ODF&W) is responsible for administering state game laws under policies established by the **Fish and Wildlife Commission**. The department issues two million sports licenses and **hunting tags** a year as well as 10,000 commercial licenses and permits, and operates a variety of facilities, including 34 **fish hatcheries** and 16 wildlife areas. Thousands of volunteers assist with management activities. 2501 SW 1st Avenue, PO Box 59, Portland 97207. 503-872-5272. Oregon Blue Book.

Fish canneries. The first successful salmon cannery was established on the **Columbia River** in 1866; by 1885 there were 55 on the river. Most of the canning crews were **Chinese**; the canning machine that replaced them was called the Iron Chink. **Chinook salmon** production peaked in 1883 with a catch of 43 million pounds, processed into 630,000 cases of 48 one-pound cans. Canneries later began taking **coho** and **sockeye**, also. The last cannery on the Columbia closed in 1980. Northwest Passage. See also **Salmon fishery**.

Fish hatcheries. Twenty-five fish hatcheries, authorized under the federal Mitchell Act, are intended to mitigate damage to fish runs from federal dams on the **Columbia River** and its tributaries. Federal hatcheries are located at Eagle Creek and Warm Springs. The Oregon Department of **Fish and Wildlife** operates a total of 34 fish hatcheries and tracks about 20 private hatcheries.

Fish ladders. Structures designed to provide migrating fish an upstream passage past an obstacle or dam. Young fish moving downstream normally do not use the ladders, and a number are killed going through power turbines or over dam spillways. A ladder at **Willamette Falls** enables salmon to spawn in the **Willamette River** and its tributaries; prior to its construction the only salmon in the upper Willamette were from the few that made it up over the falls during spring floods. Every fish using the Willamette Falls ladder is counted and identified.

Fish Lake (Jackson County). A 483-acre lake on Highway 140 at the foot of **Mount McLoughlin** high in the southern Oregon **Cascade Range**. Originally a small natural lake, it was enlarged by a dam on the North Fork of Little Butte Creek in 1915 to supply irrigation water and now has a maximum depth of 31 feet. The Medford Irrigation District operates the lake which was renovated in 1956 as part of the **Rogue River Basin Project**. Water from Fourmile Lake on the east side of the divide is carried by canal to a lava field a mile and a half from Fish Lake where it is dumped. The water reappears as springs at the head of the lake, supplying much of its flow. The lake, surrounded by federally owned forest land, is heavily used for recreation. Facilities include campgrounds, boat launches, and a resort. Atlas of Oregon Lakes.

Fish wheels. Giant waterwheel-like devices built over narrow channels in the **Columbia River**. Each bucket on the wheel scooped up **salmon** and dumped them into a deep box. The wheels, which took an average of 20,000 pounds of fish a day, first appeared on the Columbia in 1879. At one time there were 76 of them along the river where they were estimated to have taken 5-7% of the total catch. Oregon outlawed them in 1926 and Washington in 1934. Northwest Passage; Organic Machine.

Fisher. A member of the **weasel** family, *Martes pennanti*, much larger than a **marten**, which it otherwise resembles, and smaller than a **wolverine**. Males average 40 inches long (including 16 inches of tail) and 10 pounds in weight, while females weigh about 5 pounds. Fishers' preferred habitat is low and mid-elevation virgin forest near water. Like martens, fishers pursue their prey both on the ground and high in the forest. They are said to be especially fond of **porcupines**. At one time extirpated from Oregon, they were reintroduced in 1961, but only a handful of sightings have been reported. The fisher is a **protected animal**. Atlas of Oregon Wildlife; Mammals and Life Zones of Oregon; Mammals of the Northwest; Oregon Wildlife 51(1):8 Spring 1994.

Fishing boats. Trollers (rhymes with rollers) are ocean **salmon** fishing boats with long outrigger poles that trail multiple lines with baited hooks; they became feasible with the development of the gasoline engine, and by 1920 there were over 1,000 trollers operating out of the mouth of the **Columbia River**. Trawlers tow a funnel shaped net 50 to 4,000 feet below the surface of the ocean and produce the bulk of Oregon's ocean fishery; trawlers using finer mesh are used for **shrimp**. Double-ended Columbia River **gillnet** boats were copied the length of the Americas; the original sails were replaced by gasoline engines about 1910. "Fish Boats and Engines, Coastal Freighters." See also **Mosquito fleet**.

Fishing - commercial. In 1995 Oregon's commercial coastal catch totaled $76 million. **Groundfish** (including **whiting**) accounted for $38.7 million, **crab** for $19 million, **shrimp** for $8.6 million, **tuna** for $3.8 million, **salmon** for $3.5 million, and other (**sturgeon**, **shad**, **smelt**, **clams**, **squid**, scallops, crayfish,...) for $2.4 million. Oregon had 3,900 licensed commercial fishermen with 2,550 vessels, and 35 fish processing plants. The **Lincoln County** ports of **Newport** and **Depoe Bay** account for 50% of the state's total seafood tonnage. **Clatsop County**, with ports in **Astoria**, **Hammond**, and **Warrenton**, is second with 33%, followed by **Charleston** in **Coos County**. The **Pacific Fishery Management Council** manages most marine fisheries in the **Exclusive Economic Zone** outside the 3-mile limit. Agriculture; 1994-1995 Oregon Agriculture. See also **Fishing boats**; **Fishing fleet losses**.

Fishing fleet losses. On May 3 and 4, 1880, a series of sudden squalls destroyed the fishing fleet at the mouth of the **Columbia River**, drowning at least 25 men. **Depoe Bay** honors all who have been lost at sea with an annual Fleet of the Flowers on Memorial Day. Oregonian 5/7/1880:3; Organic Machine. See also **Mosquito fleet**.

Fishing - sport. Nearly 800,000 Oregon fishing licenses are sold each year to fresh and salt water anglers, equal to about a third of the state's over-16 population. Anglers have their choice of 62,000 miles of fishing streams in the state, 1,600 lakes and reservoirs, the Pacific Ocean, and salt-water estuaries. The first fishing license was established in 1909 with a $1 fee for residents and for $5 for non-residents. The Oregon Department of **Fish and Wildlife** publishes <u>Oregon Sport Fishing Regulations</u>, available at sporting goods stores and marinas. Fishing Forecasting Line 503-229-5222. The Oregon **Health Division** has issued consumption advisories about elevated levels of **mercury** in fish from the **Willamette** and **Snake** rivers, **Brownlee**, **Cottage Grove**, **Dorena**, **Owyhee**, Jordan Creek, and Antelope (Malheur County) reservoirs and **East Lake**, about organic chemicals in fatty fish from the Lower **Columbia River** (below Bonneville), and about PCBs and other compounds in fish from **Columbia Slough**. The advisories are listed in the state fishing regulations. In some places Indians have treaty fishing rights. <u>Fishing in Oregon</u>; <u>Oregon Blue Book</u>; <u>Oregonian</u> 6/17/95:D1.

Fishtrap. An organization in **Wallowa County**, founded in 1988, that sponsors summer and winter workshops and other gatherings and programs focusing on policy issues and literature in the West. PO Box 457, Enterprise 97828. 541-426-3623.

Flag. See **State flag**.

Flash floods. Floods in eastern Oregon that result from summer thunderstorm cloudbursts. The worst, the **Heppner flood** on **Willow Creek** on June 14, 1903, killed 247 persons. Most of **Arlington** was destroyed after a cloudburst on July 23, 1927. **Mitchell** has been devastated three times by sudden summer floods, in 1884 (three deaths), 1904 (two deaths), and on July 13, 1956, when 4" of rain fell nearby in 50 minutes. That 1956 flood and another, in Lane Canyon (tributary to the **Umatilla River**) on July 26, 1965, are among the largest flash floods ever observed in the U.S. The Lane Canyon flood formed a wall of water estimated to be 200 feet across and over eight feet high. <u>National Water Summary 1988-89</u>.

Flatheads. A tribe of Indians native to the west slope of the Rocky Mountains in Montana. The Indians of the Pacific coast and lower **Columbia River** were sometimes also called Flatheads because of their custom of binding the foreheads of their infants. Because the resulting flattened brow was considered a mark of superiority, **slaves** were not allowed to flatten their infants' heads. <u>Astoria</u>.

Flax. The plant from which linen is made. It was grown commercially in the **Willamette Valley** between 1844 and 1955; some was processed at the Miles Linen Mill in Salem. The short fiber went into tablecloths and napkins, the long fiber into line used for fishnetting until replaced by nylon. Efforts are being made to reintroduce it as a commercial crop for its fiber, its seed meal, and its oil. "Flax and Linen."

Fleas. Fleas were such a pest for Indians that they would move their villages to escape them. The largest flea known, *Hystrichopsylla schefferi*, lives on **boomers**. Ten times the size of usual fleas, it is over a quarter of an inch long. <u>Great Pacific Northwest Nature Factbook</u>.

Floating homes. In 1997 the **Portland** area had 1,100 floating homes docked at some 37 moorages. Once thought of as cheap **housing**, floating homes have become an expensive life style. A person buys his home through a specialized agent, then buys, leases or rents a slip, and pays a monthly moorage fee. Services to the floating homes include sewer, water, electric, and, sometimes, natural gas connections. Some moorages offer other amenities, such as garages and covered boat slips. Oregonian 1/15/95:H1, 9/14/97:H1.

Flood control. Structural flood-plain management is provided by the **Corps of Engineers**, which operates 11 flood-control reservoirs in the **Willamette River** basin, two in the **Rogue River** basin, and one on **Willow Creek**. The Corps also monitors flood control activities for four **Bureau of Reclamation** projects in Oregon. The River Forecast Center of the National Weather Service is responsible for flood warnings, while the U.S. Geological Service operates river gauging stations. The state **Emergency Management Division** works with the Federal Emergency Management Agency to respond to floods. National Water Summary. See also **Dams**.

Flood of 1813, Willamette River. The first major documented flood in Oregon. Records of the Northwest Fur Company show that water reached the house of their chief factor above the river near **Champoeg**. After the record-setting **flood of 1861** Indians said that there had been a far greater flood some time earlier, but it is not known whether it was the flood of 1813, 1844, or some other unknown flood. National Water Summary 1988-89.

Flood of 1844, Willamette River. Early settlers reported that the greatest flood they ever saw on the Willamette was in November 1844, though fur company records indicate that the **flood of 1813** may have been higher.

Flood of 1861, Willamette River and western Oregon. The "great flood" of December 1861 followed two weeks of warm heavy rain and rapid snowmelt. Waters rose 57 feet above mean low water at **Oregon City**, poured through the streets four feet deep, and carried away its mills and breakwaters. Below **Willamette Falls** the water rose 75 feet, and on Dec. 5 the steamship *St. Clair* was successfully brought down river over the falls. At **Albany** the river was 19 feet over its banks. Several Willamette Valley communities were destroyed, including **Champoeg**, Orleans (population 400) opposite **Corvallis**, and Syracuse, site of the first ferry across the **Santiam River**. There was heavy loss of livestock and property, but the number of lives lost is unknown. The Willamette flooded 353,000 acres, and had a flow of 635,000 cubic feet per second (cfs) at **Portland**, the highest ever recorded. The **lighthouse** at the mouth of the **Umpqua River** was destroyed. The **Rogue River** had an estimated flow at **Grants Pass** of 175,000 cfs. A bitter winter, the coldest since the first trappers had arrived 50 years before, followed the flood, along with deep, long-lasting snow. Army Engineers; Champoeg; St. Paul. See also **Cold spells**.

Flood of 1890, western Oregon. In late January and early February of 1890 nearly every large bridge in the **Willamette Valley** was washed downstream by the flooding river; steamboats docked in **St. Paul**, two miles from the river, high water at **Champoeg** was within 2 inches of the **1861 flood**, and in **Portland** the river reached 22.3 feet. Rivers in southern Oregon also flooded, and much of **Gold Hill** was destroyed.

Flood of 1894. On June 4, 1894, the greatest **Columbia River** flood in historic times inundated **Umatilla** and flowed past **The Dalles** at a rate of 1,200,000 cubic feet per second. It also backed up the **Willamette River** so that it rose to an all-time record high of 33.6 feet at **Portland**. A line on the inner side of the most northern arch of the Haseltine Building, 133 SW Second Avenue, marks the top of the flood, 12 feet above street level. There was, however, little current. The event, dubbed "A Carnival of Waters," created more festivity than havoc as documented in the many photos of people boating and larking through the flooded streets, but extensive damage was revealed when the waters receded after a month. The flood was caused by heavy snow melt in the Rocky Mountain headwaters of the Columbia. Round the Roses.

Flood of 1903. See **Heppner flood**.

Flood of 1948, Columbia River. The flood of May and June, 1948, sometimes called the Vanport flood, was not the highest but was the most destructive flood in the Columbia River basin in the 180 years since settlement. The river carried more than 900,000 cubic feet per second (cfs) for nearly three weeks with a peak flow of one million cfs. The 20-day flood took the lives of at least 32 people, caused 50,000 people to evacuate their homes, destroyed the city of **Vanport** (population 18,500), and caused $100 million in economic losses. Rapid snow melt in the upper reaches of the river caused the flood. Army Engineers; Vanport. See also **Flood of 1894**.

Flood of 1964. Floods throughout Oregon and in neighboring states in December 1964 led to 47 deaths, 15 of them in Oregon, and $400 million ($700 million in 1996 dollars) in damage. The flooding was caused by a deluge of warm rain on top of a heavy snow pack. Record river levels were recorded on the **Willamette, Rogue, Umpqua**, and **Coquille** rivers on December 22, 1964. **Dams** on tributaries of the **Willamette** were calculated to have reduced flood levels at **Eugene** 14.8 feet, at **Salem** by 7.5 feet, and at **Portland** by 4.5 feet. See also **Green Peter Reservoir**.

Flood of 1996. Warm rains on top of heavy snow led to major floods in northern Oregon in February, 1996. Twenty-six Oregon rivers, plus rivers in Washington and Idaho, reached or exceeded flood stage between February 7 and 10, and seven of them reached record highs. The **Willamette River** crested at 28.6 feet at the top of the **Portland** harbor wall on February 9. Dams were said to have reduced crests by 6 feet in Portland, by 7 feet in **Salem**, and by 9 feet in **Eugene**. In Oregon, the flood caused seven deaths and $400 million in damage. Twenty-two Oregon counties were declared disaster areas, 2,166 dwellings were damaged or destroyed, 22,000 persons were evacuated and 6,000 were housed in shelters, and hundreds of roads were closed by slides or high water, including **Interstate 84** and **Interstate 5** in both Washington and Oregon. Water supplies were contaminated in some 15 water districts and use was restricted in the **Portland** metropolitan area. Oregonian 2/18/96:E1. See also **Flood of 1894**.

Flood stage. The height at which water begins to cause damage. On the **Willamette River** at **Eugene** normal river level is 12 feet and flood stage is 23 feet; at **Salem** normal river level is 14 feet and flood stage is 28 feet; at **Portland** normal level is 9.2 feet and flood stage is 18 feet. Oregonian 2/9/96:A1.

Floods. Floods in western Oregon result from winter rainstorms, especially if it falls on snowpack, while floods in eastern Oregon may be caused by winter rainstorms, spring snowmelt runoff, or summer thunderstorms. An unusual flood resulted when the headwall of Polallie Creek on the northeast flanks of **Mount Hood** collapsed on Christmas day,1980, creating a debris flow that rushed down East Fork Hood River, causing one death and $13 million in damage. Some floods are broadly regional while others are remarkably localized. National Weather Summary 1988-89. See also **Pleistocene floods**.

    Floods, coastal rivers. Flooding in coastal rivers occurs in mid-winter as the result of heavy winter rains. High winter tides sometimes exacerbate the effects of flooding in the lower reaches. The **Umpqua River** flooded in 1853, 1861 (toppled the **lighthouse**), 1893 (destroyed **Elkton**), 1927, and 1964 (both devastated **Reedsport**). All coastal Oregon rivers overflowed in the **flood of 1861** and the **flood of 1964/65**. Record levels were reached by some northwest Oregon rivers in January 1972 and by others during the **flood of 1996**. See also **Tsunamis**.

    Floods, Columbia River. The Oregon reach of the **Columbia River** reaches peak flows in May and June as snowmelt from the distant Rocky Mountains pours down the river. The average annual peak discharge of the Columbia is about 583,000 cubic feet per second (cfs), but the flood of 1876, the **flood of 1894**, and the Vanport **flood of 1948** each had flows of a million or more cfs. Other notable historic floods were in 1862, 1880, the **flood of 1964** and the **flood of 1996**; the latter two were winter floods in which warm rains had caused heavy snowmelt. The major Columbia River flood plain is the flat lands on both sides of the river from **Bonneville Dam** down to its mouth. Dams built on the Columbia and its tributaries by the **Corps of Engineers** have lowered floods at Vancouver, Washington from the 37-foot level of the **flood of 1894** to 26.5 feet for an equivalent situation, and the Corps has also built levees to protect much of the area. Army Engineers. See also **Pleistocene floods**.

    Floods, eastern Oregon. Floods in eastern Oregon are sometimes the result of winter rainstorms or spring snowmelt, but are more often the result of summer thunderstorms (often with **hail**) and cloudbursts that lead to destructive **flash floods** in the canyons.

    Floods, southern Oregon. Southern Oregon has shared Oregon's major region-wide floods, including the **floods of 1861** (the most extreme), **1890**, **1964**, and **1996**. Other major area floods were in 1892 and in 1955; the latter led to the **Rogue Basin Project** for flood control. Some areas have had local floods, including **Eagle Point** in 1962, and **Ashland** and the Applegate River in 1974, and Ashland had significant floods in 1948 and 1997. **Bear Creek** flooded **Medford** in 1927. Mail Tribune 1/2/97:6A.

    Floods, Willamette River. Floods in the Willamette Valley usually occur between November and February following heavy rainfall, especially if the rains are warm enough to melt mountain snows. The greatest on record was the **flood of 1861**. Other major basin-wide floods were the **floods of 1813, 1844, 1890, 1964**, and **1996**, though there have been significant floods about every 10 years, and some tributary drainages have flooded on other occasions. Dams control less than a third of the drainage area. It has been proposed that restoring 50,000 acres of wetlands could slow the peak by six hours and reduce the flow by 18% and the crest by 1.9 feet. The original meandering, braided river has been channeled into about half of its original length. Oregonian 3/11/96:A1; Roofs over Rivers.

Flora. A book that describes the plants of a given area. The basic flora for Oregon in current use is Flora of the Pacific Northwest by Hitchcock. Others include Manual of Higher Plants of Oregon by Peck, Handbook of Northwestern Plants by Gilkey, and Illustrated Flora of the Pacific States by Abrams. Some plants of southwest Oregon are found only in the Jepson Manual. Less formal guides include Wildflowers of the Columbia Gorge; Wildflowers of the West; and Wildflower Genetics.

Floras Lake. A natural lake near the ocean nine miles north of **Port Orford**. It is separated from the ocean by sand dunes; a 1908 scheme to develop the lake into an ocean port produced the short-lived town of **Lakeport**. The lake has a maximum depth of 35 feet, and is, at 236 acres, the largest lake in **Curry County** and a prime wind-surfing area. It was named for an 1852 gold miner named Fred Flora or Florey. Atlas of Oregon Lakes. See also *Bawnmore*; **New River**.

Florence. A **Lane County** tourist town and fishing port on the **Siuslaw River** four miles from its mouth. It is located 61 miles west of **Eugene** at the junction of Highway 128 and **Highway 101**. The name board of the French ship *Florence* was found after an 1875 shipwreck at the mouth of the river and was nailed on a building that became the post office. The city was incorporated in 1893. Population 1980 4,411; 1995 6,185. Elevation 11'. PO Box 340, 97439. 541-997-3436. Oregon Geographic Names.

Flour mills. See **Gristmills**.

Flowers. In addition to the many **wildflowers** of Oregon, flowers are found in profusion in home gardens. Commercial growers in the **Willamette Valley** raise fields of **dahlias**, **irises**, and **tulips** for their bulbs, and Easter **lilies** are grown at **Brookings** on the south coast. Some flowers are grown commercially for **seeds**, and many other flowering plants, including **azaleas** and **roses**, are grown by the greenhouse and **nursery industry**.

Flu. See **Influenza**.

Flumes. Water-filled wooden channels used to transport logs or **lumber** to a mill or shipping point. They were widely used throughout the timbered regions of the west. One in California was 55 miles long. A lumber flume at Bridal Veil on the **Columbia River**, used for over 25 years, dropped 2,200 feet in four miles. Logging Transportation.

Fluoride. An ion that reduces the incidence of tooth decay. Thirty of Oregon's **drinking water** systems adjust the level of fluoride in the water and another 21 have naturally-occurring fluoride. The systems with fluoride serve 546,000 people. **Portland**'s Bull Run water supply is not fluoridated. Oregon Drinking Water; Oregonian 1/29/94:A13.

Flying saucers. See **UFOs**.

Flying squirrel. The Northern flying squirrel, *Glaucomys sabrinus*, is a small, strictly nocturnal **squirrel** found throughout Oregon's conifer forests. It is less than a foot long with almost half its length in tail. Its "flight" consists of long downward glides which it steers by using its tail and the membranes between its outstretched legs. Common, though seldom seen, it is a **protected animal**. The

Northern spotted owl is its chief predator. Atlas of Oregon Wildlife; Mammals and Life Zones of Oregon; Mammals of the Northwest. See also **Truffles**.

Fog. Fog is created when air temperature falls below the dew point. The droplets in fog or a cloud are about 1/1000th inch in diameter; if the several million droplets in a quart of space were all brought together they would make only one raindrop. Fogs are most common on the coast in the late fall and early winter when **ocean temperatures** are comparatively high, though fog also moves in off the ocean in summer as hot air inland rises, pulling in the cooler marine air. Inland, persistent winter valley fogs may combine with air pollutants, especially from wood-burning stoves, to create air quality problems. Winter fogs also interfere with holiday plane travel; since the 1960s airports have, under some conditions, cleared fog by seeding it with dry ice. Weather in Oregon. See also **Inversion**; **Weather modification**.

Folk literature. Myths, legends, tall tales, anecdotes, poems, songs, jokes, proverbs, word-games, and such that have been passed down orally. Three of the state's legendary tall-tale spinners were Hathaway Jones, the teller of tall tales from the canyons of the **Rogue River**; Benjamin Franklin, who claimed to be the original Huckleberry Finn and the biggest liar on the **McKenzie River**; and Tebo Ortega, yarn-spinner of **Harney County**. Oregon's first anthology of folk literature is The Stories We Tell, part of the **Oregon Literature Series**.

Follyfarm. A long-vanished eastern Oregon farm and post office in **Malheur County** that was located near the junction of Folly Farm Road (Fields Road), Crowley Road, and Highway 78. It was named by struggling farmer J. H. Neal who established a post office at his home in the sagebrush in 1909. Oregon Geographic Names.

Food Bank. See **Oregon Food Bank**.

Food Innovation Center. See **Agricultural Marketing Center**.

Food processing. Food processing in Oregon is a $2 billion industry with 27,500 employees. Products include canned and frozen fruits and vegetables, **sake**, **vodka**, **beer** and **wine**, and baked goods. Frozen french fries, dehydrated potato flakes, skim milk powder, and baking mix are among the state's top agricultural exports. Gourmet specialties from an array of producers include jams, condiments such as pickled vegetables and wheat berry caviar, flavored oils and vinegars, and nut candies. The state is working to increase the amount of food processing done in the state. Agriculture. See also **Canneries, history**; **Sauerkraut**.

Food stamps. In Oregon in 1996 $20 million was distributed in Food Stamps per month, but federal withdrawal of food stamps for some categories of low-income people withdrew the equivalent of $40 million (40 million pounds of food) of grocery purchases during its first year. The state planned to replace paper stamps with plastic debit cards in 1998, with the recipient's amount credited to the card account. Oregonian 3/25/96:B4, 12/17/97:D15. See also **Oregon Food Bank**.

Footbag. A golf-ball-size filled sack used in footbagging, a sport that includes, among other things, singles and doubles competitions over a 5-foot net. Though Chinese were said to have kicked around a hair-filled bag thousands of years ago, John Stalberger of **Oregon City** invented the modern footbag in 1972, and patented it in 1979 as Hacky Sack. The sport of footbagging has grown since then, and two Oregonians, Tricia George and Kenny Shults, were the 1996 world champions. Sole Purpose Footbag Club of Portland, 503-236-0939. Oregonian 6/15/96:E1.

Football. College football in Oregon began in the 1890's with teams at the State Normal College at Monmouth and Portland University. Oregon Agricultural College (now OSU) first fielded a team in 1893, and the University of Oregon in 1894. In 1962, Terry Baker, quarterback for the **Oregon State University** Beavers, was awarded the Heisman Trophy. Mel Renfro, who played for Jefferson High and the **University of Oregon** before joining the Dallas Cowboys in 1964 for 14 years, was inducted into the Pro Football Hall of Fame in 1996. The only professional football team in Oregon is the Portland Forest Dragons, an Arena (indoor) Football League team that began play in 1997. Oregonian 7/25/96:D8. See also **Linfield College; Rose Bowl; Women in sports.**

Forecourt Fountain. See **Ira C. Keller Fountain.**

Foreign languages. See **Languages.**

Foreign trade offices. See **Trade offices.**

Foreign Trade Zones. A zone that allows goods from overseas to enter the United States without paying duty, as long as they are consumed in the zone or shipped outside the U.S. The zones must have a **Customs Service** inspector. **Medford** and **Klamath Falls** have foreign trade zones.

Forensics Laboratory. The federal Clark R. Bavin National Fish and Wildlife Forensics Laboratory, opened in **Ashland** in 1989, uses a full range of crime lab techniques to solve national and international wildlife crimes. 1490 E Main, 97520. 541-482-4191.

Forest Conference. See **Northwest Forest Conference.**

Forest Ecosystem Management. See **FEMAT.**

Forest education and research. See **Canopy Trail; Forest Talk Radio; Hopkins Memorial Tree Farm; Magness Tree Farm; McDonald/Dunn Forest; Oregon Forest Resources Institute (OFRI); Starkey Experimental Forest and Range; World Forestry Center.**

Forest fires. Wild fires that burn forested areas are recognized as part of historic forest ecology. In eastern Oregon, frequent, low-intensity fires are thought to have burned under the dry forests about every 15 years, destroying brush and many small trees, but leaving the more fire resistant **ponderosa pine.** In western Oregon, forests of the **Coast** and **Cascade** ranges burned in high-intensity stand-replacement fires on average about every 150 years. Indians in western Oregon valleys burned extensive areas annually, creating a patchwork of prairies, forest, and oak savanna, in order to enhance animal browse and encourage certain food plants. Now, the 187,000 homes built in or near forest areas are of concern to both insurers and fire fighters, and in 1996 alone 44 Oregon homes were destroyed by wildfire. Major historic forest fires include

1848 Nestucca, south of **Tillamook**, 295,000 acres.
1849 **Siletz**, between **Siletz** and **Siuslaw** rivers, 800,000 acres.
1853 Yaquina, between **Yaquina Bay** and **Corvallis**, 480,000 acres.
1865 **Silverton**, 990,000 acres. (The largest known Oregon fire.)
1868 **Coos Bay**, 295,000 acres.

1868 **St. Helens** fire, 300,000 acres.

1902 Columbia fire near **Mount Hood**, 170,000 acres, several deaths.

1933 **Tillamook Burn**, 240,000 acres.

1936 **Bandon fire**, 145,000 acres, including the city of **Bandon**, 11 deaths.

1939 Second Tillamook Burn (**Saddle Mountain** fire), 190,000 acres.

1945 Third Tillamook Burn, 180,000 acres.

1966 Oxbow Burn, west of **Eugene**, 43,000 acres.

1987 Silver complex, **Siskiyou National Forest**, 96,500 acres (the largest of 550 fires that season).

1990 Awbrey Hall fire near **Bend**, 3,400 acres and 22 homes.

1996 Simnasho fire, 109,000 acres and 11 homes on the **Warm Springs Reservation**.

1996 Skeleton fire, 15,000 acres and 19 homes near **Bend**.

Fire Ecology; Oregon Blue Book 1993; Oregon Oddities. See also **Fire fighters**; **Fire lookouts**; **Keep Oregon Green**; **Prescribed burning**; **Slash burning**; **Smoke jumpers**; **Smokey the Bear**.

Forest Grove. "Ballad Town, U.S.A." A historic **Washington County** agricultural city in the northwest **Willamette Valley** eight miles west of **Hillsboro** and 26 miles west of **Portland**. In 1851 the community was given the name of J. Quinn Thornton's homestead, though the post office was called Tualatin until 1858. The city was incorporated in 1872. In 1996 the city used the **charette** process to produce a new city center plan. Forest Grove is home to **Pacific University**. The "All Northwest Original Barbershop Ballad Contest" is held annually in March and the **Concours d'Elegance** antique car show in July. Several wineries and a **sake** brewery are nearby. Population 1980 11,499; 1995 14,755. Elevation 210'. PO Box 326, 97116. 503-359-3200. Chamber of Commerce 503-357-3006. Oregon Geographic Names; Oregonian 11/17/96:L1.

Forest health. Insects and diseases kill approximately 1.6 billion **board feet** of lumber annually in Oregon, exceeding the damage caused by **forest fires**. Trees are damaged by various fungal infections (including root rots), mistletoe, and insects, including western **spruce budworm**, Douglas-fir tussock moth, mountain pine beetle, and fir engraver beetle. Insects that burrow under bark can't be fought with insecticides because the bark protects them. Damage is worse in forests already stressed by crowding or drought. Oregon Blue Book. See also **Gypsy moth**.

Forest land. Oregon's forests cover 27.7 million acres (the Atlas of the Pacific Northwest says 30.6 million acres), almost half of the state's land area. Of that, **timberland**, land physically capable of growing a commercial crop of timber, totals 21.9 million acres. Pre-settlement forests covered about 30 million acres; most of the decrease has come since 1970 and is due to clearing for agriculture, urbanization, home sites, roads, and power lines. 57% of Oregon's forest land is owned by the federal government (primarily the **Forest Service** and the **Bureau of Land Management**), the state owns 3%, Indian tribes and other governmental units 2%, individuals 16% in small parcels, and the timber industry 21%. Oregon's Forests. See also **Land use**; **Tree farms**.

Forest management agencies. See **Bureau of Land Management** (U.S.); **Forest Service** (U.S.); **Forestry, Oregon Department of**.

Forest management assistance. See **Extension Service**; **Forestry, Oregon Department of**; **Forest Resource Trust**.

Forest Park. A 4,718-acre, seven-mile-long **Portland** park, the nation's largest park within a city. It lies along **Tualatin Mountain** above **Highway 30**, stretching roughly from Cornell Road north to Newberry Road. A few roads provide access to 50 miles of forest trails; Wildwood Trail meanders 25 miles from the **World Forestry Center** to Germantown Road. Maps are available at **Hoyt Arboretum**. The park was dedicated in 1948 after 45 years of effort, and has had more recent additions. One City's Wilderness.

Forest policy. See **Federal Forest and Resource Policy Team**; **Forest Practices Act, 1971**; **Northwest Forest Conference**.

Forest Practices Act, 1971. A state law adopted in 1971 and amended since that regulates logging practices, road construction, **reforestation**, scenic corridors along highways, application of **pesticides**, wildlife habitat, and **riparian areas** on 11.7 million acres of Oregon's nonfederal lands. The provisions are among the strictest in the nation. The Oregon Department of **Forestry** administers the act.

Forest products industry. An industry based on products of **forest land**, including **lumber, plywood, pulp**, paper, **special forest products**, composite board, engineered wood products, poles, piling, and shakes. It represents about 6% of Oregon's total employment, and 31% of its manufacturing jobs. Employment in the industry has decreased from 91,000 in 1979 to around 50,000 in 1996, because of increased mechanization and decreasing timber supply. **Willamette Industries** is the largest forest products employer in Oregon, with over 3,000 employees. Legacy and Promise. See also **Louisiana Pacific Corporation**; **Lumber production, history**; **Timber harvest**; **Timber workers**.

Forest resource organizations. See **Applegate Partnership**; **Oregon Forest Resources Institute (OFRI)**.

Forest Resource Trust. A state program begun in 1993 to provide financial assistance for landowners who are converting underproductive lands into healthy forests. The landowner receives a loan for planting trees, then pays the loan, plus interest, back at the time of harvest. The **Oregon Department of Forestry** administers the program. See also **Extension Service**.

Forest Service (USFS). An agency within the U.S. Department of Agriculture that administers the thirteen **national forests** in Oregon, covering 15.5 million acres, as well as the **Columbia River Gorge National Scenic Area, Hells Canyon National Recreation Area, Oregon Dunes National Recreation Area**, interpretive centers including **Cape Perpetua Visitor Center, Lava Lands Visitor Center**, Wallowa Valley Visitors Center in **Enterprise**, and centers at **Multnomah Falls** and **Timberline Lodge**. It also operates research facilities in **Portland** and **Corvallis**. Between 1990 and 1996 regional Forest Service employment was cut by 29%. Pacific Northwest Regional Office, 333 SW First Avenue, P.O. Box 3623, Portland 97208-3623. 503-808-2971. See also **Federal Forest and Resource Policy Team, Governor's**.

Forest Talk Radio. A system of three low-power radio transmitters that broadcast forest information at 1610 AM. They are located on **Highway 26** at Camp 18, on **Highway 101** south of **Coos Bay**, and on **Interstate 5** at Pass Creek south of **Eugene**. The program is funded by the **Oregon Forest Resources Institute**.

Forestry Building. A massive log building at the 1905 **Lewis and Clark Centennial Exposition** that was billed as "The largest log cabin in the world," the "Timber Temple," and the "Wood Parthenon." The central hall was supported by 52 perfectly matched Douglas fir logs, with bark, 54 feet high and 6 feet in diameter at the base. The designer, A. E. Doyle, was later the architect for many **Portland** buildings and for **Multnomah Falls Lodge**. After the fair the building continued to be used for exhibits until it burned in 1964. Its loss prompted the construction of the **World Forestry Center**. Great Extravaganza; Round the Roses.

Forestry, Oregon Department of (ODF). The Oregon department responsible for regulating forest practices on private and state lands, researching Oregon's forest resource future, managing the **State Forests**, operating a tree nursery at **Elkton**, and providing assistance to Oregon's private forest owners on forest health, tree improvement, urban forestry, and small woodland management. It administers the Oregon **Forest Practices Act**, and is responsible for fire protection on 15.8 million acres of Oregon's private, state, and **Bureau of Land Management** forest lands. The seven-member Board of Forestry, established in 1907, makes policy. Members are appointed by the Governor. 2600 State Street, Salem 97310. 503-945-7211. Oregon Blue Book. See also **Arbor Day**; **Board of Forestry Lands**; **Common School Fund**; **Tree City USA**.

Forests. Oregon's forest trees include 30 species of conifers and 37 species of hardwoods, plus at least 8 shrub species that sometimes reach tree height. The first trees appeared in Oregon about 200 million years ago; subtropical forests that included palms, avocados, dawn redwoods, and figs appeared about 70 million years ago. About 13 million years ago the climate cooled and dried, and the subtropical trees were gradually displaced by more temperate species. By one million years ago, forests resembled those of today, but vast areas of forest died during the ice age. The forests are still recovering, 10,000 years after the last glacial period. **Forest fires**, too, have played an important role in the development of Oregon forests. Oregon now has three major types of forests, the **Douglas-fir** forests west of the crest of the Cascades, the **ponderosa pine** forests to the east, and the mixed forests of the **Siskiyou Mountains** in the southwest part of the state. Noncommercial forests are found along the crest of the **Cascade Range** and in some areas of eastern Oregon. Natural Vegetation; Trees to Know in Oregon. See also **Canopy trail**; **Forest land**; **Log**; **Lost Forest**; **Old growth forest**; **Riparian areas**; **Reforestation**; **Special forest products**; **Timber supply**; **Vegetation**.

Fort. See **Forts**.

Fort Astor. See **Astoria**.

Fort Birdseye. A log stockade built before the 1855-56 **Rogue River War** by David Birdseye on his land claim on the **Rogue River** near the mouth of Birdseye Creek. On one occasion some 500 persons "forted up" in it. Later a cabin was built using logs from the stockade. Dictionary of Oregon History.

Fort Clatsop National Memorial. A replica of the stockaded camp where the **Lewis and Clark Expedition** spent a sodden three months in 1805-06 before leaving on March 23 for their return east. The exact site of their camp is, as of

1997, unknown though being sought. The fort, located south of the mouth of the **Columbia River**, was the first U.S. military outpost on the Pacific Ocean. The 130-acre site and the replica fort, built by volunteers in 1955, were donated to the federal government in 1958 and are now part of the National Park System. The site also includes a visitors center and picnic area; special demonstrations and activities are frequently scheduled. Route 3, Box 604-FC, Astoria 97103. 503-861-2471.

Fort Dalles, 1850-1868. A military post and supply depot, probably unfortified, built in 1850 on Mill Creek in **Wasco County** in what is now **The Dalles**. It replaced the **Wascopam** Mission building which the military had used the two previous years. Fort Dalles was used as military headquarters during the **Indian wars**. The only remaining building is now a museum. Dictionary of Oregon History; Picturesque Frontier.

Fort George. The name given by the British **North West Company (NWC)** to the fort (Fifteenth and Exchange streets in **Astoria**) that had been called Astoria before the NWC and the British navy took it over from the **Pacific Fur Company** in late 1813. The NWC enlarged the fort to about 150 by 200 feet and fortified it. At the end of the war with Britain, three years of negotiation resulted in an ambiguous agreement in which the fort was restored to America and the American flag flew over it, but the NWC remained in possession of it. After **Hudson's Bay Company** merged with the NWC in 1821 it continued to operate the fort, but made **Fort Vancouver** its headquarters post in 1825. Americans began using the name Astoria again some years later. In 1850 the U.S. Army built another Fort George at a different location (First and Duane streets) in Astoria and operated it for two years. Dictionary of Oregon History; Empire of the Columbia.

Fort Harney, 1867-1880. A fort established 16 miles east of **Burns** on Rattlesnake Creek to protect miners and settlers traveling through the area. It was known variously as Camp on Rattlesnake Creek, Camp Steele, and Camp Crook before being named for General William Selby Harney. It was last of importance during the 1878 **Bannock War**, was no longer manned after 1880, and was abandoned by the government in 1889. The village of Harney, now gone, grew up two miles to the south. Dictionary of Oregon History; Oregon Geographic Names; Other Side of Oregon.

Fort Henrietta, 1855-56. A 100-foot square stockade with two blockhouses built in 1855 during the **Yakima War** on the west bank of the **Umatilla River** at the **Oregon Trail** crossing. The fort was built on the still-smoldering ruins of the Umatilla Indian Agency which had occupied the site from 1851-55. A replica of a period blockhouse is located in Fort Henrietta Park, just across the river in **Echo**.

Fort Hoskins, 1856-1865. An army fort built in **Kings Valley** on the Luckiamute River in **Benton County** to guard the new **Coast Reservation**. Lieutenant Charles Hoskins was killed in Mexico in 1846. Oregon Geographic Names; Oregon Ghost Towns; Other Side of Oregon. See also **Civil War**.

Fort Klamath, 1863-1889. A military post established about a mile southeast of the present community of Fort Klamath and 35 miles north of **Klamath Falls**. It was an important post during the **Modoc** and **Bannock wars**. Dictionary of Oregon History; Old Fort Klamath. See also **Klamath Reservation**.

Fort Lane, 1853-1856. A large, strongly-built military fort established in southern Oregon at the confluence of **Bear Creek** and the **Rogue River** near **Gold Hill**. It was a center of military activity during the **Rogue River War**. In 1855, the fort commander stood off a demand by 200 citizens from Yreka, California, for the surrender of Indians suspected of murdering 11 miners. Nothing now remains of the fort which was named for General Joseph Lane (1801-1881), first governor of the **Oregon Territory**. Dictionary of Oregon History.

Fort Orford, 1851-1856. A fort established in September, 1851, with some 15 buildings and 90 troops to protect the growing community of settlers at **Port Orford**. It was located about 300 feet from **Battle Rock** where Indians had attacked the first settlers in June of that year, but there were no further Indian troubles. Dictionary of Oregon History.

Fort Rains. A blockhouse near the present location of **Bonneville Dam** that served for years as a local landmark. It was built by Major Gabriel Rains in 1856 during the **Yakima War** for the protection of settlers. Dictionary of Oregon History.

Fort Rock. An isolated volcanic tuff ring remnant rising 325' above the surrounding desert near the community of Fort Rock, 38 miles southeast of La Pine in **Lake County**. The ring is a **maar**, created by an explosion in the early **Pleistocene**. Later wave action from a huge **Pleistocene lake**, Fort Rock Lake, eroded through the south side and cut wave terraces on the sides. It is home to a number of species of birds. Fort Rock State Monument has been designated as a **National Natural Landmark**. Fort Rock Valley, now sparsely populated, was heavily settled by **homesteaders** between 1905 and 1915, and was estimated to have had over 1,000 residents at that time. A reunion is held the second weekend in September. "Fort Rock Basin"; "Fort Rock Cave"; Geology of Oregon; High Desert.

Fort Rock Cave. A cave, originally called Cow Cave, near **Fort Rock**, first excavated in 1938 by **University of Oregon** archeologist Luther Cressman. Some 75 well-preserved **sagebrush** bark **sandals** were uncovered beneath a layer of **Mt. Mazama** ash, establishing that human settlement existed at least 7,000 years ago, at a time when the area around Fort Rock was a large, shallow **Pleistocene lake**. In 1951 carbon-14 dating of one of the sandals established an age of 9,000 years, and in 1968 charcoal from the cave, perhaps from a hearth, was carbon dated to 13,200 years ago. In 1998 the owner, Gordon Wanek, donated the cave and 20 surrounding acres to the **Archaeological Conservancy**. Archaeology of Oregon; Oregonian 1/18/98:A1; Sandal and the Cave. See also **Indians, prehistoric**.

Fort Stevens, 1864-1947. Fortifications established to guard the south entrance to the **Columbia River** (Forts Canby and Columbia guard the Washington side). Isaac Ingalls Stevens, for whom it was named, was an Army Engineer and former governor of Washington Territory who was killed in the Civil War. The fort, reconstructed in the 1890s, served as an active defense facility until the end of **World War II**. It was the site of the only hostile shelling of a military base on the U.S. mainland since the War of 1812 when, at 11:30 p.m. on June 21, 1942, a Japanese submarine fired 17 rounds into the area, thinking that they were firing at a submarine base on the Columbia. The fire was not returned as the sub was thought to be out of range of the fort's guns. The area is now a large **state park**.

Army Engineers; Fort Stevens; Silent Siege.

Fort Stevens State Park. A **state park** near the mouth of the **Columbia River** 10 miles west of **Astoria**. Its attractions include a historic military area with museum, miles of hiking and biking trails, freshwater swimming in Coffenbury Lake, wildlife viewing, and several miles of ocean beach with the remains of the 1906 shipwreck of the *Peter Iredale*. The 604-site campground is open all year. Reservations, 800-452-5687. Hammond 97121. 503-861-1671.

Fort Umpqua. Two forts, widely separated, have been called Fort Umpqua. **Hudson's Bay Company** built a fur **trading post** near the present site of **Elkton** in 1836 and used it until the 1850s; it is said to have been the first non-Indian settlement in **Douglas County** though Fort McKay (sometimes also known as Fort Umpqua) had been built near the mouth of Calapooya Creek by 1828. Later, in 1856, the Army built a Fort Umpqua on the west bank of the **Umpqua River** two miles from its mouth to guard the Indians who had been rounded up to live in the area. The remaining Indians were marched off to **Yachats** after several years, and the fort was abandoned in 1862 after a visiting paymaster found all officers away on a hunting trip. Oregon Geographic Names; Requiem for a People. See also **Coos, Lower Umpqua, and Siuslaw Indians**.

Fort Vancouver, 1825-1860. A stockaded **trading post** on the north shore of the **Columbia River**, opposite the mouth of the **Willamette River**, built by the British fur company **Hudson's Bay Company** (HBC), as a regional headquarters. The stockade encompassed 7 acres; inside were quarters for 35 men and some of their families, as well as shops, offices, and storehouses. Several hundred other persons lived outside the fort. A sawmill, grist mill, and extensive livestock and farming operations at the fort supplied the 24 other western HBC posts. Dr. John McLoughlin, 1784-1857, called the Father of Oregon because of his assistance to **Oregon Trail** pioneers, was chief factor until 1846 when he moved to **Oregon City**. The present fort, a National Historic Site operated by the National Park Service, is a partial reconstruction, the original having burned in 1866 after it had been abandoned. 612 East Reserve Street, Vancouver WA 98661-3897. 800-832-3599, 206-696-7655. Fort Vancouver.

Fort William. A **trading post** established by Nathaniel Wyeth on **Sauvie Island**, near Warrior Point, in 1834. The next spring he moved it south to a location opposite the Logie Trail into the Tualatin Valley, but it was soon abandoned. He noted about the island that "a mortality has carried off to a man its inhabitants, and there is nothing to attest that they ever existed except their decaying houses, their graves and their unburied bones, of which there are heaps. So you see, as the righteous people of New England say, providence has made room for me, and without doing them more injury than I should if I had made room for myself, viz., killing them off." General History of Oregon. See also **Malaria**.

Fort Yamhill, 1856-1865. A blockhouse built by settlers on Fort Hill near Valley Junction in **Polk County** as protection against the Indians of the area. In 1856 it was manned by one of four garrisons established by the army to police the new **Grande Ronde Reservation** and was named for the nearby river. The fort was in use for about 10 years. The blockhouse was later moved to the Grand Ronde Agency and used for a jail, and moved again in 1912 to **Dayton** where it stands in a city park. All Quiet on the Yamhill, Oregon Geographic Names; Oregonian 3/8/98:C2. See also **Civil War**.

Forts. The first fort in the Oregon country was **Fort Clatsop**, built by the **Lewis and Clark Expedition** in 1805. **Astoria** (1811), apparently never called Fort Astor, and renamed **Fort George** (1813-1818) by the British, was the second, and the **Hudson's Bay Company**'s **Fort Vancouver** (1825-1860) was the third. Later, during **Indian wars**, the U.S. Army established a series of forts, including **Fort Dalles** (1850-1866), **Fort Orford** (1851-1856), **Fort Lane** (1853-1856), **Fort Henrietta** (1855-1856), **Fort Hoskins** (1856-1865), **Fort Umpqua** (1856-1862), and **Fort Yamhill** (1856-1865), **Fort Klamath** (1863-1889), **Fort Stevens** (1864-1947), and **Fort Harney** (1867-1880). Many were connected by **military wagon roads**. "Fort" was also the name given by pioneers to a place of refuge during Indian raids, whether a military encampment, with or without a blockhouse, or a neighborhood home where a stockade had been built. Some military establishments of that era were called **camps**. Dictionary of Oregon History; Oregon Geographic Names. See also **Mount Vernon**.

Fortune 500. See **Corporations**.

Fossil. A north central Oregon town 90 miles southeast of **The Dalles** on Highway 19. It is the county seat of **Wheeler County**. The post office was established in 1876 and named by Thomas B. Hoover for some fossils he had just found on his ranch; the city was incorporated in 1891. Collecting fossils is allowed behind the high school where leaf prints are found by splitting the host rock. Population 1980 535; 1995 485. Elevation 2,654'. PO Box 467, 97830. 541-763-2698. Oregon Geographic Names.

Fossil Beds National Monument. See **John Day Fossil Beds National Monument**.

Fossil Lake. A normally dry lakebed northeast of **Christmas Lake**, once part of the **Pleistocene lake** known as Fort Rock Lake. It has been the source of many **Pleistocene** vertebrate fossil remains, including fish, water birds, elephants, camels, cats, wolves, dogs, peccaries, bears, and a variety of rodents. So many bones of early horse species were found that it was sometimes known as Equus Beds. Fossil Lake, Oregon. See also **Fossils, animal**.

Fossils, animal. A wide variety of animal fossils have been found in Oregon. The oldest are 380-million-year-old marine fossils found in eastern **Crook County**. Remnants of Jurassic ichthyosaurs, a marine reptile from 160 million years ago, have been found in **Wheeler County** and **Curry County**, but only one **dinosaur** fossil has been found. The most abundant fossils date from 45 million years ago (the **Eocene**) through the **Pleistocene**. The animals of eastern Oregon 35 million years ago included tiny four-toed horses, several kinds of primitive rhinoceroses, hog-like oreodonts, tapirs, and crocodiles, plus other less familiar species. The animals 20 million years ago included bear-like forms and various ancestral dogs, saber tooth tigers, weasels, raccoons, rodents, rabbits, elephants, antelopes, camels, peccaries, deer, and more advanced types of rhinoceroses and horses. A number of large mammals, including horses, camels, mammoths, mastodons, giant bison, sloths, and various carnivores, became extinct about the time humans first appeared 11,000 years ago. Fossil Shells; Handbook of Oregon Plant and

Animal Fossils; Reconstructions. See also **Clam burgers**; **Egg**; **Fossil Lake**; **Jaguars**; **John Day Fossil Beds National Monument**.

Fossils, plant. The oldest Oregon plant fossils, between 270 and 315 million years old, have been found in eastern **Crook County**. The subsequent plant fossil record is sparse, however, until 47 million years ago. The oldest fossils at **John Day Fossil Beds National Monument** date from about 44 million years ago. A number of **Eocene, Oligocene**, and **Miocene** locations around the state have yielded fossil plants, many similar to contemporary plants. Tree ferns, ferns, cycads, and ginkgoes have been found in eastern Oregon. Some fossils indicate warmer periods, such as the palm, fig, and magnolia tree fossils found in the **Coos Bay** area. Handbook of Oregon Plant and Animal Fossils; Reconstructions. See also **Banana**.

Foster care. Temporary care provided to children who are not safe in their own homes. Some children are able to return to their families, and some are eventually placed for **adoption**. In 1995, 7,900 children were placed in foster care, 1,421 of them classed as severely troubled. Three years after placement in foster care, 30% will have been returned to their original homes. Information on being a foster parent, 800-331-0503. Oregonian 10/29/95:L5, 3/8/96:C1. See also **Adult foster homes**.

Foster Farm. See **Philip Foster Historical Farm**.

Foster Reservoir. A lake three miles east of **Sweet Home** at the confluence of the Middle and South Forks of the **Santiam River**. It was formed in 1967 by a 126-foot high, rock fill dam built by the **Army Corps of Engineers** for flood control, for moderating the releases from **Green Peter Reservoir**, and for power generation (61 **megawatts**). At high water, the 3.5-mile-long lake covers 1,220 acres to a maximum depth of 110 feet. The lake is drawn down in the fall in preparation for flood runoff. It is popular for boating, water skiing, fishing, and camping. The nearby community of Foster was named for a father and son who operated a sawmill and grist mill there in the 1890s. Army Engineers; Atlas of Oregon Lakes; Oregon Geographic Names.

Foundations. In 1994 four Oregon foundations had assets over $100 million. They were the Meyer Memorial Trust ($296 million), Ford Family Foundation ($113.6 million; Kenneth "Pappy" Ford, 1908-1997, was the founder of Roseburg Forest Products), the Collins Foundation ($109.6 million) and the **Oregon Community Foundation** ($103 million). Sixty other foundations had assets over $1 million. Guide to Oregon Foundations; Oregon Foundation DataBook. See also **Charitable giving**; **McKenzie River Gathering**.

Fountains. See **Portland fountains**.

Four Rivers Cultural Center. A museum on the campus of **Treasure Valley Community College** in **Ontario**, opened in 1997, with displays honoring **Japanese** Americans and other significant ethnic groups of the area, including **Northern Paiute** Indians, **Basques**, and **Hispanics**. The center includes a conference center, a performing arts theater, and a Japanese garden.

Foxes. Wild members of the dog family. Three species of fox are native to Oregon. The widely distributed "red" fox, *Vulpes vulpes*, may be yellow, gray, or black, but always has a white tip on its bushy tail. It weighs about 10 pounds, and dens in rocky areas. Its varied diet includes small rodents and berries and enough farm animals that it is classed as a **predator** and managed by the Department of **Agriculture**. The gray fox, *Urocyon cinereoargenteus*, is found in western Oregon. It is a bit smaller than the red fox, and always has a black tail tip. Its curved nails enable it to climb trees readily. The large-eared, 4-pound kit fox, *Vulpes macrotis*, of far southeast Oregon, is now listed as an **endangered species**. Its soft, silky fur is buff colored with a black tail tip. Sometimes called the "desert swift", its sprinting ability enables it to feed on **kangaroo rats** and other rodents and **rabbits**. It lives in dens at the end of deep burrows. A 1991 survey found 7 kit foxes. In 1994-95 fur trappers took 142 gray foxes with an average value of $8 and 227 red foxes with an average value of $18. Atlas of Oregon Wildlife; Mammals and Life Zones of Oregon; Mammals of the Northwest.

Foxglove. A tall flowering biennial weed, *Digitalis purpurea*, originally native to the western Mediterranean. It was introduced to Oregon as a garden flower and has since naturalized throughout the **Coast Range** where the leaves are picked commercially as a source of the heart stimulant, digitalis. Plants and Animals; Wildflower Genetics.

Frank Lloyd Wright buildings. At least two homes by famed architect Frank Lloyd Wright (1867-1959) were built in Oregon. The Gordon House near **Wilsonville**, between Charbonneau and the Willamette River, was designed in 1957 but not built until 1963. In **Eugene** the Fogelson House was constructed about 1959 from plans sold and mailed by Wright to the original owners; a second floor was added later. Oregonian 2/22/98:F1; Style & Vernacular.

Fraud. See **Land fraud; Melridge, Inc.**

Fred Meyer. A **Portland**-based retail chain with stores in seven western states. Fortune 500 listed it with 1996 sales of $$3.725 billion. It has about 27,000 employees. 3800 SE 22nd Ave., Portland 97202. 503-232-8844. Oregonian 4/9/96:B14, 6/30/96:R20; Round the Roses. See also **Corporations**.

Free Emigrant Road. A **wagon road** that crossed Oregon from **Vale** to **Eugene** via the Malheur River and the Middle Fork of the **Willamette River**. It was promoted and developed in 1852 as an alternative to the **Oregon Trail** by settlers in the south end of the Willamette Valley who wished to encourage more immigration to their area. In 1853 Elijah Elliott brought a wagon train from **Vale** over the route, but an almost impassable trail and snows in the **Cascade Range** created severe hardship and necessitated a rescue of the "Lost Wagon Train". In 1854 William Macy successfully led a **wagon train** along the route, but Indian troubles limited further use. The route across the **Cascades** is now followed by Highway 58 and the main **Union Pacific** line. "Cutoff Fever;" East of the Cascades. See also **Natron cut-off**.

Free thought. See **Oregon State Secular Union**.

Free Willy. See **Keiko**.

Freezing rain. A condition that occurs as rain falls on freezing cold surfaces so that it, too, freezes, coating the world with ice. Freezing rains, sometimes called ice storms or silver thaws, occur in the **Portland** area as rains coming in from the ocean meet cold air moving down the **Columbia River Gorge**. Freezing rain is accompanied by sounds of tinkling ice, dropping power lines, breaking branches, falling trees, and crunching fenders. One of Oregon's most severe hit the **Willamette Valley** in 1979. Other significant freezing rains occurred in December 1955 in **Redmond** and January 1956 in **Pendleton**. Weather Almanac. See also **Sleet**.

Freight. See **Transportation**; **Trucking**.

Freighting outfits. Commercial, horse-drawn wagons that carried freight in the days before **railroads** and **trucks**. Some had six-horse teams pulling two tandem wagons, and others used eight and twelve-horse teams pulling three or four wagons. Whenever one outfit met another on a one-track road on a mountain side, one team had to back up, a complicated business. The drivers were known as teamsters. Twenty-mule teams pulled **borax** wagons from **Alvord Basin** to Winnemucca, Nevada. Gold and Cattle Country. See also **Pack string**; **Wagon roads**..

Fremont Highway. See **Highway 31**.

Fremont National Forest. A 1,714,693 acre national forest located in **Lake** and **Klamath** counties. It includes the Gearhart Mountain Wilderness. 524 North G Street, P.O. Box 551, Lakeview 97630. 541-947-2151.

Fremont Point. See **Winter Ridge**.

Fremont Power House. A 1908 **hydroelectric** generating station in the **Blue Mountains**. Water for its turbines came through a wooden penstock from Olive Lake, some 8 miles away. It operated until October 1967, supplying power to local **gold** mines, including those at **Granite** and Bourne. A similar plant west of **Haines** has operated even longer, generating .8 **megawatt** of power.

French Canadians in Oregon. Freemen and retired **Hudson's Bay Company** French-Canadian fur trappers, some of whom, with their Indian wives, settled on **French Prairie** before the 1830s. Legend says that a trapper named Montour settled about 1812 and planted a "few seeds". When another settler arrived in 1826, Montour left since "there was scarcely room enough in the **Willamette Valley** for two farmers of the fur-hunting order." By 1834 there were 26 French-Canadian families, centered around **Saint Paul** and **Saint Louis**. After **Willamette Mission** was established by the **Methodists** in 1834, tensions grew between **Catholics** and Protestants, exacerbated by the question of national loyalties. By the 1850s most of the French-Canadians had left, many joining the California **gold rush**. Champoeg; Guide to Early Oregon Churches.

French Pete. A creek that flows into the South Fork of the **McKenzie River**. A long battle over the fate of the **old growth** forests of the valley ended in 1978 when the area was added to the **Three Sisters Wilderness Area**. A trail into the valley begins two miles south of Cougar Reservoir. Walking Guide to Oregon's Ancient Forests.

French Prairie. An area of early white settlement in Oregon on an open prairie that lay between the **Willamette River** and the Pudding River and extended south from **Wilsonville** nearly to **Salem**. Land and river routes converged there, but more importantly, it was the first place where those heading up the Willamette came to open land that they could plow without clearing. Former **French-Canadian** (hence the name) trappers from the **Pacific Fur Company** and **Hudson's Bay Company** began farming there sometime before 1830. **Willamette Mission** was established near the south end of French Prairie in 1834 and Oregon's first government was organized in 1843 at **Champoeg**, the first **settlement**. Champoeg; Oregon Geographic Names. See also **Saint Paul**.

Frenchglen. A tiny unincorporated community at the foot of **Steens Mountain** 59 miles south of **Burns** near the south end of the **Malheur National Wildlife Refuge**. It was named for Pete French and Dr. H. J. Glenn, partners in the famous P Ranch of the area. The Frenchglen Jamboree is held in early August. On summer mornings and evenings a flock of vultures gathers on a tall observation tower east of the road; most years the flock returns to Frenchglen on March 19. A private operator leases the small, state-owned, 1924 Frenchglen Hotel and offers lodging and meals except in winter. 541-493-2825. Offbeat Oregon; Oregonian 8/31/97:D4.

Frogs. Tailless, leaping **amphibians** that differ from **toads** in having smoother skins and in being more aquatic. Eight species of frogs are found in Oregon, including the tiny, 2-inch-long primitive tailed frog, *Ascaphus truei*, that lives in cold mountain and coastal streams; the "tail" is the male copulatory organ. Several Oregon populations of the normally resilient Pacific tree frog developed excess legs in 1996, due perhaps to an outbreak of a parasitic flatworm. The number of frogs has been declining significantly because of habitat loss and increased ultraviolet radiation caused by thinning of the ozone layer. Atlas of Oregon Wildlife; Field Guide to Western Reptiles and Amphibians; Oregonian 1/29/97:A1; Plants and Animals of the Pacific Northwest. See also **Bullfrog**.

From Hellgate to Portland. A much-publicized first **transcontinental** auto crossing in which two Oldsmobile Runabouts raced from New York City to **Portland**. Olds Motor Works sponsored the 1905 race at a time when there were only 141 miles of paved roads in the entire country. Because there were no roads in the west, the route followed the **Oregon Trail**, still in use by covered wagons, for much of the way, and a covered wagon had to rescue one of the cars on **Santiam Pass**. After 40 days of brutal driving through flood, mud, sagebrush, and boulders, the first car, Old Scout, driven by Dwight Huss, reached the **Lewis and Clark Exposition** moments before the **Good Roads** Convention opened. Oregon History 39(1):14; Oregonian 7/3/95:B2.

Frozen rivers. The **Willamette River** is said to have frozen over at **Portland**, usually in January, in 1854, 1855, 1862, 1868, 1875, 1879, 1884, 1888, 1890 (ice four inches thick at Portland), 1909, 1919, 1930, and 1937. The **Columbia River** was recalled to have frozen in 1862, 1868, 1869, 1875, 1888, 1909, 1919, 1930, and 1937. On Jan. 9, 1862, the steamer *Multnomah* was trapped in the ice near Cathlamet, Washington. In January 1868 people and horses crossed to Vancouver on the ice. In 1869 the Columbia froze on November 18. The Columbia froze all the way to **Astoria** in January 1875, and in 1909 it was frozen from January 4 to 11. In December 1919 both rivers froze and cars crossed the Willamette on the ice. After the Columbia froze in late January 1930, a **Coast Guard** icebreaker was brought from San Francisco to open a route (with mixed success) for supplies and mail to isolated communities on the Washington side of the lower river. In January 1937 the rivers froze for the last time since the hydroelectric **dams** built after that resulted in higher winter flows, needed for generating electricity for winter heat and lights. Oregonian 12/27/47:7, 1/6/69:16; Weather Almanac. See also **Ocean temperature**.

Fruit crops. See **Apples**; **Berries**; **Cherries**; **Grapes**; **Peaches**; **Pears**; **Prunes and plums**.

Fruit crops history. The first non-native fruit in the Oregon Country was grown at **Fort Vancouver** beginning in 1825. In 1840 apple trees grew from seeds at **Oregon City**. Henderson Luelling brought 700 fruit trees over the plains in a covered wagon in 1847 (about half survived) and established the first **nursery** in Oregon. Oregon's bounty was displayed at the 1876 Centennial Exposition in Philadelphia with 12 varieties of **apples**, 13 of plums and prunes, and 13 of **pears**, and the quality was commended in the press. However, the booming market for Oregon's fruit faded as California orchards came into production and as diseases and pests appeared in Oregon. Markets revived with the opening of a transcontinental **railroad** connection in 1883. Oregon Oddities; This Day in Oregon 11/9. See also **Berries**; **Cherries**.

Fruit puree. Sabroso Co. in **Medford** has become the international leader of fruit puree and concentrate production and marketing, processing 90,000 tons of fruit a year. The products are used in baby food, fruit juices and nectars, snacks, including fruit rollups and Gummi snacks, and dipping sauces. Mail Tribune 6/9/96:1E.

Fun Run Express. See **Excursion trains**.

Fur trade. Two major fur trades were pursued in the Pacific Northwest. The first, which began with Captain Cook's 1778 voyage, was a triangular maritime trade in sea **otter** pelts in which the ships traded beads and other goods to the Northwest Indians for pelts, then traded the pelts in China for tea and silk which were, in turn, sold in their home ports of London or Boston. Sea otters were never plentiful off the Oregon coast, and by the 1820s had diminished everywhere. The second major fur trade was in **beaver** pelts; the fur was shaved off and felted to make men's beaver hats, popular until the 1840s. This was primarily an overland trade; the mountain men trapped and/or traded with the Indians for pelts which were carried back to St. Louis or to the **Hudson's Bay Company (HBC)** in Canada. The most extensive beaver trapping in Oregon was during the 1820s when the HBC intentionally trapped out the area that is now Oregon in order to discourage American incursions. During the 1830s a number of ex-trappers, both **French Canadian** and American, began farming at **French Prairie**. See also **Astoria**; **Pacific Fur Company**; **North West Company**; **Trading post**.

Furbearing mammals. Mammals that are protected by the Oregon Department of **Fish and Wildlife** so that surplus animals can be trapped for their furs include **beaver**, **bobcat**, **foxes** (red and gray), **marten**, **mink**, **muskrat**, **otter**, and **raccoon**. Non-protected furbearing animals that are taken in the state include **badger**, **coyote**, **nutria**, **possum**, **skunks**, and **weasel**. In 1994-95 a total of 40,552 furbearing animals were taken.

Gambling. Oregon's legal gambling industry includes Indian **casinos** (some offering sports betting), charitable gambling (**bingo and raffles**), **social gambling**, the Oregon **lottery**, and **pari-mutuel racing**. In fiscal year 1995-96, $1,086 million cash ($347 per capita) was wagered on the state lottery and $111 million ($35 per capita) was wagered on pari-mutuel racing. Oregonians authorized pari-mutuel racing in 1933, voted to allow charitable bingo in 1976, established the state lottery in 1984, and authorized charitable raffles in 1986. Before whites arrived, gambling was a favorite sport among the coastal Indians. Both men and women gambled, though they did it separately, and the men sometimes gambled away everything they owned, including themselves, so that they became slaves. Gambling; Oregonian 10/22/95:A18. See also **Casinos**.

Gambling addiction. A 1997 study estimated that 70% of Oregon adults gambled during the previous year and that 3.3% were current problem gamblers. Young, single, male minority residents were most at risk, and problem gamblers were most attracted to casinos and video poker. 60% of those surveyed reported spending less than $10 a month on gambling, 31% spent between $10 and $99 a month, and 9% were spending $100 or more a month. The 78,000 problem gamblers each spent an average of $335 a month ($4,020 a year) for a total of $313.6 million annually. The state's treatment programs served about 550 problem gamblers a year at a cost of $2 million annually. Gamblers Anonymous chapters increased from 3 in 1992 when video poker was introduced to 34 in 1997. Oregon Gambling Addiction Treatment Foundation, 1201 Court Street NE, Salem 97301. 503-399-7201. Gambling; Oregonian 8/27/97:A1.

Game animals. Animals that have been so designated by the Oregon legislature and are managed by the Oregon Department of **Fish and Wildlife**. They may or may not be hunted, depending upon their numbers. See also **Big game**; **Game birds**; **Hunting**.

Game birds. Native and introduced birds managed by the Oregon Department of **Fish and Wildlife**. They include waterfowl (duck, merganser, coot, **geese**, brant, snipe), and upland game birds (band-tailed pigeon, dove, **pheasant**, **quail**, **partridge**, **grouse**, and wild **turkey**). Oregon Hunting Guide. See also **Protected animals**.

Game fish. Oregon Sport Fishing Regulations define game fish as all **trout**, **steelhead**; Atlantic salmon; whitefish; grayling; **coho**, **chinook**, **sockeye**, chum, and pink **salmon**; largemouth and smallmouth bass; catfish; crappie; sunfish; yellow perch; mullet; shad; striped bass; **sturgeon**; **walleye**; and **bullfrogs**. See also **Warmwater fish**.

Gangs. Youth gang activity started in Portland in 1989 and by 1993 was found in half of Oregon counties. Some, but not all, of the gangs are ethnic or racial in identity. In 1993, Portland gangs included the Irish Mob, the Asian Pride, and the Skinheads. Gazette Times 11/7/93:A10. See also **Motorcycle gangs**.

Garbage. See **Hazardous waste**; **Landfills**; **Recycling**; **Solid waste**.

Gardens. **Portland** gardens include **Berry Botanic Garden**; **Crystal Springs Rhododendron Gardens**; **Elk Rock**; **International Rose Test Gardens**; **Japanese Garden**; **Leach Botanical Garden**; and **Sunken Rose Garden**. Gardens elsewhere in the state include **Connie Hansen Garden and Interpretive Center** (Lincoln City); **Martha Springer Botanical Garden and Rose Garden** (Salem); **Oregon Botanical Garden** (Silverton); and **Shore Acres State Park** (Charleston). See also **Arboretums**; **Farming history**.

Gardiner. An unincorporated community located on **Highway 101** across the **Umpqua River** from **Reedsport**. It was named for a Boston merchant whose ship wrecked at the mouth of the river in 1850. Oregon Geographic Names.

Garibaldi. A coastal fishing town 10 miles north of **Tillamook** on **Highway 101** in **Tillamook County**. It is on the site of an ancient Tillamook Indian fishing and whaling village on the shore of **Tillamook Bay**. The Garibaldi Memorial Lumberman's Park museum displays early logging and railroading equipment. The city, named in the 1860s by Daniel D. Bayley for the Italian patriot of the era, Giuseppe Garibaldi, was incorporated in 1946. Population 1980 999; 1995 950. Elevation 10'. Rainfall 90". PO Box 708, 97118. 503-322-3327. Oregon Geographic Names.

Garrison Lake. A small, shallow lake on the north edge of **Port Orford** in Curry County, Garrison Lake is separated from the ocean by a low ridge of sand dunes. The lake consists of two basins. The larger, the north basin, has a maximum depth of 26 feet while the south basin has a maximum depth of 12 feet. The lake, nearly surrounded by residences, is used for recreational boating, fishing, and swimming. Two public boat ramps are available. Water quality problems are severe and complex, due both to the natural character of the lake (shallow with poor circulation), and to the impact of human activities on it. The lake is named for a pioneer settler, John B. Garrison. Atlas of Oregon Lakes.

Gas shortage. See **Energy shortage**.

Gas tax. In 1998 the federal gas tax was 18.4¢ a gallon and Oregon's state gas tax was 24¢ a gallon for a total of 42.4¢, sixteenth highest in the country. However, because of low vehicle registration fees and lack of other taxes, in 1996 Oregon ranked between 9th and 13th lowest (depending on the vehicle's value) in overall car taxes. Trucks, however, paid a weight-mile tax that was, for heavy trucks, the highest in the nation. Before voters removed them in 1980, **state parks** and **state police** were also funded by the gas tax. Now 24% of the State Highway Fund (gas tax, weight-mile fees, and vehicle registrations) is distributed to counties, 16% to cities, and the remaining 60% is used for state **highways**. Oregon was the first state to adopt a gas tax to pay for highway construction and maintenance (1919), an idea later copied by all the other states. Dictionary of Oregon History; Oregonian 1/29/97:E2, 2/16/98:D4. See also **Motor vehicle fees**.

Gasoline. In 1994 motor gasoline supplied 17% of Oregon's total **energy** needs, with 33.8 million barrels (177.8 trillion Btu) used at a total cost of $1,784,200,000. Oxygenated gasoline with an oxygen content of 2.7% is mandated for use November through February in the **Portland** area and in southern Oregon (**Grants Pass**, **Jackson County**, and **Klamath Falls**) in order to reduce **air pollution** from **carbon monoxide**. Mail Tribune 10/31/97:A1; State Energy.

Gasoline storage tanks. The number of underground gasoline storage tanks in Oregon dropped from 30,000 to 18,000 as a result of the federal Resource Conservation and Recovery Act, passed by Congress in 1984 to decrease ground-water contamination. Rural areas, especially, have seen a decline in the number of service stations where business did not justify the expense of tank replacement, though Oregon Lottery grants have allowed installation of above-ground tanks in some communities. Oregonian 5/22/96:C1.

Gaston. A northwest **Willamette Valley** community on Highway 47 twelve miles southwest of **Hillsboro** in **Washington County**. It was named for Joseph

Gaston, a railroad promoter and historian who came to Oregon in 1862. The city was incorporated in 1914. Population 1980 471; 1995 625. Elevation 300'. PO Box 129, 97119. 503-985-3340. Oregon Geographic Names.

Gatch Falls. See **Gooch Falls.**

Gates. A timber community at the western foot of the **Cascade Range** 33 miles east of **Salem** on **Highway 22** near **Mill City.** Because it straddles the North **Santiam River** it is in both **Marion** and **Linn** counties. The post office was first called Henness, then Rock Creek, and finally changed to Gates in 1892 in honor of Mrs. Mary Gates, a pioneer settler. The city was incorporated in 1950. Population 1980 455; 1995 525. Elevation 941'. PO Box 577, 97346. 503-897-2669. Oregon Geographic Names.

Gazelle. A side-wheeler passenger **steamboat** that operated briefly on the **Willamette River** above **Willamette Falls.** While it was preparing for departure upriver from **Canemah** on April 8, 1854, its boiler exploded, killing 28 and injuring 32 persons in Oregon's first serious steamboat accident. The chief engineer had run from the boat moments before and was never heard from again. The sunken hulk was raised, floated over **Willamette Falls,** and rebuilt as the *Senorita.* Shipwrecks of the Pacific Coast.

Gearhart. A north Oregon beach resort town on **Highway 101** just north of **Seaside** and 14 miles south of **Astoria** in **Clatsop County.** It was named for Philip Gearhart, who took a donation land claim in the area in 1850, and was incorporated in 1918. Population 1980 967; 1995 1,170. Elevation 16'. PO Box 2510, 97138. 503-738-5501. Oregon Geographic Names.

Gearhart Mountain. A 8,364' mountain of south central Oregon, about 40 miles northwest of **Lakeview** near the **Lake/Klamath County** line. It is a volcano of **basalt** covered with **andesite** that erupted in the later **Miocene.** The brothers James P. and William H. Gearhart were early cattlemen of the area. Geology of Oregon.

Geer House. See **R. C. Geer Farmhouse.**

Geese. Large, long-necked waterfowl that feed on vegetation and grain. Several species pass through Oregon on their annual spring and fall migrations. About 4,000 pair of Canada geese breed in the state, and seven subspecies winter in the **Willamette Valley** in increasing numbers (165,000 in 1996). This includes about 11,000 dusky Canada geese, a subspecies that is declining due to the effects of the 1964 Alaska earthquake on its nesting grounds. Efforts to protect the dusky have reduced goose hunting in general, resulting in growing numbers and increased damage to farmers' fields. Oregonian 2/13/94:B1, 8/15/97:D4. 11/10/97:E6.

Geisel Monument. A marker enclosed by an iron fence near **Nesika Beach,** seven miles north of **Gold Beach,** that commemorates the massacre of John Geisel and his three young sons on February 22, 1856, during the **Rogue River War.** Mrs. Geisel was injured, and she and her two daughters were taken prisoner but later released. Though she escaped death then, in 1899 Mrs. Geisel, who was living alone near Gold Beach, was robbed and burned to death in her home by parties unknown. Dictionary of Oregon History; Requiem for a People.

Geiser Grand Hotel. An 1889 hotel in **Baker City,** restored and reopened in 1997. The hotel, which features Italian Renaissance Revival architecture, was the grandest hotel between Salt Lake City and Portland when it opened, but it fell on hard times and closed in 1969. The $6 million renovation was enlivened by some two dozen **ghosts**. 1996 Main, 97814. 541-523-1889. Oregonian 10/26/ 97:B4.

Gemstones. Stones gathered in Oregon include bloodstone, jasper including a green jasper known as "Oregon jade", nephrite, rhodonite, mesolite, idocrase, garnet, pink rhodonite, opal, quartz, **agate**, **thunderegg** (Oregon's **state rock**), **sunstone** (Oregon's **state gemstone**), **obsidian**, **fossils**, and **petrified wood**. Gem Trails of Oregon; Gemstones of North America.

Gender. See **Population distribution, gender**.

Genealogy. Genealogical Forum of Portland, 2130 SW Fifth, Suite 220, Portland OR 97201. 503-227-2398.

General election. An election held on the first Tuesday following the first Monday in November of even numbered years. It is the election at which national, state, and local officials are elected. See also **Ballot measures**; **Elections**; **Presidential primary**; **Primary election**; **Voter turnout**.

General fund expenditures. The general fund is the basic operating fund for Oregon's state government. Since the state **budget** is for a two-year period, the figures are usually given that way rather than as annual costs. For the 1995-97, the general fund budget totaled $7.372 billion (excluding **lottery** revenues) for two years, or $1,177 per capita per year. Of the total, 47% was spent for support of local K-12 education, 9% went for higher education, 25% for human resources, 14% for public safety and courts, and 5% for other expenditures. Spending for K-12 education increased from $1.3 billion in 1989-91 to $3.5 billion in 1995-97 due to **Measure 5**. Oregon Blue Book.

General fund revenues. Estimated revenues for the state general fund in the 1995-97 biennium totaled $8.1 billion, including **lottery**. The personal **income tax** generated $6.22 billion in revenue for the two years ($993 per person per year), and made up 72% of general fund revenues. Of the rest of the income, 8% came from the lottery, 6% from corporate income taxes, 2% from cigarette taxes, 2% from insurance taxes, 4% from other sources, and 6% from the beginning balance. Oregon Blue Book. See also **Budget.**

General Land Office (GLO). A federal office that was responsible for surveying and disposing of **public domain** lands through the **Donation Land Act of 1850**, the **Homestead Act of 1862**, mining entries, Indian allotments, and other federal land programs. In 1946 it and the Grazing Service were merged as the **Bureau of Land Management**. The GLO opened its first Oregon **land office** in 1851. Dictionary of Oregon History. See also **Oregon Manual**; **Public Land Survey**.

General Warren. A passenger and freight steamer that left **Portland** January 1852 with a capacity load of wheat and 52 persons aboard. The ship was battered by gale winds soon after reaching the ocean on January 28, and efforts to return to the river were hindered by both the tide and huge swells. The ship ran aground on **Clatsop Spit** and only 10 persons survived. Two years later the stern frame of the ship was found 60 miles to the north. Pacific Graveyard.

Geoduck. A large clam, *Panopea generosa*, said to live 130 years and reach

35 pounds in weight, though five-year-old geoducks are about 2 feet long (including the large neck) and weigh up to two pounds. In Oregon they are found only at Netarts Bay, but they are being raised commercially in Washington. The name is pronounced gooeyduck, despite the spelling. Bay Clams of Oregon; Great Pacific Northwest Nature Factbook; Oregonian 5/6/97:FD1.

Geographic center of the state. The geographic center of Oregon lies near Roberts, south of **Prineville Reservoir** and about 25 miles southeast of **Prineville**. The State Service Center for **Geographic Information Systems** identifies the co-ordinates as 44°11'29"N and -120°45'23"W. National Atlas.

Geographic center of the United States. The geographic center of the 50 United States, measured north to south, east to west, lies on the side of China Cap Peak in the **Wallowa Mountains** in southeast **Union County**. History of Union County.

Geographic Information Systems, State Service Center for (GIS). A center that provides GIS coordination and services to federal, state, and local governments as well as to private and non-profit organizations. A fee is charged. The center's library of GIS data is available free of charge through its web site, www.sscgis.state.or.us. 503-378-4163. Oregon Blue Book. See also **Oregon Geographic Names Board**.

Geographic names. See **Place names**.

Geography. Geographers recognize nine physiographic provinces in Oregon: the complex **Klamath Mountains** of the southwest part of the state; the wet, heavily forested **Coast Range** along the Pacific Ocean; the populated and agriculturally productive **Willamette Valley**, which drains to the north between the Coast Range and the high, volcanic, north-south **Cascade Range**; the north central **Deschutes-Columbia plateau** wheat country; the diverse **Blue Mountains** of the northeast with gold, cattle, and timber; the central sagebrush-covered **high lava plains**; the arid south-central **basin and range** cattle country; and the dry canyon **Owyhee uplands** of the far southeast. Perversely, the eastern two-thirds of the state feels more "Western" than does the western third, due to the aridity created by the Cascade Range rain shadow. Geology of Oregon; Making of Oregon; Rare, Threatened, and Endangered.

Geologist Examiners, State Board of. A six member board that sets qualifications, examines, and registers geologists, certifies those with an engineering specialty, and disciplines and revokes registration when warranted. 750 Front St. NE #240, Salem 97310. 503-378-4180. Oregon Blue Book.

Geology. 400 million years ago Oregon was under a great bay in the ocean; the shoreline curved east from Washington through Idaho and Nevada. The dynamics of the westward moving North America plate and the eastward moving oceanic plate explain much of the subsequent geology of the state. The oceanic plate sometimes carried along chains of volcanic islands or crustal blocks. These attached to the continent, forming the **Blue Mountains** and the **Klamath Mountains** and later the foundation of the **Coast Range**. Ocean sediments that were scraped and jammed from the oceanic plate as it slides under the mainland North America plate pushed up the Coast Range. As the oceanic plate slides deeper, down to about 90 miles below the continental surface, the leading edge melts;

some of this lighter magma rises to emerge in **volcanoes** and **lava** flows of the **Cascade Range**. The western part of the state has gradually been rotating clockwise, pivoting around a point near Puget Sound in Washington. This created an area in central Oregon that was pulled thin and through which massive **basalt** flows poured. Geology of Oregon. See also **Geography**; **Plate tectonics**.

Geology and Mineral Industries, Department of (DOGAMI). An Oregon department formed in 1937 to provide geologic information to the state and the public, and to promote and regulate mining and other geologic activities. It is governed by a board of three persons appointed by the governor for four year terms. The board appoints the State Geologist. The department has field offices in **Baker City** and **Grants Pass**, and operates the **Nature of the Northwest Information Center** in **Portland** in cooperation with the U.S. **Forest Service**. 800 NE Oregon St. #28, Ste 965, Portland 97232. 503-731-4100. Oregon Blue Book.

George Fox University. An accredited private college in **Newberg** that enrolled 1,712 students in 1995. It grew from a secondary school, Friends Pacific Academy, founded by the Friends (Quaker) Church in 1885, and in 1891 was raised to college level and renamed Pacific College. It became George Fox College in 1949, and in 1997 merged with Western Evangelical Seminary to become George Fox University. George Fox (1624-1691) was the founder of the Society of Friends. 414 Meridian, Newberg 97132. 503-538-8383. Dictionary of Oregon History; Oregon Blue Book.

Geothermal energy. Energy derived from the heat of the earth's interior. **Klamath Falls** lies over an extensive hot-water reservoir, and the mineralized water has been used to heat homes, public buildings, swimming pools, sidewalks, and streets, and to pasteurize milk. Although geothermal resources are limited in the **Blue Mountains**, **Hot Lake** (150°-205°F) near **La Grande** was developed as a spa in 1880, and **Cove** and **Union** each built facilities to exploit thermal springs and wells, though water temperatures were less than 100°F. The **Vale** region, **Alvord Basin**, **Warner Valley**, and the **Lakeview** area are known to have potential geothermal resources. Anadarko Petroleum Corporation has proposed drilling 25 wells in the Alvord Basin in preparation for a 22.9 megawatt generating plant to be completed by 1999. Plans for a 33 **megawatt** plant for the side of **Newberry Volcano** were abandoned in 1996 after further drilling found insufficient resources to support the plant; temperatures of 400°F were needed. Oregonian 9/6/96:B6. See also **Hot springs**.

Gerber Reservoir. A large irrigation impoundment 36 miles east of **Klamath Falls** in an area of open forest and rangeland. It was formed in 1925 by a dam across Miller Creek as part of the **Klamath Project**. The **Bureau of Reclamation** constructed and operates the reservoir which, when full, is three miles long with three narrow arms, covers 4,047 acres, and has a maximum depth of 65 feet. Warm water fishing is popular, especially in the spring, and there are several campgrounds and boat launching sites. Louis Gerber owned much of the area covered by the reservoir. Atlas of Oregon Lakes.

Germans in Oregon. Some of the early German settlers in Oregon became dairymen in north **Washington County** in the area around Germantown Road. "Dutch" place names in central and southern Oregon commemorate German settlers in those areas. By 1890 **Portland** had a large number of Germans, including whole villages of Germans who had lived in Russia for several generations. The German Aid Society sponsors the Liedertafel Harmonie, a singing group founded as an all-male choir in 1858 but which has included women since it reorganized in 1951. 714 SW 11th Avenue, Portland 97205. 503-223-3592. Round the Roses. See also **Immigration**; **Metolius**; **Tourism**.

Germplasm. See **Seed bank**.

Gervais (JER-vus). A historic mid-**Willamette Valley** agricultural town in **Marion County** ten miles northeast of **Salem** and three miles south of **Woodburn**. It was named in honor of Joseph Gervais, who first came to Oregon in 1811 as a fur trapper and then stayed as one of the earliest settlers. The city was platted in the early 1870s when the railroad came through and incorporated in 1878. Population 1980 799; 1995 995. Elevation 184'. PO Box 348, 97026. 503-792-4222. Oregon Geographic Names; Oregonian 3/9/97:H1.

"Get Oregon Out of the Mud". A widespread slogan that prompted the 1913 legislature to establish the Oregon State Highway Department (now the Oregon Department of **Transportation**). Except for a few **plank roads**, the **wagon roads** in use at the time were impassable in the winter. First 75 Years. See also **Highways, history**.

Geyser. A spring that erupts intermittently, often emitting steam as well as water. Oregon's geyser, "Old Perpetual", was created when a shallow well was drilled in October 1923 at Hunter's Hot Springs north of **Lakeview**. It erupts 180°F water 60 feet into the air about twice a minute. In 1955 Charles Crump drilled a 100 foot well in the **Warner Valley** north of Adel that erupted about every 12 hours until, in 1959, he drilled another nearby to 1,684 feet deep, looking for steam for generating electricity. It erupted 260°F steam periodically (300° was needed) until vandals blocked it with rocks. In recent years the **Bureau of Land Management** discovered a little 6- to 8-foot geyser of 200ºF water at **Mickey Hot Springs** in the **Alvord Basin**. It jets intermittently every minute or two in the spring but dries up in the summer. Geology of Oregon; Oregonian 8/9/60:1, 3/13/97:E8.

Ghost towns. In Oregon's brief history of white settlement, hundreds of communities have sprung up only to disappear; **Linn County** alone counts over 50. Many towns boomed and faded in the **gold-mining** areas of northeast and southwest Oregon. A number of towns in central and eastern Oregon existed only during the desert homesteading boom of the 1910s. Timber communities have been abandoned as timber was cut out and mills were closed. Some trading centers died after new forms of transportation developed. A few long-gone towns, such as **Bayocean**, **Imperial**, **Lakeport**, and **Ortley**, were unsustainable promotions. **Greenhorn** is the only incorporated Oregon city operating under state law as a "historic ghost town." Oregon Ghost Towns; Other Side of Oregon; This Side of Oregon; Tracking down Oregon. See also **Auburn**; **Follyfarm**; **Granite**; **Kinzua**; **Shaniko**; **Shevlin**; **Sumpter**; **Valsetz**.

Ghosts. Oregon's fabled ghosts include those at the **Yaquina Bay Lighthouse**, Heceta House near **Heceta Head Lighthouse**, the Applegate house near **Yoncalla**, the **Geiser Grand Hotel** in **Baker City**, and at **Hot Lake Resort**.

Oregon's Ghosts and Monsters; Oregonian 10/26/97:B4; Skookum.

Giardiasis. A **waterborne disease** caused by a microscopic protozoan parasite that is found in unfiltered surface waters throughout the state, even in **wilderness areas**. Once introduced to a watershed through human waste, it is passed along by wildlife. 925 cases were reported in the state in 1996.

Gilbert Village. See **A. C. Gilbert's Discovery Village**.

Gilchrist. A one-time **company town**, the last in Oregon, located on **Highway 97** in northern **Klamath County** 45 miles south of **Bend**. In 1997 the unincorporated community of some 130 homes was sold piecemeal to residents and others. Gilchrist Timber Company, which had relocated from Mississippi in 1938, built the town to provide housing and services for its mill employees. The tidy community was sometimes called Brown Town because all of the buildings were painted "Gilchrist brown", but in 1995 the owners began replacing the brown wood siding with pastel vinyl. The adjacent unincorporated community to the south is called Crescent. "Gilchrist, Oregon;" Oregonian 1/4/97:C1.`

Gilliam County. A northern-tier wheat county along the **Columbia River**, bounded by Washington State across the river on the north (the closest bridge is a few miles west at **Biggs**), and by **Morrow**, **Wheeler**, **Wasco**, and **Sherman** counties. Incorporated cities are **Condon** (county seat), **Arlington**, and **Lonerock**. Elevations range from 265' along the river to 3,000-foot ridges in the south. The economy is based on agriculture, livestock, recreation, and hunting. Taxable assessed value in 1995 was $205,000,000, or $117,000 per capita, the highest in the state. The county was created in 1885 from **Wasco County** and was named for Colonel Cornelius Gilliam (1798-1848) who was accidentally killed while commanding the forces of Oregon's **Provisional government** during the **Cayuse War**. It is the state's second smallest county in population; only Wheeler County has fewer. Population 1980 2,057; 1995 1,750. Area 1,223 square miles. Density 1/sq.mi. Annual precipitation 15"; average temperature January 30°F, July 67°F. Courthouse, 221 S Oregon, Condon 97823. 541-384-6351. History of Gilliam County; Oregon Blue Book.

Gillnets. Nets up to 1/4 mile long used in the **Columbia River** to catch **salmon**. Their mesh size and use is regulated. They are not to be confused with the miles-long driftnets formerly used in ocean fishing but now outlawed in the north Pacific. See also **Mosquito fleet**.

Gin. See **Vodka**.

Gin Lin trail. Gin Lin, a 19th century **Chinese** miner, reportedly took up to $2 million in gold from his claims in the Applegate Valley. The results of his hydraulic operation can be seen from the trail, located fifteen miles south of **Jacksonville**.

Glacial erratics. See **Erratics**.

Glacial floods. See **Pleistocene floods**.

Glaciation. During the ice ages of the **Pleistocene** the continental ice shield did not reach Oregon; its southern limit was the Puget Sound region of Washington. However, extensive glacier complexes formed in the **Cascade Range** beginning about 2 million years ago, and as recently as 15,000 years ago **glaciers** were nearly continuous down the high Cascades from **Mount Hood** south to **Mount**

McLoughlin. At one time glacial ice stretched from the peak of Mt. Hood down the Sandy River almost to the **Columbia River**. During the Pleistocene the **Wallowas** had nine glaciers averaging 1,000' thick (one was 22 miles long), **Steens Mountain** was heavily glaciated, and there were small isolated glaciers in the **Klamath Mountains** and the **Coast Range**. Geology of Oregon; "Glaciation in the central Coast Range". See also **Glaciers**; **Moraine**.

Glacier Lake. A much-photographed high-mountain lake lying in a glacial cirque in the **Eagle Cap Wilderness Area** of the **Wallowa Mountains**. The lake, accessible only by trail, is at 8,200 feet elevation, with Eagle Cap rising steeply behind it to 9,595 feet. The lake covers 47 acres and has a maximum depth of 125 feet. The water in the deepest part of the lake stays near 39°F (the temperature of maximum density) and even the surface water seldom warms above 50° F. There is some late summer fishing for brook trout. Atlas of Oregon Lakes.

Glaciers. Dense masses of ice, formed by the compaction of snow on land, that gradually slip downhill, tearing and grinding the bedrock they slide over. There are presently several glaciers in Oregon on the high peaks of the **Cascade Range**, all of them retreating. **Mount Hood** has nine glaciers with a total volume of 12.2 billion cubic feet of ice and snow (equal to the flow of the **Columbia River** for 18 hours), and the **Three Sisters** have five major glaciers, including the 300' thick Collier glacier between **North** and **Middle Sister**. Collier Glacier has receded a mile since 1912, and may split due to thinning. Rock Creek Glacier lies in the **Elkhorn Mountains** of northeast Oregon. Permanent snow fields, not thick enough to form ice, are found on several Oregon peaks. Geology of Oregon. See also **Glaciation**.

Gladstone. A **Portland**-area suburban city two miles north of **Oregon City** in **Clackamas County**. It lies on the north side of the Clackamas River at its junction with the **Willamette River**; city parks provide two miles of river access. Other area attractions include the Pow-Wow Maple Tree where the Clackamas and Multnomah Indian Tribes would meet, and an annual **Chautauqua** festival the first weekend of August. Gladstone was named for British statesman William E. Gladstone by developer Harvey Cross. The post office was established in 1890, and the city was incorporated in 1911. Population 1980 9,500; 1995 11,475. Elevation 57'. 525 Portland Ave., 97027. 503-656-5225. Oregon Geographic Names.

Glass Butte. A mountain of **obsidian**, elevation 6385', located south of **Highway 20** about 75 miles east of **Bend**. The mountain is part of a 12-mile series of low domes that erupted over a million-year period about 5 million years ago. Some of the obsidian is streaked with red or brown, or is iridescent silver, rather than being the usual clear black. Geology of Oregon. See also **High lava plains**.

Gleaning. An Oregon program that encourages growers to donate excess agricultural produce for harvest and use by low-income families and groups. A commercial grower may receive a tax credit, and a home gardener is eligible for a tax-deductible donation receipt.

Glendale. A southwest Oregon timber town on the **Southern Pacific Railroad** 50 miles south of **Roseburg** in **Douglas County**. It was established as a railroad station in the early 1880s. The town was originally named Julia but for unknown reasons it was changed to Glendale in a subsequent controversy. A **Rus-**

sian Jewish colony was established in 1882 and lasted five years. The city was incorporated in 1901. A fire on July 11, 1928, destroyed much of the business district. Population 1980 712; 1995 730. Elevation 1,418'. PO Box 361, 97442. 541-832-2106. Oregon Geographic Names.

Gleneden Beach. An unincorporated beach community just south of Siletz Bay 18 miles north of **Newport**. It is known primarily as the location of Salishan resort. Oregon Geographic Names.

Glide. An unincorporated community on the North **Umpqua River** 18 miles northeast of **Roseburg** that is noted for its annual spring **wildflower** show. It was named by the first postmistress in 1890 after she heard her small son singing "The River Goes Gliding Along." Oregon Geographic Names.

Gliding. In 1997 four Oregon glider operations provided rides to the public: commercial operations at the **McMinnville** and **Hood River** airports and clubs at **North Plains** and **Madras/Bend**. Oregonian 9/17/97:D9.

Goats. Pygora goats, pygmy/angora goats sometimes called Oregon teddy bears, were developed in the 1980s by Katharine Jorgenson of **Oregon City**. (Goats hold their tails up, the tails of sheep droop.) Pygora Breeders Association, PO Box 51, Clackamas 97015. Oregonian 1/19/97:D5. See also **Weather goats**.

Goble. A community on the **Columbia River** in **Columbia County**. It was the location of a ferry to Kalama, Washington on which the **Northern Pacific Railroad** transported their trains across the river until a **railroad bridge** was completed at **Portland** in 1908.

God Squad. A federal committee, formally known as the **Endangered Species** Committee, that has the authority to decide whether the costs of protecting a species from extinction are too high, in which case the species should be allowed to go extinct. The committee is made up of the secretaries of Interior, Agriculture, and Army, plus the heads of the Council of Economic Advisers, the Environmental Protection Agency, the National Oceanic and Atmospheric Administration, and a representative of each affected state. Tree Huggers.

Gold. Gold is most often found in Oregon around the edges of massive **granitic** intrusions in northeast Oregon in the **Blue** and **Wallowa mountains** and in southwest Oregon's **Siskiyou Mountains**, though lesser amounts have also been found around small intrusions in the **Cascade Range**. **Silver**, **copper**, and other minerals are frequently found associated with it. **Lode gold** is found in veins in rock where it formed by the deposition from hot, mineralized water. Gold that has weathered free and been concentrated in stream or beach deposits is called **placer gold**. Gold and Silver in Oregon.

Gold Beach. A south Oregon coast tourist and timber town located on **Highway 101** at the mouth of the **Rogue River**; it is the county seat of **Curry County**. The community, originally called Ellensburg, sprang up in the 1850's as a gold mining camp as hundreds of placer miners separated gold from beach sands until the **flood of 1861** washed away the sands. The city was incorporated in 1945. Attractions include the beaches, the scenic drive south to the California border, and jet boat trips on the Rogue River. Population 1980 1,515; 1995 2,080. Elevation 60'. 29592 Ellensburg Ave., 97444. 541-247-7029. Chamber of Commerce 800-525-2334. Oregon Geographic Names. See also **Science education**.

Gold Beach massacre. See **Rogue River War**.

Gold dredging. The process of removing **placer gold** by using a floating dredge to hoist buckets of soil and rock from a valley floor. The gravel is then washed to sort out the heavier **gold**. The dredge digs out the deposits in front of it and dumps the leftover rock (tailings) behind it, so that the dredge floats along on its own moving pond. Piles of rock tailings can still be seen along many streams of northeast and southwest Oregon; the topsoil was washed down the river. A steam dredge, one of the first, began operation in 1903 in southern Oregon. A large electric dredge that operated on Grave Creek in **Josephine County** in the 1930's could dredge 5,000 cubic yards a day. By 1954, when it closed down, the 125-foot-long **Sumpter Valley dredge,** the largest ever used in Oregon, had taken out $4.5 million in gold from an eight-mile stretch along the Powder River; the site, along with the old dredge, is being made into a **state park**. "As a county we ended without the land, without the money, and without the gold," wrote Herman Oliver in Gold and Cattle Country about dredging in **Grant County**. Dredging for Gold; Gold and Silver.

Gold Hill. A southern Oregon town 20 miles northwest of **Medford** in **Jackson County**. It is located at a rocky narrows of the **Rogue River** where toll bridges were built in the 1850s. The town was established in 1884 as a rail station, commercial center, and mining town named for the nearby hill on which gold had been discovered in 1860. The **flood of 1890** swept away most of the town, but it rebuilt and was incorporated in 1895. Attractions include the Oregon Vortex House of Mystery 5 miles north. Population 1980 904; 1995 1,235. Elevation 1,085'. 420 6th Ave., PO Box 308, 97525. 541-855-1525. Land in Common.

Gold mining. The first report of **gold** in Oregon was by members of Meek's 1845 **Lost Wagon Train** who found some nuggets, later identified as gold, in a small stream, leading to the legend of the **Blue Bucket Mine**. Gold was discovered in southwest Oregon in 1851 by miners from Illinois and in northeast Oregon in 1861, leading to **gold rushes**, mining camps, and boom towns. Miners adopted their own regulations in **mining districts**. Most of the early gold mining in Oregon was of **placer gold** in river deposits; this required labor but little capital. Hard rock mining of **lode gold** developed where veins of ore were rich enough to justify the expense. A total of 5.8 million troy ounces of **gold** had been mined in Oregon by 1965, most of it before 1942. Little gold has been mined since then, though the development of **heap-leach mining** increased the potential of low-grade ores. Gold and Silver in Oregon; Oregon's Golden Years. See also **Ashwood; Auburn mining district; Blue Bucket Mine; Bohemia mining district; Canyon City mines; Cornucopia Mine; Gold rushes; Grassy Mountain; Mining districts; Powder River mining district**.

Gold mining law. See **Mining law**.

Gold nuggets. While most gold found in **placer gold** deposits is in pieces the size of wheat grains or smaller, larger nuggets are occasionally found. The largest reported from Oregon was found in the **Greenhorn** district of western **Baker County** and weighed 677 troy ounces (about 46 pounds avoirdupois). The **Armstrong nugget** from **Grant County** weighs 80.4 troy ounces. In 1859 a nugget was discovered on the east fork of Althouse Creek in **Josephine County** that weighed 204 troy ounces, and another almost as large was found soon after in the same general area. (A troy ounce weighs about 10% more than an avoirdupois ounce.) Gold and Silver in Oregon.

Gold panning. The simplest method of **gold mining**, using only a hand-held gold pan to swirl out a slurry of sand, gravel, and water, leaving the denser **gold** behind. The gold pan itself is like a large pie pan. Some recreational miners use **dredges** to pull up bottom deposits; these require a permit from the Department of **Environmental Quality.** The **Bureau of Land Management** and **Forest Service** have identified several areas on federal lands for recreational gold mining, but recreational mining is prohibited along state-designated scenic waterways. Department of **Geology and Mineral Industries**, 503-229-5580. Gold Mining in Oregon; Oregon's Heritage: Recreational Gold Panning.

Gold rush, Alaska (1897). News of the discovery of gold in the Klondike gold fields reached **Portland** in the summer of 1897, and the city became a major outfitting port for the hordes rushing north. Merchants and farmers prospered both from the demand for goods and from the gold the successful miners brought back. Dictionary of Oregon History.

Gold rush, British Columbia (1857). After gold was discovered on the Fraser River in 1857 hundreds of Oregonians joined the stampede to the north. For a couple of years the demand for foodstuffs and goods provided a significant boost to the economy of the Oregon Territory. Dictionary of Oregon History.

Gold rush, California (1848). Word of the discovery of gold in California reached Oregon in August 1848. Two-thirds of Oregon's men promptly headed for the gold fields. The **Linn County** court was in session when the news arrived and all - judge, jury, prisoners, and spectators - left for the diggings, some by boat and some down the **Siskiyou Trail.** In 1849 Oregon's **Provisional Government** was unable to muster a quorum. Many miners eventually brought back significant amounts of gold, and the gold rush also provided, for a few years, a profitable market for Oregon's lumber, wheat and produce. Sheep sold for $16 and wheat for $6 per bushel. Dictionary of Oregon History.

Gold rush, eastern Oregon. In 1861 and 1862 gold was discovered in **Baker** and **Grant Counties.** Over $20 million was mined in 1862 alone. Boom towns included **Auburn** (1862), **Canyon City** (1862), **Granite** (1862), **Greenhorn** (1860s), **Jordan Valley** (1863), **Prairie City** (1870), **Sparta** (1862), and **Sumpter** (1861). **The Dalles** served as a major supply point for the Oregon mines as well as for Idaho where a gold rush had also begun in 1861. Dictionary of Oregon History. See also **Mint; The Dalles Military Wagon Road.**

Gold rush, southern Oregon. In 1851 some ship deserters discovered gold on the headwaters of the **Illinois River** in the **Siskiyou Mountains.** Soon other discoveries led to a number of sudden camps, the largest at Waldo, near **Cave Junction** in **Josephine County.** In the winter of 1851-52 gold was discovered near **Jacksonville** which quickly became the largest city between **Portland** and **San Francisco.** Other mining centers included **Gold Beach** (1850s), and **Gold Hill** (1860), and gold was also being mined on the south side of the Siskiyous along the **Klamath River** and in the Yreka area of northern California. **Scottsburg** at the head of navigation on the **Umpqua River**, and Crescent City, California, were supply points. Dictionary of Oregon History; Oregon's Golden Years. See also **Gin Lin trail**.

Gold rushes. The California gold rush of 1849 all but emptied Oregon of able-bodied men, but it also created a market for Oregon **wheat** and other products, and provided capital for those Oregonians who were successful. It was followed by a rush in southern Oregon in 1851-1852, on the Fraser River in British Columbia in 1857, in Idaho and eastern Oregon in 1862, and Alaska in 1897. The gold rushes led to settlement of areas little explored, to conflicts with **Indians**, to demands for goods and transportation, to instant if usually temporary cities, and to wealth, some of which was later invested. Dictionary of Oregon History. See also **Gold mining**; **Gold rush** entries.

Golden and Silver Falls. Two waterfalls in an **old-growth** forest up the Millicoma River 24 miles northeast of **Coos Bay**. Golden Falls is a **horsetail falls**, estimated to be over 125 feet high, that can be viewed at the end of a quarter-mile trail. It was named for Dr. C. B. Golden, First Grand Chancellor of the Knights of Pythias of Oregon who visited the falls soon after they were discovered. Silver Falls, 80 feet high, can be seen from the end of another quarter-mile trail. The falls are located in a day-use **state park**. Waterfall Lover's Guide.

Golden eagle. See **Eagles**.

Golf. Oregon has over 180 golf courses listed and shown on a map available from Fiddlers Green in **Eugene**, 800-548-5500. The Oregon **Tourism Commission** publishes the free Oregon Golf Directory, 800-547-7842. Eastmoreland, completed in 1916, was **Portland**'s first public golf course. The Fred Meyer Challenge, a two-day August tournament with a $1,000,000 purse founded in 1986, features 24 of the top names in golf. In 1998 it was moved to the new Reserve Vineyards and Golf Club in **Aloha**. The 1997 U.S. Women's Open, held at Pumpkin Ridge Golf Club near **North Plains**, was attended by 123,850. Oregonian 8/11/96:R1, 7/15/97:B1.

Gooch Falls. A wide 75-foot waterfall on Marion Creek, part of the headwaters of the North **Santiam River**, four miles southeast of Marion Fork, off **Highway 22**. The falls are named for Nathan Gooch who lived near them in the 1880s. They had originally been named Gatch Falls in honor of Thomas M. Gatch, who was president of **Willamette University** and later president of the University of Washington and Oregon Agricultural College (now **Oregon State University**). The name Gatch Falls has been transferred upstream to lower Marion Falls. Oregon Geographic Names; Waterfall Lover's Guide.

"Good citizens are the riches of a city." The inscription on the **Skidmore Fountain**. It was written by Colonel Charles Erskine Scott Wood, Oregon lawyer and author who was instrumental in securing the design and placement of the fountain. Portland, An Informal History.

Good Government Congress. A **depression**-born inflammatory populist political insurgency in **Jackson County**, 1930-33. Orchardist Llewellyn Banks led the movement through his newspaper with the assistance of Earl Fehl. Fehl and some of their other candidates were apparently elected to county office in 1932, but the ballots were stolen from the Courthouse after a public call for a recount. When Constable George Prescott attempted to serve Banks with a warrant for his arrest in connection with the theft, Banks killed him with a gun blast. The movement soon fell apart, and Banks spent the rest of his life in prison. The **Medford** Mail Tribune was awarded the **Pulitzer Prize** in 1934 for its "leadership in pleading for straight-thinking and peace" while under 24-hour armed guard due to constant threats of violence. "Jackson County Rebellion."

Good Roads movement. A movement that began in the 1890's when bicyclists began demanding better roads. By 1910, as cars became popular, the movement included both cyclists and drivers pressing for road improvements and new routes. Some of the slogans were "Put every county seat on a highway" and "**Get Oregon Out of the mud**." In 1917 Oregon voters provided $6,000,000 for roads to be repaid from auto license moneys over a 25 year period. "History of Transportation in the Pacific Northwest." See also **Highways, history**.

Goose Lake. A large alkaline lake, the largest lake rising in Oregon. It straddles the Oregon-California border in a broad, dry basin south of **Lakeview** with one third of its length in Oregon. When full, it is 28 miles long and covers 97,391 acres to a maximum depth of 12 feet. Though it has at times overflowed south into the Pit River, normally it is landlocked and loses water only through evaporation. Its size depends on the amount of local precipitation (averaging 13 inches per year) and the amount diverted for irrigation. In 1926 the lake was entirely dry. As its name indicates, the lake provides important habitat for nesting and migrating waterfowl. Recreation use is not extensive though there is a campground near the state line on the east side. Atlas of Oregon Lakes.

Gophers. See **Pocket gophers**.

Gordo block. See **Plate tectonics**.

Gorge Discovery Center. A 48,000 square-foot interpretive center and museum at Crate's Point three miles west of **The Dalles** with displays of the geologic, natural, and cultural history of the **Columbia River Gorge**. Thomas Hacker and Associates Architects, designers of the **High Desert Museum**, designed the center. An **Oregon Trail** Living History Park and **Wasco County** Historical Museum are adjacent. 5000 Discovery Center Lane, The Dalles, 97058. 541-296-8600. See also **Columbia Gorge Interpretive Center**.

Gorge Games. A series of competitions in outdoor sports, including windsurfing, paragliding, kite skiing, kayaking, snowboarding, climbing, mountain biking, and trail running, held in the **Columbia River Gorge**. The first games were held in July 1996. 541-386-7774. Oregonian 7/11/96:C1.

Gorges. See **Columbia River Gorge**; **Crooked River Gorge**; **Dry River**; **Hells Canyon**.

Gorse. A spiny **shrub**, *Ulex europaeus*, native to Europe, covered with butter-yellow flowers in early summer. It was introduced at **Bandon** by Lord Bennett in 1893, perhaps for use as hedgerows to contain livestock, but has since become a serious pest, spreading over 55,000 acres along the Oregon coast. Impenetrable thickets of the oily plant were a major factor in the destructive **Bandon fire** of 1936. Gorse seeds will stay viable in the soil for 80 years. Experimental biological controls include tiny gorse-specific red spider mites, introduced from New Zealand. Oregonian 8/8/96:C2.

Gouge Eye. The name by which Drewsey in **Harney County** was known in1883, apparently commemorating a frontier altercation. The postal authorities disapproved of so lusty a name, so it was changed to honor the daughter of a local rancher. Oregon Geographic Names; Other Side of Oregon.

Government. In 1997 Oregon had some 1,400 units of **local government** in addition to the state government. State government includes legislative, executive, and judicial branches. The legislative or law-making authority is vested in the people of the state through the **initiative** and **referendum** and in the two houses of the **legislature** which meets every two years. The **governor** heads the **executive** branch, which administers the laws. The **judicial system** resolves conflicts about the law through the **courts**. The state has about 45,000 **employees**. In addition to adopting the **Oregon System**, the state was among the first to ban no deposit, no return beverage bottles, to guarantee public access to all beaches, to clean up its rivers, and to protect farm lands from urban sprawl. Oregon is one of five states without a **sales tax**, one of two without self service gas pumps, one of two to offer comprehensive health insurance to low-income citizens, and the first to legalize physician-assisted suicide for the terminally ill. Oregonian 11/13/94:A16. See also **Better Government Competition; Bills; Government history; Legislature; Oregon Story.**

Government Camp. An unincorporated community and skiing center at an elevation of 3,888 feet on the slopes of **Mount Hood** on **Highway 26**. It was named for the remains of the 45 army wagons abandoned there by the First U.S. Mounted Rifles. The troops had crossed the plains in 1849 and were ordered to continue on from **The Dalles** to **Oregon City** over the grueling **Barlow Road** even though their horses and mules were in poor condition. Two-thirds of the animals died in the attempt. Oregon Geographic Names.

Government history. There was no governmental authority for the first white settlers in the **Oregon Country** until 1821 when the **Hudson's Bay Company** assumed authority over the British subjects, but there was still no comparable authority for the American settlers - who weren't convinced that they needed any, though they were concerned about whether their land ownership would be recognized by other settlers if there were no government. It was also unclear whether the area would eventually be British, American, or independent. The **Willamette Mission** group encouraged local government and American allegiance. After unsuccessful attempts to organize at the **wolf meetings**, in 1843 a series of meetings ended, after a close vote between American and British subjects, with the formation of a **provisional government** at **Champoeg**. British interests pulled back to Canada after the **Oregon Treaty of 1846**. Oregon residents lost the right to govern themselves when Oregon became a U.S. **territory** in 1848, but those rights were restored with **statehood** in 1859. General History. See also **Independence party; Oregon System.**

Government Standards and Practices Commission. A seven-member commission established in 1974 in response to the Watergate scandal as the Oregon Government Ethics Commission; the name was changed in 1993. Three members are appointed by the governor and four by the legislature (one each from the majority and minority offices of the House and the Senate). All elected officials and candidates for elected state office are required to file an annual Statement of Economic Interest with the Commission. A number of appointed officials are also required to file reports. Elected officials are prohibited from accepting gifts over $100. **Lobbyists** must register with the Commission. 100 High St. SE, Suite. 220, Salem 97310. 503-378-5105.

Governor. Oregon's top official, elected for a four-year term. He or she must be a U.S. citizen at least 30 years old and an Oregon resident for three years before taking office. The governor, who is also commander in chief of the **Oregon Air and National Guard**, is elected in November (1994, 1998, 2002, ...) and takes office the following January. The governor's duties include providing policy leadership for the state, providing administrative leadership for state government, representing Oregon to the federal government (owner of half of the state), preparing a two-year **budget** for the state, signing or vetoing legislation, calling **special sessions**, granting reprieves, pardons, and commutations, chairing the **State Land Board** and the **Progress Board**, filling vacancies in offices, and appointing department heads and members of 200 boards and commissions. Most gubernatorial appointments must be confirmed by the **Senate** before the appointees can take office. The governor's official residence is **Mahonia Hall** in **Salem**. The governor's salary in 1999 was $88,300, less than that of 200 other state employees. A total of 1,221,010 votes were cast for candidates for governor in 1994. 254 State Capitol, Salem 97310. 503-378-3111. Governing Oregon; Oregon Blue Book. See also **Administrative Services; Elected officials; Governors, history; Recall; Succession; Term limits**.

Governor Tom McCall Waterfront Park. A **Portland** city park, the site of many of Portland's festivals, located on the west bank of the **Willamette River** between the Hawthorne and Burnside bridges. The park was installed in the 1970s, replacing two five-lane streets. It includes Salmon Street Springs fountain, popular for water play. Tom McCall (1913-1983) led a campaign to clean up the heavily polluted Willamette River while he was governor, 1967 to 1975. Oregonian 9/21/96:D1. See also **Harbor Drive**.

Governor's Arts Award. The state's major art award, presented annually by the Oregon Arts Advocates Foundation and the Oregon **Arts Commission** to honor significant contributions to the arts within the state.

Governors, history. In 1843 the **provisional government**, the first organized government in what is now Oregon, established a three-man committee as the executive branch. That was found unworkable and in 1845 the provisional legislature elected George Abernethy as governor. He served until 1849 when Joseph Lane became the first of seven presidentially-appointed governors of the **Oregon Territory**. In July 1858 voters adopted a state constitution and elected and inaugurated John Whiteaker as governor of the new state, but Congress dallied until February 14, 1859, about officially admitting Oregon, so George Curry, the last territorial governor, continued in office, thus giving Oregon two governors during those months. Barbara Roberts, the state's 34th governor, serving from 1991 to 1995, was the first woman governor. All of Oregon's governors are listed in the Oregon Blue Book. Oregon Cattleman, based on the memoirs of one-time governor Walter Pierce (1861-1954), recounts tales of Oregon politics from before 1900 to the 1940s. Fire at Eden's Gate focuses on the 1967-1975 governorship of

Tom McCall (1913-1983). Governors' wives' inaugural gowns are on display at the **Robert Newell House** Museum. See also **Hillsboro**.

Governors' School. A private (despite the name) three-week summer program at **Willamette University** that trains Oregon high school students to be community leaders. After the students return to their own high schools they initiate programs, ranging from recycling to pregnancy-prevention. The program, founded in 1992, is supported by grants, donations, and tuition. Over half of the participants receive partial or full scholarships.

Grain. See **Barley**; **Grain elevators**; **Gristmills**; **Oats**; **Wheat**.

Grain elevators. Tall, 100-foot structures built next to railroads to hold bulk grain for shipment. They came into use in the 1930s, replacing burlap bags of **wheat**. Originally built of wood, many exploded and burned when wheat dust combusted. Newer elevators are built of concrete, many with computerized controls to separate wheat according to protein content. Oregonian 6/18/95:T5.

Grand Ronde and Grande Ronde. Two valleys on the opposite sides of Oregon having the same name, though spelled slightly differently. The name is French for large circle, meaning open valley. Grand (without an "e") Ronde is a valley in the **Coast Range** drained by the South Yamhill River. It is also the name of an unincorporated community on Highway 18 in that valley and the nearby reservation of the Confederated Tribes of the **Grand Ronde Community**. Grande (with an "e") Ronde is a large valley in northeast Oregon between the **Blue** and **Wallowa** mountains. It is drained by the **Grande Ronde River** which flows into the **Snake River**. **La Grande** is the major city in the valley. Oregon Geographic Names.

Grand Ronde, Confederated Tribes of. A confederation with 3,500 enrolled members representing a number of tribes. In 1857 (or 1856?) the government established a 69,000-acre reservation in the Grand Ronde valley on the east slope of the **Coast Range**, drained by the south Yamhill River. Members of 22 western Oregon and northern California tribes were forcibly marched to it, primarily from the Shasta, Molalla, Tillamook, Clatsop, Chinook, **Kalapuya**, **Klickitat**, **Umpqua**, and **Rogue** tribes. Through the years government actions reduced the size of the reservation, and the tribes were terminated as a nation in 1954 with only their cemetery left. In 1983 tribal status was reinstated and in 1988 Congress restored 9,811 acres 32 miles west of **Salem** where the tribes operate various enterprises, including Spirit Mountain **Casino**. 9615 Grand Ronde Road, Grand Ronde 97347. 503-879-5211. American Indian Reservations; First Oregonians; Native Peoples; Oregonian 10/22/95:A19, 9/22/96:D2. See also **Fort Yamhill**; **Reservations, history**.

Grande Ronde River. A 205-mile long river in northeast Oregon that heads in the **Blue** and **Wallowa Mountains** and flows northeast to join the **Snake River** in Washington. Its 4,130 square mile drainage basin has an average annual flow of 2,170,000 acre feet or 1 acre foot/acre, as measured at Troy. The river was named for the valley through which it flows. Oregon Geographic Names.

Grandmother Rock. A huge haystack rock, also called Tupper Rock, of hard blue schist that stood at the mouth of the **Coquille River** until dynamited in 1903 by the **Army Corps of Engineers** to provide rock for building the two **jet-**

ties. In 1990 the Port of **Bandon** returned an acre of ground where the rock used to stand to the **Coquille Indians**. There the tribe has built a three-story assisted living facility for grandparents. Native Peoples.

Grange. A fraternal organization with secret rituals that was organized in 1867 in Boston by Patrons of Husbandry to promote the interests of farmers and to heal the scars of the **Civil War**. Membership now is open to any. The Oregon State Grange includes representatives of the Subordinate (local) and Pomona (county) granges. In 1996 there were 252 granges with 25,497 members in Oregon. Grange halls dot the state, some abandoned, but many still being used for meetings, potlucks, dances, and community activities. 1125 SE Madison #102, Portland 97214. See also **State Agricultural Society**; **Union Party**.

Granite. A historic mining and ghost town in northeast Oregon that is Oregon's second-smallest incorporated city. Only nearby **Greenhorn** is smaller. Granite sprang up in 1862 in the **Blue Mountains**, 47 miles west of **Baker City**, following the discovery of gold on Granite Creek in **Grant County**, and was incorporated in 1901. Attractions include old buildings, hunting, fishing, and snowmobiling. Gold is still mined in the area. The city has no telephone service, no city taxes, and no paid employees. Population 1980 17; 1995 20. Elevation 4,700'. HCR 87, Box 1, Sumpter 97877. 541-379-3517 (cellular). Granite and Gold.

Granitic. A broad term describing an array of rocks formed when **andesite** magma cools slowly beneath the surface. **Gold mining** in Oregon is largely associated with granitic intrusions, such as those found in the **Siskiyou** and **Blue Mountains**. The largest intrusion in Oregon is the 324-square-mile core of the **Wallowa Mountains**. Granites are also exposed along the south end of the **Steens Mountain** fault. Circular granitic intrusions, a mile or more across, dot the Western **Cascade Range**, the remnant cores of long-since eroded volcanoes, and are at the centers of small gold mining districts. Granitic rock has been mined for building and monument stone near **Ashland** and in the **Blue Mountains**.

Grant County. A ranching and timber county in eastern Oregon on the headwaters of the **John Day River**, bounded by **Morrow**, **Umatilla**, **Union**, **Baker**, **Malheur**, **Harney**, **Crook**, and **Wheeler** counties. Incorporated cities are **Canyon City** (county seat) **John Day** (commercial center), **Dayville**, **Granite**, **Long Creek**, **Monument**, **Mount Vernon**, **Prairie City**, and **Seneca**. Elevations range from 1,830' in the northwest where the John Day River leaves the county to 9,038' **Strawberry Mountain** in the center of the county. The summit ridge of the rugged **Blue Mountains**, with some peaks over 8,000', forms the eastern boundary of the county. The first whites to settle in the area came in the 1862 **gold rush**. The county was created in 1864 out of **Wasco County** and named for General (later President) Ulysses S. Grant (1822-1885). The economy is based on forestry, agriculture, livestock, hunting, and recreation. Taxable assessed value in 1995 was $284,000,000, or $36,000 per capita. Population 1980 8,210; 1995 7,950. Area 4,528 square miles. Density 2/sq.mi. Annual precipitation 14"; average temperature January 31°F, July 68°F. Courthouse, 200 S Canyon Blvd., Canyon City 97820. 541-575-1675. "Emmet White, Part III"; History of Grant County; Oregon Blue Book.

Grants Pass. "It's the Climate." A southwest Oregon timber, commercial, and recreation center on the **Rogue River**, 30 miles west of **Medford** on **Interstate 5**. It is the county seat of **Josephine County** and headquarters for the **Siskiyou National Forest**. The name apparently honors General Ulysses S. Grant's capture of Vicksburg during the Civil War. The post office was established in 1865 and the city was incorporated in 1887. The downtown G Street Historic District has been placed on the National Register of Historic Places. Other attractions include the Museum of Art, Schmidt House Museum, a Growers Market, boat trips on the Rogue River including trips to Hellsgate Canyon and white water rafting, Boatnik Festival on Memorial Day weekend, Step Back in Time to the 50s Festival on the last weekend in July, and Heritage Days in October. Rubtsovsk, Russia, is its sister city. Population 1980 15,032; 1995 19,660. Elevation 960' 101 NW "A" St., 97526. 541-474-6360. Visitors Bureau 800-547-5927. Grants Pass; Oregon Geographic Names. See also **Nature Man**.

Grapes. In 1995 Oregon's 396 vineyards produced 14,000 tons of wine grapes, worth $13.4 million, from 5,600 acres. **Yamhill County** produced 4,423 tons, followed by **Polk** and **Washington** counties. The leading varieties were Pinot Noir, planted on 2,744 acres, and Chardonnay on 1,512 acres. 1995 Oregon Vineyard Report. See also **Wine**.

Grass seed. Oregon produces about 60% of the world's cool-season grass seed. In 1994, Oregon growers produced 229,000 metric tons of turf and pasture grass seed, worth $183 million, on 355,000 acres, primarily in the **Willamette Valley**, though some is also grown around **Madras** and **La Grande**. Much of it is grown on soils with a high winter water table which other crops will not tolerate. A certification program developed with **Oregon State University** supports Oregon grass seed's reputation for quality and purity. **Field burning** has been used since the 1940's to rid fields of diseases, weeds, and straw residues, but alternatives are being sought because of air quality concerns. Some straw is baled and sold to Japan. In 1994 grass seed production totaled:

Bentgrass	2,400 tons	$9.5 million	14,000 acres
Bluegrass	5,700 tons	$11.3 million	18,200 acres
Orchardgrass	7,300 tons	$11.9million	20,000 acres
Tall fescue	33,500 tons	$28.0 million	68,500 acres
Annual ryegrass	105,000 tons	$55.6 million	123,300 acres
Perennial ryegrass	82,500 tons	$78.3 million	131,100 acres

Native grass seed is also being grown for planting areas damaged by roads, fire, logging, and overgrazing. Rogue Institute, 541-482-6031. Oregon Agriculture. See also **Alfalfa seed**; **Clover seed**; **Meadowfoam**.

Grass Valley. A north-central Oregon community in **Sherman County** named for the tall grass that grew there. The name was adopted in 1900 by popular vote and the city was incorporated the next year. In 1996 the community held the first annual Grass Valley Wheat Festival; proceeds are used to preserve some of the town's historic buildings. The town is located 50 miles southeast of **The Dalles** on **Highway 97**. Population 1980 164; 1995 155. Elevation 2,269'. PO Box 191, 97029. 541-333-2434. "Grass Valley"; Oregon Geographic Names; Oregonian 6/20/97:C1.

Grasshoppers. In 1994 a subspecies of clear-winged grasshoppers called Camnula reached a density of 10,000 per square foot around **Burns** and north of **Chiloquin**. Each grasshopper consumes the equivalent of its own body weight every 16 hours, stripping grazing pastures of grass. In the past ranchers have sprayed with malathion but more recently found that baiting with carbaryl bran was also effective and of less toxicity to fish and bees. Oregonian 6/27/97: B2.

Grassy Mountain gold mine. An 80-acre, 700-foot deep, open-pit mine proposed in the 1990s by Newmont Mining Corporation for an area near **Owyhee Reservoir** 20 miles southwest of **Vale**. The mine, with probable reserves of 31,000 kilograms (995,900 ounces) of **gold** and 76,700 kilograms (2.4 million ounces) of **silver**, would have used **heap-leach** cyanidation to extract the metals. The company, after spending $3.6 million on the previous election in a successful campaign to defeat stiffer mining standards, abandoned the project in January 1996 as being too expensive. Mineral Industry of Oregon; Oregonian 8/13/96:A11.

Gravel. See **Sand and gravel**.

Gravestone, oldest. See **Cemeteries**.

Graveyard of the Pacific. See **Clatsop Spit**; **Peacock Spit**; **Shipwrecks**.

Gray whale. The most commonly sighted whale along the Oregon coast, *Eschrichtius robustus*, a baleen whale that grows up to 45 feet in length and may weigh 45 tons. There are now an estimated 23,000; the species was removed from the **endangered species** list in 1994. Though increasing numbers of them are becoming year-round residents, most gray whales migrate 12,000 miles twice a year from their summer waters off Alaska to their winter calving grounds in Baja California. **Whale watching** is popular during these migrations.

Grazing. See **Rangeland**.

Great Basin. A large area of the American west with no drainage to the sea. It encompasses most of Nevada, large portions of western Utah and southern California, and, in Oregon, most of **Harney** and **Lake** counties. See also **Basin and range**.

Great Basin history. The first white men to see the **High Desert** lands of the northwestern Great Basin were probably three Frenchmen who left their ship near San Diego in about 1750 and set out overland for Quebec. Two are known to have reached southern Idaho where they settled and lived with Indians. In 1808 the survivors of the wreck of the *Sea Otter* probably traversed the area in traveling by foot from near the mouth of the **Umpqua River** to Louisiana by way of **Santiam Pass**. In 1825 Peter Skene Ogden led a **Hudson's Bay Company** fur trapping party along the **Snake River** and its tributaries. Near the mouth of the **Malheur River**, Antoine Sylvaille was dispatched with five men to trap and explore the Malheur. Early in 1826 the small group reached a river that Ogden was to name the Sylvaille River, later shortened to Silvies. The Sylvaille party was apparently the first group of white men to enter the Harney Basin. When robbed of furs and other valuables by Indians, Sylvaille's party selected the French adjective *malheur*, meaning misfortune, as a name for the Malheur River. Ogden made other trips through the area as did fellow trapper John Work. In 1843 government explorer John C. Fremont and party passed through. Oregon's Great Basin Country. See also **Lost Wagon Train**.

Great blue heron. A common wading bird, *Ardea herodias*, found throughout most of Oregon. The adult bird weighs only 6 to 8 pounds, though it may stand 4' tall and has a 6' wingspan. Herons feed on fish, frogs, snakes, and rodents. In western Oregon they nest in rookeries in tall trees, but in eastern Oregon they sometimes nest on the ground. **Portland** has named the great blue heron the city's official bird. Atlas of Oregon Wildlife; Great Northwest Nature Factbook.

Great Depression. See **Depression**.

Great flood. See **Flood of 1861**.

Great Migration. The name given to the 1843 Oregon Emigrating Company **wagon train** of nearly 900 men, women, and children. Its crossing of the **Oregon Trail** was the first with wagons and the first major overland migration of settlers to Oregon. It tripled the non-Indian population of the **Oregon Country**. See also **Cow Column**.

Great Northern Railway. A railroad company that was controlled by James Jerome Hill (1838-1916) at the time that it completed a northern line between Washington state and Minnesota in 1893. By the turn of the century Hill also controlled the **Northern Pacific Railroad**. In 1907, Hill, who lived in Minnesota, purchased the **Astoria and Columbia River Railroad**, which he combined with the **Spokane, Portland and Seattle Railway** system. He purchased the **Oregon Electric Railway** in 1910, and competed with the **Southern Pacific** by running steamships to California from **Astoria**. Great Northern also owned the **Oregon Trunk Line**, which won the **Battle of the Gorge** to extend a line up the **Deschutes River** from the **Columbia River** to **Bend** in 1911, and later continued the line on south from Bend, connecting through to California in 1928, a route now owned by **Burlington Northern**. Dictionary of Oregon History; East of the Cascades.

Great Oregon Steamup. An annual event since 1970, held at **Antique Powerland** near **Brooks** on weekends in late July and early August. It features steam-powered binding, threshing, flour milling, log sawing, and tractor pull, plus exhibits, flea market, demonstrations, and food. 3995 Brooklake Road NE, Brooks 97303. 503-393-2424.

Great Plank Road. See **Canyon Road**.

Great Reinforcement. A term applied to a party of 50 (32 adults and 18 children) **Methodists** who arrived by ship in 1840. They had been recruited to join the earlier Methodist missionaries at the **Willamette Mission**. With their coming, the influence of the **Hudson's Bay Company** began to wane. Empire of the Columbia.

Great Sandy Desert. See **High lava plains physiographic province**.

Greeks in Oregon. Numbers of young Greek men came to the U.S. after 1890 to earn money to pay for their families' debts and their sisters' dowries. Most then returned to Greece. In 1910 there were 2,000 Greeks in **Portland** and Greeks made up 40% of the crew building the **Natron Cut-off** rail line between **Eugene** and **Klamath Falls**. A Greek Festival, begun in 1952, is held in early October at Holy Trinity Greek Orthodox Church in **Portland** . "Point Lookout"; Surge to the Sea.

Green Peter Reservoir. A two-pronged, ten-mile long reservoir 11 miles east of **Sweet Home** on the Middle **Santiam River**. It was formed in 1966 by a 360-foot high concrete dam built for power generation (80 **megawatts**) and flood control by the **Army Corps of Engineers**. Water surges from power generation are moderated by **Foster Reservoir** downstream. Construction began 1961; the **flood of 1964** caused $900,000 damage at the dam construction site. The lake covers 3,720 acres to a maximum depth of 315 feet, and has 38 miles of forested shoreline. A county campground and boat launch sites are located on the north side. Green Peter is named for a nearby peak and creek; "peter" (which means "rock") is a name sometimes given to rocky buttes. Army Engineers; Oregon Geographic Names.

Greenhorn. A one-time 1860s **gold mining** town that is now the smallest incorporated city in Oregon with a 1995 population of 3. It is the only municipality that exists under Oregon's "Ghost town" law, which allows an incorporated city whose population drops below the number of people needed to fill elected city offices to remain incorporated as a "historic ghost town." It lies in the **Blue Mountains** of northeast Oregon 50 miles west of **Baker City** on the western edge of **Baker County**. The post office was established in 1902 and the city was incorporated in 1912. That year the U.S. government granted the town a patent for 53.58 acres, in effect making the town a law unto itself. It was named for the Green-Horn, a 300' monolith of green serpentine on the slopes of **Vinegar Hill**. Tempska, a fossilized fern or palm, is found nearby. Elevation 6,270'. 911 Laurel Lane, Oregon City 97045. 503-656-7945. Governing Oregon; Oregon Geographic Names; Oregon's Golden Years.

Greenhorn Mountains. A range of mountains in northeast Oregon, part of the **Blue Mountains**, drained by the North and Middle forks of the **John Day River**. **Vinegar Hill**, an 8,131-foot peak, is one of the highest points.

Greenhouse and nursery products. See **Nursery industry**.

Greenhouse gases. Gases that are increasing in the atmosphere due to human activities and that have the potential to alter the climate by trapping heat. The major contribution from Oregon is of **carbon dioxide** (CO_2) (89%), followed by **methane** (9%), and nitrous oxide and PFCs (2%). Every gallon of gasoline burned releases about 20 pounds of CO_2. Oregon released 12.5 tons of CO_2 per capita in 1994, less than the U.S. average of 21.5 tons per capita, primarily because **hydroelectric power** does not generate greenhouse gases. The Oregon Department of **Energy** has concluded that the state cannot achieve its target of holding greenhouse gas emissions to 1990 levels unless there are additional federal efforts, and even 1990 emission levels would result in a doubling of CO_2 by 2100. Oregonian 11/28/97:C4; Report on Reducing.

Greenway. A corridor of protected open space managed for conservation and recreation purposes. A greenway often follows a natural land or water feature. Some greenway areas, but not all, are publicly owned and open to the public. Pacific Greenway. See also **Bear Creek Greenway**; **Willamette River Greenway**.

Gresham. "Oregon's Most Livable City." A rapidly growing Portland-area suburban city in **Multnomah County** 12 miles east of downtown **Portland**; it is Oregon's fourth largest city. The heavily forested area was first settled in 1852. The post office, established in 1884, was named for distinguished Civil War soldier and statesman Walter Quinton Gresham who was U.S. postmaster general at the time. The city was incorporated in 1905. Boeing, Fujitsu Microelectronics, and U.S. Bancorp are major employers, and headquarters for the **Mount Hood National Forest** are located in the city. Attractions include the Scottish **Highland Games** in mid-July, **Mount Hood Festival of Jazz** in August, and nearby hiking, fishing, boating, and skiing. **MAX** light rail runs from Gresham to **Portland**. Its sister cities are Ebetsu, Japan; Sok-Cho, S. Korea; and Owerri, Nigeria. Population 1980 33,005; 1995 77,240. Elevation 110'. 1333 NW Eastman Pkwy, 97030. 503-661-3000. Chamber of Commerce 503-665-1131. Gresham; Oregonian 4/5/98:H1.

Greyhound racing. See **Multnomah Greyhound Park**.

Gristmills. The first gristmill (a mill for grinding grain) in the **Willamette Valley** was built by Webley **Hauxhurst** at **Champoeg** in 1835. The first in Oregon east of the Cascades was built in 1865 in **John Day**. In 1996 Butte Creek Mill in **Eagle Point** was the only water-powered, stone-ground gristmill operating in Oregon. Gold and Cattle Country. See also **Stone-ground flour**.

Grizzly bear. See **Bears**; **Old Reelfoot**.

Grotto. The popular name for the National Sanctuary of Our Sorrowful Mother, a **Catholic** center located in a 62-acre wooded area at 8840 NE Skidmore Street in northeast **Portland**. During the summer, mass is celebrated at an outdoor sanctuary focused on a grotto at the base of a 110-foot cliff. A chapel, visitors center, and gift shop are also on the lower grounds. At the top of the cliff, reached by an elevator, are additional paths, garden areas, the architecturally distinctive Marilyn Moyer Meditation Chapel with a 180° view, plus the monastery of the Order of Servants of Mary (Servites), the order that has been responsible for the Sanctuary since 1924. The Sanctuary is open daily with no fee except for the elevator. The area is lighted at Christmas. PO Box 20008, Portland 97220. 503-254-7371.

Ground squirrels. Small to medium-sized mammals that live in rock piles or extensive burrows in which they hibernate in winter. Green vegetation is the preferred diet. Among Oregon's eight species of ground **squirrels** are the chipmunk-sized white-tailed antelope squirrel, *Ammospermophilus leucurus*, a **protected species** of southeast Oregon; the Washington ground squirrel of northeast Oregon, *Spermophilus washingtoni*, which is also protected; the golden-mantled ground squirrel, *S. lateralis*, which is often confused with a **chipmunk**; and the large California ground squirrel or gray digger, *S. beecheyi*, of western and south central Oregon, which does damage to grain and other crops, as do related ground squirrels of eastern Oregon. Atlas of Oregon Wildlife; Mammals and Life Zones of Oregon; Mammals of the Northwest.

Ground water. See **Groundwater**.

Groundfish. See **Bottom fish**.

Groundhog. See **Marmot**.

Groundwater. By 1990 seven billion gallons of water were being withdrawn daily from Oregon's groundwater **aquifers**. 75% was used for irrigation, 11% for livestock watering and rural domestic uses, 7% for industry, and 7% for public water supplies. 88% (3,500) of Oregon's public water suppliers rely at least in part on groundwater as their permanent or emergency supply. There were also an estimated 300,000 domestic **wells**, leading to concern that over pumping from the aquifers is leading to falling water tables and failing wells. Regulations are designed to protect groundwater from contamination, to conserve it, and to protect it from loss of artesian head. Efforts to reduce **nitrate pollution** in groundwater are focused on 350,000 acres in the lower **Umatilla River** basin and 150,000 acres in northern **Malheur County**. The **water rights** doctrine of prior appropriation applies to groundwater as well as to surface water. The Oregon Department of **Water Resources** monitors the state's groundwater supplies. Oregon Drinking Water; Oregon's 1994 Water Quality. See also **Aquifer**; **Drinking water**; **Water supply**; **Wells**.

Grouse. Native ground-dwelling **game birds** with feathered legs. The males perform elaborate courtship displays on strutting grounds called leks. The five species in Oregon include three found in forests and two in **sagebrush** deserts. The forest species are the ruffed grouse, *Bonasa umbellus*, spruce grouse, *Dendragapus canadensis*, and blue grouse, *D. obscurus*. The desert species are the sharp-tailed grouse, *Tympanuchus phasianellus*, which has been reintroduced into the state, and the sage grouse, *Centrocercus urophasianus*. The sage grouse grows up to 28" long, while the others are from 16 to 20" long. Atlas of Oregon Wildlife; Fish and Wildlife on the Oregon Trail.

Growth. At a two-day anti-growth conference on October 17-18, 1997, it was reported that each new three-bedroom house adds $24,502 to a community's capital expenses, including $11,377 for school construction, $5,089 for sanitary sewers, and $4,193 for roads. Oregonian 10/19/97:A1. See also **Budget growth**; **James G. Blaine Society**; **Population growth**; **Society of Native Oregon Born**; **Ungreeting cards**; **"Visit, but don't stay"**.

Guano Lake. See **Mud cracks**.

Guild Lake. See **Lewis and Clark Centennial Exposition**.

Gulf War. See **Operation Desert Storm, 1991**.

Gun dealers. Oregon had 2,578 registered gun dealers in January 1996, down from 5,331 in 1993. Dealers are registered with the U.S. Treasury Department's Bureau of Alcohol, Tobacco and Firearms. 9828 E. Burnside, Portland 97216. 503-231-2331. Oregonian 1/30/97:A6.

Guns. Handgun purchases require a thumb-print, a $10 fee, and a police background-check on the purchaser. No background check is needed for the purchase of a rifle. No permit is required to own a gun unless it will be concealed. In 1997 over 86,000 Oregonians had concealed-weapon permits issued by county sheriffs' departments under state law, up from 745 in 1990. In 1997 it was estimated that 51% of Oregon households have guns. In 1995 12 people died in unintentional firearm accidents at home, and it was estimated that there were about three times as many nonfatal firearm injuries. In 1982 the city of **Chiloquin** passed a mandatory gun ownership measure. Handguns have a range of up to a mile and rifles up to two miles. Oregonian 7/16/97:B5, 6/25/97:B1.

Gypsy moth. A European tussock moth, *Porthetria dispar*, which was introduced into the U.S. in 1869. The mottled hairy caterpillar has devastated many Eastern forests by eating the leaves of trees and shrubs. The moth first appeared in

Oregon in 1979, but intensive monitoring and controls have so far prevented extensive damage. See also **Forest health**.

Hacky Sack. See **Footbag**. .

Hafnium. A metallic element that is produced at Wah Chang in **Millersburg** as a byproduct of **zirconium** production. It is used in nuclear reactor control rods, ceramics, refractories, aerospace alloys, and optical fibers. Mineral Industry in Oregon.

Hail. Pellets formed of concentric rings of ice. They form as water droplets are carried up into cold areas of thunderstorm clouds, and then are coated and recoated with super-cooled water as they are swirled up and down in the cloud. Hail-producing thunderstorms are most common in the **Wallowa Mountains**, but occur occasionally over most of the state. A 10-minute storm on July 9, 1995, dropped hailstones the size of tennis balls in **Gilliam** and **Morrow** counties, causing millions of dollars worth of damage to crops, buildings, and vehicles from **Condon** east to **Hermiston**. In **Ashland** a 30-minute hail storm with 2" hailstones on July 13,1964, made it necessary to replace many of the roofs and windows in town. On June 23, 1900, a devastating storm with 6" hailstones was reported on Bridge Creek near **Mitchell**, and a storm on May 11, 1901 dropped 1 1/2" hail on **Canyon City** for half an hour, causing damage and flooding. For a time hail damage to **pear** trees in the **Medford** area was so frequent that in the 1950s summer clouds were seeded with silver iodide crystals to precipitate rain before it could develop into hailstones. See also **Heppner flood**; **Weather modification**.

Haines. "Biggest Little City in Oregon." A northeast Oregon timber and ranching community located in **Baker County**, 11 miles north of **Baker City** on **Highway 30**. It lies at the foot of the **Elkhorn Mountains**. The town was named in 1883 for "Judge" I. E. Haines who owned the land on which it was located, and was incorporated in 1909. Attractions include the annual Haines Stampede with **rodeo**, held on the 4th of July weekend, the Eastern Oregon Museum, historic buildings, markers, park, and Elkhorn Drive National Scenic Byway. Population 1980 341; 1995 420. Elevation 3,333'. PO Box 208, 97833. 541-856-3366. Oregon Geographic Names.

Hairball. A 2 1/2 pound hairball, found in the belly of a hog killed at a Portland meat-packing plant in 1954, is on display in the basement museum of the Abbey House at **Mount Angel Abbey**.

Hake. See **Whiting**.

Halfway. A far eastern Oregon city at the foot of the **Wallowa Mountains** in **Baker County**, 55 miles east of **Baker City**. The post office was established in 1887, though originally at a different location. There is some question as to what it was half way between, though it may have been between Cornucopia and the mouth of the Powder River. The city was incorporated in 1909. Population 1980 380; 1995 345. Elevation 2,663'. PO Box 738, 97834. 541-742-4741. Oregon Geographic Names.

Halibut. A large ocean bottom fish, *Hippoglossus stenolepsis*, that is caught commercially off **Newport,** though the major fishery is off Alaska. The record Pacific halibut was 8 feet long and weighed 450 pounds dressed. The females begin reproducing at age 12 and may live over 40 years. Sport anglers are required to have a halibut tag from the Oregon Department of **Fish and Wildlife**. Great Pacific Northwest Nature Factbook.

Halsey. A mid-**Willamette Valley** city in **Linn County** 18 miles south of **Albany** on **Highway 99E**. It was named for William L. Halsey, vice-president of the Willamette Valley Railway Company which built a line through the area in 1871. The city was incorporated in 1876. The Fort James Corporation paper mill is a major employer. Population 1980 693; 1995 725. elevation 280'. 773 W 1st St., 97348. 541-369-2522. Oregon Geographic Names.

Hammond. A community near the mouth of the **Columbia River** in **Clatsop County** that merged with **Warrenton** on December 6, 1991. It was named for Andrew B. Hammond, a noted turn-of-the-century west-coast business man. Oregon Geographic Names.

Handbill. See **Broadside**.

Hanford Nuclear Reservation. A 560-square-mile site in southeast Washington state established by the federal government in 1943 to produce plutonium for atomic bombs. Production has stopped, but the nuclear wastes remain, necessitating a cleanup estimated to cost more than $50 billion. Oregon's concerns include the potential for radioactive contamination of the **Columbia River** and of **groundwater** aquifers that extend under the river to Oregon, as well as for potential spills as wastes are transported across Oregon to other storage sites. The Oregon Hanford Waste Board in the state Office of **Energy** is the state's watchdog. The Northwest's only functioning **nuclear power** plant is also located at Hanford. Hanford; Organic Machine. See also **Downwinders**; **Energy Facility Siting Council**.

Hang gliding. A non-motorized, self-launched form of flight. High bluffs along the Oregon coast are popular spring and fall sites, while inland sites with thermal updrafts are used in the summer. **Lakeview**, where the state distance record of 155 miles was set, is known as the hang gliding capital of the west and has been the site of national championship meets in 1993 and 1997. Other popular launch sites are Woodrat Mountain near Ruch southwest of **Medford**, Pine Mountain east of **Bend**, Chehalem Mountain in **Yamhill County**, the Coburg Hills northeast of **Eugene**, and **Cape Kiwanda** on the central coast. Dick Gammon of **Hood River** built the first foot-launched hang glider in Oregon in 1971. Oregon Hang Gliding Association, 17792 NW Anastasia Drive, Portland 97229. 503-614-0178. Oregonian 5/13/96:D1.

Hanna Mining Company. A company that operated a **nickel** mine and smelter at **Riddle** from 1954 until 1987. Between 1961 and 1964 the company was the subject of investigations and lawsuits involving its activities under a government-sponsored program to stockpile strategic minerals. Because some of President Eisenhower's cabinet members were involved, the affair received national publicity.

Hansen Garden. See **Connie Hansen Garden**.

Hantavirus. A recently-identified virus, carried by deer mice, that causes a human disease characterized by fever, muscle aches, coughing, and headaches. It can lead to death from fluid accumulation in the lungs. Oregon has had one documented fatality, a 16-year-old boy in **The Dalles** in 1992.

Happy Canyon Pageant. A pageant depicting the history of the frontier performed during the evening at the **Pendleton Round-Up**. 800-457-6336.

Happy Valley. A **Portland**-area suburban community 7 miles north of **Oregon City** in **Clackamas County**. It is said that the name came from a group of young men who drank hard cider to keep warm on their walk to church meeting; they were known as "the boys from Happy Holler." The city was incorporated in 1965. Population 1980 1,499; 1995 2,660. Elevation 497'. 12915 SE King Road, 97236. 503-760-3325. Oregon Geographic Names.

Harbor Drive. An expressway built along **Portland**'s waterfront about 1940. In order to build it, much of the historic **cast iron architecture** of the old Front Street business district was demolished. By 1974, the city had decided that it was more important to have its waterfront accessible to the city, so the expressway was removed and replaced by **Governor Tom McCall Waterfront Park**.

Harbors. See **Ports**.

Hard winters. See **Cold spells**.

Hares. Members of the **rabbit** family. Oregon hares include the **jackrabbits** of the desert and the secretive **snowshoe hare** of timbered areas. Unlike rabbits, the young are born fully haired, with their eyes open, and ready to run. Instead of living in burrows hares rest and give birth in shallow basins, called forms, under bushes. Mammals and Life Zones of Oregon; Mammals of the Northwest.

Harlow House. The Troutdale Historical Society Museum, housed in a 1900 farmhouse built by the city's founder. 726 E. Historic Columbia River Highway, Troutdale. 503-661-2164.

Harney. See **Fort Harney**.

Harney Basin. A land-locked basin of 5,300 square miles, larger than Connecticut, located in central Oregon. The **Brothers fault zone** crosses through it; **Burns**, **Malheur Lake**, and **Harney Lake** (the lowest point in the basin) are located within it. Ten thousand years ago much of the basin was filled by a shallow **Pleistocene lake** that drained into the **Malheur River**. Archeological sites document that the basin, much of it now cattle country, has been for over 10,000 years a center of human activity focused on the vast flocks of water birds around the lakes. Archeology of Oregon; Feelin' Fine; Geology of Oregon. See also **Sod House**.

Harney County. Oregon's largest county, located in arid southeast Oregon where it is bounded by **Lake**, **Deschutes**, **Crook**, **Grant**, and **Malheur** counties and on the south by the state of **Nevada**. In 1890 night riders stole the county records from the county seat at Harney, a community ten miles east of **Burns** and moved them to Burns, which remains the county seat. Neighboring **Hines** is the county's only other incorporated city. Elevations rise from 3,400' at **Warm Springs Reservoir** on the eastern edge to 9,733' **Steens Mountain**. Pine forests are found in the **Ochoco Mountains** in the northern end of the county, and much of the rest of the county is vast **sagebrush** rangeland. The economy is based on forestry, manufacturing, livestock, and agriculture. Taxable assessed value in 1995 was $281,000,000, or $40,000 per capita. The county was created in 1889 from **Grant County** and named for Major General William S. Harney (1800-1889) who, as commander in Oregon in 1858-1859 was instrumental in opening areas of eastern

Oregon for settlement. Population 1980 8,314; 1995 7,050. Area 10,228 square miles. Density 1/sq.mi. Annual precipitation 10"; average temperature January 28°F, July 69°F. Courthouse, 450 N Buena Vista, Burns 97720. 541-573-6356. Feelin' Fine; Oregon Blue Book; William "Bill" W. Brown.

Harney Lake. A shallow salt lake of variable size 20 miles south of **Burns**, believed by geologists to occupy a large, low, ancient caldera. At one time the waters of Harney Lake Basin drained to the Pacific via the **Malheur River**. However, lava flows blocked the outlet, so that Harney Lake is now the lowest point in the landlocked basin. For years at a time Harney Lake is a salt flat; at other times the lakebed fills to cover 25,000 acres or more; the water then becomes increasingly saline as the lake evaporates again. **Malheur National Wildlife Refuge** encompasses Harney Lake as well as **Malheur Lake**. Harney Lake was named in 1859 for Brigadier-General W. S. Harney who was in charge of the Army Department of Oregon. Atlas of Oregon Lakes.

Harper. An unincorporated eastern Oregon ranching community on the **Malheur River** 22 miles west of **Vale** on **Highway 20**. The name was that of an early settler whose Harper Ranch is where the post office (1913) is situated. The community operates a **boarding high school**. Oregon Geographic Names.

Harris Beach State Park. A **state park** on the south coast two miles north of **Brookings**. Its campground, open all year, has 156 campsites. Reservations, 800-452-5687. 1655 Highway 101, Brookings 97415. 541-469-2021.

Harrisburg. A **Willamette River** city 27 miles south of **Albany** on **Highway 99E** in **Linn County**. The original town, called Crow's Nest, was a mile from the **Willamette River**, but during the **flood of 1861** the river relocated to its present location on the town's doorstep. Harrisburg post office was established in 1855, presumably named for the Pennsylvania capital, and the city was incorporated in 1866. Historic commercial buildings from the late 1800s are still in use, as are some of the oldest surviving houses in Oregon. Population 1980 1,881; 1995 2,130. Elevation 309'. 354 Smith St., 97446. 541-995-6655. Chamber of Commerce 541-998-6154. Oregon Geographic Names.

Hart Lake. A six-mile long, shallow lake, the lowest and most permanent of the 40-mile chain of lakes in the land-locked **Warner Valley**, though even it is sometimes pumped dry for irrigation. When full, it covers 7,234 acres to a maximum depth of 11 feet. Despite having no outlet, it is not especially alkaline. Since most of the shoreline is in private ownership there is little recreational use other than some fishing, especially for catfish. Atlas of Oregon Lakes.

Hart Mountain. A 7,710' mountain on the east side of **Hart Lake** in **Lake County**. A 25-mile long ridge, the best defined **fault**-block mountain in the U.S., extends north from Hart Mountain past Warner Peak (8,065') to end in Poker Jim Ridge. A steep, 3,000' scarp rising from **Warner Valley** forms Hart Mountain's western face; the eastern slope of the block is more gradual. The name derives from a heart cattle brand used by a ranch at its base. **Hart Mountain National Antelope Refuge** covers most of the mountain. Geology of Oregon.

Hart Mountain National Antelope Refuge. A 275,000-acre federal refuge in southern **Lake County** established in 1936 for the protection of **pronghorn antelope**. The reserve is also home to **bighorn sheep**, **deer**, small mammals, and

213 species of birds. It extends from the marshes of **Warner Valley** up over **Hart Mountain** and down long sagebrush slopes to the east. In 1994 the U.S. Fish and Wildlife Service ordered a 15-year ban on cattle grazing in the refuge. Camping is permitted only at Hot Springs Campground. PO Box 21, Plush 97637. 541-947-3315. Oregon Wildlife Viewing Guide; Oregon's Great Basin Country. See also **Order of the Antelope**.

Harvest. See **Migrant labor**.

Hatcheries. See **Fish hatcheries**.

Hate crimes. See **Crimes, bias**.

Hatfield Marine Science Center. See **Mark O. Hatfield Marine Science Center**.

Hauxhurst Beach. A name sometimes used for a portion of the spit at **Tillamook Bay**. It was named for Webley Hauxhurst (1809-1874) who helped drive horses to Oregon in 1834 with Ewing Young. He was the first white convert at Jason Lee's **Willamette Mission**, and became active in **Salem** and Oregon civic affairs. After his Yamhill Indian wife told him she was going to return to her people and take their children with her so as not to be a hindrance to his political future, Hauxhurst moved her and his family to the isolated Tillamook area and became captain of a schooner. Dictionary of Oregon History; Tillamook. See also **Gristmills**.

Hawaiians in Oregon. The 1990 census counted 2,000 Hawaiians in Oregon. Native Hawaiians, called **Kanakas**, were in Oregon during the early 1800s, employed as sailors, fur trappers, and lumber workers by the **Hudson's Bay Company**. Some became settlers. Place names such as Kanaka Flat in **Jackson County** and **Owyhee** (Hawaii) **River** in **Malheur County** indicate their wide dispersal. During the 19th century Hawaii was called the Sandwich Islands. Siskiyou Trail. See also **Intermarriage**; **Poll tax**.

Hawks. HawkWatch International coordinates volunteers at two stations in Oregon to count migrating raptors (hawks, **eagles**, vultures, and **osprey**) in the fall. Some of the birds are captured and banded. Visitors are welcome at the stations, located at Bonney Butte, east of **Mount Hood** and on Dutchman Peak south of **Medford**. 800-726-4295. Oregonian 10/8/97:F1.

Hay. In 1995, Oregon growers produced 1.9 million tons of alfalfa hay, worth $174.4 million, on 406,000 acres. Ranchers also produced 1.5 million tons of other hay, worth $98.5 million, on another 636,000 acres. **Lake County** led in total production with 300,000 tons, followed by **Malheur**, **Klamath**, **Baker**, and **Harney** counties. Oregon Agriculture.

Hayden Island. A one and a half mile long, low sandy island of about 1,200 acres in the **Columbia River** partly within **Portland** city limits. In 1960 dredging joined it to Tomahawk Island to the east. Oregon Slough and the North Portland Harbor separate it from low areas to the south. **Interstate 5** crosses the island, and **Jantzen Beach** is located on it, as are several residential neighborhoods, 320 **floating homes**, and three yacht clubs. It is named for 1850 pioneer Gay Hayden who owned it at one time. Oregon Geographic Names; Oregonian 7/13/97:H1.

Haystack Rock. A huge, much-photographed, rock that rises 235' above the surf off **Cannon Beach**, said to be the world's third-largest free-standing monolith. A higher Haystack Rock is offshore southwest of **Cape Kiwanda**; it is 327' high. A third Haystack Rock is located in **Wallowa County**. Oregon Atlas; Oregon Geographic Names.

Hazardous wastes. Over 20,000 tons of hazardous wastes are generated in Oregon each year, nearly all of it from electronic, metal, and petroleum industries in the **Willamette Valley**. A hazardous waste disposal facility near **Arlington** annually buries over 100,000 tons of hazardous wastes. 70% is from Washington and 25% from Oregon, with the rest from Idaho, Canada, Hawaii, Guam, and northern California. Radioactive wastes are not accepted. In 1993, 35% of the state's hazardous waste sites were yet to be cleaned up, while the Oregon **benchmark** goal is to have all but13% cleaned up by the year 2000. Oregon had the first state-administered hazardous waste program in the nation, developed after a private contractor accumulated 25,000 barrels of pesticide manufacturing wastes at a site near Alkali Lake in **Lake County** in 1969. His plans to treat the waste failed and the state inherited the problem. Oregon: A Statistical Overview; Oregon Environmental Atlas. See also **Hanford Nuclear Reservation**; **Spills**; **Superfund cleanup**; **Toxic pollutants**; **Umatilla Chemical Depot**.

Hazelnut. A smooth round nut, *Corylus avellana*, also called European hazelnut or filbert, that has been designated the **state nut**. Oregon produces 99% of the nation's commercial crop, nearly all in the **Willamette Valley**. Eastern hazelnut blight has been moving south through the orchards at about two miles a year, and by 1997 had reached **Woodburn** and killed a third of the state's orchards. In 1995 Oregon production totaled 17,850 tons of nuts, worth $31.4 million, from 28,690 acres. The usual harvest totals 20,000 to 25,000 tons, compared to Turkey's production of over 400,000 tons. America's first commercial hazelnut orchard, the Dorris Ranch in **Springfield**, has been operating since 1892 and is now a living history farm open to the public. The native western hazelnut, *C. cornuta*, which grows west of the **Cascade Range**, has edible nuts that were gathered by the **Indians**. Oregon Agriculture; Oregonian 1/9/97:C4, 2/26/97:B4.

HBC. The **Hudson's Bay Company**; it was popularly claimed that the initials stood for "Here Before Christ".

Head Start. See **Oregon Prekindergarten Program (OPP)**.

Head tax. See **Poll tax**.

Health Council. The Oregon Health Council identifies and analyzes significant health care issues and makes policy recommendations to the governor, legislature, and Oregon **Health Plan** administrator. It also revises the Oregon Health Plan annually and guides a statewide clearinghouse on health care data. 255 Capitol St. NE, Salem 97310. 503-378-2422 ext 402. Oregon Blue Book.

Health Division. A division of the Oregon Department of **Human Resources** that works with 34 local health departments to prevent health hazards and promote public health. It focuses on the community rather than the individual and on prevention rather than cure by licensing providers, monitoring water supply and hospitals, preventing communicable disease through immunizations, supporting family planning and **teen pregnancy** prevention, and promoting prenatal care. 800 NE Oregon St., #21, Suite. 925, Portland 97232, 503-731-4000. Oregon Blue Book. See also **Health Division Licensing Programs**.

Health Division Licensing Programs. An office within the state **Health Division** that oversees the licensing of **athletic trainers; barbers and hairdressers; body piercing** facilities and technicians; **denturists; electrologists, permanent color technicians and tattoo artists; hearing aid dealers; midwives;** and **sanitarians.** 700 Summer St. NE, Suite 100, Salem 97310-1351. 503-378-8667. Oregon Blue Book.

Health insurance. A 1997 survey found that 10.6% of Oregonians had no health insurance. The rates ranged from 7.6% in the north **Willamette Valley** to 15.9% in far eastern Oregon. Oregonian 10/29/97:B11. See also **Oregon Health Plan; Senior Health Insurance Benefits Assistance.**

Health Plan Administrator. A person who advises the state legislature on implementing universal health care as delineated in the **Oregon Health Plan** and who coordinates the work of the state agencies that implement the plan. 255 Capitol S. NE, Salem 97310. 503-378-2422. Oregon Blue Book. See also **Medical Assistance Programs.**

Heap-leach mining. A process for extracting low grade ore by percolating a weak sodium-cyanide solution through piles of rock to extract minute particles of **gold** and **silver.** The process, developed in the 1940s, has made it profitable to mine low-grade deposits and has resulted in 40,000 new mining claims in eastern Oregon since the mid-1980s. Newmont Mining Corporation abandoned plans for a heap-leach mine at **Grassy Mountain** in **Malheur County,** but is doing exploratory work at Quartz Mountain in western **Lake County** near the summit of **Highway 140.** Oregonian 5/1/95:B10, 11/25/95:C1

Hearing Aid Dealers, Advisory Council for. A seven-member council that, under the **Health Division,** advises on licensing for hearing aid dealers, investigates complaints, issues civil penalties, and suspends or revokes licenses. In 1996 Oregon had about 350 licensed hearing aid dealers. 700 Summer Street NE, Suite 100, Salem 97310-1351. 503-378-8667. Oregon Blue Book. See also **Deaf.**

Heat. Most of Oregon's records for the hottest days have occurred during the last two weeks of July and the first two weeks of August, though **Portland** reached 107°F on July 2, 1942, and again on July 30,1965, and August 8 and 10, 1981. 108°F was recorded in **Salem** twice, (July 23, 1927, and July 15,1941), in **Eugene** (August 9, 1981), and in **Corvallis** (August 10, 1981). **Medford** reached 115°F on July 20, 1946. **Pendleton** had a high of 113°F on Aug. 4, 1961, but on August 10, 1938, it had matched the state record of 119°F, first set in **Prineville** on July 29, 1898. Oregonian 8/18/77:1.

Heating oil. In 1994, 933,000 barrels of heating oil were used in Oregon at a total cost of $34.8 million. The amount has been declining steadily from a high of 3,321,000 barrels in 1972. State Energy. See also **Petroleum.**

Heating-oil tanks. In 1997 it was estimated that Oregon had 270,000 buried home-heating-oil tanks, 140,000 of them no longer in use. About one third of the abandoned tanks probably leak, and tanks in active use can also leak. Clean-up costs average $5,000. The presence of an underground tank must be disclosed when selling a house. Oregonian 3/14/97:B2.

Heaven. See **Embassy of Heaven Church; Kingdom of Heaven.**

Heaven's Gate. A cult whose members believed that they could achieve an androgynous immortality via a UFO. They recruited at a meeting in Wonder, west of **Grants Pass** and on September 14, 1975, the leaders, Texans Bo (Marshall Herff Applewhite) and Peep (Bonnie Nettles) held a recruiting session at Bayshore Inn in **Waldport**, which over 200 attended. They encouraged attendees to leave all worldly goods, including family, and follow them to a higher level of being that they would reach via a space ship. Some 20 Oregonians followed them, at least for a time, to Colorado and other points. None of those recruits was known to be among the 39 members of Heaven's Gate, as the group was later known, who committed suicide in San Diego in March 1997, though the dead included an Oregon woman, LaDonna Brugato, who had joined the group in recent years. Mail Tribune 4/6/97:13A; Oregonian 3/28,29,30/97, 4/13/97:A1.

Heceta Head. A headland on the central Oregon coast 12 miles north of **Florence**. It and the shallow banks offshore are named for Captain Bruno Heceta, who sailed along the coast in August 1775. One of Oregon's most photographed **lighthouses** is on the brow of the cape, and a **state park** picnic area is at its south base at the mouth of Cape Creek. The rock just offshore is known as the Devil's Elbow. The name is locally pronounced HEH-kuh-tah or Heh-SAY-tah though the Spanish pronunciation would be closer to Ay-THAY-tah.

Heceta Head Lighthouse A frequently-photographed, operating **lighthouse** 12 miles north of **Florence**. It and the **Umpqua River Lighthouse** were built from the same plans and were both completed in 1894. The light, automated in 1963, is the most powerful light on the Oregon coast. Its 1,000-watt bulb, rated at 4.5 million candle-power, flashes every 10 seconds and can be seen 21 miles offshore. The 56' tower, with its light 205' above the ocean, can be reached by trail from Devil's Elbow State Park. The **State Parks** Department offers summer tours. Nearby Heceta House, the former keepers' house, is being operated as a bed and breakfast; there is said to be a **ghost**. 541-997-3851. Heceta House; Oregon Lighthouses; Oregon Parks 2(3):54, Nov/Dec 1994; Oregon's Seacoast Lighthouses.

Helix. "In the Center of the Wheat Belt." A farming community 20 miles north of **Pendleton** in **Umatilla County** that ships out a million bushels of wheat a year. The Helix post office was established in 1880, its name, according to legend, inspired by a resident's infection in the helix (spiral) of his ear. The city was incorporated in 1919. Population 1980 155; 1995 170. Elevation 1,754'. PO Box 323, 97835. 541-457-2521. Oregon Geographic Names.

Hell Hole. A half-mile-long, 200-foot-deep mossy rift in the forest floor in the **Willamette National Forest** north of **Oakridge**. The crumbling walls make it so dangerous that few have ventured into the rift, and its location is not publicized. Oregonian 8/5/97:B5.

Hells Canyon. A canyon through which the **Snake River** flows along the border between northeast Oregon and Idaho. It is the deepest river-cut gorge in North America, dropping 8,430 feet from the summit of He Devil Peak in Idaho to the river. (Arizona's Grand Canyon is 5,696' deep.) Hat Point, Oregon, is 5,632' above the Snake, and the canyon averages 5,500' deep for more than 40 miles. The overflow from a large **Pleistocene lake** in southwest Idaho may have cut a spillway that the Snake River then eroded down through the plateau of **Columbia River basalt** and into the much older sedimentary rocks below, creating the gorge.

The edges of the canyon are higher than the surrounding plateau because, as the weight of material in the canyon was eroded out, the earth's crust (which is floating) rose higher in that area. Grasses and small plants grow on the steep arid slopes of the canyon in places where they can get a toehold. **Hells Canyon National Recreation Area** covers 67 miles of the canyon. The name originally applied to a side canyon; in 1950 it was applied to the main canyon as a promotional effort. Geology of Oregon; Hells Canyon; Oregon Geographic Names; Oregonian 10/5/95:E2.

Hells Canyon Dam. A dam built by the **Idaho Power Company** for power generation on the **Snake River**, 23 miles down river from **Oxbow**. The concrete dam, completed in 1967, is 300 feet high and 1,000 feet long, and has a nameplate capacity of 391.5 **megawatts**. A visitor's center is located on the Oregon side, reached by crossing the dam. **Bighorn sheep** also use the dam to cross the river. Idaho Power operates Hells Canyon Park on the Idaho shore of the reservoir. The area is noted for its spring wildflowers, including shooting stars, phlox, balsam root, bleeding heart, and biscuit root. Recreation update 800-422-3143. The dam's name comes from its location at the upper end of **Hells Canyon**. Hells Canyon. See also **High Mountain Sheep Dam**.

Hells Canyon National Recreation Area. A remote 652,488 acre reserve encompassing the 7,900-foot-deep gorge of **Hells Canyon**. The largely undeveloped area offers scenic views, 900 miles of trails, and boating, both jet and non-motorized, on the **Snake River**. It was designated as a recreation area by Congress in 1975, and is administered by the **Wallowa-Whitman National Forest**. P.O. Box 699, Clarkston, WA 99403. 509-758-0616.

Helmets. Oregon requires helmets for motorcycle operators and passengers and for bicyclists younger than 16.

Hemlock. Conifer **trees** with short needles, droopy tops, and small cones. Two species are native to Oregon. Mountain hemlock, *Tsuga mertensiana*, is found near timberline in the **Cascade Range**. The commercially important western hemlock, *T. heterophylla*, grows in the wetter areas of the **Coast Range** and the Cascades, especially where annual rainfall exceeds 60 inches. It is shade tolerant, and frequently makes thick stands under other trees. Because it has no pitch, its lumber is valued for interior work, and it also provides high-quality fiber for pulp and rayon. Indians made a coarse bread from the inner bark. Trees to Know.

Hemlock Society USA. A national right-to-die organization headquartered in **Eugene**. It began as an organization promoting individuals' right to commit suicide, and published a book, Final Exit, of techniques. However, in 1994 it shifted focus to advocating **physician-assisted suicide** as an option for terminally ill persons. PO Box 11830, Eugene 97440. 1-800-247-7421.

Hemp. See **Indian hemp**.

Henline Falls. A plunge waterfall, estimated to be at least 70 feet high, on a tributary to the Little North **Santiam River**. The entrance to the old Silver King Mine is near the base of the falls. Henline Falls and several other falls can be reached via North Fork Road which joins **Highway 22** a mile east of Mehama. Henline Falls is up a 3/4 mile dirt track to the left of the road after 17 miles. Seven other smaller falls can be reached by scrambling up the creek. Treasures of the

Oregon Country; Waterfall Lover's Guide.

Henry Hagg Lake. A multipurpose reservoir six miles southwest of **Forest Grove**, created when the **Bureau of Reclamation** completed an earth fill dam on Scoggins Creek in 1975 as part of the **Tualatin Project**. The reservoir provides flood control, irrigation, municipal and industrial water supply, improved water quality in the Tualatin River, and recreation. There are day use facilities but no campground. At full pool the lake is three miles long and covers 1,153 acres to a maximum depth of 110 feet. It is named for a **Washington County** official and dairyman who died in 1971. Atlas of Oregon Lakes.

Heppner. "Irish Capital of Oregon." A north-central Oregon farming and mill town 60 miles southwest of **Pendleton**; it is the county seat of **Morrow County**. It was founded in 1873 and named for Henry Heppner, co-owner of the first store; it was incorporated in 1887. The 1903 **Heppner flood** destroyed much of the town; **Willow Creek dam** now controls the creek. Attractions include a museum, Saint Patrick's Day Celebration, and Morrow County Fair and **Rodeo**. Population 1980 1,498; 1995 1,480. Elevation 1,955'. PO Box 756, 97836. 541-676-9618. Chamber of Commerce 541-676-5536. Oregon Geographic Names.

Heppner flood. On June 14, 1903, a thunderstorm created a 20-foot wall of water, mud, and debris that rushed down **Willow Creek** past **Heppner** where it destroyed most of the town plus two miles of railroad, and took the lives of 247 people, one fourth of the town's population. The flood continued downstream past **Lexington** and **Ione**, but two horsemen outraced the torrent and warned the people in both towns in time for them to flee. Heavy **hail** had accompanied the thunderstorm, and even five days after the flood some bodies were found preserved in large drifts of hail. The flood, one of Oregon's worst **disasters**, prompted a nation-wide outpouring of assistance. See also **Flash floods**; **Willow Creek Dam**.

Herbaria. Collections of dried plant materials kept for reference and research. Oregon's major herbarium is at **Oregon State University** (OSU). The collection includes 330,000 specimens, 55,000 of them fungi and lichens, and 2,000 more are added each year. Both the **University of Oregon**'s herbarium and **Willamette University's** Peck collection are now housed at OSU.

Heritage Tree Program. A state program that identifies Oregon trees notable for their size and history. The first four, selected in 1997, were the Munkre pear at the junction of **Highway 22** and **Interstate 5**; the nation's largest **Sitka spruce** tree near **Seaside**; the Hinds walnut, located off **Highway 138** about 12 miles north of **Sutherlin**; and a grove of 120-year-old giant sequoias in front of the **Washington County** Courthouse in **Hillsboro**. Five trees selected in 1998 were the 136-year-old Britt sequoia in **Jacksonville**, the Waldo Park sequoia in **Salem**, the Foster lilac in Eagle Creek, the Frazier shagbark hickory in **Milton-Freewater** and the "lonesome" shagbark hickory near **Shady Cove**. The program is operated by volunteers under the aegis of the **Travel Information Council**. Oregonian 3/30/97:B4, 4/7/98:E14.

Hermiston. A city in north-central Oregon near the **Columbia River**, 28 miles northwest of **Pendleton** in **Umatilla County**. Its name was taken from Robert Louis Stevenson's The Weir of Hermiston, and has had the advantage of not being in use by any other U.S. post office. The city was incorporated in 1907. The agribusiness economy of the city is based on the irrigated agriculture of the surrounding area, with J.R. Simplot, Lamb-Weston, and Hermiston Foods as the largest employers. Attractions include the Umatilla County Fair, National Horse Sale, State Horseshoe Competition, outdoor recreation, and the area's famous watermelons. 20% of the population is **Hispanic**. Population 1980 8,408; 1995 10,605. Elevation 450'. 180 NE 2nd St., 97838. 541-567-5521. Chamber of Commerce 541-567-5521. Oregon Geographic Names. See also **D. Boone tree**.

Heron. See **Great blue heron**.

Hewlett-Packard Company. A company based in Palo Alto, California, that manufactures computer, communications, and test and measurement products. It opened a plant in **Corvallis** in 1976 that employs 5,000 workers, part of its worldwide work force of 108,300, and it also has offices in **Beaverton** and **McMinnville**. Oregonian 6/30/96:R20.

High Desert. An area of Oregon's **sagebrush** plains southeast of **Bend** covering parts of **Deschutes**, **Crook**, **Harney**, and **Lake Counties**. Part of the High Desert lies within the **basin and range** and part within the **high lava plains** physiographic provinces. Elevation is over 4,000' and annual precipitation averages 10 inches or less, with surface water only at springs near **Wagontire Mountain**. Prior to settlement frequent fires restrained the sagebrush and **juniper** that has since taken over much of the bunchgrass range. The High Desert was first settled in 1863, and then heavily -and briefly - **homesteaded** between 1906 and 1916. Drought, freezes, and **jackrabbits** quickly ended most farming hopes. The term High Desert is also used more broadly to cover the entire northern-most portion of the **Great Basin** that lies in southeastern Oregon and northwestern Nevada. East of the Cascades; Oregon Desert; Fish and Wildlife on the Oregon Trail; Oregon Desert. See also **Desert**; **Great Basin history**.

High Desert Museum. A private, non-profit museum four miles south of **Bend**. Interactive displays, walk-through exhibits, and live presentations focus on the natural and cultural heritage of the arid regions of the west, including two-thirds of Oregon. 59800 S. Highway 97, Bend 97702. 541-382-4754. Oregon Blue Book; Oregonian 10/5/97:B4.

High lava plains physiographic province. An approximately rectangular area lying northwest to southeast across the center of Oregon, roughly along **Highway 20** from **Bend** to east of **Burns**. The area, about 50 miles north/south by 150 miles east/west, is bordered by the **Cascade Range** on the west, the **Deschutes Columbia plateau** and the **Blue Mountains** on the north, the **Owyhee uplands** to the east, and the **basin and range** province to the south. Volcanic activity along **Brothers fault zone** over the past 10 million years formed the area, producing such features as **lava tubes, cinder cones, maars, Glass Butte, Newberry Volcano, Hole-in-the-Ground, Crack-in-the-Ground**, and **Lava Cast Forest**. Volcanic activity has been moving northwest at about 1 mile every 100,000 years (.7" a year). The high point is **Paulina Peak** at 7,984'; the low is **Harney Lake** at 4,080'. Some old maps call the area Great Sandy Desert, a name that is not now used. Geology of Oregon.

High-lead logging. A method of logging in which a loop of cable is stretched from a pulley on a high spar to a pulley at a distant point. A clutch of logs is attached by cable to the loop, and an engine reels in the loop, carrying the logs through the air to the landing, avoiding the damage to soil that comes from dragging them over the land. The system, which came into use about 1911, is used especially on ground too steep for tractor logging.

High Mountain Sheep Dam. A 670-foot-high dam proposed at one time for the **Snake River** in **Hells Canyon** a half mile above the mouth of the Salmon River. The Pacific Northwest Power Company, (a consortium made up of **Pacific Power and Light, Portland General Electric**, Montana Power & Light, and Washington Water Power) applied for a license in 1958 after years of controversy between proponents of public and private power, and between proponents of a single high dam versus several smaller dams. Further controversy followed before Congress, in 1975, authorized **Hells Canyon National Recreation Area**, finally eliminating the possibility of High Mountain Sheep or any other dam being built in Hells Canyon below **Hells Canyon Dam**. Hells Canyon.

High schools. In 1994-95, there were198 public high schools in Oregon. Sunset High in **Beaverton** is the largest with 2,186 students in 1997-98. At the time the high school law passed in 1900 there were just four high schools, located in **Astoria, Baker City, Portland**, and **The Dalles**. Nine years later there were 115. Oregonians with a high school diploma increased from 20.5% in 1947 to 30% in 1990. Oregon Oddities; Oregonian 10/29/97:A10. See also **Schools, public**.

High speed rail. See **Northwest High-Speed Rail Corridor**.

High-tech industry. Industry based upon, and/or producing sophisticated equipment. Oregon's high-tech industry began in 1946 in a neighborhood garage in **Portland** where Howard Vollum and Jack Murdock formed **Tektronix** to build oscilloscopes. In 1976 **Intel** built a factory in **Aloha** and **Hewlett-Packard** in **Corvallis**. The industry grew further in the mid 1980s, and had an $11 billion boom in the mid 1990s. By the end of 1995 employment in technology (60,860) had surpassed employment in the timber and paper industries (60,416). A 1996 survey of 65 high-tech companies found that they had a total payroll of $2.3 billion (54,000 employees), a median wage of $43,700, total revenues of $18 billion (up 59% from 1993), and export revenues of $4.3 billion. Oregonian 1/17/96:A1, 9/11/96:C1. See also **CAPITAL Center; Semi-conductor industry; Silicon Forest**.

Higher education. The per cent of Oregonians with a college or advanced degree increased from 12.1% in 1947 to 20.2% in 1990. Oregonian 10/29/97:A10.

Higher education endowment funds. In 1997 **Reed College** led Oregon colleges with an endowment fund of $213 million, followed by **Oregon Health Sciences University** $194 million, **Oregon State University** $158 million, **Willamette University** $147 million, **University of Oregon** $140 million, **Lewis and Clark College** $89.5 million, **University of Portland** $42 million, and **Portland State University** $7.7 million. For comparison, Harvard University had an endowment of $10.9 billion. Endowment funds are made up of donated funds that are permanently invested. The income from the funds is used by the schools for a variety of purposes. Oregonian 3/3/98:B4.

Higher education, private. In 1997 privately funded higher education in

Oregon was provided by 31 independent degree-granting colleges and universities. They enroll over 25 percent of all upper-division and graduate students in the state and award 30% of the state's bachelor's and graduate degrees. Nineteen of the colleges are accredited by the Northwest Association of Schools and Colleges. These (and their fall 1995 enrollment) are **Bassist College** (103), **Concordia University** (976), **George Fox University** (1,712), **Lewis and Clark College** (3,188), **Linfield College** (2,814); **Marylhurst College** (1,286), **Mount Angel Seminary** (156), **Northwest Christian College** (408), **Oregon Graduate Institute** (530), **Pacific Northwest College of Art** (257); **Pacific University** (1,850), **Reed College** (1,290), **University of Portland** (2,630), **Walla Walla College School of Nursing** (101); **Warner Pacific College** (670), **Western Baptist College** (694), **Western Seminary** (469), **Western States Chiropractic College** (458), and **Willamette University** (2,568). The other 12 are Cascade College, ITT Technical Institute, Multnomah Bible College, National College of Naturopathic Medicine, Oregon College of Arts and Crafts, Oregon College of Oriental Medicine, Process Work Center of Portland, and Western Business College, all in **Portland**, Pioneer Pacific College in **Wilsonville**, **Salem** Bible College, **Eugene** Bible College, and Dove Bible Institute in **Medford**. Oregon Independent Colleges Association, 7150 SW Hampton St. #101, Portland 97223, 503-639-4541. Oregon Blue Book. See also **University of Phoenix**.

> **Higher education, public.** See **University System, Oregon**.
> **Highest point.** The highest point in Oregon is **Mount Hood** at 11,240'. Mount Rainier is Washington's highest point at 14,410' and Mount Whitney is California's highest point at 14,494'. Mount Shasta in northern California is 14,162'.
> **Highest road.** See **Highways, highest**.
> **Highest temperature.** See **Heat; Temperature records**.
> **Highland games.** Festivals with a Scottish focus, featuring bagpipes, Highland dancing, food and gift booths, caber tossing, and other athletic events. The Scottish Highland Games are held in mid July at **Mount Hood Community College** in **Gresham**. 503-790-2109. Highland games are also held at **Athena** in July and **Myrtle Creek** in late August.
> **Highway 6.** A 50-mile state highway between **Tillamook** and **Highway 26** north of **Forest Grove**, usually known as the Wilson River Highway. A **toll road** along the Wilson River was completed in 1893, but portions of it were often in disrepair. After decades of controversy, the state took over the route and opened it in 1941 as Oregon Highway 6, thus providing a reasonable route between Tillamook and **Portland**. Tillamook.
> **Highway 20.** A U.S. route from **Newport** east across Oregon through **Albany**, up the South **Santiam River**, over the **Santiam Pass**, and through **Bend** and **Burns** to **Ontario**. The highest spots are Tombstone Summit (4,236') and Santiam Pass (4,817') in the **Cascade Range**, and Stinkingwater Pass (4,848') and Drinkwater Pass (4,212') east of Burns. Work began on the section between Bend and Burns in 1929 after Bend businessmen contributed about $600 for the survey and improvement of a road to Burns. East of the Cascades. See also **Stinkingwater Creek**.
> **Highway 22.** A state highway that goes from Hebo on **Highway 101** (the Coast Highway) through **Salem** and up the North **Santiam River** to connect with

Highway 20 just west of **Santiam Pass**. Its **Coast Range** summit is at elevation 672'. A ten-mile stretch between **Highway 99W** and the **Willamette River** west of Salem has been designated as a **safety corridor**.

Highway 26. A U.S. route that crosses Oregon from **Highway 101** south of **Seaside** southeast through the **Tillamook Burn** and over historic **Canyon Road** to **Portland**, on past **Mount Hood** and through **Madras**, **Prineville**, and **John Day** to **Ontario**. High points are two summits in the **Coast Range** (1,309' and 1,174'), Blue Box Summit (4,025') in the **Cascade Range**, Ochoco Pass (4,722') and Keyes Creek Summit (4,372') on each side of **Mitchell**, and five passes east of **Prairie City**, of which Dixie Pass (5,279') is the highest. The first ten miles east of Highway 101 have been designated as a **safety corridor**. The 77 mile-stretch between the coast and Portland is also known as the **Sunset Highway**, and the 61 miles from Mount Hood to Madras is known as the Warm Springs Highway.

Highway 30. A historic U.S. route across northern Oregon that followed the **Columbia River** east from **Astoria** through **Portland** and on up the river 168 miles to **Boardman**, then angled southeast along the **Oregon Trail** over the **Blue Mountains** to **Ontario**. The portion from **Portland** east has been supplanted by **Interstate 84**. See also **Columbia River Scenic Highway**.

Highway 31. A state highway that runs 120 miles along the edge of the high desert in south-central Oregon, from **Highway 97** near **La Pine** southeast to **Highway 395** at Valley Falls. Picture Rock Pass, elevation 4,830', is the highest point. It is known as the Fremont Highway for Captain John C. Fremont who explored the region during the winter of 1843-44. East of the Cascades.

Highway 34. A state highway across the **Coast Range** from **Highway 101** at **Waldport** east through **Corvallis** to **Highway 20** at **Lebanon**. The 11-mile stretch from **Corvallis** east to **Interstate 5** has been designated as a **safety corridor**. Alsea Summit, elevation 1,231', is the high point.

Highway 58. A state highway that runs from **Interstate 5**, just south of **Eugene**, southeast over **Willamette Pass** (elevation 5,128') to **Highway 97**. The 92-mile route follows approximately the route of the 1853 **Free Emigrant Road**. A rail line, called the **Natron cut-off**, follows much the same route.

Highway 62. A 100-mile long state highway that loops north up the **Rogue River** from **Interstate 5** at **Medford**, crosses the **Cascade Range** (6,016') south of **Crater Lake** and drops south to join **Highway 97** south of **Chiloquin**. The turnoff to **Crater Lake National Park** is 72 miles from **Medford**.

Highway 95. A U.S. route that crosses the vast **sagebrush** spaces of southeast Oregon on its way from Mexico to Canada. It enters Oregon at McDermitt, travels north over 5,293-foot Blue Mountain Pass to Burns Junction, veers east through **Rome** and **Jordan Valley**, and then turns north into Idaho.

Highway 97. A U.S. route, the major north-south highway in central Oregon. It runs from **Biggs** on the **Columbia River** south through **Bend** and **Klamath Falls** to connect with **Interstate 5** at Weed, California. Though the mostly two-lane route crosses no major passes in Oregon, it runs through high country, and in winter snow and **black ice** contribute to a high accident rate. The 70-mile stretch from Chemult to **Klamath Falls** has been designated as a **safety corridor**. See also **Highway signs**.

Highway 99. A north-south state highway from **Portland** to **California** first known as the **Pacific Highway**. When the 345-mile route was completed in 1924, Oregon became the first state west of the Mississippi to have a paved highway the entire length of the state. Between Portland and **Junction City**, the route is divided into east and west portions, with 99E traveling down the east side of the **Willamette River** through **Oregon City**, **Salem**, **Albany**, and **Harrisburg**, and 99W down the west side through **McMinnville**, **Corvallis**, and **Monroe**. **Interstate 5** follows much of the route of Highway 99 and has replaced portions of it. First 75 Years. See also **Siskiyou Trail**; **Stumbo Strip**.

Highway 101. A U.S. route along the Oregon coast that runs 363 miles from **Astoria** to the California border, south of **Brookings**. Begun in 1914, it was completed in 1933 except for five major **bridges**. After their completion in 1936, travelers could for the first time move readily along the coast. Notable bridges include the state's highest, 345', over Thomas Creek nine miles north of **Brookings**, the mile-long McCullough Memorial Bridge over **Coos Bay**, and the four-mile-long bridge across the **Columbia River** at Astoria. The route was designated the Roosevelt Highway from 1917 to 1931, but is now more commonly known as the Coast Highway. First 75 Years; Oregonian 9/23/96:B1. See also **Three Capes Scenic Loop**.

Highway 126. A 206-mile state highway that runs from **Highway 101** on the coast at **Florence** east through **Eugene**, up the **McKenzie River**, over the **Clear Lake Cutoff** and **Santiam Pass** (4,817') and through **Sisters** to connect with **Highway 26** at **Prineville** in central Oregon. Scenic **Highway 242** over **McKenzie Pass**, closed in the winter, provides a 12 mile shorter but slower connection between the McKenzie River and Sisters.

Highway 138. A state highway that runs from **Elkton** on **Highway 38** through **Roseburg** and east up the North **Umpqua River** past **Diamond Lake** to **Highway 97**. Cascade Summit, 5,920', is crossed by a 10-mile straight stretch through lodgepole pines growing in deep **pumice** from the **Crater Lake** explosion. The route provides access to 18 waterfalls described in Waterfall Lover's Guide, including **Toketee Falls**, **Watson Falls**, and **Lemolo Falls**. See also **Colliding Rivers**.

Highway 140. A state highway in southern Oregon, part of the "**Winnemucca to the Sea**" route. It runs from **White City**, near **Medford**, east through **Klamath Falls** and **Lakeview** to **Highway 95** north of Winnemucca, Nevada. In Oregon the route includes five passes over 5,000 feet, the highest being Warner Summit, 5,846', near the Nevada line. Portions of the route are sometimes closed by snow in winter.

Highway 197. A U.S. route that goes from **The Dalles** 64 miles south to join **Highway 97** twenty-five miles north of **Madras**. It passes through **Dufur**, Tygh Valley, and **Maupin**. It crosses a 2,665' summit north of Tygh Valley but the highest point, Criterion Summit, 3,360', is near the south end.

Highway 242. A seasonal state highway over the **McKenzie Pass** east of **Eugene**. The narrow, twisting, scenic route leaves **Highway 126** at Belknap Springs and crosses raw **lava** fields at the pass, elevation 5,325', to **Sisters**. It served as the highway east from Eugene until **Clear Lake Cutoff**, opened in 1962, provided a faster, all-season route over the Cascades.

Highway 395. A north-south U.S. route that jogs its way from southern California north through eastern Oregon and Washington to the Canadian border. The 390-mile length in Oregon travels through **Lakeview, Burns, John Day, Pendleton**, and **Hermiston**. Passes include Hogback Summit, 5,039', north of Lakeview, Sagehen Summit, 4,596', west of Burns, Canyon Creek Summit, 5,152', south of John Day, and five passes between John Day and Pendleton, with the highest, Long Creek Summit, at 5,101'. The route was authorized in 1932.

Highway conditions. See **Road conditions**.

Highway Department. See **Transportation, Oregon Department of**.

Highway passes. The mountain ranges of Oregon are major barriers to transportation and were diligently searched by pioneers, sometimes following Indian trails, for reasonable crossings for **wagon roads**. Many of the wagon routes later became the present paved highways. Major highway passes across the **Cascade Range** include Blue Box Summit (4,025') on **Highway 26** south of **Mount Hood, Santiam Pass** (4,817') on **Highway 20, McKenzie Pass** (5,325') on **Highway 242**, Willamette Pass (5,128') on **Highway 58**, Cascade Summit east of **Diamond Lake** (5,920') on **Highway 138**, the summit on **Highway 140** (5,105'), and Hayden Mountain Summit on Highway 66 (4,695'). Other major highway passes include Siskiyou Summit (4,310') on **Interstate 5** near the California border, the **Interstate 84** pass (4,193') in the **Blue Mountains**, Dixie Pass (5,279') east of **John Day** on **Highway 26**, and Quartz Mountain Pass (5,306') east of **Klamath Falls** on **Highway 140**. See also **Highways, highest**, and entries for individual highways.

Highway signs. In the first part of the 20th century, the first arterial highway routes in Oregon were each designated with a color. For example, the route from **The Dalles** to **Klamath Falls** (now **Highway 97**) was designated as the "White and Blue" road, and local clubs painted white and blue bands on telephone poles, posts, and trees. The bands were visible for years. East of the Cascades.

Highways. Oregon has over 97,000 miles of roads and highways. In 1997 the Oregon Department of **Transportation** maintained 7,448 miles of state highways and 729 miles of **interstate highways**, with 22% rated poor. Counties had 15,432 miles of paved county roads (40% in poor shape) and 8,879 miles of gravel roads (nearly half rated poor). Cities had 8,258 miles of streets and roads (nearly a fourth rated poor). The average traffic lane is 11 feet wide; trucks may haul **manufactured homes** up to 16-feet wide. Mail Tribune 8/17/97:A1; Oregonian 3/6/98:D8, 3/15/98:A1. See also **Bridges; Gas tax; Rest areas**.

Highways, highest. The highest maintained road in Oregon is the **Steens Mountain** loop road, an unpaved road that goes nearly to the 9,733' summit. Paved high-elevation highways include those over **highway passes** and to ski areas, as well as the highway around **Crater Lake** to Cloudcap viewpoint (7,950') and the road to **Timberline Lodge** (6,000').

Highways, history. The first crude **wagon roads** in Oregon were laboriously built by pioneers, often following Indian trails. The builder might charge a toll, as on the **Barlow Road, Siskiyou Toll Road**, and at **Sherars Bridge**. **Military wagon roads** were financed with federal **land grants**. The **territorial government** (1849-1859) provided for the construction of the first public wagon roads. Some, still called Territorial Roads, later became county roads. In 1859 the new state of Oregon required all men between 21 and 50 to work two days a year on county roads or pay a tax. Later, bicyclists and early automobilists who wanted decent road surfaces prompted the **Good Roads movement** early in the 20th century. In 1906, the new Portland Automobile Club raised $10,000 to oil Linnton Road (now part of **Highway 30**), the first oiled road on the west coast. The **Columbia River Scenic Highway**, 1913-1922, was the first major project of the Oregon State Highway Department (now the Department of **Transportation**), founded in 1913. During the **Depression** of the 1930s, the government provided jobs through highway construction, resulting in the present highways across the Coast and Cascade ranges and along the Oregon coast. The Oregon portions of the federal **Interstate highway system** were completed between 1966 and 1988. First 75 Years. See also **From Hellgate to Portland**; **Transportation history**;

Highways, scenic. The **Columbia River Scenic Highway** and the highway around **Crater Lake** are both on the American Automobile Association's list of North America's 10 Most Beautiful Highways. The **Cascades Lake Highway** was named in 1995 as one of the nation's 10 most important scenic byways.

Hijacking. On November 24, 1971, the day before Thanksgiving, Northwest Airlines Flight 305 was hijacked on a flight from **Portland** to Seattle by passenger D. B. (Dan) Cooper. He claimed to have a bomb, and demanded that in Seattle the plane be refueled, that he be furnished with four parachutes and $200,000 cash, and that the plane then fly to Mexico City. He allowed the passengers to disembark in Seattle. As the plane traveled south he apparently parachuted out during a nighttime storm over rugged country a few miles north of Portland and was never heard from again. In 1980 decomposing marked bills totaling nearly $6,000 were found along the **Columbia River** nine miles downriver from Vancouver, Washington. Norjak.

Hiking. See **Trails**; **Trails Club of Oregon**; **Volkssports**; **Wilderness areas**.

Hilgard Junction State Park. A **state park** on the banks of the **Grande Ronde River**, just off **Interstate 84** eight miles west of **La Grande**. The park includes an **Oregon Trail** exhibit shelter, river rafting access, and a year-round campground with 18 primitive sites.

Hills Creek Reservoir. A 2,735 acre, multipurpose lake in a steep canyon on the Middle Fork of the **Willamette River** five miles southeast of **Oakridge**. It was formed in 1961 when the **Army Corps of Engineers** built a 340-foot earth- and gravel-fill dam where Hills Creek joins the Middle Fork. The lake, with a maximum depth of 299 feet, is over seven miles long. Recreation uses includes boating, fishing, and camping. Hills Creek was named for John Hill, a local rancher during the 1870's. Atlas of Oregon Lakes.

Hillsboro. A rapidly-growing suburban city 18 miles west of downtown **Portland** that is home to burgeoning **high-tech** industry and is also the county seat of **Washington County**. It was named for David Hill who had settled there in 1842. He was elected chair of the executive committee at **Champoeg** in 1843, so was, in effect, Oregon's first governor. The city was incorporated in 1876. Attractions include an annual air show during the **Rose Festival**, the Washington County Fair, a **rodeo**, free Thursday evening concerts in the park, a weekly farmers' market, and area wineries. Population 1980 27,664; 1995 46,160. Elevation 196'. 123 W Main St., 97123. 503-681-6100. Chamber of Commerce 503-648-1102. Oregon Geographic Names.

Hines. An eastern Oregon town two miles southwest of **Burns** on **Highway 20** in **Harney County**. It was named for Edward Hines who had bought the Herrick mill in 1928 and changed the name to Edward Hines Lumber Company; the city was incorporated in 1930. During the 1980s the mill was operated by Snow Mountain Pine, which, until it closed, provided half of the county's basic industry. In 1996 a motor-home company opened a manufacturing plant in the former sawmill. Population 1980 1,632; 1995 1,445. Elevation 4,155'. PO Box 336, 97738. 541-573-2251. Oregon Geographic Names. See also **Basques**.

Hispanic Affairs, Commission on. An 11-member commission created by the 1983 legislature to work for economic, social, legal, and political equality of Hispanics in Oregon. Public Service Building, 255 Capitol St. NE, Salem 97310. 503-378-3725, ext. 4184. Oregon Blue Book.

Hispanics. Persons of Central American, South American, or Spanish culture or origin. In 1993 Oregon's Hispanic population was estimated to be 147,300, up from 112,708 in 1990, and it is increasing at a rate four times that of the state's overall population increase. Hispanics are Oregon's largest ethnic minority, accounting for 4.8% of the state's population (compared to California's 26%). Three fourths have come from Mexico, with the rest from Central and South America and Spain. 31% of Oregon's Hispanics are foreign born, primarily in Mexico. In 1996 there were estimated to be more than 100,000 Mexican nationals living in the state and a Mexican consulate was opened in **Portland**. In 1990 over 18,000 Hispanics lived in **Multnomah County** and another 18,000 in **Marion County**, **Washington County** had 14,000, and **Clackamas**, **Jackson**, **Lane**, **Malheur**, and **Umatilla** counties each had over 5,000. Hispanics made up 48% of the population in **Nyssa**, 31% in **Woodburn**, 24% in **Independence**, and 21% in **Ontario**. Celebrations include **fiestas** on Mexican Independence Day on September 16 (freed from Spain in 1810), Guadalupe Day on December 12, and **Cinco de Mayo** on May 5. Nosotros; Oregonian 6/6/96:A1. See also **Four Rivers Cultural Center**; **Migrant labor**; **Mixtecs**; **Undocumented workers**.

Hispanics in Oregon, history. The first explorers off the Oregon coast, from 1542 to the 1800s, were Spanish. Mexicans came to Oregon in the mid-19th century as miners, skilled mulepackers, and **vaqueros**. Beginning in the 1920s, more came to work in agriculture and on railroad maintenance crews, some as migrants and as settlers. **Braceros** provided farm labor during **World War II**. The numbers of Hispanics who settled in Oregon increased after the war, as did the number working as migrant laborers. The Chicano Movement of the 1960s and 1970s worked to improve political, social, and economic conditions. Today increasing numbers of Hispanics are entering professions, establishing businesses, and pursuing the arts. Nosotros. See also **Colegio Cesar Chavez**; **Spanish coins**.

Historian Laureate. Thomas Vaughan, director of the Oregon Historical Society for some years, was named historian laureate of Oregon by the 1989 legislature. Oregon Blue Book.

Historic Preservation, Advisory Committee on. A committee of nine members, appointed by the governor, that reviews nominations to the **National Register of Historic Places** and works with the State Historic Preservation Office in the **Parks and Recreation Department** to implement the Statewide Comprehensive Historic Preservation Plan. 1115 Commercial St. NE, Salem 97310-1001. 503-378-6508. Oregon Blue Book.

    Historical markers. About 100 information boards, sometimes called Beaver Boards, have been placed along Oregon's highways to provide travelers with information about Oregon history. The program began in the 1930s as a **WPA** project; in 1991 responsibility was transferred from the Oregon Department of **Transportation** to the **Travel Information Council.** A list of markers with a map is part of the Pocket Guide to Oregon Museums and Historical Markers brochure, available at museums throughout the state.

    History. See timeline below and also **Archives; Disasters; Discoverers; Fur trade; Government history; Indians; Oregon Country; Oregon Territory; Settlement; Wars.** Empire of the Columbia; General History of Oregon Through Early Statehood; Landscapes of Promise; Oregon: A Bicentennial History; That Balance So Rare.

    History time line.

To 1818

15,500 to 12,800 years ago: **Pleistocene floods** at end of ice age.

9,000 years ago: Sandals from **Fort Rock Cave** have been dated to 9,000 years ago.

1542: Spanish **explorer** Bartolome Ferrelo (of Cabrillo's expedition) sails north as far as the **Rogue River** but is prevented from landing by fierce storms.

1579: The English buccaneer Sir Francis Drake sails north to at least the southern part of Oregon, may have landed at Whale Cove in Lincoln County. He comments on **weather**.

1603: Spanish sailor Martin d'Aguilar sails north along Oregon coast but is unable to land.

1707: The Spanish ship, *San Francisco Xavier*, may have wrecked on **Neahkahnie Mountain** with a load of beeswax.

1775: Spanish explorer Bruno Heceta locates the mouth of the **Columbia River** but the crew is too weak with scurvy to cross the bar.

1778: England's Captain Cook sails north along the coast; he misses the **Columbia River** but initiates the **fur trade**.

1781-82: Smallpox sweeps through the Oregon country, killing many **Indians**.

1788. The first Americans set foot in Oregon when Captain Robert Gray lands at **Tillamook Bay**; natives murder his black cabin boy.

1792: On May 11 the American ship, *Columbia Rediviva*, captained by Robert Gray, is the first ship to sail into the **Columbia River**. In the fall British Lieutenant William Broughton of Vancouver's expedition spends three weeks exploring the Columbia as far as the **Columbia Gorge** and is the first to describe the area, writing "The most beautiful landscape that can be imagined."

1801: Was Daniel Boone in Oregon? An inscription, reading "**D. Boone** 1801," has been found on a tree in eastern Oregon.

1804-06: The **Lewis and Clark Expedition** leaves St. Louis, winters 1805-06 at

Fort Clatsop near **Astoria,** and returns to St. Louis in September 1806.

1810: Three Winship brothers and 30 men arrive on their sailing ship, the *Albatross*, and unsuccessfully attempt a settlement, the first in the Oregon country, near **Rainier**. They leave after eight days.

1811: A fur post called **Astoria** is established near the mouth of the **Columbia River** by the Pacific Fur Company (American).

1814: The **North West Company** brings in the first cattle, by ship.

Joint occupancy, 1818-1846

1818: The U.S. and Great Britain sign a treaty of **joint occupancy** for the area west of the Rocky Mountains.

1820s: **Fur trade** in sea otter pelts peaks and declines, while the beaver trade prospers.

1824: The **Hudson's Bay Company** (British), establishes its western headquarters at **Fort Vancouver** with **Dr. John McLoughlin** as chief factor, and later systematically traps out all of the beaver in eastern Oregon and the Snake River region in order to discourage Americans.

1825: Botanist David Douglas first visits **Fort Vancouver**.

1826: Fur brigade leader Peter Skene Ogden takes first whites over **Siskiyou Pass**, helping to establish a route which eventually becomes **Interstate 5**.

1828: Jedediah Smith and 3 companions reach Fort Vancouver, the first whites to travel overland from central California. 15 of their party were massacred by Indians near the mouth of the **Umpqua River**.

1829: Hall Jackson Kelley of Boston organizes the **American Society for Encouraging the Settlement of the Oregon Territory**.

1830: **Malaria** epidemic decimates the Indians of western Oregon.

1830s: **Hudson's Bay Company** retired French-Canadian trappers start farming at **French Prairie** west of **Woodburn**.

1832: American Nathaniel Wyeth's first overland expedition from Boston arrives at Fort Vancouver.

1834: Nathaniel Wyeth's second expedition arrives in Oregon, includes naturalist John K. Townsend, botanist Thomas Nuttall, and **Methodist** missionary Jason Lee who settles north of **Salem**. **Hudson's Bay Company** receives 98,288 **beaver** skins at Fort Vancouver.

1838: Francois Blanchet and Modeste Demers, the first **Catholic** missionaries, arrive at Fort Vancouver.

1840: **Population** of Americans fewer than 200. **Great Reinforcement** of 50 **Methodists** arrives. The **Oregon Country** is promoted in the east as being nearly tropical, where citrus and cotton flourish and oat stalks can be used as walking sticks.

1841: An unsuccessful series of three meetings is held at **Champoeg** by settlers trying to establish some form of government in order dispose of the property of Ewing Young, who died without a will or an heir. *Star of Oregon* is launched.

1842: Dr. Elijah White leads a party of 114 persons overland to settle in Oregon.

Provisional government, 1843-1848

1843: Willamette Valley settlers (missionaries, other Americans, and French-Canadians) hold several **wolf meetings** at **Champoeg**, and on May 2 establish a **Provisional government**. In the fall the **Great Migration**, the first major **wagon train** to cross the **Oregon Trail**, arrives with 875 immigrants. John C. Fremont leads a government-sponsored exploration south across central Oregon.

1844: The Provisional government passes laws prohibiting **slavery** but also forbidding the residence of free **blacks**.

1845: The Provisional legislature elects George Abernethy first **governor** of the **Oregon Country**.

1846: Treaty of 1846 ends **joint occupancy**, assigns area south of 49°, the present Canadian border, to the U.S., and the area north to Great Britain.

1847: **Whitman Massacre**.

Oregon Territory, 1848-1858

1848: The **Oregon Territory** is created by Congress. Joseph Lane of Indiana is appointed first territorial governor.

1849: The California **gold rush** draws most Oregon men and provides a market for Oregon wheat and lumber.

1850: Population 12,093. **Donation Land Act** grants 9,000 settlers title to 2.5 million acres (without, however, prior cession of title by Indians.)

1851-56: **Rogue River War** .

1853: **Willamette University** established.

1854: First **telegraph** service established in Oregon.

1857: A convention of 60 delegates draws up Oregon's **Constitution**.

Statehood, 1859-

1859: Oregon achieves **statehood** on February 14 when Congress ratifies the state constitution and President Buchanan signs the **Admission Act**.

1860:   **Population** 52,465. Daily **stage line** service begins to California.

1861: **Gold** discoveries in eastern Oregon lead to first settlement there and to the search for routes east from the Willamette Valley. The worst **flood** in western Oregon's history destroys Orleans, **Champoeg**, and much of **Oregon City**, is followed by severe cold and prolonged snow.

1862. **Homestead Act** passes Congress. Congress also grants millions of acres during the 1860s to promote construction of **military wagon roads** and **railroads**.

1864: Voters name **Salem** as the state **capital**. Transcontinental **telegraph** reaches **Portland** via California.

1870: Population 90,923.

1872-73: **Modoc War**.

1877: **Nez Perce War**.

1878: **Bannock War**.

1880: Population 174,768.

1883: First transcontinental **railroad** connection to Oregon completed. (California was connected in 1869.)

1887: **Railroad** connection to California completed.

1890: **Population** 317,704. The value of Oregon cities and industry for the first time surpasses that of its farms.

1893-97: National economic depression abruptly slows Oregon's growth.

1900: Population 413,536

1902: Oregon adopts the **initiative** and **referendum** laws.

1905: Lewis and Clark Centennial Exposition is held in **Portland**. Oregon booms.

1910: Population 672,765.

1912: Oregon men give Oregon women the vote.

1920: Population 783,389.

1921: Employment drops 31% in two years as **World War I** boom ends.

1929-41. Depression leaves many Oregonians out of work.

1930: Population 953,786

1933: First **Tillamook burn** destroys 240,000 acres of timber.

1935: State **capitol**, built in 1876, burns.

1937: Bonneville Dam completed.

1940: Population 1,089,684

1941-45. World War II brings shipbuilding boom and changes, including an influx of people.

1947: Governor, Secretary of State, and **President of the Senate** killed in small plane crash.

1948: Columbia River **flood** destroys **Vanport**.

1950: Population 1,521,341

1960: Population 1,768,687

1962: Columbus Day storm causes deaths, destruction.

1966: Interstate 5 opens to California. Five-mile-long **Astoria** bridge replaces ferry.

1967: Beach bill adopted.

1970: Population 2,091,533

1971: Oregon adopts nation's first **bottle bill**.

1973: Oregon adopts state-wide **land use planning**.

1980: Population 2,633,321. **Mount St. Helens** erupts.

1980-83: Slump in national housing market causes economic **recession** in state.

1986: MAX light rail service begins in **Portland**.

1990: Population 2,842,321. Voters adopt **Measure 5**, leading to prolonged crisis in school finance.

1993: Oregon holds the country's first statewide vote-by-mail election.

1995: Tax incentives create boom in **electronics** industry.

2000: Population 3,400,000 (projected).

HIV. See **AIDS**.

Hockey. See **Winter Hawks**.

Hogg Rock. A landmark bluff that **Highway 20** skirts just west of **Santiam Pass**. The rock is named for Colonel T. Egenton Hogg (1836-1896), a **railroad** promoter who, shortly after the route was surveyed for a road in 1880, rushed a crew of Chinese laborers to the pass. They built several hundred yards of railroad so that Hogg could claim the right-of-way for his **Oregon Pacific Railroad**. A small boxcar was built at the site and was pushed monthly the length of the rails in order to strengthen his claim. The company went bankrupt before the line was connected from **Idanha** to the pass. Parts of the stonework and hand hewn road cuts can still be seen by climbing the west face above the highway. Treasures of the Oregon Country.

Hogs and pigs. Hog and pigs in Oregon have declined from a 1915 high of 330,000 animals in the state to 61,500 in 1995 after 99,400 were marketed with a total value of $9.6 million. **Marion** and **Yamhill** counties each had 11,000 head. 1995 Oregon. See also **Hairball**.

Holdup session. The 1897 Oregon **House of Representatives** legislative session, which failed to organize, even after complex political maneuverings by the **Republicans, Democrats**, and **Populists**. At that time, **U.S. Senators** were elected by the state **legislature**, and the House was divided on the reelection of Senator John Mitchell (convicted of **land fraud** felony in 1904) and adoption of the **initiative** and **referendum**. Since the House was not organized members could collect no pay and the legislature could not elect a Senator, so for nearly two years Oregon was represented by only one Senator. Governing Oregon.

Hole-in-the-Ground. A circular **maar** depression nearly a mile across and 500 feet deep located two miles east of Highway 31 in the northwestern corner of **Lake County**. It was created by violent steam explosions; however, unlike the explosion that created **Fort Rock**, little magma was ejected, so an ash ring was not formed. Nearby **Big Hole** is similar, but is less obvious because it is forested. A 5-mile wide basin near the dam at **Lake Owyhee** is also called Hole-in-the-Ground. Geology of Oregon.

Holiday for Lips. A **Corvallis** festival for whistlers that was held for several years during the 1980s. The sponsor, professional whistler Mitch Hider, described it as "quite a blowout." Offbeat Oregon.

Holidays. Oregon's legal holidays include all Sundays plus nine others: New Year's Day (January 1), Martin Luther King Jr.'s Birthday (third Monday in January), Presidents Day (third Monday in February), Memorial Day (last Monday in May), Independence Day (July 4), Labor Day (first Monday in September), Veterans Day (November 11), Thanksgiving Day (fourth Thursday in November), and Christmas (December 25). Oregon Blue Book.

Holocaust Memorial. See **Oregon Holocaust Memorial**.

Holt International Children's Services. An organization formed in 1956 by Harry and Bertha Holt of **Creswell** to bring orphans from Korea to the U.S. for adoption. It is now an international adoption and child services agency serving the U.S, Romania, Russia, Asia, and Latin America. 1195 City View, Eugene 97405. 541-687-2202.

Home businesses. The 1990 census reported 120,000 home businesses in Oregon. There is general agreement that it is one of the fastest-growing job categories in the state. Statewide 4.3% of Oregonians worked at home. Rates were significantly higher in some rural farming counties such as **Wheeler** and **Sherman** (11%), and **Morrow** (9%). Oregon: A Statistical Overview; Oregonian 7/8/96:B1. See also **Small business**.

Home heating. The 1990 census found that 28% of Oregon homes were heated with **natural gas**, 45% with **electricity**, 17% with **wood**, and 13% with **heating oil** or some other fuel. Oregon: A Statistical Overview. See also **Heating oil**; **Heating-oil tanks**; **Wood**; **Wood stoves**.

Home ownership. In 1996, 67% of Oregon homes were owner-occupied. They had a median value of $120,000. Oregonian 10/29/97:B1. See also **Housing**.

Home rule - cities. A state constitutional provision, Article XI, Section 2, adopted in 1906, that gives cities the power to enact their own **charters**. Prior to home rule, city charters could only be enacted or amended by the state **legislature**.

Home rule - counties. In 1958 voters adopted an amendment to the state **constitution** that allowed counties to adopt "home rule" **charters** under which they were broadly empowered to control their own affairs and could adopt **ordinances**. In 1973 the legislature extended broader powers to all counties. By 1996 nine of Oregon's 36 **counties** had adopted home rule form of **county government**: **Lane** and **Washington** 1962; **Hood River** 1964; **Multnomah** 1967; **Benton** 1972; **Jackson** 1978, **Josephine** 1980; **Clatsop** 1988; and **Umatilla** 1993. Oregon Blue Book.

Home schooling. Educating school-age children at home is legal in Oregon if the children are registered with the local **Education Service District**, and if they perform among the top 15% on annual tests. In 1995, 10,493 students, or 1.8% of all Oregon school-age children, were being educated at home. Three groups offer assistance: Oregon Home Education Network in **Beaverton**, 503-321-5166; Oregon Christian Home Education Association Network in **Portland**, 503-288-1285; and Home School Information and Service Network of Oregon in **Lake Oswego**, 503-699-9241. Home-schooling in Oregon. See also **School enrollment**.

Homestead Act of 1862. An act of Congress that enabled the head of a family to claim 160 acres of public land for a filing fee of $10 and after five years of residence or cultivation a patent (ownership) would be granted. Since most of the choice land had already been taken by **Donation Land Act** claims, only 4,617 homesteads actually passed into private ownership during the next 21 years. After that most lands left were either desert grazing lands where 160 acres was not enough to support a family or heavily timbered lands. The commutation clause of the act authorized sale for cash in lieu of the residence requirements so some timber buyers acquired homesteads in that way. In 1909 a new Homestead Act entitled homesteaders to 320 acres (increased in 1916 to 640 acres) of non-irrigable land. Thousands flocked to the Oregon desert, with women accounting for 20% of the claims, but by 1921 most of the new dry-land farmers had starved out and left. The **Taylor Grazing Act of 1934** withdrew public lands from homesteading, and the Homestead Acts themselves were repealed in 1976 by the Federal Land Policy and Management Act. A total of 11,097,982 acres of land passed to private ownership in Oregon under the Homestead Act. Circular; East of the Cascades; Disposition; High Desert; Oregon Desert. See also **Land fraud**; **Land grants**.

Homicides. In 1996 there were 119 homicides in the state. Two thirds of the homicide victims were men. 77 of the victims were white, 16 were blacks, 16 were Hispanic, 8 were Asian, and 2 were Indian. 50 of the homicides were by handgun, 4 by rifle, 4 by shotgun, 21 by knife, 10 by blunt object, 10 by physical force, and

20 by other (arson, asphyxiation, drowning, poison, strangling, unknown). There were also 10 negligent (non-traffic) homicides, 6 of them by gun. Report on Criminal Offenses. See also **Death penalty**; **Murders**.

Homosexuals. In 1987 the governor issued a ruling barring state agencies from discriminating against homosexuals. In a 1988 **initiative** voters overturned the ruling, but the state **Court of Appeals** ruled the initiative unconstitutional. In 1992 (Ballot Measure 9) and 1994 voters defeated measures that would have required state and local governments to discourage homosexuality. In Oregon as of 1996 a gay man or lesbian woman may be fired for sexual orientation except in **Ashland**, **Corvallis**, **Eugene**, and **Portland**, all of which have adopted anti-discrimination codes. Governing Oregon. See also **Domestic partnerships**; **Oregon Citizens' Alliance**.

Homowo Festival of African Arts. An annual **Portland** event inspired by Ghanaian harvest celebrations. It is held on an August weekend in Cathedral Park under the St. Johns Bridge. The festival, founded in 1990 by master drummer Obo Addy, features African music, dance, and crafts.

Honey. See **Bees.**

Honeyman State Park. See **Jessie M. Honeyman State Park**.

Hood River. A river that drains an area of 339 square miles on the north slopes of **Mount Hood** northeast to the **Columbia River**, with an average annual flow of 724,100 acre feet or 4 acre feet/acre. At one time the river was called Dog River because some early travelers arrived in the area so hungry that they ate dog meat, but a local campaign changed the name to honor the mountain at its head. The river valley has long been noted for its apple and pear orchards. Oregon Geographic Names.

Hood River (town). A city and port on the **Columbia River** 63 miles east of **Portland** on **Interstate 84**, widely known as a recreation destination. The economy is based on tourism, timber, apples, and winter pears. Attractions in addition to windsurfing on the Columbia River and skiing on **Mount Hood** include the Hood River County Historical Museum, Hood River Expo Center, Mount Hood Railroad, and tours of the Luhr Jensen plant where fishing lures are made. Hood River is the county seat of **Hood River County**. **Japanese** farmers have been important in the area and Tsuruta, Japan, is the city's sister city. The post office was established in 1858 and the city was incorporated in 1894. Population 1980 4,329; 1995 4,940. Elevation 154'. PO Box 27, 97031. 541-386-1488. Chamber of Commerce 541-386-2000. Legacy.

Hood River Apple Jam. An annual outdoor, one-day music festival held at Port Marina Park in **Hood River** in mid-August. 541-387-7529.

Hood River County. A small, northern-tier county along the **Columbia River** that encompasses the famed orchards of Hood River valley. Incorporated cities are **Hood River** (county seat), and **Cascade Locks**. The county is bounded by Washington State on the north across the Columbia (reached by bridges at Cascade Locks and Hood River), and by **Wasco**, **Clackamas**, and **Multnomah** counties. Elevations range from 72' above **Bonneville Dam** to 11,240' **Mount Hood**. The area is famous world-wide for **windsurfing**. The economy is based on agriculture, food processing, lumber, and recreation. An average of 188,000 tons of

apples, **pears**, and **cherries** are produced annually, including over 30% of the country's winter pears. Taxable assessed value in 1995 was $954,000,000, or $51,000 per capita. The county was created in 1908 from **Wasco County** and named for the river, which, in turn, had been named for Mount Hood. Population 1980 15,835; 1995 18,700. Area 533 square miles. Density 35/sq.mi. Annual precipitation 31"; average temperature January 34°F, July 67°F. Courthouse, 309 State St., Hood River 97031-2093. 541-386-3970. History of Hood River County; Oregon Blue Book.

Hood to Coast Relay. The world's largest and longest relay race, covering 195 miles from **Mount Hood** (**Timberline Lodge**) to **Seaside**. Since the first race in 1982 it has grown to over 17,000 participants who run in 875 12-person teams starting at Timberline Lodge or in 600 12-person teams running from Portland. The race is run on a late August weekend, beginning on Friday and continuing through the night. Each team member usually runs three five-mile legs. A record time of 15:44:55 was set in 1995 . Oregonian 8/25/96:C1.

Hoodoo Ski Area. A ski area on **Santiam Pass** 86 miles southeast of **Salem** and 42 miles west of **Bend**. Top elevation is 5,703 feet with a 1,035-foot vertical drop. The area has four chair lifts and a 7.5K Nordic track. Box 20, Highway 20, Sisters 97759. 541-822-3799; snow conditions 541-822-3337. Oregonian 11/16/97:T7.

Hoover-Minthorn House. An 1881 house in **Newberg** that was the boyhood home of President Herbert Hoover. 115 S. River Street, Newberg. 503-538-6629.

Hopkins Memorial Tree Farm. A demonstration **tree farm** south of **Oregon City** operated by a non-profit group, Forests Forever, Inc., for forestry-related education. Tours may be arranged by calling the OSU Extension Office in Oregon City, 503-655-8631.

Hops. Vines, *Humumlus lupulus*, with papery, cone-like seed heads that are used for flavoring beer. They are grown commercially in the central **Willamette Valley** on wire trellises 18 feet high. They were first planted in the valley around 1865. By 1879 Oregon was producing 240,00 pounds of hops annually in the area around **St. Paul**, and in the 1910s was the nation's top producer, a title now held by Washington. In 1995 Oregon's 25 growers produced 14 million pounds, worth $28 million, on 8,650 acres, about 18% of U.S. production. In 1997 Willamette Valley farmers were decreasing their acreage because new varieties that produced more hops were being grown in semi-arid central Washington. Oregon Hop Commission, 152 Chemawa Road, Salem 97303-5356. 503-393-0368. 1995 Oregon; Oregon Agriculture; Oregonian 8/4/97:B2; St. Paul. See also **Prohibition**.

Horse and buggy. Some 200 Oregonians belong to horse and buggy clubs. Two of them are: Horse and Carriage Society of Klamath Falls, 20556 Webber Road, Klamath Falls 97603; Harness and Pleasure Driving Assoc., 18555 S. Lyons Road, Oregon City 97045. Oregonian 6/22/95:B10.

Horse racing. In 1997 both thoroughbred and quarter horse races were scheduled on the one-mile track at **Portland Meadows**, Oregon's only commercial horse racing track, from October through April. Six other meets were held around the state, at **Grants Pass** mid-May to early July, three days at the Eastern Oregon

Livestock Show in **Union** in June, four days at the Crooked River Roundup in **Prineville** in July, three days at the **Tillamook County** Fair in early August, nine days at the **State Fair** in **Salem** (Lone Oak track) in late August and early September, and two days at the **Harney County** Fair in **Burns** in early September. **Parimutuel** wagering at those races and off-track betting on races held elsewhere in the country is regulated by the **Racing Commission**. Horse racing was popular among the **Indians** as soon as they had **horses**, and pioneers, too, raced horses. **Grant County** alone was said to have had a half dozen race tracks by the late 1800s. Gold and Cattle Country.

Horse Ridge Natural Area. A 600-acre area of undisturbed **juniper** forest south of **Highway 20**, 16 miles southeast of **Bend**. It has been designated as a **National Natural Landmark** as representing a distinctive climax community. Oregon Atlas.

Horse sculptures. Three bronze horses created in 1995 by Debra Butterfield of Bozeman, Montana, are located at the approach to **Portland International Airport**. They cost $350,000, the most ever paid for a piece of public art in Oregon. Oregonian 8/23/95:A1. See also **Neon horses**.

Horseback rides, historic. In February 1855 Louis Remme rode 665 miles from Knight's Landing in California's Sacramento Valley to Portland in 143 hours in order to cash a certificate of deposit for $12,500 before word reached Portland by ship from San Francisco that the banking company had failed. On December 26, 1897, cowhand David Crow rode 180 miles to carry the news of the murder of rancher Pete French from **Sod House** Ranch to Winnemucca, Nevada. The 48-hour ride took 10 horses. Crow then rode on to Red Bluff, CA to tell French's family. On December 24, 1894, a rider raced 100 miles to **Lakeview** to get a doctor for the victims of the **Silver Lake fire**. On June 14, 1903, during the **Heppner flood**, two riders successfully outran the wall of water to warn downstream communities. Cattle Country of Peter French; East of the Cascades; It Happened in Oregon; Tales out of Oregon. See also **Bigfoot**.

Horses. Horses first evolved in North America, and fossils of some of those early horses have been found in Oregon. They disappeared about 8,000 years ago but were reintroduced when the **Cayuse** and **Nez Perce** Indians got Spanish horses from the Shoshones about 1750. The Cayuse had so many horses that any Indian pony came to be called a Cayuse. In 1805 Lewis and Clark found that the Nez Perce had already developed their own breed, the **Appaloosa**, in the Palouse area of Washington. Between 1882 and 1941 the eccentric and generous William Walter (Bill) Brown was the "Horse King" of the West, grazing livestock 150 miles in every direction from his ranch headquarters between **Bend** and **Burns**. Oregon's horse population reached over 400,000 during World War I, not counting the thousands that ran wild. In 1996 the state had about 126,000 domestic horses, mules, and ponies, and about 2,000 **wild horses**. 1995 Oregon; Gold and Cattle Country; Oregon Desert; Oregon's Great Basin Country; William "Bill" W. Brown. See also **Horse racing**; **Ranches**; **Rodeos**; **Vaqueros**.

Horsetail falls. A kind of waterfall, one that maintains some contact with a rock face while descending. Horsetail Falls, named for that reason, is a 176-foot falls that can be viewed from the **Columbia River Gorge** Scenic Highway two and a half miles east of **Multnomah Falls**. Upper Horsetail Falls, sometimes called Ponytail Falls, is .4 mile up Trail #438 from the highway. Waterfall Lover's Guide.

Hospice care. Services provided by professional and volunteer caregivers to persons with terminal illnesses who have been given six months or less to live. The care may be at home or in a residential hospice. In 1996 52 hospice programs in Oregon served 8,000 persons, or 29% of Oregonians who died. Oregon Hospice Association, PO Box 10796, Portland 97210. 503-228-2104. Oregonian 9/29/97:A1. See also **Physician-assisted suicide**.

Hospitals. In 1996 there were 63 hospitals in Oregon. Even though that was fifteen fewer than in 1980, 48% of the 3,356 hospital beds in the **Portland** metro area were empty on any given day. The average hospital stay has declined 24% in 11 years, from 5.52 days in 1983 to 4.19 days in 1993. **Property taxes** help support many of the 15 rural hospitals owned by local taxing districts. Oregon Association of Hospitals and Health Systems, 4000 Kruse Way Place, Building 2, Suite 100, Lake Oswego 97035. 503-636-2204. Oregonian 4/24/95:B7, 4/16/95:D1, 12/23/96:A12.

HOST. A **Portland** nonprofit program, Home Ownership a Street at a Time, that began in 1991 by renovating or building two or more houses on a block, and then selling them at prices low and middle-income families could afford. There are no income restrictions for buyers, but they are required to live in the home, maintain the property, take a homeowner education class, and donate 50 hours of community work each year for five years. 1818 NE Martin Luther King Jr. Blvd., 503-331-1752.

Hostages. Two Oregon hostage takings have resulted in deaths. In **Springfield** in November, 1993, Allen McGuire smothered his two-year-old daughter and killed himself, and in January, 1992, **Portland** police killed Bryan French and his 12-year-old hostage, Nathan Thomas. On January 4, 1996, a gunman shot two persons (not fatally) and held four others hostage at the KOIN Center in downtown Portland for five hours before police captured him. Oregonian 1/5/96:A1.

Hot Lake. A small, natural, privately-owned lake eight miles southeast of **La Grande** that is fed by a daily flow of 2.5 million gallons of 205°F mineral water, making it Oregon's largest hot spring. The Indians had decreed the area as a place of peace, rest, and cure, and pioneers on the **Oregon Trail** utilized the warm waters. A resort hotel was built on the site in 1864, a larger one was built in 1900, and a luxurious hospital, Hot Lake Sanitarium, was added in 1906. During the 1920s there were 175 employees at the luxury spa, and over 2,000 meals were served daily. A fire in 1934 destroyed much of the resort which is now abandoned and said to be haunted. History of Union County; Oregon Cattleman; Oregon's Ghosts and Monsters.

Hot springs. Volcanic forces have endowed Oregon with a number of hot springs in the **Cascade Range** and in southern and eastern Oregon. Some of the larger and more accessible are described in Hot Springs and Hot Pools of the Pacific Northwest. Several remote hot springs are among the 11 described in The Hiker's Guide to Hot Springs in the Pacific Northwest. Many warm springs, averaging 60°F, emerged around the edges of **Lake Billy Chinook** after it filled. Geology of Oregon. See also **Geothermal energy**; **Hot Lake**; **Mickey Hot Springs**.

Hotels and lodges, historic. In 1843 Sidney Walter Moss built Main Street House, the first American hotel west of the Missouri, on the corner of Third and Main in **Oregon City**. It was a cabin, 14'x17', with no furniture except a table to serve food (no benches). Over time he improved the accommodations and built a two-story hotel across the street. He advertised with verse and by striding through town ringing a cowbell before dinner was served. Dictionary of Oregon History; This Side of Oregon. See also **Crater Lake Lodge**; **Frenchglen Hotel**; **Geiser Grand Hotel**; **Multnomah Falls Lodge**; **Multnomah Hotel**; **Oregon Caves Chateau**; **Portland Hotel**; **Timberline Lodge**; **Umatilla House**; **Wolf Creek Inn**.

House of Mystery. See **Oregon Vortex**.

House of Representatives, Oregon. The lower chamber of the Oregon **legislature**, established by the state **constitution** with 60 members elected for two-year terms. The members elect a Speaker of the House who presides, assigns **representatives** to committees, appoints committee chairs, refers measures to committee, and oversees the functioning of the House. All revenue **bills** must originate in the House. Oregon Capitol, Salem 97310. 503-986-1187. 800-332-2313 during the session. Governing Oregon; Oregon Blue Book; Oregon Legislative Guide. See also **Holdup session**; **Legislative committees**; **Succession**.

Houseboats. See **Floating homes**.

Households. The 1990 census found that Oregon had 1,103,313 households, 32% of them with children under 18 years of age, and 8.4% of them single-parent households with one or more children. Oregon: A Statistical Overview.

Houses, historic. **Amazon**; **Brunk House**; **Bush House**; **Bybee-Howell House**; **Cooley House**; **Deepwood**; **Frank Lloyd Wright buildings**; **Gilbert House Children's Museum**; **Harlow House**; **Hoover-Minthorn House**; **Hughes House**; **Jason Lee House**; **Mahonia Hall**; **McLoughlin House**; **Monteith House**; **Nunan House**; **Pauling House**; **Philip Foster Historical Farm**; **Pittock Mansion**; **R. C. Geer Farmhouse**; **Shelton-McMurphey House**; **Simpson estate**. See also **Barns**; **Buildings, historic**; **Fences**.

Housing. Between 1980 and 1990 the number of housing units in Oregon increased 10.2% (to 1,193,567) while the population grew 7.9% (to 2,842,321) during the same period. The size of the average house increased from 1,385 square feet in 1970 to 1,950 square feet in 1996. The 1990 census found that the median value of owner-occupied housing in Oregon was $67,100. The values ranged from $31,00 in **Gilliam**, **Sherman**, and **Wheeler** counties to over $85,000 in **Clackamas** and **Washington** counties. By fall 1994 average prices ranged from lows of $31,610 in **Gilliam County** and $58,210 in **Grant County** to highs of $138,580 in **Corvallis** and $167,027 in **Curry County**. The **Portland** area average was $134,200. In Portland, while the population increased by 15%, housing prices increased by 40%, and a 1995 national survey found it among the 10 least affordable cities in the country for housing. The 1997 price per square foot was $87 in **Clark County**, Washington, $99 in **Beaverton**, $102 in **Hillsboro**, and $121 in **Lake Oswego-West Linn**. Oregon: A Statistical Overview; Oregonian 4/4/96:B1, 10/19/97:B1, 2/16/98:D11. See also **Floating homes**; **Home heating**; **Home ownership**; **HOST**; **Manufactured homes**; **Street of Dreams**; **Tree houses**.

Housing and Community Service Department. A state department that works with community organizations to build affordable housing and provide services to alleviate the causes of poverty in Oregon. It has revenue bonding authority of $1.03 billion and general obligation bonding authority of about $854.7 million (equal to one-half of 1% of Oregon's taxable property true cash value). Housing policy is made by the seven-member State Housing Council. 1600 State St., Salem 97310-0302. 503-986-2000. Oregon Blue Book.

Housing starts. Housing starts in Oregon increased from 15,800 in 1991 to 24,400 in 1995, but were forecast to fall gradually to 20,000 by the year 2000. Oregon Economic and Revenue Forecast.

Housing, subsidized. The **Portland** region had 16,822 subsidized apartments in 1997. **Metro** predicts that 50,000 more will be needed in the next 15 years. Oregonian 7/13/97:A23.

Howard Prairie Lake. A large irrigation reservoir 22 miles east of **Ashland** formed in 1958 by an earth fill dam on Grizzly Creek that flooded a broad meadow. The reservoir, part of the **Rogue River Basin Project**, is operated by the Talent Irrigation District. It lies on the east side of the **Cascade Range** crest; the water is run through a tunnel to make it available for use in irrigating lands on the west side of the divide. When full, the 2,070 acre reservoir is six miles long with a maximum depth of 80 feet. Recreation use is heavy, and includes fishing as well as boating of all kinds. Facilities include campgrounds and a fishing resort. Atlas of Oregon Lakes.

Howell Territorial Park. A 130 acre park on **Sauvie Island** managed by **Metro**. It is the site of the **Bybee-Howell House** and an Agricultural Museum. Plans have been made for further developing the park over a ten-year period. Oregon History Magazine 40(4):5. June/July 1997.

Hoyt Arboretum. A 175-acre arboretum in **Portland**'s **Washington Park** with nine miles of trails. Its 700 species include one of the largest collections of conifers in the U.S., plus rare and endangered plants from Oregon. The arboretum offers maps, self-guiding tour brochures, guided tours, classes, and other educational programs from its Tree House Visitor Center, open daily 9-4. The arboretum itself is open daily during daylight hours. 4000 SW Fairview Boulevard, Portland 97221. 503-823-3655.

Hubbard. A **Willamette Valley** agricultural and manufacturing town on **Highway 99E** three miles north of **Woodburn** in **Marion County**. It was named for pioneer farmer Charles Hubbard who gave land for a station when the railroad came through in 1870. The city was incorporated in 1891. The Hubbard **Hop** Festival in July celebrates an important area crop. Nordic Enterprises (clothing and sports wear manufacturing), John Barth, Inc. (hop drying and transportation), Schrock Trucking (agricultural transportation), and Black Gold (potting soil) are major employers. Hubbard Mineral Springs was a spa resort at the turn of the century. Population 1980 1,640; 1995 2,045. Elevation 182'. PO Box 380, 97032. 503-981-9633. Oregon Geographic Names.

Huckleberry. A wild **shrub** of the genus *Vaccinium*, related to blueberries. The berries have always been an important and sacred food for Indians. Several species much prized for their flavorful blue or black **berries** grow in high open places in the **Cascade Range**. An evergreen species with black berries grows along the coast, and red huckleberry, a tall deciduous bush with tart red berries, grows in the **Coast Range**. Researchers estimate that at least 1 million acres of huckleberry habitat, supporting 12 species, exist in the Cascades, but that the numbers of plants and productive fields have diminished. Oregonian 9/21/97:B1.

Hudson's Bay Company (HBC). A company, officially "The Governor and Company of Adventurers of England Trading into Hudson's Bay," organized in London in 1670. It was given a crown charter to exclusive trading rights to Prince Rupert's Land (the Canadian area draining into Hudson's Bay). After HBC amalgamated with the **North West Company** in 1821, the crown granted the company exclusive British rights to trade with the Indians in the region west of the Rockies. HBC then dominated the **fur trade** in the **Oregon Country** from its post at **Fort Vancouver** until the **Oregon Treaty of 1846**, when it moved its operations to Canada. The company was, in effect, the government of the Oregon Country until American settlers established the **provisional government**. The HBC strongly discouraged use of alcohol by the **Indians**, and its operations were efficient, firm, and fair. Though company policy actively discouraged American competition, Dr. John McLoughlin, chief factor at Fort Vancouver from 1824 until 1846, gave significant aid to American settlers. In 1870 HBC sold much of its territory to Canada and continues today as a major Canadian retail firm. See also **Boundary question**; **Fort Umpqua**; **Siskiyou Trail**; **Umpqua Brigade**.

Hughes House. A historic 1898 Eastlake Victorian house that is part of **Cape Blanco State Park**. The 11-room, two-story house, built of old-growth Port-Orford-**cedar**, was the center of a 2,000-acre ranch. 541-332-0248. Port Orford.

Hult Center for the Performing Arts. **Eugene's** major performance center, located on Willamette Street between 6th and 7th. The center includes the 2,500-seat Silva Concert Hall and the 500-seat Soreng Theatre. Recorded information 541-342-5746; ticket office 541-687-5000.

Human Resources, Department of. Oregon's health and social services agency. Its objective, to help all Oregonians be independent, healthy, and safe, is carried out through 200 programs. Its six divisions are **Adult and Family Services**, **Children and Families**, **Health**, **Mental Health**, **Senior and Disabled**, and **Vocational Rehabilitation**. Volunteers help meet human service needs. 500 Summer St. NE, Salem 97310-1012. 503-945-5944. Oregon Blue Book.

Humanities, Oregon Council for. An organization founded in 1941 to stimulate public appreciation for and participation in the humanities, including history, philosophy, literature, and languages. Each year it awards over $150,000 in grants, publishes Oregon Humanities, and sponsors the **Oregon Chautauqua**. It is affiliated with and partially funded by the National Endowment for the Humanities. Other funding comes from donations from individuals, corporations, and foundations in Oregon. The Council has a 21 member board, five of whom are appointed by the Governor. 812 SW Washington St., Suite 225, Portland 97205. 503-241-0543; 800-735-0543.

Humbug Mountain. A 1,756-foot headland six miles south of **Port Orford** that is the highest point on the south Oregon coast. It was once known as Sugarloaf

Mountain, but, when an exploring company sent out by Captain Tichenor in 1851 got lost, it was renamed Tichenor's Humbug, and later became known just as Humbug Mountain. **Highway 101** follows Brush Creek around its east side, as did the Indian trail, which crossed the creek 17 times. A three mile trail leads to the top from a **state park** that has 108 campsites. Century of Coos and Curry; Oregon Geographic Names.

Hungarian partridge. See **Partridges**.

Hunger. An **Oregon Food Bank** survey found that 400,000 Oregonians needed emergency food supplies in 1995. Over a third of those receiving assistance were employed, 16% with full-time jobs. A U.S. Census Bureau study found that 15.4% of Oregon households were food insecure (not assured access to enough food for an active, healthy life) and 6.2% experienced moderate or severe hunger, compared to 4% nationwide. Oregonian 10/16/96:B1, 10/18/97:D8. See also **Food stamps**.

Hunt Railroad. A proposed **rail line**, never completed, that was to run from Walla Walla, Washington, south into the **Grande Ronde** Valley of northeast Oregon, around the south side of the **Wallowa Mountains**, and on to Boise, Idaho. Construction began in 1890 after residents in northeast Oregon had given rights of way and a cash subsidy of $180,000, but the only portion graded was between **Union** and **Summerville**. History of Union County.

Hunting. Over 300,000 persons, or about 16% of Oregon's population over the age of 16, are licensed hunters. All **big game** hunting requires a hunting license as well as the appropriate tag. A resident license cost $15 in 1995, and tags ranged from $11 for a general deer tag to $976 for a nonresident **bighorn sheep** tag. Wildlife programs are funded almost entirely from hunting fees. Hunting regulations are published annually by the Oregon Department of **Fish and Wildlife** and distributed free through sporting goods stores. 5,309 fish and game violations were reported in 1996. Oregonian 9/12/96:C1-10. See also **Animals**; **Bounty**; **Game birds**; **Poaching**; **Predators**; **Protected animals**.

Hunting accidents. In 1996 there were 14 hunting accidents, including one fatality, down from a 1987 high of 26 accidents and six fatalities. The 10-year average was 17 accidents and 3 fatalities, making it one of the safest forms of outdoor recreation. Mail Tribune 9/20/97. Special section 10.

Hunting, history. The first general game law, limiting the season for hunting **deer** and **elk**, went into effect in 1872, though with no funding for enforcement until 1893. The first hunting license, a $10 non-resident license, was established in 1901, and the first resident hunting license, costing $1, was established in 1905. Women were first licensed to hunt or fish in 1924. Big Game History;

Huntington. "Catfish Capital of Oregon." A historic railroad community on the eastern edge of Oregon in **Baker County**. It is located 45 miles southeast of **Baker City** between **Interstate 84** and the **Snake River** on the original **Oregon Trail**. It was named for the Huntington brothers who bought the original Miller stage station in 1882. The "last spike" ceremonies, giving Oregon a second rail **transcontinental connection** to the east, were held in Huntington on November 10, 1884. The city was incorporated in 1891. The economy is based on the Union Pacific Railroad, Ash Grove Cement Company, cattle, grain, hay, and tourism.

Fishing (in **Brownlee** Reservoir on the Snake River) and hunting attract many to the area, and the Catfish Tournament is held on Memorial Day weekend. Population 1980 539; 1995 565. Elevation 2,108'. PO Box 369, 97907. 541-869-2202. Oregon Geographic Names.

Hurricanes. A strong tropical storm over the north Atlantic Ocean, generated near the equator, with a calm central eye and winds over 74 miles per hour that comes ashore (if at all) on the east coast of North America. Hurricanes have never reached Oregon. Tropical cyclonic storms over the Pacific Ocean (called typhoons) come ashore on the east coast of Asia. Occasionally a former typhoon will meander over the Pacific, regather energy, and strike the west coast, as happened with the **Columbus Day storm**. Other Oregon storms may have wind speeds over 74 mph, but they usually originate over the North Pacific and lack the characteristics of a tropical storm. Weather of the Pacific Coast. See also **Storms**.

Hydraulic mining. A method of mining for **placer gold** in which a stream of water was forced through a long, narrowing nozzle, called a giant or monitor, to create an enormously high-pressured jet. The jet was played against banks of soil and gravel to loosen the material so that **gold** could be recovered from it. Hydraulic operations worked on Sterling Creek south of **Jacksonville** and at other sites in southwest Oregon. Because of the damage done to downstream farmlands and riverbeds from the volume of soil, trees, and debris washed down, the method was eventually outlawed. Dredging for Gold; Geology of Oregon.

Hydroelectric power. In 1992, hydropower supplied about 75% of the average electrical energy used in the Pacific Northwest. The **Columbia river** provides a major share of Oregon's electricity through generating plants built by the **Army Corps of Engineers** at **Bonneville Dam** (1093 **megawatts**), **The Dalles** (1819.7 MW), **John Day** (2,160 MW), and **McNary** (990.5 MW). (The largest, Grand Coulee in Washington, has a capacity of 6,180 MW.) The Corps also operates dams on tributaries of the **Willamette River**. On the **Snake River**, **Idaho Power** has three major dams, **Hells Canyon** (391.5 MW), **Oxbow** (190 MW), and **Brownlee** (585.4 MW). **Portland General Electric** has projects on the **Deschutes**, **Bull Run**, and **Clackamas** rivers, and **PacifiCorp** has several projects, most of them in southern Oregon on the North **Umpqua**, the upper **Rogue**, and the **Klamath**. Smaller projects are operated by **Ashland**, **Eugene**, Northern Wasco County PUD, Oregon Trail Electric Consumers Co-op, and the **Bureau of Reclamation**. Hydropower costs about 0.2 cent per kilowatt-hour to generate as compared with approximately 2.4 cents for **nuclear power**. Inventory; Oregonian 2/21/97:D2. See also **Bonneville Power Administration**; **Fremont Power House**; **Greenhouse gases**; **Northwest Power Planning Council**.

I-5. See **Interstate 5**.

I Have a Dream. A national program designed to inspire at-risk grade-school students to aim for a college education. The **Portland** program began in 1990 when 108 fifth-graders were selected at Martin Luther King Jr. Elementary School. In 1994-95 students from that class made up 10% of the freshman class at Jefferson High School but claimed half of the honors positions. Community members who sponsored that class will have invested over $850,000 by the end of their 10-year commitment. In 1995 **Portland** had five I Have a Dream classes in three elementary schools. <u>Oregonian</u> 8/6/95:L1.

Ice age. See **Pleistocene**.

Ice caves. The caves known as ice caves in Oregon are not caves in ice but **lava tubes** in which ice persists at the bottom; they are more correctly called glacieres. Examples include **Arnold Ice Cave** north of **Newberry Crater**, and South Ice Cave six miles southeast of Newberry Crater. Ice caves have a single high opening so that the only air circulation occurs when the outside air is colder - and thus heavier - than the inside air and so sinks into the cave. The lava tube ice caves are also well insulated, maintaining their temperature so that any ice that forms persists from year to year. Settlers quarried the ice. <u>Central Oregon Caves</u>. See also **Lava tubes**.

Ice skating. In 1997 indoor ice skating rinks in Oregon included two in **Portland**, at **Lloyd Center** (503-288-6073) and at Clackamas Town Center (503-786-6000), plus the Valley Ice Arena in **Beaverton** (503-297-2521), and a rink at the Lane County Fairgrounds in **Eugene** (541-687-4ICE). The Rink (541-770-1177) opened in **Medford** in 1998. Tonya Harding, Oregon's most famous ice skater, was involved in an attack on a rival skater at the 1994 national competition for which she was barred from membership in the U.S. Figure Skating Association, fined $160,000, and assigned 500 hours of community service. <u>Oregonian</u> 3/22/96:B1.

Ice storms. See **Freezing rain**.

Idaho. The state that bounds Oregon's entire eastern edge. The border follows the **Snake River** south from Oregon's border with Washington (the 46th parallel) through **Hells Canyon** to the mouth of the **Owyhee River**, then drops due south to meet **Nevada** at the 42nd parallel. Idaho, 85% the size of Oregon, has about a third of Oregon's population and a third of its gross domestic product. The area was at one time part of the **Oregon Territory** and then the Washington Territory, but was redesignated the Idaho Territory in 1863 during the Idaho **gold rush**. From the beginning of white exploration, much of the overland travel to and from Oregon has crossed Idaho, including the **Lewis and Clark Expedition**, the **Oregon Trail**, **railroads**, and **Interstate 84**.

Idaho Power Company. A large investor-owned private utility formed in 1915. It supplies electricity to parts of eastern Oregon, southern Idaho, and northern Nevada. After years of controversy, it built and operates **Brownlee**, **Oxbow**, and **Hells Canyon** dams on the **Snake River**, along with four campgrounds on the reservoirs. 1520 State Street, Boise, Idaho 83702. 208-383-2200. Recreation info: 800-422-3143. <u>Hells Canyon</u>.

Idanha. A **Cascade Range** timber community on the North **Santiam River**, 55 miles east of **Salem** on **Highway 22**, and four miles east of **Detroit**. It lies in both **Marion** and **Linn** counties. It was originally called Camp 11 or Muskrat Camp, but by the time the post office was established in 1895, the community was identified with the Idanha Hotel, which had, in turn, been named for a brand of Idaho mineral water. The **Oregon Pacific Railroad** from **Newport** and **Albany** reached Idanha in 1889 and the town became a popular tourist destination and lumber town, but, as of 1995, two of the town's three mills had closed. The city was incorporated in 1949. Population 1980 319; 1995 290. Elevation 1,718'. PO

Box 430, 97350. 503-854-3313. Oregon Geographic Names.

Illegal aliens. See **Undocumented workers**.

Illinois River. A tributary to the **Rogue River** in southern Oregon. It heads in the **Siskiyou Mountains** near the California border, flows north through the historic **gold mining** districts around **Cave Junction**, and then twists to the northwest through deep canyons to join the Rogue at Agness. It was named for the home state of the three gold-mining Althouse brothers. Old timers pronounce the "s" at the end. Oregon Geographic Names.

Imago. An internationally renowned performance ensemble now headquartered in **Portland** that mixes mime, mask, and illusionary theater. It stages both adult and children's shows at its theater in a renovated Masonic Lodge at 17 SE 8th Street. P.O. Box 15182, 97215. 503-231-9581.

Imbler. A northeast Oregon agricultural community in **Union County** 12 miles northeast of **La Grande** on Highway 82. The **Oregon Railway and Navigation Company** built a train station on the Imbler farm in 1890, and a post office was established there the next year. The city was incorporated in 1922. For a time the economy was based on lumber, then later on apple and grass seed production. Population 1980 292; 1995 310. Elevation 2,732'. PO Box 40, 97841. 541-534-6095. History of Union County.

Immigrants. The U.S. Immigration and Naturalization Service reported a total of 7,554 immigrants to Oregon from foreign countries in fiscal 1996. The most, 1,942, came from Mexico, followed by 888 from Vietnam, 444 from the Ukraine, 434 from the People's Republic of China, 341 from the former Soviet Union, 338 from the Philippines, 233 from Korea, and 207 from India. Oregonian 1/1/98:A1. See also **Population growth**.

Immigration history. The first immigrants to Oregon are thought to have come across a land bridge from Asia, perhaps over 13,000 years ago. Fur trappers established first white settlement in Oregon at **Astoria** in 1811, and more followed. In 1843, the first **wagon train** of 875 settlers reached the **Willamette Valley**, and nearly 12,000 had arrived by 1850. In 1870 **Irish** made up the largest group of foreign born in **Portland**. In 1890 the percent of the city's foreign born residents peaked at 37.4%, while another 22% had at least one foreign-born parent; the largest groups were **Chinese**, **Germans**, British, Irish, and Swedes. "Other Portland;" Pacific Slope. See also **Discoverers**; **Knappton Cove Heritage Center**; **Population growth**; **Undocumented workers**.

Immunization. Oregon law requires immunization for all preschool children unless exempted for medical or religious reasons. A child entering kindergarten needs to have had five doses against diphtheria and tetanus, four doses of polio vaccine, and one dose of measles, mumps, and rubella vaccine. Officials encourage immunization by age 2 for the child's protection. Each year children who have not been immunized by a given date (Exclusion Day) are excluded from school until they are immunized. Oregonian 8/24/94.

Imnaha. An unincorporated ranching community in northeast Oregon at the bottom of the deep grassy canyon of the **Imnaha River**. It is in **Wallowa County**, 30 miles northeast of **Joseph**; Hat Point Lookout over **Hells Canyon** is 24 miles beyond the town. An annual rattlesnake and bear meat feed held in September and a spring cow chip lottery raises money for college scholarships. The name comes from the river. History of Wallowa County; Oregonian 9/24/96:B6.

Imnaha River. A 73-mile long river in northeast Oregon that flows north from the **Wallowa Mountains** to the **Snake River** through a deep gorge parallel to **Hells Canyon** and just west of it. It drains 855 square miles. Imnaha is an Indian word meaning the land ruled over by Imna, a sub-chief. Oregon Geographic Names. See also **Eureka**.

Imperial. An early 1900s real estate promotion located in the desert on **Highway 20** sixty miles east of **Bend** and just west of Hampton. The promoter sold lots across the country on the promise that the desert would bloom like the Imperial Valley of California. East of the Cascades.

Imports. Portland is the fourth-largest U.S. auto port, handling over 22% of the total U.S. auto imports in 1992, thanks to freedom from salt air and ample, secure facilities. Nearly $6 billion of imports came through the Oregon **Customs Service** District in 1993 with vehicles and parts accounting for $2.74 billion, followed by electrical and electronic goods for $.6 billion. Oregon Blue Book.

In-line skating. See **Skating**.

Incendiary bombs. In 1942, during **World War II**, a Japanese pilot named Nobuo Fujito flew two bombing runs over southwest Oregon in a tiny plane launched from a submarine. The intention was to start great forest fires with incendiary bombs and thus pressure the U.S. Navy to retreat from the Pacific to protect the Pacific Coast. The bombs did start fires but they were quickly suppressed in the foggy forest. In 1962 the ashamed Fujito visited **Bookings**, eight miles from the areas he had bombed. Fearful of the reception he might get, he carried the family's 400-year-old samurai sword with him so that he could kill himself if Oregonians were angry with him. Deeply moved by the hospitality shown by the people of Brookings, he presented the sword to the town, which now displays it in the town library. Oregonian 10/5/97:B1. See also **Balloon bombs**.

Income distribution. Oregon, once marked by a relatively flat income distribution, has outpaced the nation in moving to a greater disparity between the richest and poorest households as the income of the wealthiest increased and the income of the poorest fell in real purchasing power. In 1993 the wealthiest 20% of Oregon families made over 7 times as much income as the poorest 20%. Oregon's ratio of 7.52 compared with national ratios ranging from 6.17 for New Hampshire to 14.47 for Louisiana. In 1994 the trend continued, with the top 20% of Oregon households taking home 55% of all pre-tax income (up from 49.5% ten years before), and the lowest 20% of households taking home 1.4%. Oregonian 8/27/95:B1, 7/11/96:A1.

Income, family. In 1996 median family income state-wide was $38,700, ranging from $22,000 in **Wheeler County** to $44,400 in **Portland** area counties. In 1949 it was $3,376. Oregonian 10/29/97:A10.

Income, personal. In Oregon 1994 average personal income per capita was $20,499, an increase of 5.2% from 1989. The averages ranged from a low of $16,203 in **Jefferson County** to a high of $24,072 in **Clackamas County**. Transfer payments (payments for which no current service is performed, such as veterans benefits, retirement, unemployment, and welfare) averaged 17.1% of total personal income statewide, and ranged from 10.4% in **Washington County** to 28.3% in **Josephine County**. Oregon's per capita income, which was at 96% of the US average in 1993, has ranged between 90 and 99% since 1980. All personal income in the state totaled $67.9 billion in 1995 and is projected to increase to $95.1 billion by 2001. Oregon: A Statistical Overview; Oregon Economic and Revenue Forecast. See also **Salaries; Wages**.

Income tax. Oregon's state income tax is the main support of state government. The rate for an individual with a taxable income over $5,250 is 9%, and the rate for corporations is 6.6%. The personal income tax is projected to raise $5,949.5 million in the 1995-97 biennium (up 11% from the previous biennium), and the corporate income tax is projected to raise $457.3 million (down 21% from the previous biennium). Personal income taxes provided 82% of 1993-95 revenue, other sources, primarily lottery funds 9%, and corporate income taxes 9%. (In the early 1950's corporations provided over 40% of the state's income tax revenue.) Taxes are collected by the Oregon Department of **Revenue**. State income tax regulations are tied closely, but not exactly, to federal tax regulations, and a copy of an individual's federal tax return must be filed along with the state tax return. Governing Oregon; Oregon Economic and Revenue Forecast December 1995. See also **Intel; Pension puzzle; Tax exemptions**.

Indego. A partnership formed in 1996 by seven Northwest electric utilities to jointly manage their transmission lines. It covers seven states and 11,000 miles of transmission lines, serving nearly 4 million customers. The two members from Oregon are **Pacific Power and Light Company** and **Portland General Electric**. The name Indego was derived from INDEpendent transmission Grid Operator. **Bonneville Power Administration**, which could possibly join the partnership, operates 15,000 miles of transmission lines in the region. Oregonian 7/16/96:B16,13. See also **Western Intertie**.

Independence. "Historic Independence." A central **Willamette Valley** pioneer city in **Polk County** 10 miles southwest of **Salem**. It was named for Independence, Missouri, at the other end of the **Oregon Trail**, by Elvin Thorp who took up a **donation land claim** at the site in 1845. The post office was established in 1852, and the city was incorporated in 1874. The **flood of 1861** wiped out the town, and the flood of 1890 again destroyed much of it. The economy is based on agriculture, timber, and manufacturing. Attractions include Riverfront Park on the **Willamette River**, the Heritage Museum, and the downtown historic district. Population 1980 4,024; 1995 4,875. Elevation 168'. PO Box 7, 97351. 503-838-1212. Chamber of Commerce 800-772-2806. Oregon Geographic Names.

Independence party. An Oregon **political party** of the 1840s that believed that the settlers formed a sovereign political body over which neither the U.S. nor Great Britain had any rights without the consent of the settlers. The American party, on the other hand, believed that the **provisional government** was just that, providing a temporary stability until the United States could take action to make the **Oregon Country** a territory. The Independence party controlled the provisional government during 1844. Empire of the Columbia. See also **Government history; Oregon Question**.

Independent. A person who has registered to vote and has checked the box marked "not a member of a party," thus choosing not to affiliate with a **political party**. Those who check "other" when they register are considered to be a party member no matter what they have written in after "other". For the November 1996 general election 400,248 voters registered as independent, 20% of the total, a percentage that has been increasing in recent decades. A voter registered as an independent (a non-affiliated voter, or NAV) may vote for party candidates in Oregon **primary elections** only if the party allows it. Julius Meier, governor 1931-35, is the only independent ever elected to state office in Oregon. See also **Voter registration**.

Indian Art Northwest. See **Northwest Indian Art Market**.

Indian burning. The Indians of the **Willamette Valley** used annual burning as an important tool in their resource management, so that much of the valley and the foothills were covered with park-line oak savannah when the settlers arrived. The burning maintained the **prairies** which produced the food plants they harvested, especially **camas** and tarweed, (*Madia sp.*). Burning also made hunting, harvesting, and travel easier, controlled **poison oak**, and provided forage for game. Indians in other parts of the state also burned for many of those reasons and sometimes for ceremonial purposes. First Oregonians. See also **Fire**.

Indian conflicts in the Willamette Valley. After **North West Company** fur trappers killed several Indians in the Willamette Valley, Alexander Ross negotiated a peace agreement (1816?) at **Willamette Falls** that held for many years. Early settlers in the valley had remarkably few conflicts with Indians, due in part to the devastating **epidemics** that by 1831 had reduced the Indian population of the area to 10% of its original numbers. The few recorded conflicts include the 1836 murder of fur trapper Alexander Carson by Indians at Alecs Butte south of **Yamhill**, the **Cockstock affair** of 1844 at **Oregon City**, a June 1846 encounter between the **Oregon Rangers** and eastern Oregon Indians on Battle Creek south of **Salem** in which one Indian was killed in a dispute about cattle, and the 1848 **Abiqua Battle**. Dictionary of Oregon History; Fur Hunters of the Far West; Oregon Geographic Names; Siskiyou Trail. See also **Indian wars**.

Indian dogs. Indians in Oregon had several kinds of dogs, some of which were eaten. The plains Indian dog was wolf-like and was thought to be a mixture of dog and **coyote**. It was used for hunting, packing, and food. A smaller, long-bodied, short-legged, sleek Indian dog, usually white with black spots, was kept as a pet and playmate for children. A good-sized brindled gray dog with a short, bushy tail was kept by the Klamath Indians. The Clallum Indian dog, a medium-sized dog with thick, woolly hair that was sheared for weaving into blankets, was especially common in the Puget Sound area and at the mouth of the **Columbia River**. Mammals and Life Zones of Oregon.

Indian hemp. A plant, *Apocynum cannabinum*, also called dogbane, that contains a strong fiber used by Indians, along with willow and other barks, for cord, nets, soft bags and **basketry**, fish line (it was strong enough to hold a **sturgeon**), and **ititamats**. Its insecticidal properties may have contributed to the preservation of food stored in containers made from it. It is not related to *Cannabis sativa*, the source of commercial hemp fiber and marijuana. Columbia River Basketry.

Indian languages. At the time of contact, Indians in what is now Oregon spoke at least 18 mutually-unintelligible languages belonging to 13 language families representing five language phyla. The oldest was perhaps the Hokan language, spoken by the Shasta Indians of **Bear Creek** Valley in southern Oregon, which was related to languages extending south into Central America. Most of the Indians in the western and northern areas of the state spoke languages of the ancient Penutian phylum, related to languages spoken from Washington south to Mexico; Chinookan, Kalapuyan, and Sahaptian were three of the nine Penutian language families spoken in Oregon. The Salish language of the Tillamooks was related to languages spoken along the coast of Washington and British Columbia. The more recent Athabaskan (Na-Dene) languages of the south coast and of the Clatskanie were also related to languages spoken to the north. The **Northern Paiutes** of southeast Oregon spoke a Uto-Aztecan language, related to languages of the Great Basin and high plains, which seems to have appeared in Oregon only within the last few hundred years. Of the rich variety of what must have been thousands of Indian stories, only some 500 have been saved; 116 of the tales are recounted in <u>Coyote Was Going There</u>. Indian names for many mammals are noted in <u>Mammals and Life Zones of Oregon</u>. Several Indian tribes are working to rekindle the use of their languages. <u>Archaeology of Oregon</u>; <u>First Oregonians</u>. See also **Chinook jargon**; **Coquille Indian Tribe**.

Indian reservations. Lands owned by a recognized Indian tribe that are not subject to local jurisdiction or taxation. A tribe may own land but the land is not recognized as reservation land until the federal government has gone through the process of placing it in trust. Currently eight of Oregon's nine recognized tribes or tribal confederations have reservations, ranging in size from the six acres that the **Coos, Lower Umpqua and Siuslaw Indians** have in **Coos Bay** to the 641,000-acre **Warm Springs** Reservation. Others are the **Burns Paiute** (11,786 acres), **Coquille Indian Tribe** (6,317 acres), **Cow Creek Band of Upper Umpqua Indians** (45 acres), Confederated Tribes of the **Grand Ronde Community** (10,051 acres), Confederated Tribes of **Siletz** (3,955 acres), and Confederated Tribes of the **Umatilla Reservation** (157,982 acres). The **Klamath Tribe** no longer has a reservation. The Fort McDermitt Indian Reservation in Nevada extends into southeast Oregon east of **Highway 95**. Some of the reservations are in several parcels, and some tribes have business or forest acreage, but no residential land. About 5,000 of Oregon's 38,500 Indians live on reservations. <u>American Indian Reservations</u>; <u>Native Peoples</u>; <u>Oregonian</u> 10/22/95:A 18.

Indian reservations, history. In 1853 Joel Palmer of the Bureau of Indian Affairs began to establish reservations for Oregon **Indians** in order to free Indian lands for white ownership, to protect Indians and whites from each other, and to encourage Indians to take up farming and a white lifestyle. Since then, 16 reservations have been established or reestablished in Oregon, of which eight remain. The first three were the Table Rock Reservation near **Medford** (1853-1856), the Cow Creek Umpqua Reservation near **Riddle** (1853-1856), and the Umpqua and Calapooia Reservation (1854-1856). After the 1856 **Rogue River War**, Indians from those reservations and from the rest of southwest Oregon were forcibly moved to the **Coast Reservation** (1855-1956), originally a 100-mile long strip of 1.4

million acres between **Cape Lookout** and **Florence**, later reduced to the Siletz reservation and then terminated. Other reservations were the **Umatilla** (1855-present), **Nez Perce** (1855-1877), **Warm Springs** (1855-present), **Grand Ronde** (1857-1904), **Klamath** (1864-1956), Malheur (1871-1882), **Coos** (1941-1956, 1984-present), Siuslaw (1948-1956), **Burns Paiute** (1935-present), **Siletz** (partially reestablished 1980-present), **Cow Creek** (1986-present), **Grand Ronde** (partially reestablished 1988-present), and **Coquille** (1989-present). In some cases several tribes, speaking different languages and perhaps of traditional enmity, were placed on one reservation. Some Indians were sent to reservations in other states. Resistance to reservation life led to several **Indian wars** so the Army established **forts** to monitor some of them. The original reservations were much reduced in size over the years by government actions, including the 1887 Dawes Act, which gave Indians individual ownership of some land and allocated the rest as surplus available for sale, which resulted in enormous loss of Indian-held lands. Later, in 1934, the sale of Indian land to non-Indians was made illegal. First Oregonians; Oregon Indians. **Indian trade**. The Indians of the Pacific Northwest had a long-established and extensive system of trade centered at Celilo near **The Dalles** where hundreds of Indians gathered annually. Lesser centers were at **Willamette Falls** and in the **Grande Ronde** valley of northeastern Oregon. The major item of trade was dried salmon; one tribe sold some 30,000 pounds of dried fish a year. Trade was also carried on in dozens of other items, including **slaves**, **obsidian**, baskets, ornaments, meat and skins of large game, **wapato** (arrowroot), **camas**, and other roots, **wocus** and other seeds, and dried berries. **Fur trade**rs found that Oregon Indians were shrewd and practiced bargainers. The use of **Chinook jargon** enabled the Indians, speakers of many different **Indian languages**, to transact business. "Property Concepts of 19th Century Oregon Indians." See also **Basketry**; **Dentalium**.

Indian tribes. There are 9 Indian tribes and confederations of tribes in Oregon that are recognized by the federal government as having sovereign right, and eight Indian **reservations**, some very small. The 9 tribes and confederations (out of 557 nationally) are the **Burns Paiute**, the Confederated Tribes of the **Grand Ronde Community**, the Confederated Tribes of **Siletz**, the Confederated Tribes of the **Umatilla Reservation**, the Confederated Tribes of **Warm Springs Reservation**, the Confederated Tribes of **Coos, Lower Umpqua, and Siuslaw Indians**, the **Coquille Indian Tribe**, the **Cow Creek Band of Upper Umpqua Indians**, and the **Klamath Tribe**. All but the Klamath have **reservations** on which a total of 5,000 Indians reside. The Fort McDermitt Indian Reservation in northern Nevada extends into southeast Oregon. See also **Cayuse Indians**; **Chetco and Tu-tut-ni Indians**; **Kalapuya Indians**; **Klickitat Indians**; **Modoc Indians**; **Nez Perce Indians**; **Northern Paiute Indians**; **Rogue River Indians**; **Wasco Indians**; **Warm Springs Indians**.

Indian Valley. See **Elgin**.

Indian wars. Much of the settlement in Oregon occurred without conflict because the Indian population had been decimated by diseases introduced by explorers and fur traders before white settlers arrived. However, especially after the 1847 **Whitman massacre**, tensions mounted and for the next 30 years a sporadic series of encounters, skirmishes, and atrocities occurred between whites and Indians, some of them intense enough to have been called wars. The first U.S. soldiers were sent to Oregon in 1848 in response to the Whitman massacre and the **Cayuse War**, and the government built **Fort Dalles**. Within a few years, Indian unrest led to the **Yakima War**, 1855-58, primarily in Washington. The **Rogue River War**, involving Indians of three linguistic groups, flared repeatedly throughout northern California and southwest Oregon until the surviving Indians were exiled to the Coast **Reservation** in 1856. Comparative quiet ensued through the 1860s except for the central Oregon depredations of the Snake River Indian, Chief Paulina, and his followers, 1866-1868. Unhappiness with reservation conditions led to the 1872-73 **Modoc War** in northern California, the **Nez Perce War** in 1877 which began in northeast Oregon and ended in Montana, and the last Indian war in the state, the **Bannock War** in 1878 in Idaho and eastern Oregon which the **Northern Paiute Indians** joined. Chronicle of the Indian Wars. See also **Forts; Indian conflicts in the Willamette Valley; Massacres**.

Indians, contemporary. The 1990 census listed 38,500 Indians in Oregon (1.4% of the state's population), of whom 16,394 were enrolled members of recognized tribes. The proportion was highest in **Jefferson County** (19.6%) and **Wasco County** (4.1%), home counties of the Warm Springs Reservation. **Klamath County** also had 4.1%. Indians were given U.S. citizenship in 1924. Affiliated Tribes of Northwest Indians (ATNI), 222 NW Davis, Suite 403, Portland 97209. 503-241-0070. First Oregonians; Native Americans; Oregonian 11/9/94:B17, 10/23/95:A8. See also **Casinos; Loud Hawk; Powwows; Reservations; Totem poles**.

Indians, historic. In 1792, in one of the first descriptions of Oregon Indians, Broughton noted "The Men at Columbia's River are strait limb'd, fine looking fellows, and the women are very pretty." The first settlers referred to Indians from west of the **Cascade Range** as Canoe Indians and those from east of the mountains as Horse Indians. The Indians of Oregon were decimated by **epidemics** following their first contact with trading ships, even before the **Lewis and Clark expedition** arrived in 1805, and by the time settlers arrived over the **Oregon Trail**, fewer than 10% of the Indians remained in western Oregon. The first **missions** were established in Oregon in 1834, and beginning in 1853 the government began moving Indians onto **reservations**. Conflicts, known as the **Indian wars**, between the Indians and settlers flared between 1847 and 1878. In 1924 Congress made Indians citizens and gave them the right to vote. In 1954 the government terminated tribal status and in 1956 terminated the reservations of the **Klamath Indians** and of all tribes west of the Cascades, but six later regained tribal recognition which meant that the government acknowledged its original treaty obligations. Oregon Indians. See also **Bigfoot (Indian); Indian wars; Johnson murder; Land ownership history; Missions; Rancheria**.

Indians, prehistoric. Indians are thought to have settled first in the interior, and then later along the Columbia River and the coast. Excavations at **Fort Rock Cave** indicate occupation perhaps 13,200 years ago, with apparently optimal conditions and maximum populations 10,000 to 8,000 years ago. Between 7,000 and 5,000 years ago there was no occupation at the site, due to the eruption of **Mt. Mazama** and to a hotter, drier climate during those years, and though the cave was occupied after that, it was by reduced numbers. The plateau Indians of northeast Oregon, **Cayuse** and **Nez Perce**, got horses from the Shoshones about 1750. They lived in teepees, while the nomadic root-gathering **Northern Paiute**s of the Great Basin built temporary small willow-dome shelters called **wickiups**, and the salmon fishing and trading tribes of the coast and along the **Columbia** and **Willamette** rivers lived at least part of the year in permanent villages of plank houses. Archaeology of Oregon; Oregon Indians; Sandal and the Cave. See also **Archeology**; **Artifacts**; **Calapooya Mounds**; **Dentalium**; **Flatheads**; **Indian languages**; **Kennewick Man**; **Middens**; **Slavery**.

Indoor Clean Air Act. See **Smoking**.

Industrial payroll. See **Payroll**.

Industrial Workers of the World (IWW). A labor organization in the timber industry in the early part of the 20th century whose members were called Wobblies. The group organized in 1905, and soon formed unions in **Portland** and **Astoria**. They agitated for the 8 hour day, better conditions in **logging** camps, and union recognition through unsuccessful strikes in Portland in 1907 and region-wide in 1917. The **Spruce Production Division**, which organized an alternative union called **Loyal Legion of Loggers and Lumbermen** (4L), effectively killed the IWW. Empire of the Columbia; Rebels of the Woods; Wildmen.

Industries, key. The legislature has designated thirteen Oregon industries as key industries. They are (with 1993 figures for employment and average wages) aerospace (4,000/$33,070); agriculture (59,000/$17,175); biotechnology (555/$34,600); environmental (22,000/$32,151); film and video (550/$31,569); fisheries 2,650/$17,524); forest products (69,280/$29,486); high technology (35,720/$39,353); metals (22,275/$31,128); plastics (5,790/$26,168); professional services (143,150/$26,753); software (8,750/$41,278); tourism (54,500/$12,537). Getting it Right. See also **Economic Development**; **Employers**; **Payroll**.

Industry Development. A division in the Department of **Economic Development** that assists the state's businesses and industries to compete locally, nationally and globally by helping to secure loans and contracts, developing training programs, and accessing export markets. The office has a number of overseas **trade offices**. 503-986-0200. Oregon Blue Book.

IndyCar Race. See **Portland IndyCar Race**.

Infant mortality. See **Births**.

Influenza. Though Oregonians, especially those over 65, are more conscientious than most in getting vaccinated, in 1996 21 cases of influenza (flu) were reported in the state plus 33 cases of H. influenza. In 1993, 1,014 Oregonians died from influenza (flu) and pneumonia. During **World War I** Spanish influenza, an especially virulent strain of viral flu, swept around the world. Between October 1918 and September 1920 Oregon recorded 48,146 cases and 3,675 flu-caused deaths. During the epidemic public gatherings were banned, schools were shut down, and stores closed early to reduce rush hour congestion. Tents, gymnasiums, and schools were pressed into service as hospitals. The spread of the influenza was exacerbated by the widespread movement of troops and other people involved in the war effort. "1918 'Spanish Influenza' Pandemic in Oregon;" Oregonian 10/11/95:B1.

Information centers. See **Visitors information centers.**

Infraction. An action that breaks the law but is less serious than a **misdemeanor** and is not considered a criminal offense. An infraction is punishable by a fine.

Initiative. A 1902 provision of the Oregon **constitution**, Art. IV Sec. 1(2), in which voters of the state gave themselves **legislative** powers by giving citizens the right to initiate and vote on constitutional amendments, state **laws**, and local **ordinances**. Prior to adoption of the initiative, only the **legislature** could enact laws. Through 1996, 288 initiated measures had qualified for the ballot, of which 99 passed. All state initiatives to date are listed in the Oregon Blue Book. Petitions for an initiative for a state law require valid signatures equal to 6% of the total number of votes cast in the last election for all candidates for **governor** (73,261 signatures 1994-1998), and 8% (97,681) are required for a constitutional amendment. Petitions for initiating a local ordinance need signatures from 15% of the areas' registered voters. It takes an estimated 14,000 hours to gather enough signatures to place a state law on the ballot. In 1982 the U.S. District Court ruled that signature gatherers may be paid. The initiative, along with the **referendum** and **recall**, is part of the famed **Oregon System**, though South Dakota in 1898 and Utah in 1900 were actually the first states to adopt the initiative. 28 states now have some version. Governing Oregon; Oregon Blue Book; Oregonian 10/19/97:B2. See also **Ballot measures; Elections Division.**

Inland Empire. A term coined in the 1880s by the Rev. George Henry Atkinson, **Congregational** missionary, for the high country east of the **Cascade Range** in Oregon and Washington. Dictionary of Oregon History.

Inmate Work Programs. A 1994 amendment to the state **constitution** requires all state prison inmates to work 40 hours a week, exempts inmate labor from state minimum wages, and exempts prison projects from competitive-bid requirements. Inmate pay starts at $1 a day. Prison industries include a farm and dairy operation, a laundry, a furniture factory, a garment factory making denims called Prison Blues, a metal shop, and services. Private partnerships have been developed using inmate labor both inside and outside the correctional facilities, and inmate work crews provide skilled and unskilled labor for contracted deployment around the state. 2585 State St., Salem 97310. 503-378-2449. Oregon Blue Book.

Insects. Oregon has some 15,000 species of insects that have been documented and an estimated 10,000 more that have yet to be discovered and described. No complete list has ever been compiled; **Oregon State University** entomologists are consolidating information into a state-wide data bank. Oregonian 2196:A16.

Institute for Sustainable Culture. A nonprofit group promoting greater environmental responsibility. It offers classes on straw-bale building, carpentry, gardening, and other subjects. 3430 SE Belmont St., Portland 97214. 503-736-1143. See also **Environmental organizations.**

Insurance agents. There were 25,123 insurance agents in Oregon in 1996.

Insurance companies New York Life Insurance Company is the oldest insurance company still operating in the state; it opened its Oregon branch in 1851.

Insurance Consumer Advocacy. An office that represents the interests of insurance consumers at rate and rule making hearings, provides public education and information to consumers, and operates the **Senior Health Insurance Benefits Assistance** volunteer outreach program. 350 Winter St. NE, Room 440, Salem 97310. 503-378-4271. Oregon Blue Book.

Insurance Division. A division of the Department of **Consumer and Business Services** that regulates insurance companies and agents. Complaints about insurance companies or agents can be made to the Consumer Protection Section at ext. 600. 50 Winter St. NE, Room 440, Salem 97310. 503-378-4271. Oregon Blue Book. See also **Insurance Consumer Advocacy; Oregon Health Plan; Senior Health Insurance Benefits Assistance**.

Intel. A semiconductor manufacturing company, headquartered in Santa Clara, California, with plants worldwide, including in **Aloha** and **Hillsboro**. In 1996 it was the state's largest **employer**, with 9,000 Oregon workers out of its total work force of 42,000. In 1994 Intel paid about 10% ($27 million) of the total corporate **income taxes** in the state. Oregonian 6/30/96:R22.

Intellectual freedom. See **Censorship**.

Intermarriage. In 1862 the Oregon legislature prohibited marriage between whites and persons of one-fourth or more Negro blood. In 1866 the prohibition was expanded to prohibit the marriage of whites with a person having one-fourth or more **Chinese** or **Kanaka** blood, or more than one-half **Indian** blood; this law was repealed in 1951. Peculiar Paradise.

Intermediate Theatre. See **Newmark Theatre**.

International Rose Test Gardens. A 4-acre garden in **Portland**'s **Washington Park** with 8,000 rose bushes representing over 500 varieties. The garden, established in 1917 through the efforts of Jesse A. Currey and the Portland Rose Society, is on three terraces with a broad view over the city to **Mount Hood**. The garden, the oldest public test garden of its type in the country, is one of the nation's 25 All-America Rose Testing Grounds, and also has beds featuring the city's Gold Medal winners, as well as a Shakespeare Garden. The roses are at their best in June and early summer and again in early fall. 611 SW Kingston. 503-227-1911. Oregonian 6/6/96:B10. See also **Sunken Rose Garden**.

International trade. See **Customs Service; Exports; Imports; Industry Development; Trade offices**.

Internment camps. See **Relocation centers**.

Interstate 5 (I-5). Oregon's major north-south freeway, part of a federal route that runs from the Mexican border near San Diego north through Sacramento, **Medford, Portland**, and Seattle, to the Canadian border near Vancouver, B.C. The Oregon portion, completed in 1966, extends 308 miles from milepost 0 at the California border to the north end of the Interstate Bridge over the **Columbia River**. It follows much of the route of the **Siskiyou Trail, Pacific Highway**, and **Highway 99**. **Siskiyou Summit** near the California border, elevation 4,310', is the highest pass on I-5 in Oregon, and is occasionally closed by snow. Four other passes lie between **Grants Pass** and **Canyonville: Sexton Mountain Pass**, 1,956', Smith Hill, 1,725', Stage Road Pass, 1,830', and **Canyon Creek Pass**, 2,015'. Volunteers place water jugs on some of the uphill stretches for motorists who have overheated radiators. See also **Baldock Freeway; Bridges, Columbia River; Commuting; Stumbo Strip**.

Interstate 82 (I-82). A 143-mile-long connector freeway between **Interstate 84** in Oregon and Interstate 90 in Washington that opened in 1988. The ten miles that lie in Oregon run north from Interstate 84 exit 179 near **Hermiston** to cross the **Columbia River** into Washington near **Umatilla.**

Interstate 84 (I-84). An east-west freeway that connects **Interstate 5** in **Portland** with Interstate 80 in Utah. It was called Interstate 80 North when it was dedicated in 1975. The Oregon portion, 378 miles long, follows from Portland east along the **Columbia River** past **Hood River** and **The Dalles**, then southeast past **Pendleton, La Grande**, and **Baker City** to cross into Idaho near **Ontario.** It lies approximately along the route of the **Oregon Trail.** Its highest point in Oregon is a 4,193-foot pass in the **Blue Mountains.** 10,000 vehicles a day travel the highway in Oregon, a fourth of them trucks. The section near Cabbage Hill east of Pendleton has been designated as a **safety corridor.** The section in Portland is known as the **Banfield Freeway.** First 75 Years.

Interstate 205 (I-205). A freeway bypass around the east side of **Portland.** It runs from exit 288 on **Interstate 5** east to **Oregon City** and then north past the **Portland International Airport**, across the **Columbia River** and north past Vancouver, Washington, to rejoin Interstate 5 nine miles north of the river. Twenty-seven of I-205's 36 miles are in Oregon. The Glenn Jackson Bridge over the Columbia was completed in 1982 and opened on May 15, 1983, with a 12-kilometer run. First 75 Years.

Interstate 405 (I-405). A four-mile freeway bypass around the west side of downtown **Portland.** It loops west and north from exit 299 on **Interstate 5** and over the Fremont Bridge to rejoin Interstate 5 at exit 302. The route, also called the Stadium Freeway, opened in 1973. First 75 Years.

Interstate highway system. A federal program established in 1956 to provide a national highway system so that troops and goods could be moved quickly for defense purposes. The last of Oregon's interstate highways was completed in 1988 with the opening of **Interstate 82. Interstate 5** (308 miles north/south) and **Interstate 84** (378 miles east/west) account for most of Oregon's 729 miles, which are 1.6% of the nation's total of 45,500 miles. Oregon's interstate highways carry 25% of the state's highway traffic. First 75 Years; Oregonian 7/9/96:B5.

Introduced species. Many of the common plant and animal species of Oregon are non-natives that have been introduced to the state since the time of white contact, either intentionally or accidentally . Examples of these naturalized non-natives include **possums**, starlings, English sparrows, garden **slugs**, honey **bees**, Himalaya **blackberries**, Scotch broom, **gorse, foxglove, Queen Anne's lace**, dandelions and most other garden weeds, tansy ragwort, various thistles, and diseases such as a root rot that is killing Port Orford **cedar.** All introduced species, including the recently arrived green **crab** and varnish **clam**, displace native species and disturb ecosystem functioning. People who are not Native Americans are, of course, also introduced. See also **Weeds.**

Inventors. Douglas Engelbart, inventor of the computer mouse and winner of the $500,000 Lemelson-MIT Prize for 1997 for American inventors, grew up in southeast **Portland** and received a degree in electrical engineering from **Oregon State University** in 1948. The hand-cranked pencil sharpener was invented in

1874 by **Albany** resident William E. Howell. A. C. Gilbert of **Salem** invented the Erector Set and other toys. Clarissa inman of Portland invented the electric curling iron. <u>Oregonian</u> 4/11/97:A1; <u>Portland's Little Red Book</u>; <u>This Day in Oregon</u>. See also **A. C. Gilbert's Discovery Village**; **Tucker Sno-Cat**.

Inversion. A weather condition that occurs when cold air is trapped near the ground by a layer of warm air above it. Inversions in the winter may persist for several days if the sun is too weak to warm the ground and heat the air so that it will rise and if there are no winds to stir the air. Inversions cause **air pollution** episodes because pollutants are trapped near the ground. Because of topography and low wind speeds, Oregon has more inversions than most other states, especially in the western valleys. The interior **Rogue River** valley (**Medford**, **Grants Pass** area) had an especially severe one in December 1985. See also **Fog**.

Investment Council. A five-member group that is responsible for investing all State of Oregon funds, including those in the **Public Employees Retirement System (PERS)**, **SAIF**, **Common School Fund**, and other trust and general funds. In 1997 those funds totaled about $30 billion. The council, guided by the "Prudent Investor Rule", seeks to make the funds as productive as possible. Three public members of the council are appointed by the governor to four-year terms. The state **treasurer** serves on the council and is chief investment officer, supported by the Investment Division. The director of PERS serves as a non-voting member. 100 Labor and Industries Bldg., 350 Winter St. NE, Salem 97310-0840. 503-378-4111. <u>Oregon Blue Book</u>. See also **Bond rating**.

ION. An acronym from the initials of Idaho, Oregon, and Nevada used for the six-million acres of **sagebrush** desert where the three states meet. The region is part of the **Great Basin**.

Ione. A north-central Oregon wheat farming community on **Willow Creek** in **Morrow County**, 18 miles northwest of **Heppner** on Highway 74. It lies some 70 miles west of **Pendleton**. It was named in 1883 for Ione Arthur, a girl who was visiting the E. G. Sperry family at the time; Sperrys owned the land that became the town. The post office was established the next year, and the city was incorporated in 1903. Population 1980 345; 1995 265. Elevation 1,080'. PO Box 361, 97843. 541-422-7437. <u>Oregon Geographic Names</u>.

Ira C. Keller Fountain. A **Portland** fountain that fills the block between SW 3rd and 4th Avenues and Clay and Market Streets in front of the **Civic Auditorium**. 13,000 gallons of water a minute flow over the huge concrete structure that was built in 1970 at a cost of $543,000. The fountain, designed by Angela Danadjieva of Halprin and Associates to entice people to explore and play in it, was described by the <u>New York Times</u> as "perhaps the greatest open space since the Renaissance." First called Forecourt Fountain, it was later named for civic leader Ira Keller. <u>Frozen Music</u>.

Iris. Two commercial **Willamette Valley** iris growers welcome visitors to their gardens during the last two weeks of May. Cooley's Gardens are located off of Silverton Road. P.O. Box 126, Silverton 97381. 503-873-5463. Schreiner's Iris Gardens are at 3625 Quinaby Road N.E., Salem 97303. 503-393-3232. Each grower issues a catalog. The nearby city of **Keizer** hosts an annual Iris Festival.

Irish in Oregon. In 1870 the largest foreign-born group in Portland was the

Irish, and elsewhere in the state they made up the bulk of the labor for railroad construction. About a thousand Irish sheepmen came from Duhallow in County Cork to **Lake County** between the 1880s and 1940s, but **Morrow County**, where Irish began immigrating in the 1860s from County Leitrim and County Longford, claims to have the largest concentration of persons of Irish descent today. In **Heppner**, where St. Patrick's Day is celebrated with a three day festival, a third of the population is Irish. Oregonian 3/14/97:B4, 9/28/97:B4. See also **Mill Ends Park**.

Iron. In Oregon in the late 1800s, locally produced iron was used for **cast-iron architecture** and **railroads**. Between 1867 and 1894, the Oregon Iron and Steel Company and its predecessor companies produced iron at a **Lake Oswego** blast furnace, using iron ore (limonite) mined from nearby **Iron Mountain** and **coal** from **Coos Bay**. The company employed several hundred men at full production, about half of them **Chinese**. Total production, 1867-1894, amounted to 93,404 tons. The 42-foot chimney of the blast furnace still stands in George Rogers Park. Grand Era of Cast Iron; Oregon Geographic Names; Oregon's Iron Dream. See also **Steel**.

Iron Mountain. A common name for Oregon mountains, often given because of rust-colored rock. Only one, north of **Lake Oswego**, was actually a source of **iron** ore. Iron Mountain in the **Cascade Range** is noted for its summer wildflowers; it is reached by a trail north of **Highway 20**, about 33 miles east of **Sweet Home**. Oregon Geographic Names.

Ironside Mountain. A prominent 7,811' mountain at the northwest edge of **Malheur County** just south of **Highway 26**. It was formed by **andesite** lava in the **Miocene**; at the mountain the flows are a mile thick. The name comes from the color of the mountain. Geology of Oregon.

Irrigation. Water supplied to croplands from stored winter rains or mountain snow melt. Because two thirds of Oregon is arid and most of the state has dry summers, irrigation markedly increases both agricultural productivity and the variety of crops that can be grown. By 1852 farmers in southern Oregon were irrigating from hand-dug **ditches**. The federal **Desert Land Act of 1877** and **Carey Act of 1894** encouraged further irrigation or reclamation projects so that by 1902, when Congress established the **Bureau of Reclamation**, 440,000 acres were irrigated. Now, 9,500 farmers irrigate 1.6 million of Oregon's 5 million acres of cropland, plus 658,000 acres of pasture and hay land. There are about 70 irrigation districts in the state. Commodities produced with irrigation represent 90% of the total value of harvested crops in Oregon. Portable sprinkler irrigation, invented in Oregon in the late 1920's, makes possible the irrigation of rolling land unsuited to flood irrigation. In 1985 an estimated 5,732 million gallons per day was used for irrigation in the state, 8% of it from **groundwater**. Over half of the water used for irrigation returns to streams or seeps into the groundwater, sometimes carrying fertilizers and pesticides. Agriculture; East of the Cascades; "Fort Rock Basin"; National Water Summary 1987; "Oregon - First in 'Portable' Irrigation". See also **Church of the Holy Water; Water rights; Water spreading; Water use**.

Irrigon. "Progress Unlimited under the Sun." A **Columbia River** town in **Morrow County** 50 miles northwest of **Pendleton** and seven miles west of

Umatilla. It was first called Grande Ronde Landing, and later Stokes, before the name Irrigon, coined from the words "irrigation" and "Oregon," was used for the post office when it was established in 1903. The city was incorporated in 1957. The town hosts an annual Walleye Tournament in April and a Watermelon Festival in August, and is on the Lewis and Clark National Historic Trail. The Umatilla Wildlife Refuge, Irrigon and Umatilla steelhead fish hatcheries, and **Umatilla Chemical Depot** are nearby. Population 1980 700; 1995 1,080. Elevation 297'. PO Box 428, 97844. 541-922-3047. Oregon Geographic Names.

Islam. Oregon has 7,000 Muslims (adherents of the Islamic faith), more than 4,000 of them in **Portland** where there are three mosques. There is also a mosque in **Corvallis**.

Island. See **The Island**.

Island City. An incorporated city two miles east of **La Grande** in **Union County**. It lies on an island formed by a slough of the **Grande Ronde River**, though the channels have been much modified, beginning with activities of the **Oregon Railway and Navigation Co.** in 1884. The city was incorporated in 1904. Population 1980 477; 1995 830. Elevation 2,743'. 10605 Island Ave., 97851. 541-963-5017. History of Union County.

Islands. Both coastal islands and river islands are found in Oregon. **Sauvie Island**, a 15 mile island in the **Columbia River**, is the largest river island; it is near **Portland**, as is **Ross Island**. Hunters Island is the largest of the 1,477 rocky islands off Oregon's coast; it is south of **Cape Sebastian** in **Curry County**. The only coastal island with a structure on it (a former **lighthouse**) is **Tillamook Rock**. Most offshore islands are included in the Three Arch Rocks and Oregon Islands **National Wildlife Refuges** to protect sea bird nesting sites.

Italians in Oregon. The first Italians in Oregon were Italian-born **Catholic** priests in the 1840s. The first Italian businessman was restaurant and hotel keeper S. N. Arrigoni who arrived with his wife in **Portland** in 1856. Many Italians came between 1890 and 1917, especially to work in railroad construction, and in 1910 Oregon had 5,538 foreign-born Italians. The first Italian district in Portland was located in what is now Duniway Park south of downtown. The first Italian church, St. Michael the Archangel, opened in 1901. Centro Vita Italiana, 4507-A SE Milwaukie Avenue, Portland 97202. 503-238-6924 "Portland Italians, 1880-1920." See also **Festa Italiana**.

Ititamat. A "counting the days" ball traditionally made by Columbia River Indian women from string spun from **Indian hemp**. A married woman would record her life's events by tying a knot as each day passed. She marked extraordinary days, such as births, with a special marker such as a shell. Columbia River Basketry.

J. A. Chanslor. An oil tanker that wrecked in the fog on rocks off **Cape Blanco** on December 18, 1919, with a loss of 36 lives and 30,000 barrels of oil. There were three survivors. Shipwrecks of the Pacific Coast.

Jackrabbits. Large **hares**. Two species occur in Oregon. The black-tailed jackrabbit, *Lepus californicus*, is common in eastern Oregon and was at one time also found in the valleys of western Oregon north to **Salem**. The larger white-tailed jackrabbit, *L. townsendii*, which grows to 24 inches long, turns white in the winter. It has been fast disappearing from the bunch-grass range in eastern Oregon as the bunch grass itself disappears, and is now classed as a **protected animal**. On the other hand, there may be as many as 5 black-tailed jackrabbits per acre in eastern Oregon for an estimated total of 20 million. In 1915 **Harney County** offered a bounty of five cents per rabbit and netted 1,029,182. Their numbers are also controlled by **coyotes** and other predators, disease, and weather. Jackrabbits' appetite for anything green makes them a major pest for ranchers, though desert homesteaders found them a ready source of meat. Jackrabbits are noted for their large ears and 45-mph speed; they can cover more than 12 feet in a single leap. As with other hares, they do not burrow, but scoop out a "form" under a **sagebrush** bush. An attempt in the early 1900s to market jackrabbit fur for hats was unsuccessful, as was a rabbit cannery in **Echo**. Three people died from **tularemia** after eating at a rabbit burger stand in southeast Oregon. Atlas of Oregon Wildlife; Experiences; Mammals and Life Zones of Oregon; Mammals of the Northwest; Oregon Desert.

Jackson County. A county in southern Oregon bounded by California on the south and by **Josephine, Douglas**, and **Klamath** counties. Incorporated cities are **Medford** (county seat), **Ashland, Butte Falls, Central Point, Eagle Point, Gold Hill, Jacksonville, Phoenix, Rogue River, Shady Cove, Talent**. The county is located where the **Siskiyou Mountains** meet the **Cascade Range**, and is bisected by the **Rogue River**. Elevations range from 964' at **Rogue River** to 7,533' **Mount Ashland** in the Siskiyous on the south and 9,495' **Mount McLoughlin** in the Cascades on the east. The economy is based on lumber, manufacturing, recreation and agriculture; the **Bear Creek Valley** is famous for its winter **pears**. Taxable assessed value in 1995 was $8,371,000,000, or $51,000 per capita. The county was created in 1852 from **Yamhill** and **Champooick** districts and originally included much of southwest Oregon. It was named for former President Andrew Jackson (1767-1845). Population 1980 132,456; 1995 164,400. Area 2,801 square miles. Density 59/sq.mi. Annual precipitation 20"; average temperature January 38°F, July 73°F. Courthouse, 10 S. Oakdale, Medford 97501. 541-776-7248. Land in Common; Oregon Blue Book. See also **Good Government Congress**.

Jacksonville. A historic southwest Oregon gold mining town five miles west of **Medford**. Gold was discovered in the winter of 1851-52, and mining tunnels were built - even under the town itself, as was learned years later when streets began to cave in. The post office was established in 1854, and the city was incorporated in 1860. It was named for **Jackson County** and served as the county seat until 1927. The 1884 courthouse, site of the sensational **DeAutremont brothers** trial, is now the county historical museum. The town declined after the new railroad bypassed it, but its 19th century buildings are now valued, and Jacksonville is one of eight National Historic Landmark Cities. "Pinto" Colvig, famed as Bozo the **Clown**, grew up in Jacksonville. The **Britt Music Festivals** are held each summer on the grounds where Peter Britt, an early photographer, had his home. Population 1980 2,030; 1995 2,010. Elevation 1,569'. PO Box 7, 97530. 541-899-1231. Jacksonville Story; Land in Common; Oregonian 6/2/96:T1. See also **Presidential visits**.

Jaguar. A fossil jaguar was discovered in **Oregon Caves** in 1995. The extinct ice-age cat, thought to be 20,000 to 40,000 years old, was about the size of a lion and had a 14-inch long skull. Oregonian 1/17/96:B3. See also **Fossils, animal**.

Jails. In 1996 there were 103 jails in the state plus 12 state prisons and one federal prison. See also **Correctional facilities; Sheridan Federal Correctional Institution**.

James G. Blaine Society. A 1940s organization without dues, members, or officers that grew in the fertile mind of writer Stewart Holbrook and was taken up by Ron Abell. Holbrook used it to sound a warning about the dangers of careless development. He suggested that members should tell prospective newcomers all the reasons they wouldn't like it here. As an example, after **Vanport** was destroyed by the **flood of 1948**, Holbrook, on a visit east, shrugged it off with the comment "have them every year. This time it just happened to get into the papers." Holbrook said that the society had no connection with the man who was once a senator from Maine and the 1884 Republican candidate for president. Blaine (1830-1893) never visited Oregon so he fit well with the "Don't come" message. Oregonian 9/14/69:NW9, 2/1/98:C5. See also **Growth**.

Jantzen Beach. A one-time **amusement park** on **Hayden Island** in the **Columbia River** just west of **Interstate 5**. The park, opened in 1929, featured four swimming pools and a natatorium, the Golden Canopy Ballroom, 25 acres of picnic grounds, and "The Big Dipper" **roller coaster**. After **Interstate 5** was built through the area, the amusement park was replaced in 1972 with a shopping **mall**, refurbished in 1996. The mall includes a 72-horse **carousel** that dates to 1917. Oregonian 7/23/95:E1, 12/15/96:C6, 1/26/97:B4.

Japan. In 1996 exports from Oregon to Japan totaled $2.1 billion. Of that, $731 million was for agricultural goods, $664 million for wood products, $550 million for high technology, $56 million for other manufactured goods, and $43 million for metals. Japan maintains an official consulate in Oregon. First Interstate Tower, 1300 SW 5th Ave., Portland 97201. 503-221-1811. Oregonian 7/30/97:C1.

Japanese American Historical Plaza. A plaza in **Portland** that honors with poems on stones the Japanese pioneers of Oregon and the Oregon Japanese-Americans who were moved to **relocation centers** during **World War II**. The plaza, dedicated in 1990, is located at the north end of **Tom McCall Waterfront Park**, just north of the Burnside Bridge, in an area that before **World War II** was a thriving Japanese American community called Nihonmachi or Japan Town. Gift; Touching the Stones.

Japanese current. See **Ocean currents**.

Japanese Garden. A five acre garden in **Washington Park** in **Portland**, designed in 1963 by Takuma Tono. It includes a pavilion and five traditional gardens: Strolling Pond Garden, Tea Garden, Natural Garden, Sand and Stone Garden, and Flat Garden. The private, non-profit Japanese Garden Society of Oregon founded the garden and maintains it. Gifts from Sapporo, Portland's **sister city**, include a pagoda and traditional tea house. The garden is open daily except Thanksgiving, Christmas, and New Year's Day. Admission. 611 SW Kingston Avenue. PO Box 3847, 97208. 503-223-1321. See also **Four Rivers Cultural Center**.

Japanese in Oregon. The 1990 census counted 12,000 persons in Oregon who identified themselves as Japanese. The first Japanese known to have been in the **Oregon Country** were three survivors whose junk washed ashore in 1834 near Cape Flattery, Washington after a year at sea. The **Hudson's Bay Company** freed the three from their Indian captors and returned them, by way of London, as far as Macao, but Japan, still closed, refused to accept them back. Japanese began moving to Oregon after the Chinese Exclusion Act of 1882. There were 25 Japanese in Oregon in 1890, 2,501 in 1900, and 4,151 in 1920. The Japanese worked in lumber, railroading, fishing, and agriculture and were important in raising specialty food crops around **Portland** and **Hood River**. There were also sizable urban populations. During **World War II**, over 4,000 Japanese-Americans from western Oregon were exiled to **relocation centers**, though many Japanese-Americans served in the much-decorated 100th Infantry Battalion and the 442nd Regimental Combat Team, which took heavy casualties in Europe. 15 died in service during the war and seven have died in service since 1945. In 1952 Congress passed legislation allowing Japanese immigrants to apply for citizenship. Japanese Americans now make up about 1.5% of Oregon's population, though in **Ontario** they account for about 4%. Gift; "Japanese in Oregon"; "Nikkei in Oregon 1834-1940"; Touching the Stones. See also **Anti-Japanese sentiment**; **Asians in Oregon**; **Four Rivers Cultural Center**; **Japanese American Historical Plaza**.

Japanese junks. Dozens of Japanese junks are known to have been found adrift on the American side of the Pacific Ocean, especially between 1636 and 1853. During those 200+ years Japan had sealed itself off from foreign influence and the emperor had decreed that all boats were to be built with a style of rudder that would break easily if a boat ventured into the rough waters of the open sea. Hundreds of boats were disabled in storms, and, caught in the Japanese current, floated across the northern Pacific and down the west coast of North America, a few with surviving crew members aboard. Nehalem tribal legend tells of a shipwrecked oriental sailor several centuries ago who became a freebooter, pillaging villages from the **Columbia River** to **Coos Bay**. A junk is reported to have grounded on **Point Adams** at the south side of the mouth of the Columbia River in 1820 with a large crew, though it is not known what happened to them. That junk is said to have carried a large cargo of **beeswax**. In 1833 three Japanese survived the wreck of their junk near Cape Flattery, Washington, after having drifted for nearly a year. They were enslaved for some months by the local Indians before being rescued by the **Hudson's Bay Company**. Japan, however, refused to let most rescued sailors return. Pacific Graveyard; Wrecked Japanese Junks.

Jason Lee House. Perhaps the oldest building in Oregon, the restored 1841 Jason Lee home has been moved to its present location in **Mission Mill Village** in **Salem**. Costumed guides offer demonstrations of 19th century lifestyles at it and two other early buildings, the Parsonage and the John D. Boon House. Jason Lee, a **Methodist**, arrived in Oregon in 1834, the first missionary in Oregon. 1313 Mill St. SE. 503-585-7012.

Jazz. **Portland** is said to be known as the best jazz city on the west coast. The Jazz Society of Oregon publishes a monthly magazine of jazz happenings in Oregon and the west called Jazzscene. PO Box 968, Portland 97207. 503-234-

1332. The **Mount Hood Festival of Jazz** is Oregon's major jazz festival. Newport also has a 3-day festival in August called Jazz on the Water (541-265-4074). Portland Guidebook. See also **Portland Art Museum**.

Jefferson. "Mint Capital of the World." A mid **Willamette Valley** farming community on the north side of the **Santiam River** in **Marion County** 18 miles south of **Salem**. Originally known as Conser's Ferry, the post office was renamed in 1861 for the Jefferson Institute. Attractions include the historic Jacob Conser House with two front doors, and the Mint Festival held the first weekend in August. Population 1980 1,702; 1995 2,020. Elevation 235'. PO Box 83, 97352. 541-327-2768. Oregon Geographic Names.

Jefferson. See **State of Jefferson**.

Jefferson County. A central Oregon county that stretches from crest of the **Cascade Range** on the west across the **Deschutes River** to the **Ochoco Mountains** on the east. It was created from **Crook County** in 1914 and named for Mount Jefferson. Location of the county seat became a rancorous tug between the county's three incorporated cities, **Metolius**, **Madras**, and **Culver**. Culver won in the short run, but in 1917 the records were moved to Madras. The county is bounded by **Wasco**, **Wheeler**, **Crook**, **Deschutes**, **Linn**, and **Marion** counties. The **Warm Springs Reservation** occupies the northwest quarter of the county. Elevations range from 1,280' where the Deschutes River leaves the county on the north to 10,495' **Mount Jefferson** on the west. The economy is based on ranching, irrigated agriculture (especially around Culver), worth over $44 million a year, forest products, and recreation. Taxable assessed value in 1995 was $803,000,000, or $50,000 per capita. The county has the state's highest birth rate, 23.3 per 1,000, and the highest infant death rate, 16.8 per 1,000. Population 1980 11,599; 1995 16,100. Area 1,791 square miles. Density 9/sq.mi. Annual precipitation 10"; average temperature January 37°F, July 70°F. 75 SE "C" St., Madras 97741. 541-475-2449. East of the Cascades; History of Jefferson County; Oregon Blue Book.

Jellyfish. Floating sea creatures, usually clear, belonging to the Cnidaria and Ctenophora phyla. About ten species are found along the Oregon coast. Most common are the small round "gooseberries" or "cat's eyes", *Pleurobrachia bachei*, which are clear marbles about a half inch in diameter with two feathery tentacles up to 5 inches long. The only common jellyfish that is potentially dangerous, especially to persons who have developed an allergic reaction to it, is the washtub-size lion's mane or sea blubber, *Cyanea capillata*, which has reddish stinging tentacles up to six feet long hanging below its clear parachute. Some jellyfish are luminescent. Moon jellyfish, *Aurelia aurita*, are featured in a display at the **Oregon Coast Aquarium**. Between Pacific Tides; Seashore Life. See also **Sail jellyfish**.

Jensen Arctic Museum. See **Paul Jensen Arctic Museum**.

Jessie M. Honeyman State Park. A **state park** on the north edge of **Oregon Dunes National Recreation Area** three miles south of **Florence**. The park includes sand dunes, portions of **Cleowax Lake** and **Woahink Lake**, each with boat ramps, swimming and picnic areas, and group facilities. It had 1.7 million visits in 1994-95, making it Oregon's most visited **state park**. The campground, with 381 spaces, is open year-round. Reservations, 800-452-5687. 84505 Highway 101 South, Florence 97439. 541-997-3641.

Jetties. Rock structures built out into the ocean at the mouths of rivers in order to direct river flow so that it will scour a channel for boats. The channels are also periodically dredged. Jetties have been built by the **Army Corps of Engineers** at the mouths of ten Oregon rivers; the longest is the 6.6-mile-long south jetty at the mouth of the **Columbia River**. Others are at the mouths of the **Nehalem, Tillamook, Yaquina, Siuslaw, Umpqua, Coos, Coquille, Rogue,** and **Chetco** rivers. The south jetty of the Coquille includes the 300' iron hull of a ship that went aground there in 1953. Construction in 1917 of the north jetty at **Tillamook Bay** blocked the sand flow, resulting in erosion at **Cape Meares** and Tillamook spit, and the destruction of the towns of Barview and **Bayocean**. Construction of a south jetty in 1974 rebalanced the sand economy. Rogue waves sometimes sweep persons off of jetties; during 1995 three persons died after being swept off the Coquille jetty. Bayocean; Oregon Coastal Harbors; Oregonian 10/9/95:B5; Tillamook. See also **Breakwaters**.

Jewish faith. The first Jewish worship service in Oregon was held in **Jacksonville** in 1856. A Jewish congregation organized in **Portland** in 1858; the first synagogue was built three years later. There are now an estimated 20,000 practicing Jews in the state with synagogues in Portland and other Oregon cities. Guide to Early Oregon Churches.

Jews-harp. See **Trump**.

Jews in Oregon. German Jewish men began arriving in Oregon in the 1840s. Two of them later each served two terms as mayor of **Portland**. The first Jewish woman, Mrs. Weinshank, arrived in 1854 and opened a boarding house. Jews from Russia and eastern Europe began arriving fifty years later. A Jewish community flourished in south Portland from the 1890s until the 1920s. Julius Meier, elected governor as an **Independent** in 1931, was a Jew. "Jews of Portland."

Job Corps. A federal residential job-training and educational program for men and women ages 16-24, begun in 1964. Oregon's camps include Angell Civilian Conservation Corps (CCC) (**Waldport**); Springdale Job Corps Center (JCC) (**Troutdale**); Timber Lake CCC (**Estacada**); Tongue Point JCC (**Astoria**); and Wolf Creek CCC (**Glide**); plus Partners in Vocational Opportunity Training (PIVOT), a day program for teen parents (**Portland**). Oregonian 9/5/95:FD1. See also **Apprenticeship and Training Division**.

JOBS. A welfare-reform program that uses state and federal welfare money to cover a portion of a person's salary in a private sector job. The program was begun as a pilot project in six counties in 1994, and expanded statewide in 1995. It is administered by the Oregon **Adult and Family Services Division**. See also **Oregon Option**.

John Day. An eastern Oregon lumber, cattle, and commercial center in **Grant County**. It is located on the **John Day River**, for which it is named, at the junction of **Highway 26** and **Highway 395** two miles north of **Canyon City**. In 1862, when Canyon City was booming from gold discoveries, John Day was known as Lower Town or Tiger Town and had a population that included some 500 **Chinese**. Now the only evidence of their presence is the **Kam Wah Chung and Co. Museum**. The post office was established in 1865, and the city was incorporated in 1901.

Headquarters for the **John Day Fossil Beds National Monument** and the **Malheur National Forest** are located in the city. Population 1980 2,012; 1995 1,900. Elevation 3,083'. 450 E. Main, 97845. 541-575-0028. Chamber of Commerce 541-575-0547. "Emmet White, Part IV"; Gold and Cattle Country; History of Grant County.

John Day Dam. A dam on the **Columbia River** 30 miles upstream from the city of **The Dalles** and 24 miles upstream from **The Dalles Dam**. It was built by the **Army Corps of Engineers** for power, flood control, navigation, and irrigation at a cost of $511 million. Construction began in 1958 with the first power generated in 1968 and the last of the 16 generators completed in 1971. The only one of the four dams on the Oregon stretch of the Columbia with significant flood control capacity, it can provide 500,000 **acre-feet** of storage. The powerhouse is 1,976 feet long, and total generating capacity is 2,160 **megawatts. Bonneville Power Administration** markets the power. Lake Umatilla, formed by the dam, extends 76 miles upstream to **McNary Dam**. There are a number of parks along the lake. PO Box 564, The Dalles 97058-9998. Army Engineers. See also **Arlington**.

John Day Formation. An extensive central Oregon geologic formation made up of vast deposits of pastel volcanic **rhyolite** ash, **andesite**, and **basalt** erupted from volcanoes between the **Blue Mountains** and the present-day **Cascade Range** during the **Oligocene**, 18 to 36 million years ago. The formation contains a rich variety of semi-tropical plant and animal **fossils**, as well as **agate** and **thunderegg** sites. It lies above the **Clarno Formation** and is, in turn, covered by the **Columbia River basalts**. Geology of Oregon. See also **Officer's Cave**; **Painted Hills**; **Steins Pillar**.

John Day Fossil Beds National Monument. A 14,000-acre national monument of three separate units in central Oregon. The Clarno unit on Highway 218 holds the oldest **fossils**, 44 million-year old tropical plants from the **Clarno Formation**. The **Painted Hills** unit near **Mitchell** contains fossils from the **John Day Formation** of 18 to 36 millions ago, including a 3-toed horse, camels, rhinoceroses, and *Metasequoia* or dawn redwood. The **Picture Gorge** area 38 miles west of **John Day** has fossils from 25 million years ago. It also includes the Cant Ranch Visitor Center at Sheep Rock on Highway 19 with exhibits of fossils. The headquarters are at 420 West Main St., John Day, 97845. 541-575-0721. Geology of Oregon; Offbeat Oregon.

John Day Lock. A single **lock**, the deepest in the world, that opened in 1968 to enable boats and barges to pass **John Day Dam**. The lock is 86' wide, 675' long, and provides 15' of water depth over the sills. It is the world's highest single-lift lock, with a maximum lift of 113'.

John Day River. A river that heads in the **Ochoco** and **Blue** mountains of north central Oregon, and flows west and north through seven counties 280 miles to the **Columbia River**, making it one of Oregon's longest rivers. Its 7,900 square mile drainage basin drops from an elevation of 9,000 feet at **Strawberry Mountain** to 200 feet at the Columbia. At river mile 20.9, annual flows average 1,499,000 acre feet, or .3 acre foot/acre. A chemical spill from a truck on February 8, 1990 dumped 3,500 gallons of hydrochloric acid into the river near Dale and affected 12 miles of the river; a $1,000,000 restoration program was undertaken by state and federal agencies, but complete fish population recovery may take years. The river was named for a member of the Astor-Hunt overland party of 1811-1812. He and a companion were robbed of everything, including their clothes, by Indians near the mouth of the river. A short river east of **Astoria** is also called the John Day River, named for the same man. Oregon Geographic Names. See also **Nook**.

Johnson City. A suburban community five miles north of **Oregon City** in **Clackamas County**. It began as a trailer court entirely owned by Delbert Johnson who instigated its incorporation in 1970. A spring-fed lake covers 5 of its 42 acres. Population 1980 378; 1995 615. Elevation 150'. 8021 SE Posey St., Milwaukie, 97267. 503-655-9710. Oregon Geographic Names.

Johnson murder. Dick Johnson, an industrious **Klickitat Indian** farmer near **Yoncalla**, and his stepfather were murdered in 1858 by eight claim jumpers who coveted his farm. Jesse Applegate attempted to bring the murderers to justice, but legal and societal opposition thwarted his efforts. Oregon, a History.

Joint Occupancy. In 1818 Great Britain and the U.S. signed a ten-year Joint Occupation Agreement for "all territories and their waters claimed by either power, west of the Rocky Mountains" to "be free and open to the vessels, citizens and subjects of both for ten years." In 1827 the countries renewed the agreement indefinitely, but later, despite President Polk's 1844 campaign slogan of "**Fifty-four Forty or Fight**," agreed to the **Oregon Treaty of 1846**, which ceded the area between the 49th parallel (the present U.S./Canadian boundary) and what was then Mexico (present-day California) to the U.S. Dictionary of Oregon History. See also **Oregon Country; Provisional government**.

Joint Ways and Means Committee. A powerful committee of the state **legislature** made up of eight members from the **Senate** and 10 from the **House of Representatives**, appointed respectively by the President of the Senate and the Speaker of the House. They each appoint one of those members to serve as co-chair of the committee. Most members serve also on the interim **Emergency Board**. All state appropriation bills, including those for the **General Fund**, grants, and fees, have to be passed by the group before being sent directly to the house and the senate floors for final votes. The Legislative Fiscal Office provides permanent support. The committee, started in 1917 and abolished only for the 1993 session, is one of Oregon's unique institutions. Governing Oregon.

Jordan Craters. An area of geologically-recent **volcanic eruptions** west of **Jordan Valley** in central **Malheur County**. Activity began about 9,000 years ago, creating a ridge of small spatter cones, and was followed after 5,000 years by fluid basalt flows, covering about 28 square miles, from the 100'-deep Coffeepot Crater. Other small shield **volcanoes** to the south erupted at about the same time. Geology of Oregon. See also **Owyhee uplands physiographic province**.

Jordan Valley. A southeast Oregon mining and ranching community in **Malheur County** on Highway 95 less than two miles from the Idaho border. A house known as the Stateline Ranch House sits astride the state line. Jordan Valley was named for Michael Jordan who led a party that discovered gold nearby in 1863; he was killed the next year in an Indian fight. The city was incorporated in 1911. **Basques** make up two-thirds of the area's population; the historic stone Pelota Court for Basque handball was built about 1916. The community hosts the

Big Loop **Rodeo** on the 3rd weekend in May. Kinross Delamar Mine is the major employer. Population 1980 473; 1995 410. Elevation 4,389'. PO Box 187, 97910. 541-586-2460. In Times Past; Oregon Geographic Names; Owyhee Trails; Tracking Down Oregon.

Jordan Valley Interagency Invasive Weed Management Project. A joint campaign, begun in 1998 by the U.S. **Bureau of Land Management**, the Oregon Department of **Transportation**, and **Malheur County**, that is designed to control noxious **weeds** on 3.6 million acres in southeast Oregon. Special efforts will focus on controlling weeds that are spread along roadsides by vehicles ("roadrunners"). Oregonian 2/24/98:C2.

Joseph. A northeast Oregon city in **Wallowa County** six miles south of **Enterprise** at the base of **Wallowa Lake** and the **Wallowa Mountains**. The town was named for the famous **Nez Perce** Indian, Chief Joseph (1837-1904), who claimed the valley as his tribe's ancestral home. The post office was established in 1880, and the city was incorporated in 1887. In 1896 a robbery of the bank by four horsemen led to a shoot-out on the main street in which one robber was killed, one escaped with the money, and two were captured; one of the captured men later became vice president of the bank. Joseph is now noted for its **bronze** foundries and its many galleries offering bronze castings and other art. Attractions include the Wallowa County Museum and the Chief Joseph Days Rodeo in July. Population 1980 999; 1995 1,190. Elevation 4,191'. PO Box 15, 97846. 541-432-3832; Chamber of Commerce 541-432-1015. From the Wallowas; History of Wallowa County.

Joseph Stewart State Park. A **state park** on **Lost Creek Lake** on the upper **Rogue River**. It is on **Highway 62**, 35 miles northeast of **Medford**. The park includes a marina, 6 miles of bike trails, 5.5 miles of hiking trails, and a campground with 201 campsites. Reservations, 800-452-5687. 541-560-3334.

Josephine County. A mountainous southwest Oregon county bounded on the south by California and by **Curry**, **Douglas**, and **Jackson** counties. The two incorporated cities are **Grants Pass** (county seat) and **Cave Junction**. Elevations range from 410', where the **Rogue River** leaves the county on the northwest, to 7,055' Grayback, near **Oregon Caves** in the **Siskiyou Mountains**. The economy is based on lumber, tourism, and agriculture. Taxable assessed value in 1995 was $3,332,000,000, or $47,000 per capita. The county was created in 1856 from **Jackson County** and named after Josephine Rollins (1833-?), whose father discovered **gold** in Josephine Creek and who was the first white woman to live in the county. Population 1980 58,855; 1995 71,100. Area 1,641 square miles. Density 43/ sq.mi. Annual precipitation 32"; average temperature January 40°F, July 72°F. Courthouse, NW 6th and C, Grants Pass 97526. 541-474-5100. Josephine County Historical Highlights; Oregon Blue Book; Oregon Geographic Names.

Juan de Fuca plate. See **Plate tectonics**.

Judges. Judges on the Supreme Court are called justices. A judge who retires from a **district court**, a **circuit court**, the **Tax Court**, the **Court of Appeals** or the Oregon **Supreme Court** may be designated a Senior Judge by the Supreme Court, and is then eligible for temporary assignment to any state court at or below the level in which the judge had served. About 80 are on the current roster. The

Judicial Conference, composed of all state and senior judges and chaired by the **Chief Justice**, studies the functioning of the Oregon **judicial system** and makes recommendations to the governor and the legislature. Governing Oregon; Oregon Blue Book. See also **Elected officials, judicial**; **Judicial Fitness and Disability**.

Judicial Conference. See **Judges**.

Judicial Fitness and Disability, Commission on. A nine-member commission that investigates complaints against judges and, if necessary, recommends disciplinary action to the Oregon **Supreme Court**. The Court may remove, suspend, or censure any Oregon court judge. PO Box 9035, Portland 97207. 503-222-4314. Oregon Blue Book.

Judicial system, state. Oregon's third branch of government, with the **executive** and **legislative** as the other two. In 1841, before there was any established government in Oregon, Dr. Ira Babcock was elected by the few settlers in the **Willamette Valley** as "supreme judge" to probate Ewing Young's estate. Oregonians have provided for a judicial system ever since. In 1981 the state took over the court system from the counties. Today the system includes **municipal courts**, **justice courts**, **county courts**, **circuit courts**, **Tax Court**, **Court of Appeals**, and the Oregon **Supreme Court**. The State Court Administrator assists the **Chief Justice** in exercising administrative authority and supervision over the courts of the state. Oregon Blue Book. See also **Courts, state**; **Judges**.

Jump-Off-Joe. A nearly-disappeared rock formation at the edge of the ocean at **Newport**. In the 19th century the rock was a large arch, but photographs show its erosion through the years to just a few remnant stones, and the coastline in the area has also been eroding significantly, by some two feet per year. The name is said to have been based on a tale of an Indian maiden who encouraged her lover to jump from the rock to escape her enraged kinsmen.

Junction City. A **Willamette Valley** town 12 miles north of **Eugene** in **Lane County**. It was named about 1870 for a planned junction of east and west side railroad lines, but plans for the west side line changed, so it was not until **Highways 99E** and **99W** came together there 50 years later that the name became appropriate. The city was incorporated in 1872. The economy is based on wood-products, agriculture, and RV and motor home manufacturing. The city's heritage is honored in an annual Scandinavian Festival held on the second full weekend in August. Population 1980 3,320; 1995 4,090. Elevation 322'. PO Box 250, 97448. 541-998-2153. Chamber of Commerce 541-998-6154. Oregon Geographic Names.

Juniper. A conifer **tree** with blue, berry-like cones on the female trees. Three species of juniper are native to Oregon, but only the western juniper, *Juniperus occidentalis*, is common, sparsely covering 5 million acres in Oregon. It is a small, aromatic, prickly tree of variable form that grows throughout the arid regions of eastern Oregon, able to survive on 8 inches of annual rainfall, too little for other trees. Though the slow-growing trees can live over 1,600 years, 97% of those in Oregon are less than 100 years old. During the past century they have more than tripled their range, which is of concern to land managers because a juniper tree 18" in diameter absorbs 40 gallons of water a day, drying up native plants and natural springs and exacerbating erosion. The wood has long been used for fence posts because it is said to be so tough that one post will outlast two post holes. Some of the wood is used for novelties, and efforts are being made to find other uses for it. Fire Ecology; Oregonian 6/17/96:B7, 10/8/97:F3; Trees to Know; Western Juniper. See also **Horse Ridge Natural Area**.

Junks, Japanese. See **Japanese junks**.

Juntura. A small eastern Oregon community and cottonwood oasis in **Malheur County** halfway between **Burns** and **Vale** on **Highway 20**. The name is Spanish for juncture, and was given because it was near the juncture of the North Fork and the **Malheur River**. The post office was established in 1890. In 1976 the city voted to disincorporate. Oregon Geographic names.

Jurassic. A geologic period between the **Triassic** and the **Cretaceous**, 140 to 200 million years ago. Oregon was still under water at the beginning of the period. Islands and crustal blocks from far to the southwest collided with North American near Idaho and were accreted to the North American plate in a series of complex maneuvers, creating the **Blue Mountains** and the **Klamath Mountains**. By the end of the period the northeast third of Oregon was dry land. Jurassic plant **fossils** such as cycads, conifers, and ginkgoes indicate a warm, moist climate. Geology of Oregon.

Juries. The basic provisions for state jury trials are established in the state **Constitution**. A grand jury (Art. VII Sec. 5) must have seven jurors of whom five must concur to find an indictment. The right to a jury trial is guaranteed in civil cases in which over $750 is at issue and in criminal cases (VII§3). The legislature may provide for juries of less than 12 but no fewer than 6 jurors (VII§9). In civil cases three-fourths of the jury may render a verdict (VII§5). In criminal cases, ten of the 12 jurors must agree on a guilty verdict in a felony case, except that all 12 must agree on a guilty verdict for first-degree murder (I§11). In 1996 jurors for state courts were drawn from voter registration and Driver and Motor Vehicle lists and were paid $10/day and 8 cents a mile, while federal jurors, drawn from voter registration lists, were paid $40/day and 31 cents a mile. In 1996 the median jury award in Oregon personal injury cases was $20,000, compared to $58,000 nationally, but a jury awarded a Gresham woman $1.25 million from Bristol-Myers Squibb for injuries caused by faulty breast implants, the largest award in the state to that time. Because of the provisions of the state **Constitution**, state courts may not reduce an excessive jury award. Governing Oregon; Oregonian 3/1/96:B1, 1/16/97:E2, 11/12/97:E5. See also **Plea bargaining**.

Justice Center. A building in **Portland** that houses retail shops, city, county, and federal offices, a 430-bed county jail, and the **Police Historical Museum**. The 1983 building, designed by Portland architect Robert Frasca of Zimmer Gunsul Frasca Partnership, has been praised by architects for its functionality, restrained Post-Modern Style, and the way in which it brings light into the building. 1120 SW Third Avenue. Frozen Music; Portland Guidebook.

Justice court. A court that is presided over by an elected justice of the peace. At the time of the **Oregon Territory** each precinct was entitled to a justice court. There are now 30 justice courts, located in 19 of Oregon's 36 counties. The boundaries of each justice court district are set by the **county commissioners**. Jurisdiction in criminal prosecutions is the same as for **circuit courts** except for felony trials, and justice courts have **small claims** and civil jurisdiction, with some exceptions, where money or damages do not exceed $2,500. Justices of the peace, who are not required to be attorneys, also perform free weddings at their offices during office hours. Oregon Blue Book. See also **Courts of record**.

Justice Department. An Oregon department created by the legislature in 1891 that functions as the legal firm for state government, doing all of the state's legal work. The department, with nearly 200 attorneys, is headed by the **attorney general**, and provides legal and enforcement services (at an hourly fee) to elected and appointed state officials, agencies, boards and commissions. The department also enforces child-support, investigates organized crime, provides consumer services, assists district attorneys, supervises charitable trusts, and arranges for crime-victim compensation. Justice Building, Salem 97310. 503-378-4400. Governing Oregon; Oregon Blue Book.

Justice of the peace. See **Justice court**.

Juvenile arrests. In 1995 47,357 juveniles were arrested in Oregon, up from 33,169 five years earlier. The arrest rate, which had been 46 arrests per 1,000 juveniles in 1990, jumped to 58.6 per 1,000 in 1995. In 1994 juvenile arrests accounted for 29% of all arrests in the state. Oregon: A Statistical Overview; Oregonian 1/29/97:E1. See also **Parental responsibility**.

Juvenile corrections. The Oregon **Youth Authority** operates correctional facilities for youths ages 12-21. These include MacLaren Youth Correctional Facility in **Woodburn** (300 beds), Hillcrest Youth Correctional Facility in **Salem** (200 beds), and four Youth Offender Work/Study Camps in **Corvallis**, **Florence**, **La Grande**, and **Tillamook** (100 beds total). Two new camps, a demonstration project, and five new state facilities, all made necessary by **Measure 11**, are being built. The five are at **Albany** (100 beds), **Burns** (50 beds), **Grants Pass** (100 beds), **Prineville** (50 beds), and **Warrenton** (100 beds). The facilities will cost about $100,000 per bed. In addition, a Youth Offender Accountability Camp (**boot camp**) opened in 1997 in Tillamook. The Oregon Department of **Education** provides educational services. Oregon Blue Book; Oregonian 10/11/95:B1. See also **Gangs**.

Juvenile Justice Advisory Committee. A committee made up of members of the Oregon Commission on **Children and Families** plus others appointed by the governor in order to meet federal requirements. It participates in the development of Oregon's Juvenile Justice plan, reviews grants, receives input from juveniles in the system, and consults with local governments - which receive two-thirds of the committee's federal funds. 530 Center Street NE, Suite 300, Salem 97310. 503-373-1283. Oregon Blue Book.

Kah-Nee-Ta. A high desert resort operated by the Confederated Tribes of the **Warm Springs Reservation**. It is located 10 miles north of **Highway 26** and Warm Springs. The resort includes a lodge that won architectural and construction awards when it opened in 1972, an 18-hole golf course, tennis courts, hiking trails, year-round heated pool, and other resort amenities. Kah-Nee-Ta Village, a mile away, opened in 1964, offers more casual facilities include teepees, camping, RV spaces, cottages, another pool, and food services. PO Box K, Warm Spring 97761. 800-554-4786. Oregonian 6/8/97:T1.

Kaiser's Oregon Ship Yard. See **Liberty ships**.

Kalapuya Indians. Indians who lived in the **Willamette Valley** upstream from **Willamette Falls** at the time of white contact. Since the falls blocked most salmon runs, their diet depended more on roots, especially **camas** and **wapato**, seeds, nuts, berries, and game. The Kalapuyas burned the valley floor and foothills annually, which gave the valley the park-like appearance that the first settlers commented on. Of an estimated population of 10,000 Kalapuya at the time of contact, fewer than 10% survived the diseases introduced by whites, especially the **malaria** epidemic of the 1830's. One survivor said that their ancestors had come from the sea and had killed the people then living in the area with large stone knives. Later a large stone knife similar to New Zealand Maori "slavekiller" was found embedded in an old tree. Kalapuyans. See also **Calapooya Mounds**; **Skyline circle**.

Kalmiopsis. A rare plant, *Kalmiopsis leachiana*, related to rhododendrons and mountain laurel, discovered in 1930 in **Curry County**. The plant is a low, many-branched shrub covered with deep-rose colored 1/2" flowers in May and June. It is named for Lilla Leach, the amateur botanist who discovered it. The plants are protected in the 180,000-acre Kalmiopsis Wilderness Area in the **Siskiyou National Forest**. Kalmiopsis 1991:3. See also **Leach Botanical Garden**.

Kam Wah Chung and Co. Museum. A museum in **John Day** that commemorates the history of the **Chinese** in the area. In the 1880s John Day had a community of over 500 Chinese gold miners. Lung On (1872-1940) and Ing "Doc" Hay (1862-1952) established a business, Kam Wah Chung and Company, in a building that had been constructed in 1866 as a trading post on **The Dalles Military Wagon Road**. Kam Wah Chung served as gathering place, store, temple, doctor's office, and dispensary for herbal medicines. The two stayed on in John Day long after the rest of the Chinese had gone, Lung On as the first automobile dealer in eastern Oregon and Doc Hay as physician, respected for his diagnostic skills and herbal treatments even after he became blind. China Doctor of John Day; Gold and Cattle Country; History of Grant County. See also **Chinese in Oregon**.

Kanakas. See **Hawaiians in Oregon**.

Kangaroo rats. Small, neat-looking nocturnal mammals, *Dipodomys sp.* Three species are found in the deserts of eastern Oregon . Like their namesake, they hop on their hind feet and use their long tails for balance. They live in burrows, closing the entrances while inside, and, like many desert dwellers, get all of their moisture from the food they eat. The kangaroo mouse and pocket **mice** are related. Atlas of Oregon Wildlife; Mammals and Life Zones of Oregon; Mammals of the Northwest.

Keeney Pass. A divide on the 15-mile segment of the **Oregon Trail** between Fort Boise on the **Snake River** and the **Malheur River**. While the one-day trek was not a difficult crossing, there was no water on the route and there was "an unusual allowance of dust to the mile", making the hot springs at what is now **Vale** especially welcome. Wagon ruts are still visible from a Bureau of Land Management viewpoint on the pass.

Keep Kids Alive. A campaign begun in 1995 to reduce the number of preventable deaths of children. In Oregon 787 young people aged 24 and younger died in 1994. Almost half of the deaths could have been prevented, including those

those from abuse and neglect (33), suicide (77), automobile accidents, fires, and bicycle accidents. The state Office for Services to **Children and Families** is involved. Oregonian 12/1/95:C3.

Keep Oregon Green. A program designed to reduce human-caused **forest fires**. 2750 State Street, Salem 97310-0627. 503-363-3606. See also **Smokey the Bear**.

Keiko (KAY ko.). An **orca** (killer whale) that starred in the movie, "Free Willy." The whale, ailing and underweight in its Mexico City amusement park home, was moved in early 1996 to a specially built 20-million gallon pool at the **Oregon Coast Aquarium** in **Newport**. The Earth Island Institute led the $9.2 million fund raising drive to build the rehabilitation tank, and United Parcel Service donated the flight. Keiko was originally captured near Iceland in 1979 when about two years old. Oregonian 6/14/95:B2, 3/14/96:D1.

Keizer. A suburban city in **Marion County** on the north edge of **Salem**. The post office was established in 1948 and the community incorporated in 1982. The name came from the Thomas. D. Keizer family, pioneer settlers of 1843. **Iris** growers in the area inspire the annual Iris Festival, and the city hosts the largest residential Christmas lighting display in the state. In 1997 the Volcanoes, a minor-league baseball team, began play in a new stadium. Population 1995 26,320. Elevation 135'. PO Box 21000, 97307. 503-390-3700. Oregon Geographic Names; Oregonian 11/3/97:E6.

Kelley, Hall Jackson. See **American Society for Encouraging the Settlement of the Oregon Territory**.

Kelp. Large brown **seaweed**s. One of the most common is bull kelp, an annual brown alga, *Nereocystis luetkeana*, that grows in 20 to 50 feet of water along the coasts of Washington, Oregon, and California. Oregon's richest beds are off **Curry County**, though it also grows off **Coos Bay** and **Depoe Bay**. The plant consists of a root-like structure called a holdfast, a long hollow stem topped with a gas-filled bladder, and two clumps of 10-foot blades, attached to the bladder, that float on the surface. Bull kelp over-winters as a minute plant, then grows as much at 120 feet the following year before being destroyed by winter storms and deposited in tangled heaps on the beach. **Indians** used kelp for food, the stem for fish line, and the float as a container for fish oil. Kelp is now used for food, pharmaceutical extracts, fertilizer, and shellfish food. A lease is required to harvest more than one ton a year or for commercial harvest; the Oregon Division of **State Lands** has leased some beds for experimental harvest. Great Northwest Nature Factbook. See also **Otters**.

Kennewick Man. A skeleton with Caucasoid features, carbon dated as 9,300 to 9,600 years old, found on July 28, 1996, in mud at the edge of the **Columbia River** near Kennewick, Washington. The skeleton, the oldest found in the Northwest and one of the oldest ever found in North America, became the focus of controversy between archaeologists who wished to study it and local **Indians** who believe that Ancient One was an ancestor of theirs and should be reburied immediately. Mail Tribune 8/17/97:3A.

Kentucky Falls. Three waterfalls located deep in the **Coast Range** 32 miles northeast of **Reedsport**. They include Upper Kentucky Falls with an estimated 80 foot drop, Lower Kentucky Falls which drops 50 feet to a pool where it splits into two 15-foot falls, and North Fork Smith Falls with a 60 foot drop. They can be viewed from a two-mile trail. Waterfall Lover's Guide.

Kicker. A 1979 state law that mandates the refund to taxpayers and corporations of all surplus **income taxes** when the total collected exceeds the budgeted amount by 2% or more. The legislature may vote to retain all or part of the kicker and has done so in 1991 and 1993. In 1995 the refund averaged 11.1% to individual taxpayers and 50.1% to corporations. Oregonian 3/16/97:A1.

Kidd Toy Museum. A museum of antique toys at 1300 SE Grand Ave., Portland 97214. 503-233-7807.

Kidney dialysis. In 1996 there were 1,658 kidney dialysis patients in Oregon. Oregonian 10/19/97:B10.

Kiger Gorge. See **Steens Mountain**.

Kiger mustangs. A protected herd of **wild horses** with unique markings known as "dun factor" that roams **Steens Mountain**. The herd is thought to be descended from the Spanish mustangs brought to North America in the early 1600's by the Conquistadors. They were first discovered by the **Bureau of Land Management** (BLM) on Beaty's Butte in 1977 and moved to an area near Kiger Gorge. Every few years the herd is thinned to maintain a balanced population, with the excess horses put up for adoption by the **Burns** office of the BLM. Breeders are now maintaining a Kiger mustang registry. Gazette Times 2/3/94:B4; Oregonian 8/18/97:B2.

Killer whale. See **Orca**.

Kindergarten. Oregon school districts must offer a minimum of 405 hours of kindergarten instruction (2 1/2 hours a day) during the **school year**, but attendance is not required. Some schools provide kindergarten for the full school day but require parents to pay for the additional half day. Oregonian 4/7/98:E4.

King City. An incorporated retirement community nine miles southwest of downtown **Portland** on **Highway 99W** in **Washington County,** next to the southwest corner of **Tigard**. Average age is 76, but a 30-year-old was elected mayor in 1996, resident of a recently annexed subdivision. The name is part of the development's royalty theme. The city was incorporated in 1966. Population 1980 1,853; 1995 2,170. Elevation 213'. 15300 SW 116th Ave., 97224. 503-639-4082. Oregon Geographic Names.

King salmon. See **Chinook**.

Kingdom of Heaven. See **Embassy of Heaven**.

Kings Valley. A **Benton County** valley and unincorporated community northwest of **Corvallis** on the **Luckiamute River** and Highway 223. It was settled in 1845 by Nahum King and family, survivors of the **Lost Wagon Train. Fort Hoskins** was located in the valley. Oregon Ghost Towns.

Kinzua. A one-time **company town** 10 miles east of **Fossil** in **Wheeler County**, founded in 1928 by the Kinzua Pine Mills Company. The town, which had 150 people at one time, was closed in 1978. Oregon Geographic Names; Oregonian 10/2/97:B1.

Kites. Kites have become increasingly popular in Oregon, especially along the coast where there are a number of kite shops and summer kite festivals. Associated Oregon Kiters, PO Box 25616, Portland 97225.

Kitty Cat. A cat to which John Bass of **Tangent** left his $250,000 estate when he died in 1983. After the cat's death in 1995 at age 19, the city inherited the 1916 farmhouse, barn, and the trust fund that had been used for feeding the cat and maintaining the estate. Oregonian 6/17/95:D1.

Kiwi fruit. In 1998 30 growers were raising baby kiwi, a grape-sized relative of the fuzzy Hayward kiwi, on 65 acres in the **Willamette Valley**, making Oregon the world's largest grower of baby kiwi. Oregonian 3/4/98:E2.

Klamath Basin. A 9,500 square-mile lake and marsh area in central southern Oregon and northern California. **Upper Klamath Lake** and Tule Lake are remnants of Lake Modoc, a 1,096 square-mile **Pleistocene** (ice ages) **lake**. Over 20,000 acres of potatoes are grown in the basin. The **Klamath Project** provided drainage and irrigation for much of the marsh area. The basin now includes 200,000 acres of irrigated cropland, pasture for 160,000 head of cattle, a large winter population of bald **eagles**, and 3.7 million waterfowl, many of them in the wildlife refuges. Projects are under way to turn some of the farmland back into marsh. Oregonian 11/16/97:A1.

Klamath Community College. A public two-year college that opened in 1996 with 445 students enrolled in the fall of that year. Classes are held throughout the community. 241 Williams Ave., Klamath Falls 97601-2704. 541-882-3521. See also **Community colleges; Small Business Development Centers**.

Klamath County. A southern Oregon ranching and timber county on the east slope of the **Cascade Range**, bounded by California on the south, and by **Jackson, Douglas, Lane, Deschutes**, and **Lake** counties. Incorporated cities are **Klamath Falls** (county seat), **Bonanza, Chiloquin, Malin**, and **Merrill**. Elevations range from 2,400' along the **Klamath River** where it leaves the county at the south to 9,178' **Mount Thielsen** north of **Crater Lake National Park**. Attractions include **Crater Lake** and **Upper Klamath Lake**. The economy is based on timber, agriculture, tourism, and recreation. Sykes Enterprises, a national computer support service, and Cell Tech, which bottles blue-green algae as a health supplement, are major employers. Taxable assessed value in 1995 was $2,650,000,000, or $43,000 per capita. The county was created in 1882 from **Lake County** and named for a local Indian tribe. Population 1980 59,117; 1995 61,600. Area 6,135 square miles. Density 10/sq.mi. Annual precipitation 14"; average temperature January 30°F, July 68°F. 403 Pine St., Suite 300, Klamath Falls 97601. 541-883-5100. Oregon Blue Book.

Klamath Falls. A southern Oregon city located at the south end of **Upper Klamath Lake** at the intersection of **Highways 97** and **140**. It is the county seat of **Klamath County**. The falls for which it is named were on the Link River, a two-mile-long stream connecting Upper Klamath Lake and Lake Ewauna, but have been drowned by a low dam built in 1917. The town was called Linkville when it was founded in 1867, but the name was changed to Klamath Falls in 1892. It was incorporated in 1905. The city, a regional commercial center that is diversifying beyond its traditional timber and agricultural base, is home to Aqua Glass, Sykes Enterprises (computer support), Cell Tech (algae harvesting), Jeld-Wen (windows, doors, resorts), **Oregon Institute of Technology**, and the **Winema National For-**

est headquarters. The **Klamath Falls earthquakes** in 1993 caused significant damage. The city uses **geothermal** heat from steam wells to heat buildings and to keep sidewalks in the downtown area ice free. Its sister city, Rotorua, New Zealand, is likewise located in an active geothermal zone. In addition to the lake and wildlife refuges for waterfowl and **eagles**, attractions include Klamath County Museum, Favell Museum of Western Art and Indian Artifacts, and the Baldwin Hotel Museum. Population 1980 16,661; 1995 18,680. Elevation 4,120' 500 Klamath Ave., 97601. 541-883-5316. Department of Tourism 800-445-6728. Oregon Geographic Names; Oregonian 9/2/97:B1.

Klamath Falls earthquakes. A series of moderate **earthquakes** centered about 12 miles northwest of **Klamath Falls** that began on September 21, 1993, with a magnitude 5.9 magnitude quake at 8:28 p.m. followed by another (6.0) at 10:45 p.m., and another (5.1) on December 4. The quakes caused two deaths and an estimated $7.5 million in damage. The courthouse had to be abandoned, two hotels and a former school had to be demolished, and the **Oregon Institute of Technology** library was severely damaged. "Looking Back."

Klamath Forest National Wildlife Refuge. A 37,600-acre marsh and forest refuge providing nesting and migration resting areas for waterfowl. It is located east of **Highway 97** 45 miles north of **Klamath Falls**. HC 63, Box 303, Chiloquin 97624. 541-783-3380. Oregon Wildlife Viewing Guide.

Klamath Indians. A southern Oregon tribe of Indians from around **Upper Klamath Lake**. Their traditional winter houses were earth-covered domes built over circular pits several feet deep. Foods included seeds of water lilies (**wocus**), fish, waterfowl, game, and roots and berries. Both tribal status and the **Klamath Reservation** were terminated in 1954. The government restored tribal status in 1986, and the tribe, with over 2,700 enrolled members, has focused on relearning its language and culture. Their Kla-Mo-Ya **casino** (named for the Klamath, **Modoc**, and Yahooskin band of **Northern Paiute** Indians) is scheduled to open at Chiloquin in 1998. PO Box 436, Chiloquin 97624. 800-524-9787; 541-783-2218. American Indian Reservations; First Oregonians; Klamath Tribe. See also **Abiqua Battle**.

Klamath Lake. See **Upper Klamath Lake**.

Klamath Marsh. See **Klamath Forest National Wildlife Refuge**; **Williamson River**.

Klamath Mountains physiographic province. A jumble of old (up to 450 million years), geologically complex coastal mountain ranges that extend from the **Coast Range** south into northern California. Forty percent of the province is in Oregon. **Cape Blanco** marks the northwest corner, while on the east the Klamaths meet the **Cascade Range**. The portion in Oregon is known as the **Siskiyou Mountains**. The Klamaths were formed by the sequential collision of at least seven separate **terranes** with the North American land mass; they were later intruded by **granitic** rocks. Deposits of **gold**, **silver**, **copper**, **nickel**, and **chromite** are found in the Siskiyous. Geology of Oregon.

Klamath Project. A project developed by the **Bureau of Reclamation**, beginning in 1905, to provide irrigation water for lands in the **Klamath Basin** of southern Oregon and northern California. It includes 185 miles of irrigation canals, eight diversion dams, and a 6,600-foot-long tunnel. **Gerber Reservoir**, the major Oregon component of the project, furnishes water to 17,400 acres in Langell Valley. Oregon and California ratified the Klamth Basin Compact in 1956. Atlas of Oregon Lakes.

Klamath Reservation. A one-time Indian reservation, established in 1864, that included **Klamath Indians**, their traditional enemies the **Modoc Indians** of northern California, and later the Yahooskin band of **Northern Paiute Indians**. It included 1,125,000 acres when established by treaty, but was significantly reduced when 86,418 acres were awarded to a timber company as part of a **wagon road** grant. The government terminated most of the reservation in 1954, transferring much of it to make up the new **Winema National Forest**. The Klamath Reservation presently covers 372 acres of land near **Upper Klamath Lake**. American Indian Reservations; First Oregonians; Native Peoples. See also **Modoc War**.

Klamath River. A long river that flows 180 miles from southern Oregon's **Upper Klamath Lake** through deep canyons in the **Cascade Range** and **Klamath Mountains** to reach the ocean in northern California. It is the first river south of the **Columbia** to cut through the Cascade Range. Its drainage basin area in the two states totals 11,850 square miles. **Pacific Power and Light** has power generating dams on the upper Klamath that create Iron Gate, Copco, and John Boyle reservoirs in California and Oregon, but the controversial **Salt Caves Project** dam proposed by the city of **Klamath Falls** was given up in 1994 after the federal government designated the last free-flowing section of the upper Klamath as a **National Wild and Scenic River**. It was named for the **Klamath Indians**. Oregonian 9/24/94:A1, 6/13/96:D7. See also **Lost River**.

Klickitat Indians. An **Indian** tribe from near **The Dalles** that traveled widely, especially into the central Coast Range. The name was said to mean "robber" or "marauder". Oregon Geographic Names.

KMX. The common name of a hybrid pine that is a cross between knobcone pine, *Pinus attenuata*, and Monterey pine, *P. radiata*. The trees, which have the fast growth of the Monterey pine and the frost-hardiness of the knobcone, have achieved spectacular growth rates in New Zealand and are being planted experimentally in Oregon.

Knappton Cove Heritage Center. A small private museum in the building that served from 1899 until 1938 as the Columbia River Quarantine Station. There immigrants suspected of having contagious diseases were confined until they no longer posed a threat and the ships that carried them were fumigated with burning sulfur pots. The center is off Washington 401, 3.2 miles upriver from the **Astoria** bridge; the residents of Astoria wanted the lazaretto some distance away from them. The museum is open limited hours and by appointment. 503-738-5206. Oregonian 6/15/97:B4.

Knievel. See **Evel Knievel**.

Knights of the Golden Circle. A pro-**slavery** secret society that was organized in California to promote a separate Pacific Coast Republic. It first appeared in Oregon in 1861 and was said to have 2,500 members in 10 lodges. By 1864 the group was openly militant and so well armed that the state began to arm pro-Union militia. In **Dallas** Senator Joseph Lane was hanged in effigy for his rumored support of the organization. The group faded away after the **Civil War**. Dictionary of

Oregon History; General History of Oregon; Peculiar Paradise.

Know Nothing Party. A 19th century political party that grew out of a national secret anti-**Catholic** organization called the Supreme Order of the Star-Spangled Banner. The party, officially the American Party, became popularly known as the Know-Nothing Party because its members, when questioned, would always reply "I know nothing about it". Its first Oregon "Wigwam" was established in 1854 in **Oregon City**. Its power in Oregon was significant but short-lived, in large part because a legislative measure adopted in December 1854 to counter their influence required audible voting in the legislature. "Bigot Disclosed."

Knowles, Joe. See **Nature Man**.

Kokanee. See **Sockeye**.

Koosah Falls. A broad 80-foot high waterfall on the upper **McKenzie River** a half-mile south of **Sahalie Falls**. The viewing area is west of **Highway 126**, 5.6 miles south of **Highway 20**. Koosah is the **Chinook jargon** word for sky. Waterfall Lover's Guide.

Korean Conflict, 1950-1953. An undeclared war in which the U.S. and 15 other member nations of the U.N. went to the aid of South Korea after it was invaded by communist North Korea. More that 54,000 Americans died in the "forgotten war" and 8,000 were missing. The 279 Oregonians who died in the conflict are listed on a memorial at Willamette National Cemetery in **Portland**. Oregonian 6/23/96:B1. See also **Women in the military**.

Koreans in Oregon. Between 1910 and 1924, a number of Korean women, expecting lives of ease, came to Oregon as picture brides only to find themselves doing hard labor as farmers' wives. The 1990 census counted 9,000 Koreans in Oregon. "Korean Women Pioneers of the Pacific Northwest". See also **Asians in Oregon**; **Holt International Children's Services**; **South Korea**.

Ku Klux Klan. An **anti-Catholic, anti-Semitic,** anti-Asian, anti-foreign born, and anti-**Black** organization, still extant, that appeared in Oregon in **Medford** in 1921 where its night riders terrorized the community, stringing up at least three persons but then cutting them down before they strangled. In the fall of 1922, with possibly as many as 25,000 members throughout Oregon, the Klan maneuvered the passage of a bill designed to close all private elementary schools and also saw many of its endorsed candidates elected to office. In 1924 nearly 10,000 people attended its annual convention in **Astoria**. Its powers soon declined, however, and by 1925 the Klan had disappeared from most of Oregon. The KKK was rumored to have been in Oregon much earlier, some speculating that the suspicious 1872 fire at the **Oregon City** woolen mill was set by the KKK as retaliation for the mill's employment of **Chinese**. "Bigot Disclosed"; Oregon Cattleman; Oregonian 12/7/97:B4; Peculiar Paradise; "Social Morality."

Kvinneakt. See **Expose Yourself to Art**.

La Grande. An agricultural, timber, and commercial center in the **Grande Ronde** valley 261 miles east of **Portland** on **Interstate 84**. It is the county seat of **Union County**. The town was briefly known as Browntown, but by the time the post office was established in 1863 it had become La Grande. It was incorporated in 1865. In 1884 the **Oregon Railway and Navigation Co**. rail line was completed through the area. **Eastern Oregon State College** opened in 1929. Attractions include outdoor sports, the Eastern Oregon Livestock Show in June, Union County Fair in July, and Oregon Trail Days and Blue Mountain **Rodeo** in August. Population 1980 11,354; 1995 12,370. Elevation 2,788'. PO Box 670, 97850. 541-962-1302. Chamber of Commerce 800-848-9969. History of Union County. See also **Anthony Lakes Ski Area; Blue Mountain University.**

La Pine State Park. A **state park** on the **Deschutes River** 27 miles south of **Bend** near **Highway 97**. The park includes 145 campsites (reservations, 800-452-5687) and the nation's co-champion **ponderosa pine** tree which is 342 inches in circumference (9 feet in diameter), and 178 feet tall.

La Pine. A fast-growing central Oregon community 30 miles south of **Bend**. It is the state's largest unincorporated community, with a population of 14,000 scattered through the general area. Many of the newcomers are retirees. Oregonian 6/24/96:B1.

Labish. See **Lake Labish.**

Labor and Industries, Bureau of. A bureau of state government, headed by the **Commissioner of Labor and Industries**, that is responsible for administering and enforcing state laws relating to employment (including **minors** and **minimum wage**) and **civil rights**. The Bureau has offices in **Bend, Coos Bay, Eugene, Medford, Pendleton, Portland**, and **Salem**. 800 NE Oregon Street, #32, Portland 97232. 503-731-4070. Oregon Blue Book.

Labor and Industries Commissioner. See **Commissioner of Labor and Industries**.

Labor College. See **Portland Labor College.**

Labor Day. A national holiday to honor working people, observed on the first Monday in September. The first was in New York City in 1882. In 1887 Oregon became the first to make it a state holiday. Oregon was also the first state to adopt an enforceable wage and hour law. Oregonian 9/3/95:D1.

Labor Department. See **Labor and Industries, Bureau of.**

Labor force participation. In 1990 Oregon's labor force participation rate for those 16 and over was 64.4%. Of the women in the labor force, 27.8% had children younger than 6, and another 40.7% had children 6-17 years. Oregon: A Statistical Overview.

Labor organizations. In 1996 the largest labor organization in Oregon was the Oregon AFL-CIO with 88,000 members, followed by the **Oregon Education Association** with 39,000 members, International Brotherhood of Teamsters with 29,000, United Brotherhood of Carpenters with 22,000, Oregon Public Employees Union with 18,000, and the American Federation of State, County and Municipal Workers with 16,000. Northwest Treeplanters and Farmworkers United (Pineros y Campesinos Unidos del Noroeste) has attempted to organize Oregon strawberry pickers, but the migrant nature of much of the work force makes organizing farm workers difficult. Oregon Business 2/96:57; Oregonian 2/25/96:A18. See also **Strikes**.

Labor organizations - history. The Typographical Society, organized in 1853, was the first labor organization in Oregon. The American Federation of Labor (AFL) appeared in **Portland** in 1887. Both the AFL and the Industrial Workers of the World (**Wobblies**) attempted, with marginal success, to organize the lumber industry between 1905 and 1917. A more successful strike in 1935 led to union recognition, but violence erupted in Portland over the next few years as the CIO and the AFL struggled for jurisdiction. The waterfronts were also the scene of labor unrest, especially between 1934 and 1941. In 1919 nearly 20,000 members of Oregon trade unions marched in **Portland** demanding withdrawal of U.S. troops from Russia and joint ownership of **railroads** by employees, operators, and the federal government. Empire of the Columbia; That Balance So Rare; This Day in Oregon.

Ladd's Addition. A neighborhood in southeast **Portland** between Hawthorne and Division, 12th and 20th. It was designed in 1891 as "a residential community for cultured people" by William Ladd, Portland's fifth mayor, and is notable for its diagonal streets and mature American elm trees. Oregonian 3/12/95:H1. See **Portland neighborhoods**.

Ladybug Theater. See **Children's theater**.

Lafayette. A historic north **Willamette Valley** town in **Yamhill County** on **Highway 99W**, five miles northeast of **McMinnville**. It was founded in 1846 by Joel Perkins who named it for Lafayette, Indiana. The city was incorporated in 1878 and was the county seat until 1889. The 1910 schoolhouse is now a mall housing more than 100 antique dealers. Population 1980 1,215 ; 1995 1,445. Elevation 160'. PO Box 55, 97127. 503-864-2451. Old Yamhill.

LaGrande. See **La Grande**.

Lake Abert. A large, 13-mile-long, shallow alkaline lake of 36,538 acres, lying at the base of **Abert Rim** 25 miles north of **Lakeview**. It and **Summer Lake** are the remnants of a large **Pleistocene lake**, **Lake Chewaucan**, that was over 350 feet deep. Lake Abert now has a maximum depth of 11 feet; in 1924 it was entirely dry. The lake is the most alkaline year-round lake in Oregon at 11,515 mg/l. **Summer Lake** is 2,649 mg/l, and **Harney Lake** 1,101 mg/l. There are no fish in the lake, but many water and shore birds feed on the brine shrimp which are also harvested commercially. The only recreational use of the lake is for bird watching. Archeologists have found evidence of human settlement, which was at times intense, back 11,000 years. Captain John C. Fremont named the lake for his chief, Colonel J. J. Abert of the U.S. Topographical Engineers in 1843; earlier explorers had called it Salt Lake. Archaeology of Oregon; Atlas of Oregon Lakes; Oregon Wildlife 49(2):8, fall 1993.

Lake Billy Chinook. A deep, three-armed Central Oregon reservoir of 3,916 acres six miles west of **Madras** at the confluence of the **Metolius, Deschutes**, and **Crooked** rivers. The lake was formed by 440-foot high Round Butte Dam, built by **Portland General Electric** for power generation in 1964. Metolius Arm, the longest, is ten miles long; maximum depth of the lake is 415 feet. The lake receives heavy recreational use; **Cove Palisades State Park** is located on the Crooked River arm. The lake was named for a **Wasco Indian** who traveled to Washington D.C. with Captain John Fremont in 1844 and was later a chief at Warm Springs. The Confederated Tribes of the **Warm Springs Reservation** applied in 1997 for the license, up for renewal in 2001, to operate the dam. Atlas of Oregon Lakes. See also **The Island**.

Lake Celilo. See **The Dalles Dam**.

Lake County. A large ranching and timber county in south-central Oregon bounded by California on the south, and by **Klamath, Deschutes,** and **Harney** counties. Incorporated cities are **Lakeview** (county seat) and **Paisley**. Elevations range from 4,147' at **Summer Lake** to 8,364-foot **Gearhart Mountain**. Most of the county has no outlet to the sea, so a number of the lakes from which it gets its name become alkaline as they evaporate. The economy is based on livestock, lumber, agriculture, recreation, and mining. Taxable assessed value in 1995 was $324,000,000, or $43,000 per capita. The county was created in 1874 from **Jackson County**. Many Irish sheepmen settled in the county. Population 1980 7,532; 1995 7,550. Area 8,359 square miles. Density 1/sq.mi. Annual precipitation 16"; average temperature January 28°F, July 67°F. Courthouse, 513 Center, Lakeview 97630. 541-947-6003. <u>Oregon Blue Book</u>; <u>William "Bill" W. Brown</u>. See also **Bernard Daly Educational Fund**.

Lake Flatulence. A name proposed after 'boiling' was noticed in an area of **Tahkenitch Lake** in 1972. Speculations as to the possible cause included a geothermal geyser or a Loch Ness-type monster in rut, but it was determined that it was most likely from an old barrel of carbide that had fallen from a train years before. Leaking carbide would react with water to produce acetylene gas. The proposal to rename the lake was rejected. <u>Atlas of Oregon Lakes</u>.

Lake Labish. A dry lakebed north of **Salem**, formerly a channel of the **Willamette River** that was cut off by a sand bar sometime in the last 2 million years and became a 10-mile-long lake. The lake gradually filled with silt and debris and a long period as a bog resulted in thick peat deposits. Bones of **Pleistocene** mammals such as mammoth, mastodon, giant sloth, and bison have been found in the peat. The area has been drained by the **Lake Labish Ditch**, and today the fertile soils grow **onions** and other crops. The area was named *la biche*, meaning elk, by French Canadians. In 1890 a train plunged through the Lake Labish trestle, killing five and injuring many. <u>Geology of Oregon</u>; <u>Oregon Geographic Names</u>.

Lake Labish Ditch. A ditch north of **Salem** dug by farmers early in the 20th century to drain **Lake Labish** bottomlands. The ditch, fed by springs, flows in two directions from its high point, west toward the **Willamette River** and east toward the Little **Pudding River**. It unexpectedly flooded new developments along its banks in 1996 and again in 1997. <u>Oregonian</u> 1/11/97:B1.

Lake of the Woods. A natural mountain lake 25 miles northwest of **Klamath Falls**. The lake is three miles long and covers 1,146 acres to a maximum depth of 55 feet. Most of the water supply into the lake is from seepage, and most of the water loss is due to evaporation, though there is occasional overflow down Seldom Creek. Summer homes, organization camps, campgrounds, and a fishing resort all testify to its popularity for swimming, boating, and fishing, and ice fishing is increasingly popular. <u>Atlas of Oregon Lakes</u>.

Lake Oswego (lake). See **Oswego Lake**.

Lake Oswego. An affluent Portland-area suburban city surrounding a lake of the same name in **Clackamas County**, eight miles south of downtown **Portland**. The community was originally named Oswego for his home town in New York state by A. A. Durham, an 1847 pioneer. The post office was established in

1853. The first **iron** produced west of the Rocky Mountains was smelted at Oswego in 1867 from locally mined ore; in 1909 a Portland **cement** plant began operations, and the city was incorporated the following year. In 1960 Oswego and Lake Grove (at the west end of the lake) voted to merge as Lake Oswego. Its sister city is Mordialloc, Australia. Population 1980 22,527; 1995 33,145. Elevation 100'. PO Box 369, 97034. 503-635-0270. Oregonian 9/21/97:H1; Oregon's Iron Dream.

Lake Owyhee. An eastern Oregon reservoir, the largest reservoir in the state, located in the barren, rugged canyons southwest of **Nyssa** in **Malheur County**. It was formed by a 417-foot-high concrete dam on the **Owyhee River**, completed in 1932 to provide irrigation water for the **Owyhee Project**, and is operated by the Owyhee Project North Board of Control. Water is released from the lake through a 3.5-mile tunnel. The lake is 52 miles long and covers 13,900 acres to a maximum depth of 117 feet. Although access is limited, the lake is popular for warm water fishing, boating, and water skiing. A state park near the north end has camping facilities. Atlas of Oregon Lakes.

Lake Simtustus. A long narrow reservoir on the **Deschutes River**, formed when **Portland General Electric** completed 205-foot **Pelton Dam** in 1958. The 637-acre lake, seven miles northwest of **Madras**, is eight miles long and 155 feet deep. A marina and campground are located near the dam. The lake is on the reservation of the Confederated Tribes of **Warm Springs** and a license to fish must be obtained from them. Simtustus was a Warm Springs Indian warrior and scout who died in 1926. Atlas of Oregon Lakes.

Lake Umatilla. See **John Day Dam**.

Lake Wallula. See **McNary Dam**.

Lakeport. A one-time town on the south Oregon coast that was briefly the largest in **Curry Country**. It was promoted in 1908 as the site of a new ocean port to be created by digging a 750' canal through the sand dunes to connect **Floras Lake** and the ocean. Six thousand lots were sold, a steam sawmill, three-story hotel, and a number of homes were built, and the town grew to 400 people before it was discovered that the lake was 9 feet higher than the ocean and would empty as soon as a canal was opened. By 1915 the town was abandoned. Lakeport; Port Orford.

Lakes. Oregon has nearly 6,000 lakes, reservoirs, and ponds. Over 1,400 are named, ranging in size from less than an acre to **Goose Lake**'s 97,000 acres. There are ten Fish Lakes, ten Clear Lakes, eleven Blue Lakes, and thirteen Lost Lakes. While lakes now cover less than 1% of the state, during the **Pleistocene** (Ice Ages), vast areas of south central Oregon were covered by large freshwater lakes. A few remnant lakes survive there, but more than half of Oregon's lakes lie in the **Cascade Range**, 100 are in the **Wallowa Mountains**, others fill depressions in the sand dunes along the coast, some are landlocked alkaline lakes of the southeast Oregon desert, and more than 60 are major manmade reservoirs. **Crater Lake** is the deepest lake in the United States (1,932 feet) and contains 14 million **acre-feet** of water. Crater Lake is also the clearest lake in the state; a Secchi disk can be seen at a depth of 142 feet. A number of other high mountain lakes have clarity readings of over 50 feet. Oregon's highest lake is in the crater of **South Sister** just below its 10,354 foot summit. Each lake is unique in its combination of type, physical characteristics, water qualities, and aquatic life. All Oregon lakes that cover more than 1,000 acres, plus a number of others, are described individually in this work Atlas of Oregon Lakes; Geology of Oregon. See also **Pleistocene lakes**.

Lakes, largest. The largest lake rising in Oregon usually is 97,000-acre **Goose Lake** - except that sometimes it is dry. It is an alkaline lake that straddles the California border; one third is in Oregon. The state's largest freshwater lake is normally **Upper Klamath Lake**, with a total surface area of 70,000 acres, but **Malheur Lake** sometimes surpasses it. In 1984 Malheur Lake swelled to cover 175,000 acres, though its normal size is closer to 50,000 acres, and sometimes it is nearly dry.

Lakeside. A western Oregon town in **Coos County** located between **Tenmile** and **North Tenmile Lakes**. A county boat launch in the town provides the only public access to the lakes. During the 1930s and '40s a resort called Currier's Village attracted the notables of Hollywood. The city was incorporated in 1974. Population 1980 1,453; 1995 1,630. Elevation 28'. 915 North Lake Road, 97459. 541-759-3011. "Starry Nights."

Lakeview. "The Tallest Town in Oregon." A high desert timber and cattle town that is also becoming known as the **hang gliding** capital of the west. It is located at the base of the **Warner Mountains** in south-central Oregon, at the junction of **Highways 140** and **395.** It is the county seat of **Lake County** and headquarters for the **Fremont National Forest**. Lakeview was founded in 1876 because local ranchers wanted a county seat closer than Linkville (later **Klamath Falls**). At the time it was named, **Goose Lake** was larger and could be seen from town. The city was incorporated in 1889. On May 22, 1900, a fire destroyed all but two businesses, but the town quickly rebuilt. Attractions include a hang gliding fly-in around the 4th of July, the Lake County Fair and Round Up on Labor Day weekend, Schminck Memorial Museum, a large Indian artifact collection at Indian Village Restaurant, and outdoor recreation in the **Fremont National Forest**. Oregon's only **geyser** is north of town at Hunters Hot Springs. Population 1980 2,770; 1995 2,645. Elevation 4,800'. 525 N 1st St., 97630. 541-947-2029. Chamber of Commerce 541-947-6040. Oregon Geographic Names.

Lakeview District, BLM. A 3,388,067-acre district of **Bureau of Land Management** grazing and forest lands, primarily in **Lake** and **Klamath** counties. 1000 Ninth Street S., P.O. Box 151, Lakeview 97630-0055. 541-947-2177. BLM Facts.

Lamb's Marketplace. See **Bell tower**.

Lambert Gardens. A 30-acre private garden that was among Portland's top tourist attractions for nearly 40 years until it closed in 1968. It was located at SE 28th and Steele. Round the Roses.

Lamprey. A primitive, eel-like **anadromous fish**, *Lampetra tridentata*. Oregon has no true eels. Unlike an eel, a lamprey has no jaws but attaches to an ocean fish with its round mouth and sucks blood and fluids from it. However, lampreys are not parasitic in fresh water. There they spawn and the young spend five or six years burrowed into the mud as filter feeders before maturing and migrating to the ocean. After several years in the ocean, they return in late spring and spend a year fasting in fresh water before spawning. Though lamprey were a rich and important food source for Indians, in the last 30 years their numbers have been plummeting to 2% or fewer returning fish, except in the **Willamette River**. In the 1990s, 9,000 to 30,000 pounds have been caught annually at **Willamette Falls**. Oregonian 5/4/97:A1, 7/19/97:A1. Oregon's Migratory Fish.

Land area. See **Size**.

Land Board. See **State Land Board**.

Land Conservation and Development Commission (LCDC). A policy making commission of seven members appointed by the governor for four year terms. The commission oversees **land use planning** in Oregon and appoints the head of the Department of Land Conservation and Development (DLCD), which administers the laws. Disputes are adjudicated by the **Land Use Board of Appeals**. 1175 Court St. NE, Salem 97310. 503-373-0050. Land Use Planning in Oregon; Oregon Blue Book; Planning the Oregon Way.

Land description. All land in Oregon is described with reference to the **Willamette Stone**. A description that reads Sec.1,T6S,R3W (read as section 1, township 6 south, range 3 west) refers to the square-mile **section** lying in the northeast corner of the sixth **township** south of the Willamette Stone and in the third range of townships west of the Willamette Stone. See also **Acre**; **Land surveys**; **Public Land survey**.

Land fraud. In the last half of the 19th century entire **sections** of **Common School Fund** lands and other **public domain** lands passed into private ownership fraudulently. George L. Woods (1832-1890), governor 1866-1870, enabled **The Dalles Military Wagon Road** to obtain 500,000 acres of prime land in the **John Day** valley by certifying that the road had been completed when it was actually an unimproved oxcart trail. William Thayer, governor, 1878-1882, Oregon Supreme Court justice, 1884-1890, and chief justice the last two years, participated in illegal land claims for 100,000 acres of land and assisted in others totaling over a million acres. Extensive tracts of Oregon timberland were obtained by large midwestern timber companies between 1901 and 1904 using a system of dummy entries under the **Homestead Act of 1862** and the **Timber and Stone Act of 1878**. Prosecution resulted in 33 convictions, including Oregon's U.S. Senator, John Mitchell (1835-1905), who died in office while his conviction was under appeal. Dictionary of Oregon History; Disposition; Empire of the Columbia; Looters of the Public Domain. See also **Corruption**; **Holdup Session**; **Military wagon roads**; **Swamp lands**; **Venal officials**.

Land grants. The title to lands in Oregon originally rested with the federal government which, through the years, granted 29 million acres to the state, tribes, corporations, and individuals in order to encourage various public benefits. Lands granted to the state of Oregon on its **admission** as a state, primarily for the support of education, totaled 4,309,435 acres (6.9% of the state). Large acreages were granted to corporations as incentive for building **railroads** (3,728,000 acres to **Oregon and California** though 2,890,000 acres were revested, and 264,520 acres to **Northern Pacific**) and **military wagon roads** (2,490,000 acres granted but 93,000 revested). Land grants to individuals were authorized by the **Donation Land Act**

of 1850 (about 2,000,000 acres);   **Homestead Act of 1862** (11,097,982 acres), **Timber Culture Act of 1873**, **Desert Land Act of 1877** (250,111 acres), **Timber and Stone Act of 1878** (3,812,303 acres),   **Carey Act of 1894**, and **mining law**. Some of the acts allowed for sale of federal land for cash, and about 6.5 million acres in Oregon were sold.   Disposition.   See also **Land fraud; Land grants, educational; Land ownership; O&C lands; Swamp lands; Tide lands**.

Land grants, educational.   Oregon has received federal **land grants** of 4,035,000 acres for education.   Congress granted Oregon section 16 and 36 in every township (two square miles out of every 36, totaling 3,399,360 **acres**) when it became a territory in 1848, (reaffirmed in the **Admission Act**); proceeds from the sale of the lands were to fund public schools and went into the **Common School Fund**.   The state also received 500,000 acres, selected primarily in **Baker**, **Union**, and **Umatilla** counties, for internal improvements under an 1841 act.   Under the Morrill Act of 1862 Oregon received 90,000 acres of **public domain** land with the proceeds from sale of the lands to be used for a college to teach agriculture, mechanical arts, and military instruction; the forerunner of **Oregon State University** became Oregon's land-grant institution.   Congress had also granted Oregon a **township** of land (23,040 acres) for a university in the act creating the **Oregon Territory** and 72 **sections** (46,080 acres) in the **Admission Act** when Oregon became a state in 1859.   Money from the sale of these lands helped found the **University of Oregon** in 1872.   Dictionary of Oregon History; Disposition; History of Oregon Land Grants.

Land office.   A local office of the **General Land Office (GLO)** where public **survey** records and claims for **public domain** land were filed.   The first in Oregon was established at **Oregon City** in 1851.   Five additional offices were later established throughout the state, though some of the offices were moved at least once. All surveys and records were transferred to the **Bureau of Land Management** in 1946.   The state of Oregon also had land offices since the federal government had given it large grants of land to dispose of.   Dictionary of Oregon History. See also **Land grants**.

Land ownership.   In 1992, 52% (32.24 million acres) of Oregon's total of 62 million acres was federally owned, 7% was owned by state and local governments and Indian tribes, and 41.2% (25.3 million acres) of the state was in private ownership. 78% of **Curry County** is publicly owned, the highest proportion in the state. More than 6 million acres of federally owned land in Oregon depends on access routes over private lands.   At the end of 1995 about 1% of the state (644,000 acres) of farm and forest land) was foreign-owned.   Oregon: A Statistical Overview.   See also **Land use; Public domain**.

Land ownership history.   **Indian** claims to the lands of the **Oregon Country** were not taken seriously by the first settlers or by the government.   A number of treaties that assigned specific lands to the Indians were signed in good faith by the Indians but were never signed by the government and other treaties were not honored. Settlers were, however, concerned about protecting their claims against other settlers since there was no government.   The first settlers, former **French Canadian** fur trappers, already had questions in 1833 about how secure their farms were, especially if the area became American.   By 1842 all settlers were worried as the prospect of floods of immigrants loomed along with the possibility that the U.S. would claim the area as **public domain** and open all of it for settlement without regard to existing claims. In 1843, the **provisional government**, as one of its first acts, adopted procedures for recording claims for 640 acres of land. Still, new settlers resented those who had arrived before 1844 and had claimed the choice sites, and claim jumping became a threat. The **Donation Land Act of 1850** finally provided a means for legalizing existing land claims. Empire of the Columbia. See also **Land grants**; **Tidelands**.

Land sailing. A recent sport that is practiced in Oregon on the dry lake bed in **Alvord Basin.**

Land surveys. Local land survey records are kept in the office of the County Surveyor. The **Bureau of Land Management**, successor to the federal **General Land Office**, is the agency authorized by Congress to determine the boundaries of public lands. See also **Engineering Examiners**; **Land description**; **Public Land Survey**.

Land trusts. Organizations that work to preserve open space, wetlands, family lands by buying land, accepting donated parcels, and accepting conservation easements. In 1998 there were nine in Oregon: Deschutes Basin Land Trust in **Bend** 541-330-0017; Greenbelt Land Trust in **Corvallis** 541-752-9609; McKenzie River Trust in **Eugene** 541-345-2799; Nature Conservancy in **Portland** 503-230-1221; North Coast Land Conservancy in **Astoria** 503-325-4059; Southern Oregon Land Conservancy in **Ashland** 541-535-7750; Three River Land Conservancy in **Lake Oswego** 503-699-9825; Trust for Public Land in **Portland** 503-228-6620; and Wetlands Conservancy in **Tualatin** 503-691-1394. Oregonian 3/16/98:B1.

Land use. Oregon has 62,120,000 **acres** of land area. In 1987, 4.3 million acres of the total land area was crop land, 1.8 million was irrigated land, 1.9 million acres was pasture, 22.3 million acres was **rangeland**; 30.6 million acres was **forest land**, .2 million acres was in **National Parks**, and .9 million was developed for urban and transportation uses. 47% of the total, or 28.9 million acres, was in non-federal ownership. As of 1992, 10.6 million acres of private land was zoned for agriculture, 8.4 million was in forest zoning, and 6.3 million acres was in other zoning. (Figures don't always add up because of differences in definitions and data-gathering methods.) Atlas of the Pacific Northwest; Oregon: A Statistical Overview; Oregon's Soil. See also **Farm land**.

Land Use Board of Appeals (LUBA). A three-member state tribunal created in 1979 to simplify and expedite the land-use appeals process and to provide consistent interpretation of state and local land-use laws, the first in the nation. LUBA doesn't review the merits of a case but bases its findings on whether the law and proper procedures were followed. Its decisions can be appealed to the state **Court of Appeals**. The three referees must be members of the Oregon State Bar. They are appointed by the governor for four-year terms. 306 State Library Bldg, 250 Winter St. NE, Salem 97310. 503-373-1265. Oregon Blue Book; Oregonian 10/5/97:B2.

Land use planning. Oregon, prompted by a desire to protect agricultural and forest land from urban sprawl and leap-frog development, has one of the most extensive programs for land use planning in the nation. Senate Bill 10 in 1969 and

Senate Bill 100 in 1973 required all of the state's cities and counties to adopt comprehensive plans consistent with 19 state-wide **planning goals** developed by the **Land Conservation and Development Commission**. Voters rejected attempts to weaken or repeal land use laws in 1976, 1978, and 1982. In perhaps the earliest planning effort in the state, **Portland**, in 1911-1912, retained Edward Bennett to draw up plans for development of the city with much of the concern centered on parks. Empire of the Columbia; Land-Use Planning in Oregon; Planning the Oregon Way. See also **1000 Friends; Urban Growth Boundaries**.

    Landfills. In 1996 Oregon had 91 landfills and 77 transfer stations operating under Department of **Environmental Quality** permits. **Portland** area garbage is hauled 140 miles to the huge **Columbia Ridge Landfill** and a nearby **hazardous waste** site, both near **Arlington**. Oregon also has 102 industrial landfills, most used to dispose of wood wastes from log decks. The first demonstration sanitary landfills were at **Milton-Freewater** and **Eugene** in 1950. A 1969 survey found that 231 Oregon communities still had community dumps and there were another 628 unclaimed dumps. Most were unattended, open-burning dumps that were leaching wastes into ground and surface waters. The state promotes the use of lined landfills managed to minimize air and water pollution. Experiences; Oregon Environmental Atlas; Solid Waste. See also **Bottle bill; Methane; Recycling; Saint Johns landfill; Solid waste**.

    Landforms. See **Geography**.

    Lands, State. See **State Lands, Division of**.

    Landscape Architect Board. A five-member board that registers landscape architects. There are about 245 in Oregon. 750 Front St. NE, Suite 260, Salem 97310. 503-378-4270. Oregon Blue Book.

    Landscape Contractors Board. A board of seven members appointed by the governor for three-year terms that licenses landscape businesses and landscape contractors and investigates complaints. Approximately 1040 landscape contractors and 780 landscaping businesses are licensed in Oregon. 700 Summer St. NE, Suite 300, PO Box 14140, Salem 97309-5052. 503-378-4621. Oregon Blue Book.

    Landslides. In western Oregon, landslides are common due to steep slopes, the character of the rocks and soils, and heavy rains. Damage from slides and stream bank erosion during the **flood of 1996**, thought to represent about 1% of the landslide potential in the state, totaled $100 million. A slide near the **Umpqua River** in November 1996 killed a woman driver, and another slide 12 miles NW of **Roseburg** destroyed a home and killed four persons. A triple-trailer dropped into a one a.m. washout of **Interstate 5** at Roseburg on November 21, 1996. Earlier landslides created lakes, such as **Triangle Lake,** in the **Coast Range**. Other old slides can be recognized by hummocky surfaces, tilted trees, small ponds, and swampy depressions. One of the largest is the mile-long Hooskanaden slide 18 miles south of **Gold Beach** that continues to drop **Highway 101** toward the ocean, and in 1996, a $4.5 million drainage system was installed at the Arizona Inn slide 14 miles north of Gold Beach. A coastal slide at **Newport** in 1942-43 took out 15 houses, and in 1961, 125 acres slid into the ocean at **Ecola State Park**. A 30-acre area in **Portland**'s **Washington Park** has been sliding for 100 years, though drainage channels have helped slow its movement. In the **Columbia River Gorge**, the

Dodson/Warrendale area is on a shelf built up from thousands of years of major slides, the most recent in 1918 and 1996. 700 years ago the massive **Cascade landslide** blocked the **Columbia River**. Geology of Oregon; Oregonian 10/19/95: B8, 2/21/96:A1, 8/20/96:A1, 8/24/96:D6, 10/7/96:C1. See also **Canyonville Slide**; **Storms**; **The Capes**; **Winter Ridge**.

Lane Community College. A public two-year college founded in 1965 that had a fall 1996 enrollment of 16,489. It offers training in 50 vocational-technical areas plus lower division transfer courses and skill upgrading for those already employed. Recently it has placed a new emphasis on training displaced workers. The college has placed among the top five community colleges in the nation for excellence of instructional programs. 4000 E 30th Ave., Eugene OR 97405-0640. 541-747-4501. Oregon Blue Book. See also **Community colleges**; **Small Business Development Centers**.

Lane County. A varied county in western Oregon that extends from the ocean over the **Coast Range**, across the **Willamette Valley**, and up to the crest of the **Cascade Range**. It includes the drainages of the Siuslaw River and the upper **Willamette River**. Incorporated cities are **Eugene** (county seat), **Coburg**, **Cottage Grove**, **Creswell**, **Dunes City**, **Florence**, **Junction City**, **Lowell**, **Oakridge**, **Springfield**, **Veneta**, and **Westfir**. The county is bounded by the ocean on the west and by **Lincoln**, **Benton**, **Linn**, **Deschutes**, **Klamath**, and **Douglas** counties. Elevations range from sea level to 10,358' at **South Sister**. The economy is based on agriculture, education, fishing, food processing, logging and wood products, recreation, and tourism. Taxable assessed value in 1995 was $14,560,000,000, or $48,000 per capita. The area was first settled by whites in 1846 when Elijah Bristow (1788-1872) staked a claim at Pleasant Hill and Eugene Skinner (1809-1864) at Eugene. The county was created in 1851 and named for Joseph Lane (1801-1881), who had been the first governor of the **Oregon Territory** and was Oregon's delegate to Congress at the time. Population 1980 275,226; 1995 301,900. Area 4,620 square miles. Density 65/sq.mi. Annual precipitation 46"; average temperature January $40\,^\circ$F, July $67\,^\circ$F. Courthouse, 125 E 8th, Eugene 97401. 541-682-4203. Lane County; Oregon Blue Book.

Languages. In 1990 92.7% of Oregonians spoke only English, 2.3% were Spanish speakers who spoke English very well, and 0.8% (21,312) spoke only Spanish. Oregonian 11/28/94:B1. See also **Chinook jargon**; **English only**; **Indian languages**.

Lapine. See **La Pine**.

Lapwai Mission. A **mission** to the **Nez Perce**, established in 1836 on the Clearwater River above what is now Lewiston, Idaho. The missionaries, the Rev. and Mrs. Henry Spalding, established a home, church, school, flour mill, sawmill, blacksmith shop, and printing press, the first in the Northwest. The mission was closed for some years following the 1847 **Whitman massacre**. Dictionary of Oregon History.

L'Arbre Seul. See **Lone Pine**.

Larch. A deciduous conifer **tree**, *Larix occidentalis*, that turns yellow in the fall before dropping its clumps of needles. It grows at mid elevations in the northern **Cascade Mountains** and in northeastern Oregon. Its decay-resistant wood is used for posts and poles, and its lumber is valuable for construction and finish work. The Oregon species is more properly called Western larch. Larch in the east is sometimes called tamarack. Trees to Know.

Larch Mountain. A 4,058' peak in eastern **Multnomah County**, accessible by a paved road, that is a favorite destination for outings from the **Portland** area. The mountain was created by an outpouring of **Boring lavas**. Despite the name there are probably no **larch** trees on the mountain. Oregon Geographic Names.

Largest lakes. See **Lakes, largest**.

Latinos. See **Hispanics**.

Latitude and longitude. From south to north, Oregon extends over four degrees of latitude, from latitude 42°N (±15" due to surveying errors) at the California border to 46°14'14"N at the edge of **Columbia River**, about 15 miles upstream from **Astoria**. Oregon's portion of the Columbia, including some islands and sand bars, extends a bit farther north. Each degree of latitude equals approximately 69 miles north/south. Oregon's mid-latitude location means that it has distinct seasonal variations in **day-length**, amount of sun, and **climate**. East/west, Oregon extends over eight degrees of longitude, from -116°27'43"W at China Bar in **Hells Canyon** to -124°33'46"W at **Cape Blanco**. Each degree of longitude equals approximately 51.4 miles east/west on the 42nd parallel (the California border), and 48.9 miles east/west on the **45th parallel** just north of **Salem**. Since the earth revolves 15° an hour, it takes 32 minutes for the sun to move across the state, so high noon in **Ontario** is about half an hour before high noon in **Coos Bay**. See also **Boundaries**; **Day Length**; **Geographic center**; **Geographic Information Systems**; **Size**.

Latourell Falls. An easily viewed, 249-foot waterfall in the **Columbia River Gorge**. It is located in Guy W. Talbot State Park 3.4 miles west of exit 28 from **Interstate 84**, and is the closest to **Portland** of the major gorge falls. Upper Latourell Falls, 75 feet high, is a mile up the trail beyond the main falls. Joseph Latourell was an early settler in the area. Tracking down Oregon; Waterfall Lover's Guide.

Latter-day Saints. See **Religion**.

Lava. Molten rock that is extruded upon the earth's surface in a **volcanic eruption**. Lavas range from fluid, low-silica **basalt** (less than 54% silica) through **andesite** (54-62% silica), silicic lava (62-64% silica), dacite (64-72% silica), to pasty **rhyolite** (72% or more silica). The more pasty a lava is, the more explosive it becomes if gas is incorporated in it. Lava flows are found throughout most of Oregon; the most recent is the 400 year old flow from Collier Cone at **McKenzie Pass**. Geology of Oregon. See also **Lunar training**.

Lava Butte. A 500' cinder cone 10 miles south of Bend on **Highway 97**. Formed some 6,000 years ago, it is among the most recent of a series of cinder cones and lava flows that have erupted along a fissure that extends about 20 miles from **Newberry Volcano** on the western end of the **Brothers fault zone**. **Lava Lands Visitor Center** is at the base, and a small observatory is perched on the edge of the crater at the top.

Lava Cast Forest. An area nine miles east of **Sunriver** where molten lava surrounded and burned live trees, leaving holes in the lava where the trees had been. There are trails through the area, which is part of **Newberry National Vol-**

canic Monument.

Lava caves. See **Lava tubes**.

Lava Lands Visitors Center. A visitor center for **Newberry National Volcanic Monument** located at the base of **Lava Butte,** 11 miles south of **Bend**. 58201 S. Highway 97, Bend 97707. 541-593-2421.

Lava River Cave. A **lava tube** in Oregon just east of **Highway 97** twelve miles south of **Bend** that has been developed for visitors by the U.S. Forest Service. The cave extends for over a mile, crossing under Highway 97. It is included in **Newberry National Volcanic Monument**. Central Oregon Caves.

Lava tube. A cave formed in a basalt lava flow when a thick crust forms over the river of molten lava and the lava drains out from under it, leaving a hollow tube behind. Many lava tube **caves** are found south of **Bend** on the broad flanks of **Newberry Volcano**, and there are a number elsewhere in the **Cascade Range** and in southeastern Oregon, including **Malheur Cave** and one of the longest, Saddle Butte Lava Tube Caves, which can be traced for 8 1/2 miles through the Saddle Butte lava field in **Malheur County**. The Saddle Butte Caves are, however, especially hazardous, both inside and on top, because of collapsing roof portions. Lava tubes were used for shelter by Indians and early settlers, and have also been used as cattle corrals, to hide stills during **Prohibition**, and, because most have a constant, cool temperature, for cold storage and for summer outings. Those in which ice persists all year are called **ice caves**. **Lava River Cave** has visitor facilities. Central Oregon Caves. See also **Arnold Ice Cave**; **Lost Crystal Cave**.

Law. Under the Oregon **constitution**, a new act (a **bill** that has become law) goes into effect on the 91st day after adjournment of a legislative session unless some other provision has been inserted into the law or it has an emergency clause. Emergency clauses are not allowed on revenue bills. The laws adopted during a session of the legislature are compiled chronologically into bound volumes called Oregon Laws. Once an act has been codified (incorporated into the subject arrangement of laws called the **Oregon Revised Statutes**), it is called a statute. Governing Oregon; Oregon Legislative Guide. See also **Ordinance**.

Law enforcement. In 1996 there were 7,195 full-time law enforcement employees in Oregon, 5,290 of them officers and 1,905 support staff. 450 of the officers were women. They were employed by the Oregon State **Police** (1,083 employees in 1996), county sheriffs (1,698 employees), city police (4,360 employees), and the Oregon **Liquor Control Commission** (54 employees). The total was up from 5,681 employees in 1987. In 1996 there were 565 assaults on law officers. There were no fatalities that year, but 15 Oregon State Police officers have been killed over the years, and as of February 1998, 25 Portland police officers have been killed in the line of duty. Oregonian 8/5/97:B1; Report of Criminal Offenses. See also **Crimes**; **Women in law enforcement**.

Law libraries. Libraries designed to support the legal research needs of attorneys. In addition to private law libraries, most counties have law libraries, as do law schools and other colleges. The **Supreme Court Library** serves the state courts. Most law libraries are also open to the public.

Law schools. See **Northwestern School of Law**; **University of Oregon**; **Willamette University**.

Lawrence Memorial Grassland Preserve. A 378-acre **Nature Conservancy** preserve near **Shaniko** that has also been designated as a **National Natural Landmark** as an excellent example of biscuit and scabland topography. The area is noted for spring **wildflowers**, including red big-headed clover, wild onion, delphinium, Columbia goldenweed, and biscuit root. Bloom lasts from April into early June. No dogs are allowed. Oregonian 4/5/95:E2.

Lawyers. See **Attorneys**; **Bar Examiners**.

LCDC. See **Land Conservation and Development Commission**.

Leach Botanical Garden. A city-owned, seven-acre **Portland** garden of 1,500 species of Pacific Northwest natives collected by John and Lilla Leach; Lilla Leach was the discoverer of *Kalmiopsis leachiana* as well as two new genera and 11 other new Oregon species. The garden is open most days and also offers tours and educational programs. 6704 SE 122nd. Avenue, Portland 97236. 503-761-9503.

Lead. A toxic heavy metal that was produced at **Cornucopia Mine**. Earlier, before 1878, **Paiute Indians** were said to have come to **Canyon City** every fall to trade, riding east out of town and returning in a couple of weeks with lead, which they traded to the settlers who made bullets from it. That source has never been found. Airborne lead levels have dropped substantially since leaded gasoline was phased out, though lead from other sources, such as old house paint, remains a source of poisoning. Gold and Cattle Country.

Lebanon. A **Willamette Valley** agricultural and lumber city in **Linn County**, 14 miles southeast of **Albany** on **Highway 20**. First settled in 1848, it was called Pinhook, Kees' Precinct, Santyam, and Washington Butte until Jeremiah Ralston dubbed it Lebanon for his Tennessee birthplace. The city was incorporated in 1878. The Strawberry Festival, begun in 1909, is held in early June. Population 1980 10,413; 1995 11,780. Elevation 347'. 925 Main St., 97355. 541-451-7421. Chamber of Commerce 541-258-7164. Oregon Geographic Names.

Lectures. See **Oregon Chautauqua**.

Left Bank. A critically acclaimed series of books published twice a year since 1991. Each volume includes poetry, prose, and illustrations by westerners, each addressing the theme of the issue. Blue Heron Publishing, 24450 NW Hansen Road, Hillsboro 97124.

Legal aid. In 1994 Oregon had 17 legal aid offices around the state that assisted 30,000 low income Oregonians. Oregonian 4/20/95:B3.

Legislative Assembly. See **Legislature**.

Legislative committees. Most of the work of the Oregon **legislature** is done by committees. The committees take testimony about specific **bills** at scheduled hearings and then at work sessions decide their fate. Committees may amend bills but the full legislature may not. All appropriations go through the **Joint Ways and Means Committee**, making it the most powerful of the committees. The number of committees changes from session to session. In addition to several joint committees, in 1997 the **Senate** had 12 committees and the **House of Representatives** had 15. Governing Oregon; Oregon Legislative Guide. See also **Emergency Board**.

Legislative Fiscal Office. The office that, under Oregon law, provides fiscal advice to the **legislature**, prepares fiscal impact statements for all proposed bills, and provides staff support for the **Emergency Board**, the **Joint Ways and Means Committee**, the Joint Legislative Audit Committee, and the Joint Information Management and Technology Committee. Oregon Blue Book; Oregon Legislative Guide. H178 State Capitol, Salem 97310. 503-986-1828.

Legislators. See **Senators, Representatives**.

Legislature. The Oregon Legislative Assembly, commonly referred to as the legislature, is the state's law-making body. It is composed of two houses, the **Senate** (30 members) and the **House of Representatives** (60 members). Regular sessions convene at the **capitol** on the 2nd Monday in January of odd-numbered years. The 70th session will convene in 1999. In recent years, regular sessions have adjourned anywhere from June 10 to August 5. The **governor** or the legislature may also convene **special sessions**. If either house has not selected a leader within five days of the start of the session, pay stops for members of that house until a leader is selected. Two house districts (with a population each of about 47,000) make up a senate district, and, since 1971, all districts are single-member districts. The **constitution** requires approval by a majority of elected (not just present) members (16 in the Senate and 31 in the House) in order to pass a **bill**. Abstentions are not allowed. **Laws** go into effect on the 91st day after the session had adjourned unless otherwise specified. Many **legislative committees** are active during the interim between sessions, especially the **Emergency Board**. The 1997 session cost $27,600 a day for a total of $4,774,800 ($1.52 per Oregonian) and passed 800 bills. State Capitol, Salem 97310. 503-986-1187, 800-332-2313 during sessions. Governing Oregon; Oregon Blue Book; Oregon Constitution, Art. IV; Oregon Legislative Guide. See also **Legislative committees**; **Referendum**.

Lemmings. See **Voles**.

Lemolo Falls (leh-MOH-loh). A 75-foot waterfall near the headwaters of the North **Umpqua River**. The falls are at the east end of Dread and Terror Ridge three miles downstream from Lemolo Dam. Lemolo is a **Chinook jargon** word meaning wild or untamed. Waterfall Lover's Guide. See also **North Umpqua Hydroelectric Project**.

Les Schwab Tire Centers. A family-owned company, headquartered in **Prineville**, that is the largest independent tire chain in the country. In 1996 it had 280 tire centers (some company-owned and others owned by dealers) located in seven western states, with sales of $712 million and 5,300 full time and 400 part time employees. 50% of a store's profits are shared with the employees of the store. Les Schwab (1917-) opened the first Les Schwab Tire Centers in 1954-55 in **Bend** and **Madras**. Oregonian 9/28/97:D1.

Leslie Gulch. A ten-mile-long canyon leading down to **Lake Owyhee**, notable for its diverse, towering, and intricately pitted rock formations. Access is via Highway 95 and Succor Creek Byway north of **Jordan Valley**; a steep unpaved road leads down the canyon. It is named for Hiram E. Leslie who was killed by lightning in the gulch in 1882. See also **Mahogany Mountain**.

Levee. An embankment built to prevent flooding. North **Portland** is protected from **Columbia River** floods by levees that extend from the Burlington Northern railroad bridge west of **Interstate 5** upstream 18 miles to the mouth of the **Sandy River**. The levees, built in the 1950s and '60s to replace older and smaller structures, are 40 to 45 feet high with clay cores and heavy rock riprap along the river side. Marine Drive runs along the top. Oregonian 2/19/36:D1.

Lewis and Clark Centennial Exposition. A highly successful promotional extravaganza held in the Guild Lake area of northwest **Portland** from June to October 1905. Noted landscape architect John Olmsted laid out the spacious 385-acres of grounds with a large lake, broad esplanades, elaborate plantings, 100,000 electric lights, and grand architecture. Oregon and other states, the federal government, and foreign countries all sponsored buildings and exhibits; Oregon's included the huge log **Forestry Building**. Other attractions included a dirigible, two diving elk, the Carnival of Venice production with a cast of hundreds, and an amusement park called The Trail. There were 1,588,000 paid admissions, and stockholders received a 21% profit. Portland's subsequent rapid growth was credited to the national attention the exposition generated. All physical evidence of the fair has disappeared. The shallow lake silted in from hillside development and was later used as a dump, and the site is now an industrial area. Great Extravaganza.

Lewis and Clark College. An accredited private liberal arts college in **Portland** that enrolled 3,188 students in 1995. Founded by **Presbyterians** as **Albany College**, it moved to **Portland** in 1938. In 1942 it was renamed Lewis and Clark College and moved to the present campus. 0615 SW Palatine Hill Rd., Portland 97219. 503-768-7000. Dictionary of Oregon History; Oregon Blue Book. See also **Northwestern School of Law**.

Lewis and Clark Expedition. An 1804-1806 military exploring expedition across America's new Louisiana Purchase and on to the Pacific Coast, the first Americans to reach the mouth of the **Columbia River** overland. The expedition was also known as the Corps of Discovery. The party of 33, capably led by Captains Meriwether Lewis (1774-1809) and William Clark (1770-1838), included 27 soldiers with frontier experience and a variety of skills, plus Clark's black manservant, an interpreter and his wife **Sacajawea**, and their baby. The expedition left Saint Louis in May 1804, traveled up the Missouri River, wintered at a Mandan Indian village in what is now North Dakota until April 1805, crossed the Rocky Mountains and reached the mouth of the Columbia in early December. There they built **Fort Clatsop** where they spent a sodden winter before leaving on March 23, 1806, for their return trip. They arrived back in Saint Louis on September 23, 1806, having established a foundation for America's claim to the west coast, and the reports of their discoveries stimulated America's interest in the vast western regions. Lewis and Clark; Original Journals. See also **Lewis and Clark Centennial Exposition**.

Lewis and Clark River. A river in northwest Oregon that flows 27 miles north along the west edge of the **Coast Range** to **Youngs Bay** west of **Astoria**. It is named for the explorers who built their 1805-06 winter camp, **Fort Clatsop**, on its banks. Oregon Geographic Names.

Lewis and Clark Trail Committee. An Oregon committee established in 1970 to promote awareness of the significance of the **Lewis and Clark Expedition** and to encourage development and protection of historical sites along their route. It is supported by the **Parks and Recreation Department**. The bicentennial of the expedition will be during the years 2004-2006. 1115 Commercial St.

NE, Salem 97310-1001. 503-378-6508. Oregon Blue Book.

Lexington. A north-central Oregon agricultural community nine miles northwest of **Heppner** on **Willow Creek** in **Morrow County**. It was named by pioneer William Penland for his Kentucky birthplace. The post office was established in 1885, and the city was incorporated in 1903. The county airport is located nearby. Population 1980 307; 1995 290. Elevation 1,454'. PO Box 587, 97839. 541-989-8508. Oregon Geographic Names.

Liars. See **Folk literature**.

Liberal University. A college dedicated to the separation of religion and education that was established in **Silverton** in 1897 by the **Oregon State Secular Union**. Despite construction of a large building (later a **Catholic** school) and the importation of noted eastern liberal Thaddeus Burr Wakeman to be president, financial problems and infighting among the supporters led to the college's demise in 1902. "Organized Free Thought in Oregon."

Liberty ships. Freighters built during **World War II** (1941-1945). Of the total 2,751 built, 322 came from Kaiser's Oregon Ship Yard (also called Oregonship), just downstream from **Portland**'s St. Johns Bridge. The first, the **Star of Oregon II**, was launched on September 27, 1941. Kaiser also built tankers at **Swan Island** and escort carriers and landing ships at Vancouver, Washington. 150,000 people were employed in the area shipyards during the war, a third of them women. The shipyards featured intensive vocational training, an innovative health maintenance organization, now called Kaiser-Permanente, round-the-clock child care, meals-to-go, mass production shipbuilding, and a focus on efficiency. A $600,000 fire on November 6, 1944, destroyed the shipyard offices at St. Johns. Oregonian 7/14/96:B3. See also **Ship building**.

Libraries. In 1992, Oregon had 125 public libraries. They owned 7.21 million volumes and served 94% of the state's population. Circulation was nearly 9 items per person served. Operating expenses were $50 million, or $19 per person served. Oregon's first library opened in 1842 at **Oregon City** with 300 volumes. The Oregon Territorial Library was authorized by Congress in 1848 and given $5,000; the collection was destroyed when the **capitol** burned in 1854. In 1864 libraries opened in **Portland, Salem, Albany**, and **Ashland**. In 1996, **Sherman County**, the last county without public library service, opened a public library. Dictionary of Oregon History. See also **Blue River; Censorship; Law libraries; Multnomah County Library; Oregon State Library**.

License plates. Oregon's official passenger car license plate features a design, selected through a contest, of dark blue letters and numbers on a light background with a tall green tree in the center. An optional **Oregon Trail** plate with a covered wagon in the background, available for an additional $5, was introduced in 1993 and raised $1.8 million for interpretive projects. A plate featuring a **salmon** was introduced in 1998 to raise money for supporting salmon habitat and Oregon parks. It costs an extra $30 every two years plus a $14 first-time fee. Group plates, which may include a logo, were also authorized by the legislature in 1993, and it has also authorized other special plates. Custom plates are also available for the regular registration fee plus $50 for two years, with the extra revenue going for litter cleanup programs. About 62,000 of the custom plates were in use in 1997, and the state Division of **Driver and Motor Vehicle Services (DMV)** receives another 300 requests each month. About 1% are turned down as offensive and another 4% are denied because they are already in use. The DMV processes 1.5 million vehicle licenses a year. Mail Tribune 7/17/97:3A; Oregonian 4/10/98:D11.

License plates, history. Oregon's first passenger car license plates, issued before 1911, were white on maroon. After that the color combination was changed nearly annually until the 1949 aluminum on black combination that was used through 1955. From 1956 through 1973 the plates were yellow on blue with "Pacific Wonderland" embossed on the plates from 1960 through 1962. Blue on yellow plates were used from 1974 through 1988. A graphic plate, the state's first, with a conifer tree in the center and a mountain range suggested across the background, was introduced in 1988 and was still in use in 1997, though the colors were modified in 1989. The arrangement of letters and numbers on the plates has changed through the years, with the first (or only) letter indicating the month of expiration from 1956 to 1985. Reining in the Horseless Carriage.

Lichens. Small plants found growing on trees, rocks, and other surfaces. Each is a symbiotic combination of a fungus, which provides the framework, and an alga, which provides the energy. About 1,000 species are known in Oregon; many are useful as indicators of air pollution. Some live to be 2000 years old. Many have herbal uses, though at least one, the chartreuse wolfbane, *Letharia volpina*, is highly toxic. Macrolichens of Pacific Northwest Forests.

Lie detector. See **Polygraph**.

Light rail. Electric passenger **railroads** serving urban areas. In **Portland**, interest in the 1970's led to the construction of **MAX**, which began operating in 1986. Construction on a western extension to **Hillsboro** began in 1993. A north-south route connecting Vancouver, WA, with **Clackamas County** has been proposed but has had mixed success at the polls. Oregonian 9/15/94:D1, 10/23/94:C1. See also **Electric railways**.

Lighthouses. The first lighthouse in the Oregon Territory was built at the mouth of the **Umpqua River** in 1857. There are now nine lighthouses on the Oregon coast, five of them still operating, at **Yaquina Head**, **Heceta Head**, **Umpqua River**, **Cape Arago**, and **Cape Blanco**. Since the lights have been automated, there are no longer lighthouse keepers, and the lighthouses themselves have been transferred from the U.S. Coast Guard to other agencies The four inactive lighthouses are located at **Tillamook Rock**, **Cape Meares** (an automated light operates nearby), **Yaquina Bay**, and **Coquille River**. All nine are on the **National Register of Historic Places**. All except the two on islands (Cape Arago and Tillamook Rock) are open for scheduled tours or visits, at least on summer weekends or by appointment. There is also a privately operated lighthouse, **"Cleft of the Rock"**, south of **Yachats**. The only active lighthouse left along the **Columbia River** is on Warrior Rock at the north tip of **Sauvie Island**, built in 1888. Lighthouses at Point Adams and Desdemona Sands have been abandoned and disappeared. Oregon chapter, U.S. Lighthouse Society, 541-271-2130. Oregon Lighthouses; Oregon Parks 2(3):54, Nov/Dec 1994; Oregon's Seacoast Lighthouses. See also **Lightships**.

Lightships. Ships with lights, anchored where navigational assistance is needed but where it is not feasible to build a lighthouse. The first on the west coast,

Columbia River Lightship No. 50, was stationed off the mouth of the **Columbia River** in 1892. It was replaced in 1909 by *No. 88*, in 1939 by *Umatilla No. 93*, in 1951 by *No. 604*, and in 1979 by an automated buoy. The buoy is 42' high and 40' in diameter. *No. 604* is now on display at the **Columbia River Maritime Museum** in **Astoria**. Earlier, during a raging storm on November 28, 1899, *No. 50* was torn from her three anchor lines and, despite rescue efforts, washed up on the beach on the north side of the Columbia. After over a year of futile attempts to refloat her, a house-moving firm was awarded the contract. They jacked her up and pulled her with horses a mile overland to Baker Bay. The move was a success, and after repairs, she returned to service on August 15, 1901. Oregon's Seacoast Lighthouses.

Lilies. Eight species of lily are native to Oregon. Easter lilies are grown at **Brookings**; in 1995 sales from 1,305 acres of bulbs brought in $13.4 million. Manual of the Higher Plants of Oregon; 1995 Oregon. See also **Melridge, Inc**.

Limestone. A sedimentary rock formed by the deposition of seashells and corals. It is composed of calcium carbonate and yields lime when burned. Limestone is found a number of places in Oregon but is mined primarily at Durkee in **Baker County** where **cement** is made from it. Mineral Industry of Oregon. See also **Oregon Caves National Monument**.

Lincoln City. "'The Beach is Just the Beginning." A beach resort community on the central Oregon coast that stretches 7 1/2 miles along **Highway 101** in **Lincoln County**. In 1964 the communities of Oceanlake, Delake, Taft, Cutler City, and Nelscott voted to combine, forming Lincoln City, which incorporated the next year; the name came from the county. Attractions include over seven miles of beach, **Devils Lake State Park**; Chinook Winds Gaming **Casino**, Factory Stores at Lincoln City, **Connie Hansen Gardens**, **Cascade Head**, and **kite** festivals. Population 1980 5,469; 1995 6,570. Elevation 11'. PO Box 50, 97367. 541-996-2152. Visitor Bureau 800-452-2151. Oregon Geographic Names. See also **Twenty Miracle Miles**.

Lincoln County. A central coastal county of long beaches, headlands, and the forested **Coast Range**. Incorporated cities are the fishing ports of **Newport** (county seat) and **Depoe Bay**, plus **Lincoln City**, **Siletz**, **Toledo**, **Waldport**, and **Yachats**. The county is bounded by the ocean on the west, and by **Tillamook**, **Polk**, **Benton**, and **Lane** counties. Elevations range from sea level to 3,359' Saddle Bag Mountain in the northeast corner. The economy is based on lumber, fishing, agriculture, and tourism. Taxable assessed value in 1995 was $3,595,000,000, or $86,000 per capita. The county was created in 1893 from **Benton** and **Polk** counties and named for President Abraham Lincoln (1809-1865). Population 1980 35,264; 1995 41,800. Area 992 square miles. Density 42/sq.mi. Annual precipitation 75"; average temperature January 43°F, July 57°F. Courthouse, 225 W Olive St., Newport 97365. 541-265-6611. First One Hundred Years; Oregon Blue Book.

Lindberg Plaza. A section of **Portland**'s Main Street between the **Arlene Schnitzer Concert Hall** and the **Portland Center for the Performing Arts** that was renamed in honor of retiring city commissioner Mike Lindberg on September 27, 1996. During his 17 years on the City Council Lindberg had played a strong role in promoting the city's cultural institutions. Oregonian 9/25/96:D5.

Lindbergh, Charles. See **Aviation history**.

Line item veto. Oregon's **governor** has "the power to veto single items in appropriation bills, and any provision in new bills declaring an emergency, without thereby affecting any other provision of such bill." Oregon **Constitution** Art. V, Sec. 15a, 1915, 1921.

Linen. See **Flax**.

Linfield College. An accredited private college in **McMinnville** that enrolled 2,814 students in 1995. It was founded by **Baptists** in 1855 as McMinnville College and was renamed in honor of George Fisher Linfield in 1922 after his widow made a large donation. As of the end of 1996, its Wildcats football team had a string of 41 consecutive winning seasons. 900 SE Baker St., McMinnville 97128. 503-434-2200. Oregon Blue Book; Oregonian 11/6/97:C1.

Linn-Benton Community College. A public two-year college that opened in 1967 in **Albany** and has another major center in **Corvallis**. In fall 1996 10,155 students enrolled. Students can work toward any of 50 associate degrees and 20 certificate programs. Any person over 18 may enroll, with or without a high school diploma. 6500 SW Pacific Blvd., Albany OR 97321-3774. 541-917-4999. Oregon Blue Book. See also **Community colleges; Small Business Development Centers**.

Linn County. A farm and forest county that extends from the **Willamette River** east to the crest of the **Cascade Range**. Incorporated cities are **Albany** (county seat), **Brownsville, Lebanon, Lyons, Harrisburg, Halsey, Mill City, Millersburg, Scio, Sodaville, Sweet Home, Tangent**, and **Waterloo**. The county is bounded by **Marion, Jefferson, Deschutes, Lane, Benton**, and **Polk** counties. Elevations range from 160' on the Willamette River on the west to 10,495' **Mount Jefferson** on the east. The economy is based on agriculture, including grass seed and sheep, food products, wood products, rare metals, and manufacturing. Taxable assessed value in 1995 was $4,446,000,000, or $45,000 per capita. The county was created in 1847 and named for Missouri Senator Lewis F. Linn (1795-1843) who authored the **Donation Land Act**. Population 1980 89,495; 1995 98,100. Area 2,297 square miles. Density 43/sq.mi. Annual precipitation 43"; average temperature January 39°F, July 66°F. Courthouse, 300 4th Ave. SW, Albany 97321. 541-967-3825. Biography; "Beyond the Ruts"; Oregon Blue Book.

Liquor Control Commission, Oregon (OLCC). A five-member citizen commission that regulates the sale, distribution, and use of alcoholic beverages in the state in order to protect Oregon's public health, safety and community livability. The commission was created in 1933 following the repeal of **prohibition**. Under Oregon law the state has the exclusive right to sell packaged hard liquor, which it does through 235 retail liquor stores operated by contracted agents. Sales in 1995-96 totaled $184 million. 56% of the net revenue ($72.4 million in the 1995-96 fiscal year) went to the state's **general fund** and most of the rest went to local governments. The state is also authorized to license private businesses that sell beer and wine by the drink or in the package. A constitutional amendment, adopted through an **initiative** in 1953, permits the sale of hard liquor by the drink in licensed establishments. Before that anyone who wanted to drink hard liquor socially had to take his own bottle to a "bottle club". The OLCC also administers the Alcohol Server Education Program and enforces the **Bottle Bill** law. 9079 SE McLoughlin Blvd, Portland 97222-7355. 503-872-5000; 800-452-6522. Oregon Blue Book; Round the Roses. See also **Alcohol** entries; **Temperance**.

Literary Arts, Inc. A nonprofit organization that sponsors Oregon Literary Fellowships for writers and small publishers, literary awards, including the **Oregon Book Awards**, and the Portland Arts and Lectures series which is the largest literary arts lecture series in the country. It is funded by memberships, donations, and grants. 720 SW Washington, Suite 745, Portland 97205. 503-227-2583.

Literature. Oregon's literary history began with the oral tales, teachings, and songs in the various **Indian languages**. Explorers' accounts, letters and diaries of pioneers and later residents, poetry, novels, short stories, and a wealth of books and articles about the state, its resources and its peoples are now all a part of Oregon's literature. Some notable Oregon writers of non-fiction include Frances Fuller Victor (1826-1902); William Kittredge (1932-); and Barry Lopez (1945-). History of Oregon Literature; Writers of West Portland. See also **Authors**; **Children's literature**; **Folk literature**; **Left Bank**; **Novels**; **National Book Awards**; **Oregon Book Awards**; **Oregon Literature Series**; **Poets**.

Lithia water. Naturally carbonated mineral water from springs on Emigrant Creek four miles east of **Ashland**. In 1911 Ashland piped the water to fountains in newly expanded and renamed Lithia Park and on the city Plaza. Some, operating on the theory that anything that tastes that bad must be good for you, claim that drinking the water has various therapeutic effects, including increased fertility. Oregonian 12/6/96:B6.

Litter. Adopt-A-River provides free garbage bags and information for persons who will help clean up a stretch of river. 800-322-3326. See also **Bottle bill**; **SOLV**.

Livestock. See **Bees**; **Cattle**; **Dairy**; **Goats**; **Hogs**; **Horses**; **Llama**; **Poultry**; **Sheep**; **Silk**; **Snails**; **Tanneries**; **Veterinary Medical Examining Board**; **Yak**.

Livestock auctions. Places where cattle and other livestock are sold to other growers or for slaughter. When livestock was being shipped by rail, the Portland Livestock Exchange in north **Portland** was the central stockyards. It closed in 1995. Livestock auctions are now located in **Ontario**, **La Grande**, **Hermiston**, **Madras**, **Woodburn**, and **Eugene**. See also **Pacific International Livestock Exposition**; **Relocation centers**.

Livestock districts. See **Open range**. Under Oregon's open range law (ORS 607) cattle may roam free and the owner is under no obligation to fence them in or retrieve them if they trespass on another's land. This is true except in cities and in areas where residents have voted to establish a livestock district.

Lizards. Dry-land **reptiles** (not to be confused with **salamanders** which are **amphibians**.) Eleven species of lizards are found in Oregon. Oregon's largest is the desert collared lizard, *Crotaphytus bicinctores*, of southeast Oregon, growing to 13 inches in length. The smallest is the four-inch short-horned lizard, *Phrynosoma douglassi*, found throughout eastern Oregon. Atlas of Oregon Wildlife; Field Guide to Western Reptiles and Amphibians; Knowing Oregon Reptiles.

Llama. A South American ruminant related to the camel. It has become popular in the U.S. as a pet, pack animal, wool producer, and guard animal for sheep herds. Llama breeding in the U.S. began in **Deschutes County** in the early 1970s and boomed in the '80s. In 1996 there were some 120 llama ranches in Central Oregon. Oregonians own at least 10% of the country's 100,000 llamas. Oregon Agriculture Summer 1994:6.

Lobbyist. A person who represents others (such as a professional, business, labor, religious, or public interest group, or a local government or government agency) at the **legislature**. A lobbyist's purpose is to secure legislation favorable to the interests he or she represents, by providing information to legislators, generating support for bills, and sometimes contributing to legislators' campaign funds via political action committees (PACs). Oregon law requires that persons who spends more than 24 hours or $100 lobbying the legislature in a 3-month period register with the state **Government Standards and Practices Commission** and file regular reports of their lobbying-related expenditures. 730 were registered in June 1997, 428 of them paid lobbyists, 82 unpaid, 168 were state employees, and 52 were other public employees. The top spenders in 1997 were the Oregon Restaurant Association $590,403, State Department of Consumer and Business Services $317,241, Associated Oregon Industries $257,681, Oregon Association of Hospitals and Health Systems $244,452, League of Oregon Cities $244,034, Portland Public Schools $232,860, Western State Petroleum Association $228,623, Oregon Medical Association $216,253, Oregon Trucking Association $215,182, and Oregon Education Association $188,585. The amount a lobbyist can give directly to a legislator as gift or entertainment is restricted. The Oregon lobby is self-regulating in that many lobbyists belong to the Capitol Club, an organization for Oregon lobbyists that establishes and enforces rules of conduct for its members. Governing Oregon; Oregonian 3/9/98:B1. See also **Campaign finance**.

Lobsters. Spiny lobsters are being raised commercially near **Paisley** and Australian red claw crayfish north of **Lakeview** in a venture begun in 1997. A **geothermal** well provides heated water and employees will harvest brine shrimp from **Lake Abert** to feed to the crustaceans. Mail Tribune 11/10/96:73. See also **Crawfish**.

Local control. A phrase used especially by advocates of community control of schools. Control is usually associated with funding, and, since the state, under the mandate of **Measure 5**, has assumed more of the funding responsibility for public schools, local control has decreased. See also **School finance**.

Local government. Oregon has over 1400 local units of government, including 36 **counties**, 240 **cities**, 220 **school districts**, and approximately 950 **special service districts**, including 23 **port districts**, nine **public transit** districts, two **boundary commissions**, and one regional government (**Metro**), as wells as fire, sewer, and water districts. Most have elected governing bodies and taxing authority. The **property tax** has been the traditional support for local governments. Governing Oregon. See also **Charter**; **Home rule**; **Ordinance**.

Locks. Bypass routes built around major obstacles to navigation. Without locks, river passage around waterfalls or rapids requires that passengers and freight be transferred to land, transported (portaged) around the obstruction, and then loaded onto another boat. **Willamette Falls Canal and Locks** was opened in 1873 to provide a water route around **Willamette Falls**. The **Cascades Canal and Locks** opened in 1896 (replaced by **Bonneville Lock** in 1938), and **The Dalles-Celilo Canal and Locks** in 1915 (replaced by **The Dalles Dam** navigation lock in 1957). **John Day Lock** opened in 1968, and **McNary Lock** in 1953. A lock on **Yamhill River** operated from 1900 until 1954. Army Engineers.

Locomotives. A steam locomotive, once owned by the **Southern Pacific** and now owned by the city of **Portland**, is fired up periodically for good-will tours. Known as No. 4449, the 1941 locomotive weighs nearly 400 tons and has a top speed of 90 mph. Oregonian 10/28/95:B2. See also **Oregon Pony**; **Prineville City Railroad**.

Lode gold. Gold found in veins in rock where it formed by deposition from hot, mineralized water. It is mined by tunneling into the rock to follow the veins and blasting the ore loose. The ore is then brought to the surface, crushed, and the **gold** is removed by some combination of physical and chemical processes, depending upon the nature of the ore. The first lode mining in Oregon began in 1862 at **Virtue Flat** east of **Baker City**. Of the total 5.8 million fine ounces of gold mined in Oregon before 1965, 2.3 million came from lode deposits. There is currently little or no lode mining in the state. Geology of Oregon; Gold and Silver in Oregon. See also **Placer gold**; **Tunnels**.

Loeb State Park. A **state park** on the **Chetco River**, eight miles inland from **Brookings**. A trail from the park, which is located in a grove of old-growth **Oregon myrtle** trees, leads to a stand of **redwoods**. The 53 campsites are open all year. No reservations.

Log. The stem of a tree once it has fallen or been felled. A log lying on the forest floor provides a variety of habitats for a sequence of diverse plant, animal, fungal, and microscopic life as it decays; a huge **old growth** log may take 300 years to disappear.

Log drives. Logs were at one time moved from the woods to the mills by floating them downstream at high water. For example, logs were brought in drives down the **McKenzie River** to the mill in **Coburg** around the turn of the century. The practice disappeared after the forests close to rivers had been cut. See also **Flumes**; **Log rafts**.

Log exports. The first log exports from Oregon were spar timbers sent to China in 1788. Now logs from private lands are exported to several Asian countries which often pay more than domestic mills. It is illegal to export logs from federal and Oregon-owned lands. See also **Lumber trade**.

Log rafts. Logs grouped inside a log boom and rafted on rivers, especially the **Willamette**, where they are sorted and moved to a mill. Ocean-going log rafts, first developed in 1906, included huge, cigar-shaped Benson rafts, built up over a period of weeks in a two-part cradle. The 900-foot-long rafts, each containing six million **board feet** of logs, plus a load of lumber on top, were towed to San Diego or some other California port. Blow for the Landing; Logging Transportation.

Loganberries. In 1994 Oregon supplied 100% of the country's loganberries from 90 acres in the **Willamette Valley**. They produced 400,000 pounds, worth $329,000. 1994-1995 Oregon Agriculture.

Logging. The process of felling trees, making logs, and getting them from the woods to a sawmill. Originally done with human and animal power, nearly all parts of the process have been mechanized, and helicopters are sometimes used to lift logs from difficult or fragile sites. Logging is the most dangerous occupation in Oregon, killing more than a dozen workers each year. See also **Clear-cut**; **Forest Practices Act**; **High-lead logging**; **Silver Fire Roundup**; **Skid roads**; **Timber carnivals**; **Timber harvest**; **Timber supply**; **Timber workers**.

Logging history. A logging museum is located at Collier State Park, 32 miles north of **Klamath Falls** on **Highway 97**. **Garibaldi** Memorial Lumberman's Park museum displays early logging and railroading equipment. Coos County Logging Museum is located in **Myrtle Creek** (541-572-2627). A free, privately-operated, outdoor museum of large logging equipment is located at Camp 18, near milepost 18 on **Highway 26** between **Portland** and the coast. Box 195, Seaside 97138. 503-755-1818. See also **Company town**; **Donkey engine**; **Flumes**; **Industrial Workers of the World (IWW)**; **Log drives**; **Logging railroads**; **Loyal Legion of Loggers and Lumbermen (4L)**; **Lumber production, history**; **Skid roads**.

Logging railroads. Until trucks came into wide use for hauling logs in the 1940s, railroads carried logs from most logging sites to a mill or river. By 1917 Oregon had some 600 miles of logging railroads. Don't Call Me Ma.

Logtown rose. A Harrison's yellow rose brought across the plains in an 1852 wagon train by Roxy Ann Bowen, and planted by her at the foot of Roxy Ann Peak near **Medford**. Ten years later the family - and the rose - moved to Logtown, six miles west of **Jacksonville**, where Roxy Ann's stepdaughter, Maryum McKee cared for the plant. Logtown, also called Log Town and Logg Town (for Francis A. Logg), sprang up around 1860 as a **gold**-mining community and soon had a population of 250 whites and 450 Chinese. The last building disappeared in 1910, but the cemetery and rose (1/2 mile closer to Jacksonville) remain on Highway 238. Ruch; Tracking down Oregon.

Lone Pine. A large **ponderosa pine** tree, called L'Arbre Seul by French Canadian trappers, that stood for years as a landmark for Indians and fur trappers on the northeast Oregon prairie near **Baker City** until a member of the first wagon train over the **Oregon Trail** cut it for firewood in 1843 - and then found that it was too green to burn. Other Side of Oregon.

Lonerock. Oregon's third-smallest incorporated city is located in north-central Oregon, 20 miles southeast of **Condon** in **Gilliam County**. The post office, named for a 100' high local landmark, was established in 1875. The city was founded in 1881 and incorporated in 1901. Population 1980 26; 1995 25. Elevation 2,800'. Lonerock Route, Condon 97823. 541-384-3196. History of Gilliam County; Oregon Ghost Towns.

Long Creek. An eastern Oregon ranching community in **Grant County** 36 miles north of **John Day** on **Highway 395**. The community, named for a nearby creek, incorporated in 1891. A **tornado** inflicted severe damage in 1894, followed by a fire the next year. In 1996 the Hua Sent Group, a Maylasian lumber company, proposed rebuilding a lumber mill that had closed earlier in the year. Population 1980 252; 1995 235. Elevation 3,754'. PO Box 489, 97856. 541-421-3601. "Family"; <u>Oregonian</u> 11/19/96:B4; <u>Tracking down Oregon</u>.

Long Narrows. See **The Dalles of the Columbia River**.

Long term care ombudsman. An office that is responsible for investigating complaints made by or on behalf of residents in long-term care facilities such as nursing homes, **adult foster-care homes**, residential care or assisted living facilities. Trained volunteers provide the service. 3855 Wolverine Street NE, Suite 6, Salem 97310. 503-378-6533, 800-522-2602. <u>Oregon Blue Book</u>. See also **Senior and Disabled Services Division**.

Long Tom River. A 55-mile long river at the south end of the **Willamette Valley** that drains 410 square miles. It flows south along the east flanks of the **Coast Range** before turning through **Fern Ridge Reservoir** and then meandering on north to join the **Willamette River** eight miles north of **Harrisburg**. As measured at river mile point 6.8, average annual flows are 536,900 acre feet, or 2.1 acre feet/acre. The name comes from that of a band of Indians, the Lung-tum-ler. The river has also been called the Lamitambuff and the Longtabuff. <u>Oregon Geographic Names</u>.

Lookout Point Dam and Reservoir. An **Army Corps of Engineers** dam across the Middle Fork of the **Willamette River** and the 14-mile-long lake it created. The dam, built in 1953 for flood control and power generation, is an embankment structure 270 feet high and 3,381 feet long, with a concrete spillway. When full, the lake covers 4,360 acres to a maximum depth of 234 feet; it is drawn down in late summer in preparation for flood runoff. The lake is popular for boating. **Dexter Reservoir**, 2.8 miles downstream, reregulates releases from Lookout Point; the two dams together can produce 135 **megawatts** of power. <u>Army Engineers</u>; <u>Atlas of Oregon Lakes</u>;

Lookout towers. See **Fire lookouts**.

Loon Lake. A lake in the **Coast Range** east of **Reedsport** that was created by a landslide 1,400 years ago. Trunks of trees that were drowned at the time are still standing on the bottom. The lake, which is gradually decreasing in size as the outlet erodes through the natural dam, covers 294 acres with a maximum depth of 105 feet. It is a popular recreation site for fishing, camping, and water skiing, and has campground and resort facilities. It was named for a loon's nest found on a floating log in 1852. <u>Atlas of Oregon Lakes</u>; <u>Oregon Geographic Names</u>.

Loons. Heavy-bodied diving birds. Three species winter along the Oregon coast. Although a pair of common loons, *Gavia immer*, spent four summers at **Devils Lake** where their calls echoed on foggy mornings, the only nest reported from Oregon was found at **Loon Lake** in 1852. <u>Birds of Oregon</u>.

Lost Creek Lake. A multi-purpose reservoir built and operated by the **Army Corps of Engineers** on the upper **Rogue River** 35 miles northeast of **Medford**. The lake was formed by the 345 foot William L. Jess dam completed in 1977 as part of the **Rogue Basin Project** for flood control, irrigation, power generation (49 **megawatts**), fish and wildlife enhancement, recreation, and water quality improvement. At full pool the lake covers 3,428 acres, is ten miles long, and has a maximum depth of 322 feet. Draw down in preparation for flood control drops the water level 60 feet. The lake is becoming increasingly popular for boating, fishing, and camping at **Joseph Stewart State Park**. <u>Atlas of Oregon Lakes</u>.

Lost Crystal Cave. A **cave** said to be located between **Bend** and **Burns**, southeast of Millican, with walls and ceiling covered with calcite crystals. It was discovered by cowboys in 1904. One of the crystals still exists, but efforts to find the cave again have failed. Where the Pavement Ends.

Lost Forest. A 9,100-acre stand of **ponderosa pine** growing 26 miles northeast of Christmas Valley in **Lake County**. The forest is a remnant of a much more extensive forest that once covered the area, but is now isolated by 40 miles of **sagebrush** from other ponderosa forests. It persists in an area with 10 inches of rainfall, considerably less than the 15 inches considered necessary for pines. A combination of factors enables it to survive, including an underlying layer of rock that holds the moisture, and fine sand on the surface that serves as a mulch. The trees are estimated to be 300-500 years old. Where the Pavement Ends.

Lost Lake, Hood River County. A lake 20 miles southwest of **Hood River** that is one of 13 lakes of that name in Oregon, all testifying to the difficulty, before the age of airplanes, of rediscovering a landmark in rugged, heavily timbered terrain. This Lost Lake is one of the most photographed lakes in Oregon, famous for the view of **Mount Hood** across its waters. It is a mile long, covers 231 acres, and has a maximum depth of 175 feet. A three-foot high spillway has been added on top of the natural lava-flow dam. No motorboats are permitted on the lake, but other boating and fishing are popular. A resort offers cabins and boat rentals, and there is a campground. Atlas of Oregon Lakes.

Lost mines and treasures. Legends abound in Oregon about buried Spanish ship treasure, gold sources found and lost, and secret Indian treasures. Lost Mines and Buried Treasures lists sources of information for 59 such legends, with the longest listings for the **Blue Bucket Mine**, the treasure of **Neahkahnie Mountain**, and the **Port Orford Meteorite**. Lost Mines and Treasures of the Pacific Northwest recounts the stories of 19 such in Oregon. Some are also recounted in Gold and Cattle Country, Oregon Oddities, and Other Side of Oregon.

Lost persons. The most frequent searches in Oregon are for lost hikers. Other searches are for lost skiers, hunters, mountain climbers, fishermen, swimmers, and for missing vehicles, including planes. Experienced searchers have found that lost children nearly always go up and go farther than expected. Oregonian 12/10/95:F1. See also **Bloodhounds**; **Emergency Management Division**; **Search and rescue**; **Search dogs**.

Lost River. A southern Oregon river that drains the highlands southeast of **Klamath Falls**. It rises in what is now Clear Lake Reservoir in northern California, loops north and west to flow south again, originally draining into **Tule Lake** but now diverted into the **Klamath River**. At one time it supported a fish run (suckers) "so thick they scared the horses when you tried to ford." The fish were an important food supply for the **Modoc Indians**. Much of the water of the river has been diverted for irrigation. The river disappears for several miles in the Langell Valley, hence the name. Feelin' Fine; Oregon Geographic Names.

Lost Wagon Train. An 1845 **wagon train** of 800 people, traveling with 200 wagons and several thousand head of livestock on the **Oregon Trail**, that accepted Stephen Meek's offer to lead them over "Meek's Cutoff" west from Fort Boise. The aim was to go west and then north around the arduous **Blue Mountains**. However, the wagon train, suffering from privation and illness, became lost in the deserts of central Oregon. A rescue party from **The Dalles** found them somewhere in the **Crooked River** area and guided them back to The Dalles where the wagons that had taken the usual route had arrived six weeks earlier. At least 24 members died of disease and hardship on the cutoff, and 20 more died soon after. An 1853 wagon train, the first to use the **Free Emigrant Road**, was also known as the Lost Wagon Train. Terrible Trail. See also **Blue Bucket Mine**.

Lostine. A ranching and recreation center in **Wallowa County** 65 miles northeast of **La Grande** on Highway 82, named for a community in Kansas. The post office was established in 1878 and the town was platted a few years later. A fire destroyed much of the business district in 1893. Telephone and electric service arrived in 1900, and the city was incorporated in 1903. Fifteen historic buildings, including the 1888 **Presbyterian Church**, are included on a self-guided walking tour. Vendors from across the west sell at the 150-space Lostine Flea Market, held the weekend after Independence Day. Population 1980 250; 1995 230. Elevation 3,200'. PO Box 181, 97857. 541-569-2415. History of Wallowa County.

Lottery, Oregon. In 1984 Oregon voters created a state lottery (**Constitution** Art. XV, Sec. 4) with profits dedicated to economic development. Scientific Games, a Georgia gambling equipment company, had commissioned a survey that showed that Oregonians would support using gambling money for economic development, and then drafted the initiative and paid for the signature gathering. The lottery and other games, including video poker (introduced in 1992), are run by the State Lottery Commission whose five members are appointed by the Governor. At least 50 percent of the revenue is to be returned as prizes, 16% may be spent for operating expenses, and the rest, about $280 million a year, goes to the state where it provides about 9% of the general budget. Between 1985 and 1997, the lottery returned $1.3 billion to the state. In 1995 voters dedicated 15% of revenue to an Education Endowment Fund for scholarships. The audit for fiscal year 1995-96 showed that the lottery took in over a billion dollars in cash (2/3rds from video poker and the rest from 7 other games) and distributed $595 million in cash prizes - plus the "churn" of $2,544 million of video poker credits won and played. Out of the $485 million that players lost ($155 per Oregon man, woman, and child), $286 million was transferred to Economic Development. The 1,840 bar, tavern, and restaurant video poker retailers received commissions of $140 million from 8,959 video machines; the rate was 35% of the first $200,000 of net receipts and 30% after that. Retailers of traditional games received 3-5% of sales plus bonuses. A 1997 poll found that 57% of Oregonians favored the lottery, 26% did not, and 18% were not sure. 500 Airport Road SE, Salem 97301. 503-540-1000. Oregon Blue Book; Oregonian 7/27/97:A1, 10/29/97:B11. See also **Burns Archive Center**; **Gambling; Gambling addiction**.

Loud Hawk. A defendant in a 13-year **Portland** court case that arose when Kenny Loud Hawk and several other Indians were arrested in eastern Oregon on charges stemming from the 1973 killing of two FBI agents at Oglala, South Dakota. After 12 years of pre-trial legal battles involving the American Indian Movement and the FBI, and a trial, the case ended with probation. Loud Hawk.

Louisiana Pacific Corporation. A **Portland**-based forest products company with plants in several states, Mexico, Canada, and Ireland, and with 1.6 million acres of timberland in Texas, Louisiana, and California. It was listed on the 1996 **Fortune 500** list with 1995 sales of $2.8 billion and has 13,000 employees. 111 SW Fifth Ave., Portland 97204. 503-221-0800. Oregonian 4/9/96:B14, 6/30/ 96:R23. See also **Salaries**.

Love seat. The world's longest love seat, located in Memphis, Tennessee, was milled by Hull-Oakes Lumber Company of **Monroe**, in 1964. It is a 28"x30" timber 110' long, with seats cut out alternately on each side.

Lovejoy Fountain. A **Portland** fountain between SW 2nd and 3rd south of Harrison. It was designed by Halprin and Associates, and constructed in 1966 as part of the **urban renewal** project that created the **Portland Center**. The full-block fountain invites sunbathing, exploring, water play, and picnics. Frozen Music.

Lowell. A south **Willamette Valley** community in **Lane County** on the north side of **Dexter Reservoir** 17 miles southeast of **Eugene**. It was named by Amos Hyland, a pioneer of the 1850s, for his home town in Maine. The post office, established in 1880, was first called Cannon for a local resident; the name was changed to Lowell in 1883. The city was incorporated in 1954. Population 1980 661; 1995 955. Elevation 741'. PO Box 490, 97452. 541-937-2157. Oregon Geographic Names.

Lower Columbia River Estuary Program. A program working to improve the **estuary** environment of the **Columbia River** from **Bonneville Dam** to the ocean. Priority issues are toxic contaminants, habitat loss and modification, conventional pollutants, biological integrity, land use and development practices and population growth, public awareness and stewardship, and institutional constraints. The program funds projects through grants. 811 SW Sixth Avenue, Portland 97204. 503-229-5247. See also **Columbia River estuary**.

Lower Klamath National Wildlife Refuge. A 53,600 acre field and wetland refuge on the California border south of **Klamath Falls**. The refuge is primarily for waterfowl, though the largest concentration of wintering bald **eagles** in the 48 states also feeds there. Rt. 1, Box 74, Tulelake CA 96134. 916-667-2231. Oregon Wildlife Viewing Guide.

Lowest point. Oregon has no land area below **sea level**.

Lowest temperature. See **Cold; Temperature, lowest**.

Lownsdale Square. See **Plaza Blocks**.

Loyal Legion of Loggers and Lumbermen (4L). An organization established by lumber operators during **World War I** to promote patriotism and undermine the **Industrial Workers of the World** (Wobblies) labor organization. Membership, which reached 100,000 in the Northwest, was to be an equal mix of employers and employees. Empire of the Columbia. See also **Spruce Production Division**.

LUBA. See **Land Use Board of Appeals**.

Luckiamute River. A 59-mile long river that flows east out of the **Coast Range** through **King's Valley**, and on to join the **Willamette River** opposite the mouth of the **Santiam River**, eight miles north of **Albany**. It drains an area of 310 square miles. The Luckiamutes were a band of **Kalapuya Indians**. Oregon Geographic Names.

Lumber production, history. The first **sawmill** in the **Oregon Country** was the **Hudson's Bay Company** mill near **Fort Vancouver**, built in 1827. By 1839 forty **Hawaiians** were working at the mill, hand sawing up to 3,000 feet of lumber daily for export. The California **gold rush** created a demand for lumber; in 1849 there were 30 sawmills along the lower **Columbia** and **Willamette Rivers**. The **railroads** provided access to timber and also boosted the demand for lumber, especially for railroad ties, which accounted for up to 50% of the production of some Oregon mills. Locally, **flumes** were often used to transport lumber from mills to shipping points. After 1890, private timber companies began acquiring large acreages of land, sometimes fraudulently. Oregon has been the leading lumber producing state in the country since 1938, producing 5.45 billion board feet in 1993 with a wholesale value of $2.55 billion. Peak production was 9 billion board feet in 1953. Encyclopedia of American Forest and Conservation History; Hard Times in Paradise. See also **Forest products industry**; **Logging, history**; **Sawmills, history**; **Spruce Production Division**; **Timber and Stone Act of 1878**; **Timber harvest**; **Timber supply**.

Lumber trade history. Lumber was exported by the **Hudson's Bay Company** from **Fort Vancouver** to Hawaii in 1828-1829, though the early export market turned out to be unpredictable. California, supplied by ship, was an early and important market. After 1883 lumber shipments by rail to Denver, Salt Lake City, and Omaha became important. Empire of the Columbia. See also **Log exports**.

Lunar training. In 1965 astronauts trained on volcanic areas south of **Bend** in preparation for the first landing on the moon in 1969.

Lyme disease. A tick-borne illness that begins with flu-like symptoms and a bulls-eye rash, which may later be followed by more rash and neurological and cardiac disorders. It is effectively treated in the early stages with antibiotics. Nineteen cases were reported in Oregon in 1996, compared with over 5,000 in New York state.

Lynchings. In the dark early hours on July 8, 1887, Oscar Kelty, who was being held for the murder of his estranged wife the month before, was dragged from his jail cell in **Dallas** and hanged from an oak tree (now gone) that stood next to the courthouse. The case against Abraham Blackburn, the man accused of leading the lynching party, was dismissed, to the satisfaction of his two hundred armed supporters who were on hand for the hearing. This Side of Oregon. On September 18, 1902, in Marshfield (now **Coos Bay**), Alonzo Tucker, a black accused of attacking a white woman, was pursued by a mob and eventually shot while trying to escape. In 1924 the mutilated body of another black resident of Marshfield was found in the bay; the murder was never solved. Peculiar Paradise. In 1910 a recluse who had killed a man, perhaps in self defense, was lynched in northern **Grant County** while being taken to **Canyon City** for trial. Several of the participants were found guilty and served time in the penitentiary. "Emmet White, Part III". See also **Vigilantes**.

Lynx. A seldom-seen, short-tailed, gray, native cat, *Lynx canadensis*. It has ear tufts and fluffy "sideburns", no spots, and large feet. Though about the same size as a **bobcat**, its longer legs and fur make it look larger. Rare in Oregon, it lives in dense conifer forests where its chief prey, the snowshoe **hare** and **grouse**, are found. Atlas of Oregon Wildlife; Mammals and Life Zones of Oregon; Mammals of the Northwest.

Lyons. A timber town on the North **Santiam River** 23 miles southeast of **Salem** in **Linn County**. It was named for the pioneer family that established the community, and was incorporated in 1958. Attractions include John Neal Memorial Park, which fronts on the river, other parks along the river, outdoor activities, and the Lyons Annual Roar in July. Population 1980 877; 1995 950. Elevation 661'. PO Box 10, 97358. 503-859-2167. Chamber of Commerce 503-897-2865. Oregon Geographic Names.

Lyric Bards. See **De Moss family**.

Maar. A type of crater created when hot magma under the surface comes into contact with ground water, building enormous steam and gas pressures that eventually burst explosively through the overlying rock. The falling fragments build a low rim, but there is usually little ejected volcanic material. **Big Hole**, **Hole-in-the-Ground**, and **Fort Rock** are maars, as are lakes such as **Blue Lake** (Linn County) and North and South Twin Lakes near Wickiup Reservoir. Atlas of Oregon Lakes.

MacArthur Fellowships. Prestigious grants, sometimes called "Genius Grants," given without any application by the recipient and with no strings attached. Jane Lubchenco, marine biologist at **Oregon State University**, received a MacArthur Fellowship in 1993 and three members of the biology department at **University of Oregon** have been recipients, Franklin W. Stahl, Phil DeVries, 1988, and Russell S. Lande, 1997. The 1997 award was for $280,000. John D. and Catherine T. MacArthur Foundation, 140 S. Dearborn St. Suite 1100, Chicago IL 60603-5285. 312-726-8000. Oregonian 6/17/97:B1.

Made in Oregon sign. A favorite **Portland** Christmas landmark located at the west end of the Burnside Bridge. Erected originally in 1940 to advertise White Satin Sugar, the 48 by 46 foot neon sign was modified in 1959 to advertise White Stag sports wear, and the stag has sported a red nose each Christmas season since then. After White Stag moved to California and refused to pay upkeep, two local businessmen, the H. Naito Corporation, which owns the building, and Ramsay Sign Company, paid electric and maintenance costs for some years. In 1996 Naito agreed to long-term support if the lettering could be changed to "Made in Oregon", the name of one of their businesses. Oregonian 12/4/96:A1, 12/24/96:A1, 4/27/97:L1.

Madras. MAD-ruhs. A high-desert town in central Oregon located where **Highways 97** and **26** meet, 90 miles south of **The Dalles** and 42 miles north of **Bend**. **Mount Jefferson** dominates the western skyline and eight other snowcapped peaks can be seen from the area. The valley was known as The Basin, but about 1903 the town was finally named Madras, perhaps for some Madras cloth in the local store. The city was incorporated in 1911. In 1917 some local residents high-handedly moved the county records from **Culver** and established Madras as the county seat of **Jefferson County**. A fire in September 1924 nearly destroyed the town. An irrigation project, completed in 1946, brought water to 100,000 acres in the area where peppermint and carrot, garlic, and onion seed are now grown. Bright

Wood Corporation (wood products) is the major employer. Area attractions include rock hounding, fly fishing and rafting on the **Deschutes River** (7 miles to the west) and fishing and boating on **Lake Billy Chinook**. The **Warm Springs Indian Reservation** is across the Deschutes River to the west and the Crooked River National Grassland is to the east. The Rockhounder's Pow Wow Rock and Gem Show and the Jefferson County Fair and **Rodeo** are both held in July. Population 1980 2,235; 1995 4,675. Elevation 2,242'. 71 SE "D" St. 97741. 541-475-2344. Chamber of Commerce 800-967-3564. East of the Cascades; Oregon Geographic Names.

Madrone. A broadleaf evergreen **tree**, *Arbutus menziesii*, that is notable for its smooth, thin, peeling red bark. It is native from British Columbia to southern California. The largest in Oregon is near **Cornelius**, and is 246 inches in circumference (6 1/2 feet in diameter) and 70 feet high. Though attractive year-round, with white flowers in spring and small orange berries in the fall, its habit of shedding bark, berries, and leaves (in their second summer) makes it messy in a lawn. Trees to Know.

Magazines. See **Periodicals**.

Magness Tree Farm. A 70-acre demonstration forest and wildlife sanctuary near **Wilsonville**. It features a visitor center, **fire lookout** tower, hiking trails, and a log bunkhouse used for summer camps . The tree farm is operated by the **World Forestry Center**. 31195 SW Ladd Hill Road, Sherwood 97140. 503-625-7471.

Magnetic declination. The angle between true north and magnetic north. Since the magnetic north pole (located in the upper Hudson Bay region) does not align directly with the true north pole, a compass reading has to be corrected for the amount of the magnetic declination. In Oregon the compass needle points to the east of true north, ranging from about 17° E in the southeast corner of the state to 20° E in northwest. Magnetic north wanders a bit from year to year; the magnetic declination that is currently accurate for a given location is available from the county surveyor's office. The earth has also reversed magnetic poles on average every 250,000 years, though it has been 780,000 years since the last reversal. Studies of lavas from **Steens Mountain** show that for a time 16 million years ago the field shifted at about 6° a day, though sometimes it may take 5,000 years for a complete reversal. Oregonian 4/22/95:B5.

Mahogany Mountain. A 6,522' mountain in far eastern Oregon 20 miles northwest of **Jordan Valley** in the **Owyhee uplands physiographic province**. The peak rises 1,000 feet above **Leslie Gulch** on the southeast rim of an ancient **Miocene** volcanic **caldera** 10 miles in diameter. The name may come from the mountain mahogany shrub, *Cercocarpus ledifolius*. Geology of Oregon.

Mahonia Hall. Oregon's governor's mansion in **Salem**, donated to the state in 1987 by private sources who had raised $1.5 million for its purchase and furnishing. Until then, the state had no official residence. The Tudor-style house, designed by Ellis F. Lawrence, founder of the **University of Oregon** School of Architecture, was built in 1924 for Salem businessman and civic leader, Thomas Livesley. One of the smallest governor's mansions in the country, it is also one of the least expensive to operate and maintain. Volunteers raised funds to redecorate it in 1998. The state provides no staffing except a security guard. Mahonia is the former scientific name for the genus of **Oregon grape**, the state flower. Oregonian 7/15/95:E1.

Mail boats. In 1895 **postal service** was begun by boat from **Gold Beach** to the isolated mining community of Illahe, 37 miles up the **Rogue River**. It took two days to sail, row, pole, and tow the 18-foot boatload of mail and freight upstream. The service has continued, but it now takes jet boats, which carry tourists as well as the mail, only two hours. Mail is also delivered by boat three times a week on **Tenmile Lakes**. Gazette Times 6/9/95:A4.

Majestic Falls. See **McDowell Creek Falls Park**.

Malaria. In 1996 24 cases of malaria were reported in Oregon. During the early 1830's an **epidemic** of "ague and fever", now thought to be malaria, killed most of the Indians of the lower **Columbia River** (**Chinook**s) and the **Willamette Valley** (**Kalapuya**s). Dr. John McLoughlin wrote in 1830 that three-fourths of the Indian population in the vicinity had died within a few weeks. Whites used quinine to control the disease and most survived, which led the Indians to believe that American traders had poisoned the river. The Indians had no experience with diseases that caused fever and their traditional treatment, using a sweat followed by a plunge into cold water, proved fatal. By the end of the epidemic, it was estimated that 2,100 Chinook and Kalapuya Indians were left of the pre-contact population of 32,000. This devastation left the Willamette Valley remarkably open for settlement without Indian confrontations. "Another Look." See also **Fort William**; **Mosquitoes**.

Malheur Cave. A 3,000' long **lava tube** south of **Burns**; it contains a lake that comes to within 1,000 feet of the entrance and totally fills the distant lower end. **Paiute Indians** used the cave as a shelter. In the early 1800's they barricaded themselves in to survive a long siege by Bannock Indians; portions of the barricades were still in place in 1902. The cave is on private land 13 miles east of Princeton, about 3 miles off Highway 78; the entrance is located in a sagebrush flat. It is owned by the Masonic Lodge in Burns which uses it ceremonially. Oregon's Great Basin Country.

Malheur County. A large county in Oregon's arid southeast corner. Incorporated cities are **Vale** (county seat), **Ontario** (commercial center), **Adrian**, **Jordan Valley**, and **Nyssa**. The county, 94% rangeland, is drained by the **Malheur** and **Owyhee** rivers, both of which flow into the **Snake River** in the productive, irrigated **Treasure Valley** area. It is bounded on the east by **Idaho**, on the south by **Nevada**, and by **Harney**, **Grant**, and **Baker** counties. Elevations range from 2,080' along the Snake to the 7,420' Blue Mountain in the southwest and 7,811' **Ironside Mountain** in the northwest corner. The economy is based on agriculture, livestock, food processing, and recreation. Taxable assessed value in 1995 was $986,000,000, or $35,000 per capita. The county was founded in 1887 and named for the Malheur River. Population 1980 26,896; 1995 28,200. Area 9,926 square miles. Density 3/sq.mi. Annual precipitation 10"; average temperature January 29°F, July 76°F. Courthouse, 251 B St. W, Vale 97918. 541-473-5124. History of Malheur Country; Oregon Blue Book.

Malheur Field Station. A private, non-profit natural science educational facility located in **Malheur National Wildlife Refuge** and operated by a consortium of 22 Oregon and Washington colleges. Lodging and food service are available to the public between March 14 and October 15. It also sponsors science camps, family weekends, and teacher education. HC 72, Box 260, Princeton OR 97721. 541-493-2629. Oregon Blue Book.

Malheur Hot Springs. Hot springs located in **Vale** that were used by pioneers as a place to bathe and wash clothes. The springs are now augmented by a thermal well; the hot water is used to heat a mushroom growing facility in Vale and then is used for year-round heating of the city swimming pool.

Malheur Lake. A huge, shallow, freshwater lake and marsh south of **Burns** in the **Harney Basin**. The only larger Oregon lakes are **Goose Lake** and **Upper Klamath Lake**. At 'normal' size, Malheur Lake covers 50,000 acres, extends twelve miles in length, and has a maximum depth of five feet, but at some point in the 1930s the lake was completely dry, while in 1984 it reached the highest levels in historic times, covering 175,000 acres. It is fed by rainfall and by the waters of the Silvies River, the Donner and Blitzen River, and Sodhouse Spring. A **Pleistocene lake** covered over ten times the area 10,000 years ago and drained into the **Malheur River** through a gap at Crane; now, however, the outflow, if any, is through The Narrows to Mud Lake and on into **Harney Lake**. The marshes of the **Malheur National Wildlife Refuge** are enormously productive of waterfowl. Atlas of Oregon Lakes.

Malheur National Forest. A 1,541,082-acre eastern-Oregon national forest located primarily in **Grant** and **Harney** counties. It includes two wilderness areas, Strawberry Mountain and Monument Rock. 139 NE Dayton Street, John Day 97845. 541-575-1731.

Malheur National Wildlife Refuge. A federal waterfowl refuge along the Donner and Blitzen River in southeast Oregon. At one time, unbelievable bird populations attracted Indians, early settlers, and later, plume hunters to **Malheur Lake**. However, after egrets were exterminated and other species were greatly diminished, President Theodore Roosevelt created the refuge. It was enlarged in 1934 after Malheur Lake dried up in a drought, and again in 1940, so that it now contains about 185,000 acres. Though it has never regained the original numbers of birds, the refuge, containing the largest fresh-water marsh in the country, attracts thousands of nesting and migratory birds. Some 227 species of birds and 57 species of mammals have been cataloged at the refuge. A 40-mile long refuge patrol road provides wildlife viewing. There is also a museum. HC 72, Box 245, Princeton 97721. 541-493-2612. See also **Diamond Craters, Malheur Field Station**. Oregon Wildlife Viewing Guide; Oregon's Great Basin Country.

Malheur Reservoir. An irrigation and flood control impoundment in rangeland on Willow Creek 14 miles west of **Huntington**. It was constructed in the late 1930s by the Orchard Irrigation District to provide irrigation water to 2,300 downstream acres. The reservoir, if full, would cover 1,282 acres to a maximum depth of 105 feet. However, due to instability of the dam, the reservoir is kept 20 feet lower than its potential full-pool height. The lake has a boat ramp but no camping facilities and receives little recreation use other than some fishing. Atlas of Oregon Lakes.

Malheur River. A river that flows east from the south slopes of the **Straw-berry Mountains** past **Vale** to join the **Snake River** at **Ontario**. It drains an area of 4,710 square miles. The name, which means "misfortune", was given to the river after fur traders discovered that a cache of supplies and furs they had left along it had been stolen by the Indians. Oregon Geographic Names. See also **Keeney Pass**.

Malin. muh LIN. A southern Oregon farming community built on land reclaimed from the Tule Lake bed near the California border in **Klamath County**, 28 miles southeast of **Klamath Falls**. It was settled in 1909 by 50 families of the Czech Colonization Club from Nebraska. A large horseradish root found growing there inspired the settlers to name the town for the famed Malin horseradish of **Czechoslovakia**. The city was incorporated in 1922. Population 1980 539; 1995 755. Elevation 4,058'. PO Box 61, 97632. 541-723-2021. Oregon Geographic Names.

Malls. Oregon's first mall was Lloyd Center in **Portland** which was, at the time it opened in 1960, the largest urban shopping center in the nation. It was notable for its covered parking and for being located near the heart of the city rather than on the outskirts. See also **Factory outlet malls**.

Mammals. Fur-covered animals that bear live young and nurse them. Many are nocturnal so are little known. Distributions within historic times are noted in Mammals and Life Zones of Oregon and present distributions are mapped in Atlas of Oregon Wildlife. See also **Animals**; **Fossils**; **Marine mammals**; and names of individual mammals.

Manhunts. One of the most electrifying manhunts in the state's history occurred during the summer of 1902 after Harry Tracy and David Merrill escaped from the Oregon State Penitentiary on June 9. During two months of bloody and audacious escapades, while pursued by several hundred militia members, the handsome and polite Tracy killed seven men, including Merrill, and, finally, when cornered on a farm near Creston, Washington, himself. Dictionary of Oregon History; It Happened in Oregon; Oregonian 12/8/96:L5. See also **DeAutremont brothers**.

Manufactured homes. In 1990 manufactured homes accounted for 11% of the **housing** in Oregon, about half of them located in mobile home parks and half on private lots. By 1997 34% of all new Oregon homes were manufactured. Manufactured homes cost about $30 a square foot while site-built homes averaged $56. In 1994 over 12,000 manufactured homes were produced at 11 plants in Oregon, employing 3,200 workers. Oregonian 7/23/95:E1, 9/24/95:H1, 3/1/98:H1. See also **Highways**.

Manufacturing. Manufacturing's share of total payroll in Oregon fell from 26% in 1985 to 21% in 1995 (service industry's share increased from 17 to 22%). High technology accounted for 32% of manufacturing payroll in 1995 while timber, which in 1955 had accounted for 60%, had declined to 27%. Major products made in Oregon include **Tektronix** oscilloscopes, Hyster lifts, Freightliner trucks, Jantzen, White Stag, and Pendleton clothing, and Tillamook cheese. The Oregon Department of **Economic Development** publishes a Directory of Manufacturers in odd-numbered years. The 1993/94 edition listed over 5,000 in the state, arranged alphabetically, by location, and by Standard Industrial Classification (SIC) code number. <u>Oregon Blue Book</u>. See also **High-tech industry**; **Payroll**; **Semi-conductor industry**.

Manzanita. A north coast beach community in **Tillamook County** that lies between **Highway 101** and the ocean 27 miles north of **Tillamook**. It was platted in 1912, the post office was established in 1914, and the city was incorporated in 1946. The name, which comes from the Spanish word for "little apple", is the common name for a western Oregon shrub, *Arctostaphylos columbiana*. Population 1980 443; 1995 715. Elevation 31'. PO Box 129, 97130. 503-368-5343. <u>Oregon Geographic Names</u>.

Maple. Deciduous **trees** and shrubs with paired, propeller-like seeds called samaras. Oregon has three native maple species. Rocky Mountain maple, *Acer glabrum*, grows in clumps across the state, sometimes in deep woods and sometimes on rocky canyon walls; a subspecies is called Douglas maple. Vine maple, *A. circinatum*, often grows in impenetrable thickets called "devil wood" by early trappers, and contributes its glowing red colors to the fall forests of western Oregon. The bigleaf maple, *A. macrophyllum*, heavily festooned with mosses, grows to be a large tree in the moist valleys of western Oregon. It is frequently planted as a shade tree along streets where, in autumn, its yellow leaves pile up like huge cornflakes. Its wood is used for furniture, and its sap can be used for maple sugar except that Oregon's mild winters usually do not stimulate an adequate sap flow. The nation's largest bigleaf maple is near Jewell in **Clatsop County**, close to the junction of highways 202 and 103. <u>Trees to Know</u>.

Maps. The Oregon Department of **Transportation** publishes the Official State Map, which includes the most recent official elevations of major mountains. The <u>Oregon Atlas and Gazetteer</u> covers the state with topographic maps with 300-foot contour intervals and a scale of 1 inch equal to 2.4 miles in western Oregon and, for eastern Oregon, 600-foot contour intervals and a scale of 1 inch equal to 4.8 miles. More detailed topographic maps and geologic maps are available from a number of bookstores and nautical supply stores as well as from **Nature of the Northwest** Information Center, Suite 177, 800 NE Oregon Street #5, Portland OR 97232. 503-731-4444. A number of early maps of the state are compiled in <u>Historical Oregon</u>. See also **Geographic Information Systems**.

Marathon. A 26.2-mile foot race. Over 6,000 runners and walkers entered the 26th annual **Portland** Marathon on Sunday, September 29, 1996, many of them raising money for a charity of their choice. In 1997 Jerome Ellison of **Talent** completed his 51st marathon, having run in every state and the District of Columbia. <u>Mail Tribune</u> 6/21/97:1A; <u>Oregonian</u> 9/29/96:B1.

Marbled murrelet. A robin-size seabird, *Brachyramphus marmoratus*. It was not learned until a nest was discovered in 1974 that it lays its single egg on a moss pad high in **old growth** hemlock and **Douglas fir** trees up to 50 miles inland from California to Alaska. The adults, which fly up to 100 mph, may make 8 trips a day to bring small fish to their young hatchling. Numbers have been declining 4-7% a year in the western U.S. The 1992 listing of the marbled murrelet as a threatened species reduced logging of coastal old growth. <u>Atlas of Oregon Wildlife</u>; <u>Birds of Oregon</u>; <u>Oregonian</u> 8/4/96:A1. See also **Endangered species**.

Marcola. An unincorporated community in **Lane County**, located in the

Mohawk Valley 12 miles north of **Springfield**. The name, first used in 1885 for the railroad station, honored Mary Cole, the wife of the town's founder, though the post office had originally been called Isabel. Oregon Geographic Names.

Mare's egg. A colonial alga, *Nostoc pruniforme*, found worldwide in low-nutrient, cold (40°F) springs, including several around **Upper Klamath Lake**. The alga forms a ball of jelly encased in a dark, leathery covering. At 10 to 15 years old, the "eggs" can be 9" in diameter and weigh 5 1/2 pounds. A species of snail cleans the outside.

Margarine. A butter substitute given a U.S. patent in 1873. During **World War II** butter was both rationed and expensive, so many families started buying margarine. Dairy farmers had persuaded most state legislatures to decree that margarine, which is naturally white, could not be colored to look like butter, but small capsules of color were packaged with it. In 1951 Oregon representative Maurine Neuberger, a Democrat, demonstrated the messy process of mixing in color in front of the state legislature's Agriculture Committee. The resulting publicity resulted in overturning the law and has also been credited with ending a long period of Republican domination of Oregon politics. Adventures in Politics; Oregonian 3/21/51:1, 11/29/94:D9.

Marijuana. Between 1986 and 1990 the per cent of Oregon 11th grade students using marijuana dropped from 29% to 13%, but it went up again to 22% in 1996. Use by Oregon 8th grade students was 12% in 1986, dropped to 5% in 1990, and increased to 15% in 1996. Oregonian 10/22/96:B1.

Marine Board, Oregon State. A board of five members, appointed by the governor for four-year terms. It promotes boating safety, education and access through regulation and by registering boats, guides, outfitters, and charter boat operators. Some of its boating safety classes are offered through correspondence. 435 Commercial St. NE, #400, Salem 97310. 800-336-2628; 503-378-8587. Oregon Blue Book.

Marine mammals. Animals that spend all or most of their lives in the ocean. Oregon's marine mammals include **seals**, **sea lions**, **elephant seals**; sea **otters**, and **whales**. All marine mammals in Oregon are **protected animals**. The Marine Mammal Hot Line, 800-452-7888, operated by the **Oregon State Police**, can be used to report stranded whales and other problems.

Marine research. See **Mark O. Hatfield Marine Science Center** (Newport); **Oregon Institute of Marine Biology** (Charleston); **Sea Grant**; **Seafood Laboratory** (Astoria).

Marion County. Oregon's most productive agricultural county and seat of state government. Incorporated cities are **Salem** (county seat and state capital), **Aumsville, Aurora, Detroit, Donald, Gates, Gervais, Hubbard, Idanha, Jefferson, Keizer, Mount Angel, Saint Paul, Scotts Mills, Silverton, Stayton, Sublimity, Turner,** and **Woodburn**. The county extends east from the **Willamette River** to the crest of the **Cascade Range**, and is bounded by **Clackamas, Wasco, Jefferson, Linn, Polk,** and **Yamhill** counties. Elevations range from 50' along the Willamette to 9,000' on the slopes of **Mount Jefferson** in the southeast corner. The economy is based on government, agriculture, food processing, lumber, manufacturing, education, and tourism. Taxable assessed value in 1995 was $10.582

billion, or $41,000 per capita. The county was created in 1843 as the **Champooick District** and renamed in 1849 to honor Revolutionary War General Francis Marion (1732?-1795), also known as the Swamp Fox, whose biography was popular at the time. Population 1980 204,692; 1995 258,000. Area 1,194 square miles. Density 216/sq.mi. Annual precipitation 40"; average temperature January 39°F, July 66°F. Courthouse, 100 High St. NE, Salem 97301-3670. 503-588-5212. Oregon Blue Book.

Marion Lake. The largest lake in Oregon not accessible by car, Marion Lake is a 261 acre natural lake 63 miles southeast of **Salem** in Mount Jefferson Wilderness Area. The lake, a little over a mile long, has a maximum depth of 185 feet. It is popular with hikers and backpackers, and there is some fishing. An annual summer algal bloom seems to be the result of naturally high levels of phosphorous entering the lake from upstream marshes rather than as a result of human activities. The lake was named in 1874 by a Marion County road locating party. Atlas of Oregon Lakes.

Maritime Museums. See **Columbia River Maritime Museum**; **Oregon Maritime Center and Museum**.

Maritime Pilots, Oregon Board of. A board of nine members, appointed by the governor for four-year terms, that licenses maritime pilots. Pilot services are used for ocean-going ships on the **Columbia** and **Willamette** rivers, across the Columbia River bar, and at **Coos Bay** and **Yaquina Bay**. 800 NE Oregon St., Suite 507, Portland 97232. 503-731-4044. Oregon Blue Book.

Mark O. Hatfield Federal Courthouse. A 17-story edifice completed in 1997 at SW Salmon and Third in **Portland** for the federal **district court**. Constructed at a cost of $106.6 million, it is the most expensive building in Oregon history and is, at 563,338 square feet, one of the largest in downtown Portland. Total cost, including purchase of the site, demolition of the Hamilton Hotel, and design, was $129 million. Bill Pedersen of New York designed the building in collaboration with John Meadows of BOORA Architects of Portland. The 15 courtrooms are in a 343-foot tower topped with an arched roof, while offices are in a lower "side-car" portion. The building contains complex security and circulation systems, with three separate sets of hallways and elevators for judges, prisoners, and the public. Art includes water features by Eric Orr, sculptures by Tom Otterness, tapestries by Judith Fawkes, and inscriptions by Sandra Stone, the latter two from Portland. Mark Hatfield was the U.S. **senator** (Republican) from Oregon from 1967 through 1996. Oregonian 5/4/97:E1, 11/9/97:L1, 11/12/97:A1. See also **Courts, federal**.

Mark O. Hatfield Marine Science Center. A **Newport** research and teaching facility, part of **Oregon State University**, that opened in 1965. The Coastal Oregon Marine Experiment Station is also located at the center, as are labs and offices of several other state and national agencies. Two research vessels, the 177-foot *Wecoma* and the 37-foot *Sacajawea*, operate from the facility. Educational programs and an aquarium are provided for teachers, school children, and the public. 2030 Marine Science Drive, 97365-5296. 541-867-0100. Oregon Blue Book.

Mark O. Hatfield Research Center. A $60 million, 16-story, 266,000-square-foot building at the **Oregon Health Sciences University**, dedicated in 1998.

It houses basic and clinical research facilities. Oregonian 2/15/98:B1.

Marmot. A large, phlegmatic member of the squirrel family. Oregon's only species is the yellow-bellied marmot, *Marmota flaviventris*, which lives in rocky places in central and eastern Oregon where it eats vegetation. It is closely related to the Eastern woodchuck (also called groundhog), *Marmota monax*. Atlas of Oregon Wildlife; Mammals and Life Zones of Oregon; Mammals of the Northwest.

Marriage. There were 25,292 marriages in Oregon in 1995 (8 per 1,000 residents) and 15,289 **divorces** (4.9 per 1,000 residents). The marriage rate has dropped from 9.1 in 1947. The median age for Oregon marriages was 27 for women and 29 for men. Oregon does not recognize common law marriage. The 1997 Legislature inadvertently dropped a phrase in a bill with the result that marriage records less than 50 years old are closed to the public. The first marriage in Oregon was that of missionaries Jason Lee and Anna Maria Pittman on July 16, 1837. Missionary History; Oregon Blue Book; Oregonian 1/26/97:A1, 10/29/97:A10, 3/11/98:D5. See also **Domestic partnerships**; **Intermarriage**; **Justice court**; **Municipal court.**

Marshes. See **Wetlands**.

Marshfield. See **Coos Bay**.

Marten. A **weasel**-like animal, *Martes americana*, up to two pounds and 26 inches long (slightly larger than a **mink** and much smaller than a **fisher**) with valuable brown fur. It pursues **squirrels** and birds in mature conifer forests and forages on the ground for rodents, insects, and berries on a hunting circuit that may take a week or more to complete. 16 were trapped in 1994-95 with an average value of $16 each. Atlas of Oregon Wildlife; Mammals and Life Zones of Oregon; Mammals of the Northwest; Oregon Wildlife 51(1):8. Spring 1994.

Martha Springer Botanical Garden and Rose Garden. A garden on the south end of the campus of **Willamette University** in **Salem**. It includes roses, both newer and historic varieties, an English perennial garden, alpine rock garden, and 12-section botanical garden.

Martini glass. A 10-foot, lighted outline of a martini glass with olive that glowed for years at **Christmas** over **Portland's** West Hills after Buddy Meadows, Jr. built it in 1978 while still in high school. It was originally his signal to his Jesuit classmates, "Parents gone, party's on." Round the Roses.

Maryhill Museum of Art. A museum on the Washington side of the **Columbia River** 17 miles east of **The Dalles.** The building, once the home of Samuel Hill, entrepreneur and Quaker pacifist, houses a collection that includes paintings, Rodin sculptures, French glass, Russian icons, Indian baskets, weapons, and a Contemporary Northwest Artists Gallery. The museum also hosts special exhibitions. 509-773-3733.

Marylhurst College. An accredited private college near **Lake Oswego** that enrolled 1,286 students in 1995. The school, operated by the Sisters of the Holy Names of Jesus and Mary, **Catholic**, opened in 1898 as the first liberal arts college for women in the Northwest. It has since become a co-educational college specializing in night and weekend courses for older and working students. PO Box 261, Marylhurst 97036. 503-636-8141. Dictionary of Oregon History; Oregon Blue

Book.

Marys Peak. A mountain off Highway 34 west of **Corvallis** that is, at 4,097', the highest point in the **Coast Range**. It is capped by a 1,000-foot-thick sill of 30-million-year-old gabbro, intruded during the **Oligocene**. The meadowed summit is notable for wild flowers, including pentstemon and tiger lilies. Noble **fir** trees surround the meadows. A path from the end of the paved road leads 1/2 mile to the top where the view extends from the **Cascade Range** on the east to the ocean on the west. A small campground is nearby. The Indians called it mouse mountain or Chintimini. **French Canadian** fur trappers are said to have called the landmark Ste. Marie, later translated to St. Marys, and finally to Marys Peak. Oregon Geographic Names.

Marys Peak Trek. A 1950s annual barbecue and entertainment, held on **Marys Peak** west of **Corvallis** for a number of years, beginning in 1946. It was sponsored by the Shrine clubs of **Benton**, **Linn**, **Lincoln**, and **Polk** counties. As many as 8,000 people would drive the then-unpaved road to the meadows near the top for the day's doings.

Marys River. A 40-mile long river that drains 299 square miles from **Marys Peak** in the **Coast Range** east to the **Willamette River** at **Corvallis**. Both Indians and early fur trappers called it the Mouse River in various languages, but by 1846 it was called the Marys River, perhaps for Mary Lloyd who crossed it that year and was said to have been the first white woman to do so. Oregon Geographic Names.

Marysville. An early name for several Oregon communities and mining camps, including **Corvallis**.

Masonic Lodge. A fraternal organization with secret rituals. In 1995 membership in Oregon was 17,600, down 700 from the year before. Nationwide membership has dropped 39% since 1959. Masonic Grand Lodge of Oregon, 3435 Pacific Avenue, Forest Grove 97116. 503-357-3158. Oregonian 3/2/96:E1. See also **Schools, private**.

Mass transit. See **Public transit**.

Massacres. See **Cascades massacre**; **Chinese massacre**; **Modoc War**; **Rogue River War**; **Smith massacre**; **Whitman massacre**.

Massage Technicians, State Board of. A board of five members appointed by the governor for four-year terms that regulates massage practitioners and businesses. The license requires 100 hours of anatomy/physiology study, 45 hours of kinesiology, 50 hours of pathology, and 135 hours of massage practice and theory. The total number of hours required will increase to 500 in 1999. In June 1997, Oregon had over 2,500 active licensed massage technicians. 800 NE Oregon St., #21, Suite 407, Portland 97232. 503-731-4064. Oregon Blue Book.

Masters Games. See **World Masters Games**.

Matsutake. A large, choice, edible wild mushroom, *Armillaria ponderosa* (also called *Tricholoma magnivelare*). It is collected commercially from Oregon forests, primarily for export to Japan because of the similarity of its distinctive spicy aroma to that of the related and highly prized Japanese matsutake. Mushrooms Demystified.

Matterhorn. A 9,832' peak of blue-white marble, in the **Wallowa Mountains** in northeastern Oregon. Glaciers carved out headwalls on several sides leaving bare vertical rock faces on the steep peak. It was named for the famous peak in the Swiss/Italian Alps. Geology of Oregon.

Maupin. MAW pin. A north-central Oregon community in **Wasco County** 44 miles south of **The Dalles** on Highway 197. It is located in the canyon of the **Deschutes River** where pioneer Howard Maupin had a ferry crossing. The city was incorporated in 1922. Maupin is now a center for **white water boating**. Population 1980 495; 1995 490. Elevation 1,041'. PO Box 308, 97037. 541-395-2698. Oregon Geographic Names.

Maury Mountains. A small, isolated mountain range southeast of **Prineville** at the **geographic center of Oregon**. The mountains, drained by the **Crooked River**, include a couple of 6,000' peaks, and are noted for moss **agates**. They are in the **Ochoco National Forest**. Colonel Maury fought in the Indian wars of central Oregon in the 1860s. Gem Trails of Oregon; Oregon Geographic Names.

MAX. A 15-mile **Tri-Met light rail** system that runs between downtown **Portland** and **Gresham**. Built for $214 million, it opened September 5, 1986. Westside MAX Roads and Rails is a six-year, $1 billion project, begun in 1993, designed to extend the line west to **Hillsboro**. The largest public works project in Oregon's history, it includes a three-mile-long tunnel 260 feet beneath the Portland area west hills. The underground Washington Park station is reached by elevator or by a staircase of 469 steps. The name MAX comes from Metropolitan Area Express.

Maywood Park. A separately incorporated city inside the **Portland** city limits that began as a 1926 subdivision northeast of **Rocky Butte**. It was named by the developer's wife who remembered how lovely the woods were in May. The residents voted to incorporate in 1967 in an effort to prevent construction of **Interstate 205** through the area. Population 1980 845; 1995 790. Elevation 77'. 4510 NE 102nd Ave., Annex #1, Portland 97220. 503-255-9805. Oregon Geographic Names.

Mazamas. A mountaineering club, Oregon's oldest, organized by 155 men and 38 women on the summit of **Mount Hood** on July 19, 1894. Membership is open to those who have "climbed on foot to the summit of a mountain on which there is a 'living' glacier..." The club conducts over 300 official climbs each year, plus hikes and other outdoor programs, maintains clubrooms in **Portland** and a lodge at **Government Camp**, and publishes Mazama, an annual. Mazama is Spanish for **mountain goat**. 909 NW 19th, Portland 97209. 503-227-2345.

McCall Preserve. See **Tom McCall Preserve**.

McCarthyism. An anti-Communist movement in the late 1940s and into the 1950s named for Senator Joseph McCarthy, Wisconsin Republican, whose tactics included indiscriminate accusations and unsubstantiated charges based on guilt by association. In Oregon, a number of businesses and agencies fired employees suspected of being Communist sympathizers, and **Reed College** fired tenured philosophy professor Stanley Moore on August 13, 1954, after he refused, on constitutional grounds, to answer a question from the U.S. House Un-American Activities Committee as to whether or not he was a Communist - though years later he revealed that he was not. "Oregon Tests Academic Freedom."

McDermitt. An unincorporated community on Highway 95 in southeast

Oregon that lies across the Oregon/Nevada border. Fort McDermitt Indian Reservation is nearby. The town was named for Lieutenant-Colonel Charles McDermit (with one t) of the Second Cavalry, California Volunteers, who was killed by Indians in 1865 while scouting along a nearby creek. The **Star City Stage Line** ran through the town. Oregon Geographic Names.

McDermitt caldera. The largest of several immense **calderas** formed by a series of **Miocene** eruptions of ash-flow tuffs in southeast Oregon 16 million years ago. Actually a series of overlapping calderas, the McDermitt complex has a combined diameter of 22 miles and lies across the Oregon-Nevada line west of Highway 95. **Mercury** was mined from three mines in the caldera from 1917 to 1957, and there are significant deposits of **uranium**. Geology of Oregon, Oregon Geographic Names.

McDonald/Dunn Forest. **Oregon State University's** 11,000-acre research and laboratory forest, located north of **Corvallis** on lands donated to the university for that purpose. What is now forest was for centuries primarily oak savanna, maintained by the **Kalapuya Indians'** annual burning. Edge Effects; Trees to Lumber. See also **Indian burning**.

McDowell Creek Falls Park. A day-use **Linn County** park eight miles north of **Sweet Home** with trails to two major waterfalls, 119-foot Royal Terrace Falls and 40-foot Majestic Falls. James McDowell was an early settler in the area. Waterfall Lover's Guide.

McIver State Park. See **Milo McIver State Park**.

McKay Reservoir. A 1,316 acre irrigation reservoir on McKay Creek five miles south of Pendleton. It was created in 1927 by a **Bureau of Reclamation** earth fill dam 165 feet high, built as part of the **Umatilla Project**, and is still operated by the Bureau. The lake, over three miles long with a maximum depth of 118 feet, provides water for the Stanfield and Westland Irrigation Districts. The lake also provides some flood control, but recreation use is limited by the summer drawdown. There are no camping facilities. The lake is surrounded by the 515-acre McKay Creek **National Wildlife Refuge**. Atlas of Oregon Lakes.

McKenzie Bridge. An unincorporated fishing and summer home community located on the **McKenzie River** 48 miles east of **Eugene**. The Log Cabin Inn has been restored to be much like the original 1886 inn, which hosted such famed guests as Herbert Hoover, Clark Gable, and the Duke of Windsor. The name comes from the historic river crossing, now bridged by **Highway 126**. Oregonian 5/31/96:A14.

McKenzie Pass. A pass, elevation 5,325', east of **Eugene**, through the central **Cascade Range** between **Mount Washington** and the **Three Sisters**. Dee Wright Observatory, built from the local **lava**, provides views of snow capped peaks and young lava flows from **Belknap Crater** and Collier Cone, and a paved interpretive trail explores the lava. The first cattle trail over the pass opened in 1862 and wagons used it soon after. **Highway 242** provides seasonal access over what was once the only route between Eugene and central Oregon, but now **Clear Lake Cutoff**, opened in 1962, provides a faster all-season route over the Cascades.

McKenzie River. A famed 90-mile long white water boating and fishing river that flows from the **Three Sisters** of the **Cascade Range** west to join the

Willamette River just north of **Eugene**. Its 1,340 square mile drainage basin includes Mohawk River, Blue River, South Fork, Horse Creek, and White Branch. Several dams have been built on the McKenzie and its tributaries for power generation, water supply, and flood control. It was named for Donald McKenzie, a member of Astor's **Pacific Fur Company**, who explored the Willamette Valley in 1812. Oregon Geographic Names. See also **Blue River Reservoir**; **Clear Lake (Linn County)**; **Eugene Water and Electric Board**; **Cougar Reservoir**; **Koosah Falls**; **Proxy Falls**; **Sahalie Falls**; **Tamolitch Falls**.

McKenzie River Gathering Foundation. A public **foundation** that funds multi-issue, social change projects in Oregon. The foundation, begun in 1976, is funded by donations. 3558 SE Hawthorne Blvd, Portland 97214. 800-489-6743; 503-233-0271.

McLoughlin House. A historic house, now located at 713 Center Street in **Oregon City**, built in 1845 by Dr. John McLoughlin (1784-1857). Dr. McLoughlin, a British citizen, was known as the Father of the **Oregon Country** because of his years as chief factor for the **Hudson's Bay Company** at **Fort Vancouver**, his activities in establishing industries and a townsite at Oregon City, and his aid to the early missionaries and pioneers, a kindness that engendered a perverse resentment among the American settlers. However, in 1851, after he became an American citizen, he was elected mayor of Oregon City. The house, originally on the lower level of town, was moved to its present site in 1909. One of the oldest buildings in Oregon, it is a National Historic Site maintained by the National Park Service and volunteers. 503-656-5146.

McMinnville. A **Willamette Valley** city 40 miles southwest of **Portland** on **Highway 99W**. It was founded in 1853 by William T. Newby who named it for his birthplace in Tennessee. The post office was established in 1855; the city was incorporated in 1882. In 1887, after a bitter fight, the **Yamhill County** seat was moved to McMinnville from **Lafayette**. The city is also home to **Linfield College**, the center of a major **wine** region, and the site of the proposed **Captain Michael King Smith Evergreen Aviation Educational Center** which will house the **Spruce Goose**. Evergreen International Aviation is a major employer. Population 1980 14,080; 1995 22,140. Elevation 157'. 230 NE 2nd St., 97128. 503-434-7301. Chamber of Commerce 503-472-6196. Old Yamhill.

McNary Dam. A 7,300 foot-long dam across the **Columbia River** six miles from **Hermiston** and 75 miles upstream from the **John Day Dam**, built for power generation (990.5 **megawatts**) and navigation. **Army Corps of Engineers** completed the dam in 1953 and operates it. **Bonneville Power Administration**, which distributes the power, canceled an unfinished 10-megawatt power project at the dam in 1995 because the electricity produced would have been too expensive. Average annual discharge is 169,800 cubic feet per second. Two 2,000-foot-long fish ladders, each 30-feet wide, enable migrating salmon to swim upstream past the dam. Lake Wallula, formed by the dam, extends upstream 64 miles. Hat Rock State Park is on the lake. McNary Project Office, PO Box 1441, Umatilla 97882. 541-922-3211.

McNary Lock. A **lock** at **McNary Dam** that enables boats and barges to bypass the dam. The lock, completed in 1953, is 86 feet wide by 675 feet long with a single maximum lift of 83 feet and a sill depth of 15 feet. Passage takes about 20 minutes.

Meacham. An unincorporated railroad community of 150 persons in the **Blue Mountains**, located on **Interstate 84** between **Pendleton** and **La Grande** at an elevation of 4,100 feet. It is one of the coldest spots in the state, said to have been minus 62°F in the 1920s. President Warren G. Harding passed through on July 3, 1923, and declared Meacham the capital of the U.S. for that one day. It is named for the Meacham brothers who operated a stage station there in the 1860s before Alfred Meacham became Superintendent of Indian Affairs in 1869. Meacham; Oregon Geographic Names; Oregonian 2/1/96:E6. See also **Temperature records**.

MEAD. A project in **Tillamook County** with plans to produce fertilizer and generate .8 **megawatt** of electricity from the manure of 10,000 cows. Each cow produces about 85 pounds of manure a day. The acronym is derived from Methane Energy and Agricultural Development

Meadow mice. See **voles**.

Meadowfoam. A small flowering plant, a hybrid of *Limnanthes alba* and *L. floccosa*, being grown for its seed oil which is used in cosmetics, plastic, and rubber production. Farmers in the **Willamette Valley** plant about 8,000 acres, using it as a rotation crop with **grass seed**. Oregonian 8/27/97:A17.

Meadowlark. See **State bird**.

Measles. In 1996 14 cases of measles were reported in Oregon. A measles epidemic, introduced from California in July 1847, killed 10% to 40% of the Indians of Oregon within a year. The **Cayuse Indians**, who lost nearly half of their tribe in the epidemic, blamed the deaths on poisoning by missionary Marcus Whitman whom they then killed in the **Whitman massacre**. The Indians had no diseases that were accompanied by fever, and their traditional healing method using a sweat lodge and cold plunge treatment was deadly when used for the febrile diseases of measles, small pox, and **malaria**. "Pacific Northwest Measles Epidemic of 1847-1848." See also **Epidemics**.

Measure 5. A **property tax** reduction ballot measure passed by the voters of Oregon in November 1990. The measure, conceived by Gresham businessman Don McIntire, required property assessments to be at actual sales values, immediately limited property tax rates for local government to $10 per $1,000 of assessed value, and phased in rate reductions for schools from an average of $16.75 per $1,000 in 1990-91 down to $5 per $1,000 in 1995-96. It also mandated that some of the school shortfall be replaced from the state **general fund**. It was estimated that by 1996 homeowners' property taxes would again be at pre-Measure 5 levels due to assessment increases, but that business property, which had increased less in value, would pay 30% less than in 1990. The effects of the measure included a shift of school support from local property tax to state **income tax** funding, cuts in state spending on other programs including **higher education**, and an increase in the **student-teacher ratio** from an average of 18 elementary students per teacher in 1990 to 23 students per teacher in 1994-95. **Local government**s have not been so hard hit as schools. For example, during the same period in which **Portland** schools lost about $50 million, city revenues increased about $80 million. Oregonian 3/19/96:A1. See also **Equalization**; **Measure 47**; **School funding**.

Measure 11. An **initiative** ballot measure passed in 1994 that mandated tough mandatory minimum prison sentences for violent crime. Sentences ranged from nearly six years for second-degree assault to 25 years without eligibility for parole or early release for murder. It applies, too, to first-time offenders and juveniles as young as 15. Results have included both a burgeoning prison population and an increase in **plea bargaining**. Oregonian 10/11/95:B1. See also **Correctional facilities**; **Juvenile corrections**.

Measure 47. An initiative constitutional amendment to reduce and limit property taxes and limit local revenues and replacement fees, authored by tax activist Bill Sizemore and adopted by voters in November 1996. In May 1997 voters replaced the measure with **Measure 50** because of the legal confusions of Measure 47.

Measure 50. A long and conplex constitutional amendment to reduce property taxes that was referred by the legislature to replace **Measure 47**. It was adopted by the voters in May 1997. Measure 50 limits **property taxes** by rolling back property assessments to 90% of the 1995-96 real market value and limiting future assessment increases to 3% a year. It also reduced each taxing district's levy by an estimated 17% except that voter-approved levies could be added back in. The tax rates were then permanently fixed, based on the 1997-98 levy. Assessed values for new and improved property can be adjusted and added to the district's value. Voters can adopt certain local option taxes. Taxing districts can increase user fees. The measure retains **Measure 5** limits but exempts voter-approved bonds and levies if approved at a general election or at one with at least a 50% turnout. The measure substitutes a tax rate system for the established **tax base** system. Voters' Pamphlet 5/20/97.

Medford. A rapidly growing commercial and transportation center in southern Oregon, 273 miles south of **Portland** on **Interstate 5** and 30 miles north of the California border. It is the county seat of **Jackson County**. The community was founded in 1884 as a stop on the new **Oregon and California Rail Road**, and was incorporated the next year, having claimed both the railroad and the county seat from **Jacksonville**. It was named for Medford, Massachusetts, appropriate because it was at the middle ford on Bear Creek. The town's growth has been based on agriculture and lumbering; at the end of **World War II** the city had 76 operating sawmills. It is home to the **Rogue River National Forest** and **Bureau of Land Management** district offices. The surrounding **Bear Creek Valley** is famous for its winter **pears**; the annual Pear Blossom Festival is held in mid-April. Attractions include the History Center, the restored Craterian Ginger Rogers Theatre, and a jazz festival held in October. Alba, Italy, is its sister city. Population 1980 39,746; 1995 55,090. Elevation 1,382'. 411 W 8th St., 97501. 541-770-4432. Visitors Bureau 800-469-6307. Land in Common. See also **Good Government Congress**; **Metropolitan Areas**; **Roxy Ann Peak**.

Medford District, BLM. An 861,012-acre district of **Bureau of Land Management** forest lands, primarily in **Jackson** and **Josephine** counties. 3040 Biddle Road, Medford 97504. 541-770-2200. BLM Facts.

Mediation. See **Dispute Resolution Commission**.

Medical Assistance Programs, Office of (OMAP). An office in the Department of **Human Resources** that administers federal and state Medicaid funds for low income Oregonians through the **Oregon Health Plan**. The 15-member Governor's Advisory Committee on Medical Assistance for the Underprivileged provides guidance. 500 Summer Street NE, Salem 97310-1014. 503-945-5772. Oregon Blue Book. See also **Health Plan Administrator**.

Medical Examiners, Oregon Board of. An eleven member board, established in 1889, that governs licensing and discipline of **physicians** (7,457 in 1997) and **physician assistants** (263), doctors of osteopathy (374), podiatrists (110), acupuncturists (244), and respiratory care practitioners (978). Board members are appointed by the governor. Seven must be MD's, two are Doctors of Osteopathy, and two are public members. The board operates on fees and fines rather than tax money. In 1996 the Board completed investigations of 309 complaints of which 68% were found not to violate Oregon's Medical Practice Act. Actions on the rest included suspension, revocation, reprimands, or letters of concern. Since 1995 the Oregonian has published quarterly lists of formal disciplinary actions taken by the Board. Reports on the status of a physician's license are available from the Board for a fee. 1500 SW 1st Avenue, Portland 97201-5826. 503-229-5770. Oregon Blue Book; Oregonian 1/30/97:B9. See also **Chiropractors**; **Naturopathic Examiners**.

Medical school. See **Oregon Health Sciences University**.

Medical Springs. A one-time spa resort named for its hot sulfur springs, located in **Union County**, 35 miles southeast of **La Grande**. It is the settlement closest to the **geographic center of the United States**. History of Union County.

Meek's Cutoff. See **Lost Wagon Train**.

Megawatt. A measure, equal to one million watts or 1,000 kilowatts, of potential electric power. A megawatt supplies sufficient power for about 1,000 people. The **hydroelectric power** dams on the **Columbia River** each have a capacity of 1,000 or more megawatts, as did **Trojan nuclear plant**. A megawatt-hour is the amount of energy used to keep 10,000 lightbulbs, each 100 watts, burning for an hour. An **electric power plant** with a nameplate capacity (a generator's maximum electrical output) of 100-megawatts has the theoretical capacity to supply 876,000 megawatt-hours a year of energy (100 megawatts x 8,760 hours in a year.) In 1994 the average Oregon residence used over 1 megawatt-hour of electricity a month and the state used a total of 40 million megawatt-hours during the year. Oregon Utility Statistics. See also **Electricity consumption**.

Melridge, Inc. An Oregon company based at **Aurora** that, during the 1970s and 80s, was the world's leading producer of **lily** bulbs. George R. Heublein bought the company in 1975 and began to sell stock to the public in 1983. Soon after Heublein resigned in 1987 the company collapsed. Heublein disappeared, but was finally arrested in 1996, pled guilty to federal tax and fraud violations, and was sentenced to five years in prison. The 5,100 investors lost $88 million, and Heublein was accused of swindling $52 million of that. A series of class action suits by 4,800 investors over nine years recovered $55.4 million, less $20 million in attorney fees. Oregonian 5/25/96:A1, 6/14/96:A1, 2/5/97:B1, 3/1/97:B5, 4/29/97:B1.

Memorial Coliseum. A multipurpose auditorium near the east end of the

Broadway Bridge that is home to the **Winter Hawks** hockey team. It was designed by Skidmore, Owings and Merrill and built in 1960. Prior to completion in 1995 of the **Rose Garden**, the income from the Coliseum had helped fund the **Portland Center for the Performing Arts**. The Blazers manages the city-owned building. 1401 N. Wheeler. 503-321-3211 (recording); 503-235-8771 office. Frozen Music.

Meningococcal disease. A life-threatening infection of the blood or the lining of the brain and spinal cord, or both, that develops when a common bacterium, *Neisseria meningitidis*, becomes active, for reasons unknown. The onset is sudden and flu-like with a developing rash, and the disease is fatal 90% of the time if left untreated. It is more common in winter, and is more common in infants and children. A new and more active strain, known from elsewhere in the world, appeared in the U.S. for the first time in Oregon in 1993. In 1994 there were 140 cases in Oregon, with eight deaths. Oregon has the highest rate in the nation. Oregonian 3/7/96:B12, 2/12/97:B2, 12/21/97:B8.

Mennonites. An Anabaptist Protestant denomination that originated in 1525 in Switzerland. Several Mennonite congregations were organized in the **Willamette Valley** in the 1890s and others congregations were added later. By 1940 there were over 1,300 Mennonites in the valley. Though many were farmers, respected for their industry and farming practices, others worked in other occupations. During **World War I**, their commitment to Pacificism and Germanic heritage made them the object of hostilities, especially in **Harrisburg** and **Albany**. "Quiet Pacifists."

Mental Health and Developmental Disability Services Division. A division of the Department of **Human Resources** that is the umbrella agency serving people with mental and developmental disabilities. Services include medicine, therapy, and social work. It oversees 33 community mental health programs and operates **Eastern Oregon Training and Psychiatric Centers**, **Fairview Training Center**, and **Oregon State Hospital**. Another of its facilities, **Dammasch State Hospital**, was closed in 1995. 2575 Bittern St. NE, Salem 97310. 503-945-9499. Oregon Blue Book.

Mercer Lake. A two-mile-long natural lake five miles north of **Florence**. Its depth of 38 feet puts the bottom six feet below sea level. The 359-acre lake has two major arms; there is a public boat ramp at the end of the northeast arm but no other public facility. The lake shore is heavily built up with private residences, resulting in decreased water quality. The lake was named for George Mercer, who surveyed the line through the lake in 1879. Atlas of Oregon Lakes; "Days at Mercer Lake."

Mercury. While there are no active mercury mines in Oregon at the present, mercury has been mined in the past, and mercury-rich cinnabar ore is found in several locations. A number of mines were scattered within a belt 20 miles wide in the **Calapooya Mountains** east of **Interstate 5** between **Cottage Grove** and **Roseburg**; Bonanza Mine in **Douglas County** produced nearly 40,000 76-pound flasks before it closed in 1961 after nearly a century of operation. Mercury mines in the **McDermitt caldera** produced a total output of 270,000 flasks, the richest supply in the western hemisphere. Mercury has also been mined on **Steens Moun-**

tain, in **Jefferson County**, and in **Lake County**, both in the Quartz Mountain area west of **Lakeview** and near Glass Buttes. The Oregon **Health Division** has issued warnings about eating fish from the **Willamette River**, **East Lake** and from **Brownlee**, **Cottage Grove**, **Owyhee**, Jordan Creek, and Antelope (Malheur County) Reservoirs because of unsafe levels of naturally-occurring mercury in the fish. Geology of Oregon; Oregonian 6/17/95:D1, 2/16/97:C9.

Mercy Flights. A subscription-supported community air ambulance, headquartered in **Medford**. At the time George Milligan founded it in 1949, it was the first community-plan air ambulance service in the U.S. Tales out of Oregon.

Merrill. A southern Oregon farming community in **Klamath County** near the California border, 20 miles southeast of **Klamath Falls**. It was named for Nathan Merrill, an 1890 settler who laid out part of the town in 1894. The city was incorporated in 1903. Population 1980 822; 1995 835. Elevation 4,064'. PO Box 487, 97633. 541-798-5808. Oregon Geographic Names.

Merry-go-rounds. See **Carousels**.

Metals. See **Aluminum**; **Copper**; **Gold**; **Hafnium**; **Iron**; **Lead**; **Mercury**; **Minerals**; **Nickel**; **Niobium**; **Silver**; **Uranium**; **Zinc**; **Zirconium**.

Meteorite. A piece of matter that has hit the earth from somewhere else in the solar system. Four have been discovered in Oregon: in Sams Valley north of **Medford**, near **Klamath Falls**, in **Salem**, and near **Oregon City**. An object that may have been a meteorite struck Jubilee Lake in northern **Union County** on September 10, 1995. See also **Fireballs**; **Port Orford Meteorite**; **Willamette Meteorite**.

Methamphetamine. An easily-made, illegal, addictive drug, made in Oregon or smuggled in from Mexico and California, and seen by some as replacing cocaine in popularity. In 1995 52 Oregon deaths were related to methamphetamines. Oregonian 6/4/96:A1.

Methane. The principal constituent of **natural gas**. It is a colorless, odorless gas created by the decomposition of organic matter in the absence of air and used for fuel and power generation. Methane emissions in the state totaled 0.279 million tons in 1995. 43% was from landfills, 36% from domestic animals (primarily cattle), and the rest from manure, natural gas production and distribution, and utility power generation. Electricity is being generated from methane collected at two landfills (Short Mountain. **Eugene** 3.2 megawatts, and Coffin Butte, **Corvallis**, 2.2 megawatts), and Project **MEAD** proposes to generate power from methane collected from dairy wastes. Report on Reducing. See also **Greenhouse gases**; **Natural gas production**.

Methodist Church. The fifth largest religious denomination in Oregon with about 30,000 members, down from a peak of 55,000 several decades ago. Methodists were the first Christian denomination to send missionaries to Oregon. A party of five, headed by the Rev. Jason Lee, came overland in 1834 and established the **Willamette Mission** and its Indian and Manual Labor School. In 1838 they established a second mission, **Wascopam**, at **The Dalles**, and in 1840 they established missions at **Clatsop Plains** and **Willamette Falls** and began mission activities at what would become **Salem**, 10 miles south of the original mission. In 1842, after disappointing results and a series of floods, they moved their educational activities south to the Salem site and focused on educating the children of white settlers. That school evolved to become **Willamette University**. The 1844 Methodist church (now gone) in **Oregon City** was the first Protestant church built on the Pacific Coast. The **Jacksonville** Methodist church, dedicated in 1855, is the oldest Methodist church still standing west of the Rockies. **Oregon State University** had **Methodist** beginnings as **Corvallis College**. Dictionary of Oregon History; Guide to Early Oregon Churches; Oregonian 10/23/96:C1. See also **Blue Mountain University; Metolius; Portland University; Religion; United Brethren Church**.

Methodist Mission. See **Willamette Mission**.

Metolius. A central Oregon agricultural community four miles southwest of **Madras** in **Jefferson County**. It is located six miles east of the confluence of the **Metolius River** and the **Deschutes River**. The area was settled in 1902 by a colony of German Methodists. The city was incorporated in 1913, after it had become a railroad division point. Irrigation has since made Metolius a farming center. Population 1980 451; 1995 630. Elevation 2,530'. 636 Jefferson Ave., 97742. 541-546-5533. East of the Cascades.

Metolius River. A 41-mile-long tributary of the **Deschutes River** that rises from the **Springs of the Metolius**. It flows at a nearly constant rate north through pine forests and then east through a deep gorge at the base of Green Ridge to **Lake Billy Chinook**, draining the eastern slopes of **Three Fingered Jack** and **Mount Jefferson**. The total drainage basin area is 450 square miles. Many of the springs feeding the Metolius are at $40°$ F, providing waters too cold for any fish but bull trout. In 1988 Congress declared the river a **National Wild and Scenic River**, managed by the **Deschutes National Forest**. The name comes from a **Warm Springs** Indian word meaning a white fish or light colored salmon. Oregon Geographic Names.

Metro. The popular name for the Metropolitan Service District, a regional government established by voters in 1978 to manage growth in the urban **tri-county** area. The **Regional Framework Plan**, adopted in 1997, is its long-range plan. Metro includes **Multnomah, Washington**, and **Clackamas** counties and 24 cities plus other governmental units. The area's 1.3 million residents account for over a third of the state's population. In addition to land use and transportation planning, Metro is responsible for operating solid-waste disposal and recycling services, former **Multnomah County** parks, golf course, and cemeteries, **Metro Washington Park Zoo, Oregon Convention Center, Portland Center for the Performing Arts, Expo Center**, and **Portland Civic Stadium**. Budgeted spending for the 1998-99 fiscal year totaled $389 million, with 28% for solid waste disposal, 25% for parks, 12% for the zoo, 11% for operating other facilities, 5% for planning, 8% for bond debt service, and 10% for general fund. **Property taxes** support a $28.8 million **bond** issue for the zoo that voters approved in 1996 and a $135 million bond issue for park acquisition approved in 1995, plus a levy that provides some operating support for the zoo. All other Metro operations are supported by fees and excise taxes, including about 28¢ a month on garbage bills. The executive officer is paid $81,600 a year. An elected seven-member Metro Council governs the district. Metro is the only elected regional government in the nation and the only one with a home-rule **charter** approved by the voters (1992). It was preceded by the Columbia Region Association of Governments (CRAG). 600 NE Grand Ave., Portland 97232-2736. 503-797-1700. Governing Oregon; Oregon Blue Book; Oregonian 12/30/96:B3, 3/10/98:A8. See also **Boundary commissions**.

Metro Washington Park Zoo. Oregon's only major zoo, operated by the three-county **Metropolitan Service District** in **Portland**. The 65-acre zoo is noted for its **elephant** breeding program, its Humboldt penguins, an African Rain Forest replica, 26 endangered and 43 threatened species and participates in 13 species survival plans. The zoo also operates a children's petting zoo and the **Center for Species Survival**, an off-site breeding and research facility. Events include a series of summer concerts on terraced lawns, the ZooBoo haunted train ride on Halloween, the Zoolights holiday lights festival, and the ZooBloom flower festival in the spring. In 1995 the zoo began disposing of its manure through Whitney Farms in **Independence**, which planned to compost and sell it, donating the profits to the zoo. 4001 SW Canyon Road, Portland 97221. 503-226-1561. Oregon Blue Book. See also **Rhythm and Zoo**; **Your Zoo and All That Jazz**; **Washington Park**; **Washington Park Fences Project**; **Zoo Railway**.

Metropolitan Areas. For the 1990 census the Bureau of the Census defined a Metropolitan Area as a city with a minimum population of 50,000 or an urbanized area of at least 100,000. A relatively free standing Metropolitan Area was defined as a Metropolitan Statistical Area (MSA). Oregon had three MSAs. The **Eugene-Springfield** MSA (282,912) included all of **Lane County**. The **Salem** MSA (178,024) included all of **Marion** and **Polk** counties. The **Medford** MSA (146,389) included all of **Jackson County**. See the **Portland-Vancouver Consolidated Metropolitan Statistical Area** (1,477,895) entry for its more complex definition.

Metropolitan Service District. See **Metro**.

Mexicans in Oregon. See **Hispanics**.

Mexico. Oregon's annual exports to Mexico have ranged from $55 million to $135 million in the 1990s, and over 100,000 Oregonians are from Mexico. It maintains a consulate in Portland at 1234 SW Morrison Street, 97205. 503-274-1442.

Mice. Oregon has 24 species of mice, each occupying its own ecological niche. Unlike **shrews**, mice are vegetarian, except for the Northern grasshopper mouse of eastern Oregon which will kill and eat not only grasshoppers but other mice its own size. Other Oregon mice include the harvest mouse, deer mouse, canyon mouse, piñon mouse, kangaroo mouse, 2 pocket mice, 2 jumping mice, 13 species of **voles**, and the introduced house mouse. Atlas of Oregon Wildlife; Mammals and Life Zones of Oregon; Mammals of the Northwest.

Mickey Hot Springs. A 20-acre site in the **Alvord Basin** that includes pools, steam vents, a **geyser**, and Oregon's only mud pot. The **Bureau of Land Management** has fenced the area to keep out cattle, but it is accessible to visitors on foot. Oregonian 3/13/97:E8.

Middens. Piles of discarded shells, bones, and other waste left by Indians near their coastal villages, easily spotted because of the white shells. One of the largest, 40 feet high, was north of **Yachats** where the Adobe Motel now stands. A midden excavated near **Tahkenitch Lake** was 500 feet long and 150 feet wide. Since rising ocean levels have drowned earlier shore lines, none of the middens is more than 5,000 years old. Most of the middens have been obliterated in recent years by erosion or development. Archaeology of Oregon.

Middle Sister. A 10,047' volcanic peak in the central Oregon **Cascade Range**. It is one of the **Three Sisters**.

Midwives. Persons other than physicians who assist at **childbirth**. Oregon midwives delivered over 5,000 babies in 1993. In 1996 Oregon had 160 certified nurse midwives who are registered nurses with a master's degree in a health profession and who work primarily in hospitals. There were also about 50 direct-entry midwives licensed by the Board of Direct Entry Midwifery, 700 Summer St. NE, Suite 100, Salem 97310, 503-378-8667. Though no formal education is required for direct-entry midwives, they must meet required levels of experience, continuing education, and peer review. They may be reimbursed by insurance. There are also unknown numbers of lay midwives, trained largely through apprenticeships, who cannot bill insurance companies. Oregonian 6/17/95:C1. See also **Nurses**; **Obstetricians**.

Migrant labor. In 1990 Oregon had 121,000 workers harvesting farm crops. Of those, 66,000 were from other countries, 29,000 were migrant American citizens who follow the harvest, and 25,000 were Oregonians, half of them children. Facts of Life. See also **Braceros**; **Farm labor**; **Hispanics**; **Undocumented workers**; **Valley Migrant League**.

Migrant workers. See **Undocumented workers**.

Military Department. An Oregon department that is headquarters for the state Army and Air **National Guard**, the **Defense Force**, and all state-owned or leased armories, posts, camps, military reservations and rifle ranges. The state provides 3% of its operating budget and the rest comes from the federal government. 1776 Militia Way SE, PO Box 14350, Salem 97309-5047. 503-945-3991. Oregon Blue Book. See also **Camp Rilea**; **Camp Withycombe**.

Military in Oregon. See **Army Corps of Engineers**; **Camps**; **Civil War**; **Forts**; **Indian wars**; **Military wagon roads**; **Oregon Rangers**; **World War I**; **World War II**.

Military wagon roads. Roads built in the 1860s after Congress granted lands totaling some 2,270,000 acres to the state to be awarded to five private Oregon companies that had agreed to construct wagon roads, many connecting military **forts**. Most of the **land grants** were comprised of the odd numbered sections (a section is a square mile) for three miles on each side of the road right of way. The five companies were **Oregon Central Military Wagon Road**, 666,656 acres (1864); **Corvallis and Aquina Bay Military Wagon Road**, 81,895 acres (1866); **Willamette Valley and Cascade Mountain Military Wagon Road**, 861,512 acres (1866); **The Dalles Military Wagon Road**, 556,627 acres (1867); and **Coos Bay Military Wagon Road**, 105,240 acres (1869). State officials fraudulently certified some of the roads as having been built so that the companies could receive their land grants. Earlier, in the 1850s, the Army had scratched out some roads so that they could move troops and supplies during the first **Indian wars**. Army Engineers; Dictionary of Oregon History; "Federal Road Building Grants for Early

Engineers; Dictionary of Oregon History; "Federal Road Building Grants for Early Oregon".

Militias. Oregon has an official volunteer militia called the **Defense Force**. There were also several organized anti-government, para-military militia organizations in central Oregon and the **Willamette Valley** at the time of the Oklahoma City bombing on April 19, 1995, but most disbanded due to the hostile publicity. In 1997 there were again reported to be 19 patriot groups and three militias in the state. In some states, militia activities, inspired by The Turner Diaries, a 1979 book written by Oregon resident William Pierce, writing under the name Andrew Macdonald, have moved from civil disobedience to violent action. Mail Tribune 4/27/97:1A; Oregonian 4/22/95:A10, 4/28/95:D3, 6/6/95:A1, 6/8/97:E7. See also **Common law courts**.

Milk. One of Oregon's top five agricultural commodities in 1994 with a total value of $222.8 million. **Tillamook County** led in production, followed by **Marion**, **Linn**, **Washington**, and **Yamhill** counties. The state's 100,000 cows produced an average of 17,140 pounds of milk per cow for a total production of 1,714 million pounds. The use of the growth hormone BST is legal in Oregon. In 1997, the state legislature designated milk as the official **state beverage**. 1994-1995 Oregon Agriculture. See also **Dairy products**.

Milk Carton Boat Race. An annual contest held at **Portland's** Westmoreland Park casting pond during the **Rose Festival**. Boats must be built of gallon and half-gallon cartons and be no longer than 13 feet. The contest attracts hundreds of entries.

Mill City. A logging community near **Gates** in the western foothills of the **Cascade Range** 30 miles southeast of **Salem**. The town lies on both sides of the North **Santiam River** so is in both **Marion** and **Linn Counties**. The post office was established in 1888, and named Mill City because a sawmill had been moved to the site from **Stayton** the year before. It was incorporated in 1947. A historic wrought-iron railroad bridge, originally used near San Jose, California, now serves as a pedestrian bridge across the river. Other attractions include the Canyon Life Interpretive Museum, Fishermen's Bend Park, fishing, and boating. Population 1980 1,565; 1995 1,610. Elevation 829'. PO Box 256, 97360. 503-897-2302. Chamber of Commerce 503-897-2865. Oregon Geographic Names.

Mill Creek Falls. A 173-foot waterfall that drops into the upper **Rogue River** near **Prospect**. Access is from Mill Creek Road which parallels **Highway 62** to the south between Prospect and Cascade Gorge. From Mill Creek Road a trail, constructed as part of Boise Cascade Corporation's Mill Creek Falls Scenic Area, leads .3 mile to the falls and, in another tenth mile, to a view of 175-foot Barr (sometimes Bear) Creek Falls. Waterfall Lover's Guide.

Mill Ends Park. A **Portland** city park, the smallest in the world. It is a 24 inch diameter circle in the median strip at SW Front Avenue and Taylor Street. The site was originally a utility pole hole out of which Oregon Journal columnist Dick Fagan, while celebrating St. Patrick's Day in 1948, claimed to have seen a leprechaun emerge. Fagan promoted it as a park in his "Mill Ends" column, and in 1976 it was transferred to the city park department. Oregonian 3/18/76:B1.

Mill pond. A pond next to a sawmill into which logs were dumped for scaling, sorting, and storage. The pond provided a comparatively easy way to move logs around in the days before heavy equipment was available.

Millersburg. A central **Willamette Valley** industrial community in **Linn County** just north of **Albany**. It incorporated in 1974 to avoid annexation with Albany, which has a higher property tax rate. Industries include Allegheny Teledyne (1,150 local employees in 1997), Willamette Industries Duraflake Division, and Georgia Pacific Resins. It was named for the pioneering Isaac Miller family which had come from Millersburg, Illinois. Population 1980 562; 1995 725. Elevation 222'. 4222 NE Old Salem Road, 97321. 541-928-4523. Oregonian 11/13/94:B5.

Millican. A hamlet 24 miles southeast of **Bend** that received national publicity in the 1940s as a "one-man town." At that time the post office, gas pump, and store were operated by the town's only citizen, bachelor William Rahn. The post office operated between 1913 and 1953. George Millican was an early stockman in the area. Oregon Geographic Names.

Million Man March. A gathering held in Washington, D.C., on October 16, 1995, as an opportunity for black men to gather for renewal and atonement. Over 200 attended from Oregon. Oregonian 10/18/95:A8.

Milltown Hill Dam. A controversial proposed 186-foot-high dam to be built by **Douglas County** on Elk Creek east of **Yoncalla**. The 6.5-mile long reservoir would flood a square mile of land and supply irrigation water to farmland through a 19-mile pipe. Concerns have been expressed about the $46 million cost, the effect on **endangered** cutthroat **trout**, and potential **mercury** contamination from natural deposits in the area. The National Marine Fisheries Service issued an assessment that the dam would block fish from spawning areas and could send toxic amounts of mercury into the water, but mitigation measures may allow its construction. Oregonian 9/24/96:B6, 12/10/96:B6, 2/21/97:A1, 4/8/97:B6.

Milo McIver State Park. A **state park** 25 miles southeast of **Portland** on the **Clackamas River**. The park includes a fish hatchery, a seven-mile equestrian trail, a four-mile hiking trail, group facilities, and a 45-unit campground. Reservations, 800-452-5687. It is located on Highway 211 five miles west of **Estacada**. McIver, a strong supporter of state parks, was a member of the Oregon Highway Commission from 1950 to 1962.

Milton-Freewater. A northeast Oregon center of diversified agriculture in **Umatilla County** 30 miles northeast of **Pendleton** in the Walla Walla Valley. Milton, possibly named for the postmaster's birthplace in New York, incorporated in 1889, while rival Freewater, settled by Milton dissidents who offered free water rights to attract residents, was incorporated in 1892. The two merged in 1950, and ten years later received an All-America City Award for the cooperative work of its citizens in combining civic and municipal operations. The area suffered a significant earthquake in 1936. Attractions include the Cinco de Mayo Fiesta in early May, the Muddy Frogwater Festival the third weekend in August, and a Harvest Festival in early October at the Frazier Farmstead Museum. Population 1980 5,086; 1995 5,985. Elevation 1,071'. Rainfall 13.6 inches. PO Box 6, 97862. 541-938-5531. Chamber of Commerce 541-938-5531. Oregon Cattleman; Oregon Geographic Names.

Milwaukie. A Portland-area suburban community on the **Willamette River**

six miles south of **Portland** and six miles north of **Oregon City** on **Highway 99E**. It was founded in 1847 by Lot Whitcomb who named it for Milwaukee, Wisconsin (which was spelled variously at the time), and grew quickly to a population of 500 by 1850. It was incorporated in 1903. Population 1980 17,931; 1995 20,015. Elevation 39'. 10722 SE Main St., 97222. 503-786-7555. Oregon Geographic Names.

Mima mounds. See **Patterned ground**.

Mimi. A German bark that was stranded at the south entrance to the **Nehalem River** on February 13, 1913. No lives were lost until an attempt was made to tow it back to sea on April 6 in the face of an approaching storm. The emptied ship rolled in the surf, and, despite several days of controversial rescue attempts while crowds watched, 17 crew members died. Shipwrecks of the Pacific Coast.

Mineral springs. See **Hot springs**; **Lithia water**.

Mineral wealth. Oregon produced nonfuel minerals in 1992 worth $214 million, 38th in the nation. The construction materials of cement, sand, gravel, and crushed stone accounted for 85% of the total. Oregon was the country's only producer of **emery** and **nickel**, was first in the production of **pumice**, third in **diatomite**, and was a significant producer of **zeolite**. In addition to the many minerals mined in the past and present in Oregon, a wealth of minerals and **metals**, including **zinc**, **iron**, **gold**, and **copper**, may be present off the Oregon coast. Mineral Industry of Oregon. See also **Asbestos**; **Bentonite**; **Borax**; **Chromite**; **Clay**; **Diatomite**; **Emery**; **Gemstones**; **Limestone**; **Metals**; **Mining**; **Ozokerite**; **Perlite**; **Potash**; **Pumice**; **Sand and gravel**; **Silicon**; **Zeolite**.

Mines (explosives). Mines have occasionally washed up on Pacific beaches. The mouth of the **Columbia River** was mined during **World War II**, and mines were also used at sea. A Soviet mine, deployed during the Korean war, washed up on a **Tillamook County** beach, hit a rock and exploded, breaking windows in nearby homes. Wrecks of Japanese Junks.

Minimum wage. In 1996 Oregonians voted to raise the minimum wage in Oregon, which had been $4.75 an hour since January 1, 1991, to $5.50 in 1997, $6 in 1998, and $6.50 an hour (the highest in the nation) in 1999. Time-and-a-half pay is required for time worked over 40 hours a week. The minimum wage must be paid even for jobs that receive tips. Some workers, especially in agriculture and domestic services, are not covered by the law. A state poster that gives information about the minimum wage and working conditions must be posted in each place of employment. In 1976 the minimum wage was $2.30, equivalent to $5.74 in 1994 dollars. The federal minimum wage was raised in September 1997 to $5.15. Bureau of Labor and Industries, Wage and Hour Division, 800 NE Oregon #32, Portland 97232. 503-731-4074.

Mining. There were 30,000 mining claims in Oregon in 1992. Mining of sand, gravel, and stone yielded $130 million in Oregon in 1992, while other metals and minerals from 31 active mines yielded $111 million. Twelve of the mines were placer **gold** mines in **Baker**, **Grant**, and **Josephine Counties**. The other mining included **clay** for bricks (**Multnomah** and **Klamath Counties**), **bentonite** (**Crook** and **Malheur Counties**), **zeolite** (**Malheur County**), **diatomite** (**Harney**, **Malheur**, **Lake**, and **Crook Counties**), **perlite** (**Baker County**), **pumice**

(**Deschutes County**), **limestone** (**Baker**, **Douglas**, and **Josephine Counties**), silica (**Coos, Douglas,** and **Jackson Counties**), **Oregon sunstone** (**Harney** and **Lake Counties**), soapstone (**Jackson County**), **copper, zinc, silver** and **nickel** (**Douglas County**). "Mining and exploration in Oregon during 1992".

Mining districts. Districts organized quickly by **gold** miners to provide basic regulation for their activities. The first three in Oregon were organized in 1852 at **Jacksonville**, Sailors Diggings, and Althouse Creek in southwest Oregon. When the Federal Mining Act of 1866 was passed it recognized local regulations if they did not conflict with existing state or federal laws. Gold and Silver in Oregon; Gold Mining in Oregon. See also **Gold mining**.

Mining law. Mining is governed by the federal 1872 Mining Act, which allows a person to stake a claim on federal lands and to live on the claim if doing $100 worth of work a year on the claim, or, since 1992, for an annual payment of $100. Once a claim has produced enough to support a "prudent man" it can be patented, and the government has to sell it to the claimant, whether individual or corporation, for $2.50 to $5.00 an acre. In 1992 the Oregon **Environmental Quality Commission** adopted the nation's most rigorous mining standards. In 1994 an **initiative** that would have tightened them even further was defeated with Newmont Mining Corporation providing $3.6 million to fund the opposition.

Mining, recreational. See **Gold panning**.

Mink. A slim, semi-aquatic, fur-bearing, carnivore, *Mustela vison*, larger than a **weasel** and smaller than a **marten**, found throughout Oregon near water. It preys primarily on aquatic animals such as **muskrats, fish,** and **frogs**. Mink are up to 24 inches long, a third of that in tail, and weigh up to four pounds. They are fierce fighters, able to damage dogs many times their size. Curved nails enable them to climb trees easily, though they are more likely to take to water to escape pursuit. In 1994-95, 370 wild mink were trapped, with pelts averaging $7 each. In 1995 Oregon's 27 commercial mink farms produced 196,000 pelts with a value of $7.7 million. Atlas of Oregon Wildlife; Mammals and Life Zones of Oregon; Mammals of the Northwest; 1995 Oregon; Oregonian 6/4/97:A1.

Minorities. See **Gender**; **Minority, Women and Emerging Small Business Office**; **Race**.

Minority, Women and Emerging Small Business, Office of. A state office responsible for promoting economic opportunities for disadvantaged minority and women-owned businesses, as well as for emerging **small businesses** that meet eligibility requirements. It distributes a list of certified businesses. 350 Winter St. NE, Salem 97310. 503-378-5651. Oregon Blue Book.

Minors. Persons under 18 years of age. Minors are no longer required to have work permits, but child labor laws apply to working young people, ages 14-17, and their employers. Provisions include the number of hours of work allowed and working conditions. Minors must be paid at least minimum wage. Younger children may work on farms under specified conditions. Bureau of Labor and Industries, Wage and Hour Division, 800 NE Oregon #32, Portland 97232. 503-731-4074.

Mint. In 1868, prompted by the **gold rush** in eastern Oregon and Idaho, a U. S. mint was completed at **The Dalles**, but by the time it was completed the gold rush had subsided, so it never actually minted coins. Its newly-appointed director had drowned in the sinking of the *Brother Jonathan* in 1865. Gold and Cattle Country; Treasures of the Oregon Country.

Mint (crop). In 1995 Oregon growers produced 3.9 million pounds of peppermint for oil, worth $57.8 million, on 51,360 acres. This is 43% of the U.S. total. Oregon also grew 6% of the nation's spearmint. 1995 Oregon. See also **National Germplasm Repository**.

Miocene. A geologic epoch between 11 and 25 million years ago, preceded by the **Oligocene** and followed by the **Pliocene**. During the Miocene western Oregon continued to rotate clockwise; Oregon's coastline moved west to near its present location, the northern **Coast Range** emerged, there was extensive volcanism and faulting which produced the **basin and range** mountains of south-central Oregon along with a line of **andesite** volcanoes stretching north from **Gearhart Mountain** to **Strawberry Mountain**, **Columbia River basalt** was extruded, and the older western **Cascade Range** was uplifted, cutting off moisture to eastern Oregon and changing its earlier wet, tropical climate to the drier one of today. Geology of Oregon. See also **John Day Fossil Beds**.

Mirror Pond. A mile-long pond on the **Deschutes River** in **Bend** formed by Steidl Dam. The dam was built in 1910 to provide electricity to the town. Parks on both sides of the river provide access to the pond. East of the Cascades.

Misdemeanor. An action that breaks a law, more serious than an **infraction**, and less serious than a **felony**. A misdemeanor is punishable by a fine, imprisonment, or both.

Missing Children Clearinghouse. See **Police, Oregon State**.

Mission Bottom. A low-lying area along the east side of the **Willamette River** across the river from **Wheatland**, about 10 miles north of **Salem**. It was the location of **Willamette Mission**.

Mission Mill Village. A five-acre complex of historic buildings in **Salem**. Tours visit the 1841 **Jason Lee House** and Methodist Parsonage, 1847 John D. Boon Home, 1858 Pleasant Grove Presbyterian Church, and 1863 Thomas Kay Woolen Mill. The Marion County Historical Society Museum is also at the Village. 1313 Mill Street SE, Salem 97301. 503-585-7012; 800-874-7012.

Missions. In 1832 the New York press reported that four Nez Perce or Flathead Indians had appeared in St. Louis seeking the "white man's Book of Heaven." Moved by the plea, five **Methodists**, led by the Rev. Jason Lee, came west in 1834 and established **Willamette Mission** north of **Salem**. Additional Methodist missions were established in 1838 at **The Dalles** (**Wascopam**), and in 1840 on the **Clatsop Plains**, at **Willamette Falls**, and at what became **Salem**. Dr. Marcus Whitman and Henry Spaulding, representing the American Board of Commissioners for Foreign Missions, established missions in 1836 near Walla Walla, Washington, and at **Lapwai**, Idaho. The first **Catholic** priest in Oregon, Father Francois Blanchet, arrived in 1838; **St. Paul**'s mission was dedicated on January 6, 1840. Dictionary of Oregon History. See also **Whitman massacre**.

Missoula floods. See **Pleistocene floods**.

Mistletoe. Semi-parasitic plants that grow on host **trees**. Oregon has nine species. *Phoradendron flavescens*, the traditional Christmas mistletoe, grows on oaks and can eventually kill them.   It has small, thick leaves and sticky white berries.   The other eight species grow on various native conifers.   Some do not seriously damage the host conifers, though mistletoe in **Douglas-fir** can cause an abnormal and damaging bushy growth called witches broom, especially in southwest Oregon.   Manual of the Higher Plants.

Mitchell. A central-Oregon community in Bridge Creek canyon in **Wheeler County**, 82 miles northeast of **Bend** on **Highway 26**. It was originally a stop on the **stage** route from **The Dalles** to **Canyon City**. The post office, established in 1873, was named for John Hipple Mitchell, Oregon's newly elected Senator. The town, rebuilt after an 1884 flood that took three lives, was incorporated in 1891. About half the town was destroyed by fire in August, 1899, though the 1894 **Baptist** Church still survives. Much of the rebuilt town was again destroyed by a **flash flood** on July 11, 1904 that took two lives. Another flood on July 13, 1956 also caused extensive damage. The community operates a **boarding high school**. The **Painted Hills** unit of **John Day Fossil Beds National Monument** is six miles northwest of town. Population 1980 183; 1995 175. Elevation 2,777' PO Box 97, 97750. 541-462-3366. Oregon Geographic Names; Oregon Ghost Towns.

Mitchell Monument. A monument near **Bly** to six people killed May 5, 1945 on Gearhart Mountain in **Lake County** by a Japanese **balloon bomb**. The six were Elsye Mitchell, the pregnant wife of the Rev. Archie Mitchell, and five children, out on a Sunday School picnic. The children were Jay Gifford, 13, Edward Engen, 13, Sherman Shoemaker, 11, Joan Patzke,13, and Dick Patzke, 14. Only the minister survived. He later became a missionary in Vietnam, working in a leper colony until he was taken prisoner by Communist guerrillas and never heard from again.   Weyerhaeuser Timber Company built the monument. Mail Tribune 7/6/97:1B; Silent Siege.

Mixtecs. A non-Spanish-speaking ethnic group from the Mexican state of Oaxaca, 3,000 miles from Oregon, from which comes much of the state's lowest-paid migrant agricultural labor. Sometimes called the "little people", they are noted for being tireless and productive.   Their linguistic isolation makes them highly dependent on labor contractors. Nosotros. See also **Hispanics**.

Mobile homes. See **Manufactured homes**.

Moby Mary. A 13-foot killer whale (**orca**) that appeared in **Columbia Slough** off **Portland**'s **Jantzen Beach** on October 12, 1931. The whale, known also as Jimmy McCool's whale for an Oregonian wildlife reporter, intrigued the thousands who came to see it cavorting in fresh water. The public was outraged when, on October 24, Ed Lessard and his son killed the whale with harpoons. Some other parties quickly hijacked the dead whale and briefly put it on exhibit. It then disappeared for a day and a half until the sheriff tracked it down in a storage shed and had the ripening animal embalmed as evidence. The Lessards were found guilty of killing a fish by illegal means, but an appeals court exonerated them when it ruled that a whale was not a fish. The Lessards then took the pickled whale on tour in Washington state while Oregon courts considered its disputed ownership. By the time the state of Oregon won possession four years later it had decided that it no longer wanted a pickled whale. The whale presently disappeared again, until discovered in 1979 by loggers deep in the forests of Clark County Washington. There, under 15 feet of dirt, they buried the still-preserved whale. Oregonian 8/29/79:E8.

Mocks Crest. A bluff above the **Willamette River** in **Portland** on the east side of the river, overlooking Mocks Landing (formerly Mocks Bottom) and **Swan Island**. Mocks Bottom was named for Henry Mock who settled there in 1852. Mocks Crest was named for his son John who settled on the bluff and gave land there for what is now the **University of Portland**. Oregon Geographic Names. See also **Waud Bluff**.

Modoc Indians. A group of Indians that lived along **Lost River** and around the lakes (Lower Klamath Lake and **Tule Lake**) that existed at one time south of **Klamath Falls**. Their opposition to being confined to the **Klamath Reservation** led to the **Modoc War, 1872-1873**. After their defeat the few survivors were shipped off to Oklahoma, though a few later returned to the Klamath Reservation. Federal recognition was reestablished for the Oklahoma Modocs in 1978. 515 G. St. SE, PO Box 939, Miami OK 74355. 918-542-1190.

Modoc War, 1872-1873. An **Indian war** along the Oregon-California border that broke out in November 1872 when troops attempted to return Modoc Indians from **Lost River** to the **Klamath Reservation** where they had been assigned to live with their traditional enemies, the **Klamath Indians**. In January 1873, after a series of fights and raids, the Modocs took refuge in lava beds south of Tule Lake, California, an area now set aside as Captain Jack's Stronghold in Lava Beds National Monument. The army was unsuccessful in routing them so held a series of peace negotiations. During one of these the Indians killed General Edward Canby. The siege continued, but in May the Indians scattered as food and water became scarce, and by June 3 the last had been captured. The four Modoc leaders were tried and hanged, and the remaining 153 Modocs were shipped to an Oklahoma reservation where many died. In 1903 some Modocs were allowed to return to the Klamath Reservation. Twenty years before the war, in one of a series encounters between Modocs and whites, a white vigilante had killed most of the 46 people in a Modoc village. Hell with the Fire Out; Klamath Tribe; Modocs and Their War. See also **Camp Warner**.

Molalla. Both moh-LAH-luh and MOH-lah-luh. A **Willamette Valley** foothills ranching and timber town 15 miles south of **Oregon City** in **Clackamas County**. Molalla post office was established in 1850 near the community of Liberal; it was moved to the present site about 1875. The city was incorporated in 1913; its shield features a bucking bronco with the slogan "Riding High for America". The Molalla Apple Festival is held in October. The Molallas were an Indian tribe of the area, related to the **Cayuse Indians**. Population 1980 2,992; 1995 4,045. Elevation 371'. PO Box 248, 97038. 503-829-6855. Oregon Geographic Names.

Molalla River. A 50-mile long river that flows from the west slopes of the **Cascade Range** into the **Willamette River** near **Canby**. The **Pudding River** joins it a mile from its mouth. The drainage basin is 878 square miles, and average annual volume, as measured near the mouth, is 1,726,500 acre feet, or 3.4 acre feet/acre. The Molalla Indians were a Waiilatpuan tribe related to the northeast Oregon Cayuse Indians whose legends say that the Molallas were driven west by hostile tribes many years before. Oregon Geographic Names.

Moles. Underground insectivores, living on earthworms, larvae, and insects that they locate by smell and vibration. Unlike **pocket gophers**, they eat little vegetation. A mole has a pointy snout, tiny eyes, no external ears, paddle-like front feet with large claws for digging, velvety black or gray fur, and a naked tail. Four species occur in Oregon. The largest, Townsend's mole, *Scapanus townsendi*, of western Oregon, grows to nine inches long and is especially abundant in the **Willamette Valley**, where a single mole can create as many as 500 one-foot mounds in a season. Atlas of Oregon Wildlife; Great Pacific Northwest Nature Factbook; Mammals and Life Zones of Oregon; Mammals of the Northwest.

Monasteries. **Catholic** monasteries in Oregon include the Brigittine **Monastery of Our Lady of Consolation** in **Amity**, the Trappist **Our Lady of Guadalupe** near **Lafayette**, the Servite Order of Servants of Mary at the **Grotto** in **Portland**, and two Benedictine orders in **Mount Angel**, **Mount Angel Abbey** and **Queen of Angels Monastery**.

Monastery of Our Lady of Consolation. A cloistered Brigittine **Catholic** monastery in **Amity** noted for the fudge and chocolate truffles sold through its gift shop. The 14 monks chant the Liturgy of the Hours seven times a day. Some services are open to the public, but guests are asked to call before attending. 23300 SW Walker Lane, Amity, 97101. 503-835-8080.

Money. The Indians of Oregon engaged primarily in barter, but **dentalium** was also used as a medium of exchange. After fur trading began, a beaver skin was used as a standard unit. After the settlers came, money was in short supply, and for several years people had to make do with barter and with substitutes such as **Abernethy rocks** and **beaver money**. During the **Depression**, sheepskin and **buckskin scrip** was used in eastern Oregon. Dictionary of Oregon History; Oregon Oddities.

Monmouth. "Hometown Pride." A central **Willamette Valley** college town on **Highway 99W** in **Polk County** 14 miles southwest of **Salem**. It was established in 1855 when members of an 1852 pioneer group from Monmouth, Illinois, gave 640 acres of land for a town and Christian Church college. The post office was established in 1859; the city was incorporated in 1880. The college became a state school in 1882 and is now **Western Oregon State College**. Monmouth is the only city in Oregon that is dry; the sale of liquor and its consumption in public have been prohibited since the city charter was adopted in 1881. Attractions include the **Paul Jensen Arctic Museum**, Western Days Parade on the 4th of July, the 1880 Gentle House, the Victorian Tea Festival in August with tours of historic homes, Baskett Slough **National Wildlife Refuge** to the north, and Sarah Helmick **State Park** to the south. Population 1980 5,594; 1995 7,225. Elevation 213'. 151 W Main, 97361. 503-838-0722. Visitor information 800-772-2806. Oregon Geographic Names.

Monroe. A south **Willamette Valley** farm town 18 miles south of **Corvallis** on **Highway 99W** in **Benton County**. It was first settled in 1853; Starr's Point was the post office name. In 1874 the name was changed to honor the fifth president of the U.S., and in 1914 the city was incorporated. Monroe Brick and Tile Company is a major local business. Many **Christmas trees** are raised in the hills west of town. Population 1980 412; 1995 495. Elevation 288'. PO Box 486,

97456. 541-847-5176. Oregon Geographic Names. See also **Love seat**; **Picnic tables**.

Monsters. Tales of monsters in Oregon include the **Conser Lake monster** as well as water monsters in **Devils Lake** and **Wallowa Lake**. Oregon's Ghosts and Monsters.

Monteith House. A historic home built in 1849 in **Albany** by brothers Thomas and Walter Monteith who had founded the city the year before. The house resembles the farmhouses around their home town of Albany, New York. Historic events associated with the house include the founding of the state **Republican** party. Architecture Oregon Style.

Monument. An isolated northeast Oregon ranching community 60 miles northwest of **John Day** in **Grant County**. It is on the North Fork of the **John Day River**. The post office, established in 1874, was named for nearby Monument Mountain, so named because it resembles a pulpit. The city was incorporated in 1947. Area attractions include scenic vistas, wildlife viewing, hunting, and fishing. Population 1980 192; 1995 170. Elevation 2,000' PO Box 426, 97864. 541-934-2025. "Emmet White, Part III"; Oregon Geographic Names; Tracking down Oregon.

Monuments. See **Astor Column**; **Bell tower**; **Oregon Holocaust Memorial**; **Stonehenge replica**; **Suzhou stone**.

Moose. A horse-sized North American deer relative, *Alces alces*, that is reported to have been native at one time in the **Blue Mountains** of northeast Oregon. In 1922 five moose were introduced at **Tahkenitch Lake** where they persisted for a few years. At least two moose have in recent years wandered into northeast Oregon where one was killed in 1993 by a hunter who thought it was a cow elk. Mammals and Life Zones of Oregon.

Moraine. A pile of glacial debris, called till, composed of a mix of rocks, gravels, and soil. A terminal moraine is the till deposited at the end of a glacier, and lateral moraines are deposited along the sides of a glacier. Some of the largest in Oregon are the lateral moraines along the sides of **Wallowa Lake**, which are 1,200 feet high from lake bottom to crest. See also **Glaciation**.

Morels. Choice edible wild **mushrooms**, *Morchella esculenta* and related species, found in the spring, especially in recently burned areas. It is sought eagerly by both amateurs and commercial gatherers, though all are notoriously secretive about their best patches. Mushrooms Demystified.

Mormon basin. A high plateau that lies across the **Baker/Malheur** county line, between Bridgeport and Rye Valley. It was named for an 1862 group of Utah prospectors who found **gold** in the area. Oregon Geographic Names.

Mormons. A popular name for members of the Church of Jesus Christ of Latter-day Saints, a church based on the Book of Mormon. See also **Religion**.

Morning Star of Tillamook*.** A **schooner** built by residents of the **Tillamook Bay** area in order to bring in supplies to their isolated area. All of the boards, iron bolts and fittings were made by hand from local timber and iron gleaned from shipwrecks. The novice builders completed it after just a few months of intense effort in 1854, and launched it on January 1, 1855. Tillamook; To Build a Ship (novel). See also ***Star of Oregon.

Moro. A north-central Oregon community that is the county seat of **Sherman County**. It is located 38 miles southeast of **The Dalles** on **Highway 97**. The area was first settled in 1868. The city, named perhaps for Moro, Illinois, was incorporated in 1899. Population 1980 336; 1995 285. Elevation 1,807'. PO Box 231, 97039. 541-565-3535. Oregon Geographic Names.

Morrow County. A northern-tier **wheat**-growing county along the **Columbia River**. Incorporated cities are **Heppner** (county seat), **Boardman** (largest), **Ione**, **Irrigon**, and **Lexington**. The county is bounded by **Washington State** on the north (the closest bridge across the Columbia is on **Interstate 82** a few miles east at **Umatilla**), and by **Umatilla**, **Grant**, **Wheeler**, and **Gilliam** counties. Elevations range from 265' along the river to 5,932' Black Mountain in the southeast. The economy is based on agriculture, food processing, power generation, lumber, livestock, and recreation. Taxable assessed value in 1995 is $944,000,000, or $109,000 per capita. The county was created in 1885 from Umatilla County and named for Jackson L. Morrow (1827-1899), area pioneer and member of the state legislature. Population 1980 7,519; 1995 8,700. Area 2,049 square miles. Density 4/sq.mi. Annual precipitation 14"; average temperature January 33°F, July 69°F. Courthouse, 100 Court St., Heppner 97836. 541-676-9061. Homesteads and Heritages; Oregon Blue Book. See also **Irish**; **Umatilla Chemical Depot**.

Mortuary and Cemetery Board. A board of eleven members appointed by the governor for four-year terms. The board licenses funeral facilities, cemeteries, and practitioners, including sales persons, and investigates complaints. The board has compiled and sells a directory of funeral homes and registered **cemeteries**. 430 State Office Building, 800 NE Oregon St., #21, Portland 97232-2109, 503-731-4040. Oregon Blue Book.

Mosier. A community on the **Columbia River** five miles east of **Hood River** and 16 miles west of **The Dalles** in **Wasco County**. It was first settled in 1853 by the J. H. Mosier family, who offered a stopping place for travelers, and was incorporated in 1914. Population 1980 340; 1995 290. Elevation 112'. PO Box 456, 97040. 541-478-3505. Oregon Geographic Names.

Mosquito fleet. The name given in the 1880s to the sailboats of the gillnet salmon fishermen of the **Columbia River**. The two-man boats were 25-feet long, single-masted, and equipped with oars. They operated primarily from **Tongue Point** to the mouth of the river; other kinds of nets were used upstream. Some 2,600 rowboats and sailboats were fishing the river between **Portland** and the ocean at that time. Butterfly Fleet; Columbia River Salmon. See also **Fishing fleet losses**.

Mosquitoes. Forty-four species of mosquitoes are found in Oregon. One species, *Anopheles freeborni*, is a potential carrier of **malaria**, and *Culex tarsalis*, the only species found in every county, transmits encephalitis from birds to horses and humans. Since 1983 **Paisley** has held an annual Mosquito Festival in late July to raise money for mosquito control because, it is said, parents got tired of putting rocks in the pockets of small children to keep them from being carried away by the "skeeters". See also **Malaria**; **Vector control districts**.

Mosser Awards. $1,000 awards given in 1965/66 for outstanding teaching at Oregon's state colleges and universities. The awards, brainchild of state legislator John Mosser (1923-1996), were authorized by the legislature. Each school was free to implement the awards as it saw fit, but, after much controversy, several schools opted not to participate. The awards did, however, lead to the development of systematic methods for evaluating teaching. Oregonian 11/4/65:22.

Mosses. Small, spore-bearing plants that need moisture for at least part of their life cycle. Moss cells are so little differentiated that almost any part can reproduce. Mosses are able to photosynthesize at a lower temperature than most plants so thrive in mild winters. They are highly specialized as to the ecological niche in which they grow; a single tree in a moist forest may have 30 species of moss on it. Huge quantities of moss are being gathered commercially for the floral trade. Plants and Animals.

Mother of Oregon. Tabitha Moffatt Brown (1780-1858) was designated by the 1987 legislature as Mother of Oregon for her courage, resourcefulness, and contributions to the state. The widow of an Episcopal minister, at the age of 66 she financed her own wagon for the difficult trip west over the **Applegate Trail** in 1846. After settling in West Tualatin she opened a boarding school for orphans that eventually became **Pacific University**. Dictionary of Oregon History. See also **Father of Oregon**.

Mother Queen of Oregon. See **Oldest known Oregonian**.

Motor Carrier Transportation. A branch of the Oregon Department of **Transportation** that regulates the commercial operations of motor carriers on Oregon's roads and highways and operates the Ports of Entry offices at the borders. On July 31, 1996, they had 32,957 carriers registered and 262,620 active plates. They collect about $215 million annually from the highway use tax and registration fees. 550 Capitol St. NE, Salem 97310-1380. 503-378-6699. Oregon Blue Book.

Motor vehicle fees. In 1996, the fee for a standard driver's license, good for four years, was $26.25. The renewal fee was $16.25. The fee for licensing a car, good for two years, was $30. Custom license plates were $80. Titles were $10. The state **gas tax** was $.24 a gallon. Oregon's fees, administered by Oregon **Driver and Motor Vehicle Services**, were among the lowest in the country.

Motor vehicle laws. As of 1997 Oregon law requires that both driver and passengers wear **seat belts**, and restraint seats are required for children under four years of age. Drivers must be 15 to obtain an instruction permit and 16 to get a driver's license. Helmets are required for motorcycle drivers and passengers and for bicyclists under 16. Radar detectors are permitted. Copies of the Oregon Driver's Manual are available from DMV (**Driver and Motor Vehicle Services**) offices.

Motor vehicles. See **Driver and Motor Vehicle Services**.

Motorcycle gangs. In 1994 nine motorcycle gangs, estimated to represent 1% of motorcycling enthusiasts, were known to have members in Oregon. Gypsy Joker, the largest, had 65 members in the Northwest with Oregon clubhouses in **Coos Bay** and **Portland**. Hells Angels, which earlier had ceded Oregon and Washington to the Jokers, was thought to be moving back into the Northwest. The gangs, which are reputed to be sophisticated crime groups, play a major role in **methamphetamine** production, and were also said to have income from **prostitution, gambling**, sale of **guns** and illegal weapons, and **murder**-for-hire. Oregonian 8/7/94:E1.

Motorcycle stunts. See **Evel Knievel**.

Motorcycles. In 1988 the Oregon legislature referred a measure requiring motorcycle helmets to the voters who adopted it. See also **Evel Knievel**.

Mount Angel. A 485' butte in the mid **Willamette Valley** known to early settlers as Lone Butte, and to Indians as Tap-a-lam-a-ho, indicating a mountain used for communion with the Great Spirit. It is a fault "pop-up", an area caught between a series of intersecting fault blocks. There have been many small earthquakes in the area over the years. Geology of Oregon; Oregon Geographic Names.

Mount Angel (town). "Justice to All, Favors to None." A mid **Willamette Valley** agricultural and Catholic center in **Marion County**, 20 miles northeast of **Salem** incorporated in 1893. It was known variously as Roy, Frankfort, and Fillmore until, in 1883, the Reverend Father Adelhelm Odermatt, O.S.B., named it in honor of Engelberg (Mount Angel), Switzerland and moved his Benedictine community there from **Gervais**. In 1903 a new **Mount Angel Abbey** was built on top of the butte southeast of town. Benedictine Sisters from Switzerland founded the Queen of Angels Monastery in 1882. The town's Swiss-German heritage is celebrated annually with an **Oktoberfest** in September which has become one of the state's largest events. The 1912 Saint Mary's Catholic Church has been restored after heavy damage from the **Scotts Mills earthquake**. Population 1980 2,876; 1995 1,010. Elevation 168'. PO Box 960, 97362. 503-845-9291. Chamber of Commerce 503-845-6882. Oregon Geographic Names.

Mount Angel Abbey. A Benedictine abbey in the town of **Mount Angel** founded in 1882 and named for the mother house in Engelberg ("angel mountain" in German), Switzerland. In 1995 the famous library, designed by Finnish architect Alvar Aalto and completed in 1970, was given a Presidential Citation by the American Institute of Architects. A collection of Old Believer artifacts is displayed in the abbey museum, and a museum of oddities in the basement of Abbey House includes 8-legged calves and a huge **hairball.** The Abbey hosts the **Abbey Bach Festival** in July. See also **Queen of Angels Monastery**. Mt. Angel Abbey; Oregonian 12/10/95:D1.

Mount Angel Seminary. An accredited private college on **Mount Angel** that enrolled 156 students in 1995. It was established as St. Anselm's Seminary in 1889. In 1933 it became a full, four-year men's college, but since 1947 has limited itself to training men for the priesthood. St. Benedict 97373. 503-845-3951. Dictionary of Oregon History; Oregon Blue Book.

Mount Ashland. A mountain eight miles south of **Ashland** that is, at 7,533 feet, the highest point in the **Siskiyou Mountains**. It is part of the 150-square-mile, 155-million-year-old Ashland pluton. The **Ski Ashland Ski Area**, owned by the city of **Ashland**, is located near the top of the mountain which lies in the **Rogue River National Forest**. Geology of Oregon.

Mount Bachelor. A 9,065' volcanic peak in the **Cascade Range** 25 miles southwest of **Bend**. Mount Bachelor Ski Area is on the north slopes of the mountain. Originally called Bachelor Butte because of its relationship to the **Three Sisters**, the name was changed to Mount Bachelor when the ski area was built. Oregon Geographic Names.

Mount Bachelor Ski Area. A ski area 22 miles west of **Bend** with a 3,365-foot vertical drop from its 9,065' peak. Facilities include 11 chair lifts and 56K of Nordic track. PO Box 1031, Bend 97709. 541-382-2607; snow conditions 541-382-7888. Oregonian 11/16/97:T7.

Mount Bailey. An 8,363-foot southern Oregon mountain in the **Cascade Range** just west of **Diamond Lake**. Proposals have been made to develop a ski area on the mountain. Until then downhill skiers reach the mountain (3,000-foot vertical drop) by snow-cat. Reservations 800-733-7593 or 541-793-3333. The origin of the name is unclear. Oregonian 11/23/95:D1.

Mount Emily. A 6,064' mountain north of **La Grande**. One story says that a small man named Leasy named it for his much larger wife because of her great size, but another says that it was named by the men of La Grande for a woman named Emily who lived on its slopes because they so frequently went up to Mount Emily. Oregon Geographic Names. See also **Prineville City Railroad**.

Mount Fanny. A 7,153' peak due east of **La Grande** in northeast Oregon. It was named for Fannie McDaniel, who, in 1862, was one of the first women to live in **Cove**. Oregon Geographic Names.

Mount Hebo. A 3,154' mountain in the **Coast Range** 20 miles southeast of **Tillamook**. It is made of the same **Columbia River basalt** as **Saddle Mountain** and **Neahkahnie Mountain**. The origin of the name is uncertain, but is possibly a distortion of Heave Ho. Winds of 170 mph were recorded on the mountain during the **Columbus Day Storm**. The U.S. Air Force operated a radar station on the mountain from the 1950s to the 1970s. Geology of Oregon; Oregon Geographic Names.

Mount Hood. An **andesite volcano** which is, at 11,240', the highest mountain in Oregon, one of the youngest, and the most active. It lies just south of the **Columbia River** at the northern end of Oregon's **Cascade Range**. Formed within the last million years, its most recent eruptive periods produced small domes and mud flows. Pyroclastic flows and extensive lahars (mud flows) have gone down the White River to the **Deschutes River** and down the **Sandy River** to the Columbia. Crater Rock, a dome near the summit, was formed in eruptions between 1760 and 1818; today an eroded remnant is all that remains. Minor eruptions were noted until 1907, and steam vents and fumaroles are present today near the top. There are nine **glaciers** on the mountain. The first documented climb was in 1857, and now, with 10,000 people a year ascending it (plus a gibbon in 1964), it is the most climbed peak in North America, second worldwide only to Japan's Mt. Fuji. Lord Hood (1724-1816), was an admiral in the British navy with a long and distinguished career. Geology of Oregon; Oregon Geographic Names; Oregonian 12/14/94:D1, 12/15/96:K1. See also **Enola Hill**; **Mount Hood National Forest**; **Mountain climbing**; **Ski areas**; **Timberline Lodge**.

Mount Hood Community College. A public two-year college in **Gresham**; satellite centers are located in Maywood Park and Lynch Park. In fall 1996 11,970 students enrolled. It offers two-year transfer and career-training programs, and serves as a resource for area residents, organizations, and businesses. 26000 SE Stark St., Gresham OR 97030-3300. 503-667-6422. Oregon Blue Book. See also **Community colleges**; **Small Business Development Centers**.

Mount Hood Festival of Jazz. An annual festival, sponsored by **Mount Hood Community College** and held in **Gresham** the first weekend in August. Since its founding in 1982, it has become the state's largest jazz festival. The annual poster is sought by collectors. 503-666-3810.

Mount Hood Loop. A popular recreational drive from **Portland** east around **Mount Hood**. If traveled counterclockwise, the route follows **Highway 26** southeast from Portland around the south side of Mount Hood (55 miles) to join Highway 35, follows it north (43 miles) to **Hood River**, and then returns west to Portland (60 miles) down the **Columbia River** along **Interstate 84**. Points of interest include an eight mile side trip up to **Timberline Lodge**, apple orchards in the Hood River valley, sailboarders on the Columbia at Hood River, **Bonneville Dam**, and **Multnomah Falls**.

Mount Hood Meadows. A ski area 67 miles east of **Portland** with 11 chair lifts and a 15K Nordic track. The area has a 2,777-foot vertical drop from a top elevation of 7,300 feet. PO Box 470, Highway 35, Mount Hood 97041. 503-337-2222; snow conditions 503-227-7669. Oregonian 11/16/97:T7.

Mount Hood National Forest. A 1,116,269-acre national forest that lies across the north-Oregon portion of the **Cascade Range** in **Multnomah**, **Clackamas**, **Hood River**, and **Wasco** counties. In includes five wilderness areas: Columbia, Mount Hood, Salmon-Huckleberry, Badger Creek, and Bull of the Woods. Four major rivers originate on the forest, the **Clackamas**, **Sandy**, **Hood**, and **White**. They provide drinking water for 40% of Oregonians. The **ski areas** on **Mount Hood** are located on the forest, and the forest also administers the **Columbia River Gorge National Scenic Area**. Annual timber harvests, which were over 400 million board feet in the mid 1980s, have declined to under 30 million board feet. 2955 NW Division, Gresham 97030. 503-666-0700. Oregonian 12/15/96:K1. See also **Bull Run**; **Timberline Lodge**.

Mount Hood Railroad. See **Excursion trains**.

Mount Hood Skibowl. See **Skibowl/Multipor**.

Mount Howard. A 8,256' peak in the **Wallowa Mountains** at the south end of **Wallowa Lake**. The **Wallowa Lake Tramway** offers gondola rides to the top where there are trails and panoramic views of the jagged Wallowas, the lake, and the broad Wallowa River valley to the north. A chair lift has been proposed for the east side. Major-General Oliver Otis Howard (1830-1909) served with distinction in the **Civil War**, the **Nez Perce War**, and the **Bannock War**. Oregon Geographic Names.

Mount Jefferson. A 10,495' volcanic peak in the central Oregon **Cascade Range**. It is Oregon's second highest peak. In February 1869 there were reports that smoke was seen ascending from the summit. First climbed in 1888, it is considered Oregon's most difficult major peak. Lewis and Clark named the mountain in1806 for President Jefferson who had sponsored their expedition. Oregon Geographic Names.

Mount Mazama. A volcanic peak remnant that had grown through a series of eruptions beginning 400,000 years ago until it was 10,000 to 12,000 feet high. However, lava flows from side vents and a series of varied and violent eruptions of **pumice** 6,900 years ago emptied six cubic miles of **rhyolite** magma from the chamber beneath the mountain, causing the unsupported top to suddenly collapse in upon itself. The resulting **caldera** is now filled by **Crater Lake**. A later eruption created Wizard Island, a **cinder cone** in the caldera. The now-vanished peak was named in 1896 for the **Mazamas** mountaineering organization; the word is Spanish for mountain goat. Geology of Oregon; Oregon Geographic Names.

Mount McLoughlin. A 9,495' volcanic peak in the **Cascade Range** south of **Crater Lake**. It has probably not erupted since the last ice age when a glacier carved a cirque on the northeast slope; a glacier survived until less than 100 years ago. The most recent flows were **andesite** lavas from fissures at the base of the mountain. Though called Mt. McLoughlin on an 1838 map, it was for years known as Mount Pitt until the state legislature restored its name in 1905, honoring Dr. John McLoughlin, chief factor for the **Hudson's Bay Company** at **Fort Vancouver** from 1824 to 1846 and founder of **Oregon City**. Geology of Oregon; Oregon Geographic Names.

Mount Pisgah Arboretum. A 200-acre private arboretum of native flora on Frank Parish Road, four miles SE of **Eugene**. It is located next to Buford Park, and together they provide large natural areas, including trails up Mount Pisgah. The area is noted for its spring **wildflowers**, including **camas, trilliums**, fawn lilies, violets, orchids, buttercups, irises, delphiniums, bleeding hearts, cat's ears, candyflower, and vetches. It is open to the public during daylight hours. PO Box 5621, Eugene 97405. 541-747-3817. Oregonian 4/5/95:E1.

Mount St. Helens. A volcano in Washington state 50 miles northeast of **Portland** that, after two months of rumblings, erupted at 8:31 a.m. on May 18, 1980, blowing off the side and top of the mountain. The mountain was 9,677' high before the eruption and 8,364' after. The eruption killed 57 people, destroyed 221 homes and 4.7 billion board feet of timber, and caused mud flows, widespread ash falls, and 150 square miles of devastation. Subsequent smaller eruptions dropped ash on northern Oregon, and created a dome 920 feet tall inside the crater. Five visitor centers, each with a different focus, are located along Highway 504 east of Castle Rock. The mountain was named for British Baron Saint Helens. Mount St. Helens National Volcanic Monument, 42218 N.E. Yale Bridge Road, Amboy, WA 98601. 206-247-5473. Mount St. Helens.

Mount Tabor Park. A city park on an extinct volcano in **Portland**. The park includes a basketball court in an old crater and a bronze statue of Harvey Scott, 1838-1910, civic leader and editor of the **Oregonian** for 33 years. The peak, with a **cinder cone** on its north side, is one of a number of **Pliocene** eruptions of **Boring lavas** in the Portland area. The name is that of a mount in Israel. Geology of Oregon; Oregon Geographic Names.

Mount Thielsen. A 9,178' peak in the south Oregon **Cascade Range** north of **Crater Lake** and east of **Diamond Lake**. The mountain, a volcanic core eroded by glaciers, is topped by a rock spire. It is sometimes known as the lightening rod of the Cascades. Lightning has created carrot-shaped "lightning tubes" and glassy rock formations at the summit. It was at onetime called Big Cowhorn, but was later named for Hans Thielsen, a pioneer railroad builder. Oregon Atlas; Oregon Geographic Names.

Mount Vernon. An eastern Oregon cattle and lumber community eight miles west of **John Day** on **Highway 26** in **Grant County**. It was named for a prize black stallion of the same name that won races throughout the state. The animal was stabled in a small stone building built to protect it that, during the **Bannock War** of 1878, became the local fort. The building still stands on the north side of Highway 26 two miles east of town. A resort at a hot springs two miles north of town was popular for decades until destroyed by flood and fire. The post office was established in 1877; the city was incorporated in 1948. A two-day timber carnival called the Cinnabar Mountain Rendezvous Days is held on Memorial Day weekend. Population 1980 569; 1995 645. Elevation 2,871'. PO Box 647, 97865. 541-932-4688. History of Grant County; Tracking down Oregon. See also **Asbestos**.

Mount Washington. A distinctive spired peak, elevation 7,794', in the central **Cascade Range**, south of **Three Fingered Jack** and north of **North Sister**. It lies in the Mount Washington Wilderness, and is drained by tributaries of the **McKenzie River** on the west and of the **Deschutes River** on the east. Six men from **Bend** were the first to reach the top in 1923. It was named for George Washington. Oregon Geographic Names.

Mountain beaver. See **Boomer**.

Mountain climbing. Oregon's highest mountain, **Mount Hood**, which 10,000 people a year climb, is the second most-frequently climbed mountain in the world. Transmitter units can be rented for climbs; when one is activated it enables rescuers to pinpoint the climber's location. On average, two climbers a year lose their lives on the mountain. The worst climbing disaster on the mountain occurred the week of May 11, 1986 when 7 students and 2 teachers from Oregon Episcopal School died on a climb. See also **Mazamas**; **Rock climbing**.

Mountain goats. Large (to 300 pounds), white animals, *Oreamnos americanus*, closely related to the European chamois. They have small, black horns that curve slightly to the rear. Young **bighorn sheep** are sometimes mistaken for mountain goats. Despite some early comments that they were native to Oregon, there are no verifiable records of them in the state prior to their successful introduction to northeast Oregon in 1951. Between 1965 and 1968 a few **hunting tags** were issued, but hunting has been closed since then. Further introductions have been made so that there are now thought to be over 80 goats in the **Wallowa** and **Elkhorn Mountains**. Mountain goats are native to the Washington Cascades and have been introduced into the Washington Olympics where they are decimating native vegetation. Big Game History; Mammals and Life Zones of Oregon; Mammals of the Northwest.

Mountain sheep. See **Bighorn sheep**.

Mountain Writers Center. A **Portland** house that serves as a resource center for area poets and as the planning center for the Mountain Writers Series. The annual series, started in 1973, sponsors area readings by notable writers and poets. In 1996-97 10,000 listeners heard 30 writers and poets through the series. 3624 SE Milwaukie Avenue, 97202. 503-236-4854. Oregonian 8/31/97:F1.

Mountains. Oregon's major mountain ranges include the **Coast Range**, the volcanic **Cascade Range**, the ancient **Siskiyou Mountains** of the southwest, and the ranges of the **Blue Mountains** of the northeast. All these mountain ranges support productive forests. The drier mountains of the **basin and range** area of the southeast include **Steens Mountain** and the **Pueblo** and **Trout Creek Mountains**.

Mouse. See **Mice**.

Movies. See **Drive-in theaters**; **Films**.

Mr. Portland. See **Allow Me**.

MSAs. See **Metropolitan Areas**.

Mud cracks. As the water level drops in Alvord Lake in the **Alvord Basin** and Guano Lake near the southeastern corner of **Lake County**, fissures up to 15 feet deep and 100 feet across develop in the drying mud. The fissures form giant polygonal patterns 50 to 1,000 feet across. Those at Guano Lake are the largest known in North America, and are so large that the patterns are not apparent from the ground. Geology of Oregon.

Mud pot. See **Mickey Hot Springs**.

Mud slides. See **Landslides**.

Muddy Frogwater Festival. See **Milton-Freewater**.

Mules. See **Enterprise**.

Multnomah Channel. A 21-mile-long secondary mouth of the **Willamette River** that flows around the west side of **Sauvie Island** to join the **Columbia River** at **Saint Helens**. The channel is popular for pleasure boating and has a number of boat launching sites, marinas, and house boat moorages along it. A bridge crosses the channel near its south end.

Multnomah County. A county at the center of the state's major metropolitan area, located on the **Willamette** and **Columbia Rivers**. Incorporated cities are **Portland** (80% of county population and county seat), **Fairview, Gresham, Maywood Park, Troutdale**, and **Wood Village**. It is the state's largest county in population and the smallest in area. The county is bounded by Washington State on the north (reached by bridges across the Columbia via **Interstate 5** and **Interstate 205**), and by **Hood River, Clackamas, Washington**, and **Columbia** counties. Elevations range from tidewater on the Columbia and Willamette up to 4,058' **Larch Mountain** and a 4,500' ridge on the east. The economy is based on manufacturing, transportation, wholesale and retail trade, and tourism. Taxable assessed value in 1995 was $34,683,000,000, or $55,000 per capita. The county was created in 1854 from parts of Washington and Clackamas counties, and named for the local Indians. It is governed by a five-member county commission with each commissioner elected from a separate district. Population 1980 562,647; 1995 626,500. Area 465 square miles. Density 1,347/sq.mi. Annual precipitation 37"; average temperature January 39°F, July 68°F. Courthouse, 1021 SW 4th, Portland 97204. 503-248-3511. Governing Oregon; Oregon Blue Book. See also **Consolidation; Metro**.

Multnomah County Library. The library system serving **Portland** through the Central Library and its multiple branches. The 1913 Central Library, designed by A. E. Doyle, reopened in April 1997 after two years of extensive renovation. The library's roots go back to the 1864 organization of the Library Association of Portland (LAP) as a subscription library, although another library group had existed even earlier. In 1902 the city, and then, in 1903, Multnomah County, contracted with the Association for free public library services. It is now the largest library system in the state. 70% of county residents have library cards. 801 SW 10th Avenue. 503-248-5234. Dictionary of Oregon History; Oregonian 5/6/97:L1, 11/2/97:E5.

Multnomah Falls. The fourth highest waterfall in the U.S., located in the **Columbia River Gorge** at exit 31 from **Interstate 84**. The upper portion of the falls drops 542 feet over a ledge of **Columbia River basalt** to a pool, then spills another 69 feet. A trail leads to viewpoints and a bridge over the lower falls. The trail to the top has been closed because of rock and slide hazards, but the top can be reached via longer trails. A school-bus-sized rock fell from the wall of the upper falls on Labor Day 1995, causing minor injuries to 22 persons, including members of a wedding party being photographed on the bridge. Some 2 million visitors a year make Multnomah Falls Oregon's top tourist attraction. Multnomah Falls Lodge provides visitor services. Waterfall Lover's Guide.

Multnomah Falls Lodge. A rustic stone building near **Multnomah Falls** with day visitor facilities. It was designed by Portland architect A. E. Doyle and built in 1925 by the city of **Portland**. Historic Highway Bridges of Oregon.

Multnomah Greyhound Park. A dog racing track in **Wood Village**, 16 miles east of **Portland**, where greyhound dogs are raced five nights a week from May until early September. One of the largest crowds shows up for the Wiener Dog Summer Nationals which features long - and slow - dachshunds. The track has a glass-enclosed grandstand and restaurants. NE 223rd at Glisan, Wood Village. 503-667-7700. Portland Guidebook. See also **Pari-mutuel racing**; **Racing Commission**.

Multnomah Hotel. A historic American Renaissance-style building that opened in 1912 as one of **Portland**'s grand hotels, with 750 rooms. However, it had a rocky history and was turned into a federal office building in the 1960s. After an extensive renovation it reopened in 1997 as the Embassy Suites hotel. 319 SW Pine St., 97204. 503-279-9000. Oregonian 11/2/97:G1. See also **Aviation history**.

Multnomah Stadium. See **Civic Stadium**.

Mumford quote. Lewis Mumford, an urban planner, spoke at the **City Club of Portland** in 1938, saying "I have seen a lot of scenery in my life, but I have seen nothing so tempting as a home for man in this Oregon country....You have here the basis for civilization on its highest scale, and I am going to ask you a question which you may not like. Are you good enough to have this country in your possession? Have you got enough intelligence, imagination and cooperation among you to make the best use of these opportunities?..." Facts of Life.

Municipal court. A court that has jurisdiction over violations of city code, such as traffic and parking ordinances, and has some authority over criminal cases occurring within the city limits. Municipal courts are not **courts of record**, so appealing a decision entails a new trial in a **circuit court**. A municipal judge, who need not be an attorney, may be either appointed or elected as determined by the city **charter**, and can perform weddings within his or her jurisdiction. Oregon Blue Book.

Municipal electric systems. Eleven Oregon cities operated **electric utilities** in 1994: **Ashland, Bandon, Canby, Cascade Locks, Drain, Eugene, Forest**

Grove, **McMinnville**, **Milton-Freewater**, **Monmouth**, and **Springfield**. The number of customers ranged from 546 at Cascade Locks to 70,000 in Eugene. Oregon Utility Statistics. See also **Eugene Water and Electric Board**; **Public Power Council**.

Munson Creek Falls. The highest waterfall in the **Coast Range** drops 266 feet in several tiers. The falls are located 1.6 miles east of **Highway 101** seven miles south of **Tillamook**. A short trail leads to the base of the falls, and the half-mile Upper Trail leads to a full viewpoint. Goran Munson was an early settler. Waterfall Lover's Guide.

Murals. Notable murals in Oregon include the Oregon history murals in the state **capitol**, painted in the 1930s by Barry Faulkner and Frank Schwarz, and the 1989 trompe l'oeil ("fool the eye") scenes by Richard Haas on the **Oregon History Center** in **Portland**. Many communities have supported the painting of murals depicting scenes of local interest on exterior walls in their business districts, such as in **Oregon City** and **Sweet Home** and Wyland's whale murals in Portland and **Newport**. Oregonian 8/7/95:C1.

Murderers Harbour. See **Tillamook Bay**.

Murders. There were 119 murders reported in Oregon in 1996, down from 129 in 1995. **Multnomah County** led with 49, or about one a week. Sensational Oregon murder trials include the 1969 trials of the three men accused of murdering Larry Peyton and his girlfriend, Beverly Ann Allan, in 1960. Other notable murders include that on May 11, 1961, when Jeannace June Freeman and her lover, Gertrude Nunez, threw Nunez's two children off the highway bridge into the **Crooked River Gorge**. Freeman was sentenced to death, the first woman to receive the **death penalty**, but, in 1964, after voters had repealed the death penalty but not made the repeal retroactive, Governor Hatfield commuted her sentence to life imprisonment. Diane Downs shot her three children in 1983, killing one and leaving the other two permanently damaged; in 1987 she escaped from prison but was captured 10 days later. Michel Francke, director of corrections, was stabbed to death outside his office on January 17, 1989. Frank Gable, an ex-convict, was found guilty in August 1991 and given a life sentence. A lawyer who had represented him married him during a brief recess in the trial. Charity Lamb, the first woman found guilty of murder in Oregon, was convicted in 1854 and sentenced to hard labor for the rest of her life. In 1852 Cyrenius Hooker was found guilty of murder and hanged at what is now **Dallas** in a case tangled in politics. Mass killings in Oregon include the murder of six people gunned down in **Klamath Falls** on July 24, 1977; a **Portland** man who shot and killed his wife and four children before taking his own life on November 20, 1983; and five persons stabbed to death near **Bandon** on May 9, 1996. Dictionary of Oregon History; Governing Oregon; "Murder"; Oregonian 9/11/96:E12; 1/28/97:B2; Report on Criminal Offenses. See also **Church of the Bride of Christ**; **Death penalty**; **Homicides**; **Suicide**.

Museum at Warm Springs. A museum opened in 1993 by the Confederated Tribes of the **Warm Springs Reservation** to document the three very different life styles and traditions of the **Warm Springs**, **Wasco**, and **Northern Paiute** tribes, and to keep alive their legacies. The museum also features live demonstrations during the summer, and has a gift shop. Warm Springs is 15 miles northwest of **Madras** and 108 miles southeast of **Portland**. 2189 Highway 26, Warm Springs 97761. 541-553-3331. Oregon Blue Book.

Museum of Art. A museum on the campus of the **University of Oregon** built with private contributions to house the Murray Warner Collection of Oriental Art. Architects for the Romanesque Style building were Lawrence & Holford. It was completed in 1933. Style and Vernacular.

Museums, art. See **Maryhill Museum of Art**; **Museum at Warm Springs**; **Portland Art Museum**.

Museums, children's. See **Children's Museum**; **Gilbert House Children's Museum**; **Kidd Toy Museum**.

Museums, historical. See **End of the Oregon Trail Interpretive Center**; **High Desert Museum**; **Museum at Warm Springs**; **Oregon History Center**; **Oregon Trail Interpretive Center**; **Police Historical Museum**; **Tamustalik Cultural Institute**.

Museums, science and natural history. See **High Desert Museum** (Bend); **Mark O. Hatfield Marine Science Center** (Newport); **OMSI** (Portland); **Oregon Coast Aquarium** (Newport); **Paul Jensen Arctic Museum** (Monmouth); **Umpqua Discovery Center** (Reedsport); **University of Oregon Museum of Natural History** (Eugene); **Wildlife Safari** (Roseburg).

Museums, transportation. See **Antique Powerland Museum**; **Captain Michael King Smith Evergreen Aviation Educational Center**; **Oregon Aviation Museum**.

Mushrooms. The visible fruiting bodies of various fungi; the plant itself is a network of microscopic threads. Oregon growers raised $31 million worth of mushrooms in 1994, with major growing facilities located in **Salem** and **Vale**. In the wild, spring species begin fruiting in late March along the coast and continue into June at higher elevations. Fall mushrooms begin after a couple of good rains and continue until frost. Only five kinds of the more than 3,000 species of wild mushrooms found in Oregon are of commercial importance: **boletes, chanterelles, matsutakes, morels**, and **truffles**. Gathering, whether on private or public lands, requires permission from the land owner. In 1997 the **Deschutes** and **Winema** national forests collected more than $365,000 in permit fees for commercial harvesting. Some mushrooms found in Oregon are deadly, especially *Amanita phalloides*, some species are toxic to a few eaters but have no effect on others, and some may not cause immediate discomfort though they cause long-term liver damage. Several mushroom clubs have October mushroom shows, including the Oregon Mycological Society. 13716 SE Oatfield Road, Milwaukie OR 97222. Mushrooms Demystified.

Music. See **Columbia River Songs**; **Jazz**; **Music festivals**; **Oregon Symphony**; **Outdoor concert sites**; **Portland Baroque Orchestra**; **Portland Opera Association**; **Portland Youth Philharmonic**; **Riverside Classics**; **Rose Garden Concerts**; **Shape note singing**; **Symphony orchestras**; **Trumpets**.

Music by Blue Lake. See **Blue Lake, Multnomah County**.

Music festivals. See **Abbey Bach Festival**; **Britt Music Festivals**; **Cascade Festival of Music**; **Cascade Head Music Festival**; **Chamber music**; **Ernest**

Bloch Music Festival; **Hood River Apple Jam**; **Mount Hood Festival of Jazz**; **North by Northwest Music and Media Conference**; **Oregon Bach Festival**; **Oregon Coast Music Festival**; **Sunriver Music Festival**; **Vortex I**; **Waterfront Blues Festival**.

Music history. See **Bands**; **De Moss Family**; **Sagebrush Symphony**.

Musicians. Carl "Doc" Severinsen (1927-), nationally-known trumpeter and band leader, grew up in **Arlington**. Johnnie Ray (1923-1990), popular rhythm and blues singer of the 1950s, grew up in **Dallas**. See also **De Moss Family**.

Muskrat. A swimming, cat-sized rodent, *Ondatra zibethicus*, that lives in marshes. Clams, turtles, and the roots of marsh plants make up its diet. Its long, naked tail is somewhat flattened vertically, unlike the **beaver's** which is flattened horizontally. Like the larger beaver, the muskrat lives in lodges in marshes or in deep burrows that may do serious damage to the banks of irrigation canals. The lodges usually rise about three feet above water with their entrances below the surface. When muskrat numbers explode, the animals strip all vegetation in what is called an "eat-out". 14,110 were trapped in Oregon in 1994-95, with an average value of $2 each. Atlas of Oregon Wildlife; Mammals of the Northwest; Mammals and Life Zones of Oregon.

Mussel. The California mussel, *Mytilus californianus*, is a black-shelled bivalve that grows in masses in the intertidal zone along rocky stretches of the coast. It was eaten by **Indians** who left the shells in great **middens**. In recent years it has become a more widely popular seafood. Harvest is regulated by the Oregon Department of **Fish and Wildlife**. During summer months mussels may accumulate deadly toxins from **red tides**; during those times the state closes the harvest. Fresh water mussels grow in some inland Oregon waters. Clam Digging and Crabbing in Oregon. See also **Shellfish poisoning**.

Myrtle Creek. A southwest Oregon town in **Douglas County**, 18 miles south of **Roseburg**. It is on the east side of the South **Umpqua River**, across a bridge from exit 108 of **Interstate 5**. Attractions include annual Celtic **Highland Games**, a Summer Arts Festival, a Bluegrass Festival, Millsite Park (a city park with, among other things, RV hookups), and an 18-hole golf course. The post office, named for the local groves of **myrtle**, was established in 1854, but the town wasn't laid out until 1862. It was incorporated in 1893, disincorporated in 1901 after it went broke, and reincorporated in 1903. Population 1980 3,365; 1995 3,290. Elevation 640'. PO Box 940, 97457. 541-863-3171. Oregon Geographic Names.

Myrtle Point. "In the Heart of the Myrtlewoods." A southwest Oregon logging and agricultural town on the **Coquille River** 26 miles south of **Coos Bay** on **Highway 42** in **Coos County**. It is the location of the Coos County Fair in August, a harvest festival in September, and the Coos County Logging Museum, housed in a 1910 domed building (with echo) that is a scaled-down replica of the Mormon Tabernacle. A brochure lists that and other historic buildings. Dairy farms and sheep ranches surround the town. The community was first called Meyersville and then Ott, but in 1876 the name was changed to Myrtle Point because of the abundance of **myrtle** trees. It was incorporated in 1887. Population 1980 2,859; 1995 2,740. Elevation 90'. 424 5th St., 97458. 541-572-2626. Oregon Geographic Names.

Myrtlewood. See **Oregon-myrtle**.

Mysteries. See **Crop circles**; **Kalapuya Indians**; **Lost Crystal Cave**; **Lost mines and treasures**; **Monsters**; **Mystery city**; **Neahkahnie Mountain**; **Oregon Vortex**; **Shipwrecks**; **Skyline Circle**; **Spanish coins**; **Squiyowhiynoof**; **UFOs**.

Mystery city. In 1881 the Port Orford Post reported that stones that looked like shaped sandstone had been revealed when a large tree uprooted near Floras Creek north of **Port Orford**. Diggers found similar stones under a number of mounds in the area, and also found what seemed to have been a ditch, walled on the lower side with the same kind of shaped stones. There were no further reports. Century of Coos and Curry.

NAFTA. An acronym for the North American Free Trade Agreement, adopted in 1994, that eliminated many trade barriers between Canada, the United States, and Mexico. As of February 1996, 341 Oregon workers had lost their jobs due to the agreement. Oregonian 2/24/96:A12.

Names. In 1996 the most popular names for girls born in Oregon were Emily (325), Jessica, Hannah, Ashley, Sarah, Samantha, Madison, Megan, Rachel, and Taylor. For boys the most popular names were Jacob (460), Austin, Tyler, Michael, Andrew, Joshua, Brandon, Nicholas, Daniel, and Matthew. In 1943 the most popular names for girls were Linda, Sharon, Mary, Judith, Patricia, Carol, Barbara, Karen, Sandra, and Nancy. For boys in 1943 the popular names were Robert, James, Richard, John, William, David, Michael, Ronald, Larry, and Donald. Oregonian 10/29/97:A10. See also **Place names**.

Narrow gauge railroads. See **Sumpter Valley Railroad**; **Zoo Railway**.

Nason. See **Celebration Family**.

National Book Awards. Prestigious national literary awards given annually in fiction, nonfiction, and poetry. The $10,000 awards are announced in November. Bernard Malamud's **novel**, The Magic Barrel, won the fiction award in 1959 while he was teaching (until 1961) at **Oregon State University**, and his later novel, The Fixer, won in 1967. William Stafford of **Lewis and Clark College** won the 1963 poetry award for Traveling Through the Dark. Ursula LeGuin won the 1973 award for **children's literature**. Barry Lopez of **Eugene** won the 1986 nonfiction award for Arctic Dreams. Portland writer Katherine Dunn's novel Geek Love was nominated in 1989, the novel Beyond Deserving, by **Ashland** writer Sandra Scofield, was nominated in 1991, and the novel Will You Please Be Quiet Please, by **Clatskanie** native Raymond Carver, was nominated in 1992. Oregonian 11/12/95:F1.

National College of Naturopathic Medicine. A four-year college in **Portland** that enrolls about 300 students in the study of healing through the use of natural remedies, changes in lifestyle, and awareness of the relationship between mind and body. The school, which grants doctoral degrees, is one of only two accredited naturopathic colleges in the country. It was founded in 1956. 11231 SE Market Street, Portland, 97216. 503-255-4860. Oregonian 6/24/96:B1.

National forests. Federally owned forests, administered by the U.S. **Forest Service** in the Department of Agriculture. National forests developed as the result of an 1891 federal law authorizing the creation of forest reserves on federal land. Oregon's first, the **Bull Run** Reserve, now part of the Mount Hood National Forest, was created in 1892. Oregon now has thirteen National Forests, covering 15.5 million acres: **Deschutes, Fremont, Malheur, Mount Hood, Ochoco, Rogue River, Siskiyou, Siuslaw, Umatilla, Umpqua, Wallowa-Whitman** (the nation's largest), **Willamette**, and **Winema National Forests**. Sixteen other National Forests have existed in Oregon at various times; for the most part they were absorbed into the present national forests, though some portions reverted to **public domain** lands. In lieu of property taxes, counties are paid 25% of national forest proceeds, with the money to be used for roads and schools. USFS Pacific Northwest Regional Office, 333 SW First Avenue, P.O. Box 3623, Portland 97208-3623. 503-808-2971. "Oregon Heritage."

National Germplasm Repository. A center located at **Corvallis** that is part of a national system to preserve the genetic diversity of crop plants. There are ten such repositories in the National Plant Germplasm System, each responsible for maintaining seeds, plants, and/or other genetic material for a different array of crops. The center at Corvallis is responsible for **blackberries, blueberries, boysenberries, mint, pears**, and **strawberries**. 33447 Peoria Road, 97333. 541-750-8712.

National Grassland. See **Crooked River National Grassland**.

National Guard. A military force of 9,000 volunteer citizen soldiers under the command of the governor. As of 1997, the state had 100 Army Guard units and 18 Air Guard units, all administered by the State of Oregon **Military Department**. Units include the 142nd Fighter Wing at **Portland** Air Base, the 114th Fighter Squadron at Kingsley Field, **Klamath Falls**, the 82nd Troop Command Brigade headquartered in **Lake Oswego**, and the 41st Enhanced Infantry Brigade headquartered in **Tigard**. During war time National Guard members can be called to active duty by the president; two Oregon units served in **Operation Desert Storm**, and the 41st Infantry Division was mobilized in 1940 and sent to Australia in 1942 during **World War II**. The Guard is the only military organization trained and equipped to act in state emergencies upon order of the governor. Guard members also provide volunteer support for community projects as part of their training activities. 97% of its funding comes from the federal government. 1776 Militia Way, Salem 97309-5047. 503-945-3991. Oregon Blue Book. See also **Camp Rilea; Camp Withycombe; Defense Force; Oregon National Guard Youth Conservation Corps**.

National Historic Oregon Trail Interpretive Center. See **Oregon Trail Interpretive Center**.

National historic trails. Oregon has four national historic trails: the **Applegate Trail, Lewis and Clark** Trail, **Nez Perce (Nee-Me-Poo) National Historic Trail**.and **Oregon Trail**. They were so designated after the National Trails System Act was adopted in 1968.

National Marine Fisheries Service. An agency of the National Oceanic and Atmospheric Administration in the U.S. Department of Commerce. It provides management, research, and services for the protection and rational use of living marine resources. 7600 Sand Point Way, NE., Bin C-15700, Bldg 1, Seattle

WA 98115. 206-526-6150. Environmental and Technical Services Division, 525 NE Oregon Street, Suite 500, Portland 97232. 503-230-5400. Directory of Organizations.

National monuments. The National Park Service administers two national monuments in Oregon, **Oregon Caves National Monument** and **John Day Fossil Beds National Monument**, as well as **Fort Clatsop National Memorial**. **Newberry National Volcanic Monument** is administered by **Deschutes National Forest**.

National natural landmarks. Sites containing outstanding examples of the geological and ecological components of the nation's landscape. Of the 587 NNL sites designated as of July 1997, six are in Oregon. They are **Crown Point**, **Fort Rock** State Monument, **Horse Ridge Natural Area, Lawrence Memorial Grassland Preserve**, Willamette Floodplain in **William L. Finley National Wildlife Refuge**, and **Newberry Crater**. The NNL program was established in 1962 and is administered by the National Park Service, 909 First Avenue, Seattle WA 98104. 206-220-4105. "National Natural Landmarks."

National parks. Oregon has one national park, **Crater Lake National Park**. The National Park Service in the U.S. Department of Interior also administers **Fort Clatsop National Memorial, John Day Fossil Beds National Monument, Nez Perce National Historical Park**, and **Oregon Caves National Monument**, for a total of 197,850 acres.

National recreation areas. Oregon has two national recreation areas, **Hells Canyon NRA** on the **Snake River**, administered by the **Wallowa-Whitman National Forest**, and **Oregon Dunes NRA** on the coast south of **Florence**, administered by the **Siuslaw National Forest**.

National Register of Historic Places. A compilation of sites registered with the federal government through state agencies. Oregon's nominations are handled through the Oregon **Parks and Recreation Department**. The state had 1313 places on the list as of January 1, 1994. Three-fourths of the national listings are for buildings. The rest include other structures (such as bridges), districts, sites, and objects (such as fountains). Most are privately owned. "Owners have no obligation to open their properties to the public, to restore them, or even to maintain them, if they choose not to do so," though there may be tax advantages to doing so. The State Historic Preservation Office maintains a listing of the historic properties that, because they have received a property-tax break, have scheduled an annual free open house. 1115 Commercial St. NE, Salem 97310-1001. 503-378-6508. Oregon Blue Book. National Register. See also **Buildings, historic; Historic Preservation; Houses, historic**.

National scenic area. See **Columbia River Gorge National Scenic Area**.

National wild and scenic rivers. A system created by Congress in 1968 to preserve designated stretches of rivers in a free-flowing condition and, where they flow through federal land, to protect corridors averaging 1/4 mile on each side. The government can also purchase land, timber, or scenic easements, but only if the landowner is willing to sell. Management decisions depend on whether the river segment has been designated as Wild, Scenic, or Recreational. Oregon has over a fourth of the nation's total, more than 40 river segments totaling 1,780 miles.

They are administered by **National Forests** and the **Bureau of Land Management**. Though federal designation does not affect private lands, if the state has also designated the river as a **scenic waterway**, private lands are governed by that designation. "National Wild and Scenic Rivers System;" Oregon Scenic Waterways Program.

National wildlife refuges (NWRs). As of 1996 Oregon had 19 U.S. **Fish and Wildlife Service** refuges. Western Oregon refuges included the offshore refuges of Three Arch Rocks (1907) and Oregon Islands, Cape Meares and Bandon Marsh Refuges on the coast, and several in the **Willamette Valley** for wintering waterfowl, including Ankeny, Baskett Slough, and William L. Finley refuges. **Hart Mountain National Antelope Refuge, Klamath Forest NWR, Lower Klamath NWR, Malheur NWR**, and **Upper Klamath NWR** are the major federal refuges east of the Cascades. Hunting is allowed in some refuges. 911 NE 11th Avenue, Portland 97232-4181. 503-231-6169. Oregon Wildlife Viewing Guide. See also **Fish and Wildlife (Oregon); South Slough National Estuarine Reserve**.

Native American literature. See **Indian literature**.

Native Americans. See **Indians, contemporary**.

Native plants. Oregon has over 3,300 species of native plants. The **Columbia River Gorge** and the **Siskiyou Mountains** contain unusual concentrations of rare plants; both are places where plants survived through the last ice age and where climate extremes meet. Native Plant Society of Oregon, 2584 NW Savier Street, Portland 97210. See also **Arboretums; Endangered plants; Flora; Introduced species; Plants; Poisonous plants; Trees; Vegetation; Wildflowers**.

Natron cut-off. A rail line, opened in 1926 across the **Cascade Range** between **Eugene** and **Klamath Falls**, that now serves as the main rail line from the **Willamette Valley** to California. It is also known also as the Pengra Pass, Cascade, or Shasta route. In 1909 the **Southern Pacific** company began construction of the route as an alternative to the steep 3.3% (far more than the standard 2.2%) grade over the **Siskiyou Summit**. At one time 1,250 men, most of them immigrants, worked on the project. The route crosses southeast over the Cascades through Pengra Pass (just south of **Willamette Pass**) to Klamath Falls, south into California and back over the Cascades to rejoin the original rail line south of Weed. A line to Nevada splits off at Klamath Falls. Natron was a railroad station just east of **Springfield**, its name inspired by a kind of rock on nearby Mount Pisgah. Oregon Geographic Names; "Point Lookout."

Natural Bridge. A spot on the upper **Rogue River** 10 miles north of **Prospect** where the rushing river disappears into a 200-foot lava tube before reappearing downstream. A 12-year-old girl was sucked through the tube in the late 1980s and survived; others have not been so fortunate. Oregon Atlas.

Natural gas. In 1994 natural gas supplied 15% of Oregon's total **energy** needs, with more than 1.2 billion therms of natural gas sold in the state. Except for the 2% produced in Oregon, it came by pipeline from Canada and from the San Juan Basin in the Rocky Mountain states. 20% was used for residential energy, 16% for commercial, 43% for industrial, 4% for transportation, and 18% for generating **electricity**. Vehicles powered by natural gas include buses in the **Medford** area, and **Jackson County** is converting its county fleet to natural gas fuel to reduce air pollution. Oregon Blue Book; State Energy Data Report. See also **Electric power plants**; **Public Utility Commission**.

Natural gas pipelines. Natural gas was first piped into the state in 1956. Pipelines now run along the **Interstate 5** and **Interstate 84** corridors as well as to Astoria and to the north-central coast. In 1961 a 36-inch natural-gas pipeline running from Alberta, Canada to San Francisco was laid through central Oregon in a six-foot trench called the "big ditch". Atlas of Oregon; East of the Cascades.

Natural gas production. In 1996, 21 natural gas wells were producing in the Mist gas field in **Columbia County**, 14 operated by Enerfin Resources and 7 by Northwest Natural Gas. They produced 1.7 billion cubic feet of gas during the year, about 2% of the natural gas used in the state, with a value of $3.4 million. The gas is almost pure **methane**. Cumulative production since the field was discovered in 1979 was 60 billion cubic feet, with a total value of about $116.2 million. Some of the depleted pools are being used for gas storage. Exploratory wells elsewhere in the state have found smaller, non-commercial quantities, except that promising areas have been located in the Tyee Basin in **Coast Range** near **Roseburg**. Hydrocarbon Exploration; "Oil and Gas"; Oregonian 11/29/96:B4.

Natural gas utilities. Three investor-owned gas utilities operate in Oregon. In 1994 they reported sales of 792 million therms in the state, with total revenues of $397 million. Northwest Natural sold 83% of the total, 8% was from Cascade Natural Gas Corporation, and 9% from WP Natural Gas. The companies had a total of 446,000 customers, 392,000 of them residential customers who used an average of 764 therms each in 1994. Many large industrial customers buy natural gas directly from producers. Oregon Utility Statistics.

Natural Heritage Advisory Council. A nine-member body that identifies areas of Oregon that contain rare plants, animals, aquatic species, and geologic features. It developed the **Natural Heritage Program**. 775 Summer St. NE, Salem 97310. 503-378-3805. Oregon Blue Book.

Natural Heritage Program. A data base, authorized by the Legislature in 1981 and 1988, of Oregon's rare, threatened, and endangered plants, animals, and ecosystems. The **Nature Conservancy**, Oregon Division of **State Lands**, and several other public agencies maintain it cooperatively. The listing is published periodically as Rare, Threatened, and Endangered Plants and Animals of Oregon. Site-specific information is available from the office. 1205 NW 25th Avenue, Portland 97210. 503-229-5078.

Natural history museums. See **Museums, science and natural history**.

Natural Resources Conservation Service. A federal agency in the Department of Agriculture, formerly known as the Soil Conservation Service. Its mission is to help farmers and the public at large make the best use of the nation's natural resources. Its main Oregon office is in **Portland**, and it has several field offices in the state. 101 SW Main St., Room 1300, 97204. 503-326-2751. Oregon Blue Book.

Nature Conservancy of Oregon. The state branch of a national conservation organization that preserves the diversity of plants, animals and natural communities by protecting the lands and waters needed for their survival. The state organization, founded in 1960, in 1997 had 23,000 members and 53 preserves and protected areas totaling over 260,000 acres. The preserves have been donated or purchased on a willing-seller basis. 821 SE 14th Avenue, Portland 97214. 503-230-1221. See also **Land trusts**.

Nature Man. A Maine forest survival enthusiast named Joe Knowles who, in order to demonstrate his survival skills, went, with much publicity, naked and unarmed from **Grants Pass** into forests of the **Siskiyou Mountains** in July 1914. He emerged after five weeks, healthy, weathered, and wrapped in animal skins, but the world, preoccupied with the outbreak of **World War I**, paid little attention to his feat. Grants Pass.

Nature of the Northwest. An information office and store in **Portland**, operated jointly by the U.S. **Forest Service** and the Oregon Department of **Geology and Mineral Resources**. In addition to free brochures, the store sells books and maps, including all 1,944 of the 71/2 minute series topographic maps for Oregon. The store is on the lobby level of the Portland State Office Building, 800 NE Oregon Street, #5, Suite 177, 97232. 503-731-4444. Oregon Blue Book.

Naturopathic Examiners, Board of. A state board of five members appointed by the governor for three-year terms. The board registers and licenses naturopathic physicians and investigates complaints. It also certifies doctors qualified to practice natural childbirth. Oregon is one of only a few states to license naturopaths as primary care providers. 407-B State Office Building, 800 NE Oregon St., #21, Portland 97232. 503-731-4045. Oregon Blue Book.

Naturopathy. See **National College of Naturopathic Medicine**.

Navigable waterways. The term "navigable" is defined differently by various government agencies. The term used in relation to ownership of the beds and banks of waterways, is "title navigability." Under the **Admission Act** Oregon became owner of all land underlying navigable waterways within the state. However, in the 1870s the legislature granted ownership of certain submersible lands (lands between ordinary low and high water) along several rivers to upland land owners, but those lands remain subject to some public use, and the public always has the right to navigate over the surface of any waters in the state. The public does not, however, have the right to trespass on privately-owned land to get to the waters. The **State Land Board** leases some state-owned banks and beds to marinas, log rafting companies, and gravel mines, with the income going into the **Common School Fund**. Oregonian 2/19/96:D2; Who Owns the Waterways?

Neahkahnie Mountain. A 1,631' mountain rising abruptly from the ocean north of the Nehalem River in **Tillamook County** 30 miles north of **Tillamook**. The old Indian trail across its cliffs, high above the ocean, was said by early travelers, settlers, and mail carriers to have been terrifying. Indians of the area told David McKay of the **Hudson's Bay Company** a long story of treasure buried by stranded sailors. According to legend, the crew of a ship dug a deep hole, lowered a chest into it, and then killed the black member of the crew and placed his body on the chest before covering it with dirt. Extensive searches since have found evidence of early white presence, including stones with carved messages, but no treasure. Some maintain that McKay, himself, recovered the treasure. Another shipwreck near Neahkahnie Mountain, possibly the *San Francisco Xavier*, was the source of the large amounts of **beeswax** that have been washing up on shore for years. The mountain's name is from the local Indian words "ne", meaning place, plus the name of a major deity who turned to stone on the mountain. Oregon Geographic Names; Stories of Nehalem; Tillamook. See also **Ozokerite**.

Necanicum River. A 21-mile long river on the north coast that drains 87 square miles before flowing into the ocean at **Seaside**. The name is derived from Ne-hay-ne-hum or Nekonikon, the name of an Indian lodge up the stream. Oregon Geographic Names.

Nehalem. A north coast community in **Tillamook County** 25 miles north of **Tillamook** on **Highway 101**. The post office, named for the local Indians, was established about 1870; the city was incorporated in 1899. Population 1980 258; 1995 235. Elevation 8'. PO Box 143, 97131. 503-368-5627. Oregon Geographic Names.

Nehalem Bay State Park. A **state park** on a sand spit between Nehalem Bay and the ocean 3 miles south of Manzanita Junction and 25 miles north of **Tillamook**. Six miles of sand beach make the park a favorite with beachcombers. The 291-site campground is open all year. The 2,400-foot Nehalem Airport is less than 1/4 mile from the campground entrance; there is a 6-site primitive camp for those who fly in. A horse camp has 17 campsites, each with a two-horse corral, that can be reserved, as can a meeting hall. Reservations, 800-452-5687. 9500 Sandpiper Lane, Nehalem 97131. 503-368-5943.

Nehalem River. A 119-mile long river that heads in the **Coast Range** fifteen miles west of **Forest Grove** and then makes a large loop north past **Vernonia** before reaching the ocean at Nehalem Bay north of **Tillamook**. **Jetties** at the mouth help maintain a channel for fishing boats. The river drains 847 square miles and is one of five rivers designated for **coho salmon** habitat restoration. The Salish Indians who lived along the lower river were called Nehalems, though the word originally may have meant "place where people live." Oregon Geographic Names. See also *Mimi*.

Neon horses. Fourteen life-size neon outlines of horses placed in farmyards along **Interstate 5** between **Salem** and **Eugene** during the winter in 1994. Some of the sculptures, by Cloverdale artist Martin Anderson, were later placed around **Pioneer Courthouse Square** in **Portland**, and several have appeared since at various places.

NERO Project. A high-speed communication system connecting five Oregon universities; the acronym stands for Network for Education and Research in Oregon. It can transmit up to 155 million bits of information a second (compared to 20,000 per second for a home computer modem) and uses Asynchronous Transfer Mode (ATM). Funding is from a National Aeronautics and Space Administration (NASA) $4.5 million grant. See also **ED-NET**.

Nerve gas. See **Umatilla Chemical Depot**.

Nesika Beach (Neh SEEK uh). An unincorporated community on the south Oregon coast seven miles north of **Gold Beach**. The **Geisel Monument** is located just south of town, and a **bronze** foundry was recently established in the community.

Nesika Illahee Pow-Wow. An annual celebration hosted by the **Siletz Reservation** on the second weekend of August. It is one of the largest **pow-wows** in the state with over 200 competitive dancers plus singing, vendors of Indian wares, and a salmon feast. Photographing some of the people and ceremonies is not allowed, but otherwise the public is welcome.

Nestucca River. A 52-mile long coastal river that drains 259 square miles of the **Coast Range** into the north end of Nestucca Bay 20 miles north of **Lincoln City**. The Little Nestucca River flows into the south end of the bay. The meaning of the Indian name is unknown. Oregon Geographic Names.

Netarts Bay. A five-mile-long bay on the north Oregon coast west of **Tillamook**. See also **Oysters**.

Networks. See **Communications networks**.

Nevada. A state that shares about 160 miles of Oregon's southern border. Although about 10% larger in area, it has less than half Oregon's population. In 1848 the U.S. acquired the area from Mexico by treaty, and after years in various territories, it became a state in 1864. The **Applegate Trail** traversed the Humboldt Valley in Nevada, and cattle were driven from eastern Oregon to the railroad at Winnemucca until closer rail lines were built in Oregon. Fort McDermitt Indian Reservation straddles the Oregon/Nevada line.

New Albion. The name given by the English pirate and explorer Francis Drake to the region of the west coast of North America that he claimed for England in 1579. Map makers applied the name to the coastal areas of what is now Oregon and Washington. Empire of the Columbia.

New England. Many of the more educated immigrants to Oregon in the early years were from New England and they exercised a disproportionate influence on the communities in which they settled, most notably in **Forest Grove**, **Portland**, and **Salem**. Empire of the Columbia.

New Era. An unincorporated **Clackamas County** community five miles south of **Oregon City** on **Highway 99E** and the **Willamette River**. Early settlers included members of the New Era Spiritualist Society, and the name seemed appropriate for the community. Oregon Ghost Towns.

New Market Theater. A **Portland** building, completed in 1873, that is noted for its **cast-iron architecture**. The market was on the ground floor where a 200-foot arcade, lined with 28 marble produce stalls, led through the building from First Avenue to Second. The floor above had a 1,200-seat theater where the great entertainers of the era performed. It has been renovated and shops again line the ground floor. 50 SW Second Avenue. Grand Era of Cast-Iron.

New River. A river next to the coast north of **Cape Blanco** that was created by pioneers to drain marsh in order to make pasture. It used to drain straight to the ocean, but after beach grass was planted around the turn of the century, the river, which dries up in the summer, annually finds a new outlet, each year about 100 yards farther north. The river now runs nine miles north from **Floras Lake** to its present outlet. The area is home to a variety of endangered species. A canoe put-in is located off of Croft Lake Road. Oregonian 12/27/94:B1.

New Theatre Building. A **Portland** building at SW Broadway and Main, part of the **Portland Center for the Performing Arts**. It includes both the 900-seat **Newmark Theatre** and the 300-seat **Dolores Winningstad Theatre**. The building, sometimes called the Performing Arts Center, was completed in 1987.

Newberg. A **Willamette Valley** city in **Yamhill County**, between **Portland** and **McMinnville** on **Highway 99W**. In early days the area was called the Grubby End of the Chehalem Valley, but in 1869 the first postmaster established the post office and named it for Neuberg, Germany. In 1881 two Quakers platted a town-site in anticipation of the arrival of a rail line. Quakers also established the first school, which later became **George Fox College**. The boyhood home of former president Herbert Hoover (1874-1964) is now the Hoover-Minthorn House Museum. Newberg was incorporated in 1889. Population 1980 10,394; 1995 15,285. Elevation 175'. 414 E. First St., 97132. 503-538-9421. Chamber of Commerce 503-538-2014. Old Yamhill.

Newberry Crater. A **caldera** formed when the summit of **Newberry Volcano** collapsed after drainage of magma had removed support for its upper slopes. The caldera floor has risen some 14 feet in the last 1,300 years and volcanologists think another eruption is likely within the next few hundred years. **Rhyolite** eruptions between 6,400 and 1,300 years ago created six large **obsidian** flows into the caldera, a **pumice** volcano in its center, and a series of **cinder cones** across the center that divide the caldera into the two basins of **East** and **Paulina Lakes**. **Paulina Peak** on the south wall is the high point; the wall of the caldera is breached on the west by Paulina Creek which drops over **Paulina Creek Falls**. It has been designated a **National Natural Landmark**. Recreation and fishing facilities are available at the lakes. Atlas of Oregon Lakes.

Newberry National Volcanic Monument. A 50,000-acre area in central Oregon set aside in 1990 to preserve the remarkable geologic landforms of the region. It includes **Newberry Volcano, Paulina and East Lakes** in **Newberry Crater**; **Lava Butte, Lava Cast Forest, Lava River Cave, cinder cones, obsidian** flows, **lava tubes**, and other volcanic features. Campgrounds and small resorts are available at the lakes. The monument is administered by **Deschutes National Forest**. Information is available at **Lava Lands Visitors Center** on **Highway 97** ten miles south of **Bend**. 58201 S. Highway 97, Bend 97707. 541-593-2421.

Newberry Volcano. A huge shield **volcano** that lies on the **Brothers fault zone** south of **Bend**; it has the largest volume of any volcano in the Northwest. Built by **basalt** lava eruptions beginning 500,000 years ago, it now covers 500 square miles. At one time it had a 10,000' summit that collapsed, forming a **caldera** known as **Newberry Crater**. The high point on the caldera rim is **Paulina Peak** at 7984'. Over 400 **cinder cones**, many **lava caves**, and other volcanic features are found on its flanks. Plans for a 33 **megawatt** geothermal energy plant on the side of the volcano were abandoned in 1996 after tests found inadequate steam. The mountain is named for geologist Dr. John Strong Newberry, an 1855 explorer for the Pacific Railroad Surveys. **Newberry National Volcanic Monument** encompasses much of the volcano. Geology of Oregon.

Newell House. See **Robert Newell House**.

Newmark Theatre. A 900-seat **Portland** theater at SW Broadway and Main in the New Theatre Building (sometimes called the Performing Arts Center) that also houses the **Dolores Winningstad Theatre**. **Portland Center Stage** is the resident company. The theater opened in 1987 as part of the **Portland Center for the Performing Arts** and was known until 1997 as the Intermediate Theatre. 503-

796-9293 for event information recording. Emergencies (during events only) 503-274-6566. Oregonian 12/10/97:A1.

Newport. "The Friendliest." A coastal tourist center on **Yaquina Bay** at the junction of **Highways 101** and **20** that is also a lumber and fishing port and the county seat of **Lincoln County**. It was part of the **Siletz Reservation** until oysters, which were in great demand in San Francisco, were discovered in the bay in 1864. Oregon's first resort hotel, the Ocean House, was built in Newport in 1865; vacationers came by stage and steamer from **Corvallis**. The post office was established in 1868, and the city was incorporated in 1882. Old Bay Front on the north side of the bay is a mix of canneries and tourist attractions, while the **Oregon Coast Aquarium** and **Hatfield Marine Science Center** are both located on the south side. The town also has a visual arts center, a performing arts center, historical museum and the **Oregon Coast Community College Service District**. The Seafood and Wine Festival is held the last full weekend in February. The name was perhaps suggested by Newport, RI. Mombetsu, Japan, is its sister city. Population 1980 7,519; 1995 9,495. Elevation 134'. 810 SW Alder St., 97365. 541-265-5331. Chamber of Commerce 541-265-8801. First One Hundred Years.

Newspapers. Oregon is essentially a one-newspaper state, dominated by the Portland **Oregonian**, which had a paid daily circulation in 1996 of 338,586. The Eugene Register Guard (75,301), and the Salem **Statesman Journal** (58,733) followed. The 1997-98 Oregon Blue Book lists over 100 newspapers published in Oregon, of which nineteen are dailies. Oregon Newspaper Publishers Assoc., 7150 SW Hampton St., Suite 111, Portland 97223. 503-624-6397. See also **Portland Observer**.

Newspapers - history. The first newspaper on the west coast was the Flumgudeon Gazette and Bumblee Bee Budget, a handwritten satirical paper that appeared semi-weekly during the 1845 session of the **provisional government** in **Oregon City**. Its motto was "Don't stroke us backwards! There is enough villainy going on to raise our bristles without that." The first printed newspaper on the west coast was the Oregon Spectator, which began February 5, 1846 at Oregon City with William G. T'Vault (1806-1869) as editor. In 1931 Portland had four daily papers. Dictionary of Oregon History; East of the Cascades; History of Oregon Newspapers. See also **Oregonian**; **Pulitzer Prize**; **Scottsburg**; **Statesman Journal**.

Newsreels. See **Films - history**.

Nez Perce Indians. An Indian tribe that lived in the area where Washington, Oregon, and Idaho meet. In 1996, the tribe, which had been moved to reservations in Kansas, Oklahoma, Idaho, and Washington, some before and some after the 1877 **Nez Perce War**, reestablished an Oregon presence by purchasing over 10,000 acres of former cattle ranches adjoining **Hells Canyon National Recreation Area** so that they could restore some of the wilderness habitat that had once sustained their culture. A group is also planning a Nez Perce Indian education and cultural center near the confluence of the Lostine and Wallowa rivers, a center that would focus on the culture of the area's native Americans for the 10,000 years before whites arrived. In 1838 Samuel Parker wrote in his Journal of an Exploring Tour Beyond the Rocky Mountains about the Nez Perce, "Probably there is no government upon earth where there is so much personal and political freedom, and the same time so little anarchy; and I can unhesitatingly say, that I have nowhere witnessed so much subordination, peace, and friendship as among the Indians in the Oregon Territory. The day may be rued when their order and harmony shall be interrupted by any instrumentality whatever." Children of Grace; Hell's Canyon; Nez Perce. See also **Lapwai Mission**.

Nez Perce National Historic Park. A park with 24 sites in four states, including four located in **Wallowa County** in northeast Oregon. The four in Oregon include Joseph Canyon Overlook north of **Enterprise**, Dug Bar Crossing in **Hells Canyon**, a summer campsite at **Wallowa**, and the Old Chief Joseph grave site and cemetery in **Joseph**. P.O. Box 93, Spalding ID 83551. 208-843-2261.

Nez Perce (Nee-Me-Poo) National Historic Trail. A 1,100-mile route followed by a band of **Nez Perce Indians** in their flight from their homeland near **Wallowa Lake** to the Bears Paw Battlefield in northern Montana during the **Nez Perce War**. Congress added the route to the National Trails System in 1986. Information is available from **Wallow-Whitman National Forest** and **Vale District, BLM**.

Nez Perce War, 1877. An **Indian war** that began in June 1877 after some embittered young **Nez Perce** warriors killed four whites to protest the coming removal of the Indians from their native **Wallowa** Valley, a valley reserved to them in an 1855 treaty. Whites fired on Indians who were approaching under a flag of truce; the Indians fired back, killing 33 with no losses of their own. General Oliver Howard then mustered 400 men and began an epic pursuit of the band of 750 Nez Perce men, women, and children who were fleeing to Canada under Young Chief Joseph. After a three month flight during which the Nez Perce had traversed 1,100 miles of rugged terrain despite 13 engagements with the army, the weakened Indians had reached the Bear Paw Mountains in Montana, just 40 miles from Canada, where, after a battle and siege, they surrendered on October 5. 122 Indians, 127 soldiers, and 50 civilians were killed in the campaign. The surviving Indians were sent to reservations in Kansas and Oklahoma and later returned to reservations in Washington and Idaho. "I Will Fight No More Forever."

Niagara. A former town site, now a county park, on the North **Santiam River** eight miles east of **Mill City**. The river gorge is so constricted at the site that even though the river is 45' deep it is only 4'3" wide. A number of efforts to dam the river at the site have been made; the first, a log dam, was built before 1890, but was washed out by floods. Despite the finding by engineers in 1913 that the site was unsuitable for a dam, efforts persisted for some years. Treasures of the Oregon Country.

Nickel. The only operating nickel mine in the United States was at Nickel Mountain west of **Riddle** in **Douglas County** until it closed in 1998. The ore at Nickel Mountain, formed by the weathering of peridotite, is about 1.4% nickel. Mining of the deposits, discovered by shepherds in 1865, began in the 1880s and has continued intermittently since. The **Hanna Mining Company** operated the mine and smelter from 1954 until 1986. Glenbrook Nickel Company operated it 1989-1993 and 1995-1998, supplementing its production with ore from New Caledonia imported via a facility at **Coos Bay**. Total potential production was 36 million pounds of nickel annually, using as much electricity as the entire city of **Eugene**. A separate plant manufactured abrasives from the leftover slag. Geology of Oregon; "Mining and exploration in Oregon during 1992"; Mail Tribune 1/31/ 98:3A; Oregonian 4/8/95:D10.

Nike. An Oregon company, the world's leading manufacturer of high quality athletic footwear and maker of sports equipment and apparel. Nike, with 12,000 employees worldwide, led the list of Oregon **corporations** on the Fortune 500 list with $6.471 billion in 1996 sales. The founder, Phil Knight (1938-), has become the richest Oregonian in history. One Bowerman Drive, Beaverton 97005. 503-671-6453. Oregonian 4/9/96:B14.

Nike shoe spill. During a storm on May 27, 1990, five containers filled with 80,000 Korean-made Nike shoes washed off a container ship 500 miles off the Aleutians. About 200 shoes were found along north Washington beaches after Thanksgiving, and more washed up later that winter and spring along Oregon beaches. Their distribution provided useful data to those studying ocean currents. Oregonian 9/24/92:B1. See also **Ship spills**.

Niobium. A gray metallic element, also called Columbium, that is used in alloys. Over a million pounds annually is produced at Wah Chang in **Millersburg**. Mineral Industry of Oregon.

Nitrate pollution. Pollution of **groundwater** caused by concentrations of nitrates in the soil, whether natural or from fertilizers, livestock wastes, wastewater applications on farm land, septic systems, or military activities. Levels above 10 milligrams per liter can cause blue baby syndrome in infants, as happened in eastern Oregon in the 1950s, and can also adversely affect the health of pregnant or nursing women. A 1995 study found levels of nitrogen in the **Willamette River** from **Eugene** to the **Columbia River** exceeded drinking-water standards. That same year, studies of **groundwater** in northeast Oregon found nitrate concentrations of 10 to 20 milligrams, and up to 70 milligrams across northern **Morrow** and **Umatilla** counties. High levels are also found in northern **Malheur County** where nitrates occur both naturally and from fertilizers leaching into irrigated soil. Experiences; Oregonian 10/31/95:B2, 4/30/97:A13.

Nitrogen dioxide. A reddish-brown gas, NO_2, that is a lung irritant and a precursor of **ozone**. It also leads to corrosion of metals, contributes to acid rain, and reduces visibility. The major human-caused source is petroleum fuel combustion in motor vehicles and in utility and industrial boilers. 1996 emissions in Oregon totaled 218,000 tons. Oregon Air Quality. See also **Air pollution**.

Nobel Prize. Two persons from Oregon have received Nobel Prizes. The first, William P. Murphy (1892-1987), was one of three who received the physiology/medicine prize in 1934 for finding a treatment for pernicious anemia. Dr. Murphy had attended school in **Condon** and graduated from the **University of Oregon**. The second winner, Linus Pauling (1901- 1994), is the only person to have received two unshared Nobel Prizes. The first was the 1954 award in chemistry for his work on molecular bonding, and the second was the 1962 Peace Prize for his work for international control of nuclear weapons and against nuclear testing in the atmosphere. The Linus Pauling Institute of Science and Medicine and his personal papers are located at **Oregon State University**, where he received his bachelor's degree. He, too, had attended school in Condon, as well as in **Portland**. Force of Nature. See also **Pauling House**.

Noble fir. See **Fir**.

Noise pollution. The state has adopted noise control standards but transferred enforcement to local governments. Earlier, when urban homes were spaced so that each family could have a cow, Oregonians legislated against cowbells at night. Oregon Oddities.

Nook. A peninsular ridge that lies between the **Columbia River** and the **John Day River** just east of their confluence. The Nook, two miles wide and eight miles long, rises steeply on both sides to the 1,200' ridge top.

Norm Thompson headquarters. A **Hillsboro** building, designed by Sienna Architects, that took top prize in a competition called "Architecture + Energy: Building Excellence in the Northwest." The building uses cement made from recycled auto glass, lighting with occupancy sensors, and flooring made from old freight cars. The contest, sponsored by the American Institute of Architects, is funded by a grant from the **Bonneville Power Administration**. Oregonian 7/7/96:D2.

Norma. The second, and last, steamboat to traverse the full length of **Hells Canyon**. It was brought from **Huntington** where it had been built (but proved to be unprofitable) down to Lewiston, Idaho, in 1895. The *Shoshone* had been brought down in 1870. Hells Canyon.

Normal schools. Colleges that offered two-year programs for training elementary and high school teachers. In the 1880s the state of Oregon designated normal schools in **Monmouth, Ashland, Weston, The Dalles**, and **Drain**, but they all were abolished in 1909 after years of controversy over state aid. Later, normal schools were reestablished at Monmouth, Ashland, and **La Grande** and became Colleges of Education in 1939. The three are now **Western Oregon University, Southern Oregon University**, and **Eastern Oregon University**. Dictionary of Oregon History.

Norpac. An Oregon farmers cooperative that processes canned and frozen vegetables under the Flav-R-Pac label. It plans a 138-acre industrial park on **Interstate 5** at the Brooks exit that will include a visitor center and gift shop featuring Oregon's agricultural products. Oregonian 5/5/95:B1.

North Bend. A western Oregon tourist, timber and fishing town on **Highway 101** just north of **Coos Bay**. Captain Asa Simpson and his son Louis Simpson founded the town in 1856 and called it Yarrow. It was incorporated in 1903 as North Bend because it sits on the "north bend" of the bay. Major employers include Weyerhaeuser Corporation, Bay Area Hospital, and CEDCO (**Coquille Indian Tribe**) which operates a **casino**. Attractions include parks, Coos County Historical Museum, and the largest shopping center on the southern Oregon coast. Population 1980 9,779; 1995 9,855. Elevation 41'. PO Box B, 97459. 541-756-8500. Chamber of Commerce 800-824-8486. Louie Simpson's North Bend.

North by Northwest Music and Media Conference. An annual October festival, begun in 1995, in which 300 groups from 12 Western states and Canada play 40-minute sets at 20 **Portland** metro-area clubs. Oregonian 10/27/96:D1.

North Macadam District. A 130-acre area of **Portland** along the west bank of the **Willamette River**, from the Marquam Bridge 1.2 miles south to Bancroft Street. A plan for the area, which includes some abandoned industrial sites, envisions a mixed neighborhood of residential, office, and retail spaces. Oregonian 5/23/97:A15.

North Pacific Industrial Association Exposition Building. A **Portland** building that was the largest on the West Coast at the time it was completed in 1889. The structure, located between Burnside and Morrison, and 18th and 20th, was 400 feet by 200 feet with a high, glass-roofed, central hall. More than 15,000 Oregonians crowded in to hear President Benjamin Harrison dedicate it on May 5, 1891. The building had housed over 250 exhibitions before fire destroyed it in 1910. 503-285-7756. Portland, An Informal History; Round the Roses.

North Plains. "City to the Sunset." A north **Willamette Valley** town in **Washington County** 20 miles west of **Portland** on **Highway 26**. Originally platted in 1910, North Plains served as a processing and shipping point for local farm and lumber products from the north plains of the Tualatin Valley. It incorporated in 1963. Major businesses include lumber, landscaping, grain processing, manufacturing, and Pumpkin Ridge Golf Course. North Plains Days is held annually in August. Population 1980 715; 1995 1,245. Elevation 176'. 31360 NW Commercial St., PO Box 537, 97133. 503-647-5555. Chamber of Commerce 503-647-2207. Oregon Geographic Names.

North Powder. A community on the Powder River in **Union County**, 25 miles south of **La Grande** on **Interstate 84**. Pioneers on the **Oregon Trail** camped in the area in the 1840s, and it was first settled in 1851. However, not until the transcontinental **Oregon Railway and Navigation Co**. rail line came through in 1884 was a town laid out. The city was incorporated in 1903. Population 1980 430; 1995 530. Elevation 3,256'. PO Box 309, 97867. 541-898-2185. History of Union County.

North Santiam Highway. See **Highway 22**.

North Sister. A 10,085' volcanic peak in the central Oregon **Cascade Range**. It is the most deeply eroded of the **Three Sisters**. Collier Cone on its north flank erupted some 400 years ago. Collier **Glacier** lies between **North** and **Middle Sister**.

North Tenmile Lake. See **Tenmile Lake**.

North Umpqua Hydroelectric Project. A series of eight **hydroelectric power** developments on the North **Umpqua River** with a total capacity of 185 **megawatts**. The eight projects are Lemolo No. 1, Lemolo No. 2, Clearwater No. 1, Clearwater No. 2, Toketee, Fish Creek, Slide Creek, and Soda Springs. Each development typically consists of a dam, waterway, penstock, and powerhouse. Two major reservoirs, Lemolo Lake and Toketee Lake, provide water storage. The project, built between 1947 and 1956, is owned by **PacifiCorp**.

North West Company. A Canadian fur trading company, organized in 1783 in Montreal as a competitor to the **Hudson's Bay Company**. In 1813 the company bought the fort called **Astoria**, plus **Wallace House** and other northern posts from the **Pacific Fur Company**, renamed Astoria **Fort George**, and began operations along the lower **Columbia River** and in the **Willamette Valley**, where they built **Willamette Post**. Though the company was singularly inept in its relations with the area **Indians** and was not particularly profitable, it dominated the fur trade of the Columbia Basin until it merged with the Hudson's Bay Company in 1821. Champoeg; Fur Hunters of the Far West. See also **Rogue River War**; **Fur trade**.

Northern lights. See **Aurora borealis**.

Northern Pacific Railroad. A railroad company that transformed Oregon by providing Oregon's first **transcontinental connection** by rail on September 11, 1883. It connected its line from Minnesota with the **Oregon Railway and Navigation Company** line that ran along the south bank of the **Columbia River** from **Portland** to Walla Walla, Washington. By the time they met, both lines were controlled by Henry Villard. In 1887 Northern Pacific built a line between **Portland** and Tacoma that crossed the Columbia by ferry between **Goble** and Kalama, Washington. The company received 264,520 acres of federal timber lands in Oregon in lieu of its lands in Mount Rainier National Park (1899) and other places. Dictionary of Oregon History; Disposition. See also **Astoria and Columbia River Railroad**; **Celebrations**; **Land grants**.

Northern Paiute Indians. Nomadic Indians of the Great Basin high deserts of southeast Oregon. Paiutes spoke a Uto-Aztecan language related to the languages of other tribes in the Great Basin. For much of the year the Northern Paiutes ranged across the arid high plateau in small bands, but in winter some gathered in groups of considerable size, as Ogden reported in 1826 from **Malheur Lake**. In 1872 the government established the 1.8 million acre Malheur Reservation but abolished it after the Indians had been moved to Washington following the **Bannock War** of 1878. Later, Northern Paiutes were assigned to six reservations in three states, including the **Burns Paiute, Klamath**, and **Warm Springs Reservations** in Oregon. First Oregonians; People of Warm Springs; Sarah Winnemucca. See also **Four Rivers Cultural Center**.

Northern spotted owl. An 18" owl, *Strix occidentalis*, that breeds in humid **old growth** conifer forests of western Oregon, Washington, and California where it feeds especially on **voles** and **flying squirrels**. It is preyed on by great horned owls. The barred owl, which was first sighted in the state in the 1970s, may be displacing it. Surveys through 1992 estimated that about 2,000 pairs nested in Oregon. In 1990 it was listed by the federal government as a threatened species, and in the following year a court injunction halted logging in areas that might be habitat for the owl, significantly reducing timber harvests on federal lands. The injunction was lifted in 1994, but the timber harvest has remained low as old growth habitat is retained. Atlas of Oregon Wildlife. See also **Endangered species**; **FEMAT Report**; **Northwest Forest Conference**.

Northwest Children's Theater. See **Children's theater**.

Northwest Christian College. An accredited private college in **Eugene** that enrolled 408 students in 1995. 828 11th Ave. E., Eugene 97401. 541-343-1641. Oregon Blue Book.

Northwest Earth Institute. An organization that offers study programs and resources for motivating individuals to accept responsibility for the Earth by transforming personal values and habits. Suite 532, 921 SW Morrison St., Portland 97205. 503-227-2807. See also **Environmental organizations**.

Northwest Electric Power and Conservation Planning Council. See

Northwest Power Planning Council.

Northwest Film and Video Center. A center in the **Portland Art Museum** that presents films five nights a week, holds classes, and sponsors events, including an annual International Film Festival and an annual Northwest Film and Video Festival. 1219 SW Park Ave., Portland 97205. 503-221-1156.

Northwest Forest Conference. A one-day meeting held in **Portland** on April 2, 1993, at which President Clinton, Vice-president Gore, and seven cabinet members listened to a series of speakers address the legal gridlock between **logging** and retention of **old growth forests**. The resulting **FEMAT report** included nine options of which Option 9 became the new Northwest federal forest policy. While addressing the **Northern spotted owl** and other **endangered species** issues, it allowed an annual cut of 1.2 billion board feet of timber from federal lands, down from an annual average of 4.3 billion board feet from federal lands in Oregon during the previous decade. Tree Huggers.

Northwest High-Speed Rail Corridor. A rail corridor from **Eugene** north through **Portland** to Vancouver, B.C., so designated for federal funding for high-speed rail systems. The ultimate goal is to provide 125 mph rail service, though 90 mph service may be more achievable in the near future.

Northwest Indian Art Market. A juried art market with works by several hundred Indian artists from across the U.S. It is planned for May 1998 and will be held at hotels throughout the **Portland** downtown area with headquarters at the Hilton Hotel. Oregonian 11/14/97:D1.

Northwest Passage. A passage, sometimes called Anian Strait, rumored to connect the Atlantic and Pacific oceans around or across the north end of North America. The search for the route influenced exploration for over 400 years, from 1497 to 1906, although the third voyage of Captain James Cook, 1776-1780, persuaded most that there was no such practicable route. An icebreaker finally managed to traverse the Arctic Ocean between the Atlantic and the Pacific in 1954. Dictionary of Oregon History; Empire of the Columbia.

Northwest Power Planning Council. A four-state organization, officially called the Northwest Electric Power and Conservation Planning Council, established by Congress in 1980 to create a 20-year energy plan for the region and to restore fish and wildlife populations affected by **hydroelectric power** development in the **Columbia River** basin. The public is to be involved extensively in the decision-making process. Eight members serve on the council, two each from Oregon, Washington, Idaho, and Montana, appointed by the state governors for three-year terms. The council has no enforcement authority. 852 SW 6th Ave., Suite 1100, Portland 97204-1348. 503-221-5161 or 800-222-3355. Oregon Blue Book. See also **Salmon management**.

Northwest Regional Style. An architectural style that developed in Oregon in the mid 1930s, inspired by the indigenous wooden barns, covered bridges, and other functional wooden structures of the region. Homes in the style were characterized by broad shingled hipped roofs, natural wood finish, much glass, and close integration of the house with its environment. Among the architects who developed the style were A. E. Doyle, John Yeon, Pietro Belluschi, and Saul Zaik. Yeon's 1936 Watzek House and The Shire, his 75-acre garden in Washington across from **Multnomah Falls**, have been given to the **University of Oregon**. Oregon Style.

Northwest Service Center. A former church in **Portland** now used for dramatic performances and other events. 1819 NW Everett Street.

Northwestern School of Law. A law school that opened in **Portland** in 1884 as a night school with two students. It was part of the **University of Oregon** until 1913, then was privately sustained by the Gantenbein family until 1965 when it merged with **Lewis and Clark College**. It is fully accredited by the American Bar Association. "Lewis and Clark Law School: Northwestern School of Law, 1884-1973."

Notary Public. A person who has been authorized by the state to administer oaths and authenticate documents and signatures. Oregon's **Corporation Division** commissions notaries, investigates complaints, and provides certifications of notarized documents. Oregon Blue Book.

Novels. Some of the notable novels of Oregon include the first, Grains, (sometimes called Ruth Rover), 1854, by Margaret Jewett Bailey (1812?-1882); Bridge of the Gods, 1890, by Frederic Homer Balch (1861-1891); Honey in the Horn, 1935, by Harold L. Davis (1894-1960) for which he received the **Pulitzer Prize**; A New Life, 1961, by Bernard Malamud (1914-1986); Sometimes a Great Notion, 1964, by Ken Kesey (1935-); Trask, 1969, by Donald Berry (Oregonian 7/27/97:L1,4,5); The River Why, 1983, by David Duncan; The Jump-Off Creek, 1989, by Molly Gloss (1944-); Sky Fisherman, 1995, by Craig Lesley; and A Sweetness to the Soul by Jane Kirkpatrick, named Outstanding Western Novel of 1995 by the Western Heritage Center. Other writings by Oregon authors include westerns by Ernest Haycox (1899-1950), Jean Auel's Clan of the Cave Bear series, and Phillip Margolin's suspense thrillers. The World Begins Here, an anthology of Oregon short fiction, includes a listing of short fiction and novels. Dictionary of Oregon History; Oregonian 3/1/96:E1, 4/22/96:A2. See also **National Book Awards**; **Prairie Flower**.

Nuclear power. **Trojan nuclear power plant**, Oregon's only nuclear power plant, was built by **Portland General Electric (PGE)** and operated from 1976 to 1992, despite unsuccessful ballot measures to force its closure in 1986, 1990, and 1992. In 1980 Oregonians adopted an **initiative** requiring voter approval of any future nuclear power plant in Oregon. Washington's only nuclear power plant operates at **Hanford Nuclear Reservation** about 40 miles north of **Hermiston**; it is owned by the **Washington Public Power Supply System** and has a capacity of 1,200 **megawatts**. **Bonneville Power Administration** underwrote much of the costs of developing it and two other never-completed plants and still carries $7.1 billion in debt from that effort. See also **Pebble Springs**.

Nuclear reactors. Research reactors, licensed by the U.S. Nuclear Regulatory Commission, are located at **Oregon State University** and at **Reed College**.

Nunan House. A Queen Anne-style house near **Jacksonville** that Jeremiah Nunan ordered from a catalog in 1890 as a Christmas gift to his family. After the family moved into the house (which had arrived in 14 boxcars), they were plagued with illness, two sons died, and Nunan eventually killed himself. It was later found that the family may have suffered from lead poisoning from lead-lined water tanks.

Oregonian 6/2/96:T2.

Nurse practitioners. Registered **nurses** with a master's degree plus additional training in a number of areas. They may prescribe from a comprehensive list of drugs, do physical examinations, order tests, and admit patients. In Oregon nurse practitioners may have their own offices or may practice with physicians. In 1996 there were 1,200 in Oregon who had been licensed by the State Board of Nursing.

Nursery industry. An industry in Oregon of nearly 2,000 plant-producing growers. In 1995 greenhouse and nursery products were Oregon's leading agricultural commodity with sales of $352 million, following only California and Florida. $70 million of the total was from greenhouse crops, while nursery crops had a value of $282 million. 90% of sales were outside Oregon. **Clackamas County** led, followed by **Washington**, **Marion**, **Yamhill**, and **Multnomah** counties. Monrovia Nursery south of **Dayton** is the largest container nursery in the world, producing 42 million plants annually. Oregonian 3/2/95:C1; 1995 Oregon. See also **Oregon Garden Project**.

Nursery industry history. Henderson Luelling (1809-1878) brought a wagon load of 700 young fruit trees (41 varieties) across the **Oregon Trail** in 1847 and the next year established the first nursery in the **Oregon Country** at **Milwaukie**. His brother and partner, Seth, who spelled his name Lewelling (1820-1896), became famed as a developer of improved varieties of fruit, including Bing and Black Republic **cherries**. In 1875 Joseph Lambert developed the Lambert cherry and gave exclusive propagation rights to the Oregon State Horticultural Society. The first ornamental shrubbery was shipped to Preston Gillette near **Astoria** in 1853. Oregon Oddities. See also **Fruit crops - history**.

Nurses. In 1996 Oregon had over 33,000 registered nurses (RNs) with a minimum of 2 years of college, 4,600 licensed practical nurses (LPNs) with one year of training, 17,000 certified nursing assistants (CNAs) with 120 hours of instruction, and 1,200 **nurse practitioners**. All were licensed or certified by the State Board of Nursing, a nine-member board, established in 1911, that regulates nursing practice and education. Board members are appointed by the governor for three-year terms. 800 NE Oregon St., Suite 465, Portland 97232-2162. 503-731-4745. Oregon Blue Book. See also **Midwives**.

Nursing Home Administrators, Board of Examiners of. A board of nine members appointed by the governor for three-year terms. The board develops and enforces nursing home standards and licenses the administrators. There were approximately 480 licensed administrators in 1996. 800 NE Oregon St., Suite 407, Portland 97232. 503-731-4046. Oregon Blue Book.

Nursing homes. See **Continuing care communities**; **Long Term Care Ombudsman**.

Nut crops. Oregon's major nut crop is **hazelnuts**, formerly called filberts. **Chestnuts** and walnuts are also grown, but on a much smaller scale.

Nutria. A large semi-aquatic rodent, *Myocaster coypus*, the size of a medium **beaver**, native to South America. Populations in Oregon are the result of releases, beginning in 1937, by disillusioned nutria fur farmers. A nutria has brown fur, webbed hind feet, a round naked tail, and dorsal mammae. It nests in floating lodges, or like beavers and muskrats, in burrows in banks, and feeds on vegetation. In 1994-95, 7,744 were trapped in Oregon with an average value of $2 each. Atlas of Oregon Wildlife; Mammals of the Pacific Northwest.

NXNW. See **North by Northwest Music and Media Conference**.

Nyssa (NISS uh). "Gateway to Oregon." An eastern Oregon agricultural town in **Malheur County** 13 miles south of **Ontario**. The origin of the name is uncertain, but one theory says that a local student was inspired by the name of St. Gregory of Nyssa . Another holds that it arose in the early days of the local sheep industry from the acronym of the New York Sheep Stock Association (NYSSA). Irrigated farming now focuses on sugar beets (there is a sugar refinery in town), sweet corn, potatoes, mint, wheat, and onions. The Nyssa Nite Rodeo is held during the last full week in June, and Thunderegg Days celebrates rock hounding beginning on the 2nd Wednesday of July. The **Oregon Trail** crossed the **Snake River** from Fort Boise just south of town. The post office was established in 1889; the city was incorporated in 1903. Population 1980 2,862; 1995 2,885. Elevation 2,178'. 14 S. 3rd St., 97913. 541-372-2264. History of Malheur Country; Oregon Geographic Names.

O&C counties. Eighteen western Oregon counties that receive money from the federal government under the **Oregon and California Railroad** Land Grant Fund. They include all Oregon counties west of the **Cascade Range** except Clatsop, plus Klamath County. After the **O&C lands** reverted from private ownership back to the federal government, Congress authorized payments of 50% of timber revenues to the counties to compensate them for the property taxes they were losing. However, to cushion the sudden drop in timber harvest income in the early 1990s due to **Endangered Species Act** constraints, Congress in 1993 allocated a ten-year, declining-% of 1986-1990 revenues to the 18 counties. BLM's Billion-Dollar Checkerboard.

O&C lands. The common designation for **Oregon and California Railroad** Revested Lands in Oregon. In 1866 Congress had authorized a **land grant** of 3.7 million acres of **public domain** land (later estimated to carry 71 billion board feet of timber) to the railroad company to encourage it to build a rail line from **Portland** to the Oregon-California border. The grant, totaling 12,800 acres per mile of railroad, consisted of all odd-numbered square-mile **sections** within the 20 miles on each side of the proposed right-of-way, or, if those lands were already owned, equivalent in-lieu lands. The law provided that the lands be sold for not more than $2.50 per acre to bona fide settlers, and that no person could buy more than 160 acres. Settlers turned out not to be interested because most of the heavily timbered land was unsuitable for farming, so much of the land was logged or sold in large tracts to timber companies. Both the O&C and its successor, the **Southern Pacific**, violated the terms set by the government, and, after a 1915 Supreme Court decision, the remaining 2.89 million acres were eventually revested. Most of those checkerboard lands are now administered by the **Bureau of Land Management** with 50% of revenues going to the 18 **O&C counties** in which they are located, though the **Forest Service** administers about 500,000 acres. The 1937 O&C Act requires that O&C lands be managed for "permanent forest production" and that they contribute "to the economic stability of local communities and industries."

BLM's Billion-Dollar Checkerboard; Disposition; Railroading in Southern Oregon. See also **Coos Bay Military Wagon Road**.

Oak. A **tree** or **shrub**, usually deciduous, that bears acorns. Seven oaks are native to Oregon, four of them rare shrubs of southwestern Oregon. The most common oak tree in the state is the Oregon white oak, *Quercus garryana*, which is the only native oak found north of **Eugene**; it was scattered over the foothills of the **Willamette Valley** at the time of settlement. **Indians** used the acorns for food, and the leaves are a high-protein animal feed. Its wood is of good quality and long-lasting, but has been little used commercially though it is being tried for wine **barrels** and flooring. Settlers used the wood to make charcoal for their forges. The "Signature" oak in the **Oregon Botanical Garden**, estimated to be over 400 years old, is thought to be the oldest left in the state. The California black oak, *Q. kelloggii*, with bristle-tipped, lobed leaves, is found in the valleys of southwest Oregon and south into California, as is the Canyon live oak, *Q. chrysolepis*, with evergreen, holly-like or smooth leaves and dense, tough wood once used for axles and mauls. Trees to Know.

Oakland. A historic southwest Oregon community in **Douglas County** 17 miles north of **Roseburg**. The first post office, established in 1852, was three miles north of the present city and was named for the oak prairie there. In 1872 the town moved itself south to be on the new **Oregon and California Railroad** and incorporated in 1878. After a fire in the 1890s destroyed its wooden buildings, the town rebuilt with brick and stone. It was at one time the state's **turkey** production center and later a timber town, but now the town's economy focuses on the tourists attracted by its historic buildings and museum. Oakland Historic Day is held the second Saturday in May, the Grand Celebration is the last weekend in June, and the Umpqua Valley Wine, Arts and Jazz Festival is held in September. Population 1980 886; 1995 870. Elevation 430'. PO Box 117, 97462. 541-459-4531. Offbeat Oregon; Oregon Geographic Names.

Oakridge. A town in the timbered **Cascade Range** in **Lane County**, 40 miles southeast of **Eugene** on the **Willamette Pass Highway**. Originally known as Hazeldell, the name was changed to Oakridge in honor of local features. The railroad reached the town in 1910, and the post office was established in 1912. The city was incorporated in 1935. Two large sawmills supported the community until the mid 1980s; it is now diversifying its economy. The town holds a Tree Planting Festival the weekend before Mother's Day and features mountain bike events at a Fat Tire Festival on the fourth weekend in July. Area attractions include Aufderheide Scenic Byway and Hills Creek Reservoir. Population 1980 3,680; 1995 3,175. Elevation 1,209' PO Box 385, 97463. 541-782-2258. Chamber of Commerce 541-782-4146. Oregonian 3/20/96:A12.

Oaks Amusement Park. An amusement park along the east bank of the **Willamette River** in south **Portland**, located at the foot of SE Spokane Street near the Sellwood Bridge. Built by Oregon Water Power & Railway Company in 1905 to create traffic for its interurban line, it is now the oldest continuously operating amusement park in the nation. The park has 29 rides including a **roller coaster**, a 96' Ferris wheel, and a 1911 **carousel**, plus the Ladybug Theater, and a roller-skating rink with the floor mounted on barrels so that it can be floated during floods. In 1997 the **Multnomah County** Fair was held at the park. A non-profit organization has operated the park since 1985. 503-233-5777. "How It Was Then." See also **Boat building**.

Oaks Pioneer Church. A small Gothic Revival Style church near the east end of the Sellwood Bridge in **Portland**. The oldest surviving Protestant church in the state, it was constructed in 1851 in **Milwaukie** as St. John's Episcopal Church, and was moved and remodeled several times. In 1961 the building, no longer in use as a church, was barged to the present site. Now owned by Portland Parks and Recreation and managed by the Sellwood-Moreland Improvement League, it is popular for weddings, with up to six a day. 503-233-1497. Century of Portland Architecture; Guide to Early Oregon Churches.

OAR. See **Oregon Administrative Rules**.

Oats. In 1995, Oregon growers produced 3.7 million bushels of oats, worth $5.7 million, on 37,900 acres. 1995 Oregon.

Obscenity. See **Censorship**; **Pornography**; **Sex industry**.

Observatories. Buildings equipped with telescopes for making astronomical observations. The Northwest's largest reflector telescope, a 24-inch Cassegrain, is housed at **Pine Mountain Observatory** east of **Bend**, and the second largest is at **Clackamas Community College**, 503-657-6958, ext. 2351. Other Oregon observatories include those at **Mount Hood Community College** Solar Observatory, 503-669-6944; and **Sunriver** Nature Center and Observatory. See also **Planetariums**.

Obsidian. A volcanic glass with a chemical composition similar to **rhyolite-andesite** lava. **Newberry Crater** contains several flows of the common shiny black form, but some of the obsidian from **Glass Butte** is streaked with reds and browns. Since the broken edges are very sharp, Indians shaped obsidian into **projectile points**, knives, and scrapers. It was an important trade item, and obsidian tools have been found hundreds of miles from the source of the rock. Geology of Oregon. See also **Perlite**; **Pumice**.

Obstetricians. Physicians specializing in childbirth. Oregon had 360 obstetrician/gynecologists who delivered more than 34,000 babies in 1993. Oregonian 6/17/95:C1. See also **Births**; **Midwives**.

OCA. See **Oregon Citizens' Alliance**.

Occupational Safety and Health Division. A division of the Oregon Department of **Consumer and Business Services** that enforces the Oregon Safe Employment Act, establishes minimum safety and health standards for all industries, consults with Oregon businesses on ways to operate a safe and healthful workplace, and fines violators. The largest fine, $1.4 million, was assessed against Oregon Steel Mills Inc. in July 1995 for selling a blasting material containing toxic substances. 350 Winter St. NE, Room 430, Salem 97310-0220. 503-378-3272. Message only, 800-922-2689. Oregon Blue Book.

Occupational Therapy Licensing Board. A board of five members appointed by the governor for four-year terms. It regulates occupational therapy through licensing its practitioners. In July 1997 the board listed 840 active licensed occupational therapists and 224 licensed OT assistants. 700 NE Oregon St., Suite 407, Portland 97232. 503-731-4048. Oregon Blue Book.

Occupations. Oregon Occupations 1994-1995 lists 335 occupations and specialties in the state.

Ocean. The Pacific Ocean, the world's largest, defines Oregon's western boundary and is also the primary determinant of Oregon's weather, spawning the storms that move across the state, and moderating both winter low and summer high temperatures in western Oregon. See also **Beaches**; **Ocean** entries; **Sea level**; **Tides**; **Waves**.

Ocean currents. The great currents of the north **Pacific Ocean** move like vast rivers around the ocean. The North Pacific gyre flows in a clockwise circle, moving swiftly north past Japan (the Kuroshio Current), cooling and slowing as it flows east toward North America (the West Wind Drift) and south along the west coast (the California Current), and, warming again, flowing back toward Japan. Part of the West Wind Drift splits off and circles counterclockwise past Alaska and the Aleutian Islands. Long-term weather changes alter the amount of the West Wind Drift that is diverted. When more of the current flows north, the ocean off Oregon becomes warmer and less productive. (Cool water off the coast in summer reduces the amount of precipitation over land since cool water evaporates less moisture than warm water.) The direction and speed of subsidiary seasonal currents depend on winds and sea level. In winter the broad, fast Davidson Current flows north. Oregon Oceanbook; Oregonian 12/8/96:A1. See also **Ocean temperatures**; **Rip currents**; **Tides**; **Upwelling**.

Ocean floor. The ocean floor off Oregon slopes gradually down across the **continental shelf** for 10 to 46 miles, then drops abruptly down the continental slope to a depth of 10,000 feet at the **Cascadia subduction zone** where the Juan de Fuca Plate is ramming down under the North American plate. Beyond the subduction zone the ocean floor rises to the volcanic Juan de Fuca Ridge, some 300 miles offshore, where upwelling magma keeps feeding the Juan de Fuca Plate on the east and the vast Pacific Plate on the west. The plates spread at rates ranging from 1 1/2 inches a year on the south to 4 inches a year on the north. The ocean floor may include valuable **mineral** deposits. Geology of Oregon; Oregon Oceanbook. See also **Columbia River plume**; **Plate tectonics**; **Sea mounts**.

Ocean life. Most life in the ocean is dependent on various single-celled plants, called phytoplankton, that grow in the lighted surface waters. The phytoplankton are eaten by a variety of drifting animals called zooplankton which are, in turn, food for small fish and filter-feeding whales, and in turn,... Organisms large enough to swim against currents are collectively called nekton. The varied habitats of the ocean floor host an array of bottom-dwelling plants and animals. Deep-ocean life forms have evolved that get their energy not from light but, via bacteria, from methane or from hydrogen sulfide ejected from hydrothermal vents, as along the Juan De Fuca Ridge. Oregon Oceanbook.

Ocean temperature. The waters of the **Pacific Ocean** off Oregon are cool; survival time is estimated to be two to four hours for a person in the ocean without an exposure suit. Temperatures range from 46°F to 64°F, though temperatures from 50°F to 57°F are most common. The ocean temperature off Oregon is warmer than the freezing point of seawater (28.4°F), so it does not freeze, nor are any bays known to have frozen. Waters are warmest in the early fall and coldest in the spring and early summer. A warming phase that began in 1976 has resulted in less sea life. Earlier another warming trend lasted from 1925 to 1947, followed by a cooling period from 1947 to 1976. Oregonian 12/8/96:A1; Weather of Oregon. See also **El Niño; Frozen rivers.**

Ochoco Mountains. Ponderosa pine-covered mountains in central Oregon east of **Prineville**; several peaks are over 6,000'. The **Ochoco National Forest** covers much of the area. Ochoco, a **Paiute** word for willows, is the name of a tributary of the **Crooked River** and of a Paiute chief, though there is dispute as to which was named first. Oregon Geographic Names. See also **Blue Mountain physiographic province; Clarno Formation; John Day Formation; Maury Mountains.**

Ochoco National Forest. A 978,907-acre, central-Oregon national forest located primarily in **Crook, Harney**, and **Wheeler** counties. It includes three wilderness areas, Mill Creek, Bridge Creek, and Black Canyon. The forest also manages the **Crooked River National Grassland.** 3000 E. Third, P.O. Box 490, Prineville 97754. 541-447-6247.

Ochoco Reservoir. A 1,100 acre, 100-foot deep irrigation impoundment six miles east of **Prineville**. It was created in 1921 when the Ochoco Irrigation District built a dam on Ochoco Creek. The dam was rehabilitated in 1950, and then again in 1994 and 1995 because of leakage that apparently has been controlled. Concerns downstream in Prineville prompted installation of a warning siren so that, if the dam fails, city residents would have perhaps 45 minutes to get to higher ground. The lake is a heavily used recreation site, with a **state park** and resort facilities; ice fishing is popular in the winter. Atlas of Oregon Lakes; Oregonian 8/29/94:B2, 6/8/95:C2, 1/15/97:B6.

Octopus. Eight-armed, soft-bodied mollusks that spend most of their time hiding in crannies in shallow water from which they emerge to capture passing crabs. One of the largest known, *Octopus dofleini*, is found in Northwest waters. It has an arm spread of up to nine feet and may weigh 100 pounds. Seashore Life. See also **Squid.**

Octopus tree. A sprawling **Sitka spruce** tree, located in **Cape Meares** State Park.

Odell Lake. A five-mile-long natural mountain lake just east of **Willamette Pass**, one of the largest lakes in the Oregon Cascades. A glacial moraine blocked Odell Creek some 10,000 years ago, creating the lake; the moraine has since been topped by a dam. The lake covers 3,582 acres to a maximum depth of 282 feet. It is heavily used for fishing, boating, and swimming; resorts and several campgrounds provide facilities. **Highway 58** lies along the east side of the lake, and the main **Southern Pacific** rail line to California goes along the west side. Local legend says that there is a locomotive on the bottom, lost when it was being barged across the lake, though a 1995 search failed to find it. William Holman Odell was an 1852 pioneer and surveyor who discovered the lake in 1865. Atlas of Oregon Lakes; Oregonian 7/23/95:L1, 8/3/95:F1.

ODF. See **Forestry, Oregon Department of.**

ODF&W. See **Fish and Wildlife, Oregon Department of**.

Odors. The pleasant smells of Oregon include the pungency of forests and sagebrush, the enticing aroma from coffee houses, the fleeting fragrance of rose hedges and hayfields along highways. The notable stinks come from pulp mills, dairy cattle manure ponds and spray irrigation using the liquid manure, mushroom raising operations, and the occasional beaching of decomposing dead **whales** and **sail jellyfish** masses.

Officer's Cave. A growing cave 11 miles south of Kimberly in **Grant County**. The cave is a maze that was 700' long when measured in 1914 but had increased to 1,500' long when examined in 1975. It develops as major storms erode the soft clays and silts of the **John Day Formation** along an underground stream in the unstable formation; large roof slabs create rock falls where they have dropped. It was named for the Floyd Officer family which homesteaded the area. Geology of Oregon.

Ogden Martin Waste-to-Energy Facility. A **Marion County** disposal facility located four miles north of **Salem** that burns garbage to make electricity. Up to 550 tons of non-recycled **solid waste** is burned daily in two combustion units, producing 13.1 **megawatts** of electricity. The plant uses 2 megawatts of the electricity and sells the rest to **Portland General Electric**. Ferrous metals are removed from the ash before it is landfilled 10 miles north. The plant, owned by Ogden Martin Systems of Marion Inc., began operating in 1987. 4850 Brooklake Road NE, PO Box 9126, Brooks 97305. 503-393-0890.

Oil. Oil supplies more of Oregon's energy than does any other source. Oregonians purchased over 2.7 billion gallons of oil products in 1994. 81% was used for transportation, and the rest for manufacturing, powering farm machinery, and heating. Most comes to the state through a pipeline from Puget Sound south to **Eugene** and another from Salt Lake City across northeast Oregon. The rest is brought in by truck, tanker, and rail. There are no refineries in Oregon, other than an asphalt refinery in **Portland**, and no producing oil wells. Beginning in 1902, exploratory wells have been drilled around the state and offshore, often accompanied by extensive promotion and local excitement but little success. Geology of Oregon; Hydrocarbon Exploration; "It's Down There Someplace;" Oregon Blue Book. See also **Gasoline; Ozokerite; Petroleum; Shale City**.

Oil tanks. See **Heating-oil tanks**.

OIT. See **Oregon Institute of Technology**.

Oktoberfest. A traditional German harvest festival. Oregon's major Oktoberfest is held in **Mount Angel** the third week in September with German sausage, music, dancing, arts and crafts booths, a farmers market, and beer and wine gardens. Over 350,000 people attend the four-day celebration which has grown from its 1966 beginnings to be the largest folk festival in the Northwest. 503-845-9440. An Oktoberfest that includes family activities and golf is held at **Oaks Amusement Park** in **Portland**.

Olallie Lake. The largest of a group of 200 natural lakes ringing Olallie Butte nine miles north of **Mount Jefferson**. Olallie Lake covers 188 acres and is a mile long, with a maximum depth of 43 feet. Despite its heavy use for boating, swimming, and fishing, the lake is still so clear that the bottom is visible even at the deepest point. A campground and resort provide facilities, but no motorboats are allowed on the lake. Olallie is from a **Chinook jargon** word for berries, meaning, in the Cascades, huckleberries. <u>Atlas of Oregon Lakes</u>.

OLCC. See **Liquor Control Commission**.

Old Aurora Colony Museum. See **Aurora Colony**.

Old Believers. See **Russians in Oregon**.

Old Church. A **Portland** church at 1422 SW 11th Avenue that is notable as an outstanding example of Victorian Carpenter Gothic. The church was designed by Warren Heywood Williams and built in 1882 by the Calvary Presbyterian Church. The Old Church Society formed in 1967 to save the building, which was no longer used, and has recently completed its restoration. The building can be rented for cultural, musical, and social events. 503-222-2031. <u>Century of Portland Architecture</u>; <u>Oregonian</u> 1/29/95:L9.

Old growth forest. Popularly, a west-side conifer forest with large, old trees. There is little agreement as to a precise definition, nor as to the original - or even present - extent. **FEMAT** defines an old growth forest as, "A forest stand usually at least 180-220 years old with moderate to high canopy closure; a multi-layered, multi-species canopy dominated by large overstory trees; high incidence of large trees, some with broken tops and other indications of old and decaying wood (decadence); numerous large snags; and heavy accumulations of wood, including large logs on the ground." 1,084 species of plants and animals (not including arthropods), have been identified as associated with old growth coniferous forests. 1.6 million acres of federal **forest land** in Oregon has multi-story forests with medium to large conifer trees. Over half is in the Western Cascades, and a fourth of the total is in areas withdrawn from harvest. Much of the wood from old conifers is of high value, close grained and knot free. <u>Ancient Forests</u>; <u>Forest Ecosystem Management</u>; <u>Forest Dreams</u>; <u>Tree Huggers</u>; <u>Walking Guide to Oregon's Ancient Forests</u>. See also **French Pete**; **Northwest Forest Conference**; **Opal Creek**; **Salvage rider**; **Silver Fire Roundup**; **Timber supply**.

Old Reelfoot. A male grizzly **bear** that limped from the effects of a steel trap. First noted in 1846, it raided southern Oregon livestock for decades before being killed in **Jackson County** at the base of **Pilot Rock** in 1891. Its eight-foot carcass was exhibited at the Columbian Exposition in Chicago in 1893. <u>Listening to Coyote</u>.

Old Scout. See **From Hellgate to Portland**.

Old Town, Portland. See **Chinatown**.

Oldest businesses. The <u>Oregonian</u>, founded in 1850, is the oldest continuously operating commercial business in Oregon. Holman Funeral Service, opened in 1854, is the oldest continuously operating family business; Meier and Frank, founded in 1857, is the oldest department store; and Huber's, established in 1879, is Oregon's oldest active restaurant. All are in **Portland**. They were among sixty businesses over 100 years old honored on April 27, 1995.

Oldest known Oregonian. Mary Ramsey Lemons Woods was born in Tennessee on May 20, 1787. In 1853 she rode a mule bareback to Oregon and lived in Oregon until she died on January 1, 1908 at the age of 120 years, 7 months, and 11 days. In her last year she was crowned "Mother Queen of Oregon." <u>This Day in Oregon</u>.

Oldest rocks. See **Rocks, oldest**.

Oleo. See **Margarine**.

Oligocene. A geologic epoch 25 to 38 million years ago between the **Eocene** and the **Miocene** during which volcanoes erupted in the Western **Cascade Range**, the **John Day Formation** was laid down in Central Oregon, and sediments several thousand feet deep were deposited in what is now western Oregon. Geology of Oregon.

Olympics. Oregonians have won at least 60 medals at the Olympic games 1906 through 1996, 32 of them gold medals. Some of the winners are listed on page 10 of the 1997-98 Oregon Blue Book, though Oregon's most famous swimmer, Don Schollander of **Lake Oswego**, winner of four gold medals in 1964 and a gold and silver in 1968, is not listed, nor is Otis Davis, winner of two gold medals in track in 1960.

Ombudsperson. See **Citizens' Representative**.

OMSI. The Oregon Museum of Science and Industry, located in **Portland** on the east bank of the **Willamette River**. It is an independent, non-tax-supported center founded in 1944 that moved to its present facilities in 1992. The museum features both permanent and changing interactive exhibits and demonstrations, the *USS Blueback* submarine, a gift shop, restaurant, OMNIMAX theater, sky theater, and auditorium, plus special events scheduled throughout the year. OMSI's Education Research Center, housed at the museum's former location in **Washington Park**, operates science camps and teacher education programs. 1945 SE Water Avenue, Portland 97214-3354. 503-797-4000. Oregon Blue Book; Oregonian 10/3/96:A1.

One Percent for Art. A program established by the state legislature in 1977 that designates that one percent of funding for all new state building and remodeling projects be for quality art works. The Oregon **Arts Commission** administers the program. Some cities in **Multnomah** and **Lane** counties also set aside money to purchase art works for public places. Oregon Blue Book.

One-room schools. Several one-room schools still operate in Oregon, including one with 11 students located at Troy at the junction of the Grande Ronde and Wenaha rivers in far northeast Oregon. The state's oldest remaining one-room school house is at Ballston, near **Sheridan** in **Polk County**. The 1855 building now houses pioneer teaching memorabilia. Oregonian 10/6/96:C6. See also **School districts**.

Oneonta Gorge. The canyon created where Oneonta Creek drops into the **Columbia River** two miles east of **Multnomah Falls**. The area around the gorge along the **Columbia River Scenic Highway** has been designated as the Oneonta Gorge Botanical Area because of the unique array of plants found there. A trail leads up the west side of the gorge past Oneonta Falls and **Triple Falls**. The origin of the name Oneonta is unknown though a side-wheel steamer named *Oneonta* operated on the **Columbia River** from 1863 to 1877. Waterfall Lover's Guide.

Onions. In 1995, Oregon growers produced 1.2 billion pounds of storage onions (16% of U.S. production) worth $53 million on 22,420 acres. **Malheur County** produced over 70% of the total, and more than any other county in the U.S. **Sherwood** hosts an Onion Festival in October. Onions are also raised in the **Lake Labish** bottom land. 1995 Oregon.

Ontario. An eastern Oregon city in **Malheur County** on the **Snake River** and **Interstate 84** that is the commercial center for productive irrigated farmland along both the Oregon and Idaho sides of the Snake River and site of the rapidly-expanding Snake River **Correctional Facility**. **Treasure Valley Community College** and the **Four Rivers Cultural Center** are located in Ontario. The town was founded in1883 as a cattle-shipping station on the new transcontinental **railroad** and named by settler James Virtue for Ontario, Canada. It incorporated in 1899. A Japanese Obon Festival is held in mid-July, the Malheur County fair is in August, and the Ontario Winter Wonderland Parade is held on the first Saturday in December. The city, with **Japanese** Americans making up about 4% of the population, has a Buddhist temple and the largest judo club in the nation. Sayama, Japan, is its sister city. Other important ethnic groups include **Basques**, **Hispanics**, and **Northern Paiute** Indians. Population 1980 8,814; 1995 9,980. Elevation 2,140'. 444 SW 4th St., 97914. 541-889-7684. Visitor Bureau 541-889-8012. History of Malheur Country.

Opal Creek Wilderness. A **wilderness area** created by Congress in 1996, after years of controversy, to preserve a 12,800-acre stand of **old growth** timber on the headwaters of the Little North Fork of the **Santiam River**. Trees up to 1,000 years in age and 10 feet in diameter cover about 7,250 acres. Though the rest of the area has never been logged, the trees are not quite so old. The Friends of Opal Creek, a preservationist group, own 225 acres of patented mining claim in the center of the disputed area, and holds another 2,000 acres of unpatented mining claims. The wilderness area and an adjacent 13,640-acre scenic recreation area will be managed by **Willamette National Forest**. Oregonian 10/2/96:D1; Showdown at Opal Creek.

Open meetings laws. "Sunshine" laws adopted by voters in 1974 and 1978 in response to the Watergate scandal. They provide that no meeting of a public body may be held without at least a twenty-four hour notice that includes the agenda and the proposed action. It also provides that decisions must be reached in the open except for personnel matters. A gathering becomes a "meeting" when there is a quorum. Governing Oregon.

Open range. As of 1997, under Oregon's 1894 open range law (ORS 607) cattle may roam free in Oregon and the owner is under no obligation to fence them in or retrieve them if they trespass on another's land. This is true except in cities, along interstate highways and a few state highways, and in areas where residents have voted to establish a livestock district. Open range exists in 26 of the state's 36 counties, and most of the areas are not posted. The 10 counties with totally closed range are **Benton**, **Clackamas**, **Clatsop**, **Coos**, **Gilliam**, **Hood River**, **Multnomah**, **Polk**, **Sherman**, and **Tillamook**. In open range, a motorist who damages livestock on the highway is liable for the damage to the livestock, and the owner of the animal has no liability for damage to the car or persons in it. About 100 motorists collide with livestock each year, and there have been five deaths. Oregonian 7/20/97:A1.

Open records law. A state law adopted in 1973 that provides that records of government actions are to be public. Since then numbers of exemptions have been established by the legislature with some of the most controversial relating to the confidentiality of disciplinary proceedings by the 23 state health licensing boards. Governing Oregon.

Opera. See **Portland Opera Association**.

Operation Desert Storm, 1991. An intense international military operation against Iraq following its August 2, 1990, invasion of Kuwait. The campaign lasted for a month, from January 17, 1991 to February 17, though many troops were stationed in the region for months longer. In addition to the Oregon members of the military, two Oregon **National Guard** units were sent to the Gulf. Six Oregonians lost their lives in the operation. See also **Women in the military**.

Operation Red Hat. In December 1969, President Nixon secretly ordered thirteen-thousand tons of munitions loaded with nerve-gas, enough to kill twice the world's human population, to be moved from Okinawa to the **Umatilla Chemical Depot**. Governor McCall led a six-month campaign, code-named Operation Red Hat, against the plan. The proposal was dropped in May, 1970. Fire at Eden's Gate.

Opossum. See **Possum**.

Opposite side of the globe. See **Geographic opposite**.

Optometry, Oregon Board of. A board that regulates optometry by licensing optometrists. Its five members are appointed by the governor for three-year terms. License fees support its activities. In May 1997 there were 577 active licensed optometrists. 3218 Pringle Rd. SE, Suite 100, Salem 97302-6306. 503-373-7721. Oregon Blue Book.

Orca. A toothed whale, *Orcinus orca*, also called killer whale or blackfish. It is the largest member of the **dolphin** family, with males reaching 28 feet. Orcas are notably ferocious, feeding not only on fish, but on other sea mammals, including seals, **sea lions**, walruses, **porpoises, dolphins**, and even the larger **whales**. They have been reported as far upstream in the **Columbia River** as Vancouver, Washington. Mammals and Life Zones of Oregon; Mammals of the Northwest. See also **Keiko; Moby Mary**.

Orchestras. See **Symphony orchestras**.

Order of the Antelope. An organization of some of Oregon's most powerful business men that worked with the **Lakeview** Chamber of Commerce in the 1930s to get President Roosevelt to establish **Hart Mountain National Antelope Refuge**. The all-male organization held an annual party on the refuge until 1992 when it was banned for rowdiness, excessive drinking, profanity, sexism, racism, and gambling. Oregonian 10/17/94:A6.

Ordinance. A measure adopted by a city or county government, a local law. State laws pertaining to **initiative** and **referendum** also apply to ordinances. See also **Charter; Home rule**.

Oregon department and agency entries. See substantive word. For example, Oregon State Police is listed as **Police, Oregon State**.

Oregon. A medium sized state of the United States of America, bounded by the Pacific Ocean on the west, California and Nevada on the south, Idaho on the east, and Washington state on the north. It is roughly rectangular in shape, about 275 miles north/south by 350 miles east/west, encompassing 97,949 square miles. Oregon was admitted to the Union as the 33rd state on February 14, 1859. **Salem**

is the capital, **Portland**, with a population of 500,000, is the largest city, and the **population** of the state passed 3,000,000 in 1994. It has about 1% of the nation's population and 3% of its land area. See also **Boundaries**; **History**; **Oregon (name)**; **Size**.

Oregon. A battleship, launched in San Francisco as America's premier warship on October 23, 1893. In 1898, while war with Spain threatened and Spanish warships were thought to be on the prowl in both oceans, she made a record and much publicized 13,879-mile dash from San Francisco around South America to Florida. She then took a leading part in the **Spanish-American War** in the Caribbean and later saw active service during **World War I**. Between 1925 and 1943 she was docked as a museum ship in **Portland**, but during **World War II** was towed to the South Pacific as a cargo hull and abandoned in Guam. Her mast was returned to Portland and is mounted at the Battleship *Oregon* Memorial near the end of Oak Street in **Tom McCall Waterfront Park**. Dictionary of Oregon History; "Race."

Oregon (name). The origin of the name Oregon is unknown, though a favored theory is that it came from a name for the Ouisconsink (Wisconsin) River, carelessly spelled and then carelessly transcribed to French maps of the early 1700s where it was written as Ouaricon-sint. The name Ouragon was used in 1765 by English Major Robert Rogers on a petition to explore the country west of the Great Lakes. Adventurer Jonathan Carver was the first to spell it Oregon in his 1778 Travels Through the Interior Parts of North America where he lists "the River Oregon, or the River of the West..." as one of the four great rivers of the continent. However, no form of Oregon was used by Captain Vancouver or Captain Gray (1792), Lewis and Clark (1804-1806) or Astor (1811). The name came into popular usage after the poet William Cullen Bryant used it in his 1817 poem "Thanatopsis". Oregon Geographic Names.

Oregon Administrative Rules. Regulations developed by Oregon's administrative departments and agencies in order to carry out legislative laws. They are edited, codified, and published by the **Archives** Division under the **Secretary of State**. Oregon Blue Book. See also **Oregon Revised Statutes.**

Oregon Agricultural Center. See **Agricultural Marketing Center**.

Oregon Agricultural College. See **Oregon State University**.

Oregon and California Railroad (O&C). A historic railroad company involved in the long and complex effort to construct a rail line between **Portland** and California. After promoter Ben Holladay came to Oregon in 1868, he managed to win control of several competing rail companies in the **Willamette Valley**, reorganized them as the Oregon and California Railroad, and captured the 3,728,000-acre **land grant** offered by Congress for the Oregon portion of a connecting line. In 1872 Holladay's line reached **Roseburg**, but by then Holladay was bankrupt. Henry Villard took over and in 1884 the line reached **Ashland**, but then Villard, too, was bankrupt. Finally, in 1887, the company that became the **Southern Pacific** took it over and completed the connection between Ashland and Redding, California, thus opening the route to California and ending the days of the **stage line**. History of the Southern Pacific. See also **O&C lands**.

Oregon and California Trail. See **Siskiyou Trail**.

Oregon Aviation Museum. A nonprofit group working to make Oregon's place in aviation history better known. As one project, members are restoring the biplane in which Dorothy Hester completed 69 consecutive outside loops in the early 1930s, setting a record that lasted until 1989. PO Box 553, Cottage Grove 97424. Mail Tribune 8/31/97:1B. See also **Captain Michael King Smith Evergreen Aviation Educational Center**.

Oregon Bach Festival. An early summer classical music festival featuring more than 50 concerts and events in **Eugene**, **Corvallis**, and **Salem**. Begun by Helmuth Rilling in 1970, it has grown to be one of the country's outstanding festivals. 541-346-5666.

Oregon Ballet Theater. A **Portland** company that mounts four productions a year at the **Civic Auditorium**, tours, and offers training and outreach programs. Its 1993/94 budget was $3.9 million. 222 SW Clay Street, 97201-5812. 503-227-6867. Business Journal 8/25/95:10; Oregonian 8/24/97:E1.

Oregon Biodiversity Project. A private sector project administered by Defenders of Wildlife that is compiling information on aspects of ecosystems in the state to be used as guidance for managing Oregon's public lands and natural resources. The computerized data base will be available in various forms, including on the Internet. Their outreach program is called NatureMapping. 1637 Laurel St., Lake Oswego 97034. 503-697-3222.

Oregon Biotechnology Innovation Center. A center opened in 1995 as an incubator for new companies based on the health sciences. It offers low cost space for offices and laboratories. 2611 SW Third Ave., Portland 97201-4952. 503-241-7802. Oregonian 10/14/95:C7.

Oregon Blue Book. A biennial publication by the state of Oregon that provides extensive information about state government. It also includes a history of the state, information about the state's economy and resources, and listings of counties, cities, media, and federal offices. The **Secretary of State**'s office publishes each edition in April or May of odd-numbered years while the **legislature** is in session. Copies are sold at bookstores around the state, at the **Capitol**, and by the Secretary of State, Attn. Oregon Blue Book, PO Box 3370, Portland 97208.

Oregon Book Awards. Annual awards presented for fiction, literary non-fiction, poetry, drama, and works for young readers. **Literary Arts, Inc.**, sponsors the annual awards; the ceremony is in October in Portland. 720 SW Washington, Suite 745, Portland 97205. 503-227-2583. The Pacific Northwest Booksellers' Association also makes annual awards. See also **Literature**; **National Book Awards**.

Oregon Botanical Garden. A series of gardens being developed on a 220-acre site near **Silverton** by the Oregon Nurserymen's Garden Foundation. It will showcase nursery products from Oregon in mature landscape designs. The site has a wide diversity of land forms and includes what may be Oregon's oldest **oak** tree. Oregonian 6/25/95:F1. See also **Nursery industry**.

Oregon Brewers Festival. The country's biggest beer festival, held on a late July weekend in **Portland**'s **Tom McCall Waterfront Park**. Some 80,000 attend the event at which 70 brewers from around the U.S. and Canada offer handcrafted beers. 503-778-5917.

Oregon Caves Chateau. A six-story lodge, opened in 1934, that nestles across a canyon at **Oregon Caves National Monument**. Oregon State University professor Arthur L. Peck had developed the original site plan in 1923 and called for sheathing the buildings with bark from local Port Orford **cedars**. **Grants Pass** builder Gust Lium designed and built the chateau, using mostly local woods and stone. The building's long, low-roofed lobby echoes the feeling of the nearby cave. Great Lodges.

Oregon Caves National Monument. A marble cave in southern Oregon, 20 miles east of **Cave Junction**. It has three miles of passages on five levels, and includes an underground stream, chambers, stalactites, stalagmites, chandeliers, draperies, soda straws, grape clusters, and popcorn formations, as well as some new species of insects and **fossil** bones of a 500-pound **jaguar** and a 46,000-year-old grizzly **bear**. The original **limestone**s were laid down on the ocean floor190 million years ago and were metamorphosed by pressure into marble before being uplifted into the **Siskiyou Mountains**. The caves themselves were carved out by acidic ground water within the last million years. The caves were discovered by a bear hunter in 1874; the National Monument was created in 1909. A 75-minute guided tour through the chilly caves is available year-round. It involves 500 stairs. 19000 Caves Hwy., Cave Junction 97523. 541-592-2100. Geology of Oregon; Oregonian 7/4/96:A22.

Oregon Center for Public Policy. A think tank established in 1997 with a grant from the Stern Family Fund to provide research on budget and tax issues affecting low-income Oregonians. 16415 Herigstad Road, Silverton 97381. 503-873-7709. Oregonian 12/21/97:B2. See also **Income distribution**.

Oregon Central Military Wagon Road. A **military wagon road** authorized by Congress to run from **Eugene** to Idaho, and as encouragement Congress granted the state 845,536 acres (odd-numbered **sections** of land for three miles on either side of the right of way) to be awarded to the builder as the road progressed. It was partially constructed between 1864 and 1867 by a private company interested in the land. The route the company selected went up the Middle Fork of the **Willamette River**, south around Diamond Peak, over lush grazing lands that had already been granted to the **Klamath Indians**, across southern Oregon past **Camp Warner** and **Jordan Valley**, and east into Idaho. The poorly maintained road was little used, and the land ended up in lengthy legal entanglements. In 1874 the California and Oregon Land Company (later Booth Kelley Lumber Company) acquired the company and its valuable timber holdings. Some small parcels of desert land had been sold to the gullible from around the country, and the lands with no value reverted to the counties in which they were located. In 1935 the government gave compensation to the Klamath Indians for the lands taken from them. Dictionary of Oregon History; Historical Oregon; Oregon Central Military Wagon Road; Pioneer Roads.

Oregon Chautauqua. An annual selection of lectures, exhibits, and films available to community groups from the Oregon Council for the **Humanities**. 812 SW Washington St., Suite 225, Portland 97205. 503-241-0543; 800-735-0543.

Oregon Children's Theatre Company. See **Children's theater**.

Oregon Citizens' Alliance (OCA). A politically-conservative organization that has promoted anti-gay-rights and anti-abortion initiatives as well as other conservative Christian positions. At its peak it had 3,400 members and 17,000 donors. It was organized in 1986 by Lon Mabon and others. Governing Oregon; Oregonian 3/10/96:A1.

Oregon City. A historic city, Oregon's first, located at **Willamette Falls**, 14 miles south of downtown **Portland** on **Highway 99E**. It was founded and named by Dr. John McLoughlin of the **Hudson's Bay Company** in 1842, and incorporated in 1844, the first incorporated U.S. city west of the Rocky Mountains. It has been the county seat of **Clackamas County** since 1843, and was the **capital** for the Oregon **Provisional** and **Territorial** governments from 1843 to 1852. The **End of the Oregon Trail Interpretive Center** commemorates its historic importance as the terminus of the **Oregon Trail**. Other attractions include **McLoughlin House**, Clackamas County History Museum, Stevens-Crawford Museum, and a cliff-side municipal elevator that carries pedestrians 90 feet between the lower and upper levels of the town. **Clackamas Community College** is located just south of the city. Tateshina, Japan, is its sister city. Population 1980 14,673; 1995 18,980. Elevation 55'. 320 Warner Milne Road, PO Box 351, 97045. 503-657-0891. Chamber of Commerce 503-656-1619. Oregon Geographic Names. See also **San Francisco**.

Oregon Climate Trust. A nonprofic organization approved by the legislature to support tree planting projects and other efforts to offset **carbon dioxide** emissions. **Electric power plants** can donate money to the trust as a way of meeting state goals for reduced emissions. Oregonian 4/10/98:D4.

Oregon Coast Aquarium. A non-profit institution on the south shore of **Yaquina Bay**, adjacent to the **Mark O. Hatfield Marine Science Center**. It has an exhibit area, four galleries replicating coastal habitats, a theater, cafe, gift shop, and outdoor exhibits that include a 2-million gallon pool for **Keiko**, the **orca** whale of Free Willy fame, plus sea otters, sea lions, harbor seals, a giant octopus, and a walk-through seabird aviary. It is open every day but Christmas. 2820 SE Ferry Slip Road, Newport 97365. 541-867-3474. Oregon Blue Book.

Oregon Coast Community College Service District. A public two-year college that has offered classes to **Lincoln County** residents since 1987. Students can take fully accredited college transfer, vocational, professional, and community education classes at centers in **Newport** and **Lincoln City**. Enrollment in fall 1996 was 763. 332 SW Coast Highway, Newport OR 97365-4928. 541-265-2283. Oregon Blue Book. See also **Community colleges; Small Business Development Centers**.

Oregon Coast Music Festival. A two-week festival held in **Coos Bay, North Bend, Reedsport**, and **Bandon** in mid-July. Events include classical, folk, and jazz music. 800-676-7563, 541-269-2720.

Oregon Coast Trail. A 362-mile trail-in-progress along the coast from the **Columbia River** south to the California border. It was first proposed by **University of Oregon** geography professor Sam Dicken in 1959. About 200 miles of the route are on sand **beaches** and portions are along roads and **Highway 101**. A guide is available from the State **Parks and Recreation Department**.

Oregon College of Education. See **Western Oregon University**.

Oregon Commonwealth Federation. A short-lived populist political organization, incorporated in 1937 with Monroe Sweetland as executive secretary. It advocated a public housing authority to cope with slum owners, low-cost public power, and briefly leaned towards establishing a third (Farmer-Labor) political party. However, the group lacked both labor and agriculture support, and by the 1938 elections it was heavily involved in the **Democratic Party**. "Toward a Farmer-Labor party in Oregon, 1933-38."

Oregon Community Foundation. A statewide nonprofit organization, founded in 1973, that administers permanent charitable funds established through gifts and bequests from individuals, businesses, and organizations. During 1996 it awarded $14.5 million in grants and scholarships from over 300 endowment funds having a total value of $148 million. In 1997 the value had grown to $190 million. 621 SW Morrison Street, Suite 725, Portland 97205. 503-227-6846. See also **Foundations**.

Oregon Conservative Convention. A one-day gathering held in May 1997 as an alternative to the **Dorchester Conference**. Its purpose was to energize the fiscal and social conservatives of the state. Pat Turnidge, the organizer, hoped that it would become an annual event. Oregonian 5/25/97:C2.

Oregon Convention Center. A center in **Portland** on the east bank of the **Willamette River** notable for its twin glass towers. The 500,000-square-foot building, designed by Zimmer Gunsul Frasca Partnership and completed in 1990, contains a half million dollars worth of public art, including a Foucault pendulum in the north tower. The building is open to the public except when scheduled events limit access. It is owned and operated by **Metro** with some support from the **Multnomah County** hotel/motel tax. The **Rose Quarter** lies just to the north. 777 NE Martin Luther King Jr Bv. 503-235-7575. Portland Guidebook.

Oregon Council for the Humanities. See **Humanities**, Oregon Council.

Oregon Country. The name given in the early 1800s to a large, poorly known, and vaguely defined area that was variously claimed by Spain, Russia, Great Britain, and the U.S. It included the vast region between the Pacific Ocean and the Continental Divide, from Russian Alaska south to Spanish California. In 1819 Spain surrendered all claims north of the 42nd parallel (the present Oregon/California border), and in 1824 Russia relinquished its claims south of what is now Alaska ($54°40"$). In 1818 Great Britain and the U.S. signed a ten-year Treaty of **Joint Occupancy** that was renewed indefinitely in 1827. Later, both countries agreed to the **Oregon Treaty of 1846**, which awarded the area south of the 49th parallel (the present U.S./Canadian boundary) to the U.S. Two years later the U.S. designated its portion as the **Oregon Territory**. Dictionary of Oregon History. See also **Boundary question**; **Champoeg**; **Fifty-four Forty or Fight**; **Hudson's Bay Company**; **Oregon Question**; **Provisional government**.

Oregon Country Fair. A '60s era festival held the second weekend of July near **Veneta** west of **Eugene**. It began as a Renaissance-type craft fair in 1969 and has become the Northwest's largest celebration of alternative lifestyles, offering free entertainment along with the food and crafts booths. The fair owns its wooded location on the Long Tom River. 541-343-6554.

Oregon Cultural Heritage Commission. A non-profit organization dedicated to honoring Oregon writers and artists of the past. PO Box 3588, Portland 97208. 503-292-6439.

Oregon department and agency entries. See substantive word. For example, Oregon Department of Transportation is listed as **Transportation, Oregon Department of,** *and Oregon State Police is listed as* **Police, Oregon State.**

Oregon Donor Program. A non-profit organization that promotes awareness of the value and need for anatomical donation. In 1997 fifty Oregonians were waiting at any one time for corneas and 700 were waiting for internal organs. In 1996 there were 70 organ donors. A million Oregonians have a donor code on their driver's licenses but their families must still sign consent forms at their time of death. There is no added cost. Though there is no age limit for eye and whole body donations, 75 is the age limit for bone and skin donations and 70 for internal organ donations. PO Box 532, Portland 97207. 503-494-7888, 800-452-1369.

Oregon Dunes National Recreation Area. A 31,566 acre area that extends from the mouth of the **Siuslaw River** near **Florence** south 38 miles, almost to the **Coos River** near **North Bend.** It includes 14,000 acres of sand **dunes,** some of them 180' high, 38 miles of beaches, hiking trails, picnic areas, 14 campgrounds, boat ramps, equestrian areas, and dune buggy areas. The **Siuslaw National Forest** administers the area. 855 Highway Avenue, Reedsport 97467. 541-271-3611.

Oregon Education Association. The second-largest **labor organization** in the state with a 1997 membership of 40,000. It was formed in 1858 "to diffuse a sound, healthful and thorough education among the mass of people." 6900 SW Haines Road, Tigard 97223. 503-684-3300.

Oregon Education Endowment. A fund, authorized as a constitutional amendment by voters in 1995, with the money to come from 15% of Oregon **Lottery** profits (perhaps $3 million a month) beginning in July 1997. The measure requires that earnings on the fund be used for education. Oregonian 6/3/97:C4.

Oregon Electric Railway. An **electric railway** company that operated a 122-mile passenger line down the east side of the **Willamette River** between **Portland** and **Eugene** from 1912 until 1933. The first 50 miles to **Salem** opened in 1908, and a side line to **Forest Grove** opened the same year. The "owl" trains, which ran at night, would drop sleeper cars at Salem, Albany, and Eugene so that businessmen heading for those destinations could sleep until morning before setting forth on their day's work. Stations West. See also **Red Electrics.**

Oregon Electric Railway Society. See **Antique Powerland Museum.**

Oregon Emigrating Company. See **Great Migration.**

Oregon Environmental Council. A statewide coalition of some 2,000 individuals and organizations. It was formed to increase understanding of the human impact on the environment and to encourage stewardship of natural resources. Earthwatch Oregon is its quarterly newsletter. 520 SW 6th, Suite 940, Portland 97204-1535. 503-222-1963.

Oregon Experiment. A project at the **University of Oregon** in the 1970s that implemented the theory that users rather than architects should have major, ongoing responsibility for campus design. Oregon Experiment.

Oregon Field Ornithologists. Oregon's principal statewide birding organization. It publishes a quarterly, Oregon Birds. PO Box 10373, Eugene 97440.

Oregon Food Bank. A nonprofit organization that provides 20 million pounds of food a year through emergency food boxes, each containing a three-to-five-day supply of groceries, to over 400,000 Oregonians annually through a network of 20 regional agencies in Oregon and southwest Washington, and 650 local hunger-relief agencies. 65% of the food they distribute comes from food industry donations, 12% from the U.S. Department of Agriculture, 15% from community food and fund drives, and 8% is purchased with state and other funds. 2540 NE Riverside Way, Portland 97211. 503-282-0555. Oregonian 10/14/97:E5, 12/17/97:D15. See also **Food stamps**; **Hunger**.

Oregon Forest Resources Institute (OFRI). An agency created by the 1991 legislature to improve public understanding of forest practices and products, and to encourage sound **forest management**. Oregon's timber producers pay a dedicated timber harvest tax to fund OFRI and its programs. 1440 SW Third Avenue, Suite 305, Portland 97201. 503-229-6718. See also **Forest education**; **Forest Talk Radio**.

Oregon Garden. See **Oregon Botanical Garden**.

Oregon Geographic Names Board. A board that supervises the naming of all geographic features within the state. It is an affiliate of the U.S. Board on Geographic Names and is associated with the **Oregon Historical Society**, which maintains its records. Lewis A. McArthur, who served on its board for 35 years, compiled Oregon Geographic Names, and his son, Lewis L. McArthur, has continued the work. The book, now in its sixth edition, is published by the Oregon Historical Society. 1200 SW Park Ave., Portland 97205. 503-306-5200. Oregon Blue Book. See also **Geographic Information Council.**

Oregon Graduate Institute. An accredited private educational institution in **Beaverton** that enrolled 530 graduate students in 1995. 19600 NW Von Neumann Dr., Beaverton 97006. 503-690-1121. Oregon Blue Book.

Oregon grape. An evergreen shrub, *Berberis* (formerly *Mahonia*) *aquifolium*, that is the **state flower**. The main stems grows several feet high with five to seven shiny, holly-like leaflets along the leaf stems. Clusters of small yellow flowers in the spring are followed by edible purple-black berries in the late summer. The berries are sometimes used for preserves, and a yellow dye can be made from the roots. Oregon grape is found wild in the western part of the state, and is widely planted as an ornamental. Five other species of *Berberis* occur in Oregon, including long-leaved Oregon grape, *B. nervosa*, a similar but less prickly plant with 15 to 19 dull leaflets along each stem. Plants and Animals; Manual of the Higher Plants.

Oregon Health Plan. A plan created by a series of 1989-1993 laws to provide health care to more low-income Oregonians than federal Medicaid rules would allow by reducing the number of medical procedures that are offered but offering them to more people. A comprehensive list of medical services and treatments has been compiled in priority order, based on criteria such as the potential to save a life or to improve quality of life. A cutoff point is then determined, with the government paying only for those procedures above the cutoff. Opponents say that the plan rations health care; proponents say that it makes basic health care available to more by eliminating nonessential procedures for the few. About 121,000 joined the plan in 1994, its first year. It is funded jointly by state and federal funds. Oregon Prison Industries handles some of provider inquiries. See also **Budget growth**; **Health Plan Administrator**; **Medical Assistance Programs**;

Oregon Health Sciences University. A university that was part of the Oregon **University System** until the legislature launched it as an independent public corporation on July 1, 1995. It is housed in 27 major buildings on top of **Portland**'s Marquam Hill (**Pill Hill**), and includes schools of dentistry, medicine, and nursing, plus University Hospital and Doernbecher Children's Hospital, dozens of primary care and specialty clinics, three research institutes, and several outreach and public service units. Enrollment in the fall of 1994 was 1,396. In 1997 it had over 8,300 employees, making it one of the state's largest employers. 10% of its budget came from state appropriations, with the rest from tuition, fees, gifts, grants, and contracts. 3181 SW Sam Jackson Park Road, Portland OR 97201. 503-494-8311. Oregon Blue Book. See also **Mark O. Hatfield Research Center.**

Oregon Historical Society. A membership organization in **Portland** that had its beginnings in 1873 as the **Oregon Pioneer Association**. It collects, preserves, exhibits, and publishes the history of Oregon, operates the **Oregon History Center**, provides an interpretive program at the restored 1856 **Bybee Howell House** on **Sauvie Island**, hosts programs for children and adults, maintains the records of the **Oregon Geographic Names Board**, and publishes monthly and quarterly publications and books about the history of Oregon and the Pacific Northwest. About 9% of its $5 million budget comes from the state of Oregon, and the rest comes from gifts, grants, memberships, endowments, and other sources. 1200 SW Park Ave., Portland 97205. 503-306-5200. Oregon Blue Book; Round the Roses.

Oregon History Center. A center in **Portland**, operated by the **Oregon Historical Society**, which has both permanent and changing exhibits, a museum store, and a research library. The five-story building, built with thousands of private contributions in 1964, was designed by Wolff and Zimmer with Pietro Belluschi as design consultant. The Society also owns the rest of the block, including the Sovereign Hotel with immense trompe l'oeil **murals**, painted by Richard Haas in 1989, depicting scenes from Oregon's history. 1200 SW Park Avenue. 503-222-1741. Frozen Music; Portland, An Informal History.

Oregon Holocaust Memorial. A proposed memorial to the 6,000,000 Jews killed by the Germans during World War II. It is to be located in **Washington Park** just off SW Wright Ave. Oregonian 12/22/96:E2.

Oregon in the world. Oregon lies half way between the equator and the north pole. It is most distant from (opposite) an area of the Crozet Basin of the Indian Ocean, between Crozet and Kerguelen Islands southeast of Madagascar. See also **45th parallel**; **Latitude and longitude.**

Oregon Institute. A school organized in 1842 by **Methodists** with the first sessions held at **Wallace House** north of **Salem**. The school moved to Salem in 1844 and affiliated with **Willamette University** in1853. It was the first school for white children in Oregon. Dictionary of Oregon History. See also **School history**.

Oregon Institute of Marine Biology. A coastal educational and research facility operated by the **University of Oregon** at **Charleston** on **Coos Bay**. Facilities include teaching and research laboratories, boathouse, dock, boats, holding tanks, and housing. PO Box 5389, Charleston 97420. 541-888-2581.

Oregon Institute of Technology. A state college established in 1947 that serves students from its main campus in **Klamath Falls** and its Portland Metro Campus in **Milwaukie**. In the fall of 1994, 2,444 students enrolled. While associate degrees and academic transfer programs are available, most students earn bachelor's degrees. OIT emphasizes hands-on experience for its students and seeks faculty members with "real-world" experience. The Klamath Falls campus is unique in being totally heated and cooled by geothermal energy; its Geo-Heat Center attracts scientists and engineers from around the world. 3201 Campus Dr., Klamath Falls OR 97601-8801. 541-885-1000. Oregon Blue Book.

Oregon Law Foundation. See **Bar**, Oregon State.

Oregon Literature Series. An award-winning, six-volume series sponsored by the Oregon Council of Teachers of English and published by Oregon State University Press between 1988 and 1994. George Venn of **Eastern Oregon State College** was general editor. The volumes are The World Begins Here: An Anthology of Oregon Short Fiction; Many Faces: An Anthology of Oregon Autobiography; Varieties of Hope: An Anthology of Oregon Prose (includes a listing of over 200 articles and books by Oregonians or about various aspects of Oregon); From Here We Speak: An Anthology of Oregon Poetry; The Stories We Tell: An Anthology of Oregon Folk Literature; and Talking on Paper: An Anthology of Oregon Letters and Diaries. Each is listed in the bibliography at the end of this book.

Oregon Maneuvers. War games for 100,000 troops held in the **High Desert** in 1943 to train soldiers during **World War II**. Major General Alexander Patch commanded troops from the 91st, 96th, and 104th Infantry Divisions. East of the Cascades. See also **Camp Abbot**.

Oregon Manual. A 47-page booklet published in 1851 by the **General Land Office**. It's official title was "Instructions to the Surveyor General of Oregon; Being a Manual for Field Operations." The full text, published in History of the Rectangular Survey System, pages 433-447, remains of interest to those dealing with land surveys and property ownership. See also **Public Land Survey**.

Oregon Maritime Center and Museum. A museum on **Portland**'s waterfront operated entirely by volunteers. Admission includes a tour of the stern-wheeler *Steamer Portland*, moored next to the museum. 113 SW Front Avenue. 503-224-7724. Portland Guidebook.

Oregon Memorial Association. A non-profit association organized in 1961. It is dedicated to sensible, low-cost mortuary, memorial, and funeral services through participating mortuaries in western Oregon. It also provides education and advocacy. PO Box 649, Madras 97741. Toll-free 888-475-5520.

Oregon Military Museum. See **Camp Withycombe**.

Oregon Museum of Science and Industry. See **OMSI**.

Oregon-myrtle. A broadleaved evergreen **tree**, *Umbellularia californica*, also known as California laurel. It grows only in California and southwestern Oregon - and not in the Holy Land, despite claims to the contrary. Myrtle trees growing in the open have a tidy, rounded appearance. The largest known, 501 inches in circumference (13.3 feet in diameter), grows about 10 miles northeast of **Gold Beach** on Jerry's Flat Road. Myrtle's aromatic leaves are sold by some spice companies as bay leaves, and its hard, colorfully grained wood is made into fine bowls, novelties, gun stocks, and paneling. Squirrels eat the nuts. Trees to Know.

Oregon Natural Heritage Program. See **Natural Heritage Program**.

Oregon Natural Resources Council (ONRC). A controversial environmental organization, founded in 1972, and now with 50 group members and 6,000 individual members. It has been active in halting the construction of Elk Creek Dam in the Rogue River drainage, in halting a number of federal timber sales, and in efforts to protect endangered plant and animal species. It has an annual budget of $700,000. 522 SW 5th, Portland 97204. 503-223-9001.

Oregon Option. A collection of innovative Oregon welfare reform and health service programs that the federal government in December 1994 authorized the state to administer if the state could provide accountability. The state does that through the Oregon **Benchmarks** program which was already in place. The agreement reduces bureaucratic requirements for Oregon applications for federal grants. The federal government also agreed to pay Oregon a dividend if its welfare caseload declined, so after the load dropped from a 1994 high of 43,617 families to 34,889 two years later, the state received an $8 million reward. Oregonian 5/26/96:F3. See also **Adult and Family Services**; **JOBS**; **Oregon Health Plan**; **Welfare**.

Oregon Pacific Railroad. A proposed **transcontinental connection** by rail, promoted by T. Edgenton Hogg in 1878, to link **Newport** (planned for development as a major deep water port) with Salt Lake City via **Santiam Pass**. It was also called the Yaquina Railroad and later the Corvallis and Eastern Railroad. By 1885 two trains a day ran between **Albany**, which was dry, and Newport where alcohol was available; the returning hangovers were called "train sickness". The line east reached **Idanha** before the company went bankrupt in 1890. In 1907 ownership passed to **Southern Pacific**, which used it as a branch line; it is now owned by **Willamette & Pacific Railroad**. Dictionary of Oregon History; Oregonian 10/25/95:C2. See also **Hogg Rock**.

Oregon PeaceWorks. Oregon's largest peace, justice, and environmental organization. It publishes a monthly newspaper, The Oregon PeaceWorker. 333 State Street, Salem 97301. 503-585-2767.

Oregon Photojournalism Day. A day, July 15, 1983, on which over 90 of Oregon's professional photographers participated in Project Dayshoot to chronicle an average day in Oregon for an exhibition at the **Oregon History Center**. Three hundred of the two thousand submitted photographs were published in One Average Day.

Oregon Pioneer Association. An organization of those who arrived in Oregon prior to 1855 (extended in 1894 to those who arrived before Oregon became a state in 1859). The group held annual meetings from 1873 until 1951 and published annual Transactions which included accounts of the meetings as well as pioneers' writings and diaries. The group was succeeded by Sons and Daughters of Oregon Pioneers and by the **Oregon Historical Society**. Dictionary of Oregon History; This Side of Oregon. See also **Pioneers**.

Oregon Plan. A plan proposed in 1997 by Governor John Kitzhaber to prevent the federal government from listing **coho** salmon runs from **Cape Blanco** north as **endangered**. The timber industry promised $13.6 million of the $30 million needed to restore and protect the fish runs. Both the state legislature and the federal government agreed to the plan. Oregonian 4/25/97:A1.

Oregon Poison Center. See **Poison Control Center**.

Oregon Pony. The first **locomotive** in Oregon, a wood-burning steam engine brought in by ship in 1862 to pull rail cars on a five-mile portage railroad around the **Cascades of the Columbia River**. The portage railroad was owned by the Oregon Steam Navigation Company (later the **Oregon Railway and Navigation Company**). The Oregon Pony is now in a park at **Cascade Locks**. Treasures of the Oregon Country.

Oregon Portage Railroad. The first railroad in Oregon, built in 1859 to provide a portage route around the **Cascades of the Columbia River**. Mules pulled the cars over the five-mile length of wooden tracks. It soon became part of the **Oregon Steam Navigation Company** which replaced the mules with the **Oregon Pony** engine.

Oregon Prekindergarten Program (OPP). A state education program that works with the federal Head Start program to provide services to low-income three- and four-year-old children and their families. The programs aim to improve the child's academic and life success and reduce long-term social costs. In 1995-96 the two programs served 6,405 children (Head Start 4,630 and OPP 1,775), or 29% of the 22,157 eligible children. Oregon Report Card.

Oregon Public Broadcasting. A non-commercial television and radio network providing educational and entertainment broadcasting to northern Oregon and southwest Washington. It operates several stations, including KOPB-TV and KOPB-FM in **Portland**, and KOAC-AM in **Corvallis**. Sixty percent of its $12 million budget comes from donations, 20% comes from the state, and 11% from federal support. The system is one of the nation's oldest and strongest public broadcasting networks, leading in per capita viewing audience and in per capita college credit enrollments. The first station, KOAC, was founded in 1922. 7140 SW Macadam Avenue, Portland 97209-3013. 503-293-1904. See also **Public broadcasting**.

Oregon Question. The name given in the 1840s to the issue of the nationality of the government of the **Oregon Country**. The early American residents had no formal government at all until a **provisional government** was adopted in 1843. Some locals hoped for British rule, some urged American, and some, who prevailed for at least the year of 1844, urged that Oregon be an independent country. American interests came to predominate, as indicated by a petition to the Congress in 1840, at a **Champoeg** decision in 1843, and especially after the **Oregon Treaty of 1846.** After the **Whitman massacre** in 1847 another petition led to Congressional creation of the **Oregon Territory** in 1848. Empire of the Columbia. See also **Boundary question; Independence party**.

Oregon Railway and Navigation Company. A company formed in 1879 by Henry Villard in order to further his vision of a transcontinental railroad line terminating in **Portland**. As first step, his company bought the Oregon Steam Navigation Company, the Oregon Steamship Company, and the Walla Walla and Columbia Railroad. In 1881 he also acquired control of the **Northern Pacific** Railroad. Rail lines were built and, on September 8, 1883, the connection was completed west of Helena, Montana, but at such cost that both Villard and the company were bankrupt. The company directors reorganized and built a second **transcontinental connection** through **Pendleton** to connect with the **Oregon Short Line** at **Huntington**. A branch line, completed in 1908, served the Wallowa Valley from **La Grande**. **Union Pacific** acquired the lines in 1889. Dictionary of Oregon History; To the Columbia Gateway.

Oregon Rangers. A mounted rifle company organized in 1844 in response to the **Cockstock affair**, but it was never called into action. It was Oregon's first military organization. Dictionary of Oregon History.

Oregon Regional Primate Research Center. A research facility, affiliated with **Oregon Health Sciences University**, located on a 250-acre campus west of **Portland**. Its 24 senior scientists and their associates focus on research in reproductive science, neuro-science, immunology, and pathobiology, using over 2,000 monkeys, primarily rhesus macaques. Federal funds support 80% of its $11 million budget. In 1997 the Center's success in producing a pair of genetically similar rhesus monkeys brought it international publicity from those comparing the feat to the recent cloning of sheep in Scotland. 505 NW 185th Avenue, Beaverton 97006. 503-645-1141. Oregonian 3/5/97:E1.

Oregon Revised Statutes. The codified **laws** of the state of Oregon as adopted by the **legislature** or by the voters of the state using the **initiative** or **referendum**. The multi-volume set, arranged by subject, is republished every two years to incorporate the most recent legislative session statutes. See also **Oregon Administrative Rules**.

Oregon Rural Development Council. A group that coordinates funding agencies dealing with rural populations and sets action priorities. It also makes community presentations to identify and help resolve barriers affecting rural community vitality. It includes the Oregon State Community Economic Revitalization Team and other governmental units. Basic funding is from the U.S. Department of Agriculture. PO Box 40204, Portland 97201. 503-326-5833.

Oregon School of Arts and Crafts. A non-profit school offering a three-year certificate program in crafts, and a four-year bachelor of fine arts in crafts. The school, established in 1906, is housed on a campus built in 1979. The campus features a variety of events, exhibits, contemporary crafts sales, and the Hands-On Cafe. It is accredited by the National Association of Schools of Art and Design. 8245 SW Barnes Road, Portland 97225. 503-297-5544.

Oregon Shakespeare Festival. An Equity repertory theater company in **Ashland** that produces 11 plays a year from February through October. The plays range from Shakespeare to newly-commissioned works. In the years since Angus Bowmer produced the first play in 1935, it has grown to be one of the largest non-profit theaters in the country, and annually attracts over 350,000 theater-goers, 88% of them from beyond the Rogue Valley. The festival has three theaters, the outdoor 1,200-seat Elizabethan theater (1935), the 500-seat indoor Bowmer Theater (1970), and the intimate 150-seat Black Swan (1977). PO Box 158, Ashland 97520. 541-482-4331. As I Remember Adam.

Oregon Shines. A strategic plan, first formulated by 16 committees in 1988, that is designed to guide Oregon's economic development for 20 years. The plan, as revised in 1996, sets the goals of achieving quality jobs for all Oregonians, safe, caring, and engaged communities, and healthy, sustainable surroundings. **Bench-marks** proposed by the plan were authorized by the 1991 legislature. The **Progress Board** monitors progress. Oregon Blue Book; Oregon Shines; Oregon Shines II.

Oregon Shores Conservation Coalition. An organization that works to preserve public access and limit development along the coast. **CoastWatch** serves as their monitoring group. PO Box 1344, Depoe Bay, 97341. 541-765-2234.

Oregon Short Line Railway. A line built by a subsidiary of the **Union Pacific** between Granger, Wyoming, and **Huntington**, where it connected with the **Oregon Railway and Navigation Company** line on November 11, 1884, to pro-vide a second, and shorter, **transcontinental connection** between **Portland** and the East. Dictionary of Oregon History.

Oregon Sports Hall of Fame. A membership organization that exhibits a collection of trophies, uniforms, memorabilia, and biographies of those who have been inducted since it began in 1980. The annual inductees are selected by the membership. Standard Insurance Center, 900 SW 5th Avenue, Suite C-80, Port-land 97204. 503-227-7466.

Oregon Star Party. A Labor Day weekend camp out, held since 1988 in some dark place for stargazing, swap meet, nature hikes, and other activities. The 1997 camp out was on the **Ochoco National Forest**. 360-892-0473; ospinc@teleport.com. Oregonian 7/2/97:D11.

Oregon State Hospital. A psychiatric hospital that provides separate treat-ment programs for children and adolescents, adults, the elderly, and criminals. It is operated by the **Mental Health and Developmental Disability Services Divi-sion**. The hospital opened in 1883 with 370 patients transferred from the Hawthorne Asylum in Portland. 2600 Center St. NE, Salem 97310. 503-945-2870. Oregon Blue Book.

Oregon State Library. A library on the Capitol Mall in **Salem** that is the information resource for state government and the center for library development in Oregon. It also provides braille, talking books, and other library materials to 38,000 Oregonians with visual or other disabilities, and provides specialized infor-mation and electronic information to all library users. A seven-member board of trustees provides guidance. 250 Winter St. NE, Salem 97310-0640. 503-378-4243. Oregon Blue Book.

Oregon State Police. See **Police, Oregon State**.

Oregon State Secular Union. A statewide organization, 1889-1901, formed by members of secular organizations from **Coos Bay**, **McMinnville**, **New Era**, **Portland**, and **Silverton**. The members held strong and varied opinions, but were united in the support of separation of church and state. Despite meager funds and dissension within the group, it decided to found **Liberal University** in Silverton. The Torch of Reason, a weekly newspaper published by the college, served as the group's major publication. "Organized Free Thought in Oregon." See also **Secu-lar churches**.

Oregon State University. Oregon's oldest state university, located in **Corvallis**. It offers 80 baccalaureate, 77 master's and 56 doctoral programs, and is the only Oregon university with colleges of agriculture, home economics, forestry, veterinary medicine, oceanography, and pharmacy. 14,131 students enrolled in fall 1994. It began as a community school in 1852, was later **Corvallis College**, became Oregon Agricultural College in 1869 as the state's designated land grant college, and became a state institution in 1886. The name was later changed to Oregon State College and then Oregon State University. During the **depression**, intense rivalries with the **University of Oregon**, located 40 miles away, led the state to sharply define the functions of the two schools and to eliminate duplicate programs; the delineations have since become blurred. Corvallis 97331. 541-737-0123. Dictionary of Oregon History; Oregon Blue Book. See also **Agricultural Experiment Station**; **Extension Service**; **Land grants, educational**; **University System, Oregon**.

Oregon Statesman. See **Statesman Journal**.

Oregon Steam Navigation Company. A highly profitable monopoly that for 20 years controlled steamship traffic on the **Columbia River** - including portage railroad traffic around the **Cascades** (5 miles) and **The Dalles of the Columbia River** (14 miles) - and on the **Snake River**. Its **Portland** dock was at the end of Ash Street, making it one of the city's busiest streets. The company, which formed in 1860 when several companies banded together, was sold in 1879 to the **Oregon Railway & Navigation Company**. Empire of the Columbia. See also **Columbia River transportation**; **Oregon Portage Railroad**.

Oregon Story. The name given to the accomplishments of Governor McCall's administration (1967-1975) and to Oregonians' assumption that government can work for the well-being of its environment and its citizens without being hobbled by politics. The model was especially appealing at that time, contrasting as it did with the Nixon Watergate hearings. Fire at Eden's Gate.

Oregon Style. The name given to the lusty and unrestrained editorial style of Oregon's early newspapers as they hurled invective at each other during the 1850s and 1860s. The **Oregonian** (**Portland**), Oregon Argus (**Oregon City**), and **Statesman** (**Salem**) were especially noteworthy. The Statesman, in one instance, described the Oregonian as a paper devoted to "...the grossest personal abuse, the most foul-mouthed slander, grovelling scurrility, falsehood and ribald blackguardism..." and then chided the Oregonian editor for ill temper and over sensitiveness. History of Oregon Newspapers; Varieties of Hope. See also **Salem Clique**.

Oregon Symphony. An orchestra in **Portland** that performs in the **Arlene Schnitzer Concert Hall**, tours, and records. Founded in 1895 as the Portland Symphony, it is the oldest orchestra west of the Mississippi, and seventh oldest in the country. James DePriest has been Music Director and Conductor since 1980. In 1993/94 the association, with a budget of $8.9 million, sponsored over 120 concerts and recitals that over 300,000 persons attended. A 15-day strike by musicians in September 1996 resulted in cancellation of several events. 711 SW Alder, Portland 97205. 503-228-1353, 800-228-7343. Business Journal 8/25/95:10; Oregon Blue Book; Oregonian 9/3/95:E1, 9/25/96:A1.

Oregon System. The name given to a series of legislative reform measures adopted between 1902 and 1908, including the **initiative** and **referendum** (1902), direct **primary** (1904), and **recall** (1908). The reforms were the **Populists'** response to the **corruption** of the 1880s and 1890s. Impetus was provided by the **People's Power League** and William U'Ren, inspired by J. S. Sullivan's book, Direct Legislation by Citizenship, through Initiative and Referendum. Empire of the Columbia.

Oregon Territory, 1849-1859. On August 14, 1848 the U.S. Congress authorized a **territorial government** for Oregon, though it was not until the newly appointed governor, General Joseph Lane (1801-1881), arrived in **Oregon City** on March 2, 1849, that it went into effect, superseding the independent **provisional government**. Territorial status became possible after the resolution of the U.S./ Great Britain **boundary question** through the **Oregon Treaty of 1846**, and was spurred when Oregonians, alarmed by the **Whitman Massacre**, petitioned Congress to become part of the U.S. The Oregon Territory included the lands west of the crest of the Rocky Mountains, and between latitudes 49°N (now the U.S./Canada border) and latitude 42°N (now the Oregon/California border). It included what is now **Oregon, Washington, Idaho**, and western **Montana**. The area north of the **Columbia River** and the 46th parallel was separated out in 1853 as the Washington territory. As a U.S. territory, the area had the benefit of U.S. military protection from Indians, assurance of land titles, and federal investment in such things as military roads, postal service, government buildings, and navigation aids and improvements. However, all territorial officials were appointed by the President, and residents of the territory had no vote or influence except for one non-voting delegate to Congress. Oregon's territorial status lasted until **statehood** was granted on February 14, 1859. Atlas of the Pacific Northwest; Empire of the Columbia. See also **Donation Land Act of 1850**; **Indian wars**; **Land grants, educational**; **Military wagon roads**; **Oregon Country**.

Oregon-Tillamook Railroad. A 91-mile rail line, built in 1911 by the **Pacific Railway and Navigation Company**, and now owned by the Port of Tillamook, that crosses the rugged **Coast Range** between **Tillamook** and the **Willamette Valley**. Part of the route along the Salmonberry River washed out in 1996, creating environmental concerns. Freight trains haul lumber, feed, and rock over the route, and **excursion trains** operate at both ends. The state gave the railroad to the Port and established an authority, made up of three state officials and two port commissioners, to oversee its operations. Oregonian 8/10/96:B1.

Oregon Tilth, Inc. A membership organization founded in 1974 that supports **organic farming** and gardening. Oregon Tilth sponsors an organic certification office (PO Box 218, Tualatin OR 97062. 503-692-4877), a research and education center in Philomath, a directory of organic farmers and retail outlets, and a newspaper, In Good Tilth. In 1997 it certified some 3,000 organic farms abroad. 31615 Fern Road, Philomath OR 97370. 541-929-6743. Oregonian 9/4/97:C1.

Oregon Trail. A 2,000-mile crude **wagon road** used by pioneer immigrants as they traveled from the Missouri River to Oregon. The general route was used by fur traders as early as 1812, but not until 1841 did a wheeled vehicle travel west of Fort Hall, Idaho. Small groups in 1841 and 1842 were followed by the 1843 **Great Migration**, a **wagon train** of nearly 900 people. was the first of many to cross to Oregon on the Trail. The California Road branched off in Idaho; Oregonians claimed that a sign marked the road to Oregon and a glittery rock marked the trail to California, so that those who could read came to Oregon and those after glitter went south. Of the 300,000 who came west on the trail between 1840 and 1860, about 53,000 came to Oregon, 10,000 of them in the peak year of 1852. The rest went to California, Nevada, and Utah. Some 20,000 emigrants died along the way, primarily from cholera. Wagons continued to use the route into the 20th century, long after the **transcontinental** railroad to Oregon was completed in 1883. Emigrants could not begin their six-month trek until May when grass along the route had grown enough to feed their livestock; they arrived in Oregon five or six months later facing a winter without land, home, or crops. The Oregon Trail was somewhat easier for the first users because they had more grass and game, the **Indians** were not yet hostile, and cholera had not yet appeared. Later travelers also had to go farther, once in Oregon, to find available land. The general route (with many variations) followed up the Platte River, across the continental divide at South Pass, down the Snake River to Fort Boise, and north through the **Blue Mountains** of NE Oregon. At **The Dalles** the emigrants either made their way down the **Columbia River** (boating their wagons down to the difficult portage around the **Cascades**, and boating again to **Fort Vancouver**, while their cattle were driven overland on the north side), or, after 1845, had the alternative of avoiding this hazardous enterprise by taking the grueling new **Barlow Road** (toll) south around **Mount Hood.** Some wagon trains attempted other routes, including Meek's Cutoff followed by the **Lost Wagon Train**, the **Free Emigrant Trail** (Elliott Cutoff), and the **Applegate Trail** (South Road). In 1906 Ezra Meeker, who had crossed the Oregon Trail with an oxcart in 1852, returned by oxcart, erecting trail markers as he went. He crossed it again by oxcart in 1910, by car in 1916, and by plane in 1924 at the age of 94. Ruts of the Oregon Trail can still be seen near the **Oregon Trail Interpretive Center** (**Baker City**), at **Keeney Pass**, and five miles west of **Echo** at Echo Meadows BLM site. Since its designation in 1978 as the National Historic Oregon Trail, the route has been marked on federal lands by concrete pillars. The **Oregon Railway and Navigation Co**. rail line was built along part of the route, and the New Oregon Trail, a graveled highway from **Portland** to the east coast, was completed in 1923. **Interstate 84** now follows much of the route in Oregon. Interpretive centers, in addition to the one at **Baker City**, include **End of the Oregon Trail Interpretive Center** in **Oregon City** and **Tamustalik Cultural Institute** near **Pendleton**. Dictionary of Oregon History; Empire of the Columbia; Oregon Trail; Plains Across.

Oregon Trail Advisory Council. A council appointed by the governor to promote, develop, and protect the historic **Oregon Trail**. It formed the Oregon Trail Coordinating Council which coordinates the development of Oregon's historic trails as a tourism resource. The state **Parks and Recreation Department** provides support. 1115 Commercial St. NE, Salem 97310. 503-399-9243. Oregon Blue Book.

Oregon Trail Interpretive Center. A museum and living-history center on Flagstaff Hill five miles east of **Baker City**. The displays, demonstrations, stage productions, trails, and outdoor programs depict development of the **Oregon Trail** and the life of those traveling westward on it. The ruts of a 13-mile segment of the trail can be seen from the museum. The **Bureau of Land Management** built and operates the museum, officially called the National Historic Oregon Trail Interpretive Center. PO Box 987, Baker City 97814. 541-523-1843. See also **End of the Oregon Trail Interpretive Center**.

Oregon Trail Pageant. An outdoor pageant held at **Clackamas Community College** in **Oregon City**. The musical drama is performed from mid-July into early August. 503-657-0988.

Oregon Trail reenactments. Commemorative **wagon trains** reenacted all or part of the **Oregon Trail** migration in 1959 (Missouri to Oregon), 1973 (Missouri to Oregon and another from **Nyssa** to **Oregon City**), and in 1993 (Wyoming to Oregon City; Missouri to Oregon). A four-day re-enactment of pioneer wagon trains is sponsored annually by the **Pendleton Round-Up** Association. See also **Aurora**; **Orlo**.

Oregon Treaty of 1846. A U.S. treaty with Britain, signed June 15, 1846, that provided that the north boundary of the western U.S. would be at $49°$ latitude (the present Canadian border), and provided protection for interests of British subjects and of the **Hudson's Bay Company** to whom the U.S. awarded $650,000 in 1869 for its rights and titles. The treaty was a compromise, as Great Britain had wished to retain the area north of the **Columbia River**, while the U.S. had claimed all the area north to $54°40'$, the border of Russian-owned Alaska. After the treaty was signed a subsequent dispute (the "pig wars") arose over ownership of the San Juan Islands that was settled in favor of the U.S. claim through arbitration by the Emperor of Germany. Empire of the Columbia. See also **Boundary question**; **Fifty-four Forty or fight**; **Joint occupancy**; **Oregon Country**.

Oregon Trunk Line. A railroad line organized in 1906 to build a rail line from **The Dalles** up the **Deschutes River** to **Bend**. It soon became part of the **Great Northern Railway** and defeated the **DesChutes** (sic) **Railroad** in the **Battle of the Gorge**. East of the Cascades.

Oregon Vortex. A commercial visitor attraction in southern Oregon near **Gold Hill** that features, especially in the House of Mystery, distortions of alignments said to be caused by a 165-foot spherical field of force. 4303 Sardine Creek Road, Gold Hill 97525. 541-855-1543.

Oregon Zoo. A name proposed in 1998 for the **Metro Washington Park Zoo**. Oregonian 3/13/98:D1.

Oregonian. Oregon's major daily **newspaper**, published in **Portland**. Daily circulation in 1996 was 338,586. The paper publishes four main editions: the Northwest for eastern and southern Oregon, which goes to press the evening before delivery; the Northwest Final for northwest Oregon, the coast, Willamette Valley, and central Oregon; the Sunrise for the Portland metropolitan area; and the Street Final (sometimes called The Screamer for its large banner headlines), available about noon at stands in the Portland area. The paper, founded by Whig (Republican) businessmen in 1850, is the oldest continuing business in Oregon. Harvey W. Scott, (1838-1910) was the paper's influential owner/editor for 45 years until his death. The paper is now owned by Advance Publications, a large, privately-held media company controlled by the Newhouse family. The Oregonian Printing Press Park near the west end of the Morrison Street bridge marks the location of the building that housed the paper's first printing press. 1320 SW Broadway, 97201.

503-221-8327. Oregonian 6/25/95:E1. See also **Films - history**; **Newspapers**; **Oregon Style**; **Strikes**.

Oregonians, character. Early Oregonians were noted as respectable people with an emphasis upon "sobriety and thrift, with confidence in the rudiments of education and in modest ambitions of competence and self-sufficiency. ...one would not often find the great risk-taker but rather the conservative personality." Portland, An Informal History, quoting Dorothy Johansen. See also **Mumford quote**.

Oregonians for Food and Shelter. An organization of agricultural and forest users of pesticides. 567 Union NE, Salem 97301. 503-370-8092.

Organic farming. Farming that uses no pesticides or chemical fertilizers and works to replenish the soil and build biological diversity. In 1994 Oregon had about 150 organic farms certified by **Oregon Tilth**. They were growing 500 products on 6,000 acres. Oregon's 1972 organic food law was the first in the nation. Oregonian 9/6/94:FD2.

Organic laws. The first laws, also called the First Organic Laws, drawn up by the **provisional government** and adopted July 5, 1843. Some of the provisions were taken verbatim from the Iowa Territorial Laws of 1839 ("Little Blue Book"). On July 26, 1845, additional laws, now known as the Second Organic Laws, were adopted by vote of the people. In 1849 some of these laws were absorbed into the laws of the **territorial government**, which also adopted certain chapters of the 1843 Revised Statutes of Iowa ("Big Blue Book"). The "Blue Book Controversy" about the status of the various sets of laws raged until adoption of a code of laws by the legislature in 1853. Dictionary of Oregon History.

Organizations. The **Portland Public Library** maintains a Portland Area Community Organizations data base. A directory of organizations in the Portland area, the Portland Metropolitan Chamber of Commerce Associations Directory, is available from them at 221 NW 2nd, 97209. 503-228-9411. The Pioneer Lyceum and Literary Club, a debating society formed at **Oregon City** in 1842, was perhaps the first Oregon organization.

Orlo Foundation. A **Portland** nonprofit art collective that uses creative arts to explore environmental themes. The group produces art exhibitions, publications, including Bear Essentials, performance work, including **Word on the Street**, and public awareness campaigns. Among its efforts have been the "Stumps of Mystery" bumper stickers and "The Promised Landfill" multi-media exhibition about the environmental effects of western expansion. The latter coincided with the **Oregon Trail** Sesquicentennial which was appropriate since the site where the Oregon Trail ended was occupied by a landfill. Orlo is an Italian word meaning "brink" or "edge". PO Box 10342, Portland 97210. 503-242-2330. Reflections Spring 1995:32. See also **Environmental organizations**.

ORS. See **Oregon Revised Statutes**.

Ortley. A one-time **Wasco County** community on the plateau above the **Columbia River** seven miles southeast of Mosier between **Hood River** and **The Dalles**. It was promoted by a land company as a European-style community with central town and outlying apple orchards. The post office opened in 1912, along with stores, a school, saloon, and fancy hotel. However, it soon became apparent that both soil and climate were unsuitable for orchards and by 1922 all but one resident had left and the post office closed. The power line was maintained to the area until the lone resident finally left in 1946. Ortley was a variety of apple. Oregon Geographic Names; Oregon Ghost Towns.

Osprey. A large, fish-eating bird, *Pandion haliaetus*, that summers throughout North America near large bodies of water. Osprey, sometimes called fish hawks, are often misidentified as bald **eagles**. The birds hunt by plunging feet-first into the water and capturing fish in their talons. The osprey population declined 30 years ago because of DDT damage, but has rebounded in the last 20 years. In Oregon there are now about 200 occupied nests, large piles on top of poles, platforms, and broken trees, especially along the **Deschutes River** and at **Crane Prairie Reservoir**. Nesting sites are protected under the Oregon **Forest Practices Act**. Osprey.

OSSHE. The acronym for the Oregon State System of Higher Education. The name was changed in 1998 to the Oregon **University System**. Oregonian 1/ 17/98:D12.

Osteopaths. See **Medical Examiners**.

Ostrich. Large flightless birds, native to Africa, that are being raised in Oregon for meat. The birds, which weigh 300 to 400 pounds and stand 9 feet high, have a low-fat meat similar to beef. Unlike the smaller **emus** and rheas, they lay their eggs in the summer. Oregon Ostrich Association, 300 NE Multnomah, Suite 29, Portland 97232. 503-234-8666.

Oswald West State Park. A **state park** on the north Oregon coast 10 miles south of **Cannon Beach**. The park, located in a rain forest with massive **spruce** and **cedar** trees, includes a 13-mile segment of the **Oregon Coast Trail** as well as a trail to the tip of **Cape Falcon**. The park has 36 walk-in primitive camp units; wheelbarrows are available. Oswald West (1873-1960) was governor 1911-1915 and was instrumental in preserving public access to Oregon beaches. No reservations.

Oswego Canal. A canal dug by hand in 1871 to connect the **Tualatin River** to Sucker Lake (now **Oswego Lake**). A proposed second canal and **lock**s connecting the lake with the **Willamette River** was never built, but the Tualatin was nonetheless an important artery of commerce for the next few decades. The full route would have enabled wheat and other water freight to be moved to and from the Tualatin Valley without having to be portaged around **Willamette Falls**. Blow for the Landing.

Oswego Lake. A lake in **Clackamas County** entirely within the city limits of the city of **Lake Oswego**. It covers 395 acres, is three miles long, and has a maximum depth of 55 feet. The lake occupies a former channel of the **Tualatin River** - which now bypasses it except for a connecting canal. The lakebed was further deeply scoured by **Pleistocene floods** 13,000 years ago. The natural lake level has been raised by the addition of a dam owned by the Oregon Iron and Steel Corporation. The Lake Oswego Shorefront Committee, made up of those owning lake frontage or access rights, owns the lake bed; there is no public access. For three weeks every year the lake level is dropped six feet so that owners can repair docks and seawalls. The lake is heavily used for recreation, especially for water skiing, though the water quality is poor, due primarily to the heavy development around it. The lake was named by an early settler for his home town of Oswego, NY. Atlas of Oregon Lakes. See also **Oswego Canal**.

Otters. Aquatic members of the **weasel** family. River otters, *Lutra canadensis*, originally occupied nearly all the permanent streams and lakes of Oregon, living on fish, frogs, or crustaceans. The otters, which grow to 45 inches long and 25 pounds in weight, are gentle, playful animals, though they can be fierce when attacked. The **High Desert Museum** has river otters on view in a pool with underwater viewing windows. The larger sea otters, *Enhydra lutris*, grow to 60 inches in length and 75 pounds in weight. They live on crustaceans and other sea animals, and their consumption of **sea urchins** is important to the health of **kelp** beds. Once common along Oregon's coast, sea otters were extirpated by fur hunters in the early 1900s, and reintroductions have been unsuccessful. They may be seen at the **Oregon Coast Aquarium**. Both river and sea otters were prized for their furs, that of the sea otter being the world's most valuable fur in the 19th century. In 1994-95, 486 river otters were trapped in Oregon with an average value of $48 each. Atlas of Oregon Wildlife; Mammals and Life Zones of Oregon; Mammals of the Northwest. See also **Fur trade**; **Water pollution**.

Our Lady of Grace Shrine. A 32-foot stainless steel sculpture of the Virgin Mary planned for a location along **Interstate 84** near the **Umatilla Chemical Depot**. Reports that people had seen an apparition of Our Lady of Guadalupe in a landscape painting in **Boardman** provided inspiration for the shrine. Charles Parks of Delaware designed the sculpture. Oregonian 12/5/96:D9.

Our Lady of Guadalupe. A cloistered Trappist abbey near **Lafayette** that moved there from New Mexico in 1955. The abbey makes and sells fruitcakes and biscotti and operates a retreat guest house. There are walking trails on the grounds, and some services are open to the public. It is located on Abbey Road three miles north of **Highway 99W**. 503-852-0107.

Outdoor concert sites. Areas in the northern **Willamette Valley** at which outdoor events are held include **Portland Meadows** (16,000-32,500 capacity); the **Commons** (3,000); **Washington Park Zoo** Amphitheatre (3,800-6,000); **Washington Park** Rose Garden Amphitheatre (4,000); **Oaks Park** (4,000); **Champoeg State Park** Amphitheater (3,000); Sokol Blosser Winery near **Dundee** (3,000); and L.B. Day Amphitheatre at the **State Fair**grounds, (8,900). Oregonian 8/6/95:C1.

Outlet malls. See **Factory outlet malls**.

Outward Bound. An organization with programs designed to help people, especially youngsters, use outdoor adventures to uncover their own hidden talents and strengths. Its west coast headquarters are in **Portland**. Pacific Crest Outward Bound School, 0110 SW Bancroft. 503-243-1993.

Ouzel. See **Water ouzel**.

Owls. Thirteen species of owls breed in Oregon, varying in size from the 7" flammulated owl to the 27" great gray owl. Most are nocturnal hunters preying on small mammals, insects, and birds, but the flammulated owl is mainly an insectivore. Atlas of Oregon Wildlife. See also **Northern spotted owl**.

Owyhee canyons. An area in the southeast corner of Oregon south of **Rome** where the **Owyhee River** and its tributaries flow through rugged canyons. **Three**

Forks is at the center.

Owyhee Project. A project developed by the U.S. **Bureau of Reclamation**, beginning in the 1920s, to supply irrigation water to 105,000 acres in Oregon and Idaho on the west side of the **Snake River**. 72% of the acreage is in Oregon. Much of the water is supplied from **Lake Owyhee** through 172 miles of canals and 500 miles of laterals. Atlas of Oregon Lakes.

Owyhee River. A long river that originates in Nevada and flows 400 miles through deep desert canyons lined with towering rock formations in southern Idaho and southeast Oregon before joining the **Snake River** near **Nyssa**. It drains 11,300 square miles, and has an average annual volume of 386,000 acre feet or .1 acre foot/acre. At some seasons, its Class IV and V rapids provide thrills for white water boaters. **Lake Owyhee** is formed by a dam on the lower river; the Oregon **Health Division** has issued warnings about eating fish from the reservoir because of high levels of **mercury**. Owyhee is an earlier spelling of Hawaii; the river was named for two Hawaiians killed near it by Indians in 1819. Oregon Geographic Names. See also **ION**; **Leslie Gulch**; **Pillars of Rome**; **Three Forks**.

Owyhee uplands physiographic province. An arid region in the southeast corner of the state bordered on the north and west by the **Blue Mountains**, the **high lava plains**, and the **basin and range** provinces. It rises from 2,100 feet elevation at its north end along the **Snake River** to 6,500 feet at the top of **Mahogany Mountain** south of **Lake Owyhee**. The deep **Owyhee canyons** expose a geologic history of **Miocene** and later volcanic eruptions. Immense **calderas** also date from the Miocene, as do **fossils** of plants and animals that indicate a moister era. The most recent volcanism, within the past 10,000 years, was at **Jordan Craters**. The **Owyhee River** drains the area. Geology of Oregon.

Oxbow Dam. An **Idaho Power Company** power generating dam on the **Snake River**. The 205-foot-high, 1,150-foot-long earth and rock fill dam, completed in 1961, is on the upstream end of a three-mile loop that the Snake River makes around a hard rock ridge. The dam diverts water through two tunnels beneath the ridge, each 42 feet in diameter and 900 feet long, to a powerhouse at the downstream end of the loop. Generating capacity is 190 **megawatts**. The first development at the site was in 1909 when a 28-foot diameter tunnel was completed, along with a generator with a capacity of .6 megawatts. Idaho Power operates McCormick Park on the Idaho shore of the reservoir as well as Copperfield Park on the Oregon side at Oxbow. **Hells Canyon Dam** is 23 miles downstream, and **Brownlee Dam** is 13 miles upstream. Recreation update 800-422-3143. Hells Canyon. See also **Oxbow Incident**.

Oxbow Incident. A series of mishaps and disasters in the fall of 1958 as attempts were made to get migrating **salmon** around the **Idaho Power Company** construction site at **Oxbow Dam** on the **Snake River**. Thousands of fish died. No satisfactory method for bypassing the dam was found, and after four years the attempts to get migrating salmon up and down stream past **Hells Canyon, Oxbow**, and **Brownlee** dams were abandoned, and the salmon run on the upper Snake River disappeared. Hells Canyon.

Oysters. The prized small Olympia oyster, *Ostrea lurida*, is native to some Oregon bays. Commercial harvest began in **Yaquina Bay** in 1863 and in **Netarts**

Bay in 1870, but the stocks were soon depleted. They had vanished from **Coos Bay** even before white settlement, but have recently reappeared there, and attempts are being made to reestablish them in Netarts, Yaquina, and **Alsea** bays. Cultivation of the much larger Pacific oyster, *Ostrea giga*, (native to Japan) began in 1930 in Netarts Bay and later expanded to **Tillamook Bay**, Yaquina Bay, Coos Bay, and **Winchester Bay** on the **Umpqua River**. Abandoned salmon ranches in Yaquina Bay and Coos Bay may also be used for oysters. Oregon now produces about 21,000 gallons of meat a year, worth $700,000. Sport harvest of oysters is banned. All Oregon shellfish should be cooked before eating to avoid illness from *Vibrio parahaemolyticus*, a bacterium that lives in estuary mud. 1994-1995 Oregon Agriculture; Oregonian 6/29/95:B7, 9/24/96:B4; Tillamook.

Ozokerite. A mineral wax. In 1893 it was proposed that the **beeswax** found on beaches near **Neahkahnie Mountain** was actually ozokerite. Despite scientific tests that showed it to be indeed beeswax, enthusiasts insisted that it was ozokerite and was an indication of petroleum. In 1909 the Necarney City Hydrocarbon Company was formed and drilled for two years with no success. Lost Mines and Treasures.

Ozone. A form of oxygen that, although desirable in the upper atmosphere, constitutes the major component of smog in the lower atmosphere. Ozone damages the human respiratory system, vegetation, and materials such as paint and rubber. It is formed in the presence of sunlight and at temperatures over 90 degrees by chemical reactions between volatile organic compounds and **nitrogen dioxide**, so is controlled by controlling emissions of those pollutants. Controls on emissions from motor vehicles and gas-powered equipment, gasoline and paint vapors, aerosol products and industry have helped decrease ozone levels in the state. Ozone from the **Portland** metropolitan area is blown to the southeast, concentrating near **Molalla**. In 1997 **Portland** moved into compliance with federal ground-level ozone rules, but areas in nonattainment status included **Salem, Eugene, Klamath Falls, Medford, Grants Pass, Oakridge, Lakeview,** and the **Pendleton - La Grande** area. Oregon Air Quality; Oregon Environmental Atlas; Oregonian 4/28/95:D9, 11/10/95:B3, 11/28/96:A1, 4/28/97:B6. See also **Air pollution**.

P. I. See **Pacific International Livestock Exposition**.

Pacific City. An unincorporated coastal community in **Tillamook County** on the south side of **Cape Kiwanda** 17 miles north of **Lincoln City**. It is the only place on the Oregon coast where boats, especially fishing dories, are launched directly from the beach into the surf. Nearby sand **dunes** provide dune buggy recreation.

Pacific Coast Republic. See **Knights of the Golden Circle**.

Pacific College. See **George Fox College**.

Pacific Crest National Scenic Trail. A trail, designated by Congress in 1968, that traverses the Sierra Nevada and **Cascade Range** between Mexico and Canada, including 441 miles in Oregon. It enters Oregon from California about 20 miles west of **Interstate 5**, travels east through the **Siskiyou Mountains** to the Cascades and then turns north, passing **Crater Lake** and other Cascade peaks and lakes to cross the **Columbia River** at **Cascade Locks**. A third of the distance is through **wilderness areas**. Motorized travel is not permitted. Maps are available from the U.S. **Forest Service**.

Pacific Crest Trail. See **Pacific Crest National Scenic Trail**.

Pacific Fishery Management Council. An agency, one of eight regional groups, established by Congress in 1976 to develop management plans for fisheries off the coasts of Washington, Oregon, and California. Eight of the 13 voting members are appointed by the Secretary of Commerce, and the remainder represent state and federal agencies. 2130 SW Fifth Avenue, Suite 224, Portland 97201. 503-326-6352. Directory of Organizations.

Pacific flyway. The name given to the routes used by birds migrating west of the Rocky Mountains between their wintering grounds (in Oregon, the southwest, and Mexico), and their breeding grounds (in Alaska and Canada). Some birds fly just offshore along the coast, others fly through the **Willamette Valley**, and huge numbers migrate across eastern Oregon. **Malheur National Wildlife Refuge** is a prime viewing spot in early April as the birds are north-bound, and again in the fall on their return migration. Oregon Wildlife Viewing Guide.

Pacific Fur Company. An American company organized in 1810 by John Jacob Astor with the intention of linking overland **fur trade** with the maritime trade with China. To this end he sent an ill-starred crew by sea to establish **Astoria** at the mouth of the **Columbia River** (at least 35 lives lost) and the misfortunate **Astor Overland Expedition** (two lives lost). In addition to Astoria, the company built **Wallace House**, a **trading post** in the **Willamette Valley**, and posts to the north. After the company sold its interests to the Canadian **North West Company** in 1813, 15 of its employees stayed to become the first known **settlers** in the **Oregon Country**. Astoria; Champoeg; Dictionary of Oregon History.

Pacific Graveyard. See **Shipwrecks**.

Pacific Highway. The original highway between **Portland** and California; it followed much of the route of the **Siskiyou** and **Applegate** trails. In 1911 the Pacific Highway Association organized to promote a Pacific Highway between Canada and Mexico, and posted "Pacific Highway" signs along the proposed route. Progress in Oregon was slower than in the other states, though **Jackson County** paved 13 miles in 1914. The route up **Siskiyou Summit** was soon relocated and paved, with one lane cement and one lane "black top" in an inconclusive comparison. The sections through **Josephine** and **Douglas** counties were especially difficult, but the full route through Oregon was finally completed when the last portion was paved in 1924, making the highway from Canada to Mexico the longest paved highway in the world. In 1923 the full route was designated as **Highway 99**. Portions were later rebuilt, and much of it was supplanted in the 1960s by **Interstate 5**. Dictionary of Oregon History; South Road.

Pacific International Livestock Exposition. A major annual trade show and social event organized in 1910 by the Portland Livestock Exchange to promote the region's livestock industry. At its peak it ran for 10 days, but began to decline in the 1960s and by 1994 had faded away. Some of the buildings were turned over to **Multnomah County** and have been transformed into the **Exposition Center**. Oregonian 6/21/95:D1.

Pacific Monthly. A **Portland** literary magazine that had a circulation of 85,000 in 1906. It evolved into California's Sunset Magazine. Portland, An Informal History.

Pacific Northwest College of Art. An accredited four-year college in **Portland** that grants a B.F.A. degree. It is housed at the **Portland Art Museum** until 1998 when it will move to 815 NW 12th Avenue. The college was founded in 1909 as the educational arm of the Museum, though it is now financially and administratively independent. 257 students enrolled in 1995. 815 NW 12th Ave., 97209. 503-226-4391. Oregon Blue Book.

Pacific Northwest Museum of Natural History. A 30,000 square foot museum in **Ashland** that opened in 1994 and then was closed in 1997 for financial reasons. Interactive exhibits featured a variety of Oregon habitats and invited the visitor to make decisions about the use of timber, rangeland, and water resources. It was located at 1500 E. Main.

Pacific Northwest Truck Museum. See **Antique Powerland Museum**.

Pacific Ocean. See **Ocean** entries.

Pacific Power and Light Company (PP&L). An investor-owned **electric utility** (a division of **PacifiCorp**). In 1994 it had 455,000 retail customers in Oregon, 70,000 of them in **Portland**. Oregon revenues totaled $826 million from sales of 17.7 million megawatt hours. Although Oregon sales accounted for 30% of PP&L revenues, less than 4% of its electricity was generated in the state. It had an installed generating capacity in the state of 325 **megawatts** from the **North Umpqua Hydroelectric Project** and other **hydroelectric** plants on the **Klamath, Rogue**, and **Deschutes** rivers. Historically, PP&L and **Portland General Electric** were rivals in providing electric service in the Portland area until a 1969 agreement allocated separate service areas, eliminating duplicated facilities. 920 SW 6th, Portland 97204-1203. 503-464-5000. Stream flow and reservoir info: 800-547-1501. Electrifying Eden; Inventory; Oregon Utility Statistics. See also **Wind power**.

Pacific Railroad Survey of 1855. A government-sponsored survey of several possible railroad routes from the midwest to the Pacific Coast as well as a north/south route through Oregon and California. Lt. R. S. Williamson (1824-1882) was in charge of the north/south survey, assisted by Lt. Henry L. Abbot (1831-1927), who later had responsibility for much of the exploration and most of the report writing. Between August 12 and November 5, 1855, the Abbott party explored north up the east side of the **Cascade Range**, crossed into the **Willamette Valley** approximately along the route that **Highway 26** now follows, and then went south along the **Siskiyou Trail/Interstate 5** route, while Williamson's party explored the **Willamette Pass** route and the east side of the **Willamette Valley**. The government printed 55,000 copes of the final 13-volume report of all the surveys, including maps, paintings, and information about the land, plants, and animals of the west. The Oregon/California route is covered in Volume 6. "Abbot Railroad Surveys, 1855"; Reports of Explorations.

Pacific Railway and Navigation Company. A 91-mile railroad line from **Hillsboro** to **Tillamook**, completed in 1911 through the rugged **Coast Range**. The line went through 13 tunnels and crossed 85 trestles and bridges on its route from sea level up over the 1,800' Cochran summit and down to **Banks**. Thirty-five of the bridges were over 100 feet long, including the highest single-pile span in the world. The Big Baldwin trestle was 167 feet high. The line was commonly known as the PR&N, or the Punk, Rotten, and Nasty. The **Southern Pacific** acquired it in 1915. It carried passengers until 1933, but then, after the **Tillamook Burn**, 90% of its business was hauling salvaged logs. It now operates as the **Oregon-Tillamook Railroad**. Tillamook; Tillamook Burn Country.

Pacific Rim Economic Conference. A regional one-day session held on June 27, 1995 at **Portland State University**. It was initiated by President Clinton, who attended along with Vice-President Gore and a number of cabinet officials. They heard from West Coast panelists who discussed the regional economy, trade, and the workplace.

Pacific States Marine Fisheries Commission. An interstate commission, authorized by Congress in 1947 to serve as a forum for discussion of coastal and national issues that affect Pacific fisheries. It has no regulatory or management authority but operates a mark processing center, an information network, and some contract services. The five member states (Alaska, Washington, Idaho, Oregon, and California) each have three members: the state fishery director plus one appointed by the governor and one by the legislature. 45 SE 82nd Avenue, Suite 100, Gladstone 97027-2522. Directory of Organizations.

Pacific University. An accredited private college in **Forest Grove** that enrolled 1,850 students in 1995. Optometry and physical therapy education are specialties. It grew from a missionary school established in 1841 by Rev. Harvey Clark for Indian children and later pioneer children, and joined with an orphan boarding school operated by Tabitha Brown, **Mother of Oregon**. Ministers from the **Presbyterian** and **Congregational** churches incorporated the Tualatin Academy (a secondary school) there in 1850, and college classes were added in 1854 under the name Pacific University. In 1863 Harvey Scott, later famed editor of the **Oregonian**, was the first graduate. 20443 College Way, Forest Grove 97116. 503-357-6151. Dictionary of Oregon History; Oregon Blue Book.

Pacific Wonderland. A slogan on Oregon **license plates** from 1960 through 1962. First 75 Years.

PacifiCorp. A diversified **electric utility** company, the parent corporation for **Pacific Power and Light Company**. It serves 1.3 million retail electricity customers in seven states but is also broadening its products and services in the U.S. and abroad. Fortune 500 listed it as having 1996 sales of $4.294 billion and over 12,000 employees. 700 NE Multnomah St., Suite 1600, Portland 97232. 503-731-2000. Oregonian 4/9/96:B14, 6/30/96:R25, 6/15/97:C1.

Pack rats. See **Wood rats**.

Pack string. A line of 15 to 20 horses or mules used to pack goods to places that had no **wagon road** access. Pack strings were used especially to haul freight to gold-mining camps between 1862 and 1885. The first pack outfits and packers came from Mexico, and most of the rigging still carries Spanish names. Where wagon roads were developed, **freighting outfits** replaced the pack strings. Gold and Cattle Country.

PACs. See **Campaign finance reform**; **Lobbyists**.

Paddle-wheel. See **Stern-wheeler.**

Painted Hills. A portion of the 30 million year old **John Day Formation** in western **Wheeler County**, northwest of **Mitchell**, in which soils have eroded and weathered to a rainbow of colors that are especially vivid when damp. The Painted Hills unit is part of the **John Day Fossil Beds National Monument**; fossil plants are found in nearby formations. Geology of Oregon.

Paisley. A south-central Oregon ranching community in **Lake County** 45 miles north of **Lakeview** on the **Fremont Highway**. The post office, named for Paisley, Scotland, was established in 1879. The city was incorporated in 1911. The community operates a **boarding high school** and sponsors the annual **Mosquito** Festival in late July. Population 1980 343; 1995 345. Elevation 4,369'. PO Box 100, 97636. 541-943-3173. Oregon Ghost Towns.

Paiute Indians. See **Northern Paiute Indians**.

Paleocene. A geologic epoch between the **Cretaceous** period and the **Eocene**, between 55 and 67 million years ago. The **Blue Mountains** were above sea level and experienced intermittent volcanic activity. The shoreline lay east of the present **Cascade Range**; the Cascades and the **Coast Range** had not yet formed. Geology of Oregon.

Paleozoic. A geologic era that lasted from the pre-Cambrian to the Mesozoic era (**Triassic** period), 250 to 600 million years ago. Oregon was covered by deep ocean; the shore line curved across Washington to Idaho and Nevada. However, volcanic archipelagos that would eventually become part of Oregon were building on the Farallon oceanic plate. Geology of Oregon. See also **Rocks, oldest**.

Panama Canal. A canal cut through central America in 1914 that brought European and eastern U.S. ports 6,000 miles closer to Oregon, making Oregon products (especially lumber) more competitive there. The increase in trade, however, was not so immediate as Oregonians had anticipated, due to the effects of **World War I**.

Panhandle. An area of **Baker County** on the south slope of the **Wallowa Mountains**. It lies between the Powder River, the **Snake River**, and the south boundary of **Wallowa County**, and includes the communities of Oxbow, **Halfway**, Cornucopia, **Richland**, **Sparta**, and Keating. Between 1864 and 1901 it was a panhandle portion of **Union County**, but was then transferred back to Baker County so that residents could have easier access to a county seat.

Paper mills. See **Pulp mills**.

Parades. See **Electrical Parade**; **Rose Festival**; **Veteran's Day**.

Paralytic shellfish poisoning. See **Shellfish poisoning**.

Parental responsibility. Under laws passed by the 1995 legislature, parents who fail to supervise their children can be ordered to take parenting classes or fined up to $1,000. Parents of youthful offenders are held responsible under a contract for their child's probation and must work with the court to devise a supervision plan for the child. Oregonian 7/17/95:B1.

Pari-mutuel racing. Greyhound and **horse racing** on which people wager against the other bettors. Total bets placed in Oregon, including those placed at 19 off-track betting outlets, were $111.1 million in fiscal year1995-96, and winnings averaged 79 cents on the dollar. The state received $1.7 million (1.5% of handle) as its share. Pari-mutuel racing has been regulated since 1933 by the Oregon **Racing Commission**. Oregonian 10/22/95:A18. See also **Multnomah Greyhound**

Park.

Park Blocks. A one-block-wide strip through downtown Portland that was originally planned to extend from the base of the hills to the **Willamette River**. The South Park Blocks are a one-block-wide park strip through downtown **Portland**, between SW Park and 9th, donated in 1852. Originally 18 blocks long, in 1865 the heirs of one donor reclaimed the six blocks between Stark and Salmon. The South Park Blocks, noted for elms and statues, now extend 12 blocks from Salmon Street south past **Portland State University** to SW Jackson, and are fronted by major buildings including the **Portland Art Museum** and the **Oregon History Center**. The North Park Blocks, between NW Park and 8th Avenues from Ankeny to Glisan, were donated in 1869 by Capt. John Couch, and the city purchased land for O'Bryant Park, between Stark and Washington, in 1971. Seven developed blocks lie between the South and North Park Blocks, including the block between Yamhill and Taylor, slated for a parking garage, that developer Tom Moyer bought for $5 million and donated to the city in 1998. Oregonian 5/20/97:A8, 3/1/98:B1.

Parks. See **Bush's Pasture Park** (Salem); **National parks**; **Portland parks**; **State parks**.

Parks and Recreation Department. The Oregon department responsible for administering Oregon's **state parks** and for establishing, in alliance with other public and private providers, integrated statewide, cooperative, non-duplicated services. The department is also responsible for administering the Federal Land and Water Conservation Fund, 360 miles of **beaches** under the Oregon Beach Bill, 221 scenic, recreational and historic areas included in the Statewide Comprehensive **Historic Preservation** Plan and other programs, 500 miles of **trails** in the Oregon Recreational Trails System, 19 state **scenic waterways**, and the **Willamette River Greenway**. The department was created in 1921 as a branch of the Highway Department, made a division in 1929 with Samuel Boardman as the first superintendent, and made a separate department in 1990. 1115 Commercial NE, Salem 97310-1001. 503-378-6305. Park information 800-551-6949. Park reservations 800-452-5687. Oregon Blue Book. See also **Gas tax**.

Parole. The conditional release of a prisoner before his or her sentence has expired. See also **Community Corrections**; **Parole and Post-Prison Supervision**; **Probation**.

Parole and Post-Prison Supervision, Board of. A full-time, paid, three-member board that determines which prison inmates are safe to release into society. Members are appointed to staggered four-year terms by the governor. The board operates under three sets of laws. The first, a discretionary system, applies to inmates who committed crimes before 1/26/77, though as of July 1997 only two inmates still qualified. The second, a matrix system in which the board sets the inmate's prison term, applies to those who committed their crimes between 1/26/77 and 11/1/89. The third, a sentencing-guidelines system, applies to those whose crimes were committed after 11/1/89; under it the parole board has no say in setting terms nor about when to release the inmate. Once a prisoner has served his term, the board cannot delay his release even if it agrees that he is not yet safe for society. **Measure 11** made sentences mandatory for the most serious crimes and made them longer. Prisoners now are also given a period (months to years) of post-prison supervision for which the Board can impose conditions. The parole officers who supervise the parolees are employed by the counties. In 1995 20% of inmates were released on parole compared to 50% a year earlier. 2575 Center Street NE, Salem 97310-0470. 503-945-0900. Oregon Blue Book; Oregonian 6/25/95:A1. See also **Community Corrections**.

Particulates. Small particles in the air. **Air pollution** caused by particles less than about 100 microns in diameter (about the diameter of a human hair) is called total suspended particulate (TSP) pollution. Although all particulates corrode buildings, damage vegetation, and reduce visibility, the fine particles, those under 10 microns (PM_{10}), are the most damaging to human health because they lodge in the lungs where they cause mechanical and chemical problems. Smoke is made up primarily of these fine particulates. Particulate emissions in Oregon have decreased in recent decades because of the elimination of **wigwam burners** and the phase out of leaded gasoline, but **slash** and **field burning**, dust from roads and agriculture, fireplace smoke, and exhaust from cars and power plants remain major sources. PM_{10} emissions in Oregon totaled 207,000 tons in 1996. In 1998 the federal government instituted tougher standards for extremely small particles, under 2.5 microns (invisible), which are especially dangerous to health, Oregon Air Quality; Oregon Environmental Atlas; Oregonian 11/28/96:A1, 3/6/98:D4. See also **Visibility Protection Plan; Wood stoves**.

Parties. See **Political parties**.

Partridges. **Game birds** somewhat larger than **quail**. There are no native partridges in Oregon, but several species have been introduced. The Hungarian or gray partidge, *Perdix perdix*, was unsuccessfully introduced into western Oregon in 1900, but populations introduced in eastern Oregon in 1912 have thrived in bunchgrass and **sagebrush** foothills where they are now hunted. Atlas of Oregon Wildlife. See also **Chukar**.

Passes. See **Highway passes**.

Patents. U.S. patents granted to Oregon residents are listed in issues of Oregon Scientist along with information on how to obtain abstracts or full copies of the patents.

Patterned ground. An area in which some geologic feature, such as mounding, is repeated. In Oregon "Mima Mounds," mounds 2 to 3 feet high and 12 to 15 feed across, are found in several places, including at Tom McCall State Park in the Columbia River Gorge and along **Highway 97** between **Grass Valley** and **Shaniko** and west along Bakeoven Road. Some speculate that such mounds are caused by the action of gophers while others maintain that they are the result of freeze/thaw cycles or earthquakes or glacial deposits or wind erosion. Similar mounds are also found in other states. Ground patterned with depressions (vernal pools) is found in the Agate Desert near **White City**. See also **Mud cracks**.

Paul Jensen Arctic Museum. A museum on the campus of **Western Oregon State College** in Monmouth, that houses artifacts from Alaskan Eskimos. It is open to the public during limited hours. 590 W. Church St., Monmouth 97361. 503-838-8468.

Paulina Creek Falls. A 100-foot waterfall formed as Paulina Creek plunges out of **Newberry Crater**. Short trails lead to viewpoints from a picnic area on the north side of Paulina Lake Road. The falls are sometimes called Upper Falls; Lower Falls are four miles downstream. Waterfall Lover's Guide.

Paulina Lake and East Lake. Two deep natural lakes occupying the caldera in **Newberry Volcano**; they were probably one lake until cinder cones and lava flows separated them 2,050 years ago. The larger of the two is Paulina Lake which is two miles in diameter, covers 1,531 acres, and is 250 feet deep. East Lake, 40 feet higher than Paulina Lake, is over a mile in diameter, covers 1,044 acres, and is 180 feet deep. A major source of water in each of the lakes is subsurface mineralized hot springs. East Lake has no surface outlet; water is lost by seepage. Paulina Lake drains out through Paulina Creek. Trout fishing is popular on both lakes, though the Oregon **Health Division** has issued cautions about eating the fish from East Lake because of **mercury** content, probably from the hot springs. Each lake has a small resort. Chief Paulina was an infamous Snake Indian believed to be responsible for a series of depredations in the area. He was killed on April 25, 1867. Atlas of Oregon Lakes.

Paulina Mountains. An isolated mountain group 25 miles south of **Bend** that consists of **Paulina Peak** on **Newberry Volcano** and its flanking volcanic cones. Some of the area is in **Newberry National Volcanic Monument**.

Paulina Peak. The high point, at 7,984', on the rim of **Newberry Crater**. It can be reached by a dirt road, and provides a view of Big **Obsidian** Flow, **Newberry Crater**, and the surrounding countryside. Paulina was a Snake Indian, believed responsible for a large number of atrocities over a wide area of eastern Oregon in the 1860's. Oregon Geographic Names.

Pauling House. A house at 3945 SE Hawthorne Boulevard in **Portland** that was the childhood home of noted scientist Linus Pauling. Pauling was a two-time winner of the **Nobel Prize**, promoted peace concerns, and advocated increased use of vitamin C. He was born February 28, 1901 in Portland, graduated in 1922 from what is now **Oregon State University** with a degree in chemical engineering, and died August 19, 1994 at Big Sur, California. Oregonian 3/7/96:B11.

Pawn shops. In 1997 Oregon had 19 state-licensed pawn shops where customers could get a short-term, high-interest loan by providing some item(s) of merchandise as security. The customer would then have 90 days to redeem the merchandise or renew the loan. About 12% of merchandise is forfeited and then sold by the pawnshop. The shops are regulated by the state Division of **Finance and Corporate Securities**. Oregonian 9/1/97:B17.

Payroll. In 1996 the semiconductor industry had an Oregon payroll of $1,157 million. It was followed by general medical and hospital ($1,132 million), medical offices, clinics ($1,079 million), eating places ($929.6 million), grocery stores ($627.3 million), temporary services ($586.9 million), new and used cars ($500.6 million), department stores ($471.2 million), sawmills, planing mills ($466.4 million), and plumbing, heating, air conditioning ($435.3 million). In 1980 sawmills and planing mills had been the top payroll at $896.8 million. In 1994 the average annual payroll for employment that was covered under the Oregon **unemployment** insurance program was $24,789, though it ranged from a high of $28,850 in **Washington County** to a low of $17,494 in **Malheur County**. Between 1980 and 1994, an average of 84.3% of total employment in the state was covered employment. Oregon: A Statistical Overview; Oregonian 12/17/97:D1. See also **Employers**; **Employment**.

PDX. The airport designation for **Portland International Airport**.

Peace Corps. In September 1996, 167 Oregonians were serving as Peace Corps volunteers, part of the total of 3,278 from the state who have served in the Peace Corps since it was founded in 1961. 2001 6th Avenue, Suite 1776, Seattle WA 98121. 800-424-8580. Oregonian 9/11/96:E10.

Peaches. In 1995, Oregon growers produced 127,000 boxes of peaches, worth $2.1 million, on 1,525 acres. The first peaches in the Oregon Country were sprouted pits brought to **Fort Vancouver** in 1829 by a sailor who had found the peaches on Juan Fernandez Island. Dictionary of Oregon History; 1995 Oregon.

Peacock Spit. An area of shallow water and shifting sands extending into the mouth of the **Columbia River** from Cape Disappointment. The spit originally lay in the mouth of the river east of the Cape, but after construction of the North Jetty in 1917, it gradually migrated seaward and around to the north to lie primarily outside the mouth. The U.S. sloop-of-war *Peacock,* part of the **Wilkes Expedition**, wrecked on the sands on July 18, 1841, one of numerous **shipwrecks** on the spit. "Delay"; Dictionary of Oregon History; Oregon Shipwrecks.

Pearl District. A 2548-acre area of northwest **Portland** that has been transforming from a warehouse area to a tony arts and residential district. It is bounded by 6th, Burnside, Interstate 405, and the Willamette River. Originally called the Northwest Triangle, in 1986 it was dubbed the Pearl District for its "crusty warehouses with the gems inside." Oregonian 8/3/97:L1.

Pears. Oregon grows about a fourth of the nation's pears. In 1995, Oregon growers produced 171,600 tons of winter pears, worth $45.6 million, on 12,545 acres, and 76,100 tons of Bartlett pears, worth $13.8 million, on 5,595 acres. **Hood River County** produces two thirds of Oregon's pears, with **Jackson County** growing most of the rest. In 1885 J. H. Stewart pioneered Jackson County's pear industry. Harry and David's Bear Creek Orchards in **Medford** began shipping gift packs of pears in 1933 and started the Fruit of the Month Club in 1937. "Cubby of Bear Creek"; 1995 Oregon; Oregon Oddities. See also **Fruit**; **National Germplasm Repository**.

Peas. Oregon grows 11% of the country's green peas for processing. In 1995 the state's growers produced 74,000 tons worth $17.6 million on 38,215 acres, primarily in **Umatilla County**. 1995 Oregon; Oregon Agriculture.

Peavy Arboretum. An 80-acre **Oregon State University** arboretum five miles north of **Corvallis**. It includes 160 species of **trees** and **shrubs**. The arboretum, established in 1925, also serves as gateway to the university's adjacent McDonald research forest. 541-737-4452.

Pebble Springs. A location three miles southeast of **Arlington** in **Gilliam Country** that was the site of a controversial proposed but never built **Portland General Electric nuclear power plant** in the late 1970s. The site, a sheep camp, was known for a Pebble Springs brand whiskey bottle that had been found there. Oregon Geographic Names.

Pelican Butte. An 8,036' conical peak in the southern Oregon **Cascade Range**, northeast of **Mount McLoughlin** in the **Winema National Forest**. Jeld-

Wen Corporation, developer of the 3,600-acre Running Y Ranch resort on **Upper Klamath Lake**, has proposed a 600-acre ski area for the mountain. The area would have 5 lifts and 3,800 feet of vertical drop. Mail Tribune 11/29/96:1B.

Pelton Dam. A 205-foot dam on the **Deschutes River**, completed by **Portland General Electric** in 1958, that created **Lake Simtustus**. It and its reregulating dam have a joint generating capacity of 116.1 **megawatts**. Because the faulty fish ladders have been abandoned, the dams block **salmon** and **steelhead** runs that once ran up the Deschutes. In 1997 the Warm Springs Indians bid for the federal license, up for renewal in 2001, to operate Pelton and **Round Butte** dams. The tribes already own the generating facilities at the Pelton reregulating dam and also receive annual payments of about $10 million from PGE because the dams lie partly on reservation land. Oregonian 7/23/97:C1.

Pencil sharpener. See **Inventors**.

Pendleton. A major commercial center of northeast Oregon, located 209 miles east of **Portland** on **Interstate 84** and **Highway 395**. It has been the county seat of **Umatilla County** since 1864 and is headquarters for the **Umatilla National Forest**. The famed **Pendleton Round-Up** is held the second full week in September. Some of the town's colorful past can be explored on an underground tour of the **prohibition** era saloons, card rooms, and other businesses. Other attractions include the 1889 glass-enclosed 57-foot-high Seth Thomas Clock Tower, Pendleton Woolen Mills, a historical museum, a **casino** four miles east, and a game refuge 7 miles south. The **Til Taylor statue** honors a legendary sheriff. Dr. William C. McKay established the first trading post at the site in 1851. Later the area was known as Marshall Station and then Middleton before the growing community was named in 1868 in honor of the 1864 Democratic candidate for vice-president, George Hunt Pendleton of Ohio. The city was incorporated in 1880 and survived a series of floods to become the nation's leading wool market by the end of the century. Marinkina, Philippines, is its sister city. Population 1980 14,521; 1995 15,930. Elevation 1,068'. PO Box 190, 97801. 541-276-1811. Chamber of Commerce 541-276-7411. Oregon Geographic Names.

Pendleton Round-Up. A 4-day **rodeo** and festival, one of the Big Four rodeos; the others are in Walla Walla WA, Ellensburg WA, and Lewiston ID. It began in 1910 as an outgrowth of annual Indian roundups held where the present grounds are located and is still a major Indian gathering. The accompanying Happy Canyon Pageant depicts an idyllic Indian world and its displacement by white settlement. PO Box 609, Pendleton 97801. 800-43-RODEO.

Pengra Pass. See **Natron cut-off**.

Peninsula Rose Garden. See **Sunken Rose Garden**.

Pension puzzle. After a 1989 U.S. Supreme Court ruling that it was illegal to exempt state and local pensions from state taxes (as Oregon state employee contracts specified) unless federal pensions were also exempt, the legislature responded by taxing state and local pensions but also giving state workers increased benefits. Voters, however, defeated the proposal in 1990. A further complex series of legislative actions and court reversals resulted in refunds to Federal retirees for 1988 and 1989 and, in 1997, $400 million in reimbursement to 50,000 retired state and local public employees from the Oregon **Public Employees Retirement Sys-**

tem (PERS) pension fund. Oregonian 11/23/97:D2.

People's Power League. A turn-of-the century reform political group led by William S. U'Ren of **Milwaukie**. It was instrumental in passing measures for the **initiative, referendum, recall**, direct **primary,** corrupt practices, **voters' pamphlet,** and **women's suffrage**. See also **Oregon System**.

People's utility district (PUD). A governmental unit that Oregon voters can establish in order to provide electricity. Six have been established in Oregon: Central Lincoln (the largest, with $54.5 million in revenues in 1994), Clatskanie, Columbia River, Emerald, Northern Wasco County, and Tillamook. Each PUD has an elected board of directors. See also **Electric utilities**; **Public power**; **Public Power Council**.

Peppermint. See **Mint**.

Peregrine falcon. A bird of prey, *Falco peregrinus*, also called duck hawk because it preys especially on water birds, though peregrines also prey on shorebirds, pigeons, and starlings. They nest on ledges on cliffs and city buildings - and on **Portland**'s Fremont Bridge. The birds, up to 18" long, are known for their swift flight, with diving speeds up to 200 mph. They fly as high as 3,500 feet, and can spot a pigeon five miles away. At one time near extinction and on the **endangered species** list, they have made a recovery in recent years. In 1980 Oregon had just one pair, at **Crater Lake**, but by 1997 there were 52 known nest sites, though not all nests were occupied. Oregonian 6/18/97:A23. See also **Falcons**.

Performance. See **Do Jump!; Imago; Oregon Chautauqua; Portland Center for the Performing Arts; Portland Institute for Contemporary Art; Portland International Performance Festival**.

Performing Arts Center. See **Portland Center for the Performing Arts**.

Periodicals. Seventy-three periodicals published in Oregon with circulation of over 1,000 are listed in the Oregon Blue Book. See also **Calyx**; **Firebrand**; **Pacific Monthly**; **West Shore**.

Perlite. A form of volcanic glass that puffs up like popcorn when it is heated and is then used in lightweight concrete and in potting mix for plants. It has been mined in **Baker County** and in the Tucker Hills south of **Paisley** and occurs elsewhere in Oregon.

PERS. See **Public Employees Retirement System**.

Pesticide Hot Line. A national toll-free pesticide information service operated at **Oregon State University**. It provides information about products, poisonings, effects, and disposal, 6:30 a.m. to 4:30 p.m. weekdays. National Pesticide Telecommunications Network, Agricultural Chemistry Extension, 333 Weniger Hall, OSU, Corvallis OR 97331-6502. 800-858-7378. Oregonian 10/17/95:B2. See also **Poison Control Center**.

Pesticides. In 1981, 31.42 million pounds of pesticides were used in Oregon. Wood preservatives accounted for over half, and soil fumigants used for potatoes, onions, and bulbs accounted for 11%. U.S. Geological Survey data found 25 pesticides in the **Willamette River**. The most common was atrazine, a weed killer, found at 90% of the 40 sample sites, but in all cases below drinking water standards. More than 400,000 pounds of atrazine were applied in the state in 1987, the last year data for pesticide use were compiled. The **Forest Practices Act** regulates the use of pesticides on state and private forest lands. Oregon Environmental Atlas; Oregonian 10/13/97:B7.

Peter Britt Festivals. See **Britt Festivals**.

Peter Iredale. A 278', four-masted British sailing ship that went aground on the beach south of the mouth of the **Columbia River** October 25, 1906. All 20 crew members reached shore safely. Remnants are still visible in the sand at **Fort Stevens State Park**. Pacific Graveyard.

Petrified wood. Wood that has been turned to stone by the gradual replacement of the wood by microcrystalline quartz. It is found through much of Oregon, especially in the central part of the state. A 60' petrified log was found in 1967 near **Lebanon**. Limb sections valued for their dendritic markings are found in **Crook County**. The amount of petrified wood that can be collected and the methods for collecting it are regulated by the government. Information is available from the **Bureau of Land Management**. Gem Trails of Oregon; Gemstones of North America, Vol. 2.

Petroglyphs and pictographs. Prehistoric designs or images. A petroglyph is cut into rock, while a pictograph is painted on rock with natural pigments. Many have been found throughout Oregon. Indian Rock Art; Pictographs and Petroglyphs. See also **Wallula Stone**.

Petroleum. In 1994, 65,358,000 barrels (362.6 trillion Btu) of petroleum products were used in Oregon at a cost of $2,843,100,000. 52% was **gasoline** for motor vehicles. The rest included asphalt and road oil (5%), distillate fuel (21%), aviation gasoline and jet fuel (7%), LPG (2%), lubricants (1%), residual fuel (7%), and other (5%). No petroleum is produced in the state. State Energy. See also **Heating oil**; **Natural gas**; **Oil**; **Ozokerite**; **Shale City**.

Petticoat Government. The term used for the city government of **Umatilla**, 1916-1920. In 1916 the wife of the incumbent mayor defeated her husband for mayor, and women were also elected as city recorder, treasurer, and to four council seats. The election received national media attention. The women provided the town with four years of solid, active government. "Umatilla's 'Petticoat Government'".

PGE. See **Portland General Electric**.

Phantom Bridge. A natural bridge, difficult to find (hence the name), located northwest of **Detroit**. It is on the French Creek Ridge Trail. The bridge is about 30 feet long and 40 feet above the ground. Treasures of the Oregon Country.

Pharmacy, State Board of. A board of seven members appointed by the governor to four-year terms. The board, created in 1891, provides information for the public, licenses pharmacists, and registers pharmacies, drug wholesalers, and manufacturers. Its activities are financed by license fees. In 1996 there were 2,484 pharmacists in the state. 800 NE Oregon St., #9, Suite 425, Portland 97232. 503-731-4032. Oregon Blue Book.

Pheasants. **Game birds**, none native to Oregon. The ring-necked pheasant, *Phasianus colchicus*, native to China, was introduced in 1882 on **Sauvie Island** and near **Lebanon** in the first successful pheasant plant in the U.S., and a hunting season was begun in 1891. However, as agricultural practices changed, its numbers have been declining. In 1993 a new strain of Chinese pheasant called the

Sichuan, more adaptable to a variety of habitats, was introduced in Oregon. <u>Atlas of Oregon Wildlife</u>; <u>Fish and Wildlife on the Oregon Trail</u>.

Phi Beta Kappa. An elite academic honor society with chapters at four Oregon colleges: **University of Oregon**, **Reed College**, **Lewis and Clark College**, and **Willamette University**. <u>Oregonian</u> 10/7/97:E4.

Philanthropy. A 1996 donation of $25 million to the **University of Oregon** from Phil Knight, cofounder of Nike, is the largest gift ever given to a northwest university. Earlier **Oregon State University** had received a gift of timberland from Kaye Richardson of **Falls City** which the university sold in 1994 for $23.8 million. <u>Oregonian</u> 5/24/96:A1. See also **Charitable giving**.

Philip Foster Historical Farm. A historic homestead in Eagle Creek, open as a living museum where visitors can participate in pioneer chores. It includes a home (1883), barn, blacksmith shop, pioneer gardens including an old-variety apple orchard, picnic tables, and a Pioneer Store. Philip Foster (1805-1884) came to Oregon by sea in 1843 and established his **donation land claim** and a store at **Oregon City**. He helped build **Barlow Road** past his farm and then sold meals and produce to those traveling the road. 29912 SE Highway 211, Estacada 97023. 503-630-5051. <u>Dictionary of Oregon History</u>.

Phillips Lake. A 1,475-acre reservoir 15 miles southwest of **Baker City** that is over four miles long and has a maximum depth of 125 feet. Part of the **Baker Project**, it was formed in 1968 by completion of Mason Dam on the **Powder River**. In addition to irrigation, the project provides flood control, fish and wildlife enhancement, and recreation, including camping, fishing, swimming, and water skiing. The lake was named for Fred Phillips, a long-time Baker City advocate of the project. <u>Atlas of Oregon Lakes</u>.

Philomath. "Lover of Learning." A **Willamette Valley** forest products town at the foot of the **Coast Range** in **Benton County**, six miles west of **Corvallis** on **Highways 20** and **34**. The town was founded in 1867 and named for the **United Brethren Church**'s then-new **Philomath College**. The city was incorporated in 1882. The annual Philomath Frolic and Rodeo is held in July and the Shrewsbury Renaissance Faire in September. The town is noted for its volunteers who have built several community facilities, including a new library. Population 1980 2,673; 1995 3,315. Elevation 279'. 980 Applegate St., 97370. 541-929-6148. Chamber of Commerce 541-929-2454. <u>Oregon Geographic Names</u>.

Philomath College. A **United Brethren Church** college that opened in 1867 and closed in 1929 due to financial problems. The name means lover of learning. Land surrounding the college was platted to form the town of **Philomath** with no grog shops, gambling saloons, or theaters allowed. The two-story building, constructed of **bricks** made on the site, now houses the Benton County Historical Museum. <u>Dictionary of Oregon History</u>.

Phoenix. A southwest Oregon town in **Jackson County** 4 miles southeast of **Medford** on **Highway 99**. Sam and Huldah Colver took up a **donation land claim** in 1851 where they built a large house of 14"-thick timbers that still stands. In 1854 a town was laid out around the house and was for some 20 years known as Gasburg in honor of the animated loquacity of the town's only available young lady. In about 1856 grist mill owner Sylvester M. Waite opened the post office. He used his fire insurance plate "Phoenix" as the name of the post office, though it was years before the name was used for the community. The phoenix is a legendary bird that consumed itself in a fire every 500 years and then rose again from the ashes. The city was incorporated in 1911. Nabari, Japan, is its sister city. Population 1980 2,309; 1995 3,615. Elevation 1,520'. PO Box 666, 97535. 541-535-1955. Land in Common; Early Days in Phoenix, Oregon.

Photographers. Early Oregon photographer Joseph Buchtel (1830-1916) arrived in **Portland** in 1852, and by 1884 had a collection of 25,000 negatives, most of them, however, destroyed while he was abroad. Benjamin Gifford, called "Dean of Oregon Photographers", did commercial, scenic, and portrait work in Portland and The Dalles, 1880s through the 1930s. Swiss-born photographer Peter Britt (1819-1905) arrived in **Jacksonville** in 1852 where he created a large collection of pioneer portraits and landscapes. Tom Cronise made over 30,000 photographs in Salem between 1892 and 1927; the **Oregon Historical Society** now has the negatives. **Pulitzer Prize** winning photojournalist David Hume Kennerly is from **Roseburg**. Ray Atkeson's Oregon (1968) was the first large-format photographic book published about a state. Dictionary of Oregon History; "Oregon Photography"; Oregonian 10/13/96: B1, 11/26/97:B2. See also **Oregon Photojournalism Day; Posters.**

Physical Therapist Licensing Board. An Oregon board of seven members appointed by the governor for four-year terms to license physical therapists and investigate complaints. In 1996 there were 2,279 physical therapists and over 600 physical therapist assistants licensed in the state. 800 NE Oregon St., Suite 407, Portland 97232. 503-731-4047. Oregon Blue Book.

Physician assistants. Persons who, following four years of college and 1/2 to 3 years of additional training, work under the supervision of physicians in offices, clinics, and hospitals. The Board of **Medical Examiners** approves the individual "practice description" that governs the work of each physician assistant. There were 263 in Oregon as of June 1997. The **Oregon Health Sciences University** operates a new training program. See also **Nurse practitioners.**

Physician-assisted suicide. Oregon was the first state in the nation to approve physician-prescribed lethal drugs for terminally ill persons who have requested them. The measure passed on November 8, 1994, with 52% in favor. The Catholic Church and the American Medical Association opposed the measure, but the Oregon Medical Association took no position at the time. Court cases blocked its implementation until November 1997, the same month that 60% of the voters refused to repeal the measure after the **legislature** had referred it for another vote. The idea was originally proposed by Governor Tom McCall in 1972 and was later promoted by the **Hemlock Society**. See also **Hospice care.**

Physicians. In 1997 Oregon had 7,457 active physicians. In 1993 the statewide ratio was 193 physicians per 100,000 residents, but **Multnomah County** had 407 physicians per 100,000 residents while **Gilliam, Sherman,** and **Wheeler** counties had none. Qualifications and disciplinary actions are governed by the Oregon Board of **Medical Examiners**. Oregon: A Statistical Overview. See also **Women's firsts.**

Physiographic province. See **Geography.**

PICA. See **Portland Institute for Contemporary Art**.

Picnic tables. Five single-plank picnic tables, each 85' long, were made from a single **Douglas fir** log by Hull-Oakes Lumber Company of **Monroe**. The tables are in parks of the area, including in Avery Park in **Corvallis**.

Pictographs. See **Petroglyphs**.

Picture Gorge. A gorge 38 miles west of **John Day** formed by erosion as the **John Day River** cut a 1500' deep canyon through **basalt**. It is named for Indian **pictographs** found in the area. One of the units of the **John Day Fossil Beds National Monument** is located in the gorge. Geology of Oregon.

Piddock. A three-inch long coastal clam, *Penitella penita*, sometimes called rock oyster. It lives tightly snugged into the bottom of a hole, up to 6 inches deep, that it has bored into soft rock. Various other animals may later inhabit the burrow it has made. Piddocks are sometimes gathered for food by breaking apart the rocks with a hammer. Seashells of the Pacific Northwest; Seashore Life.

Pika. (Pronounced PEE ka.) A small relative of the **rabbit**, *Ochotona princeps*, also called cony, that lives in mountain rock slides made up of rocks at least a foot in diameter. The pika scurries around the rocks on fur-padded feet, squeaking out an alarm call at intruders. It makes hay from most of the green plants in its environs; the haystacks lie deep in burrows under the rock slides where they provide winter food. **Martens** are a major predator. Several races are found in Oregon, with coloring to match the rocks in which they live. The pika is classed as a **protected animal**. Atlas of Oregon Wildlife; Mammals and Life Zones of Oregon; Mammals of the Northwest.

Pill Hill. The popular name given to Marquam Hill in southwest **Portland** because it is home to three major medical centers: the **Oregon Health Sciences University**, Shriners Hospital for Crippled Children, and Veterans Affairs Medical Center. Oregonian 10/5/94:D10; Round the Roses. See also **Skybridge**.

Pillars of Rome. Ornamented cliffs and columns, up to 100 feet high, that formed in tuffaceous sediments along the deep canyon where Jordan Creek merges with the **Owyhee River**. They are located four miles northwest of **Rome** in **Malheur County**. Geology of Oregon.

Pilot Butte. A prominent lone **cinder cone** east of **Bend** that served as a landmark for pioneers. It rises 500 feet above the surrounding area and provides a panoramic view from the overlook on top. It has been an undeveloped **state park** since 1927 . Geology of Oregon.

Pilot Rock. A 5,910' monolith in southern Oregon that rises above the ridge line three miles southeast of **Siskiyou Summit**. The landmark was noted at least as early as 1841 as a guide to the **Siskiyou Trail**. Oregon Geographic Names.

Pilot Rock (town). A northeast Oregon agricultural and lumber town in **Umatilla County**, located 13 miles south of **Pendleton** in the western foothills of the **Blue Mountains**. It is named for a nearby high bluff. The post office was established in 1868. The city was platted about 1876 and was incorporated in 1912. Population 1980 1,630; 1995 1,560. Elevation 1,637'. PO Box 130, 97868. 541-443-2811. Oregon Geographic Names; Tracking down Oregon.

Pilots. In 1995, the Oregon **Aeronautics Section** had nearly 9,000 pilots registered.

Pine. A conifer **tree** with woody cones and needles borne in bunches. Oregon has eight native pines. Lodgepole pine, *Pinus contorta*, has two needles per bunch and grows both in the mountains and along the coast where it is called shore pine. Oregon's three-needle pines include the wide-spread **ponderosa pine**, *P. ponderosa*; the similar Jeffrey pine, *P. jeffreyi*, of southern Oregon; and knobcone pine, *P. attenuata*, in the southwestern interior. The five needle pines include Western white pine, *P. monticola*, which grows in scattered mid-elevation sites; **sugar pine**, *P. lambertiana*, with its foot-long cones, in southern Oregon; limber pine, *P. flexilis*, above 7,000 feet in the **Wallowa Mountains**; and whitebark pine, *P. albicaulis.*, which grows near timberline in the **Cascade Mountains** and in a few high spots in eastern Oregon. Trees to Know. See also **KMX**.

Pine Mountain Observatory. A **University of Oregon** astronomical observatory on 6,395' Pine Mountain, 34 miles southeast of **Bend**, that opened in 1967. It houses 15, 24, and 32-inch telescopes, with the largest used for computer-stored electronic images. The observatory is open to the public on summer weekend evenings. **Deschutes County**, in which the observatory is located, has adopted an ordinance limiting light pollution in the night sky. 541-683-1381. Oregonian 4/27/97:D4.

Pink elephant. On May 18, 1961, promoter and boater Jack Matlack pulled Miss Bimbo, a live, water-skiing, pink-painted elephant outfitted in a purple bikini, down the **Willamette River** through **Portland**. Oregonian reporter Linda Lampman, also in a purple swimsuit, managed to stay atop Miss Bimbo for part of the ride. The stunt was undertaken to publicize a circus. "Pink Elephants on the Willamette."

Pioneer Courthouse. An 1873 downtown **Portland** building, designed by A. B. Mullett, that was the first major federal building constructed in the Northwest. It was built oddly distant from the city center which was along the river front at that time, but the city has since grown around it. Refurbished in 1973, it now serves the 9th U.S. Circuit Court of Appeals. The second floor courtroom is open to the public when court is not in session. 520 SW Morrison. Oregonian 2/23/96:C3; Portland, An Informal History.

Pioneer Courthouse Square. "Portland's living room" is a European-style plaza occupying the downtown city block between Morrison and Yamhill, Sixth and Broadway. Once the site of the **Portland Hotel** and then for 30 years a parking lot, the square, an **urban renewal** project, was designed by Will Martin and opened in 1984 as a public space and center for many Portland events. Bricks paving the square carry the names of over 64,000 contributors. Other attractions include a coffee shop, an iron gate left from the Portland Hotel, terra cotta columns echoing nearby buildings, a waterfall, amphitheater, sculptures, including the **Weather Machine** and **Allow Me**, a travel bookstore, and rest rooms. The **Transit Mall** and **MAX** meet at the square, and **Tri-Met** has a transit information office there. 701 SW 6th Avenue. 503-223-1613. Frozen Music; Portland, An Informal History.

Pioneer Place. An upscale four-block commercial mall, opened in 1990, in downtown **Portland** between Third and Fifth Avenues and Morrison and Taylor Streets. The area includes a four-level pavilion housing over 70 specialty stores,

Saks Fifth Avenue department store, a 16-story office building, a parking structure, and a vacant block being held for future construction. $32 million of the $134.5 million cost came from city and state funds. 700 SW 5th Av. Oregonian 6/18/95:E1.

Pioneer Spirit. A 10-ton statue of a horse and rider emplaced in **Springfield** for the 1959 Oregon Centennial. The blocky, impressionistic, white-washed, cement statue, also known as the White Horse, has been criticized for its lack of artistic merit but has gained adherents as a civic symbol. Oregonian 5/11/97:D4.

Pioneers. Those who came to Oregon before Oregon became a state in 1859; nearly all came by land rather than by sea. During the 1840's Oregon's population included the native **Indians** (much decimated by **epidemics**); the **French Canadians** (former **Hudson's Bay Company** trappers) and their Indian wives around **Saint Paul**; the "Rocky Mountain Boys" (former American **fur trappers**) in the Tualatin valley; the **Methodist** community near **Salem**; the midwestern American farmers who had come over the **Oregon Trail** and who settled throughout the **Willamette Valley**; and the shop keepers, many of them from **New England**. The 1850 census showed that 53% of the adults had been born north of the Mason-Dixon line and 46% south of it, while 80% of the children had been born in the frontier midwest states. Only 7% of the total **population** of 12,093 was over 45 years old. The pioneers had been encouraged to come by the promise of economic opportunity and free land, reports of a benign and healthful climate, patriotism, and restlessness. Dictionary of Oregon History; "Origins of the Population of Oregon in 1850;" That Balance So Rare. See also **Oregon Pioneer Association**; **Oregonians, character**.

Pipelines. See **Natural gas pipelines**; **Oil**.

Pittock Mansion. A city-owned, 22-room French Renaissance chateau located nearly 1,000 feet above **Portland** with views east over the city to the **Cascade Range**. Designed by San Francisco architect Edward Foulkes for Henry and Georgiana Pittock, the house, completed in 1914, featured a personal shower, an elevator, an intercom, a central vacuum system, and a walk-in freezer. It was rescued from demolition by a community group in 1964 and the 46-acre grounds were made part of a chain of parks in the West Hills. The Gate Lodge Restaurant serves lunch. Admission fee. 3229 N.W. Pittock Drive, Portland 97210. 503-823-3623. Century of Portland Architecture; Oregonian 2/2/97:L9; Portland Guidebook.

Place names. As of 1992, the U.S. Geological Survey's Geographic Names Information System listed about 45,000 names for Oregon. Oregon Geographic Names lists over 5,400 of the most significant and mentions some 2,000 more. Oregon's colorful but little-known place names include Hawksy Walksy, a dry lake bed, and Oregon End Table, a mesa, both in southwest **Harney County**; Mugwump Lake in **Warner Valley**; Helloff in **Tillamook County**; Hell-for Slim Draw and Unnecessary Mountain north of **Klamath Falls**; and Tom Dick and Harry Mountain southwest of **Government Camp**. Long-gone communities or post offices in eastern Oregon include Follyfarm, Lonely, Lonesomehurst, Voltage, and Whorehouse Meadows. A number of place names that sound descriptive are actually derived from personal names, such as **Boring**, Drinkwater Pass (though nearby

Stinking Water Pass is descriptive), Fields, Goodpasture Island, Golden Falls, Officer's Cave, Pleasant Valley, **Reedsport**, **Riddle**, **Roseburg**, Savage Rapids, **Spray**, Sterling Mine, Vineyard Mountain, Virtue Flats, **Westport**, and Woods. Two Oregon towns, **Coburg** and **Mount Vernon**, are named for horses, and one, **Malin**, is named for a kind of horseradish. Oregon Geographic Names; Oregon Oddities; Tracking down Oregon. See also **Gouge Eye**; **Lakes**.

Placer gold. Gold that has weathered free from the rocks in which it was formed (in the rocks it is called **lode gold**) and concentrated in stream deposits or, on the coast, in **black sand**. It is mined by **gold panning**, sluicing, **gold dredging**, or **hydraulic mining**. Placer gold usually ranges in size from tiny flakes up to grains of wheat, though larger **gold nuggets** have been found. Long **ditches** were often dug to carry water to placer mines. Of Oregon's total gold production of 5.8 million fine ounces before 1965, 3.5 million was from placer deposits. Some small placer operations are currently in operation. Gold and Silver in Oregon.

Plague. A disease, caused by a bacterium, *Yersinia pestis*, that occurs in several forms, one of which swept through Asia and Europe in the 14th century. It is transmitted by fleas from **ground squirrels**, **pocket gophers**, **chipmunks**, **rats**, and **rabbits**, and is found throughout Oregon except in the northwest counties. Thirteen cases have been reported in the state since 1934, including in **Deschutes County** in 1995. It can be fatal if untreated. It is not contagious unless pneumonia develops. Oregonian 10/7/95:D2.

Plains of Abraham. See **Cove Island**.

Plane crashes. On October 28, 1947, a plane crash west of **Lakeview** killed the pilot and three Republican state leaders: **Governor** Earl Snell, **Secretary of State** Robert Farrell, Jr., and Senate President Marshall Cornett. (John Hall, Speaker of the House, became Governor.) On December 28, 1978, United Airlines Flight 173, a DC-8, crashed near East Burnside and 157th Avenue in **Portland**, killing 10. On November 22, 1996, an Air Force HC-130 crashed at sea off California, killing 10 of the 11 Portland-area reservists aboard. Oregonian 11/3/97:E12. See also **Crater Lake**; **Disasters**; **World War II**.

Planes. See **Aircraft**.

Planetariums. Buildings in which images of the night sky are projected onto a domed ceiling. Oregon's planetariums include those at **OMSI**, 503-797-4000; **Mount Hood Community College**, 503-667-7297; **Chemeketa Community College**, 503-399-5161; Lane Education Service District 541-689-6500, ext. 227, and North Medford High School, 541-776-8726. See also **Observatories**.

Plank roads. The first surfacing for Oregon **wagon roads** was made of split logs or wooden planks, laid crosswise, and sometimes topped with lengthwise boards. These plank roads made possible year-round travel on roads that were otherwise impassable in winter mud. The first plank road in Oregon was **Canyon Road**, built in 1851-53 by **Portland** entrepreneurs. A plank road built in 1899 provided the first year-round route between **Tillamook** and **Nestucca**. First 75 Years; Tillamook. See also **"Get Oregon Out of the Mud"**.

Planning goals. Oregon has 19 statewide goals with which local comprehensive plans must be consistent. The goals deal with 1: Citizen Involvement, 2: Land Use Planning, 3: Agricultural Land, 4: Forest Lands, 5: Open Space, Scenic and Historic Areas, and Natural Resources, 6: Air, Water, and Land Resources Quality, 7: Areas Subject to Natural Hazards and Disasters, 8: Recreational Needs, 9: Economic Development, 10: Housing, 11: Public Facilities and Services, 12: Transportation, 13: Energy Conservation, 14: Urbanization, 15: Willamette River Greenway, 16: Estuarine Resources, 17: Coastal Shorelands, 18: Beaches and Dunes, 19: Ocean Resources. Oregon Statewide Planning Goals; Planning the Oregon Way. See also **Land Use Planning**.

Plants, non-native. See **Introduced species**.

Plants, wild. See **Algae**; **Ferns**; **Flora**; **Introduced species**; **Lichens**; **Mosses**; **Mushrooms**; **Native plants**; **Shrubs**; **Trees**; **Vegetation**; **Weeds**; **Wildflowers**.

Plate tectonics. A geologic theory that the earth's surface is made up of about a dozen large moving plates. **Earthquakes** and **volcanic eruptions** are characteristic of the zones where the plates are moving past each other either horizontally, vertically, or both. Along the **Cascadia subduction zone** off the coast of Oregon, the Juan de Fuca Plate, which lies under the Pacific Ocean off most of the coast of Oregon, is pushing under the North America Plate on which Oregon rests at a rate of about 1.5 inches per year (24 miles in a million years), slower than the 3-inch per year rate of 35 million years ago. The leading edge of the Juan de Fuca plate melts after it has been rammed some 90 miles down under the continental plate. This melted rock, or magma, is lighter than the solid rock above it and so pushes its way up toward the surface. Thus the **Cascade Range**, with its line of volcanic peaks 100 miles from the coast, marks the melting edge 90 miles below. From the time the plate subducts until some of it reemerges on the surface as lava takes about 20 million years. The geology becomes more complex south of **Cape Blanco**, both offshore and onshore. Geology of Oregon; Oregon Oceanbook. See also **Ocean floor**; **Volcanoes**.

Playa. The flat floor of an undrained desert basin, sometimes covered by a shallow lake. A number of playas are found in eastern Oregon, including in **Alvord Basin**. See also **Mud cracks**.

Plaza Blocks. A line of three **Portland** park blocks fronted by many public buildings, extending from Salmon Street south to Jefferson between 3rd and 4th avenues. Lownsdale Square, north of the **elk statue** in Main Street, and Chapman Square to the south were dedicated in 1852 as courthouse squares. They have been the scene of political speeches, anti-**Chinese** riots in the 1880s, and the great 1883 **celebration** of the first transcontinental train. In 1924 "undesirable male elements" led to Chapman Square being reserved for women. William Chapman (1808-1892) and Daniel Lownsdale (1803-1862) were pioneer Portland businessmen. The third block was developed in 1974 and named for Terry D. Schrunk (1913-1975), long-time Portland mayor. The **Suzhou stone** was placed in Schrunk Plaza in 1997. Portland, An Informal History; Dictionary of Oregon History; Round the Roses.

Plea bargaining. A procedure used when a **court** case against a defendant is virtually airtight and, instead of going to an expensive trial, the court accepts a plea bargain in which the defendant pleads guilty and the charges and penalties are negotiated. About 80 to 90% of cases "plead out." Oregonian 6/29/97:L5. See also **Polygraph**.

Plea for the Indians. A small book in which John Beeson (1803-1889), formerly from southern Oregon, argued against the prevailing treatment of Indians. The views of Beeson, an 1853 pioneer with farm and family near **Talent**, had made him so unpopular during the **Rogue River War** that he had to flee the area. He spent most of the rest of his life traveling and speaking on behalf of Indians, with, however, little to show for his efforts. Other Side of Oregon.

Pleistocene. The current geologic epoch, which includes the two million years since the end of the **Pliocene**, though the most recent 10,000 years is sometimes called the Holocene epoch. During the Pleistocene, **volcanic eruptions** are creating the high **Cascade Range**, and there have been eruptions along the **Brothers fault zone**. At least four ice ages have occurred during the Pleistocene, periods of cool, wet weather with extensive **glaciation** separated by very dry periods. Massive walls of water rushed down the **Columbia River** in the **Pleistocene floods**. Large **Pleistocene lakes** filled many of the valleys of eastern Oregon as recently as 10,000 years ago. Geology of Oregon.

Pleistocene floods. Between 15,500 and 12,800 years ago a number of floods rushed down the **Columbia River** as an ice dam on the Clark Fork River in Montana repeatedly formed and ruptured, releasing up to 400 cubic miles of water in each catastrophic deluge. There were perhaps 100 of these floods, averaging one every 27 years. These were the world's largest known floods, emptying the earth's largest known lake, Glacial Lake Missoula. The wall of water would pour across eastern Washington and down the Columbia River, scouring basins as it went and then backing up in several temporary lakes: Lake Lewis north of **Wallula Gap**, Lake Condon from Wallula Gap west to **The Dalles**, and Lake Allison in the **Willamette Valley** south nearly to **Eugene**. The floodwaters, blocked by the **Coast Range** north of **Portland**, were 400 feet deep at Portland. They deposited 100 feet of silt and gravel in the Willamette Valley, along with **erratics** (boulders from the Rockies that had been frozen in ice floes). An **Indian** stone knife has been found in the gravels of the flood. The floods are sometimes called the Missoula floods or the Bretz floods for Harlen Bretz who first described the process in the 1920s. Geology of Oregon; Sandal and the Cave.

Pleistocene lakes. Vast pluvial lakes that covered much of south central Oregon during the wet periods of the **Pleistocene**, most recently until about 11,000 years ago. The largest were Fort Rock Lake at 1,400 square miles (900,000 acres, or 42 miles across if round), Lake Modoc (**Upper Klamath Lake** is a remnant) which stretched 75 miles and covered 1,096 square miles, and Malheur Lake (**Malheur** and **Harney lakes** are remnants) covering 900 square miles. Others included Alvord Lake (491 square miles), Lake Coleman (**Warner Lakes**) 483 square miles, Lake Chewaucan (**Lake Abert** and **Summer Lake**) 461 square miles, **Goose Lake**, Catlow Lake, and Alkali Lake. The ancient shorelines can be seen in many places. Geology of Oregon.

Pliocene. A geologic epoch between the **Miocene** and the **Pleistocene**, from 2 to 11 million years before the present. During the Pliocene the climate was cool and dry, especially east of the **Cascade Range**. Oregon's coastline was about where it is now. The **basin and range** area of southeastern Oregon was stretched, resulting in block faulting and eruptions of **basalt** and **rhyolite**; **volcanic erup-**

tions also formed buttes in the **Portland** area, continued to build the high Cascades, and produced small cones over a large area around **Bend**. **Uplift** continued in the Cascades and the **Coast Range** with some folding and faulting. Extensive deposits of soil and gravel filled valleys over much of the state. Geology of Oregon. See also **Portland geology**.

Plover. See **Snowy plover**.

Pluvial lakes. See **Pleistocene lakes**.

Plywood. A building material created by laminating thin sheets of veneer (shaved from logs) together with the grain alternating. The first plywood in Oregon was created in 1901; it became common in the 1920s after better glues were developed. The number of plywood plants in Oregon declined 42% between 1980 and 1990. See also **Forest products industry**.

Poaching. Poaching, the illegal killing of game animals, can be reported by calling 800-452-788; rewards are offered. The U.S. and Canadian wildlife crime hot line is 800-800-WARDEN or 719-576-1564. See also **Forensics Laboratory**.

Pocket gopher. A medium sized rodent that excavates underground burrows using its incisors as well as its front paws. Pocket gophers live primarily on the roots they encounters as they dig, which they carry in their external cheek pouches (pockets). The five species found in Oregon, all genus *Thomomys*, are from 8 to 12 inches long. The Camas pocket gopher of the **Willamette Valley** is the largest. Atlas of Oregon Wildlife; Mammals and Life Zones of Oregon; Mammals of the Northwest.

Podiatrists. See **Medical Examiners**.

POE. Port of entry. See **Motor Carrier Transportation**.

Poets laureate. In 1923 the Oregon Authors' Club selected, and Governor Pierce proclaimed, Edwin Markham (1852-1940), born in **Oregon City**, as Oregon's first poet laureate. In 1951 Ben Hur Lampman (1886-1954) was appointed as the second. Ethel Romig Fuller (1883-1965) was poet laureate from 1957 to 1965. William Stafford (1914-1993), professor at **Lewis and Clark College**, was appointed in 1975 but resigned in 1987 in an unsuccessful effort to encourage the legislature to involve the poet laureate in the active encouragement of poetry, especially in the schools. It remains an honorary position established by legislation which requires that the governor appoint a poet laureate for four years and that the person be a poet who has lived in the state for at least 10 years, is publicly recognized and well regarded as a poet, and who captures the beauty and spirit of the state through verse. Dictionary of Oregon History; Writers of West Portland.

Poets. Some of Oregon's notable poets, in addition to those named as Oregon **poet laureate**, include Sam Simpson (1846-1899); Cincinnatus Hiner (Joaquin) Miller (1834-1913) of **Canyon City**; Charles Erskine Scott Wood (1852-1944), corporation lawyer and reformer; H. L. Davis (1894-1960) of **Yoncalla** who won the Levinson Prize in 1919; and **Pulitzer Prize** winner Phyllis McGinley (1905-1978). Oregon State Poetry Association, PO Box 602, West Linn 97068. Dictionary of Oregon History; From Here We Speak; Tracking down Oregon. See also **Astoria; Camp Angell; Literature; National Book Award**.

Point Adams. A low forested peninsula on the south side of the mouth of the **Columbia River**. It is, at 46°12'44"N, not quite the most northerly point in Oregon. It was named by Captain Robert Gray in 1792 in honor of John Adams, later elected president. Earlier, in 1775, Captain Bruno Heceta had called it Cabo Frondoso, or Leafy Cape, because of the number of trees on it. **Fort Stevens State Park** occupies much of the point. **Clatsop Spit** extends from the point north into the mouth of the river. Oregon Geographic Names. See also **Latitude and longitude**.

Poison Control Center. Toll-free telephone assistance in case of suspected poisoning is available 24 hours a day from the Oregon Poison Control Center. In Portland call (503) 494-8968. Elsewhere in Oregon call 800-452-7165. 3181 SW Sam Jackson Park Road, Portland 97201.

Poison oak. A plant, *Rhus diversiloba*, with three-part leaves, white berries, and variable growth habit. In forests it grows as both a low ground cover and as a vigorous vine, while in the open it becomes a large sturdy **shrub** thicket. It is a member of the cashew family. Though honey made from its flowers is choice, the leaves, stems, and roots contain an oil, urushiol, that causes dermatitis in 80% of the population. The leaves turn red in the fall, tempting some to gather it for decoration. Smoke from burning poison oak twigs can cause serious bronchial irritation, and some have been hospitalized after using the stems for roasting hot dogs. Poison ivy is a closely related species found in eastern Oregon. Stories that the **Indians** were immune to poison oak and ivy would seem belied by the number of Indian cures that are also found in folklore. Research at the **Oregon Health Sciences University** has found Stokogard Outdoor Creme to be the only effective protection against poison oak, ivy, and sumac. Oregonian 7/2/95:C2; Plants and Animals. See also **Indian burning**.

Poisonous animals. Animals with toxins that cause illness or death to humans. Those in Oregon include **rattlesnakes**, three **spiders**, a **salamander**, and eggs of the cabezon fish (sculpin). **Clams** and **mussels** can be deadly during periods of **red tide**. Bee stings cause more deaths in the U.S. than do snakes. Punctures from fin spines of scorpion fish and rockfish can cause painful wounds, though they are not fatal. Oregon Wildlife 48(4):14 July/August 1992.

Poisonous plants. At least three dozen genera of native and naturalized plants found in Oregon are poisonous to humans. Among the most dangerous are death camas, *Zigadenus venenosus*, poison hemlock, *Conium maculatum*; water hemlock, *Cicuta sp*; nightshades, *Solanum sp*; *Letharia*, a fluorescent green lichen, and some **mushrooms**. **Poison oak** is a common cause of dermatitis. Name Your Poison.

Poles in Oregon. A number of people from Poland came to Oregon in the 1890s. Since 1994, **Portland**'s Polish community has sponsored an annual festival in late September at St. Stanislaus Polish Catholic Church. Oregonian 9/29/96:B4.

Police. See **Law enforcement**.

Police Academy. See **Public Safety Standards and Training Board**.

Police Historical Museum. A museum on the 16th floor of the **Justice Center** that displays vintage police equipment. 1120 SW 3rd Avenue. 503-823-0019. Portland Guidebook.

Police, Oregon State (OSP). The state's comprehensive **law enforcement**

agency. In 1980 Oregon voters changed funding for state police from the **gas tax** to the **general fund**. Since then the number of state police has dropped and the focus changed from patrol to crime investigation. The department operates crime laboratories around the state, houses all fingerprint records, and has been assigned responsibility for, among other things, the **Emergency Management Division**, office of the **Fire Marshal**, the **Boxing and Wrestling Commission**, Drug Abuse Reduction through Education (D.A.R.E.), Missing Children Clearinghouse, Wildlife Protection; and the Law Enforcement Data Systems. Since the agency was created in 1931, 15 Oregon State Police officers have been fatally shot. 400 Public Service Bldg., Salem 97310. 503-378-3720. Oregon Blue Book; Oregonian 10/17/96:C2. See also **Law enforcement**.

Polio. A viral disease, poliomyelitis (earlier called infantile paralysis), that attacks nerve cells. Epidemics swept the U.S. periodically until vaccines were developed in the 1950s. In two weeks in 1953 **Mercy Flights** transported 23 cases from **Medford** to larger hospitals. The disease caused permanent nerve damage to about half of those known to have had it and was fatal to 8%. In Oregon about 2,500 of the 10,000 polio survivors have developed post-polio syndrome as their surviving muscle-control nerves wear out from overwork. Easter Seal Society, 5757 SW Macadam Avenue, Portland 97201. 503-228-5108 or 800-556-6020. Oregonian 5/11/95:C10.

Political parties. Oregon political parties that met the qualifications for placing candidates on 1995 ballot were the **Democrat, Republican**, Libertarian, Pacific, American, and New Alliance parties. At each **primary election** registered voters in each party elect two persons from the precinct (precinct committee workers) to serve on the party's county committee. Delegates from the county committee make up the party's state central committee. Parties are not particularly powerful in Oregon and many precinct positions are vacant. State party conventions tend to be more extreme than the party's registered voters. Historically, Oregon's early Democrats tended to be southern sympathizers who favored statehood, while the Whigs, forerunners of the Republicans, opposed it. Though Oregon from 1900 to 1970 was fairly solidly Republican, party loyalties before and since have been more evenly divided. **Independent**s have been the fastest growing group. Governing Oregon. See also **Communists; Independence party; Know Nothing party; Oregon Commonwealth Federation; Populist; Third party candidates; Union party; Voter registration; Voter turnout**.

Politics. Oregon's first settlers came from a frontier tradition of democracy, states' rights, antimonopoly and anti-British sentiment, and self-determination. Political **corruption** in the 19th century led to **Populists'** reforms and the **Oregon System** of **initiative, recall**, and **referendum**. Politics in the 20th century have been characterized by an urban/rural split, an assumption that the political debate is open to everyone and that the people should have the last word on public policy, a remarkable lack of corruption, and a tradition of innovation. Empire of the Columbia; Governing Oregon. See also **Political parties; Western States Center**.

Polk County. A farm and forest county that extends from the **Willamette River** at **Salem** across the western **Willamette Valley** up into the **Coast Range**. Incorporated cities are **Dallas** (county seat), **Falls City, Independence, Monmouth**, and **Willamina**. The county is bounded by **Yamhill, Marion, Linn, Benton, Lincoln** and **Tillamook** counties. Elevations range from 100' along the Willamette to 3,589' Laurel Mountain in the west. The county was created in 1845 from **Yamhill District** and named for then newly-elected president James K. Polk (1795-1849). The economy is based on agriculture, forest products, manufacturing, and education. Taxable assessed value in 1995 was $2,236,000,000, or $40,000 per capita.. Population 1980 45,203; 1995 55,400. Area 745 square miles. Density 74/sq.mi. Annual precipitation 51"; average temperature January 39°F, July 66°F. Courthouse, 850 Main St., Dallas 97338. 503-623-8173. History of Polk County; Oregon Blue Book.

Poll tax. The 1862 session of the legislature adopted a one dollar poll tax "to be paid by each and every male person over twenty-one and under fifty years of age." It also adopted a measure requiring "That each and every negro, Chinaman, **kanaka**, and mulatto residing within the limits of this state shall pay an annual poll tax of five dollars for the use of the County...". The law was accidentally repealed in 1864 and attempts to repass it were unsuccessful. **Union County** had at one time a "poll tax" that required each adult man to furnish two days of labor each year for road work. History of Union County; Peculiar Paradise; "Unwelcome Settlers."

Pollution. The U.S. Environmental Protection Agency list of Oregon's polluters includes companies that release toxic chemicals to the air, land, or water. These releases may be done under permit and don't necessarily violate the law. In 1993 the top 10 were 3M in **White City**, 1,389,650 pounds; Boise Cascade in **Saint Helens** 1,127,060 pounds; Glenbrook Nickel, **Riddle** 1,123,708 pounds; Rexham Graphics, **Portland** 950,000 pounds; Simpson Investment, **Portland**, 887,220 pounds; Weyerhaeuser, **Springfield** 768,369 pounds; Pope & Talbot, **Halsey** 741,550 pounds; Georgia-Pacific Resins, **Albany** 655,100 pounds; James River Paper, **Clatskanie** 601,178 pounds; and Wah Chang, **Albany** 548,100 pounds. Oregonian 3/28/95:B8. See also **Air pollution; Toxic pollutants; Water pollution**.

Polygraph. A machine designed to measure the body's involuntary responses, such as blood pressure, heart rate, and sweat. A semiannual seven-week accredited polygraph course offered through the Board on **Public Safety Standards and Training** at **Western Oregon University** is one of seven in the nation. Polygraph results are not admissible in Oregon courts, though polygraphs are used for monitoring some parolees, evaluating candidates for **plea bargaining**, and for screening suspects. Some polygraph studies report an accuracy level of 97%, depending upon the skill of the operator. Oregonian 4/10/95:B4.

Pompous Twit awards. Awards that were given by political columnist Ron Blankenbaker of the Salem **Statesman Journal** to politicians for offenses such as spending a record amount of money to get elected. At Christmas the twits were invited to atone for their deeds by contributing to a charity drive called "Pompous Twits Anonymous." From their inception until Blankenbaker retired in 1996, every Oregon governor and member of Congress managed to earn an award. Governing Oregon.

Ponderosa pine. A **pine**, *Pinus ponderosa*, that is the major timber tree of eastern Oregon and is also found in the Willamette Valley and southern Oregon. Its lumber is prized for interior work, and its fiber is used for pulp and fiberboard. Usually ponderosa requires at least 15 inches of annual rainfall, but in the **Lost Forest** it grows with only 10 inches a year because the ground structure traps moisture. Large old trees with their glowing golden bark are known as yellow bellies. The largest, a national co-champion, is in **La Pine State Park**. It is 342 inches in circumference (9 feet in diameter), and 178 feet tall. Stands of ponderosa pine do best with low-intensity ground fires every 10 to 15 years which burn competing vegetation while the ponderosas survive, protected by their thick bark. A **Winema National Forest** interpretive site called Desert Forest Journeys, located 10 miles east of **Diamond Lake**, shows ponderosa pine forest ecology. Trees to Know. See also **L'Arbre Seul**.

Pony Express. A legendary and financially troubled transcontinental private mail service operated by Russell, Majors, and Waddell between St. Joseph, Missouri, and Sacramento, California, from April 3, 1860 until displaced by the telegraph in October 1861. More generally, any **express service** of the time that used horseback riders. (Freight was carried by **pack strings**.) Oregon had a number of such routes in the 1850s and '60s that served gold camps until displaced by **stage lines** after **wagon roads** were opened. A 225-mile pony express route from **Canyon City** to **The Dalles** took 28 hours; the charge was fifty cents for a letter or 3% of the weight for gold dust. Dictionary of Oregon History.

Poplar. See **Cottonwood**.

Population. Oregon's population on July 1, 1997, was 3,217,000 as estimated by the **Center for Population Research and Census**. Oregon has about 1% of the nation's population while California's has about 10%. **Multnomah County** is the most populous county in the state with over 600,000 people, while **Wheeler County** had fewer than 1,400 in 1995. **Portland**, with nearly 500,000 people, was the largest incorporated city and **Greenhorn**, population 3, was the smallest, while **Moro** in **Sherman County**, with a population of 290, was the smallest county seat. See also **Census; Metropolitan Areas; Portland-Vancouver Consolidated Metropolitan Statistical Area; School enrollment**.

Population density. In 1996 Oregon had a population density of 33.4 per square mile, up from 27.4 per square mile in 1980. The national average in 1996 was 75 per square mile and California had over 200 per square mile. Density in Oregon ranged from fewer than 1 person per square mile in **Harney, Lake**, and **Wheeler** counties to 1,440 per square mile in **Multnomah County**. Oregon: A Statistical Overview; Oregonian 1/1/98:A1.

Population distribution, age. In 1995 persons from birth through age 17 accounted for 26% of the state's total population of 3,132,000. Ages 18 through 64 accounted for 60%, and those 65 and older accounted for 14% - but are expected to account for 22% by 2040 when the state's median age will have increased from the present 35.9 to 41.1. **Malheur** and **Jefferson** counties led in the percent of children, with 31% of their population 17 and younger, while the lowest percent of children were in **Benton County** (22%) and **Curry County** (21%). On the other hand Curry County led with the highest percent of those 65 and older (25%), though Benton County had the lowest percent of seniors (10%), and the highest percent of adults ages 18-64 (68%). In the retirement community of **King City**, 84% were 65 or over. Oregon: A Statistical Overview.

Population distribution, gender. The 1990 census counted 1,445,248 women in Oregon and 1,397,073 men. There were 105.3 men per 100 women under the age of 18, while over the age of 80 the ratio was 51.6 men per 100 women.

Population distribution, geographic. Oregon's population is concentrated along the **Interstate 5** corridor and especially in the **Willamette Valley**. Eighty-seven percent of Oregon's population live west of the **Cascade Range** with 70% in the **Willamette Valley**. Twenty percent of the people of the state live in **Multnomah County**, 10% in neighboring **Clackamas County** and 12% in **Washington County**. The 1990 census found that 71% of the state's population was urban. The entire southeast quarter of the state holds only 1% of the state's population. Oregon: A Statistical Overview; Oregon Environmental Atlas.

Population distribution, racial and ethnic. The 1990 census found that 4% of Oregon's population identified itself as **Hispanic**, 1.4% as **Indian**, 1.6% as African American, and 2.4% as Asian or Pacific Islander. The counties with the highest percentage of Hispanics were **Malheur** (20%), **Hood River** (16%), and **Jefferson** and **Morrow**, (11% each). Counties with the highest percent of Indians were **Jefferson** (20%), and **Wasco** and **Klamath** (4% each). **Multnomah County** had 6% African American, the only county with more than 1%. **Benton County** had 5.5% Asian, followed by **Multnomah** (4.7%) and **Washington** (4.3%) By 1995 Oregon had a total population of 3,141,000. Of that, 2,929,000 (93.3%) were white, 151,000 (4.8%) were Hispanic, 111,000 (3.5%) were Asian or Pacific Islander, 54,000 (1.7%) were Black, and 47,000 (1.5%) were American Indian. By the year 2010, the U.S. Census Bureau estimates that Oregon's total population will be 3,876,000, and that the composition will be 3,508,000 (90.5%) white, 265,000 (6.8%) Hispanic, 238,000 (6.1%) Asian or Pacific Islander, 70,000 (1.8%) Black, and 60,000 (1.5%) American Indian. Oregon: A Statistical Overview; Oregonian 6/16/96:C4.

Population growth since 1980. Oregon's population grew 7.9% between the 1980 and 1990 census though the state's **Hispanic** population grew 71.2%. Twelve counties lost population, while five counties each grew more than 15%. Then, between 1990 and 1995 the state's population grew an estimated 10.2%, and it is expected to grow a total of 18.1% between 1990 and the year 2000. The state's population has been increasing by approximately 50,000 persons annually. The excess of **births** over **deaths** accounts for 15,000 of those, and the rest of the increase, about 35,000, is because more people are moving in than moving out, about half of them from California. It has been estimated that about a fourth of the state's 1997 residents did not live in the state seven years earlier. The **Portland** metropolitan area and **Bend** area are the fastest growing areas of the state. Metro area population is expected to increase by 440,500 to a total of 1,800,000 by 2015, and the state's population is expected to increase to 3,500,000 by 2003 and 5,190,000 by 2040. Facts of Life; Oregon: A Statistical Overview; Oregonian 4/26/95:E1, 1/23/97:A1, 10/17/97:D1, 11/7/97:A1, 4/7/98:E11. See also **Economic Analysis Office**; **Housing**; **Immigrants**.

Population history, Oregon. During the first decade of settlement between

1840 and 1850, Oregon grew by 12,000 new residents at the same time that, for comparison, Wisconsin added 275,000.

1840   150   Estimated white population.
1850   12,093   U.S. Census (<u>Oregon Blue Book</u>)
1860   52,465   "
1870   90,923   "
1880   174,768   "
1890   317,704   "
1900   413,536   "
1910   672,765   "
1920   783,389   "
1930   953,786   "
1940 1,089,684   "
1950 1,521,341   "
1960 1,768,687   "
1970 2,091,533   "
1980 2,633,321   "
1990 2,842,321   "
1995 3,132,000   estimate, **Center for Population Research**.
2000 3,400,000 projected
2025 4,556,000 projected
2040 5,190,000 projected

Population projections. Various population projections have estimated that Oregon will have 3,400,000 people by the year 2000, 4,556,000 by 2025, and 5,190,000 by 2040. By 2025 it is estimated that 21% of the population will be over 65 (up from 14% in 1997), and that 81% will be white (down from 89% in 1997), 10% **Hispanic** (up from 5% in 1997), 5% **Asian** (up from 3% in 1997), 2% **Black** (2% in 1997), and 2% American **Indian** (1% in 1997). <u>Oregonian</u> 11/23/97:F2.

Populist. A member of the People's Party, organized nationally in 1891 and the next year in Oregon. Populists advocated free silver, direct government, an income tax, and banking reform. Four Populists served in the 1893 Oregon legislature and ten in 1895. Planks of the party platform were eventually taken over by the **Republican** and **Democratic** parties, and the reform impulse led to adoption of the **Oregon System**. <u>Dictionary of Oregon History</u>; <u>Empire of the Columbia</u>. See also **Union Party**.

Porcupine. A large, slow-moving rodent, *Erethizon dorsatum*, weighing 20 to 30 pounds. It is nearly covered with coarse hair interspersed with long, hollow quills that make it an efficient swimmer. A porcupine will drive the barbed tail quills into an attacking animal with a blow of its tail where the quills embedded in the attacking animal's face may cause it to die of starvation. Porcupines occur widely throughout Oregon, especially in open conifer forests, though also in sagebrush far from trees. They eat the buds, leaves, and bark of trees, sometimes killing them, and also gnaw on buildings, tools, auto tires, and electrical insulation. The **fisher** is the primary predator. Annual porcupine races in **Baker City** ended in 1991 after animal rights activists discovered that they were illegal under an obscure state law. <u>Atlas of Oregon Wildlife</u>; <u>Mammals and Life Zones of Oregon</u>;

Mammals of the Northwest; Oregonian 7/14/95:D2.

Pornography. In 1994 the **Oregon Court of Appeals** ruled that under the 1987 State vs. Henry decision child pornography is protected as free speech. Oregonian 5/7/95:D1. See also **Censorship**; **Sex industry**.

Porpoises. Small toothed whales of the **dolphin** family, usually with blunt heads. The harbor porpoise, *Phocoena phocoena*, up to 6 feet long, is the most common porpoise in the Northwest, and sometimes enters the lower reaches of the **Columbia River**. It does not playfully gambol as do the larger porpoises. Mammals and Life Zones of Oregon; Mammals of the Northwest.

Port districts. Districts created under state law to promote commercial development of port facilities. The Oregon Ports Division, 503-986-0243, in the Department of **Economic Development** provides assistance. Each of Oregon's 23 port districts (listed in the Oregon Blue Book) has taxing authority and is governed by elected commissioners. The **Port of Portland** is the largest, and the Port of **Brookings** Harbor, established in 1959, is the newest. The port districts along the **Columbia River** serve barge and container shipping, and some provide recreation facilities as do many coastal ports. Oregon Public Ports Association, 727 Center St. NE, Suite 208, Salem 97301. 503-585-1250.

Port of entry. See **Motor Carrier Transportation**.

Port of Portland. A **port district** created in 1891 to improve port facilities, port services, and navigation on the **Willamette** and lower **Columbia** rivers. Its creation was a response to the concern that **Portland** would not thrive if either land or water carriers monopolized the wharves. The Port operates five marine terminals (including a new mineral export terminal) plus the Portland Ship Repair Yard (**Swan Island**), the **Portland International Airport**, and general aviation airports in **Troutdale**, **Hillsboro**, and Mulino. Some $9 billion worth of cargo pass through the port's facilities each year, over half of it to and from **Japan**. It is the nation's largest grain port, is sixth in auto handling, and the port's floating dry dock is the largest in the Americas. The port plans to develop 825 acres on the west end of **Hayden Island** into three large grain and container terminals in a $657 million project. Its 10,000 acres in the Portland area also include Rivergate Industrial District, Swan Island Industrial Park, Mocks Landing, Portland International Center, Troutdale Industrial Park, and Brookwood Corporate Park. PO Box 3529, Portland 97208. 800-547-8411. 503-231-5000. Governing Oregon; Oregonian 3/7/97:A1. See also **Exports**.

Port Orford. A fishing port on the south Oregon coast in **Curry County**, 28 miles north of **Gold Beach** on **Highway 101**, that bills itself as the most westerly incorporated city in the continental U.S. The name comes from Cape Orford, an early name for **Cape Blanco**, seven miles to the north. Sea Captain William Tichenor established the town as mining camp in 1851. **Fort Orford**, 1851-1856, protected the booming community from Indians until the end of the **Rogue River War**. The post office was established in 1855. In 1868 a 300,000-acre **forest fire** destroyed the town, and there was significant damage on November 23, 1873, from an **earthquake** that was felt from Portland to San Francisco and estimated at 6.3. The city was incorporated in 1935. Since the harbor offers little protection other than a **breakwater**, fishing boats are hoisted from the ocean and stored on the docks.

Population 1980 1,061; 1995 1,050. Elevation 59'. PO Box 310, 97465. 541-332-3681. Chamber of Commerce 541-332-8055. Port Orford; Tracking down Oregon. See also **Battle Rock**.

Port-Orford-cedar. A conifer tree, *Chamaecyparis lawsoniana*, native to **Coos** and **Curry Counties**. It is widely-planted as an ornamental, but both native stands and ornamentals are threatened by an introduced root rot. The wood is used for arrow shafts and is also valued, especially by the Japanese, for finish lumber. The nation's largest grows in a picnic area 9.8 miles southeast of Powers on the Elk Creek Road. It is 219' tall and 37'7" in circumference (12 feet in diameter). Oregon Blue Book. See also **Cedars**.

Port Orford Meteorite. A large meteorite that John Evans reported finding in 1856 in **Curry County** and from which he had a fragment. Many and extensive searches failed to locate it. Recent studies have documented that the entire story was a hoax, perpetrated by Evans in an attempt to solve his financial woes, and his piece of meteorite was actually from a meteorite that fell in Chile in 1820. Port Orford, Oregon, Meteorite Mystery.

Portages. Land routes for boat passengers and freight between waterways or around water obstacles. The most important in Oregon history have been those around the **Cascades of the Columbia River** and **The Dalles of the Columbia River**. In southern Oregon mules pulled a train across a two-mile portage between Isthmus Slough of **Coos Bay** and Beaver Slough of the **Coquille River** from 1869 until replaced in 1874 by a steam railroad. Blow for the Landing. See also **Locks**; **Oregon Portage Railroad**.

Portland. Oregon's largest city (132 square miles and, in 1995, 497,600 people, one sixth of the state's population), as well as its commercial and cultural center. It lies in northwest Oregon on both sides of the **Willamette River** near its confluence with the **Columbia River**, 110 miles from the ocean. Vancouver, Washington (population 53,000), lies directly north across the Columbia River. Portland is the county seat of **Multnomah County**, though portions of the city also lie in **Clackamas** and **Washington Counties**. About 75% of the residents live on the east side of the Willamette. The city is governed by four elected commissioners and a mayor, each with assigned departments. Its nine **sister cities** are Ashkelon, Israel; Corinto, Nicaragua; Guadalajara, Mexico; Kaohsiung, Taiwan; Khabarovsk, Russia; Sapporo, Japan (the first, 1959); Suzhou, China; Ulsan, Korea; and Mutare, Zimbabwe (the latest, 1991). Elevation 77'. Population 1980 366,383; 1995 497,600. 1221 SW Fourth Ave., 97204. 503-823-4000. Visitors Association 503-222-2223 or 800-962-3700. See also **Consolidation**; **Metropolitan Service District**; **Portland City Hall**; other **Portland** entries.

Portland. See *Steamer Portland*.

Portland address tiles. Black house numbers, each on a 2 1/4 by 3 1/2 inch white ceramic tile, set in an aluminum frame. They were manufactured in Portland and distributed to 94,000 homes throughout the city during a massive re-addressing program in the 1930s. They are being reproduced in Portland by Fernill Pottery and sold through restoration specialty stores nationally. Oregonian 5/22/97:H&G22.

Portland addresses. For address purposes, Portland is divided by Burnside the Willamette), North (the peninsula west of Williams Avenue between the Willamette and Columbia rivers), NE (north of Burnside and east of Williams Avenue), SW (south of Burnside and west of the Willamette), and SE (south of Burnside and east of the Willamette). Avenues run north/south and are (mostly) numbered, while streets run east/west. There are 100 numbers per block. Round the Roses.

Portland and Western. See **Willamette and Pacific**.

Portland Area Theatre Alliance. An organization that serves members with information about thirty area theaters. Members receive Play-by-Play (a magazine of theater news), ticket discounts, audition information, and an annual theater directory. 1436 SW Montgomery St., 97201-2557. 503-241-4902.

Portland Art Association. A private, non-profit association organized in 1892. It built the first public art museum in the Northwest in 1905, established the Museum Art School in 1909, and built the present **Portland Art Museum** in the 1930s.

Portland Art Museum. A museum designed by Pietro Belluschi and built by the **Portland Art Association** in the 1930s. It houses both permanent and special painting and sculpture exhibits, the Gilkey Print Center, a museum shop and cafe, the Berg Swann Auditorium, and, until 1998, the **Pacific Northwest College of Art**. The North Wing, located in a former Masonic Temple, houses the **Northwest Film and Video Center** and the Rental Sales Gallery. A sculpture mall lies between the buildings. In 1995, a $2.5 million, six-month renovation added climate control. Museum After Hours is a series of Wednesday evening **jazz** concerts. In 1993/94 the budget was $5.9 million, and 240,000 attended its exhibits and events. 1219 SW Park Avenue, 97205. 503-226-2811. Business Journal 8/25/95:10: Oregon Blue Book. See also **Evening at Giverny**.

Portland Baroque Orchestra. A group founded in 1984 that plays a series of concerts of music from the Baroque period (1600 to 1750 A.D.) at Trinity Episcopal Cathedral, 147 NW 19th. Its performances have been nationally broadcast. The office is at 610 SW Broadway, Suite 602, 97205-3407. 503-224-7908. Tickets 503-222-6000.

Portland bridges. Nineteen **bridges** carry cars and railroads across the **Willamette** and **Columbia** rivers in the Portland area between **Sauvie Island** and **Oregon City**. Morrison Street bridge was the first, built in 1887 as a privately-owned toll bridge and replaced in 1905 and 1958. From north to south they are, plus the year built (and replaced) and type of opening (if any),

Columbia River -

Burlington Northern RR	1908	turntables
Interstate 5 southbound	1958	vertical lift
Interstate 5 northbound	1917	vertical lift
Glenn Jackson (I 205)	1984	

Willamette River -

Sauvie Island	1948	
St. Johns	1931	
St. Johns RR	1989	vertical lift

Broadway	1913 bascule
Steel	1889, 1912 compound vertical lift
Burnside	1894, 1926 bascule
Morrison Street	1887, 1905, 1958 bascule
Hawthorne	1891, 1910 vertical lift
Marquam	1966
Ross Island	1926
Sellwood	1925
Southern Pacific RR	1910
West Linn	1970
Oregon City	1922

Oregonian 8/10/97:C4, 8/27/97:A19. See also **Bridges** entries.

Portland Building. A controversial 1982 downtown **Portland** building at 1120 SW Fifth Avenue that houses city and county offices. It was designed by Princeton architect Michael Graves and was the nation's first major Post Modern Style building. **Portlandia**, a 35-foot tall statue of a kneeling woman, is above the Fifth Avenue entrance. The building cost $22.4 million, or $51 per square foot, less than the cost at the time of building a house. Cracks that developed in 1995 led to the discovery of structural flaws requiring some $3.5 million to rectify, including seismic upgrades. Frozen Music; Oregonian 9/15/95:A1, 2/2/97:G1.

Portland Center. A 54-block area of **Portland** that was redeveloped as the South Auditorium **Urban Renewal** Project of the 1960s by the firm of Skidmore, Owings and Merrill. 1,500 residents and 200 businesses were relocated before the deteriorating ethnic neighborhood, bounded by SW Market Street, Harbor Drive, Arthur Street, and Fourth Avenue, was leveled. The area was rebuilt with three apartment towers, garden apartments, commercial buildings, Pettygrove Square, and **Lovejoy Fountain**. Frozen Music; Portland, An Informal History.

Portland Center for the Performing Arts. A complex owned by the city of **Portland** that includes four theaters in three buildings: the **Arlene Schnitzer Concert Hall** on Broadway; the 1987 New Theatre Building (sometimes called the Performing Arts Center), also on Broadway, that houses both the **Newmark** and the **Dolores Winningstad** theaters, and the **Civic Auditorium** at SW 3rd and Clay. The Center sells over a million tickets a year. It was managed by **Metro** for several years, but the city resumed operations in 1997. While a $19 million bond issue in 1981 helped create the Center, there was no stable source of operating funds until 1997 when **Multnomah County** agreed to contribute $1.2 million a year from the lodging tax and the city agreed to contribute $600,000 a year. 1111 SW Broadway, 97205-2999. 503-248-4335. 503-796-9293 for event information recording. Facts of Life; Oregonian 9/14/97:E1.

Portland Center Stage. An Equity theater company that was once affiliated with **Ashland**'s **Oregon Shakespeare Festival** but became independent in 1994. It produces classic and contemporary works at the **Newmark Theatre**. 1111 SW Broadway, 97205-2999. 503-274-6588. Portland Guidebook.

Portland City Hall. **Portland**'s historic Italian Renaissance style City Hall was designed by the firm of Widden and Lewis and built in 1895, remodeled in the 1930s and given a $30 million restoration and seismic upgrade in the 1990s. 1221

SW Fourth Ave., 97204. 503-823-4000. Oregonian 3/30/98:C1; 4/12/98:F1.

Portland Community College (PCC). A public two-year college that serves students from **Multnomah** and **Washington** counties and from parts of **Clackamas, Columbia**, and **Yamhill** counties. In fall 1996 PCC enrolled 35,108 at its three campuses and two special-purpose centers. It offers two-year college transfer programs as well as one- and two-year career programs in 80 occupational and technical areas. It also participates in the Portland Area Vocational and Technical Education Consortium which is a partnership between it and 27 public high schools in the district. After seven years of operation under the Portland School District, the community college became an autonomous district in 1968. PO Box 19000, Portland OR 97280-0990. 503-244-6111. Oregon Blue Book. See also **Community colleges; Small Business Development Centers**.

Portland density. In 1998 **Portland**'s density was 3,100 persons per square mile, down from more than 5,000 in 1960. The change reflects changing urban borders, more people living alone, more single-parent families, and fewer families with children. Oregonian 2/16/98:D11.

Portland downtown. Portland's downtown area was laid out with 200-foot-long blocks and 60-foot-wide streets. The short blocks were designed because they produced the maximum number of valuable corner lots, but they also resulted in an open downtown that invites exploration. Since 1850, the business area has moved several blocks west of its riverfront beginnings and has evolved from forest to cabins to cottages to townhouses to commercial buildings to the present high-rise office buildings. Each stage was razed to make way for the next. Portland, An Informal History.

Portland Exposition Building. See **North Pacific Industrial Association Exposition Building**.

Portland fire. On August 2, 1873 a fire, perhaps incendiary, began at 4:30 a.m. in a furniture-store workroom near First and Taylor streets. It spread quickly to the adjoining wooden buildings to the river, then north and west, consuming 22 blocks despite the efforts of Portland and Salem firemen. The latter and their equipment had been rushed to Portland by train in a record time of an hour and fifteen minutes. The losses, estimated at $1.25 million, included much of the business district as well as housing and employment, and were felt in the city for some time. Another major fire had burned a number of downtown blocks the previous December. Oregon Oddities; Round the Roses.

Portland fountains. Portland's many fountains include **Ira C. Keller Fountain, Lovejoy Fountain, Salmon Street Springs**, and **Skidmore Fountain**. Some have earned alternative names. The large metal rainbow at SW 5th and Ankeny that spurts jets of water is known as "The Car Wash," and the three nudes at the entrance to the Georgia Pacific Building at 900 SW Fifth, officially called "The Quest," are more often called "Family Night at the Y" or "Three Groins in a Fountain." Oregon Parks 2(1):62-64. July/August 1994; Portland's Public Art. See also **Benson fountains; Essential Forces**.

Portland General Electric Company (PGE). An investor-owned **electric utility**, formed in 1891, that, in 1996, served 45% of Oregon's population (650,000 retail customers) in northwest Oregon. Total 1994 revenues were $959 million from the sale of 19.5 million **megawatt** hours. About a fourth of its electricity was generated at company-owned facilities. In 1996 its installed generating capacity, most of it in Oregon, totaled 2,180 **megawatts**. In Oregon PGE built **Trojan** (nuclear, closed), **Boardman** (coal, 560 MW), three natural gas plants, **Beaver** (583 MW), **Bethel** (113 MW),and **Coyote Springs** (346 MW), as well as **hydroelectric** facilities on the **Deschutes** (363 MW), **Bull Run** (58 MW), and **Clackamas** (158 MW) rivers. It operates recreation facilities on the reservoirs. Enron Corporation of Houston, Texas, acquired PGE in 1997. One World Trade Center, 121 SW Salmon, Portland 97204. 503-228-6322, 800-542-8818. Electrifying Eden; Inventory; Oregon Utility Statistics; Oregonian 6/8/97:D1. See also **Lake Billy Chinook**; **Lake Simtustus**; **Pebble Springs**; **Timothy Lake**.

Portland geology. The oldest rocks in the Portland area are the fossil-laden, 22-million-year-old Scappoose Formation deposits, laid down under the shallow seas that covered the area at that time. Later the **Columbia River Basalts** flooded through the area from eastern Oregon, laying down a thousand feet of basalt on top of the Scappoose Formation. The nearby **Coast Range** was uplifted thirteen million years ago, creating the Portland and Tualatin basins and **Tualatin Mountain**. During the **Pliocene** great lakes filled the basins and deposited silts that became "Sandy River mudstone." The lakes were breached and the ancestral **Columbia River** deposited pebbles and rocks from the Canadian Rockies creating the "Troutdale Formation." Pliocene eruptions created volcanoes in the area, including **Mount Tabor**, **Rocky Butte**, and several in **Forest Park**. During dry interglacial periods in the last 700,000 years, yellowish dust from Columbia River flood plains blew in, creating soils known as Portland Hills Silt, up to 55 feet thick in Forest Park. Repeated **Pleistocene floods** between 15,000 and 12,800 years ago flooded the area, sometimes nearly to the top of Mount Tabor, and deposited sediments in the valleys. Geology of Oregon. See also **Earthquakes**.

Portland government. Portland is governed by four elected commissioners and a mayor, each elected at large and then assigned responsibility for a specific area of city government. The mayor has little extra authority other than to assign the responsibilities to the commissioners. Portland has had three women mayors, Dorothy McCullough Lee, 1948, Connie McCready, 1979, and Vera Katz, 1994. City voters adopted the commission system in 1913 to replace a 15-member council/ward system which had been plagued with corruption. Round the Roses.

Portland Historical Races. Over 100 classic race cars race at **Portland International Raceway** in July. 503-224-4400.

Portland history. Portland was founded in 1844, a year after the first **wagon train** arrived at **Oregon City** on the **Oregon Trail**. The first cabin was located at Front and Washington. A post office opened in 1849, and in 1851 the **territorial government** incorporated the city. The residents built a jail as the first public building. The investment in a **plank road** led to its rapid growth as a deep-water **wheat** shipping port, and it was later called "a city built by gravity" as boats floated grain down the **Willamette** and **Columbia** rivers to its wharves. By 1890 manufacturing was valued at $25,400,000, foreign export trade amounted to $6,600,000, and four **railroads** served the city and spurred growth across the river in East Portland. The **Lewis and Clark Exposition** in 1905 boosted the city's growth, and it received another boost when 70,000 new workers arrived to work in the shipyards of **World War II**. Major weather events include the **floods of 1861, 1894, 1948, 1964**, and **1996**, and the **Columbus Day Storm** of 1962. Portland titles; Round the Roses. See also **Oregonian**; other **Portland** entries.

Portland Hotel. A million dollar, eight floor, 326 room grand hotel that, after its completion in 1890, was for decades the center of business and social life of Portland. It occupied the block between Yamhill, Sixth, Morrison, and Broadway, an area that had earlier been the site of Portland's first real schoolhouse. The hotel was razed in 1951; the site became a parking lot before being turned into **Pioneer Courthouse Square** in 1983. Portland, An Informal History.

Portland IndyCar Race. An annual June **auto race** run since 1984 at the **Portland International Raceway** as part of the **Rose Festival**. The CART (Championship Auto Racing Teams) 198.9-mile race covers 102 laps on the 1.95-mile track. Winning speeds have ranged from 96.3 mph (Fittipaldi in 1993) to 115.208 mph (Michael Andretti in 1991). The race, along with its qualifying events, is the largest spectator sports event in Oregon; 164,000 attended over three days in 1995. Oregonian 6/26/95:D10.

Portland Institute for Contemporary Art. An institute begun in 1995 that sponsors performances by artists and ensembles in dance, music, theater, and visual arts. Since it first had no space of its own, the events were scheduled at various venues around Portland, but Wieden & Kennedy offered space in its refurbished building at 12th and Everett, beginning in 1998. 503-242-1419. Oregonian 9/10/95:E1, 4/12/97:B8.

Portland International Airport. Oregon's major **airport**, symbol PDX. It is the 33rd busiest airport in North America, with 11.9 million passengers through it in 1995, up from 7.2 million in 1992. Fourteen passenger airlines provided service to 120 cities worldwide, and 16 cargo carriers handled over 250,000 tons annually. During a major 1997 expansion and remodel that added, among other things, a 266-foot control tower, two steelworkers were killed when a partially-built steel superstructure collapsed. The airport, owned and operated by the **Port of Portland**, opened in 1940 near Marine Drive. The present terminal has been much enlarged since it opened in 1958. Oregonian 1/26/96:D1, 9/24/97:D1; Round the Roses.

Portland International Performance Festival. A summer festival sponsored by **Portland State University** that includes performances, readings, workshops, films, and lectures. 503-725-8500.

Portland International Raceway. A 12-turn, 1.95-mile city-owned, self-supporting **auto racing** track in West Delta Park. It opens in April for a variety of summer motor sports events. Highlights are the **Portland IndyCar Race**, the Rose Cup/TRANS AM, and the IMSA Grand Prix. At Christmas time lighted displays are mounted around the track for drive-by viewing. 1940 N. Victory Boulevard, west of exit 306B from **Interstate 5**. 503-285-6635. Oregonian 12/18/97:E9.

Portland Labor College. An evening school for adults, sponsored by the Portland Central Labor Council, that operated 1922-1929 in the Labor Temple at Fourth and Jefferson. As many as 125 students were enrolled during a term. The

College also sponsored the Labor College Players, the country's only workers' theater and for several years Portland's only local theater. "Labor and Education."

Portland Marathon. See **Marathon.**

Portland Meadows. Oregon's major **horse racing** track. It is a glass-enclosed, heated facility with an indoor paddock where the horses can be inspected. 1001 N. Schmeer Road. 503-285-9144. Portland Guidebook.

Portland Memorial Coliseum. See **Memorial Coliseum.** **Portland/Multnomah County consolidation.** Proposals to consolidate **Portland** and **Multnomah County** were considered in 1997, though voters had rejected the idea four times between 1913 and 1974. In 1983 the city and county eliminated many duplicated services when they passed Resolution A. This divided functions so that Multnomah County now focuses on human services while Portland focuses on urban services. About a dozen areas of duplication remain, including planning and transportation. The potential effects of consolidation on the other five cities in Multnomah County remain in question. Oregonian 5/15/97:D1.

Portland name. Portland was founded in 1844 by William Overton and Asa Lovejoy but Overton sold his interest almost immediately to Francis Pettygrove. Lovejoy, from Massachusetts, wanted to call the new town Boston, but Pettygrove, from Maine, won the coin toss and named it Portland, an appropriate choice given the continuing importance of its deep-vessel port in the city's economy. For some years the town was also derisively known as Stumptown for the stumps in the middle of its mud streets. In 1953 writer Stewart Holbrook proposed changing Portland to Multnomah, an effort that received national attention but no support from the City Council. Again, in preparation for Oregon's statehood centennial in 1959, Holbrook proposed a song, "Meet me in Multnomah, Nomah" that also garnered considerable publicity, especially after an Oregon woman actually named Nomah appeared. In 1995 Oregonian writer Jonathan Nicholas proposed again that Portland deserved a more distinctive name. Portland is also known as the **City of Roses** and **Rip City.** Its airport designation is PDX. Facts of Life; Oregon Geographic Names; Oregonian 5/31/95:C1.

Portland neighborhoods. Portland is made up of 94 identified neighborhoods, each with a neighborhood association encouraged by the city's Office of Neighborhood Associations. Portland Names and Neighborhoods; Round the Roses. See also **Albina; Chinatown; Hayden Island; Ladd's Addition; Mocks Crest; North Macadam District; Pearl District; River District; Rivergate; Swan Island.**

Portland Observer. A weekly paper founded in 1970 that is the state's oldest continuing black publication. Paid circulation in 1994 was 30,000. 4747 NE M. L. King Blvd., 97211. 503-288-0033. Oregon Blue Book.

Portland Opera Association. An opera company in **Portland** that presents five operas a year at the **Civic Auditorium** with international casts performing with the Portland Opera orchestra and chorus. English translations are projected for foreign language operas. The company also has a year-round education and outreach program, and sponsors Broadway Theater Season that brings nationally touring Broadway productions to Portland. In 1993/94 its budget was $4.5 million. 1516 SW Alder, Portland 97205. 503-241-1407. Business Journal 8/25/

95:10; Oregon Blue Book.

Portland parks. Portland's **Forest Park** is the nation's largest city park and **Mill Ends Park** the smallest. **Washington Park** includes the **Metro Washington Park Zoo**, the **International Rose Test Garden**, the **Japanese Gardens**, **Hoyt Arboretum**, and the **Viet Nam Memorial. Governor Tom McCall Waterfront Park** is the location of many of Portland's festivals. Mt. Tabor Park is on an extinct volcano. In 1904 Portland engaged John C. Olmsted to recommend a long-range park plan and authorized a $1,000,000 bond issue to carry it out. His plan for a connected, comprehensive system, including natural areas, is still referred to, though much of the riverfront land that he had planned for parks went to industry and airports. The **Park Blocks** were the first city park. Oregonian 5/20/97:A1. See also **Metro; Plaza Blocks**.

Portland population history.

1850	800
1860	2,874
1870	8,293
1880	17,577
1890	46,385
1900	90,426
1910	207,214
1920	258,288
1930	301,815
1940	305,394
1950	373,628
1960	372,676
1970	379,967
1980	366,383
1990	437,319

Facts of Life.

Portland Public Library. See **Multnomah County Library**.

Portland Repertory Theater. A **Portland** Equity theater company that had produced six well-received contemporary plays a season. In 1998 the board closed the company due to its large debt. It had been located at 2 World Trade Center, 25 SW Salmon. Oregonian 2/1/98:B1.

Portland Rose Festival. See **Rose Festival**.

Portland Speedway. An oval **auto racing** track, one of the oldest circle tracks in the nation, located at 9727 N. Martin Luther King Jr. Boulevard (Highway 99E) in north Portland. 503-282-2883.

Portland stairs. The City of Portland maintains over 165 outdoor stairways. The longest is a flight of 287 steps to the top of Mount Tabor. Portland's Little Red Book of Stairs.

Portland State University. One of Oregon's three major state research universities, located on a downtown Portland campus. It began in 1946 as the **Vanport Extension Center**, opened to serve returning **World War II** veterans. Now it offers 32 bachelor's, 38 master's, and eight doctoral programs. It enrolled 14,428 students in the fall of 1994. A number of centers and institutes offer service programs, including the **Center for Population Research and Census**. 630 SW Mill St., PO Box 751, Portland 97207-0751. 800-547-8887 ext. 5256; 503-725-3000. Oregon Blue Book. See also **University System, Oregon**.

Portland Traction Company. A 15-mile **electric railroad** that operated from Portland to **Oregon City** between 1893 and 1958. Built as the East Side Railway Company, it had three other names before becoming the Portland Traction Company. Between 1915 and 1933 service was offered on a connecting line to **Mount Angel** as well. Stations West.

Portland University. A one-time **Methodist** college that opened for classes in 1891 and closed, after factional and financial difficulties, in 1900. The property was sold to the **Catholic** Church that operated it as Columbia University, before renaming it the **University of Portland** in 1935. Dictionary of Oregon History.

Portland Youth Philharmonic. The country's oldest youth orchestra, organized by Mary Dodge in 1924. Jacob Gershkovitch was the first conductor, and Jacob Avshalomov was conductor from 1955 until 1995. 1119 SW Park, Suite 197, 97205-2495. 503-223-5939. Concerts Reviewed. See also **Sagebrush Symphony**.

Portland-Vancouver Consolidated Metropolitan Statistical Area (PVCMSA). A designation used in the 1990 census that included **Clark County** in Washington, plus **Multnomah**, **Washington**, **Clackamas**, and **Yamhill** counties in Oregon. The PVCMSA had a total population of 1,477,895, 27th largest in the nation. Of those, 1,239,842 were in the four-country area in Oregon that was called the Portland Primary Metropolitan Statistical Area. The population in the PVCMSA increased almost 14% in the 10 years since 1980. The 10-year growth rates, by county, were Clark 24%, Washington 26.7%, Yamhill 18.5%, Clackamas 15.3%, and Multnomah 3.8%. Facts of Life.

Portlandia. A 35-foot statue of a kneeling woman, also known as Queen Kong or Trident over Tri-Met, emplaced in 1985 above the Fifth Avenue entrance of the **Portland Building**. She represents Lady Commerce, seen on Portland's official seal. The $348,000 **sculpture** is the world's second-largest hammered copper statue; only the Statue of Liberty is larger. The sculptor was Raymond Kaskey who still owns the copyright. Oregonian 9/24/95:D1.

Ports. Oregon's four deep-water ports are at **Portland** and **Astoria** (both on the **Columbia River**), **Newport** (**Yaquina Bay**), and **Coos Bay**. Ports serving fishing fleets are at **Hammond** and **Warrenton** (Columbia River), **Wheeler** (**Nehalem River**), **Garibaldi** (**Tillamook Bay**), **Depoe Bay**, **Florence** (**Siuslaw River**), **Reedsport** and **Winchester Bay** (**Umpqua River**), **Charleston** (**Coos Bay**), **Bandon** (**Coquille River**), **Port Orford**, **Gold Beach** (**Rogue River**), and **Brookings** (**Chetco River**). All of these ports are protected by **jetties** or **breakwaters**. Oregon ports serving commercial traffic on the Columbia River above Portland include those at **Cascade Locks**, **Hood River**, **The Dalles**, **Arlington**, and **Umatilla**. See also **Port districts**.

Portuguese man-of-war. See **Sail jellyfish**.

Possum. A primitive, cat-sized, gray marsupial, *Didelphis virginiana*, native to the southeastern U.S. It was first introduced into northeast Oregon about 1912, and is now common in both western and northeastern Oregon. The possum has a pointy face, clawed feet for climbing, and a long, naked, prehensile tail. The nocturnal animal is omnivorous, feeding on, among other things, road kill to which it contributes its own numbers. In 1994-95, 1,028 were taken for skins with an average value of $1.40 each. Atlas of Oregon Wildlife; Mammals and Life Zones of Oregon; Mammals of the Northwest.

Postal Service. The United States Postal Service serves Oregon through the Portland District. There are 500 Oregon Post Offices and delivery units, staffed by 9,850 employees, that deliver mail to 1,578,600 households and businesses. In 1995 the state generated $581,774,000 in postal revenue. PO Box 4029, 97208-4029. 503-294-2344. See also **Astoria Post Office**; **Dune Mushers Mail Run**; **Mail boats**.

Postal service history. Mail in Oregon was carried by private parties until Oregon's **provisional government** established postal routes in the **Willamette Valley** in 1846, but the routes were abandoned within a year as unprofitable. Federal postmasters were appointed in 1847 for **Astoria** (the first American post office on the Pacific coast) and **Oregon City**. By 1860 Oregon had 96 post offices, and by 1900 there were 890. There are now 500. Monthly steamship postal service from California was begun in 1850, providing 40-day service from the Atlantic coast. Daily mail service by **stage line** to Sacramento, taking seven days en route, began in 1861. Mail delivery continued to be a problem for the remote areas of the state until they were served by **railroads**. **Express services** competed with the postal service until the competition was outlawed in 1895. Between 1955, when the last passenger train was taken off the **Southern Pacific** line, and 1971, a long white truck called the Highway Post Office, or HyPO, operated between **Medford** and **Portland**. Mail was sorted as it traveled. Dictionary of Oregon History; Mail Tribune 2/18/98:2A; Oregon Geographic Names; "Portland: Wells Fargo's Hub"; This Day in Oregon. See also **Astoria post office**; **Pony Express**.

Posters. See **Expose Yourself to Art**; **Mount Hood Festival of Jazz**.

Pot hunting. A term used for removing cultural **artifacts**, whether Indian or white, without authority. See also **Archeology**.

Potash. A mineral that is an important source of potassium for agriculture. In 1997 the **Port of Portland** opened a mineral export terminal with the expectation that potash would become the port's third largest bulk **export**, accounting for shipments of at least 1.5 million tons a year. The potash is mined in the Canadian plains provinces and shipped by rail to Portland where it is loaded on ships bound for Pacific ports. Oregonian 3/25/97:C1.

Potatoes. In 1995 Oregon's 500 commercial potato growers produced 2.7 billion pounds, worth $143.9 million, on 53,000 acres, primarily in **Morrow**, **Umatilla**, **Malheur**, and **Klamath** counties. Potatoes are Oregon's top value-added crop, with many of them processed into frozen french fries (some exported to Asia), and into potato flakes. Potatoes were being grown at **Fort Vancouver** by 1825; in 1832 they harvested 15,000 bushels. Oregon Potato Commission, 700 NE Multnomah, Suite 460, Portland 97232-4104. 503-731-3300. 1995 Oregon.

Pottery. Pottery works in Oregon during the 19th century included the Oregon Pottery Company in **Buena Vista**, 1866-1897, and the Hannah Pottery near **Shady Cove**, 1870-1900.

Poultry. See **Chickens**; **Eggs**; **Emu**; **Ostrich**; **Turkeys**.

Poverty. In 1989, 12.1% of Oregon households and 12.4% of the state's population were below the poverty line. The percentages ranged from 6% in **Washington County** to 21% in **Wheeler County**. In 1995 3% of the population received Aid to Dependent Children and 9% received food stamps. Oregon: A Statistical Overview. See also **Income**.

Powder River. A river in eastern Oregon's **Baker County** that drains an area of 1,720 square miles of **Elkhorn Ridge** and the south slopes of the **Wallowa Mountains** east to the **Snake River**. It has an average annual volume of 386,000 acre feet or .4 acre feet/acre. It was named for the powdery soil along the stream. **Baker City** and **North Powder** are located along it. Oregon Geographic Names.

Powder River mining district. An area east of **Baker City** where **gold** was first discovered near **Virtue Flat** in 1862. The development of the Sparta mines to the northeast soon followed. The **Auburn mining district** and the **gold mining** areas of **Sumpter**, **Greenhorn**, and **Granite** are west of **Baker City**. Oregon's Golden Years.

Power. See **Basketball, women's**.

Powers. An isolated southwest Oregon timber community in the mountains of **Coos County**, about 50 miles south of **Coos Bay** and 24 miles south of **Myrtle Point**. The community was named in 1914 for Albert Powers, manager of a local logging company. The railroad to the mill was completed that year, and the post office was established the next year. The city was incorporated in 1947. Population 1980 819; 1995 680. Elevation 286'. PO Box 250, 97466. 541-439-3331. Oregon Geographic Names.

Powwows. Traditional Indian gatherings held for spiritual, social, and economic reasons. The **Siletz Tribes** host the annual **Nesika Illahee Pow-Wow**, the largest powwow in the state. The **Klamath**, **Grand Ronde**, **Umatilla**, and **Warm Springs** Indians also host powwows, and Indians in the **Portland** area host one at East Delta Park in June. Respectful non-Indians are welcome to attend. Native Peoples. See also **Pendleton Round-Up**.

PP&L. See **Pacific Power and Light Company**.

Prairie City. An eastern Oregon ranching community 13 miles east of **John Day** on **Highway 26** in **Grant County**. The town site and post office were established in 1870 as a **gold-mining** center. During the **Bannock War** in 1878 a local flour mill and a gold mining hole were used for forts. The city was incorporated in 1891. The **Sumpter Valley Railroad** carried freight and passengers between **Baker City** and Prairie City from 1910 to 1947; the DeWitt Museum (open summers) is located in the old depot. Population 1980 1,106; 1995 1,170. Elevation 3,539'. PO Box 370, 97869. 541-820-3605. Gold and Cattle Country; History of Grant County.

Prairie Flower. An early **novel** of the Oregon Country, one of the most widely read books of the time, published in Cincinnati in 1849. Emerson Bennett, a popular novelist, was listed as the author, though **Oregon City** hotelier Sidney Walter Moss claimed to have written all or parts of it. Dictionary of Oregon History.

Prairies. Open grasslands. Those in the **Willamette Valley** were the sites of the earliest farms in Oregon. These prairies and the adjacent oak savannah foothills resulted from years of annual fall burning by the Indians; as soon as the burning ceased, any area left unplowed or ungrazed grew up in brush and **Douglas fir**. Most of the Willamette Valley prairie soils are heavy clay, suitable only for pasture, grains and **grass seed** crops. However, other areas in the valley, including the rich soils of the flood plains (wooded when pioneers arrived), now support a diversity of crops. "Changing Geography of the Willamette Valley Woodlands". See also **French Prairie**; **Indian burning**; **Tombstone Prairie**; **Zumwalt Prairie**.

Precipitation. Moisture that reaches the earth, including mist, rainfall, snow, hail, and sleet. Measurable precipitation is defined as at least 1/100th of an inch. Annual precipitation along the coast is about 75", increases to 165" in the **Coast Range**, decreases to about 40" in the **Willamette Valley**, increases again on the western slopes of the **Cascade Range** to 150" (mostly as snowfall), and decreases again east of the Cascades to 5" to 15", except for mountainous areas; the western slopes of the **Blue Mountains** receive 40" to 50" annually. Precipitation in Oregon correlates strongly with elevation. The wettest spots in the state, found in the **Coast Range** and in the **Klamath Mountains** northeast of **Brookings**, receive over 165" annually, and Sugarloaf Mountain east of **Lincoln City** may average over 200" a year, but the rain gauge keeps washing away. The driest area, with 5" annually, is the **Alvord Basin** in southeast Oregon. The most dramatic rain shadow in the entire 48 states is on the east side of **Santiam Pass**, where, in an elevation drop of just 1,500 feet, annual precipitation drops from 100" to 14". In western Oregon precipitation is heaviest from November through January, while the lowest probability of rain, an 8% chance, is in the last half of July and first half of August. The rainfall pattern in northeast Oregon is more uniform throughout the year because of frequent summer thunderstorms. Rainfall in Portland demonstrates an average 18-year cycle. A precipitation map of Oregon is available for purchase from the **Oregon Climate Service**, 326 Strand Hall, OSU, Corvallis 97331. 541-737-5705. Oregon Wet, High, and Dry. See also **Drought**; **Hail**; **Rainfall records**; **Snowfall**; **Snowfall records**.

Predators. Animals designated by the state as predators are managed by the Oregon Department of **Agriculture**. Only two animals are so designated, **coyotes** and red **foxes**. **Bear** and **cougar**, formerly classed as predators, are now classed as **game animals**.

Prefontaine Classic. An annual track meet named for the legendary Oregon runner, Steve Prefontaine (1951-1975). The meet is held in June at Hayward field in **Eugene** where Prefontaine won seven individual NCAA championships while at the **University of Oregon**. At the time of his death in a one-car crash in Eugene, he held every American record between 2,000 and 10,000 meters and between two and six miles. Two films about him, "Pre" and "Prefontaine", were released in 1997. Oregonian 5/28/95:C1.

Pregnancy. A 1997 study estimated that 11% of the pregnant women in Oregon used illegal drugs, affecting 4,760 infants, and a total of over 10,00 infants had been subjected to harmful substances (drugs, alcohol, tobacco) while still in the womb. Oregonian 8/27/97:A21. See also **Abortions**; **Births**; **Teen pregnancy**.

Presbyterian Church. William Gray and the Rev. Lewis Thompson organized the first Presbyterian church in Oregon on the **Clatsop Plains** about 1845. In 1852 two churches south of **Albany**, representing two branches of Presbyterianism, formed the United Presbyterian Church (soon established nationally) and the next year founded a church in Albany, the first under the new name. In 1867 Presbyterians sponsored **Albany College** which later became **Lewis and Clark College**. Dictionary of Oregon History; Guide to Early Oregon Churches. See also **Old Church**; **Religion**.

Prescott. "The Quiet City." A northwest Oregon residential community on the **Columbia River** in **Columbia County** 18 miles north of **Saint Helens** on **Highway 30**. It was named about 1905 for the owners of the sawmill. A post office, long-since closed, was established two years later, and the city was incorporated in 1948. Population 1980 73; 1995 60. Elevation 26'. 72742 Blakely St., Rainier 97048. 503-556-8440. Oregon Geographic Names.

Prescribed burning. Burning of forested areas to reduce the fuel load, reduce harmful insects and diseases, and thin heavy stands of young trees. It is a technique used especially in areas east of the **Cascade Range** where frequent, low intensity fire had once been a natural part of the ecosystem and fire suppression has led to crowded, unhealthy forests. Fire Ecology. See also **Forest fires**.

Presidential cabinet members from Oregon. George Williams (1823-1910) of **Portland** was appointed U.S. Attorney General by President Grant in 1873; he had been chief justice of the Supreme Court of the Oregon territory 1853-1858 and U.S. senator from Oregon 1865-1871. Douglas McKay (1893-1959) of **Salem** was appointed Secretary of the Interior by President Eisenhower in 1953 after having served as governor, 1949-1952. Neil Goldschmidt (1940-) of **Portland** was appointed Secretary of Transportation in 1979. He later served as governor 1987-1991. Donald Hodel (1935-), also from Portland, was appointed by President Reagan as Secretary of Energy in 1982 and as Secretary of the Interior in 1985. Oregon Blue Book.

Presidential candidates from Oregon. Two Oregonians have been on a major party's national ticket. General Joseph Lane, first governor of the **Oregon Territory** and later the first U.S. Senator from Oregon, was the 1860 Democratic candidate for vice-president with John Breckinridge. Senator Charles McNary was the 1940 Republican candidate for vice-president with Wendell Willkie. Neither was on the winning ticket. In 1972 Tonie Nathan ran as the Libertarian Party's first vice-presidential nominee and became the first woman to receive an Electoral College vote. In 1996 Winona LaDuke, raised in **Ashland**, was the Green Party candidate for vice-president as Ralph Nader's running mate. Dictionary of Oregon History.

Presidential primary. A state election held every four years on the second Tuesday in March to nominate candidates for U.S. President. Candidates who receive at least 10% of the vote are given a proportional share of the state party convention delegates. From the 1940s until the early 1970s Oregon's May primary was treated as a significant contest by presidential candidates, but then other states scheduled earlier primaries. In an attempt to increase its national significance, the 1995 legislature separated the presidential primary from the rest of the state's **primary election** and moved it to March, with mail-in ballots allowed. Under Oregon law the **Secretary of State** is responsible for deciding which presidential candidates are listed on the ballot. A listed candidate may not remove his or her name. Governing Oregon.

Presidential visits. At least nine U.S. presidents have visited Oregon while in office. Rutherford B. Hayes was the first, stopping at towns from **Jacksonville** (where his party disputed a huge hotel bill by announcing that they had not intended to buy the hotel) to **Portland** in September and October, 1880. Benjamin Harrison visited by train in May of 1891, stopping first in **Ashland** and then heading north to dedicate the new **North Pacific Industrial Association Exposition Building** in **Portland**. Theodore Roosevelt followed much the same route before he laid the corner stone for the **Lewis and Clark Centennial Exposition** on May 21, 1903. In October, 1909, William Howard Taft visited Portland and several cities to the south. Woodrow Wilson spoke in Portland in 1919. Warren G. Harding dedicated the Old **Oregon Trail** and declared **Meacham** the capital of the U.S. for a day when he passed through on July 3, 1923, just a month before he died. Franklin Delano Roosevelt visited Portland in June, 1934, dedicated **Bonneville Dam** and **Timberline Lodge** on September 28, 1937, and visited Portland's **World War II** shipyards on October 1, 1942. Harry Truman visited in April, 1945, just after assuming the presidency, and again in June, 1948, to view damage from the **Vanport** flood. Bill Clinton visited **Portland** on April 2, 1993, for the **Northwest Forest Conference**, on June 27, 1995, for the **Pacific Rim Economic Conference**, on February 14, 1996, to view damage from the **flood of 1996**, and on September 20, 1996, to campaign. Herbert Hoover spent five years of his boyhood in **Newberg** and **Salem** and returned to Oregon several times in later years to fish. Ulysses S. Grant made an extensive tour of the state in October 1879, two years after he left the White House. Dictionary of Oregon History; Jacksonville.

Presidents' Range. A name proposed in 1839 for the **Cascade Range** by Hall Kelley of the **American Society for Encouraging the Settlement of the Oregon Territory**. Each of the peaks would be named for a president. Though the botanist David Douglas had used the name Cascade Mountains in the 1820s, there wasn't general agreement on the name at the time of Kelley's proposal. Confusion reigned for some time, but eventually other names prevailed. **Mount Jefferson** had already been named in 1806. Kelly proposed Mount Washington for a peak in Washington state; Oregon's **Mount Washington** was apparently named independently of his efforts. Oregon Geographic Names.

Primary election. An election held on the third Tuesday in May of even numbered years, except that the **presidential primary** is held the second Tuesday in March. At a primary election voters select their party's candidates for office. Oregon primaries have traditionally been, by party choice, closed primaries in which only voters registered in a party could vote for that party's candidates. However, the **Republican party** allowed independents to vote in primaries in 1990 and 1992, and the **Democratic party** opened its 1998 primary to independents. A person who is registered as an **independent** may always vote on **ballot measures**. Oregon's direct primary was adopted in 1904 as Oregon's first **initiative**. Oregonian 10/27/97:E1. See also **General election**.

Primate Center. See **Oregon Regional Primate Research Center**.

Prineville. A central Oregon lumber town 35 miles northeast of **Bend**. It is located where Ochoco Creek joins the Crooked River and at the junction of **Highways 26** and 126. A high rim to the west provides a view over the town. Prineville is the county seat of **Crook County** and site of the headquarters for the **Ochoco National Forest**, a **Bureau of Land Management** district, and **Les Schwab Tire Centers**. Attractions include a historical museum, 1909 courthouse, city-owned and operated railroad, an 18-hole municipal golf course, rock hounding, hunting, fishing, and other outdoor recreations. Barney Prine, the namesake, is said to have built, during one day in 1870, the first house, store, saloon, and blacksmith shop - all under one roof. The town, incorporated in 1880, was the first incorporated town in central Oregon. Later in the 1880's, nine deaths were attributed to masked **vigilantes**. The town boomed in the 1930s after lumber mills were established. Population 1980 5,276; 1995 6,095. Elevation 2,868'. 400 E 3rd St., 97754. 541-447-5627. Chamber of Commerce 541-447-6304. East of the Cascades.

Prineville City Railroad. A railroad built by the city of **Prineville** after city voters authorized bonds in 1916. The line extends 19 miles down the **Crooked River** to Prineville Junction where it joins the north-south **Burlington Northern Union Pacific** line. The line languished, with little freight for the small "Galloping Goose" engine to pull, until a sawmill opened in 1937. Sometimes a 95-ton **steam locomotive**, "Mount Emily Shay No. 1", leased from the **Oregon Historical Society**, is used to reenact a **logging railroad** run. East of the Cascades; Oregonian 1/28/97:B3.

Prineville District, BLM. A 1,581,745-acre district of **Bureau of Land Management** grazing and forest lands in the drainages of the **Deschutes** and **John Day Rivers**. 185 E 4th Street, P.O. Box 550, Prineville 97754. 541-447-4115. BLM Facts.

Prineville Reservoir. An 18-mile long, serpentine irrigation impoundment on the **Crooked River**, 15 miles southeast of **Prineville**. The lake, which covers 3,136 acres to a maximum depth of 130 feet, was formed by Arthur R. Bowman Dam in 1961 and is a major component of the **Crooked River Project**. A resort and **Prineville Reservoir State Park** offer facilities for the many boaters and fishermen. Water transparency of the lake is usually limited because of suspended fine soil particles. Atlas of Oregon Lakes.

Prineville Reservoir State Park. A central Oregon **state park** 17 miles southeast of **Prineville**. The park has a boat ramp and docks, plus 70 campsites and three cabins. Reservations, 800-452-5687. 916777 Parkland Drive, Prineville 97754. 541-447-4363.

Printing. See **Book publishing**; **Broadside**; **Newspapers**; **Periodicals**.

Prison Blues. A line of blue jeans and T-shirts made by inmates at the Eastern Oregon Correctional Institution. They are sold in stores and by mail-order. 800-597-7472. See also **Correctional facilities**.

Prison costs. See **Corrections, costs**.

Prisons, federal. See **Sheridan Federal Correctional Institution**.

Prisons, state. See **Correctional facilities**.

Private investigators. In 1996 there were 800 private investigators in Oregon, a number that is expected to increase by 6.9% a year to 1,238 in the year 2005. Beginning in 1998, private investigators will have to take an ethics test, pay for a license, and get 16 hours of training a year. Felons will not be licensed. Oregonian 10/5/97:C1.

Private schools. See **Schools, private**.

Prizes. See **Andre Berger Awards**; **Drammy awards**; **Earle A. Chiles Award**; **Governor's Arts Award**; **MacArthur Fellowships**; **National Book Awards**; **Nobel Prize**; **Oregon Book Awards**; **Pulitzer Prize**.

Probation. A suspended sentence given to a convicted offender who serves no prison time so long as he meets the prescribed conditions of good behavior. See also **Community Corrections**; **Parole**.

Professional sports teams. See **Baseball, professional**; **Basketball, men's**; **Basketball, women's**.

Professional Technical Education. An office in the Oregon Department of **Education** that, among other things, works to create employment training opportunities for Oregon high school and **community college** students. 37% of high school students enroll in professional technical courses. More than 100 Tech Prep/ Associate Degree programs combine high school and community college training, serving 31,000 students. The number of schools and businesses forming education partnerships has been increasing, prompted by Oregon's **Education Act for the 21st Century**. Oregon Report Card.

Progress Board. A nine-member board created in 1989 to monitor the state's strategic plan for economic development, **Oregon Shines**, and to be the major state agency monitoring long term trends. It reports biennially to the legislature on progress toward the **benchmark** goals. The Board is within the Oregon Department of **Economic Development**. 503-986-0033. Oregon Blue Book. See also **Economic Analysis Office**.

Prohibition. The sale of alcohol was an early and acrimonious issue in Oregon, beginning with the **provisional government**, which outlawed the sale of liquor between 1844 and 1849. Under a local option law adopted in 1904, some towns were "dry" and some were "wet" - even within counties that were dry. During **Pendleton**'s dry periods saloons went literally underground. Two years after Oregon women got the vote, the state, by **initiative**, prohibited the manufacture, transport, or sale of alcoholic beverages in 1914 (effective January 1, 1916). Eastern brewers retaliated by boycotting Oregon **hops**. Home brewing, moonshining, and bootlegging were prevalent during prohibition. Prohibition, adopted nationally in 1920, was repealed by both the state and nation in 1933. The sale of liquor by the drink was authorized in 1952. Brewed in the Pacific Northwest; East of the Cascades. See also **Alcohol**; **Children's Farm Home**; **Oregon Pacific Railroad**; **Temperance**; **Whiskey Local**.

Project Dayshoot. See **Oregon Photojournalism Day**.

Project Vote Smart. A national project headquartered in Oregon that provides free non-partisan information on issues and candidates to citizens and the media. Grants and memberships provide funding. Volunteers and student interns do much of the work, including staffing the phone banks. Center for National Independence in Politics, 129 NW 4th Street, Suite 204, Corvallis 97330. 800-

622-7627.

Projectile points. Sharp points that **Indians** made of shaped stone to use as tips on arrows, spears, and atlatl (throwing stick) darts. Pioneers found them in great numbers throughout Oregon; archeologists have identified certain styles with specific time periods. Enthusiasts who have studied the ancient techniques now make replicas. Archaeology of Oregon. See also **Archeology**; **Artifacts**.

Promised Land. A larger-than-life bronze sculpture that portrays a pioneer family, Bible in hand, on the **Oregon Trail**. The sculpture, by David Manuel of **Joseph**, was commissioned by the Oregon Trail Coordinating Council for $100,000 as a gift for **Portland**. After controversy erupted over the quality of the work and its lack of recognition of contributions by other races and cultures to Oregon's early history, it was decided that the sculpture, temporarily emplaced at several sites around Portland, would be permanently placed in Chapman Square in the **Plaza Blocks**. Oregonian 8/25/95:A1, 5/18/97:E8.

Pronghorn antelope. A deer-size game animal, *Antilocapra americana*, often called just antelope though it is not a true antelope. Pronghorns were originally found throughout eastern Oregon, in the southern **Cascade Range**, and in the **Rogue Valley**. They were much reduced by 1912, but numbers are now increasing in the **sagebrush** areas of eastern Oregon to over 22,000 in 1990. When running, they are able to attain speeds up to 70 miles per hour in short bursts, and to cruise at 35 mph. Both males and females have horns; only the black outer sheath is shed annually. Their hollow hair provides excellent insulation for cold weather. A white rump patch can be flashed at will; when the hairs lie down the patch all but disappears. **Hunting tags** are issued for central and eastern Oregon. Atlas of Oregon Wildlife; Big Game History; Mammals and Life Zones of Oregon; Oregon's Great Basin Country. See also **Hart Mountain National Antelope Refuge**.

Property tax. An annual tax that traditionally funded public schools, community colleges, and local governments. State government has received no property taxes since 1940. Before 1996, the amount of property tax was determined by multiplying the market value of real property and business personal property by the local government tax rates necessary to raise the amount needed. The amount needed was determined by the **tax base** plus any voter-approved serial levies (to provide additional operating funds for a limited time) and bond measures (for capital projects). that voters had authorized outside the tax base. Growth of the tax base without further voter authorization was limited to 6% a year, no matter how much population and inflation grew. Property tax assessments and collections are handled by counties. They were required to physically reappraise property every six years. In intervening years values were based on sales figures for comparable property. Oregonians defeated property tax limitations eight times before adopting **Measure 5**, limiting rates, in 1990. **Measure 47**, adopted in 1996 and amended by Measure 50 in 1997, limits increases in assessed value. Home values have increased faster than commercial property values, resulting in a shift of tax burden from business property to residential property. Governing Oregon; Oregonian 10/16/94:A18, 12/7/97:B2. See also **Assessed value**; **Strategic Investments Program**; **Tax exemptions**; **Tax increment financing**; **Taxes**.

Prospect. An unincorporated lumbering community in southwest Oregon on the upper **Rogue River** in **Jackson County**, located 44 miles northeast of **Medford** on Highway 42. The Prospect Hotel, opened in 1893 and restored in 1991, has hosted Jack London, Zane Gray, and Herbert Hoover, all of whom came to fly fish. Land in Common.

Prostitution. The Council for Prostitution Alternatives says that about 500 women are employed in the sex trade in **Portland** as prostitutes, dancers, lingerie models, and escorts. Portland has a forfeiture ordinance that allows the city to confiscate the car of a prostitution customer, and other cities are considering such ordinances. 1811 NE 39th Ave., 97212. 503-282-1082. Oregonian 10/16/97:F4. See also **Sex industry**.

Protected animals. Species that are protected by Oregon law and may not be taken without a Scientific Taking Permit from the Oregon Department of **Fish and Wildlife** - except for rabbits and rodents which may be taken if they are destroying agricultural crops or products. Protected animals include Columbian white-tailed **deer**, several **bats**, **pika**, pygmy **rabbit**, white-tailed **jack rabbit**, **chipmunk**, white-tailed antelope **squirrel**, Washington **ground squirrel**, chickaree (pine squirrel), **flying squirrel**, white-footed **vole**, **ringtail**, **fisher**, all **marine mammals**, and all non **game birds** except European starling, house sparrow, and rock dove. See also **Endangered animals**.

Provisional government, 1843-1849. An independent government in Oregon, answering to neither the U.S. nor Britain. It was the first government in the **Oregon Country**, formed as the result of a close vote May 2, 1843 at **Champoeg**. Since the **Hudson's Bay Company** had authority over the **French Canadian** and **British** residents, the provisional laws governed only the small American community in the **Willamette Valley**. Further, since the U.S./British **boundary question** had not yet been resolved, there was uncertainty about whether Oregon would eventually be independent, part of the U.S., or part of Britain. The provisional government established the usual three branches of government though with an executive committee instead of a governor, land laws, and **taxes** - which were made voluntary. The code of laws was based on the laws of the Territory of Iowa. In 1845 the provisional legislature elected a **governor**, George Abernethy, to replace the executive committee, and made Willamette Falls (**Oregon City**) the capital. Bitter antagonisms, centering around economic problems, **prohibition**, **land ownership**, and the **Hudson's Bay Company**, characterized the sessions of the provisional legislature. The provisional government continued until March 2, 1849 when the Oregon Country became part of the U.S. as the **Oregon Territory**. Dictionary of Oregon History; Empire of the Columbia. See also **Independence party**; **Joint Occupancy**; **Oregon Question**; **Organic laws**.

Proxy Falls. A 200-foot high waterfall on a tributary of the **McKenzie River**. A half mile hike from McKenzie Pass **Highway 242** six miles east of its junction with **Highway 126** leads to both Proxy Falls and Upper Falls, a waterfall that cascades over 100 feet from springs on the canyon wall. Nearby Proxy Point was named by surveyors looking for a possible triangulation station. Waterfall Lover's Guide.

Prunes and plums. A crop grown at one time over much of the **Willamette Valley**. In 1995 Oregon growers produced 3,500 tons of prunes and plums worth

$671,000, down from the 1935 high of 125,000 tons. The first prune orchard in Oregon was established in 1858 by Seth Lewelling. 1995 Oregon; Oregon Oddities; Oregonian 11/8/96:C4.

Psychiatric Security Review Board. A board of five members, appointed by the governor for three-year terms, that has jurisdiction over persons found by a court to be "guilty except for insanity." The board's jurisdiction is limited to the maximum time the person could have been incarcerated had the person been found responsible. The board may commit a person to a state hospital, conditionally release a person to a community-based program, revoke a conditional release, or discharge a person from its jurisdiction. 620 SW 5th Ave., Suite 907, Portland 97204. 503-229-5596. Oregon Blue Book.

Psychologist Examiners, State Board of. A seven member board appointed by the governor to license and regulate psychologists in Oregon. As of June 1997 there were about 970 licensed. 3218 Pringle Road SE, Suite 130, Salem 97302-6309. 503-378-4154. Oregon Blue Book.

Public broadcasting. The Oregon radio and television broadcasting stations that are funded by listeners, governments, educational institutions, and/or corporate sponsors instead of through paid advertising are listed in the Oregon Blue Book. **Bend**, **Corvallis**, **La Grande**, **Medford**, and **Portland** have public television stations, and twenty-five communities have public radio stations. KSOR Jefferson Public Radio in **Ashland** has the largest translator network of any public radio station in the U.S. See also **Oregon Public Broadcasting**.

Public domain. Lands owned by the federal government, especially those that are not reserved for some specific use. All of Oregon was federally-owned public domain land in 1846 (though nearly all without treaty agreement from **Indians**), but since then half of it has been transferred to tribal, state, or private ownership through treaties, the **Admission Act** and other acts of Congress, and **land grants** designed to encourage settlement and the construction of roads and railroads. Of Oregon's total area of 62 million acres, the federal government now owns 31.3 million acres. Of that, half (15.6 million acres) is managed by the **Forest Service** and half (15.7 million acres) by the **Bureau of Land Management**. Disposition of the Public Domain in Oregon.

Public Employees Retirement System (PERS). A retirement program serving some 800 Oregon governmental units. It has over 146,000 active members, 30,000 inactive members, and 66,000 retirees and beneficiaries. Forty percent of its members are school employees, 28% are state employees, and 32% are employees of other governmental units. It is funded by contributions from employers and employees plus income from investments, and provides retirement income, death benefits, and disability benefits. A board of nine members, appointed by the governor to three-year terms, guides it. 11410 SW 68th Parkway, Tigard 97223. 503-598-7377. Oregon Blue Book. See also **Employees, state**; **Investment Council**; **Pension puzzle**.

Public Instruction, Superintendent of. See **Superintendent of Public Instruction**.

Public Land Survey. A federal survey of western lands under the auspices of the U.S. **General Land Office**, based on the U.S. Land Ordinance of 1785, that called for marking land into six-mile square **townships**, each made up of 36 square-mile **sections**. The survey in Oregon began in 1851 with the establishment of the point now known as the **Willamette Stone** as the reference point. It is complete over most of the state except for some rugged areas of public land. The original surveyors' descriptive notes are useful to those interested in the vegetation cover at the time of the original survey. History of the Rectangular Survey System. See also **Land description; Land surveys; Oregon Manual; Standard parallels.**

Public Officials Compensation Commission. A commission authorized by the **legislature** to biennially review salaries of all **elected officials** and to recommend salary adjustments to the legislature. 155 Cottage St. NE, Salem 97310. 503-378-2766. Oregon Blue Book.

Public power. Concerns in the 1920's about the high rates charged by the private **electric utilities** led to protests by the **Grange**, George Joseph, and Governor Julius Meier, and eventually, in 1930, to voter approval of **people's utility districts**. (**Constitution** Article XI, Sec. 12) Disputes over public versus private development of dams on the **Snake River** continued into the 1950's. Hells Canyon.

Public Power Council. An organization of the 114 publicly-owned utilities that buy power and transmission services from **Bonneville Power Administration.** Members are from six Northwest states, including Oregon. 500 NE Multnomah Street, Portland 97232. 503-232-2427.

Public Safety Standards and Training, Board on. A 21-member board that sets standards for police and fire personnel, agencies, and for equipment. It also licenses **polygraph** examiners, and operates the public safety training facility at **Western Oregon State College**, sometimes called the Police Academy. 550 N. Monmouth Ave., Monmouth 97361. 503-378-2100. Oregon Blue Book.

Public schools. See **Schools, public.**

Public spaces, Portland. See **Commons; Outdoor concert sites; Pioneer Courthouse Square; Plaza Blocks.**

Public transit. In 1997 Oregon had ten public transportation districts providing scheduled bus service, and **Tri-Met** in **Portland** also provided **MAX** light rail. The other districts served **Astoria, Corvallis, Eugene, Hood River, John Day, Medford, Klamath Falls, Oregon City**, and **Salem**. Some other cities and counties provided scheduled service without having a transportation district, such as **Wilsonville** (South Metro Area Rapid Transit, or SMART) which operates free busses, including a commuter route to Salem. In 1990, 70% of Oregon commuters drove to work alone; the **Benchmark** goal is to reduce that to 50% by the year 2000. Coordination of public transit and some funding is available through the Public Transit Section in the Department of **Transportation**. 555 13th St. NE, Salem 97310. 503-986-3300. See also **Amtrak; Bus lines; Commuting; Light rail; Streetcars.**

Public Utility Commission (PUC). A three-member Oregon board that regulates customer rates and services of investor-owned utilities, including **telephone, natural gas**, and **electric utilities**, and some water companies. It does not regulate **people's utility districts**, cooperatives, or municipally-owned utilities, and its Transportation Program was transferred to the **Motor Carrier Transportation** branch in 1996. 550 Capitol St. NE, Salem 97310-1380. 503-378-6611. Oregon Blue Book. See also **Citizens Utility Board**.

Publishing. See **Book publishing**; **Broadside**; **Newspapers**; **Periodicals**.

PUD. See **People's utility district**.

Pudding River. A river that flows north 63 miles from the area east of **Salem** up through the central **Willamette Valley** to join the **Molalla River** a mile before the Molalla joins the **Willamette River** near **Canby**. It drains an area of 530 square miles and has an average annual volume of 883,900 acre feet, or 2.9 acre feet/acre. The near connection of a headwater creek with **Lake Labish** suggests that at some time in the distant past the Pudding may have been a channel of the Willamette. The river was christened in honor of a blood pudding enjoyed by fur trappers on its banks in about 1822. Oregon Geographic Names.

Pueblo Mountains. A 20-mile long range of desert mountains near the Nevada border of **Harney County**, south of **Steens Mountain**. High point is Pueblo Mountain at 8,725'. The range contains some of the oldest exposed rocks in southeast Oregon, thought to be 150 million years old. Miners in 1863 knew the area as the Puebla Mining District. The Pueblo Valley lies east of the mountains. Oregonian 7/20/95:E1; Oregon Geographic Names.

Pulitzer Prize. In 1934, the Pulitzer Prize in journalism for meritorious public service was awarded to the **Medford** Mail Tribune for its coverage of Jackson County's **Good Government Congress** turmoil. It is the only Oregon newspaper ever awarded the prize. Oregon author Harold Lenoir Davis (1894-1960) won the Pulitzer Prize for fiction in 1936 for his **novel**, Honey in the Horn. In 1939 Ronald Callvert of the **Portland** Oregonian received a Pulitzer for editorial writing, and in 1957 Wallace Turner and William Lambert of the Oregonian received Pulitzers for reporting on organized crime. Phyllis McGinley (1905-1978), born in **Ontario**, won the 1961 Pulitzer Prize for poetry. David Hume Kennerly, a photojournalist from **Roseburg**, received a Pulitzer Prize in 1972 for his coverage of Vietnam. Oregon Blue Book. See also **State of Jefferson**.

Pulp mills. Mills that physically or chemically break down wood to produce fibrous pulp from which paper is made. The first paper mill in the Pacific Northwest began operation in 1867 at **Oregon City** and the first pulp mill in Oregon opened near **Astoria** in 1884. Simpson's mill at **Willamette Falls** in **West Linn**, begun in 1889, was the oldest continuously operating pulp mill in Oregon when it closed in 1996; it reopened under new owners the next year. As of 1995 there were 13 pulp and/or paper plants in Oregon, seven of them using the odor-producing Kraft process to make pulp. The various specialized plants produce coated and uncoated printing papers, newsprint, tissue, paper bags, and corrugated layers and linerboard for cartons. Several of the mills utilize recycled paper. Encyclopedia of American Forest and Conservation History; Lockwood-Post's Directory. See also **Forest products industry**.

Pumice. A frothy form of **obsidian** ejected explosively from volcanoes and so full of air bubbles that pieces will float. The massive explosions of **Mount Mazama** blew pumice as far as Montana. Pumice is valued for making lightweight concrete aggregate with excellent structural, insulating, and soundproofing qualities, and is also used in the manufacture of stone-washed jeans. It is mined commercially in **Deschutes County**. Mineral Industry of Oregon. See also **Rhyolite**.

Pumpkins. The record for the largest pumpkin grown in Oregon is held by Kirk Mombert of **Coburg** who raised an 866-pound monster. Giant pumpkins add about 10 pounds a day as they near maturity. Oregonian 10/23/97:B1.

Pupil/teacher ratio. See **Student/teacher ratio**.

Puppets. See **Children's theater**.

Pursuit of the Nez Perce. The name given by the military to the campaign of 1877 against the non-treaty **Nez Perce** Indians. See **Nez Perce War**.

Quail. Small upland **game birds**. The three species found in Oregon include valley or California quail, *Callipepla californica*, with a teardrop-shaped plume arching forward, which was native to the southern edges of the state but has been introduced throughout; mountain quail, *Oreortyx pictus*, a secretive quail with a long, thin plume streaming up and back; and bob white, *Coolinus virginianus*, a plumeless quail introduced into northeast areas of the state. Atlas of Oregon Wildlife.

Quakers. See **George Fox College**.

Quaking aspen. See **Cottonwood**.

Queen Anne's lace. One of western Oregon's most common summer **weeds**, Queen Anne's lace, *Daucus carota*, is the wild version of the cultivated carrot. A biennial, it blooms and sets seed its second year and then dies. It was introduced from Europe. Plants and Animals.

Queen of Angels Monastery. A Benedictine Sisters **Catholic** convent in **Mount Angel** with 50 resident sisters. The community was established in 1882. The center wing of the 1887 monastery building and adjoining Howard Hall were damaged by the 1993 **Scotts Mills earthquake**. 840 Main Street, Mount Angel, 97362. 503-845-2556. Oregonian 5/16/95:B2.

Quicksand. Sand that is saturated with water and will no longer support weight. It is found in low places throughout Oregon's coastal sand **dunes**. Since it occurs near the top of the water table, it is more frequently found in winter months when the water table is higher. A person will normally not sink farther than hip deep.

Quicksand Bay. See **Tillamook Bay**.

Quotations. See **Broadside**; **"Good citizens are the riches of a city"**; **Mumford quote**; **"Visit, but don't stay"**.

R. C. Geer Farmhouse. A historic house east of **Salem**, open for visitors. Pioneer Ralph Carey Geer (1816-1895) started a nursery business in 1847, imported sheep from England, and was an early flax grower. 12390 Sunnyview Road NE, 97301. 503-873-3406. Dictionary of Oregon History.

Rabbits. Small furry mammals. Three species are native to Oregon, the brush rabbit, *Sylvilagus bachmani*, of western Oregon; Nuttall's cottontail, *S. nuttallii*, of eastern Oregon, and the smaller pygmy rabbit, *Brachylagus idahoensis*, of southeast Oregon which is now classed as a **protected animal**. The Eastern cottontail, *S. floridanus*, was introduced to **Linn County** in 1939 and has spread throughout the **Willamette Valley**. All rabbits will use burrows, but only the pygmy rabbit digs its own. Rabbit young are born naked and helpless. **Hares**, including

jackrabbits, are closely related, though the young of hares are born able to run, and hares don't use burrows. Atlas of Oregon Wildlife; Mammals and Life Zones of Oregon; Mammals of the Northwest. See also **Pika**; **Tularemia**.

Rabies. A virus disease of the nervous system, transmitted primarily by bites from infected animals, that is fatal in humans unless treated. Rabies is now comparatively rare in Oregon with no human cases reported in the 1990s. Five animal cases were reported in 1996 and 14 in 1997. Bats are the only reservoir species, though other animals can occasionally become infected as a result of contact with an infected bat. Oregon had a major outbreak of rabies between 1914 and 1920 that spread from coyotes to livestock and humans. In January 1936 in **Portland** there were 55 rabies cases, and in May of that year 85 persons were treated for dog bites. Mammals and Life Zones of Oregon.

Raccoon. A common, heavy-bodied nocturnal animal, *Procyon lotor*, up to 32 inches long and weighing about 20 pounds when full grown, with a black eye mask and bushy tail with alternating black and gray rings. It is found throughout most of Oregon except in high-mountain and arid areas. Raccoons are omnivorous, with much of their food gathered in or near water. They are good swimmers and climbers. Some people enjoy feeding these nightly marauders, though others find their damage to gardens, orchards, and poultry less captivating. In 1997 there were estimated to be about 200,000 in the **Portland** area, about one per family, though their numbers are decimated about every five years by distemper. In 1994-95, 3,584 were trapped with an average pelt value of $6 each. Atlas of Oregon Wildlife; Mammals and Life Zones of Oregon; Mammals of the Northwest. See also **Ringtail**.

Race. In the 1990 census, 94.6% of Oregonians identified themselves as white (compared with 69% in California), 2.4% as **Asian** or Pacific Islander, 1.6% as **black**, and 1.4% as American **Indian**, Eskimo, or Aleut. During the 1980s the black population grew 23.2%, Native American 26.2%, and Asian 69%. In 1990, 4% identified themselves as **Hispanic** (an ethnic rather than racial identify), and the number had increased 71.3% from 1980. See also **Bigotry**; **Minority, Women and Emerging Small Business Office**; **Population distribution, racial and ethnic**; **Segregation**.

Race for the Cure. A national series of races to raise money for breast cancer research, education, treatment, and screening. The 5k run/walk in **Portland** attracted 22,000 women participants in 1996 and raised $473,000, second only to the race in Washington, D.C. 75% of the money raised locally is spent locally. Oregonian 9/17/97:C1.

Racial and ethnic prejudice. See **Bigotry** .

Racing Commission. A five-member commission, appointed by the governor, that regulates **pari-mutuel racing**. It administers one greyhound and 11 horse meets conducted annually at various locations throughout Oregon. 800 NE Oregon St., #11, Suite 405, Portland 97232. 503-731-4052.

Radio stations. KGW in **Portland** began broadcasting in 1922, the first commercial station in Oregon. Oregon has 181 commercial stations listed in the 1997-98 Oregon Blue Book plus another 34 public or educational stations. See also **Forest Talk Radio**; **Public broadcasting**.

Radiologic Technology, Board of. A board of seven members, appointed by the governor for three-year terms, that licenses persons who use ionizing radiation on human beings for medical diagnosis or therapeutic purposes. In 1996 there were 2,122 licensed in Oregon. 407 State Office Building, 800 NE Oregon St., Portland 97232-2162. 503-731-4088. Oregon Blue Book.

Radon. A natural radioactive gas, formed by the decay of radium in the soil, that can lead to lung cancer, especially if it concentrates indoors. The concentration depends upon type of soil, closeness to the soil (radon is more concentrated in basements) and the air tightness of the building. Oregon averages 1.3 picoCuries per liter of air, well below the recommended safe level of 4 picoCuries. However, tests in northwest Oregon in 1994 found that 22% of the homes tested exceed the guideline, and West Salem averaged 10.2 picoCuries. Radon is highest in areas built on sediments or granite. Oregon Health Division, Suite 705, 800 NE Multnomah Street, Portland 97232, 503-731-4272. EPA 800-767-7236. Oregon Environmental Atlas; Oregonian 10/24/94:B2.

Raffles. See **Bingo**.

Rafting. See **White water boating**.

Rafts. See **Log rafts**.

Rail banking. An arrangement enacted by Congress in 1983 that enables a community to keep an abandoned railroad right-of-way intact while using it for other purposes, such as for a trail. See also **Rails to Trails**.

Rail biking. A sport that involves riding specially-fitted bicycles on railroad tracks. While all rail companies vigorously discourage unauthorized use, the Port of **Tillamook Bay** is exploring the possibility of organized rail bike tours over their tracks in the **Coast Range**. Oregonian 11/21/95:B2.

Rail lines, contemporary. See **Burlington Northern**; **Central Oregon and Pacific**; **Oregon-Tillamook**; **Prineville City Railroad**; **Union Pacific**; **Willamette and Pacific**.

Rail lines, historic. See **Astoria and Columbia River**; **Daddy Trains**; **DesChutes Railroad**; **Great Northern**; **Hunt Railroad**; **Northern Pacific**; **Oregon and California**; **Oregon Electric**; **Oregon Pacific**; **Oregon Railway and Navigation Co.**; **Oregon Short Line**; **Oregon Trunk Line**; **Pacific Railway and Navigation Co.**; **Southern Pacific**; **Spokane, Portland and Seattle**; **Sumpter Valley**; **W.C.T.U.**; **Whiskey Local**.

Rail lines, passenger. See **Amtrak**; **Light rail**; **Northwest High-Speed Rail Corridor**; **Zoo railway**.

Railroad bridges. **Portland**'s Steel Bridge, opened in 1887 (replaced in 1912) was the first railroad bridge across the **Willamette River**. Until it was built, east-bound passengers were ferried across the river to catch the train. Trains northbound from Portland were themselves ferried across the **Columbia River** between **Goble** and Kalama, Washington, until the **Spokane, Portland and Seattle Railroad** completed a double-track bridge from Portland across **Hayden Island** to Vancouver in 1908. The Booth-Kelly Railroad Bridge (the Hayden Bridge) across the **McKenzie River** at **Springfield** is thought to be the oldest remaining bridge in Oregon; it was built in Utah in 1882 and moved to the McKenzie in 1900. The railroad bridge over the **Crooked River Gorge** is 320 feet above the river, 25 feet higher than the nearby highway bridge, and was one of the highest bridges in the world at the time of its construction in 1910. Stations West.

Railroad land grants. See **Northern Pacific; O&C lands**.

Railroad Survey. See **Pacific Railroad Survey.**

Railroads. A $400 million industry that transports more than 40% of the Oregon products that leave the state, and, through **Amtrak**, provides passenger service on major routes. In 1992 rail freight in and out of Oregon totaled 53.8 million tons, with a fourth of it originating in the state. Farm products were the largest commodity shipped by rail, followed by lumber and wood products. The state's rail system includes about 2,600 route-miles of track (down from a 1930 peak of over 4,000 miles), operated by two class-one lines (**Union Pacific** and **Burlington Northern**) and about twenty **shortline railroads**. Union Pacific provides most of Oregon's railroad service, operating a main line to the east out of **Portland** as well a the main line from Portland south to California. The rail corridor between Portland and **Eugene** is part of the federal **Northwest High-Speed Rail Corridor**. Transportation Development Branch, Oregon Department of Transportation. 555 13th St. NE, Salem 97301. 503-986-3420. Oregon Blue Book; Oregonian 9/30/97:C3. See also **Excursion trains; Light rail; Rail banking; Union Station.**

Railroads, history. The first railroad in Oregon was a wooden tramway, built to connect Abernethy Island in the **Willamette River** to **Oregon City**. The first steam engine in Oregon, the **Oregon Pony**, arrived by ship in 1862 for use on iron-faced rails on a 5-mile portage around **Cascades of the Columbia River**. Regular rail service began in the Willamette Valley in 1870. The first **transcontinental connection** between **Portland** and the east coast opened in 1883 (California had connected in 1869) via the **Oregon Railway and Navigation Company** and the **Northern Pacific** through Montana. It provided an alternative to **wagon trains**. In 1884 a connection at **Huntington** with the **Oregon Short Line** from Wyoming provided another transcontinental link. The **Oregon and California/ Southern Pacific** line from Portland to San Francisco was finally completed through in 1887. The **Battle of the Gorge**, 1909-1911, resulted in rail service up the **Deschutes River** to **Bend** and eventually on south to California. The railroads led to **population growth** and expansion of the **economy**; they also played a major, and frequently corrupting, role in Oregon politics at the end of the 19th century. **Logging railroads** that used geared locomotives on steep grades carried logs from forests to mills during the first half of the 20th century. In 1919 nearly 20,000 members of Oregon trade unions marched in **Portland** demanding joint ownership of **railroads** by employees, operators, and the federal government. Atlas of Oregon; Backwoods Railroads; Oregon Oddities; This Day in Oregon. See also **Celebrations; Excursion trains; De Autremont brothers; Electric railways; Locomotives; Pacific Railroad Survey; Rail lines; Train wrecks; Venal officials; Whiteaker's Ride.**

Rails to Trails. A nationwide but locally-funded effort to convert abandoned rail lines to trails. Oregon has eight trails, with more possible as rail lines are abandoned. The eight are **Banks-Vernonia Linear State Park** (21 miles); Springwater Corridor (16.8 miles) in southeast **Portland**; Row River (13 miles) east of **Cottage Grove**; OC&E and Woods (110 miles) from **Klamath Falls** to Bly, and from Beatty north to Thompson Reservoir; **Deschutes River** (16 miles) at the mouth of the river; Wallula Lake (4.8 miles) from two miles upstream from **McNary Dam** to Hat Rock State Park; Sumpter Valley (.2 mile) at Dixie Summit on **Highway 26** east of **Prairie City**; and Malheur (12 miles) from Summit Prairie to Murray Camp south of Strawberry Mountain Wilderness Area. Oregonian 5/11/95:D1. See also **Rail banking**.

Rainbow Family. An informal group that has gathered annually on some **National Forest** across the country every Fourth of July since 1972. The group camped in Oregon in 1978 and 1991, and in 1997 the 20,000 campers gathered south of **Prineville**. The group is noted for its alternative life style, clean camps, and post-event rehabilitation of its sites.

Rainfall. See **Precipitation**; **Rainfall records**.

Rainfall records. As of the end of 1996, Oregon's record 24-hour rainfall was 10.65", recorded at Elk River Fish Hatchery, 5 miles east of **Port Orford** on November 19, 1996. **Portland** received more than 10" in two days, December 12 and 13, 1882, and more than 7.5" of that fell in 24 hours. The record amount for a month, 52.78", was recorded at Glenora Station (now Lees Camp) at the mouth of the North Fork of the **Wilson River** in **Tillamook County** in December 1917. Oregon's record for a single year is 204" (17 feet), recorded at Laurel Mountain in western **Polk County** in 1996. The previous record had been 169", recorded at nearby **Valsetz** in 1937. Oregonian 2/12/96:B7, 1/13/97:A17; Weather of Oregon. See also **Precipitation**.

Rainier. "Spirited City on the Mighty Columbia." A river town in **Columbia County** about half way between **Portland** and **Astoria** on **Highway 30**. The town and post office were established by Charles Fox in 1851, and named Eminence. The following year the name was changed to Rainier for the Washington mountain that can be seen from the area. The city was incorporated in 1885. The town has several homes over 100 years old. The 1930 Lewis and Clark **bridge** across the **Columbia River** connects Rainier to Longview, Washington. In September 1995 the town was featured on the national MacNeil/Lehrer Newshour as example of a community where citizens are actively involved in improving economic stability and quality of life. Population 1980 1,655; 1995 1,720. Elevation 23'. PO Box 100, 97048. 503-556-7301. Oregon Geographic Names.

Rainmaking. See **Weather modification**.

Rajneeshpuram. A onetime city and commune in north central Oregon's **Wasco County**. In 1981 the red-clad followers of Bhagwan Shree Rajneesh bought the 64,000 acre **Big Muddy** Ranch on a tributary of the **John Day River**, and immediately built and incorporated the commune where the Bhagwan, with a fleet of Cadillacs, presided. During their four years there, the commune spent $60 million developing a community for 3,000 people, including a water and sewer system, two lakes, an airport, a hotel, 88,000-square-foot meeting hall, residences (the Bhagwan's house burned in a 1996 wildfire), shops, and the Rajneesh International Meditation University. The community was incorporated in 1982 as **Rajneeshpuram**, an action the U.S. District Court invalidated as a violation of the separation of church and state. In 1984 the 4,000 followers took over the city of

Antelope and renamed it Rajneesh. That same year members of the commune spread *Salmonella* organisms in restaurant salad bars in **The Dalles** and 750 people became ill. Later that year the commune brought bus loads of homeless people to the commune and registered them to vote in an apparent attempt to take over county government. An investigation implicated the group in arson, attempted murder, and a large wiretapping network. The Bhagwan's main assistant, Ma Anand Sheela, fled to Germany in 1985 where she was arrested on a variety of U.S. charges. After the Bhagwan attempted an escape the same year, he was fined $400,000 and deported to India where he died in 1990, having changed his name to Osho. Oregon Geographic Names; Oregonian 6/5/95:B1, 9/19/95:B2.

Rancheria. An Indian village, especially in southwest Oregon. Requiem for a People.

Ranches. The largest cattle ranch in Oregon is the **ZX Ranch** at **Paisley**, owned by Idaho potato baron J.R. Simplot; it covers 1.3 million acres, including rented land. Famous historic ranches include the P Ranch developed by Peter French (1849-1897) beginning in 1871. The ranch eventually covered 150,000 acres, from the Catlow Valley north to **Malheur Lake**, and ran 45,000 head of cattle. Although an excellent rancher, French was drawn into numerous disputes with other settlers in the area and was killed by one of them. Henry Miller (1827-1916) and his Pacific Land and Livestock Company owned over a million acres and a million head of cattle in five states, including the former **Whitehorse Ranch** and Alvord Ranch in Oregon. Bill Brown (1855-1941), "Horse King of the Northwest," owned 34,000 acres and more than 10,000 horses in the **Wagontire Mountain** area. Cattle Country of Peter French; Feelin' Fine (Bill Hanley); Gold and Cattle Country (Herman Oliver); Oregon Cattleman (Walter Pierce); Oregon's Great Basin Country; William "Bill" W. Brown. See also **Big Muddy**; **Cattle**; **Horseback rides**; **Horses**; **Range wars**; **Resort ranches**; **Sheep**.

Range (land description). See **Township**.

Range wars. Disputes between sheepmen and cattlemen over the use of Oregon's open range led cattlemen to form the Crook County Sheep Shooting Association in 1896. The members had to swear to secrecy and agree to lie, if necessary, on the witness stand. Between 1903 and 1906 over 10,000 eastern-Oregon sheep were killed, and hay and sheep camps were destroyed with impunity. Public outrage was aroused by a letter the group sent to the Oregonian in 1906 bragging about what they had done, and was aroused further when a **Silver Lake** storekeeper who might have been able to identify buyers of ammunition was found dead. There was never any prosecution, but the wars ended when the U.S. **Forest Service** instituted grazing permits and range allotments in late 1906. However, the **Wagontire Mountain** Range Feud over access to water holes led to the deaths of five men between 1925 and 1930. Antelope; East of the Cascades; William "Bill" W. Brown.

Rangeland. Lands used for cattle grazing. 22.3 million acres of Oregon lands (36% of the state) are classed as rangeland, 9.2 million acres of it privately owned and 13.1 million acres owned by the federal government. Most of central Oregon was a grass prairie just 120 years ago. After the **gold rush** died out in the 1870s, some miners turned to ranching and brought in thousands of **cattle** and

sheep. Within a few decades much of the bunchgrass was gone, and **sagebrush** and **juniper** began to spread across the rangeland; the transition time can be marked by counting the rings in large sagebrush bushes. Wild rye, the **High Desert**'s largest bunchgrass, once made a lush cover but could not survive mowing, grazing, and declining water tables. Range conditions are now rated, depending upon the per cent of the original plant community that is present and the amount of soil erosion. In 1995, 31% of the **Bureau of Land Management** (BLM) rangeland in Oregon and Washington was rated excellent or good. Non-native noxious **weeds** have taken over about 9% of the rangeland. In 1906 the new **National Forests** began charging a grazing fee, and since the 1934 **Taylor Grazing Act**, grazing on 13 million acres of other eastern Oregon **public domain** rangeland has been managed by the BLM. In 1993 its grazing fees were $1.92 per AUM (Animal Unit Month, equal to one cow per month) in the winter and $1.86 in the summer for some 700,000 AUMs. Atlas of the Pacific Northwest; BLM Facts; Crossing the Next Meridian; "Fort Rock Basin"; Gold and Cattle Country; (High Desert Museum); Listening to Coyote; Oregon Desert; Oregonian 10/28/96:A1; Prairie Keepers; Public Grazing Lands; Sacred Cows. See also **Cow Cops**; **Crooked River National Grassland**; **Livestock districts**; **Range wars**; **Vale Project**.

Rare animals and plants. See **Endangered animals**; **Endangered plants**.

Raspberries. In 1995, growers in the **Willamette Valley** produced 20,000 pounds of red raspberries (a third of the nation's crop), worth $12.8 million, on 3,820 acres. Oregon also produces 100% of the nation's black raspberries, sometimes called black caps, which brought in $2 million in 1995. 1995 Oregon.

Rats. The rats of Oregon include **wood rats**, **kangaroo rats**, and the Norway rat, *Rattus norvegicus*, introduced from ships in early 1800s. It is a vector for **plague**, typhus, **tularemia**, and ectoparasites and also causes damage by consuming and contaminating food. It is omnivorous and semi aquatic, and is closely associated with human activity. Atlas of Oregon Wildlife; Mammals and Life Zones of Oregon; Mammals of the Northwest.

Rattlesnake. The only reptile native to Oregon that is poisonous to humans, and the only pit viper found in the state. The Western rattlesnake, *Crotalus viridis*, is of variable color and pattern, and two to five feet in length. It hibernates in dens during the winter and emerges when outdoor temperatures rise above 70° F. It lives on rodents and other small animals, killed by venom injected through its pair of hollow fangs. Each time it sheds its skin, once a year or more often, a new segment is added to the rattle on the end of its tail. Few people have actually died from a rattlesnake bite. In case of a bite, the patient should be kept quiet with the bite and his heart as close to the same level as possible, and a call placed to the Oregon **Poison Center**, 800-452-7165 (225-8968 in **Portland**). Atlas of Oregon Wildlife; Field Guide to Western Reptiles and Amphibians; Knowing Oregon Reptiles. See also **Imnaha**.

Razor clam. A clam, *Siliqua patula*, with a thin oval shell up to 6" long, that is found on ocean sand beaches of the Pacific Northwest from the low-tide line out about a mile. In Oregon they are found near **Seaside** and on several beaches south to Myers Creek in **Curry County**. Razor clams can dig themselves down into the sand (9" a minute) until they are several feet deep. Razor clams should be avoided when they contain paralytic saxitoxins; razor clamming in Oregon was closed from 1991 until 1994 because of toxins. Clamming is regulated by the Oregon Department of **Fish and Wildlife** which sets catch limits, but no license is required. Clam Digging and Crabbing in Oregon. See also **Shellfish poisoning**.

Real Estate Agency. The state agency responsible for the licensing, education, and enforcement mandated by Oregon's real-estate laws, regulating escrow agents, registering subdivisions, condominiums, timeshares and campgrounds, and investigating complaints. It processes some 5,000 license applications and monitors 4,700 escrow and real estate offices a year. In 1996 there were 1,300 real estate appraisers and 6,172 real estate brokers in the state. 1177 Center St. NE, Salem 97310-2503. Licensing and Information 503-378-4170. Regulation and enforcement 503-378-8414. Oregon Blue Book.

Real estate promotions. See **Christmas Valley**; **Imperial**.

Rebecca at the Well. A sculpture in **Portland**'s **Park Blocks** given to the city in 1926 by Joseph Shemanski, a grateful immigrant. Oliver Barrett was the sculptor. Portland, An Informal History; Portland's Public Art.

Recall. The power of the Oregon electorate to vote a state or local elected official out of public office between elections; it does not apply to U.S. senators or representatives. The recall was made part of the Oregon **constitution**, Article II, Section 18, in 1908 by voters using their new **initiative** powers. It has been used sparingly, being normally reserved for instances of malfeasance or flagrant incompetence. The request for a recall election for a statewide office requires petition signatures equal to 15% of the votes for **governor** in the official's district at the most recent election. For a statewide elective office, 183,152 signatures would be required, 1994-1998. Oregon Blue Book. See also **Elections Division**.

Recessions. A major Oregon recession was triggered in 1980-1983 when national mortgage interest rates rose to 15%, resulting in the collapse of the home-building market. In less than a year Oregon lost 13,519 timber jobs, or one in seven. In three years the state lost a total of 100,000 jobs, and by January 1983, the state's unemployment rate had reached 12.5%. That year, for the first time since 1830, the state's population decreased. By 1986 the state was producing as much lumber as before the recession, but with nearly thirty thousand fewer workers. Various national economic downturns have also affected Oregon, including those in 1907, 1913-15 (20% unemployment in **Portland**), 1921 (employment dropped 31% as the **World War I** boom ended), and 1991. Fire at Eden's Gate. See also **Depressions**.

Reclamation. See **Bureau of Reclamation**.

Recreational vehicles (RVs). In 1994, there were a dozen major brands of RVs manufactured in Oregon, and 7,782 motor homes and trailers were produced. Some 191,000 RVs were registered in the state. Oregonian 9/13/95:C1.

Recycling. In 1995, 34.7% of disposed material in Oregon was recycled. This totaled 1.3 million tons, or 804 pounds per person. Rates ranged from lows of 9% and 10% in **Lake** and **Wallowa** counties to a high of 39% in the **Metro** area. Curbside recycling is mandated by an 1983 law, and a 1991 Oregon law, the first of its kind in the country, mandated recycling 25% of plastic containers; Oregon actually recycles about 32%. Oregon law mandates a statewide 50% recycling level by the year 2000. <u>Oregon Environmental Atlas</u>; <u>Oregonian</u> 11/8/96:C1; <u>Solid Waste</u>. See also **Bottle Bill**; **Landfills**; **Solid waste**.

Red Electrics. Red electric passenger trains operated by the **Southern Pacific** from 1914 to 1929 on a loop down the **Willamette Valley** from **Portland** to **Corvallis**. The east side of the loop went south through Oswego (now **Lake Oswego**), **Sherwood**, and **Newberg**; the west side went through **Beaverton**, **Forest Grove**, and **Gaston**. <u>Red Electrics</u>. See also **Electric railways**; **Oregon Electric Railway**.

Red fir. See **Douglas-fir**; **Fir**.

Red Hat. See **Operation Red Hat**.

Red tide. A term for a "bloom" of oceanic phytoplankton (single-celled algae). The numbers of algae increase to such an extent that they color the sea red - or brown or green, and some blooms do not color the water at all. Some blooms are bioluminescent. Sometimes the bloom is that of a species that produces toxins which accumulate in the "filter-feeders," clams and oysters that feed on the plankton. It does not seem to harm them but may be fatal to humans. See also **Shellfish poisoning**.

Redmond. "The Hub of Central Oregon." A rapidly-growing central Oregon city 16 miles northeast of **Bend** on **Highway 97** in **Deschutes County**. Its economy is based on agriculture, wood products, services, and recreation. The Redmond Air Center is a regional center for U.S. **Forest Service** fire management activities, including smoke jumpers. Area attractions include rock climbing at **Smith Rock State Park**, skiing, fishing and boating, golf, a reindeer ranch, Peterson Rock Garden, Fantastic Museum, Crooked River Dinner Train, and Eagle Crest destination resort. The Redmond post office was established in 1905 and named for Frank Redmond, the first settler to acquire **Carey Act** land in an 85,000-acre area proposed for irrigation. The town was platted in 1906, incorporated in 1910, and the **Oregon Trunk Line** railroad arrived in 1911. Whangarei, New Zealand, is its sister city. Population 1980 6,452; 1995 10,585. Elevation 2,996'. 716 SW Evergreen, PO Box 726, 97756. 541-923-7710. Chamber of Commerce 800-574-1325. <u>East of the Cascades</u>; <u>Redmond</u>.

Redwood. A tall coastal California conifer **tree**, *Sequoia sempervirens*, that is also native to the southwest corner of Oregon. At one time, before the **Cascade Range** emerged, redwood, the related giant sequoia, *Sequoiadendron*, and the dawn redwood, *Metasequoia*, were all found throughout warmer, moister Oregon. They are now planted as ornamentals, though they sometimes outgrow urban gardens. Redwoods have flat rows of needles, inch-long, thick-scaled cones, and wood that is extremely resistant to decay. <u>Trees to Know</u>.

Reed College. An accredited four-year liberal arts college in **Portland** that is renowned for its high academic standards; it has more **Rhodes scholars** for its size than any other school in the U.S. (The school fight song is "Hegel, Kant, Marx, Spinoza! C;mon Reed, hit 'em in the nosa!") Reed was established by a $3,000,000 bequest from the widow of Portland businessman Simeon G. Reed; classes began in 1911. Enrollment in fall 1995 was 1,290. 3202 SE Woodstock Blvd., Portland 97202. 503-771-1112. <u>Dictionary of Oregon History</u>; <u>Oregon Blue Book</u>. See also **McCarthyism**.

Reedsport. A western Oregon city on **Highway 101** in **Douglas County**, located ten miles upstream from the mouth of the **Umpqua River**. Area attractions include **Oregon Dunes National Recreation Area**, **Umpqua River Lighthouse**, Dean Creek **Elk** Viewing Area, and the **Umpqua Discovery Center**. Beginning in 1877 large crews of Chinese were brought in annually to can **salmon** caught by Scandinavian fishermen. The city was platted about 1900 and named for Alfred W. Reed, a pioneer resident of the area. The post office was established in 1912, the same year the railroad was built, and the city was incorporated in 1919. After floods devastated the city in 1927 and 1964, a dike wall, some of it now featuring murals, was built around the lower area. Population 1980 4,984; 1995 4,860. Elevation 10'. 451 Winchester Ave., 97467. 541-271-3603. Chamber of Commerce 800-247-2155. Oregon Geographic Names.

Referendum. A provision in the Oregon **constitution** that allows the **legislature** or the voters themselves to refer an act of the **legislature** for a vote by the people. The referendum was adopted in 1902 and is part of the **Oregon System**. Through 1996, the voters have referred 61 measures of which 25 passed. The legislature itself has referred 363 measures of which 206 passed. (The legislative referrals include constitutional amendments, which, by law, must be referred.) Voters who wish to refer a legislative measure to the ballot must file a petition within 90 days of the date the legislature adopted the measure. The petition must be signed by 4% of the number of electors who voted in the most recent regular election for **governor** (48,841 valid signatures, 1994-1998). Local **ordinances** may also be referred with signatures from 10% of the registered voters in that jurisdiction. Governing Oregon; Oregon Blue Book. See also **Ballot measures**; **Elections Division**.

Reforestation. Oregon has required reforestation following timber harvesting since 1941. Compliance is over 97%. See also **Forest Practices Act**.

Refuges. See **National Wildlife Refuges**.

Region 2040 plan. A plan for guiding growth in the **Metro** area for 50 years. It was adopted by the Metro Council in 1994 after years of work and public input. The plan is designed to prevent sprawl into farmland by accommodating most of the anticipated 700,000 new residents within the existing 365-square mile **urban growth boundary** and adding 18,500 acres to it. The **Regional Framework Plan**, completed in December 1997, laid out the specifics. Oregonian 12/8/94:C6, 3/19/97:A15.

Regional Development. A division in the Oregon Department of **Economic Development** that assists local cities, counties, and port districts to meet their economic development needs, especially in accessing federal programs. 503-986-0210. Oregon Blue Book.

Regional Framework Plan. A comprehensive plan adopted by **Metro** in 1997 to guide and manage area growth to the year 2040. The plan was mandated by the Metro charter that voters adopted in 1992. It sets guidelines for land use in order to minimize the impact of metropolitan growth on surrounding farmlands, deals with housing, schools, transportation, parks, water, and hazards and establishes measures for gauging the success of the plan. One chapter addresses coordination with neighboring Clark County, Washington. Oregonian 12/11/97:A21.

Registration. See **Voter registration**.

Religion. About a third of Oregonians are members of some organized religion, ranking in the bottom three states, and Oregon is also near the bottom in church attendance, with only a third attending regularly - although 290,000 people attended the 1992 Billy Graham crusade in **Portland**. **Marion County** led the state in the 1990 census with 48% of its population as church adherents (nearly half of them Catholic), while **Wheeler County**, with 20%, had the fewest. A 1990 study found that Oregon had the highest percent (17%) of nonbelievers of any state. The largest Christian denomination in the state is **Catholic** with, in 1995, 309,000 adherents, almost 10% of the state's population. Other major denominations included Church of Jesus Christ of Latter-day Saints with 130,000 Oregon members, Evangelical Lutheran 49,000, Assemblies of God 47,000, United **Methodist** 42,000, **Presbyterian** Church (USA) 38,000, Christian Churches/Churches of Christ 37,000, **Seventh Day Adventist** 34,000, Southern **Baptist** Convention 31,000, plus dozens of denominations with fewer than 30,000 members. Non-Christian religious groups in Oregon include the **Jewish faith** (20,000 members), **Islam** (7,000), **Baha'i Faith, Church of Scientology**, and Buddhist. Facts of Life; Oregonian 1/21/96:C2. See also **Church of the Bride of Christ; Church of the Holy Water; Disciples of Christ; Episcopal Church; Mennonites; Unitarian Universalist Church; United Brethren Church; United Church of Christ**.

Relocation centers. In 1942, during the early days of **World War II**, the U.S. government moved 123,000 resident West Coast **Japanese** Americans, 75,000 of them American citizens, to ten inland relocation centers and 18 isolation centers. The numbers included 4,043 Japanese from western Oregon who were first detained several months at the Portland International Livestock Yards (called the North Portland Assembly Center) where they were housed in the animal pens. **Ontario** was a "free zone" where Japanese Americans could work without living in a camp. Following the war, **anti-Japanese** sentiment, such as ads and petitions in the **Hood River** newspaper, discouraged many from returning to their farms; a number settled in Ontario and **Portland** instead. The **Four Rivers Cultural Center** honors those displaced during the war, as does the **Japanese American Historical Plaza** in **Portland**. "The Japanese in Oregon;" Touching the Stones.

Renewable energy. In Oregon **hydroelectric power** and **wood** together provide nearly a fourth of Oregon's total **energy**, a higher proportion of renewable energy than in any other state. Geothermal and solar energy are used primarily for home and business heating. Biomass technology, using such things as garbage, animal wastes, and wood residues produces about 105 trillion Btu per year in Oregon, about 16% of the state's non-transportation energy. See also **Biofuels; Wind power**.

Reported diseases. See **Diseases**.

Representatives, Oregon. Sixty representatives serve in the Oregon **House of Representatives**, each elected from a single-member district for a two-year term. A candidate must be 21, a U.S. citizen, and have resided in the district for a year prior to election. In the 1990s each house district includes over 47,000 people; the districts are redrawn every 10 years after the census. Representatives are limited to 6 years (3 terms) of service in the House after 1992; the record service is 14 terms, from 1969 through 1997, served by Republican Bill Markham from **Riddle**. The pay for Representatives, last raised in 1997, is $14,496 a year. Oregon Capitol, Salem 97310. 503-986-1187. 800-332-2313 during the session. Oregon Blue Book; Oregon Legislative Guide. See also **Campaign finance**; **Ethics**; **Legislature**; **Recall**; **Term limits**.

Representatives, U.S. Representatives to the U.S. Congress are elected for two-year terms. Since the reapportionment following the 1980 census, Oregon has had five representatives in the U.S. House of Representatives. The state had just one in 1860, but as the state grew, the number increased to 2 after the 1890 census, to 3 in 1910, to 4 in 1940, and then to 5 in 1980. Some who served the longest in Washington were Willis Hawley (R) of **Salem**, 13 terms, 1907-1933, Al Ullman (D) of Baker, now **Baker City**, 12 terms, 1957-1981; Walter Norblad, Jr. (R) of **Astoria**, 10 terms, 1946-1964; Edith Green (D) of **Portland**, 10 terms, 1955-1975; and Les AuCoin (D) of **Portland**, nine terms, 1975-1993. The Oregon Blue Book lists all of Oregon's past and present U.S. representatives. See also **Congressional districts**; **Felony**; **Scandals**; **Term limits**; **Whiteaker's Ride**.

Reptiles. 28 species of reptiles are found in Oregon: two **turtles**, eleven **lizards**, and fifteen **snakes**. Knowing Oregon Reptiles. See also **Animals**.

Republican party. One of Oregon's two major **political parties**, and one that has frequently dominated Oregon politics, especially during the first 70 years of the 20th century. For the November 1996 election 714,548 Oregonians (36%) registered as Republican, compared to 805,286 (41%) as **Democratic** and 400,248 (20%) as **Independent**. The Republican party grew from Whig and American Party members who were united in their opposition to **slavery**. Dubbed "Black Republicans" and backed by the Oregonian, they were decisive in nominating Abraham Lincoln for the presidency in 1860. Republican State Central Committee of Oregon, 8196 SW Hall Blvd, Suite 101, PO Box 1450, Beaverton 97075-1450. 503-520-1996. Dictionary of Oregon History; Oregon Blue Book; This Day in Oregon. See also **Dorchester Conference**; **Oregon Conservative Convention**; **Political parties**; **Voter registration**.

Rescissions Act of 1995. See **Salvage rider**

Reservations. See **Indian reservations**.

Reservoirs. Man-made lakes, usually constructed by placing a **dam** across a river, that are designed to provide irrigation water during dry summer months, generate power, provide flood control, supply municipal water, enhance wildlife habitat, and/or provide recreation opportunities. Oregon has over 60 man-made lakes having 5,000 **acre-feet** or more of storage capacity, and the state's largest, **Lake Owyhee**, stores over one million acre-feet of water. Irrigation reservoirs are usually drawn down during the summer as water is needed for crops, whereas flood-control reservoirs are drawn down in the fall to make room for winter storm flows and later snowmelt runoff. Power generation may lead to fluctuating stream flows downstream from a reservoir, though the fluctuations are sometimes modified by a second dam downstream.

Resort ranches. Ranches, also called dude ranches, that give visitors a taste of ranch life. There are several in Oregon, located in nearly all parts of the state. Information is available from the **Tourism Commission**.

Resorts. Destination resorts in Oregon that offer a variety of recreational facilities, including **golf**, include Salishan south of **Lincoln City** 800-452-2300; Resort at the Mountain at Welches 800-669-7666; Kah-Nee-Ta on the **Warm Springs Reservation** 800-554-4786; Black Butte Ranch near **Sisters** 800-452-7455; Eagle Crest near **Redmond** 800-682-4786; Inn of the Seventh Mountain west of **Bend** 800-452-6810; Sun River south of **Bend** 800-547-3922; and the newest, Running Y Ranch Resort near **Klamath Falls** 888-797-2624.

Resource and Technology Development Fund. A state fund chartered in 1985 to invest in early-stage businesses and applied research projects with the goal of turning them into wealth-creating enterprises anchored in Oregon. In 9 years it has invested $11.3 million of **lottery** funds in 42 ventures. Returns from investments are used to cover operating expenses and for reinvesting in new businesses. A six member board appointed by the governor guides the investments. Cascadia Pacific Management, 4370 NE Halsey Street, Suite 233, Portland 97213-1566. 503-282-4462. Oregon Blue Book.

Respiratory care practitioners. See **Medical Examiners**.

Rest areas. Areas established along **highways** that are designed to improve highway safety by giving motorists a place to take a break from driving. They usually include rest rooms. The first in Oregon were built in the early 1920s. Ten pairs are located along **Interstate 5** about 30 miles apart. The first, north of **Eugene**, opened in 1962. Rest areas along **Interstate 84** are spaced somewhat farther apart. In 1995 Oregon had a total of 53 roadside rest areas plus 49 state parks that served as rest areas, and spent $4.6 million on utilities and maintenance at the areas. Oregonian 7/2/96:A1.

Retail sales. In 1992 Oregon retail sales per capita averaged $8,114, though they ranged from a low of $2,260 in **Morrow County** to a high of $10,346 in **Deschutes County**. Sales statewide, adjusted for inflation, rose 16.3% from 1987-1992. Oregon: A Statistical Overview.

Retirement homes. See **Continuing care communities**.

Revenue, Oregon Department of. A department that administers the state's tax programs, including income, corporation, excise, gift, inheritance, tobacco, and amusement device **taxes**. It also collects revenues for some local governments, including **Tri-Met,** and collects delinquent accounts for state agencies and community colleges. Though the department does not collect **property taxes**, it provides training and assistance for county assessors and tax collectors, and appraises utility property, timberland, and most large industrial property. It also collects timber severance taxes for distribution to local districts. 457 Revenue Bldg., 955 Center St. NE, Salem 97310. 503-945-8214. Oregon Blue Book. See also **Budget; General Fund**.

Revenues, local governments. See **Property tax; Special service districts**.

Revenues, state government. The **income tax** provides most of the discretionary income for state government. In the 1995-97 biennium, the personal income tax provided $6.22 billion, corporate income tax $.52 billion, the **lottery** $.73 billion, federal funds $5.37 billion, other funds $13.19 billion, and beginning balance (including trust funds such as **PERS**) $23.46 billion. Federal funds include human resource grants such as for Medicaid, welfare, and nursing homes, education grants, and transportation grants. "Other" includes dedicated funding such as income from college tuition, hunting licenses, interest on state bonds for veterans home loans, unemployment insurance, gas taxes, and park user fees. Oregon Blue Book. See also **Budget**; **General fund**.

Rhodes scholars. Students who have received scholarships to pursue graduate work at Oxford University in England; 32 are selected annually in the U.S. as part of the world-wide total of about 200. Between the time the program was founded in 1903 and 1996, 78 scholarships had been awarded to candidates submitted by the Oregon committee, 56 of them from Oregon colleges, including 30 from **Reed**, 18 from the **University of Oregon**, three each from **Linfield** and **Willamette**, and two from **Oregon State University**. In 1997 **Lewis and Clark** had its first Rhodes scholar. Rhodes Scholarship Trust, American Secretary, Pomona College, Claremont CA 91711-6305. 909-621-8138.

Rhododendron. A group of evergreen or deciduous **shrubs** with showy flowers. Oregon has three native rhododendrons: the white-flowered rhododendron, *R. albiflorum*, of the high **Cascade Range** and **Blue Mountains**, the pink-flowered western rhododendron, *R. macrophyllum*, found along the coast and at mid-elevation in the western mountains, and the deciduous, fragrant Western **azalea**, *R. occidentale*, of Southwestern Oregon. Oregon hobby and commercial growers raise other species, plus thousands of hybrids; over 2,000 can be seen at the **Crystal Springs Rhododendron Gardens**. Manual of the Higher Plants.

Rhyolite. A pasty, light-colored volcanic rock, rich in silica, formed by the melting of continental crust. It is so stiff when molten (like peanut butter) that it extrudes as plug domes, or as **obsidian**. If formed with steam it blasts out violently as ash or **pumice**, as happened with **Mount Mazama**. Rhyolites are found in south central and eastern Oregon, and are found farther north as **John Day Formation** ash.

Rice. Rice is being grown in southern Oregon near **Central Point** as a seed crop and in northeast Oregon around **Hermiston**. See also **Wild rice**.

Richest Oregonians. See **Wealthiest Oregonians**.

Richland. A community in far eastern Oregon located near the confluence of the Powder and **Snake Rivers** in **Baker County**, 41 miles east of **Baker City**. It was named by founder W. R. Usher in honor of its productive soil. The post office was established in 1897, and the city was incorporated in 1917. Population 1980 181; 1995 185. Elevation 2,213'. PO Box 266, 97870. 541-893-6141. Oregon Geographic Names.

Rickreall. An unincorporated farming community on Rickreall Creek, ten miles west of **Salem**. The origin of its name has been much debated. According to one story, La Creole, an exceptionally beautiful woman of **Kalapuya** and Mexican parentage, lived in an Indian village on the creek which became known for her. The name was corrupted by frontiersmen. Recollections; Oregon Geographic Names.

Riddle. A southwest Oregon city in **Douglas County** on the **Southern Pacific Railroad** 22 miles south of **Roseburg**. It was named for William H. Riddle, an 1851 pioneer of the area. The city was incorporated in 1893. Major employers include lumber mills and, until it closed in 1998, the Glenbrook Nickel Mine (formerly **Hanna Mining Company**). Population 1980 1,265; 1995 1,160. Elevation 706'. PO Box 143, 97469. 541-874-2571. Oregon Geographic Names.

Rifts. See **Crack-in-the-Ground**; **Hell Hole**.

Rimrock. A rock formation characteristic of much of central and southeastern Oregon. Rimrock is formed by partial erosion in areas originally covered by volcanic flows, leaving cliffs of rimrock with grass-and **sagebrush**-covered talus slopes below.

Rimrock (resort). A controversial $500 million, 1,800 acre destination resort proposed in the 1990s for a location next to **Smith Rock** State Park, north of **Redmond** in central Oregon.

Ringtail. A buff-colored, large-eared, nocturnal **protected animal**, *Bassariscus astutus*, that is related to the **raccoon**. Half of its 28 inch length is a bushy tail ringed with alternating dark and light bands. In Oregon ringtails are found only in the southwest corner of the state, where miners tamed them to catch mice and rats. Atlas of Oregon Wildlife; Mammals and Life Zones of Oregon; Mammals of the Northwest.

Rip City. A term invented by **Trail Blazer** announcer Bill "the Schonz" Schonely for a basketball shot that touches nothing but net on its way through the hoop. The term has since been sometimes used for the city of **Portland**. Facts of Life in Portland.

Rip current. An **ocean current** leading directly away from the shore and out through the breakers, usually with an embayment at the shore end. Between the embayments, longshore currents flow parallel to the shore. Rip currents are dangerous for swimmers since they sweep them out to sea, and the embayments hollowed out by the currents leave the shore vulnerable to erosion. The locations of rip currents change for unknown reasons. "Ocean processes and hazards along the Oregon coast;" Oregon Oceanbook.

Riparian areas. Areas along the banks of streams and rivers, usually rich with plant and animal species. A healthy riparian area also moderates water temperatures and provides nutrients and structural elements needed by aquatic life. Riparian areas in Oregon's **forests** are protected by the **Forest Practices Act**, but there is no similar legal protection for agricultural and urban stream banks.

Rite Aid. See **Thrifty PayLess**.

River basin areas. The Oregon Department of **Water Resources** has divided the state into 18 river basin areas. These are North Coast, Mid Coast, South Coast, Rogue, Umpqua, Willamette, Sandy, Hood, Deschutes, Klamath, Goose and Summer, Malheur Lake, John Day, Umatilla, Grande Ronde, Powder, Malheur, and Owyhee.

River District. A 250-acre triangle of land on the west side of the **Willamette River** in **Portland**, north of Burnside, between the river and **Interstate 405**. It includes the **Pearl District** and the Old Town/**Chinatown** neighborhoods, as well as **Union Station** and old railroad yards. The **Port of Portland** owns about 100 acres of undeveloped industrial land. To encourage development, especially the construction of the 5,500 new housing units needed to provide housing inside the **urban growth boundary**, the city has considered promoting a Central City Streetcar, spending $140 million of public money to eliminate the Lovejoy Street Ramp and build a new ramp to the Broadway Bridge, and developing Tanner Creek Park and water feature projects. Oregonian 7/24/97:A1. See also **Agricultural Marketing Center**.

River levels. Current conditions are available by calling the National Weather Service river line at 503-261-9246.

Rivergate. A **Port of Portland** industrial district that wraps around the northwest end of a peninsula that lies between the mouth of the **Willamette River** and the **Columbia River**. Kelly Point Park is on the tip and **Columbia Slough** drains the interior of the area.

Rivergrove. A Portland-area suburban community In **Washington** and **Clackamas Counties** that lies just east of **Interstate 5** seven miles south of downtown **Portland**. It was named for the **Tualatin River** on its south and the old community of Lake Grove (now part of **Lake Oswego**) to the north. The city was incorporated in 1971 in order to avoid annexation to Lake Oswego. Population 1980 314; 1995 300. Elevation 132'. PO Box 1104, Lake Oswego 97035. 503-639-6919. Oregon Geographic Names.

Rivers. The Oregon Department of **Water Resources** reports that the state has 112,640 miles of rivers and **streams**. The **Willamette River** and the rivers of northern Oregon flow into the **Columbia River**, either directly or through major tributaries, including the **Snake**. The rivers of the **Coast Range** flow directly into the Pacific Ocean. The **Umpqua** and **Rogue** rivers of southwestern Oregon break through the Coast Range to drain from the **Cascade Range** to the Pacific. The **Klamath**, like the Columbia, breaks through both the Coast Range and the Cascades to the ocean. The rivers and steams of southeastern Oregon drain into landlocked lakes with no outlet to the ocean. Most **navigable waterways** are owned by the people of Oregon up to ordinary high water line. See also **Frozen rivers**; **National Wild and Scenic Rivers**; **Scenic waterways**.

Riverside Classics. A series of outdoor, late-summer Tuesday night concerts given in **Portland**'s **Governor Tom McCall Waterfront Park** by the **Oregon Symphony** and **Portland Youth Philharmonic**. Food is available.

Road agents. Stagecoach robbers. They were said to be numerous in **The Dalles** area in 1871. This Day in Oregon 10/28.

Road conditions. See **Road reports**.

Road construction. In 1997 the Department of **Motor Vehicles** had a brochure and hot line with information on road construction delays. The hot line, at 1-503-976-7277, was updated weekly, and the average call cost $.30.

Road reports. In Oregon 800-977-6368; outside 503-588-2941. Washington 800-695-7623; NW Washington 206-368-4499. California 916-445-7623. Idaho 208-336-6600. Montana 406-444-6339.

Roads. See **Highways**.

Roadside rest areas. See **Rest areas**.

Robert Newell House. A house west of **Champoeg State Park** that is used as a museum. The original house was built in 1852; the present house is a replica built in 1959. In addition to furnishings from the 1860s, the museum contains Indian artifacts, needlework, and a collection of inaugural gowns worn by the wives of Oregon's governors. The Newell home survived the **flood of 1861** and provided refuge for many of the survivors after nearby **Champoeg** was swept away. 8089 Champoeg Road NE, St. Paul 97137. 503-678-5537.

Rock climbing. A sport pursued by a number of Oregonians, though the state has surprisingly few quality rock climbing sites. **Smith Rock State Park** near **Redmond** is the most famous. In urban areas climbers use rock climbing gyms. See also **Beacon Rock**; **Rooster Rock**.

Rock oyster. See **Piddock**.

Rockaway Beach. A north coast community 15 miles north of **Tillamook** on **Highway 101** in **Tillamook County**. The town, located on a seven-mile stretch of sand beach, was developed as a resort in 1910 and named Rockaway for a resort on Long Island in New York state. The name was later changed to Rockaway Beach. A fire destroyed the main business block in 1934. The city was incorporated in 1942. Population 1980 906; 1995 1,160. Elevation 17'. PO Box 5, 97136. 503-355-2291. Oregon Geographic Names.

Rockhounding. A recreation that includes searching for polishable rocks such as **agate**, jasper, and **obsidian**, collecting them, cutting and polishing them at home, and sometimes setting them as jewelry. Rockhounding was especially popular in the 1950s and 60s, and is again on the rise. There are 32 clubs in Oregon; **Geology and Mineral Industries** has a list. Gem Trails of Oregon. See also **Gemstones**; **Nyssa**.

Rocks, oldest. The oldest rocks in Oregon are a 200 foot thick Devonian **limestone** deposit in the Grindstone **terrane** in eastern **Crook County** in an area called the Berger Ranch. The deposit contains microfossils and fossil corals dating back 380 million years. Ancient rocks are also found in the **Klamath Mountains**, but the oldest are in the northern California portion. Geology of Oregon.

Rocks, youngest. Crater Rock on **Mount Hood** was created between 1760 and 1818; today only an eroded remnant remains. The lava flow at **McKenzie Pass** from Collier Cone is 400 years old. Geology of Oregon.

Rocky Butte. A 612' extinct volcano in **Portland** formed about 1.2 million years ago. A stone structure was built on the top by the Works Progress Administration in the 1930s and lighted in 1995. Rock from a quarry on the east side was used to build the Multnomah County Jail at the east base in 1941. The jail was displaced by **Interstate 205** in 1983. Geology of Oregon; Oregon Geographic Names; Oregonian 10/8/95:D4.

Rocky Mountain Retreat. A historic area on the Tualatin Plains, located near present-day **Highway 26** north of **Hillsboro**. The first whites in the area were former Rocky Mountain fur trappers who, with their families, settled there in 1840. The group included Joe Meek, Caleb Wilkins, John Larison, Robert Newell, and a man named Nicholas. Ewing Young.

Rodents. See **Beaver**; **Boomer**; **Mice**; **Muskrat**; **Nutria**; **Pocket gopher**; **Porcupine**; **Rats**; **Plague**; **Tularemia**.

Rodeos. An exhibition of cowboy skills featuring some or all of seven PRCA events: saddle bronc riding, bull riding, steer wrestling, bareback riding, calf roping, steer roping, and team roping. In 1995 there were 19 PRCA rodeos in the state. The top five (with dates and purses) were the **Pendleton Round-Up** (9/13-9/16, $85,925), and in **Eugene** (6/30-7/04, $54,600); **Saint Paul** (7/01-7/04,

$54,000); **Hermiston** (8/09-8/12, $44,100); **Sisters** (6/09-6/11, $36,000). Professional Rodeo Cowboys Assn., 101 Pro Rodeo Drive, Colorado Springs, CO 80919-9989. 719-593-8840.

Rogue Basin Project. A controversial project authorized by Congress in 1962 for three multi-purpose dams in southern Oregon to be built by the **Army Corps of Engineers**. The first, completed in 1977, created **Lost Creek Lake** on the **Rogue River**. The second, the dam that created **Applegate Lake**, 30 miles southwest of **Medford**, was completed in 1980. Construction on the third, **Elk Creek Dam** northwest of Lost Creek Lake, was begun in 1986 but halted the next year by public concern over potential water turbidity and the dismal cost-benefit analysis. The similarly named **Rogue River Basin Project** was a **Bureau of Reclamation** irrigation project. Army Engineers.

Rogue Community College. A public two-year college, located in **Grants Pass**, that serves **Josephine** and **Jackson** counties with transfer courses and vocational programs. In fall 1996 enrollment was 4,783. The college was founded in 1970. 3345 Redwood Highway, Grants Pass OR 97527-9298. 541-471-3500. Oregon Blue Book. See also **Community colleges; Small Business Development Centers**.

Rogue River. A major river in southwestern Oregon that rises at Boundary Springs on the slopes of **Crater Lake** in the **Cascades** and drops 5,000' in 216 miles before reaching the ocean at **Gold Beach** where **jetties** help maintain a channel for fishing boats. The river drains an area of 5,180 square miles and has an average annual volume of 6,597,000 acre feet, or 1.823 acre feet/acre. It is one of five rivers designated for **coho salmon** habitat restoration. In 1968, the section between Galice and Foster Bar was designated as a **National Wild and Scenic River**, the first in the country. A limited number of permits for floating that section are issued by the **Siskiyou National Forest** Visitor Center in Galice, 541-479-3735. Because the river was first reported (1827) by **Hudson's Bay Company** trapper Alexander McLeod, some called it McLeod's River. However, it was more commonly called it "La Riviere aux Coquins," or Rogue River, because of the troublesome local Indians. Geology of Oregon; Oregon Geographic Names; This Side of Oregon. See also **Natural Bridge; Rogue River Gorge**.

Rogue River (town). A southwest Oregon mill and recreation town in **Jackson County** 25 miles northwest of **Medford** on **Interstate 5**. It is located where Evans Creek flows into **Rogue River** from the north. Before a bridge was built across the Rogue, people would wade or swim across while holding onto their horse's tail and the community became known as Tailholt. The first post office, established in 1876 with John Woods as postmaster, was called Woodville. The city was incorporated in 1911, and the next year its name was changed to Rogue River. Attractions include the National Rooster Crowing Contest in late June, a timber festival, Jet Boat River Excursions during the summer, a historic museum, and Palmerton Arboretum. Population 1980 1,308; 1995 1,950. Elevation 1,001'. PO Box 1137, 97537. 541-582-4401. Chamber of Commerce 541-582-0242. Land in Common.

Rogue River Basin Project. A 1956-1961 U.S. **Bureau of Reclamation** project in southern Oregon that increased irrigation water supplies to the **Rogue**

River valley by tapping water from both sides of the **Cascade Range**. The water from the east slopes (**Klamath River** drainage) is carried by canal and tunnel to the Rogue drainage. The Bureau built **Howard Prairie Lake** (operated by Talent Irrigation District) and Agate Lake, operated by the Rogue River Valley Irrigation District, and rehabilitated four reservoirs, two operated by the Talent Irrigation District (**Emigrant Lake** and Hyatt Reservoir, originally built in 1923), and two operated by the Medford Irrigation District (**Fish Lake** and Fourmile Lake, built in 1922.) The similarly named **Rogue Basin Project** was an **Army Corps of Engineers** flood control project. Atlas of Oregon Lakes.

Rogue River Gorge. A slot gorge through which the upper **Rogue River** roars just above Union Creek, 12 miles north of **Prospect**. A short trail leads to an overlook from a parking lot on the north side of **Highway 62**. Oregon Atlas.

Rogue River Indians. Various bands and tribes of Indians native to southwest Oregon, including groups that spoke Kusan, Athabaskan, Talkelman, and Shastan **Indian languages**. The **Coos Indians** were to the north of the Rogue River Indians and the **Klamaths** and Modocs to the east. They all had similar life styles, living in plank houses built over house pits and using salmon and acorns as staple foods. In 1851 the Rogues were estimated to number 9,500, but many died in the **Rogue River War**, and the last 1,200 were moved to the **Coast Reservation** in 1856. Requiem for a People.

Rogue River National Forest. A 685,986-acre national forest in southern Oregon, located primarily in **Jackson County**. The section in the **Siskiyou Range** includes **Mount Ashland** (7,533'), and the larger area in the **Cascade Range** includes **Mount McLoughlin** (9,495'). The forest includes three wilderness areas: Sky Lakes, Rogue-Umpqua Divide, and Red Buttes. 333 West 8th Street, P.O.Box 520, Medford 97501. 541-776-3600.

Rogue River War, 1851-53, 1855-1856. An **Indian war** in southern Oregon and northern California that involved the various groups loosely known as the **Rogue River Indians**. Hostilities between whites and Indians actually started years earlier, beginning with the massacre of at least 14 Indians by **North West Company** trappers in the Umpqua River area in about 1817. Conflicts continued, intensifying as the number of settlers and gold miners increased in the early 1850s, and led to the Table Rock Treaty on September 10, 1853 - but both parties soon violated its provisions. The second round of fighting began in earnest when local gold miners and settlers killed 23 sleeping Indians, including 16 women and children, on the **Table Rock** Reservation on October 8, 1855. The conflict spread down the **Rogue River** canyon, involved a **massacre** of 23 settlers on February 22, 1856, a month-long siege by the Indians of settlers at **Gold Beach**, and a series of encounters between the Army and Indians before the last Indians surrendered on June 29, 1856. Some 200 whites and soldiers - and probably more Indians - had been killed. The 2,000 surviving Indians were moved to the Coast **Reservation**. Dictionary of Oregon History; Fur Hunters of the Far West; Indian Battles Along the Rogue River; Requiem for a People. See also **Battle Rock**; **Fort Lane**; **Geisel Monument**; **Plea for the Indians**.

Roller coasters. Oregon's only permanent roller coaster opened in 1996 in **Oaks Amusement Park** in **Portland**. Riders speed over 1,200 feet of track, including a full loop, in 70 seconds, traveling at 50 mph. Earlier, Oaks Amusement Park had the wooden Whirlwind, one of the country's first roller coasters, built in 1905. During the 1920s there was a somewhat roller-coaster like scenic railway circling the top of **Council Crest**. The famed Big Dipper roller coaster at **Jantzen Beach** had operated for 42 years before it was closed in 1970 to make way for the expansion of **Interstate 5**. "How It Was Then;" Oregonian 5/31/96:A18.

Roller skating. See **Skating**.

Romanians. In 1997 there were 40,000 Romanians in Oregon, most of whom arrived after 1970. The Romanian community in **Portland** was estimated at 12,000 persons in 1994, and a number of them operate **adult foster homes** for the elderly. Oregonian 10/10/94:A10, 10/17/97:D13.

Rome. An unincorporated southeast Oregon community on the **Owyhee River** in **Malheur County**. It is 33 miles west of **Jordan Valley** on Highway 95. The **Pillars of Rome** lie four miles northwest.

Roosevelt Highway. See **Highway 101**.

Rooster Crowing Contest. See **Rogue River (town)**.

Rooster Rock. At least four major Oregon rock outcrops are called Rooster Rock. The most prominent is a 200 foot pillar of **basalt**, a favorite for rock climbers, located along the **Columbia River** east of **Crown Point.** The rock slid as a mass from the nearby canyon wall where the scar is still visible. Its name dates from at least 1876 and is of phallic significance. The day-use **state park** in which it is located includes a boat basin, a sandy beach, and 3.2 miles of hiking trails. Another notable Rooster Rock, also popular with climbers, looms high on the north side of **Highway 20** twenty-three miles east of **Sweet Home**. It lies in the Menagerie Wilderness Area, along with Chicken Rock, Cockatoo Tower, Beetle Dome, Turkey Monster, and Camel's Hump. Geology of Oregon; Oregon Geographic Names.

Ropes course. A course of physical obstacles designed to test group teamwork and problem solving abilities. The only publicly owned course in Oregon is **Eugene**'s Spencer Butte Challenge Course that opened in 1995. Reservations are required. 541-682-5329. Oregonian 5/22/95:B2.

Rose Bowl. An invitational college football game played in Pasadena, California, on New Year's Day. The **University of Oregon** Ducks played in 1958 (Ohio State 10, Oregon 7) and in 1995 (Penn State 38, Oregon 20). **Oregon State University** played in 1957 (Iowa 35, OSU 19) and 1965 (Michigan 34, OSU 7). In earlier years, when it was called the Tournament of Roses, Oregon played in 1917 (Oregon 14, Penn 0) and 1920 (Harvard 7, Oregon 6.) Oregonian 9/8/95:D4.

Rose City Astronomers. An **astronomy** club, the largest in the Pacific Northwest, affiliated with the national Astronomical League. It meets monthly at **OMSI** in **Portland**. 503-255-2016.

Rose Festival. **Portland**'s major festival since1907, a month-long series of June events held from **Hillsboro** to **Mount Hood.** Over 350,000 attend the Grand Floral Parade on the second weekend in June, making it the largest spectator event in Oregon and the nation's second-largest all-floral parade. The festival also includes the nation's oldest and largest children's parade plus other parades, a rose show, cultural and sporting events, a carnival, a fleet of Canadian and American navy vessels, a queen's court representing area high schools, fireworks, hot air balloons, an air show, the **Portland IndyCar Race**, and the **Milk Carton Boat Race**. In 1996 the Junior Court was replaced with a community service program for children called Rose Festival Kids. Portland Rose Festival Association, 220 NW Second Avenue, 97209. 503-227-2681. Portland Gateway; Portland Rose Festival; Round the Roses.

Rose garden. See **Gardens; International Rose Test Gardens; Martha Springer Botanical Garden and Rose Garden; Sunken Rose Garden**.

Rose Garden (arena). A multi-purpose arena in **Portland**, opened in 1995, that was built by the **Trail Blazers** for their games. The 785,000 square-foot arena seats 20,000 people, has 677 televisions screens, and features a fountain called **Essential Forces**. It is located in the **Rose Quarter** between the east ends of the Steel and Broadway bridges. The building and associated developments cost $262 million, including a $34.5 million loan from the city to be repaid from user fees. Oregonian 10/8/95:Special section.

Rose Garden Children's Park. A playground in **Portland** located just below the **International Rose Test Gardens** in **Washington Park**. Portland Guidebook.

Rose Garden Concerts. A series of outdoor concerts featuring a variety of music, held at the **Washington Park**'s **International Rose Test Garden** over Labor Day weekend. Seating is on the lawn; sand chairs are allowed but not full-size chairs, nor is food or drink allowed. Oregonian 8/27/97:C1.

Rose Quarter. A 37-acre area on the east side of the **Willamette River** in **Portland** located between the east ends of the Steel and Broadway bridges. It includes the **Rose Garden** arena, the **Memorial Coliseum**, the **Commons**, One Center Court (a building housing restaurants and businesses), **Essential Forces** (a fountain), four parking garages, and a transit center served by **Tri-Met** buses and **MAX** light rail. The **Oregon Convention Center** is across the street. Oregonian 10/8/95:Special section.

Roseburg. "Timber Capital of the Nation." A southwest Oregon city on the South **Umpqua River**, 185 miles south of **Portland** on **Interstate 5**. It is situated at the intersection of three geologic provinces: the **Klamath Mountains** to the south, the **Cascade Range** to the east, and the **Coast Range** to the west. The community was called Deer Creek for a few years before it became known for the 1851 settler and tavern keeper, Aaron Rose. It became the **Douglas County** seat in 1854, and was incorporated in 1872. The economy is based on timber, tourism, and agriculture. The headquarters of both the **Umpqua National Forest** and a **Bureau of Land Management** district are in the city. Area attractions include the Douglas County Museum, Wildlife Safari, wineries, white water boating, fishing, and the waterfalls of the North Umpqua River. In 1997 volunteers planted halfmile rows of red roses up the bluffs of Mount Nebo along I-5. Durango, Mexico, is its sister city. Population 1980 16,644; 1995 19,220. Elevation 479'. 900 SE Douglas Ave, 97470. 541-672-7701. Chamber of Commerce 800-444-9584. Oregon Geographic Names.

Roseburg District, BLM. A 423,758-acre district of **Bureau of Land Management** forest lands, primarily in **Douglas County**. 777 NW Garden Valley Blvd,

Roseburg 97470. 541-440-4930. BLM Facts.

Roseburg explosion. A blast in **Roseburg** at 1:15 a.m. on Friday, August 7, 1959, that killed nine persons, injured 50 others, and destroyed 12 square blocks of downtown Roseburg. A truck loaded with 6 1/2 tons of ammonium nitrate and gelatin had been parked on Pine Street between Washington and Oak streets while the driver spent the night at the Umpqua Hotel, four blocks away. During the night, the building next to the truck caught fire. The driver was awakened by the fire sirens and was racing to the truck when he was knocked flat by the blast while still a block from it. (Roseburg) News Review 8/7/59. See also **Disasters**.

Roses. Commercial rose growers in Oregon include Edmunds' Roses, 6235 SW Kahle Road, Wilsonville 97070. 503-682-1476; Heirloom Old Garden Roses, 24062 NE Riverside Drive, St. Paul 97137. 503-538-1576; and Jackson and Perkins, PO Box 1028, Medford 97501. 800-292-4769. See also **Logtown rose**.

Roslyn Lake. See **Bull Run Lake**.

Ross Island. A mile-long island in the **Willamette River** at **Portland**; it can be seen to the south from the Ross Island Bridge. It was named for Sherry Ross, an early settler on it. Blue Ruin, a famous whiskey of pioneer days, was said to have been made on the island. It and its small neighboring islands were the moorages for free-living houseboaters around 1905. Oregon Geographic Names; Portland, An Informal History.

Round Butte Dam. A **hydropower** dam built on the **Deschutes River** by **Portland General Electric** in 1964, creating **Lake Billy Chinook**. It has a nameplate generating capacity of 247.2 **megawatts**.

Roxy Ann Peak. A 3,573' butte just east of **Medford**. An unpaved road to Prescott Park (no facilities) and around the top provides views of the area. See also **Log Town rose**.

Royal Terrace Falls. See **McDowell Creek Falls Park**.

Ruch (roosh). An unincorporated community in the **Applegate River** valley of southwest Oregon, 8 miles south of **Jacksonville**. It was named for C. M. Ruch who bought land there in 1896 and opened the post office the next year. Oregon Geographic Names; Ruch.

Rudolph. See **Made in Oregon sign**.

Rufus. A north Oregon community in **Sherman County** on the **Columbia River** 29 miles east of **The Dalles** on **Interstate 84**. It was named for Rufus Wallis, who settled in the area sometime before 1876. The city was incorporated in 1965. **John Day Dam** is two miles east. Population 1980 352; 1995 295. Elevation 180'. PO Box 27, 97050. 541-739-2321. Oregon Geographic Names.

Running. See **Hood to Coast**; **Marathon**; **Prefontaine Classic**; **Race for the Cure**.

Rural communities. See **Oregon Rural Development Council**.

Rural community boundary. An optional boundary drawn around an unincorporated community by the county under **Land Conservation and Development Commission** authorization. Once such a boundary has been established, the unincorporated community has more land use options, such as allowing some urban uses, developing at higher densities, and installing water and sewer systems. Several hundred communities would qualify, based primarily on existing zoning.

See also **Urban growth boundary**.

    Rural development. See **Enterprise Zones**; **Regional Development**.

    Rural Oregon Coalition. See **Sagebrush Coalition**.

    Russians in Oregon. In 1808 Russians planned to found a settlement on the **Columbia River** but the founding ship was wrecked. In 1882 a group of young Russian Jewish exiles from Odessa founded a commune at **Glendale** in southern Oregon. The New Odessa Colony lasted only until 1887, but the members, nearly all professionals, were notable for their continued activism. Groups of **Germans** who had lived in Russia for several generations came to **Portland** in the 1890s. More than 7,000 Russian Jewish refugees presently live in the **Portland** area. Old Believers, members of a conservative religious sect that resisted changes to Russian Orthodoxy 300 years ago, settled near **Woodburn** beginning in the 1960s. Many of them left Russia at the time of the Russian Revolution in 1917 and lived for some years in China and later in Brazil. There are now about 10,000 in Oregon. **Springfield** hosts an annual Ukrainian Day Celebration. Beaver, Kings, and Cabins; Dictionary of Oregon History; In Search of Western Oregon; Oregonian 10/17/95:B1; Round the Roses.

    Sabroso Co. See **Fruit purees**.

    Sacajawea Peak. A **granitic** peak that is, at 9,839', the highest in the **Wallowa Mountains** of northeast Oregon. See also **Sacajawea statue**.

    Sacajawea statue. A **Portland** statue by Alice Cooper that honors Sacajawea (ca 1787-1812), a Shoshone Indian who was the only woman on the **Lewis and Clark Expedition**. The statue was commissioned for the 1905 **Lewis and Clark Centennial Exposition** and later moved to **Washington Park**. Sacajawea's husband was an interpreter for the expedition, and she also interpreted and guided. She was said to have contributed a full man's share to the success of the expedition, besides taking care of her baby, "Pomp" (Jean Baptiste Charbonneau, 1805-1866), who is buried at Inskip's Ranch, 15 miles west of **Jordan Valley**. Great Extravaganza; Other Side of Oregon; Portland's Public Art.

    Sacred Harp Singers. See **Shape note singing**.

    Saddle Mountain. A 3,283' peak, composed of **Columbia River Basalt**, located east of **Seaside** in the northern **Coast Range**. It is the highest point in the county, and from the top, reached by a 2.5 mile trail, are views of the coastline, the **Columbia river**, and the **Cascade Range**. According to Indian tradition, a great chief who had been killed by enemies turned into an eagle on the top of Saddle Mountain and became the creator of thunder and lightning. The mountain is noted for its wildflowers. A few primitive campsites are located at the trailhead. Moontrap (novel); Oregon Geographic Names.

    Safety belts. In 1996, 82% of Oregonians used seat belts. Oregon law (an **initiative** adopted by state voters in 1990) requires that each driver and passenger use a safety belt or be in an approved child-restraint system at all times. (A child-restraint system is required for children less than four years of age and weighing 40 pounds or less.) 800-772-1315. Oregonian 10/13/97:B4.

    Safety corridors. Stretches of highway that have proven to be especially dangerous, so are designated for special enforcement attention. They have been posted with large speed limit signs and signs advising motorists to turn on headlights. There are 10 or more state-designated safety corridors in Oregon; the longest is 70 miles of **Highway 97** from **Klamath Falls** north to Chemult.

Sagebrush. Aromatic desert **shrubs** of the genus *Artemisia*. Tall sage, *A. tridentata*, grows from one to eight feet tall, and is now, as a result of grazing, the most common plant on the desert **rangeland** of eastern Oregon, though it constituted only 20% of the original bunchgrass community. Despite its high protein content, domestic livestock prefer almost any other feed. At higher elevations, tall sage is replaced by short sages, *A. rigida* and *A. arbuscula*. **Playas** that are covered with *A. cana* are known as "cana flats"; these were esteemed by sheepmen and continue to provide important forage for cattle. Natural Vegetation; Oregon's Great Basin Country.

Sagebrush Coalition. A group organized in 1991 to give Oregon's sparsely settled eastern counties a greater voice in Salem. The name was changed in 1995 to Rural Oregon Coalition as part of a plan to include representatives of some western Oregon rural areas. Oregonian 1/25/95:B4.

Sagebrush Symphony. An orchestra established by Mary Dodge for school children in **Burns**. The **Oregon Historical Society** sells prints of a 1915 photo of the white-clad children, perched ready to play on a large violin-shaped float in the midst of endless **sagebrush**. Dodge was later the founder of the **Portland Youth Philharmonic**. That Balance So Rare.

Sagittaria. See **Wapato**.

Sahalie Falls. Two Oregon waterfalls are named with the **Chinook jargon** word meaning high. One, on the East Fork Hood River near Mount Hood Meadows Ski Area, is a **horsetail falls** over 60 feet high, while the other is a 140-foot high torrent on the upper **McKenzie River**. It can be seen from a viewpoint off **Highway 126** located 5.2 miles south of **Highway 20**. Waterfall Lover's Guide.

SAIF Corporation. A state-owned, independent public corporation that sells **workers' compensation** insurance to Oregon employers. Created to be competitive in the marketplace by the legislature in 1979 as successor to the State Accident Insurance Fund, it is governed by a board of five members appointed by the governor for four-year terms. Operating income comes from premiums and investments. Some 200 private companies also offer workers' compensation insurance in the state. SAIF has about 35% of the market, private insurers 48%, and 17% of Oregon employers are self insured. 400 High St. SE, Salem 97312-1000; 503-373-8000. Oregon Blue Book. See also **Investment Council**; **Occupational Safety and Health**.

Sail jellyfish. A floating sea creature, *Velella velella*, that sometimes washes up on Oregon beaches in great drifts on strong southerly or westerly winds. Each bluish jellyfish consists of a flat oval about two inches long with a cellophane-like sail diagonally across it; those from the other side of the ocean have their sails on the opposite diagonal. Sail jellyfish are sometimes called by-the-wind sailors or, mistakenly, Portuguese men-of-war. Between Pacific Tides; Seashore Life.

Saint Helens. A northwest Oregon wood-products city on the **Columbia River**, 30 miles north of **Portland** on **Highway 30**. In 1845 founder Captain H.M. Knighton called the town Plymouth, but in 1850 the name was changed to Saint Helens, apparently because of the proximity of **Mount St. Helens** across the river.

Part of the present town was first known as Milton and later as Houlton. Saint Helens is the county seat of **Columbia County**, with county offices in a 1906 black stone courthouse on the riverfront. Population 1980 7,064; 1995 8,080. Elevation 42'. PO Box 278, 97051. 503-397-6272. Chamber of Commerce 503-397-0685. Oregon Geographic Names.

Saint John's Episcopal Church. See **Oaks Pioneer Church**.

Saint Johns landfill. A one-time **landfill** that was, for 50 years, the largest garbage dump in western Oregon. It occupied 236 acres in north **Portland**, filling a pond between **Columbia Slough** and **Bybee Lake**. In 1966 smoke from a 10-day fire at the dump drifted 50 miles south to **Salem** where there were complaints about the odor. By the time it closed in 1991, 14 million tons of garbage had been dumped there from half the population of the state. **Metro** is responsible for restoring the site to prevent water pollution. Portland garbage is now hauled 140 miles to **Columbia Ridge Landfill** at **Arlington**. Experiences; Oregonian 8/24/95:F6.

Saint Louis. An old **settlement** on **French Prairie** in the **Willamette Valley**, west of **Interstate 5** and four miles southwest of **Woodburn**. A Jesuit missionary, the Reverend Aloysius Verecuysee, built a log church there in 1845. The parish, named for Saint Louis, King of France, was organized in 1847. The area was earlier called Grand Prairie. Oregon Geographic Names.

Saint Patrick's Day. See **Irish in Oregon**; **Mill Ends Park**.

Saint Paul. A **Willamette Valley** farming community, one of the oldest in the state, located in **Marion County** on **French Prairie**, 21 miles north of **Salem**. It grew up around the first Catholic Church in Oregon, **Saint Paul Catholic Church**, named in 1839 for the apostle Paul by Father Blanchet, its first priest. The post office was established in 1874, and the city was incorporated in 1901. Saint Paul is noted for its annual 4th of July **rodeo**. Population 1980 312; 1995 355. Elevation 169'. PO Box 7, 97137. 503-633-4971. Saint Paul.

Saint Paul Catholic Church. The first church in the Pacific Northwest was a log church built at what is now **Saint Paul** in 1836 by the local **French Canadians** in anticipation of positive response to their request for **Catholic** missionaries. In 1846 the log church was replaced by a **brick** church that was later enlarged. The church's two-foot-thick walls, severely damaged by the 1993 **Scotts Mills earthquake**, were rebuilt brick by brick. In the process, a box was found that had been placed in the wall when the church was built; it contained a corroded coin, a blackened medal and an old newspaper, The Tablet, of which the only legible parts were the name, an ad for a toothbrush, and a recipe for mango sauce. See also **Missions**.

Saint Peters Dome. A 775' basalt monolith in the **Columbia River Gorge** on the side of Yeon Mountain, south of exit 35 from **Interstate 84**. It was first climbed in 1940. Oregon Geographic Names.

Sake. (Pronounced SOCK-ee.) A Japanese rice wine, usually served warm. Japan America Beverage Company began building a sake brewery in **Forest Grove** in 1996. Although the company had originally hoped to use Oregon **rice**, it was found that the kind needed didn't ripen in Oregon. Oregonian 3/19/96:B14.

Salamanders. Amphibians that differ from frogs in having tails and in crawling rather than hopping. Some are fully terrestrial, some spend most of their lives in water, but most live as adults in moist places, especially under logs. At least fifteen species are found in Oregon, including the Pacific giant, *Dicamptodon tenebrosus*, which, at 12 inches, is the world's largest terrestrial salamander. It relishes banana **slugs** and can climb trees, as can the slender clouded salamander, *Aneides ferreus*. The related rough-skinned newt or water dog, *Taricha granulosa*, is bright orange underneath. Its skin secretions (tetrodotoxin) and flesh are deadly to humans and animals if eaten; legend says that a camper died after drinking coffee made in a pot of water in which a water dog had taken refuge. Atlas of Oregon Wildlife; Field Guide to Western Reptiles and Amphibians; Plants and Animals of the Pacific Northwest.

Salaries. Oregon's highest paid executives during the 1993 fiscal year were Harry Merlo, chief executive of **Louisiana-Pacific Corporation** who was paid $12.2 million in cash and long-term compensation, Walden Rhines of Mentor Graphics who received $5.9 million, including stock options, and Delbert Yocum of **Tektronix** who received $3.4 million. Business Journal 7/29/94:40. See also **Minimum wage**; **Wages**.

Salaries, public employees. The 1997 legislature set the salary for the **Governor** at $88,300, for **Secretary of State**, **Treasurer**, and **Superintendent of Public Instruction** at $67,900, and for **Attorney General** at $72,000. (ORS 292.313) Over a hundred other state employees had higher salaries, including the three state university presidents who each made $116,964 in 1995. An annual salary survey by the American Association of University Professors shows faculty salaries at Oregon's public colleges and universities remain below the national average. In 1996, the salary for the mayor of **Portland** (a full-time position) was $88,472, and the city commissioners each earned $79,359. Twenty eight other city employees earned more than the mayor. Salaries of state **elected officials**, including judges, account for less than 1/2 of 1% of the state **general fund** budget. Governing Oregon; Oregonian 10/8/95:D8, 2/5/97:B1.

Salem. Oregon's capital and third largest city, Salem lies in the **Willamette Valley** 51 miles south of **Portland** on **Interstate 5**. It is the county seat of **Marion County**, though the portion west of the **Willamette River** lies in **Polk County**. It was first settled in 1840-41 when Jason Lee's **Methodist Mission** moved to Mill Creek and established a school that became **Willamette University**. The townsite, laid out in 1844, was probably named for Salem, Massachusetts; the word means peace. The post office was established in 1849, and the city was incorporated in 1857. Attractions include the **Capitol, Mission Mill Village, Deepwood Estate, Bush's Pasture Park, Gilbert House Children's Museum**, Marion County Historical Society Museum, Prewitt-Allen Archaeological Museum, the 1871 First United Methodist Church, the 1926 Elsinore Theatre, the 1905 Grand Theatre, **Salem Art Fair and Festival** in July, Oregon **State Fair** in August, the nearby 1861 **Brunk House** and **R. C. Geer Farmhouse**, and area wineries. Its four sister cities are Kawagoe, Japan; Salem, India; Simferopol, Ukraine; and Vaxjo, Sweden. Population 1980 89,091; 1995 118,355. Elevation 154'. 555 Liberty St. SE, 97301. 503-588-6255. Chamber of Commerce 800-874-7012. Oregon Geographic Names. See also **Metropolitan Areas**.

Salem Art Fair and Festival. A free, annual art and crafts festival, begun in

1949, held at **Bush Pasture Park** in **Salem** on the third full weekend in July. It is the largest juried fair of its kind in Oregon, attended by over 100,000, with 200 artists, plus food, entertainment, demonstrations, and hands-on crafts events for children and adults. Salem Art Association, 600 Mission Street, 97302-6203. 503 581-2228.

Salem clique. A powerful group of **Salem** Democrats that controlled the Oregon **legislature** during the period of **territorial government** in the 1850's. Asahel Bush, publisher of the Oregon Statesman, was an influential member of the group. The clique was instrumental in eliminating the effectiveness of the **Know Nothing Party**. They also championed General Joseph Lane as Governor and later as delegate to Congress until his pro-slavery views lost him their support. Dictionary of Oregon History.

Salem District, BLM. A 401,288-acre district of **Bureau of Land Management** forest lands in northwest Oregon. 1717 Fabry Road, SE, Salem OR 97306. 503-375-5646. BLM Facts.

Sales tax. In 1997 Oregon was one of five states with no state sales tax; the others were Alaska, Delaware, Montana, and New Hampshire. Sales tax proposals have been before the voters nine times, most recently in November 1993, and have been soundly defeated each time. Some cities have instituted sales taxes on motel rooms and restaurant meals. Oregonian 9/20/93:A8. See also **Taxes**.

Salmon. Large anadromous fish. Oregon has three common species. The largest is the **chinook** or king salmon, *Oncorhynchus tshawytscha*; which usually spawns in the main stem of the rivers, while the **coho** or silver salmon, *O. kisutch*, spawns in smaller tributaries. The third is the less tasty chum or dog salmon, *O. keta*. Two other salmon species are less common, though pink salmon, *O. gorbuscha*, is harvested commercially offshore, and the much smaller **sockeye** or red salmon, *O. nerka*, migrates up the **Columbia River** to its spawning grounds in Washington. All salmon hatch in freshwater gravel beds (the newly hatched salmon are called alevin), migrate after varying amounts of time downstream to the ocean where they spend one to five years, depending on the species, and then return to their home streams to spawn and die. Before the Columbia River dams were built, chinook salmon returned as far as 1,200 miles up the Columbia, which is the more remarkable since they don't eat once they leave the ocean on their spawning run. Historically, 12 to 16 million salmon returned to the Columbia River basin each year, though by 1995, fewer than 150,000 appeared. Dams have created major problems for salmon passage both up- and down-stream, and salmon runs are blocked completely on the Columbia by the Grand Coulee Dam in Washington, and on the **Snake River** by **Hells Canyon Dam**. Oregon record sizes are 83 pounds for chinook, 25 for coho, 19 for chum, and 4 pounds for kokanee (land-locked sockeye). **Indians** may legally sell salmon along the Oregon banks of the **Columbia River**. Columbia River Salmon; Fishing in Oregon; Oregonian 1/29/94:E1, 10/29/95:S1, 8/29/97:C4; Organic Machine; Salmon of the Pacific. See also **Oxbow Incident**; **Salmon recovery**; **Steelhead**.

Salmon fishery. The **Hudson's Bay Company** first exported salmon (salted) from **Fort George** in 1823. The **territorial** constitution of 1848 prohibited dams without salmon passage. The first salmon cannery on the **Columbia River** opened in 1866 and ten years later the first salmon hatchery was built. In 1883, forty-three million pounds of **chinook** salmon were caught in the Columbia. The annual catch of chinook began to decline after 1885, but **fish canneries** began utilizing **coho** and **sockeye** as well, so that the total annual salmon fishery on the Columbia still averaged over 41 million pounds a year between 1916 and 1920. By 1956, however, the total catch had declined to less than 10 million pounds, and the last Columbia cannery closed in 1980. **Fish wheels** could each take in 20,000 to 50,000 pounds of fish a day. Dependable gas motors made possible commercial ocean trolling beginning about 1912. Many fishermen were immigrants, and the type of gear they used corresponded with their ethnicity. Gillnets, traps, and horse seines were used primarily by Scandinavians, purse seines by Austrians, and trollers by western Europeans, while the Indians used dip nets. Empire of the Columbia; Northwest Salmon Crisis; Organic Machine; Salmon Fishers of the Columbia.

Salmon Harbor. See **Winchester Bay**.

Salmon management. Between 1981 and 1997, $3 billion was spent on salmon recovery in the Columbia basin but the number of **salmon** and **steelhead** fell from 1.1 million in 1981 to 909,000 in 1996. It has been the world's most expensive attempt to save a wild creature. Federal law requires **Bonneville Power Administration** to pay the ongoing costs, capped at $435 million a year. Though the **Northwest Power Planning Council** was ostensibly given authority in 1980, management of the dwindling salmon populations has been complicated by a confusing web of governmental jurisdictions and agencies, as well as scientific uncertainty. Normative River, a 1996 scientific study requested by the NWPPC, proposed new ways to restore the productivity of the **Columbia River**. In 1998 a Three Sovereigns Forum was proposed that would include federal, state, and tribal leaders and would have final say on recovery measures. Northwest Salmon Crisis; Oregonian 7/27/97:A1, 2/2/98:E1. See also **Columbia Basin Fish and Wildlife Authority; Columbia River Inter-Tribal Fish Commission; National Marine Fisheries Service; Oregon Plan; Pacific Fishery Management Council; Pacific States Marine Fisheries Commission**.

Salmon ranching. Private corporations started more than a dozen salmon ranches in Oregon estuaries in the 1970s and 1980s but abandoned them as unprofitable after too few fish returned. There were also environmental impacts from fish wastes. In 1997 a three year, $212,000, joint attempt by a sport fishing group, Northwest Steelheaders, the Oregon Department of **Fish and Wildlife**, and the Port of **Coos Bay**, was abandoned after only 5 **coho** returned. The Port of **Newport** is considering using abandoned salmon ranches to increase the coho sports fishery in **Yaquina Bay** or for **abalone** or **oyster** farming. Oregonian 6/29/97:B4.

Salmon recovery effort. See **Salmon management**.

Salmon River (Lincoln County). A 25-mile long river that drains a 75 square mile valley in the **Coast Range** to the ocean south of **Cascade Head**. A wagon road along the river operated as a **toll road** from 1908 until 1920. Today State Highway 18 from **McMinnville** follows the river down the west slope of the Coast Range west to **Highway 101**, some of it in the **Van Duzer Forest Corridor**.

Salmon Street Springs. A fountain in **Portland**'s **Governor Tom McCall Waterfront Park** that was designed by Portland landscape architect Robert Per-

ron. Its100 water jets are computer controlled to make changing patterns. Portland Guidebook.

Salt Caves Project. A controversial proposal to build a dam on the upper
Klamath River. **Pacific Power and Light** first proposed the project in 1980, and
then, after they abandoned it in 1982, the city of **Klamath Falls** took it up. Concerns about the effect on fish and wildlife habitat, and questions about the financial feasibility of the project were ended when the eleven-mile stretch of river
between J. C. Boyle Dam and the California border was declared a **National Wild
and Scenic River** in September 1994. Oregonian 9/24/94:A1.

Salt Creek Falls. A 286-foot plunge waterfall, Oregon's highest outside the
Columbia River Gorge, that is visible from **Highway 58** about five miles west of
Willamette Pass. Five other falls can be seen along three miles of Diamond Creek
Falls Trail which leaves from the Salt Creek Picnic Area. These include Lower
Diamond Creek Falls, a tiered falls estimated to be over 200 feet high, and Dia-
mond Creek Falls, over 70 feet high. Salt Creek was named for the salt springs
along the creek that are used by deer as salt licks. Waterfall Lover's Guide.

Salt springs. In order to prevent a private monopoly on such a basic neces-
sity as salt, Congress, in the 1859 Oregon **Admission Act**, granted the state up to
12 salt springs along with up to six sections of land adjoining each. However,
since Oregon fronted the ocean and had a ready source of salt, the grant was not
important and lapsed with no claims being made. History of Oregon Land Grants.

Salvage rider. A Congressional addition to a federal 1995 budget bill that
contained three provisions: it certified that the Clinton forest plan met all legal
tests (meaning that there could be no legal challenge to it); that salvage logging of
dead and dying trees be accelerated, and that 150 **Forest Service** on-hold timber
sales would be released for logging even if logging would damage **endangered
species**. The rider was to expire at the end of 1996. Opposition grew after it was
found that many of the released timber sales involved logging **old growth** timber.
In September 1996 the government swapped 3,800 acres of the old growth forests
for younger stands of equal value. Oregonian 3/11/96:A1, 9/19/96:B1.

Samuel H. Boardman State Park. A ten-mile-long **state park** that lies
along the coast from 4 miles north of **Brookings** north nearly to Pistol River. Beach
access and picnic facilities are provided at several places, but there is no camping.

San Francisco. San Francisco was known as Yerba Buena while California
was Mexican. The name was changed to San Francisco in 1847. At that time
Oregon City was the seat of American government on the west coast, so the original plat map for the city of San Francisco was filed there in 1850. The map still
hangs in the office of the county clerk of **Clackamas County**. **Sandstone** quarried
in the **Coast Range** east of **Toledo** was used for the San Francisco mint and post
office. Oregon Ghost Towns; This Day in Oregon.

San Francisco Xavier. A Manila galleon that disappeared on a 1705 voyage
from the Philippines to Acapulco, Mexico. Its route would have been the one in
use since 1564 for annual trading voyages, crossing the Pacific to Cape Mendocino
in northern California and then turning south to Mexico. It is possible that the *San
Francisco Xavier* was blown off course and wrecked on the Oregon coast, becoming the source of the **beeswax** that has been found on the beach at **Neahkahnie**

Mountain. Oregon Shipwrecks.

Sanctuary of Our Sorrowful Mother. See **Grotto**.

Sand and gravel. Over 16 million tons of sand and gravel are used annually in Oregon as is about the same amount of crushed rock. Construction materials - sand, gravel, rock, and Portland cement - account for 85% of the total mineral production value of the state. Silica sand is mined north of **Coos Bay** for use in making glass. Mineral Industry of Oregon. See also **Mineral wealth**.

Sand dunes. See **Beaches**; **Dunes**.

Sand in the City. A **Portland** event in July at **Pioneer Courthouse Square**, held as a benefit for Kids on the Block Awareness Program. In 1997, 100 tons of sand were trucked in and 18 corporate teams sculpted creations from it.

Sand spit. A point of sand that develops at the mouth of a river where a projecting headland deflects the river current. Sand spits are the least stable land form in Oregon, yet, despite the lessons of the vanished city of **Bayocean**, commercial development continues on them. Erosion of the Siletz Spit in 1972/73 exposed, within the heart of the spit, drift logs that had been cut by saws; Salishan homes had been built above them. Nestucca Spit was breached during a storm in 1978. The Alsea Spit development eroded for three years, beginning during high 1982/83 **El Niño sea levels** and culminating in September 1985 when shifting currents widened the normally narrow bay entrance to 1,900 feet in 5 weeks. Netarts Spit was also severely eroded during the 1982/83 El Niño, and has had recurring problems since. Geology of Oregon. See also **Beaches**; **Clatsop Spit**; **Peacock Spit**.

Sandals. Oregon's most famous sandals are the 75 found in **Fort Rock Cave** in 1938. Made of twisted sagebrush bark rope, they were carbon-dated to 9,000 years ago. Sandals made of sagebrush bark or from tule have also been found at other archeological excavations in south central Oregon. Sandal and the Cave. See also **Artifacts**; **Fort Rock Cave**.

Sandcastle Day. An annual **Cannon Beach** sand sculpture contest, held since 1965 on the beach north of Haystack Rock on a June Saturday morning between tides. It attracts some 1,000 entrants and 20,000 spectators. 503-436-2623.

Sandhill crane. A tall bird, *Grus canadensis*, similar to the **great blue heron**. The sandhill crane is the tallest bird in the Northwest, over 44" tall with a 7-foot wingspan. It eats roots, berries, grain, mice, frogs, snakes, and insects. The cranes, which nest in the western U.S., including about 1,000 pairs in **Klamath**, **Lake**, and **Harney Counties**, are noted for their courting dance. Some migrate between Alaska and California, resting at **Sauvie Island** and nearby areas. Their raucous calls can sometimes be heard as a single-file flight passes high overhead. Atlas of Oregon Wildlife; Birds of Oregon; Sandy.

Sandstone. Sandstone from a quarry in **Lincoln County** east of **Toledo** was used for building the San Francisco mint and post office. The **Polk County** courthouse in **Dallas** is built of sandstone quarried three miles west of town. Oregon Ghost Towns. See also **Clam burgers**.

Sandwich Islands. The name given by Captain Cook to what are now known as the Hawaiian Islands when he discovered them in 1778. See also **Hawaiians in Oregon**.

Sandy. "Gateway to Mount Hood." A northwest Oregon town located in **Clackamas County**, 24 miles southeast of **Portland** on **Highway 26**. The historic **Barlow Road** passed through the area. The post office was established in 1873 and named for the nearby **Sandy River**, originally called the Quicksand River by **Lewis and Clark**. The city was incorporated in 1913. Attractions include a historical museum, Jonsrud Viewpoint overlooking the Sandy River gorge, Meinig Memorial Park, including Fantasy Forest Playpark, Sandy Fish Hatchery, and the Sandy Mountain Festival on the 2nd weekend in July. Population 1980 2,905; 1995 4,685. Elevation 1,000'. 39250 Pioneer Boulevard, 97055. 503-668-5533. Chamber of Commerce 503-668-4006. Oregon Geographic Names; Sandy Pioneers; Whistle Punks.

Sandy River. A 56-mile-long river that drains 508 square miles of the west slope of **Mount Hood**, flowing into the **Columbia River** near **Troutdale**. The river is heavily used for recreation, and a steep-sided, 12.5-mile section between Dodge and Dabney parks has been designated a **National Wild and Scenic River**. **Bull Run** and Salmon River are major tributaries. For some years the river was called the Quicksand for the immense amounts of sand at its mouth, but the name has since been shortened to Sandy. Oregon Geographic Names; Oregonian 7/4/95:A1.

Sanitarians. In 1997 the Oregon **Health Division Licensing Programs** office had 350 sanitarians and trainees registered. A seven-member board, appointed by the governor, establishes policy. Oregon Blue Book.

Sanitary landfills. See **Landfills**.

Santa Clara. A passenger steamer with nearly 60 persons aboard that struck an uncharted shoal at the entrance to **Coos Bay** on November 2, 1915. One of the lifeboats flipped over in the high seas and 16 lives were lost. The boat's whistle was one of the few things saved and was used for years by a mill in the area. Shipwrecks of the Pacific Coast.

Santiam Pass. A pass, elevation 4,817', through the central **Cascade Range**. All highway travel heading east from central and southern Willamette Valley is funneled across it. Travelers from **Eugene** cross the pass via the McKenzie River (**Highway 126**), those from the **Albany** area via the South Santiam (**Highway 20**), and from the **Salem** area via the North Santiam (**Highway 22**). The area was first known as Wiley Pass for Andrew Wiley who blazed a route up the west side in 1859, and later as Hogg Pass for T. Egenton Hogg who built a section of the **Oregon Pacific Railroad** across it past **Hogg Rock**. The route was first opened as a toll road for moving herds of cattle to eastern Oregon, and then in 1866 as a **wagon road**, sometimes called the Santiam Toll Road, that crossed the pass about three miles south of the present highway. East of the Cascades. See also *Sea Otter*; **Willamette Valley and Cascade Mountain Military Wagon Road**.

Santiam River. A major river that drains 1,830 square miles of the western slope of the **Cascade Range** east of **Albany**. At river mile point 9.6, it has an average annual volume of 5,536,000 acre feet, or 4.8 acre feet/acre. Major tributaries are the North, Middle, South, Little North Santiam, and Breitenbush rivers, and Thomas, Crabtree, and Quartzville Creeks. Flood control and power dams have been built on both the North and South Santiam. The river was named for the

Santiam Indians, a tribe of **Kalapuya Indians** who lived along it. <u>Oregon Geographic Names</u>.

Santiam State Forest. A 48,000-acre **state forest** in **Clackamas, Marion** and **Linn** counties made up of **Board of Forestry Lands**. ODF Santiam Unit Office, 22965 N. Fork Road SE, Lyons 97358. 503-859-2151. See also **Shellburg Falls**.

Sasquatch. See **Bigfoot**.

SAT. A nation-wide test of verbal and mathematical skills given annually to college-bound high school seniors, formerly called the Scholastic Assessment or Scholastic Aptitude Test. In 1996-97,Oregon scores averaged 1049 (525 verbal and 524 math) out of a possible 1600. Oregon students ranked first among the 20 states in which at least 50% of the students took the test. In 1996 Oregon students who ranked in the top 10% of their class posted scores 23 points below the national average for top students. In Oregon boys scored 36 points higher than girls, whites scored 210 points higher than blacks and 155 points higher than Mexicans and Mexican-Americans, and students from families earning more than $100,000 scored 117 points higher than those from families earning $10,000-$20,000. <u>Oregonian</u> 8/23/96:A1, 8/27/97:A1. See also **ACT**.

Saturday Academy. A private program that operates science-oriented summer school sessions in **Portland** and four other centers in Oregon for 4th to 12th graders. The **Oregon Graduate Institute of Science and Technology** provides guidance, and a variety of groups and individuals help support it. As of 1997, over 44,000 students had been served by the program since it began in 1983. <u>Oregonian</u> 6/24/97:C11.

Saturday markets. Craft markets. **Portland**'s, begun in 1974, is held Saturdays and Sundays, March through December, under the west end of the Burnside bridge; it has over 270 booths. See also **Farmers markets**.

Sauerkraut. A food made from fermented cabbage. Steinfeld's Products in **Scappoose**, a family owned company founded in 1922, operates the only major sauerkraut plant west of the Mississippi and sponsors an annual October festival. 503-285-6076. See also **Verboort**.

Sauvie Island. A long low island, one of the largest river islands in North America. It is about three miles wide and over 15 miles long, from **Portland** north to **St. Helens** between the main channel of the **Columbia River** on the east and **Multnomah Channel**, a secondary mouth of the **Willamette River**, on the west. The south half of the island lies in **Multnomah County** and is primarily farm land, protected from seasonal flooding by dikes completed in 1941. The north end, in **Columbia County**, is a maze of waterways and lakes, including **Sturgeon Lake**. Much of the north end was acquired in 1947 by the Oregon Department of **Fish and Wildlife**. Half of the waterfowl wintering in the **Willamette Valley** stay on Sauvie Island, and some 220 species of birds are known to be present at some time during the year. A bridge near the south end provides access from **Highway 30**. The island's flat, quiet roads are popular for bicycling. A significant earthquake shook the island in 1964. In 1805 **Lewis and Clark** called it Wappatoo Island for the abundant **wapato** that grew there, and estimated that 2,400 Multnomah Indians lived on it with another 1,800 just across the channel. However, by the time

Nathaniel Wyeth established **Fort William** trading post in 1834, **epidemics**, especially the 1830 **malaria** epidemic, had killed them all. "Sauvie" honors Laurent Sauve, a French-Canadian who operated a large **Hudson's Bay Company** dairy farm on the island 1838-1844. Atlas of Oregon Lakes; Birds of the Pacific Northwest; Oregon Geographic Names; Story of Sauvies Island. See also **Black walnut**; **Bybee-Howell House**.

Savage Rapids Dam. A low dam, built in 1921 on the **Rogue River** five miles upstream from **Grants Pass**, owned by the Grants Pass Irrigation District. Because it damages fish runs, the Oregon **Water Resources** Commission and the **Bureau of Reclamation** proposed eliminating it and substituting pumps. In 1995 the legislature authorized an 18-member task force to come up with alternatives. Oregonian 8/11/95:B2.

Sawmills, history. The **Hudson's Bay Company** (HBC) built the first sawmill in the **Oregon Country** in 1827 near **Fort Vancouver** in what is now Washington State. Early lumber mills in what is now Oregon included Ewing Young's 1838 mill on lower Chehalem Creek and one built by Dr. McLoughlin at **Oregon City** in 1842-43. The 1848/49 California **gold rush** created a sudden demand for Oregon lumber, giving impetus to the timber industry. By the turn of the century, mill capacity exceeded demand, and even in 1917 they operated at only 62% of capacity. Post **World War II** demand beginning in 1945 again prompted rapid growth of the industry. However, about half of Oregon's mills have closed since 1980 due to improvements in mill efficiency and cut-backs in logging on federal lands. Hull-Oakes Lumber Company of **Monroe** operates the only steam sawmill left in the state. See also **Cold deck**; **Flumes**; **Lumber production, history**; **Wigwam burners**.

Scandals. Unsavory antics by Oregonians have made national news in recent even numbered years. In 1992 U.S. Senator Bob Packwood left the Senate because of revelations about his unwanted advances to women. In 1994 Olympic figure skater Tonya Harding was disgraced for her association with an attack on rival Nancy Kerrigan's knee. In 1996 U.S. Representative Wes Cooley left Congress after publicity about his questionable claims of, among other things, military service in Korea. In 1998 recent Lewis and Clark graduate Monica Lewinsky was at the center of a sex scandal involving President Clinton. See also **Corruption**; **Land swindles**; **Swamp lands**; **Venal officials**.

Scandinavians in Oregon. Scandinavians, persons of Danish, Finnish, Norwegian, and Swedish descent, were by 1910 the largest ethnic group in Portland. The nearly-vanished communities of Denmark near **Bandon** and Norway near **Myrtle Point** mark other areas settled by Scandinavians. In June a Midsummer Scandinavian Festival is held in **Astoria** (503-325-6311), where many **Finns** settled, and **Junction City** (541-998-6154) celebrates in mid-August with a four-day Scandinavian Fest with each day dedicated to one of the Nordic nationalities. A Nord Fest has been held in **Portland** in recent years at First Immanuel Lutheran Church, NW 19th and Irving. 503-226-3659. Scandinavian Heritage Foundation, Portland State University, PO Box 751, Portland 97207-0751. 503-725-3064.

Scappoose (ska-POOS). A northwest Oregon town in **Columbia County** 20 miles northwest of **Portland** on **Highway 30**. The post office was established in 1872 and named Scappoose, a Chinook Indian word meaning gravelly plain. The city was incorporated in 1921. Major employers include OS Systems, Steinfeld Products, and West Coast Shoe Company. The 1902 Watts House serves as city hall and museum. The Sauerkraut Festival is held in October. Population 1980 3,213; 1995 3,845. Elevation 61'. PO Box P, 97056. 503-543-7146. Chamber of Commerce 503-397-0685. History of Scappoose.

Scenic areas. See **Columbia River Gorge National Scenic Area**.

Scenic Byways. A program established by the Oregon Department of **Transportation** in 1997 that designated 11 highway routes as scenic routes worth exploring. The routes must have a "corridor management plan" that provides for maintenance of the view, an interpretive plan, and no billboard additions. The longest is the 350-mile coast **Highway 101**, the shortest the 66-mile **Cascade Lakes Highway** out of **Bend**. A brochure describes the routes and their historical, recreational, and scenic points of interest. Mail Tribune 3/29/97:2A; Scenic Driving. See also **Back Country Byways**.

Scenic waterways. 1,150 miles of 19 Oregon rivers, plus all of **Waldo Lake**, are now covered by the Scenic Waterways Act, an initiative passed by Oregon voters in 1970 and administered by the state **Parks and Recreation Department**. The act prohibits any dams, reservoirs, impoundments or placer mining on a scenic waterway, and places restrictions on the activities of landowners within 1/4 mile of the waterways in order to protect scenic values as seen from the river. However, public use of private property, including river shores, is prohibited without the explicit consent of the landowner. Except for Waldo Lake and the Nestucca River, the scenic waterways are also protected as **National Wild and Scenic Rivers**. Oregon Scenic Waterways Program.

SCF. See **Children and Families, Services to**.

Schnitzer Concert Hall. See **Arlene Schnitzer Concert Hall**.

Scholarship Commission. An Oregon commission that administers a variety of state, U.S., and privately funded scholarship and financial aid programs for Oregonians attending post secondary institutions. Its seven members are appointed by the governor for four-year terms. 1500 Valley Dr., Suite 100, Eugene 97401. 541-687-7400; 800-452-8807. Oregon Blue Book. See also **Bernard Daly Educational Fund**, **Oregon Community Foundation**; **Western Interstate Commission for Higher Education**

Scholastic Assessment Test. See **SAT**.

School buses. Oregon law requires that schools transport elementary students living more than one mile from school and high school students living more than one and a half miles; about half of Oregon **public school** children ride a school bus to school. The state funds 70% of student transportation costs. State law requires all motorists in both directions to stop and stay stopped anytime a school bus is flashing its red lights. This is true no matter how many lanes, except on a divided highway that has an unpaved median strip. Oregon Driver's Manual; Oregon Report Card.

School districts. In 1995-96 Oregon had 237 school districts (down from 2,556 in 1918). Of these, 168 were unified districts, 9 union high districts, 39 elementary districts, and 21 unified districts without an operating high school.

The total has been decreasing as the result of a 1991 state law requiring independent elementary school districts to merge with high school districts and had declined to 220 in 1997. **Portland** School District, with 57,000 students, is the largest school district in the state, though four other high school districts within Portland (Centennial, David Douglas, Parkrose, and Reynolds) serve another 15,000 students. Oregon School Directory 1995-96. See also **One-room schools; Schools, public**.

School enrollment. In 1995, 576,557 students attended **schools** in Oregon, up 7.5% from 1991. 527,914 (91.6%) were in public schools, 38,150 (6.6%) in private schools, and 10,493 (1.8%) were receiving **home schooling**. Enrollments are projected to increase to a total of 610,000 by 2006. The percentage of Oregon children aged 5 to 19 enrolled in school increased from 79.3% in 1950 to 87.9% in 1990. Oregonian 4/9/96:A1, 8/23/96:C3, 10/29/97:A10. See also **Schools; Students**.

School finance. In 1994-95 Oregon public schools spent $2.9 billion, 83.5% of it on salaries and benefits and 11.5% on buildings and grounds. The cost per student in 1994 was $5,015, up from $3,908 (in 1994 dollars) in 1975. However, the money available for public schools has declined about 15% per student since **Measure 5** was adopted in 1990 to reduce local **property taxes** (the traditional support for schools and local government). Before Measure 5 the state supplied 26% of funding, and supported the so-called state "safety net", adopted after several school districts closed down in 1985 for lack of funds. After Measure 5, state funding for schools increased, and by 1995-96 the state supplied two thirds of school funding, using **income tax** and **lottery** proceeds. The transfer of major responsibility for school funding from the local level to state government resulted in the transfer of much local control to the state level as well as cuts in much of the rest of the state budget. In 1996 Oregonians spent 3.86% of their personal income on public schools, down from 4.5% in 1982. Governing Oregon; Oregonian 5/31/96:B6, 6/25/96:A8, 2/18/97:A1. See also **Common School Fund; Equalization**.

School history. The first formal education west of the Rockies took place when John Ball taught at **Fort Vancouver** in 1832-33. In 1834 Solomon Smith taught the first school in what is now Oregon in the home of Joseph Gervais at **French Prairie**. The **Methodists** organized the **Oregon Institute** in 1842, the same year that the first **Catholic** school in Oregon opened at **Saint Paul**. The first school for girls began at Saint Paul two years later. The first **public school** in Oregon opened in 1852 in **Portland** with 20 students, taught by John Outhouse (pronounced O'-thus). The first secondary-level education in Oregon was carried out in private schools, often called academies or institutes. Among the earliest were Oregon Institute (1842), Clackamas County Female Seminary (1847), Tualatin Academy (1848), Santiam Academy (1854), and La Creole Academy (1855). What is now Lincoln High in **Portland** was the state's first public high school, established with 45 students in 1869 despite opposition from the Oregonian; it has had various names and occupied six sites since then. Dictionary of Oregon History; Oregon Oddities. See also **High schools**.

School lands. See **Common School Fund**.

School reform. See **Education Act for the 21st Century**.

School uniforms. In 1995 students at Lake Labish Elementary School (K-5) in the Salem-Keizer School District became the first public school students in Oregon to wear uniforms.

School year. State law requires a minimum of 405 hours of instruction for **kindergarten**, 810 hours for first through third grade, 900 hours for fourth through eighth grade, and 990 hours for ninth through twelfth grade, spread over a span of 265 consecutive calendar days, but districts may schedule the hours as they wish. Some schools schedule longer days but for just 4 days a week. Up to 30 hours a year of instruction time may be used for in-service staff development activities. The average number of school days in the state is 169, compared with 240 days in Japan and Germany. A 1991 law that would have extended the school year to 200 days by 2000 was repealed by the 1995 legislature. Oregonian 12/10/96:B2, 12/24/96:B2.

Schools, private. In 1995, 342 private and parochial schools made reports to the Oregon Department of **Education**, though, since they are not required to use certified teachers and do not need to be licensed or registered, the actual number is not known. The reported enrollment at those schools grew 28% from 1990-91 to 38,150 in 1995-96. In 1922 an **initiative** measure to outlaw private (**Catholic**) schools, promoted by the **Masonic Lodge** and **Ku Klux Klan**, was adopted by the voters of Oregon. The measure was overturned by a unanimous decision of the U.S. Supreme Court in 1925. Oregon Oddities; Oregonian 3/3/96:A17. See also **School enrollment**.

Schools, public. In fall 1996 **school enrollment** in Oregon's public schools totaled 537,854. In 1994-95, Oregon had 1,208 tax-supported public schools, including 896 elementary schools, 44 junior high schools, and 198 high schools, plus 70 combined or alternative schools. The graduation rate in 1993-94, as for the previous several years, was 71.7%. Danebo Elementary School in **Eugene** is one of 13 U.S. schools selected for participation in a three-year project to institute changes in elementary school education. The first tax-supported schools in the state opened in 1851. A compulsory attendance law passed in 1889. **High schools** were added in 1900. Oregon Oddities; Oregon Report Card. See also **ACT**; **Boarding schools**; **Charter schools**; **Common School Fund**; **Dropouts**; **Education** entries; **One-room schools**; **SAT**; **School** entries; **Science education**; **SMART**; **Students**.

Schooner. Traditionally, a two-masted sailing ship, though after 1884 small wooden steam schooners served the Pacific coast lumber trade until the 1940s. It is estimated that 75% of the fleet of over 200 were shipwrecked due to the hazardous conditions in which they worked. Shipwrecks of the Pacific Coast. See also *Morning Star of Tillamook*; *Star of Oregon*.

Schrunk Plaza. See **Plaza Blocks**; **Suzhou stone**.

Science education. **Gold Beach** High School was co-champion of the 1996 International Science and Engineering Fair, and placed in the top 10 in each of the previous four years. Oregonian 6/8/96:D1.

Science, Technology and Society Lecture Series. An annual series of lectures in **Eugene** and **Portland** sponsored by the Institute for Science, Engineering and Public Policy. 503-232-2300.

Scientists. Award-winning Oregon scientists include chemist Linus Pauling, twice winner of the **Nobel Prize**, and marine biologist Jane Lubchenco, professor at **Oregon State University**, who was awarded a **MacArthur Fellowship** in 1993, and who served as president of the American Association for the Advancement of Science in 1995-96.

Scientology. See **Church of Scientology**.

Scio. (SIGH-oh) "Covered Bridge Capital of the West." A mid-**Willamette Valley** timber and farming community in **Linn County** 17 miles northeast of **Albany**. The area was known as Santyam Forks when first settled in 1844, and then as McDonalds Precinct, before William McKinney, owner of the flour mill, renamed it Scio for his home town in Ohio. The post office was established in 1860, and the city was incorporated in 1866. A **Czechoslovakian** influx, beginning in the late 1800s, is marked by the historic ZCJB Gymnastics Hall. Events include the Linn County Fat Lamb and Wool Fair, and the Northwest Championship Sheep Dog Trials, both on the 3rd weekend in May. Population 1980 579; 1995 655. Elevation 317'. PO Box 37, 97374. 503-394-3342. Oregon Geographic Names; Scio.

Scott-Applegate Trail. See **Applegate Trail**.

Scottish Highland games. See **Highland games**.

Scotts Mills. A foothill community in **Marion County** on the eastern edge of the **Willamette Valley** 21 miles northeast of **Salem**. It was named about 1860 for the sawmill and flour mill owned by Robert and Thomas Scott. The post office was established in 1887, and the city was incorporated in 1916. Population 1980 249; 1995 310; Elevation 420'. PO Box C, 97375. 503-873-2065. Oregon Geographic Names.

Scotts Mills earthquake. A magnitude 5.6 (Richter scale) **earthquake**, sometimes called the Spring Break quake, that struck at 5:35 a.m. on March 25, 1993, three miles east of **Scotts Mills**. It did an estimated $28 million in damage to bridges, the state **capitol** dome in **Salem**, churches in **Mount Angel** and **Saint Paul**, and other buildings. "Looking Back"; "Scotts Mills Earthquake."

Scottsburg. A historic unincorporated community and one-time port at the head of navigation on the **Umpqua River** in **Douglas County**. It is 17 miles east of **Reedsport** on Highway 38. Levi Scott, for whom the community is named, built a hotel there in 1850 and then established the Umpqua Gazette, the first Oregon newspaper south of **Salem**. The hotel was managed by Daniel Lyons, a totally blind pioneer who also was first editor of the paper. The community flourished briefly as the supply center for the southern Oregon **gold** mines until much of the trade moved to Crescent City, California. The **flood of 1861** obliterated a large part of the community. Dictionary of Oregon History; Oregon Geographic Names.

Sculpture. See **Sandcastle Day**; **Our Lady of Grace Shrine**.

Sculptures, non-Portland. See **Black Bird** (Medford); **Caveman**. (Grants Pass); **Neon horses**; **Pioneer Spirit** (Springfield); **Til Taylor statue** (Pendleton).

Sculptures, Portland. See **Abraham Lincoln**; **Allow Me**; **Beverly Cleary Sculpture Garden**; **Birds on a Wire**; **Colossus of Portland**; **Elk statue**; **Expose Yourself to Art**; **Horse sculptures**; **Portlandia**; **Promised Land**; **Rebecca at the Well**; **Sacajawea statue**; **Weather Machine**.

Sea anemones. Tentacled sea creatures that somewhat resemble flowers. The green sea anemone, *Anthopleura xanthogrammica*, is found in tide pools along Oregon's rocky shores, as is the small aggregating anemone, *A. elegantissima*, which divides in half each year. As their colony grows, the anemones around the outside produce specialized weapons while those on the interior concentrate on growing and reproducing. Anemones can move 3 to 4 inches an hour, though they can also attach firmly to rocks. The tentacles are effective at seizing prey which is then paralyzed by stinging darts before being eaten. They may live for several hundred years. The name is frequently mispronounced as 'anenome'. Great Northwest Nature Factbook; Seashore Life.

Sea birds. Petrels, auklets, grebes, murrelets, pelicans, and scoters nest on Oregon's coast and rocky offshore **islands**. Many of the offshore islands are now included in **National Wildlife Refuges**. "It has been estimated that Oregon was home to more than two million sea birds as recently as 1940, but the development of the coast has trimmed that number by a factor of ten." Listening to Coyote; Oregon Wildlife Viewing Guide.

Sea creatures. See **Barnacles**; **Crabs**; **Jellyfish**; **Octopus**; **Sail jellyfish**; **Sea anemones**; **Sea cucumbers**; **Sea urchins**; **Seashells**; **Shellfish**; **Squid**; **Starfish**.

Sea cucumbers. Ocean bottom sea creatures that have long, muscular bodies. The edible California sea cucumber, *Parastichopus californicus*, grows up to 18 inches in length. Though valued for food by Indians and some contemporary Oregonians, it is not gathered commercially. Great Northwest Nature Factbook; Seashore Life.

Sea Grant. **Oregon State University** is one of 29 national Sea Grant Colleges, supporting applied research on marine resources. Two-thirds of its funding comes from the National Oceanic and Atmospheric Administration, and one third is from the state. Sea Grant also supports education and **extension service** programs. 500 Administrative Services, Oregon State University, Corvallis 97331. 541-737-2714.

Sea level. The sea level along the Oregon coast was 300 to 500 feet lower than at present 17,000 years ago because so much of the earth's water was tied up in ice during **Pleistocene** glaciation. Much of the **continental shelf** was exposed and rivers cut channels across it. As the glaciers melted, the sea level rose until, by 10,000 years ago, the level was about 200 feet lower than now. The sea level continues to rise about 8" per century, but the effect on the Oregon coast is not uniform because of differential **uplift**. Sea level is also affected by other forces; for example, during the El Niño of 1982-83 the sea level at **Newport** was about 14 inches above its average winter level. It has been predicted that the sea level will rise perhaps 3 inches over the next 50 years; rising sea levels result in increased shoreline erosion. Holocene Sea Level Changes in the Pacific Northwest; "Ocean processes and hazards along the Oregon coast." See also **Waves**.

Sea Lion Caves. The world's largest natural sea cave, formed by wave action eroding fracture zones in a **basalt** headland north of **Florence** on the central Oregon coast. The central chamber is over 50 feet high and covers an acre. Ledges in the cave provide the only mainland breeding site for Steller **sea lions**. Three partners bought the caves and built a path and stairs down to them in 1932; a gravel road provided the only access. The same families still operate the facility, now with an elevator, gift shop, and **Highway 101** at its front door. <u>Oregon Coast</u> 11(1):28 Jan/Feb 1992.

Sea lions. Fish-eating **marine mammals**, larger than **seals**, with external ears. Two species are found along the Oregon coast, the California sea lion, *Zalophus californianus* (the circus "seal"), and the larger northern or Steller's sea lion, *Eumetopias jubata*, which breeds at **Sea Lion Caves** and on offshore rocks. The Steller's males may reach 13 feet in length and a ton in weight; each controls a harem of 10 or more females. **Cape Arago** provides a good viewpoint. All **marine mammals** are **protected animals**. <u>Great Northwest Nature Factbook</u>.

Sea mounts. Underwater shield **volcanoes** on the **ocean floor**. There are over 60 off the south Oregon coast, and nearly 50 off the mouth of the **Columbia River**.

Sea Otter. An English fur-trading **schooner** that wrecked near the mouth of the **Umpqua River** on August 22, 1808, with six (some sources say four) survivors. At least three are said to have made it over the **Santiam Pass** and overland through the then unexplored west to the Red River of Louisiana. It was Oregon's first recorded **shipwreck**, though **beeswax** evidence indicates at least one earlier Spanish shipwreck, perhaps the *San Francisco Xavier* in 1705. <u>Shipwrecks of the Pacific Coast</u>.

Sea urchins. Tennis-ball-size spiny creatures of rocky ocean shores that feed primarily on seaweeds. Purple urchins, *Strongylocentrotus purpuratus*, excavate pits in solid rock in which they are somewhat protected from the force of the surf. A few are gathered commercially. Red urchins, *S. franciscanus*, have been harvested commercially by divers in the ocean off **Port Orford** since 1986. Their gonads, called uni, are exported to Japan where they are eaten raw as a delicacy. The harvest declined from 9.3 million pounds in 1990 to 1.5 million pounds in 1995 (worth $1.2 million to the fishermen), or about 5% of the total west coast harvest. Sea urchins are also harvested off **Gold Beach**, **Brookings**, and **Depoe Bay**. <u>Between Pacific Tides</u>; <u>Oregonian</u> 7/16/96:B1; <u>Pacific States</u>; <u>Seashore Life</u>.

Seafood. About half of Oregon's annual $60 million commercial catch of **fish** and **shellfish** is exported, especially to Japan. <u>Oregonian</u> 7/5/95:B8,7.

Seafood Laboratory. A Coastal Oregon Marine Experiment Station laboratory established by **Oregon State University** in **Astoria** in 1940 to undertake research in the utilization of marine and related resources. The lab focuses on research in value-added product development, seafood biochemistry and quality, seafood safety, and waste utilization. Federal, state, and private sources provide funding. One of its projects, research on processing methods for **whiting**, led for a fishery that in 1996 accounted for over half of all Oregon seafood landings and sales of $30 million a year. 250 36th Street, Astoria 97103. 503-325-4531. <u>Oregonian</u> 12/10/96:B4. See also **Agricultural Experiment Station**.

Seal Rock. An unincorporated **Lincoln County** coastal community and state park 10 miles south of **Newport** on **Highway 101**. At the park the large rock with eroding access is known as Tourist Rock; the monolith just to the south of it is Elephant Rock. The Seal Rocks themselves are a partially submerged ledge one half mile out in the ocean that runs parallel to the coast for two and a half miles. These rocks are the southernmost extension of the **Columbia River basalt** flows.

Seals. **Marine mammals** smaller than **seal lions** and without external ears. The spotted harbor seal, *Phoca vitulina*, which is seen along beaches and bays, formerly ventured up the **Columbia River** as far as **The Dalles**. The immense **elephant seal**, *Mirounga angustirostris*, is also seen along the Oregon coast. **Cape Arago** provides a good viewpoint. All **marine mammals** are **protected animals**. Great Northwest Nature Factbook.

Search and rescue. In Oregon county sheriffs are responsible for searches for **lost persons** and vehicles with two exceptions. The U.S. **Coast Guard** is responsible for searches on federally defined navigable waterways; in 1993 the Portland unit conducted 300 operations in the **Columbia** and **Willamette** rivers. The U.S. National Park Service is responsible for searches in **National Parks**. The Air Force Reserve's 304th Rescue Squadron of the 939th Rescue Wing, based in Portland, has no mandate to assist with civilian searches, and doing so disrupts its training schedules for reservists. Much of the cost of searches is borne by volunteer groups. Under a 1995 Oregon law, hikers, hunters, and mountain climbers who have not exercised reasonable care are billed up to $500 of search costs. Oregonian 12/10/95:F1. See also **Bloodhounds**; **Emergency Management Division**; **Search dogs**.

Search dogs. In 1997 the Oregon State Sheriffs Association had 11 certified volunteer dogs available to assist in searches. The dogs, of various breeds, must pass a test every 2 years. Oregon set standards for volunteer search dogs in 1992, the first state to do so. Oregon Search Dog Council, 503-795-9464. Oregonian 9/17/97:E2. See also **Bloodhounds**; **Emergency Management Division**.

Seashells. Shells of a variety of snails, chitons (actually eight crosswise plates), sand dollars, and bivalves can be gathered along the Oregon coast. Many of the shells, however, are broken by the force of the waves. The Oregon hairy triton has been designated the **state seashell**. Seashells of the Pacific Northwest.

Seaside. Oregon's oldest beach resort town, named for railroad entrepreneur Ben Holladay's luxurious 1860s Seaside House. Seaside is on the north coast in **Clatsop County**, 15 miles south of **Astoria** on **Highway 101**. Here the **Lewis and Clark Expedition** boiled down enough sea water to net four bushels of salt early in 1806. The first post office was established in 1871, and the city was incorporated in 1899. Attractions include the broad sand beach, the Promenade along the beach, the Annual Beach Volleyball Tournament on the 2nd weekend in August, the Seaside Aquarium, and Seaside Museum. Population 1980 5,193; 1995 5,750. Elevation 13'. 989 Broadway, 97138. 503-738-5511. Chamber of Commerce 800-444-6740. Oregon Geographic Names.

Seastars. See **Starfish**.

Seat belts. See **Safety belts**.

Seawalls. Walls built to prevent erosion or to keep ocean, river, or lake waters from flooding onto the adjacent land. **Portland**'s mile-long, 27-foot- high harbor wall on the west bank of the **Willamette River** was begun in 1929 after waterfront wharves had outlived their usefulness, and completed in 1933. Plywood panels were hurriedly emplaced between the fence pillars during the **flood of**

1996 but the flood crested just below the top of the wall. In 1997, 382 steel plates were fabricated to have in readiness for the next flood. In 1996 a developer proposed building a 450-foot long, 26-foot high seawall at **Lincoln City** that would extend 150 feet out toward the ocean and be backfilled to create room for an 88-unit condominium. Oregonian 6/19/96:C3, 1/10/97:D1.

Seaweed. An ocean-growing plant that is an alga rather than a seed-bearing plant. A number of species are found along the Oregon coast, especially on rocky shores between high and low **tide** lines. Many are edible or used as sources of vegetable gums. Sea Vegetables; Seashore Life; Seaweeds at Ebb Tide. See also **Algae; Kelp**.

Secession. See **Daylight saving time; Separatism; State of Jefferson**.

Second-largest city. While **Portland** has been the largest city in Oregon from soon after its founding, the honor of being second largest has been claimed by a number of the state's communities, especially in the days of **gold-rush** boom towns (**Auburn** and **Canyon City**, about 1864) and during **World War II** (**Camp Adair** in 1943 and **Vanport**, 1944-45.) **Eugene** has been the state's second-largest city in recent years.

Secretary of State. Oregon's second-ranking elected official, elected to a four year term in November of years divisible by four. Annual salary for the position in 1998 was $67,900. The Secretary of State is chief **elections** officer and auditor of public accounts, keeps the official records of the **legislature** and of the **executive Department**, is custodian of the **state seal**, is responsible for the state **archives**, is a member of the **State Land Board**, publishes the **Oregon Blue Book**, chairs the Historic Properties Commission, is head of the Corporation Division, and oversees the State Boards of Accountancy, Appraiser Certification and Licensure, and Tax Service Examiners. In addition to authorizing financial audits, the Secretary of State has the authority to conduct program audits that go beyond financial matters. 136 State Capitol, Salem 97310. 503-986-1500. Governing Oregon; Oregon Blue Book. See also **Recall; Succession; Term limits**.

Section. A square mile of land, containing 640 **acres**, though surveying errors have occasionally resulted in larger or smaller sections. There are 36 sections in a **township**. See also **Land description**.

Secular Churches. The First Secular Church of **Portland** was established on January 29, 1893, with Katie Kehm Smith as lecturer. A similar group was organized in **Silverton** at about the same time, headquartered in Liberal Hall, which displayed across its facade, "Universal Mental Liberty." The movement, including the **Oregon State Secular Union** and its affiliated groups, seems to have disappeared by 1903. "Organized Free Thought in Oregon." See also **Liberal University**.

Securities. The Business Journal publishes an annual issue devoted to a description of the top public companies headquartered in Oregon or with a strong local presence. As of January 1, 1995, the state Division of **Finance and Corporate Securities** had registered 4,147 securities and licensed 1,160 broker-dealers and 516 investment advisers.

Seed bank. See **National Germplasm Repository**.

Seed crops. Oregon's seed crops include **grass seed, alfalfa seed, clover**

seed, and **sugar beet** seed. In addition, vegetable and flower seeds worth $16.7 million are grown on 8,900 acres. 1995 Oregon. See also **Field burning**.

Segregation, education. **Salem** and **Portland** each opened a separate school for **blacks** and mulattos in 1867. After parents of students in the Portland school demanded better funding for their school, the community ended segregated schooling in 1871. That same year, after two black girls had attempted to enroll, **Pendleton** closed its public school and didn't reopen until the black family moved away several years later. "Unwelcome Settlers."

Segregation, employment. Employment for **blacks** in Oregon was limited to railroad, hotel, or domestic work both by **labor unions** and by employers until **World War II** when skilled positions were opened in the shipyards for the duration of the war. In 1949 the state legislature passed the Oregon Fair Employment Practices Act.

Segregation, housing. Prior to the 1920s, **blacks** in **Portland** had found housing throughout the city, but in 1919 the Portland Realty Board added to its code of ethics a provision prohibiting its members from selling property in white neighborhoods to blacks or Orientals. A white neighborhood was defined as one without a black-occupied residence within four blocks. The position was officially repealed in 1952. After **World War II** blacks who had worked in wartime shipyards and were left homeless by the 1948 **Vanport flood** crowded into the Albina district since housing in other areas was closed to them. In 1950 the Portland Housing Authority officially integrated. The **University of Oregon** refused to allow black women to room in the college dorms in the 1930s and 40s. A public accommodations bill was passed by the **legislature** in 1953. Peculiar Paradise. See also **Sundown laws**.

Segregation, school. During the 1860s and 1870s **black** children were not allowed to attend **public schools** in **Portland**, **Salem**, and **Pendleton**. Portland and Salem set up separate schools for a time, but by 1874 the black children were enrolled in the public schools. School segregation was also practiced briefly in **Coos County** in 1903, and in **Vernonia**, Maxville, and **Portland Catholic** schools during the 1920s. Peculiar Paradise.

Seismic Safety Policy Advisory Commission, Oregon. A commission responsible to the governor and legislature for reviewing, coordinating, and advising on all plans and proposals addressing seismic hazards, and for implementing and maintaining an appropriate emergency services system. 595 Cottage St. NE, Salem 97310. 503-378-2911. Oregon Blue Book. See also **Earthquakes**.

Seismological station. See **Blue Mountain Observatory**.
Sellwood Church. See **Oaks Pioneer Church**.

Semi-conductor industry. An industry that manufactures the chips that serve as the brains of computers. In1996 it had the greatest industrial **payroll** in Oregon. **Intel** (headquartered in California), the state's largest manufacturer, opened its first Oregon plant in **Washington County** in 1976; by 1997 its six facilities there employed some 9,000 people. The growth of the industry has also attracted supporting businesses to locate in the area. The semi-conductor chip and wafer plants in the **Portland** metropolitan area are valued at more than $10 billion, five times the $2 billion value of real estate in downtown Portland. In 1996-97 Hyundai

Semiconductor America built a $1.3 billion, 1-million-square-foot plant on the outskirts of **Eugene** that was controversial because it involved filling 21 acres of wetlands. Oregonian 10/13/95:C1, 3/7/96:D1, 3/28/97:D1. See also **High-tech**; **Silicon Forest**; **Strategic Investment Program**.

Senate, Oregon. The upper chamber of the Oregon **legislature**. It has 30 members elected for four-year terms. The members elect a President of the Senate who presides, assigns **senators** to committees, appoints committee chairs, refers measures to committee, and oversees the functioning of the Senate. In addition to considering **bills**, the Senate confirms the governor's appointments to certain offices, boards, and commissions. Oregon Capitol, Salem 97310. 503-986-1187. 800-332-2313 during the session. Oregon Blue Book; Oregon Legislative Guide. See also **Legislative committees**; **Succession**.

Senators, Oregon. Thirty senators serve in the Oregon **Senate**, each elected from a single-member district for a four-year term, with half elected every two years. Senators are limited to 8 years of service in the Senate. A candidate must be 21, a U.S. citizen, and have resided in the senatorial district for a year prior to election. In the 1990s each senate district contains about 95,000 people; the districts are redrawn every 10 years after the census. Their pay, last raised in 1997, is $14,496 a year. The average election campaign for a seat in the Oregon Senate cost $5,549 in 1972 and $52,756 in 1992. Oregon Blue Book; Oregon Legislative Guide. See also **Campaign finance**; **Ethics**; **Legislature**; **Recall**; **Term limits**.

Senators, U.S. Oregon's two U.S. senators were elected by the Oregon legislature until 1908 when, in response to **corruption**, a state **initiative** authorized non-binding statewide election. A 1913 amendment to the U.S. Constitution allowed for direct elections nation-wide. Thirty-three men and one woman (Maurine Neuberger, 1960-'67) have served as U.S. senators from Oregon, 16 of them **Democrats** and 19 **Republicans** (Wayne Morse served two terms for each party.) The longest serving senators have been: Charles L. McNary (R), 1917-1944; Wayne Morse, 1945-1969; Mark Hatfield (R), 1967-1996; and Robert Packwood (R), 1969-1995. The Oregon Blue Book lists Oregon's past and present U.S. senators. U.S. senators are elected at state-wide elections for six-year terms. The next regular election for first position, filled by Gordon Smith in the 1996 election, will be in 2002. The next regular election for second position, filled by Ron Wyden in a 1996 special election, will be in 1998. See also **Felony**; **Holdup session**; **Scandals**; **Term limits**; **Venal officials**; **Vote by mail**.

Seneca. An eastern Oregon timber and ranching community 25 miles south of **John Day** on **Highway 395** in **Grant County**. The post office was established in 1895 and named for the postmistress' brother-in-law, Portland Judge Seneca Smith. Seneca was for a time a company town for the Edward Hines Lumber Company, which came to the area in 1926. The city was incorporated in 1970. Population 1980 285; 1995 230. Elevation 4,666' 106 A St., 97873. 541-542-2161. Oregon Geographic Names.

Senior and Disabled Services Division. A division of the Department of **Human Resources** that encourages independence, dignity, and quality of life for seniors and the disabled. It is the designated State Unit on Aging. Services are delivered through local Area Agencies on Aging and state field offices. Referral services, 800-282-8096. Protective services, 800-232-3020. 500 Summer St. NE, Salem 97310-1015, V/TTY 503-945-5811. Oregon Blue Book. See also **Adult foster care**; **Continuing care communities**; **Long Term Care**.

Senior Health Insurance Benefits Assistance (SHIBA). A program of the **Insurance Division** that uses volunteers to assist Medicare beneficiaries in making health insurance decisions, filing claims, and making appeals. 503-378-4484, 800-722-4134. Oregon Blue Book.

Separatism. In 1861 pro-slavery forces proposed an independent nation, the Pacific Coast Republic, an idea promoted by the **Knights of the Golden Circle**. Earlier, in 1854, a separate state had been proposed for southern Oregon and northern California, an idea revived in 1941 as the **State of Jefferson**.

Serial levy. See **Property tax**.

Serpentinite. A soft, dark, greenish, greasy-looking metamorphic rock. It is formed by the reaction of peridotite (the rock of the earth's interior) with water, and is an important component of the oceanic crust. It is found in the **Blue Mountains** and the **Siskiyou Mountains** where unique species of plants are found growing on the serpentine outcrops.

Service districts. See **Special service districts**.

Services to Children and Families. See **Children and Families, Services to**.

Settlement. The first non-Indian settlement in Oregon was the **Astoria** fur **trading post**, established by Americans in 1811. Former members of the company who settled in Oregon after 1813 are thought to have been the first settlers in the **Willamette Valley**. **Fort Vancouver** was established by the **Hudson's Bay Company** in 1825. Their fur trappers began settling on **French Prairie** and at what is now **Oregon City** in 1829. The **Methodist Mission** was established near **Salem** in 1834. The first major influx of settlers came over the **Oregon Trail** in 1843 to the **Willamette Valley**. **Gold** discoveries in southwest Oregon in 1851 and in northeast Oregon in 1861-62 led to the settlement of those areas. Central Oregon was first settled in 1863. See also *Albatross*; **Pioneers**.

Settlement patterns. The first few farmers in Oregon settled on the open lands of **French Prairie** and the Tualatin plains where they were joined by those arriving on the 1843 **wagon train**. The immigrants of 1845 had to push to the middle of the **Yamhill, Luckiamute**, and **Pudding River** valleys to find available land. By 1847 settlers had to go to the head of the **Willamette Valley**, and by the 1850s they were settling in the **Umpqua, Rogue**, and coastal valleys. East of the **Cascade Range** settlement had centered at **The Dalles** until **gold** discoveries led to the establishment of **Canyon City** in 1862. See also **Donation Land Claims**.

Settlements. The pioneer communities in the **Willamette Valley** were known as settlements until about 1850. In the 1840s the settlements included **Oregon City, Canemah** (just above the **Willamette Falls**), La Butte (**Butteville**), **Champoeg**, St. Paul Catholic Mission (**Saint Paul**), Methodist Mission (**Willamette Mission**), Chemeketa (**Salem**), **Dayton**, Yamhill Falls (**Lafayette**), and Grand Prairie (**Saint Louis**). The earliest white settlements were along waterways since rivers provided the easiest transportation, and the pattern continued after **steamships** were introduced in 1850. However, with the construction of the first **railroad** line in 1870, new communities clustered along the rail lines. After **gold** was discovered in southern and eastern Oregon in the 1850s and 1860s, mining camps sprang up in areas far distant from either rivers or rails, and transportation was by horseback or, after rudimentary **wagon roads** were built, by horse-drawn **stage lines**. After 1900, the automobile again changed transportation patterns, making possible more dispersed settlement and sprawling suburbs. Champoeg.

Seven Devils. The name given to the area along the **coast** between the **Coquille** and **Coos** rivers because of the deep ravines that made travel and road building through the area arduous. Century of Coos and Curry.

Seventh Day Adventist Church. A denomination founded in 1844. Its first Oregon churches were established in the mid 1870s in **Salem** and **Milton**. The first camp meeting was held near Salem in 1878. Through the years the church has operated a number of academies, including the Rogue Valley Adventist School since 1926, and Milo Academy on the South **Umpqua River**. Oregon Conference, 13455 SE 97th Avenue, Clackamas 97015. 503-652-2225. Dictionary of Oregon History.

Sewage treatment. Five hundred sewage treatment plants serve two thirds of Oregon's population, and the Department of **Environmental Quality** regulates another 3,250 industrial and agricultural sources. About 30% of Oregonians use septic tanks for sewage disposal. Though the first sewage treatment plant in Oregon was built in **Baker City** in 1936, most treatment plants were not built until the 1950s and 60s, and they provided just primary treatment, removing 30% of the organic waste. **Portland**'s first plant opened in 1952. By 1977 all municipalities along the **Willamette River** were providing secondary treatment, removing at least 85% of organic wastes. Chronic overflows of raw sewage are a concern at twelve Oregon cities, including Portland, and disposal of the sludge and toxic wastes remaining after sewage treatment are also of concern. Experiences in Environmental Sanitation; Oregon Environmental Atlas; Oregon's 1994 Water Quality.

Sewellel. See **Boomer**.

Sex industry. After the state **Supreme Court**'s unanimous 1987 interpretation of the state constitution in State vs Henry, Oregon became one of the most permissive states in the nation for sex-related businesses. Metropolitan area businesses include adult book and video stores, stores selling sex toys, live peek booths, lingerie modeling shops, adult tanning parlors, topless bars, strip clubs, escort services, and street walkers. In 1995 **Portland** had 20 times the number of nude entertainment spots that Los Angeles had, and **Multnomah County** police made 400 prostitution arrests, including prostitutes and their customers. Oregonian 5/7/95:D1, 6/16/96:D1. See also **Censorship; Pornography; Prostitution; Tin Plate Law**.

Sexton Mountain Pass. A pass on **Interstate 5**, elevation 1,956'. Though about the same elevation as much of **Ashland**, the pass is noted for treacherous winter driving conditions as well as for the expansive view south over **Grants Pass** and the Rogue valley.

Sexual harassment. In recent years about 235 charges of sexual harassment have been filed each year with the **Civil Rights Division** of the Oregon **Bureau of Labor and Industries**. Though most of the charges are employment related, charges may also be related to public accommodations or housing. Complaints of sexual harassment may be filed with either the state Civil Rights Division, 503-731-4075, or with the U.S. Equal Employment Opportunity Commission at 1-800-669-4000. Oregonian 11/6/94:C1.

Sexually transmitted diseases. Oregon law requires health care prividers to report the following sexually transmitted diseases (STDs) to a local health department (reports are confidential): **AIDS**, 293 cases and 90 deaths in 1997; chancroid, a bacterial infection, 1 case; **clamydia**, 5,254 cases; gonorrhea, a bacterial infection, 773 cases in 1997, down from over 11,000 in 1980; lymphogranuloma venereum (LGV), 0,; pelvic inflammatory disease (PID), 719; and syphilis, 24. Oregonian 4/8/98:B12.

Shad. An introduced **anadromous fish**, *Alosa sapidissimia*, related to herring, that grows to 30" long. Shad lose their teeth when they enter the ocean and feed by straining plankton through their gill rakers. First introduced from the eastern U.S. in 1871, up to four million now migrate up the **Columbia River** where there is a commercial shad fishery; at times, some 60,000 a day pass **McNary Dam**. Major shad runs also occur in the Coos, Umpqua, and Siuslaw Rivers. Oregon Wildlife 48(4):8 July/August 1992; Oregon's Migratory Fish.

Shady Cove. "Meet the Rogue in Shady Cove." A southwest Oregon town in **Jackson County**. It is 24 miles north of **Medford** where Highway 62 crosses the **Rogue River**. The name comes from a cove in the east bank of the river several hundred yards upriver from the highway bridge. The post office was established in 1939; the city was incorporated in 1972. Population 1980 1,097; 1995 1,950. Elevation 1,349'. PO Box 1210, 97539. 541-878-2225. Land in Common.

Shakespeare. See **Oregon Shakespeare Festival**; **Tygres Heart Shakespeare Company**.

Shale City. A short-lived community based on an **oil** extraction scheme 12 miles northeast of **Ashland**. In 1922 a promoter arrived in Ashland with a model of a retort he proposed to build for extracting petroleum from shale beds east of town. Much of the community invested, and a 250-ton retort was built. It soon broke down, the state investigated his syndicate, and the promoter disappeared, but local investors persisted. After two years of effort they got the machine restarted - and watched as it melted into a pile of junk. In 1961 shale was again briefly mined from the area for use as a soil amendment. Daily Tidings 10/16/61; "Shale City".

Shanghaied. See **Crimp**.

Shaniko (SHAN ih ko). A **Wasco County** community 36 miles northeast of **Madras** on **Highway 97**. The site, with its dependable water supply, had for a time been a stagecoach stop called Cross Hollows. In 1898-1900 Columbia Southern laid a rail line south from **Biggs** to Shaniko and built a station there as the shipping point for central Oregon **wool**. The booming community was incorporated the next year. By 1903 Shaniko was known as the "Wool Shipping Capital of the World" and thrived until its shipping business vanished after rail lines reached **Bend** in 1911. The community lingers as a picturesque ghost town featuring antiques and old buildings. The community sponsors Shaniko Days, Pioneer Days, and a Halloween Spook House. The name Shaniko came from the Indian pronunciation of the name of August Scherneckau, an early rancher and stage station operator. Population 1980 30; 1995 30. Elevation 3,340'. PO Box 17, 97057. 541-489-3317. Chamber of Commerce 541-395-2529. East of the Cascades; Oregon Geographic Names; Shaniko People.

Shape note singing. Unaccompanied four-part hymn singing using music in which notes of the scale are indicated by different shapes. The basic hymn book, The Sacred Harp, was published in 1844. The **Portland** members of the Pacific Northwest Sacred Harp Singers gather monthly for a sing. 503-232-6371. Oregonian 6/27/95:C1.

Sharks. Primitive fish with cartilaginous skeletons. Ten species are found in the waters off Oregon. They are the sevengill (9'), thresher (25'), white (21'), basking (45'), shortfin mako (12'), soupfin (6'), blue (12'), leopard (6'), spiny dogfish (5'), and Pacific angel shark (5'). The huge basking shark is one of the most benign, feeding on plankton, while the white shark is the most vicious of sharks, feeding on fish, **seals**, and other **marine mammals** and munching the occasional surfer. None of the eleven attacks on surfers recorded off Oregon since 1976 has been fatal. The attacks were at **Cannon Beach** 11/27/79, 10/23/88; **Oswald West State Park** 9/21/94; **Cape Kiwanda** 8/20/83; **Neskowin** 9/30/84, 2/24/91; **Winchester Bay** 8/24/76, 10/27/80, 3/8/92; Bastendorff Beach (near **Coos Bay**)1/2/93; **Gold Beach** 9/13/92. Audubon Society Field Guide; Oregonian 9/26/95:C1.

Shasta Route. See **Natron cut-off**.

Shedd. An unincorporated community 18 miles south of **Albany** on **Highway 99E**. It was founded when the residents of Boston, a mile to the east, moved their houses down the road to Frank Shedd's land next to the new railroad. **Boston Roller Mills** is the only remnant of Boston. Oregon Geographic Names.

Sheep. Oregon had 394,000 sheep and lambs in 1995. Sales of sheep and lambs for slaughter grossed $25.8 million, and **wool** sales brought another $1.8 million. **Douglas** and **Linn** counties led with 70,000 animals each. The first sheep in Oregon were those of the **Hudson's Bay Company** in the 1830's. Sheep arrived in eastern Oregon soon after cattle; between 1895 and 1936 annual inventories were over 2 million. On **Steens Mountain** alone there were estimated to have been over 140,000 sheep in 1901; they were banned from Steens Mountain in 1972. Many eastern Oregon towns began as sheep camps, and the growth of **Heppner**, **Pendleton**, and **Condon** was based on sheep. **Irish**, **Basques**, and **Portuguese** from the Azores all played an important role in developing the industry. Oregon Sheep Growers Assoc., 1270 Chemeketa St. NE, Salem 97301. 503-364-5462. "Sheep Husbandry in Oregon", Oregon's Great Basin Country, 1995 Oregon. See also **Guard dogs**.

Sheep drives. Sheep were moved overland into Oregon from California in 1842 and over the **Oregon Trail** beginning in 1844. As the sheep multiplied, the sheep drives went the other direction. In 1882 three bands totaling more than 20,000 sheep were driven from eastern Oregon to Laramie, Wyoming. After the transcontinental railroad reached Oregon in 1883, the sheep were sent by rail. East of the Cascades.

Sheepshooters War. See **Range wars**.

Shellburg Falls. An 80-foot plume waterfall, one of several in an area south of **Silver Falls State Park**. The falls, located on **Santiam State Forest** land, are three miles north of **Highway 22** at Mehama. Vandalism, garbage, and damage from off-road vehicles resulted in a two-year road closure, beginning in late 1997, but the falls can be reached by a one-mile hike. Oregonian 10/7/97:E2; Waterfall Lover's Guide.

Shellfish. Clams, crabs, abalone, mussels, and **piddocks** (rock oysters) may be gathered along the Oregon coast following the regulations listed in Oregon Sport Fishing Regulations. **Oysters,** however, are raised by private growers and may not be taken without the grower's permission. Shellfish are gathered commercially in **Coos, Netarts, Nehalem, Tillamook, Umpqua,** and **Yaquina** bays. See also **Seafood; Shrimp.**

Shellfish poisoning. Toxins produced by single-celled algae may cause poisoning in humans who eat shellfish. One kind, paralytic shellfish poisoning, is caused by saxitoxins produced by *Alexandrium (Gonyaulax) cantenella,* that have been accumulated in filter-feeding shellfish (clams, muscles, scallops, oysters). Symptoms begin with tingling lips, face and/or fingers. About 10% of the cases are fatal, with death resulting from respiratory paralysis within 12 hours. Treatment includes vomiting and respiratory care. Another illness, amnesic shellfish poisoning, is caused by domoic acid, a toxin produced by a diatom, *Nitzchia pseudoseriata (Pseudonitzchia australis).* Symptoms range from vomiting to permanent short-term memory loss, respiratory failure, and death. There is no known treatment. Outbreaks have occurred in the fall. The Oregon Health Division monitors coastal shellfish, and closes areas to shellfish harvest when evidence of toxins appear. The toxins can be avoided by following instructions about harvesting closures announced by the Oregon Department of **Agriculture** on its shellfish information line at 503-986-4728. See also **Red tides.**

Shells. See **Seashells.**

Shelton-McMurphey House. An imposing 1880 Queen Anne Style house that overlooks downtown **Eugene** from the slopes of **Skinner Butte.** At Christmas the decorated house is opened for tours. 303 Willamette Street. Style & Vernacular.

Sherars Bridge (SHERZ). A bridge over the **Deschutes River** nine miles downstream from **Maupin.** It is located below Sherars Falls, an important Indian fishing spot where, in 1826, explorer Peter Skene Ogden lost five horses when he tried to cross the river on an Indian bridge. John Todd built a toll bridge in 1860 that served stagecoach traffic and travelers on the **Oregon Trail.** Joseph Sherar bought the bridge in 1871, spent $75,000 improving the roads leading to it, and built a 33-room hotel and other businesses. Now no buildings remain and the only facility is a takeout spot for river rafts just above the falls. East of the Cascades; Oregon Ghost Towns; Sweetness to the Soul (novel).

Sheridan. A town in **Yamhill County** 15 miles southwest of **McMinnville** that lies near the west edge of the **Willamette Valley.** The town and the post office were established in 1866 and named for General Philip Henry Sheridan who had by then distinguished himself in the **Civil War.** Sheridan had been stationed at nearby **Grand Ronde Agency** in 1856 as a lieutenant, and then at **Fort Hoskins** in 1857. The city was incorporated in 1880. A fire on July 18, 1913, razed the entire business district and many homes. The frame buildings were replaced with larger brick structures. The **Sheridan Federal Correctional Institution**, built in 1989, is a major employer. Population 1980 2,249; 1995 4,615. Elevation 189'. 120 SW Mill St., 97378. 503-843-2347. Chamber of Commerce 503-843-2322. Old Yamhill.

Sheridan Federal Correctional Institution. The only federal prison in Oregon. It was built in **Sheridan** in 1989 to house 1,126 inmates though it had 1,757 prisoners in June of 1994. Riots in September 1993 resulted in $208,000 damage; causes were not released. Oregonian 6/20/96:A10.

Sherman County. A northern-tier county along the **Columbia River**. Incorporated cities are **Moro** (county seat), **Grass Valley**, **Rufus**, and **Wasco**. The county is bounded by Washington State (reached by a bridge on **Highway 97** at **Biggs**), and by **Gilliam** and **Wasco** counties. The borders are also marked by the deep canyons of the **Deschutes River** on the west and the **John Day River** on the east, the Columbia River on the north, and Buck Hollow Creek along much of the south. The rolling land rises from 160' along the Columbia to 3,000' in the south. The economy is based on wheat, barley, and cattle. Taxable assessed value in 1995 was $151,000,000, or $79,000 per capita. The county, first settled by whites in the 1870s, was created in 1889 from **Wasco County** and named for Civil War leader General William Tecumseh Sherman (1820-1891). Population 1980 2,172; 1995 1,900. Area 831 square miles. Density 2/sq.mi. Annual precipitation 11"; average temperature January 30°F, July 68°F. Courthouse, 500 Court St., PO Box 365, Moro 97039. 541-565-3606. They Paved the Way; Oregon Blue Book.

Sherwood. A **Willamette Valley** city in **Washington County** 15 miles southwest of downtown **Portland**. The town was laid out in 1889 and named Smockville by founder James Smock. Two years later the residents voted to change the name to Sherwood because the heavy forests put them in mind of England's Sherwood Forest, and the city was incorporated in 1893. The Robin Hood Festival, begun in 1955, features an archery tournament competition with archers in Nottingham, England, which Sherwood archers have won 21 times in 40 years. The Onion Festival is held in October. The Tualatin River Wildlife Refuge is now being created next to the city. Population 1980 2,386; 1995 5,320. Elevation 193'. 20 NW Park St., 97140. 503-625-5522. Oregon Geographic Names; Oregonian 3/16/97:C9.

Shevlin. A one-time post office and company town owned by the Shevlin-Hixon Company. It was moved from place to place in **Deschutes** and **Klamath Counties** as needed for logging operations. The post office was in service from 1931 to 1951. Oregon Geographic Names.

Ship building. In 1826 the **Hudson's Bay Company** built a 60-ton **schooner** and a 30-ton sloop at **Fort Vancouver**, but then gave up ship building because of the lack of skilled labor, iron, and seasoned timber. The first ship built in what is now Oregon was the *Star of Oregon*, a **schooner** launched in 1842. In 1848 settlers near **Astoria** built a schooner, loaded it with produce, and sailed it to California where both schooner and cargo were sold. Settlers at **Tillamook** built the *Morning Star of Tillamook* in 1854. In 1874 the 186' clipper, *Western Shore*, was built in **Coos Bay**. **Steamboats** were built on the **Willamette** and **Columbia** rivers, beginning in 1850, and later on a number of coastal bays. During **World**

War I wooden ships, including a number of schooners for carrying lumber and other bulk freight, were built in **Astoria, Columbia City, Portland**, and **Tillamook**, and steel ships were built in Portland. Ship building then faded again until **World War II** when 150,000 workers, a third of them women, flooded into the Portland/ Vancouver area to work in Kaiser's shipyards where, working three shifts a day, they built 750 ships, including 322 **Liberty ships** and 99 Victory ships. Blow for the Landing; Marine History. See also **Cow scow**; **Vanport**.

Ship spills. Spills from container ships have led to interesting **beach combing** on Oregon beaches. Mixed consumer goods in 49 containers washed off the *Hyundai Seattle* on December 9, 1994 near the International Date Line. Some of the goods started coming ashore on Oregon beaches in early 1996, and are predicted to swirl around to the Philippines by about 1999. Oregonian 3/20/96:D1. See also **Nike shoe spill**.

Ships, large. The huge 791' *Crystal Harmony* docked at **Portland**'s harbor wall in May 1996, but largest ship to dock in Portland was the *Ever Ultra*, a 931' long container ship brought in on June 28, 1996. It was loaded carefully - and successfully - though there was concern that its loaded depth might exceed the river's 40' channel depth. The ship can carry 3,300 twenty-foot long containers. Such super ships normally require a 43'-deep channel, a possibility being studied for the **Columbia River**. Oregonian 6/27/96:A1.

Shipwrecks. Thousands of boats, including **Japanese junks**, Spanish ships, fur trading vessels, **schooners**, fishing boats, passenger liners, oil tankers, and others, have wrecked along the Oregon coast. Weather, malfunctions, and shifting sandbars caused wrecks, as did occasional incompetence, as with the *Glenesslin* when the drunk captain and crew sailed her full speed into the foot of **Neahkahnie Mountain** on the sunny afternoon of October 1, 1913. The causes of some shipwrecks, such as the *Blanco* in 1864, *Uncle Sam* in 1876, and the *Fearless* in 1889, remain unknown because the ships drifted ashore with no crews on them. At the mouth of the **Columbia River**, known as the Graveyard of the Pacific, more than 200 ships, 2,000 small craft, and 1,500 lives have been lost. Remnants of the *Sujamico*, a 325-foot steamer that ran aground (without loss of life) in 1929, resurfaced in the sand north of **Coos Bay** in 1997. Guide to Shipwreck Sites along the Oregon Coast; Oregon Shipwrecks; Oregonian 3/26/97:D6; Pacific Graveyard; Shipwrecks of the Oregon Coast. See also *Alaskan*; *Bawnmore*; **Boiler Bay**; *Brother Jonathan*; **Camp Castaway**; *Czarina*; *Erria*; **Disasters**; **Fishing fleet**; *General Warren*; *J. A. Chanslor, Mimi*; *Peter Iredale*; *San Francisco Xavier*; *Santa Clara*; *Sea Otter*; *William and Ann*.

Shipyards. See **Liberty ships**; **Ship building**; **Swan Island**.

Shoes. See **Nike shoe spill**.

Shore Acres State Park. A 743-acre day-use **state park** located on the former Louis **Simpson estate** 13 miles southwest of **Coos Bay**. The Simpson buildings are gone, but 7 acres of formal gardens have been restored. The gardens are now a major year-round attraction and are lighted with 120,000 lights in December. The park also has a glass-enclosed observation shelter with a 180-degree view of the coastal bluffs where winter storms generate spectacular wave action. 541-888-3778.

Shortline railroads. Feeder rail lines, many originally part of the **Southern Pacific** system, now owned by about 20 companies of which **Central Oregon and Pacific** and **Willamette and Pacific** are the largest. Various shortline companies serve the **Willamette Valley**. Others cross the Coast Range from **Hillsboro** to **Tillamook**, from **Corvallis** to **Newport**, and from **Eugene** to Mapleton and **Coos Bay**, another connects from Eugene south through **Medford** to California, and in northeast Oregon a shortline travels between **La Grande** and **Enterprise**. Backwoods Railroads; Railroads down the Valleys.

Shoshone. A **steamboat** owned by the **Oregon Steam Navigation Company** that had been in unprofitable service on the upper **Snake River**. The company decided to bring it down to Lewiston, Idaho, and in 1870 it completed the trip, having run the full length of **Hells Canyon**, including over Copper Ledge Falls. Hells Canyon. See also *Norma*.

Shoshone. The name given by Oregon's first geologist, Thomas Condon, to the area now known as the **Blue Mountains**. He hypothesized that it and the southwest corner of the state were at one time islands; the southwest island he called Siskiyou. East of the Cascades.

Shrews. The smallest mammals, nocturnal insectivores related to **moles** rather than to the vegetarian **mice**. Ten species are found in Oregon, two of them in **sagebrush** regions and the others in damp areas with dense vegetation. The water shrew, *Sorex palustris*, is an adept swimmer. Shrews range from 3.5 to 6 inches long, with a third of the length in a nearly furless tail. They have pointed noses, tiny eyes, and thick brown or gray coats. Active and voracious feeders, they consume twice their weight each 24 hours, and will kill mice larger than they. Atlas of Oregon Wildlife; Mammals and Life Zones of Oregon; Mammals of the Northwest.

Shrimp. Oregon's commercial ocean fishermen annually harvest an average of 27 million pounds of tiny pink shrimp, *Pandalus jordani*, about a third of the total Pacific coast catch. Brine shrimp are harvested commercially from **Lake Abert**. Pacific States. See also **Fishing boats**.

Shrubs, wild. See **Blackberry**; **Gorse**; **Huckleberry**; **Poison oak**; **Rhododendron**; **Sagebrush**.

Siding. A composite siding, made of compressed wood chips and resin by **Portland**-based Louisiana-Pacific Corporation, was introduced in 1985 and used on hundreds of thousands of homes nationwide before some of it was found to be defective. An April 1996 class-action settlement is projected to cost L-P $425 million or more by the time all claims are paid, even though the average award is significantly less than the cost of replacing the siding. Oregonian 11/10/97:E6.

Silcox Hut. A Cascadian-style stone and timber bunkhouse located at the 7,000' level on **Mount Hood** near the upper end of the Magic Mile ski lift. The building, constructed in 1939, was later abandoned for some years before it was renovated and reopened for meals and lodging in 1992. It was named for Ferdinand A. Silcox, chief of the U.S. Forest Service at the time it was built. **Timberline Lodge** handles reservations. Oregon Geographic Names.

Siletz (sih LETS). A central **Coast Range** town 12 miles northeast of **Newport** in **Lincoln County**. The area became home to Indians from various Western

Oregon tribes when the Siletz Reservation was established in the 1850s. The city, incorporated in 1946, sponsors the annual **Nesika Illahee Pow-Wow**. The word "Siletz" is a **Rogue River Indian** name for black bear. Population 1980 1,001; 1995 1,110. Elevation 130'. PO Box 318, 97380. 541-444-2521. Oregon Geographic Names.

Siletz River. A 72-mile long river that twists through the **Coast Range** to broad, shallow Siletz Bay at the south end of **Lincoln City**. It drains an area of 308 square miles. The bay is part of a **National Wildlife Refuge**, and the river is one of five rivers designated for **coho salmon** habitat restoration. The river was named for the local Indians, the southernmost Salishan tribe on the coast, though it is said to come from the Rogue River Indian word, Silis, meaning black bear. Oregon Geographic Names.

Siletz Terrane. A piece of oceanic crust that collided with the North American continent about 50 million years ago. Too buoyant to be overridden by the continental crust, it joined with it to form the foundation for the **Coast Range** and **Willamette Valley**. The terrane is 15 to 20 miles thick under the Coast Range, but thins to 3 miles thick under Vancouver Island. Oregonian 10/14/94:B6.

Siletz Tribes and Reservation, Confederated Tribes of. A confederation of Indians from 24 bands and tribes from northern California, western Oregon, and southern Washington, and speaking a variety of languages. The first of the Indians were forcibly marched to the 100-mile-long **Coast Reservation** in 1856. A series of government actions whittled away at the reservation until it was essentially gone by 1890, and in the 1950s the tribes, themselves, were officially terminated by the government. Congress once again recognized the Siletz in 1977, and a few years later some lands were returned. The tribes now have over 2,200 enrolled members and a **reservation** of 3,955 acres in several parcels near **Siletz.** The tribes operate several enterprises, including a **casino**, Chinook Winds Gaming Center, in **Lincoln City**. The Nesika Illahee **Powwow** is held annually on the second weekend in August in Siletz. PO Box 549, Siletz 97380. 541-444-2532. First Oregonians; Native Peoples; Oregonian 10/22/95:A19.

Silicon. The most abundant element in the earth's crust after oxygen. It is used especially in alloys and electronics. A silicon metal plant in **Springfield** is capable of producing 9,000 metric tons annually. Mineral Industry of Oregon.

Silicon Forest. A name in use since at least 1981 to describe the cluster of **high-tech industries** in Oregon, especially the **semi-conductor industry** in the southwest **Metro** area. Oregonian 12/3/95:G1, 6/23/96:C1.

Silk. From 1893 to 1897 the Southern Oregon Silk Station operated at **Coquille** to investigate the practicability of establishing silk culture in the area. The station developed a new breed of silk worm, published A Handbook in Silk Culture, and distributed over 2,000 mulberry trees. Output at the end of the four years was 76 pounds of raw silk. Century of Coos and Curry.

Siltcoos Lake. The largest lake on the Oregon coast, Siltcoos Lake is a shallow natural lake 7 miles south of **Florence**. Shaped like a lumpy starfish, the lake is over three miles from tip to tip, covers 3,164 acres, and has a maximum depth of 22 feet, at which point the bottom is 14 feet below sea level. Salt water intrusions up the Siltcoos River led, in 1963, to the construction of a small dam on the river by the International Paper Company in order to provide a year-round supply of fresh water to their pulp mill in **Gardiner**. The dam also raised the lake level slightly. The lake is popular for all kinds of fishing, especially for bass. Six resorts provide services, and there is a campground near the outlet. The origin of the Indian name is uncertain. Atlas of Oregon Lakes.

Silva Concert Hall. See **Hult Center for the Performing Arts**.

Silver. A metal, often found with **gold**, that is currently being mined in **Douglas County**. Over a quarter of a million ounces of silver was produced at Copperfield and Homestead in **Baker County** between 1910 and the 1930's. See also **Cornucopia Mine**; **Mining**.

Silver Falls State Park. An 8,000-acre park 26 miles east of **Salem** that includes 10 major waterfalls, five of them over 100 feet high. Highest is South Falls which drops 177 feet over a basalt ledge. A short trail leads to an overlook; a longer trail goes behind the waterfall. All of the waterfalls are accessible by a seven-mile trail, and there are also bicycle, jogging, and equestrian trails. The park includes a conference center, nature lodge, group facilities, and campsites. 503-873-8681. Waterfall Lover's Guide.

Silver Fire Roundup. A large demonstration in **Grants Pass** in the summer of 1988 by timber industry workers and supporters protesting the lack of salvage logging after the Silver Complex Fire. The fire had burned 100,000 acres in a roadless area north of the **Kalmiopsis Wilderness Area**. The crowds wore yellow ribbons to symbolize support for timber, and 1,500 log trucks convoyed to the county fairgrounds. Even before the fire, debate had been strident between those wishing to preserve **old growth forests** and the roadless character of the North Kalmiopsis and those wanting to utilize the timber resource. In Timber Country.

Silver Lake. An unincorporated ranching community of weathered buildings in the high desert of **Lake County**. It is 96 miles northwest of **Lakeview** on Highway 31. It was named for the lake of variable size six miles to the east. The post office was established in 1875. In 1894 about 50 people lived in the town when it suffered one of Oregon's major **disasters**, the **Silver Lake fire**. High Desert.

Silver Lake fire. A fire in the tiny community of **Silver Lake** on December 24, 1894. Two hundred people from the area had crowded into the second floor of a frame building for a Christmas eve program. Someone knocked over a kerosene lamp, which started a fire, panic ensued, and 43 people died. Their ashes were buried in one coffin. Every person in the area lost relatives in the fire. A rider on horseback summoned Dr. Daly from **Lakeview**, 100 miles away, to care for the burned and injured. East of the Cascades. See also **Disasters**; **Horseback rides**.

Silver thaw. See **Freezing rain**.

Silverton. A foothill town on the edge of the **Willamette Valley** in **Marion County** 17 miles east of **Salem**. The town was established in 1854 and named for Silver Creek by Polly Crandall Coon who owned the town site. The post office was established in 1855, and the city was incorporated in 1885. Attractions include the Silverton Historic Museum and **Silver Falls State Park** 12 miles southeast of town. Population 1980 5,168; 1995 6,405. Elevation 249'. 306 S Water St., 97381. 503-873-5321. Oregon Geographic Names.

Silverton Bobbie. Bobbie, a collie dog owned by Frank and Elizabeth Brazier of **Silverton**, was lost by them in Wolcott, Indiana on August 15, 1923, while they were on a vacation trip. Six months later, on February 15, 1924, the thin and exhausted dog appeared back home in Silverton. The fame of the dog, dubbed Silverton Bobbie, spread, and Bobbie played the starring role in a movie, "Bobbie the Wonder Dog"; Tracking down Oregon.

Silvies River. An eastern Oregon river that rises on the south slopes of the **Aldrich** and **Strawberry Ranges** and flows south past **Seneca** and **Burns** into **Malheur Lake**, draining 1,310 square miles. It was named for Antoine Sylvaille, a fur trapper who in 1826 reported it as a stream rich in beaver. Oregon Geographic Names.

Simple living. See **Institute for Sustainable Culture**; **Northwest Earth Institute**.

Simpson estate. A famed one-time estate southwest of **Coos Bay** built by lumberman Louis Jerome Simpson. His mansion, built near the turn of the century, contained a 26 by 52 foot heated indoor swimming pool, a ballroom that ran the length of the mansion's third floor, a hallway paneled in wood from the **Oregon-myrtle**, and Tiffany glass chandeliers. There were also extensive formal gardens. The mansion burned to the ground on July 4th, 1921, and Simpson lost his fortunes during the Depression in the 1930s. The state now owns the site and has restored the gardens which are featured at **Shore Acres State Park**. There has been some talk of rebuilding the mansion. Oregonian 9/29/97:E2.

Simpson Gardens. See **Shore Acres State Park**.

Siskiyou Mountains. Ancient, rugged, and geologically complex mountains of southwestern Oregon and northern California that are part of the **Klamath Mountains**. The highest peak in the Oregon Siskiyous is **Mount Ashland** at 7,533'. The Siskiyous are drained by the **Rogue River** and several coastal rivers and streams. The **Rogue River National Forest** and **Siskiyou National Forest**, including the **Kalmiopsis Wilderness Area**, cover much of the area in Oregon. **Gold** and **mercury** have been mined in some areas. The Siskiyous are noted for unusual plants. The name derives from a Cree Indian word for bob-tailed horse, bestowed by Canadian packers in 1828 when a noted bob-tailed race horse was among the pack horses lost in a snow storm in the area. Oregon Geographic Names. See also **Eight Dollar Mountain**; **Nature Man**; **Serpentinite**.

Siskiyou National Forest. A 1,163,986-acre national forest in the extreme southwest corner of Oregon. It includes all or part of five wilderness areas, **Kalmiopsis**, Grassy Knob, Wild Rogue, Siskiyou, and Red Buttes, as well as the Illinois and Rogue Wild and Scenic Rivers. The forest is noted for its unusual plant communities, and includes the country's largest **Oregon-myrtle** tree. 200 NE Greenfield Road, P.O.Box 440, Grants Pass 97526. 541-471-6500.

Siskiyou Summit. A pass, elevation 4,310' on **Interstate 5**, the highest point on I-5 between Canada and Mexico. There, eleven miles south of **Ashland**, the highway crosses the **Siskiyou Mountains** a mile north of the California border. The pass also marks the area where the ancient Siskiyous on the west meet the more recent volcanic **Cascade Range** on the east. The pass was used by the Shasta Indians who lived on both sides of it. The first whites known to have crossed it were Peter Skene Ogden's party of **Hudson's Bay Company** fur trappers in February 1827. A railroad line crosses through Tunnel 13, site of the sensational **DeAutremont brothers** train robbery in 1923. The highway is sometimes closed by winter snows; signs are posted at Ashland if chains are required. First Over the Siskiyous. See also **Pilot Rock**; **Siskiyou Trail**.

Siskiyou Toll Road. The first **wagon road** over **Siskiyou Summit**. It was authorized by the Oregon legislature and built in 1857-58. Private parties, including Lindsay Applegate from 1861 to 1868, operated the road until the state bought it from the Dollarhide family in 1913 and built **Pacific Highway (Highway 99)** along the route. Dictionary of Oregon History; This Day in Oregon. See also **Siskiyou Trail**.

Siskiyou Trail. A route between the **Willamette Valley** and **California** (Mexican until 1846), that was explored and established in the late 1820s by fur trappers from the **Hudson's Bay Company**. In addition to its use by the **Umpqua Brigade** of trappers, in the 1830s herds of Mexican horses, sheep, and cattle were driven up the route to the **Oregon Country** and parties of emigrants used it to move on to California in the 1840s. In 1841 a detachment from the **Wilkes Expedition** traveled south from **Fort Vancouver** to **Yerba Buena** over the trail. In 1846 portions of it were included in the **Applegate Trail** and used for the first time by wagons. The California **gold rush** drew hordes of gold seekers along the trail in 1848-49. In 1860 the first **stage line** followed much of the route, and in 1887 the **Southern Pacific** railroad was completed along it. Later **Highway 99** and **Interstate 5** followed close to the same route. Siskiyou Trail.

Sister Cities. A people-to-people program that encourages the exchange of information and visitors between American and foreign cities. The programs are usually privately financed. In 1996 Oregon towns with sister cities were **Albany**, **Ashland**, **Astoria**, **Beaverton** (4), **Canby**, **Coos Bay**, **Corvallis**, **Eugene** (4), **Grants Pass**, **Gresham** (3), **Hood River**, **Klamath Falls**, **Lake Oswego**, **Medford**, **Newport**, **Ontario**, **Oregon City**, **Pendleton**, **Portland** (9), **Redmond**, **Roseburg**, **Salem** (4), and **Winston**. Information is available from the International Division of Oregon's Economic Development Department, One World Trade Center, 121 SW Salmon Suite 300, Portland 97204. 800-448-7512.

Sister States. Oregon has three Sister State arrangements. The first, with Fujian Province in the People's Republic of China, was inaugurated in 1984. Fujian is on the Formosa Strait opposite Taiwan; it's capital is Fuzhou. The second, with Taiwan, is one of 32 sister-state relationships that Taiwan has established with U.S. states. Oregon's third and most active sister-state relationship is with Toyama Prefecture in Japan, across Honshu Island from Tokyo. The Prefecture government allocates $150,000 a year to support exchanges but all Oregon participation is privately organized and financed. The Sister State program is coordinated by the International Division of the Oregon Economic Development Department, One World Trade Center, 121 SW Salmon Suite 300, Portland 97204. 800-448-7512.

Sisters. An 1880s western theme town in central Oregon's **Deschutes County**, 22 miles northwest of **Bend** on **Highway 20**. It is named for the nearby **Three Sisters** peaks. The town grew up near **Camp Polk**, and thrived between 1880 and 1908 when large bands of sheep were driven to and from summer pasture in the

Cascade Range. The post office was established in 1888, the townsite plat was filed in 1901, and the city was incorporated in 1946. The town is now supported by tourism. Attractions include Sisters **Rodeo** on the 2nd weekend in June, an outdoor Quilt Show on the 2nd Saturday in July, High Mountain Dixieland Jazz Festival in September, the Museum of the Fantastic, and **llama** farms. Nearby mountains, lakes, and rivers offer year-round recreation and scenery. Population 1980 696; 1995 775. Elevation 3,182'. 150 N Fir, PO Box 39, 97759. 541-549-6022. Chamber of Commerce 541-549-0251. Oregon Geographic Names.

Sitka Center for Art and Ecology. A center near **Cascade Head** designed to foster creativity that connects to nature. It sponsors workshops and residencies. Cascade Head Ranch, Otis 97368. 541-994-5485. Oregonian 9/12/97:D2. See also **Environmental organizations**.

Sitka spruce. A tall conifer **tree**, *Picea sitchensis,* with stiff, sharp needles, that grows in a narrow belt along the coast, one of three **spruce** species native to Oregon. Its wood has the highest strength-to-weight ratio of any known wood, making it stronger than steel, pound-for-pound. The wood was in demand for airplane wing and fuselage frames during both World Wars; the largest spruce mill in the world was built in **Toledo** during **World War I**. The wood is used today for pulp, lumber specialties, and for sounding boards in musical instruments. The nation's co-champion for largest Sitka spruce is in Klootchy Creek Park on **Highway 26** one mile east of **Highway 101**; it is 206 feet tall, 673 inches in circumference (nearly 18 feet in diameter), and is thought to be 700 years old. Trees to Know. See also **Octopus tree; Spruce Production Division**.

Siuslaw (sigh YOU slaw) **National Forest**. An 835,875-acre national forest along the central Oregon **Coast Range**. It includes three wilderness areas, Drift Creek, Cummins Creek, and Rock Creek. It also administers the **Cascade Head** Scenic Research Area, **Cape Perpetua** Visitor Center, and the **Oregon Dunes National Recreation Area**. 4077 Research Way, P.O. Box 1148, Corvallis 97339. 541-750-7000.

Siuslaw River. A 109-mile long river that drains 773 square miles of the central **Coast Range** west to the ocean where **jetties** help maintain a channel for the **Florence** fishing fleet. Only a low pass and short distance separates its headwaters from the **Willamette Valley** at **Cottage Grove**. The North Fork and Lake Creek are major tributaries. The name is derived from that of a local tribe of Yakonan Indians. Oregon Geographic Names.

Siuslaw Tribe. See **Coos, Lower Umpqua, and Siuslaw Indians**.

Siwash. A **Chinook jargon** term for Indian that was in general use in the late 1800s. It may have come from the French word "sauvage."

Size of Oregon. The state of Oregon is close to rectangular in shape, about 275 miles north/south and 350 miles east/west. It covers 97,060 square miles of land area (62,120,000 acres, larger than the United Kingdom) plus 889 square miles of inland water area for a total area of 97,949 square miles. It is the 10th largest state, larger than Utah and slightly smaller than Wyoming. The coastline is variously reported to be 296 to 362 miles long. The most northerly point may be **Point Adams**, 46°12'44"N, at the south side of the mouth of the **Columbia River**, though sand bars and islands in the river are more northerly, and the state reaches its southernmost extents along the 42nd parallel, the Oregon/California border. **Cape Blanco** at 124°33'46"W is the most westerly point of mainland Oregon though some rock islands lie farther west, while the easternmost point is along the **Snake River** in the China Bar area, at 116°27'43"W. Oregon Blue Book. See also **Boundaries**; **Geographic center**; **Latitude and longitude**.

Skateboarding. Burnside Skatepark under the east end of **Portland's** Burnside Bridge is a favorite spot for skateboarding. In 1998 skate parks were being constructed in several other Oregon communities, especially in southern Oregon.

Skating. An old-fashioned roller rink with a Wurlitzer Pipe Organ is located at **Oaks Amusement Park** in **Portland**. It is the oldest continuously- used skating rink in America and has the largest wood skating floor on the West Coast. Roller skates and inline skates are available. In **Portland** skaters enjoy **Governor Tom McCall Waterfront Park**, and ICU Skate Company sponsors inline skating weekly at the **Memorial Coliseum** and during the summer at the **Portland International Raceway**. Portland Guidebook. See also **Ice skating**.

Ski areas, downhill. Oregon has ten downhill ski areas with chair lifts: **Anthony Lakes** near La Grande, **Hoodoo** on Santiam Pass, **Mount Bachelor** (the largest) near Bend, **Mount Hood Meadows** (second largest), **Ski Ashland** in southern Oregon, **Skibowl/Multorpor** on Mount Hood, **Summit** on Mount Hood, **Timberline** on Mount Hood, and **Willamette Pass** southeast of Eugene. Three other areas offer T-bar lifts: **Cooper Spur** south of Hood River, **Ferguson Ridge** in the Wallowa Mountains, and **Warner Canyon** near Lakeview. Timberline offers year-round skiing, and Mount Bachelor usually opens in November. The rest open as soon as snow conditions permit. Ski report update: 503-222-9128. Avalanche update: 503-326-2400. Oregonian 11/23/95:D1. See also **Mount Bailey**; **Pelican Butte**; **Sno-Park permits**; **Wallowa Lake Tramway**.

Ski areas, Nordic. Ski areas with groomed Nordic (cross-country) ski tracks include **Anthony Lakes** near La Grande, **Cooper Spur** south of Hood River, **Hoodoo** on Santiam Pass, **Mount Bachelor** near Bend, **Mount Hood Meadows**, **Summit** on Mount Hood, and **Willamette Pass**. Oregonian 11/23/95:D1. See also **Sno-Park permits**.

Ski Ashland Ski Area. A southern Oregon ski area on **Mount Ashland** 15 miles south of **Ashland**. It has four chair lifts with a 1,150-foot vertical drop from the top elevation of 7,530 feet. The City of **Ashland** bought the area in 1992. PO Box 220, Ashland 97520. 541-482-2897; snow conditions 541-482-2754. Oregonian 11/16/97:T7.

Skibowl/Multorpor. A ski area 53 miles east of **Portland** on **Highway 26**. The area has a Snow Tube Park plus four chair lifts with a top elevation of 5,026 feet and a vertical drop of 1,500 feet. "Multorpor" was coined from Multnomah, Oregon, and Portland. 87000 E. Highway 26, Government Camp 97028. 503-272-3206; snow conditions 503-222-2695. Oregonian 11/16/97:T7.

Skid roads. Roads on which logs are dragged out of the forest. The first had logs (skids) laid crosswise about ten feet apart. The skids were greased, and sometimes would smoke or burn as the teams of oxen hauled the logs across them. Later skid roads had the skids laid parallel to form a trough along which logs were hauled by cable from a **donkey engine**. Today's skid roads are usually not surfaced, and the logs are hauled out over them with a tractor skidder. <u>Tillamook</u>. "Careless reporters with dirt in their ears have written skidrow or skid row so often that this miserable, phony term is accepted by the ignorant. There's no such damn thing as skidrow and there never was..." <u>Woods Words</u>.

Skidmore Fountain. A **Portland** fountain erected in 1888 in the then busy heart of the city at SW 1st and Ankeny. Its inscription reads "**Good citizens are the riches of a city.**" As the center of the city moved, the area declined, but since its designation as a Historic District in 1975 it is reviving, with the **Saturday Market** and events in **Governor Tom McCall Waterfront Park** bringing many to the area near the west end of Burnside Bridge. Stephen Skidmore was a pioneer druggist who left $5,000 to build a fountain for "thirsty horses, men and dogs". The balance of its $18,000 cost was donated. The city rejected Henry Weinhard's offer to pump beer through the fountain at its unveiling. <u>Portland, An Informal History</u>; <u>Portland's Public Art</u>.

Skinner Butte. An isolated 681-foot hill located in a **Eugene** city park between the downtown business area and the **Willamette River**. A road spirals to the top of the butte which was for years topped by a controversial **cross**. Skinner Butte and the city of Eugene are both named for Eugene Skinner who settled at its base in 1846 and who donated the land to the city. See also **Shelton-McMurphey House**.

Skunk cabbage. A large-leaved perennial, *Lysichitum americanum*, whose early yellow spathes light up western Oregon's bogs. The plant, used by **Indians**, is edible if properly cooked; otherwise its calcium oxalate crystals are intensely irritating. However, animals browse the plants, apparently without harm. <u>Great Northwest Nature Factbook</u>.

Skunks. Cat-sized black and white members of the **weasel** family. Two species are found in Oregon, both nocturnal. The striped skunk, *Mephitis mephitis*, occurs near water throughout much of the state except in areas of heavy timber. It grows to 24 inches long, including its fluffy tail, weighs up to 14 pounds, and is glossy black with a white stripe down its back. It is noted for its ability to spray a well-aimed nauseating liquid 15 feet in any direction, including over its head, from glands at the base of its tail. The smaller spotted skunk, *Spilogale gracilis*, sometimes called civet cat, grows to 16 inches long, is black intricately patterned with white, and has a white plume at the end of its tail. Though it weighs less then two pounds, its self defense is nearly as powerful as that of the striped skunk; **owls** are its main predator. Both species are able diggers, and live primarily on the insects and small rodents they uncover. Skunks may carry rabies, leptospirosis, and **tularemia**. In 1994-95, 321 spotted skunks were trapped with an average value of $5 each, and 547 striped skunks with an average value of $4.40 each. <u>Atlas of Oregon Wildlife</u>; <u>Mammals and Life Zones of Oregon</u>; <u>Mammals of the Northwest</u>.

Sky diving. At least 14 sky divers have been killed in parachuting accidents in Oregon. <u>Oregonian</u> 3/6/98:D1.

Skybridge. The 660-foot-long Veterans Hospital skybridge on **Pill Hill** in **Portland** is the longest air-conditioned pedestrian bridge in the country. <u>Portland's Little Red Book of Stairs</u>.

Skyline Circle. A stone circle 35 feet in circumference, found on the John Cunningham farm six miles south of Salem in 1924. The oblong stones were 18 inches to four feet in length, and had been crudely carved to resemble phalli. The stones were upright when found but nearly completely buried; they were removed. Kalapuyans.

Skyscrapers. See **Tallest buildings**.

Slash burning. The disposal of logging debris, such as tops and branches, by burning. It prepares the ground for planting, but its use has been much restricted by smoke management concerns. See also **Air pollution**; **Fire**; **Visibility**.

Slavery, Indian. Most of the Indians of Oregon kept slaves, primarily Indians from other tribes. Many tribes conducted raids for the express purpose of securing slaves, while other slaves were children of slaves, and some had become slaves through sale or to pay off their owner's - or their own - gambling debts. Slaves were valuable trade items. Customs regulating how slaves were treated, who could own them, whether they could marry, and whether they could ever gain their freedom varied from tribe to tribe. Oregon Oddities; "Property Concepts of 19th Century Oregon Indians."

Slavery, Negro. Although Oregon's early settlers were anti-Negro they were split on the slavery issue. Oregon's **provisional government** voted in 1844 not to allow slavery, and in 1853 Robin Holmes and his family, brought to Oregon as slaves, sued for their freedom and were granted it. After the US Supreme Court decided, in their 1857 Dred Scott decision, that a territorial government could not legislate on slavery, Oregonians, intent upon deciding the question for themselves, quickly voted for statehood. In the 1857 vote adopting the state **constitution**, 74% of Oregon voters rejected slavery, while at the same time 89% approved excluding blacks from the state. Peculiar Paradise, "Slaves and Free Men"; This Side of Oregon. See also **Blacks in Oregon**; **Exclusion laws**; **Knights of the Golden Circle**.

Sled dogs. The largest dog sled racing event in Oregon is held near Chemult in January, sponsored by the community, the **Winema National Forest**, and several sled-dog clubs. 541-365-7001. Races are also held near **Sumpter**, and sled dogs race in the annual **Dune Mushers Mail Run** from **North Bend** to **Florence** in early March.

Sleet. Snow that melts as it is falling and then refreezes as it hits a long stretch of colder air, so has turned to ice before it hits the ground. A **freezing rain** doesn't turn to ice until it hits the ground.

Slides. See **Landslides**.

Slugs. Shell-less land mollusks related to **snails**. They abound in western Oregon where humidity is high and soils are low in the calcium needed for snail shells. The native banana slug, *Ariolimax columbianus*, of the coastal forests may grow to 8 inches in length during its average six-year life span. Nearly a dozen other species now live in Oregon, most of them non-native garden pests. Most are vegetarian, but one species eats earthworms. Field Guide to the Slug.

Small Business. See **Business Information Center**; **Business Retention Service**; **Home businesses**; **Minority, Women and Emerging Small Business**

Office; **Oregon Biotechnology Innovation Center**; **Resource and Technology Development Fund**.

Small Business Development Centers. Centers established at **community colleges** and three regional colleges to assist local businesses and potential entrepreneurs. They are linked by a statewide network created in 1983 by the legislature in cooperation with the U.S. Small Business Administration, which joins with the Oregon **Economic Development** Department to fund the centers. A fourth of the funding comes from **lottery** dollars. The SBDC Advisory Council provides policy guidance to the 20 centers and advises on the grants program. Oregon Small Business Development Centers Network Office, 44 W. Broadway, Suite 501, Eugene, 97401. 541-726-2250.

Small Business Ombudsman for Workers Compensation. See **Worker's Compensation Ombudsman**.

Small Claims Courts. A system of Oregon courts established by the **legislature** to settle claims for amounts under $3,500. The courts were formerly administered by Oregon's **district courts**, but as of 1998, the **circuit courts** have jurisdiction. Claims forms are available in every county courthouse and filing fees are under $100. Some Small Claims Courts require that the parties try mediation first. Hearings are informal, with just the parties to the claim and the judge present; no lawyers are allowed and there are no juries. The decisions are final with no appeals. Nearly 57,000 Oregonians filed small claims in 1993. A "Small Claims Reference Manual" is available for $2 at the **Multnomah County** Civil Courts Department. 503-378-6046.

Smallpox. See **Epidemics**.

SMART. A **Portland**-area program, Start Making A Reader Today (SMART), that recruits volunteers to read with kindergarten, first, and second-grade pupils who need extra help, and which gives books to students. The Oregon Children's Foundation, an organization created in 1991 by then governor Neil Goldschmidt and the law firm of Ater Wynne Hewitt Dodson & Skerritt sponsor the program. The law firm received the first National Civic Literacy Award from the American Bar Association in 1995 for its efforts. Oregonian 8/7/1995:B1.

Smelt. Small fish, about 8 inches long, found in large schools. Both river and ocean smelt are caught in Oregon. The river smelt are **anadromous**, living in the ocean but returning to a freshwater river to spawn and die. The sea smelt spend their entire lives in the ocean, and can spawn more than once. The runs of both are unpredictable as to both time and place. River smelt usually spawn in March along the Sandy River east of **Portland** but a decade or more may go by with none. Ocean smelt spawn on beaches characterized by "smelt sand", a coarse sand found in just a few places, including at Smelt Sands State Park just north of **Yachats**. Smelt are usually caught by either a dip net or, in the ocean, an A-frame net. The limit is 25 pounds; no license is required. The oil of a species known as eulachon or candle fish was used by Indians for lamps, and the dried fish were used as candles. In Search of Western Oregon; Oregon's Migratory Fish; Treasures of the Oregon Country.

Smith massacre. In June 1828 Jedediah Smith led a party of 19 fur trappers and nearly 300 horses up the coast from Mexican California (which had expelled them) north towards the protection of the British **Hudson's Bay Company (HBC)** at **Fort Vancouver**. At the mouth of the Smith River where it flows into the **Umpqua River**, they were attacked by Indians. Four survived, including Smith, and managed to make their way to Fort Vancouver. The HBC later recovered their furs from the Indians. Dictionary of Oregon History.

Smith Rock. A large, colorful assemblage of cliffs and crags located in a sharp bend of the **Crooked River** nine miles northeast of **Redmond**. It and adjacent areas are included in **Smith Rock State Park**. The area with its hundreds of climbing routes is a center for rock climbers. Guidebooks are available locally. The rocks, composed of volcanic debris ejected 10 to 18 million years ago, are part of the **John Day Formation**. John Smith, **Linn County** sheriff 1855-1859, was the white discoverer. Geology of Oregon; Oregon Geographic Names.

Smith Rock State Park. A **state park** nine miles NE of **Redmond** on the **Crooked River** famed as a rock climbing site. The park's seven miles of hiking trails provide access to climbing routes and to a year round, walk-in bivouac camp.

Smog. See **Ozone**.

Smoke. See **Field burning**; **Fire**; **Forest fires**; **Indian burning**; **Slash burning**.

Smoke jumpers. **Fire fighters** who parachute to isolated forest fires throughout the west. The **Deschutes National Forest** established Oregon's only present smoke jumper base, the Redmond Air Center, in 1964. It houses about 50 smoke jumpers. Earlier, a smoke jumper base operated at **Cave Junction** from 1943 to 1981, and another at **La Grande** from 1964 to 1982. Pictorial History.

Smokey the Bear. A black bear introduced by the U.S. **Forest Service** in 1944 as the symbol for its fire prevention efforts. A bear cub rescued from a **forest fire** in 1950 and dubbed Smokey then became the living symbol. The number of man-caused fires dropped by half between 1950 and 1980, testifying to the effectiveness of Smokey the Bear's slogan, "Only you can prevent forest fires." Woodsy Owl was introduced in 1971 with the slogan "Give a hoot - Don't pollute."

Smoking. A 1994 survey found that over 6% of Oregon sixth graders and 18% of eighth graders reported having smoked during the previous month. By 11th grade one fourth of the students smoked, while one in six chewed smokeless tobacco. 21% of Oregon residents call themselves smokers. A third of workers earning less than $10,000 a year smoke, the unemployed smoke more than the employed, and 72% of high school dropouts have smoked at least 100 cigarettes in their lifetime compared to 36% of college graduates. In 1994, 6,181 deaths in Oregon (23% of all deaths) were tobacco related. The Oregon Indoor Clean Air Act provides that no public place may be declared in its entirety a smoking area except for stores selling primarily alcohol and tobacco, any place closed to minors by law, and lounges and taverns. In 1997 **Corvallis** and **Benton County** further banned smoking in all workplaces and enclosed public places. Smoking is banned in all of the state's **correctional facilities**. In 1996 Oregon voters authorized a tobacco tax increase to pay for anti-smoking ads, and in 1997 the state filed a $1 billion lawsuit against seven tobacco companies; the case was expected to go to trial in 1999. Oregon: A Statistical Overview; Oregonian 1/1/3/95:A1, 1/26/96:A13, 1/29/97:E1 4/10/98:A24; Tobacco and Oregonians.

Snails. Land mollusks with shells. Native species are found in Oregon's forests; those in gardens are introduced species, including one that is edible. All Northwest land snails are turbinate (the shell grows at an angle along a spiral screw), and all are dextral, with the bulk of the shell on the soft body's right side. Edible french snails, *Helix aspersa*, also called escargot, are being raised commercially by a grower in **Marcola**. The fresh snails will compete with canned snails imported from France. Field Guide to the Slug; Mail Tribune 12/8/96:2E.

Snake River. A 1,038-mile-long river that rises in Jackson Lake, Wyoming, and flows through southern Idaho before turning north through **Hells Canyon** to join the **Columbia River** at Pasco, Washington. It defines the northern half of the Oregon-Idaho border. The only part of Oregon lying east of the Snake is an area of some 30 square miles south of **Nyssa**. There are 10 dams on the river in Idaho, 3 along the Oregon/Idaho border, and 4 on the Washington stretch. The dams have eliminated the spawning runs of some 40,000 **salmon** on the upper Snake. River trips into Hells Canyon leave from Clarkston, Washington and Lewiston, Idaho. Indians of the area were called the Snake Indians by early fur trappers because of their facility at concealing themselves. Hells Canyon; Oregon Geographic Names. See also **Brownlee Dam**; **Hells Canyon Dam**; **Oxbow Dam**.

Snake River Indians. See **Indian wars**.

Snakes. Legless **reptiles**. Fifteen species of snakes are found in Oregon; only the western **rattlesnake** is poisonous. Three species are constrictors: gopher snake, rubber boa, and king snake. The sharp-tailed snake, *Contia tenuis*, which feeds on slugs, is a protected species. Atlas of Oregon Wildlife; Field Guide to Western Reptiles and Amphibians; Knowing Oregon Reptiles.

S.N.O.B. See **Society of Native Oregon Born**.

Sno-Cat. See **Tucker Sno-Cat**.

Sno-Park permit. A permit to park at designated winter recreation areas between November 15 and April 30. The permits help pay for snowplowing. Both one-day and annual permits are sold at **Driver and Motor Vehicle Services** (DMV) offices, sporting goods stores and ski areas.

Snowfall. In western Oregon, average annual snowfall ranges from less than 1 inch on the south coast and 5" at **Astoria** to 6 to 12" in the **Willamette Valley**. Higher elevations receive much more, with **Mt. Hood** receiving on average 465" (39 feet) at **Timberline Lodge** (6,000' elevation), and **Crater Lake** (6,475' elevation) averaging 540" (45 feet). East of the **Cascade Range** snowfall averages range from 10 to 50" in most places, with up to 200" in the **Blue Mountains**. The winter snowpack in Oregon's mountains serves as a great reservoir, releasing water in the spring and summer when it is needed for agriculture and streamflows.

Snowfall records. **Bonneville Dam** holds the state record for a one-day snowfall of 39", January 9, 1980, and it had a total of 63" in four days. **Hood River** had a monthly total of 84.5" of snow that same month. **Crater Lake** received the state's record season snowfall with a total of 879" (73 feet 3 inches) in 1932-33. **Portland** records include a 24-hour snowfall of 15.5" on January 20-21, 1943, and a season total of 61" during the winter of 1892-93. Other notable snowfalls in Portland were in 1862, December 19-21, 1892 (27.5"), December 9-11, 1919 (17.5"), January 31-Feb. 1, 1937 (16"), January 9-18, 1950 (22"), and December 1969 - January 1970 (24"). In January1969, **Eugene** had 34" on the ground, **Astoria** had 18", and **Roseburg** had 27". A severe blizzard is defined as a snowstorm with winds 45 mph or higher, a temperature of 10°F or lower, and visibility near zero due to falling or blowing snow. Oregonian 2/13/69. See also **Cold spells**.

Snowmobiling. Oregon has 3,550 miles of groomed snowmobile trails and another 3,000 miles of marked but ungroomed trails. **Diamond Lake** is a popular center. The Oregon State Snowmobile Association has 32 member clubs. PO Box 435, La Pine OR 97739. 800-682-7669. Oregonian 3/8/95:E1. See also **Sno-Park permit**.

Snowshoe hare. A medium-sized **hare**, *Lepus americanus*, of conifer forests of western and northeast Oregon. Its name comes from its large hind paws. At higher elevations in the winter the normally brownish hare turns white except for its black ear tips. It is the preferred prey of the **lynx**. Atlas of Oregon Wildlife; Mammals and Life Zones of Oregon; Mammals of the Northwest.

Snowy plover. A six-inch, sand-colored shore bird, *Charadrius alexandrinus*, "the pale little ghost of the sand dunes". Oregon has two distinct populations, one nesting along the coast, and the other on inland alkali lake beds. It was federally listed as threatened in 1993. A major problem has been the encroachment on its beach habitat by introduced European beach grass. The grass not only eliminates the open sand on which it lays its eggs, but also provides cover for predators, such as cats and coyotes. Critical habitat areas have been proposed for 28 sites in the west, including seven in Oregon. Atlas of Oregon Wildlife; Birds of Oregon; Oregon Wildlife 51(4):12 Spring 1995. See also **Endangered animals**.

Soap Box Derby. Young people from Oregon took top awards at the national Soap Box Derby in 1978 (Darren Hart), 1990 (Sami Jones), 1992 (Carolyn Fox), and 1997 (Dolline Vance). All were from **Salem** which has the oldest (1951) soap box course west of the Mississippi, located in **Bush's Pasture Park**. Other tracks are located in **Lincoln City**, on Mount Tabor in **Portland** (unused) and in **Sandy** (also unused). The Akron, Ohio, event, for ages 8-16, began in 1934. Oregonian 9/8/97:C1.

Soapstone. A soft rock used for art carving, also called talc and steatite. High quality soapstone in a variety of colors is mined in **Jackson County**. Mineral Industry in Oregon.

Soccer. The Portland Pride is a professional soccer team that plays in the Continental Indoor Soccer League. It has been playing at the **Memorial Coliseum** since 1993.

Social gambling. Under a 1974 state law, city and county governments may legalize **gambling** in such places as taverns so long as only the players, and not the businesses, profit. Eleven counties and 33 cities have done so. However, social gambling is entirely unregulated, and investigations into social gambling have found that the house has been getting a share of the pot. Oregonian 10/22/95:A18.

Social workers. See **Clinical Social Workers**.

Society for Creative Anachronism. An organization founded in California in 1966 to re-create the Middle Ages. Within the organization, the Pacific Northwest exists as the Kingdom of An Tir. The Society, with a worldwide membership of 30,000, stages mock combats with elaborate rules of dress and conduct. Oregonian 8/17/97:L1.

Society of Native Oregon Born (S.N.O.B.) A society with some 5,000 members formed by Jim Cloutier of **Eugene** in 1979. For a modest membership fee those who were born in Oregon receive a handsome, frameable certificate. "Naturalized" Oregonians, those who have lived in the state for at least 50 years, may also apply, but a SNOB must sponsor the application. S.N.O.B. has on occasion held membership picnics at **Champoeg**. PO Box 5406, Eugene 97405. 541-342-3797. Oregonian 2/1/98:C5.

Sockeye. A species of **salmon**, *Oncorhynchus nerka*, also called red salmon, now found in Oregon only as passing migrants in the **Columbia River**, where runs once totaled 4 million, and as a landlocked form called kokanee in some mountain lakes, including **Wallowa Lake**. Historic runs to Wallowa Lake and **Suttle Lake** have been blocked by dams, and Columbia River runs now are under 50,000 a year. At maturity, ocean-going sockeye weigh from 2 to 12 pounds and are 19-21 inches in length. The Oregon record is 4 pounds. The sockeye is distinguished from other salmon by its tail without spots and its small eye pupil; at spawning the fish become crimson with a green head. They spawn in streams, usually near lakes in which the juvenile fish grow for a year or more before migrating to the ocean. After one to four years in the ocean, each fish returns to its home river to spawn. Columbia River Salmon; Oregonian 7/14/97:E1; Salmon of the Pacific.

Sod House. The site of the first permanent residence in the **Harney Basin**, located near the headquarters of **Malheur National Wildlife Refuge**. The original sod house was built in 1862 by two sets of brothers named Chapman and Stenger. The Sod House Ranch was later part of Peter French's famous P Ranch, and was the site of his murder. Cattle Country of Peter French; Oregon's Great Basin Country. See also **Horseback rides; Ranches**.

Soda ash. A mineral, sodium carbonate, that is used in making glass. Some 2.4 million tons a year are shipped through the **Port of Portland**, making it the port's second largest bulk **export**. The soda ash comes by rail from Green River, Wyoming, and is shipped to several Pacific ports.

Sodaville. A **Willamette Valley** community four miles southeast of **Lebanon** in **Linn County**. The cold mineral spring for which it is named was discovered in 1848 and by 1890 the town had grown into a thriving health spa resort. The spring and an area around it measuring 198'x198' were at one time the smallest **state park**, but the park is now owned by the city. The town was incorporated in 1880 . Population 1980 171; 1995 245. Elevation 125'. 30723 Sodaville Road, 97355. 541-258-8882. "Beyond the Ruts."

Soil. Soils worldwide have been classed into ten orders; six are represented in Oregon. Information about Oregon's soils is available in books of county soil surveys from the **Natural Resources Conservation Service**. The NRCS has also created a land capability classification based on the land's ability to grow crops that divides the state into eight classes. Class I is the best for growing crops with few or no limitations, while Class VIII is unsuitable for any crops. Oregon has 1.9 million acres of prime farmlands (3% of the state), and 10.7 million acres of farmlands classed as important. Atlas of the Pacific Northwest; Manual for Judging

Oregon Soils; Oregon's Soil. See also **Erosion**.

Soil and Water Conservation Districts. There are 45 soil and water conservation districts in Oregon, each with a locally elected board of directors. The districts' main concerns are with the conservation and wise use of the soils, waters, wildlife habitats, and productive agriculture of the state. They are funded with local funds matched by state funds and, under Oregon law, may establish a local tax base or operating levy or issue improvement bonds. Soil and Water Conservation Commission, 635 Capitol St. NE, Salem 97310-0110. 503-986-4705. Oregon Blue Book.

Soil Conservation Service. See **Natural Resources Conservation Service**.

Solar eclipses. A full solar eclipse was visible across north-west Oregon on February 26, 1979, and another was seen across northern Oregon on June 8, 1918. The next solar eclipse visible in the Northwest will be in the year 2068.

Solar energy. In 1994 solar energy supplied the equivalent of 121,000 **megawatt** hours of electricity in Oregon, nearly all of it for residential use. The total represented less than .4 of 1% of residential **energy** consumption. State Energy.

Solid waste. In 1995 Oregonians sent 2.4 million tons (1,500 pounds per person) of garbage to landfills and recycled another 804 pounds per person. Oregon had 47,746 million tons of municipal waste in place in 1990, an amount projected to increase to 55,474 million tons by 2015 (not including wastes imported from other states to Oregon landfills). Garbage is incinerated in **Coos** and **Curry Counties**, and the **Ogden Martin Waste-to-Energy facility** in **Marion County** generates electricity from burning garbage. Laws passed in 1971 called for eliminating open burning dumps, consolidating disposal sites, preparing environmentally sound **landfills**, and promoting **recycling**. Oregon's solid waste disposal priorities are first to reuse, then to reduce, recycle, recover energy, and, as a final resort, to dump in a landfill. Oregon: A Statistical Overview; Oregon Environmental Atlas; Report on Reducing; Solid Waste. See also **Bottle bill**; **Hazardous waste**; **Pollution**; **Sewage treatment**; **Superfund cleanup**.

SOLV. A non-profit organization, Stop Oregon Litter and Vandalism, founded in 1969 by Governor Tom McCall to bring government, businesses, and citizens together to keep Oregon livable. Over 50,000 volunteers help with annual projects, including "Paint the Town Clean" in **Portland**, beach cleanups, and Earth Day cleanups that gather over 3.5 million pounds of waste. During the spring and fall Great Beach Cleanups, begun in 1984, thousands of volunteers help pick up tons of debris (5,500 volunteers and 28,000 tons in spring 1997). A number of agencies, organizations, and corporations coordinate and cosponsor the event, including the Oregon Department of **Fish and Wildlife**, and the Oregon State **Parks and Recreation Department**. 111 SE Washington, PO Box 1235, Hillsboro 97123. 800-322-3326, 503-844-9571. Oregonian 4/18/97:B1, 10/1/97:E9. See also **Environmental organizations**.

Soreng Theatre. See **Hult Center for the Performing Arts**.

South Beach State Park. A **state park** two miles south of **Newport**. The park, near a long beach, has a nature trail as well as a trail to the south **jetty** of Yaquina Bay. The campground has 254 sites and is open all year. Reservations, 800-452-5687. 5580 S. Coast Highway, South Beach 97366. 541-867-4715.

South Falls. See **Silver Falls State Park.**

South Road. See **Applegate Trail.**

South Santiam Highway. See **Highway 20.**

South Sister. A central Oregon volcanic peak which is, at elevation 10,358', the highest of the **Three Sisters.** It has a crater on top with a small lake in it. An extensive **lava** flow on the south and southwest flanks, along with the dome at Rock Mesa, developed 2,300 years ago. Smoke was noted from the summit in 1853. Geology of Oregon.

South Slough National Estuarine Reserve. A 4,400-acre fresh and salt-water reserve established in 1974 to protect the biological resources of **Coos Bay**'s South Slough. The reserve is administered cooperatively by the state and federal governments with the **State Land Board** providing policy guidance. The interpretive center is located 5 miles south of **Charleston** on Seven Devils Road and is open all year; there are also hiking and canoe trails, with some guided canoe trips. The area had been logged over, beginning in the 1870s, **oyster** beds were planted in 1874, and homesteaders settled in 1875; the area was notorious during **Prohibition** for its stills and moonshine. PO Box 5417, Charleston 97420. 541-888-5558. Oregon Coast 13(5):28 Sept./Oct. 1994; Oregonian 9/19/96:E10.

Southern Expedition. See **Umpqua Brigade.**

Southern Oregon Barter Fair. An annual October fair to exchange organic produce and handicrafts, held in the Applegate Valley south of **Medford.** The three-day, alternative-lifestyle festival was not held in 1997, the first miss since it began in 1979.

Southern Oregon University. A four year college and graduate school in **Ashland** that enrolled 4,535 students in fall 1994. One of Oregon's three state-supported regional universities, it offers bachelor programs through 22 departments as well as some master's degrees. **Oregon Health Sciences University** offers a baccalaureate nursing program on campus. The Oregon **University System** has designated SOU as the state system center for the performing arts, and the Schneider Museum of Art focuses attention on visual arts. The beginnings of the college can be traced to the Ashland Academy, founded in 1869 by **Methodists.** The school changed its name several times, and ceased to exist at all between 1890 and 1895 and again between 1909 and 1926. It then reopened as Southern Oregon State Normal School and was later Southern Oregon College of Education and then Southern Oregon State College. 1250 Siskiyou Blvd., Ashland 97520. 541-552-6111. Oregon Blue Book.

Southern Oregon Visitors Association. 800-448-4856.

Southern Pacific (SP). A **railroad** line, now owned by **Union Pacific,** that serves the southwestern U.S. in a crescent from **Portland** through California to New Orleans. Its main line provided Oregon's only rail link south to California. Because the original 3.3% grade over the **Siskiyou Summit** was too steep, the company opened the **Natron cut-off** in 1926. SP's feeder lines have been sold to **shortline railroad** companies. History of the Southern Pacific; Oregonian 7/4/96:C1. See also **Central Oregon & Pacific; Oregon and California Railroad.**

Southwestern Oregon Community College. A public two-year college in **Coos Bay** founded in 1961 to serve **Coos** and western **Douglas** counties with college transfer courses, occupational programs, and adult enrichment courses. In fall 1996 3,215 students enrolled. 1988 Newmark, Coos Bay OR 97420-2912. 541-888-2525. Oregon Blue Book. See also **Community colleges; Small Business Development Centers**.

Soy sauce. In 1995 a plant in **Salem** owned by Yamasa Corporation began manufacture of soy sauce for sale in North America. The plant, which uses a six-month fermentation period, has a capacity of 1.7 million gallons of sauce. Western markets are growing 10% a year; consumption in Japan is 10 liters a person per year. Oregonian 4/21/95:C2, 7/4/95:D1.

Spanish-American War, 1898-1899. A war in which the U.S. supported Cuban rebels against Spain. Oregon supplied 1,630 volunteers who served in one complete regiment of infantry and two batteries of field artillery. The artillery units remained in the U.S., but the infantry served in the Philippines. Sixty-four Oregonians died, two-thirds of them from disease. A monument to them is located in Lownsdale Square in downtown **Portland** on SW 4th between Main and Salmon. See also *Oregon* **(battleship)**.

Spanish coins. A Spanish coin dated 1784 was found in a sluice box in the **Illinois Valley** in 1916. **Gold** miners of the area felt that it and other findings confirmed that Spanish gold-seekers from California had been in the area long before Americans began finding gold there. This Day in Oregon:7/2.

Sparta. A ghost town on the south slopes of the **Wallowa Mountains**. After gold was discovered there in 1862, the town boomed and by the 1870s had 3,000 people. At one time the population included 1,000 **Chinese** who had been brought in to dig a 30-mile ditch from Eagle Creek. It was named for Sparta, Illinois. History of Union County.

Special education. Education for children and youths with disabilities. About 11% of Oregon's public school **students** receive special education, with 97% of them (compared with a national average of 71%) in regular public schools. Others attend the School for the **Blind**, the School for the **Deaf**, or are being served in other programs. Oregon Report Card. See also **Talented and gifted (TAG) students**.

Special forest products. A term used for non-timber products from **forests**. It includes florist greens (moss, ferns, bear grass, vine maple, salal, huckleberry), Christmas evergreen boughs, edibles (watercress, mushrooms, berries); medicinals (cascara bark, yew bark, prince's pine root, devil's club root, St. John's wort), and cones for seeds. Total market value is not known, though it is thought to be at least $100 million annually. The industry has recently burgeoned, leading to concerns about theft, sustainability, and Indian treaty rights.

Special service districts. Any of 28 types of local districts authorized by state law, including those for irrigation, fire, water supply, cemetery, park and recreation, road, **vector control**, transportation, and soil and water conservation. All have the power to levy **property taxes** inside their boundaries to finance the services they provide, and all are directed by elected boards. There are about 950 in Oregon, many of them overlapping. Special Districts Association of Oregon, PO Box 12613, Salem 97309. 503-371-8667. Oregon Blue Book. See also **Local government; Property tax**.

Special session. A session of the **legislature** that meets to address a specific matter sometime after the regular session has adjourned. As of 1997 all special sessions had been called by the **governor** even though a 1976 constitutional amendment gave the legislature the power to call itself into special session. Through 1996 there have been 30 special sessions, three of them in 1982 alone, but there have also been 20-year stretches with none. Several have lasted for just one day, though the longest, in 1982, lasted for 37 days. All are listed in the Oregon Blue Book.

Speech-Language Pathology and Audiology, State Board of Examiners for. A board of seven members appointed by the governor for three-year terms. It regulates the practices of speech pathologists and audiologists, licenses them, and investigates violations. In 1996 there were 1,014 licensed in Oregon. 800 NE Oregon St., Suite 407, Portland 97232. 503-731-4050. Oregon Blue Book.

Speed limits. The 1995 repeal of federal speed limits left much of Oregon again under the state's **basic rule** speed law, which requires that a driver must not drive at a speed greater than is reasonable and prudent. Under the basic rule a driver may not be convicted for exceeding the posted speed if he can convince a judge that driving conditions at the time made the higher speed reasonable and prudent. In a confusing web of laws, the basic rule still (1996) apparently applies to rural **interstate highways** that have a 65-mph limit, in counties with over 100,000 population, and to some streets with posted limits. Trucks and buses, however, remain subject to maximum speed limits. Oregonian 1/10/96:D7. See also **Traffic fines**.

Spencer Butte. A 2,065' butte just south of **Eugene** that rises 1,600 feet above the city. It was named in 1845 for John Spencer who was Secretary of War at the time. In the late 1930s Eugene voters adopted a measure to save it from logging. A trail leads to the top. "Searching."

Spiders. Silk-spinning arachnids (not insects). Oregon has three spiders with bites that are poisonous to humans, the black widow, hobo, and brown recluse. The female of the black widow spider, *Latrodectus mactans*, has a shiny, spherical black abdomen marked with red, often in the form of an hourglass underneath. The smaller male does not bite, and is eaten by the female after mating. The aggressive or hobo house spider, *Tegenaria agrestis*, is a fast-moving, long-legged brown spider up to 1 3/4" long that makes funnel-shaped webs around woodpiles and building foundations. It closely resembles the larger giant house spider (up to 3" long) which does not bite humans but does eat the hobo spider. The third, the violin or brown recluse spider, *Loxosceles reclusa*, found in California, is rare in Oregon. A bite from it or the hobo spider is occasionally fatal and may create a deep festering crater that takes weeks to heal, as well as nausea, headache, and other neurological problems. Oregonian 5/31/96:B5.

Spills. The state charged those responsible $275,000 for spilling a load of hydrochloric acid into the **John Day River** on February 8, 1990. **Southern Pacific** paid the state $250,000 for damages resulting from diesel fuel spilled into Yoncalla and Elk creeks during a 1993 derailment. The state charged Talent Irrigation District $400,000 for flushing an herbicide into **Bear Creek** on May 8, 1996, that killed 92,000 **steelhead** plus other fish. The Department of **Environmental**

Quality maintains a toll-free number for reporting spills and other **hazardous waste** emergencies. 800-452-0311. Oregonian 1/19/95:B10, 8/21/96:C3.

Spirit of Oregon. See **Excursion trains**.

Spirit of the Rogue Nature Center. A proposed center to be built along the **Rogue River** in McGregor Park, just below **Lost Lake**, 30 miles north of **Medford**. The center, envisioned as a coastal river version of the **High Desert Museum**, hopes to open early in the 21st century. Mail Tribune 9/6/97:1C.

Spokane floods. See **Pleistocene floods**.

Spokane, Portland and Seattle Railroad. A rail line that, with the secret agreement of **Great Northern** and **Northern Pacific** railways, built a **railroad bridge** over the **Columbia River** at Portland and a 230-mile line from **Portland** up the north side of the Columbia to Pasco and Spokane. The expensive line, completed in 1908, entailed creating 13 tunnels by boring through a total of five miles of solid rock. The route, coupled with the Northern Pacific line to Astoria, provided a route for transporting Inland Empire wheat to tidewater ports and also supplied another **transcontinental connection** for **Portland**. **Burlington Northern** now operates the line. Dictionary of Oregon History.

Sports Hall of Fame. See **Oregon Sports Hall of Fame**.

Sports meets. See **Gorge Games**; **Olympics**; **State Games of Oregon**; **World Masters Games**.

Spotted owl. See **Northern spotted owl**.

Spouting horn. A periodic spout of water on a rocky shoreline where the pressure from waves forces water from an underwater cave out through a hole in the top. Oregon's most notable are north of the **Depoe Bay** bridge and, during high surf, at the Devil's Churn at **Cape Perpetua**, but spouts occur on other rocky shorelines when the conditions of tide and wave are right.

Spray. A central Oregon community on the **John Day River** in **Wheeler County**, 35 miles southeast of **Fossil** on Highway 19. John and Mary Spray platted the town and established the post office in 1900. The city was incorporated in 1958. The community operates a **boarding high school** and sponsors the annual Spray **Rodeo** and Eastern Oregon Half-Marathon on Memorial Day weekend. Hunting, fishing, and river rafting are popular pursuits. Population 1980 155; 1995 165. Elevation 1,772'. PO Box 83, 97874. 541-468-3391. Oregon Geographic Names.

Spring break quake. See **Scotts Mills earthquake**.

Springfield. A south **Willamette Valley** city that extends from **Eugene** east 8 miles along Highway 126 in **Lane County**. Founded by **Oregon Trail** pioneers Elias and Mary Briggs in 1848, Springfield was named for their fenced-off spring in an open field. The post office was established in 1868, and the city was incorporated in 1885. Sony Disc Manufacturing, Kingsford Charcoal, and Weyerhaeuser are the major employers. Attractions include Washburne National Historic District, Springfield Museum, "Splash" indoor wave pool, the annual Filbert Festival, the state's oldest Christmas parade, and a Ukrainian Day Celebration, as well as boating and fishing on the **Willamette** and **McKenzie** rivers. Population 1980 41,621; 1995 49,005. Elevation 459'. 225 5th St., 97477. 541-726-3700. Chamber of Commerce 541-746-1651. Oregon Geographic Names.

Springs of the Metolius. The Metolius River issues as a full river from springs at the north base of Black Butte near Camp Sherman, 11 miles NE of **Sisters**. The springs produce a year-round steady flow of 50,000 gallons a minute of 46 to 48°F water.

Spruce. A conifer **tree** with stiff, prickly needles and papery cones. Three species are native to Oregon, **Sitka spruce** (*Picea sitchensis*) along the coast, Engelmann spruce (*P. engelmannii*) in the **Cascade Range**, and the rare Brewer's weeping spruce (*P. breweriana*) in a few isolated places high in the **Siskiyou Mountains**. Trees to Know.

Spruce budworm. An insect that is the most destructive defoliator of **Douglas-fir** and **spruce** stands in North America, though it also feeds on other species. The damage shows up as reduced growth and top kill, leading to multiple tops; repeated attacks finally kill the trees. During the 1950s, 3 million acres in the Northwest were sprayed with DDT to halt outbreaks; a severe outbreak between 1980 and 1993 infested over 7 million acres in Oregon and Washington. The adult form of the budworm is a mottled orange-brown moth, with a 1" wing span, that lays its eggs in mid-summer. Oregonian 4/23/95:A18. See also **Forest health**.

Spruce Goose. A 219-foot-long, all-wood flying boat with a wingspan of 320 feet, the broadest in the world. It was built by Howard Hughes in 1942 on a U.S. government war contract to carry 700 combat troops during **World War II**. However, after just one 70-second flight, it ended up as a tourist attraction. In 1992 the legendary plane was moved, first by ship and then overland seven miles to the proposed **Captain Michael King Smith Evergreen Aviation Educational Center** in **McMinnville**. Oregonian 3/23/97:C8.

Spruce Production Division. A **World War I** division of the U.S. Army Signal Corps, organized in 1917 to increase production of **Sitka spruce** lumber for use in military aircraft. The 30,000 men of the division were put to work in the lumber industry at civilian wages, and huge new mills were built, including one at **Toledo**. One result was the effective destruction of the **Industrial Workers of the World** (Wobblies) union. Dictionary of Oregon History; Encyclopedia of American Forest and Conservation History. See also **Loyal Legion of Loggers and Lumbermen**.

Squawfish. A fish, *Ptychocheilus oregonensis*, a large minnow, native to Northwest pools and sluggish water, which has thrived in the reservoirs behind dams. Because each fish may eat up to 10 juvenile **salmon** a day, in the 1990s **Bonneville Power Administration** paid $3-5 for every squawfish over 11 inches long which was turned in from the **Columbia River**. Some anglers caught over 2,500 in a year. In 1995 a total of 200,000 were caught, estimated to be 16% of the population. The program is thought to have reduced predation over 30% since it was begun in 1990. Information, 800-622-4520 or 800-858-9015. Oregonian 7/6/95:D6, 10/18/95:C8.

Squid. Ten-armed, soft bodied mollusks. One small species, *Loligo opalescens*, grows up to two feet long and is of commercial value; it appears periodically off the Oregon coast. A larger species, *Moroteuthis robusta*, the northwest squid, grows up to 20 feet long and is sometimes pulled in by fishermen, but it tastes too strongly of iodine to be palatable. A single 225 pound specimen of giant squid, *Architeuthis sp.*, was caught off the Oregon coast in 1978, the only one ever caught north of Chile. Great Northwest Nature Factbook; Seashore Life. See also **Octopus**.

Squirrels. Eight species of **ground squirrels** are found in Oregon, plus three species of **chipmunks**, one **flying squirrel**, and three native species of tree squirrels. The tree squirrels include the western gray squirrel, *Sciurus griseus*. of western Oregon; the **protected** smaller, brown, Douglas squirrel, also called pine squirrel or orange-bellied chickaree, *Tamiasciurus douglasii*, of western and central Oregon; and the red squirrel, *T. hudsonicus*, with dark tail and white belly, found in conifer forests in northeast Oregon. The eastern fox squirrel, *S. niger*, has been introduced to some urban areas of the state and spread into nearby woodlands. Hunting of gray squirrels is controlled by the Oregon Department of **Fish and Wildlife**. Atlas of Oregon Wildlife; Mammals and Life Zones of Oregon; Mammals of the Northwest. See also **Tularemia**.

Squiyowhiynoof. (Squee-oh-whee-noof) A white man in a long black robe who was said by the **Yoncalla** Indians to have appeared alone and lived with them for a while until killed by hostile Indians. The earliest settlers calculated that it must have been sometime between 1750 and 1800, well before any other whites were known to have been inland in the **Oregon Country**. He was said to have carried a book with illustrations of hell and heaven, and to have been the source of the names for three Yoncallas who were named John, Jacob, and Paul (Be-el). Recollections; Skookum. See also **Great Basin history**.

Stadium Freeway. See **Interstate 405**.

Stadiums. Major Oregon stadiums include **Civic Stadium** in **Portland**, Parker Stadium at **Oregon State University** in **Corvallis**; and Autzen Stadium at the **University of Oregon** in **Eugene**.

Stage lines. Businesses that transported passengers in horse-drawn coaches over **wagon roads**. The stage lines also carried **express services**, displacing the **Pony Express**, but most freight was carried by **freighting outfits**. The first scheduled stage service in Oregon began operation between **Oregon City** and **Salem** in 1850, and additional lines were soon established in the **Willamette Valley**. Routes were extended to northern California during the 1851-1855 **gold rush**, and, after a wagon road was connected through to Sacramento in 1860, the **California Stage Company** operated seven (later six) day runs between Sacramento and **Portland** until the railroad link was completed in 1887. After gold was discovered in eastern Oregon, a stage line, the first of an extensive network throughout the **Blue Mountain** area, began operating in 1863 between **The Dalles** and **Salt Lake City**. The next year, a 197-mile, three-day line began operating between The Dalles and **Canyon City**. Horses were changed and meals were served about every 15 to 20 miles. **Railroads** displaced most stages, but some of the isolated stage lines operated into the 20th century until replaced by motor vehicles. Dictionary of Oregon History; Gold and Cattle Country; Oregon's Golden Years; "Portland: Wells Fargo's Hub"; South Road; This Day in Oregon. See also **California Stage Company**; **Road agents**; **Star City Stage Line**.

Stairs. See **Portland stairs**.

Standard parallels. Survey correction lines, authorized by the **Oregon**

Manual, established during the **Public Land Survey**. North of the **Columbia River** the standard parallels were to be every four **townships** (24 miles) apart while south of the river they were to be every five townships (30 miles) apart. History of the Rectangular Survey System.

Stanfield. A northeast Oregon agricultural town in **Umatilla County** five miles southeast of **Hermiston** and 23 miles west of **Pendleton** on **Interstate 84**. The community was known as Foster, for a local landowner, when the post office was established in 1883. In 1907 the name was changed to honor another local landowner, Robert Stanfield, who was elected U.S. Senator from Oregon in 1920. The city was incorporated in 1910. Population 1980 1,568; 1995 1,700. Elevation 592'. PO Box 369, 97875. 541-449-3831. Oregon Geographic Names.

Star City Stage Line. A **stage line** that carried the gold and silver from Silver City, Idaho, to Chico, California, and from there it was carried to the U.S. Mint in San Francisco. Three stage drivers were killed even though the government protected the route from Confederate sympathizers and Indians during the **Civil War** because the gold and silver were needed to help pay for the war. The line ran over 100 miles through southeast Oregon from near **Jordan Valley** to **McDermitt**, and operated until the **Oregon Short Line Railway** opened in 1884. Oregonian 5/8/95:B1.

Star of Oregon. A 53-foot **schooner**, the first ship built in Oregon. She was launched in 1841 after intense work by a small group of American settlers, led by Joseph Gale, working on **Swan Island** and Oak Island in the **Willamette River**. After Lt. Wilkes of the **Wilkes Expedition** supplied informal master's papers, navigating instruments and an American flag, the group sailed the *Star* to San Francisco where, as planned, they traded it for cattle that they then drove back overland to Oregon in order to break the cattle monopoly of the **Hudson's Bay Company** and **Willamette Mission**. One hundred years later, the *Star of Oregon II* , a 441' **Liberty ship**, was the first ship launched by Kaiser's Oregon Ship Yard in **Portland**. Dictionary of Oregon History; Stars of Oregon.

Starfish. Star-shaped ocean creatures that attach themselves to seashore rocks by a multitude of tiny suction-tube feet. Several species live along the Oregon coast. The most frequently seen is the purple (so called, though it is sometimes brown or orange) starfish, *Pisaster ochraceus*, which lives in the intertidal zone. It feeds on **mussels** and other shellfish by using its suction tubes to pull the shells apart far enough for it to extrude its stomach into the shell where it dissolves the soft body and absorbs the liquid. Oregon Department of **Fish and Wildlife** regulations limit the taking of starfish. Between Pacific Tides; Seashore Life.

Starkey Experimental Forest and Range. An area 28 miles southwest of **La Grande** on the **Wallowa-Whitman National Forest** that has been dedicated for research since 1940. In 1987, four intensive ten-year-long research projects were begun in a 40-square-mile area surrounded by an eight-foot-high fence. One project studies the relationship of the age of breeding bull elk to the survival of elk calves. Others look at the responses of **elk, deer**, and **cattle** (a number of them with tracking collars) to forest management activities, to motorized traffic, and to each other. The only entry is off route 244. 1401 Gekeler Lane, La Grande 97850. 541-963-7122.

Starvation Creek Falls. A 186-foot waterfall in Starvation Creek State Park in the **Columbia River Gorge** near exit 56 from **Interstate 84**. Railroad passengers, stranded for three hungry weeks during snowstorms in December 1884, called the area Starveout, though no one died during the incident. The creek has been called Starvation Creek since then. Waterfall Lover's Guide.

State Accident Insurance Fund. See **SAIF Corporation**.

State Agricultural Society. A non-political organization formed in 1860 by delegates from Oregon's county agricultural societies. It was instrumental in promoting agricultural knowledge and encouraging superior production. The first **State Fair** in 1861 grew from the efforts of the group. The **Grange** gradually absorbed the interest; by 1912 the county agricultural societies had ceased to exist. Dictionary of Oregon History.

State animal. The 1969 legislature designated the **beaver** as the state animal due to its role in early Oregon history and to its fabled ingenuity and industriousness, and Oregon is known as the Beaver State. The beaver is also the emblem of **Oregon State University**. Oregon Blue Book.

State beverage. The 1997 legislature designated **milk** as the official state beverage.

State bird. The western meadowlark (*Steunella neglecta*) selected by Oregon's school children in 1927 to be the official state bird. The brownish, robin-size bird has a yellow breast with a distinctive black V below its throat. Its song is a flute-like warble. A year-round resident, it is found in meadows and open lands throughout the state. Oregon Blue Book.

State colors. The state colors are navy blue and gold. See also **State flag**.

State Court Administrator. See **Chief Justice**.

State dance. The square dance, a combination of steps and figures danced by four couples grouped in a square, was designated by the 1977 legislature as the official state dance. It is a lively dance of pioneer origins. Oregon Blue Book.

State Fair. An annual 12-day celebration held in **Salem** from late August through Labor Day weekend. The first, in 1861, was held in what is now **Gladstone**, but the event was moved to Salem the next year. Over 600,000 attend, making it one of the largest fairs in the nation. The fair includes farm, home garden, and hobby exhibits, **4-H** and FFA exhibitions, livestock and horse shows, commercial displays, a carnival, and entertainment, including daily big-name attractions in the L. B. Day Amphitheatre. From the beginning the fair has celebrated Oregon's agriculture, and it continues to feature the bounty of the state, including giant **pumpkins** and 13-foot-high corn, nearly 6,000 animal entries, and one of the 10 largest horse shows in the nation. Attendance has dropped in recent years from a 1991 high of over 800,000. Facilities on the 185-acre fairgrounds, some of them aging, are rented out during the year for other events. The governor appoints the five member State Fair Advisory Commission. 2330 17th St. NE, Salem 97310. 503-378-3247. Oregon Blue Book. See also **County fairs**.

State fish. The **chinook salmon** was designated state fish by the 1961 legislature. It is the largest species of Pacific salmon, with some weighing over 100 pounds. Oregon Blue Book.

State flag. Oregon's flag is navy blue and gold (the state's colors). On the face is the **state shield** with STATE OF OREGON written above it and 1859 written below it. A beaver is pictured on the reverse side; Oregon is the only state that has a different pattern on the reverse side of its flag. The parade version of the flag has a gold fringe. Oregon Blue Book.

State flower. The **Oregon grape**, *Berberis aquifolium*, was adopted as Oregon's state flower in 1899. Oregon Blue Book.

State forests. The Oregon Department of **Forestry** manages 789,000 acres of forest land, over half of it in **Tillamook** and **Clatsop** counties. Of this, 654,000 acres are managed for the counties, and 132,000 acres are **Common School Fund** forest lands, managed for the **State Land Board**. There are five major state forests - **Tillamook**, **Clatsop**, **Santiam**, **Elliott**, and **Sun Pass** - plus scattered tracts. Oregon law requires that state lands be managed to produce sustainable revenue for counties, schools, and local taxing districts. Oregon Forests Report. See also **Board of Forestry Lands**.

State Games of Oregon. A multi-sport competition held in July at **Mount Hood Community College**. In 1996, the eleventh year of the games, over 10,000 athletes, both recreational and elite, competed in over 40 sports. An additional 6,000 had participated in local and regional qualifying events. Oregonian 7/13/96:E1.

State gemstone. The Oregon **sunstone** or heliote was designated as the Oregon gemstone by the 1987 legislature. It is a transparent feldspar, sometimes with color and a metallic shimmer ("schiller" or "aventurescence") that glints from within the stone. The stones are found in limited areas of **Lake** and **Harney Counties**. While not unique to Oregon, those found in Oregon are valued for their clarity and range of colors. Learning about Oregon; Oregon Blue Book. See also **State rock**.

State hat. At present Oregon has no official state hat, though cowboy hat, hard hat, baseball cap, and sunbonnet have all been suggested.

State Hospital. See **Oregon State Hospital**.

State insect. The Oregon swallowtail butterfly (*Papilio oregonius*), was designated state insect by the 1979 legislature. The yellow and black butterfly is native to the **sagebrush** canyons of the **Columbia River** and its tributaries. Oregon Blue Book.

State Land Board. A three-member board comprised of the **governor**, who serves as chair, the **secretary of state**, and the state **treasurer**. The board's primary responsibility is management of the **Common School Fund** lands and money, though it is also responsible for **submerged lands**. The Division of **State Lands** is its administrative arm. 775 Summer Street, Salem 97310-1337. 503-378-3805. Oregon Blue Book.

State Lands, Division of. The administrative agency for the **State Land Board** and the **Natural Heritage Advisory Council**. The agency also administers the **South Slough National Estuarine Reserve**, **Tongue Point Marine Industrial Site**, wetland resources, coastal resources below mean high tide line, the removal-fill law for waterways, and a student loan program; leases state-owned mineral rights and state lands; maintains historical land records; and acts as trust agent for abandoned funds and as personal representative for the estates of persons who die leaving no will or known heirs. 775 Summer Street, Salem 97310-1337. 503-

378-3805. Oregon Blue Book.

State motto. "She Flies With Her Own Wings." It was first used, in Latin, *Alis Volat Propiis*, on the seal of the Oregon **territory**. However, for 30 years between 1957 and 1987 the official motto was "The Union," which still appears on the **state seal**. Oregon Blue Book.

State nut. In 1989 the legislature named the **hazelnut** as the state nut. Oregon Blue Book.

State of Jefferson. A proposed state to be made up of the counties of northwest California and southwest Oregon. Various such proposals had simmered since before Oregon became a state, but they gathered steam in the 1930s during the **Depression** when the isolated communities in the rugged **Klamath Mountains** were frustrated by the lack of roads and lack of resource development. The movement, which had as its emblem a gold pan overlain with a double cross, peaked in late 1941 with weekly rallies in Yreka, California. It was cut short by the sudden death of the mayor of **Port Orford**, a major leader, on December 2, and by the entry of the U.S. into **World War II** later that week following the Japanese bombing of Pearl Harbor on December 7. A reporter from the San Francisco <u>Chronicle</u> received a **Pulitzer Prize** for his coverage of the effort. "Short Happy History."

State of Oregon department and agency entries. See substantive word. For example, State Police is listed as **Police, Oregon State**.

State parks. Oregon has 225 developed state parks, 50 of them with **campgrounds**. Day use visitors outnumber campers by 20 to 1. Day-use fees and camping fees are charged at many of the parks, replacing the **gas tax** money that had supported the parks until voted out in 1980. The legislature has decreased state support from 22% of the parks budget to 11% while visits have increased. Annual permits are sold at state park offices and by many sporting goods stores. Campsites can be reserved by calling 800-452-5687. In 1993-94, park attendance totaled 42 million, fifth highest in the nation. 1.7 million visited **Jessie. M. Honeyman State Park** on the coast, the most popular park in the system. Oregon parks have 465 visitors per acre, compared with 182 per acre in Washington and 49 per acre of parks in California. A number of the parks have facilities that meet the Americans with Disabilities Act standards, and several have horse trails and facilities. The first land deeded to the State Highway Commission for park purposes was Sarah Helmick State Park (south of **Monmouth**) in 1922. One hundred eighty one state parks, most of them donated to the state by civic minded citizens, were created during the administration (1929-1950) of Sam Boardman, Oregon's first park superintendent. The parks are now administered by the state **Parks and Recreation Department**, which cooperates in the publication of <u>Oregon Parks Magazine</u>. 1115 Commercial St. NE, Salem 97310-1001. State park information 800-551-6949. State park reservations 800-452-5687. <u>Oregonian</u> 6/19/96:A16, 6/20/96:A1, 6/1/97:E1; <u>Oregon's Highway Park System</u>. See also **Rails to Trails**; **Sodaville**; **Yurt camping**.

State parks, listings. The following state parks have separate entries in this work. They are listed regionally. Those with campgrounds are marked with a *. There are many other state parks, including some with campgrounds.

State parks, coast. See **Fort Stevens***; **Oswald West***; **Nehalem Bay***;

Cape Meares; Cape Lookout*; Devils Lake*; Beverly Beach*; South Beach*; Beachside*; Carl Washburne*; Jessie M. Honeyman*; Sunset Bay*; Shore Acres; Bullards Beach*; Cape Blanco*; Samuel H. Boardman; Harris Beach*; Loeb*.

State parks, Willamette Valley. See **Banks-Vernonia**; **Tryon Creek**; **Milo McIver***; **Champoeg***; **Willamette Mission**; **Silver Falls***.

State parks, southern Oregon. See **Joseph Stewart***; **Valley of the Rogue***.

State parks, Cascade Range. See **Detroit Lake***.

State parks, central Oregon. See **Cove Palisades***; **Prineville Reservoir***; **Smith Rock**; **La Pine***; **Collier***.

State parks, northeast Oregon. See **Emigrant Springs***; **Hilgard Junction***; **Wallowa Lake***; **Farewell Bend***.

* - State parks with campgrounds

State Police. See **Police, Oregon State**.

State rock. The **thunderegg** was adopted as state rock by the legislature in 1965. Oregon Blue Book. See also **State gemstone**.

State seal. Oregon's state seal consists of a shield topped with an eagle. On the shield the Pacific Ocean is pictured in the distance with a departing British man-of-war, an arriving American merchant ship, and the setting sun. In the foreground is a covered wagon and clump of conifers, below that a ribbon that reads "The Union", and at the bottom a pickax, plow, and sheaf of wheat representing mineral and agricultural resources. 33 stars set around the shield honor Oregon as the 33rd state admitted to the union. In the circular band surrounding the shield is printed "STATE OF OREGON 1859". The seal was authorized by the state Constitutional Convention in 1857. Oregon Blue Book.

State seashell. The 1991 legislature named the Oregon hairy triton, *Susitriton oregonensis*, the state seashell. Named in 1848 for the Oregon Territory, it is the only shell that carries the name of a state. Oregon Blue Book.

State song. "Oregon, My Oregon," with words by J. A. Buchanan and music by Henry B. Murtagh, was adopted as the state song in 1927 after having won a state-wide competition in 1920. "Land of the empire builders, land of the golden west, conquered and held by free men, fairest and the best. Onward and upward ever, forward and on and on. Hail to thee, land of heroes, my Oregon./ Land of the rose and sunshine, land of the summer's breeze, laden with health and vigor, fresh from the western seas. Blest by the blood of martyrs, land of the setting sun. Hail to thee, land of promise, my Oregon." Words and music are in the Oregon Blue Book. Earlier, the song "Sweet Oregon" by Henry **De Moss**, was popular. The words to it are in Oregon Oddities.

State System of Higher Education. See **University System, Oregon**.

State treasurer. See **Treasurer**.

State tree. The legislature designated the **Douglas-fir** as the state tree in 1939 because of its economic importance to Oregon. It is found in all Oregon counties except **Sherman County**. State trees from nearly all of the 50 states are growing in an arboretum at the south-bound rest area on **Interstate 5** south of **Wilsonville**. Oregon Blue Book.

State Unit on Aging. See **Senior and Disabled Services Division**.

Statehood. Oregonians, dismayed that, as residents of the **Oregon Territory** they were not allowed to make their own decision on **slavery**, finally agreed in 1857 to call a constitutional convention and thus start the movement toward statehood. Congress, however, was in no hurry, and did not admit the Oregon to the union until February 14, 1859. It became the 33rd state, signified on the **state seal** by 33 stars. The portion of the Oregon Territory that was not included within the state's boundaries was added to the **Washington** Territory and became part of the **Idaho** Territory in 1863. Empire of the Columbia. See also **Admission Act**; **Constitution**; **Territorial government**.

Statesman Journal. A daily paper published in **Salem** with a 1996 circulation of 58,733. It was founded as the Oregon Statesman, a strongly Democratic paper, in **Oregon City** in 1851 with Asahel Bush (1824-1913) as editor. Bush was a practitioner of the colorful **Oregon Style**. In 1853 the paper moved to **Salem** where it served as the voice of the **Salem Clique**. For some years beginning in 1929 it was edited by Charles A. Sprague who was Republican governor 1938-42. PO Box 13009, 97309. 503-399-6611. Dictionary of Oregon History; History of Oregon Newspapers. See also **Newspapers**; **Pompous Twit awards**.

Statues. See **Sculpture**.

Statute. See **Law**; Oregon Revised Statutes.

Stayton. A town on the east edge of the **Willamette Valley** 15 miles southeast of **Salem** in **Marion County**. The townsite, named for founder Drury Stayton, was platted in 1872, the same year the post office was established. It was incorporated in 1901. Attractions include the Santiam Historical Museum. Population 1980 4,396; 1995 5,905. Elevation 448'. 362 N 3rd Ave., 97383. 503-769-3425. Chamber of Commerce 503-769-3464. Oregon Geographic Names.

Steam engines. See **Great Oregon Steamup**; **Locomotives**; **Sawmills, history**; **Steamboats**.

Steamboats. The first steamboat on the **Columbia River** was the **Hudson's Bay Company**'s *Beaver*, a combination sailing ship/side-wheeler brought to **Fort Vancouver** in 1836. The 90' *Columbia*, also a side-wheeler, was built in **Astoria** in 1850. It provided the first scheduled service on the river, replacing sail power which had been undependable on the river's winding channel. Another side-wheeler, the 160' *Lot Whitcomb*, was launched at **Milwaukie** on Christmas day in 1850, the first of over 50 steamboats, most of them **stern-wheelers**, built on the **Willamette River**. Steamboats burned an average of four cords of wood an hour, consuming much of the accessible forest along the rivers. During the **flood of 1861** a steamboat, the *St. Clair*, was successfully taken down the **Willamette River** over **Willamette Falls**. Two steamboats were brought down through **Hells Canyon**, the *Shoshone* in 1870 and the *Norma* in 1895, and several made it over **Celilo Falls** and through the **Cascades of the Columbia River**. The *Swan* ascended the **Umpqua River** to Roseburg in 1870, prompting Congress to appropriate $70,000 for channel clearance, but the run was never made again. Blow for the Landing; Dictionary of Oregon History; "History of Transportation in the Pacific Northwest", Hells Canyon; Marine History; Southern Oregon Mosquito Fleet. See also *Bailey Gatzert*; *Gazelle*; **Oregon Steam Navigation Company**; **Ship building**; *Steamer Portland*.

Steamer Portland. A **stern-wheeler** steam tugboat built in 1947 by the **Port of Portland** to replace its earlier boat of the same name. At the time it was retired in 1981 it was the last commercially operated steam-driven stern-wheeler in the world. In 1989 the **Oregon Maritime Center and Museum** rescued the abandoned boat and volunteers restored it. It now makes occasional runs and races, and was seen in the 1993 movie "Maverick". Blow for the Landing; Oregonian 10/23/95:B1.

Steel. A malleable alloy of **iron**. A steel rolling mill operates in **McMinnville**, and a steel slab and plate plant in **Portland**. Mineral Industry of Oregon.

Steelhead. A fish, once named *Salmo gairdneri*, but now put in the same genus as **salmon** and called *Oncorhynchus mykiss*. Those that spend their entire lives in rivers are called rainbow **trout**, while those that spend one or more years in the ocean and return to freshwater to spawn are called steelhead. Unlike other salmon that die after spawning, some steelhead may repeat this cycle. Steelhead average 28 inches long and about 10 pounds at maturity, though the Oregon record is 35 1/2 pounds. Healthy runs of wild summer steelhead return to the North **Umpqua River** and to the **John Day River**, and some coastal rivers have healthy runs of wild winter steelhead, but **Snake River** stocks have been listed as threatened, and other Oregon stocks may be also be listed. **Indians** may legally sell steelhead along the Oregon banks of the **Columbia River**. Fishing in Oregon; Oregonian 4/1/96:B6, 8/29/97:C4; Salmon of the Pacific.

Steens Mountain. A 50-mile long, north-south **fault**-block ridge south of **Burns** that rises above the surrounding desert to 9,733', the highest point in southeast Oregon. The long, gradual, **sagebrush**-covered western slopes have been deeply eroded by **glaciers**, while the east slope drops abruptly 4,100 feet to the **Alvord Basin**. The mountain formed when vast volcanic flows from the **Miocene** were later broken by north-south **faults**, and a large block tilted up between the faults. Glaciers carved away at the ridge from both east and west, eroding through the crest above Kiger Gorge to produce a gap called The Big Nick or the Gunsight. Plants include 78 species classified as rare, including six not found anywhere else. An unpaved loop road from Frenchglen passes two campgrounds in the 241,730-acre Steens Mountain High Desert Recreation Area and goes nearly to the summit. The road is usually open from June 30 to November 1, if snow permits. The **Bureau of Land Management** administers the area for grazing and tourism, and over 40,000 persons visit annually. "Unique Botany." See also **Frenchglen**; **Kiger mustangs**; **Malheur National Wildlife Refuge**; **Pueblo Mountains**.

Steins Pillar. The largest of several crags 20 miles east of **Prineville**, Steins Pillar is 350 feet high and 120 feet in diameter. It looms over a forested slope above Mill Creek, north of **Ochoco Reservoir**. Successive volcanic deposits of the **Clarno** and **John Day Formations** have eroded along vertical fracture joints to form the crags. They are dangerous to climb because of the friable rock; Steins Pillar was first climbed in 1950. The name is pronounced Steens, and tradition says that it, like **Steens Mountain**, was named for Major Enoch Steen, commander of an 1860 expedition against Indians of the area. Geology of Oregon; Oregon Geographic Names. See also **Twin Pillars**.

Stern-wheeler. A boat propelled by a paddle-wheel mounted at the rear, more maneuverable in fast currents than a side-wheeler. The first stern-wheeler constructed in Oregon was the *Jennie Clark* in 1854. The *Ohio*, launched in 1874, had a loaded draft of only 10 inches which permitted her to haul freight to **Eugene** when no other boat could make it that far upriver. In the 19th century, the stern-wheeler *Telephone* would make the 100 mile round trip to **Astoria** and back to **Portland** in a day and the *Bailey Gatzert* would complete its round trip between Portland and **The Dalles** in a day. Now, a fleet of stern-wheeler excursion boats operates out of Portland, two diesel-electric stern-wheelers owned by the Port of **Cascade Locks** make daily cruises, and stern-wheelers operate and/or offer lodging on several coastal rivers, including at **Winchester Bay**, **Florence** and **Bandon**. Most are now diesel powered, but in 1994 the *Steamer Portland* narrowly won the first annual Great American Stern-wheeler Race on the **Willamette River** through **Portland**, the first such race since 1952. Blow for the Landing. See also **Cow scow**; **Ship building**; **Steamboats**.

Stewart State Park. See **Joseph Stewart State Park**.

Stinkingwater Creek. A creek in **Harney County** that flows north into the **Malheur River**. **Highway 20** crosses it and the Malheur between Stinkingwater Pass and Drinkwater Pass. Stinkingwater was named for the stench from some mineral springs along the creek. Drinkwater, however, was named for a family from Drewsey. Oregon Geographic Names.

Stocks. See **Securities**.

Stone-ground flour. In 1996 two **gristmills** in Oregon ground flour on stone grindstones. Butte Creek Mill in **Eagle Point** is water powered while Bob's Red Barn (Moore Natural Foods, Inc.) in **Milwaukie** uses electric power.

Stonehenge replica. A 1918 monument built by entrepreneur Samuel Hill across the **Columbia River** from **Biggs** as a memorial to local men killed in **World War I**. The reproduction is not exact. Free.

Stop Oregon Litter and Vandalism. See **SOLV**.

Storms. Major storms in Oregon include those of

May 4, 1880:	A sudden gale destroyed the **fishing fleet** at the mouth of the **Columbia River**, drowning 25 men.
December 21, 1889:	High winds. There were also bad floods that winter as well as **landslides** that caused 5 deaths in the **Cottage Grove** area.
January 29, 1920:	Winds at the mouth of the **Columbia River** were officially estimated at having been 160 miles per hour; the anemometer was reading 132 mph when it was destroyed.
April 21-22, 1931:	A **dust storm** on an east wind blasted across the northwest and 600 miles out to sea.
October 12, 1962:	The **Columbus Day Storm** hit with winds of 170 mph at **Mount Hebo** and 116 mph in **Portland**. There were 24 deaths in Oregon.
November 13, 1981:	A storm with wind gusts over 120 mph hit the central Oregon coast. There were five deaths in Oregon, and power outages even in the Portland area.
January, 1990:	Winds measured at over 100 mph at Netarts west of

Tillamook blew down 55 million board feet of timber.

December 12, 1995:   Wind gusts were registered of 110 mph at **Cape Blanco**, 119 mph at **Sea Lion Caves**, 107 mph at **Newport**, 101 mph at **Astoria**, and 61 mph at **Portland**. A **barometric pressure** of 28.51" at **Astoria** was the lowest ever recorded in the state. See also Hurricanes; Tornadoes; **Wind**.

Strategic Investment Program (SIP). A measure adopted by the legislature in 1993 that allows local governments to cap the **property tax** value of new plants at $100 million for 15 years in order to attract expensive high-tech plants. In 1994 **Washington County** gave the tax break three times: a $74.3 million tax break to **Intel** Corporation for a $500 million expansion of its Aloha chip plant (355 new jobs) and for its $2.3 billion Ronler Acres project (1,400 jobs), and a $15.2 million tax break to Integrated Device Technology for a new $801 million plant (400 jobs). In 1995 **Multnomah County** gave Fujitsu Microelectronics a $32.6 million break on its $1 billion expansion (445 jobs) and LSI Logic Corporation a $113 break on its $4 billion chip complex in Gresham (467 jobs). **Yamhill County** rejected a tax break for Sumitomo Sitex for a $912 million wafer plant that would have created 734 jobs in Newberg. Oregonian 4/6/97:C1. See also **Enterprise Zones**.

Straw-bale buildings. Oregon's first legal straw-bale structure is a studio built nine miles from **Sisters** in 1995. A demonstration straw bale house was built later in 1995 in **Eugene**. The Institute for Sustainable Culture, 503-736-1143, is proposing to build the first in **Portland**, at SE 21st and Clinton. Oregonian 12/15/96:E6.

Strawberries. In 1995, Oregon growers produced 61.9 million pounds of strawberries, worth $28.8 million, on 6,100 acres; this is about 4% of the nation's production. Harvest depends on some 24,000 migrant workers. Strawberries were cultivated at **Fort Vancouver** as early as 1831, though wild strawberries were found in abundance in western Oregon through the 1870s. Production peaked in 1957 with 18,000 acres in berries. Most are now grown in **Washington County**. **Lebanon** has held an annual strawberry festival since 1909. Dictionary of Oregon History; 1995 Oregon.

Strawberry Mountains. A range in central Oregon formed by volcanic eruption of **andesite** during the time of the **Columbia River Basalt** flows. The flows covered 1,500 square miles and are over 1 mile thick at **Ironside Mountain** in Malheur County. Strawberry Mountain, at 9,038', is the high point. The south side drains into landlocked **Harney Lake**, the north side into the **John Day River**. Gold has been mined on the north side, and the mountains provide grazing, timber, and recreation. Some of the range is covered by the Strawberry Mountain Wilderness Area. The name came from the wild strawberries along Strawberry Creek. Geology of Oregon, Oregon Geographic Names. See also **Clarno Formation**; **John Day Formation**.

Streams. See **Rivers**.

Street of Dreams. An annual month-long summer tour of several custom homes in the **Portland** area. Special events and concession stands are also included. It is sponsored by the Home Builders Association of Metropolitan Portland which organized the first one in 1976. Over 100,000 attend. Fee. Oregonian 8/3/95:R2.

Streetcars. Passenger vehicles operating on rails, usually within a city. The rails are in the traffic lanes, unlike **light rail** which normally has an exclusive travel lane, making light rail faster but more expensive. Light rail also incorporates more complex technology, including a better connection to the power line. In 1997 the only streetcars operating in Oregon were those that ran on a regular schedule between **Portland** and **Lake Oswego** on the **Willamette Shore Railway**. As of early 1998, Portland was considering a streetcar line between **Portland State University** and the **Pearl District**, and perhaps another across Hawthorne Bridge and out Hawthorne Boulevard. **Astoria** has proposed a six-mile streetcar line on an unused railroad along the waterfront from **Tongue Point** to Youngs Bay Bridge, and there was talk in **Salem** of a streetcar connection to West Salem using a railroad bridge across the **Willamette River**. See also **Public transit**.

Streetcars, history. Streetcars operated in **Portland** from 1872 to 1950, the first ones pulled by horses. Later, a small steam engine replaced the horse, and, as early as 1889 in Salem, electric cars were used, powered through trolleys running on overhead power lines. In 1910, when **Portland** had a population of 200,000, streetcars crossed Burnside Bridge 1,000 times a day. That year the women of the city held a successful mass meeting demanding that the steps be lowered so that they could step up and down without being leered at by passing males. By 1918 Portland had a 197-mile streetcar system, but it was abandoned after cars became popular. In 1986, after several decades with no street cars, the **Tri Met** began operating a **light rail** system. In **Curry County** streetcars rescued from the 1895 wreck of the *Bawnmore* were used as outbuildings. Fares, Please; Oregonian 9/24/96:B5; Portland, An Informal History; Round the Roses; Stations West. See also **Electric railways**; **Electrical Parade**.

Strikes, private employees. Major labor strikes since 1945 include a timber-industry-wide strike begun in September 1945 in the Pacific Northwest at the end of **World War II** that lasted, in some places, 6 months. The stereotypers' union struck the **Oregonian** and the Portland Journal on November 10, 1959; the bitter dispute lasted five and a half years, until April 24, 1965. A 50-day strike against Greyhound Bus Lines ended on December 21, 1983. An 88-day strike by 7,000 grocery workers against a group of **Portland** stores lasted from August 19 to November 13, 1994, with picketing only at Fred Meyer stores; it was estimated that the strike cost Fred Meyer, Inc., at least $60 million. In 1995 Boeing machinists struck, including 1,044 workers in **Gresham**, for 69 days, ending on December 15. A 15-day strike by **Oregon Symphony** musicians ended on September 24, 1996. A 33-day strike by 2,000 employees of Kaiser Permanente ended on October 6, 1997. See also **Employment Relations Board**; **Labor organizations**.

Strikes, public employees. Public employees were given the right to strike in 1973. By 1996 there had been 31 strikes (and 3,957 mediated disputes). Members of the Oregon Public Employees Union struck state offices from May 8 through May 14, 1995. In 1987 state employees called a rolling strike, and in 1980 **Multnomah County** workers had struck for 38 days. The first strike by teachers was in **Hillsboro** in 1973; in 1987 the longest teachers' strike lasted 22 days in **Eugene**. A 1997 strike by **Sandy** teachers lasted 7 days. Oregonian 3/3/96:D3, 4/1/96:A1. See also **Employment Relations Board**; **Labor organizations**.

Studded tires. In 1997 tires with embedded metal studs, used for improved traction on snow and ice, were estimated to cause $40 million in annual damage to Oregon roads, mainly in the form of ruts on heavily traveled highways. As of 1997, the weight of new studs was limited to 1.5 grams for cars, 2.3 grams for light trucks, vans, and sport utility vehicles, and 3 grams for large trucks and buses. Owners of older studded tires may use them until they wear out. Studded tires may be used only between November 1 and April 1. Oregonian 11/1/97:A1.

Student/teacher ratio. In 1995 Oregon had 527,914 public school students and 26,680 teachers, for a ratio of 19.8 students per teacher, up from the 1990-91 ratio of 17.7. The ratio increased as the number of students went up while the number of teachers remained the same following **Measure 5** and **equalization**. Average class size is larger than the student ratio because the ratio also includes teachers of music, art, physical education, and compensatory education. The state does not gather information on class size. Oregon Report Card; Oregonian 3/3/96:A1.

Students. Average Oregon **public school** daily attendance in 1994-95 was 492,000 students. Cumulative public school enrollment that year was 547,200, up from 510,000 in 1990-91, and enrollment is projected to increase to 576,800 in 1998-99. Two-thirds of the students lived in the metropolitan areas of **Portland**, **Salem**, **Eugene**, and **Medford**. Nearly half rode school buses. 16% were from families with incomes below the federal poverty level and 37% received free or reduced-price lunches. Minorities made up 14.1% of the total, with 52% of the students who entered the public schools since 1990 from minority populations, especially Hispanic. In 1996-97 6.4% of the students spoke little or no English, up from 3.1% in 1992-93. Oregon Report Card; Oregonian 10/14/97:E4. See also **School enrollment**; **Special education**; **Student/teacher ratio**; **Talented and gifted students**.

Stumbo Strip. A 16-foot-wide strip, owned by the Stumbo family, that crossed **Highway 99** north of **Glendale** in southern Oregon. It was near the present Milepost 85 on **Interstate 5**. On Sunday afternoon, August 12, 1956, three Stumbo brothers and their cousin blockaded the highway for nearly an hour, backing up several hundred cars, trucks, and buses, because the state had neglected to purchase the strip from them before building the highway across it nine years before. To further tweak the state, they petitioned to operate their strip as a toll road, encouraged truckers to file for a partial rebate of their public highway use tax, talked of building a drainage ditch across the highway, and listed the land for sale as "an ideal home site for a family with children at the end of the longest dead-end street in the west" and with "highway frontage on two sides." After they had subdivided the strip into 2" squares and sold 290 of them to the public for $2 each, the county jailed one of the brothers for having sold the properties without getting county approval of the subdivision. The state later condemned the strip and paid the brothers $125. Josephine County Historical Society.

Stump farms. Farms established by cutting a forest. The stumps were often laboriously burned out so the area could be plowed, but if the area was to be used for grazing, the stumps would be left and the livestock would graze around them.

Stumptown. See **Portland**.

Sturgeon. The white sturgeon is a huge, ancient, migratory fish, *Acipenser transmontanus*, found in the **Columbia**, **Snake**, **Willamette**, **Umpqua**, **Rogue**, and **Klamath Rivers** and in **Lake Oswego**. It is primarily a freshwater fish but some undertake extensive ocean travels. The largest known, caught in the Snake River in 1898, was 20 feet long and weighed 1,500 pounds. A 12-foot specimen weighing 1,285 pounds was taken from the Columbia River near Vancouver, Washington, in 1929. The slow-growing fish may live to be 100 years old. Sturgeon were fished almost to extinction between 1885 and 1895 when 25 million pounds were harvested each year from the Columbia. Now, in order to protect the large females with their millions of eggs, white sturgeon over a given size (66 inches in most rivers) may not be taken. The green sturgeon, *A. medirostris*, is found in bays and lower rivers, but is less tasty. <u>Fishing in Oregon</u>; <u>Great Northwest Nature Factbook</u>; <u>Oregonian</u> 3/7/96:E6.

Sturgeon Lake. A 3,000-acre lake in the center of **Sauvie Island**, the largest of the shallow floodplain lakes located just downstream from the confluence of the **Willamette** and **Columbia Rivers**. Though Sturgeon Lake is over five miles long, at no point is it over three feet deep. The water is murky, and, since levees were built, a sediment deposition rate of an inch per year threatens its value as bird habitat. The lake is used for fishing, canoeing, and bird watching. The origin of the name is unclear though local folklore says that in pioneer days a **sturgeon** picked apples from nearby trees. <u>Atlas of Oregon Lakes</u>.

Subduction zone. See **Cascadia Subduction Zone**.

Sublimity. "More Than a City...A State of Mind." A rural residential and agricultural community located in the low foothills of the **Cascade Range** in **Marion County** 13 miles southeast of **Salem**. It was established by James Denny who named it "for the sublime scenery in the hills around the town." The post office was established in 1852, making it one of the oldest in the state. Sublimity College, a secondary school sponsored by the United Brethren in Christ, was chartered in 1858 and operated into the 1870s. Milton Wright, father of Wilbur and Orville Wright, was the first teacher. The city was incorporated in 1903. Christmas trees, grass seed, and timber support the economy. Population 1980 1,077; 1995 1,915. Elevation 547'. PO Box 146, 97385. 503-769-5475. Chamber of Commerce 503-769-3464. <u>Sublimity</u>.

Submarines. See *Blueback*; **World War II**.

Submerged lands. The state of Oregon has title to all submerged land under navigable waterways, given to it by the federal government at statehood. The state charges rental fees for docks, boathouses, marinas and other uses that float over the state-owned submerged land. The lands are managed by the **State Land Board**. <u>Oregonian</u> 9/24/97:D7. See also **Wetlands**.

Substance abuse. See **Alcohol**; **Drug abuse**; **Smoking**.

Succession. Oregon has no lieutenant governor. If the office of the **governor** becomes vacant, the office passes, in order, to the **Secretary of State**, **Treasurer**, President of the **Senate**, and Speaker of the **House of Representatives**.

Voters adopted this line of succession in 1972 as Article V, Section 8a, of the state **constitution**. Prior to 1972 the President of the Senate was first in line of succession, followed by the Speaker of the House. In 1947 Governor Earl Snell, Secretary of State Robert Farrell Jr., and President of the Senate Marshall Cornett were killed in a private **plane crash**, and John Hall, Speaker of the House, became governor.

Sucker. A fish of genus *Catostomus* that feeds primarily on algae. A sucker's mouth is small, turned down, and works like a suction cup. Its teeth are located in its throat. Suckers in **Upper Klamath Lake**, considered sacred by the **Klamath Indians** and historically important to them as a food source, were declared an **endangered species** in 1988. Oregonian 9/25/96:D8.

Sugar beets. In 1995, Oregon growers produced 434,000 tons of sugar beets, worth $17.2 million, on 18,100 acres in the **Ontario** area. They were processed in **Nyssa**. In 1898 a sugar beet factory was built at **La Grande** with 500 acres of sugar beets under contract to it, but lack of irrigation led to low yields and the plant closed in 1912. Sugar beet seed worth over $5 million is raised in the **Willamette Valley**. 1995 Oregon.

Sugar pine. A tall **pine**, *Pinus lambertiana*, found scattered in mixed stands in southwestern Oregon and up the **Cascade Range** nearly to **Mount Hood**. Sugar pine's long branches are distinctive, and the cones, over a foot long, are the longest in the world. They are carried at the tips of the long branches where they dangle when ripe. The seeds are edible, as is the sweet but laxative pitch that drips from wounds. The cones are gathered for decoration but need to be baked (a hot oven for 15 minutes) or dipped into boiling water to reduce the stickiness. Trees to Know.

Suicide. Five hundred twenty five Oregonians killed themselves in 1995, up from 472 in 1993, and Oregon's suicide rate reached an all-time high of 17 out of every 100,000 persons, compared to the national rate of 12.4 per 100,000. The rates were especially high among those over 75 (33.2 per 100,000) and among young people aged 25-34 (24.1 per 100,000). Suicide is the second leading cause of death among 10-17 year olds, behind accidents. More people killed themselves with guns than all other methods combined. There were three times as many suicides as murders. Oregon: A Statistical Overview; Oregonian 2/7/96:A1, 1/29/97:E1, 8/29/97:A1. See also **Physician-assisted suicide**.

Sulfur dioxide. A colorless, pungent gas, SO_2, that is a lung and eye irritant. It also damages plants and building materials, contributes to acid rain and reduces visibility. In 1996 Oregon emissions totaled 64,000 tons. Burning high-sulfur coal is not allowed in Oregon, so the major sources were from burning diesel fuel and **heating oil**. Oregon Air Quality. See also **Air pollution**.

Summer camps. Residential and day summer camps for children are listed in an annual spring edition of the Oregonian at about the time that fairs featuring camp information are held in the **Portland** area.

Summer Lake. A sometime-lake lying in the desert at the eastern base of **Winter Ridge** seven miles northwest of **Paisley**. It and **Lake Abert** are remnants of a huge **Pleistocene** lake, **Lake Chewaucan**. During wet years Summer Lake may be15 miles long by 5 miles wide, covering 38,000 acres to a maximum depth of 5 feet, while in other years it dries up to just a channel surrounded by marshes. The lake has no outlet, so becomes alkaline as it evaporates. The area serves as important waterfowl habitat; the northern end is managed as the Summer Lake Wildlife Area. Atlas of Oregon Lakes.

Summerville. An agricultural community 18 miles north of **La Grande** in **Union County**. The post office was established in 1865. One account says that it was named by the postmaster for a friend, Alexander Sommerville, but another says that it was so named because the snow melted there earlier than at the competing town of Winter. The city was incorporated in 1885. Population 1980 143; 1995 150. Elevation 2,705'. PO Box 92, 97876. 541-534-2035. History of Union County. See also **Hunt Railroad**.

Summit Ski Area. A ski area 54 miles east of **Portland** on **Highway 26** with a 306-foot vertical drop from a top elevation of 4,306 feet, one chair lift, a rope tow, 12K of Nordic track, and tube-sliding hills. PO Box 459, Government Camp 97067. 503-272-0256. Oregonian 11/16/97:T7

Sumpter. A northeast Oregon gold-mining community in **Baker County** 29 miles west of **Baker City**. A cannonball-like rock, found in 1861 when attention was focused on **Civil War** news from Fort Sumter, South Carolina, suggested the name. The Sumter post office was established in 1874; in 1883 postal officials said that the name Sumter could not be used, so it was changed to Sumpter, which means a pack animal. The city was incorporated in 1901. At one time the town had a population of 3,500, but it faded after gold returns dwindled and a fire in 1917 destroyed most of the town. A small day-use **state park** includes the **Sumpter Valley dredge**, and the **Sumpter Valley Railroad** has a depot in the town. Population 1980 133; 1995 175. Elevation 4,388'. PO Box 68, 97877. 541-894-2314. Gold and Cattle Country.

Sumpter Valley dredge. A state-owned historic **gold-mining** dredge now resting as the focal point of a day-use **state park** at **Sumpter**, 30 miles west of **Baker City**. The125-foot-long, five-story dredge , the largest ever used in Oregon, mined $4.5 million worth of gold from an eight-mile stretch along the **Powder River**, churning bottom land into barren rock piles. It operated 24 hours a day from 1935 to 1954, closing down only for the 4th of July and Christmas. Dredging for Gold. See also **Gold dredging**.

Sumpter Valley Railroad. An 80-mile, narrow-gauge railroad begun in 1889 in **Baker City** to carry logs, passengers, and freight down from the **Blue Mountains**. The line, known locally as the Stump Dodge, reached **Prairie City** in 1910, but by 1947 all the tracks had been pulled up. A five-mile stretch through an area of **gold-dredging** tailings (now a wildlife refuge) between **Sumpter** and McEwen, has been restored and trips are offered over it during the summer. 541-894-2268. Gold and Cattle Country.

Sumpter Wildlife Area. A designated area of 36,000 acres owned by **Baker County** that extends 11 miles upstream from **Phillips Lake** to the town of **Sumpter**. The area is an old dredge site, where, in the early years of this century, hydraulic gold mining turned the valley bottom into piles of rock and ponds. It has since become prime wildlife habitat, enhanced by some artificial nesting snags. Oregon Wildlife Viewing Guide.

Sun Pass State Forest. A **state forest** in **Klamath County**, comprised primarily of some 20,000 acres of **Board of Forestry Lands**. ODF Klamath Lake District Office, 3400 Green Springs Drive, Klamath Falls 17601. 541-883-5681.

Sundown laws. City ordinances that prohibited **blacks** from spending the night in town. **Grants Pass** is said to have had signs posted on the bridge into town that said "Nigger don't let the sun set on you here." In Timber Country. See also **Blacks in Oregon history**.

Sunfish. See **Warmwater fish**.

Sunken Rose Garden. One of the country's finest rose gardens, located in **Portland's** Peninsula Park. Its 15,000 roses represent 700 varieties. The garden was established in 1907, with horse-drawn scrapers creating the sunken beds of the formal garden. It is open daily. N. Ainsworth and N. Albina Streets. 503-823-3636.

Sunny Valley. A valley north of **Grants Pass**, at Exit 71 **Interstate 5** between **Sexton Pass** and Smith Hill Summit. The post office name was changed to Sunny Valley from Grave Creek in 1945, and had earlier been Leland before Leland station was established on the railroad four miles to the west. Grave Creek, which flows through the valley, was named for the burial there in 1846 of a girl, Martha Leland Crowley, a member of the first wagon train to use the **Applegate Trail** through the area. Among the many deaths on that train were those of her father, her sister, an older brother, the brother's wife, and his child. Oregon Geographic Names.

Sunriver. An unincorporated 3,300-acre central-Oregon destination resort community on the **Deschutes River** with a population between 3,000 and 15,000, depending on season. It is located 15 miles south of **Bend** in **Deschutes County** on the site of **Camp Abbot**. The post office and resort facilities opened in 1969 with the name coined by the developers. Visitor information 800-800-8334. Governing Oregon.

Sunriver Music Festival. A 10-day classical music festival held in the Great Hall at **Sunriver** in August. 541-593-1084

Sunrise, sunset. See also **Day length; Twilight**.

	June 21	(DST)	December 21	(PST)
	Sunrise	Sunset	Sunrise	Sunset
Portland	5:22 a.m.	9:03 p.m.	7:48 a.m.	4:30 p.m.
Medford	5:35 a.m.	8:52 p.m.	7:38 a.m.	4:42 p.m.

Sunset Bay State Park. A coastal **state park** located in a sheltered cove 12 miles southwest of **Coos Bay**. The park includes 138 campsites. Reservations, 800-452-5687. 10965 Cape Arago Highway, Coos Bay 97420. 541-888-4902.

Sunset Highway. A 77-mile portion of **Highway 26** between the coast and **Portland**. Known as Wolf Creek Highway when it opened in 1938, it was renamed in 1946 for the Sunset (41st) Division of the U.S. Army which had many members from the Pacific Northwest and had played an important role in both **World Wars I** and **II**.

Sunset Strip. See **Daylight saving time**.

Sunshine laws. See **Open meeting law; Open records law**.

Sunstone. A semi-precious clear feldspar, also called heliolite, that varies in color from yellow or red to green and blue, though much of what is called sunstone is more accurately labradorite. It occurs as large crystals in **basalt** at four limited locations in Oregon, three on private land and the fourth on **Bureau of Land Management** land in **Lake County** where the stones are known as "Plush diamonds" for the nearby community. The stones are being mined commercially near **Hines** in **Harney County**. Some are priced at over $100 per caret. It was designated the **state gemstone** in 1987. Gem Trails of Oregon; Geology of Oregon.

Superfund cleanup. Oregon has nine sites on the National Priority List that makes them eligible for federal Superfund cleanup funds. The nine include Allied Plating (chromium) and Gould Battery (lead) in **Portland**, Joseph Forest Products in **Joseph**, Martin Marietta (cyanide and fluoride) and Union Pacific Railroad in **The Dalles**, Wah Chang Albany (radioactive wastes) in **Millersburg**, **Umatilla Chemical Depot** (nitrates and explosives) near **Hermiston**, United Chrome Products (hexavalent chrome) in **Corvallis**, and Northwest Pipe and Casing in **Clackamas**. The Oregon Department of **Environmental Quality** has identified an additional 200 **hazardous waste** sites across the state that don't qualify for federal Superfund dollars but where cleanup is necessary. Oregon Environmental Atlas; Oregon Scientist Spring 1994 p.7.

Superintendent of Public Instruction. An elected, state-wide, nonpartisan office filled at elections held every four years on the same schedule as election for **governor** (1994, 1998, 2002,...) Salary in 1998 was $67,900. The superintendent heads the Oregon Department of **Education**, carries out the policies of the Oregon State Board of Education, implements the **Education Act for the 21st Century**, and is responsible for providing leadership for public preschool, elementary, and high school education. Responsibility for education beyond high school rests with the commissioner of **community colleges** (who answers to the Board of Education) and the State Board of **Higher Education**. 255 Capitol St. NE, Salem 97310. 503-378-3573. Governing Oregon; Oregon Blue Book; Oregonian 12/7/96:A1. See also **Education, Oregon State Board of**; **Elected officials**; **Recall**; **Succession**; **Term limits**.

Supreme Court. Oregon's highest court, with seven justices elected on state-wide nonpartisan ballots to six-year terms. The members of the court elect one of their number to serve as **Chief Justice** for a six-year term. The court is primarily a court of review, hearing appeals from the decisions of the **Court of Appeals**. If it decides not to review a case, the decision by the Court of Appeals becomes final. The Supreme Court hears direct appeals in death penalty cases and **Tax Court** cases, and may accept original jurisdiction in a few areas. In 1995, 424 cases were filed with the court, up from 263 in 1990, but fewer than 10% of the number filed with the Court of Appeals. The Supreme Court also admits lawyers to practice law in Oregon, based on recommendations from the Board of **Bar Examiners**, and may reprimand, suspend, or disbar lawyers upon investigation and trial by the Oregon State **Bar**. It may also censure, suspend, or remove judges upon investigation and recommendation by the Commission on **Judicial Fitness and Disability**. Supreme Court Bldg., 1163 State St., Salem 97310. 503-986-5555. Governing Oregon; Oregon Blue Book.

Supreme Court Library. A **law library**, first authorized in 1848, that supports the research needs of the **Supreme Court** and **Court of Appeals**. It also serves state agencies, and is open to attorneys and the general public. Supreme Court Bldg., 1163 State St., Salem 97310. 503-986-5640. Oregon Blue Book.

Surface water. See **Drinking water**; **Lakes**; **Rivers**.

Surfing. A sport pursued by some along the Oregon coast, despite the average ocean temperature of 48° F that makes wet suits necessary all year. Surf shops, scattered along the coast, are concentrated at **Lincoln City** where the Pacific Northwest Surfing Museum is located (541-996-3957). See also **Sharks**.

Surimi. A fish paste made at plants in **Astoria** and **Newport** from **whiting**. The paste is made into imitation **crab**, Japanese fish cakes called kamaboko, and other imitation seafoods elsewhere in the world. Oregonian 7/28/97:D2.

Surveys. See **Land surveys**.

Sustainable Northwest. A nonprofit organization whose "Founders of the New Northwest" program in 1997 honored people whose efforts had contributed to a more sustainable ecosystem in the Northwest. 1020 SW Taylor, Portland 97205. 503-221-6911. See also **Environmental organizations**.

Sutherlin. "Gateway to Recreation." A historic southwest Oregon timber town in **Douglas County** 12 miles north of **Roseburg** on **Interstate 5**. It was named for Fendel Sutherlin and his family who settled in the area in 1851 and were active in its development. The city was incorporated in 1911. Annual events include Timber Days, the Blackberry Festival, Sutherlin Stampede **Rodeo**, and parades for Halloween and Christmas. Population 1980 4,560; 1995 5,830. Elevation 518'. PO Box 459, 97479. 541-459-2856. Visitors Center 541-459-5829. History of Sutherlin.

Suttle Lake. A well known and heavily used natural mountain lake located along **Highway 20** forty miles northwest of **Bend**. It lies in a glacial trough in which water is held behind **moraines**. The lake covers 253 acres and is over a mile long, with a maximum depth of 75 feet. The lake is popular for fishing, boating, swimming, and water skiing. There are campgrounds and a resort. It was (mis)named for John Settle who discovered it in the 1860s while involved with building the **Willamette Valley and Cascade Mountain Military Wagon Road**. Atlas of Oregon Lakes.

Suzhou stone. A 22-foot, 16-ton limestone rock located in Terry D. Schrunk Plaza in downtown **Portland**, across Fourth Avenue from the city hall. Since a parking garage is located under the plaza, the stone and surrounding reflecting pool were carefully sited above a supporting column. It was given to Portland by Suzhou, China, one of its sister cities, in 1997. Oregonian 10/29/97:B1.

Swamp Lands Act of 1860. An act in which Congress granted to Oregon **public domain** swamp lands that the state could then sell. Oregon required applicants to pay $1.00 an acre and reclaim the land or grow crops successfully for three years. Confusion and state expenses in designating swamp lands, problems with conflicting land claims, and the limited success of private construction in creating **irrigation** projects reduced the value of the act, though land sales continued for several decades. However, the state's dealings in swamp lands were never quite according to the law. In the 1870s lands in southern and eastern Oregon were surveyed and sold as swamp lands when the nearest water was 30 feet below the surface. Later it was revealed that the governor, treasurer, and secretary of state were in league with the speculators. William Thayer (1827-1899), governor 1878-1882, who was himself an applicant for 100,000 acres of swamp land, ignored provisions of the law and helped others to acquire large acreages for little or nothing. In the end, a total of 73,442 acres was patented to the state. Disposition; Empire of the Columbia; "Financial History"; History of Oregon Land Grants. See also **Land frauds**; **Land grants**.

Swan Island. Oregon's shipbuilding center, a lowland (no longer an island) on the east side of the **Willamette River** in **Portland**. The *Star of Oregon*, the first ship built in Oregon, was built on the island. In 1921 the **Port of Portland** purchased it, dredged a new west channel, and used the dredgings to quadruple its size. The Portland **airport** operated on Swan Island from 1927 to 1940, and during **World War II** (1941-1945), Kaiser's Swan Island Shipyard built 147 T-2 tankers there. In 1976 Tri-county voters passed a $84 million bond issue to build one of the world's largest floating dry docks and the nation's only publicly owned commercial shipyard on the site. After business declined the port leased the shipyard to Cascade General in 1995. Oregonian 10/19/94:A1, 5/25/95:C1.

Sweet Home. A **Willamette Valley** timber town in **Linn County**, 27 miles southeast of **Albany** on **Highway 20**. It is on the South **Santiam River** at the western edge of the **Cascade Range**. The town was originally called Buckhead because of a saloon that had a deer's head over its door. The Sweet Home post office was established in 1874, and the city was incorporated in 1893. Klondike Kate (1876-1957) of Yukon dance hall fame retired to Sweet Home in the early 1950s. Population 1980 6,921; 1995 7,350. Elevation 537'. 1140 12th Ave., 97386. 541-367-5128. Oregon Geographic Names.

Swifts. Flocks of Vaux's swifts, *Chaetura vauxi*, small birds closely related to chimney swifts, stop in **Portland** for several days in late September on their fall migration. Hundreds can be seen near sunset swirling down into the large chimney at Chapman Grade School, NW Pettygrove and 27th. Portland Audubon Society, 503-292-6855.

Sycan Marsh. A 36-square-mile wetland at the head of the **Klamath River** basin, much of which was drained for pasture in the 19th century. The Nature Conservancy bought 24,000 acres in 1980 and has worked together with **ZX Ranch**, holder of a 40-year grazing lease, to restore the marsh. The area is important habitat for birds and other wildlife, and is a nesting area for **sandhill cranes**. Oregonian 6/30/96:L1.

Symphony orchestras. Symphony orchestras in Oregon include four in the **Portland** area: **Oregon Symphony** 503-228-1353, **Portland Youth Philharmonic** 503-223-5939, Columbia Symphony Orchestra 503-244-8338, and the Metropolitan Youth Symphony 503-228-9125. Others in the state include Oregon East Symphony 800-880-NOTE in **Pendleton**; Central Oregon Symphony 541-317-3941 in **Bend**; Rogue Valley Symphony 541-488-2521 in **Ashland**; and the **Eugene** Symphony 541-687-9487. See also **Sagebrush Symphony**.

Table Rock Treaty. See **Rogue River War**.

Table Rocks. Two prominent mesas eight miles north of **Medford**. Upper and Lower Table Rocks each stand approximately 800 feet above the valley floor and are capped with 125 feet of **basalt**. They are remnants of lava flows from a million years ago that have long since eroded away except where the flows were especially thick in a river bottom; the horseshoe shape of each rock is the preserved shape of an ancient river meander. The **Nature Conservancy** and the **Bureau of Land Management** own portions of the rocks and have built trails to the flat grassy tops. The Table Rocks are noted for their unique flora and carpets of goldfields in April. "As Long As the World Goes On"; Geology of Oregon; Table Rocks; "Upper and Lower Table Rocks".

TAG. See **Talented and gifted students**.

Tahkenitch Lake. A lake of complex shape ten miles north of **Florence**; its name is an Indian word meaning "many arms". It is over two miles long and covers 1,674 acres to a maximum depth of 23 feet. The outlet has been modified with a low dam built in 1963 by the International Paper Company in order to provide a year-round supply of fresh water to its pulp mill in **Gardiner**. Nearly the entire shoreline is privately owned by small lot owners and a timber company. The lake is very productive of fish, but introduced water plants interfere with fishing. There is a small resort and a nearby campground. Atlas of Oregon Lakes. See also **Lake Flatulence**; **Moose**.

Talent. "A Growing City of Friendly People." A southwest Oregon town in **Jackson County** seven miles southeast of **Medford**. Though first settled in 1852 by Jacob Wagner, the town was named for A. P. Talent who platted it in the early 1880s. The city was incorporated in 1911. Major employers in 1996 were Fabricated Glass and Micro Trains. The **Bob Day Festival** was held in July for several years. Population 1980 2,577; 1995 4,530. Elevation 1,635'. PO Box 445, 97540. 541-535-1566. Land in Common; Talent.

Talented and gifted students (TAG). About 8% of Oregon school students have been identified as having exceptional academic, intellectual, artistic, or leadership talents and gifts. Average school district funding for special programs for TAG students was $161 per student in 1994, down from $445 in 1992. Oregon Handbook; Oregon Report Card. See also **Special education**; **Students**.

Tallest building. See **Buildings, tallest**.

Tamanawas Falls. A waterfall estimated to drop over 100 feet from a rock ledge on the east slopes of **Mount Hood**. It can be reached by a two-mile trail from Highway 35 near Sherwood Campground. The name is a **Chinook jargon** word for friendly spirit. Waterfall Lover's Guide.

Tamolitch Falls. A 60-foot dry falls with a spring-fed punchbowl at the base. The falls originally carried the **McKenzie River**, but the river was diverted for power generation. The pool is reached by a two- mile hike from the McKenzie River Trailhead north of Trail Bridge Reservoir. Tamolitch is the **Chinook jargon** word for tub or bucket. Waterfall Lover's Guide.

Tamustalik Cultural Institute. (ta-MUST-ah-luck) A center on the **Umatilla Indian Reservation** that provides an American Indian perspective on the history of the **Oregon Trail**. It is one of five interpretive centers to be located along the trail. The 45,800-square-foot project includes exhibits, gift shop, auditorium, and classrooms. Oregonian 4/25/97:D8.

Tangent. A rural **Willamette Valley** agricultural community six miles south of **Albany** on **Highway 99E** in **Linn County**. The town grew up around a railroad station built in 1871 and was named for the 20-mile-long straight tangent of the rail line through the town. It was incorporated in 1893. Jenks Hatchery, Oregon's largest and oldest **chicken** hatchery, is near Tangent, and it is also a **grass seed** shipping center. In 1983 a Tangent farmer died and left his house and estate to his cat, **Kitty Cat**; the city inherited the estate when the cat died in 1995. Population 1980 478; 1995 695. Elevation 248'. PO Box 251, 97389. 541-928-1020. Oregon Geographic Names.

Tanneries. The Muir-McDonald Tannery in **Dallas** has been in operation since 1863.

Tansy ragwort. A plant, *Senecio jacobaea*, native to Europe, that has become a naturalized weed in Oregon. In 1974, 8,850 head of cattle and 58 horses died after eating the toxic plant. The cinnabar moth and ragwort flea beetle were introduced to control it, and by 1995 cattle deaths were estimated to be fewer than 200 a year. Oregonian 7/18/96:B8.

Tantalum. A hard acid-resistant metallic element. It is produced by Wah Chang of **Millersburg**, and is used primarily for aerospace engine components. Mineral Industry of Oregon.

Tar balls. Sticky small black balls that periodically wash up on the **beaches**. They are created when oil from natural oozes off California, spills, leaks, and roads collects bits of detritus. Winds and ocean currents sometimes drive them ashore. Kerosene will clean them off. Oregonian 4/25/97:D8.

Tattoo artists. According to results of a nationwide survey, Oregon has the nation's most comprehensive laws for preventing infectious disease and ensuring that tattoo artists are trained. The **Electrologists, Permanent Color Technicians and Tattoo Artists** Advisory Council advises the **Health Division** on administration and enforcement of the laws. About 60 facilities and 80 tattoo artists had been licensed as of 1996. Oregonian 7/11/95:C1.

Tax base. Prior to **Measure 50**, the amount of money to be provided for a governmental unit (such as a city, county, school district) from **property taxes**. Voters could authorize property taxes beyond the tax base for temporary serial levies (for operating funds) and **bonds** (for capital projects). The state **constitution** provided that no **property tax** could be levied without first having a tax base authorized by a vote of the people. Prior to **Measure 5** growth in the tax base was limited to 6% a year. Measure 50 replaced the tax base with a tax rate system in which taxing districts have a fixed rate they can apply to the assessed value within their district, and the amount of assessed value may increase only 3% a year except for additions (new and improved property). Governing Oregon.

Tax breaks. See **Strategic Investment Program**.

Tax Court. A state court that hears all questions arising under state tax laws. The judge is elected for a six-year term on a statewide, nonpartisan ballot. There is no jury. Each trial is scheduled, when possible, in the county where the taxpayer resides. In 1997 a Magistrate Division was established that hears cases informally, either in person or by phone. Unless the taxpayer has elected to file as a **small claims** procedure, the magistrate's decision may be appealed to the Regular Division of the Tax Court. Appeals from the Tax Court go to the **Supreme Court**. Around 400 tax cases are filed each year. Supreme Court Bldg, 1163 State St.,

Salem 97310. 503-986-5645. Oregon Blue Book.

Tax exemptions. Exemptions from **income tax** and/or **property tax** authorized by governments in order to encourage certain activities or to provide a benefit for certain classes of taxpayers. The total amount of Oregon state and local exemptions ($14.5 billion for the 1995/97 biennium) almost equals the total amount of taxes collected ($14.6 billion). Leading categories of exemptions to the property tax are intangible personal property such as bank accounts and stocks ($4.3 billion); federal property ($2.1 billion); privately owned timber that is taxed at harvest instead of as property ($919 million); and state and local government property ($575 million). The major income tax exemption is the personal exemption on the state income tax ($600 million). Oregonian 4/6/97:D2. See also **Assessed value**.

Tax increment financing. A method of financing **urban renewal** districts that, before **Measure 5**, used the increased **property tax** revenues resulting from increased property values to pay off bonds that had been issued to finance the improvements. The system worked by freezing the assessed property values (and hence the tax revenue to the city from that area) within a designated area for a defined period of time, such as ten or fifteen years. Bonds were then sold to provide money for improvements in the area, and as investments were made and property values increased, property taxes on the increased value were used to pay off the improvement bonds. At the expiration of the time period the area was entered on the property-tax rolls at its new, higher value. The effect of **Measure 47** and Measure 50, adopted by voters in 1996 and 1997, on urban renewal bonds is uncertain. Oregonian 11/22/96:B1; 2/24/98:C1.

Tax rate. See **Measure 50**; **Tax base**.

Tax Service Examiners, Board of. A board of seven members appointed by the governor to three-year terms. It examines and licenses persons who, for a fee, assist in the preparation of personal income tax returns. Licensed tax preparers are apprentice-level practitioners who must work under the supervision of licensed tax consultants. There were 1,840 tax preparers in the state in 1996. 3218 Pringle Road SE, Suite 120, Salem 97302-6308. 503-378-4034. Oregon Blue Book.

Tax Supervising and Conservation Commission. A state commission of four members appointed by the governor for four-year terms to provide oversight over the 40 taxing districts within **Multnomah County**. It was established in 1919, and is funded by Multnomah County. 724 Mead Bldg., 421 SW 5th Ave., #724, Portland 97204-2189. 503-248-3054. Oregon Blue Book.

Taxes. Oregon traditionally has relied on the state **income tax** to support state government and on the **property tax** to support local government. **Measure 5** moved school support from reliance on local property tax towards reliance on state income taxes. The state has no **sales tax** and no gift tax. An inheritance tax return must be filed if a federal estate tax return is required. In 1993 Oregonians paid on average $2,217, which is less than the U.S. average of $2,310, and the state ranked 22nd in the country in the total amount of state and local taxes paid. However, the per cent of personal income paid for state and local taxes was higher than average, 12.1% compared with the U.S. average of 11.6%, because Oregon incomes are lower than the national average. Individuals have been paying an increasing share of taxes and businesses a decreasing share, according to a 1997 study. For every $1.00 that individuals paid, businesses paid $0.99 in 1978-79, $0.79 in 1990-91, and $0.64 in 1995-96. The effect of the **initiative** and **referendum** is that no major tax legislation can be passed without a vote of the people. The first tax levied in Oregon was a voluntary levy agreed to at an 1843 meeting of settlers in order to pay a bounty on **wolves**. Governing Oregon; Oregonian 10/20/95:D1. See also **Business taxes; Head tax; Poll tax; Wolf meetings**.

Taxol. See **Yew**.

Taylor Grazing Act of 1934. A 1934 federal law that for the first time regulated grazing on the 13,000,000 acres of eastern Oregon **rangeland** administered by the **Bureau of Land Management**. A system of permits and fees was established. Until then the use of the range had been free and open to any. Oregon Desert.

TB. See **Tuberculosis**.

Teacher pay. In 1995-96 Oregon **public school** districts paid teachers an average annual salary of $39,575, that ranked 14th in the nation. Averages ranged from $50,254 in Connecticut to $26,346 in South Dakota, with the national average at $37,685. Oregon figures include a 6% pension contribution by employers. Starting pay for teachers in 1994-95 ranged from $20,700 to $23,911, while top pay ranged from $33,083 in smaller districts to $47,114 in larger districts. Teachers' pay is at the bottom when compared with other licensed Oregon professions. Oregonian 9/2/96:A1, 2/25/97:E2.

Teacher Standards and Practices Commission. A 17-member commission with members appointed by the governor for three-year terms. It approves teacher preparation programs offered by Oregon colleges and universities, licenses teachers, administrators, and other school employees, and takes disciplinary actions. Some 70,000 Oregonians hold licenses as educators. 2555 Capitol St. NE, Suite 105, Salem 97310. 503-378-6813. Oregon Blue Book.

Teachers. The average Oregon **public school** teacher has 14.3 years of teaching experience and is 41 years old. 65% of teachers are female, and 3.8% are minorities (compared with 14.1% of the **students**). Oregon Report Card; Oregonian 4/12/95:C1. See also **Teacher pay**.

Tears of Joy Theater. See **Children's theater**.

Tectonic plates. See **Plate tectonics**.

Teen pregnancy. In Oregon in 1994, 3,214 teenagers (1.9% of females ages 10-17), became pregnant and 2,022 gave birth. Oregon: A Statistical Overview. See also **Births; Health division**.

Teepee burners. See **Wigwam burners**.

Teeth. See **Fluoride**.

Tektronix. A company that began manufacturing oscilloscopes in a basement in 1946 and led the way to **Washington County's high-tech industry** boom. At its peak in 1981 it employed 24,000 people, down to 4,520 in 1995. See also **Salaries**.

Tel-Law. Tapes on legal topics that telephone callers can listen to by calling 503-620-3000. The system is sponsored by the Oregon State **Bar**.

Telegraph. Oregon's first wire link to the east coast came via the completion of the telegraph system between **Portland** and California on March 1, 1864, an occasion marked by a message from the mayor of Portland to the mayor of Portland, Maine. Local telegraph service had been introduced in Portland in 1854. Dictionary of Oregon History. See also **Transcontinental connections**.

Telephone. In 1996 Oregon had 5 major telephone companies providing local service, each fully regulated by the state **Public Utility Commission**. Complaints about phone service can be filed with the commission at 800-522-2404. There were also 19 smaller, partially-regulated companies and 11 unregulated telephone cooperatives. The state's 250 long-distance services are not state regulated. In 1994 gross operating revenues totaled $1,151 million from 1.6 million access lines. US West accounted for 63% of revenues, and GTE Northwest for 24%. Oregon Utility Statistics. See also **Communication networks**; **Fiber optics**.

Telephone history. **Portland**'s first telephone service began on August 7, 1878, with teen-aged boys as the operators. Local exchanges opened in **Astoria** and **Salem** in 1884, **Pendleton** in 1889, and in other cities soon after. In 1898 service was established to San Francisco where the first transcontinental long distance call was made in 1915. Dictionary of Oregon History; Proud of Our Past; This Day in Oregon.

Television. Thirteen Oregon cities have one or more commercial and/or public television stations: **Beaverton** (1), **Bend** (3), **Brookings** (1), **Coos Bay** (2), **Corvallis** (1), **Eugene** (5), **Klamath Falls** (2), **La Grande** (1), **Medford** (5), **Ontario** (1), **Portland** (8), **Roseburg** (3), and **Salem** (1). The public stations are in Bend, Corvallis, La Grande, Medford, Ontario, and Portland. Television arrived in Oregon in 1952 when KPTV went on the air, making **Portland** the last major city in the U.S. to have a television station. Oregon Blue Book.

Temperance. Moderation in, or abstinence from, the use of alcoholic beverages has been promoted in Oregon since the first **Methodist missionaries** arrived in 1834. The **Portland** Washingtonian Total Abstinence Society met for the first time in 1851. Women crusaders invaded saloons in Portland in 1874. The Women's Christian Temperance Union (W.C.T.U.) founded the **Children's Farm Home**. This Day in Oregon. See also **Prohibition**.

Temperature. Temperatures in Oregon are moderate along the coast and increase in range with distance from the coast and with elevation. **Brookings** on the southwest coast has the mildest climate; its monthly mean minima range through the year from $36°F$ to $53°F$, and maxima range from $48°F$ to $69°F$. **Portland**'s monthly mean minima range from $34°F$ to $57°F$ and maxima from $45°F$ to $80°F$, while at **Baker City** in northeast Oregon monthly mean minima range from $17°F$ to $49°F$ and maxima from $34°F$ to $85°F$. See also **Cold**, **Heat**.

Temperature changes. One of Oregon's most sudden temperature changes occurred in **Heppner** on December 11, 1995 when, beginning at 4:30 p.m., the temperature dropped $20°F$ in four minutes. In western Oregon dramatic temperature changes occurred during February 1995, February 1990, and, most notably, in December 1919, when unseasonably warm weather was followed suddenly, beginning on December 9, by eight days in the low teens and 15" of snow - but by Christmas temperatures were back in the 50s. Oregonian 2/18/95:A1.

Temperature inversions. See **Inversions**.

Temperature records. The lowest temperature officially recorded in Oregon is -54°F (-48°C), recorded on February 9, 1933 in **Ukiah** and on the next day at **Seneca**. Residents of **Meacham** claim an unofficial record of -62°F in the 1920s. The highest temperature recorded in Oregon is 119°F, from **Prineville** on July 29, 1898 and **Pendleton** on August 10, 1938. Oregon Blue Book. See also **Cold spells**; **Heat**.

Tenino Indians. See **Warm Springs Indians**.

Tenmile Lake and **North Tenmile Lake**. Two natural, multi-armed lakes near the coast south of **Reedsport**. They are linked by a 1/2 mile navigable canal, widened in 1997 from 28 to 50 feet. The town of **Lakeside** lies between them with docks and a public launch on Tenmile Lake. Tenmile Lake covers 1,627 acres and North Tenmile Lake covers 1,098 acres. Each has arms stretching at least four miles from Lakeside, and each has a maximum depth of about 22 feet. They are among the most popular lakes in the state for boating and fishing, though the fishery has had a complex history. Private land and homes surround the lakes; the only public access is the Lakeside boat launch. Tenmile was the name given to the creek that drains Tenmile Lake to the ocean because early settlers estimated it to be ten miles from the settlement of **Winchester Bay**. Atlas of Oregon Lakes.

Term limits. Oregon's **Governor**, **Secretary of State**, and **Treasurer** each serve four-year terms, and each is limited by the original state **constitution** to serving eight years in any twelve years (1859). In 1992 voters adopted an amendment to the state constitution (Art. II, Sec. 19) that limits all statewide elected officials, except **judges**, to a lifetime total of eight years in each office. This includes **Attorney General**, **Commissioner of Labor and Industries**, and **Superintendent of Public Instruction**. Under the 1992 amendment, Oregon **senators** have a lifetime limit of eight years, and **Oregon representatives** have a lifetime limit of six years; total service in the Oregon **legislature** is limited to twelve years. Only terms of service beginning after December 3, 1992, are counted in the limits. The limits for state legislators are being challenged in court, and in 1995 the U.S. Supreme Court struck down limits that Oregon voters had set in 1992 for its **U.S. senators** (12 years) and **U.S. representatives** (6 years).

Terraces. Old shorelines marked by deposits of sand and gravel 20 to 50 feet thick, occur along the **coast** between **Coos Bay** and **Port Orford**. Some of the more recent coastal terraces are obvious, such as Pioneer Terrace (103,000 years old) along which **Highway 101** is located. However, others are higher, older, and more eroded. Terrace development was complex, reflecting varying rates of coastal uplift, fluctuating sea levels, deformation, faulting, and erosion. Terraces created by wave action are also visible around several of Oregon's vanished **Pleistocene lakes**. Geology of Oregon.

Terrane. A group of rocks, bounded by fault surfaces, that has been displaced from its point of origin. Each group has its own layered sequence of rocks and **fossils** by which it is recognized. Oregon has been the site of multiple collisions with ocean islands, large and small, that rafted to Oregon on the oceanic plates and were accreted to North America. It is estimated that two-thirds of the state is composed of rocks and sediments that originated elsewhere in the Pacific basin. The **Blue** and **Klamath Mountains** have especially complex accumulated terranes. <u>Geology of Oregon</u>. See also **Siletz terrane.**

Territorial government, 1849-1859. During the ten-year duration of the **Oregon Territory**, residents were frustrated by their lack of influence on U.S. policy (the territory had a single, non-voting delegate to Congress) and by Presidential appointments of outsiders, some of them corrupt, as territorial judges and officials. Strident political discord in the territorial legislature and the local newspapers swirled around land laws, political appointments, and the location of the **capital**. Following the Dred Scott decision that denied the right of territories to decide for themselves whether they wished to be slave or free, outraged Oregonians decided that they would control their own destinies and finally, after having defeated the measure in three previous attempts, voted in 1857 for a constitutional convention and **statehood**. Politics in Congress were such, however, that it was not until February 14, 1859, that Oregon was admitted as a state. <u>Dictionary of Oregon History</u>; <u>Empire of the Columbia</u>. See also **Constitution; Donation Land Act of 1850; Rogue River War; Oregon Question; Oregon Style; Organic laws; Salem Clique.**

Territorial Sea. See **Exclusive Economic Zone.**

Territory of Oregon. See **Oregon Territory; Territorial government**.

Terry D. Schrunk Plaza. See **Plaza Blocks; Suzhou stone.**

The Capes. A high-end gated subdivision built in the 1990s on a 150-foot-high sand bluff above the beach near Oceanside, west of **Tillamook**. In the winter of 1997-98 winter storms eroded away the protecting basal dune and the bluff began to fall away, threatening 32 townhomes. The residents' request to place riprap rock along the base, illegal under Oregon law, was denied by **Tillamook County** and the governor. <u>Oregonian</u> 2/22/98:C1. See also **Beaches - geology.**

The Dalles. A historic **Columbia River** city 81 miles east of **Portland** on **Interstate 84**. It is the county seat of **Wasco County**. The area around **The Dalles of the Columbia River** was long a center of Indian fishing, settlement and trade. In 1838 **Methodists** established the **Wascopam** Mission, and the military operated Fort Dalles from 1850 to 1868. The first post office, called Dalles, was established in 1851. In 1853 the name was changed to Wascopum, and in 1860 it was changed to The Dalles. The city was incorporated in 1857. It was an important river shipping point and supply center for the **gold rushes** of eastern Oregon and Idaho. Attractions include the **Gorge Discovery Center, Oregon Trail** Living History Park, Wasco County Historical Museum, 1850 **Fort Dalles** Museum, 1859 Wasco County Courthouse, St. Peter's Landmark (an 1897 Gothic church), art center, and children's museum. Population 1980 10,820; 1995 11,355. Elevation 98'. 313 Court St., 97058. 541-296-5481. Visitors Bureau 800-255-3385. <u>Oregon Geographic Names</u>.

The Dalles Canal and Locks. An 8 1/2 mile canal with five **locks**, each with eight-foot lift, on the **Columbia River,** completed in 1915 by the **Army Corps of Engineers**. It replaced a 13-mile portage railroad around **The Dalles of the Columbia River**, including **Celilo Falls**. Very little commercial traffic actually used the **locks** until after completion of **Bonneville Lock** in 1938. After the reservoir behind **The Dalles Dam** flooded the canal and locks in 1957, traffic was routed through a new single lock that has a maximum lift of 87.5', is 675' long and 86' wide, and is 15' deep over the sills. <u>Army Engineers</u>; <u>Oregon Historical Quarterly</u> 16(2): entire issue, June 1915.

The Dalles Dam. A dam on the **Columbia River** completed in 1957 by the **Army Corps of Engineers** for power generation and navigation. It is two miles east of **The Dalles** and 45 miles upstream from **Bonneville Dam**. The L-shaped structure includes a 1,380-foot spillway across the river and a 2,089-foot-long powerhouse parallel to the shore. Generating capacity was increased in 1973 to the present total of 1,819.7 **megawatts**. The dam and generators are operated by the Corps, while **Bonneville Power Administration** distributes the power. Lake Celilo, formed by the dam, extends 24 miles upstream to **John Day Dam**. The lake covered **The Dalles Canal and Locks** as well as **Celilo Falls** and necessitated moving a nearby ancient Indian community. The Corps operates a number of recreation facilities and campgrounds along the lake. PO Box 564, The Dalles 97058-9998. <u>Army Engineers</u>.

The Dalles Military Wagon Road. A **military wagon road** authorized to go from **The Dalles** to Fort Boise in Idaho by way of **Canyon City**. A private company built a minimal roadway along the heavily used 180-mile route from The Dalles to the gold camps of Canyon City, but the rest of the route to Fort Boise was never constructed. Despite this, Governor Woods attested in 1869 that he had examined the road and it was completed, thus clearing the way for the company to receive a Congressional **land grant** of 556,627 (or 592,558; sources vary) acres located in the odd numbered **sections** for three miles on each side of the route. The Eastern Oregon Land Company ended up with much of the land. <u>Dictionary of Oregon History</u>; <u>Historical Oregon</u>; <u>In the Ruts</u>; <u>Oregon Ghost Towns</u>; <u>Pioneer Roads</u>. See also **Kam Wah Chung**.

The Dalles of the Columbia River. A swift and turbulent eight-mile stretch of the Columbia that contained three major impediments to navigation: **Celilo Falls**, the Little Narrows or Ten Mile Rapids, and the Long Narrows, also called The Dalles or Five Mile Rapids (which ended in the Big Eddy.) A number of craft managed to negotiate the run downstream at high water. The entire stretch is now under Lake Celilo behind **The Dalles Dam**. The river above the falls was called the Upper Columbia, while the 40 miles of river downstream to the **Cascades of the Columbia** (Bonneville) was known as the Middle Columbia. The Dalles/ Celilo area was an important Indian fishing and trading center with 11,000 years of continuous occupation. Since all river travelers had to portage, the resident Indians collected tolls from those passing through. A later railroad portage served until completion in 1915 of the 8.5-mile-long **The Dalles Canal and Locks**. Fur-trading voyageurs used the word "dalles" to describe a river flowing swiftly through a narrow channel. The later names of Five and Ten Mile Rapids marked distances from the city of **The Dalles**. <u>Blow for the Landing</u>; <u>Dictionary of Oregon History</u>; <u>Oregon Geographic Names</u>; "Wishram."

The Island. A distinctive high, flat, steep-sided point between the **Crooked River** and the **Deschutes River** that rises 900 feet above the canyon floor and 450 feet above the waters of **Lake Billy Chinook**. Pioneers called it the "Plains of Abraham," and some call it Cove Island. The lava-flow ridge is a remnant of the last lava flows from Horse Butte, near **Newberry Volcano**. A lower section connects it on the south to a broader plain known as The Peninsula. Due to overuse, the **Bureau of Land Management** now permits only research or educational access to the area. A similar formation north of the Warm Springs River and east of Highway 26 is also called The Island. Geology of Oregon.

Theater. Theater in Oregon is anchored by one of the nation's largest repertory companies, the **Oregon Shakespeare Festival** in **Ashland**, and by **Portland**'s two major Equity companies, **Portland Center Stage** and **Portland Repertory Theatre.** The first known theatrical performance in the Oregon country, "Three Weeks of Marriage," was presented by the crew of a British sloop at **Fort Vancouver** on February 19, 1846. The first theater built in Oregon opened in Portland on November 23, 1858, presenting "Honeymoon" and "Betsy Baker." Dictionary of Oregon History; This Day in Oregon. See also **Artists Repertory Theatre; Children's theater; Imago; Northwest Service Center; Portland Area Theatre Alliance.**

Think tanks. See **Cascade Policy Institute; Oregon Center for Public Policy.**

Third party candidates. In 1990, the **Oregon Citizen's Alliance** candidate Al Mobley got 13% of the vote for governor, which probably altered the outcome of the election. In 1992 Ross Perot's American Party qualified as a major political party when Perot polled 24%, well over the required 20% (now 15%) of the vote. Four years later, in 1996, Perot polled 11%. Governing Oregon. See also **Political parties; Voter registration.**

Thompson Valley Reservoir. A large irrigation impoundment located 32 miles northwest of **Paisley** in **Lake County.** At full pool it covers 1,800 acres and is 22 feet deep. However, by September it may be nearly dry because of irrigation drawdown. The lake was constructed about 1930 for the Silver Lake Irrigation District. There are two campgrounds in the pine forests around the lake, but recreation use is light. Atlas of Oregon Lakes.

Threatened species. See **Endangered species.**

Three Capes Scenic Loop. A 38-mile loop west from **Tillamook** past the locale of **Bayocean,** south over **Cape Meares,** past Netarts Bay, **Cape Lookout,** sand **dunes,** Sand Lake, and **Cape Kiwanda** to **Pacific City,** and back to **Highway 101,** 25 miles south of Tillamook.

Three Fingered Jack. A 7,841' craggy peak in the central **Cascade Range,** south of **Mount Jefferson** and north of **Mount Washington.** It lies within the Mount Jefferson Wilderness, and is drained by the **Metolius River** on the east and the North **Santiam River** on the west. Origin of the name is uncertain, though the summit has three rock spires. It was first climbed in 1923.

Three Forks. A remote basin in the **Owyhee Canyons** near the Idaho border in the southeast corner of the state. There the North and Middle Fork join the **Owyhee River** which continues north through a deep canyon.

Three Sisters. Three major volcanic peaks in the central Oregon **Cascade Range.** Known in the 1840s as Faith, Hope, and Charity, the peaks are now known as **North Sister** (10,085'), **Middle Sister** (10,047'), and **South Sister** (10,358'). **Broken Top** (9,152') to the southeast, completes the group. They lie some 45 miles east of **Bend,** in the Three Sisters Wilderness Area.

Three Sisters Wilderness Area. A 287,000-acre wilderness area in the **Deschutes** and **Willamette National Forests**. It is extended to the south by the Waldo Lake Wilderness and to the north by the Mount Washington Wilderness. The area includes the three volcanic peaks of the Three Sisters, each over 10,000 feet high, with snow fields and lava flows, and numerous small lakes in the central and southern parts of the area. The **old growth** forests of **French Pete** Creek were incorporated into the west side in 1978.

Thrifty PayLess. A chain of drug stores that was the second-largest Oregon-based public **corporation** until it was acquired by Rite Aid Corporation in late 1996. Thrifty, with 35,500 employees, was listed on the Fortune 500 list as having sales of $4.8 billion in 1996. PayLess began as a single drugstore in La Grande in 1939. 9275 SW Peyton Lane, Wilsonville 97070-9200. 503-682-4100. Oregonian 4/9/96:B14, 10/15/96:B16.

Thundereggs. Agate-filled round geodes found as knobby brown balls, which, when cut in half, often reveal star-shaped designs, crystals, plumes, zeolites, or banding, all in a variety of colors. Thundereggs are usually about the size of tennis-balls, though they may range in size from less than an inch to over 3 feet in diameter. The largest known, 5 x 4 feet and estimated to weigh 3,500 pounds, was found near **Maupin** in 1970 and is on display on the state **capitol** grounds in **Salem**. Thundereggs are found at a number of localities in Oregon and elsewhere, especially in light-colored volcanic ash such as the **John Day Formation**. Geologists do not agree on the processes forming them. In 1965 the thunderegg was designated Oregon's **state rock**. Gemstones of North America; Oregon's Heritage: Thundereggs. See also **Nyssa**.

Tidal waves. See **Tsunamis**.

Tide pools. Pools of sea water that persist in rock or sand basins between high and low tides. They support a unique array of life, much of which has been destroyed by thoughtless collecting. An old rock quarry on **Yaquina Head** north of **Newport** has been converted into a handicapped-accessible tide pool by the **Bureau of Land Management**.

Tidelands. Oregon's 500,000 acres of tidelands (those lands lying between high and low tide except along the sea shore) were, under the U.S. Constitution, the property of the state rather than of the federal government. In 1872 the state legislature provided for the sale of tidelands. However, in an earlier confusion, the federal government had already awarded some settlers title to tidelands, a problem addressed by an 1885 law. History of Oregon Land Grants. See also **Wetlands**.

Tides. Tides along the Oregon coast range from highs of nearly 10 feet to lows of minus 2 feet, for a maximum difference of about 12 feet. They are highest in December when the sun is closest to the earth. "Spring tides," tides with the greatest difference between high and low, occur around the time of the new moon and full moon, while "neap tides," those with the least difference, occur in between. Since a full tidal cycle is about 12 and a half hours long, there are usually two high and two low tides a day. Tide tables are available from sporting goods stores and are also printed in many western Oregon newspapers. Since tides vary in both height and time from place to place along the coast (tides at **Coos Bay** are 23 to 30 minutes earlier than those on the **Columbia River**), correction tables are usually published along with the tide tables. Oregon Oceanbook. See also **Rip current**; **Tsunami waves**.

Tidewater. In Oregon usage, the head of tide; the place on a river that is the most upstream spot at which the effects of ocean tides can be discerned. The tide affects some of the coastal rivers for 20 to 30 miles inland, the **Columbia River** up to **Bonneville Dam**, and the **Willamette River** up to **Willamette Falls**.

Tigard. A fast-growing suburban city in **Washington County** nine miles southwest of **Portland**. It was first called Tigardville for Wilson Tigard who settled there in 1852. The city was incorporated in 1961. Population 1980 14,799; 1995 35,000. Elevation 169'. 13125 SW Hall Blvd., 97223. 503-639-4171. Oregon Geographic Names.

Til Taylor statue. A 1929, life-sized statue in **Pendleton** of legendary Sheriff Til Taylor, mounted on his horse. Taylor was credited with more than 2,500 arrests, brought in 26 of the 28 men who broke out of the **Umatilla County** jail, shot it out with a robber while holding another struggling outlaw with his free hand, and, in 1915, tracked three jail-breakers for 20 miles through the **Blue Mountains** before capturing them single-handedly. He had been sheriff for 18 years when, in 1920, at age 54, he was killed during a jail break. Oregonian 7/23/97:C2.

Tillamook. A northwest Oregon city on **Tillamook Bay** at the junction of Highway 6 and **Highway 101**, the county seat of **Tillamook County**. In the early days it was called Hoquarton, The Landing, or Lincoln before the Tillamook post office was established in 1866, and the city was incorporated in 1891. An arson fire on June 18, 1893, destroyed much of the business district, and the courthouse burned on November 14, 1904. The economy is based on tourism, dairying, and timber. Attractions include the Tillamook **Cheese** Factory, Tillamook Naval Air Station Museum featuring **World War II** aircraft and **blimps** in a huge hangar, Latimer Quilt and Textile Center, Tillamook County Museum, **Munson Creek Falls**, **Three Capes Scenic Loop**, and outdoor sports and recreation including fishing, crabbing, and clamming. The Tillamook County **Rodeo** is held on the last weekend in June, the Bayberry Faire in July, and the Tillamook County Fair in August. Population 1980 3,991; 1995 4,245. Elevation 22'. 210 Laurel Ave., 97141. 503-842-2472. Chamber of Commerce 503-842-7525. Tillamook.

Tillamook Bay. A large bay on the north Oregon coast into which Miami Creek and Kilchis, **Wilson**, **Trask**, and Tillamook rivers drain. The Tillamook River is one of five rivers designated for **coho salmon** habitat restoration. In recent years cooperative efforts have controlled contamination from dairy farm manure that earlier had damaged **oyster** harvesting, and the National Estuary Program operates a cleanup program. **Jetties** now help maintain channel to the ocean for fishing boats, but when the bay was sighted by Captain John Meares on July 6, 1788 he recorded that a sand bar closed its mouth and named it Quicksand Bay. However, a month later, on August 14, the American Captain Robert Gray, on his voyage around the world in the *Lady Washington* , entered the bay in what is thought to be the first landing by Europeans in Oregon. Grays cabin boy was killed by Indians after he and some others had gone ashore, prompting Gray to name it Murderers Harbour. Tillamook. See also **Bay Ocean**; **Jetties**; *Morning Star of Tillamook*.

Tillamook Bay Community College Service District. A public two-year college founded by **Tillamook County** voters in 1981. In fall 1996 enrollment was 1,063. It offers a full range of community college programs including a complete two-year transfer program. 6385 Tillamook Ave., Bay City 97107-9641. 503-842-8222. Oregon Blue Book. See also **Community colleges; Small Business Development Centers**.

Tillamook Burn. A rugged area in the north Oregon **Coast Range** that was burned and partially reburned by major forest fires in 1933, 1939, and 1945, and by a smaller fire in 1951. The 1933 fire started on August 14. In 10 days the fire burned 40,000 acres, but then exploded in a giant firestorm that, in just 20 hours, burned an additional 200,000 acres and over 11 billion board feet of finest timber. The mushroom cloud of smoke and ash rose to 40,000 feet and was visible in Montana; ash fell on ships 400 miles at sea and was two feet deep on the streets of **Tillamook**. The fires burned and reburned a total of 355,000 acres, killing, in all, 13 billion board feet of timber; of that, 7.5 billion board feet was salvaged. One firefighter died in the 1933 fire, and another in the 1951 burn. In 1948 Oregon voters authorized a $13 million bond issue to pay for reforestation. Although 99% of the reforestation was done by contract laborers and prison inmates, 25,000 school children and other volunteers also planted trees on the burn, and the rehabilitation program, completed in 1973, used helicopters for the first time for forest work. Much of the area is now in the **Tillamook State Forest**. Tillamook Burn Country.

Tillamook County. "Tillamook, the Land of Trees, Cheese, and Ocean Breeze." A county on the north coast, created in 1853 from portions of Clatsop and Yamhill counties. The name was that of the local Indian tribe, and is said to mean "land of many waters." Incorporated cities are **Tillamook** (county seat), **Bay City, Garibaldi, Manzanita, Nehalem, Rockaway Beach**, and **Wheeler**. The county is bounded by the Pacific Ocean on the west, and by **Clatsop, Washington, Yamhill, Polk**, and **Lincoln** counties. Elevations range from sea level to 3,226' Kings Mountain in the **Coast Range**. The first white settler, Joe Champion, arrived in 1851 and lived in a hollow spruce tree he called his castle. The area was long isolated by rugged mountains and treacherous bays until the railroad arrived in 1911. Swiss settlers began the now-famous dairying and **cheese** making; the county now has 23,000 cows, nearly one cow per person. Timber, fishing, and tourism are also important to the economy. Taxable assessed value in 1995 was $2,119,000,000, or $91,000 per capita. Population 1980 21,164; 1995 23,300. Area 1,125 square miles. Density 21/sq.mi. Annual precipitation 91"; average temperature January $42°$F, July $58°$F. Courthouse, 201 Laurel Ave, Tillamook 97141. 503-842-3403. Oregon Blue Book; Tillamook. See also **Blimps**; *Morning Star of Tillamook*.

Tillamook Head. A promontory on the north Oregon coast 20 miles south of **Astoria** between **Seaside** and **Cannon Beach** that rises to 1,136'. Captain William Clark of the **Lewis and Clark expedition** crossed the point January 7, 1806 on his way to view a beached whale to the south. The point at the top where he commented on the fine view is known as Clarks Point of View, and the stream to the south where the whale lay he named Ecola (**Chinook jargon** for whale) Creek. The Tillamooks were the local Indian tribe. Oregon Geographic Names.

Tillamook Rock Lighthouse. An inactive **lighthouse** on an offshore rock located in turbulent ocean waters one mile off **Tillamook Head**. It can be seen from **Seaside** and **Cannon Beach**. The light was put into service in 1881 after a harrowing construction effort and the death of a surveyor who was swept from the rock by a wave. The building is 62' high, and the light is 133' above the water. Waves smashed the lens in 1934 and storms have sent rocks crashing through the glass, leading to its nickname, Terrible Tilly. The **Coast Guard** abandoned the light in 1957, and the lighthouse is now a privately owned columbarium, used for storing ashes of the dead. Oregon Lighthouses; Oregon's Seacoast Lighthouses.

Tillamook State Forest. Oregon's largest **state forest**, 364,000 acres in size, covering much of **Tillamook County** and parts of **Washington County**. Established in 1973, it is comprised of **Board of Forestry Lands** administered by the **Oregon Department of Forestry**. After the **Tillamook Burn**, 255,000 acres came into state ownership when private landowners stopped paying taxes on their devastated lands. Reforestation was paid for by Oregon taxpayers who narrowly authorized $13 million in bonds for the purpose. Revenues from forest harvests after the year 2000 are expected to be about $100 million a year; by law, 2/3 of this revenue is to be returned to Tillamook and Washington counties for distribution to local governments and school districts. ODF Tillamook District Office, 4907 E. 3rd Street, Tillamook 97141-2999; ODF Forest Grove District Office, 801 Gales Creek Road, Forest Grove 97116-1199. 503-357-2191. Oregonian 7/1/97:C11; Tillamook Burn to Tillamook State Forest.

Tilth. See **Oregon Tilth**.

Timber and Stone Act of 1878. A federal law that allowed ranchers to purchase 160 acres of non-arable **public domain** land at $2.50 an acre in order to provide timber and stone for construction. Few took advantage of the act until the early 1900s when timber interests paid the way for trainloads of "entrymen" to come from the East. The entrymen applied for land claims, which were then illegally transferred to the timber companies. The resulting **land fraud** cases attracted national attention. The practice came to an end after forest reserves (which later became **national forests**) were placed with the U.S. Department of Agriculture and withdrawn from entry in 1905, but by then 3,812,303 acres had been transferred to private ownership. Disposition; East of the Cascades. See also **Land grants**.

Timber Carnivals. See **Albany World Championship Timber Carnival**; **Estacada Timber Festival**.

Timber Culture Act of 1873. A federal act that provided that a person could claim **public domain** lands by planting the land with at least 2,700 trees per acre (a tree every four feet). The act was repealed in 1891. Circular. See also **Land grants**.

Timber harvest. About 570 billion **board feet** of timber have been harvested in Oregon since white settlement. Oregon's highest timber harvest, in 1952, was 9.8 billion board feet. The annual average between 1883-87 was 8 billion board feet, 4.3 from federal land and 3.7 from non-federal land. The forecast for total annual harvests through 2001 is about 4.2 billion board feet. In 1995 4.3 billion board feet were harvested, enough to build over 500,000 three-bedroom homes. Of that, industrial forest lands supplied 2.7 billion board feet, or nearly two thirds of the total, while **National Forests** supplied 515 million board feet, **Bureau of Land Management** 139 million, **state forests** 109 million, Bureau of Indian Affairs 79 million, city and county forests 30 million, and small woodlands 703 million board feet. An estimated 1.6 billion board feet is lost annually to insects and disease. Legacy and Promise; Oregon Economic and Revenue Forecast; Oregonian 10/23/96:C6. See also **Forest products industry**; **Logging history**; **Lumber production, history**; **Northwest Forest Conference**.

Timber industry. See **Forest products industry**.

Timber rider. See **Salvage rider**.

Timber Summit. See **Northwest Forest Conference**.

Timber supply. As of 1992, standing timber in Oregon totaled 205 billion board feet, down 28% from 1952 due to the replacement of logged large **old growth** trees with young reforestation. 85 billion board feet of the total, growing at 3 billion board feet per year, is on nonfederal **timberlands**, and 120 billion board feet, growing at 2.4 billion board feet per year, is on higher, less-productive federal lands. A 1989 study reported that Oregon's forests have the capacity to produce a sustainable harvest level for the next 100 years of 7.5 billion board feet per year (3.8 billion from federal lands and 3.7 from state and private lands). However, various restrictions may reduce **timber harvest** to 4.5 billion board feet or less. Hard Times in Paradise; Legacy and Promise; Oregon Economic and Revenue Forecast.

Timber workers. In 1972 one of every 11 workers made a living directly from the timber industry. By 1995 one of every 26 nonagricultural workers worked in lumber and wood products, and by the year 2000 the ratio is expected to be one in 33. Fire at Eden's Gate; Oregon Economic and Revenue Forecast. See also **Company town**; **Forest products industry**.

Timberland. Land capable of annually producing 20 cubic feet or more of industrial wood per acre. Forests west of the **Cascade Range** average 147 cubic feet of growth per year. Timberlands account for 21.9 million acres, or 79%, of Oregon's **forest lands**. However, only 60% of the timberland is available for full-yield timber production because of set-asides for **wilderness areas**, wildlife habitat, **riparian areas**, research, and other such uses. Oregon's Forests.

Timberline Lodge. A massive, Cascadian-style stone and timber building at the 6,000-foot-level on the south side of **Mount Hood** that opened on February 4, 1938, two years after the first drawings. It had been dedicated on September 28, 1937, by President Franklin Roosevelt. A team of architects designed the building, and the Works Progress Administration built it and hired the crafts workers who designed and created the handmade furnishings and decorations. The decaying building was saved when Richard Kohnstamm reopened it in 1955. Volunteers led an effort to refurbish the lodge for its 40th anniversary. Great Lodges; Timberline Lodge.

Timberline Ski Area. A ski area on **Mount Hood** six miles north of Government Camp, 60 miles east of **Portland**. Six chair lifts serve the area which drops 3,590 vertical feet from its top elevation of 8,540'. It is Oregon's highest ski area and the only one offering summer skiing. Timberline Lodge 97028. 503-231-

7979; snow conditions 503-222-2211. Oregonian 11/16/97:T7. The Magic Mile chair lift, opened in 1939 (later replaced), was the second in the country. From January 3, 1951 to January 2, 1956, an aerial tramway carried skiers the three miles between **Government Camp** and **Timberline Ski Area**. Its two cars (actually buses) could each carry 24 people.

Time Traveler. A $30 million theme park proposed to open in 1998. Euro Center Productions Limited plans to build it someplace in the Pacific Northwest, possibly in the **Portland** area, using private financing. Oregonian 3/1/96:D1.

Time zones. Time zones were established by the railroads in 1883. Oregon lies within the Pacific Time Zone, except for the area around **Ontario** in northern **Malheur County**, which is in the Mountain Time Zone (one hour ahead of the rest of the state). See also **Daylight saving time**.

Timothy Lake. A reservoir 48 miles southeast of **Portland** formed in 1956 when **Portland General Electric** dammed Oak Grove Fork of the **Clackamas River** for power generation. The lake, which covers 1,282 acres, flooded Timothy Meadows where sheepherders had supplemented the natural grasses by spreading the seed of Timothy grass. The main lake is over a mile across; it has a narrow arm reaching another mile back into the hills. Maximum depth is 80 feet. Since there is no irrigation draw-down, the lake remains popular all summer for fishing; boat speed is limited to 10 miles per hour. There are several campgrounds. Atlas of Oregon Lakes.

Tin Plate Law. A **Portland** city ordinance adopted in response to a famous vice report of 1912 that found that the city had nearly 400 "immoral" places. The ordinance required each building owner to inscribe his name and address on a tin plate and attach it to his building. The intention was to shame the city fathers who owned most of the brothels. They, however, discovered a loophole in that the ordinance did not specify the language, so plates were mounted in everything from Urdu to Hebrew. Portland, An Informal History. See also **Sex industry**.

Tires. See **Cement**; **Les Schwab Tire Centers**; **Studded tires**; **Traction devices**.

Titanium. A strong, light-weight **metal** used in aircraft engines and frames, drilling products, and golf heads. One of the nation's three top producers, Oregon Metallurgical Corporation in **Albany** (bought by Allegheny Teledyne in 1997), has a capacity of over 6,000 metric tons a year. Mineral Industry in Oregon; Oregonian 3/5/96:B14.

Toads. Tailless **amphibians** that differ from **frogs** in having a drier, warty skin, being less aquatic, and, usually, walking instead of hopping. Three species are found in Oregon, the western toad, *Bufo boreas*, which has disappeared from some areas where it was once common, Woodhouse's toad, *B. woodhousii*, along the southeast edge of the state, and the Great Basin spadefoot toad, *Scaphiopus intermontanus*, which has a spade on each hind foot that it uses to dig itself backwards into a burrow. Field Guide to Western Reptiles and Amphibians.

Tobacco. Two species of tobacco, *Nicotiana attenuata* and *N. quadrivalvis* (also called *N. bigelovii*), are native to eastern and southern Oregon. **Indians** of the **Willamette Valley** and the south Oregon coast cultivated them, and also smoked the dried leaves of kinnikinnick, *Arctostaphylos uva-ursi*. Commercial tobacco,

N. tabacum, has been cultivated in western Oregon; in 1865 over 3,400 pounds was raised in **Polk County** alone. Champoeg; Century of Coos and Curry; Handbook of Northwestern Plants; Oregon Oddities. See also **Smoking**.

Toketee (TOE-keh-tee) **Falls**. A two-tiered waterfall on the North Umpqua River that drops 30 feet, then plunges 90 feet over a solid wall of basalt. They are about 60 miles east of **Roseburg** up **Highway 138**. The falls, impressive even though a portion of the river has been diverted through a 12-foot pipeline for power generation, can be seen by hiking .6 mile down the north side of the river from a spur off Road #34. Toketee is the **Chinook jargon** word for graceful. Oregon Geographic Names; Waterfall Lover's Guide. See also **North Umpqua Hydroelectric Project**.

Toledo. A western Oregon city in **Lincoln County**, six miles east of **Newport** on **Highway 20**. The post office, established in 1868, was named for the Ohio hometown of the homesteading John Graham family. Toledo was incorporated in 1905. It was home for many years to the world's largest **Sitka spruce** sawmill, and was the county seat until 1954. A pulp and paper mill is the town's largest employer, but the town is also diversifying into tourism and antiques. Population 1980 3,151; 1995 3,400. Elevation 64'. PO Box 220, 97391. 541-336-2247. Chamber of Commerce 541-336-3183. First One Hundred Years; Pictorial Recollections.

Toledo incident. See **Anti-Japanese sentiment**.

Toll roads. Roads paid for by user fees. Oregon presently has no toll roads, but the 1995 legislature authorized two toll roads to be built and operated by private companies, one a bypass around **Newberg** and **Dundee**, and the other between **Sherwood** and **Tualatin**. The **Barlow Road** was Oregon's first toll road, and during the pioneer period and until the 1920s many other bridges and roads, especially over passes, were privately built and paid for by tolls. The maintenance was usually better than on public roads or **military wagon roads**. The state, itself, has used tolls to pay for bridges but never for roads. South Road. See also **Sherars Bridge**; **Siskiyou Toll Road**.

Tom McCall Preserve. An area in the **Columbia River Gorge** that is noted for its spring wildflower displays. The site, owned by the **Nature Conservancy**, is on the **Columbia River Highway** east of the **Mosier** exit 69 off **Interstate 84**. Bloom begins in March and continues through a changing assortment of flowers until early summer. No dogs are allowed. Oregonian 4/5/95:E2.

Tom McCall Waterfront Park. See **Governor Tom McCall Waterfront Park**.

Tombstone Prairie. A meadow on **Highway 20** just east of Tombstone summit and seven miles west of the junction with **Highway 126**. Its name comes from a tombstone on the south edge of the meadow that bears the inscription "James A., son of J. W. & C. M. McKnight. From an Accidental Shot. Oct. 17, 1871. Aged 18 Y's 9 M's 9 D's," plus eight verses of poetry. Oregon Geographic Names.

Tongue Point. A point that projects into the **Columbia River** just east of **Astoria**. It was named for its shape in 1792 by Lieutenant William Broughton. In the 1920s a submarine base was authorized for the point but never completed. Shortly before **World War II**, the base was redesignated as a U.S. Naval Air Station and rapidly completed by 1940. The station was declared surplus in 1961. A federal Job Corps center was established there in 1965. The state bought North Tongue Point in 1980 as an investment for the **Common School Fund**, but attempts to create a car-importing center came to naught. Oregon Geographic Names; Oregonian 7/4/96:B2. See also *Erria*.

Tornadoes. Oregon usually has about one tornado a year, but few actually touch down or do serious damage. Family stories report that in the early 1870s a devastating windstorm or tornado struck the **St. Paul** area north of **Salem**. On January 15, 1887, a tornado caused heavy damage both west and east of **Cottage Grove**, though a ridge bumped it over the town itself. In north central Oregon a tornado that touched down at **Lexington** on June 14, 1888, left a 20-mile trail of destruction and caused four deaths, and on June 3, 1894, a tornado with winds said to be over 200 mph destroyed homes at **Long Creek** and killed three people. A tornado in April 1972 in the **Portland**-Vancouver area killed six people in Vancouver and caused $5 million of damage. In December 1993 a moderate tornado caused $600,000 damage in Saint Paul. Oregonians have sometimes called tornadoes cyclones. Cottage Grove; Oregonian 9/4/55:16, 4/6/95:D1, 6/3/97:C1; St. Paul. See also **Waterspout**.

Totem poles. Carved poles depicting family lineage or events that were placed before dwellings by some Northwest Indian tribes. No Oregon tribes carved or used totem poles, but several have been placed in Oregon. Notable is a 50-foot totem pole at the **Washington Park Zoo**, carved by Lelooska (1933-1996) in 1959 to celebrate Oregon's role in the scientific study of Antarctica. He also carved a massive pole that is located on Portland's Terwilliger Boulevard. Oregonian 9/6/96:B9.

Tourism. One of Oregon's major industries with visitor spending in 1995 totaling $4.16 billion, up 5.5% from the year before. A third of the money was spent in the **Portland** area. About two-thirds of the state's tourists are Oregonians. The industry employed 65,000 workers, up 33% since 1990, with a payroll of $831.2 million, a 61% increase since 1990. State room tax receipts were $112.7 million, up 67% from 1990. In 1994 expenditures per capita averaged $1,279, but ranged from a low of $465 in **Columbia County** to a high of $8,163 in **Lincoln County**. Foreign tourists spend $96 a day, compared with an average of $84 a day spent by domestic tourists. In 1995, 38,000 German tourists visited Oregon, staying an average of 21 days. Oregon: A Statistical Overview; Oregonian 3/9/96:B1.

Tourism Commission. A commission that works with the Oregon Department of **Economic Development** to promote Oregon as a visitor destination and to encourage increased visitor expenditures in the state. 775 Summer Street NE, Salem 97310. 800-547-7842; 503-986-0000. See also **Travel Information Council**; **Visitors information centers**.

Tourist attractions. In 1994, the most-visited attractions in Oregon were **Multnomah Falls**, 2,000,000 visitors; **Timberline Lodge**, 1,500,000; **D River** Wayside, 1,400,000; **Metro Washington Park Zoo**, 1,000,000; and **Oregon Museum of Science and Industry** (OMSI), 1,000,000. Oregonian 9/6/95:A4.

Towns. See **Cities**.

Township. An area of land six miles by six miles, made up of 36 **sections**, totaling 23,040 **acres**. The sections are numbered boustrophodonically, beginning at the NE corner, west across the top row, east across the row below, west on the next, and so on, back and forth, ending with section 36 in the SE corner. If there were already **Donation Land Claims** in a township at the time it was surveyed, each DLC was given a section number, beginning with section 37, in the order in which they were surveyed. While east/west rows of townships are called townships, north/south columns of townships are called ranges. Every township in Oregon is described with respect to the Willamette Meridian (which runs north/south) and the Willamette Base Line (which runs east/west), all referenced to the **Willamette Stone**. In Oregon, unlike northeastern states, a township is not a governmental unit. History of the Rectangular Survey System. See also **Land description**; **Public Land Survey**.

Toxic pollutants. From 1990-1994 discharges of all types of toxic chemicals in Oregon totaled 2.5 million pounds, including 84,019 pounds of cancer-causing chemicals. Pulp and paper mills were the primary sources with methanol and ammonia making up the bulk of the releases. In 1988 the most common toxic air pollutant was acetaldehyde from field, forest, and heating fires. It was followed by toluene, formaldehyde, pesticides, phenol, benzene, lead, and xylene. Cigarette smoke and asbestos fibers are other airborne pollutants. Oregon Environmental Atlas; Oregonian 9/25/96:D1, 4/30/97:A13. See also **Air pollution**; **Hazardous wastes**; **Pollution**; **Spills**; **Water pollution**.

Toxic spills. See **Spills**.

Toy Hall of Fame. See **A. C. Gilbert's Discovery Village**.

Track. See **Prefontaine Classic**; **Women in sports**.

Traction devices. Oregon law defines traction devices as chains, cable chains or **studded tires**. They may be required during snow conditions on some highways.

Trade offices. Oregon has trade offices in Tokyo, Japan; Seoul, South Korea; and Taipei, Taiwan. Oregon also has contract representatives in Germany and Mexico. The representatives are part of the **Industry Development** office in the Oregon Department of **Economic Development**. Oregonian 7/14/95:C1.

Trading post. A building or cluster of buildings built by fur trading companies as a center where they could trade with **Indians** and other trappers for furs and food. The first in Oregon was **Astoria**. The first in the **Willamette Valley** was the **Pacific Fur Company**'s **Wallace House** near **Salem**, established in 1812. The **Willamette Post** near **Champoeg** was probably established the next year by the **North West Company**. There may have been a post on the **Umpqua River** near the present site of **Roseburg**, and there is some evidence that one was briefly established at the lower end of the **McKenzie River**. The **Hudson's Bay Company** established **Fort Vancouver** in 1825 as their Columbia District headquarters and trading post. In 1836 they built **Fort Umpqua** near the junction of Elk Creek and the **Umpqua River** and maintained it until the 1850s. Champoeg. See also **Fort William**; **Fur trade**.

Traffic. See **Commuting**.

Traffic accidents. Oregon's traffic fatality rates average 1.7 per 100 million vehicle miles traveled, compared to the national average of 1.6. In 1996 there were

53,253 accidents in the state with damage over $500 and 522 deaths, including 29 motorcycle fatalities. Alcohol or drugs were a factor in 41% of the fatal crashes. Oregon's most dangerous stretches of highway include Highway 62 near **Medford**; **Highway 97** through **Deschutes** and **Klamath** counties; **Highway 22** between **Santiam Pass** and the coast; **Highway 126** from **Eugene** to central Oregon; **Highway 101** along the Oregon coast; a 3.4-mile stretch of Highway 238 near **Jacksonville**; a 5.5-mile stretch of Highway 211E near the Clackamas Highway junction; and a 10-mile stretch of **Highway 20** near **Sweet Home**. **Interstate 84** through **Hood River** is one of the 10 safest in the nation. Accidents have not increased so fast as the traffic on the state's highways, many of them built in the 1930s. Oregonian 11/26/95:A20, 8/19/96:A1.

Traffic fines. The state bail amounts in 1996 were $89 for driving 1 to 10 mph over the posted limit, $134 for driving 11 to 20 mph over, $267 for 21 to 30 mph over, and $519 for driving more than 30 mph over the limit. Fines are doubled in work zones and, beginning in 1998, in school zones. Oregonian 1/13/96:A10. See also **Basic rule**; **Speed limits**.

Trail Blazers. An NBA professional basketball team that plays at the **Rose Garden** in **Portland**. On June 5, 1977, the team won the NBA championship over Philadelphia in a home game, and the city erupted in the culminating display of "Blazermania". 503-231-8000. Oregonian 3/30/97:C1. See also **Rip City**.

Trailhead parking passes. The U.S. **Forest Service** sells trailhead parking passes for certain designated trails. The passes, instituted in 1997, must be purchased ahead of time from a Forest Service office, sporting goods store, or other recreational outlet; they are not available at the trailhead. Both day and seasonal passes are available. Oregonian 2/2/98:E2.

Trails. In 1995 there were 8,245 miles of public non-motorized trails in Oregon, 80% of them on **National Forests**. The longest is the **Pacific Crest National Scenic Trail** along the **Cascade Range** between Washington and California. Other trails are partially completed, including the **Oregon Coast Trail** and the Desert Trail, completed from the Nevada border north across **Steens Mountain**. The **Rails to Trails** program creates trails along abandoned railroad right of way. The Oregon **Parks and Recreation Department** coordinates recreational trail programs in the state. Many hiking trails are described in guidebooks and agency publications. Oregon Recreation Trails Plan; Pacific Greenway. See also **Bear Creek Greenway**; **Canopy trail**; **Gin Lin trail**; **Hiking**; **Lost persons**; **Parks**; **Trailhead Parking Passes**; **Willamette River Greenway**.

Trails Club of Oregon. A hiking club that sponsors a variety of hikes year-round. It also owns two lodges. 503-233-2740.

Trails, pioneer. Pioneers used waterways, Indian trails, and animal trails in their travels in Oregon. Many of these routes were later used for **wagon roads** and **highways**. Some of the trails are documented in Pioneer Trails of the Oregon Coast. See also **Oregon Trail**; **Siskiyou Trail**.

Train stations. See **Union Station**.

Train wrecks. One of Oregon's worst train wrecks occurred in 1890 when the trestle over **Lake Labish** collapsed under a south-bound **Southern Pacific** passenger train. Five people were killed and one hundred others were injured. In

December 1884 floods in western Oregon were followed by cold and heavy snow, and a train with 150 passengers was stranded seven miles west of **Hood River** from December18 until January 6. Railroading in Southern Oregon. See also **DeAutremont brothers**.

Tramways. See **Timberline Ski Area; Wallowa Lake Tramway**.

Transcontinental auto race. See **From Hellgate to Portland**.

Transcontinental connections. The first whites to reach Oregon overland were the members of the **Lewis and Clark Expedition** who traveled by horse, boat, and foot to reach the Pacific coast in the winter of 1805-1806. The first overland wagons reached the area in 1841. The first **telegraph** connection to the east coast was completed on March 1, 1864, via California. The first transcontinental **railroad** connection between Oregon and the east was established on September 11, 1883 by the **Oregon Railway and Navigation Company/Northern Pacific**. A second was established on November 11, 1884 with **Union Pacific** through **Huntington**, and a third in 1908 via the **Spokane, Portland and Seattle Railroad**. The first automobiles to reach Oregon overland were participants in the 1905 **From Hellgate to Portland** race.

Transit malls (Portland). Two downtown Portland streets dedicated to pedestrians and public transportation. The areas, Fifth and Sixth avenues north of Madison, were designed in 1975 and feature patterned pavements, plantings, fountains, sculptures, and covered bus stops. Portland, An Informal History. See also **Fareless Square**.

Transmission lines. See **Bonneville Power Authority; Indego; Western Intertie**.

Transportation. 90% of all person-trips to destinations within Oregon are by automobile or truck. Vehicles in the state were driven 27 billion miles in 1990, a number expected to increase to 34 to 44 billion by the year 2010. The state spends 80% of its total transportation capital investment on **highways**. **Public transit** carried 65 million passengers in 1990, and is projected to carry 108 million in 2010. Seventy-six million tons of freight originated in Oregon and was transported a total of 22,200 million ton/miles. Water transport is predominantly on the **Columbia River** and includes ocean-going freighters docking in **Portland** and large barges carrying wheat and other cargo from as far upriver as Lewiston, Idaho. Other deep water **ports** are at **Astoria, Newport,** and **Coos Bay**. Two major **railroads** now serve the state, radiating out from Portland, **Union Pacific** and **Burlington Northern**. Atlas of the Pacific Northwest. See also **Commuting; Pipelines**.

Transportation energy. In 1994 transportation in Oregon used 52.3 million barrels of petroleum products (up from 37.6 million barrels in 1974), and 6 billion cubic feet of **natural gas**. 63% of the petroleum was **gasoline**, 20% diesel fuel, 9% jet fuel, 7% heavy fuel, and the rest was lubricants, LPG, and aviation gasoline. State Energy. See also **Oil**.

Transportation history. The first humans into what is now Oregon are thought to have come by foot over a land bridge from Asia some 10,000 or more years ago. Later visitors arrived by sea, some from **shipwrecks** and some on long voyages of exploration and trade. Meanwhile Indians made good use of their canoeing prowess on rivers and the ocean, and marked the first trails, many later developed by pioneers into **wagon roads**. Horses and boats, especially **steamships**, moved people and freight until the **railroads** were built; the first **transcontinental connection** by rail from Oregon was completed in 1883. After the automobile arrived in **Portland** in 1899, cars, buses, and trucks took over most of the transportation needs of the state and changed the state's development pattern. The first commercial air flight was in 1928. "History of Transportation." See also **Aviation history; Highways, history; Railroads, history**.

Transportation, Oregon Department of (ODOT). The state agency responsible for building and maintaining state highways, roads, and bridges, and for driver and vehicle licensing, motor carriers, aviation, bicycle paths, public transit, rail passenger and freight systems, ports and marine transportation, pipelines, transportation safety, and transportation planning. Some responsibilities are carried out through **Driver and Motor Vehicle Services, Motor Carrier Transportation**, and the **Aeronautics Section**. The five members of the Transportation Commission, appointed by the governor, establish policy. The Department dates from 1913 when the legislature, determined to **"Get Oregon Out of the Mud"**, created the Oregon State Highway Department. 135 Transportation Building, Salem 97310. 503-986-3200. Oregon Blue Book. See also **Highways, history**.

Trappers' Trail. See **Siskiyou Trail**.

Trappist monastery. See **Our Lady of Guadalupe**.

Trask River. An 18-mile long river that drains 176 square miles of the **Coast Range** into **Tillamook Bay** south of the **Wilson River**. It is named for Elbridge Trask of Massachusetts who first came to Oregon in 1834 and later, in 1852, settled in **Tillamook County**. Oregon Geographic Names; Trask (novel).

Travel Information Council. A semi-independent agency, established in 1972, that installs tourist information and business logo signs as well as travel information centers and kiosks along the state's highways. A business pays $200 per exit to have its logo put on freeway signs. The money supports the council which receives no state funding. 229 Madrona Avenue SE, Salem 97302. 503-378-4508. Oregonian 6/16/95:D2. See also **Heritage Tree Program; Historical markers; Tourism**.

Treasure Valley. The irrigated area along the **Snake River** around **Ontario** in northeastern **Malheur County**.

Treasure Valley Community College. A public two-year college located in **Ontario** that has served both Oregon and Idaho residents of the Treasure Valley region of the **Snake River** valley since 1962. The college offers college transfer courses, vocational programs, and community-education programs. Fall 1996 enrollment was 3,007. 650 College Blvd., Ontario OR 97914-3498. 541-889-6493. Oregon Blue Book. See also **Community colleges; Small Business Development Centers**.

Treasurer. An **elected official** who is responsible for all money paid into the state **treasury** and is the state's chief investment officer. The four-year position is filled in the state-wide election held in November of years divisible by four. Salary in 1998 was $67,900 a year. The state treasurer heads the state **treasury** and serves on the **State Land Board**. 159 State Capitol, Salem 97310-0840. 503-378-4329.

<u>Oregon Blue Book</u>. See also **Investment Council**; **Recall**; **Succession**; **Term limits**.

Treasury. A department of Oregon government, headed by the state **treasurer**, that invests the state's trust funds, operates an investment pool for local governments, oversees the issuance and retirement of bonds, receives and deposits all funds acquired by state agencies, and maintains the necessary accounting records. 159 State Capitol, Salem 97310-0840. 503-378-4329. <u>Oregon Blue Book</u>. See also **Investment Council**.

Treaty of Joint Occupancy. See **Joint Occupancy**.

Tree City USA. A program begun in 1976 through which cities can obtain Tree City USA status by adopting a tree ordinance, appointing a commission to advise the city on tree issues, spending $2 per capita on community forestry activities, and holding an **Arbor Day** celebration. In Oregon 27 cities were named Tree Cities in 1995 with **Salem** certified for the 20th straight year. The Oregon Department of **Forestry** administers the program in the state. <u>Forest Log</u> March/April 1996.

Tree farm. A piece of land on which the landowner is growing trees as a crop, whether for Christmas trees or for timber. By state law, trees must be planted after **clear-cutting** so that there are, after five years, at least 200 free-to-grow trees per acre. Much of the lower elevation **forest land** in Oregon is in small, family-owned tree farms. Tree farms that meet stewardship standards may become certified Tree Farms and are also eligible for annual awards. Oregon Tree Farm System, 1701 Liberty Street SE, Salem 97302-5158. 503-588-1813.

Tree houses. A tree-house resort, begun in 1990 near Takilma, south of **Grants Pass**, was the subject of court actions because the owner, Michael Garnier, refused to get building permits and was in violation of zoning laws. One of the tree houses was given an informal stress test in 1997 when 86 people and assorted pets, weighing a total of 11,000 pounds, crowded into it. Garnier let people stay in the tree houses in exchange for buying a special T-shirt for $75 to $125. Garnier had earlier traveled the fair circuit as Dr. Birch's Traveling Medicine Show, selling such items as empty boxes of breakfast cereal called Fantasy Flakes. <u>Mail Tribune</u> 7/25/97:2A, 8/10/97:3B.

Trees. See **Abernethy elm**; **Alder**; **Big trees**; **Cascara**; **Cedar**; **Cottonwood**; **Douglas-fir**; **Fir**; **Hemlock**; **Heritage Tree Program**; **Juniper**; **Larch**; **Madrone**; **Maple**; **Mistletoe**; **Oak**; **Oregon-myrtle**; **Pine**; **Redwood**; **Spruce**; **Tree City U.S.A.**; **Yew**.

Trestles. See **Pacific Railway and Navigation Company**.

Tri City. An unincorporated community in **Douglas County** 20 miles south of **Roseburg** on **Interstate 5**. Its name apparently originated with the Tri City School District that includes **Canyonville**, **Myrtle Creek**, and **Riddle**. <u>Oregon Geographic Names</u>.

Tri-county area. The **Portland** metropolitan area of **Multnomah**, **Clackamas**, and **Washington** counties. In 1995 the three counties had 1,305,100 people, or 46% of the state's population, and paid (1994) $1,139 million, or 48.4%, of the state's **income taxes**. <u>Oregonian</u> 4/15/96:B5. See also **Metro**.

Tri-County Metropolitan Transportation District. See **Tri-Met**.

Tri-Met. The popular name for the Tri-County Metropolitan Transportation District of Oregon which operates **buses** and **MAX** light rail in the **Portland** metropolitan area of **Multnomah**, **Washington**, and **Clackamas** counties. It was named America's Best Large Transit Agency in 1989. 4012 SE 17th Avenue, Portland 97202. 503-238-4915. Facts of Life. See also **Transit malls**; **Fareless Square**.

Trials. See **Juries**; **Plea bargaining**.

Triangle Lake. One of the few natural lakes in the **Coast Range**, a triangular lake that formed after a giant landslide blocked Lake Creek 25 miles west of **Junction City**. The lake covers 279 acres, is less than a mile across, and has a maximum depth of 95 feet. It is surrounded by private land except for a small county day-use park that provides public access. The lake is popular for water skiing, swimming, and fishing. Atlas of Oregon Lakes.

Triassic. A geologic period, 200 to 250 million years ago, that came before the **Jurassic** period. The **Paleozoic** era preceded it. During the Triassic, Oregon was still under a deep sea. The North American plate was moving west, opening the Atlantic Ocean, while the Farallon plate under the Pacific was moving east, carrying long chains of islands on it. Over millions of years, a series of these archipelagos collided with the mainland and some of these are now the **Blue** and **Klamath Mountains**. Triassic **fossils** include coral reefs and huge fish-like reptiles called ichthyosaurs. Geology of Oregon.

Trillium. A foot-high plant of the forest floor. The western trillium, *Trillium ovatum*, is a favorite wild flower and is often used as a symbol and name for Oregon products. Its three white petals appear above the three green leaves in early spring. If the leaves are picked the plant will be unable to make food for next year's bloom. There are several other species of trilliums in the state; one in northeast Oregon has dark red flowers. Wildflowers of the West.

Triple Falls. A segmented waterfall in **Oneonta Gorge**, estimated to be at least 100 feet high, that is split into three ribbons, hence the name. The falls can be reached by hiking 1.7 miles up Oneonta Trail. Waterfall Lover's Guide.

Trojan nuclear power plant. Oregon's only nuclear power plant, now closed, operated for 16 years from May 1976 until November 1992 on the banks of the **Columbia River** near **Rainier**, 42 miles downstream from **Portland**. Its looming, 499-foot-tall, flaring cooling tower remains as a notable landmark. **Portland General Electric** built the 1,130 **megawatt** plant and **Eugene Water and Electric Board** owned 30%. The closed plant has been put to other uses as a facility to manufacture products used in cleaning up hazardous waste and air pollution and as a science education center. The Facility Regulation Division of the Oregon Department of **Energy** oversees its decommissioning.

Trolleys. See **Electric railways**; **Streetcars**.

Trout. Fish of the **salmon** family, though usually smaller than salmon, that live in cool, clear, fresh water. Two species of native trout, rainbow, *Oncorhynchus mykiss*, and cutthroat, *Salmo clarki*, are found in Oregon. Lahontan cutthroat trout and Umpqua River cutthroat trout have been declared as **endangered species**. Redband trout are rainbow trout found east of the Cascade crest; some have adapted to desert streams where water temperatures are up to 83° F. **Steelhead** are rainbow trout that have spent one or more years in the ocean and then returned to freshwater to spawn. Cutthroat trout may also go to sea. Brown trout, *S. trutta*, and Atlantic salmon, *S. salar*, have been introduced, as have several fish of the Char family, genus *Salvelinus,* including brook trout and Mackinaw or lake trout. Char have smaller scales and lighter spots than native trout, and have no teeth in the roof of the mouth. Bull trout (Dolly Varden) is an **endangered** native char, thriving in 40°F water which is too cold for other fish. The golden trout, *Oncorhynchus aguabonita*, has been introduced from the Sierra. Oregon trout records are 36 lb. 8 oz. for Mackinaw, 28 lb. for rainbow; 27 lb. 12 oz. for brown; 23 lb. 2 oz. for bull; 9 lb. 6 oz. for brook; 7 lb. 10 oz. for golden; and 6 lb. 4 oz. for sea-run cutthroat. Trout fishing season opens at many lakes in late April and on streams in late May. For years many small-town Oregon businesses closed for the opening of trout fishing season. Trout worth $970,000 are being raised commercially on fish farms in Oregon. Fishing in Oregon; Great Northwest Nature Factbook; Oregonian 12/26/94:A1, 7/10/95:A1, 5/23/96:D9.

Trout Creek Mountains. Mountains that rise 4,500 feet from the desert in the southeast corner of **Harney County**. The highest point, 8,506', is Orevada View in Nevada. Open grassy plateaus with patches of mountain mahogany are cut by deep canyons lined with aspen and willow. Summer wildflowers can be spectacular. Trout Creek drains to the north into the **Alvord basin**. Oregonian 7/20/95:E1.

Trout farming. Oregon's 37 rainbow **trout** farms sold about $1.2 million worth of trout in 1997 (compared with Idaho's $31 million.) Oregonian 11/7/97:C1.

Troutdale. "Gateway to the Columbia Gorge." A fast-growing **Columbia River** city 17 miles east of **Portland** on **Interstate 84** in **Multnomah County**. It was originally called Sandy when the post office was established in 1854, but about 1880 the post office was reestablished as Troutdale, named by Captain John Harlow for his fish pond. The city was incorporated in 1907. Attractions include **Edgefield**, Columbia Gorge Factory Stores, the annual AeroFair, and the **Columbia Gorge**. Population 1980 5,908; 1995 11,450. Elevation 73'. 104 SE Kibling Av., 97060. 503-665-5175. Oregon Geographic Names. See also **Harlow House**.

Trucking. The trucking industry employs 90,000 people in Oregon, or 1 in 12 workers, according to the Oregon Trucking Association. The truckers move 180 million tons of freight a year, or more than 80% of the total freight moved in the state. Oregonian 12/4/94:L1. See also **Gas tax**; **Motor Carrier Transportation**.

Trucks. In 1995 trucks accounted for over half of the new vehicles sold by Oregon dealers. **Portland**'s Freightliner Corporation (owned by Daimler-Benz) is the country's leading manufacturer of heavy trucks, selling 52,890 trucks in 1995. Oregonian 1/17/96:B14, 3/10/96:F1. See also **Antique Powerland Museum**.

Truffles. Fruiting bodies of fungi that mature under ground. About 300 species are known from Oregon, a few of them choice edibles, including the Oregon white truffle, *Tuber gibbosum*, and the Oregon black truffle, *Picoa carthusiana*. The fungi form symbiotic mycorrhizal relationships with other plants, including forest trees, in which the fungus provides mineral nutrients, water, and protection against toxins and pathogenic fungi, while the plant supplies sugars to the fungus.

Truffles are eaten and the spores dispersed by animals, especially **voles** and **flying squirrels**. North American Truffling Soc., PO Box 296, Corvallis OR 97339. See also **Mushrooms**.

Trump. A small, lyre-shaped musical instrument, also called Jew's-harp, that is played by holding the frame between the teeth and plucking a projecting piece of metal with the fingers. Bill Gohring, one of two makers in America, makes them in his mountain cabin home near **Sumpter**. Jew's-Harp Guild, PO Box 92, Sumpter 97877. Oregonian 4/7/98:E2.

Trumpets. The David G. Monette Corporation in **Portland** makes trumpets for national clients, including the Boston Symphony and Wynton Marsalis. David Monette's inventions include the STC ("Sheldon the Cat") mouthpiece, the $15,000 Raja Samadhi trumpet, and the flumpet, a cross between a trumpet and flugelhorn. Willamette Week 4/12-18/95:38; Oregonian A&E 1/10/97:38.

Tryon Creek State Park. A forested day-use **state park** in southwest **Portland** and **Lake Oswego** off Terwilliger Boulevard. It includes a nature center, 8 miles of hiking trails, 3.5 miles of horse trails, and a 3-mile bike path, plus an all-abilities/barrier-free trail. There are no picnic or camping facilities. 11321 SW Terwilliger Boulevard, Portland 97219. 503-653-3166.

Tsalila. (sah-lee-lah). An Indian name for the **Umpqua River**. A Tsalila Festival was first held in September 1997 in **Reedsport**.

Tsunami waves. A series of ocean **waves**, usually triggered by an **earthquake**, that are sometimes inaccurately called tidal waves. A tsunami can travel up to 600 mph; waves from a **subduction zone** earthquake near the Oregon coast could reach land within five to 30 minutes. On March 27 and 28, 1964, waves nine to ten feet high, generated by a magnitude 9.2 earthquake in Alaska's Prince William Sound, hit the Oregon coast, drowning 4 children who had been sleeping on the beach at **Beverly Beach State Park**, flooding parts of **Cannon Beach** and causing $1 million in property damage in Oregon and $8 million in Crescent City, California, where 11 persons were killed. Coastal marshes preserve evidence of more massive tsunamis associated with large subduction zone earthquakes, such as a 30-foot wave that hit the coast 300 years ago, probably, according to tsunami records in Japan, on January 26, 1700. A Center for the Tsunami Inundation Mapping Effort (TIME) has been established at the **Mark O. Hatfield Marine Science Center** in **Newport**. Maps of the coastal tsunami inundation line designed to discourage major public facilities in areas of danger are available from **Nature of the Northwest**. Property damage from a tsunami may be covered by flood insurance. Oregon Coast 14(5):42 Sept./Oct. 1995; Oregonian 10/22/95:B4.

Tu-tut-ni Indians. See **Chetco Indians**.

Tualatin (two AH lah tin). A rapidly-growing Portland-area residential suburb in **Clackamas** and **Washington Counties** 12 miles south of **Portland**. It is located on the Tualatin River for which it is named. The post office was established in 1869, and the city was incorporated in 1913. The city has hosted an August Tualatin **Crawfish** Festival since 1950. Population 1980 7,483; 1995 18,750. Elevation 123'. PO Box 369, 97062. 503-692-2000. Oregon Geographic Names; Tualatin.

Tualatin Mountain. A 15-mile long timbered ridge between the Tualatin

Valley and the **Willamette River/Multnomah Channel** that extends northwest from **Portland**'s **West Hills**. Skyline Boulevard follows along near the crest, and **Forest Park** covers much of the steep eastern slope. Though it has been heavily logged, the ridge has been a transportation barrier and its unstable soils have created construction problems. One City's Wilderness. See also **Portland geology**.

Tualatin Project. A 1975 project in which the U.S. **Bureau of Reclamation** built and continues to operate **Henry Hagg Lake** plus pumping plants and 86 miles of piped lateral distribution system. The project provides irrigation water, recreation, flood control, supplemental water for four communities, and increased summer flows in the **Tualatin River**, thus improving its water quality. Atlas of Oregon Lakes.

Tualatin River. An 84-mile long river that drains 715 square miles of the east slopes of the **Coast Range** and the north Willamette Valley to join the **Willamette River** upstream from **Willamette Falls**. Average annual flow at mile 1.5 is 1,075,000 acre feet, or 2.4 acre feet/acre. The Tualatin Valley was one of the first areas of the state to be settled, with **wheat** as the pioneers' major crop, but the farmers soon diversified into fruits and other crops. From the 1860s until about 1890, a **steamboat** operated 60 miles upstream to Emerick's Landing, carrying passengers, wheat, and other freight, but a portage was required at either Willamette Falls or at Sucker Lake (now **Oswego Lake**). The Tualatin Valley now is one of Oregon's most rapidly growing regions with most of the agriculture displaced by a dozen incorporated cities, including **Beaverton** and **Hillsboro**. The origin of the Indian name is uncertain, though it may have meant "sluggish," which would describe the river. Blow for the Landing; Oregon Geographic Names. See also **Canyon Road**; **Oswego Canal**.

Tuberculosis. A lung disease caused by a bacillus. The rate in Oregon is about 6 cases per 100,000 people, lower than the national rate of over 9 cases per 100,000. In 1996, 190 cases were identified in the state, half of them in foreign-born persons. American Lung Association of Oregon, 9320 SW Barbur Blvd, Suite 140, Portland 97219-5481. 800-586-4872, 503-246-1997.

Tucker Sno-Cat. A machine that rides over the top of snow on four broad tracks, invented by Emmitt Tucker who began manufacturing them near **Medford** in 1946. The machines are used for utility work, snow surveys, snow trail grooming, and transportation in Antarctica. 2872 S Pacific Hwy, 97501. 541-779-3731. Mail Tribune 2/2/97:1E.

Tuition. In 1996/97, the full-time tuition at the **University of Oregon** was $3,541 a year for Oregon residents (up from $112.50 in 1947) and $11,665 for nonresidents. Other state colleges were slightly lower. With room, food, books, and other costs added in, the average annual bill is about $11,000 for state residents. Tuition at **community colleges** was about a third of that at state institutions of **higher education**.

Tularemia. An infectious disease of wild animals, especially **rabbits** and rodents, caused by a bacterium, *Francisella tularensis*. Humans contract the disease via tick and deer fly bites, by handling infected animals, or by eating partially cooked meat, and it may be fatal if not treated by a physician. A number of persons became ill and three died after eating at a rabbitburger stand in southeast Oregon some years ago. Experiences.

Tule (TOO-lee) **Lake**. A large shallow, marshy lake that once existed in southern Oregon and northern California south of **Klamath Falls**. **Lost River**, which fed the lake, has been diverted, and most of the drained lakebed is now farmland. Tule is a kind of large rush. Oregon Geographic Names.

Tulips. Tulip bulbs are grown commercially in the **Willamette Valley**; visitors are welcome at the 30 acres of blooming fields of the Wooden Shoe Bulb Company where the Woodburn Spring Tulip Show is held in April. 33814 S. Meridian Road, 6 miles east of **Woodburn**, 97071. 503-634-2243; 800-711-2006.

Tumalo Falls. A 97-foot waterfall on Tumalo Creek 15 miles west of **Bend**. The origin of the name is unknown. Waterfall Lover's Guide.

Tumalo Irrigation District. A district with a complex legal and financial history that serves 7,300 irrigated acres north of **Bend** on the west side of the **Deschutes River**. It was the first irrigation district to be taken over and operated by the state (1904) under provisions of the federal **Carey Act of 1894** and became the focus of vigorous land promotion efforts at that time. Tumalo Dam, the 72-foot high centerpiece of the district, was completed in 1914, but massive leaks and sink holes developed in the reservoir over the next few years, making it unusable; the dry dam still stands at Bull Flat. "Tumalo—Thirsty Land."

Tuna. In 1994 4.7 million pounds of tuna (albacore, yellowfin, and skipjack) worth $3.7 million were landed at Oregon ports. Over the past 10 years, Oregon's commercial fishermen have landed an average of 2.8 million pounds of albacore, about a fourth of the total Washington, Oregon and California catch of 10.8 million pounds. Most were 10 to 12 pounds in weight. Earlier, from 1970 through 1974 Oregon's catch averaged 18 million pounds of the total three-state catch of 52 million pounds. 1994-1995 Oregon Agriculture; Pacific States...

Tunnel Falls. A 100-foot waterfall six miles up **Eagle Creek** trail in the **Columbia River Gorge**. Waterfall Lover's Guide.

Tunnels. Tunnels have been excavated in Oregon for light rail, railroads, highways, irrigation, and **lode gold** mines. Some of the most extensive were the 36 miles of underground passages dug at the **Cornucopia Mine** in the **Wallowa Mountains** north of **Halfway**; a restaurant for miners was located a mile and a quarter back in the mountain. At the North Pole-Columbia complex of mines in the **Blue Mountains** north of **Sumpter** 50,000 feet of tunnels were developed along a 12,000 foot vein. Ashland Mine in the **Siskiyou Mountains** had 11,000 feet of tunnel. Gold and Silver in Oregon.

Turkeys, domestic. At Thanksgiving 1949 Oregon promoter Eugene Malecki flew to Istanbul, Turkey, with a 37-pound live turkey that he presented to the president; they then dined on frozen Oregon turkey. Earlier, in 1937, 3.9 million pounds of dressed turkeys were produced in the state, three-fourths of them in **Douglas County** where **Oakland** was home to the Northwestern Turkey Show. Domestic turkeys are no longer raised in Oregon on a commercial scale. "Gobbler Glory Days"; Oregonian 4/4/96:D6.

Turkeys, wild. Turkeys were first released in Oregon in 1899 and have now been successfully introduced throughout the state. Since pen-reared wild turkeys do not thrive in the wild, a trap-and-transplant program is used. The first limited hunting was allowed in 1965, and there is now a state-wide season. Atlas of Oregon Wildlife.

Turner. A **Willamette Valley** town in **Marion County** 7 miles southeast of **Salem**. It was named for pioneer Henry Turner at the time the railroad station was built. The city was incorporated in 1905. Mill Creek **Correctional Facility** is located near the town. Population 1980 1,116; 1995 1,320. Elevation 285'. PO Box 456, 97392. 503-743-2155. Oregon Geographic Names.

Turnips. See **Gardens**.

Turtles. **Reptiles** with shells; they may be terrestrial or aquatic. Two species, both aquatic, are found in Oregon, the western pond turtle, *Clemmys marmorata*, and the painted turtle, *Chrysemys picta*. Their numbers have been declining significantly, due, perhaps, to predation by introduced bass and **bullfrogs**. Oregon has no native tortoise. Sea turtles have sometimes come ashore on Oregon beaches. Atlas of Oregon Wildlife; Field Guide to Western Reptiles and Amphibians; Knowing Oregon Reptiles.

TV Highway. The Tualatin Valley Highway, Highway 8, through **Forest Grove**, **Hillsboro**, and **Beaverton**.

Twality District. The northwest of the four original **districts** (later, **counties**) into which the **Oregon Country** was divided by the **Provisional government** on July 5, 1843, and from which the counties of northwest Oregon were later created. The Twality District was the part of the **Oregon Country** lying north of the Yamhill River between the **Willamette River** and the ocean. It was renamed **Washington County** in 1849 by the legislature of the **Oregon territory**. Twality, an Indian word of disputed meaning, was also spelled Tualatin, Falatine, Nefalatine, and Quality. The three other districts were **Champooick** to the southeast, **Clackamas** to the northeast, and **Yamhill** to the southwest. "Oregon Counties"; Oregon Geographic Names.

Twenty Miracle Miles. A 1960s chamber of commerce slogan for **Highway 101** through **Lincoln City** in north **Lincoln County**. The traffic jams, haphazard development, and gaudy commercialism of the area prompted then-Governor Mark Hatfield to dub it the Twenty Miserable Miles. Fire at Eden's Gate; Oregonian 7/7/97:A7.

Twilight. The period in the evening between sunset and the moment when the sun is six degrees below the horizon, or, in the morning from the moment the sun is six degrees below the horizon until sunrise. At 45° north latitude (**Salem**) twilight is at its maximum (35 minutes morning and evening) at winter solstice while day length is at its minimum of about 9 hours.

Twin Pillars. A 200-foot rock pillar with a split top located in the Mill Creek Wilderness of **Ochoco National Forest**, about six miles airline northeast of **Steins Pillar**. Oregon Atlas.

Tygres Heart Shakespeare Company. A theater company that produces Shakespeare plays in the **Dolores Winningstad Theatre**. 1111 SW Broadway. 503-222-9220. Portland Guidebook.

Typhoons. See **Hurricanes**.

U.S. See rest of name.

U.S. Bancorp Tower. See **Big Pink**.

UFOs. The nation's first flying saucer sighting was reported by the **Pendleton** paper on June 24, 1947, after private pilot Kenneth Arnold reported that he had seen nine bright objects flying in formation over the Washington Cascades at 1,600 mph. The first photographs ever made of a flying saucer were taken near **Sheridan** on May 11, 1950. Oregon sightings are reported in The Observer, published quarterly by Oregon MUFON (Mutual Unidentified Flying Object Network), PO Box 83632, Portland 97203. Oregon Stater 79(5):27 October 1995; Oregonian 6/22/ 97:A1. See also **Heaven's Gate**.

Ukiah. A ranching community in a broad valley 48 miles south of **Pendleton** at the junction of **Highway 395** and 244 in **Umatilla County** notable for the antler-covered Antler Inn. The town was platted in 1890 and named by E. B. Gambee for the town in California where he had once lived. When lands in the Ukiah area were going to be opened for settlement in 1905, applicants at the **La Grande** land office held their places in line night and day for six weeks. Ukiah was incorporated in1969. The community operates a **boarding high school**. Population 1980 249; 1995 270. Elevation 3,400'. PO Box 265, 97880. no phone. History of Union County; Oregonian 3/8/98:C4.

Ukrainians. See **Springfield**.

Umatilla. A transportation center, originally called Umatilla Landing, in **Umatilla County**, located 40 miles northwest of **Pendleton** where the Umatilla River joins the **Columbia River**. The town sprang up as a transportation and trading center during the gold rushes of the 1860s, with the post office established in 1863, and the city incorporated the following year. Several decades later it became a railroad center. In 1894 a significant earthquake hit the area. The **Petticoat Government** brought it national attention in 1916. The economy is supported by irrigated farming, river barging, the **Union Pacific Railroad**, business from **Interstate 82** and **84**, and power transmission from **McNary Dam**. Population 1980 3,199; 1995 3,250. Elevation 296'. PO Box 130, 97882. 541-922-3226. Chamber of Commerce 800-542-4944. "Umatilla's 'Petticoat Government'"; Oregonian 10/26/94:A1.

Umatilla Chemical Depot. A 30-square-mile chemical weapons storage facility built in 1942 in **Morrow** and **Umatilla** counties near **Umatilla**, between **Interstate 84** and the **Columbia River**. In 1997, 11.6% of the U.S. supply of obsolete chemical weapons were still stored there. The stockpile included 4.7 million pounds of mustard gas stored in 1,635 one-ton steel tanks, plus another 2.5 million pounds of the lethal nerve gas VX, which is a contact poison, and GB (sarin), designed to be inhaled as a poisonous aerosol spray. The poisons were stored in 220,604 deteriorating rockets, mines, artillery shells, and bombs housed in concrete bunkers called igloos. Of the original 1,001 igloos, 89 were still used for nerve gas. Concerns about security and disposal of the chemicals were ongoing. The Army has proposed incinerating the chemicals, beginning in July 2000. Oregonian 3/21/95:A6, 8/25/96:A1, 6/21/97:D1. See also **Operation Red Hat**; **Superfund cleanup**.

Umatilla County. A northern-tier county of rolling wheat fields. Incorporated cities are **Pendleton** (county seat), **Adams**, **Athena**, **Echo**, **Helix**, **Hermiston**, **Milton-Freewater**, **Pilot Rock**, **Stanfield**, **Ukiah**, **Umatilla**, and **Weston**. The county is bounded by the **Columbia River** and Washington State on the north, and by **Wallowa**, **Union**, **Grant**, and **Morrow** counties. Elevations range from 265' on the **Columbia River** to 6,850' Tower Mountain in the **Blue Mountains** in the southeast corner. The economy is based on agriculture (wheat and cattle, as well as irrigated crops such as peas and onions), food processing, wood products, tourism, manufacturing, and recreation. Taxable assessed value in 1995 was $2,462,000,000, or $38,000 per capita. The county was created from **Wasco County** during the 1862 **gold rush**. Population 1980 58,861; 1995 65,200. Area 3,231 square miles. Density 20/sq.mi. Annual precipitation 12"; average temperature January 34°F, July 73°F. Courthouse, 216 SE 4th, Pendleton 97801. 541-276-7111. Oregon Blue Book; Umatilla County.

Umatilla House. A famed 19th century hotel built on the **Columbia River** waterfront at **The Dalles** in 1857, a favorite with gold miners, cowboys, and freighters, as well as the steamboat, stage, and rail passengers who landed on its doorstep. Rebuilt after fires in 1877 and 1879, it grew to 141 rooms and a dining room that seated 250. In 1929 the outdated building, known at one time as the best hotel west of Minneapolis and north of San Francisco, was torn down. Dictionary of Oregon History; Oregon Oddities.

Umatilla Indian Reservation, Confederated Tribes of the. A confederation with some 1,630 enrolled Umatilla, Walla Walla, and **Cayuse** Indians. After the **Whitman massacre** in 1847, the three tribes were forced in 1855 to cede 6 million acres to the U.S. government and in return were given a reservation of 512,000 acres. Government actions since that have reduced the reservation, located five miles east of **Pendleton**, to its present 158,000 acres. Over half of it is owned by non-Indians, and 2,000 non-Indians live on the reservation. The confederation operates a number of businesses, including the Wildhorse Gaming Resort that includes a **casino**, a 100-room hotel, and an 18-hole golf course. The nearby **Tamustalik** (ta-MUST-ah-luck) **Cultural Institute** tells the story of the **Oregon Trail** from the Indian point of view. **Crow's Shadow Institute,** located next to St. Andrews Mission, is a nonprofit arts facility that features local Indian artists. PO Box 638, Pendleton 97801. 541-276-3165. American Indian Reservations; First Oregonians; Native Peoples; Oregonian 10/22/95:A18.

Umatilla National Forest. A 1,512,833-acre national forest in the **Blue Mountains** of northeast Oregon. Most of it is in **Umatilla** and **Grant** counties, although 300,000 acres lies in Washington. The forest includes three Wilderness areas, Wenaha-Tucannon, North Fork Umatilla, and North Fork John Day. 25117 SW Hailey Avenue, Pendleton 97801. 541-276-3811.

Umatilla Project. A project for irrigating lands along the **Umatilla River** undertaken by the **Bureau of Reclamation** following a 1903 study. The Bureau completed **Cold Springs Reservoir** near **Hermiston** in 1908 and **McKay Reservoir** near **Pendleton**, which it still operates, in 1927. The project furnishes a full supply of water to 17,348 acres and supplemental water to another 13,235 acres, and also has some flood control and recreation benefits. Atlas of Oregon Lakes.

Umatilla River. A river in northeast Oregon that flows from the **Blue Mountains** northwest past **Pendleton** to join the **Columbia River** at the town of **Umatilla**. It drains 2,540 square miles, and has an average annual volume of 331,800 acre feet at mile point 2.1, or .2 acre feet/acre. Butter Creek is a major tributary. Dams, including Three Mile Falls, Westland, and Stanfield dams, divert water for irrigation, and by the 1920s the diversions had eliminated **salmon** runs. However, salmon runs were restored in the 1980s through the Umatilla Basin Project, a cooperative effort that gave irrigators water from the Columbia River in order to decrease diversions from the Umatilla. Umatilla is an Indian word of unknown meaning. Oregon Geographic Names; Oregonian 4/25/97:D4, 9/15/97:B9.

Umpqua Brigade. An annual fur-trapping expedition sent south along the **Siskiyou Trail** from the **Hudson's Bay Company** headquarters at **Fort Vancouver** between 1825 and the early 1840s to trap furs in what is now southern Oregon and California. The brigade, composed of trappers, their families, and 200 or more horses, would make a colorful passage up the **Willamette Valley**. It was sometimes called the Southern Expedition or the California Brigade. Champoeg. See also **Fur trade**.

Umpqua Community College. A public two-year college that has served most of **Douglas County** since 1964. It enrolled 5,497 students in fall 1996. Students may take college transfer courses, vocational-technical education, developmental studies, and community education. The college's campus is located four miles north of **Roseburg** on a hillside overlooking the North **Umpqua River**. PO Box 967, Roseburg OR 97470-0226. 541-440-4600. Oregon Blue Book. See also **Community colleges; Small Business Development Centers**.

Umpqua County. A county created by the **Territorial** legislature in 1851. Its 5,000+ square miles covered the length of the Umpqua River valley. **Douglas County** was created from the eastern portion in 1852, some of the western end was added to **Coos County** in 1853, and in 1862 the rest of the western part was added to Douglas County and Umpqua County ceased to exist. "Oregon Counties"; Umpqua: The Lost County.

Umpqua Discovery Center. A natural and cultural history museum and gift shop on the **Reedsport** waterfront. A gazebo on top offers a full 360° degree periscope view of the river and town. The retired Antarctic research vessel *Hero* has been moored adjacent to the center but operated separately, though the museum devotes a room to the Antarctic experience. In 1998 the fate of the ship was uncertain. 409 Riverfront Way, Reedsport 97467. 541-271-4816.

Umpqua Indians. See **Coos, Lower Umpqua, and Siuslaw Indians**, and **Cow Creek Band of Umpqua Indians**.

Umpqua National Forest. A 1,028,879-acre national forest in the **Cascade Range**, primarily in **Douglas County**. It includes three wilderness areas, Rogue-Umpqua Divide, Mount Thielsen, and Boulder Creek. 2900 NW Stewart Parkway, P.O.Box 1008, Roseburg 97470. 541-672-6601.

Umpqua River. A 112-mile long river in southwest Oregon that drains 4,560 square miles, much of it in **Douglas County**. The North Umpqua and South Umpqua head on the west slopes of the **Cascade Range** north of **Crater Lake** and join west of **Roseburg**. The river then cuts through the **Coast Range** past the historic port of **Scottsburg** at the head of tidewater, 28 miles from the mouth, and flows past **Reedsport** and **Winchester Bay** to the ocean where **jetties** help maintain the channel for fishing boats. **Cow Creek** is a major tributary of the South Umpqua, and Smith

River joins the Umpqua near Reedsport. **Interstate 5** lies in the Umpqua drainage for 90 miles, from Stage Road Pass north past Roseburg to a low divide south of **Cottage Grove**. The river's cutthroat **trout** have been declared as endangered, and the North Umpqua is one of five watersheds targeted for **coho salmon** habitat restoration. The river's name came from a word used for the general area by the local **Indians**, an Athabascan tribe. Oregon Geographic Names. See also **Floods, coastal rivers; Fort Umpqua; Lemolo Falls; North Umpqua Hydroelectric Project;** *Sea Otter*; **Smith massacre; Steamboats; Toketee Falls; Tsalila; Watson Falls**.

Umpqua River Lighthouse. An operating **lighthouse** near **Winchester Bay** six miles south of **Reedsport**. It was put into service in 1894, as was the **Heceta Head Lighthouse,** built from the same plans. It replaced the first lighthouse in the Oregon Territory which had been built at the mouth of the **Umpqua River** in 1857 but was destroyed by the **flood of 1861**. The masonry tower rises 65' above the ground and the light is 165' above sea level. The 2-ton lens is 72 inches in diameter and rotates four times a minute; its alternate red and white flashes are visible 20 miles at sea. The light was automated in 1966, and the lighthouse is now managed by the Douglas County Parks Department. Limited summer tours are offered. 541-271-4631. Oregon Lighthouses; Oregon Parks 2(3):54 Nov/Dec 1994; Oregon's Seacoast Lighthouses.

Undocumented workers. The U.S. Immigration and Naturalization Service estimated in 1996 that about 20,000 undocumented workers (illegal immigrants) live year-round in Oregon. An additional 20,000 to 40,000 come for seasonal agricultural and forestry work. Oregonian 3/26/96:A6. See also **Farm workers**.

Unemployment. In March 1995, unemployment in Oregon stood at 4.5%, below the national rate of 5.5% and the lowest it had been in over 15 years, but by November 1997 it had inched up to 5.3%, above the national rate of 4.6%. Unemployment rates have been higher in rural areas than in cities; **Wheeler County** had a 23.6% unemployment rate in 1991, and in March 1997 **Grant County** reached 22.1%. During the 1982-83 **recession** the statewide unemployment rate was 12.5%. Oregon Labor Trends; Oregonian 4/24/96:C2, 12/17/97:E1. See also **Employment Department; Payroll**.

Ungreeting cards. A series of humorous cards developed by Frank Beeson and Jim Cloutier of **Eugene** in the early 1970s, ostensibly to discourage **growth**. They carried such messages as "Last year in Oregon, 677 people fell off their bikes - and drowned." Cloutier also published a series of four "Orygone" cartoon books plus the Best of Orygun, and founded the **Society for Native Oregon Born** (SNOB). Oregonian 2/1/98:C5.

Uniform State Laws, Commission on. An Oregon commission of three members appointed by the governor for four-year terms. It works with a national commission to promote uniformity in laws among states on matters where uniformity is desirable, such as the Uniform Commercial Code. 520 SW Yamhill, Suite 800, Portland 97204-1383. 503-226-6151. Oregon Blue Book.

Uniforms. See **School uniforms**.

Union. An agricultural town in **Union County** 14 miles southeast of **La Grande** on Catherine Creek. It was founded in 1862 during the **Civil War**, its name inspired by patriotism. The first business was a nursery selling fruit trees, and Union was also a supply center for mines off in the mountains. The post office was established in 1863, and the city was incorporated in 1878. From 1872 to 1904 it served as the county seat. Attractions include an 1869 Gothic mansion and other Victorian homes and the Union County Museum. Population 1980 2,062; 1995 1,920. Elevation 2,789'. PO Box 529, 97883. 541-562-5197. History of Union County; Union.

Union County. A county in northeast Oregon centered on the broad and productive valley of the **Grande Ronde** River between the **Blue Mountains** and the **Wallowa Mountains**. Incorporated cities are **La Grande** (county seat), **Cove, Elgin, Imbler, Island City, North Powder, Summerville**, and **Union**. The county is bounded by **Wallowa, Baker, Grant**, and **Umatilla** counties. Elevations range from 2,120' along the Grande Ronde in the north to 9,595' **Eagle Cap** on the east in the Wallowas. The economy is based on agriculture, lumber, and education. Taxable assessed value in 1995 was $917,000,000, or $38,000 per capita. The county was created in 1864 from **Baker County**. Its name came from the town of Union, which had been established two years before, though La Grande was the first county seat. However, Union won a 1874 challenge, and the county jail was moved (literally) to Union and a new brick courthouse was built. In 1904, La Grande successfully re-challenged, and the county seat has been there since. Population 1980 23,921; 1995 24,400. Area 2,038 square miles. Density 12/sq.mi. Annual precipitation 19"; average temperature January $31°$ F, July $70°$ F. 1106 K Ave., La Grande 97850. 541-963-1001. History of Union County; Oregon Blue Book. See also **Panhandle**.

Union Pacific Corporation (UP). A major **railroad** company that, since its 1996 purchase of **Southern Pacific**, controls 90% of Oregon's rail traffic. In 1884 a UP subsidiary, the **Oregon Short Line** from Wyoming, connected at **Huntington** with the **Oregon Railway and Navigation Company** line from **Portland**, opening Oregon's second **transcontinental connection** by rail. Union Pacific now owns the entire line and provides Oregon's most direct rail connection to the east (along much the same route as **Interstate 84**) as well as the state's major connection south to California (from **Portland** to **Eugene** along the east side of the **Willamette Valley**, across the **Cascade Range** via the **Natron cut-off** near Willamette Pass, and south through **Klamath Falls**). An office in Boise serves Oregon. 208-338-6288. Oregonian 7/4/96:C1, 10/12/97:C1. See also **Battle of the Gorge**.

Union Party. A **political party** organized in 1889 at a Salem convention of members of the **Grange** and Knights of Labor. It advocated a reform program, including **prohibition**, and measures to decrease the power of banks and end land speculation. It faded after a few years as its members turned to the **Populists**. Empire of the Columbia.

Union Station. Portland's railroad station, located at the north end of 6th Avenue, serving all rail lines coming into the city. It is the only major **railroad** station in the state and is the oldest big-city train depot west of St. Louis. The building, notable for its 140-foot tower with giant clock, was designed by the Kansas City firm of Van Brunt and Howe and built on filled-in Couch Lake. The station has been flooded several times since being built; during one flood a 15" steelhead was caught in the building. It opened February 14, 1896 and was extensively remodeled in the 1930s. In 1987 the building and 31 acres were bought by the Portland Development Commission. Its complex 100-year-old metal-tile roofing was replaced in 1998. Century of Portland Architecture; History of Portland Union Station Structures; "How It Was Then"; Oregonian 5/9/96:C1, 2/21/98:B1 .

Unions. See **Labor organizations**.

Unitarian Universalist Church. The first Unitarians in Oregon met in homes from 1855 until a church was built in **Portland** in 1867. Dr. Thomas Lamb Eliot (1845-1936) was pastor from 1867 until 1893. An active promoter of education and other community interests, he served as director of the Portland Library Association and Superintendent of Schools, was principal founder of the parks system, the Humane Society, the Boys and Girls Aid Society, and **Reed College**. One of his sons was pastor from 1906 until 1934. Guide to Early Oregon Churches,

United Brethren Church. A wagon train of 98 United Brethren came over the **Oregon Trail** in 1853. Most settled in **Benton County** where they later established **Philomath College** and the town of **Philomath**. A church schism in 1889 eventually led the more liberal branch to merge with the Evangelical Church which, in turn, joined with the **Methodist Church** in 1958 to form the United Methodist Church. Guide to Early Oregon Churches. See also **De Moss Family**.

United Church of Christ. A Protestant denomination formed in 1957 by the merger of the **Congregational Church** with the Evangelical and Reformed churches. Guide to Early Oregon Churches.

United States. See rest of name.

United States Exploring Expedition. See **Wilkes Expedition**.

Unity. A northeast Oregon community on the east side of the **Blue Mountains** in **Baker County** 49 miles east of **John Day** on **Highway 26**. In 1891 settlers met to find a more convenient location for the local post office and commemorated their agreement on a new site by naming it Unity. The city was incorporated in 1972. Nearby attractions include the Monument Rock Wilderness to the south and Unity Lake State Park to the north. Population 1980 115; 1995 115. Elevation 4,029'. PO Box 7, 97884. 541-446-3544. Oregon Geographic Names.

Unity Reservoir. An irrigation impoundment on the Burnt River in **Baker County** completed in 1939 as part of the **Burnt River Project**. The lake lies five miles north of **Unity**. At full pool it covers 974 acres to a maximum depth of 50 feet, though by late summer irrigation withdrawals have lowered it significantly. Recreation use is heavy, especially for fishing. A **state park** provides camping facilities. Atlas of Oregon Lakes.

University of Oregon (UO). A state liberal arts college and major research university located in **Eugene**. It is Oregon's largest university, with a fall 1994 enrollment of 16,680 students. In addition to programs in sciences, social sciences, humanities, and a four-year Honors College, it has six professional programs: business, education, architecture and allied arts, journalism and communications, law, and music. Facilities include the **Oregon Institute for Marine Biology** in **Charleston** and **Pine Mountain Observatory** near **Bend**. It opened with state support in 1876 after **Eugene** raised the money to build Deady Hall. Eugene

97403. 541-346-1000. Dictionary of Oregon History; Oregon Blue Book. See also **Land grants, educational**; **Oregon Experiment**; **Tuition**; **University System, Oregon**.

University of Oregon Museum of Natural History. A museum in **Eugene**, founded in 1936, that produces exhibits and programs relating to anthropology, archaeology, zoology, and geology. The Oregon State Museum of Anthropology, created by the legislature in 1935, is now part of it and is responsible for curating anthropological materials belonging to the state as well as doing contract archaeological work. 1680 E 15th Ave., Eugene 97403-1224. 541-346-3024. Oregon Blue Book.

University of Phoenix. A university, headquartered in Arizona, with campuses in 10 states. It opened a branch in **Tigard** in 1997 that will offer bachelor's and master's degrees through concentrated night classes. Classes are aimed at professional working adults age 23 and older, and graduate students must have three years of work experience. 13190 SW 68th Parkway, Tigard. 503-670-0590.

University of Portland. An accredited **Catholic** college overlooking the **Willamette River** in north **Portland.** 2,630 students enrolled in 1995. The school opened as Columbia University, a Catholic school for young men, in 1901. In 1935 the name was changed to University of Portland, and in 1951 women were admitted. 5000 N Willamette Blvd., Portland 97203. 503-283-7911. Dictionary of Oregon History; Oregon Blue Book. See also **Portland University**.

University System, Oregon. Oregon's system of state-operated colleges and universities, organized in 1932 and known until 1997 as the Oregon State System of Higher Education (OSSHE). Its seven schools include three major research universities: **Oregon State University** (Corvallis), **Portland State University**, and **University of Oregon** (Eugene); three regional universities (known as state colleges until 1997): **Eastern Oregon University** (La Grande), **Southern Oregon University** (Ashland), and **Western Oregon University** (Monmouth); and the **Oregon Institute of Technology** (Klamath Falls). Head count enrollment in 1995-96 totaled 96,305 for credit courses. In 1996, the state **general fund** provided 28% of operating costs, 22% came from tuition, 18% was from fees for services such as housing, 15% from federal funds, 7% from donations and grants, 2% from the lottery, and 8% from other sources. State support has been declining in recent years due to **Measure 5**. The governor appoints the 11-member State Board of Higher Education which in turn appoints the chancellor and establishes system-wide policy. PO Box 3175, Eugene 97403. 541-346-5700. Oregon Blue Book. See also **Central Oregon University Center**; **Community colleges**; **Malheur Field Station**; **Mosser Awards**; **NERO Project**; **Oregon Health Sciences University**; **Tuition**; **Western Interstate Commission for Higher Education**.

Uplift. Recent studies confirm that the western edge of the **Coast Range** is rising while the slopes along the **Willamette Valley** are sinking. The rates of uplift are greatest close to the **Cascadia Subduction Zone**, and are higher from **Newport** south and from **Tillamook** north. **Cape Blanco** shows the highest rate, at 1" in 3 years. **Astoria** is rising 1" in 36 years, while the town of **Rainier** is sinking proportionately. Geology of Oregon.

Upper Klamath Lake. The largest freshwater lake in Oregon (**Goose Lake** is larger but saline, and is not all within Oregon), covering 61,543 acres in the main lake plus another 9,298 acres in its northeast arm (called Agency Lake) for a total of over 70,000 acres. The lakes extend 22 miles north from **Klamath Falls**, west of **Highway 97**. Agency Lake averages just 3 feet deep. Upper Klamath Lake averages 14 feet deep, though a small area near the west edge drops to 50 feet. Water level is controlled by a low dam built on the Link River in 1917 by the U.S. **Bureau of Reclamation**. The lake and marshes provide important waterfowl habitat and are a major stop on the migration flyway. The lake is used for irrigation, fishing, and boating, though poor water quality limits water contact sports. The lake is naturally rich in nutrients. These, together with the shallow character of most of the lake, make possible great swarms of midges, large areas of water plants, and a growth of **algae** that is harvested commercially. In some places the fall decay of algae creates offensive odors. The lake is named for the **Klamath Indians**; the origin of their name is uncertain. Atlas of Oregon Lakes. See also **Klamath Basin**; **Pleistocene lakes**.

Upper Klamath National Wildlife Refuge. A 14,900 acre marsh refuge on the west shore of **Upper Klamath Lake**. A canoe trail from Rocky Point Resort provides viewing, though access into nesting areas is restricted. Rt.1, Box 74, Tulelake CA 96134. 916-667-2231. Oregon Wildlife Viewing Guide.

Upwelling. A summer ocean condition along the Oregon coast that occurs as north winds, in combination with the Coriolis effect, set up a spiral of water movement within the upper 100 feet of the ocean. This results in a slow movement of this surface layer seaward, at right angles to the wind direction. The surface waters are replaced by an onshore flow of colder water that rises from depths of several hundred feet and may be as much as 16°F colder than the surface water found several hundred miles west. Active upwelling is strongest along the central and south coast and is restricted to a narrow band ranging from 6 to 18 miles from shore. As warm marine air passes over the cool water it forms fog that is pulled landward by warm air rising inland. Upwelling brings up cold, nutrient-rich water that feeds the food chain, and when upwelling fails, as during an **El Niño** event, fish and bird life suffers from a lack of food. Oregon Oceanbook. See also **Ocean currents**.

Uranium. A heavy radioactive metal. Small amounts were produced between 1958 and 1965 at a mill in **Lakeview**; the ore came from a mine northwest of the town. Significant uranium deposits have been located in the **McDermitt caldera**. Geology of Oregon.

Urban growth boundary (UGB). The designated boundary of the area around an Oregon city which is expected to meet that city's growth needs for 20 years. The boundaries are designed to prevent urban sprawl into agricultural and forest lands and to encourage development where urban services, including utilities and transportation, can be most economically provided. State law requires that any possible expansion areas outside the UGB must be able to provide water and sewer services, must not be zoned for exclusive farm use, and must be near jobs or land currently zoned for industrial or commercial use. In the **Portland** metropolitan area where **Metro** is responsible for land use planning, the urban growth boundary was increased in 1997 by about 4,500 acres, enough for 29,350 homes. Oregonian 10/24/97:A1. See also **Boundary commissions**; **Land use planning**; **Region 2040 plan**; **Rural community boundary**.

Urban renewal. A program for renewing America's decaying urban areas that was spurred by the Federal Housing Act of 1949. The state had 56 urban renewal districts in 1998. The **Portland** Development Commission was the first, starting with a series of efforts that led to the award-winning South Auditorium Renewal Project (1961, 1966) by Skidmore, Owings and Merrill (SOM). The project cleared a 44-block area of ethnic neighborhoods on the south edge of downtown and replaced them with the **Portland Center**. That project was followed by Portland State Urban Renewal Project(1965), Portland Waterfront Renewal Plan (1975) and Portland Transit Mall (1978), all by SOM. **Pioneer Courthouse Square** and the lake in Tualatin Commons were also urban renewal projects. Frozen Music; Oregonian 1/19/97:G1, 2/24/98:C1. See also **1972 Downtown Plan**; **Tax increment financing**.

U.S. See rest of name.

Vale. A historic eastern Oregon agricultural town and the county seat of **Malheur County**. It is located 17 miles west of **Ontario** at the junction of **Highways 20** and **26**. **Oregon Trail** wagon trains made a welcome laundry stop at **Vale Hot Springs** on the **Malheur River**; the hot springs now heat the city swimming pool and a **mushroom** plant. **Cattle**, **onions**, **potatoes**, **sugar beets**, and **wheat** are also raised in the area. Historic sites include the 1872 Stone House Museum, Meek's Cutoff (route of the **Lost Wagon Train**), and the Henderson grave where pioneers died of thirst just out of sight of the river. The Duck Race and **Rodeo** are held in July, and hunting and fishing are popular. The post office was established in 1883, and the city was incorporated in 1889. The source of the name, French for valley, is unknown. Population 1980 1,558; 1995 1,495. Elevation 2,243'. Rainfall 9". 252 B Street West, 97918. 541-473-3133. Chamber of Commerce 541-473-3800. History of Malheur Country.

Vale District, BLM. A 4,961,123-acre **Bureau of Land Management** district of grazing and forest land in **Malheur County** and northeast Oregon. 100 Oregon Street, Vale 97918. 541-473-3144. BLM Facts. See also **Jordan Valley Interagency Invasive Weed Management Project**.

Vale Project (BLM). An 11-year project undertaken by the **Vale District Office** of the **Bureau of Land Management** to improve **rangeland** in southeast Oregon. 267,193 acres were seeded, primarily with crested wheatgrass (native to Turkestan), and fences, cattle guards, roads, and water systems were installed. The project began in 1963. Sacred Cows.

Vale Project (Bureau of Reclamation). An **irrigation** project through which the U.S. **Bureau of Reclamation** purchased 1/2 interest in the **Warm Springs Reservoir** in 1926, built Agency Valley Dam and **Beulah Reservoir** in 1935, and built **Bully Creek** Dam and Reservoir in 1963. The project is owned by the Vale Oregon Irrigation District which irrigates 35,000 acres around **Vale**. The project also offers coordinated flood control, and, at Beulah Reservoir, recreation. Atlas of Oregon Lakes.

Valley Migrant League. An organization formed from the Migrant Ministry in 1964 in **Woodburn** in order to better serve Mexican **migrant labor** on farms in the **Willamette Valley**. It addressed problems in education, health, and housing, and later moved into political activities. It was succeeded by Oregon Rural Opportunities. Nosotros.

Valley of the Rogue State Park. A southern Oregon **state park** between **Interstate 5** and the **Rogue River** 12 miles southeast of **Grants Pass**. The park includes a boat ramp, group facilities, and 173 year-round camp sites. Reservations, 800-452-5687. It is the state's second most visited park, with 1.5 million visits in 1994-95. 541-582-1118.

Valsetz. A now-obliterated company logging town in the **Coast Range** in **Polk County**, 16 miles west of **Falls City**. It was built in 1919 by William W. Mitchell Company and named for the Valley and Siletz Railroad; the post office opened the next year. The timber lands, town, and sawmill were owned by several companies before Boise Cascade Corporation bought them in 1959. In 1984, after the timber had been cut, Boise Cascade closed down the mill, demolished the buildings, tore up the streets, took out the dam, and planted a forest where the town and log pond had once been. Oregonian 7/1/84: special section.

Van Duzer Forest Corridor. A narrow forest corridor along a ten-mile stretch of Highway 18 through the **Coast Range** between **Lincoln City** and **Grand Ronde**. Murphy Hill, elevation 760 feet, is the high point, The corridor includes a rest area with picnic tables.

Vanport. A city that was located on a floodplain between **Portland** and the **Columbia River** between 1942 and 1948. Constructed as a temporary government housing project for shipyard workers during **World War II**, it was the largest housing project ever built in the United States, and, with 40,000 residents by the end of 1943, was the **second-largest city** in Oregon. Vanport College later developed into **Portland State University**. The city, located north of **Columbia Slough** and west of Denver Boulevard (now **Interstate 5**), was surrounded by high dikes. At 4:17 p.m. on Sunday, May 30 (Memorial Day), during the **flood of 1948**, the Columbia River breached the railroad dike at the west end and flooded Vanport with 15 feet of water, destroying the city (which housed 18,000 people at the time), and taking 15 lives. Nonetheless, Vanport's "Water Babies" float entered the **Rose Festival** parade two weeks later. The city, however, was never rebuilt, and the land is now designated for commercial and recreational uses, including the **Portland International Raceway**. Vanport.

Vanport flood. See **Flood of 1948**.

Vaqueros. Mexican cowboys. In the 1870s, vaqueros came to eastern Oregon from California (which was Mexican until 1848) to work on the huge cattle **ranches** and brought with them skills, equipment, and terms still in use. The Dos Coronas Charro Association in **Hood River** keeps the skills alive. "Buckaroo" derives from "vaquero". Nosotros.

Vector control districts. Districts that control disease-spreading organisms. Though they have legal authority to deal with a range of vectors, from rats to flies, in 1997 all of the districts dealt only with **mosquitoes**. There are 16 in Oregon, established under state law as **special service districts**. Most are small, though **Jackson County**'s is county-wide. In **Multnomah County** the county health department does mosquito control. Both the state **Health Division** and Oregon Department of **Fish and Wildlife** must approve vector control programs.

Vegetable crops. Vegetable and truck crops grown in Oregon, including **beans**, **broccoli**, **carrots**, **cauliflower**, **corn**, **onions**, **peas**, **potatoes**, **pumpkins**, **rice**, and **wild rice**, had a total value in 1995 of $248 million. Vegetable **seeds** are also grown. 1995 Oregon.

Vegetation. Oregon's diversity of geography, soil, and climate results in distinctively different plant communities. These may be categorized as 1) the north coastal strip under ocean influence, with dune vegetation, shore **pines**, **Sitka spruce**, and impenetrable brush; 2) the south coastal strip, from the **Coquille River** south, with sphagnum bogs and **Oregon-myrtle**; 3) the heavily forested **Coast Range** with stands of **Douglas-fir**; 4) the ancient **Siskiyou Mountains** with a variety of unique species, including Brewer's **spruce** and **kalmiopsis**; 5) the interior valleys of the **Rogue** and **Umpqua Rivers**, characterized by quickly-maturing spring flowers and mixed forests; 6) the **Willamette Valley**, now mostly cultivated, but originally a mix of **oak** savannah that the **Indians** maintained with annual burning, and brushy, thickly wooded areas along the river flood plains; 7) the **Cascade Range**, heavily forested with mixed conifers; 8) dry eastern Oregon, with vast areas of **sagebrush**, and scattered **juniper** and **ponderosa pine** stands; and 9) the ancient **Blue Mountains** where species from the Cascades as well as from the Rocky Mountains are found. Each of these areas includes a further diversity of habitats, and some botanists divide eastern Oregon into east Cascades, Columbia basin, high plains, basin and range, and Owyhee uplands. **Introduced plants** are displacing much of the native vegetation in some areas. Manual of the Higher Plants of Oregon; Natural Vegetation of Oregon and Washington. See also **Geography**; **Native plants**.

Vehicle inspection. A program operated by the Department of **Environmental Quality** in the **Portland** and **Medford** areas. Vehicles are tested every two years for excessive exhaust emissions. Federal EPA tests found that cars in the **Portland** area produce 34% less **carbon monoxide** and 24% less hydrocarbons than do cars in **Eugene** where there is no auto emissions testing. Oregonian 5/6/95:D4. See also **Air pollution**.

Venal officials. The last part of the 19th century was notable for the corruption of Oregon's officials. Joseph N. Dolph, U.S. Senator, 1883-1895, was simultaneously vice-president of a major Oregon railroad company. John H. Mitchell, U.S. Senator for four terms between 1873 and 1905 was legal counselor for two Oregon railroads; he was convicted of **land fraud** in 1905. Napoleon Davis, Clerk of the State Land Board 1887-1891, and his predecessor, E. P. McCormack, controlled the sale of **Common School Fund** lands; they extracted a fee of $1.25 per acre, plus a final deposit of $100,000, for their personal use. Looters of the Public Domain. See also **Corruption**; **Land frauds**; **Swamp lands**.

Veneta. A south **Willamette Valley** city in **Lane County** 15 miles west of **Eugene** on Highway 126. It was begun in 1912 by E. E. Hunter who named it for his five-year-old daughter. The post office opened two years later, and the city was incorporated in 1962. Fernridge Fun Daze is held the last weekend in June, and the **Oregon Country Fair** in July. There is a Pioneer Museum in nearby Crow. Population 1980 2,449; 1995 2,785. Elevation 409'. PO Box 458, 97487. 541-935-2191. Oregon Geographic Names.

Venture capital. See **Resource and Technology Development Fund.**

Verboort. A small, unincorporated community in **Washington County** two miles northeast of **Forest Grove,** named for William Verboort who owned land in the area. It is noted for the early November Verboort Sausage and Kraut Feed and Bazaar, held annually since 1935. 503-357-3860. Oregon Geographic Names.

Vernonia. A northwest Oregon logging town deep in the **Coast Range** in **Columbia County,** 23 miles west of **Saint Helens**. It was first settled in 1873 and named for the daughter that settler Ozias Cherrington had left in Ohio. The post office was established in 1878, and the city was incorporated in 1891. In 1996 the community was hard hit by flooding from the Nehalem River. Attractions include the Columbia County Historical Society Museum, Lake Vernonia, a former mill pond that is now a fishing and recreation area, and the Friendship Jamboree and Logging Show on the first full weekend in August. Population 1980 1,785; 1995 2,110. Elevation 620'. 919 Bridge St., 97064. 503-429-5291. Chamber of Commerce 503-429-3021. Oregon Geographic Names; This Side of Oregon.

Veterans Affairs, Department of. A department of state government that serves Oregon's military veterans with counseling and claims services, administers an extensive veterans' home and farm loan program, and is establishing a 151-bed state veterans' home scheduled to open in late 1997 at **The Dalles**. 700 Summer St. NE, Salem 97310-1201. 503-373-2000. The Claims Program represents veterans before the U.S. Department of Veterans Affairs. 1220 SW Third Ave., Suite 1509, Portland 97204. 503-326-2611. Oregon Blue Book. See also **Women in the military**.

Veterans Day. A legal holiday on November 11 that commemorates the veterans who have served in America's wars. **Albany** has one of the nation's largest Veteran's Day parades. 541-928-5094

Veterinary Medical Examining Board. A board of seven members appointed by the governor for four-year terms that licenses veterinarians, veterinary technicians, and animal euthanasia technicians, investigates complaints, and imposes penalties. There were 1,300 veterinarians in Oregon in 1996. 800 NE Oregon St., Suite 407, Portland 97232. 503-731-4051. Oregon Blue Book.

Veto. Oregon's **governor** has the authority under the state **constitution** Article V, Section 15, to exercise a **line-item veto** in appropriation bills, to veto any emergency clause provision, and to veto any **bill** passed by the **legislature**. The governor has 5 working days to veto a bill after receiving it during a legislative session and 30 days for bills received at the end of the session - but then must give 5 days notice of possible intent to veto a bill. A 2/3 vote of each house is required to override a veto. Governor Oswald West is thought to hold the veto record with a total of 58 vetoes in 1911. Governor Vic Atiyeh vetoed 40 in 1983, and Governor John Kitzhaber vetoed 57 in 1995.

Video. See **Northwest Film and Video Center**.

Vietnam Veterans Living Memorial. An 11-acre site in **Washington Park** dedicated in 1987 to the 57,000 Oregonians who served in the **Vietnam War**. The names of the 751 Oregonians who died in the war are listed on six polished black granite alcoves. There is also a companion chronology of events in Oregon from 1959 to 1976. Fallen Warriors Foundation, 333 S. State Street, Suite 241, Lake Oswego 97034. Portland Guidebook.

Vietnam War, 1950-1975. A war between South Vietnam (and later its allies, including the U.S.) and communist North Vietnam (supported by China). U.S. involvement escalated rapidly in the early 1960s. By 1968 the U.S. had 525,000 troops in Vietnam, and protests were increasing nation-wide and in Oregon, especially at the **University of Oregon**. President Nixon ordered an invasion of Cambodia on April 30, 1970, which, along with the killing of four student protesters at Kent State University in Ohio, reignited the protests. Classes were canceled at several Oregon colleges, and in **Portland**, on May 11, 1970, city police moved in on protesters in the South Park Blocks, injuring 31. The last American soldiers left Vietnam on April 29, 1975. In 1993 Katherine Power, alias Alice Metzinger, of the **Lebanon** area, confessed to having been a participant in a 1970 war-protest Boston bank robbery in which a policeman was killed. She was sentenced to 8 to 12 years in a Massachusetts prison. Oregonian 7/10/97:D1. See also **Vortex I; Women in the military**.

Vietnamese in Oregon. The 1990 census counted 9,000 Vietnamese in Oregon. In 1997 it was estimated that over 20,000 persons of Vietnamese heritage lived in the **Portland** area. An annual Tet Festival there celebrates the Vietnamese New Year for three days beginning on the new moon following January 20. Oregonian 2/2/97:D7. See also **Asians in Oregon**.

Vigilantes. A group of masked riders that ruled **Crook County** with lynchings and shootings between 1882 and 1884. After nine men had been killed or disappeared, the Vigilantes were defied by a law-abiding group called the Moonshiners, so called because they watched for the masked riders at night. Earlier, between 1863 and 1865, less organized vigilantes had killed 32 outlaws along the trails leading from **The Dalles** to **Canyon City** and the Idaho gold mines. East of the Cascades; Oregon's Golden Years. See also **Lynchings**.

Vinegar Hill. An 8,131' peak in the **Greenhorn Mountains** between the Middle and North Forks of the **John Day River** in eastern **Grant County**. The Green-Horn, a 300' foot high monolith of green serpentine, is on its slopes at the head of Salmon Creek. Oregon's Golden Years.

Virtue Flat. A four-mile-long area eight miles east of **Baker City**. The **Oregon Trail** crossed the flat and then wound on down Flagstaff Hill to the Powder River valley. Virtue Mine, the first **lode gold** mine in northeast Oregon, is nearby. Both were named for James W. Virtue, a prominent resident and one-time sheriff. Oregon Geographic Names.

Visibility. The Oregon Department of **Environmental Quality** operates a Visibility Monitoring Program in selected Class I (or pristine) areas from July 1 to September 15 under the federal Clean Air Act. The goal of the regulations is to reduce the frequency of visibility impairment in **wilderness areas** and **Crater Lake National Park** by 60 to 90% over 1982-84 levels. Thanks to regulation of major new sources of industrial emissions plus restrictions on summer **slash** and **field burning**, visibility in the north and central **Cascade Range** had improved 65 to 75% by 1992. Oregon Air Quality

"**Visit, but don't stay**". The shorthand version of a much-publicized statement made by then Governor Tom McCall on CBS evening news on January 12, 1971. His full statement, made during an interview about Oregon's environmental gains, was "Come visit us again and again. This is a state of excitement. But for heaven's sake, don't come here to live." Despite his admonition, Oregon's population grew 25% during his eight years in office. Fire at Eden's Gate. See also **Growth; James G. Blaine Society.**

Visitors information centers. The Oregon Department of **Economic Development** operates nine welcome centers, located in **Astoria, Seaside, Brookings, Ashland, Klamath Falls, Lakeview, Ontario, Umatilla,** and **Portland**. Banners greet tourists in Italian, French, Spanish, German, Korean, Japanese, Mandarin Chinese, and English. In Portland a center operated by the Portland/Oregon Visitors Association provides information about accommodations, attractions, conventions, events, interpreters, maps, tours, transportation, and weather conditions at 28 SW Salmon, Portland OR, 97204. 503-222-2223; 800-962-3700. See also **Tourism Commission**.

Vital records. Birth and death records are available from Oregon Vital Records Unit of the **Health Division**. Marriage and divorce records are available from them or from the appropriate county. There is a fee. 800 NE Oregon St., Suite 205, PO Box 14050, Portland 97293-0050. 503-731-4095.

Vital statistics. Oregon Vital Statistics Annual Report is published in two volumes. Volume one includes data on births, marriages, divorces, unmarried mothers, teen pregnancy, low birthweight infants, and induced abortions. Volume two include data on deaths, including infant and neonatal deaths, maternal deaths, and adolescent suicide attempts. Center for Health Statistics, 800 NE Oregon Street, Suite 215, Portland 97232.

Vocational Rehabilitation Division. A division of the Department of **Human Resources** that helps disabled Oregonians achieve and maintain employment and independence. 500 Summer St. NE, Salem 97310. 503-945-5880. Oregon Blue Book.

Vodka. A distilled liquor being produced by Bendistillery, a microdistillery in **Bend**. In addition to Crater Lake vodka the company also makes Cascade Mountain gin. Oregonian1/2/97:B10,8.

Volcanic eruption. The movement of molten material (magma) from the earth's interior to the surface. An eruption may be a quiet flow or an explosive event; it may be from a fissure, the flank of a **volcano**, or straight up or laterally from a central volcanic conduit. The erupted matter may be fluid (**lava**), gaseous, and/or solids, such as ash, rock, and **pumice**. Two-thirds of Oregon's landforms are volcanic in origin, though some of the activity took place elsewhere in volcanic archipelagos before they were accreted to North America as **terranes**. The most recent volcanic activity in the state has been along **Brothers fault zone** and the **Cascade Range**. While the magnitude of volcanism and volume of extrusions has been decreasing steadily since the middle **Miocene**, geologists say that many of Oregon's **Cascade Range** peaks are dormant (potentially active) rather than extinct, with **Newberry Crater** a likely spot for the next eruption. See also **Cinder cone; Crater Lake; Columbia River basalt; Diamond Craters; High lava**

plains; **Jordan Craters**; **McKenzie Pass**; **Mount Hood**; **Rocks, youngest**; **South Sister**.

Volcano. A vent in the earth from which molten rock, ash, and/or gases issue. A mountain of erupted material often forms around the vent. The eruption may be comparatively gentle or violently explosive depending upon the type of magma and whether moisture is present; water expands more than 1,000 times when it vaporizes, providing the explosive force in volcanic eruptions. The erupted magma may come from the leading edge of a subducting plate when it reaches a depth of about 90 miles below the surface where it melts, or it may come from the earth's magma chambers, from which it oozes up through cracks as the crust (land surface) is thinned by stretching. Volcanic cones in Oregon are of three types: **cinder cones**, shield volcanoes (**Newberry Volcano**), and composite or stratovolcanoes that form the high peaks of the **Cascade Range**. Fire Mountains. See also **Andesite**; **Basalt**; **Caldera**; **Lava**; **Lava tubes**; **Obsidian**; **Plate tectonics**; **Pumice**; **Rhyolite**; **Sea mounts**.

Voles. Various stocky, short-tailed **mice**. Thirteen species are found in Oregon in a variety of habitats, some living in trees and some in burrows. In 1958 an explosion of montane voles (also called montane meadow mice), *Microtus montanus*, overran much of eastern Oregon, spreading from the irrigated fields out into the desert itself. Numbers were said to be up to 6,400,000 in a square mile. A **Klamath County** grower "offered to bet all comers that if they threw a silver dollar out into his field of alfalfa, it would fall into an open mouse hole. He nearly always won." The plague was one of the largest in world history. Voles consume their own weight in food in a day, and can destroy an alfalfa field in short order. The white-footed vole is a **protected animal**. The California red-backed vole, which lives largely on **truffles**, is a favorite of the **Northern spotted owl**. Lemmings, which are related to voles, are not found in Oregon. Atlas of Oregon Wildlife; Mammals of the Northwest; Oregon Desert; "Searching."

Volkssports. Inexpensive organized physical recreations, including walking, bicycling, cross-country skiing, and swimming, offered in Oregon through 40 local Volkssports clubs. The most popular activities are the 10-kilometer (6.2-mile) walks. Oregon Trail State Volkssport Association, PO Box 1422, Tualatin 97062. 503-243-5725.

Volunteers. A 1997 study for the **Progress Board** found that 55% of Oregonians said they gave some volunteer time, compared with 49% nationwide. About 33% volunteer an hour a week; the Progress Board goal is to increase that to 50% by 2010. The study found that college graduates volunteer more than those with high school education, 45% to 21%; home owners volunteer more than renters, 36% to 26%, and married Oregonians volunteer more than singles, 38% to 24%. Oregonian 8/29/97:C1.

Vortex I. A free, state-sponsored rock music festival held in McIver State Park 30 miles southeast of Portland, August 28-30, 1970. It was designed to decrease the possibility of violent confrontation between students protesting the **Vietnam War** and 25,000 members of the American Legion at their national convention in **Portland** with President Nixon as the scheduled speaker. The festival was pushed through by Governor Tom McCall despite much opposition. It proved to be effective, with some 35,000 attending Vortex I and only a small group of protesters in Portland. Police were stationed at the entrance but not within the park; there was no violence and few injuries. Fire at Eden's Gate; Vortex I.

Vote by mail. A process first authorized by the 1981 legislature. Oregon held the nation's first vote-by-mail **election** for a federal office during the January 1996 special election to replace **Senator** Bob Packwood. The 65.8% turnout was the highest in any state-wide special election of the century. Vote by mail eliminates the expense, estimated to have been $2,000,000 a year, of setting up polling places in each precinct. Oregonian 2/1/96:E4.

Vote Smart. See **Project Vote Smart**.

Voter registration. Oregonians may register to vote by mail or in person up to 21 days before an **election**. Forms are available from county election offices, in many public buildings, and from many state agencies, including **Driver and Motor Vehicle Services**. For the November 1996 general election, 1,962,155 voters were registered in Oregon, 805,286 (41%) as **Democrat**, 714,548 (36%) as **Republican**, 400,248 (20%) as **Independent** (up from 11% in 1990), and 2% in other parties. Republicans held a majority in most counties, except **Multnomah County** where registrations were 50% Democrat and 26% Republican, the coastal counties from **Coos** north and then east along the **Columbia River** through **Wasco County**, and in the central Willamette Valley counties of **Benton**, **Linn**, and **Lane**. In 1970, only 2% of the voters were registered as something other than Democrat or Republican, but the percent has been increasing steadily since 1970. Voter registration was adopted by the state in 1898. Prior to 1986 Oregonians could register up to and on election day, but that was changed after the Bhagwan Shree Rajneesh tried to take over **Wasco County** government by bringing in homeless people at the last minute to vote. Governing Oregon; Oregon Blue Book.

Voter turnout. In the 1996 **general election**, 1,399,180 Oregonians, or 71% of all registered voters, voted. That compared with 68% in 1994 and 82% in 1992. The 1996 turnout included 75% of registered **Democrats** (604,147 voted), 79% of registered **Republicans** (561,376), 45% of those registered in other parties (18,814), and 54% of those registered as **Independent** (214,843). Oregonian 7/13/97:D2.

Voters' Pamphlet. A pamphlet of information about candidates and **ballot measures** that is assembled by the state **Elections Division** and mailed to each household in Oregon prior to **primary** and **general elections** and most statewide special elections. The space in the pamphlet is bought by candidates and by supporters or opponents of measures, except that the legislature may furnish an argument for each measure it refers. Regulations include a provision that a candidate's picture may not be more than a year old and may not show lapel pins or a uniform. Counties may issue voters' pamphlets for local elections. Many states don't have voters' pamphlets; Oregon was one of the first, authorizing it in 1903. Governing Oregon; Oregon Blue Book.

Voting. See **Elections**.

Wage and Hour Division. A division of the Oregon Bureau of **Labor and Industries** that administers and enforces state laws concerning working conditions, **minimum wage**, overtime, employment of minors, wage collection, and wage rate. It also licenses farm/forest labor contractors, farm-worker camp operators, shorthand reporters, private employment agencies, and consumer-electronic/ entertainment-equipment service providers. A commission of three-members, appointed by the governor to four-year terms, sets policies. 800 NE Oregon St. #32, Portland 97232, 503-731-4074. Oregon Blue Book.

Wages. In October 1995, average hourly earnings for Oregon industrial production workers were $12.79, ranging from $7.72 in apparel manufacturing to $18.80 in construction. An Oregon **Employment Department** 1996 survey found that wages in Oregon had increased 142% since 1976 while inflation rose 169%, resulting in a real-wage decrease of about 10%. Most of the loss was attributed to the **recession of 1980-1983**. In 1996 the annual wage averaged $27,031 in Oregon and $28,945 nationally. Wages were lower across eastern Oregon, with **Sherman County** on the bottom at $17,903. Oregon Economic and Revenue Forecast; Oregon Labor Trends; Oregonian 9/28/96:D1, 3/24/97:B12, 11/12/97:E2. See also **Income**; **Minimum wage**; **Salaries**; **Wealthiest**.

Wagon roads. Prior to development of roads over which wheeled vehicles could travel, freight was carried by back, boat, or **pack string**. In 1836, the Whitman missionary caravan traveled west with wagons, though their heavy wagon was abandoned at Fort Laramie, and only a light wagon, reduced to a two-wheeled cart, was taken through to Fort Boise, the first wheeled vehicle to go so far on the western trail. The first wagon to reach the **Willamette Valley** was one of the Newell party's wagons in 1841, and in 1843 the first of many **wagon trains** came through on the **Oregon Trail**, which meant that goods could be transported to Oregon via a land route, at least as far as **The Dalles**. The **Applegate Trail**, a wagon route from Fort Hall, Idaho, into the south end of the Willamette Valley, was opened in 1846. In 1848 the Oregon end was used in the other direction by the first wagons to travel south from Oregon to California, following the Applegate Trail to Tule Lake, California, and then heading southwest along a new route to the Sacramento Valley. By 1860 a shorter route to California was opened to the west of Mount Shasta. The first wagons to travel south from **The Dalles** through central Oregon were those of an Army caravan laden with supplies for **Fort Klamath** in the fall of 1867. Some wagon roads were developed as **military wagon roads** and others were built by private parties as **toll roads** . East of the Cascades; Empire of the Columbia; In the Ruts; Pioneer Roads; Roads of Yesterday; South Road. See also **Free Emigrant Road**; **Freighting outfits**; **"Get Oregon Out of the Mud"**; **Highways, history**; **Military wagon roads**; **Siskiyou Trail**; **Stage lines**; **Yreka Trail**.

Wagon trains. Though some Oregon immigrants arrived by ship, most, especially farmers with livestock, families, and household goods, came by wagon 2,000 miles over the **Oregon Trail** until the **railroad** connection opened in 1883. The first major wagon train was that of the 1843 Oregon Emigrating Company (the **Great Migration**). At a time when wages were $1.50 a day and land in Illinois was selling for $3 to $6 per acre, immigrants needed $800 to $1,200 to prepare for the trip. Supplies at the few supply forts along the way cost $1/pound for coffee, sugar, and flour. The wagons were prairie schooners with a 4'x10' bed, wide wooden wheels, and a cloth top. Each wagon could carry about 2,000 pounds of supplies. Women and children walked most of the way in order to lighten the load for the oxen that were pulling the wagons.

Wagontire Mountain. A long 6,504' central-Oregon mountain in the **high lava plains** between **Highways 20** and **395**. It was a landmark for early travelers who camped by a large spring on its north side and named it for an iron wagon tire rim abandoned by an early immigrant party. Earlier it had been known as Mountain Spring and Ram's Peak. Legendary horse rancher Bill Brown (1855-1941) owned over 30,000 acres in the area. One of the sheep slaughters of the **range wars** took place on its slopes in 1904, and later, from 1925 to1930, the mountain was the site of the Wagontire Mountain Range Feud in which five men died. East of the Cascades; Oregon Geographic Names; William "Bill" W. Brown.

Wah Gwin Gwin Falls. A 207-foot waterfall on Phelps Creek west of **Hood River**, just before the creek reaches the **Columbia River**. The falls are on the grounds of the Columbia Gorge Hotel, reached via exit 62 from **Interstate 84** and west on Westcliff Drive for .2 mile The Indian name is said to mean tumbling waters. Waterfall Lover's Guide.

Wahclella Falls. A waterfall in the **Columbia River Gorge** that drops 95 feet in two tiers into a pool on Tanner Creek, a mile up a trail from the **Bonneville Dam** exit from **Interstate 84**. Wahclella was the **Indian** name for an area near **Beacon Rock**. Waterfall Lover's Guide.

Wahkeena Falls. An easily viewed, 242-foot tiered waterfall in the **Columbia River Gorge** one half mile west of **Multnomah Falls**. Originally called Gordon Falls, the name was changed in 1915 to the Yakima Indian word meaning "most beautiful." Waterfall Lover's Guide.

Waldo Lake. A natural large, deep, high mountain lake of exceptional clarity located at the head of the North Fork of the **Willamette River**, 55 miles southeast of **Eugene**. It covers 6,298 acres in a glacial basin enclosed by moraines, is almost six miles long, and has a maximum depth of 420 feet. The cobalt blue lake is among the purest in the world, though the lack of nutrients limits fish production. Canoeing and sailing are popular, but there is a 10 mph limit for motor boats. The only facilities are three campgrounds with boat ramps. A onetime project to route water from the lake down through a tunnel to a west-side power plant was partially built; some evidence remains. The lake is now protected under the state's **Scenic Waterways** law. It was named for Judge John B. Waldo (1844-1907) who sought his recreation in the Cascades. Atlas of Oregon Lakes.

Waldport. A coastal **Lincoln County** tourist and retirement town at the mouth of the Alsea River where Highway 34 meets **Highway 101**. The town was founded, and the post office established, in 1881 by David Ruble of Alsea who named it using the German word for forest plus "port." There was no wagon road to the town until 1888. The city was incorporated in 1911. The hazardous bar at the mouth of the river has discouraged use as an ocean port, but fishing is popular in the river and bay. The handsome 1936 bridge over the bay was replaced in 1991, an event documented at the state's Alsea Bay Bridge Interpretive Center, 541-563-2002. Population 1980 1,274; 1995 1,705. Elevation 12'. PO Box 1120, 97394. 541-563-3561. First One Hundred Years; Oregonian 9/7/97:H1. See also **Heaven's Gate**.

Walking. See **Hiking**; **Volkssports**.

Walla Walla College School of Nursing. An accredited private college in

Portland that enrolled 101 students in 1995. 10355 SE Market, 97216. 503-251-6115. Oregon Blue Book.

Walla Walla River. A river that rises in the **Blue Mountains** of northeast Oregon and flows northwest into Washington State and west to join the **Columbia River** just north of the Oregon border. Its waters are used to irrigate productive farmlands north of **Milton-Freewater**. Walla is a **Nez Perce** word meaning running water; repeating it indicates a diminutive, so that Walla Walla means a small rapid river. Oregon Geographic Names.

Wallace House. A **trading post** built in 1812 by members of the **Pacific Fur Company**. The post, located on Wallace Prairie about three miles north of what is now **Salem**, was the first structure built by whites in the **Willamette Valley**. The building passed through the hands of the **North West Company** and the **Hudson's Bay Company** before becoming the first home for the **Oregon Institute**, a **Methodist** school that was the forerunner of **Willamette University**. Dictionary of Oregon History.

Walleye. A sport fish, *Stizostedion vitreum*, introduced into the upper **Columbia River** in the 1940s which has since spread down the river past **Portland**. The Oregon record is a 19-pound, 15-ounce fish caught in 1990 near **Rufus**. Walleye, so called because of its apparently opaque eye, is also called pike perch. **Indians** may legally sell walleye along the Oregon banks of the **Columbia River**. Oregonian 4/18/96:C1, 8/29/97:C4.

Wallowa. A **Wallowa County** ranching community 47 miles northeast of **La Grande** and 18 miles northwest of **Enterprise** on Highway 82. The post office was established in 1873 and the city was incorporated in 1899. See **Wallowa River** for the origin of the name. Population 1980 847; 1995 755. Elevation 2,923'. PO Box 487, 97885. 541-886-2422. History of Wallowa County.

Wallowa County. A rugged county in the northeast corner of Oregon with the **Wallowa Mountains** in the south, the Wallowa River valley in the center, and deep grassy canyons in the north draining to the **Snake River** and **Hells Canyon**. Elevations range from 870' along the Snake up to 9,839' **Sacajawea Peak**. Incorporated cities are **Enterprise** (county seat), **Joseph**, **Lostine**, and **Wallowa**. The county is bounded by Washington State on the north, Idaho on the east, and by **Baker**, **Union**, and **Umatilla** counties. Wallowa County was created in 1887 from **Union County** by residents who felt too far removed from the county seat. The next year, in a bitterly contested election, Enterprise defeated Joseph for the county seat. The first wagon road into the area was built in 1879, and the **Oregon Railway and Navigation Co**. rail line in 1908. The Wallowa County Chieftain, a weekly established in 1884, is the county's general circulation newspaper and oldest business. The economy is based on ranching, lumber, bronze casting and art, and recreation. Taxable assessed value in 1995 was $428,000,000, or $59,000 per capita. Population 1980 7,273; 1995 7,250. Area 3,153 square miles. Density 2/sq.mi. Annual precipitation 13"; average temperature January 24°F, July 63°F. Courthouse, 101 S River, Enterprise 97828. 541-426-4543. History of Wallowa County; Oregon Blue Book.

Wallowa Lake. A large oval lake in northeastern Oregon in a spectacular setting at the base of the **Wallowa Mountains**. The 1,508-acre lake lies in a glaciated valley flanked on each side by smooth lateral **moraines** that rise 900 feet above the water; a terminal moraine encloses the end of the lake. Water level is controlled by a dam, the latest in a series dating back to1884. Maximum depth in the 3.5-mile-long lake is 299 feet. Fishing is excellent. Over half of the land around the lake is in private ownership. **Wallowa Lake State Park** is located at the south end and the town of **Joseph** lies just to the north. A monster is said to live in the lake. Atlas of Oregon Lakes; Oregon's Ghosts and Monsters. See also **Alpenfest**; **Sockeye**.

Wallowa Lake State Park. A **state park** at the south end of **Wallowa Lake** that includes a marina, a one-mile nature trail, and a 210-site campground with a **yurt**. Reservations, 800-452-5687. 72214 Marina Lane, Joseph 97846. 541-432-4185.

Wallowa Lake Tramway. A service offering 15-minutes rides in four-passenger aerial gondola cars from 4,100' up to 8,140', near the top of **Mount Howard** in the **Wallowa Mountains**. Views from the top encompass broad fields to the north, **Wallowa Lake**, and the high peaks and steep canyons of the Wallowas. A deli operates at the top of the tramway, and there are two miles of alpine trails. It opened in 1970. A proposed chair lift on the east side of the mountain would offer 2,000 vertical feet of downhill skiing. Skiers would reach it from the top of the tramway. 541-432-5331. Oregonian 10/14/97:E13.

Wallowa Mountains. A mountain mass in northeastern Oregon, called the Switzerland of North America, that continues in Idaho as the Seven Devils Mountains; **Hells Canyon** cuts between. The Wallowas are part of a five-mile thick **terrane** from the **Paleozoic**, once part of a volcanic island chain. A large **granitic** intrusion from about 150 million years ago now makes up the resistant core of the higher parts. **Sacajawea Peak** at 9,839' is the highest peak. Other high peaks include the **Matterhorn**, at 9,832', Aneroid Mountain, 9,702', Pete's Point, 9,675', Twin Peaks, 9,673', and Eagle Cap, 9,595. Three episodes of **glaciation** also shaped the area. Ore bodies around the margins of the granite have been commercially mined for **gold**, **copper**, and **silver**. There are nearly 100 lakes in the Wallowas; **Wallowa Lake** is the largest. Most of the area is within the **Wallowa Whitman National Forest**; the central area is in the **Eagle Cap Wilderness Area**. The **Wallowa Lake Tramway** offers rides up **Mount Howard** near **Wallowa Lake**. Geology of Oregon. See also **Geographic center of the United States**; **Mount Fanny**.

Wallowa River. A river in northeast Oregon that rises in the **Wallowa Mountains** and flows north through **Wallowa Lake** and west into the **Grande Ronde River**. Hay fields and pastures in its high valley are irrigated from the river, which drains an area of 1,750 square miles. Wallowa is a **Nez Perce** word for a fish trap made of a structure of stakes set in a triangle to support a network of sticks. The structures were placed in the river just below Wallowa Lake. Oregon Geographic Names.

Wallowa-Whitman National Forest. A 2,396,934-acre national forest, the nation's largest, in the northeast corner of Oregon. It includes four wilderness areas, North Fork John Day, Monument Rock, **Eagle Cap**, and **Hells Canyon**, as well as **Starkey Experimental Forest and Range** and **Hells Canyon National**

Recreation Area. 1550 Dewey Avenue, P.O.Box 907, Baker City 97814. 541-523-6391.

Wallula Gap. A narrow, 12-mile-long, cliff-lined gap in the Horse Heaven Hills through which the **Columbia River** flows as it reaches Oregon. A pair of large side-by-side basalt columns, the Twin Sisters, were noted by **Lewis and Clark**. Columbia.

Wallula Stone. A 10-ton block of **Columbia River basalt**, covered with carvings thought to date from about 1500 AD. Originally located near the confluence of the Walla Walla and Columbia Rivers at a site now flooded, in 1910 it was brought to Portland where it was displayed at the City Hall until it was returned to the **Umatilla Indian Reservation** in 1996. The stone is said to have marked the area where the territories of several tribes came together. Oregonian 7/27/96:B2, 8/1/96:D2..

Wapato. A plant, *Sagittaria latifolia*, with a fleshy root and large, arrowhead-shaped leaves that grows in shallow ponds. It is also called arrowhead or wild potato. The roots, harvested year-round, were an important food source for Indians. After **carp** were introduced, the plant was all but eliminated in areas where it had formerly grown thickly, as on **Sauvie Island**. Story of Sauvies Island.

Wapiti. See **Elk**.

Warm Springs Highway. See **Highway 26**.

Warm Springs Indians. A tribe of Indians, also called Tenino, whose members originally lived in a 10 million acre area from the **Columbia River** to south of **Bend**, between the **Cascade Range** and the **Blue Mountains**, except for an area controlled by the **Wasco Indians** in the northwest corner. The Warm Springs Indians spoke Sahaptian, and moved between summer and winter villages. **Sherars Falls** on the **Deschutes** was an important fishing spot for **salmon**, and they also depended on game, roots, and berries. They were moved to the **Warm Springs Reservation** in 1855. PO Box 1299, Warm Springs 97761. 541-553-3257. First Oregonians; People of Warm Springs.

Warm Springs Reservation, Confederated Tribes of the. A confederation of some 3,600 members of the **Warm Springs**, **Northern Paiute**, and **Wasco** tribes. Each of the three tribes came from a different area, had a different lifestyle, and spoke a totally different language. About 3,100 members live on the 641,035-acre reservation, the largest in Oregon, established in 1855 northwest of **Madras**. Most of the reservation lies in **Wasco** and **Jefferson** counties, and extends from the crest of the **Cascade Range** east down to the arid lands along the **Deschutes River**. The confederation operates several businesses, including a sawmill and **Kah-Nee-Ta** Resort and Indian Head Gaming Center, as well as the **Museum at Warm Springs**. PO Box C, Warm Springs 97761. 541-553-3257. American Indian Reservations; First Oregonians; Native Peoples; Oregonian 10/22/95:A18; People of Warm Springs.

Warm Springs Reservoir. A large irrigation impoundment 14 miles southwest of **Juntura** in sparsely vegetated land on the line between **Harney** and **Malheur Counties**. The lake was formed in 1919 by the construction of a 106-foot high, concrete arch dam by the Warm Springs Irrigation District. The **Vale Project** now owns half of the storage. The lake covers 4,195 acres when full with a maximum depth of 140 feet, but is much reduced by late summer. Recreation use is limited by difficult access. Atlas of Oregon Lakes.

Warmwater fish. Fish species native or introduced to Oregon's ponds, lakes, reservoirs, and main rivers. Records kept by the Oregon Bass and Panfish Club include largemouth bass, 11 lb. 9.6 oz; smallmouth bass 7 lb. 4.6 oz; bluegill 2 lb. 5.5 oz; warmouth 1 lb. 14.2 oz; black crappie 4 lb. 6.1 oz; white crappie 4 lb. 12 oz; yellow perch 2 lb. 2 oz; bullhead catfish 3 lb. 6 oz; channel catfish 36 lb. 8 oz; white-striped hybrid bass 18 lb. 8 oz; flathead catfish 42 lb.; white catfish 15 lb.; green sunfish 11 oz; redear sunfish 1 lb. 15.5 oz; pumpkinseed sunfish 6.6 oz. Oregon Bass and Panfish Club, PO Box 1021, Portland 97207. Oregonian 5/23/96:D9. See also **Walleye**.

Warner Canyon. A ski area 10 miles northeast of **Lakeview**, owned by **Lake County**, with a T-bar and a 730-foot drop from a 6,000-foot top elevation. PO Box 1204, Lakeview 97630. 541-947-5001. Oregonian 11/16/97:T7.

Warner Mountains. A mountain range in northeastern California that extends into Oregon just east of **Lakeview**, between **Goose Lake** on the west and the **Warner Valley** on the east. Two of the Oregon peaks, Crane Mountain and Drake Peak, are over 8,400' high. **Abert Rim** is at the northern end of the range. There is also a Warner Mountain in the **Cascade Range** southeast of **Oakridge**.

Warner Pacific College. An accredited private college in **Portland** that enrolled 670 students in 1995. 2219 SE 68th Ave., Portland 97215. 503-775-4366. Oregon Blue Book.

Warner Valley. A fault-block basin in southeastern **Lake County** lying at the western base of **Hart Mountain** and Poker Jim Ridge. It is lined with a 40-mile chain of a dozen lakes and marshes, all remnants of **Pleistocene** Lake Warner, sometimes called Lake Coleman. Crump Lake at the south is 13 feet higher than Bluejoint Lake at the north end. The largest lakes are **Hart Lake** and Crump Lake which may each cover over 7,000 acres, though there are years when all the lakes dry up. Hot springs are common, and Crump **Geyser**, created by well drilling, erupted periodically for several decades. A significant earthquake shook the area in 1968. The community of Adel is on **Highway 140** where it crosses the valley. Brevet Captain William Warner was killed by Indians in 1849 just south of the valley. Oregon Geographic Names; Hole in the Sky.

Warrenton. Oregon's most northwesterly town, located in **Clatsop County** across the two-mile-long **Youngs Bay** Bridge from **Astoria**. D. K. Warren platted the town in 1891, and it grew to include Lexington (the original county seat, founded in 1848) and Flavel. Warrenton was incorporated in 1899, and **Hammond** merged with it in 1991. In land area the city is the fourth largest in the state, much of it on former tide flats protected by dikes built by **Chinese** labor. The town includes the county airport and 80% of the industrial area of the county. The economy is supported by a sawmill, seafood processing plant, fishing, a large **Coast Guard** base, and tourism. Area attractions include **Fort Stevens State Park**, Historical Area and Military Museum, the wreck of the *Peter Iredale*, **Fort Clatsop National Monument** (the 1805-1806 wintering site of the **Lewis and Clark Expedition**), and the south **jetty** and sand spit at the mouth of the **Columbia River**, plus fishing, clamming, and the annual Astoria-Warrenton Crab and Seafood Festival in April.

Population 1980 2,493; 1995 3,845. Elevation 5'. PO Box 250, 97146. 503-861-2233. Warrenton.

Wars. See **Indian wars**; **Civil War, 1861/65**; **Spanish American War, 1898/99**; **World War I, 1914/18**; **World War II, 1941/45**; **Korean Conflict, 1950/53**; **Vietnam War, 1950/75**; **Operation Desert Storm, 1991.**

Wasco. A north Oregon community in **Sherman County** 30 miles east of **The Dalles** on **Highway 97**. It is located at the historic intersection of a route from the Deschutes country to the south with the **Oregon Trail**. The first post office, established in 1870, was called Spanish Hollow, but in 1882 the name was changed to Wasco for the county which at that time encompassed it. The city was incorporated in 1898. Population 1980 415; 1995 385. Elevation 1,271'. PO Box 26, 97065. 541-442-5515. Oregon Geographic Names.

Wasco County. A northern-tier county on the **Columbia River** just east of the **Cascade Range** that includes the east slopes of **Mount Hood** and the lower **Deschutes River**. Incorporated cities are **The Dalles** (county seat), **Antelope, Dufur, Maupin, Mosier, Shaniko**. The county is bounded by Washington State (reached by a bridge at The Dalles) on the north, and by **Sherman, Gilliam, Wheeler, Jefferson, Marion, Clackamas**, and **Hood River** counties. Elevations range from 72' along the Columbia to 5,599-foot Mount Wilson on the crest of the Cascades in the **Warm Springs Reservation.** When it was created in 1854 from **Champooick District**, Wasco County included all of the **Oregon Territory** between the **Cascade Range** and the Rocky Mountains, some 130,000 square miles. It was named for the local tribe of Indians. The economy is based on agriculture (wheat, cherries, apples, livestock), lumber, manufacturing, electric power, transportation, and aluminum. Northwest Aluminum in **The Dalles** employs 500 workers, making it the county's largest private employer. Taxable assessed value in 1995 was $1,075,000,000, or $48,000 per capita. Population 1980 21,732; 1995 22,600. Area 2,396 square miles. Density 9/sq.mi. Annual precipitation 13"; average temperature January 33°F, July 73°F. Courthouse, 511 Washington, The Dalles 97058. 541-296-2207. History of Wasco County; Oregon Blue Book.

Wasco Indians. A tribe of Indians whose members originally lived along the south shore of the **Columbia River** from the **Cascades** east to **Celilo Falls**, but who were moved to the **Warm Springs Reservation** in 1855. The eastern-most group of Chinookan-speaking Indians, they remained at their village sites throughout the year, fishing for **salmon** and trading. People of Warm Springs.

Wascopam. A **Methodist** mission at **The Dalles** organized in 1838 by the Rev. Daniel Lee, nephew of the Rev. Jason Lee of **Willamette Mission**. Pulpit Rock, the focal point of the mission, can be seen behind the present high school. The mission was abandoned in 1847, and the buildings were used for a few years as a military garrison called Fort Lee. Dictionary of Oregon History; Guide to Early Oregon Churches.

Washburne State Park. See **Carl Washburne State Park**.

Washington. The state that borders Oregon on the north. The **Columbia River** forms the boundary between Oregon and Washington from the ocean upriver until it turns north near **Pendleton**. The border then follows the 46th parallel east to the **Snake River** and the border with **Idaho**. Washington is 70% the size of

Oregon and has 1.7 times its population. At one time it was part of the **Oregon Territory**, contested for by Britain and the U.S. After the treaty of 1846 established the present U.S./Canadian boundary, settlement in Washington increased rapidly. It became Washington Territory in 1853 and a state in 1889. Seattle developed as the major Northwest port because it could be reached without the dangerous bar crossing that faced ships at the mouth of the **Columbia River**. Oregon and Washington have always been closely tied by the proximity of populated areas and by similar interests, problems, and environment.

Washington County. A rapidly growing metropolitan and agricultural county in northwest Oregon just west of **Portland**. Incorporated cities are **Hillsboro** (county seat), **Banks, Beaverton, Cornelius, Durham, Forest Grove, Gaston, King City, North Plains, Sherwood, Tigard, Tualatin**, and **Wilsonville**. The county is bounded by **Columbia, Multnomah, Clackamas, Yamhill**, and **Tillamook** counties. Elevations range from 100' along the Tualatin River up to 3,300' Saddle Mountain on the **Coast Range** on the west. The economy is based on high-tech industry, agriculture, lumber, and food processing. Taxable assessed value in 1995 was $22,280,000,000, or $60,000 per capita. The county was created in 1843 as one of the original four counties, called **Twality District** at the time. The name was changed in 1849 to honor the country's first president. Population 1980 245,860; 1995 370,000. Area 727 square miles. Density 509/sq.mi. Annual precipitation 38"; average temperature January 39°F, July 67°F. 155 N 1st Ave., Hillsboro 97124. 503-648-8611. Oregon Blue Book. See also **Metro**.

Washington Park. A 145-acre park in the west hills of **Portland**. In an act of forethought the city fathers purchased the land in 1871 when it lay far from the city, which had a population of 8,000. Washington Park now anchors the south end of a chain of parks that extends a green belt for nine miles to the northwest through **Forest Park**. In the 1880s the German Songbird Society of Portland imported starlings, nightingales, thrushes, and finches for the park which contributed to its popularity for carriage drives. Park facilities now include **Metro Washington Park Zoo, World Forestry Center, International Rose Test Garden, Rose Garden Children's Park, Japanese Garden, Hoyt Arboretum, Vietnam Memorial**, an outdoor theater, a narrow gauge railway, an archery range, tennis courts, and picnic areas. Portland, An Informal History.

Washington Park Fences Project. A 1995 project in which 16 artists turned 13,000 square feet of plywood fence around a **light rail** construction site at **Metro Washington Park Zoo** into giant murals. Kristy Edmunds was curator of the "Fences" project which was documented in a 1996 catalog.

Washington Park Zoo. See **Metro Washington Park Zoo**.

Washington Public Power Supply System (WPPSS). A consortium of 19 **people's utility districts** and 4 municipal electric systems in the state of Washington. The group organized in 1957, and in the 1960s began construction of five **nuclear power** plants. Only plant number 2 at **Hanford Nuclear Reservation** in Washington was completed (1,200 **megawatts**). **Bonneville Power Administration (BPA)** markets its costly power. The other plants were mothballed after costs soared from the expected $4 billion to $24 billion ($4,800 each for Washington's 5,000,000 residents). BPA had backed the bonds for Plants 1, 2, and 3 and still carries $7.1 billion of that debt. In 1983 WPPSS defaulted on $2.25 billion in investor-owned bonds for uncompleted Plants 4 and 5, which was the largest default in the history of the municipal bond market. The resulting court battle was finally resolved in 1995. Illusions of Power; Oregonian 1/27/95:B2; Organic Machine.

Water law. Under Oregon law all waters in the state, both surface and groundwaters, belong to the public and are managed by the **Water Resources** Department under polices established by the Water Resources Commission.

Water ouzel. A small, nondescript gray bird, *Cinclus mexicanus*, that frequents rapidly-flowing streams year round. It is unusual in being as much at home under water as on land as it walks about hunting among pebbles for food, even on the bottom of rushing torrents. Because it bobs constantly as it moves about, it is also called dipper. It sings all year, and builds its moss-covered nests near water, sometimes in the spray. Birds of Oregon.

Water pollution. In 1997 the two most common chemical pollutants in the **Willamette River** were atrazine and diuron, both pesticides that drain into the river from farmland. The greatest concentration of atrazine was .2 parts per billion, well below the EPA safety standard of 3 parts per billion, and the largest concentration of diuron was .24 parts per billion, much less than the EPA standard of 10 parts per billion. From 1990 through 1994, industries legally discharged more cancer-causing chemicals into the **Columbia River** than into any other river in the nation. The Columbia received over 4.3 million pounds of legal toxic emissions annually and the Willamette River 1.2 million pounds. A 1995 study found that half of the river **otters** trapped on the lower Columbia River exhibited physical deformities caused by pollution. Pollutants being released into a river or along its shores can be reported to the Oregon Department of **Environmental Quality** at 800-452-0311. Information about **Portland**'s combined sewer and storm drain overflow into the **Willamette River** is available from the River Alert Info Line, 503-823-2479. Oregonian 3/1/96:B1, 9/25/96:D1, 4/30/97:A13, 12/12/97:C8. See also **Dioxins**; **Environmental Quality Department**; **Groundwater**; **Nitrate pollution**; **Pollution**; **Spills**; **Water quality**.

Water quality. **Crater Lake** has the purest water in the state. Four Oregon cities, **Baker City**, **Bend**, **Portland**, and **Reedsport**, get their **drinking water** from sources so pure they do not have to filter the water. In 1998 the Oregon Department of **Environmental Quality** identified 1,163 river segments, totaling 13,800 miles (out of 112,000 miles of river in the state), plus 32 lakes as failing to meet federal clean water standards because of high temperatures (over half the streams), fecal coliform bacteria, toxic residues from farms and industries, excess nutrients, and/or excess sediments. DEQ Water Quality Division, 811 SW 6th Ave., Portland 97204. 503-229-5279. Mail Tribune 2/20/98:1A; Oregon Environmental Atlas; Oregonian 7/18/96:C1; Oregon's 1994 Water Quality. See also **Groundwater**; **Sewage treatment**; **Waterborne diseases**; **Willamette River water quality**.

Water Resources, Oregon Department of. The department that authorizes diversions and appropriations of surface and groundwater, assures the safety of dams, issues permits for water use, establishes instream water rights, determines critical groundwater areas, and monitors water supplies and quality in Oregon's 18 river basin areas. The department has 17 districts throughout the state, each with a watermaster in charge. The seven-member Water Resources Commission oversees the activities of the department, sets water policy, and determines how unallocated water will be used. Commerce Bldg., 158 12th St. NE, Salem 97310. 503-378-8455; 800-624-3199. Oregon Blue Book. See also **Groundwater**; **Irrigation**; **Rivers**.

Water rights. Disputes over allocation of water rights resulted in 1909 legislation that gave the authority to control water rights to the state. Rights are based of the principle of "prior appropriation" which means that, when supplies are limited, users with the most recent water rights are the first to get shut off so those with prior rights can continue to have water. In low flow years there may not be any water left in some streams after existing rights are exercised, especially for portions of the **Walla Walla**, **Umatilla**, **Rogue**, and **Umpqua** rivers. Any water rights granted after 1955 may be used only for water amounts in excess of the minimum stream flows established at that time. A water right is a property right attached to the land so goes to the new owner if the land is sold. The principle of prior appropriation also applies to **groundwater**. Oregon Environmental Atlas. See also **Irrigation**.

Water spreading. The practice of irrigating crop lands outside irrigation district boundaries, also defined as the unauthorized use of federal water. It is known to have occurred in recent years on some 17,000 acres near **Hermiston**. Farmers say the practice was condoned by the **Bureau of Reclamation** and resulted from improved irrigation efficiency which freed up more water. Environmentalists are concerned that, if it removes more water from streams, it damages **salmon** runs. Oregonian 4/24/96:C2.

Water supply. Oregon's water supply comes primarily from precipitation which averages 124 billion gallons a day, and another 1.3 billion gallons arrives in the state as surface-water inflow. Of the total 125.3 billion gallons, 44.2 billion gallons evaporates, 78.5 billion leaves as surface-water outflow, and 2.6 billion is consumed, mostly by agriculture. There is, in addition, a daily boundary river flow of 118 billion gallons. Oregon's water supply varies both by region and season. Oregon receives 75% of its precipitation between October and March but demand is highest in the summer. Snow provides natural storage of winter precipitation, and reservoirs store additional amounts for summer use, especially for irrigation. National Water Summary 1987. See also **Groundwater**; **Precipitation**.

Water table. See **Groundwater**.

Water use. In 1985 some 6,540 million gallons a day of water was withdrawn for use in Oregon, 88% of it for **irrigation** and the rest for domestic, commercial, industrial, and mining uses. Ninety percent of the total came from surface water and 10% from **groundwater**. Of the total, 40% was actually consumed and 60% returned. "Instream" uses, such as for fish, hydropower, or recreation, do not consume water but can nonetheless lead to conflicts, as on the **Columbia River** where the need for adequate flows for **salmon** conflicts with the need for maintaining high pools for hydropower and navigation. National Water Summary 1987.

Waterborne disease. In 1992 an outbreak of **Cryptosporidiosis** in **Medford**

caused 15,000 residents to become ill with diarrhea and abdominal cramps; it was traced to inadequately filtered **drinking water**. In 1975 some 2,200 people became ill from an *E. coli* bacterial infection at **Crater Lake National Park** that was caused by sewage seeping into the water supply. Smaller outbreaks in the state have resulted from *Shigella* in an unchlorinated well, and unfiltered surface water led to an enterovirus outbreak and at least six outbreaks of **giardiasis**. A typhoid fever epidemic in **Eugene** in 1906 was traced to the water supply, prompting formation of the **Eugene Water and Electric Board**. Oregon Drinking Water.

Waterfalls. Oregon has more than 400 identified waterfalls of an array of types, including plunge falls which fall free and horsetail falls which fall vertically while maintaining contact with the cliff face. Some 30 of the highest or most notable falls are described individually in this work, but all are appealing. The Oregon side of the **Columbia River Gorge** is lined with 71 waterfalls, 11 of them over 100 feet high, including **Multnomah Falls**, the state's highest at 620 feet. **Munson Creek Falls** is the highest in the **Coast Range** at 267 feet. **Silver Falls State Park** features ten major falls. Waterfalls at lower elevations are at their best in the winter and early spring, while high elevation falls are most spectacular after snowmelt has filled their streams in early summer. Waterfall Lover's Guide.

Waterfront Blues Festival. A **Portland** festival held annually in early July at **Governor Tom McCall Waterfront Park**, the largest blues festival on the west coast. Proceeds benefit the Oregon Food Bank. 503-282-0555.

Waterfront Park. See **Governor Tom McCall Waterfront Park**.

Waterloo. A **Willamette Valley** community in **Linn County** on the South **Santiam River** 18 miles southeast of **Albany** and 5 miles southeast of **Lebanon**. A grist mill located at the falls of the South Santiam River supported the nearby thriving community of Kees Mill until it burned; Waterloo County Park is near the site. The name Waterloo was suggested after a one-sided court decision in an estate settlement following Kees' death. The post office was established in 1875; the city was incorporated in 1893. Population 1980 211; 1995 220. Elevation 410'. 31140 First St., Lebanon, 97355. 541-451-2245. Oregon Geographic Names.

Watermaster. See **Water Resources, Oregon Department of**.

Watershed Enhancement Board, Governor's (GWEB). A board established by the state legislature in 1987 to help Oregonians improve the quality of the state's watersheds. (A watershed is the area drained by a distinct stream or river system and separated from other similar systems by ridgetop boundaries.) GWEB is also responsible for supporting local, county-established watershed councils and for granting funds to assist with local projects. There were 80 recognized councils in Oregon in 1998. Governor's Natural Resources Offices, Public Service Building, Salem 97310. 503-378-3589. Oregon Blue Book.

Waterspout. A **tornado** spawned over water that sucks up water and perhaps fish, sometimes dropping them later over land. On October 24, 1996, a waterspout was spotted over the ocean off **Cape Foulweather** that touched down two miles offshore and was shooting out lightning bolts as it came in. It dissipated as it hit land. In **Grant County** the term waterspout is used to mean a cloudburst and the resulting **flash flood**. Gold and Cattle Country; Oregonian 11/3/96:C6.

Watson Falls. A 272-foot plunge waterfall on Watson Creek, near the North

Umpqua Highway. The turn south off **Highway 138** is 2.2 miles east of Toketee Lake onto Fish Creek Road. The falls can be seen fully from a bridge across Watson Creek a quarter mile up the trail from the Watson Falls Picnic Ground. Waterfall Lover's Guide.

Waud Bluff. A bluff along the east shore of the **Willamette River** north of **Swan Island**, site of the **University of Portland** and the farthest upriver landing of the **Lewis and Clark Expedition**. Oregon Geographic Names. See also **Mocks Crest**.

Wave terraces. See **Terraces**.

Waves. Ocean waves off the Oregon **coast** are measured by a microseismometer at **Newport**. Ocean breakers average about 7 feet high in the summer and 13 feet in the winter, but individual storm waves are commonly 40-50 feet high, and the record is 95 feet. These storm waves have powerful erosion potential. An unexpectedly high wave is called a sneaker wave; such waves can wash the unwary out to sea. "Ocean processes and hazards along the Oregon coast." See also **Ocean currents**; **Sea level**; **Tsunami waves**.

Ways and Means Committee. See **Joint Ways and Means Committee**.

W.C.T.U. A 13-mile-long rail line, the White City Terminal and Utility Railroad, that operates in White City industrial park near **Medford**. White City was **Camp White** during **World War II**. W.C.T.U. also stands for the Women's Christian Temperance Union, an anti-drinking organization that was especially active during the first part of the 20th century. Railroading in Southern Oregon.

Wealthiest Oregonians. In 1997 Forbes Magazine listed three Oregonians among the 400 richest people in the country. They were #17, Philip Knight of **Portland** (**Nike** founder) $5.4 billion; # 361, Robert Boisseau Pamplin, Jr., of **Lake Oswego** (head of R. B. Pamplin Corporation textile mills and other interests) $525 million; and #388, Les Schwab of **Prineville** (**Les Schwab Tire Centers**) $500 million. Mail Tribune 9/29/97:5A.

Weapons depot. See **Umatilla Chemical Depot**.

Weasel. Small, short-legged, long-bodied furry carnivores noted as ferocious killers, sometimes apparently killing just for sport. Two species occur in Oregon. The long-tailed weasel, *Mustela frenata*, is up to 16 inches long, while the short-tailed weasel or ermine, *M. erminea*, is up to 10 inches long and has brown fur that, in colder areas, turns white in winter except for the black tip of the tail. Both live primarily on rodents, and are especially effective at catching them in burrows. The weasel is related to (in increasing size) **mink**, **marten**, **fisher**, and **wolverine**. Other members of the weasel family are the **badger**, **skunks**, and **otters**. 49 weasels were trapped in Oregon in 1994-95. Atlas of Oregon Wildlife; Mammals of the Northwest.

Weather. Oregon's earliest weather records are rainfall records from **Astoria** dating from 1850. The state's basic weather data set began in 1880, and information is now collected at 384 cooperative weather data sites, many of them staffed by volunteers who collect, at a minimum, high and low temperature for the date plus precipitation data. Earl Stewart in **Cottage Grove** was given the first Earl Stewart award in 1992 for 75 years of daily weather reporting, the longest in the country. See also **Climate**; **Rainfall records**; **Snowfall records**; **Storms**; **Tem-**

perature records; **Wind records**.

Weather Globe. A lighted globe on top of **Portland**'s Standard Plaza at 1100 SW 6th Ave. It shines white when colder weather is expected, red for warmer weather, and green if no change is forecast. The globe blinks if rain is coming but shines steadily for a dry forecast. It has been lighted since 1962. Oregonian 9/24/96:B1.

Weather goats. A one-time flock of feral goats that was often visible from **Roseburg** on the bluffs of Mount Nebo above **Interstate 5**. It was said that you could tell what the weather was going to do by how high up the bluffs the goats were browsing. In the 1970s a radio station broadcast an official goat report twice each morning. Among the reports "variable high goats" indicated good weather, "widely scattered goats" indicated partly sunny, and "low goat pressure" indicated an approaching storm. Oregonian 5/24/71:Sec.3:20.

Weather Machine. A 25-foot tall kinetic sculpture in **Pioneer Courthouse Square** in **Portland** that opens each day at noon with a puff of mist to make the weather forecast: a sun for clear weather, a dragon for rain, and a **great blue heron** (Portland's city bird) if uncertain. The device was designed in 1988 by Oman Design Group. Portland Guidebook.

Weather modification. In the early 1950s orchardists in the **Medford** area promoted seeding clouds with silver iodide as a way to reduce **hail** damage to their pear trees. The controversial practice generated opposition from other farmers who felt that it reduced their rainfall. Measures to control rain making in general were hotly debated in the legislature. The practice faded in the 1970s after environmental impact studies were required.

Weaving. Oregon's 27 weaving and fiber craft guilds belong to Weaving Guilds of Oregon (WeGO) which publishes lists of guilds, classes, and suppliers. Information is available from local arts centers or from the Portland Handweavers Guild, PO Box 6676, Portland 97228.

Wedderburn. An unincorporated community on the north bank of the **Rogue River** across from **Gold Beach**. It was established in 1895 to support a nearby salmon cannery, and since then has also been the home port for mail boat service up the Rogue. The name came from founder R. D. Hume's ancestral home in Scotland. Oregonian 9/1/95:B2.

Weddings. See **Justice court**; **Marriages**; **Municipal court**.

Weeds. Plants that are a nuisance because they are growing where they are not wanted. Nearly all of the agricultural, range, and garden weeds of Oregon are non-native **introduced species**, some brought in intentionally and some by accident. The following noxious weeds are toxic to livestock and big game and are controlled by law in eastern Oregon: leafy spurge (*Euphorbia esula*), knapweed (*Centaurea sp.*), yellow starthistle (*Centaurea solstitialis*), **tansy ragwort** (*Senecio jacobaea*), white-top (*Cardaria draba*), Dalmation toad flax (*Linaria dalmatica*), Scotch thistle (*Onopordum acanthium*), and rush skeletonweed (*Chondrilla juncea*). Other weeds especially troublesome in Oregon include **gorse** (*Ulex europaeus*) with its spiny stems, common crupina (*Crupina vulgaris*), and purple loosestrife (*Lythrum salicaria*), which is taking over some wetlands. Specific biological controls, such as beetles and weevils, are being introduced for some of the troublesome weed species, including tansy ragwort, gorse, and purple loosestrife. Plants and Animals; Weeds. See also **Jordan Valley Interagency Invasive Weed Management Project**.

Welfare. Assistance offered by the state to families in financial need, using a combination of state and federal money. Welfare recipients in the state are required to search for work and to participate in work programs and job training and, if needed, in mental health or drug addiction programs. Oregon's program operates under a seven-year federal waiver dating from the 1996 federal welfare reform law. The waiver allocates money to the state based on its 1994 level when Oregon had 44,000 families on welfare. By December 1997, the state's welfare rolls had shrunk to 19,542, the lowest number since 1970, because of the state's focus on helping recipients become self sufficient. The extra federal money was being used for programs to help needy families, including day-care and job-training. Oregonian 2/25/97:E1. See also **Adult and Family Services Division**; **Oregon Option**; **JOBS**.

Wells. The Oregon Department of **Water Resources** estimates that there are 300,000 wells in Oregon. About 3,800 of those serve regulated domestic water systems. A 1989 law requires the seller of any real estate that includes a well for domestic water to have the water tested and to report the results to the **Health Division**. The Division maintains a list of labs approved for **drinking water** testing. See also **Groundwater**.

Welsh in Oregon. By 1890 a number of Welsh families were farming in the area around Beaver Creek, south of **Oregon City**, where they built Bryn Seion Welsh Congregational Church. The church, still in use, has been the site of an annual Welsh singing festival. A number of people from Wales had also settled in **Portland**. "Wiliiam D. Davis."

West Hills. The area of **Portland** lying west of the downtown area. The hills, the south end of **Tualatin Mountain**, are graced with extensive parks and handsome neighborhoods.

West Linn. A rapidly-growing **Clackamas County** residential city 12 miles south of **Portland** on the west bank of **Willamette River** opposite **Oregon City**. It was established as Robins Nest by Robert Moore, a pioneer of 1840 who ran a ferry across the Willamette. In 1845 the name was changed to Linn in honor of Senator Lewis Linn of Missouri who was an early advocate for settlement in the **Oregon country**, and became West Linn in 1854. The community was destroyed by the **flood of 1861** but rebuilt, and incorporated in 1913. Population 1980 11,358; 1995 19,370. Elevation 105'. 22825 Willamette Falls Drive, 97068. 503-657-0331. Chamber of Commerce 503-656-6744. Oregon Geographic Names.

West Shore. A widely circulated monthly magazine (later a weekly), published in Portland 1876-1891 by Leopold Samuel. Designed to encourage immigration, West Shore was the first illustrated magazine published in the Northwest. "L. Samuel and the West Shore."

Western Baptist College. An accredited private college in **Salem** that enrolled 694 students in 1995. 5000 Deer Park Dr. SE, Salem 97301. 503-581-8600. Oregon Blue Book.

Western Evangelical Seminary. See **George Fox University**.

Western Interstate Commission for Higher Education (WICHE). An interstate agency created in 1953 by 13 western states to provide cost-effective college programs through three cooperative student exchange programs. The Professional Student Exchange Program provides financial assistance to selected students who wish to enroll in professional programs not available in the student's home state. The Western Regional Graduate Program provides students access to over 100 graduate programs at resident rates of tuition. Western Undergraduate Exchange enables undergraduates to enroll in designated programs in other states on a space-available basis at 150% of resident tuition. Each state has three commissioners appointed by the governor. PO Box 3175, Eugene 97403. 541-346-5729. Oregon Blue Book.

Western Intertie. A network of high-voltage power transmission lines that links power plants and substations in 14 western states as well as in parts of Canada and Mexico. It is overseen by the Western System Coordinating Council, headquartered in Salt Lake City, which is one of nine North American regional councils. The web, which can carry 4,800 **megawatts**, grew piecemeal as utilities connected their lines, but massive power outages in 1996 led to calls for a single authority to operate the grid. Some also see the need for additional transmission lines, at a cost $1 million a mile. Oregonian 7/4/96:C1. 8/18/96:A1. See also **Bonneville Power Administration**; **Indego**.

Western Oregon University. A state liberal arts college in **Monmouth** that enrolled 3,871 students in fall 1994. The school offers 30 bachelor's and three master's degrees and is noted for its teaching research program. The Oregon Police Academy and the Oregon Military Academy are both affiliated with the school. Western is the oldest university in the Oregon **University System**, tracing its history to Monmouth College, founded in 1853 by the Christian Church (**Disciples of Christ**). In 1882 it became Oregon State **Normal School** at Monmouth, then Oregon College of Education and later Western Oregon State College. Monmouth 97361. 503-838-8000. Oregon Blue Book.

Western Seminary. An accredited private college in **Portland** that enrolled 469 students in 1995. 5511 SE Hawthorne Blvd., Portland 97215. 503-233-8561. Oregon Blue Book.

Western States Center. A **Portland** organization founded by Jeff Malachowsky in 1987 with the aim of reinvigorating democracy in the west. It provides research, policy analysis, and training camps aimed at encouraging new leaders to run for political office. 522 SW 5th Suite 1390, Portland 97204. 503-228-8866. Oregonian 10/13/95:E1.

Western States Chiropractic College. An accredited private college in **Portland** that enrolled 458 students in 1995. 2900 NE 132nd Ave., 97230. 503-256-3180.

Western System Coordinating Council. See **Western Intertie**.

Westfir. A former mill town in **Lane County** in the **Cascade Range** 41 miles southeast of **Eugene**. The name came from its origin in 1923 as a **company town**, established by the Western Lumber Company which sawed fir lumber. The operations were later taken over by Edward Hines Lumber Company which closed the mill in 1977 and sold the town. In 1979 residents voted to incorporate so that the utilities could be in public ownership. Population 1980 312; 1995 280. Elevation 1,114'. PO Box 296, 97492. 541-782-3733. Oregon Geographic Names.

Westlake. See **Dunes City**.

Weston. A northeast Oregon farming town in **Umatilla County** three miles from **Athena** and 20 miles northeast of **Pendleton** on Highway 11. The post office was established in 1869 and named by postmaster T. T. Lieuallen for his home town in Missouri. The city was incorporated in 1878. Population 1980 719; 1995 655. Elevation 1,796'. PO Box 427, 97886. 541-566-3313. Oregon Geographic Names.

Westport. An unincorporated community in **Clatsop County,** 27 miles east of **Astoria** on **Highway 30**. It was founded by John West about 1850, and was the site of an early salmon cannery in 1869. The community is the Oregon terminus for the only **ferry** across the **Columbia River**. Oregon Geographic Names.

Wetlands. Lands in which water saturation is the dominant factor governing soil development and plant and animal communities. Seasonal wetlands are saturated for only short periods of time, while other wetlands, such as marshes, may be inundated for most of the year. Fens originate from groundwater or runoff and are nutrient-rich, while bogs derive from precipitation and are nutrient-poor. Once regarded as wasteland, wetlands are now recognized as highly productive wildlife habitat, and are also valuable for flood protection, pollution abatement, and water flow regulation. It is estimated that 1.4 million of the 2.26 million acres of wetlands in the state have been lost to drainage and development. There are also 20,000 acres of tidal wetlands in Oregon. Wetlands are regulated by the state Division of **State Lands**, the Oregon Department of **Environmental Quality**, and the federal government. Atlas of the Pacific Northwest; Oregonian 10/17/97:A1; Oregon's 1994 Water Quality. See also **Klamath Forest National Wildlife Refuge; Lower Klamath National Wildlife Refuge; Sycan Marsh; Submerged lands; Swamp Lands Act; Tidelands**.

Whale strandings. An unusual stranding of sperm **whales**, *Physeter catodon*, occurred in June 1979 when 41 went aground on a sand beach at **Florence** for unknown reasons; all died despite rescue efforts. The bodies were pushed into trenches and burned. Earlier, in January 1903 a wounded 54-foot sperm whale beached near **Astoria**. A dead beaked whale washed ashore at **Lincoln City** June 6, 1994. Dead or stranded gray whales are not uncommon. In addition to burning (using alumagel and/or tires), dead whales have been disposed of by towing to an island, burying, or blowing them up. Reports of stranded whales can be made to the Marine Mammal Hot Line, 800-452-7888. Oregonian 6/21/79:D1; This Day in Oregon. See also **Exploding whale**.

Whale watching. Gray **whales** pass Oregon on their 6,000-mile winter migration between the Bering Sea and Baja California and on their return in the spring. They travel at about 5 mph with the pregnant females leading the southbound procession in December, followed by mature adults and then immature animals. The young animals lead the return north in March, followed by males and females without calves, and the females with new calves usually pass by during May. The whales stay within two miles of the coast while migrating, so whale watching is popular. Whale Watching Week, sponsored by the Oregon Department of **Parks**

and Recreation, is scheduled between Christmas and New Year's and again in March, with trained volunteers stationed midday at many viewing sites along the coast to assist the public. Charter boats also offer trips. Whales have occasionally made their way up the **Columbia River** to **Portland**, to the delight of thousands. See also **Moby Mary**.

Whales. Twenty three species of whales, **dolphins**, and **porpoises** visit Pacific Northwest waters. The most commonly sighted whale is the once-endangered gray whale, *Eschrichtius robustus*, a baleen whale that grows up to 45 feet in length and may weigh 45 tons. The species has rebounded to an estimated 22,000 and was removed from the **endangered species** list in 1994. Most gray whales migrate twice a year though increasing numbers of them are becoming year-round residents, and **whale watching** is popular, especially during the migrations. All marine mammals are **protected animals**. "Gray Whales" See also **Keiko**; **Marine mammals**; **Moby Mary**; **Whale strandings**.

Wheat. In 1995, Oregon growers harvested 59 million bushels of wheat, worth $278 million, from 881,000 acres (17% of it irrigated), making it one of Oregon's top five crops. Some 4,800 Oregon farmers, over a third of them in **Umatilla County**, received federal subsidy payments in 1994 totaling $25.3 million, down from $42.2 million in 1993. 90% of the wheat is exported to Asia, much of it shipped by barge down the **Columbia River** to **Portland**; one barge carries as much as 140 trucks. In 1996 43% of all exported U.S. grain was shipped from the Portland area. 1995 Oregon. See also **Grain**.

Wheat, history. In Oregon wheat was first raised in the **Willamette Valley**, but since the 1880s most production has been of soft white winter wheat raised on deep loess soils in the Oregon Columbia Basin counties of **Umatilla**, **Morrow**, **Sherman**, **Gilliam**, and **Wasco**. Wheat was Oregon's first cash crop and was made legal tender for a time in 1846 because coin was in such short supply. The **Hudson's Bay Company** bought much of the early production, shipping it to Alaska, Hawaii, and California, and England. The first wheat was harvested east of the **Cascade Range** in 1863. High freight costs by rail, barge, and ship have been a problem for Oregon growers since pioneer days. Wheat straw has been tried as an alternative for wood fiber in making fiber board. Dictionary of Oregon History.

Wheatland. An unincorporated community on the west bank of the **Willamette River** 10 miles north of **Salem**. It was at one time an important wheat shipping point and is now in an area of diversified agriculture. The Wheatland **ferry** crosses the river to **Mission Bottom**..

Wheeler. A **Tillamook County** community on Nehalem Bay in northwest Oregon, 24 miles north of **Tillamook** on **Highway 101**. It was named for Coleman Wheeler who operated a sawmill in the community. The city was incorporated in 1914. The economy is based on tourism and recreation. Population 1980 319; 1995 360. Elevation 18'. PO Box 177, 97147. 503-368-5767. Chamber of Commerce 503-368-5100. 100 Years of the Nehalem Country.

Wheeler County. A sparsely populated, arid, rugged, ranch and timber county in north central Oregon. Incorporated cities are **Fossil** (county seat), **Mitchell**, and **Spray**. The county is bounded by **Gilliam**, **Morrow**, **Grant**, **Crook**, **Jefferson**, and **Wasco** counties. Elevations range from 1,150' in the canyon of the **John Day River** in the northwest, to 5,892-foot Baldy, part of the **Ochoco Mountains**, in the center of the county. The economy is based on ranching, timber, and tourism. Taxable assessed value in 1995 was $69,000,000, or $45,000 per capita. In November 1996, by a vote of 445 to 418, voters increased the **tax base** from $180,000 to $580,000, thereby avoiding bankruptcy of the county government. Attractions include the **John Day River** and the Clarno and **Painted Hills** units of **John Day Fossil Beds National Monument**. The county was created in 1899 from parts of Grant, Gilliam, and Crook counties and named for Henry H. Wheeler (1826-1915), an early stage operator noted for his narrow escape from an Indian attack in 1866. Population 1980 1,513; 1995 1,550. Area 1,713 square miles. Density 1/sq.mi. Annual precipitation 14"; average temperature January 38°F, July 66°F. Courthouse, 701 Adams St., Fossil, 97830. 541-763-2911. Glimpses of Wheeler County; History of Wheeler County; Oregon Blue Book.

Whiskey Local. A passenger service operated by the **Southern Pacific** between **Grants Pass** and **Ashland** sometime between 1908 and 1933. It used McKeens, self-contained, streamlined cars with round windows that operated on 200 horsepower gasoline truck engines. Early in the operation of the service Ashland was "wet" and Grants Pass was "dry"; travelers could take the Whiskey Local to Ashland for a weekend fling. Railroading in Southern Oregon.

Whistlers. See **Holiday for Lips**.

White City. An unincorporated southwest Oregon community six miles north of **Medford** in **Jackson County**, located on part of the **World War II** site of **Camp White**. After the war, part of the site became an industrial park with lumber mills and manufacturing plants. It also includes a Veterans Administration Domiciliary, shopping areas, and a residential community made possible when tractors were developed that could rip the hardpan so that septic tank disposal fields could be installed. County urban renewal funds are being used for improvements. Land in Common; Oregonian 10/17/96:C6.

White Horse. See **Pioneer Spirit**.

White River. A river that heads on the south slopes of **Mount Hood** and flows south and east to join the **Deschutes River** five miles north of **Maupin**. Three miles above the junction White River Falls, a 70-foot double waterfall with two lower plunges, can be seen at Tygh Valley State Wayside on Highway 216 , and a quarter-mile trail leads to a view of the falls from below. Remnants of an old electric power station persist. The name comes from the color given by the load of glacial silt it carries. Oregon Geographic Names.

White Stag sign. See **Made in Oregon sign**.

White sturgeon. See **Sturgeon**.

White water boating. Oregon rivers famous for white water boating include the **McKenzie**, **Deschutes**, **Rogue**, **Owyhee**, and **Sandy** rivers, and many others have memorable stretches. Surf kayaking also has its advocates. River level information is available from the National Weather Service, 503-261-9246. Tourism, 775 Summer St. NE, Salem OR 97310. 503-986-0000. Oregon River Tours; Rivers of the West; Soggy Sneakers.

Whiteaker's Ride. A record-setting train trip by Oregon's U.S. **Represen-**

tative-elect, John Whiteaker (1820-1902). He left his home near **Eugene** by train on Saturday evening, March 8, 1879, for **Portland**, where he boarded the steamship *Elder* the next morning. Congressional Democrats needed his vote on March 17 in order to elect a speaker, so as soon as the boat docked in San Francisco on the 12th they had him ferried to Oakland and speeded cross-country by special train. The trip set a cross-country record, and he arrived at 10 a.m. on Monday the 17th in time to cast the deciding vote. The trip took just 207 hours from the time he left home, but the expense of it led to sarcastic commentary in the press. Whiteaker, who led a wagon train over the **Oregon Trail** in 1852, had served as Oregon's first state **governor** and in several other positions. Dictionary of Oregon History; Oregonian 3/18/1879: 3.

Whitehorse Ranch. The first **ranch** in eastern Oregon, established in 1869 by frontier aristocrat John S. Devine in southeastern **Malheur County**. He later developed the Alvord Ranch as well. He died in 1901, after having declared bankruptcy following disastrous stock losses in the terrible winter of 1889. Oregon's Great Basin Country.

Whiting. A **groundfish**, *Merluccius productus*, also called Pacific hake, caught commercially off California, Oregon, and Washington. Fewer than 500 metric tons were harvested prior to 1990, but, thanks to research at the **Seafood Laboratory** into better ways of keeping the fish fresh and into uses for it, Pacific whiting has become the Oregon fleet's largest catch. The total for 1997 was estimated to be over 200,000 metric tons. The **Pacific Fishery Management Council** allocates the catch between vessels bringing the catch to shore, factory trollers that process their own catch, and boats that take their catch to mother ships for processing. The mild white meat is used for making **surimi**. Byproducts include organic fertilizers, supplemental animal feed, and composted materials for remediation of soils contaminated with toxic wastes. Agriculture; Oregonian 6/24/96:A1, 10/26/96:D5. Pacific States.

Whitman massacre. A massacre of 14 persons, including the **Presbyterian** missionaries Marcus and Narcissa Whitman, by **Cayuse Indians** on November 29, 1847, at Whitman's mission at Waiilatpu in southeastern Washington. The Indians also took forty-seven other persons captive but a **Hudson's Bay Company** relief party rescued them. The five murderers voluntarily surrendered in 1850 and were tried and hanged in **Oregon City**. The Indians, decimated by **measles**, had thought they were being poisoned by the missionaries, not knowing that some of them had themselves carried the disease back from a recent trip to California. The massacre led to the **Cayuse War** and to a petition to the U.S. Congress for territorial status. Empire of the Columbia. See also **Epidemics**; **Lapwai Mission**; **Missions**; **Oregon Territory**.

WICHE. See **Western Interstate Commission for Higher Education**.

Wickiup. A rounded temporary Indian dwelling made of poles covered by brush, used by the nomadic **Northern Paiute Indians** east of the **Cascade Range**.

Wickiup Reservoir. A large irrigation reservoir on the upper **Deschutes River** 10 miles west of **La Pine**. It was formed in 1949 when work was completed on the 100' high, earth-filled dam as part of the **Deschutes Project**. The lake covers 10,334 acres at full pool, is five miles long, and 70 feet deep at maximum.

It is extensively used for fishing and boating, even at times of maximum draw-down. There are several campgrounds. Early rangers named the area for the **wickiup** structures found there. Atlas of Oregon Lakes.

Wigwam burners. Old-style sawmill waste burners that were tall metal cones with rounded tops. Prior to the use of wigwam burners the waste was burned in open piles. The wigwam burners were an innovation to prevent the spread of fire but did nothing to mitigate the smoke and ash, so were phased out under the state's air pollution control laws.

Wild and Scenic Rivers. See **National Wild and Scenic Rivers**; **Scenic waterways**.

Wild horses. There are approximately 44,000 wild horses in the U.S., half of them in Nevada, and about 2,000 of them in two herds in eastern Oregon. Though in some areas **cougars** are major predators, killing 75% of the foals, the Oregon herds have been increasing at 20% a year, quickly exceeding the carrying capacity of the available range. The **Bureau of Land Management** periodically rounds up the excess horses, as well as wild burros, and sells them to the public for adoption. Some of the adopted horses end up being sold for slaughter; the meat is exported. BLM District Office, HC 74-12533 Highway 20 West, Hines, 97738. 541-573-4400. Oregonian 1/29/97:A1. See also **Kiger mustangs**.

Wild rice. A cereal grain being grown commercially by several farmers in the Willamette Valley. One follows the traditional method, sowing the seed in shallow water near Ankeny Game Refuge south of **Salem**, while another grows it "dry" near **Brownsville**. Oregonian 6/8/97:C4. See also **Rice**.

Wild turkeys. See **Turkeys**.

Wilderness areas. Areas within **National Forests** that have been set aside under the Wilderness Act of 1964 to be maintained as wilderness. Only foot and horse travel is allowed (no motors, no wheels). Overuse has led to restrictions in some areas, including campfire prohibitions, designated campsites, and, in at least two areas, limited entry. In 1997 Oregon had over two million acres in 36 designated wilderness areas. The largest were **Eagle Cap** in the **Wallowa Mountains** (360,000 acres), **Three Sisters** in the **Cascade Range** (287,000 acres), and Kalmiopsis in the **Siskiyou Mountains** (180,000 acres). The controversial **Opal Creek Wilderness**, 12,800 acres, was created in 1996 along with an adjacent 13,000-acre scenic recreation area. Each wilderness area is administered by the National Forest in which it is located. The **Bureau of Land Management** also administers four wilderness areas totaling 16,703 acres, plus 87 wilderness study areas totaling 2.8 million acres. Oregonian 10/1/96:A1.

Wildflowers. Oregon's many wildflowers begin blooming in early spring in western Oregon, and the season then moves up and east with the peak bloom in high mountain meadows in July and August. A few of the state's noted wildflower viewing areas are **Blair Lake Meadows, Hoyt Arboretum, Iron Mountain, Lawrence Memorial Grassland Preserve, Marys Peak, Mount Pisgah Arbo-retum, Tom McCall Preserve**, all in northwest Oregon; **Eight Dollar Mountain, Table Rock**, and **Castle Crest** in southwest Oregon; and **Anthony Lake, Eagle Cap Wilderness**, and **Hells Canyon Dam** in northeast Oregon. Wildflower shows are held several places, including at **Glide**. Field Guide to Pacific States Wildflowers; Oregonian 4/5/95:E1; Wildflower Genetics; Wildflowers of the West. See also **Camas**; **Carnivorous plants**; **Endangered plants**; **Flora**; **Gardens**; **Herbaria**; **Indian hemp**; **Kalmiopsis**; **Native plants**; **Oregon grape**; **Plants**; **Skunk cabbage**; **Trillium**; **Wapato**; **Wocus**.

Wildlife refuges. See **National Wildlife Refuges**.

Wildlife Safari. A private drive-through wild-animal park off **Highway 42** near **Winston**, south of **Roseburg**. A variety of animals from around the world can be observed by motorists as the animals roam free on the 600-acre reserve. Other services and attractions are also offered. PO Box 1600, Winston OR 97496-0231. 541-679-6761, 800-355-4848.

Wildlife Services. A part of the U.S. Department of Agriculture, formerly called the Animal Damage Control program. The agency works with people who are having problems with wildlife, including **deer**, **bear**, **cougar**, **beaver**, birds at airports, **endangered species**, and **rabies** suppression. In addition to the state office in **Portland**, there are district offices in **John Day, Roseburg**, and **Salem**. Field specialists are funded jointly by federal, state, and county funds. 6135 NE 80th Suite A8, Portland 97218. 503-231-6184.

Wiley Pass. See **Santiam Pass**.

Wilkes Expedition. The United States Exploring Expedition, a government sponsored scientific and exploring expedition to the Pacific and Antarctic, 1838-1843. Lt. Charles Wilkes (1798-1877) commanded the expedition, including six ships and a number of scientists, which visited the **Columbia River** and the **Willamette Valley** between May and October 1841. One of his sloops, the *Peacock*, wrecked on **Peacock Spit** at the mouth of the Columbia. In the **Oregon Country** Wilkes met with **Hudson's Bay Company** officials and with American settlers, provided assistance to the *Star of Oregon*, sent a party overland to California, and later published accounts of the expedition's findings. Americans in the area had hoped that he would encourage local government so were disappointed with his advice that the time was inopportune, but his reports did arouse interest in Oregon. "Delay"; Dictionary of Oregon History. See also **Siskiyou Trail**.

Willamette (wih LAMB eht). A community, now part of **West Linn**, at the confluence of the Tualatin and **Willamette** rivers. The name is from an Indian word for the local area, and has been variously spelled, including Wal-lamt, Wallamet, and Wilarmet. Oregon Geographic Names.

Willamette and Pacific Railroad. A **shortline railroad**, headquartered in **Albany**, that operates lines in the **Willamette Valley** and from Albany to the coast. Its sister company, Portland and Western, operates lines in the north end of the valley. 800-677-4875. See also **Oregon Pacific Railroad Company**.

Willamette Cattle Company. See **Corporations**.

Willamette County. A county proposed in 1997 that would include **Multnomah, Clackamas**, and **Washington** counties. Oregonian 10/27/97:E10.

Willamette Falls. A horseshoe-shaped falls where the **Willamette River** drops 41 feet over a ledge of **Columbia River basalts** at **Oregon City**, 26 miles upstream from the confluence of the Willamette and the **Columbia River**. Though the falls blocked most salmon runs, the area was an important Indian fishing and trading site. Settlers channeled the water to power a lumber mill in 1842, a flour mill in 1844, a woolen mill in 1864, a paper mill in 1867, and electric generators beginning in 1867. Willamette Falls was also the name used for the **settlement** that later became Oregon City. Before the locks were built, boats were sometimes lifted over falls with ropes in a process known as cordelling.

Willamette Falls (city). An earlier name for **Oregon City** that persisted for some years as an expression of settlers' resentment towards Dr. John McLoughlin, of the **Hudson's Bay Company**. McLoughlin, who had extended much kindness to the immigrants to Oregon, had platted and named Oregon City in 1842. The resentment focused on his Catholicism and his affluence.

Willamette Falls Canal and Locks. A 1,200' long series of four **locks** around 41' high **Willamette Falls** on the **Willamette River** at **West Linn**. The locks, which opened January 1, 1873, enabled passengers and freight for the first time to travel up and down the river without having to portage and change boats. The locks were constructed with walls of shaped stone assembled without mortar. In 1915 the company then operating the locks sold them for $375,000 to the **Army Corps of Engineers** which operates them as a free service; boaters need to allow an hour for passage. In 1974 the locks were put on the **National Register of Historic Places**. A small museum and picnic area are on the west side of the locks. Lockmaster, Willamette Falls Locks, U.S. Army Corps of Engineers, West Linn 97068. 503-656-3381. Army Engineers.

Willamette Greenway. See **Willamette River Greenway**.

Willamette House. See **Willamette Post**.

Willamette Industries. A **Portland**-based wood products company that, in 1996, owned 1.8 million acres of timberland and had 12,000 employees in 21 states. Fortune 500 listed it as having 1996 sales of $3.425 billion. 1300 SW Fifth Ave., Suite 3800, Portland 97201. 503-227-5581. Oregonian 4/9/96:B14, 6/30/96:R31. See also **Corporations**.

Willamette Meridian. See **Willamette Stone**.

Willamette Meteorite. A 15-ton nickel-iron meteorite, the largest ever found in the U.S., and the 6th largest in the world. It measures 10' by 7' by 4'. Ellis Hughes discovered it in 1902 near **Willamette**, though it may have been an **erratic** originally fallen in Montana and rafted to Oregon on an ice floe during **Pleistocene floods**. Hughes spent months digging it out and winching it 3/4 mile to his own property. A series of lawsuits begun by the owners of the property on which it was found finally awarded it to them. They sold it to a New Yorker for $20,600; she gave it to the American Museum of Natural History where it still remains. A replica plus a half pound of the original are at the **University of Oregon** Museum of Natural History, and another replica is on the grounds of the **West Linn** United Methodist Church. Geology of Oregon; Oregon History Magazine 40(1):27 Summer 1996.

Willamette Mission. A mission established by **Methodist** missionary Jason Lee and four associates in 1834 on the **Willamette River** 10 miles north of **Salem**. In 1836 thirteen additional men and women were sent as helpers, and in 1840 the "**Great Reinforcement**" of 32 additional adults and 18 children arrived by ship, allowing more missions to be established. The Willamette Mission opened a store in 1840, the first alternative to the **Hudson's Bay Company**. In 1841 the mission moved to **Salem** where a school was founded that later became **Willamette University**. Prior to the formation of the **Provisional government** the mission served the American settlers as an informal court of justice. It was also an important agricultural, economic, and educational center, but had less success in converting Indians. In 1844 Lee was recalled, and the mission was closed. Most buildings were destroyed in the **flood of 1861**. Dictionary of Oregon History; Grains. See also **Mission Mill Village**.

Willamette Mission State Park. A day-use **state park** eight miles north of **Salem** at the site of **Willamette Mission**, built by the **Methodists** in the 1830s. The buildings themselves were destroyed in the **flood of 1861**. In addition to a mission monument, the park includes picnic areas, the nation's largest black **cottonwood** tree, boat ramp, fishing docks, wildlife viewing area, and trails for hikers, bikes, and horses.

Willamette National Forest. A 1,800,381-acre national forest in Oregon's central **Cascade Range**, primarily in **Lane**, **Linn**, and **Marion** counties. It includes eight wilderness areas: Bull of the Woods, Middle Santiam, **Mount Jefferson**, Menagerie, **Mount Washington**, **Three Sisters**, **Waldo Lake**, and Diamond Peak. The forest budget dropped from $56.5 million in 1990 to $29.6 million in 1996, and the staff dropped from 767 to 409. 211 East 7th Avenue, P.O.Box 10607, Eugene 97440. 541-465-6521.

Willamette Pass. See **Highway passes**.

Willamette Pass Ski Area. A ski area 69 miles southeast of **Eugene** on **Highway 58**. It has a top elevation of 6,683 feet with a 1,563-foot vertical drop. Facilities include five chair lifts and a 20K Nordic track. PO Box 5509, Eugene 97405. 800-444-5030; snow conditions 541-345-7669. Oregonian 11/16/97:T7.

Willamette Post. A combination dwelling and fur **trading post** established in 1813 by the **North West Company** at the north end of **French Prairie** a few miles west of **Champoeg**. Dictionary of Oregon History.

Willamette River. A river that drains a major valley in northwest Oregon between the **Coast Range** and the **Cascade Range**. The longest river entirely within Oregon, it officially rises where the Middle Fork leaves Timpanogas Lake in the high Cascades, and flows 261 miles north to the **Columbia River**. The Middle Fork is considered navigable beginning at River Mile 203 below **Dexter Reservoir**. The Willamette River itself begins at **Eugene** where the Coast Fork joins with the Middle Fork at River Mile 187, and by **Portland** the river is 900 feet wide. The watershed of 11,440 square miles represents 12% of the state's land area. Average annual volume is 22,730,000 acre feet (3.2 acre feet/acre) at Oregon City. Between Eugene and tidewater below **Willamette Falls** at **Oregon City** it drops 420 feet, or about 4 feet a mile. There are no dams on the main stem. Tributaries from the **Coast Range** on the west include the **Long Tom**, **Marys**, **Luckiamute**, **Yamhill**, and **Tualatin** rivers. From the **Cascade Mountains** on the east, the major tributaries are the Coast Fork, and the **McKenzie**, **Calapooia**, **Santiam**, **Molalla**, and **Clackamas** rivers. The **Willamette Valley** has been the most populated drainage basin in the state since the beginning of white settlement. The name Willamette apparently derives from the Indian word for a place on the west bank near **Oregon City**; a controversy flourished for years about the appropriate spelling. Oregon Geographic Names; Oregonian 10/25/95:C1, 3/1/96:A1; Water Resources; Willamette River Recreation Guide. See also **Frozen rivers**; **Pleistocene floods**.

Willamette River channel. Geologic evidence indicates that the channel of the **Willamette River** has been shifted through time by lava flows, such as from Highland Butte south of **Oregon City**, by glacial outwash, and probably by the **Pleistocene floods**. For example, at one time it went east around the Salem Hills rather than west as it does at present, and at some time it probably flowed through **Lake Labish** and the present **Pudding River** area. When whites arrived, the Willamette was a meandering river marked with sand bars and snags, flowing through a wooded floodplain, up to 6 miles wide, laced with multiple and changing channels, oxbows, wetlands, and sloughs. Sandbars and snags in the Willamette between **Portland** and the **Columbia River** so limited navigation that the city bought a dredge in 1865, but turned it over to the **Army Corps of Engineers** the next year. The Corps has since maintained a 40-foot deep channel from the Columbia upstream to Portland's Broadway Bridge, and eight feet deep from there upstream to **Willamette Falls** where **Willamette Falls Canal and Locks** were opened in 1873. For steamboats and pole boats a depth of 3.5 feet was maintained to **Corvallis** and at 2.5 feet from there to **Eugene**. In 1932 Congress took no action on a proposal to canalize the river with dams and locks from Oregon City to Eugene at a cost of $23.5 million. Army Engineers; Geology of Oregon; Oregonian 11/6/31:1. See also **Willamette River transportation**.

Willamette River dams. There are no dams on the main stem of the Willamette River, but the **Army Corps of Engineers** has built 11 dams and two reregulating dams on the tributaries which control runoff from 27% of the river's drainage basin. The 11 dams, with the dates they were placed in service for flood control, are **Fern Ridge** (1941), **Cottage Grove** (1942), **Dorena** (1949), **Detroit/**Big Cliff (1953), **Lookout Point**/Dexter (1953), **Hills Creek** (1961), **Cougar** (1963), **Fall Creek** (1965), **Green Peter** (1966), **Foster** (1967), and **Blue River** (1968). Army Engineers. See also **Floods, Willamette River**.

Willamette River Greenway. A program created by the Oregon legislature in 1967 to maintain and enhance the scenic, recreational, historic, natural, and agricultural qualities along over 200 miles of the **Willamette River**, from **Dexter Reservoir** and **Cottage Grove Reservoir** to its mouth. The greenway legislation applies to lands lying within 150 feet of the river on each side. Originally envisioned by Karl Onthank, UO administrator and conservationist, as a corridor of green with trails along both sides of the river, the program was later reduced in scope. In the 1970s the state legislature gave regulatory authority to local governments. Most of the 170 parcels of land now dedicated to the greenway were acquired before 1980 when voters removed parks from **gas tax** funding. Greenway programs are coordinated by the Oregon **Parks and Recreation Department**. 503-378-6305. Willamette River Recreation Guide.

Willamette River transportation. Even though two-thirds of Oregon's population lives within 20 miles of the Willamette River, it no longer serves as the transportation artery that it was both for Indians and early settlers. The first white settlements were along the river which, especially after steamboats came into use in the 1850s, carried most of the valley's freight and passenger traffic. Portaging was necessary around **Willamette Falls** until **Willamette Falls Canal and Locks** opened in 1873. It was only after railroads were built down the valley in the 1870s that sizable settlements grew up away from the river, and, since the advent of cars and trucks in the 20th century, river traffic above the falls has been mostly barges, log rafts, and pleasure boats, plus **ferries** at **Canby, Wheatland**, and **Buena Vista**. Willamette River Recreation Guide.

Willamette River water quality. In 1938, after the Willamette River had become so polluted that fish died within minutes of contact with the water, Oregon voters created the State Sanitary Authority, now called the Department of **Environmental Quality**, to clean it up. Water quality improved as federally-funded sewage treatment facilities and industrial pollution controls were built after **World War II**, and the river was declared safe for swimming in 1972. Today, 80% of the pollution comes from agricultural runoff of pesticides, fertilizers, and animal wastes. Between 1990 and 1994 over 1.2 million pounds of chemicals were released into the river. In 1997 a citizen task force proposed a series of 100 steps to be taken to restore water quality. Oregonian 10/17/97:A1, 12/17/97:A1. See also **Oregon Plan**.

Willamette Shore Railway. A seven-mile stretch of former **Southern Pacific** railroad between Lake Oswego and Portland. In 1988 six partners, **Lake Oswego, Portland, Multnomah County, Clackamas County, Tri-Met**, and **Metro**, bought the right of way for $1.2 million to hold as part of a regional transportation network. Lake Oswego manages the line and the **streetcar**, powered by a generator car, that volunteers from the Oregon Electric Railway Historical Society operate on a regular schedule. Oregonian 8/18/97:B6.

Willamette Stone. A point, set with a cedar stake in 1851, that was the starting place for the **Public Land Survey** in Oregon and Washington. All land in Oregon and Washington is legally described in reference to the point. The stake was replaced by the Willamette Stone in 1885, and the vandalized stone was replaced in 1988 with a stainless steel marker. The north/south line surveyed through the marker is called the Willamette Meridian and the east/west line is the Willamette Base Line. Stark Street east of the Willamette River in Portland lies on the Base Line but most of Baseline Road in Washington County does not. A small **state park** now surrounds the Willamette Stone site near Skyline Boulevard west of **Portland**, at north latitude 45°31'10.831", west longitude 122°44'33.551". Oregon Geographic Names; Oregon Surveyor 16(4):18 July/August 1988; Oregonian 6/24/67:6; Round the Roses. See also **Land description**.

Willamette University. An accredited private four-year liberal arts college in **Salem** that enrolled 2,568 students in 1995. Established in 1853, it is the oldest institution of higher learning in the Northwest. The **Oregon Institute**, organized in 1842 by the **Methodists** of **Willamette Mission**, was its forerunner and associated school. Its college of law, founded in 1883, is the second oldest **law school** west of the Rockies; only Hastings in San Francisco, founded in 1878, is older. 900 State Street, Salem 97301. 503-370-6300. Dictionary of Oregon History; Oregon Blue Book. See also **Governors' School**.

Willamette Valley. A 130-mile-long valley of 11,440 square miles (12% of

Oregon's land area) drained by the **Willamette River** as it flows north to the **Columbia River** between the **Coast** and **Cascade** ranges. **Interstate 5** connects most of the cities of the valley, from **Cottage Grove** at the south end to **Portland** at the north. In 1995, 75% of the state's people and 75% of the state's jobs were located in the valley, and 2,000,000 people, two-thirds of Oregon's population, lived within 20 miles of the river. The valley is also the state's most diversified agricultural area, producing nearly half of the state's total value in agriculture from such high-value specialty crops as **grass seed, hazelnuts, hops,** wine **grapes, nursery** products, and **berries.** Originally home to the **Kalapuya Indians,** it was the first area in the state to be settled by whites, whose initial crop was **wheat.** Z Magazine 8(10):13 Oct. 1995. See also **Settlements.**

Willamette Valley and Cascade Mountain Military Wagon Road. A **military wagon road** authorized to run 448 miles from **Albany** over the **Santiam Pass** to Fort Polk near **Sisters,** and on to **Prineville** and Fort Harney near **Burns** to end at Fort Boise in Idaho. Though much of the road east of Fort Harney was not completed, the company nonetheless received a Congressional **land grant** in 1866, authorized by the governor, of 861,512 acres. A section known as the Old Santiam Wagon Road or Santiam Toll Road operated as a toll road until 1914. It crossed the Cascade summit three miles south of the present **Santiam Pass** on **Highway 20.** Dictionary of Oregon History; Historical Oregon; History of the Willamette Valley...Road; Pioneer Roads.

Willamette Valley land use. No single government plans for the future of the 14,000 square miles of land in the Willamette Valley. Lands are regulated by 10 counties, 101 cities, three regional planning agencies, one tribal government, and 10 state and federal agencies. **Metro** is the only regional government with planning authority. Oregonian 10/12/97:A1.

Willamette Valley physiographic province. An area that lies between the **Coast Range** and the **Cascade Range,** and extends from the **Columbia River** 130 miles south to **Cottage Grove.** The valley, which occupies the southern end of a basin created by **uplift** of the **Coast Range,** is drained by the **Willamette River.** Elevation drops an average of 3 feet per mile, from 400' near **Eugene** to sea level near **Portland.** It is underlain by **Eocene** volcanoes that erupted before the Coast Range uplift. These were then buried by over a mile of ocean sediments. **Columbia River Basalt** later flowed in through the north end and up the valley to **Salem,** 1000' thick in some places. **Pliocene** eruptions 5 million years ago created many of the buttes around Portland. Later, **Pleistocene floods** repeatedly covered the valley, sometimes to 400' above present sea level, dropping up to 100' of gravel and silt, along with boulders from Montana (**erratics**) that were carried in on ice floes. Geology of Oregon. See also **Boring lavas; Calapooya Mountains; Chehalem Mountains; Mount Angel (butte); Siletz Terrane; Skinner Butte; Spencer Butte.**

Willamina (will uh MINE uh). "Timber Town USA." A western **Willamette Valley** town in **Yamhill** and **Polk** counties 17 miles southwest of **McMinnville.** It is on the banks of Willamina Creek, named for the first white woman, Willamina Maley (later Williams), to cross it (in 1846). The Willamina post office was established in 1855, but the town didn't develop until a grist mill and sawmill were built in 1878. A **brick** plant operated for over 60 years before closing in 1971. Two major fires, in 1919 and 1924, each destroyed much of the business district. Area attractions include the Coastal Hills Art Tour in November, the 1907 Dr. Andrew Kershaw House, Huddleston Park, Blackwell County Park, and Willamina Falls. The city was incorporated in 1903. Population 1980 1,749; 1995 1,775. Elevation 225'. PO Box 629, 97396. 503-876-2242. Old Yamhill.

William and Ann. A British bark owned by the **Hudson's Bay Company** (HBC) that went aground on **Clatsop Spit** during a storm in March 1829 with the loss of all 46 crew members. The ship carried a load of provisions for **Fort Vancouver**. Disputes between the Clatsop Indians, who had recovered much of the goods, and the HBC led the HBC to attack the Indian village several months later. HBC recovered the goods; one Indian was killed and several were injured. Pacific Graveyard.

William L. Finley National Wildlife Refuge. A refuge established in 1964 twelve miles south of **Corvallis**. Part of the refuge has been designated as Willamette Floodplain **National Natural Landmark**. The landmark area, though not adjacent to the river, represents the largest remaining native and unplowed example of bottomland interior valley grasslands in the area. The 1857 Fiechter House is on the refuge and is sometimes opened by volunteers. 26208 Finley Refuge Road, Corvallis 97333. 541-757-4730. Oregon Wildlife Viewing Guide.

Williamson River. A river that drains 3,030 square miles of central Oregon east of **Highway 97**, flowing through Klamath Marsh and south into **Upper Klamath Lake**. Sprague River joins it near its lower end. It has average annual flows of 750,700 acre feet at mile point 10.3, or .4 acre foot/acre. Robert Williamson explored central Oregon for the 1855 Pacific Railroad Surveys. Oregon Geographic Names. See also **Klamath Forest National Wildlife Refuge**.

Willow Creek. A stream in **Gilliam** and **Morrow** counties that flows north from the **Blue Mountains** through rolling wheat country to join the **Columbia River** nine miles east of **Arlington**. It drains 881 square miles with an average annual volume of 22,680 acre feet at mile point 3.7, or .04 acre feet/acre. A flash flood on the creek caused the devastating **Heppner flood** of 1903; **Willow Creek Dam** was later built to prevent more such disasters. Another of Oregon's many Willow Creeks flows southeast through an intensively irrigated valley to join the **Malheur River** at **Vale**.

Willow Creek Dam. A flood-control dam built by the **Army Corps of Engineers** above **Heppner** to prevent another **Heppner flood**. The dam is 169 feet high and 1,780 feet long. The first roller-compacted concrete dam in the country, it was built in just five months in1983 at a cost of $34.7 million. There was concern in 1989 that leaching of the concrete was weakening the dam. The Corps reported that the dam has prevented several floods, including one on May 11, 1995 and again in February 1996. Oregon Geographic Names; Oregonian 6/19/95:B2, 2/19/96:D2.

Wilson River. A 33-mile long river that drains 193 square miles of the **Coast Range** and flows into the south end of **Tillamook Bay**. It was apparently named for Henry Wilson, an English printer who, in about 1851, was the first to drive cows into the area from the north, thus founding **Tillamook County**'s dairy industry. <u>Oregon Geographic Names</u>.

Wilson River Highway. See **Highway 6**.

Wilsonville. A recent and rapidly growing city on the **Willamette River** in **Clackamas** and **Washington** counties, located 19 miles south of **Portland** on **Interstate 5** - and within 60 minutes of 80% of Oregon's population. The first post office, established in 1876, was called Boons (not Boones, for reasons unknown) Ferry for the ferry operated by Daniel Boone's great-grandson just west of the present I-5 bridge. The name was changed to honor Charles Wilson, the postmaster, in 1880. The city was incorporated in 1969. Major employers are Tektronix (1,338), Mentor Graphics (888), and Hollywood Entertainment (646). Over half of the daytime population consists of workers who come from other cities. Population 1980 2,920; 1995 9,765. Elevation 175'. 30000 SW Town Center Loop East, 97070. 503-682-1011. <u>Oregon Geographic Names</u>; <u>Oregonian</u> 8/11/97:A1.

Winchester. A historic unincorporated community on the North **Umpqua River** 10 miles north of **Roseburg**. It was founded in 1850 by members of an exploring expedition and named for Heman (not Herman) Winchester, the expedition captain. Winchester was for some years the largest settlement in the Umpqua region, and was the county seat of **Douglas County** until 1854. <u>Oregon Geographic Names</u>.

Winchester Bay. An unincorporated **Douglas County** fishing community near the mouth of the **Umpqua River**. It is Oregon's largest sport fishing port, with a 750-slip boat basin called Salmon Harbor, charter fishing boat services, and county camping and RV parks. **Umpqua River Lighthouse** is two miles south. 541-271-3407. It was named for Heman Winchester, as was **Winchester** near Roseburg. <u>Oregon Geographic Names</u>.

Wind. Oregon's winds generally blow in from the ocean. In the winter and spring they blow from the southwest as storm fronts move in, while summer winds are usually from the northwest and are associated with fair weather. An east wind usually means clear, dry weather with low humidity, and sometimes results in a **dust storm**. East winds in late summer and fall create high fire danger, while a wintertime east wind will bring cold arctic air sweeping down the **Columbia River Gorge** that can result in **freezing rain** in the **Portland** area if it meets rain. The Oregon Chapter of the American Meteorological Society sponsored a "name the East Wind" contest in 1997 and "Coho" was the winner. Mountains slow winds, and sheltered valleys have a higher potential for **inversions** and **air pollution** buildup. **Portland** airport has calm winds (less than three miles per hour) 10% of the year, while **Medford** has calm winds 37% of the year. Lowest wind speeds tend to occur in the evening and early morning hours of fall and winter. Generally, Oregon has more calm days than in other areas of the country. <u>Oregonian</u> 10/31/97:D5, 12/1/97:B1. See also **Chinook wind**; **Hurricanes**; **Storms**; **Tornadoes**; **Wind speed records**.

Wind power. In 1996 there were no commercial wind power generating installations in Oregon. A 1970s experimental installation by **Pacific Power and Light** on the coast at Whiskey Run north of **Bandon** was dismantled after corrosion destroyed the parts. A 1993 proposal would place 50 wind turbines on Sevenmile Hill, a bluff west of **The Dalles** and just east of the **Columbia River**

Gorge National Scenic Area. In 1995 Kenetech Windpower proposed placing 100-foot wind towers on Vansycle Ridge in north **Umatilla County**. The wind plant would generate about 50 **megawatts**, to be expanded later to 100 megawatts. In 1997 **PacifiCorp** and the **Eugene Water & Electric Board** began construction of a 41.4 megawatt project (enough to light 30,000 homes) near Arlington, Wyoming. Oregonian 9/27/97:B8.

Wind speed records. Oregon's highest wind speeds were recorded during the **Columbus Day Storm** on October 12, 1962 with gusts of 170 miles per hour at the Air Force station on **Mt. Hebo**, 116 mph at the Morrison Street Bridge in **Portland**, and 106 mph at **Troutdale**. See also **Storms**; **Tornadoes**.

Windsurfing. A sport that became popular in Oregon, especially on the **Columbia River** in the **Hood River** area, soon after it started in about 1980. Hood River Chamber of Commerce, 800-366-3530. See also **Gorge Games.**

Wine. In 1995 Oregon had 75 wineries and over 350 vineyards located in five regions: the **Willamette**, **Umpqua**, **Rogue River**, **Columbia**, and Walla Walla valleys. In 1995 the wineries crushed nearly 10,000 tons of wine grapes, a third of it Pinot Noir, and produced 636,000 cases of wine. In 1994 Bridgeview Vineyards in **Cave Junction** led production with over 100,000 gallons, followed closely by Willamette Valley Vineyards in **Turner**, Oregon's only publicly owned winery. King Estate west of **Cottage Grove** and Flynn Vineyards are other leading producers. Over 25% of production was sold out of state. A few specialty wineries produce wine from berries and other fruits. Oregon has the nation's strictest wine labeling regulations. Oregon Wine Center 1200 NW Front Avenue, Suite 400, Portland 97209. 503-228-8403. Business Journal 4/21/95:22; 1995 Oregon Winery Report. See also **Barrels**; **Grapes**.

Winema National Forest. A 1,097,324-acre national forest along the eastern base of the **Cascade Range** in southern Oregon's **Klamath County**. It includes three wilderness areas, Mountain Lakes, Sky Lakes, and Mount Thielsen. Much of the Winema was originally part of the **Klamath Reservation**. 2819 Dahlia Street, Klamath Falls 97601. 541-883-6714.

Winnemucca to the Sea. A route promoted by local businessmen that runs from Winnemucca, Nevada, located on Interstate 80, north and west to reach the ocean at Crescent City, California. The route follows **Highway 95** and **Highway 140** to **Medford**, **Interstate 5** to **Grants Pass**, and Highway 199 to Crescent City.

Winnie. See **Dolores Winningstad Theatre**.

Winningstad Theatre. See **Dolores Winningstad Theatre**.

Winston. A southwest Oregon city in **Douglas County**, on the South **Umpqua River**, nine miles south of **Roseburg** on Highway 42. The post office, named for Elijah Winston, the first postmaster, was established in 1893. The city was incorporated in 1955. Tokora, New Zealand, is its sister city. Population 1980 3,359; 1995 4,075. Elevation 534'. 201 NW Douglas Blvd., 97496. 541-679-6739. Oregon Geographic Names.

Winter. See **Cold spells**; **Snowfall records**; **Storms**; **Temperature**.

Winter Hawks. An ice hockey team in the Junior Western Hockey League that plays at the **Memorial Coliseum**, October through March. 503-238-6366. Portland Guidebook.

Winter Ridge. A **rimrock** west of Summer Lake in **Lake County** underlain by volcanic ash deposits. The weak deposits to the east of the ridge were unable to support the weight of the massive **basalt** flows on top and collapsed in a series of giant **landslides** that slumped toward **Summer Lake**. Captain John Fremont named both the ridge and **Summer Lake** on December 16, 1843, while looking down from the ridge at Fremont Point, elevation 7,135', to the green grass surrounding the lake. Oregon Geographic Names.

Wintering-In Harvest Festival. See **Bybee-Howell House**.

Witches broom. See **Mistletoe**.

Woahink Lake. A many-fingered, two-mile-long coastal lake five miles south of **Florence** that covers 820 acres. At its maximum depth of 68 feet the bottom of the lake is 30 feet below sea level. Fifteen percent of the shoreline lies in **Jessie M. Honeyman State Park**; the rest is in private ownership, with many homes along the shoreline. Water quality has remained quite high despite the amount of development. Recreation includes fishing for both warm and cold water species, boating, and swimming. A campground is located on **Cleowax Lake** across **Highway 101**. The origin of the name is unknown. Atlas of Oregon Lakes.

Wobblies. See **Industrial Workers of the World**.

Wocas. A common yellow water-lily, *Nuphar polysepalum*, that once covered 10,000 acres in the **Upper Klamath Lake** area. The **Klamath Indians** used the seeds for food after a complex process of preparation that involved gathering the pods into canoes, fermenting them, and roasting and grinding the seeds.

Wolf. A large, wild dog, *Canis lupus*, once found throughout Oregon but extirpated, probably by the 1930s. Though they weigh about half as much as **cougars**, wolves hunt **deer**, **elk**, and, when available, **cattle**. They were so damaging to the livestock of early settlers that the need to control them prompted the first attempt to form a government in Oregon at the **wolf meetings**. Mammals and Life Zones of Oregon; Mammals of the Northwest.

Wolf Creek Highway. See **Sunset Highway**.

Wolf Creek Inn. A historic southern Oregon **stage line** stop, built, according to legend, in 1857 and rebuilt, after it burned (perhaps 1873), with hand-hewn and pegged beams. Jack London, Sinclair Lewis, Mary Pickford, and Clark Gable have been among its guests. The state bought the inn, sometimes called Wolf Creek Tavern, in 1975 and restored it. A concessionaire operates it, offering food and lodging year-round. The inn is located at Wolf Creek, an unincorporated community off **Interstate 5** at exit 76, 20 miles north of **Grants Pass**. 541-866-2474. In Search of Oregon; Oregonian 2/2/97:C1.

Wolf meetings. Early settlers in the **Willamette Valley** found that predators, especially wolves, were doing serious damage to their livestock. In early 1843 the settlers met twice and voted for a bounty, to be paid for through a voluntary tax. The meetings went so well that it was further decided (as some had planned all along) that "a committee be appointed to take into consideration the propriety of taking measures for the civil and military protection of the colony." The committee report was presented at a later meeting at **Champoeg**. Champoeg. See also **Provisional government**.

Wolverine. The largest member of the **weasel** family, *Gulo gulo*, though it looks more like a small bear. It is a solitary, slow, fierce, and powerful animal that grows to 40 inches long and 30 pounds in weight. The fearless wolverine will kill animals as large as **moose** though it lives primarily on small mammals and carrion. Its Oregon range was thought to be the forests of the **Cascade Range** and **Blue Mountains**, but one was seen near **Cape Lookout** in 1969, another was killed on **Interstate 84** near **The Dalles** in 1990, and one was sighted on **Steens Mountain** in 1994. Wolverines are rare and fully protected by law. Atlas of Oregon Wildlife; Mammals and Life Zones of Oregon; Mammals of the Northwest.

Wolves. See **Wolf**.

Women. See **Gender**.

Women in business. In 1997 women made up 44% of Oregon's labor force. Reports on the number of women-owned businesses in the state vary from 88,000 to 121,000. In 1996 in the **Portland**-Vancouver area, 40% of the firms were owned by women and women hired 28% of the workers and accounted for 25% of business sales. In May 1996 Working Woman magazine included two Oregon women on their list of the top 50 women business owners in the U.S., Gertrude Boyle of Columbia Sportswear and Helen Jo Whitsell of Copeland Lumber Yards, both **Portland**-based companies. Oregonian 3/27/96:D13, 4/24/96:D1, 8/12/97:E11, 10/5/97:C1. See also **Minority, Women and Emerging Small Business Office**.

Women in government. In 1914 Abigail Scott Duniway, Oregon's premier suffragette, became the first woman to officially vote in Oregon. Nan Wood Honeyman (D) was elected to the U.S. House of Representatives in 1936, as was Edith Green (D), for 10 terms, 1954-1972, and Elizabeth Furse (D) 1992-. Maurine Neuberger (D) served in the U.S. Senate from 1960-1967. Statewide positions filled by women include **Governor** Barbara Roberts (D), 1990-1994; **Secretary of State** Norma Paulus (R), 1976-1984, and Barbara Roberts (D), 1984-1990; **Treasurer** none; **Attorney General** none; **Commissioner of Labor and Industries** Mary Wendy Roberts (D), 1978-1994; **Superintendent of Public Instruction** Norma Paulus, 1990-1998; **Supreme Court** Justices Betty Roberts, 1982-1986, Susan Graber 1990- (nominated to U.S. 9th **Circuit Court** of Appeals in 1998), and Susan Leeson 1998-; **Appeals Court** Judges Betty Roberts 1977-1982, Mary Deits 1986- (chief judge 1997-), Susan Graber 1988-1990, Susan Leeson 1993-1998, and Virginia Lynn Linder, 1997-; Oregon **Tax Court** none. Ann Aiken became a U.S. **District Court** judge in 1998. Dorothy McCullough Lee served as the first woman in the Oregon House of Representatives, 1928-1932, served in the state Senate 1932-1940, and was elected mayor of **Portland** in 1948. Connie McCready served as Portland's mayor in 1979, and Vera Katz was elected mayor in 1994. See also **Petticoat Government**; **Presidential candidates**; **Women's suffrage**.

Women in law. See **Attorneys**.

Women in law enforcement. In 1908 Lola Baldwin of **Portland** became the nation's first paid municipal policewoman. She worked to prevent conditions that might lure young women into prostitution or crime. At least two women have been killed in police work in the state, Alice Mae Moran, a matron with the Josephine County Sheriff's Office in 1971, and Portland police officer Colleen Waibel in 1998. Municipal Mother; Oregonian 1/28/98:A5. See also **Law enforcement**.

Women in sports. Mary Slaney of **Eugene** has been the country's most successful female distance runner with 20 years of records in distances from 800 to 3,000 meters. Liz Heaston became the first woman to play in a college **football** game when she kicked two points after touchdowns for **Willamette University** on 10/18/97. See also **Basketball, women's**.

Women in the military. In 1997, the records of the Oregon Department of **Veterans' Affairs** showed that 18,600 women veterans lived in the state. Of those, 4,200 had served during **World War II**, 1,500 during the **Korean War**, 3,900 during the **Vietnam War**, and 2,900 during Operation Desert Storm in 1991. The 1997 state legislature contributed $18,200 to a national memorial for women in the military. Oregonian 10/18/97:A8.

Women, Oregon Commission for. An eleven-member commission established by the legislature in 1983 to work for women's equality through advocacy and legislation. It sponsors an annual "Women of Achievement" dinner and issues several publications, including Oregon Women and the Law. PO Box 751-CW, Portland 97207. 503-725-5889. Oregon Blue Book.

Women's firsts. The first white woman in Oregon was Jane Barnes, an English barmaid who was brought to **Fort George** in 1814 by its new governor and who left shortly, after his death. This Side of Oregon. In 1880, Bethenia Owens-Adair (1840-1926), an 1843 pioneer, became the first woman graduate physician on the Pacific Coast, practicing in Portland and Yakima. Dictionary of Oregon History. In 1885 Mary Gysin Leonard, acquitted in 1878 of murdering her estranged husband, became the first woman admitted to the practice of law in Oregon. "Discovered"; Governing Oregon; Tracking down Oregon. In 1886 Minnie Hill became the first licensed female steamboat captain west of the Mississippi. Blow for the Landing. The Salem firm of Lord-Schryver, famed for early 20th century landscaping, was the first women's landscape architecture firm in the Northwest.

Women's suffrage. The attempt by Oregon women to get the right to vote began in 1870. Male voters defeated the proposal five times (1884, 1900, 1906, 1908, 1910) before passing it in 1912, eight years before the Nineteenth Amendment to the U.S. Constitution gave all U.S. women the vote. Abigail Scott Duniway was the persistent leader of the struggle in Oregon. She was opposed by her brother, Harvey Scott, editor of the **Oregonian,** the most influential newspaper in the state. The first woman to actually vote in Oregon was tobacco-chewing One-eyed Charlie Parkhurst, a stage line driver for 30 years who voted in 1868. After his death in 1878, One-eyed Charlie Parkhurst was found to have been a woman. Little Joe Monahan, a cowhand and rancher who voted in the **Jordan Valley** area, was also found to be a woman after her death in 1904. Oregon History 38(4):6 Winter 1994-95; Oregon's Golden Years; Tracking down Oregon. See also **Prohibition**.

Wood. In 1994 Oregon residences burned 459,000 cords of wood for **home heating**. A cord is a stack of wood 4x4x8 feet. State Energy Data Report. See also **Wood stoves**.

Wood burners. See **Wigwam burners**.

Wood products industry. See **Forest products industry**.

Wood rats. Wild rats, often called pack rats, that are known for their habit of collecting all manner of objects on their nightly forays and incorporating them into the large, musky-smelling piles in which they nest. Three species of wood rats, all vegetarian and from 12 to 16 inches long, are found in the state, the desert wood rat, *Neotoma lepida*, of southeast Oregon, the dusky-footed wood rat, *N. fuscipes*, of western Oregon, and the bushy-tailed wood rat, *N. cinerea*, throughout the state. They use the same urinating stations repeatedly, creating large white deposits of urine residues on desert rimrock. Atlas of Oregon Wildlife; Mammals and Life Zones of Oregon; Mammals of the Northwest.

Wood stoves. The 1990 census found that 17% of Oregon homes were heated partly or entirely with **wood**. During the 1970s the use of fireplaces and wood stoves for home heating had increased as a response to a rapid rise in oil costs. This resulted in increased **particulate** and **carbon monoxide** air pollution. In 1983 Oregon passed the nation's first law restricting wood stove emissions and all stoves sold after July 1, 1986, must be certified as "clean burning." This has resulted in major reductions in **air pollution**, especially in southern Oregon. Oregon Environmental Atlas. See also **Home heating**.

Wood Village. "Home of Greyhound Racing." A **Multnomah County** residential community 16 miles east of **Portland** on **Interstate 84** between **Fairview** and **Troutdale**. Built as a housing project for Reynolds Aluminum Company workers during **World War II**, it was named for building contractor Lester Wood. The city was incorporated in 1951. Major employers are **Multnomah Greyhound Park**, Krueger's Truck Stop, Willamette Greystone, and Magnetic Specialties. Population 1980 2,253; 1995 2,965. Elevation 130'. 2055 NE 238th Drive, 97060. 503-667-6211. Oregon Geographic Names.

Woodburn. A **Willamette Valley** city in **Marion County** 17 miles north of **Salem** on **Interstate 5**. It was platted by J. A. Settlemeier in 1871 along the forthcoming railroad, and the post office was established the same year. The name commemorates a fire that escaped after being set to burn brush and felled timber along the railroad right-of-way. The city was incorporated in 1889. It is a town of remarkable diversity for its size, containing a retirement community, a growing Hispanic population, a sizable group of Russian Old Believers, and a number of Mennonites. Attractions include the 1890s Settlemeier House. The Woodburn Spring **Tulip** Show is held in April. Population 1980 11,196; 1995 15,475. Elevation 182'. 270 Montgomery St., 97071. 503-982-5222. Oregon Geographic Names.

Woodchuck. See **Marmot**.

Wool. Wool production in Oregon in 1995 was 2.6 million pounds, sheared from 374,000 **sheep**, worth $1.8 million. **Shaniko** was at one time the largest wool-shipping rail station in the world. East of the Cascades; 1995 Oregon. See also **Weaving**; **Woolen mills**.

Woolen mills. The first woolen mill in Oregon began operation in Salem in 1858 after several years of effort led by Joseph Watt. By 1890 there were 10 in the state, and by the early 1900s cities in all areas of Oregon had woolen mills. Pendleton Woolen Mills, established in **Pendleton** in 1909 to make Indian blankets, now has 14 plants in five states making 100% virgin wool blankets, fabric, and garments. In 1997 Mt. Jefferson Woolen Mill in **Jefferson** was Oregon's other surviving woolen mill. Pioneer Woolen Mills in Oregon; Later Woolen Mills in Oregon. See also **Mission Mill Village**; **Weaving**.

Word on the Street. A day, October 3, 1997, sponsored by **Orlo** and dedicated to celebrating literature "out loud and on street corners" as an Earth Day for literature. 503-242-1047. Oregonian 8/15/97:B1.

Workers' compensation. A system for compensating workers for work-related injuries. Oregon's once cumbersome and expensive system was reformed by the legislature in 1990, resulting in a steady decline in rates such that by 1996 the state had dropped from 6th to 34th highest nationally. Work-related deaths had dropped from 144 in 1973 to 48 in 1995; 14 of the 1995 fatalities were in construction. Of the 348 fatalities resulting in claims between 1988 and 1992, 17 were homicides. **Logging** is the most dangerous occupation in the state; in 1988-1990 it had a payroll of $478 million and losses of $107 million. Violence in the Workplace; "Workers' Compensation Reform." See also **SAIF Corporation**; **Vocational Rehabilitation**; **Workplace fatalities**.

Workers' Compensation Division. A division of the Oregon Department of **Consumer and Business Services** that administers and enforces the Workers' Compensation Law. 350 Winter St. NE, Salem 97310. 503-945-7514. Oregon Blue Book. See also **SAIF**.

Workers' Compensation Ombudsman. An independent advocate for injured workers in their dealings with the **workers' compensation** system. Information about the office is included in notices sent out to injured workers. 800-927-1271, or 503-378-3351. The **Small Business** Ombudsman for Workers Compensation advocates for small businesses at workers' compensation rate-making and rule-making hearings and develops educational materials for small business operators. 503-378-4209. Both are in the Labor and Industries Building, 350 Winter St. NE, Salem 97310. Oregon Blue Book.

Workplace fatalities. The number of Oregon workplace deaths totaled 63 in 1992, 64 in 1993, 55 in 1994, 48 in 1995, and 54 in 1996. Transportation accounted for nearly half. The most dangerous occupations were transport operators with a total of 50 deaths in five years, and forestry, logging, and fishing with a total of 47 in five years. Oregonian 8/2/97:A10.

World Championship Timber Carnival. See **Albany World Championship Timber Carnival**.

World Forestry Center. A private, non-profit **forest education** center near the **Metro Washington Park Zoo** in **Portland**. The World Forest Institute (an information clearinghouse for international forestry), an exhibit hall, and a gift shop, are located at the Center, which also sponsors classes, tours, and demonstrations, operates **Magness Tree Farm**, and publishes a quarterly journal, Forest Perspectives. 4033 SW Canyon Road, Portland 97221. 503-228-1367. Oregon Blue Book.

World Masters Games. The largest multi-sport event in the world is scheduled for Oregon, August 9-22, 1998. The 25 sports competitions for athletes over age 30 will be held at sites from **Hood River** and **Portland** to **Eugene**. Some 25,000 participants are expected. Oregonian 8/10/97:D1.

World War I, 1914-1918. A war that began in Europe with Austria and Germany as the aggressors. The U.S. entered the war in 1917. Oregon became known as the volunteer state; **Portland's National Guard** unit was the first in the country to mobilize. Patriotism also led to vigilante groups that searched out dissidents. The U.S. Army built logging rail lines and a **Sitka spruce** mill in **Toledo** to produce lightweight wood for fighter planes. See also **Spruce Production Corporation**.

World War II, 1941-1945. A war that involved the U.S. in both Europe (against Germany) and the Pacific (against Japan). 148,039 Oregonians served in the military; of those 5,314 were injured and 2,826 died. During the war Oregon's population ballooned by 194,000 people, many arriving to build **Liberty ships** in Henry Kaiser's **Portland** shipyards and living in **Vanport**. Women joined the work force in unprecedented numbers, and teenagers were employed to harvest farm crops. **Pendleton** Air Base trained Doolittle's Raiders for their historic bombing mission over Tokyo, and training camps were established at **Camp Abbot**, **Camp Adair**, and **Camp White**. Some of the soldiers who trained in the camps later returned to settle in Oregon. Timber workers were 'frozen" in their jobs. Many Oregonians raised Victory Gardens and volunteered for air raid watches and coast patrols, and everyone was affected by censorship, rationing, and blackouts. About 4,500 **Japanese** Americans, two thirds of them American citizens, were moved from western Oregon to **relocation centers** in Idaho, California, and Wyoming. 15,000 **braceros** were brought in to do farm work. **Mines** were laid in the mouth of the **Columbia River**. In anticipation of a possible Japanese invasion, dynamite was placed under all the coast bridges and roads leading inland, road signs were removed, lights were turned out or covered in blackouts, and the coastline was patrolled by the Coast Guard foot, horseback, and boat and by Navy **blimp** patrols. On June 21, 1942, a Japanese submarine shelled the area around **Fort Stevens.** On September 9 and 19 the same submarine launched a small plane that dropped **incendiary bombs** on the forests of **Curry County**. A B-17F crashed on **Cape Lookout** in August 1943 with ten men aboard; only the bombardier survived. On January 31, 1945, a Navy PBY bomber crashed east of **Brookings**; all eight aboard were killed. Six persons were killed by a **balloon bomb** on May 5, 1945. Oregon Coast 3-4/94:80; Silent Siege; "WW II at Home." See also **Camp Angell**; **Oregon Maneuvers**; **Women in the military**.

World's Electrical, Industrial, and Highways Exposition. See **Atlantic Pacific Highways and Electrical Exposition**.

World's fairs. See **Atlantic Pacific Highways and Electrical Exposition**; **Expositions**; **Lewis and Clark Centennial Exposition**.

World's Shortest River. The designation given by the Guinness Book of World Records to the 120-foot long **D River** in **Lincoln City**.

WPPSS. See **Washington Public Power Supply System**.

Wrestling. The first professional wrestling match in Oregon was held on August 9, 1883, when world champion Donald Dinny was defeated by D.A. McMillan. This Day in Oregon. See also **Boxing and Wrestling Commission**.

Wright Point. A six-mile long, flat-topped ridge 12 miles south of **Burns** that extends east from a mesa into **Harney Basin**. It rises 250 feet above the desert floor and averages 1,200 feet wide. The ridge is actually a fossilized river, an example of inverted topography. It is the remnant of a river valley filled by lava flows in the late **Pliocene**; the resistant lava remained as the area around it eroded.

Highway 205 crosses the ridge. The name came from Camp Wright which had been named in October 1865 for Brigadier-General George Wright who, with his wife, had been drowned in the wreck of the **Brother Jonathan** a few months earlier. The site of Camp Wright at the base of the eastern end is now the location of Island Ranch, one of the area's historic cattle **ranches**. Geology of Oregon; Oregon's Great Basin Country; Oregon Geographic Names. See also **Camps, military**.

Wyeth. See **Camp Angell**.

Yachats (yah-hots). "Gem of the Oregon Coast." An ocean-side tourist community on the central Oregon coast in **Lincoln County**, 23 miles south of **Newport** on **Highway 101**. Originally the site of an Alsea Indian village whose last residents had died of smallpox in 1853, it was included in the **Coast Reservation** from 1860 to 1875 and was home to some 300 **Coquille, Coos**, and Lower Umpqua Indians until they were removed to allow white settlement. The post office, established in 1887, was called Ocean View. In 1916 it was renamed Yachats for the local river and Indian village; the name is said to mean "at the foot of the mountain." The city was incorporated in 1966. Attractions include the Little Log Church (museum), an Arts and Crafts Fair in March, **Smelt** Fry in July, Kite Festival in October, and **Cape Perpetua** Visitor Center 3 miles south of town. Population 1980 482; 1995 645. Elevation 23'. PO Box 345, 97498. 541-547-3565. Chamber of Commerce 541-547-3530. Oregon Geographic Names; She's Tricky.

Yak. A large, long-haired ox, *Bos grunniens*, of Tibet and central Asia. Livestock operators, including 10 in Oregon, have been experimenting with yak crossbred cattle because yaks are hardy and have meat that is low in fat and high in protein. Oregonian 2/26/97:B4.

Yakima War, 1855-58. An **Indian war** in Washington state that grew out of the unrest following the **Whitman massacre** and the subsequent **Cayuse War** of 1847-1850. Open warfare began in 1855 with encounters throughout much of the state, including a siege of Seattle and the **Cascades massacre**, an attack on a white settlement on the north shore of the **Columbia River** near Bonneville. Some Oregon residents took part in the conflict, and it prompted the building of **Fort Henrietta,** but none of the engagements was on Oregon soil. Dictionary of Oregon History. See also **Fort Rains**.

Yamhill. "A Small Taste of Oregon." A **Willamette Valley** farming town in **Yamhill County**, 13 miles north of **McMinnville** on Highway 47. The North Yamhill River is close to town which was called North Yam Hill when the post office opened in 1851. The city was incorporated in 1891, and its name changed to Yamhill in 1908. The Yamhills were a local Indian tribe. Population 1980 690; 1995 940. Elevation 182'. PO Box 9, 97148. 503-662-3511. Old Yamhill.

Yamhill County. A county in northwest Oregon extending from the **Willamette River** west up into the **Coast Range**. Incorporated cities are **McMinnville** (county seat), **Amity, Carlton, Dayton, Dundee, Lafayette, Newberg, Sheridan**, and **Yamhill**. The county is bounded by **Washington, Clackamas, Marion, Polk**, and **Tillamook** counties. Elevations rise from 50' along the Willamette to 3,423' Trask Mountain on the west. The economy is based on agriculture, lumber, education, international aviation, dental equipment, manu-

factured homes, pulp and paper, and steel. Taxable assessed value in 1995 was
$3,311,000,000, or $44,000 per capita. **Yamhill District** was one of Oregon's
original four counties, created in 1843. It was named for the local Yamhelas band
of **Kalapuya Indians**. Population 1980 55,332; 1995 74,600. Area 718 square
miles. Density 104/sq.mi. Annual precipitation 44"; average temperature January
39°F, July 65°F. Courthouse, 535 NE 5th, McMinnville 97128. 503-472-9371.
Old Yamhill; Oregon Blue Book.

Yamhill District. The southwest of the four original districts (later, **counties**) into which the **Oregon Country** was divided by the **Provisional government** on July 5, 1843, and the one from which the counties of southwest Oregon
were later created. Yamhill District was that part of the **Oregon Country** lying
between the **Willamette River** and the ocean, from the Yamhill River south to 42°
latitude (the present Oregon/California border). The three other districts were
Champooick to the southeast, **Clackamas** to the northeast, and **Twality** to the
northwest. "Oregon Counties."

Yamhill River. A river that, with its two main branches, the North Yamhill
and the South Yamhill, drains 770 square miles from the east slopes of the **Coast
Range** to the **Willamette River** six miles south of **Newberg**. In 1900 a small dam
with a 16-foot lift navigation lock was completed eight miles up the river near
Lafayette. It operated until 1954. "Yamhill" was apparently derived from the
name of a local band of **Kalapuya Indians**. Army Engineers; "From Dream to
Demolition"; Oregon Geographic Names.

Yamsay Mountain. A prominent peak, elevation 8,242', in south central
Oregon, important in the lore of the **Klamath Indians**. It is in the **Winema Na-
tional Forest** near the **Klamath/Lake County** line 40 miles east of **Crater Lake**.
The mountain was formed in the **Pliocene** as a **basalt** shield volcano with later
rhyolite lavas. Yamsay is a Klamath name referring to the north wind. Geology of
Oregon; Oregon Geographic Names.

Yaquina (yuh KWIN uh) **Bay**. The bay at the mouth of the **Yaquina River**
on the central Oregon coast. **Newport** is located on its north bank. It is a major
fishing port and ocean freighters come into the bay to pick up loads of lumber; it is
the only deep-water port between **Astoria** and **Coos Bay**. The Yaquinas were the
local Indians. See also **Oysters**.

Yaquina Bay Lighthouse. A frame **lighthouse** on the north shore of Yaquina
Bay that was in service only from 1871 until supplanted by **Yaquina Head Lighthouse** in 1873. The light itself, restored in 1996, is officially listed as a private
navigational beacon. The building, which includes both the keeper's quarters and
the light, is owned by the State **Parks and Recreation Department** and is kept
open most afternoons by volunteers. It is also used for weddings, despite its legendary **ghost**. 541-265-5679. Oregon Lighthouses; Oregon Parks 2(3):54 Nov/
Dec 1994; Oregon's Seacoast Lighthouses; Oregonian 9/30/96:B4.

Yaquina Head Lighthouse. An active **lighthouse** three miles north of **Newport** that has been in operation since 1873. Legend claims, perhaps erroneously,
that it was originally planned for **Cape Foulweather** seven miles to the north, but
was built instead on Yaquina Head after construction materials were mistakenly
landed there. Its light is 162' above the ocean, and the 93-foot tower makes it the

tallest Oregon lighthouse. The tower, located in the **Yaquina Head Outstanding Natural Area**, is open on a limited schedule for tours. 541-265-2863. Oregon Lighthouses; Oregon Parks 2(3):54 Nov/Dec 1994; Oregon's Seacoast Lighthouses.

Yaquina Head Outstanding Natural Area. A **Bureau of Land Management** area on Yaquina Head, an ocean headland three miles north of **Newport**. The area includes **Yaquina Head Lighthouse**, an interpretive center that opened in 1997 with exhibits about the lighthouse and the natural history of the area, trails on the headland, and wheel-chair accessible trails to and around a 3.5 acre **tide pool** that was created in 1994 by opening an abandoned quarry to the sea. 541-564-3100.

Yaquina Railroad. See **Oregon Pacific Railroad**.

Yaquina River. A 59-mile long river that drains 122 square miles of the central **Coast Range** to the ocean at **Newport** where **jetties** at the mouth help maintain a channel for deep-water boats. The Yaquinas were a small band of Yakonan Indians who lived in the area. Oregon Geographic Names.

Yellow fir. See **Douglas-fir**.

Yerba Buena. See **San Francisco**.

Yew. A scraggly, slow-growing, understory conifer **tree**, *Taxus brevifolia*, found in forests throughout the west. Though it has needle-like leaves, its seeds are in small red berries (arils) rather than in cones; the berries are poisonous to humans, though not to birds. Yew trees were important to Indians and pioneers because of the tough, resilient wood, but the trees had little modern commercial value until they were found to contain paclitaxel (Taxol$^{\circledR}$), a substance that is effective in the treatment of several kinds of cancer. Paclitaxel is extracted primarily from the bark, but is also found in the needles. About 60 pounds of wet bark, equivalent to the bark from three 120-year-old trees 8" in diameter, is needed to treat a case of ovarian cancer. Weyerhauser Company planted 15 million cuttings in its Northwest nurseries in 1993 for harvest in three to five years and research continues on raising related species. Synthesized paclitaxel is too expensive to meet the demand. Report on the Pacific Yew.

Yoncalla. yahn-kahl-luh. A southwest Oregon community in **Douglas County**, 28 miles north of **Roseburg**. The Yoncalla Valley was noted for many years as the home of the Applegate brothers; Jesse Applegate is said to have named the community for the prominent mountain to the northwest that Indians called Yoncalla, "home of the eagles." The 1856 Charles Applegate house northeast of town is one of Oregon's notable haunted houses. Yoncalla's post office was established in 1851, and the city was incorporated in 1901. The community was awarded President Bush's 53rd "Point of Light" for volunteerism. Population 1980 805; 1995 960. Elevation 354'. PO Box 508, 97499. 541-849-2152. Oregon Geographic Names; Oregon's Ghosts and Monsters; Skookum. See also **Milltown Hill Dam**.

Youngs Bay. A large bay on the south side of the **Columbia River** near its mouth. **Astoria** is located on its east bank, linked to **Warrenton** on its west bank by a two-mile-long bridge. Both the **Lewis and Clark River** and **Youngs River** flow into the bay. The bay and river were both named by British Lieutenant William Broughton of Captain Vancouver's 1792 expedition for Sir George Young (later Admiral) of the royal navy. Oregon Geographic Names.

Youngs River. A 23-mile long river that drains 122 square miles of the **Coast Range** north into **Youngs Bay**.

Youth Authority (OYA). An Oregon department created by the 1995 legislature to administer the state's **juvenile corrections** facilities for youths ages 12-21 and to supervise their parole and probation. In 1996 approximately 2,000 youth offenders were under their supervision, 1,000 of them at an out-of-home facility or foster home. 530 Center St. NE, Suite 200, Salem 97301-3740. 503-373-7205.

Youth Conservation Corps. See **Oregon National Guard Youth Conservation Corps**.

Yreka Trail. A wagon road used by California **gold** miners to get to **Canyon City** following gold strikes there in 1861 and 1862. Though the exact route is obscure in many places, it is known that it went from Yreka, California to Canyon City by way of the **Klamath Falls** area, across the **High Desert** of central Oregon, and across the South Fork of the **John Day River**. "Juniper Stumps."

Yurt camping. Oregon **state parks** rent yurts (82 in 1997) for year-round camping in many coastal parks as well as at **Champoeg**, **Valley of the Rogue**, and **Wallowa Lake** state parks. The yurts are domed, circular, 16-foot diameter insulated tents on plywood floors with lockable doors. They have electricity and space heaters, but cooking must be done outside. Cabins are available at **Prineville Reservoir**. Reservations, 800-452-5687.

Zebra mussel. A small striped freshwater shellfish, *Dreissena polymorpha*, that is native to Russia. It was accidentally introduced into the Great Lakes area in 1988. Within a few years it spread there and in the Mississippi River system in such numbers that it clogged pipelines and disabled water systems. Some biologists say that its spread to the west is all but inevitable; there is no known control. Oregonian 8/27/95:A21.

Zeolites. A group of minerals found in rocks of volcanic origin. They are notable for their ability to exchange ions so are used in water softeners and similar applications. At least 23 zeolite minerals have been identified in Oregon, and some are mined in **Malheur County** near the Idaho border for use as a carrier for agricultural chemicals. "Zeolites."

Zigzag. An unincorporated community southwest of **Mount Hood** on **Highway 26**. It is at the confluence of the Zigzag and the Sandy rivers which are separated by Zigzag Mountain. The name apparently comes from an entry that Joel Palmer made in his journal on October 11, 1845, describing his descent that day of a deep ravine (now called Zigzag Canyon) near timberline. "The manner of descending is to turn directly to the right, go zigzag for about one hundred yards, then turn short round, and go zigzag until you come under the place where you started from; then to the right, and so on, until you reach the base." Oregon Geographic Names.

Zinc. Zinc and **copper** are mined at the Silver Peak Mine south of **Riddle**. The ore is concentrated for shipment to Japan where it is processed. Mineral Industry of Oregon.

Zirconium. A strong metallic element that is resistant to corrosion. Highly refined zirconium is used in nuclear reactors and chemical processing, while less pure forms are used in cluster bombs. Wah Chang in **Millersburg** is one of the world's leading processors. In January 1995 the company pleaded guilty to having illegally exported cluster bomb components in the 1980s for use by Iraq, and agreed to a $13 million fine.

Zoning. See **Land use planning**.

Zoo. See **Metro Washington Park Zoo**.

Zoo Railway. A 30-gauge rail line in **Portland**'s **Washington Park**. During the summer it makes regular 25-minute, 3/4-mile trips along steep, forested hillsides between the Zoo Station near the **International Rose Test Gardens** and the **Metro Washington Park Zoo**. Round-trip fare includes admission to the zoo.

Zumwalt Prairie. A 200-square-mile area north of **Wallowa Lake** that is notable for its flourishing native grasslands and raptor population. Most of the area is owned by local ranchers and is used for grazing. Prairie Keepers.

ZX Ranch. One of the largest ranches in the west, owned by J. R. Simplot of Idaho. The ranch, headquartered in **Paisley**, runs 10,000 head of cattle on 1.3 million acres of owned and leased lands, including **Sycan Marsh**. Oregonian 6/30/96:L1.

BIBLIOGRAPHY

"1918 'Spanish Influenza' Pandemic in Oregon," by Ivan M. Wooley. Oregon Historical Quarterly 64(3):246-258 September 1963.

1994-1995 Oregon Agriculture and Fisheries Statistics. U.S. Department of Agriculture and Oregon Department of Agriculture, 635 Capitol St. NE, Salem 97310-0110, 1995. 84 pp.

1995 Oregon County and state Agricultural Estimates. Special Report 790. Oregon State University Extension Service, Corvallis, rev. January 1996. 13 pp.

1995 Oregon Foundation DataBook, by Craig McPherson. C&D Publishing, Portland, 1995. 282 pp.

1995 Oregon Vineyard Report. Oregon Agricultural Statistics Service, 1735 Federal Building, 1220 SW 3rd, Portland 97204. 800-338-2157. 4 pp.

1995 Oregon Winery Report. Oregon Agricultural Statistics Service, 1735 Federal Bldg, 1220 SW 3rd, Portland 97204. 503-326-2131. 4 pp.

AAA TourBook. See Oregon Washington AAA TourBook.

"Abbot Railroad Surveys, 1855", by Robert W. Sawyer. Oregon Historical Quarterly 33(1):1-24 March 1932; 33(2)115-135 June 1932.

Adventures in Politics: We Go to the Legislature, by Richard L. Neuberger. Oxford University Press, New York, 1954. 210 pp.

Agriculture: Oregon's Leading Industry. Oregon Department of Agriculture, Salem, [1995?] 23 pp.

All Quiet on the Yamhill: The Civil War in Oregon, by Royal A. Bensell. University of Oregon Books, Eugene, 1959. 226 pp.

American Indian Reservations and Trust Areas, by Veronica E. Velarde Tiller. Economic Development Administration, U.S. Department of Commerce, Washington, D.C., 1996. Oregon entries, pp. 539-549.

Amerikanuak, by William A. Douglass and Jon Bilbao. University of Nevada Press, Reno, 1975. 519 pp.

"Ancient Caldera Complex Revealed," by Frank R. Hladky and Thomas J. Wiley. Oregon Geology 55(3):70 May 1993.

Ancient Forests of the Pacific Northwest, by Elliott A. Norse. Wilderness Society. Island Press, Washington, D.C., 1990. 327 pp.

"Another Look at the 'Fever and Ague' of Western Oregon," by Robert T. Boyd. Ethnohistory 22(2):135-154 Spring 1975.

Antelope: The Saga of a Western Town, by Arthur H. Campbell. Maverick, Bend, 1900. 326 pp.

"Anti-Japanese Legislation in Oregon, 1917-1923," by Daniel P. Johnson. Oregon Historical Quarterly 97(2):176-210 Summer 1996.

Applegate Trail of 1846: A Documentary Guide to the Original Southern Emigrant Route to Oregon, by William Emerson. Ember Enterprises, PO Box 1343, Ashland 97520-0045, 1996. 158 pp.

Archaeology of Oregon, by C. Melvin Aikens. Bureau of Land Management, 1300 NE 44th Avenue, Portland 97213, 1993. 302 pp.

"Architecture in Oregon, 1845-1895," by Marion D. Ross. Oregon Historical

Quarterly 57(1):4-64 March 1956. (Illustrations p. 4-32, text p. 33-64)

Architecture Oregon Style. See Oregon Style.

Army Engineers and the Development of Oregon: A History of the Portland District U.S. Army Corps of Engineers, by William F. Willingham. [The District, Portland, 1983]. 258 pp.

Artists of the Pacific Northwest: A Biographical Dictionary, 1600s-1970, by Maria Sharylen. McFarland & Company, Box 611, Jefferson, NC 28640, 1993. 252 pp.

As I Remember Adam: An Autobiography of a Festival, by Angus L. Bowmer. Oregon Shakespearean Festival Association, Ashland, 1975. 272 pp.

"'As Long As the World Goes On': The Table Rocks and the Takelma," by Kay Atwood. Oregon Historical Quarterly 95(4):516-533 Winter 1994-95.

Ashland, the First 130 Years, by Marjorie O'Harra. Southern Oregon Historical Society, Jacksonville,1981. 200 pp.

"Ashwood on Trout Creek: A Study in Continuity and Change in Central Oregon," by Peter G. Boag. Oregon Historical Quarterly 91(2):116-153 Summer 1990.

Astoria, by Washington Irving. Binfords & Mort, Portland 97242, (1836) 1967. 475 pp.

Astoria and Empire, by James Ronda. University of Nebraska Press, Lincoln, 1990. 400 pp.

Atlas of Oregon, by William Loy, Stuart Allan, Clyde P. Patton, and Robert D. Plank. University of Oregon Books, Eugene, 1976. 215 pp.

Atlas of Oregon Lakes, by Daniel M. Johnson, et. al. Oregon State University Press, Corvallis, 1985. 317 pp.

Atlas of Oregon Wildlife: Distribution, Habitat, and Natural History, by Blair Csuti, et al. Oregon State University Press, Corvallis, 1997. 492 pp.

Atlas of the Pacific Northwest, by Philip L. Jackson and A. Jon Kimerling. Eighth edition. Oregon State University Press, Corvallis, 1993. 152 pp.

Audubon Society Field Guide to North American Fishes, Whales, and Dolphins. Alfred A. Knopf, New York, 1983. 848 pp.

Backwoods Railroads: Branchlines and Shortlines of Western Oregon, by D. C. Jesse Burkhardt. Washington State University Press, Pullman, 1994. 168 pp.

"Bandon-by-the-Sea Revisited," by Thomas C. McClintock. Oregon Historical Quarterly 75(4):339-343 December 1974.

Barlow Road, by Walter Meacham. Oregon Council, American Pioneer Trails Association, place not given, 1947. 19 pp.

"Basque Folklore in Southeastern Oregon," by Sarah Baker Munro. Oregon Historical Quarterly 76(2):153-174 June 1975.

Bay Clams of Oregon: Their Identification, Relative Abundance, and General Distribution. by Lowell D. Marriage. Fish Commission of Oregon, [Portland], 1958. 29 pp.

Bayocean: The Oregon Town that Fell into the Sea, by Bert and Margie Webber. Webb Research Group/Pacific Northwest Books Company, Medford, 1989. 206 pp.

Beachcombing and Camping along the Northwest Coast, by Bert & Margie Webber. Ye Galleon Press, Fairfield WA, 1978. 190 pp.

Beachcombing the Pacific, by Amos L. Wood. Henry Regnery Company, Chicago, 1975. 225 pp.

Beaver, Kings and Cabins by Constance Lindsay Skinner. Macmillan, New York, 1933. 273 pp.

"Beginnings of the Credit-Union Movement in Oregon," by Patricia Duffy and John P. Farrell. Oregon Historical Quarterly 87(4):388-406 Winter 1986.

Between Pacific Tides, by Edward F. Ricketts, et al. Fifth edition. Stanford University Press, Stanford CA, 1985. 652 pp.

"Beyond the Ruts," by Bill and Ellen Lilja. Oregon History Magazine 39(1):8-9,23 Spring/Summer 1995.

Big Blow: The Story of the Pacific Northwest's Columbus Day Storm, by Ellis Lucia. Storm Book, 1835 N. Highland St., Portland, 1963. 66 pp.

Big Game History 1890-1990, by Robert Mace, Ralph Denney, and Rod Ingram. Oregon Department of Fish and Wildlife, Salem, 1995. 40 pp.

"Bigot Disclosed: 90 Years of Nativism," by Malcolm Clark, Jr. Oregon Historical Quarterly 75(2):108-190 June 1974.

Biography of John McCoy with a Brief History of Linn County, by Fred McCoy. Richard R. Milligan, Albany, 1983. 64 pp.

Birder's Guide to Oregon, by Joseph E. Evanich, Jr. Portland Audubon Society, 1990. 288 pp.

Birds of Oregon, by Ira N. Gabrielson and Stanley G. Jewett. Oregon State College, Corvallis, 1940. Republished as Birds of the Pacific Northwest, Dover, New York, 1970. 650 pp.

Birds of Oregon: Status and Distribution, ed. by Jeff Gilligan et al., Cinclus Publications, PO Box 284, McMinnville 97128, 1994. 330 pp.

BLM Facts, Oregon and Washington 1993. Bureau of Land Management, Portland. 58 pp.

BLM's Billion-Dollar Checkerboard: Managing the O & C Lands, by Elmo Richardson. Forest History Society, Santa Cruz, CA,1980. 200 pp.

Blow for the Landing: A Hundred Years of Steam Navigation on the Waters of the West, by Fritz Timmen. Caxton Printers, Caldwell, Idaho, 1973. 235 pp.

Brewed in the Pacific Northwest: A History of Beer Making in Oregon and Washington, by Gary and Gloria Meier. Fjord Press, Seattle. 1991. 216 pp.

Bridge of the Gods: A Romance of Indian Oregon, by Frederic Homer Balch. 1890, republished by Binfords and Mort, Portland, 1965. 318 pp.

Brownsville, Linn County's Oldest Town, by Margaret Carey and Patricia Hainline. Calapooia Pub., Brownsville, 1976. 44 pp.

"Bull Run Watershed: Portland's Enduring Jewel," by Rick Harmon. Oregon Historical Quarterly 96(2/3):242-270 Summer/Fall 1995.

Business Journal, Serving Greater Portland. Weekly. PO Box 14490, Portland 97214. 503-274-8733.

Butterflies of Oregon, by Ernst J. Dornfeld. Timber Press, Forest Grove, 1980. 276 pp.

Butterfly Fleet: Salmon, Sails and Oars on the Columbia River, by Dena Johnson.

Bookpartners, PO Box 922, Wilsonville 97070, 1997. 343 pp.

Camp Adair, 50 Years Ago, World War II. Polk County Museum, 187 SW Court Street, Dallas 97338. 1992. 109 pp.

Camp White, by Chris Hald, M.D. Webb Reserarch Group, Medford, 1994. 124 pp.

Capitol Names: Individuals Woven into Oregon's History, by Philip Cogswell, Jr. Oregon Historical Society, Portland, 1977. 140 pp.

Capitol's Who's Who for Oregon: The State Reference. Capitol Publishing Company, Portland. At least three volumes, 1936, 1942, 1948.

Casual and Factual Glimpses at the Beginning and Development of Oregon's Roads and Highways, by Ralph Watson. Oregon State Highway Commission, Salem, [195?]. 62 pp.

Cattle Country of Peter French, by Giles French. Binfords and Mort, Portland, 1964. 167 pp.

Central Oregon Caves, by Charlie and Jo Larson. ABC Publishing, Vancouver WA, 1987. 44 pp.

Century of Coos and Curry, by Emil R. Peterson and Alfred Powers. Binfords & Mort, Portland. 1952. 599 pp.

Century of Portland Architecture, by Thomas Vaughan and George McMath. Oregon Historical Society, Portland, 1967. 226 pp.

Chakeipi, the Place of the Beaver, by Virginia Mapes. City of Beaverton, 1993. 163 pp.

Champoeg: Place of Transition, by J. A. Hussey. Oregon Historical Society, Portland, 1967. 404 pp.

"Changing Geography of the Willamette Valley Woodlands," by Jerry C. Towle. Oregon Historical Quarterly 83(1):66-87 Spring 1982.

Children of Grace: The Nez Perce War of 1877, by Bruce Hampton. Henry Holt and Co., New York, 1994. 407 pp.

Child's World: Children's Books: A Bibliography of Oregon Illustrators and Authors of Children's Books in the 20th Century, compiled by Juanita B. Price. Price Productions, 373 Altadena, Astoria 97103, 1995. 62 pp.

China Doctor of John Day, by Jeffrey Barlow and Christine Richardson. Binford & Mort, Portland, 1979. 118 pp.

Chinook, a History and Dictionary, by Edward Harper Thomas. Metropolitan Press, Portland, 1935. 181 pp.

Chronicle of the Indian Wars, by Alan Axelrod. Prentice Hall, New York, 1993. 280 pp.

Circular from the General Land Office Showing the Manner of Proceeding to Obtain Title to Public Lands under the Pre-Emption, Homestead, and Other Laws. Government Printing Office, Washington D.C., 1892. 256 pp.

City on the Willamette: The Story of Portland, Oregon, by Percy Maddux. Binfords & Mort, Portland, 1952. 229 pp.

Clam Digging and Crabbing in Oregon, by John A. Johnson. Adventure North Publishing Co., PO Box 101, Gardiner 97441.

Clatsop County, Oregon, a History, by Emma Gene Miller. Binfords and Mort, Portland [1958]. 291 pp.

Climatological Data for Oregon Agricultural Regions, by George H. Taylor, et al.

Special Report 912, Agricultural Experiment Station/ Oregon Climate Service, Oregon State University, Corvallis, 1993. 68 pp.

Columbia: Great River of the West, by Earl Roberge. Chronicle Books, San Francisco, [1985]. 160 pp.

Columbia River Basketry: Gift of the Ancestors, Gift of the Earth, by Mary Dodds Schlick. University of Washington Press, Seattle, 1994. 232 pp.

Columbia River Salmon and Steelhead Trout: Their Fight for Survival, by Anthony Netboy. University of Washington Press, Seattle. 1980. 180 pp.

Concerts Reviewed: 65 Years of the Portland Youth Philharmonic, by Jacob Avshalomov. Amadeus Press, Portland, 1991. 387 pp.

"Coos Bay Fireball of February 24, 1992 - Oregon's brightest." Oregon Geology 55(1):22 January 1993.

Coquille Indians: Yesterday, Today and Tomorrow, by Roberta L. Hall. Smith, Smith, and Smith Pub., Lake Oswego, 1984. 203 pp.

Cottage Grove: Golden Was the Past, 1850-1970, by Writers Discussion Group, Cottage Grove, 1970. 224 pp.

"Cow Creek Band of the Umpqua Tribe in Douglas County Oregon." Douglas County Planning Department. n.d. brochure.

Coyote Was Going There: Indian Literature of the Oregon Country, compiled and edited by Jarold Ramsey. University of Washington Press, Seattle, 1977. 295 pp.

"Crimping and Shanghaiing on the Columbia River," by Denise M. Alborn. Oregon Historical Quarterly 93(3): 262-291 Fall 1992.

Crossing the Next Meridian: Land, Water and the Future of the West, by Charles F. Wilkinson. Island Press, Washington, D.C., 1992. 367 pp.

"Cubby of Bear Creek - The Harry and David Story," by Bill Alley. Southern Oregon Heritage 1(3):22-28 Winter 1995.

"Cutoff Fever," by Leah Collins Menefee and Lowell Tiller. Oregon Historical Quarterly 77(4):308-340 December 1976; 78(1):41-72 March 1977; 78(2):121-157 June 1977; 78(3): 207-250 September 1977; 78(4):293-331 December 1977; 79(1):4-50 Spring 1978.

"Cynthia Stafford and the Lost Mining Town of Auburn," by Virginia Duffy McLoughlin. Oregon Historical Quarterly 98(1): 6-55 Spring 1997.

Day with the Cow Column, by Jesse A. [sic] Applegate. Ye Galleon Press, Fairfield WA, 1990. 225 pp. It includes A Day with the Cow Column in 1843 (20 pp) by Jesse Applegate (1811-1888), originally published in the Overland Monthly in 1868, and Recollections of My Boyhood (167 pp) by his nephew, Jesse A. (Applegate) Applegate (1835-1918), originally published in 1914 in Roseburg.

"Days at Mercer Lake," by Robert D. Clark. Oregon Historical Quarterly 75(4):300-308 December 1974.

"Delay and Wreck of the Peacock: An Episode in the Wilkes Expedition," by Constance Bordwell. Oregon Historical Quarterly 92(2):119-198 Summer 1991.

Dictionary of Oregon History, by Howard McKinley Corning. Binfords & Mort, Portland, 1956. 284 pp.

Directory of Organizations. Northwest Power Planning Council, Portland, 1995. 72 pp.

"Discovered: A Photo and More Facts About Mary Leonard, Oregon's First Woman Lawyer," by Fred W. Decker. Letter to the Editor, Oregon Historical Quarterly 78(2): 174-177 June 1977.

Disposition of the Public Domain in Oregon: Memorandum of the Chairman to the Committee on Interior and Insular Affairs, United State Senate, Transmitting a Dissertation Submitted to the Department of History and the Committee on Graduate Study of Stanford University, [by Jerry A. O'Callaghan]. U.S. Government Printing Office, Washington, D.C., November 1960. 113 pp.

Don Coyote, by Dayton O. Hyde. Arbor House, New York, 1986. 245 pp.

"Donation Land Act and the Making of Modern-Day Oregon," by David A. Johnson. Oregon Humanities: p. 8-11 (no vol. #) Winter 1994.

Don't Call Me Ma, by Sam Churchill. Doubleday, Garden City, 1977. 201 pp.

Dredging for Gold, by Bert Webber. Webb Research Group, Medford 97501. 1994. 100 pp.

Dropout Rates in Oregon High Schools 1993-1994. Oregon Department of Education, Salem, March 1995. 41 pp.

Early Days in Phoenix, Oregon, by Marjorie Neill Helms. Printed by Bulletin Publishing Company, Grants Pass, 1954. 39 pp.

East of the Cascades, by Phil F. Brogan. Binford & Mort, Portland, 1977. 304 pp.

"Economics of Dentalium," by R. B. Clark. The Veliger 6(1):9-19, 1963.

Ecotopia: The Notebooks and Reports of William Weston, by Ernest Callenbach. Banyan Tree Books, Berkeley CA, 1975. 187 pp.

Eden Seekers: The Settlement of Oregon, 1818-1862, by Malcolm Clark, Jr. Houghton Mifflin, Boston, 1981. 327 pp.

Edge Effects: Notes from an Oregon Forest, by Chris Anderson. University of Iowa Press, Iowa City, 1993. 185 pp.

Electrifying Eden: Portland General Electric 1889-1965, by Craig Wollner. Oregon Historical Society Press, Portland,1990. 325 pp.

Elliott State Forest. Oregon Department of Forestry, Salem. Undated. 4 pp.

"Ellison-White Chautauqua," (Letter to the Editor) by Donald P. Abbott. Oregon Historical Quarterly 85(3):304-307 Fall 1984.

"Emmet White: Reminiscences of a Rimrocker," edited by Annette White Parks. Oregon Historical Quarterly Part I, 85(3):228-252 Fall 1984. Part II, 85(4):375-386 Winter 1984. Part III, 86(1):23-46 Spring 1985. Part IV, 86(2):183-215 Summer 1985.

Empire of the Columbia, by Dorothy O. Johansen and Charles M. Gates. Harper & Brothers, New York, 1957. 685 pp.

Encyclopedia of American Forest and Conservation History, edited by Richard C. Davis. Macmillan Publishing Company, New York, 1983. Two volumes.

Encyclopedia of Western Railroad History: Volume III, Oregon, Washington, by Donald B. Robertson. Caxton Printers, Caldwell, Idaho, 1995. 338 pp. (Oregon p. 39-171)

"Engineering the Cascades Canal and Locks, 1876-1896," by William F.

Willingham. <u>Oregon Historical Quarterly</u> 88(3):228-257 Fall 1987.

"Ethnicity and Radicalism: The Finns of Astoria and the <u>Toveri</u>, 1890-1930," by P. G. Hummasti. <u>Oregon Historical Quarterly</u> 96(4):362-393 Winter 1995-96.

"Eugene in the Depression 1929-1935," by Paul L. Shinn. <u>Oregon Historical Quarterly</u> 86(4):340-369 Winter 1985.

<u>Ever After</u>, by William Wharton. Newmarket Press, New York, 1995. Originally published as <u>Wrongful Deaths</u>, Granta Books, London, 1994.

<u>Ewing Young, Master Trapper</u>, by Kenneth L. Holmes. Binfords & Mort, Portland, 1967. 180 pp.

"Exhibition Era of Early Aviation in Oregon, 1910-1915," by Patrick Harris. <u>Oregon Historical Quarterly</u> 87(3):245-276 Fall 1986.

<u>Experiences in Environmental Sanitation</u>, by William B. Culham. Vantage Press, New York, 1994. 152 pp.

<u>Facts of Life in Portland Oregon</u>, by Elaine S. Friedman. Portland Possibilities, Portland, 1993. 386 pp.

<u>Fall of the House of WPPSS</u>, by Daniel Jack Chasan. Sasquatch Publishing, Seattle, 1985. 111 pp.

"Family and Community on the Eastern Oregon Frontier," by William F. Willingham. <u>Oregon Historical Quarterly</u> 95(2):176-204 Summer 1994.

<u>Fares Please!: Those Portland Trolley Years</u>, by John T. Labbe. Caxton Printer, Caldwell ID, 1980. 164 pp.

<u>Fast Facts 1996</u>. Bonneville Power Administration, Portland, 1997. 16 pp.

"Federal Road Building Grants for Early Oregon," by W. Turrentine Jackson. <u>Oregon Historical Quarterly</u> 49(1):3-29 March 1948.

<u>Feelin' Fine!: Bill Hanley's Book</u>, "put together" by Anne Shannon Monroe. Doubleday, Doran & Co., Garden City, NY, 1930. 304 pp.

<u>Ferryboats on the Columbia River Including the Bridges and Dams</u>, by Robert H. Ruby and John A. Brown. Superior Pub. Co.: Seattle, 1974. 176 pp.

<u>Field Guide to Pacific States Wildflowers</u>, by T. F. Niehaus and C. L. Ripper. Houghton Mifflin Company, Boston. 1976. 432 pp.

<u>Field Guide to the Slugs</u>, by David George Gordon. Sasquatch Books, Seattle,1994. 48 pp.

<u>Field Guide to Western Reptiles and Amphibians</u>, by Robert C. Stebbins. 2nd Edition. Peterson Field Guide Series. Houghton Mifflin Company, Boston, 1985. 336 pp.

"Field Trip Guide to Cascadia Paleoseismic Evidence Along the Northern Oregon Coast: Evidence of Subduction Zone Seismicity in the Central Cascadia Margin," by Curt D. Peterson, Mark E. Darienzo, Scott F. Burns, and William K Burris. <u>Oregon Geology</u> 55(5):99-114 September 1993.

"Financial History of Oregon," by F. G. Young. <u>Quarterly of the Oregon Historical Society</u>. "Chapter 2, Oregon's Public Domain" 10(4):366-389 December 1909; "Chapter 2, continued, Sale of Oregon's Lands" 11(2):121-161 June 1910; "Part 5, Treasury Administration in Oregon" 12(1):89-110 March 1911.

<u>Fire at Eden's Gate: Tom McCall and the Oregon Story</u>, by Brent Walth. Oregon

Historical Society: Portland, 1994. 564 pp.

Fire Ecology of Pacific Northwest Forests, by James K. Agee. Island Press, Washington, D.C., 1993. 493 pp.

Fire Lookouts of the Northwest, by Ray Kresek. Ye Galleon Press, Fairfield WA, 1984. 412 pp.

Fire Mountains of the West: The Cascade and Mono Lake Volcanoes, by Stephen L. Harris. Mountain Press Publishing Co., Missoula MT, 1988. 379 pp.

First Duty: A History of the United States District Court for Oregon, ed. by Carolyn M. Buan. U.S. District Court of Oregon Historical Society, Portland, 1993. 332 pp.

"First Fifty-Five in Fairview," by Melvin K. Moller. Oregon Historical Quarterly 84(1):56-92 Spring 1983.

First One Hundred Years in Lincoln County, Oregon, 1893 to 1993. Lincoln County Centennial Committee, Lincoln County Historical Society, Newport, 1993. 200 pp.

First Oregonians, edited by Carolyn M. Buan and Richard Lewis. Oregon Council for the Humanities, Portland, 1991. 128 pp.

First Over the Siskiyous: Peter Skene Ogden's 1826-1827 Journey Through the Oregon-California Borderlands, by Jeff LaLande. Oregon Historical Society Press, Portland, 1987. 149 pp.

First 75 Years. State Highway Division, Salem, 1988. 16 pp.

Fish and Wildlife on the Oregon Trail: Then and Now, by Pat Wray. Oregon Department of Fish and Wildlife, Salem, undated. 15 pp.

"Fish Boats and Engines, Coastal Freighters," by Truman B. Cook. Oregon Historical Quarterly 83(1):53-65 Spring 1982.

Fishing in Oregon, by Madelynne Diness Sheehan and Dan Casali. Eighth Edition. Flying Pencil Publications, 33126 SW Callahan Road, Scappoose 97056, 1995. 280 pp.

Fishwheels of the Columbia, by Ivan J. Donaldson and Frederic K. Cramer. Binfords and Mort, Portland, 1971. 124 pp.

"Flax and Linen: An Uncertain Oregon Industry," by Steve M. Wyatt. Oregon Historical Quarterly 95(2):150-175 Summer 1994.

Flora of the Pacific Northwest: An Illustrated Manual, by C. L. Hitchcock and A. Cronquist. University of Washington Press, Seattle, 1976. 730 pp.

"For the Love of the Game," by Jack Cleaver. Oregon History Magazine 39(1):19-21 Spring/Summer 1995.

Force of Nature, by Thomas Hager. Simon & Schuster, New York, 1995. 721 pp.

Forest Dreams, Forest Nightmares: The Paradox of Old Growth in the Inland West, by Nancy Langston. University of Washington Press, Seattle, 1995. 368 pp.

Forest Ecosystem Management: An Ecological, Economic, and Social Assessment: Report of the Forest Ecosystem Manangement Assessment Team, July 1983. U.S. Forest Service, National Marine Fisheries Service, Bureau of Land Managment, Fish and Wildlife Service, National Park Service, and Environmental Protection Agency, Washington, D.C. About 800 pp.

Forest Log. Oregon Department of Forestry, Public Affairs Office, 2600 State

Street, Salem 97310. Bimonthly. Free.

"Fort Rock Basin: Valley in Transition," by Merritt Y. "Bud" Parks. Oregon Historical Quarterly 98(1):56-90 Spring 1997.

"Fort Rock Cave: Monument to the 'First Oregonians'," by Constance Bordwell. Oregon Historical Quarterly 88(2):117-147 Summer 1987.

Fort Stevens: Oregon's Defender at the River of the West, by Marshall Hanft. Oregon State Parks Division, Salem, 1980. 360 pp.

Fort Vancouver. Handbook 113. Superintendent of Documents, Washington D.C. 1981. 143 pp.

Fossil Lake, Oregon: Its Geology and Fossil Faunas, by Ira S. Allison. Oregon State University Press, Corvallis, 1966. 48 pp.

Fossil Shells from Oregon Beach Cliffs, by Ellen J. Moore. Chintimini Press, 3324 SW Chintimini Avenue, Corvallis 97333. 1994. 88 pp.

"Frederic Homer Balch and the Romance of Oregon History," by Stephen L. Harris. Oregon Historical Quarterly 97(4):390-427 Winter 1996-97.

Free Land for Free Men: A Story of Clackamas County, by Vera Martin Lynch. Publisher not given. 1973. 680 pp.

"Free Love and Free Speech on the Pacific Northwest Frontier," by Carlos A. Schwantes. Oregon Historical Quarterly 82(3):271-293 Fall 1981.

"From Dream to Demolition: The Yamhill Lock and Dam," by Suann Murray Reddick. Oregon Historical Quarterly. Part I, 91(1):43-80 Spring 1990; Part II, 91(2):154-202 Summer 1990.

From Here We Speak: An Anthology of Oregon Poetry, ed. by Ingrid Wendt and Primus St. John. Vol. 4 of the Oregon Literature Series. Oregon State University Press, Corvallis, 1993. 332 pp.

From the Wallowas, by Grace Bartlett. Pike Press, Enterprise, 1992. 144 pp.

Frontier Doctor, by Urling C. Coe. Macmillan Company, New York, 1940. 264 pp.

Frozen Music: A History of Portland Architecture, by Gideon Bosker and Lena Lencek. Oregon Historical Society, Portland, 1985. 331 pp.

Fur Hunters of the Far West, by Alexander Ross. 1855, republished by the University of Oklahoma Press, Norman, 1956. 304 pp.

Gambling and Problem Gambling in Oregon: Report to the Oregon Gambling Addiction Treatment Foundation, by Rachel A. Volberg. Gemini Research, 310 Poplar Street, Roaring Spring, PA 16673. 8/26/97. 88 pp.

Gem Trails of Oregon, by James P. Mitchell. Gem Guides Book Co., 315 Cloverleaf Drive, Suite F, Baldwin Park CA 91706,1989. 119 pp.

Gemstones of North America, by John Sinkankas. Van Nostrand, New York. Volume 1, 1959. 675 pp. Volume 2, 1976. 494 pp.

General History of Oregon Through Early Statehood, by Charles H. Carey. Third edition. Binfords & Mort, Portland, 1971. 916 pp.

Generating Failure: Public Power Policy in the Northwest, by David Shapiro. University Press of America, Lanham MD, 1989. 114 pp.

Geology of Oregon, 4th edition, by Elizabeth L. Orr, William N. Orr, and Ewart Baldwin. Kendall/Hunt Publishing Company, Dubuque IO, 1992. 254 pp.

Getting it Right in Oregon: Biennial Report, Oregon Economic Development Commission. February 1995. 56 pp.

Gift: The Oregon Nikkei Story Retold, by Deena K. Nakata. Japanese American Citizens League, 1429 SE 110th Ave, Portland 97216, 1995. 175 pp.

"Gilchrist, Oregon, A Company Town," by John Driscoll. Oregon Historical Quarterly 85(2):135-153 Summer 1984.

"Glaciation in the Central Coast Range of Oregon," by Ewart M. Baldwin. Oregon Geology 55(4):87-89. July 1993.

"Gladstone Chautauqua: Education and Entertainment, 1893-1928," by Donald B. Epstein. Oregon Historical Quarterly 80(4):391-403 Winter 1979.

Gladstone, Oregon - A History. Part One: Earliest Times to the Civil War's Eve, by Herbert K. Beals. Gladstone Historical Society, 7005 Valley View Drive, Gladstone 97027. 1992. 148 pp.

Glimpses of Wheeler County's Past: An Early History of North Central Oregon. Ed. by F. Smith Fussner. Bindford & Mort (for Wheeler County Historical Commission), Portland, 1975. 134 pp.

"Gobbler Glory Days," by Tricia Jones. Oregon History 40(1):4-7 Summer 1996.

Gold and Cattle Country, by Herman Oliver. Binfords & Mort, Portland, 1961. 312 pp.

Gold and Silver in Oregon, by Howard C. Brooks and Len Ramp. Bulletin 62. Oregon Department of Geology and Mineral Industries, Portland, 1968. 37 pp.

Gold in the Woodpile: An Informal History of Banking in Oregon, by O. K. Burrell. University of Oregon, Eugene, 1967. 335 pp.

Gold Mining in Oregon. Bert Webber, editor. Webb Research Group Publishers, Medford 97501. 1995. 332 pp.

Golden Was the Past. See Cottage Grove.

Governing Oregon: An Inside Look at Politics in One American State, by Thomas L. Mason. Kendall/Hunt Pub. Co., Dubuque, Iowa, 1994. 251 pp.

Governors of Oregon, by George S. Turnbull. Binfords & Mort, Portland, 1959. 107 pp.

Grains, or Passages in the Life of Ruth Rover, with Occasional Pictures of Oregon, Natural and Moral, by Margaret Jewett Bailey. Oregon State University Press, Corvallis. (1854) 1986. 338 pp.

Grand Era of Cast-Iron Architecture in Portland, by Willam John Hawkins III. Binford & Mort, Portland 1976. 211 pp.

Grants Pass, the Golden Years, 1884-1984, by Percy T. Booth. Grants Pass Centennial Commission, Grants Pass, 1984. 113 pp.

"Grass Valley, 1901," by Giles French. Oregon Historical Quarterly 75(1):43-48 March 1974.

Gray Whales, by B. R. Mate. Extension Service, Oregon State University, Corvallis, 1989. 2 pp.

Great Extravaganza: Portland and the Lewis and Clark Exposition, by Carl Abbott. Oregon Historical Society, Portland, 1981. 81 pp.

Great Lodges of the West, by Christine Barnes. W. W. West, 20875 Sholes Road, Bend 97702, 1997. 136 pp.

Great Northwest Nature Factbook by Ann Saling. Alaska Northwest Books, PO

Box 3007, Bothell WA 98041, 1991. 198 pp.

Gresham: Stories of Our Past, Campground to City, by Wynferd Chilton. Gresham Historical Society, Davis Fox Printing, Gresham, 1993. 344 pp.

Guide to Early Oregon Churches, by Olga Samuelson Freeman. Freeman, Eugene, 1976. 88 pp.

Guide to Historic Barns in Douglas County Oregon. Douglas County Planning Department, Roseburg. Undated brochure

Guide to Historic Bridges in Douglas County Oregon. Douglas County Planning Department, Roseburg. Undated brochure.

Guide to Oregon Foundations. Sixth Edition. United Way of the Columbia Willamette, Information & Referral, 619 SW 11th Avenue, Suite 300, Portland 97205-2646, 1995. 184 pp.

Guide to Shipwreck Sites along the Oregon Coast, by R. E. Wells and Victor C. West. Wells & West, 1166 Windsor, North Bend 97459. 77 pp.

Handbook of Northwestern Plants, by H. M. Gilkey and L. J. Dennis. Oregon State University Bookstores, Corvallis, 1973. 507 pp.

Handbook of Oregon Plant and Animal Fossils, by William Orr and Elizabeth Orr. William Orr, P.O. Box 5286, Eugene 97405, 1981. 285 pp.

Hanford: Issues That Concern Oregon. Oregon Department of Energy, Nuclear Waste Program, Salem, 1995. Various paging.

Hard Times in Paradise: Coos Bay, Oregon, 1850-1986, by William G. Robbins, University of Washington Press, Seattle, 1988. 194 pp.

Heceta House: A Historical and Architectural Survey, by Stephanie Finucane. Waldport District, Siuslaw National Forest, 1980. 109 pp.

Hell with the Fire Out: A History of the Modoc War, by Arthur Quinn. Faber and Faber, Boston, 1997. 200 pp.

Hells's Canyon: The Deepest Gorge on Earth, by William Ashworth. Hawthorn Books: New York. 1977. 246 pp.

Hero of Battle Rock, by Bert Webber. Ye Galleon Press, Fairfield, Washington, 1973. 25 pp.

High Desert of Central Oregon, by Raymond R. Hatton. Binford and Mort, Portland, 1977. 148 pp.

Hiker's Guide to Hot Springs in the Pacific Northwest, by Evie Litton. Falcon Press, P.O.Box 1718, Helena MT 59624. 1993. 299 pp.

Historic Highway Bridges of Oregon, by Dwight Smith, James Norman, and Pieter Dykman. Oregon Historical Society Press, Portland. 1986, 1989. 323 pp.

"Historical Earthquakes in and around Portland, Oregon," by Jacqueline D. J. Bott and Ivan G. Wong. Oregon Geology 55(5):116-122 September 1993.

Historical Oregon. Treasure Chest Maps, Box 1013, Corvallis 97330. 1970. 34 pp.

History of Baker County, Oregon. Baker County Historical Society [Baker], 1986. 360 pp.

History of Benton County, Oregon, by David D. Fagan. A. G. Walling, Portland, 1885. 532 pp.

History of Crook County, Oregon. Crook County Historical Society, Prineville, 1981. 304 pp.

History of Gilliam County, Oregon. Gilliam County Historical Society, Condon,

1981. 320 pp.

History of Grant County, Oregon, 1862-1983. Grant County Oliver Museum, Canyon City, 1983. 211 pp.

History of Hood River County, Oregon 1852-1982, by Lewis A. Merz. Hood River County Historical Society, Hood River 1982. 558 pp. Volume II, 523 pp.

History of Jefferson County Oregon, 1914-1983. Jefferson County Historical Society, Madras, 1984. 168 pp.

History of Malheur Country. Malheur County Historical Society, place not given, 1988. 200 pp.

History of Oregon Land Grants, by Charles MacC. Snow. University of Oregon, Eugene, 1909. Copy of typescript. 22 pp.

History of Oregon Literature, by Alfred Powers. Metropolitan Press, Portland, 1935. 809 pp.

History of Oregon Newspapers, by George S. Turnbull. Binfords & Mort, Portland, 1939. 560 pp.

History of Polk County, Oregon. Polk County Historical Society, Monmouth, 1987. 301 pp.

History of Portland Union Station Structures: Buildings, Architects and Clients, by Patricia C. Erigero. P. C. Erigero, place not given, 1987. 81 pp.

History of Scappoose between the Years 1852-1930, by James Loring Watts. Compiled by the Grant Watts Parent Organization, 1984. Reprinted 1992, Columbia Education Service District. 52 pp. Available ($4) from Scappoose Public Library, PO Box 400, Scappoose 97056.

History of Sutherlin, Oregon, by G. H. Lee. C. Giles Hunt Memorial Library, Sutherlin, 1988. 70 pp.

History of the Deschutes Country in Oregon. Deschutes County Historical Society, Bend, 1985. 530 pp.

History of the Rectangular Survey System, by C. Albert White. Bureau of Land Management, U.S. Department of the Interior, Washington D.C., [1983]. 774 pp.

History of the Southern Pacific, by Bill Yenne. Bison Books, Greenwich CT, 1985. 127 pp.

History of the Willamette Valley and Cascade Mountain Wagon Road, by Cleon L. Clark. Deschutes County Historical Soc., Bend, 1987. 118 pp.

"History of Transportation in the Pacific Northwest," by Randall V. Mills. Oregon Historical Quarterly 47(3):281-312 September 1946.

History of Union County, Oregon, by Bernal D. Hug. Union County Historical Society, La Grande, 1961. 247 pp.

History of Wallowa County, Oregon. Wallowa County Museum Board, Joseph, 1983. 424 pp.

History of Wasco County, Oregon, by William H. McNeal. Publisher not given, The Dalles, 1950. 471 pp.

History of Wheeler County, Oregon, by Janet L. and McLaren E. Stinchfield. Times-Journal, place not given, 1983. 256 pp.

Hole in the Sky: A Memoir by William Kittredge. Alfred A. Knopf, New York, 1992. 238 pp.

Holocene Sea Level Changes in the Pacific Northwest: A Catalogue of Radiocarbon Dates and an Atlas of Regional Sea Level Curves, by Ian Hutchinson. Institute for Quaternary Research, Simon Fraser University, Burnaby B.C., 1992. 100 pp.

Home-schooling in Oregon: The Handbook, by Ann Lahrson. Out of the Box Publishing, PO Box 80214, Portland 97280. 1994. 282 pp.

Homes in the Oregon Forest: Settling Columbia County, 1870-1920, by Egbert S. Oliver. Calapooia Publications, Brownsville, 1983. 230 pp.

Homesteads and Heritages: a History of Morrow County, Oregon, by Giles French. Binfords and Mort, Portland, 1971. 127 pp.

Honey in the Horn, by H. L. Davis. Harper & Brothers, London, 1935. 380 pp.

Hot Springs and Hot Pools of the Northwest, by Jayson Loam and Marjorie Gersh. Aqua Thermal Acess, 55 Azalea Lane, Santa Cruz CA 95060, 1992. 191 pp.

"How It Was Then: The Pacific Northwest In the Twenties," by Frederick Bracher. Oregon Historical Quarterly 85(2):155-180 Summer 1984.

Hyas Tyee: the United States Customs Service in Oregon, 1848-1989, by Harvey Steele. U.S. Customs Service Historical Study #14, U.S. Treasury Department, Washington, D.C., 1990. 128 pp.

Hydrocarbon Exploration and Occurrences in Oregon, by R.E. Stewart, V. C. Newton, Jr., and D. L. Olmstead. Oregon Department of Geology and Mineral Industries, Portland, 1989. 78 pp.

I Will Fight No More Forever: Chief Joseph and the Nez Perce War, by Merrill D. Beal. University of Washington Press, Seattle, 1963. 366 pp.

Illusions of Power: A History of the Washington Public Power Supply System (WPPSS), by D. Victor Anderson. Praeger, New York, 1985. 159 pp.

Illustrated Flora of the Pacific States: Washington, Oregon, and California, by L. R. Abrams and R. Ferris. Stanford University Press, Stanford CA, 1923-1960. Four volumes.

Illustrated History of Baker, Grant, Malheur and Harney Counties with a Brief Outline of the Early History of the State of Oregon. Western Historical Publishing Co., [Spokane], 1902. 788 pp.

In Search of Western Oregon, by Ralph Friedman. Caxton Printers, Caldwell ID, 1990. 782 pp.

In the Ruts of the Wagon Wheels: Pioneer Roads in Eastern Oregon, by Lawrence E. Nielsen. Maverick Publications, Bend, 1987. 126 pp.

In Timber Country: Working People's Stories of Environmental Conflict and Urban Flight, by Beverly A. Brown. Temple University Press, Philadelphia, 1995. 300 pp.

In Times Past: A History of the Lower Jordan Valley Communities, by Hazel R. Fretwell-Johnson. The Print Shoppe, PO Box 29, Filer ID 83328, 1990. 212 pp.

Indian Battles Along the Rogue River 1855-56 by Frank K. Walsh. Te-Cum-Tom Publications, 2618 Sand Creek Road, Grants Pass 97526, 1972. 28 pp.

Indian Rock Art of the Columbia Plateau, by James D. Keyser. University of Washington Press, Seattle, 1991. 138 pp.

Inventory of Power Plants in the United States as of January 1, 1996. Energy Information Administration, U.S. Department of Energy, Washington, DC, 1996. 409 pp.

"Iron into Gold," by Joanne B. Mulcahy. Oregon History 38(3):Cover,6-7,24-25 Autumn 1994.

It Happened in Oregon, by James A. Crutchfield. Falcon, Helena MT, 1994. 111 pp.

"'It's Down There Someplace': Oil Exploration in Harney County," by Dorsey Griffin. Oregon Historical Quarterly 93(1):4-25 Spring 1992.

"'Jackson County Rebellion': Social Turmoil and Political Insurgence in Southern Oregon during the Great Depression," by Jeff LaLande. Oregon Historical Quarterly 95(4):406-471 Winter 1994-95.

Jacksonville: Biography of a Gold Camp, by Francis D. Haines, Jr. Gandee Printing Center, [Medford], 1967. 164 pp.

Jacksonville, Oregon: The Making of a National Historic Landmark, by Bert and Margie Webber. Ye Galleon Press, Fairfield WA, 1982. 143 pp.

Jacksonville Story, by Richard H. Engeman. Southern Oregon Historical Society, Jacksonville, 1980. 47 pp.

James Beard: A Biography, by Robert Clark. HarperCollins, New York, 1993. 357 pp.

"Japanese in Oregon". Oregon Historical Quarterly 94(4):309-447 Winter 1993-94.

Jepson Manual: Higher Plants of California, edited by J.C. Hickman. University of California Press, Berkeley, 1993. 1,400 pp.

"Jews of Portland, Oregon: A Statistical Dimension, 1860-1880," by Scott Cline. Oregon Historical Quarterly 88(1):4-25 Spring 1987.

Josephine County Historical Highlights. Josephine County Library System: Josephine County Historical Society, Grants Pass, 1976. 127 pp.

Journey Back: Eagle Point, Brownsboro, Lake Creek and Climax, by Barbara Hegne, 421 Stevens Road #9, Eagle Point 97524, 1990. 126 pp.

Jump-off Creek, by Molly Gloss. Houghton Mifflin, Boston, 1989. 186 pp.

"Juniper Stumps on the Yreka Trail of 1862-1864," by Lawrence E. Nielsen. Oregon Historical Quarterly 88(1):49-51 Spring 1987.

Kalapuyans: A Sourcebook on the Indians of the Willamette Valley, by Harold Mackey. Mission Mill Museum Assoc., 180 Commerical St NE, Salem 97301. 165 pp.

Kalmiopsis. Published annually by the Native Plant Society of Oregon, PO Box 902, Eugene 97440.

Klamath Tribe: A People and Their Reservation, by Theodore Stern. University of Washington Press, Seattle, 1965. 356 pp.

Knowing Oregon Reptiles, by Alan D. St. John. Salem Audubon Society, PO Box 2013, Salem 97308. 36 pp.

"Korean Women Pioneers of the Pacific Northwest," by Sonia S. Sunoo. Oregon Historical Quarterly 79(1):51-63 Spring 1978.

"L. Samuel and the West Shore: Images of a Changing Pacific Northwest," by J. D. Cleaver. Oregon Historical Quarterly 94(2/3):166-224 Summer/Fall 1993.

"Labor and Education: Portland Labor College, 1921-1929," by Jerry Lembcke.

Oregon Historical Quarterly 85(2):116-134 Summer 1984.

Lakeport: Ghost Town of the South Oregon Coast, An Oregon Documentary, by Bert and Margie Webber. Webb Research Group, Medford, 1990. 191 pp.

Lancaster's Road: The Historic Columbia River Scenic Highway, by Oral Bullard. TMS Book Service, Beaverton, 1982. 62 pp.

Land in Common: An Illustrated History of Jackson County, Oregon. Joy B. Dunn, editor. Southern Oregon Historical Society, Medford, 1993. 178 pp.

Land of the Umpqua: A History of Douglas County Oregon, by Stephen Dow Beckham. Douglas County Commissioners, Roseburg, 1986. 285 pp.

Land-Use Planning in Oregon: A No-Nonsense Handbook in Plain English, by Mitch Rohse. Oregon State University Press, Corvallis, 1987. 286 pp.

Landscapes of Promise: The Oregon Story 1800-1940, by William G. Robbins. University of Washington Press, Seattle, 1997. 392 pp.

Lane County: An Illustrated History of the Emerald Empire, by Dorothy Velasco, Dianne Donovan, and the Lane County Historical Society. Windsor Publications, Northridge CA, 1985. 168 pp.

Later Woolen Mills in Oregon, by Alfred L. Lomax. Binfords & Mort, Portland, 1974. 301 pp.

Learning about Oregon: Symbols, Legends, and Facts, by Marvin L. and Marjorie A. Covey. Oregon Department of Education, 700 Pringle Parkway SE, Salem 97310. 1988. 110 pp.

Legacy. Hood River News, 1995. 143 pp.

"Letter to the Editor," by Fred W. Decker. Oregon Historical Quarterly 78(2):174-177 June 1977.

"Lewis and Clark Law School: Northwestern School of Law, 1884-1973," by John Clinton Geil. Oregon Historical Quarterly 84(4):389-408 Winter 1983.

Lewis and Clark: The Journey of the Corps of Discovery, an Illustrated History, by Dayton Duncan and Ken Burns. Knopf, New York, 1997. 248 pp.

Life-History and Growth of the Razor Clam by Harvey C. McMillin. Washington State Dept. of Fisheries, Olympia, 1924. 52 pp.

Listening for Coyote: A Walk Across Oregon's Wilderness, by William L. Sullivan. William Morrow and Company, New York, 1988. 239 pp.

Lockwood-Post's Directory of the Pulp, Paper and Allied Trades. Miller Freeman, San Francisco. Annual.

Logging Transportation, by Nelson C. Brown. J. Wiley & Sons, New York, 1936. 327 pp.

"Look Back at Oregon's Earthquake History, 1841-1994," by Ivan Wong and Jacqueline Bott. Oregon Geology 57(6):125-139 November 1995.

Looters of the Public Domain, by S. A. D. Puter. Portland Printing House, Portland, 1908. Reprinted by Arno Press, New York, 1972. 495 pp.

Lost Mines and Buried Treasures of the West, by Thomas Probert. University of California Press, Berkeley. 1977. 593 pp.

Lost Mines and Treasures of the Pacific Northwest, by Ruby El Hult. Binfords & Mort, Portland. 1957. 257 pp.

Loud Hawk: The United States versus the American Indian Movement, by Kenneth S. Stern. University of Oklahoma Press, Norman, 1994. 373 pp.

Louie Simpson's North Bend, by Dick Wagner. North Bend News, North Bend,1986. 60 pp.

Macrolichens of Pacific Northwest Forests, by Bruce McCune and Linda Geiser. Oregon State University Press, Corvallis, 1997. 386 pp.

Magnificent Gateway: a Layman's Guide to the Geology of the Columbia River Gorge, by John Eliot Allen. Timber Press, Forest Grove, 1979. 144 pp.

Mail Tribune. PO Box 1108, Medford, 97501. Daily.

Making of Oregon: A Study in Historical Geography, by Samuel Dicken and Emily Dicken. Oregon Historical Society, Portland, 1979. 208 pp.

Mammals and Life Zones of Oregon, by Vernon Bailey. USDA Bureau of Biological Survey, Washington DC, 1936. 416 pp.

Mammals of the Northwest, by Earl J. Larrison. Seattle Audubon Society, 1976. 256 pp.

Mammals of the Pacific Northwest, by James R. Christensen and Earl J. Larrison. University Press of Idaho, Moscow ID, 1982. 167 pp.

Manual for Judging Oregon Soils, by J. H. Huddleston and G. F. Kling. Oregon State University Extension Service in cooperation with the Department of Soil Science, Corvallis, 1984. 81 pp.

Manual of Oregon Trees and Shrubs, by Warren R. Randall, Robert F. Keniston, Dale N. Bever, and Edward C. Jensen. OSU Book Stores, Corvallis, 1985. 305 pp.

Manual of the Higher Plants of Oregon, by Morton Eaton Peck. Second edition. Oregon State University Press, Corvallis, 1961. 936 pp.

Many Faces: An Anthology of Oregon Autobiography, ed. by Stephen Dow Beckham. Vol. 2 of the Oregon Literature Series. Oregon State University Press, Corvallis, 1993. 330 pp.

"March 24, 1993, Scotts Mills earthquake—western Oregon's wake-up call," by Ian P. Madin, George R. Priest, Matthew A. Mabey, Steve Malone, Tom S. Yelin, and Dan Meier. Oregon Geology 55(3):51-57 May 1993.

Marine History of the Pacific Northwest. The short title for a series of books. The first, Lewis & Dryden's Marine History of the Pacific Northwest, was published in 1895. (494 pp.) It was updated by The H. W. McCurdy Marine History of the Pacific Northwest in 1966 (706 pp.), and by The H. W. McCurdy Marine History of the Pacific Northwest, 1966-1976, in 1977 (255 pp.)

Meacham: A Wide Spot on the Oregon Trail Where the Meadowlark Still Sings, by Betty Booth Stewart. Crossroad Books, Tigard, 1996. 192 pp.

"Memories of the Grant Park Neighborhood," by Beverly Cleary. Oregon History Magazine 39(3/4):18-20 Winter-Spring 1996.

Mineral Industry of Oregon, by Rodney J. Minarik. Published as the Bureau of Mines 1992 Annual Report for Oregon, U.S. Department of the Interior, Washington D.C., 1994. 11 pp.

"Mineral Tree," by Brian O'Brian. Forest Log 63(6):30-31 May-June 1994.

"Mining and exploration in Oregon during 1992," by Frank R. Hladky. Oregon Geology 55(2):27-34 March 1993.

Missionary History of the Pacific Northwest, Containing the Wonderful Story of

Jason Lee..., by H. K. Hines. H. K. Hines, Portland, 1899. 510 pp.

Modocs and Their War, by Keith A. Murray. University of Oklahoma Press, Norman, 1959. 346 pp.

Mt. Angel Abbey: A Centennial History of the Benedictine Community and its Library 1882-1982, by Lawrence J. McCrank. Scholarly Resources, Wilmington Delaware, 1983. 176 pp.

Mount St. Helens: The Eruption and Recovery of a Volcano, by Rob Carson. Sasquatch Books, Seattle, 1990. 160 pp.

Municipal Mother: Portland's Lola Greene Baldwin, America's First Policewoman, by Gloria E. Myers. Oregon State University Press, Corvallis, 1995. 232 pp.

"Murder of Cyrenius C. Hooker," by Thomas Branigar. Oregon Historical Quarterly 75(4):344-359 December 1974.

Mushrooms Demystified, by David Arora. Second edition. Ten Speed Press, Berkeley, 1986. 959 pp.

"Mysterious Journey: The Catholic Ladder of 1840," by Kris A. White and Janice St. Laurent. Oregon Historical Quarterly 97(1):70-88 Spring 1996.

Name Your Poison: A Guide to Cultivated and Native Oregon Plants Toxic to Humans, by La Rea J. Dennis. Oregon State University, Corvallis, 1972. 76 pp.

National Atlas of the United States. U.S. Geologic Survey, Washington D.C., 1970. 417 pp.

"National Natural Landmarks Program in the Pacific Northwest," by Stephen Gibbons. Oregon Geology 59(5):123-124 Sept/Oct 1997.

National Register of Historic Places 1966 to 1994. Preservation Press, National Trust for Historic Preservation, Washington, D.C., 1994. 923 pp.

National Water Summary, 1983. U.S. Geological Survey, Water-Supply Paper 2250, Washington, D.C.. 243 pp.

National Water Summary, 1986: Ground-Water Quality. U.S. Geological Survey, Water-Supply Paper 2325, Washington, D.C.. 560 pp.

National Water Summary, 1987: Water Supply and Use. U.S. Geological Survey, Water-Supply Paper 2350, Washington, D.C.. 553 pp.

National Water Summary, 1988-89: Hydrologic Events and Floods and Droughts. U.S. Geological Survey, Water-Supply Paper 2375, Washington, D.C., 1991. 591 pp.

National Water Summary, 1990-91: Stream Water Quality. U.S. Geological Survey, Water-Supply Paper 2400, Washington, D.C.. 590 pp.

National Wild and Scenic Rivers System, December 1992 (map). U.S. Geological Survey, Denver, 1993.

Native Peoples of the Northwest: A Traveler's Guide to Land, Art, and Culture, by Jan Halliday and Gail Chehak. Sasquatch Books, Seattle, 1996. 292 pp.

Natural Vegetation of Oregon and Washington, by J. F. Franklin and C. T. Dyrness. Oregon State University Press, Corvallis, 1988. 452 pp.

Nectar and Pollen Plants of Oregon and the Pacific Northwest, by D. M. Burgett, B. A. Stringer, and L. D. Johnston. Honeystone Press, PO Box 511, Blodgett 97326, 1989. 151 pp.

New Life, by Bernard Malamud. Farrar, Straus and Cudahy, New York, 1961. 367 pp.

Nez Perce Indians and the Opening of the Northwest, by Alvin M. Josephy, Jr. Yale University Press, New Haven, 1965. 705 pp.

"Nikkei in Oregon, 1834-1940," by Barbara Yasui. Oregon Historical Quarterly 76(3):225-257 September 1975.

No Silence! A Library Life, by William R. Eshelman. Scarecrow Press, Lanham MD, 1997. 340 pp.

Norjak: The Investigation of D. B. Cooper, by Ralph P. Himmelsbach and Thomas K. Worcester. Norjack Project, West Linn, 1986. 135 pp.

Normative River: An Ecological Vision for the Recovery of Columbia River Salmon. Northwest Power Planning Council, 1996. 500 pp.

Northwest Originals: Oregon Women and Their Art, ed. by Ellen Nichols. In UNISON Publication, Portland, 1989. 101 pp.

Northwest Passage: The Great Columbia River, by William Dietrich. Simon & Schuster, New York,1995. 448 pp.

Northwest Salmon Crisis: A Documentary History. Edited by Joseph Cone and Sandy Ridlington. Oregon State University Press, Corvallis, 1996. 374 pp.

Nosotros: The Hispanic People of Oregon. Essays and Recollections, edited by Erasmo Gamboa and Carolyn M. Buan. Oregon Council for the Humanities, Portland, 1995. 159 pp.

"Ocean processes and hazards along the Oregon coast," by Paul D. Komar. Oregon Geology 54(1):3-19 January 1992.

Offbeat Oregon: A Connoisseur's Collection of Travel Discovery in Oregon, by Mimi Bell. Chronicle Books, San Francisco, 1983. 129 pp.

"Oil and Gas Exploration and Development in Oregon, 1996," by Dan E. Wermiel. Oregon Geology 59(2):39-40 March/April 1997.

Old Fort Klamath: An Oregon Frontier Post 1863-1890, by Buena Cobb Stone. Webb Research Group, Medford, 1990. 112 pp.

Old Yamhill: The Early History of Its Towns and Cities. Yamhill County Historical Society, Lafayette, 1976. 106 pp.

On the Home Front: The Cold War Legacy of the Hanford Nuclear Site, by Michele S. Gerber. University of Nebraska Press, Lincoln, 1997. 334 pp.

One Average Day: Oregon Project Dayshoot Photographs/15 July 1983. Western Imprints, Oregon Historical Society, Portland,1984. 133 pp.

One City's Wilderness: Portland's Forest Park, by Marcy Cottrell Houle. Oregon Historical Society Press, Portland, 1996. 152 pp.

One Hundred Years of the Nehalem Country. Nehalem Bay United Methodist Church, Nehalem, 1970.

Oregon, by Ray Atkeson and Carl Gohs. [C. H. Belding, Portland, 1968.] 187 pp.

Oregon: A Bicentennial History, by Gordon B. Dodds. W. W. Norton & Company, New York, 1977. 240 pp.

Oregon: A Statistical Overview 1996, by Rebecca L. Reid and Willam R. Flagg. Southern Oregon Regional Services Institute, Southern Oregon State College, Ashland, July 1996. 140 pp.

Oregon Agriculture: Facts and Figures. Oregon Department of Agriculture, Salem, 1995. Brochure.

Oregon Air Quality Annual Data Summary 1996. Department of Environmental Quality, Portland, 1997. 62 pp.

Oregon Airport Directory. Oregon Department of Transportation Aeronautics Division, Salem, [1990?]. 109 pp.

Oregon Almanac and Book of Facts. Binfords & Mort, Portland, 1961. 607 pp.

Oregon Atlas and Gazetteer. Second edition. DeLorme Mapping, Freeport Maine, 1996. 88 pp.

Oregon Bicycle and Pedestrian Plan: An Element of the Oregon Transportation Plan. Oregon Department of Transportation, Salem, 1995. 245 pp.

Oregon Biography Index, edited by Patricia Brandt and Nancy Guilford. Oregon State University, Corvallis, 1976. 131 pp.

Oregon Blue Book. Published biennially in the spring of odd-numbered years by the Secretary of State, State Capitol, Salem 97310. 503-378-4139. ca. 460 pp. Available in many bookstores or from the above office.

Oregon Business: Helping Oregon Companies Grow. Monthly. 610 SW Broadway, Suite 200, Portland 97205. 503-223-0304, 800-367-3466.

Oregon Cattleman/Governor Congressman: Memoirs and Times of Walter M. Pierce. Edited and expanded by Arthur H. Bone. Oregon Historical Society, Portland, 1981. 500 pp.

Oregon Central Military Wagon Road: A History and Reconnaissance, by Stephen Dow Beckham. Willamette National Forest, Eugene, 1981. Two volumes.

Oregon Coast. Published bimonthly by Oregon Coast Magazine, PO Box 18000, Florence 97439-0130. Subscription.

Oregon Coastal Harbors. U.S. Army Corps of Engineers, PO Box 2946, Portland 97208-2946, 1986. Pamphlet.

Oregon Constitution. 1859 plus later amendments. Copies are in the Oregon Blue Book and Oregon Revised Statutes.

Oregon Constitution, and Proceedings and Debates of the Constitutional Convention of 1857, by Charles H. Carey. Oregon State Printing Department, Salem, 1926. 543 pp.

"Oregon Counties, Their Creations and the Origins of Their Names," by Frederick V. Holman. The Quarterly of the Oregon Historical Society 11(1):1-81 March 1910.

Oregon Covered Bridges, by Bert and Margie Webber. Pacific Northwest Book Co., Medford, 1991. 162 pp.

Oregon Desert, by E. R. Jackman and R. A. Long. Caxton Printers, Caldwell ID, 1964. 407 pp.

Oregon Drinking Water Program, Biennial Report, July 1, 1992 - June 30, 1994. Oregon Department of Human Resources, Health Division, Drinking Water Program, Portland. 41 pp.

Oregon Driver's Manual 1993-95. Department of Transportation, Salem. 84 pp.

Oregon Earthquake Handbook, by Vern Cope. PO Box 19843, Portland 97280. 1993.

Oregon Economic and Revenue Forecast. Quarterly. Office of Economic Analysis, Department of Administrative Services, 155 Cottage Street NE, Salem 97310. March 1996 issue had 80 pp.

Oregon: End of the Trail, compiled by workers of the Writers' Program of the Works Projects Administration in the State of Oregon. American Guide Series. Binfords & Mort, Portland, 1940, 1951. 549 pp.

Oregon Environmental Atlas, edited by Carolyn Young and Joseph Poracsky. Oregon Department of Environmental Quality, Portland, 1988. 64 pp.

Oregon Experiment, by Christopher Alexander, et al. Oxford University Press, New York, 1975. 191 pp.

Oregon Express Companies, by Dale E. Forster. Raven Press, Eugene, 1985. Distributed by Pacific Northwest Books, Medford. 231 pp.

"Oregon - First in 'Portable' Irrigation," by E. H. Davis. Oregon Historical Quarterly 78(4):351-354 December 1977.

Oregon for the Curious, by Ralph Friedman. Caxton Printers., Caldwell ID, 1972 (Third edition). 246 pp.

Oregon Forests Report. Oregon Department of Forestry, Salem, 1993. 24 pp.

Oregon Geographic Names, by Lewis A. McArthur. Sixth edition revised and enlarged by Lewis L. McArthur. Oregon Historical Society Press, Portland, 1992. 957 pp.

Oregon Geology. Published bimonthly by the Oregon Department of Geology and Mineral Industries, Suite 965, 800 NE Oregon Street #28, Portland 97232. Subscription.

Oregon Ghost Towns, by Lambert Florin. Superior Publishing Company, Seattle, 1970. 96 pp.

Oregon Handbook, by Stuart Warren and Ted Long Ishikawa. Moon Publications, PO Box 3040, Chico CA 95927, Third edition, 1995. 520 pp.

Oregon Handbook for Parents of Talented and Gifted Children, by Jerry Fuller and Karen Brazeau. Oregon Department of Education, Salem, 1990. 69 pp.

"Oregon Heritage: National Forests," by J. Herbert Stone. Oregon Historical Quarterly 76(1):28-38 March 1975.

Oregon Hunting Guide, by John A. Johnson. Adventure North Publishing Co., PO Box 1402, Newport 97365, 1991. 176 pp.

Oregon Indians: Culture, History and Current Affairs. An Atlas and Introduction, by Jeff Zucker, Kay Hummel, and Bob Høgfoss. Western Imprints, Oregon Historical Society, Portland, 1983. 229 pp.

Oregon Labor Trends. Published monthly by the Oregon Employment Department, Workforce Analysis Section, Room 206, 875 Union Street NE, Salem 97311. 503-378-6487.

Oregon Legislative Guide. Published biennially by the Legislative Administration Committee, Publications/Distribution, Room 49 State Capitol, Salem 97310. 503-986-1180. 164 pp. in 1995.

Oregon Lighthouses, by Sharlene and Ted Nelson. (Umbrella Guide to Oregon Lighthouses). Epicenter Press, Box 82368, Kenmore Station, Seattle WA 98028, 1994. 118 pp.

Oregon Main Street: A Rephotographic Survey, by James Norman. Oregon Historical Society Press, Portland, 1994. 100 pp.

Oregon Occupations 1994-1995. Oregon Career Information System, 1244 University of Oregon, Eugene 97403-1244. 566 pp.

Oregon Oceanbook, by Tish Parmenter and Robert Bailey. Oregon Department of Land Conservation and Development, Salem, 1985. 85 pp.

Oregon Oddities: A Partial Collection of the Series Produced by the Federal Writers' Project and Historical Records Survey of the Works Progess Administration of Oregon 1939-1941. Typescript. (Jackson County Library System.) 208 pp.

Oregon Parks Magazine. Bimonthly. Educational Publications Foundation in cooperation with the Oregon Parks and Recreation Department, PO Box 18000, Florence 97439-0130.

"Oregon Photography: The First Fifty Years," by Terry Toedtemeier. Oregon Historical Quarterly 94(1):37-76 Spring 1993.

Oregon Post Offices, by Richard W. Helbock. La Posta, Las Cruces NM, 1982. 160 pp.

Oregon Recreation Trails Plan 1995. Oregon Department of Parks and Recreation, Salem, 1996. 58 pp. plus map.

Oregon Report Card. Annual. Oregon Department of Education, 255 Capitol Street NE, Salem 97310-0203. 503-378-3310, ext. 485.

Oregon River Tours, by John Garren. Binford & Mort, Portland, 1974. 120 pp.

Oregon Scenic Waterways Program: A Landowner's Guide. Oregon State Parks and Recreation Department, Salem, [1990?]. 15 pp.

Oregon School Directory 1995-96. Oregon Department of Education, Salem.

Oregon Scientist, The Quarterly Review of Science, Research, Technology, Related Business, and Education. PO Box 230220, Tigard, 97223. 503-292-8460.

Oregon Shines: An Economic Strategy for the Pacific Century, by Neil Goldschmidt, Governor. Oregon Economic Development Department, Salem, 1989. 213 pp.

Oregon Shines II: Updating Oregon's Strategic Plan. A Report to the People of Oregon. Oregon Progress Board and the Governor's Oregon Shines Task Force, 775 Summer St. NE, Salem 97310. 1997. 98 pp. Highlights, 19 pp.

Oregon Shipwrecks, by Don Marshall. Binford & Mort Publishing, Portland, 1984. 235 pp.

Oregon Sport Fishing Regulations. Oregon Department of Fish and Wildlife. Annual. Available free at sporting goods stores. 48 pp.

Oregon Style: Architecture from 1840 to the 1950s, by Rosalind Clark. Professional Book Center, Portland, 1983. 231 pp.

"Oregon Tests Academic Freedom in (Cold)Wartime: The Reed College Trustees versus Stanley Moore," by Michael Munk. Oregon Historical Quarterly 97(3):262-354 Fall 1996.

"Oregon Trail in the Columbia Gorge, 1843-1855: The Final Ordeal," by G. Thomas Edwards. Oregon Historical Quarterly 97(2):134-175 Summer 1996.

Oregon Trail Memorial Half-Dollar (1926-1939), by Bert Webber. Webb Research Group/Pacific Northwest Books Company, Medford, 1986. 53 pp.

Oregon Trail: Yesterday and Today, a Brief History and Pictorial Journey Along the Wagon Tracks of Pioneers, by William E. Hill. Caxton Printers, Caldwell, Idaho, 1992. 179 pp.

Oregon Utility Statistics. Annual. Public Utility Commission, 550 Capital Street, Salem 97310-1380. (96 pp. in 1994.)

Oregon Vital Statistics Annual Report. Center for Health Statistics, 800 NE Oregon Street, Suite 215, Portland 97232. Two volumes.

Oregon Washington AAA TourBook. American Automobile Assoc, 1000 AAA Drive, Heathrow FL 32746-5063, 1997. 194 plus 252 pp

Oregon: Wet, High and Dry, by John O. Dart and Daniel M. Johnson. Portland State University, Portland, 1981. 365 pp.

Oregon Wildlife. Quarterly, published by the Oregon Department of Fish and Wildlife, 2501 SW 1st, Portland 97201.

Oregon Wildlife Viewing Guide, by Julia Goodnight and Sara Vickerman. Defenders of Wildlife, 333 S. State Street, Suite 173, Lake Oswego 97034. 1988. 80 pp.

Oregon Women and the Law. Oregon Commission for Women, PO Box 751-CW, Portland 97207. 1997. 283 pp.

Oregonian. Daily newspaper. 1320 SW Broadway, Portland 97201. 503-221-8327.

Oregon's Agricultural Progress. Quarterly, published by the Oregon Agricultural Experiment State, OSU, Administrative Services A422, Corvallis 97331-2119.

Oregon's Captivating Clams, by R. W. Jacobson, P. Heikkila, and K. S. Hilderbrand. Oregon State University Extension Service, Corvallis, July 1987. Brochure.

Oregon's Forests: 1994 Fact Book. Evergreen Magazine, 4025 Crater Lake Highway, Medford 97504. 1994. 24 pp.

Oregon's Ghosts and Monsters, by Mike Helm. Rainy Day Press, Eugene, 1983. 157 pp.

Oregon's Golden Years: Bonanza of the West, by Miles F. Potter. Caxton Printers, Caldwell, Idaho, 1982. 181 pp.

Oregon's Great Basin Country, by Denzel and Nancy Ferguson. Gail Graphics, Burns, 1978. 178 pp.

Oregon's Heritage: Recreational Gold Panning. Oregon's Heritage Brochure II. Oregon Department of Geology and Mineral Industries, Portland. Undated brochure.

Oregon's Heritage: Thundereggs, by Paul F. Lawson. Oregon's Heritage Brochure I, Oregon Department of Geology and Mineral Industries, Portland, 1989. Brochure.

Oregon's Highway Park System 1921-1989: An Administrative History, by Lawrence C. Merriam, Jr., and David G. Talbot. Oregon Parks and Recreation Department, Salem, 1992. 310 pp.

Oregon's Iron Dream: A Story of Old Oswego and the Proposed Iron Empire of the West, by Mary Goodall. Binfords & Mort, Portland, 1958. 156 pp.

Oregon's Migratory Fish, by Pat Wray. Oregon Department of Fish and Wildlife,

Salem, 1989. 6 pp.

Oregon's 1994 Water Quality Status Assessment Report: 305(b) Report. Department of Environmental Quality, Portland, 1994. Various pagings.

Oregon's Seacoast Lighthouses, by James A. Gibbs. Webb Research Group, Medford, 1992. 265 pp.

Oregon's Soil: A Resource Condition Report. U.S.D.A. Soil Conservation Service, Portland, 1985. 26 pp.

Oregon's Statewide Planning Goals: 1994 Edition. Department of Land Conservation and Development, 1175 Court Street NE, Salem 97310. 47 pp.

Organic Machine, by Richard White. Hill and Wang, New York, 1995. 130 pp.

"Organized Free Thought in Oregon," by Patricia Brandt. Oregon Historical Quarterly 87(2):167-204 Summer 1986.

Original Journals of the Lewis and Clark Expedition, 1804-1806, ed. by Reuben G. Thwaites. Antiquarian Pess, New York, 1959. Eight volumes.

"Origins of the Population of Oregon in 1850," by Jesse S. Douglas. Pacific Northwest Quarterly 41:95-108 April 1950.

Osprey. Forest Practice Notes #10, Oregon Department of Forestry, Salem, September 1992. 6 pp.

"'Other Portland': A Statistical Note on Foreign-Born, 1860-1910," by Paul G. Merriam. Oregon Historical Quarterly 80(3):258-268 Fall 1979.

Other Side of Oregon, by Ralph Friedman. Caxton Printers, Caldwell ID, 1993. 425 pp.

Owyhee Trails: The West's Forgotten Corner, by Mike Hanley and Ellis Lucia, Caxton Printers, Caldwell ID, 1988. 314 pp.

Pacific Coast Fern Finder, by Glenn Keator and Ruth M. Heady. Illustrated by Valerie R. Winemiller. Nature Study Guild, Box 972, Berkeley, CA 94701, 1981. 61 pp.

Pacific Graveyard: A Narrative of Shipwrecks Where the Columbia River Meets the Pacific Ocean, by James A. Gibbs. Binfords & Mort, Portland, 1954, 1960. 173 pp.

Pacific Greenway: A Vision for Northwest Oregon, by Marc Smiley. The Conservation Fund. Undated. 52 pp.

Pacific Northwest Economic Indicators. Published bimonthly by the First Interstate Bank Northwest Region, PO Box 3131, Portland 97208.

"Pacific Northwest Measles Epidemic of 1847-1848," by Robert Boyd. Oregon Historical Quarterly 95(1):6-47 Spring 1994.

Pacific States Marine Fisheries Commission 47th Annual Report for the Year 1994. 45 SE 82nd Dr., Suite 100, Gladstone 97027-2522. 33 pp.

Peculiar Paradise: A History of Blacks in Oregon, 1788-1940, by Elizabeth McLagan. Georgian Press, Portland, 1980. 230 pp.

People of Warm Springs. Confederated Tribes of the Warm Springs Reservation of Oregon, 1984. 80 pp.

Picket Fence in Oregon: An American Vernacular Comes West, by Philip Dole. Cultural-Technical Booklet Number One. Historic Preservation Program, School of Architecture and Allied Arts, University of Oregon, Eugene, 1986. 52 pp.

<u>Pictographs and Petroglyphs of the Oregon Country</u>, by J. Malcolm Loring and Louise Loring. Monograph XXI, Institute of Archaeology, University of California, Los Angeles, 1982. Part 1, Columbia River and Northern Oregon. 325 pp. Part 2, Southern Oregon. 355 pp.

<u>Pictorial History of Smokejumping</u>, by Stan Cohen. Pictorial Histories Publishing Company, Missoula, MT, 1983. 172 pp.

<u>Pictorial Recollections of Toledo, Oregon</u>, by Evelyn Parry. Lincoln County Historical Society, Newport, 1983. 50 pp.

<u>Picturesque Frontier: The Army's Fort Dalles</u>, by Priscilla Knuth, Oregon Historical Soceity, Portland, 1987. 114 pp.

<u>Pietro Belluschi: Modern American Architect</u>, by Meredith Clausen. MIT Press, Cambridge MA, 1994. 469 pp.

"Pink Elephants on the Willamette: The Life and Times of Jack 'Thanks a Million' Matlack," by Paul C. Pitzer. <u>Oregon Historical Quarterly</u> 96(2/3):136-191 Summer-Fall 1995.

<u>Pioneer Catholic History of Oregon</u>, by Edwin V. O'Hara. St. Anthony Guild Press, Paterson NJ. 1939. 234 pp.

<u>Pioneer Roads in Central Oregon</u>, by Lawrence E. Nielsen, Doug Newman, and George McCart. Maverick Publications, Bend, 1985. 200 pp.

<u>Pioneer Trails of the Oregon Coast</u>, by Samuel N. Dicken. Portland: Oregon Historical Society, 1971. 77 pp.

<u>Pioneer Woolen Mills in Oregon</u>, by Alfred L. Lomax. Binfords & Mort, Portland, 1941. 312 pp.

<u>Plains Across: The Overland Emigrants and the Trans-Mississippi West, 1840-1860</u>, by John D. Unruh, Jr. University of Illinois Press, Urbana, 1979. 565 pp.

<u>Planning the Oregon Way: A Twenty-Year Evaluation</u>, edited by Carl Abbott, Deborah Howe, and Sy Adler. Oregon State University Press, Corvallis, 1994. 328 pp.

<u>Plants and Animals of the Pacific Northwest</u>, by Eugene N. Kozloff. University of Washington Press, Seattle, 1978. 264 pp.

<u>Plea for the Indians with Facts and Features of the Late War in Oregon</u>, by John Beeson. John Beeson, No. 15 Laight Street, New York, 1857. Republished by Ye Galleon Press, Fairfiled WA, 1982. 148 pp.

"Point Lookout, the Natron Cut-off, and the Changing Face of Lane County," by Jerold Williams. <u>Oregon Historical Quarterly</u> 93(4):419-435 Winter 1992-93.

<u>Port Orford: A History</u>, by Patrick Masterson. BookPartners, PO Box 922, Wilsonville 97070. 203 pp.

<u>Port Orford, Oregon, Meteorite Mystery</u>, by Roy S. Clarke, Jr., Howard Plotkin, and V. F. Buchwald. Smithsonian Contributions to the Earth Sciences, no. 31, Washinton D.C., 1993. 43 pp. Reprints are available from the Oregon Department of Geology and Mineral Industries in Portland.

<u>Portland: A Historical Sketch and Guide</u>, by Terence O'Donnell and Thomas Vaughan. Oregon Historical Society, Portland, 1976. 161 pp.

<u>Portland: An Informal History & Guide</u>, by Terence O'Donnell & Thomas Vaughan.

Oregon Historical Society, Portland, 1984. 211 pp.

Portland Bridge Book, by Sharon Wood and Jay Dee Alley. Oregon Historical
Society, Portland, 1989. 96 pp.

Portland, Gateway to the Northwest, by Carl Abbott. Windsor Publications,
Northridge CA, 1985. 270 pp.

Portland Guidebook: An Insider's Guide to Portland, Oregon, by Carolyn Wiecks.
6th edition. GloveBox GuideBook, The Authors Communication Team,
PO Box 25211, Portland 97225, 1995. 160 pp.

"Portland Italians, 1880-1920," by Charles F. Gould. Oregon Historical Quarterly
77(3):239-260 September 1976.

Portland Names and Neighborhoods: Their Historic Origins, by Eugene E. Snyder.
Binford & Mort, Portland, 1979. 256 pp.

Portland Rose Festival: For You a Rose in Portland Grows, by Mike Donahue.
American & World Geographic Pub., place not given, 800-654-1105, 1996.
104 pp.

"Portland: Wells Fargo's Hub for the Pacific Northwest," by W. Turrentine Jackson. Oregon Historical Quarterly 86(3):228-267 Fall 1985.

"Portlander John Reed Remembers Lee Sing, His Family's Chinese Servant," by
Fred DeWolfe, Oregon Historical Quarterly 97(3):356-371 Fall 1996.

Portland's Little Red Book of Stairs: The City's Ultimate Guide to More than 150
Curious and Colorful Outdoor Stairways, by Stefana Young. Coobus Press,
PO Box 15085, Portland 97239, 1996. 207 pp.

Portland's Public Art: A Guide and History, by Norma Catherine Gleason and
Chet Orloff. Western Imprints, Oregon Historical Society. Press, Portland, [1983]. 71 pp.

Prairie Keepers: Secrets of the Grasslands, by March Houle. Addison-Wesley
Publishing Company, Reading, Massachusetts, 1995. 266 pp.

Pronunciation Guide of Oregon Place Names, by Robert Monagham. Oregon Association of Broadcasters, Eugene, 1961. 81 pp.

"Property Concepts of 19th Century Oregon Indians," by James Arneson. Oregon
Historical Quarterly 81(4):391-422 Winter 1980.

Proud of Our Past, Planning for Your Future: A History of the Telephone Industry
in Oregon. Oregon Independent Telephone Association, 555 Union Street
NE, Salem 97301, 1990. 80 pp.

Public Grazing Lands, by William Voigt. Rutgers University Press, New Brunswick
NJ, 1976. 359 pp.

"Quiet Pacifists: Oregon's Old Mennonites, 1914-1945, by David Peterson. Oregon Historical Quarterly 93(2):116-146 Summer 1992.

"Race Of the Oregon," by Ralph E. Shaffer. Oregon Historical Quarterly 76(3):269-
298 September 1975.

Railroading in Southern Oregon and the Founding of Medford, by Bert and Margie
Webber. Ye Galleon Press, Fairfield WA, 1985. 255 pp.

Railroads down the Valleys: Some Short Lines of the Oregon Country, by Randall
V. Mills. Pacific Books, Palo Alto CA, 1950. 151 pp.

Rare, Threatened and Endangered Plants and Animals of Oregon. Oregon Natural
Heritage Program, 1205 NW 25th Avenue, Portland 97210. 503-229-

5078. 1993. 79 pp.

Rebels of the Woods: The I.W.W. in the Pacific Northwest, by Robert L. Tyler. University of Oregon Books, Eugene, 1967. 230 pp.

Recollections of My Boyhood, by Jesse A. Applegate, included in A Day with the Cow Column, by Jesse A. [sic] Applegate. Ye Galleon Press, Fairfield WA, 1990. 225 pp. The book includes A Day with the Cow Column in 1843 (20 pp) by Jesse Applegate (1811-1888), originally published in the Overland Monthly in 1868, and Recollections of My Boyhood (167 pp) by his nephew, Jesse A. (Applegate) Applegate (1835-1918), originally published in 1914 in Roseburg.

"Reconstructions of Eocene and Oligocene Plants and Animals of Central Oregon," by Gregory Retallack, Erick Bestland, and Theodore Fremd. Oregon Geology 58(3):51-69 May 1996.

Record Book for Oregon's Big Game Animals, by David Morris. 1997. (541-352-HUNT)

Red Electrics: Southern Pacific's Oregon Interurban, by Tom Dill and Walter R. Grande. Pacific Fast Mail, Edmonds WA, 1994. 135 pp.

Redmond: Rose of the Desert, by B. Elizabeth Ward. B. Elizabeth Ward, [Redmond], 1975. 104 pp.

Redmond: Where the Desert Blooms, by Keith Clark. Western Imprints, Oregon Historical Society, Portland, 1985. 120 pp.

Reining in the Horseless Carriage: the History of Regulating Motor Vehicles in Oregon. Driver and Motor Vehicle Services Branch, Oregon Department of Transportation, Salem, [1994?]. 48 pp.

"Reminiscence: Arthur E. Harder on Pioneer Persistence." Oregon Historical Quarterly 93(2):187-196 Summer 1992.

"Reminiscence: John Fahey on 'Reeducating' German Prisoners During World War II." Oregon Historical Quarterly 93(4):368-393 Winter 1992-93.

Report of Criminal Offenses and Arrests 1996. Oregon State Police, Law Enforcement Data System, Salem, 1997. Various paging.

Report on Reducing Oregon's Greenhouse Gas Emissions. Oregon Department of Energy, Salem, 1995. 79 pp. Appendix D, 75 pp.

Report on the Pacific Yew (*Taxus brevifolia*) to the Sixty-seventh Oregon Legislative Assembly by Kenneth Wiensz. Oregon Department of Forestry, Salem, 1993. 30 pp.

Reports of Explorations and Surveys, to Ascertain the Most Practicable and Economical Route for a Railroad from the Mississippi River to the Pacific Ocean. U.S. War Department, Washington D.C., 1855-1861. 12 volumes in 13. (Volume VI, Routes in Oregon and California.)

Requiem for a People: The Rogue Indians and the Frontiersmen, by Stephen Dow Beckham. University of Oklahoma Press, Norman, 1971. 214 pp. Reissued with new introduction by the author, Oregon State University Press, Corvallis, 1996.

River Why, by David James Duncan. Sierra Club Books, San Francisco, 1983. 294 pp.

Rivers of the West, by Elizabeth L. Orr and William N. Orr. PO Box 5286, Eugene

97405. 1985. 334 pp.

Roads of Yesterday in Northeast Oregon, by Lawrence E. Nielsen. Maverick Publications, Bend, 1990. 143 pp.

Roosevelt's Forest Army: A History of the Civilian Conservation Corps 1933-1942, by Perry H. Merrill. 200 Elm Street, Montpelier Vermont 05602, 1981. 208 pp.

Round the Roses, Portland Past Perspectives: A Collection of Columns Published in This Week Magazine Between May 1983 and November 1987, by Karl Klooster. Published by the author, PO Box 15173, Portland 97215, 1987. 255 pp.

Ruch and the Upper Applegate Valley (An Oregon Documentary), by John and Marguerite Black. Webb Research Group, Medford, 1989. 238 pp.

S. P. & S.: The Spokane, Portland, & Seattle Railway, by Ed Austin and Tom Dill. Pacific Fast Mail, Edmonds WA, 1996. 375 pp.

Sacred Cows at the Public Trough, by Denzel and Nancy Ferguson. Maverick, Bend, 1983. 250 pp.

Saint Paul, Oregon: 1830-1890, by Harvey J. McKay. Binford & Mort, Portland, 1980. 242 pp.

Salmon Fishers of the Columbia, by Courtland L. Smith. Oregon State University Press, Corvallis, 1979. 117 pp.

Salmon of the Pacific, by Adam Lewis. Sasquatch Books, Seattle, 1994. 96 pp.

Sandal and the Cave: The Indians of Oregon, by L. S. Cressman. Oregon State University Press, Corvallis, 1962, 1981. 81 pp.

Sandy Pioneers, Early Settlers and Barlow Road Days, ed. by Elizabeth Hartman and Marie Schwartz. Sandy Pioneer and Historical Association, PO Box 652, Sandy 97055, 1993. 252 pp.

Sandy: The True Story of a Rare Sandhill Crane Who Joined Our Family, by Dayton O. Hyde, 1968. Dial Press, New York, 1968. 215 pp.

Sarah Winnemucca of the Northern Piutes, by Gae Whitney Canfield. University of Oklahoma Press, Norman OK, 1988. 306 pp.

Scenic Driving Oregon, by Tom Barr. Falcon, Helena MT, 1993. 277 pp.

Scio in the Forks of the Santiam, by Carol Bates. C. Bates, [Scio?], printed by Gates Graphics, Gates, 1989. 529 pp.

"'Scooping the Local Field': Oregon's Newsreel Industry, 1911-1933," by Ellen S. Thomas. Oregon Historical Quarterly 90(3):228-304 Fall 1989.

Sea Vegetables: Harvesting Guide and Cookbook, by Evelyn McConnaughey. Naturegraph, Happy Camp, CA, 1985. 239 pp.

"Searching for the Tree Vole: An Episode in the 1914 Biological Survey of Oregon," by George A Jobanek. Oregon Historical Quarterly 89(4):369-400 Winter 1988.

Seashells of the Pacific Northwest, by James Seeley White. Binford & Mort, Portland, 1976. 127 pp.

Seashore Life of the Northern Pacific Coast, by Eugene N. Kozloff. University of Washington Press, Seattle, 1993. 370 pp.

Seaweeds at Ebb Tide, by Muriel Lewin Guberlet. University of Washington Press, Seattle, 1956. 182 pp.

"Shale City: A story of oil, greed and failure", by Marjorie O'Harra. Ashland Gazette Monthly 6(11):10,11 December 1995.

Shaniko People, by Helen Guyton Rees. Binford & Mort, Portland, 1983. 245 pp.

"Sheep Husbandry in Oregon," by John Minto. The Quarterly of the Oregon Historical Society 3(3):219-247 September 1902.

She's Tricky Like Coyote: Annie Miner Peterson, an Oregon Coast Indian Woman, by Lionel Youst. University of Oklahoma Press, Norman, 1997. 307 pp.

Shipwrecks of the Pacific Coast, by James A. Gibbs. Binfords & Mort, Portland, 1962. 316 pp.

"Short Happy History of the State of Jefferson," by Richard Reinhardt. Journal of the Shaw Historical Society 4(2):1-7 Spring 1990.

Short History of Portland, by Gordon De Marco. Lexikos, San Francisco, 1990. 159 pp.

Showdown at Opal Creek: The Battle for America's Last Wilderness, by David Seideman. Carol & Graf Publishers, New York, 1993. 419 pp.

Silent Siege: Japanese Attacks against North America in World War II by Bert Webber. Ye Galleon Press, Fairfield WA, 1984. 396 pp.

Siskiyou Trail: The Hudson's Bay Company Route to California, by Richard Dillon. McGraw-Hill Book Company, New York, 1975. 381 pp.

Skookum, An Oregon Pioneer Family's History and Lore, by Shannon Applegate. Quill/William Morrow, New York, 1988. 460 pp.

Sky Fisherman, by Craig Lesley. Houghton Mifflin, Boston, 1995. 304 pp.

"Slaves and Free Men: Blacks in the Oregon Country, 1840-1860," by Quintard Taylor. Oregon Historical Quarterly 83(2):153-170 Summer 1982.

"Social Morality and Personal Revitalization: Oregon's Ku Klux Klan in the 1920s," by David A. Horowitz. Oregon Historical Quarterly 90(4):364-384 Winter 1989.

Soggy Sneakers: Guide to Oregon Rivers. Willamette Kayak and Canoe Club, Corvallis, 1986. 208 pp.

Solid Waste. Full title: Oregon State Integrated Resource and Solid Waste Management Plan 1995-2005. Oregon Department of Environmental Quality, Portland, 1994. 348 pp.

Sometimes a Great Notion, by Ken Kesey. Viking Press, New York, 1964. 628 pp.

South Road: Its Development and Significance, by Claude W. Nichols, Jr. Master's thesis, University of Oregon, Eugene, June 1953. 252 pp.

Southern Oregon Mosquito Fleet: Stories about Coos County Boats, 1853 to 1948, by Victor C. West. Victor West, North Bend, 1986. 42 pp.

"Starry Nights in Lakeside circa 1930s - The Hollywood Connection," by Greg Wasson. Umpqua Post: Dune Country Travel Companion, Reedsport. 1997. pp 27-29.

State Energy Data Report 1994. Energy Information Administration, Department of Energy, Washington, D.C. Annual, about 500 pp.

Stations West, the Story of the Oregon Railways, by Edwin D. Culp. Caxton, Caldwell ID,1972. 265 pp.

Stories of Nehalem by S. J. Cotton. M.A.Donohue & Company: Chicago. [1915]. 147 pp.

Stories We Tell: An Anthology of Oregon Folk Literature, ed. by Suzi Jones & Jarold Ramsey. Vol. 5 of the Oregon Literature Series. Oregon State University Press, Corvallis, 1993. 326 pp.

Story of Eugene, by Lucia Moore, Nina McCornack (sic), and Gladys McCready. Lane County Historical Society, PO Box 11532, Eugene, 1995 reprint of 1949 work. 277 pp.

Story of Sauvies Island, by Omar C. Spencer. Oregon Historical Society/Bindfords & Mort, Portland, 1950. 134 pp.

Study of the Historic Columbia River Highway. Oregon Department of Transportation, Salem, 1987. 159 pp.

Style & Vernacular: A Guide to the Architecture of Lane County, Oregon. Southwestern Oregon Chapter, American Institue of Architects. Oregon Historical Society, Portland, 1983. 159 pp.

Sublimity, the Story of an Oregon Countryside, 1850-1950, by Mark Joseph Schmid. Library Bookstore, St. Benedict, 1951. 159 pp.

Surge to the Sea: The Greeks in Oregon, by Thomas Doulis. Jack Lockie & Associates, [Portland?], 1977. 87 pp.

"Susie Jessel, the Faith Healer of Ashland," by Louise A. Watson. Southern Oregon Heritage 2(4):4-7, 1997.

Sweet Oregon: The DeMoss Family Lyric Bards - The West's Favorite Entertainers, by Elbert Oliver DeMoss. DeMoss Publishing Co., PO Box 22754, Eugene 97402. 140 pp. Republished by Maverick Publications, Bend, 1995. 146 pp.

Sweetness to the Soul, by Jane Kirkpatrick. Questar Publishers, PO Box 1720, Sisters 97759, 1995. 425 pp.

Table Rocks of Jackson County: Islands in the Sky, by Chris Reyes. Last Minute Publications, Ashland, 1994. 142 pp.

Talent: Worth Its Weight in Gold, by Yvonne Reynolds. Lolot Publishing, 207 Jacob Circle, Talent 97540, 1996. 164 pp.

Tales out of Oregon, by Ralph Friedman. Pars Publishing Company, 2845 NE 56th Avenue, Portland 97213. 1967. 248 pp.

Talking on Paper: An Anthology of Oregon Letters & Diaries, ed. by Shannon Applegate and Terence O'Donnell. Vol. 6 of the Oregon Literature Series. Oregon State University Press, Corvallis, 1993. 324 pp.

Terrible Trail: The Meek Cutoff, 1845, by Keith Clark and Lowell Tiller. Caxton Printers, Caldwell ID. 1966. 244 pp.

That Balance So Rare: The Story of Oregon, by Terence O'Donnell. Portland: Oregon Historical Society Press, 1988. 135 pp.

They Paved the Way, by Bertha Belshe. Belshe, place not given, 1976. 303 pp.

This Day in Oregon: Daybook of Oregon History Featuring Hugh Wetshoe, by James Cloutier. Image West Press, Eugene, 1982. [126 pp.]

This Side of Oregon, by Ralph Friedman. Caxton Printers, Caldwell ID, 1983. 316 pp.

Tillamook Burn to Tillamook State Forest. Oregon Department of Forestry, Salem, 1993. 24 pp.

Tillamook: Land of Many Waters, by Ada M. Orcutt. Binfords & Mort, Portland,

1951. 272 pp.

Tillamook Burn Country: A Pictorial History, by Ellis Lucia. Caxton Printers, Caldwell ID, 1984. 307 pp.

Timberline Lodge, edited by Rachael Griffin and Sarah Munro. Friends of Timberline, Box 37, Mount Hood 97041, 1978. 90 pp.

To Build a Ship, by Don Berry. Viking Press, New York, 1963. 209 pp.

To the Columbia Gateway: The Oregon Railway and the Northern Pacific, 1879-1884, by Peter J. Lewty. Washington State University Press, Pullman, 1987. 202 pp.

Tobacco and Oregonians: A Legacy of Illness and Death. Center for Health Satistics, Oregon Department of Human Resources Health Division, 800 NE Oregon Street, Portland 97232, 1992. 166 pp.

Touching the Stones: Tracing One Hundred Years of Japanese American History. Oregon Nikkei Endowment, PO Box 3458, Portland 97208, 1994. 112 pp.

"Toward a Farmer-Labor Party in Oregon, 1933-38," by Hugh T. Lovin. Oregon Historical Quarterly 76(2):135-151 June 1975.

Tracking down Oregon, by Ralph Friedman. Caxton Printers, Caldwell ID, 1978. 306 pp.

Trask, by Don Berry. Viking Press, New York, 1960. 373 pp.

Treasures of the Oregon Country, by Maynard C. Drawson. Dee Publishing, Salem, 1973, 1975. 147 pp.

Tree Huggers: Victory, Defeat and Renewal in the Northwest Ancient Forest Campaign, by Kathie Durbin. Mountaineers, Seattle, 1996. 304 pp.

Trees to Know in Oregon, by Edward C. Jensen and Charles R. Ross. Oregon State University Extension Service and Oregon Department of Forestry, Corvallis, 1994. 128 pp.

Trees to Lumber. McDonald-Dunn Forest: A Historic Look at Sawmilling, by George B. Wisner. OSU Book Stores, Corvallis, 1992. 48 pp.

Tualatin: From the Beginning, by Loyce(sic) Martinazzi and Karen Lafky Nygaard. Tualatin Historical Society, Tualatin, 1994. 192 pp.

"Tumalo—Thirsty Land," by Martin T. Winch. Oregon Historical Quarterly 85(4):340-374 Winter 1984; 86(1):47-79 Spring 1985; 86(2):153-182 Summer 1985; 86(3):268-297 Fall 1985; 86(4):370-418 Winter 1985; 87(1):21-66 Spring 1986.

Umatilla County, a Backward Glance, by Umatilla Historical Society. E.O. Master Printers, Pendleton, 1980. 270 pp.

"Umatilla's 'Petticoat Government,' 1916-1920," by Shelley Burtner Wallace. Oregon Historical Quarterly 88(4):385-402 Winter 1987.

Umbrella Guide to Oregon Lighthouses. See Oregon Lighthouses.

Umpqua: The Lost County of Oregon, by Jerry Winterbotham, 753 Templeton St., Brownsville 97327, 1994. 156 pp.

Umpqua Valley, Oregon, and Its Pioneers. Binfords & Mort, Portland, 1967. 290 pp.

Uncle Mike's Guide to the Real Oregon Coast, by Michael Burgess. Illustrated by Steve McLeod. 2nd ed., Saddle Mountain Press, Cannon Beach, 1997. 87 pp.

Union, Oregon, City of Victorian Heritage: Union Centennial Album 1878-1978, by Rick Steber and Jerry Gildemeister. Union Centennial Productions, Union, 1978. 100 pp.

"Unique Botany of Steens Mountain: The Rare and Endemic Plants," by Donald Mansfield. Kalmiopsis 5:10-17, 1995.

"Unwelcome Settlers: Black and Mulatto Oregon Pioneers," by K. Keith Richard. Oregon Historical Quarterly Part I, 84(1):29-55 Spring 1983. Part II, 84(2): 172-205 Summer 1983.

"Upper and Lower Table Rocks, Jackson County," by Joan Seevers and Darren Borgias. Kalmiopsis 3:1-9, 1993.

Vanport, by Manly Maben. Oregon Historical Society Press, Portland, 1987. 152 pp.

Varieties of Hope: An Anthology of Oregon Prose, ed. by Gordon B. Dodds. Vol. 3 of the Oregon Literature Series. Oregon State University Press, Corvallis, 1993. 330 pp.

Visionaries, Mountain Men & Empire Builders, by Fred Lockley. Rainy Day Press, Eugene, 1982. 397 pp.

Vortex I, by Ron Cooper and Gerry Lewin. Adolphson's Printing, Salem, 1970. 50 pp.

Walking Guide to Oregon's Ancient Forests, by Wendell Wood. Oregon Natural Resources Council, Portland, 1991. 317 pp.

"Walter M. Pierce and the Birth Control Movement," by Gerald Schwartz. Oregon Historical Quarterly 88(4):370-383 Winter 1987.

Warrenton, by Lyle Anderson. Published by the author, 1993. 189 pp.

Water Power in the "Wilderness": The History of Bonneville Lock and Dam, by William F. Willingham. U.S. Army Corps of Engineers, Portland District, s.l., [1987]. 74 pp.

Water Quality Status Assessment Report. Full title: Oregon's 1994 Water Quality Status Assessment Report: 305(b) Report. Department of Environmental Quality, Portland, 1994. Various pagings.

Water Resources. Appendix V, Volume 2 of the Columbia-North Pacific Region Comprehensive Framework Study of Water and Related Lands. Pacific Northwest River Basins Commission, Vancouver, Washington, 1970. 1,022 pp.

Waterfall Lover's Guide to the Pacific Northwest, by Gregory A. Plumb. 2nd ed. The Mountaineers, Seattle, 1989. 249 pp.

Weather Almanac of Oregon and Southwest Washington. Weather Almanac, PO Box 13, Marylhurst 97036, 1979. 80 pp.

Weather of Oregon, by Fred W. Decker. Science Series 2, Oregon State College, Corvallis, 1960. 41 pp.

Weather of the Pacific Coast, by Walter Rue. Writing Works, Mercer Island WA, 1978. 208 pp.

Weeds of the Pacific Northwest, by Helen M. Gilkey. Oregon State College, Corvallis, 1957. 441 pp.

Weeds of the West. Western Society of Weed Science and University of Wyoming, 1991. 630 pp.

Western Juniper: Its Impact and Management in Oregon Rangelands, by T. E. Bedell, L. E. Eddleman, T. Deboodt, and C. Jacks. EC 1417. Oregon State University Extension Service, Corvallis, 1993.

Who Has Seen: A History of Violence against Wives, by David Peterson del Mar. Harvard University Press, Cambridge MA, 1996. 244 pp.

Where the Pavement Ends, by the Christmas Valley Women's Club. Christmas Valley, 1968. 33 pp.

Whistle Punks and Misery Whips: An Album of the Early Sandy Area, by Elizabeth Hartman and Phil Jonsrud. Sandy Pioneer and Historical Association, Sandy, 1989. 215 pp.

Who Owns the Waterways? Information About Public Ownership of Oregon's Waterways. Oregon Division of State Lands, Salem, 1992. 4 pp.

Who's Who in Oregon. Oregon City Enterprise, Oregon City, 1929.

Who's Who in the West. Marquis Who's Who, Inc, Chicago, 1949-.

Wildflower Genetics: A Field Guide for British Columbia and the Pacific Northwest, by Anthony J. F. Griffiths and Fred R. Ganders. Flight Press, Vancouver, B.C., 1983. 215 pp.

Wildflowers of the Columbia Gorge: A Comprehensive Field Guide, by Russ Jolley. Oregon Historical Society Press, Portland, 1988. 331 pp.

Wildflowers of the West, by Mabel Crittenden and Dorothy Telfer. Celestial Arts, Millbrae, California, 1975. 199 pp.

Wildmen, Wobblies, and Whistle Punks: Stewart Holbrook's Lowbrow Northwest. Ed. by Brian Booth, Oregon State University Press, Corvallis, 1992. 313 pp.

Willamette River Recreation Guide. Oregon State Marine Board and Oregon Parks and Recreation Department, Salem, 1995. 34 pp.

William "Bill" W. Brown, 1855-1941: Legend of Oregon's High Desert, Including a History of the "Wagontire Mountain Range Feud," by Edward Gray. Edward Gray, 58 E. 24th Place, Eugene, 97405, 1993. 222 pp.

"William G. Davis Visits the Oregon Welsh in 1891," by Phillips G. Davies. Letter to the Editor, Oregon Historical Quarterly 83(1):88-90 Spring 1982.

"Wishram," by Henry J. Biddle. Oregon Historical Quarterly 27(1):113-130. March 1926.

Woods Words, by Walter F. McCulloch. Oregon Historical Society, Portland, 1958. 219 pp.

Woody Guthrie, Roll on Columbia: The Columbia River Collection, edited by Bill Murlin. Sing Out Publications, PO Box 5253, Bethlehem PA 18015-0253, 1991. 93 pp.

Wool Story, from Fleece to Fashion. Seventh edition. Pendleton Woolen Mills, Portland, 1991. 35 pp.

"Workers' Compensation Reform: Helping Sell Oregon to New Business," by Robert L. Hill. AOI Business Viewpoint 33(6): entire issue (16 pp.) June 1993.

World Begins Here: An Anthology of Oregon Short Fiction, ed. by Glen A. Love. Vol. 1 of the Oregon Literature Series. Oregon State University Press, Corvallis, 1993. 293 pp.

World of the Bison, by Ed Park. J. B. Lippincott, Philadelphia, 1969. 161 pp.

Wrecked Japanese Junks Adrift in the North Pacific Ocean, by Bert Webber. Ye

Galleon Press, Fairfield, WA, 1984. 201 pp.

Writer's Northwest Handbook. Blue Heron Publishing, Hillsboro. Annual.

Writers of West Portland: A Guide to Portland's Literary Past. Oregon Cultural Heritage Commission, PO Box 3588, Portland 97208, 1996. Brochure.

"WWII At Home," by Sala Horowitz. Oregon History Magazine 38(2):6-7,26-27 [Spring 1994].

"Zeolites in the Cascade Range of Northern Oregon," by Keith Bargar and Robert Oscarson. Oregon Geology 59(5):107-122, Sept/Oct 1997.

Zimmer Gunsul Frasca: Building Community, by Mildred F. Schmertz. Rockport Pub., Rockport Massachusetts, 1995. 208 pp.